The Oxford
Color
Italian
Dictionary

With new word-games supplement

ITALIAN – ENGLISH
ENGLISH – ITALIAN

ITALIANO – INGLESE
INGLESE – ITALIANO

OXFORD
UNIVERSITY PRESS

OXFORD
UNIVERSITY PRESS

Great Clarendon Street, Oxford OX2 6DP

Oxford University Press is a department of the University of Oxford.
It furthers the University's objective of excellence in research, scholarship,
and education by publishing worldwide in

Oxford New York

Athens Auckland Bangkok Bogotá Buenos Aires Calcutta
Cape Town Chennai Dar es Salaam Delhi Florence Hong Kong Istanbul
Karachi Kuala Lumpur Madrid Melbourne Mexico City Mumbai
Nairobi Paris São Paulo Singapore Taipei Tokyo Toronto Warsaw

with associated companies in Berlin Ibadan

Published in the United States
by Oxford University Press Inc., New York

First published as the Oxford Paperback Italian Dictionary, second edition 1997
First two-color edition published 1997
First published in this format with new material added 1999

British Library Cataloguing in Publication Data

Data available

Library of Congress Cataloging in Publication Data

Data available

ISBN 0–19–860251–0

10 9 8 7 6 5 4 3 2 1

Typeset in Nimrod and Arial
by Lexus Ltd.
Printed in Great Britain by
The Bath Press

Contents/Indice

Editors/Redazione

Debora Mazza   Jane Goldie
Donatella Boi   Francesca Logi
Sonia Tinagli-Baxter   Carla Zipoli
Peter Terrell

Copy Editors/Segreteria di redazione

Jacqueline Gregan   Daphne Trotter

Project management by/A cura di
LEXUS

Word games/Giochi enigmistici
Loredana Riu

Preface/Prefazione

This revised edition of the *Oxford Color Italian Dictionary* is an updated and expanded version of the *Oxford Italian Minidictionary* edited by Joyce Andrews. Colloquial words and phrases figure largely, as do neologisms. Noteworthy additions include terms from special areas such as computing and business that have become a familiar feature of current language. This revised edition also includes word games specifically designed to develop skills in the effective use of the dictionary, and to help improve users' knowledge of Italian vocabulary and usage in a fun and entertaining way.

Questa edizione riveduta, in colore, è il risultato di un lavoro di ampliamento e aggiornamento della precedente edizione curata da Joyce Andrews. Un'attenzione particolare è stata rivolta a vocaboli ed espressioni colloquiali di coniazione recente e a termini relativi a settori specifici, quali l'informatica e il commercio, divenuti ricorrenti nella lingua di tutti i giorni. Questa edizione riveduta contiene inoltre dei giochi enigmistici ideati espressamente per sviluppare l'abilità nell'usare efficacemente il dizionario e per consolidare la conoscenza dell'italiano in modo stimolante e divertente.

Proprietary terms/Marchi registrati

This dictionary includes some words which are, or are asserted to be, proprietary names or trademarks. Their inclusion does not imply that they have acquired for legal purposes a non-proprietary or general significance, nor is any other judgement implied concerning their legal status. In cases where the editor has some evidence that a word is used as proprietary name or trademark this is indicated by the symbol ®, but no judgement concerning the legal status of such words is made or implied thereby.

Questo dizionario include alcune parole che sono o vengono considerate marchi registrati. La loro presenza non implica che abbiano acquisito legalmente un significato generale, né si suggerisce alcun altro giudizio riguardo il loro stato giuridico. Qualora il redattore abbia trovato testimonianza dell'uso di una parola come marchio registrato, quest'ultima è stata contrassegnata dal simbolo ®, ma nessun giudizio riguardo lo stato giuridico di tale parola viene espresso o suggerito in tal modo.

Introduction/Introduzione

In order to give the maximum information about English and Italian in the space available, this new dictionary uses certain space-saving conventions. A swung dash ~ is used to replace the headword within the entry. Where the headword contains a vertical bar | the swung dash replaces only the part of the headword that comes in front of the | . For example, **efficien|te** *a* efficient. ~**za** *nf* efficiency (the second bold word reads **efficienza**). Indicators are provided to guide the user to the best translation for a specific sense of a word. Types of indicator are:

field labels (see the list on pp vii–viii), which indicate a general area of usage (commercial, computing etc);

sense indicators, eg: **bore** *n* (*of gun*) calibro *m*; (*person*) seccatore, -trice *mf*;

typical subjects of verbs, eg: **bond** *vt* (*glue*:) attaccare;

typical objects of verbs, placed after the translation of the verb, eg: **boost** *vt* stimolare (*sales*); sollevare (*morale*);

nouns that typically go together with certain adjectives, eg: **rich** *a* ricco; (*food*) pesante.

A solid black circle means that the same word is being translated as a different part of speech, eg: **partition** *n* ... ● *vt* ... Italian stress is shown by a ' placed in front of the stressed syllable in a word. Square brackets are used around parts of an expression which can be omitted without altering the sense.

Allo scopo di fornire il maggior numero possibile di informazioni in inglese e in italiano, questo nuovo dizionario ricorre ad alcune convenzioni per sfruttare al massimo lo spazio disponibile. Un trattino ondulato ~ è utilizzato al posto del lemma all'interno della voce. Qualora il lemma contenga una barra verticale | , il trattino ondulato sostituisce solo la parte del lemma che precede | . Ad esempio: **dark|en** *vt* oscurare. ~**ness** *n* buio *m* (la seconda parola in neretto va letta **darkness**). Degli indicatori vengono forniti per indirizzare l'utente verso la traduzione corrispondente al senso voluto di una parola. I tipi di indicatori sono:

etichette semantiche (vedi la lista pp vii–viii), indicanti l'ambito specifico in cui la parola viene generalmente usata in quel senso (commercio, informatica ecc);

indicatori di significato, es.: **redazione** *nf* (*ufficio*) editorial office; (*di testi*) editing;

soggetti tipici di verbi, es.: **trovarsi** *vr* (*luogo*:) be;

complementi oggetti tipici di verbi, collocati dopo la traduzione dello stesso verbo, es.: **superare** *vt* overtake (*veicolo*); pass (*esame*);

sostantivi che ricorrono tipicamente con certi aggettivi, es.: **solare** *a* (*energia, raggi*) solar; (*crema*) sun.

Un pallino nero indica che la stessa parola viene tradotta come una diversa parte del discorso, es.: **calcolatore** *a* ... ● *nm* ... La pronuncia inglese è data usando l'Alfabeto Fonetico Internazionale. Delle parentesi quadre racchiudono parti di espressioni che possono essere omesse senza alterazioni di senso.

Pronunciation of Italian

Vowels :

a   is broad like *a* in *father*: **casa**.
e   has two sounds: closed like *ey* in *they*: **sera**; open like *e* in *egg*: **sette**.
i   is like *ee* in *feet*: **venire**.
o   has two sounds: closed like *o* in *show*: **bocca**; open like *o* in *dog*: **croma**.
u   is like *oo* in *moon*: **luna**.
When two or more vowels come together each vowel is pronounced separately:
buono; baia.

Consonants:

b, d, f, l, m, n, p, t, v are pronounced as in English. When these are double they are
sounded distinctly: **bello**.
c   before **a, o,** or **u** and before consonants is like *k* in *king*: **cane**.
     before **e** or **i** is like *ch* in *church*: **cena**.
ch   is also like *k* in *king*: **chiesa**.
g   before **a, o,** or **u** is hard like *g* in *got*: **gufo**.
     before **e** or **i** is like *j* in *jelly*: **gentile**.
gh   is like *g* in *gun*: **ghiaccio**.
gl   when followed by **a, e, o, u** is like *gl* in *glass*: **gloria**.
gli is like *lli* in *million*: **figlio**.
gn   is like *ni* in *onion*: **bagno**.
h   is silent.
ng   is like *ng* in *finger* (not *singer*): **ringraziare**.
r   is pronounced distinctly.
s   between two vowels is like *s* in *rose*: **riso**;
     at the beginning of a word it is like *s* in *soap*: **sapone**.
sc   before **e** or **i** is like *sh* in *shell*: **scienza**.
z   sounds like *ts* within a word: **fazione**; like *dz* at the beginning: **zoo**.
The stress is shown by the sign ' printed before the stressed syllable.

Pronuncia inglese

Simboli fonetici
Vocali e dittonghi

iː	*see*	ɔː	*saw*	eɪ	*page*	ɔɪ	*join*	ɒ	*got*
ɪ	*sit*	ʊ	*put*	əʊ	*home*	ɪə	*near*	ə	*ago*
e	*ten*	uː	*too*	aɪ	*five*	eə	*hair*	aʊə	*flour*
æ	*hat*	ʌ	*cup*	aɪə	*fire*	ʊə	*poor*	ɑː	*arm*
ɜː	*fur*	aʊ	*now*						

Consonanti:

p	*pen*	tʃ	*chin*	s	*so*	n	*no*
b	*bad*	dʒ	*June*	z	*zoo*	ŋ	*sing*
t	*tea*	f	*fall*	ʃ	*she*	l	*leg*
d	*dip*	v	*voice*	ʒ	*measure*	r	*red*
k	*cat*	θ	*thin*	h	*how*	j	*yes*
g	*got*	ð	*then*	m	*man*	w	*wet*

Note: ' precede la sillaba accentata. La vocale nasale in parole quali *nuance* è indi-
cata nella trascrizione fonetica come õ: njuːõs.

Abbreviations/Abbreviazioni

adjective	*a*	aggettivo
abbreviation	*abbr*	abbreviazione
administration	*Admin*	amministrazione
adverb	*adv*	avverbio
aeronautics	*Aeron*	aeronautica
American	*Am*	americano
anatomy	*Anat*	anatomia
archaeology	*Archaeol*	archeologia
architecture	*Archit*	architettura
astrology	*Astr*	astrologia
attributive	*attrib*	attributo
automobiles	*Auto*	automobile
auxiliary	*aux*	ausiliario
biology	*Biol*	biologia
botany	*Bot*	botanica
British English	*Br*	inglese britannico
chemistry	*Chem*	chimica
commerce	*Comm*	commercio
computers	*Comput*	informatica
conjunction	*conj*	congiunzione
cooking	*Culin*	cucina
definite article	*def art*	articolo determinativo
	ecc	eccetera
electricity	*Electr*	elettricità
et cetera	*etc*	
feminine	*f*	femminile
familiar	*fam*	familiare
figurative	*fig*	figurato
formal	*fml*	formale
geography	*Geog*	geografia
geology	*Geol*	geologia
grammar	*Gram*	grammatica
humorous	*hum*	umoristico
indefinite article	*indef art*	articolo indeterminativo
interjection	*int*	interiezione
interrogative	*inter*	interrogativo
invariable (no plural form)	*inv*	invariabile
law	*Jur*	legge/giuridico
literary	*liter*	letterario
masculine	*m*	maschile
mathematics	*Math*	matematica
mechanics	*Mech*	meccanica
medicine	*Med*	medicina

masculine or feminine	*mf*	maschile o femminile
military	*Mil*	militare
music	*Mus*	musica
noun	*n*	sostantivo
nautical	*Naut*	nautica
pejorative	*pej*	peggiorativo
personal	*pers*	personale
photography	*Phot*	fotografia
physics	*Phys*	fisica
plural	*pl*	plurale
politics	*Pol*	politica
possessive	*poss*	possessivo
past participle	*pp*	participio passato
prefix	*pref*	prefisso
preposition	*prep*	preposizione
present tense	*pres*	presente
pronoun	*pron*	pronome
psychology	*psych*	psicologia
past tense	*pt*	passato
	qcno	qualcuno
	qcsa	qualcosa
proprietary term	® *	marchio registrato
rail	*Rail*	ferrovia
reflexive	*refl*	riflessivo
religion	*Relig*	religione
relative pronoun	*rel pron*	pronome relativo
somebody	*sb*	
school	*Sch*	scuola
singular	*sg*	singolare
slang	*sl*	gergo
something	*sth*	
technical	*Techn*	tecnico
telephone	*Teleph*	telefono
theatrical	*Theat*	teatro
television	*TV*	televisione
typography	*Typ*	tipografia
university	*Univ*	università
auxiliary verb	*v aux*	verbo ausiliare
intransitive verb	*vi*	verbo intransitivo
reflexive verb	*vr*	verbo riflessivo
transitive verb	*vt*	verbo transitivo
transitive and intransitive verb	*vt/i*	verbo transitivo e intransitivo
vulgar	*vulg*	volgare
cultural equivalent	≈	equivalenza culturale

Aa

a (ad *before vowel*) *prep* to; (*stato in luogo, tempo, età*) at; (*con mese, città*) in; (*mezzo, modo*) by; **dire qcsa a qcno** tell sb sth; **alle tre** at three o'clock; **a vent'anni** at the age of twenty; **a Natale** at Christmas; **a dicembre** in December; **ero al cinema** I was at the cinema; **vivo a Londra** I live in London; **a due a due** two by two; **a piedi** on *o* by foot; **maglia a maniche lunghe** long-sleeved sweater; **casa a tre piani** house with three floors; **giocare a tennis** play tennis; **50 km all'ora** 50 km an hour; **2 000 lire al chilo** 2,000 lire a kilo; **al mattino/alla sera** in the morning/evening; **a venti chilometri/due ore da qui** twenty kilometres/two hours away

a'bate *nm* abbot

abbacchi'ato *a* downhearted

ab'bacchio *nm* (young) lamb

abbagli'ante *a* dazzling ● *nm* headlight, high beam

abbagli'are *vt* dazzle. **ab'baglio** *nm* blunder; **prendere un ~** make a blunder

abbai'are *vi* bark

abba'ino *nm* dormer window

abbando'na|re *vt* abandon; leave (*luogo*); give up (*piani ecc*). **~rsi** *vr* let oneself go; **~rsi a** give oneself up to (*ricordi ecc*). **~to** *a* abandoned. **abban'dono** *nm* abandoning; *fig* abandon; (*stato*) neglect

abbassa'mento *nm* (*di temperatura, acqua, prezzi*) drop

abbas'sar|e *vt* lower; turn down (*radio, TV*); **~e i fari** dip the headlights. **~si** *vr* stoop; (*sole ecc*) sink; *fig* demean oneself

ab'basso *adv* below ● *int* down with

abba'stanza *adv* enough; (*alquanto*) quite

ab'batter|e *vt* demolish; shoot down (*aereo*); put down (*animale*); topple (*regime*); (*fig: demoralizzare*) dishearten. **~si** *vr* (*cadere*) fall; *fig* be discouraged

abbatti'mento *nm* (*morale*) despondency

abbat'tuto *a* despondent, down-in-the-mouth

abba'zia *nf* abbey

abbel'lir|e *vt* embellish. **~si** *vr* adorn oneself

abbeve'ra|re *vt* water. **~toio** *nm* drinking trough

abbi'ente *a* well-to-do

abbiglia'mento *nm* clothes *pl*; (*industria*) clothing industry, rag trade

abbigli'ar|e *vt* dress. **~si** *vr* dress up

abbina'mento *nm* combining

abbi'nare *vt* combine; match (*colori*)

abbindo'lare *vt* cheat

abbocca'mento *nm* interview; (*conversazione*) talk

abboc'care *vi* bite; (*tubi*) join; *fig* swallow the bait

abboc'cato *a* (*vino*) fairly sweet

abbof'farsi *vr* stuff oneself

abbona'mento *nm* subscription; (*ferroviario ecc*) season-ticket; **fare l'~** take out a subscription

abbo'na|re *vt* make a subscriber. **~rsi** *vr* subscribe (**a** to); take out a season-ticket (**a for**) (*teatro, stadio*). **~to, -a** *nmf* subscriber

abbon'dan|te *a* abundant; (*quantità*) copious; (*nevicata*) heavy; (*vestiario*) roomy. **~te di** abounding in. **~te'mente** *adv* (*mangiare*) copiously. **~za** *nf* abundance

abbon'dare *vi* abound

abbor'da|bile *a* (*persona*) approachable; (*prezzo*) reasonable. **~ggio** *nm* Mil boarding. **~re** *vt* board (*nave*); approach (*persona*); (*fam: attaccar bottone a*) chat up; tackle (*compito ecc*)

abbotto'na|re *vt* button up. **~'tura** *nf* [row of] buttons. **~to** *a fig* tight-lipped

abboz'zare *vt* sketch [out]; **~ un sorriso** give a hint of a smile. **ab'bozzo** *nm* sketch

abbracci'are *vt* embrace; hug, embrace (*persona*); take up (*professione*); *fig* include. **ab'braccio** *nm* hug

abbrevi'a|re *vt* shorten; (*ridurre*) curtail; abbreviate (*parola*). **~zi'one** *nf* abbreviation

abbron'zante *nm* sun-tan lotion

abbron'za|re *vt* bronze; tan ⟨pelle⟩. **~rsi** *vr* get a tan. **~to** *a* tanned. **~'tura** *nf* [sun-]tan

abbrusto'lire *vt* toast; roast ⟨caffè ecc⟩

abbruti'mento *nm* brutalization. **abbru'tire** *vt* brutalize. **abbru'tirsi** *vr* become brutalized

abbuf'fa|rsi *vr* fam stuff oneself. **~ta** *nf* blowout

abbuo'nare *vt* reduce

abbu'ono *nm* allowance; *Sport* handicap

abdi'ca|re *vi* abdicate. **~zi'one** *nf* abdication

aber'rante *a* aberrant

aberrazi'one *nf* aberration

a'bete *nm* fir

abi'etto *a* despicable

a'bil|e *a* able; ⟨idoneo⟩ fit; ⟨astuto⟩ clever. **~ità** *nf inv* ability; ⟨idoneità⟩ fitness; ⟨astuzia⟩ cleverness. **~'mente** *adv* ably; ⟨con astuzia⟩ cleverly

abili'ta|re *vt* qualify. **~to** *a* qualified. **~zi'one** *nf* qualification; ⟨titolo⟩ diploma

abis'sale *a* abysmal. **a'bisso** *nm* abyss

abi'tabile *a* inhabitable

abi'tacolo *nm* Auto passenger compartment

abi'tante *nmf* inhabitant

abi'ta|re *vi* live. **~to** *a* inhabited ● *nm* built-up area. **~zi'one** *nf* house

'abito *nm* (da donna) dress; (da uomo) suit. **~ da cerimonia/da sera** formal/evening dress

abitu'al|e *a* usual, habitual. **~'mente** *adv* usually

abitu'ar|e *vt* accustom. **~si** *a vr* get used to

abitudi'nario, -a *a* of fixed habits ● *nmf* person of fixed habits

abi'tudine *nf* habit; **d'~** usually; **per ~ out of habit; avere l'~ di fare qcsa** be in the habit of doing sth

abnegazi'one *nf* self-sacrifice

ab'norme *a* abnormal

abo'li|re *vt* abolish; repeal ⟨legge⟩. **~zi'one** *nf* abolition; repeal

abomi'nevole *a* abominable

abo'rigeno, -a *a & nmf* aboriginal

abor'rire *vt* abhor

abor'ti|re *vi* miscarry; ⟨volontariamente⟩ have an abortion; *fig* fail. **~'vo** *a* abortive. **a'borto** *nm* miscarriage; ⟨volontario⟩ abortion. **~sta** *a* pro-choice

abrasi'one *nf* abrasion. **abra'sivo** *a & nm* abrasive

abro'ga|re *vt* repeal. **~zi'one** *nf* repeal

'abside *nf* apse

abu'lia *nf* apathy. **a'bulico** *a* apathetic

abu'sare *vi* **~ di** abuse; over-indulge in ⟨alcol⟩; ⟨approfittare di⟩ take advantage of; ⟨violentare⟩ rape. **~ivo** *a* illegal

a'buso *nm* abuse. **~ di confidenza** breach of confidence

a.C. *abbr* **(avanti Cristo)** BC

'acca *nf fam* **non ho capito un'~** I understood damn all

acca'demi|a *nf* academy. **A~a di Belle Arti** Academy of Fine Arts. **~co, -a** *a* academic ● *nmf* academician

acca'dere *vi* happen; **accada quel che accada** come what may. **~uto** *nm* event

accalappi'are *vt* catch; *fig* allure

accal'carsi *vr* crowd

accal'da|rsi *vr* get overheated; *fig* get excited. **~to** *a* overheated

accalo'rarsi *vr* get excited

accampa'mento *nm* camp. **accam'pare** *vt fig* put forth. **accam'parsi** *vr* camp

accani'mento *nm* tenacity; ⟨odio⟩ rage

acca'nirsi *vr* persist; ⟨infierire⟩ rage. **~to** *a* persistent; ⟨odio⟩ fierce; *fig* inveterate

ac'canto *adv* near; **~ a** *prep* next to

accanto'nare *vt* set aside; *Mil* billet

accaparra'mento *nm* hoarding; *Comm* cornering

accapar'ra|re *vt* hoard. **~rsi** *vr* grab; corner ⟨mercato⟩. **~'tore, ~'trice** *nmf* hoarder

accapigli'arsi *vr* scuffle; ⟨litigare⟩ squabble

accappa'toio *nm* bathrobe; ⟨per spiaggia⟩ beachrobe

accappo'nare *vt* **fare ~ la pelle a qcno** make sb's flesh creep

accarez'zare *vt* caress, stroke; *fig* cherish

accartocci'ar|e *vt* scrunch up. **~si** *vr* curl up

acca'sarsi *vr* get married

accasci'arsi *vr* flop down; *fig* lose heart

accata'stare *vt* pile up

accat'tivante *a* beguiling

accatti'varsi *vr* **~ le simpatie/la stima/l'affetto di qcno** gain sb's sympathy/respect/affection

accatto'naggio *nm* begging. **accat'tone, -a** *nmf* beggar

accaval'lar|e *vt* cross *(gambe)*. ~**si** *vr* pile up; *fig* overlap

acce'cante *a (luce)* blinding

acce'care *vt* blind ●*vi* go blind

ac'cedere *vi* ~ **a** enter; *(acconsentire)* comply with

accele'ra|re *vi* accelerate ●*vt* speed up, accelerate; ~**re il passo** quicken one's pace. ~**to** *a* rapid. ~'**tore** *nm* accelerator. ~**zi'one** *nf* acceleration

ac'cender|e *vt* light; turn on *(luce, TV ecc)*; *fig* inflame; **ha da ~e?** have you got a light?. ~**si** *vr* catch fire; *(illuminarsi)* light up; *fig* become inflamed

accendi'gas *nm inv* gas lighter; *(su cucina)* automatic ignition

accen'dino *nm* lighter

accendi'sigari *nm* cigar-lighter

accen'nare *vt* indicate; hum *(melodia)* ●*vi* ~ **a** beckon to; *fig* hint at; *(far l'atto di)* make as if to; **accenna a piovere** it looks like rain. **ac'cenno** *nm* gesture; *(con il capo)* nod; *fig* hint

accensi'one *nf* lighting; *(di motore)* ignition

accen'ta|re *vt* accent; *(con accento tonico)* stress. ~**zi'one** *nf* accentuation. **ac'cento** *nm* accent; *(tonico)* stress

accentra'mento *nm* centralizing

accen'trare *vt* centralize

accentu'a|re *vt* accentuate. ~**rsi** *vr* become more noticeable. ~**to** *a* marked

accerchia'mento *nm* surrounding

accerchi'are *vt* surround

accerta'mento *nm* check

accer'tare *vt* ascertain; *(controllare)* check; assess *(reddito)*

ac'ceso *a* lighted; *(radio, TV ecc)* on; *(colore)* bright

acces'sibile *a* accessible; *(persona)* approachable; *(spesa)* reasonable

ac'cesso *nm* access; *(Med: di rabbia)* fit; **vietato l'~** no entry

acces'sorio *a* accessory; *(secondario)* of secondary importance ●*nm* accessory; **accessori** *pl (rifiniture)* fittings

ac'cetta *nf* hatchet

accet'tabile *a* acceptable

accet'tare *vt* accept; *(aderire a)* agree to

accettazi'one *nf* acceptance; *(luogo)* reception. ~ **[bagagli]** check-in. **[banco]** ~ check-in [desk]

ac'cetto *a* agreeable; **essere bene ~** be very welcome

accezi'one *nf* meaning

acchiap'pare *vt* catch

ac'chito *nm* **di primo** ~ at first

acciac'ca|re *vt* crush; *fig* prostrate. ~**to, -a** *a* **essere** ~**to** ache all over. **acci'acco** *nm* infirmity; *(pl: afflizioni)* aches and pains

acciaie'ria *nf* steelworks

acci'aio *nm* steel; ~ **inossidabile** stainless steel

acciden'ta|le *a* accidental. ~**l'mente** *adv* accidentally. ~**to** *a (terreno)* uneven

acci'dente *nm* accident; *Med* stroke; **non capisce/non vede un ~** *fam* he doesn't understand/can't see a damn thing. **acci'denti!** *int* damn!

accigli'a|rsi *vr* frown. ~**to** *a* frowning

ac'cingersi *vr* ~ **a** be about to

acci'picchia *int* good Lord!

acciuf'fare *vt* catch

acci'uga *nf* anchovy

accla'ma|re *vt* applaud; *(eleggere)* acclaim. ~**zi'one** *nf* applause

acclima'tar|e *vt* acclimatize. ~**si** *vr* get acclimatized

ac'clud|ere *vt* enclose. ~**so** *a* enclosed

accocco'larsi *vr* squat

accogli'en|te *a* welcoming; *(confortevole)* cosy. ~**za** *nf* welcome

ac'cogliere *vt* receive; *(conpiacere)* welcome; *(contenere)* hold

accol'larsi *vr* take on *(responsabilità, debiti, doveri)*. **accol'lato** *a* high-necked

accoltel'lare *vt* knife

accomia'tar|e *vt* dismiss. ~**si** *vr* take one's leave *(da of)*

accomo'dante *a* accommodating

accomo'dar|e *vt* *(riparare)* mend; *(disporre)* arrange. ~**si** *vr* make oneself at home; **si accomodi!** come in!; *(si sieda)* take a seat!

accompagna'mento *nm* accompaniment; *(seguito)* retinue

accompa'gna|re *vt* accompany; ~**re qcno a casa** see sb home; ~**re qcno alla porta** show sb out. ~'**tore**, ~'**trice** *nmf* companion; *(di comitiva)* escort; *Mus* accompanist

accomu'nare *vt* pool

acconci'a|re *vt* arrange. ~'**tura** *nf* hair-style; *(ornamento)* head-dress

accondiscen'den|te *a* too obliging. ~**za** *nf* excessive desire to please

accondi'scendere *vi* ~ **a** condescend; comply with *(desiderio)*; *(acconsentire)* consent to

acconsen'tire *vi* consent

accontentare | acronimo

acconten'tar|e *vt* satisfy. **~si** *vr* be content (**di** with)

ac'conto *nm* deposit; **in ~** on account; **lasciare un ~** leave a deposit

accop'pare *vt fam* bump off

accoppia'mento *nm* coupling; (*di animali*) mating

accoppi'ar|e *vt* couple; mate (*animali*). **~rsi** *vr* pair off; mate. **~ta** *nf* (*scommessa*) bet placed on two horses for first and second place

acco'rato *a* sorrowful

accorci'ar|e *vt* shorten. **~si** *vr* get shorter

accor'dar|e *vt* concede; match (*colori ecc*); *Mus* tune. **~si** *vr* agree

ac'cordo *nm* agreement; *Mus* chord; (*armonia*) harmony; **andare d'~** get on well; **d'~!** agreed!; **essere d'~** agree; **prendere accordi con qcno** make arrangements with sb

ac'corgersi *vr* **~ di** notice; (*capire*) realize

accorgi'mento *nm* shrewdness; (*espediente*) device

ac'correre *vi* hasten

accor'tezza *nf* (*previdenza*) forethought

ac'corto *a* shrewd; **mal ~** incautious

accosta'mento *nm* (*di colori*) combination

acco'star|e *vt* draw close to; approach (*persona*); set ajar (*porta ecc*). **~si** *vr* **~si a** come near to

accovacci'ar|si *vr* crouch, squat down. **~to** *a* squatting

accoz'zaglia *nf* jumble; (*di persone*) mob

accoz'zare *vt* **~ colori** mix colours that clash

accredita'mento *nm* credit; **~ tramite bancogiro** Bank Giro Credit

accredi'tare *vt* confirm (*notizia*); *Comm* credit

ac'cresc|ere *vt* increase. **~ersi** *vr* grow larger. **~i'tivo** *a* augmentative

accucci'arsi *vr* (*cane:*) lie down; (*persona:*) crouch

accu'dire *vi* **~ a** attend to

accumu'la|re *vt* accumulate. **~rsi** *vr* pile up, accumulate. **~ tore** *nm* accumulator; *Auto* battery. **~zi'one** *nf* accumulation. **ac'cumulo** *nm* (*di merce*) build-up

accura'tezza *nf* care

accu'rato *a* careful

ac'cusa *nf* accusation; *Jur* charge; **essere in stato di ~** *Jur* have been charged; **la Pubblica A~** *Jur* the public prosecutor

accu'sa|re *vt* accuse; *Jur* charge; complain of (*dolore*); **~re ricevuta di** *Comm* acknowledge receipt of. **~to, -a** *nmf* accused. **~ tore** *nm Jur* prosecutor

a'cerbo *a* sharp; (*immaturo*) unripe

'acero *nm* maple

a'cerrimo *a* implacable

ace'tone *nm* nail polish remover

a'ceto *nm* vinegar

A.C.I. *abbr* (**Automobile Club d'Italia**) Italian Automobile Association

acidità *nf* acidity. **~ di stomaco** acid stomach

'acido *a* acid; (*persona*) sour ● *nm* acid

a'cidulo *a* slightly sour

'acino *nm* berry; (*chicco*) grape

'acne *nf* acne

'acqua *nf* water; **fare ~** *Naut* leak; **~ in bocca!** *fig* mum's the word!. **~ di Colonia** eau de Cologne. **~ corrente** running water. **~ dolce** fresh water. **~ minerale** mineral water. **~ minerale gassata** fizzy mineral water. **~ naturale** still mineral water. **~ potabile** drinking water. **~ salata** salt water. **~ tonica** tonic water

acqua'forte *nf* etching

ac'quaio *nm* sink

acquama'rina *a* aquamarine

acqua'rello *nm* = **acquerello**

ac'quario *nm* aquarium; *Astr* Aquarius

acqua'santa *nf* holy water

acqua'scooter *nm inv* water-scooter

ac'quatico *a* aquatic

acquat'tarsi *vr* crouch

acqua'vite *nf* brandy

acquaz'zone *nm* downpour

acque'dotto *nm* aqueduct

'acqueo *a* **vapore ~** water vapour

acque'rello *nm* water-colour

acqui'rente *nmf* purchaser

acqui'si|re *vt* acquire. **~to** *a* acquired. **~zi'one** *nf* attainment

acqui'st|are *vt* purchase; (*ottenere*) acquire. **ac'quisto** *nm* purchase; **uscire per ~i** go shopping; **fare ~i** shop

acqui'trino *nm* marsh

acquo'lina *nf* **far venire l'~ in bocca a qcno** make sb's mouth water

ac'quoso *a* watery

'acre *a* acrid; (*al gusto*) sour; *fig* harsh

a'crilico *a* acrylic

a'crobata *nmf* acrobat. **~'zia** *nf* acrobatics *pl*

a'cronimo *nm* acronym

acu'ir|e *vt* sharpen. **~si** *vr* become more intense

a'culeo *nm* sting; *Bot* prickle

a'cume *nm* acumen

acumi'nato *a* pointed

a'custic|a *nf* acoustics *pl.* **~o** *a* acoustic

acu'tezza *nf* acuteness

acutiz'zarsi *vr* become worse

a'cuto *a* sharp; *(suono)* shrill; *(freddo, odore)* intense; *Gram, Math, Med* acute ●*nm Mus* high note

adagi'ar|e *vt* lay down. **~si** *vr* lie down

a'dagio *adv* slowly ●*nm Mus* adagio; *(proverbio)* adage

adattabilità *nf* adaptability

adatta'mento *nm* adaptation; **avere spirito di ~** be adaptable

adat'ta|re *vt* adapt; *(aggiustare)* fit. **~rsi** *vr* adapt. **~'tore** *nm* adaptor. **a'datto** *a* suitable (**a** for); *(giusto)* right

addebita'mento *nm* debit. **~ di'retto** direct debit

addebi'tare *vt* debit; *fig* ascribe *(colpa)*

ad'debito *nm* charge

addensa'mento *nm* thickening; *(di persone)* gathering

adden'sar|e *vt* thicken. **~si** *vr* thicken; *(affollarsi)* gather

adden'tare *vt* bite

adden'trarsi *vr* penetrate

ad'dentro *adv* deeply; **essere ~ in** be in on

addestra'mento *nm* training

adde'strar|e *vt* train. **~si** *vr* train

ad'detto, -a *a* assigned ●*nmf* employee; *(diplomatico)* attaché; **addetti** *pl* **ai lavori** persons involved in the work. **~ stampa** information officer, press officer

addiaccio *nm* **dormire all'~** sleep in the open

addi'etro *adv* *(indietro)* back; *(nel passato)* before

ad'dio *nm & int* goodbye. **~ al celibato** stag night, stag party

addirit'tura *adv* *(perfino)* even; *(assolutamente)* absolutely; **~!** really!

ad'dirsi *vr* **~ a** suit

addi'tare *vt* point at; *(in mezzo a un gruppo)* point out; *fig* point to

addi'tivo *a & nm* additive

addizio'nal|e *a* additional. **~'mente** *adv* additionally

addizio'nare *vt* add [up]. **addizi'one** *nf* addition

addob'bare *vt* decorate. **ad'dobbo** *nm* decoration

addol'cir|e *vt* sweeten; tone down *(colore)*; *fig* soften. **~si** *vr fig* mellow

addolo'ra|re *vt* grieve. **~rsi** *vr* be upset (**per** by). **~to** *a* pained, distressed

ad'dom|e *nm* abdomen. **~i'nale** *a* abdominal; [**muscoli**] **addominali** *pl* abdominals

addomesti'ca|re *vt* tame. **~'tore** *nm* tamer

addormen'ta|re *vt* put to sleep. **~rsi** *vr* go to sleep. **~to** *a* asleep; *fig* slow

addos'sar|e *vt* **~ a** *(appoggiare)* lean against; *(attribuire)* lay on. **~si** *vr* *(ammassarsi)* crowd; shoulder *(responsabilità ecc)*

ad'dosso *adv* on; **~** *prep* on; *(molto vicino)* right next to; **mettere gli occhi ~ a qcno/qcsa** hanker after sb/sth; **non mettermi le mani ~!** keep your hands off me!; **stare ~ a qcno** *fig* be on sb's back

ad'durre *vt* produce *(prova, documento)*; give *(pretesto, esempio)*

adegua'mento *nm* adjustment

adegu'a|re *vt* adjust. **~rsi** *vr* conform. **~to** *a* adequate; *(conforme)* consistent

a'dempiere *vt* fulfil. **~'mento** *nm* fulfilment

ade'noidi *nfpl* adenoids

ade'ren|te *a* adhesive; *(vestito)* tight ●*nmf* follower. **~za** *nf* adhesion. **~ze** *npl* connections

ade'rire *vi* **~ a** stick to, adhere to; support *(sciopero, petizione)*; agree to *(richiesta)*

adesca'mento *nm* *Jur* soliciting

ade'scare *vt* bait; *fig* entice

adesi'one *nf* adhesion; *fig* agreement

ade'sivo *a* adhesive ●*nm* sticker; *Auto* bumper sticker

a'desso *adv* now; *(poco fa)* just now; *(tra poco)* any moment now; **da ~ in poi** from now on; **per ~** for the moment

adia'cente *a* adjacent; **~ a** next to

adi'bire *vt* **~ a** put to use as

'adipe *nm* adipose tissue

adi'ra|rsi *vr* get irate. **~to** *a* irate

a'dire *vt* resort to; **~ le vie legali** take legal proceedings

'adito *nm* **dare ~ a** give rise to

adocchi'are *vt* eye; *(con desiderio)* covet

adole'scen|te *a & nmf* adolescent. **~za** *nf* adolescence. **~zi'ale** *a* adolescent

adom'brar|evt darken; fig veil. ~si vr (offendersi) take offence

adope'rar|evt use. ~si vr take trouble

ado'rabilea adorable

ado'ra|revt adore. ~zi'one nf adoration

ador'narevt adorn

adot't|arevt adopt. ~ivo a adoptive. **adozi'one**nf adoption

adprep = **a**(davanti a vocale)

adrena'linanf adrenalin

adri'aticoa Adriatic ●nm **l'A~** the Adriatic

adu'la|revt flatter. ~'tore, ~'trice nmf flatterer. ~zi'one nf flattery

adulte'ra|revt adulterate. ~toa adulterated

adul'terionm adultery. a'dultero, -aa adulterous ●nm adulterer ●nf adulteress

a'dulto, -a a & nmf adult; (maturo) mature

adu'nanzanf assembly

adu'na|revt gather. ~ta nf Mil parade

a'duncoa hooked

ae'rarevt air (stanza)

a'ereoa aerial; (dell'aviazione) air attrib ●nm aeroplane, plane

ae'robic|anf aerobics. ~o a aerobic

aerodi'namic|a nf aerodynamics sg. ~o a aerodynamic

aero'nautic|a nf aeronautics sg; Mil Air Force. ~o a aeronautical

aero'plano nm aeroplane

aero'porto nm airport

aero'scalo nm cargo and servicing area

aero'sol nm inv aerosol

'afa nf sultriness

af'fabil|e a affable. ~ità nf affability

affaccen'da|rsi vr busy oneself (a with). ~to a busy

affacci'arsi vr show oneself; ~ alla finestra appear at the window

affa'ma|revt starve [out]. ~to a starving

affan'na|re vt leave breathless. ~rsi vr busy oneself; (agitarsi) get worked up. ~to a breathless; dal respiro ~to wheezy. af'fanno nm breathlessness; fig worry

af'fare nm matter; Comm transaction, deal; (occasione) bargain; affari pl business; non sono affari tuoi fam it's none of your business. affa'rista nmf wheeler-dealer

affasci'nante a fascinating; (persona, sorriso) bewitching

affasci'narevt bewitch; fig charm

affatica'mentonm fatigue

affati'car|e vt tire; (sfinire) exhaust. ~si vr tire oneself out; (affannarsi) strive

af'fattoadv completely; **non... ~**not... at all; **niente ~!**not at all!

affer'ma|re vt affirm; (sostenere) assert. ~rsivr establish oneself

affermativa'mente adv in the affirmative

afferma'tivoa affirmative

affermazi'one nf assertion; (successo) achievement

affer'rare vt seize; catch (oggetto); (capire) grasp; **~ e al volo**fig be quick on the uptake. ~sivr **~si a**grasp at

affet'ta|re vt slice; (ostentare) affect. ~toa sliced; (sorriso, maniere) affected ●nm cold meat, sliced meat. ~zi'one nf affectation

affet'tivo a affective; **rapporto ~** emotional tie

af'fetto¹ nm affection; **con ~** affectionately

af'fetto²a **~ da** suffering from

affettuosità nf inv (gesto) affectionate gesture

affettu'osoa affectionate

affezio'na|rsi vr **~rsi a** grow fond of. ~to a devoted (a to)

affian'car|e vt put side by side; Mil flank; fig support. ~si vr come side by side; fig stand together; ~si a qcnofig help sb out

affiata'mentonm harmony

affia'ta|rsi vr get on well together. ~to a close-knit; **una coppia ~ta** a very close couple

affibbi'arevt **~ qcsa a qcno** saddle sb with sth; **~ un pugno a qcno**let fly at sb

affi'dabile a dependable. ~ità nf dependability

affida'mento nm (Jur: dei minori) custody; **fare ~ su** qcno rely on sb; **non dare ~** not inspire confidence

affi'dar|e vt entrust. ~si vr ~si a rely on

affievo'lirsivr grow weak

af'figgere vt affix

affi'larevt sharpen

affili'ar|evt affiliate. ~si vr become affiliated

affi'nare vt sharpen; (perfezionare) refine

affinché *conj* so that, in order that

af'fin|e *a* similar. **~ità** *nf* affinity

affiora'mento *nm* emergence; *Naut* surfacing

affio'rare *vi* emerge; *fig* come to light

af'fisso *nm* bill; *Gram* affix

affitta'camere *nm inv* landlord ● *nf inv* landlady

affit'tare *vt* (*dare in affitto*) let; (*prendere in affitto*) rent; **'af'fittasi'** 'to let', 'for rent'

af'fitt|o *nm* rent; **contratto d'~o** lease; **dare in ~o** let; **prendere in ~o** rent. **~u'ario , -a** *nmf Jur* lessee

af'fligger|e *vt* torment. **~si** *vr* distress oneself

af'fli|tto *a* distressed; **~tto da** suffering from. **~zi'one** *nf* distress; *fig* affliction

afflosci'arsi *vr* become floppy; (*accasciarsi*) flop down; (*morale:*) decline

afflu'en|te *a & nm* tributary. **~za** *nf* flow; (*di gente*) crowd

afflu'ire *vi* flow; *fig* pour in

af'flusso *nm* influx

affo'ga|re *vt/i* drown; *Culin* poach; **~re in** *fig* be swamped with. **~to** *a* (*persona*) drowned; (*uova*) poached. **~to al caffè** *nm* ice cream with hot espresso poured over it

affol'la|re *vt*, **~rsi** *vr* crowd. **~to** *a* crowded

affonda'mento *nm* sinking

affon'dare *vt/i* sink

affossa'mento *nm* pothole

affran'ca|re *vt* redeem (*bene*); stamp (*lettera*); free (*schiavo*). **~rsi** *vr* free oneself. **~tura** *nf* stamping; (*di spedizione*) postage

af'franto *a* prostrated; (*esausto*) worn out

af'fresco *nm* fresco

affret'ta|re *vt* speed up. **~rsi** *vr* hurry. **~ta'mente** *adv* hastily. **~to** *a* hasty

affron'tar|e *vt* face; confront (*il nemico*); meet (*le spese*). **~si** *vr* clash

af'fronto *nm* affront, insult; **fare un ~ a qcno** insult sb

affumi'ca|re *vt* fill with smoke; *Culin* smoke. **~to** *a* (*prosciutto, formaggio*) smoked

affuso'la|re *vt* taper [off]. **~to** *a* tapering

afo'risma *nm* aphorism

a'foso *a* sultry

'Africa *nf* Africa. **afri'cano, -a** *a & nmf* African

afrodi'siaco *a & nm* aphrodisiac

a'genda *nf* diary

agen'dina *nf* pocket-diary

a'gente *nm* agent; **agenti** *pl* **atmosferici** atmospheric agents. **~ di cambio** stockbroker. **~ di polizia** policeman

agen'zia *nf* agency; (*filiale*) branch office; (*di banca*) branch. **~ di viaggi** travel agency. **~ immobiliare** estate agency

agevo'lare *vt* facilitate. **~zi'one** *nf* facilitation

a'gevol|e *a* easy; (*strada*) smooth. **~'mente** *adv* easily

aggancia're *vt* hook up; *Rail* couple. **~si** *vr* (*vestito:*) hook up

ag'geggio *nm* gadget

agget'tivo *nm* adjective

agghiacci'ante *a* terrifying

agghiacci'ar|e *vt fig* **~ qcno** make sb's blood run cold. **~si** *vr* freeze

agghin'da|re *vt fam* dress up. **~rsi** *vr fam* doll oneself up. **~to** *a* dressed up

aggiorna'mento *nm* up-date

aggior'na|re *vt* (*rinviare*) postpone; (*mettere a giorno*) bring up to date. **~rsi** *vr* get up to date. **~to** *a* up-to-date; (*versione*) updated

aggi'rar|e *vt* surround; (*fig: ingannare*) trick. **~si** *vr* hang about; **~si su** (*discorso ecc:*) be about; (*approssimarsi*) be around

aggiudi'car|e *vt* award; (*all'asta*) knock down. **~si** *vr* win

aggi'un|gere *vt* add. **~ta** *nf* addition. **~tivo** *a* supplementary. **~to** *a* added ● *a & nm* (*assistente*) assistant

aggiu'star|e *vt* mend; (*sistemare*) settle; (*fam: mettere a posto*) fix. **~si** *vr* adapt; (*mettersi in ordine*) tidy oneself up; (*decidere*) sort things out; (*tempo:*) clear up

agglomera'mento *nm* conglomeration

agglome'rato *nm* built-up area

aggrap'par|e *vt* grasp. **~si** *vr* **~si a** cling to

aggra'vante *Jur nf* aggravation ● *a* aggravating

aggra'var|e *vt* (*peggiorare*) make worse; increase (*pena*); (*appesantire*) weigh down. **~si** *vr* worsen

aggrazi'ato *a* graceful

aggre'dire *vt* attack

aggre'ga|re *vt* add; (*associare a un gruppo ecc*) admit. **~rsi** *vr* **~rsi a** join. **~to** *a* associated ● *nm* aggregate; (*di case*) block

aggressi'one *nf* aggression; (*atto*) attack

aggres'sivo *a* aggressive. **~ività** *nf* aggressiveness. **~ore** *nm* aggressor

aggrin'zare, aggrin'zire *vt* wrinkle

aggrot'tare *vt* **~ le ciglia/la fronte** frown

aggrovigli'are *vt* tangle. **~rsi** *vr* get-entangled; *fig* get complicated. **~to** *a* entangled; *fig* confused

agguan'tare *vt* catch

aggu'ato *nm* ambush; (*tranello*) trap; **stare in ~** lie in wait

agguer'rito *a* fierce

agia'tezza *nf* comfort

agi'ato *a* (*persona*) well off; (*vita*) comfortable

a'gibile *a* (*palazzo*) fit for human habitation. **~ità** *nf* fitness for human habitation

'agile *a* agile. **~ità** *nf* agility

'agio *nm* ease; **mettersi a proprio ~** make oneself at home

a'gire *vi* act; (*comportarsi*) behave; (*funzionare*) work; **~ su** affect

agi'tare *vt* shake; wave (*mano*); (*fig: turbare*) trouble. **~rsi** *vr* toss about; (*essere inquieto*) be restless; (*mare*) get rough. **~to** *a* restless; (*mare*) rough. **~tore, ~'trice** *nmf* (*persona*) agitator. **~zi'one** *nf* agitation; **mettere in ~zione** qcno make sb worried

'agli = a + **gli**

'aglio *nm* garlic

a'gnello *nm* lamb

agno'lotti *nmpl* ravioli *sg*

a'gnostico, -a *a & nmf* agnostic

'ago *nm* needle

ago'nia *nf* agony. **~z'zare** *vi* be on one's deathbed

ago'nistica *nf* competition. **~o** *a* competitive

agopun'tura *nf* acupuncture

a'gosto *nm* August

a'graria *nf* agriculture. **~o** *a* agricultural ● *nm* landowner

a'gricolo *a* agricultural. **~tore** *nm* farmer. **~tura** *nf* agriculture

agri'foglio *nm* holly

agritu'rismo *nm* farm holidays, agrotourism

'agro *a* sour

agroalimen'tare *a* food *attrib*

agro'dolce *a* bitter-sweet; *Culin* sweet-and-sour; **in ~** sweet and sour

agrono'mia *nf* agronomy

a'grume *nm* citrus fruit; (*pianta*) citrus tree

aguz'zare *vt* sharpen; **~ le orecchie** prick up one's ears; **~ la vista** look hard

aguz'zino *nm* slave-driver; (*carceriere*) jailer

ahimè *int* alas

'ai = a + i

'Aia *nf* L'**~** The Hague

'aia *nf* threshing-floor

Aids *nmf* Aids

ai'rone *nm* heron

ai'tante *a* sturdy

aiu'ola *nf* flower-bed

aiu'tante *nmf* assistant ● *nm* *Mil* adjutant. **~ di campo** aide-de-camp

aiu'tare *vt* help

ai'uto *nm* help, aid; (*assistente*) assistant

aiz'zare *vt* incite; **~ contro** set on

al = a + **il**

'ala *nf* wing; **fare ~** make way

ala'bastro *nm* alabaster

'alacre *a* brisk

a'lano *nm* Great Dane

'alba *nf* dawn

Alba'nia *nf* Albania. **a~ese** *a & nmf* Albanian

albeggi'are *vi* dawn

albe'rato *a* wooded; (*viale*) tree-lined. **~'tura** *nf Naut* masts *pl*. **albe'rello** *nm* sapling

al'bergo *nm* hotel. **~o diurno** *hotel where rooms are rented during the daytime*. **~a'tore, ~a'trice** *nmf* hotel-keeper. **~hi'ero** *a* hotel *attrib*

'albero *nm* tree; *Naut* mast; *Mech* shaft. **~ genealogico** family tree. **~ maestro** *Naut* mainmast. **~ di Natale** Christmas tree

albi'cocca *nf* apricot. **~o** *nm* apricot-tree

al'bino *nm* albino

'albo *nm* register; (*libro ecc*) album; (*per avvisi*) notice board

'album *nm* album. **~ da disegno** sketch-book

al'bume *nm* albumen

'alce *nm* elk

'alcol *nm* alcohol; *Med* spirit; (*liquori forti*) spirits *pl*; **darsi all'~** take to drink. **al'colici** *nmpl* alcoholic drinks. **al'colico** *a* alcoholic. **alco'lismo** *nm* alcoholism. **~iz'zato, -a** *a & nmf* alcoholic

alco'test® *nm inv* Breathalyser®

al'cova *nf* alcove

al'cun, al'cuno a & pron any; **non ha ~ amico** he hasn't any friends, he has no friends. **alcuni** pl some, a few; **~i suoi amici** some of his friends

alea'torio a unpredictable

a'letta nf Mech fin

alfa'betico a alphabetical

alfabetizzazi'one nf **~ della popolazione** teaching people to read and write

alfa'beto nm alphabet

alfi'ere nm (scacchi) bishop

al'fine adv eventually, in the end

'alga nf seaweed

'algebra nf algebra

Alge'ri|a nf Algeria. **a~no, -a** a & nmf Algerian

ali'ante nm glider

'alibi nm inv alibi

alie'na|re vt alienate. **~rsi** vr become estranged; **~rsi le simpatie di qcno** lose sb's good will. **~to, -a** a alienated ● nmf lunatic

a'lieno, -a nmf alien ● a **è ~ da invidia** envy is foreign to him

alimen'ta|re vt feed; fig foment ● a food attrib; (abitudine) dietary. **~ri** nmpl food-stuffs. **~ tore** nm power unit. **~zi'one** nf feeding

ali'mento nm food; **alimenti** pl food; Jur alimony

a'liquota nf share; (di imposta) rate

ali'scafo nm hydrofoil

'alito nm breath

'alla = a + la

allaccia'mento nm connection

allacci'ar|e vt fasten (cintura); lace up (scarpe); do up (vestito); (collegare) connect; form (amicizia). **~si** vr do up, fasten (vestito, cintura)

allaga'mento nm flooding

alla'gar|e vt flood. **~si** vr become flooded

allampa'nato a lanky

allarga'mento nm (di una strada, delle ricerche) widening

allar'gar|e vt widen; open (braccia, gambe); let out (vestito ecc); fig extend. **~si** vr widen

allar'mante a alarming

allar'ma|re vt alarm. **~to** a panicky

al'larme nm alarm; **dare l'~** raise the alarm; **falso ~** fig false alarm. **~ aereo** air raid warning

allar'mis|mo nm alarmism. **~ta** nmf alarmist

allatta'mento nm (di animale) suckling; (di neonato) feeding

allat'tare vt suckle (animale); feed (neonato)

'alle = a + le

alle'anza nf alliance. **~to, -a** a allied ● nmf ally

alle'ar|e vt unite. **~si** vr form an alliance

alle'gare[1] vt Jur allege

alle'ga|re[2] vt (accludere) enclose; set on edge (denti). **~to a** enclosed ● nm enclosure; **in ~** attached, appended. **~zi'one** nf Jur allegation

allegge'rir|e vt lighten; fig alleviate. **~si** vr become lighter; (vestirsi leggero) put on lighter clothes

allego'ria nf allegory. **alle'gorico** a allegorical

allegra'mente adv breezily

alle'gria nf gaiety

al'legro a cheerful; (colore) bright; (brillo) tipsy ● nm Mus allegro

alle'luia int hallelujah!

allena'mento nm training

alle'na|re vt, **~rsi** vr train. **~ tore, ~ trice** nmf trainer, coach

allen'ta|re vt loosen; fig relax. **~si** vr become loose; Mech work loose

aller'gia nf allergy. **al'lergico** a allergic

al'lerta nf o nm inv **stare ~** be on the alert

allesti'mento nm preparation. **~ scenico** Theat set

alle'stire vt prepare; stage (spettacolo); Naut fit out

allet'tante a alluring

allet'tare vt entice

alleva'mento nm breeding; (processo) bringing up; (luogo) farm; (per piante) nursery; **pollo di ~** battery hen or chicken

alle'vare vt bring up (bambini); breed (animali); grow (piante)

allevi'are vt alleviate; fig lighten

alli'bito a astounded

allibra'tore nm bookmaker

allie'tar|e vt gladden. **~si** vr rejoice

alli'evo, -a nmf pupil ● nm Mil cadet

alliga'tore nm alligator

allinea'mento nm alignment

alline'ar|e vt line up; Typ align; Fin adjust. **~si** vr fall into line

'allo = a + lo

al'locco nm tawny owl; fig dunce

al'lodola nf [sky]lark

alloggi'are vt (persona:) put up; (casa:) provide accommodation for; Mil billet ● vi put up, stay; Mil be billeted.

al'loggio nm (appartamento) flat; Mil billet

allontana'mento nm removal

allonta'nar|e vt move away; (licenziare) dismiss; avert (pericolo). ~si vr go away

al'lora adv then; (in quel tempo) at that time; (in tal caso) in that case; d'~ in poi from then on; e ~? what now?; (e con ciò?) so what?; fino ~ until then

al'loro nm laurel; Culin bay

al'luce nm big toe

alluci'na|nte a fam incredible; sostanza ~nte hallucinogen. ~to, -a nmf fam space cadet. ~zi'one nf hallucination

alluci'nogeno a (sostanza) hallucinatory

al'ludere vi ~ a allude to

allu'minio nm aluminium

allun'gar|e vt lengthen; stretch [out] (gamba); extend (tavolo); (diluire) dilute; ~ il collo crane one's neck. ~e le mani su qcno touch sb up. ~e il passo quicken one's step. ~si vr grow longer; (crescere) grow taller; (sdraiarsi) lie down

allusi'one nf allusion

allu'sivo a allusive

alluvio'nale a alluvial

alluvi'one nf flood

al'meno adv at least; [se] ~ venisse il sole! if only the sun would come out!

a'logeno nm halogen ● a lampada alogena halogen lamp

a'lone nm halo

'Alpi nfpl le ~ the Alps

alpi'nis|mo nm mountaineering. ~ta nmf mountaineer

al'pino a Alpine ● nm Mil gli alpini the Alpine troops

al'quanto a a certain amount of ● adv rather

alt int stop

alta'lena nf swing; (tavola in bilico) see-saw

altale'nare vi fig vacillate

alta'mente adv highly

al'tare nm altar

alta'rino nm scoprire gli altarini di qcno reveal sb's guilty secrets

alte'ra|re vt alter; adulterate (vino); (falsificare) falsify. ~rsi vr be altered; (cibo:) go bad; (merci:) deteriorate; (arrabbiarsi) get angry. ~to a (vino) adulterated. ~zi'one nf alteration; (di vino) adulteration

al'terco nm altercation

alter'nanza nf alternation

alter'na|re vt, ~rsi vr alternate. ~'tiva nf alternative. ~'tivo a alternate. ~to a alternating. ~'tore nm Electr alternator

al'tern|o a alternate; a giorni ~i every other day

al'tero a haughty

al'tezza nf height; (profondità) depth; (suono) pitch; (di tessuto) width; (titolo) Highness; essere all'~ di be on a level with; fig be up to

altezzos|a'mente adv haughtily. ~ità nf haughtiness

altez'zoso a haughty

al'ticcio a tipsy, merry

altipi'ano nm plateau

alti'tudine nf altitude

'alto a high; (di statura) tall; (profondo) deep; (suono) high-pitched; (tessuto) wide; Geog northern; a notte alta in the middle of the night; avere degli alti e bassi have some ups and downs; ad alta fedeltà high-fidelity; a voce alta, ad alta voce in a loud voice; (leggere) aloud; essere in ~ mare be on the high seas. alta finanza nf high finance. alta moda nf high fashion. alta tensione nf high voltage ● adv high; in ~ at the top; (guardare) up; mani in ~! hands up!

alto'forno nm blast-furnace

altolà int halt there!

altolo'cato a highly placed

altoparl'ante nm loudspeaker

altopi'ano nm plateau

altret'tanto a & pron as much; (pl) as many ● adv likewise; buona fortuna! grazie, ~ good luck! thank you, the same to you

altri'menti adv otherwise

'altro a other; un ~, un'altra another; l'altr'anno last year; domani l'~ the day after tomorrow; l'ho visto l'~ giorno I saw him the other day ● pron other [one]; un ~, un'altra another [one]; ne vuoi dell'~? would you like some more?; l'un l'~ one another; nessun ~ nobody else; gli altri (la gente) other people ● nm something else; non fa ~ che lavorare he does nothing but work; desidera ~? (in negozio) anything else?; più che ~, sono stanco I'm tired more than anything; se non ~ at least; senz'~ certainly; tra l'~ what's more; ~ che! and how!

altroi'eri nm l'~ the day before yesterday

al'tronde adv d'~ on the other hand

al'trove adv elsewhere

al'trui a other people's ●nm other people's belongings pl

altru'is|mo nm altruism. ~ta nmf altruist

al'tura nf high ground; Naut deep sea

a'lunno, -a nmf pupil

alve'are nm hive

al'za|re vt lift, raise; (costruire) build; Naut hoist; ~re le spalle shrug one's shoulders; ~re i tacchi fig take to one's heels. ~rsi vr rise; (in piedi) stand up; (da letto) get up; ~rsi in piedi get to one's feet. ~ta nf lifting; (aumento) rise; (da letto) getting up; Archit elevation. ~to a up

a'mabile a lovable; (vino) sweet

a'maca nf hammock

amalga'mar|e vt, ~si vr amalgamate

a'mante a ~ di fond of ●nm lover ●nf mistress, lover

ama'rena nf sour black cherry

ama'retto nm macaroon

a'mar|e vt love; be fond of, like (musica, sport ecc). ~to, -a a loved ●nmf beloved

ama'rezza nf bitterness; (dolore) sorrow

a'maro a bitter ●nm bitterness; (liquore) bitters pl

ama'rognolo a rather bitter

ama'tore, -'trice nmf lover

ambasci'a|ta nf embassy; (messaggio) message. ~'tore, ~'trice nm ambassador ●nf ambassadress

ambe'due a & pron both

ambien'ta|le a environmental. ~ li-sta & nmf environmentalist

ambien'tar|e vt acclimatize; set (personaggio, film ecc). ~si vr get acclimatized

ambi'ente nm environment; (stanza) room; fig milieu

ambiguità nf inv ambiguity; (di persona) shadiness

am'biguo a ambiguous; (persona) shady

am'bire vi ~ aspire to

'ambito nm sphere

ambiva'len|te a ambivalent. ~za nf ambivalence

ambizi'o|ne nf ambition. ~so a ambitious

'ambra nf amber. **am'brato** a amber

ambu'lante a wandering; venditore ~ hawker

ambu'lanza nf ambulance

ambula'torio nm (di medico) surgery; (di ospedale) out-patients' [department]

a'meba nf amoeba

'amen int amen

a'meno a pleasant

A'merica nf America. ~ del Sud South America. **ameri'cano, -a** a & nmf American

ame'tista nf amethyst

ami'anto nm asbestos

ami'chevole a friendly

ami'cizia nf friendship; fare ~ con qcnomake friends with sb; amicizie pl (amici) friends

a'mico, -a nmf friend; ~ del cuore bosom friend

'amido nm starch

ammac'ca|re vt dent; bruise (frutto). ~rsi vr (metallo:) get dented; (frutto:) bruise. ~to a dented; (frutto) bruised. ~tura nf dent; (livido) bruise

ammae'stra|re vt (istruire) teach; train (animale). ~to a trained

ammai'nare vt lower (bandiera); furl (vele)

amma'lar|si vr fall ill. ~to, -a a ill ●nmf sick person; (paziente) patient

ammali'are vt bewitch

am'manco nm deficit

ammanet'tare vt handcuff

ammani'cato a essere ~ have connections

amma'raggio nm splashdown

amma'rare vi put down on the sea; (nave spaziale:) splash down

ammas'sar|e vt amass. ~si vr crowd together. **am'masso** nm mass; (mucchio) pile

ammat'tire vi go mad

ammaz'zar|e vt kill. ~si vr (suicidarsi) kill oneself; (rimanere ucciso) be killed

am'menda nf amends pl; (multa) fine; fare ~ di qcsa make amends for sth

am'messo pp di ammettere ●conj ~ che supposing that

am'mettere vt admit; (riconoscere) acknowledge; (supporre) suppose

ammic'care vi wink

ammini'stra|re vt administer; (gestire) run. ~'tivo a administrative. ~'tore, ~'trice nmf administrator; (di azienda) manager; (di società) director. ~'tore delegato managing director. ~zi'one nf administration; fatti di ordinaria ~zione fig routine matters

ammi'ragli|o nm admiral. ~'ato nm admiralty

ammi'ra|re vt admire. ~to a restare/

essere ~**to** be full of admiration. ~**tore**, ~**trice** nmf admirer. ~**zi'one** nf admiration. **ammi'revole** a admirable

ammis'sibile a admissible

ammissi'one nf admission; (approvazione) acknowledgement

ammobili'a|re vt furnish. ~**to** a furnished

am'modo a proper ● adv properly

am'mollo nm in ~ soaking

ammo'niaca nf ammonia

ammoni'mento nm warning; (di rimprovero) admonishment

ammo'ni|re vt warn; (rimproverare) admonish. ~**tore** a admonishing. ~**zi'one** nf Sport warning

ammon'tare vi ~ **a** amount to ● nm amount

ammonticchi'are vt heap up

ammorbi'dente nm (per panni) softener

ammorbi'dir|e vt, ~**si** vr soften

ammorta'mento nm Comm amortization

ammor'tare vt pay off (spesa); Comm amortize (debito)

ammortiz'za|re vt Comm = **ammortare**; Mech damp. ~**tore** nm shock-absorber

ammosci'ar|e vt make flabby. ~**si** vi get flabby

ammucchi'a|re vt, ~**rsi** vr pile up. ~**ta** nf (sl: orgia) orgy

ammuf'fi|re vi go mouldy. ~**to** a mouldy

ammutina'mento nm mutiny

ammuti'narsi vr mutiny

ammuto'lire vi be struck dumb

amne'sia nf amnesia

amni'stia nf amnesty

'amo nm hook; fig bait

amo'rale a amoral

a'more nm love; **fare l'~** make love; **per l'amor di Dio/del cielo!** for heaven's sake!; **andare d'~ e d'accordo** get on like a house on fire; ~ **proprio** self-respect; **è un ~** (persona) he/she is a darling; **per ~ di** for the sake of; **amori** pl love affairs. ~**ggi'are** vi flirt.

amo'revole a loving

a'morfo a shapeless; (persona) colourless, grey

amo'roso a loving; (sguardo ecc) amorous; (lettera, relazione) love

ampi'ezza nf (di esperienza) breadth; (di stanza) spaciousness; (di gonna) fullness; (importanza) scale

'ampio a ample; (esperienza) wide; (stanza) spacious; (vestito) loose; (gonna) full; (pantaloni) baggy

am'plesso nm embrace

amplia'mento nm (di casa, porto) enlargement; (di strada) widening

ampli'are vt broaden (conoscenze)

amplifi'ca|re vt amplify; fig magnify. ~**tore** nm amplifier. ~**zi'one** nf amplification

am'polla nf cruet

ampol'loso a pompous

ampu'ta|re vt amputate. ~**zi'one** nf amputation

amu'leto nm amulet

anabbagli'ante a Auto dipped ● nmpl **anabbaglianti** dipped headlights

anacro'nis|mo nm anachronism. ~**tico** a **essere** ~ be an anachronism

a'nagrafe nf (ufficio) registry office; (registro) register of births, marriages and deaths

ana'grafico a **dati** nmpl **anagrafici** personal data

ana'gramma nm anagram

anal'colico a non-alcoholic ● nm soft drink, non-alcoholic drink

a'nale a anal

analfa'be|ta a & nmf illiterate. ~**tismo** nm illiteracy

anal'gesico nm painkiller

a'nalisi nf inv analysis; Med test. ~ **grammaticale/del periodo/logica** parsing. ~ **del sangue** blood test

ana'lista nmf analyst. ~**tico** a analytical. ~**z'zare** vt analyse; Med test

anal'lergico a hypoallergenic

analo'gia nf analogy. **a'nalogo** a analogous

'ananas nm inv pineapple

anar'chi|a nf anarchy. **a'narchico, -a** a anarchic ● nmf anarchist. ~**smo** nm anarchism

A.N.A.S. nf abbr (Azienda Nazionale Autonoma delle Strade) national road maintenance authority

anato'mia nf anatomy. **ana'tomico** a anatomical; (sedia) contoured, ergonomic

'anatra nf duck

ana'troccolo nm duckling

'anca nf hip; (di animale) flank

ance'strale a ancestral

'anche conj also, too; (persino) even; ~ **se** even if; ~ **domani** tomorrow also o too, also tomorrow

anchilo'sato a fig stiff

an'cora *adv* still, yet; (*di nuovo*) again; (*di più*) some more; ~ **una volta** once more

'ancora *nf* anchor; **gettare l'~ra** drop anchor. ~'raggio *nm* anchorage. ~'rare *vt* anchor

anda'mento *nm* (*del mercato, degli affari*) trend

an'dante *a* (*corrente*) current; (*di poco valore*) cheap ●*nm* Mus andante

an'dare *vi* go; (*funzionare*) work; ~ **via** (*partire*) leave; (*macchia:*) come out; ~ |bene| (*confarsi*) suit; (*taglia:*) fit; **ti va bene alle tre?** does three o'clock suit you?; **non mi va di mangiare** I don't feel like eating; ~ **di fretta** be in a hurry; ~ **fiero di** be proud of; ~ **di moda** be in fashion; **va per i 20 anni** he's nearly 20; **ma va' |là|!** come on!; **come va?** how are things?; ~ **a male** go off; ~ **a fuoco** go up in flames; **va spedito |entro| stamattina** it must be sent this morning; **ne va del mio lavoro** my job is at stake; **come è andata a finire?** how did it turn out?; **cosa vai dicendo?** what are you talking about?. ~**rsene** go away; (*morire*) pass away ●*nm* going; **a lungo** ~**re** eventually

'andito *nm* passage

an'drone *nm* entrance

a'neddoto *nm* anecdote

ane'lare *vt* ~ **a** long for. a'nelito *nm* longing

a'nello *nm* ring; (*di catena*) link

ane'mia *nf* anaemia. a'nemico *a* anaemic

a'nemone *nm* anemone

aneste'sia *nf* anaesthesia; (*sostanza*) anaesthetic. ~'sta *nmf* anaesthetist. ane'stetico *a & nm* anaesthetic

an'fibi *nmpl* (*stivali*) army boots

an'fibio *nm* (*animale*) amphibian ●*a* amphibious

anfite'atro *nm* amphitheatre

'anfora *nf* amphora

an'fratto *nm* ravine

an'gelico *a* angelic

'angelo *nm* angel. ~ **custode** guardian angel

angli'cano *a* Anglican. ~**ismo** *nm* Anglicism

an'glofilo, -a *a & nmf* Anglophile

an'glofono, -a *nmf* English-speaker

anglo'sassone *a & nmf* Anglo-Saxon

ango'lare *a* angular. ~**zi|one** *nf* angle shot

'angolo *nm* corner; Math angle. ~ |di| cottura kitchenette

ango'loso *a* angular

an'goscia *nf* anguish. ~**are** *vt* torment. ~**ato** *a* agonized. ~**oso** *a* (*disperato*) anguished; (*che dà angoscia*) distressing

angu'illa *nf* eel

an'guria *nf* water-melon

an'gustia *nf* (*ansia*) anxiety; (*penuria*) poverty. ~**are** *vt* distress. ~**arsi** *vr* be very worried (**per** about)

an'gusto *a* narrow

'anice *nm* anise; Culin aniseed; (*liquore*) anisette

ani'dride *nf* ~ **carbonica** carbon dioxide

'anima *nf* soul; **non c'era ~ viva** there was not a soul about; **all'~!** good grief!; **un'~ in pena** a soul in torment. ~ **gemella** soul mate

ani'male *a & nm* animal; ~**li domestici** *pl* pets. ~'lesco *a* animal

ani'mare *vt* give life to; (*ravvivare*) enliven; (*incoraggiare*) encourage. ~**rsi** *vr* come to life; (*accalorarsi*) become animated. ~**to** *a* animate; (*discussione*) animated; (*strada, paese*) lively. ~'tore, ~ **trice** *nmf* leading spirit; Cinema animator. ~**zi|one** *nf* animation

'animo *nm* (*mente*) mind; (*indole*) disposition; (*cuore*) heart; **perdersi d'~** lose heart; **farsi ~** take heart. ~**sità** *nf* animosity

ani'moso *a* brave; (*ostile*) hostile

'anitra *nf* = anatra

annac'qua|re *vt anche fig* water down. ~**to** *a* watered down

annaffi'a|re *vt* water. ~**toio** *nm* watering-can

an'nali *nmpl* annals

anna'spare *vi* flounder

an'nata *nf* year; (*importo annuale*) annual amount; (*di vino*) vintage

annebbia'mento *nm* fog build-up; *fig* clouding

annebbi'a|re *vt* cloud (*vista, mente*). ~**si** *vr* become foggy; (*vista, mente:*) grow dim

annega'mento *nm* drowning

anne'ga|re *vt/i* drown

anne'rir|e *vt/i* blacken. ~**si** *vr* become black

annessi'one *nf* (*di nazione*) annexation

an'nesso *pp di* annettere ●*a* attached; (*Stato*) annexed

an'nettere vt add; (accludere) enclose; annex (Stato)

annichi'lire vt annihilate

anni'darsi vr nest

annienta'mento nm annihilation

annien'tar|e vt annihilate. **~si** vr abase oneself

anniver'sario a & nm anniversary. **~ di matrimonio** wedding anniversary

'anno nm year; **Buon A~!** Happy New Year!; **quanti anni ha?** how old are you?; **Tommaso ha dieci anni** Thomas is ten [years old]. **~ bisestile** leap year

anno'dar|e vt knot; do up (cintura); fig form. **~si** vr become knotted

annoi'a|re vt bore; (recare fastidio) annoy. **~rsi** vr get bored; (condizione) be bored. **~to** a bored

anno'ta|re vt note down; annotate (testo). **~zi'one** nf note

annove'rare vt number

annu'a|le a annual, yearly. **~rio** nm year-book

annu'ire vi nod; (acconsentire) agree

annulla'mento nm annulment; (di appuntamento) cancellation

annul'lar|e vt annul; cancel (appuntamento); (togliere efficacia a) undo; disallow (gol); (distruggere) destroy. **~si** vr cancel each other out

annunci'a|re vt announce; (preannunciare) foretell. **~tore, ~trice** nmf announcer. **~zi'one** nf Annunciation

an'nuncio nm announcement; (pubblicitario) advertisement; (notizia) news. **annunci** pl **economici** classified advertisements

'annuo a annual, yearly

annu'sare vt sniff

annuvo'lar|e vt cloud. **~si** vr cloud over

'ano nm anus

anoma'lia nf anomaly

a'nomalo a anomalous

anoni'mato nm **mantenere l'~** remain anonymous

a'nonimo, -a a anonymous ● nmf (pittore, scrittore) anonymous painter/writer

anores'sia nf Med anorexia

ano'ressico, -a nmf anorexic

anor'mal|e a abnormal ● nmf deviant, abnormal person. **~ità** nf inv abnormality

'ansa nf handle; (di fiume) bend

an'sare vi pant

'ansia, ansietà nf anxiety; **stare/essere in ~ per** be anxious about

ansi'oso a anxious

antago'nis|mo nm antagonism. **~ta** nmf antagonist

an'tartico a & nm Antarctic

antece'dente a preceding ● nm precedent

ante'fatto nm prior event

ante'guerra a pre-war ● nm pre-war period

ante'nato, -a nmf ancestor

an'tenna nf Radio, TV aerial; (di animale) antenna; Naut yard. **~ parabolica** satellite dish

ante'porre vt put before

ante'prima nf preview; **vedere qcsa in ~** have a sneak preview of sth

anteri'ore a front attrib; (nel tempo) previous

antiade'rente a (padella) nonstick

antia'ereo a anti-aircraft attrib

antial'lergico a hypoallergenic

antia'tomico a **rifugio ~** fallout shelter

antibi'otico a & nm antibiotic

anti'caglia nf (oggetto) piece of old junk

antica'mente adv in ancient times, long ago

anti'camera nf ante-room; **far ~** be kept waiting

antichità nf inv antiquity; (oggetto) antique

antici'clone nm anticyclone

antici'pa|re vt advance; Comm pay in advance; (prevedere) anticipate; (prevenire) forestall ● vi be early. **~ta'mente** adv in advance. **~zi'one** nf anticipation; (notizia) advance news

an'ticipo nm advance; (caparra) deposit; **in ~** early; (nel lavoro) ahead of schedule

an'tico a ancient; (mobile ecc) antique; (vecchio) old; **all'antica** old-fashioned ● nmpl **gli antichi** the ancients

anticonceziona'nale a & nm contraceptive

anticonfor'mis|mo nm unconventionality. **~ta** nmf nonconformist. **~tico** a unconventional, nonconformist

anticonge'lante a & nm anti-freeze

anti'corpo nm antibody

anticostituzio'nale a unconstitutional

anti'crimine a inv (squadra) crime attrib

antidemo'cratico a undemocratic

antidolo'rifico nm painkiller

an'tidoto nm antidote

anti'droga a inv (campagna) anti-drugs; (squadra) drug attrib

antie'stetico a ugly

antifa'scismo nm anti-fascism

antifa'scista a & nmf anti-fascist

anti'forfora a inv dandruff attrib

anti'furto nm anti-theft device; (allarme) alarm ● a inv (sistema) anti-theft

anti'gelo nm antifreeze; (parabrezza) defroster

antigi'enico a unhygienic

An'tille nfpl le ~ the West Indies

an'tilope nf antelope

antin'cendio a inv allarme ~ fire alarm; porta ~ fire door

anti'nebbia nm inv Auto [faro] ~ foglamp, foglight

antinfiamma'torio a & nm anti-inflammatory

antinucle'are a anti-nuclear

antio'rario a anti-clockwise

anti'pasto nm hors d'oeuvre, starter

antipa'tia nf antipathy. **anti'patico** a unpleasant

an'tipodi nmpl antipodes; essere agli ~ fig be poles apart

antiquari'ato nm antique trade

anti'quario, -a nmf antique dealer

anti'quato a antiquated

anti'ruggine nm inv rust-inhibitor

anti'rughe a inv anti-wrinkle attrib

anti'scippo a inv theft-proof

antise'mita a anti-Semitic

anti'settico a & nm antiseptic

antisoci'ale a anti-social

antista'minico nm antihistamine

anti'stante a prep in front of

anti'tarlo nm inv woodworm treatment

antiterro'ristico a antiterrorist attrib

an'titesi nf inv antithesis

antolo'gia nf anthology

'antro nm cavern

antropolo'gia nf anthropology. **antro'pologo, -a** nmf anthropologist

anu'lare nm ring-finger

'anzi conj in fact; (o meglio) or better still; (al contrario) on the contrary

anziani'tà nf old age; (di servizio) seniority

anzi'ano, -a a old, elderly; (di grado ecc) senior ● nmf elderly person

anzi'ché conj rather than

anzi'tempo adv prematurely

anzi'tutto adv first of all

a'orta nf aorta

apar'titico a unaligned

apa'tia nf apathy. **a'patico** a apathetic

'ape nf bee; **'nido** nm di api honeycomb

aperi'tivo nm aperitif

aperta'mente adv openly

a'perto a open; **all'aria aperta** in the open air; **all'**~ open-air

aper'tura nf opening; (inizio) beginning; (ampiezza) spread; (di arco) span; Pol overtures pl; Phot aperture; ~ **mentale** openness

'apice nm apex

apicol'tura nf beekeeping

ap'nea nf immersione in ~ free diving

a'polide a stateless ● nmf stateless person

a'postolo nm apostle

apostro'fare vt (mettere un apostrofo a) write with an apostrophe; reprimand (persona)

a'postrofo nm apostrophe

appaga'mento nm fulfilment

appa'ga|re vt satisfy. ~**rsi** vr ~**rsi di** be satisfied with

appai'are vt pair; mate (animali)

appallotto'lare vt roll into a ball

appalta'tore nm contractor

ap'palto nm contract; **dare in** ~ contract out

appan'naggio nm (in denaro) annuity; fig prerogative

appan'na|re vt mist (vetro); dim (vista). ~**si** vr mist over; (vista:) grow dim

appa'rato nm apparatus; (pompa) display

apparecchi'a|re vt prepare ● vi lay the table. ~**tura** nf (impianti) equipment

appa'recchio nm apparatus; (congegno) device; (radio, TV ecc) set; (aeroplano) aircraft. ~ **acustico** hearing aid

appa'ren|te a apparent. ~**te'mente** adv apparently. ~**za** nf appearance; **in** ~**za** apparently.

appa'ri|re vi appear; (sembrare) look. ~ **scente** a striking; pej gaudy. ~**zi'one** nf apparition

apparta'mento nm flat, apartment Am

appar'ta|rsi vr withdraw. ~**to** a secluded

apparte'nenza nf membership

apparte'nere vi belong

appassio'nante a (storia, argomento) exciting

appassio'na|re vt excite; (commuovere) move. ~**rsi** vr ~**rsi a** become excited by. **~to** *a* passionate; **~to di** *(entusiastico)* fond of

appas'sir|e *vi* wither. **~si** *vr* fade

appel'larsi *vr* **~ a** appeal to

ap'pello *nm* appeal; *(chiamata per nome)* rollcall; *(esami)* exam session; **fare l'~** call the roll

ap'pena *adv* just; *(a fatica)* hardly ●*conj* [non] **~** as soon as, no sooner... than

ap'pendere *vt* hang [up]

appendi'abiti *nm inv* hat-stand

appen'dice *nf* appendix. **appendi·cite** *nf* appendicitis

Appen'nini *nmpl* **gli ~** the Apennines

appesan'tir|e *vt* weigh down. **~si** *vr* become heavy

ap'peso *pp di* **appendere** ●*a* hanging; *(impiccato)* hanged

appe'ti|to *nm* appetite; **aver ~to** be hungry; **ouon ~to!** enjoy your meal!. **~'toso** *a* appetizing; *fig* tempting

appezza'mento *nm* plot of land

appia'nar|e *vt* level; *fig* smooth over. **~si** *vr* improve

appiat'tir|e *vt* flatten. **~si** *vr* flatten oneself

appic'care *vt* **~ il fuoco** set fire to

appicci'car|e *vt* stick; **~e a** *(fig: appioppare)* palm off on ●*vi* be sticky. **~si** *vr* stick; *(cose:)* stick together; **~si a qcno** *fig* stick to sb like glue

appiccica'ticcio *a* sticky; *fig* clingy

appicci'coso *a* sticky; *fig* clingy

appie'dato *a* **sono ~** I don't have the car; **sono rimasto ~** I was stranded

appi'eno *adv* fully

appigli'arsi *vr* **~ a** get hold of; *fig* stick to. **ap'piglio** *nm* fingerhold; *(per piedi)* foothold; *fig* pretext

appiop'pare *vt* **~ a** palm off on; *(fam: dare)* give

appiso'larsi *vr* doze off

applau'dire *vt/i* applaud. **ap'plauso** *nm* applause

appli'cabile *a* applicable

appli'ca|re *vt* apply; enforce *(legge ecc)*. **~rsi** *vr* apply oneself. **~'tore** *nm* applicator. **~zi'one** *nf* application; *(di legge)* enforcement

appoggi'ar|e *vt* lean (**a** against); *(mettere)* put; *(sostenere)* back. **~si a** a lean against; *fig* rely on. **ap'poggio** *nm* support

appollai'arsi *vr* *fig* perch

ap'porre *vt* affix

appor'tare *vt* bring; *(causare)* cause. **ap'porto** *nm* contribution

apposita'mente *adv* *(specialmente)* especially

ap'posito *a* proper

ap'posta *adv* on purpose; *(espressamente)* specially

apposta'mento *nm* ambush; *(caccia)* lying in wait

appo'star|e *vt* post *(soldati)*. **~si** *vr* lie in wait

ap'prend|ere *vt* understand; *(imparare)* learn. **~i'mento** *nm* learning

appren'di|sta *nmf* apprentice. **~'stato** *nm* apprenticeship

apprensi'one *nf* apprehension; **essere in ~ per** be anxious about. **appren'sivo** *a* apprehensive

ap'presso *adv* & *prep (vicino)* near; *(dietro)* behind; **come ~** as follows

appre'star|e *vt* prepare. **~si** *vr* get ready

apprez'zabile *a* appreciable. **~'mento** *nm* appreciation; *(giudizio)* opinion

apprez'za|re *vt* appreciate. **~to a** appreciated

ap'proccio *nm* approach

appro'dare *vi* land; **~ a** *fig* come to; **non ~ a nulla** come to nothing. **ap'prodo** *nm* landing; *(luogo)* landing-stage

approfit'tare *vi* take advantage (**di** of), profit (**di** by). **~tore**, **~'trice** *nmf* chancer

approfondi'mento *nm* deepening; **di ~** *(fig: corso)* advanced

approfon'dire *vt* deepen. **~rsi** *vr (divario:)* widen. **~to** *a (studio, ricerca)* in-depth

appropri'arsi *vr* take possession (**di** of); *(essere adatto a)* suit. **~to a** appropriate. **~zi'one** *nf* Jur appropriation. **~zione indebita** *Jur* embezzlement

approssi'ma|re *vt* **~re per eccesso/difetto** round up/down. **~rsi** *vr* draw near. **~tiva'mente** *adv* approximately. **~'tivo** *a* approximate. **~zi'one** *nf* approximation

appro'va|re *vt* approve of; approve *(legge)*. **~zi'one** *nf* approval

approvvigiona'mento *nm* supplying; **approvvigionamenti** *pl* provisions

approvvigio'nar|e *vt* supply. **~si** *vr* stock up

appunta'mento *nm* appointment, date *fam*; **fissare un ~** make an appointment; **darsi ~** decide to meet

appun'tar|e *vt (annotare)* take notes; *(fissare)* fix; *(con spillo)* pin; *(appuntire)*

appun'ti|re vt sharpen. ~**to** a (mento) pointed

ap'punto[1] nm note; (piccola critica) niggle

ap'punto[2] adv exactly; **per l'~!** exactly!; **stavo ~ dicendo...** I was just saying...

appu'rare vt verify

a'pribile a that can be opened

apribot'tiglie nm inv bottle-opener

a'prile nm April; **il primo d'~** April Fools' Day

a'pri|re vt open; turn on (luce, acqua ecc); (con chiave) unlock; open up (ferita ecc). ~**si** vr open; (spaccarsi) split; (confidarsi) confide (**con** in)

apri'scatole nf inv tin-opener

aqua'planing nm andare in ~ aquaplane

'**aquila** nf eagle; **non è un'~a!** he is no genius!. ~**lino** a aquiline

aqui'lone nm (giocattolo) kite

ara'besco nm arabesque; hum scribble

A'rabia Sau'dita nf l'~ Saudi Arabia

'**arabo, -a** a Arab; (lingua) Arabic ●nm Arab ●nm (lingua) Arabic

a'rachide nf peanut

ara'gosta nf lobster

a'rancia nf orange. ~ **ata** nf orangeade. ~**o** nm orange-tree; (colore) orange. ~'**one** a & nm orange

a'ra|re vt plough. ~**tro** nm plough

ara'tura nf ploughing

a'razzo nm tapestry

arbi'tra|re vt arbitrate in; Sport referee. ~**ietà** nf arbitrariness. ~**io** a arbitrary

ar'bitrio nm will; **è un ~** it's very high-handed

'**arbitro** nm arbiter; Sport referee; (nel baseball) umpire

ar'busto nm shrub

'**arca** nf ark; (cassa) chest

ar'ca|ico a archaic. ~ '**ismo** nm archaism

ar'cangelo nm archangel

ar'cata nf arch; (serie di archi) arcade

arche|olo'gia nf archaeology. ~**o'logico** a archaeological. ~'**ologo, -a** nmf archaeologist

ar'chetto nm Mus bow

architet'tare vt fig devise; **cosa state architettando?** fig what are you plotting?

archi'tet|to nm architect. ~**'tonico** a architectural. ~**'tura** nf architecture

archivi'are vt file; Jur close

ar'chivio nm archives pl; Comput file

archi'vista nmf filing clerk

ar'cigno a grim

arci'pelago nm archipelago

arci'vescovo nm archbishop

'**arco** nm arch; Math arc; (arma, Mus) bow; **nell'~ di una giornata/due mesi** in the space of a day/two months

arcoba'leno nm rainbow

arcu'a|re vt bend. ~**rsi** vr bend. ~**to** a bent, curved; (schiena di gatto) arched

ar'dente a burning; fig ardent. ~'**mente** adv ardently

'**ardere** vt/i burn

ar'desia nf slate

ar'di|re vi dare. ~**to** a daring; (coraggioso) bold; (sfacciato) impudent

ar'dore nm (calore) heat; fig ardour

'**arduo** a arduous; (ripido) steep

'**area** nf area. ~ **di rigore** (in calcio) penalty area. ~ **di servizio** service area

a'**rena** nf arena

are'narsi vr run aground; (fig: trattative) reach deadlock; **mi sono arenato** I'm stuck

'**argano** nm winch

argen'tato a silver-plated

argente'ria nf silver[ware]

ar'gento nm silver

ar'gil|la nf clay. ~'**loso** a (terreno) clayey

argi'nare vt embank; fig hold in check, contain

'**argine** nm embankment; (diga) dike

argomen'tare vi argue

argo'mento nm argument; (motivo) reason; (soggetto) subject

argu'ire vt deduce

ar'gu|to a witty. ~**zia** nf wit; (battuta) witticism

'**aria** nf air; (aspetto) appearance; Mus tune; **andare all'~** fig come to nothing; **avere l'~...** look...; **corrente** nf **d'~** draught; **mandare all'~** qcsa fig ruin sth

aridità nf dryness

'**arido** a arid

arieg'gia|re vt air. ~**to** a airy

ari'ete nm ram. **A~** Astr Aries

ari'etta nf (brezza) breeze

a'ringa nf herring

ari'oso a (locale) light and airy

aristo'cra|tico, -a a aristocratic ●nmf aristocrat. ~**zia** nf aristocracy

arit'metica nf arithmetic

arlec'chino nm Harlequin; fig buffoon

'arma nf weapon; **armi** pl arms; (forze armate) [armed] forces; **chiamare alle armi** call up; **sotto le armi** in the army; **alle prime armi** fig inexperienced, fledg[e]ling. **~ da fuoco** firearm. **~ impropria** makeshift weapon. **~ a doppio taglio** fig double-edged sword

armadi'etto nm locker, cupboard

ar'madio nm cupboard; (guardaroba) wardrobe

armamen'tario nm tools pl; fig paraphernalia

arma'mento nm armament; Naut fitting out

ar'ma|re vt arm; (equipaggiare) fit out; Archit reinforce. **~rsi** vr arm oneself (di with). **~ta** nf army; (flotta) fleet. **~tore** nm shipowner. **~tura** nf framework; (impalcatura) scaffolding; (di guerriero) armour

armeggi'are vi fig manoeuvre

armi'stizio nm armistice

armo'ni|a nf harmony. **ar'monica** nf **~ [a bocca]** mouth organ. **ar'monico** a harmonic. **~oso** a harmonious

armoniz'zar|e vt harmonize ●vi match. **~si** vr (colori:) go together, match

ar'nese nm tool; (oggetto) thing; (congegno) gadget; **male in ~** in bad condition

'arnia nf beehive

a'roma nm aroma; **aromi** pl herbs. **~tera'pia** nf aromatherapy

aro'matico a aromatic

aromatiz'zare vt flavour

'arpa nf harp

ar'peggio nm arpeggio

ar'pia nf harpy

arpi'one nm hook; (pesca) harpoon

arrabat'tarsi vr try, do all one can

arrabbi'a|rsi vr get angry. **~to** a angry. **~tura** nf rage; **prendersi un'~tura** fly into a rage

arraf'fare vt grab

arrampi'ca|rsi vr climb [up]. **~ta** nf climb. **~tore, ~trice** nmf climber. **~tore sociale** social climber

arran'care vi limp, hobble; fig struggle, limp along

arrangia'mento nm arrangement

arrangi'ar|e vt arrange. **~si** vr manage; **~si alla meglio** get by; **ar'rangiati!** get on with it!

arra'parsi vr fam get randy

arre'care vt bring; (causare) cause

arreda'mento nm interior decoration; (l'arredare) furnishing; (mobili ecc) furnishings pl

arre'da|re vt furnish. **~tore, ~trice** nmf interior designer. **ar'redo** nm furnishings pl

ar'rendersi vr surrender

arren'devo|le a (persona) yielding. **~lezza** nf softness

arre'star|e vt arrest; (fermare) stop. **~si** vr halt. **ar'resto** nm stop; Med, Jur arrest; **la dichiaro in [stato d']arresto** you are under arrest; **mandato di arresto** warrant. **arresti** pl **domiciliari** Jur house arrest

arre'tra|re vt/i withdraw; pull back (giocatore). **~to** a (paese ecc) backward; (Mil: posizione) rear; **numero** nm **~to** (di rivista) back number; **del lavoro ~to** a backlog of work ●nm (di stipendio) back pay

arre'trati nmpl arrears

arricchi'mento nm enrichment

arric'chi|re vt enrich. **~rsi** vr get rich. **~to, -a** nmf nouveau riche

arricci'are vt curl; **~ il naso** turn up one's nose

ar'ringa nf harangue; Jur closing address

arrischi'arsi vr dare. **~to** a risky; (imprudente) rash

arri'va|re vi arrive; **~re a** (raggiungere) reach; (ridursi) be reduced to. **~to, -a** a successful; **ben ~to!** welcome! ●nmf successful person

arrive'derci int goodbye; **~ a domani** see you tomorrow

arri'vismo nm social climbing; (nel lavoro) careerism. **~ta** nmf social climber; (nel lavoro) careerist

ar'rivo nm arrival; Sport finish

arro'gan|te a arrogant. **~za** nf arrogance

arro'garsi vr **~ il diritto di fare qc** take it upon oneself to do sth

arrossa'mento nm reddening

arros'sar|e vt make red, redden (occhi). **~si** vr go red

arros'sire vi blush, go red

arro'stire vt roast; toast (pane); (ai ferri) grill. **ar'rosto** a & nm roast

arroto'lare vt roll up

arroton'dar|e vt round; Math ecc round off. **~si** vr become round; (persona:) get plump

arrovel'larsi *vr* ~ il cervello rack one's brains

arroven'ta|re *vt* make red-hot. ~rsi *vr* become red-hot. ~to *a* red-hot

arruf'fa|re *vt* ruffle; *fig* confuse. ~to *a* ⟨*capelli*⟩ ruffled

arruffianarsi *vr* ~ qcno *fig* butter sb up

arruggi'ni|re *vt* rust. ~rsi *vr* go rusty; *fig* ⟨*fisicamente*⟩ stiffen up; ⟨*conoscenze:*⟩ go rusty. ~to *a* rusty

arruola'mento *nm* enlistment

arruo'la|re *vt/i,* ~si *vr* enlist

arse'nale *nm* arsenal; ⟨*cantiere*⟩ [naval] dockyard

ar'senico *nm* arsenic

'arso *pp di* ardere ●*a* burnt; ⟨*arido*⟩ dry. ar'sura *nf* burning heat; ⟨*sete*⟩ parching thirst

'arte *nf* art; ⟨*abilità*⟩ craftsmanship; le belle arti the fine arts. arti figurative figurative arts

arte'fa|re *vt* adulterate ⟨*vino*⟩; disguise ⟨*voce*⟩. ~tto *a* fake; ⟨*vino*⟩ adulterated

ar'tefice   *nmf*   craftsman; craftswoman; *fig* author

ar'teria *nf* artery. ~ [stradale] arterial road

arterioscle'rosi *nf* arteriosclerosis, hardening of the arteries

'artico *a & nm* Arctic

artico'la|re *a* articular ●*vt* articulate; ⟨*suddividere*⟩ divide. ~rsi *vr fig* ~rsi in consist of. ~to *a Auto* articulated; *fig* well-constructed. ~zi'one *nf Anat* articulation

ar'ticolo *nm* article. ~ di fondo leader

artifici'ale *a* artificial

arti'fici|o *nm* artifice; ⟨*affettazione*⟩ affectation. ~'oso *a* artful; ⟨*affettato*⟩ affected

artigia'nal|e *a* made by hand; *hum* amateurish. ~'mente *adv* with craftsmanship; *hum* amateurishly

artigia'nato *nm* craftsmanship; ⟨*ceto*⟩ craftsmen *pl.* ~'ano, -a *nm* craftsman ●*nf* craftswoman

artigli'ere *nm* artilleryman. ~e'ria *nf* artillery

ar'tiglio *nm* claw; *fig* clutch

ar'tist|a *nmf* artist. ~ica'mente *adv* artistically. ~ico *a* artistic

'arto *nm* limb

ar'trite *nf* arthritis

ar'trosi *nf* rheumatism

arzigogo'lato *a* fantastic, bizarre

ar'zillo *a* sprightly

a'scella *nf* armpit

ascen'dente *a* ascending ●*nm* ⟨*antenato*⟩ ancestor; ⟨*influenza*⟩ ascendancy; *Astr* ascendant

ascensi'one *nf* ascent; l'A~ the Ascension

ascen'sore *nm* lift, elevator *Am*

a'sce|sa *nf* ascent; ⟨*al trono*⟩ accession; ⟨*al potere*⟩ rise

a'scesso *nm* abscess

a'sceta *nmf* ascetic

'ascia *nf* axe

asciugabianche'ria *nm inv* ⟨*stenditoio*⟩ clothes horse

asciugaca'pelli *nm inv* hair dryer, hairdrier

asciuga'mano *nm* towel

asciu'ga|re *vt* dry. ~si *vr* dry oneself; ⟨*diventare asciutto*⟩ dry up

asci'utto *a* dry; ⟨*magro*⟩ wiry; ⟨*risposta*⟩ curt; essere all'~ *fig* be hard up

ascol'ta|re *vt* listen to ●*vi* listen. ~'tore, ~'trice *nmf* listener

a'scolto *nm* listening; dare ~ a pay attention to; mettersi in ~ *Radio* tune in

asfal'tare *vt* asphalt

a'sfalto *nm* asphalt

asfis'si|a *nf* asphyxia. ~'ante *a* ⟨*caldo*⟩ oppressive; ⟨*fig: persona*⟩ annoying. ~'are *vt* asphyxiate; *fig* annoy

'Asia *nf* Asia. asi'atico, -a *a & nmf* Asian

a'silo *nm* shelter; ⟨*d'infanzia*⟩ nursery school. ~ nido day nursery. ~ politico political asylum

asim'metrico *a* asymmetrical

'asino *nm* donkey; ⟨*fig: persona stupida*⟩ ass

'asma *nf* asthma. a'smatico *a* asthmatic

asoci'ale *a* asocial

'asola *nf* buttonhole

a'sparagi *nmpl* asparagus *sg*

a'sparago *nm* asparagus spear

asperità *nf inv* harshness; ⟨*di terreno*⟩ roughness

aspet'ta|re *vt* wait for; ⟨*prevedere*⟩ expect; ~re un bambino be expecting [a baby]; fare ~re qcno keep sb waiting ●*vi* wait. ~rsi *vr* expect. ~'tiva *nf* expectation

a'spetto¹ *nm* appearance; ⟨*di problema*⟩ aspect; di bell'~ good-looking

a'spetto² *nm* sala *nf* d'~ waiting room

aspi'rante *a* aspiring; ⟨*pompa*⟩ suction *attrib* ●*nmf* ⟨*a un posto*⟩ applicant;

(al trono) aspirant; **gli aspiranti al titolo** the contenders for the title

aspira'polvere nm inv vacuum cleaner

aspi'ra|re vt inhale; Mech suck in ● vi ~**re a** aspire to. ~**tore** nm extractor fan. ~**zi'one** nf inhalation; Mech suction; (ambizione) ambition

aspi'rina nf aspirin

aspor'tare vt take away

aspra'mente adv (duramente) severely

a'sprezza nf (al gusto) sourness; (di clima) severity; (di suono) harshness; (di odore) pungency

'aspro a (al gusto) sour; (clima) severe; (suono, parole) harsh; (odore) pungent; (litigio) bitter

assag'gia|re vt taste. ~**gini** nmpl Culin samples. **as'saggio** nm tasting; (piccola quantità) taste

as'sai adv very; (moltissimo) very much; (abbastanza) enough

assa'li|re vt attack. ~**tore**, ~'**trice** nmf assailant

as'salto nm attack; **prendere d'~** storm (città); fig mob (persona); hold up (banca)

assapo'rare vt savour

assassi'nare vt murder, assassinate; fig murder

assas'sin|io nm murder, assassination. ~**o, -a** a murderous ● nm murderer ● nf murderess

'asse nf board ● nm Techn axle; Math axis. ~ **da stiro** ironing board

assecon'dare vt satisfy; (favorire) support

assedi'are vt besiege. **as'sedio** nm siege

assegna'mento nm allotment; **fare ~ su** rely on

asse'gna|re vt allot; award (premio). ~'**tario** nmf recipient. ~**zi'one** nf (di alloggio, denaro, borsa di studio) allocation

as'segno nm allowance; (bancario) cheque; **contro ~** cash on delivery. ~ **circolare** bank draft. **assegni** pl **familiari** family allowance. ~ **non trasferibile** cheque made out to 'account payee only'

assem'blea nf assembly; (adunanza) gathering

assembra'mento nm gathering

assen'nato a sensible

as'senso nm assent

assen'tarsi vr go away; (da stanza) leave the room

as'sen|te a absent; (distratto) absentminded ● nmf absentee. ~**te'ismo** nm absenteeism. ~**te'ista** nmf frequent absentee. ~**za** nf absence; (mancanza) lack

asse'r|ire vt assert. ~'**tivo** a assertive. ~**zi'one** nf assertion

asses'sorato nm department

asses'sore nm councillor

assesta'mento nm settlement

asse'st|are vt arrange; ~**e un colpo** deal a blow. ~**si** vr settle oneself

asse'tato a parched

as'setto nm order; Naut, Aeron trim

assicu'ra|re vt assure; Comm insure; register (posta); (fissare) secure; (accertare) ensure. ~**rsi** vr (con contratto) insure oneself; (legarsi) fasten oneself; ~**rsi che** make sure that. ~'**tivo** a insurance attrib. ~'**tore**, ~'**trice** nmf insurance agent ● a insurance attrib. ~**zi'one** nf assurance; (contratto) insurance

assidera'mento nm exposure. **asside'rato** a Med suffering from exposure; fam frozen

assidua'mente adv assiduously. ~**ità** nf assiduity

as'siduo a assiduous; (cliente) regular

assil'lante a (persona, pensiero) nagging

assil'lare vt pester

as'sillo nm worry

assimi'la|re vt assimilate. ~**zi'one** nf assimilation

as'sise nfpl assizes; **Corte d'A~** Court of Assize[s]

assi'sten|te nmf assistant. ~**te sociale** social worker. ~**te di volo** flight attendant. ~**za** nf assistance; (presenza) presence. ~**za sociale** social work

assistenzi'ale a welfare attrib. ~'**lismo** nm welfare

as'sistere vt assist; (curare) nurse ● vi ~ **a** (essere presente) be present at; watch (spettacolo ecc)

'asso nm ace; **piantare in ~** leave in the lurch

associ'a|re vt join; (collegare) associate. ~**rsi** vr join forces; Comm enter into partnership. ~**rsi a** join; subscribe to (giornale ecc). ~**zi'one** nf association

assogget'tar|e vt subject. ~**si** vr submit

asso'lato a sunny

assol'dare vt recruit

as'solo nm Mus solo

as'solto pp di **assolvere**

assoluta'mente adv absolutely

assolu'tismo nm absolutism

asso'luto a absolute. **~zi'one** nf acquittal; Relig absolution

as'solvere vt perform (compito); Jur acquit; Relig absolve

assomigli'ar|e vi **~e a** be like, resemble. **~si** vr resemble each other

assom'marsi vr combine; **~ a qcsa** add to sth

asso'nanza nf assonance

asson'nato a drowsy

asso'pirsi vr doze off

assor'bente a & nm absorbent. **~ igienico** sanitary towel

assor'bire vt absorb

assor'da|re vt deafen. **~nte** a deafening

assorti'mento nm assortment

assor'ti|re vt match (colori). **~to** a assorted; (colori, persone) matched

as'sorto a engrossed

assottigli'ar|e vt make thin; (aguzzare) sharpen; (ridurre) reduce. **~si** vr grow thin; (finanze:) be whittled away

assue'fa|re vt accustom. **~rsi** vr **~rsi a** get used to. **~tto** a (a caffè, aspirina) immune to the effects; (a droga) addicted. **~zi'one** nf (a caffè, aspirina) immunity to the effects; (a droga) addiction

as'sumere vt assume; take on (impiegato); **~ informazioni** make inquiries

as'sunto pp di **assumere** ● nm task. **assunzi'one** nf (di impiegato) employment

assurdità nf inv absurdity; **~ pl** nonsense

as'surdo a absurd

'asta nf pole; Mech bar; Comm auction; **a mezz'~** at half-mast

a'stemio a abstemious

aste'n|ersi vr abstain (**da** from). **~si'one** nf abstention

aste'nuto, -a nmf abstainer

aste'risco nm asterisk

astig'ma|tico a astigmatic. **~ tismo** nm astigmatism

asti'nenza nf abstinence; **crisi di ~** cold turkey

'asti|o nm rancour; **avere ~o contro qcno** bear sb a grudge. **~oso** a resentful

a'stratto a abstract

astrin'gente a & nm astringent

'astro nm star

astrolo'gia nf astrology. **a'strologo, -a** nmf astrologer

astro'nauta nmf astronaut

astro'nave nf spaceship

astrono'mia nf astronomy. **~o'nomico** a astronomical. **a'stronomo** nm astronomer

astrusità nf abstruseness

a'stuccio nm case

a'stu|to a shrewd; (furbo) cunning. **~zia** nf shrewdness; (azione) trick

ate'ismo nm atheism

A'tene nf Athens

'ateo, -a a & nmf atheist

a'tipico a atypical

at'lant|e nm atlas. **~ico** a Atlantic; **l'[Oceano] A~ico** the Atlantic [Ocean]

at'let|a nmf athlete. **~ica** nf athletics sg. **~ica leggera** track and field events. **~ica pesante** weight-lifting, boxing, wrestling, etc. **~ico** a athletic

atmo'sfer|a nf atmosphere. **~ico** a atmospheric

a'tomic|a nf atom bomb. **~o** a atomic

'atomo nm atom

'atrio nm entrance hall

a'troc|e a atrocious; (terrible) dreadful. **~ità** nf inv atrocity

atrofiz'zarsi vr Med, fig atrophy

attaccabot'toni nmf inv [crashing] bore

attacca'brighe nmf inv troublemaker

attacca'mento nm attachment

attacca'panni nm inv [coat-]hanger; (a muro) clothes hook

attac'ca|re vt attach; (legare) tie; (appendere) hang; (cucire) sew on; (contagiare) pass on; (assalire) attack; (iniziare) start ● vi stick; (diffondersi) catch on. **~si** vr cling; (affezionarsi) become attached; (litigare) quarrel

attacca'ticcio a sticky

at'tacco nm attack; (punto d'unione) junction

attar'darsi vr stay late; (indugiare) linger

attec'chire vi take; (moda ecc:) catch on

atteggia'mento nm attitude

atteggi'ar|e vt assume. **~si** vr **~si a** pose as

attem'pato a elderly

at'tender|e vt wait for ● vi **~e a** attend to. **~si** vr expect

atten'dibil|e a reliable. **~ità** nf reliability

atte'nersi vr **~ a** stick to

attenta'mente *adv* attentively

atten'ta|re *vi* ~re a make an attempt on. ~to *nm* act of violence; *(contro politico ecc)* assassination attempt. ~'tore, ~'trice *nmf* *(a scopo politico)* terrorist

at'tento *a* attentive; *(accurato)* careful; ~! look out!; stare ~ pay attention

attenu'ante *nf* extenuating circumstance

attenu'a|re *vt* attenuate; *(minimizzare)* minimize; subdue *(colori ecc)*; calm *(dolore)*; soften *(colpo)*. ~rsi *vr* diminish. ~zi'one *nf* lessening

attenzi'one *nf* attention; ~! watch out!

atter'ra|ggio *nm* landing. ~re *vt* knock down ●*vi* land

atter'rir|e *vt* terrorize. ~si *vr* be terrified

at'tes|a *nf* waiting; *(aspettativa)* expectation; in ~a di waiting for. ~o *pp di* attendere

atte'sta|re *vt* state; *(certificare)* certify. ~to *nm* certificate. ~zi'one *nf* certificate; *(dichiarazione)* declaration

'attico *nm* attic

at'tiguo *a* adjacent

attil'lato *a* *(vestito)* close-fitting; *(elegante)* dressed up

'attimo *nm* moment

atti'nente *a* ~ a pertaining to

at'tingere *vt* draw; *fig* obtain

atti'rare *vt* attract

atti'tudine *nf* *(disposizione)* aptitude; *(atteggiamento)* attitude

atti'v|are *vt* activate. ~ismo *nm* activism. ~ista *nmf* activist. **attività** *nf inv* activity; *Comm* assets *pl*. ~o a *a* active; *Comm* productive ●*nm* assets *pl*

attiz'za|re *vt* poke; *fig* stir up. ~'toio *nm* poker

'atto *nm* act; *(azione)* action; *Comm, Jur* deed; *(certificato)* certificate; atti *pl* *(di società ecc)* proceedings; mettere in ~ put into effect

at'tonito *a* astonished

attorcigli'ar|e *vt* twist. ~si *vr* get twisted

at'tore *nm* actor

attorni'ar|e *vt* surround. ~si *vr* ~si di surround oneself with

at'torno *adv* around, about ●*prep* ~ a around, about

attrac'care *vt/i* dock

attra'ente *a* attractive

at'tra|rre *vt* attract. ~rsi *vr* be attracted to each other. ~t'tiva *nf*

charm. ~zi'one *nf* attraction. ~zioni turistiche tourist attractions

attraversa'mento *nm* *(di strada)* crossing. ~ pedonale pedestrian crossing, crosswalk *Am*

attraver'sare *vt* cross; *(passare)* go through

attra'verso *prep* through; *(obliquamente)* across

attrez'za|re *vt* equip; *Naut* rig. ~rsi *vr* kit oneself out; ~'tura *nf* equipment; *Naut* rigging

at'trezzo *nm* tool; attrezzi *pl* equipment; *Sport* appliances *pl*; *Theat* props *pl*

attribu'ir|e *vt* attribute. ~si *vr* ascribe to oneself; ~si il merito di claim credit for

attri'buto *nm* attribute. ~zi'one *nf* attribution

at'trice *nf* actress

at'trito *nm* friction

attu'abile *a* feasible

attu'al|e *a* present; *(di attualità)* topical; *(effettivo)* actual. ~ità *nf* topicality; *(avvenimento)* news; programma di ~ità current affairs programme. ~iz'zare *vt* update. ~mente *adv* at present

attu'a|re *vt* carry out. ~rsi *vr* be realized. ~zi'one *nf* carrying out

attu'tire *vt* deaden; ~ il colpo soften the blow

au'dac|e *a* daring, bold; *(insolente)* audacious;. ~ia *nf* daring, boldness; *(insolenza)* audacity

'audience *nf inv* *(telespettatori)* audience

'audio *nm* audio

audiovi'sivo *a* audiovisual

audi'torio *nm* auditorium

audizi'one *nf* audition; *Jur* hearing

au'gento *nm* height; essere in ~ be popular

augu'rar|e *vt* wish. ~si *vr* hope. **au'gurio** *nm* wish; *(presagio)* omen; auguri! all the best!; *(a Natale)* Happy Christmas!; tanti auguri best wishes

'aula *nf* classroom; *(università)* lecture-hall; *(sala)* hall. ~ magna *(in università)* great hall. ~ del tribunale courtroom

aumen'tare *vt/i* increase. au'mento *nm* increase; *(di stipendio)* [pay] rise

au'reola *nf* halo

au'rora *nf* dawn

auscul'tare *vt Med* auscultate

ausili'are *a* & *nmf* auxiliary

auspicabile *a* è ~ **che...** it is to be hoped that...

auspi'care *vt* hope for

au'spicio *nm* omen; **auspici** (*pl: protezione*) auspices

austerità *nf* austerity

au'stero *a* austere.

Au'strali|a *nf* Australia. **a~'ano, -a** *a & nmf* Australian

'Austria *nf* Austria. **au'striaco, -a** *a & nmf* Austrian

autar'chia *nf* autarchy. **au'tarchico** *a* autarchic

autenti'c|are *vt* authenticate. **~ità** *nf* authenticity

au'tentico *a* authentic; (*vero*) true

au'tista *nm* driver

'auto *nf inv* car

'auto+ *pref* self+

autoabbron'zante *nm* self-tan ● *a* self-tanning

autoambu'lanza *nf* ambulance

autoartico'lato *nm* articulated lorry

autobio'gra'fia *nf* autobiography. **~'grafico** *a* autobiographical

auto'botte *nf* tanker

'autobus *nm inv* bus

auto'carro *nm* lorry

autocommiserazi'one *nf* self-pity

autoconcessio'nario *nm* car dealer

auto'critica *nf* self-criticism

autodi'datta *nmf* self-educated person, autodidact

autodi'fesa *nf* self-defence

auto'gol *nm inv* own goal

au'tografo *a & nm* autograph

autolesio'nis|mo *nm fig* selfdestruction. **~tico** *a* self-destructive

auto'linea *nf* bus line

au'toma *nm* robot

automatica'mente *adv* automatically

auto'matico *a* automatic ● *nm* (*bottone*) press-stud; (*fucile*) automatic

automatiz'za|re *vt* automate. **~zi'one** *nf* automation

auto'mezzo *nm* motor vehicle

auto'mobi|le *nf* [motor] car. **~'lismo** *nm* motoring. **~'lista** *nmf* motorist. **~'listico** *a* (*industria*) automobile *attrib*

autonoma'mente *adv* autonomously

autono'mia *nf* autonomy; *Auto* range; (*di laptop, cellulare*) battery life. **au'tonomo** *a* autonomous

auto'psia *nf* autopsy

auto'radio *nf inv* car radio; (*veicolo*) radio car

au'tore, -'trice *nmf* author; (*di pittura*) painter; (*di furto ecc*) perpetrator; **quadro d'~** genuine master

auto'revo|le *a* authoritative; (*che ha influenza*) influential. **~'lezza** *nf* authority

autori'messa *nf* garage

autori'tà *nf inv* authority. **~'tario** *a* autocratic. **~ta'rismo** *nm* authoritarianism

autori'tratto *nm* self-portrait

autoriz'za|re *vt* authorize. **~zi'one** *nf* authorization

auto'scontro *nm inv* bumper car

autoscu'ola *nf* driving school

auto'stop *nm* hitch-hiking; **fare l'~** hitch-hike. **~'pista** *nmf* hitch-hiker

auto'strada *nf* motorway

autostra'dale *a* motorway *attrib*

autosuffici'en|te *a* self-sufficient. **~za** *nf* self-sufficiency

autotraspor'ta|tore, ~'trice *nmf* haulier, carrier

auto'treno *nm* articulated lorry, roadtrain

autove'icolo *nm* motor vehicle

auto'velox *nm inv* speed camera

autovet'tura *nf* motor vehicle

autun'nale *a* autumn[al]

au'tunno *nm* autumn

aval'lare *vt* endorse, back (*cambiale*); *fig* endorse

a'vallo *nm* endorsement

avam'braccio *nm* forearm

avangu'ardia *nf* vanguard; *fig* avantgarde; **essere all'~** be in the forefront; *Techn* be at the leading edge

a'vanti *adv* (*in avanti*) forward; (*davanti*) in front; (*prima*) before; **~!** (*entrate*) come in!; (*suvvia*) come on!; (*su semaforo*) cross now, walk *Am*; **va' ~!** go ahead!; **andare ~** (*precedere*) go ahead; (*orologio:*) go fast; **~ e indietro** backwards and forwards ● *a* (*precedente*) before ● *prep* **~ a** before; (*in presenza di*) in the presence of

avanti'eri *adv* the day before yesterday

avanza'mento *nm* progress; (*promozione*) promotion

avan'za|re *vi* advance; (*progredire*) progress; (*essere d'avanzo*) be left [over] ● *vt* advance; (*superare*) surpass; (*promuovere*) promote. **~rsi** *vr* advance; (*avvicinarsi*) approach. **~ta** *nf* advance. **~to** *a* advanced; (*nella notte*) late; **in età ~ta** elderly. **a'vanzo** nm remainder; *Comm* surplus; **avanzi** pl *(rovine)* remains; *(di cibo)* left-overs

ava'ri|a nf *(di motore)* engine failure. **~'ato** a *(frutta, verdura)* rotten; *(carne)* tainted

ava'rizia nf avarice. **a'varo, -a** a stingy ●nmf miser

a'vena nf oats pl

a'vere vt have; *(ottenere)* get; *(indossare)* wear; *(provare)* feel; **ho trent'anni** I'm thirty; **ha avuto il posto** he got the job; **~** *(fame/freddo* be hungry/cold; **ho mal di denti** I've got toothache; **cos'ha a che fare con lui?** what has it got to do with him?; **~ da fare** be busy; **che hai?** what's the matter with you?; **nei hai per molto?** will you be long?; **quanti ne abbiamo oggi?** what date is it today?; **avercela con qcno** have it in for sb ●*v aux* have; **non l'ho visto** I haven't seen him; **lo hai visto?** have you seen him?; **l'ho visto ieri** I saw him yesterday ●nm **averi** pl wealth sg

avia'tore nm flyer, aviator. **~zi'one** nf aviation; *Mil* Air Force

avidità nf avidness. **'avido** a avid

avio'getto nm jet

'avo, -a nmf ancestor

avo'cado nm inv avocado

a'vorio nm ivory

Avv. abbr **avvocato**

avva'lersi vr avail oneself **(of** di)

avval'la'mento nm depression

avvalo'rare vt bear out *(tesi)*; endorse *(documento)*; *(accrescere)* enhance

avvam'pare vi flare up; *(arrossire)* blush

avvantaggi'ar|e vt favour. **~si** vr **~si di** benefit from; *(approfittare)* take advantage of

avve'dersi vr *(accorgersi)* notice; *(capire)* realize. **~uto** a shrewd

avvelena'mento nm poisoning

avvele'na|re vt poison. **~rsi** vr poison oneself. **~to** a poisoned

avve'nente a attractive

avveni'mento nm event

avve'nire[1] vi happen; *(aver luogo)* take place

avve'ni|re[2] nm future. **~'ristico** a futuristic

avven'ta|rsi vr fling oneself. **~to** a *(decisione)* rash

av'vento nm advent; *Relig* Advent

avven'tore nm regular customer

avven'tu|ra nf adventure; *(amorosa)* affair; **d'~** *(film)* adventure attrib.

~'rarsi vr venture. **~ri'ero, -a** nm adventurer ●nf adventuress. **~'roso** a adventurous

avve'ra|bile a *(previsione)* that may come true. **~rsi** vr come true

av'verbio nm adverb

avver'sa|re vt oppose. **~io, -a** a opposing ●nmf opponent

avversi'one nf aversion. **~tà** nf inv adversity

av'verso a *(sfavorevole)* adverse; *(contrario)* averse

avver'tenza nf *(cura)* care; *(avvertimento)* warning; *(avviso)* notice; *(premessa)* foreword; **avvertenze** pl *(istruzioni)* instructions

avverti'mento nm warning

avver'tire vt warn; *(informare)* inform; *(sentire)* feel

avvez'za|re vt accustom. **~si** vr accustom oneself. **av'vezzo** a **avvezzo a** used to

avvia'mento nm starting; *Comm* goodwill

avvi'a|re vt start. **~rsi** vr set out. **~to** a under way; **bene ~to** thriving

avvicenda'mento nm *(in agricoltura)* rotation; *(nel lavoro)* replacement

avvicen'darsi vr take turns, alternate

avvicina'mento nm approach

avvici'na|re vt bring near; approach *(persona)*. **~si** vr come nearer, approach; **~si a** come nearer to, approach

avvi'lente a demoralizing; *(umiliante)* humiliating

avvili'mento nm despondency; *(degradazione)* degradation

avvi'li|re vt dishearten; *(degradare)* degrade. **~rsi** vr lose heart; *(degradarsi)* degrade oneself. **~to** a disheartened; *(degradato)* degraded

avvilup'par|e vt envelop. **~si** vr wrap oneself up; *(aggrovigliarsi)* get entangled

avvinaz'zato a drunk

avvin'cente a *(libro ecc)* enthralling. **av'vincere** vt enthral

avvinghi'ar|e vt clutch. **~si** vr cling

av'vio nm start-up; **dare l'~ a qcsa** get sth under way; **prendere l'~** get under way

avvi'sare vt inform; *(mettere in guardia)* warn

av'viso nm notice; *(annuncio)* announcement; *(avvertimento)* warning; *(pubblicitario)* advertisement; **a mio ~**

avvi'stare vt catch sight of

avvi'tare vt screw in; screw down ⟨coperchio⟩

avviz'zire vi wither

avvo'ca|to nm lawyer; fig advocate. ~ **tura** nf legal profession

av'volgere vt wrap [up]. **~si** vr wrap oneself up

avvol'gibile nm roller blind

avvol'toio nm vulture

aza'lea nf azalea

azi'en|da nf business, firm. ~ **agricola** farm. ~ **di soggiorno** tourist bureau. **~'dale** a ⟨politica, dirigente⟩ company attrib; ⟨giornale⟩ in-house

azio na'mento nm operation

azio'nare vt operate

azio'nario a share attrib

azi'one nf action; Fin share; **d'~** ⟨romanzo, film⟩ action[-packed]. **azio'nista** nmf shareholder

a'zoto nm nitrogen

azzan'nare vt seize with its teeth; sink its teeth into ⟨gamba⟩

azzar'd|are vt risk. **~arsi** vr dare. **~ato** a risky; ⟨precipitoso⟩ rash. **az'zardo** nm hazard; **gioco d'azzardo** game of chance

azzec'care vt hit; ⟨fig: indovinare⟩ guess

azzuf'farsi vr come to blows

az'zurro a & nm blue; **il principe ~** Prince Charming. **~'rognolo** a bluish

Bb

bab'beo a foolish ● nm idiot

'babbo nm fam dad, daddy. **B~ Natale** Father Christmas

bab'buccia nf slipper

babbu'ino nm baboon

ba'bordo nm Naut port side

'babysitter nmf inv baby-sitter; **fare la ~** babysit

ba'cato a wormeaten

'bacca nf berry

baccalà nm inv dried salted cod

bac'cano nm din

bac'cello nm pod

bac'chetta nf rod; ⟨magica⟩ wand; ⟨di direttore d'orchestra⟩ baton; ⟨di tamburo⟩ drumstick

ba'checa nf showcase; ⟨in ufficio⟩ notice board. **~ elettronica** Comput bulletin board

bacia'mano nm kiss on the hand; **fare il ~ a qcno** kiss sb's hand

baci'ar|e vt kiss. **~si** vr kiss [each other]

ba'cillo nm bacillus

baci'nella nf basin

ba'cino nm basin; Anat pelvis; ⟨di porto⟩ dock; ⟨di minerali⟩ field

'bacio nm kiss

'baco nm worm. ~ **da seta** silkworm

ba'cucco a **un vecchio ~** a senile old man

'bada nf **tenere qcno a ~** keep sb at bay

ba'dare vi take care (**a** of); ⟨fare attenzione⟩ look out; **bada ai fatti tuoi!** mind your own business!

ba'dia nf abbey

ba'dile nm shovel

'badminton nm badminton

'baffi nmpl moustache sg; ⟨di animale⟩ whiskers; **mi fa un baffo** I don't give a damn; **ridere sotto i ~** laugh up one's sleeve

baf'futo a moustached

ba'gagli nmpl luggage, baggage. **~'aio** nm Rail luggage van; Auto boot

ba'gaglio nm luggage; **un ~** a piece of luggage. ~ **a mano** hand luggage, hand baggage

baggia'nata nf **non dire baggianate** don't talk nonsense

bagli'ore nm glare; ⟨improvviso⟩ flash; ⟨fig: di speranza⟩ glimmer

ba'gnante nmf bather

ba'gna|re vt wet; ⟨inzuppare⟩ soak; ⟨immergere⟩ dip; ⟨innaffiare⟩ water; ⟨mare, lago:⟩ wash; ⟨fiume:⟩ flow through. **~rsi** vr get wet; ⟨al mare ecc⟩ swim, bathe

bagnasci'uga *nm inv* edge of the water, waterline

ba'gnato *a* wet

ba'gnino, -a *nmf* life guard

'**bagno** *nm* bath; (*stanza*) bathroom; (*gabinetto*) toilet; (*in casa*) toilet, bathroom; (*al mare*) swim, bathe; **bagni** *pl* (*stabilimento*) lido; **fare il ~** have a bath; (*nel mare ecc*) [have a] swim or bathe; **andare in ~** go to the bathroom or toilet; **mettere a ~** soak. **~ turco** Turkish bath

bagnoma'ria *nm* **cuocere a ~** cook in a double saucepan

bagnoschi'uma *nm inv* bubble bath

'**baia** *nf* bay

baio'netta *nf* bayonet

'**baita** *nf* mountain chalet

bala'ustra, balaus'trata *nf* balustrade

balbet't|are *vt/i* stammer; (*bambino:*) babble. **~io** *nm* stammering; babble

bal'buzie *nf* stutter. **~'ente** *a* stuttering ● *nmf* stutterer

Bal'can|i *nmpl* Balkans. **b~ico** *a* Balkan

balco'nata *nf Theat* balcony, dress circle

balcon'cino *nm* **reggiseno a ~** underwired bra

bal'cone *nm* balcony

baldac'chino *nm* canopy; **letto a ~** four-poster bed

bal'dan|za *nf* boldness. **~zoso** *a* bold

bal'doria *nf* revelry; **far ~** have a riotous time

Bale'ari *nfpl* **le |isole| ~** the Balearics, the Balearic Islands

ba'lena *nf* whale

bale'nare *vi* lighten; *fig* flash; **mi è balenata un'idea** I've just had an idea

bale'niera *nf* whaler

ba'leno *nm* **in un ~** in a flash

ba'lera *nf* dance hall

'**balia** *nf* wetnurse

ba'lìa *nf* **in ~ di** at the mercy of

ba'listico *a* ballistic; **perito ~** ballistics expert

'**balla** *nf* bale; (*fam: frottola*) tall story

bal'labile *a* good for dancing to

bal'la|re *vi* dance. **~ta** *nf* ballad

balla'toio *nm* (*nelle scale*) landing

balle'rino, -a *nmf* dancer; (*classico*) ballet dancer; **ballerina** (*classica*) ballet dancer, ballerina

bal'letto *nm* ballet

bal'lista *nmf fam* bull-shitter

'**ballo** *nm* dance; (*il ballare*) dancing;

sala da ~ ballroom; **essere in ~** (*lavoro, vita:*) be at stake; (*persona:*) be committed; **tirare qcno in ~** involve sb

ballonzo'lare *vi* skip about

ballot'taggio *nm* second count (*of votes*)

balne'a|re *a* bathing *attrib*. **stagione ~** swimming season. **stazione ~** seaside resort. **~zione** nf **è vietata la ~zione** no swimming

ba'lordo *a* foolish; (*stordito*) stunned; **tempo ~** nasty weather

'**balsamo** *nm* balsam; (*per capelli*) conditioner; (*lenimento*) remedy

'**baltico** *a* Baltic. **il |mar| B~** the Baltic [Sea]

balu'ardo *nm* bulwark

'**balza** *nf* crag; (*di abito*) flounce

bal'zano *a* (*idea*) weird

bal'zare *vi* bounce; (*saltare*) jump; **~ in piedi** leap to one's feet. **balzo** *nm* bounce; (*salto*) jump; **prendere la palla al balzo** seize an opportunity

bam'bagia *nf* cotton wool; **vivere nella ~** *fig* be in clover

bambi'nata *nf* childish thing to do/say

bam'bi|no, -a *nmf* child; (*appena nato*) baby; **avere un ~no** have a baby. **~'none, -a** *nmf pej* overgrown child

bam'boccio *nm* chubby child; (*sciocco*) simpleton; (*fantoccio*) rag doll

'**bambo|la** *nf* doll. **~'lotto** *nm* male doll

bambù *nm* bamboo

ba'nal|e *a* banal; **~ità** *nf inv* banality; **~iz'zare** *vt* trivialize

ba'nan|a *nf* banana. **~o** *nm* banana-tree

'**banca** *nf* bank. **~ |di| dati** databank

banca'rella *nf* stall

ban'cario, -a *a* banking *attrib*; **trasferimento ~** bank transfer ● *nmf* bank employee

banca'rotta *nf* bankruptcy; **fare ~** go bankrupt

banchet'tare *vi* banquet. **ban'chetto** *nm* banquet

banchi'ere *nm* banker

ban'china *nf Naut* quay; (*in stazione*) platform; (*di strada*) path; **~ non transitabile** soft verge

ban'chisa *nf* floe

'**banco** *nm* (*di scuola*) desk; (*di negozio*) counter; (*di officina*) bench; (*di gioco, banca*) bank; (*di mercato*) stall; (*degli imputati*) dock; **sotto ~** under the counter; **medicinale da ~** over the counter medicines. **~ informazioni** information desk. **~ di nebbia** fog bank

banco'mat® *nm inv* autobank, cashpoint; (*carta*) bank card, cash card

ban'cone *nm* counter; (*in bar*) bar

banco'nota *nf* banknote, bill *Am*; **banco'note** *pl* paper currency

'banda *nf* band; (*di delinquenti*) gang. **~ d'atterraggio** *Aeron* landing strip. **~ rumorosa** rumble strip

bande'ruola *nf* weathercock; *Naut* pennant

bandi'era *nf* flag; **cambiare ~ra** change sides, switch allegiances. **~rina** *nf* (*nel calcio*) corner flag. **~rine** *pl* bunting *sg*

ban'dire *vt* banish; (*pubblicare*) publish; *fig* dispense with (*formalità, complimenti*). **~to** *nm* bandit. **~tore** *nm* (*di aste*) auctioneer

'bando *nm* proclamation; **~ di concorso** job advertisement (*published in an official gazette for a job for which a competitive examination has to be taken*)

bar *nm inv* bar

'bara *nf* coffin

ba'rac|ca *nf* hut; (*catapecchia*) hovel; **mandare avanti la ~ca** keep the ship afloat. **~'cato** *nm* person living in a makeshift shelter. **~'chino** *nm* (*di gelati, giornali*) kiosk; *Radio* CB radio. **~'cone** *nm* (*roulotte*) circus caravan; (*in luna park*) booth. **~'copoli** *nf inv* shanty town

bara'onda *nf* chaos; **non fare ~** don't make a mess

ba'rare *vi* cheat

bar'atro *nm* chasm

barat'tare *vt* barter. **ba'ratto** *nm* barter

ba'rattolo *nm* jar; (*di latta*) tin

'barba *nf* beard; (*fam: noia*) bore; **farsi la ~** shave; **è una ~** (*noia*) it's boring

barbabi'etola *nf* beetroot. **~ da zucchero** sugar-beet

bar'barico *a* barbaric. **bar'barie** *nf* barbarity. **'barbaro** *a* barbarous ● *nm* barbarian

'barbecue *nm inv* barbecue

barbi'ere *nm* barber; (*negozio*) barber's

barbi'turico *nm* barbiturate

bar'bone *nm* (*vagabondo*) vagrant; (*cane*) poodle

bar'boso *a fam* boring

barbu'gliare *vi* mumble

bar'buto *a* bearded

'barca *nf* boat; **una ~ di** *fig* a lot of. **~ a motore** motorboat. **~ da pesca** fishing boat. **~ a remi** rowing boat, rowboat *Am*. **~ di salvataggio** lifeboat. **~ a vela** sailing boat, sailboat *Am*. **~i'olo** *nm* boatman

barcame'narsi *vr* manage

barcol'lare *vi* stagger

bar'cone *nm* barge; (*di ponte*) pontoon

bar'dar|e *vt* harness. **~si** *vr hum* dress up

ba'rel|la *nf* stretcher. **~li'ere** *nm* stretcher-bearer

'Barents: il mare di ~ the Barents Sea

bari'centro *nm* centre of gravity

ba'rile *nm* barrel. **~ lotto** *nm fig* tub of lard

ba'rista *nm* barman ● *nf* barmaid

ba'ritono *nm* baritone

bar'lume *nm* glimmer; **un ~ di speranza** a glimmer of hope

'barman *nm inv* barman

'baro *nm* cardsharper

ba'rocco *a & nm* baroque

ba'rometro *nm* barometer

ba'rone *nm* baron; **i baroni** *fig* the top brass. **baro'nessa** *nf* baroness

'barra *nf* bar; (*lineetta*) oblique; *Naut* tiller. **~ spazio** *Comput* space bar. **~ strumenti** *Comput* tool bar

bar'rare *vt* block off (*strada*)

barri'care *vt* barricade. **~ta** *nf* barricade

barri'era *nf* barrier; (*stradale*) roadblock; *Geol* reef. **~ razziale** colour bar

bar'rire *vi* trumpet. **~to** *nm* trumpeting

barzel'letta *nf* joke; **~ sporca** *o* **spinta** dirty joke

basa'mento *nm* base

ba'sar|e *vt* base. **~si** *vr* **~si su** be based on; **mi baso su ciò che ho visto** I'm going on [the basis of] what I saw

'basco, -a *nmf & a* Basque ● *nm* (*copricapo*) beret

'base *nf* basis; (*fondamento*) foundation; *Mil* base; *Pol* rank and file; **a ~ di** containing; **in ~ a** on the basis of. **~ dati** database

'baseball *nm* baseball

ba'setta *nf* sideburn

basi'lare *a* basic

ba'silica *nf* basilica

ba'silico *nm* basil

ba'sista *nm* grass roots politician; (*di un crimine*) mastermind

'basket *nm* basketball

bas'sezza *nf* lowness; (*di statura*) shortness; (*viltà*) vileness

bas'sista *nmf* bassist

'basso *a* low; (*di statura*) short; (*acqua*) shallow; (*televisione*) quiet; (*vile*) despicable; parlare a bassa voce speak quietly, speak in a low voice; la bassa Italia southern Italy ● *nm* lower part; *Mus* bass. guardare in ~ look down

basso'fondo *nm* (*pl* bassi fondi) shallows *pl*; bassifondi *pl* (*quartieri poveri*) slums

bassorili'evo *nm* bas-relief

bas'sotto *nm* dachshund

ba'stardo, -a *a* bastard; (*di animale*) mongrel ● *nmf* bastard; (*animale*) mongrel

ba'stare *vi* be enough; (*durare*) last; basta! that's enough!, that'll do!; basta che (*purchè*) provided that; basta così that's enough; basta così? is that enough?, will that do?; (*in negozio*) will there be anything else?; basta andare alla posta you only have to go to the post office

Basti'an con'trario *nm* contrary old so-and-so

basti'one *nm* bastion

basto'nare *vt* beat

baston'cino *nm* (*da sci*) ski pole. ~ di pesce fish finger, fish stick *Am*

ba'stone *nm* stick; (*da golf*) club; (*da passeggio*) walking stick

ba'tosta *nf* blow

bat'tagli|a *nf* battle; (*lotta*) fight. ~'are *vi* battle; *fig* fight

bat'taglio *nm* (*di campana*) clapper; (*di porta*) knocker

battagli'one *nm* battalion

bat'tello *nm* boat; (*motonave*) steamer

bat'tente *nm* (*di porta*) wing; (*di finestra*) shutter; (*battaglio*) knocker

'batter|e *vt* beat; (*percorrere*) scour; thresh (*grano*); break (*record*) ● *vi* (*bussare, urtare*) knock; (*cuore*) beat; (*ali ecc*) flap; *Tennis* serve; ~e a macchina type; ~e gli occhi blink; ~e le mani clap [one's hands]; ~e le ore strike the hours. ~si *vr* fight

bat'teri *nmpl* bacteria

batte'ria *nf* battery; *Mus* drums *pl*

bat'terio *nm* bacterium. ~'logico *a* bacteriological

batte'rista *nmf* drummer

bat'tesimo *nm* baptism, christening

battez'zare *vt* baptize, christen

battiba'leno *nm* in un ~ in a flash

batti'becco *nm* squabble

batticu'ore *nm* palpitation; mi venne il ~ I was scared

bat'tigia *nf* water's edge

batti'mano *nm* applause

batti'panni *nm inv* carpetbeater

batti'stero *nm* baptistery

batti'strada *nm inv* outrider; (*di pneumatico*) tread; *Sport* pacesetter

battitap'peto *nm inv* carpet sweeper

'battito *nm* (*del cuore*) [heart]beat; (*alle tempie*) throbbing; (*di orologio*) ticking; (*della pioggia*) beating

bat'tuta *nf* beat; (*colpo*) knock; (*spiritosaggine*) wisecrack; (*osservazione*) remark; *Mus* bar; *Tennis* service; *Theat* cue; (*dattilografia*) stroke

ba'tuffolo *nm* flock

ba'ule *nm* trunk

'bava *nf* dribble; (*di cane ecc*) slobber; aver la ~ alla bocca foam at the mouth

bava'glino *nm* bib

ba'vaglio *nm* gag

'bavero *nm* collar

ba'zar *nm inv* bazaar

baz'zecola *nf* trifle

bazzi'care *vt/i* haunt

be'arsi *vr* delight (di) in

beati'tudine *nf* bliss. be'ato *a* blissful; *Relig* blessed; beato te! lucky you!

beauty-'case *nm inv* toilet bag

bebè *nm inv* baby

bec'caccia *nf* woodcock

bec'ca|re *vt* peck; *fig* catch. ~rsi *vr* (*litigare*) quarrel. ~ta *nf* peck

beccheggi'are *vi* pitch

bec'chino *nm* grave-digger

'becco *nm* beak; (*di caffettiera ecc*) spout. ~'cuccio *nm* spout

be'fana *nf* Epiphany; (*donna brutta*) old witch

'beffa *nf* hoax; farsi beffe di qcno mock sb. bef'fardo *a* derisory; (*persona*) mocking

beffar|e *vt* mock. ~si *vr*~si di make fun of

'bega *nf* quarrel; è una bella ~ it's really annoying

be'gonia *nf* begonia

beige *a & nm* beige

be'la|re *vi* bleat. ~to *nm* bleating

'belga *a & nmf* Belgian

'Belgio *nm* Belgium

'bella *nf* (*in carte, Sport*) decider

bel'lezza *nf* beauty; che ~! how lovely!; chiudere/finire in ~ end on a high note

'belli|co *a* war *attrib*. ~**'coso** *a* warlike. ~**ge'rante** *a* & *nmf* belligerent

'bello *a* nice; *(di aspetto)* beautiful; *(uomo)* handsome; *(moralmente)* good; **cosa fai di ~ stasera?** what are you up to tonight?**;oggi fa ~** it's a nice day; **una bella cifra** a lot;**un bel piatto di pasta** a big plate of pasta; **nel bel mezzo** right in the middle; **un bel niente** absolutely nothing;**bell'e fatto** over and done with;**bell'amico** [a] fine friend he is/you are!;**questa è bella!** that's a good one!; **scamparla bella** have a narrow escape ● *nm (bellezza)* beauty; *(innamorato)* sweetheart; **sul più ~** at the crucial moment;**il ~ è che...** the funny thing is that...

'belva *nf* wild beast

be'molle *nm Mus* flat

ben *vedi***bene**

ben'ché *conj* though, although

'benda *nf* bandage; *(per occhi)* blindfold. **ben'dare** *vt* bandage; blindfold *(occhi)*

'bene *adv* well;**ben ~** thoroughly; ~**!** good!;**star ~** *(di salute)* be well; *(vestito, stile:)* suit; *(finanziariamente)* be well off;**non sta ~** *(non è educato)* it's not nice;**sta'va ~!** all right!;**ti sta ~!** [it] serves you right!;**ti auguro ~** I wish you well;**di ~ in meglio** better and better;**fare ~** *(aver ragione)* do the right thing;**fare ~ a** *(cibo:)* be good for; **una persona per ~** a good person;**per ~** properly;**è ben difficile** it's very difficult;**come tu ben sai** as you well know;**lo credo ~!** I can well believe it! ● *nm* good;**per il tuo ~** for your own good.**beni** *nmpl (averi)* property *sg*;**un ~ di famiglia** a family heirloom

bene'detto *a* blessed

bene'di|re *vt* bless. ~**zi'one** *nf* blessing

benedu'cato *a* well-mannered

benefat'|tore, -'trice *nm* benefactor ● *nf* benefactress

benefi'care *vt* help

benefi'cenza *nf* charity

benefici'a|re *vi.*~**e di** profit by. ~**io, -a** *a* & *nmf* beneficiary.**bene'ficio** *nm* benefit.**be'nefico** *a* beneficial; *(di beneficenza)* charitable

bene'placito *nm* consent, approval

be'nessere *nm* well-being

bene'stante *a* well-off ● *nmf* well-off person

bene'stare *nm* consent

benevo'lenza *nf* benevolence. **be'ne'volo** *a* benevolent

ben'fatto *a* well-made

'beni *nmpl* property *sg; Fin* assets; ~ **di consumo** consumer goods

benia'mino *nm* favourite

be'nigno *a* kindly; *Med* benign

benin'for'mato *a* well-informed

benintenzio'nato, -a *a* well-meaning ● *nmf* well-meaning person

benin'teso *adv* needless to say, of course

benpen'sante *a* & *nmf* self-righteous

benser'vito *nm***dare il ~ a** qcno give sb the sack

ben'sì *conj* but rather

benve'nuto *a* & *nm* welcome

ben'visto *a* essere ~ go down well *(da* with)

benvo'lere *vt***farsi ~ da** qcno win sb's affection; **prendere qcno in ~** take a liking to sb;**essere benvoluto da tutti** to be well-liked by everyone

ben'zina *nf* petrol, gas *Am*;**far ~** get petrol. ~ **verde** unleaded petrol.**benzi'naio, -a** *nmf* petrol station attendant

'bere *vt* drink; *(assorbire)* absorb; *fig* swallow ● *nm* drinking; *(bevande)* drinks *pl*

berga'motto *nm* bergamot

ber'lina *nf Auto* saloon

Ber'lino *nm* Berlin

ber'muda *nfpl (pantaloni)* Bermuda shorts

ber'noccolo *nm* bump; *(disposizione)* flair

ber'retto *nm* beret, cap

bersagli'are *vt fig* bombard. **ber'saglio** *nm* target

be'stemmi|a *nf* swear-word; *(maledizione)* oath; *(sproposito)* blasphemy. ~**are** *vi* swear

'besti|a *nf* animal; *(persona brutale)* beast; *(persona sciocca)* fool;**andare in ~a** *fam* blow one's top.~**ale** *a* bestial; *(espressione, violenza)* brutal; *(fam: freddo, fame)* terrible. ~**alità** *nf inv* bestiality;*fig* nonsense.~**ame** *nm* livestock

'bettola *nf fig* dive

be'tulla *nf* birch

be'vanda *nf* drink

bevi'|tore, -'trice *nmf* drinker

be'vuta *nf* drink.~**o** *pp di***bere**

bi'ada *nf* fodder

bianche'ria *nf* linen. ~ **intima** underwear

bi'anco *a* white; *(foglio, pagina)* blank

●*nm* white; **mangiare in** ~ not eat fried or heavy foods; **andare in** ~ *fam* not score; **in** ~ **e nero** (*film, fotografia*) black and white, monochrome; **passare una notte in** ~ have a sleepless night

bian'core *nm* (*bianchezza*) whiteness

bianco'spino *nm* hawthorn

biasci'care *vt* (*mangiare*) eat noisily; (*parlare*) mumble

biasi'mare *vt* blame. **bi'asimo** *nm* blame

'Bibbia *nf* Bible

bibe'ron *nm inv* (baby's) bottle

'bibita *nf* [soft] drink

'biblico *a* biblical

bibliogra'fia *nf* bibliography

biblio'te|ca *nf* library; (*mobile*) bookcase. ~**'cario, -a** *nmf* librarian

bicarbo'nato *nm* bicarbonate. ~ **di sodio** bicarbonate of soda

bicchi'ere *nm* glass

bicchie'rino *nm fam* tipple

bici'cletta *nf* bicycle; **andare in** ~ ride a bicycle

bico'lore *a* two-coloured

bidè *nm inv* bidet

bi'dello, -a *nmf* janitor, [school] caretaker

bido'nata *nf fam* swindle

bi'done *nm* bin; (*fam: truffa*) swindle; **fare un** ~ **a qcno** *fam* stand sb up

bien'nale *a* biennial

bi'ennio *nm* two-year period

bi'etola *nf* beet

bifo'cale *a* bifocal

bi'folco, -a *nmf fig* boor

bifor'c|arsi *vr* fork. ~**azi'one** *nf* fork. ~**uto** *a* forked

biga'mia *nf* bigamy. **'bigamo, -a** *a* bigamous ●*nmf* bigamist

bighello'nare *vi* loaf around. **bighel'lone** *nm* loafer

bigiotte'ria *nf* costume jewellery; (*negozio*) jeweller's

bigliet't|aio *nm* booking clerk; (*sui treni*) ticket-collector. ~**e'ria** *nf* ticket-office; *Theat* box-office

bigli'et|to *nm* ticket; (*lettera breve*) note; (*cartoncino*) card; (*di banca*) banknote. ~**to da visita** business card. ~**'tone** *nm* (*fam: soldi*) big one

bi'gnè *nm inv* cream puff

bigo'dino *nm* roller

bi'gotto *nm* bigot

bi'kini *nm inv* bikini

bi'lanci|a *nf* scales *pl*; (*di orologio, Comm*) balance. **B**~**a** *Astr* Libra. ~**'are**

vt balance; *fig* weigh. ~**o** *nm* budget; *Comm* balance sheet; **fare il** ~**o** balance the books; *fig* take stock

bile *nf* bile; *fig* rage

bili'ardo *nm* billiards *sg*

'bilico *nm* equilibrium; **in** ~ in the balance

bi'lingue *a* bilingual

bili'one *nm* billion

bilo'cale *a* two-room

'bimbo, -a *nmf* child

bimen'sile *a* fortnightly

bime'strale *a* bimonthly

bi'nario *nm* track; (*piattaforma*) platform

bi'nocolo *nm* binoculars *pl*

bio'chimica *nf* biochemistry

biodegra'dabile *a* biodegradable

bio'etica *nf* bioethics

bio'fisica *nf* biophysics

biogra'fia *nf* biography. **bio'grafico** *a* biographical. **bi'ografo, -a** *nmf* biographer

biolo'gia *nf* biology. **bio'logico** *a* biological. **bi'ologo, -a** *nmf* biologist

bi'ond|a *nf* blonde. ~**o** *a* blond ●*nm* fair colour; (*uomo*) fair-haired man

bio'sfera *nf* biosphere

bi'ossido *nm* ~ **di carbonio** carbon dioxide

biparti'tismo *nm* two-party system

'birba *nf*, **bir'bante** *nm* rascal, rogue. **bir'bone** *a* wicked

biri'chino, -a *a* naughty ●*nmf* little devil

bi'rillo *nm* skittle

'birr|a *nf* beer; **a tutta** ~**a** *fig* flat out. ~**a chiara** lager. ~**a scura** brown ale. ~**e'ria** *nf* beer-house; (*fabbrica*) brewery

bis *nm inv* encore

bi'saccia *nf* haversack

bi'sbetic|a *nf* shrew. ~**o** *a* bad-tempered

bisbigli'are *vt/i* whisper. **bi'sbiglio** *nm* whisper

'bisca *nf* gambling-house

'biscia *nf* snake

bi'scotto *nm* biscuit

bisessu'ale *a* & *nmf* bisexual

bise'stile *a* **anno** ~ leap year

bisetti'manale *a* fortnightly

bi'slacco *a* peculiar

bis'nonno, -a *nmf* great-grandfather; great-grandmother

biso'gn|are *vi* ~**a agire subito** we must act at once; ~**a farlo** it is necessary to do it; **non** ~**a venire** you don't have to come. ~o nm need; (povertà) poverty; aver ~o di need. ~oso a needy; (povero) poor; ~oso di in need of

bi'sonte nm bison

bi'stecca nf steak

bisticci'are vi quarrel. bi'sticcio nm quarrel; (gioco di parole) pun

bistrat'tare vt mistreat

'bisturi nm inv scalpel

bi'torzolo nm lump

'bitter nm inv (bitter) aperitif

bi'vacco nm bivouac

'bivio nm crossroads; (di strada) fork

bizan'tino a Byzantine

'bizza nf tantrum; fare le bizze (bambini:) play up

biz'zarro a bizarre

biz'zeffe adv a ~ galore

blan'dire vt soothe; (allettare) flatter. 'blando a mild

bla'sone nm coat of arms

blate'rare vi blether, blather

'blatta nf cockroach

blin'da|re vt armour-plate. ~to a armoured

blitz nm inv blitz

bloc'ca|re vt block; (isolare) cut off; Mil blockade; Comm freeze. ~si vr Mech jam

blocca'sterzo nm steering lock

'blocco nm block; Mil blockade; (dei fitti) restriction; (di carta) pad; (unione) coalition; in ~ Comm in bulk. ~ stra-dale road-block

bloc-'notes nm inv writing pad

blu a & nm blue

blue-'jeans nmpl jeans

bluff nm inv (carte, fig) bluff. bluf'fare vi (carte, fig) bluff

'blusa nf blouse

'boa nm boa [constrictor]; (sciarpa) [feather] boa ● nf Naut buoy

bo'ato nm rumbling

bo'bina nf spool; (di film) reel; Electr coil

'bocca nf mouth; a ~ aperta fig dumbfounded; in ~ al lupo! break a leg!; fare la respirazione ~ a ~ a qcno give sb mouth to mouth resuscitation or the kiss of life

boc'caccia nf grimace; far boc-cacce make faces

boc'caglio nm nozzle

boc'cale nm jug; (da birra) tankard

bocca'porto nm Naut hatch

boc'cata nf (di fumo) puff; prendere una ~ d'aria get a breath of fresh air

boc'cetta nf small bottle

boccheggi'are vi gasp

boc'chino nm cigarette holder; (di pipa, Mus) mouthpiece

'bocc|ia nf (palla) bowl; ~e pl (gioco) bowls sg

bocci'a|re vt (agli esami) fail; (respingere) reject; (alle bocce) hit; essere ~to fail; (ripetere) repeat a year. ~ tura nf failure

bocci'olo nm bud

boccon'cino nm morsel

boc'cone nm mouthful; (piccolo pasto) snack

boc'coni adv face downwards

'boia nm executioner

boi'ata nf fam rubbish

boicot'tare vt boycott

bo'lero nm bolero

'bolgia nf (caos) bedlam

'bolide nm meteor; passare come un ~ shoot past [like a rocket]

Bo'livi|a nf Bolivia. b~'ano, -a a & nmf Bolivian

'bolla nf bubble; (pustola) blister

bol'la|re vt stamp; fig brand. ~to a fig branded; carta ~ta paper with stamp showing payment of duty

bol'lente a boiling [hot]

bol'let|ta nf bill; essere in ~ta be hard up. ~'tino nm bulletin; Comm list

bol'lino nm coupon

bol'li|re vt/i boil. ~to nm boiled meat. ~tore nm boiler; (per l'acqua) kettle. ~ tura nf boiling

'bollo nm stamp

bol'lore nm boil; (caldo) intense heat; fig ardour

'bomba nf bomb; a prova di ~ bomb-proof

bombarda'mento nm shelling; (con aerei) bombing; fig bombardment. ~ aereo air raid

bombar'd|are vt shell; (con aerei) bomb; fig bombard. ~i'ere nm bomber

bom'betta nf bowler [hat]

'bombola nf cylinder. ~ di gas gas bottle, gas cylinder

bombo'lone nm doughnut

bombo-ni'era nf wedding keep-sake

bo'naccia nf Naut calm

bonacci'one, -a nmf good-natured person ● a good-natured

bo'nario a kindly

bo'nifica nf land reclamation. bonifi-'care vt reclaim

bo'nifico nm Comm discount; (bancario) [credit] transfer

bontà *nf* goodness; *(gentilezza)* kindness

'**bora** *nf* bora *(cold north-east wind in the upper Adriatic)*

borbot'tare *vi* mumble; *(stomaco:)* rumble. ~io *nm* mumbling; *(di stomaco)* rumbling

'**borchi**|**a** *nf* stud. ~'**ato** *a* studded

bor'da|re *vt* border. ~'tura *nf* border

bor'deaux *a inv (colore)* claret

bor'dello *nm* brothel; *fig* bedlam; *(disordine)* mess

'**bordo** *nm* border; *(estremità)* edge; a ~ *Naut, Aeron* on board

bor'gata *nf* hamlet

bor'ghese *a* bourgeois; *(abito)* civilian; in ~ in civilian dress; *(poliziotto)* in plain clothes

borghe'sia *nf* middle classes *pl*

'**borgo** *nm* village; *(quartiere)* district

'**bori**|**a** *nf* conceit. ~'**oso** *a* conceited

bor'lotto *nm* [**fagiolo**] ~ borlotto bean

boro'talco *nm* talcum powder

bor'raccia *nf* flask

'**bors**|**a** *nf* bag; *(borsetta)* handbag; *(valori)* Stock Exchange. ~a dell'acqua calda hot-water bottle. ~a frigo coolbox. ~a della spesa shopping bag. ~a di studio scholarship. ~ai'olo *nm* pickpocket. ~el'lino *nm* purse. bor-'sista *nmf Fin* speculator; *Sch* scholarship holder

bor'sello *nm (portamonete)* purse; *(borsetto)* man's handbag. ~tta *nf* handbag. ~tto *nm* man's handbag

bo'scaglia *nf* woodlands *pl*

boscai'olo *nm* woodman; *(guardaboschi)* forester

'**bosco** *nm* wood. bo'scoso *a* wooded

bossolo *nm* cartridge case

bo'tanic|a *nf* botany. ~o *a* botanical ●nm botanist

'**botola** *nf* trapdoor

'**botta** *nf* blow; *(rumore)* bang; fare a botte come to blows. ~ e risposta *fig* thrust and counter-thrust

'**botte** *nf* barrel

bot'te|ga *nf* shop; *(di artigiano)* workshop. ~'**gaio, -a** *nmf* shopkeeper. ~'**ghino** *nm Theatr* box-office; *(del lotto)* lottery-shop

bot'tiglia *nf* bottle; in ~a bottled. ~e'ria *nf* wine shop

bot'tino *nm* loot; *Mil* booty

'**botto** *nm* bang; di ~ all of a sudden

bot'tone *nm* button; *Bot* bud

bo'vino *a* bovine; bovini *pl* cattle

box *nm inv (per cavalli)* loosebox; *(recinto per bambini)* play-pen

'**boxe** *nf* boxing

'**bozza** *nf* draft; *Typ* proof; *(bernoccolo)* bump. boz'zetto *nm* sketch

'**bozzolo** *nm* cocoon

brac'care *vt* hunt

brac'cetto *nm* a ~ arm in arm

bracci'a|le *nm* bracelet; *(fascia)* armband. ~'letto *nm* bracelet; *(di orologio)* watch-strap

bracci'ante *nm* day labourer

bracci'ata *nf (nel nuoto)* stroke

'**bracci**|**o** *nm (pl nf* braccia) arm; *(di fiume, pl* bracci) arm. ~'olo *nm (di sedia)* arm[rest]; *(da nuoto)* armband

'**bracco** *nm* hound

bracconi'ere *nm* poacher

'**braci**|**e** *nf* embers *pl*; alla ~e chargrilled. ~'ere *nm* brazier. ~'ola *nf* chop

'**brado** *a* allo stato ~ in the wild

'**brama** *nf* longing. bra'mare *vt* long for. bramo'sia *nf* yearning

'**branca** *nf* branch

'**branchia** *nf* gill

'**branco** *nm (di cani)* pack; *(pej: di persone)* gang

branco'lare *vi* grope

'**branda** *nf* camp-bed

bran'dello *nm* scrap; a brandelli in tatters

bran'dire *vt* brandish

'**brano** *nm* piece; *(di libro)* passage

Bra'sil|e *nm* Brazil. b~i'ano, -a *a & nmf* Brazilian

bra'vata *nf* bragging

'**bravo** *a* good; *(abile)* clever; *(coraggioso)* brave; ~! well done!. bra'vura *nf* skill

'**breccia** *nf* breach; sulla ~ *fig* very successful, at the top

bre'saola *nf* dried, salted beef sliced thinly and eaten cold

bre'tella *nf* shoulder-strap; bretelle *pl (di calzoni)* braces

'**breve** *a* brief, short; in ~ briefly; tra ~ shortly

brevet'tare *vt* patent. bre'vetto *nm* patent; *(attestato)* licence

brevità *nf* shortness

'**brezza** *nf* breeze

'**bricco** *nm* jug

bric'cone *nm* blackguard; *hum* rascal

'**bricio**|**la** *nf* crumb; *fig* grain. ~o *nm* fragment

'**briga** *nf (fastidio)* trouble; *(lite)* quarrel; attaccar ~ pick a quarrel;

prendersi la ~ di fare qcsa go to the trouble of doing sth

brigadi'ere nm (dei carabinieri) sergeant

bri'gante nm bandit; hum rogue

bri'gare vi intrigue

bri'gata nf brigade; (gruppo) group

briga'tista nmf Pol member of the Red Brigades

'briglia nf rein; **a ~ sciolta** at breakneck speed

bril'lante a brilliant; (scintillante) sparkling ●nm diamond

bril'lare vi shine; (metallo:) glitter; (scintillare) sparkle

'brillo a tipsy

'brina nf hoar-frost

brin'dare vi toast; **~ a qcno** drink a toast to sb

'brindisi nm inv toast

bri'tannico a British

'brivido nm shiver; (di paura ecc) shudder; (di emozione) thrill

brizzo'lato a greying

'brocca nf jug

broc'cato nm brocade

'broccoli nmpl broccoli sg

bro'daglia nf pej dishwater

'brodo nm broth; (per cucinare) stock. **~ ristretto** consommé

'broglio nm **~ elettorale** gerrymandering

bron'chite nf bronchitis

'broncio nm sulk; **fare il ~** sulk

bronto'l|are vi grumble; (tuono ecc:) rumble. **~io** nm grumbling; (di tuono) rumbling. **~one, -a** nmf grumbler

'bronzo nm bronze

bros'sura nf **edizione in ~** paperback

bru'care vt (pecora:) graze

bruciacchi'are vt scorch

brucia'pelo adv **a ~** point-blank

bruci'a|re vt burn; (scottare) scald; (incendiare) set fire to ●vi burn; (scottare) scald. **~rsi** vr burn oneself. **~to** a burnt; fig burnt-out. **~tore** nm burner. **~'tura** nf burn. **bruci'ore** nm burning sensation

'bruco nm grub

'brufolo nm spot

brughi'era nf heath

bruli'c|are vi swarm. **~hio** nm swarming

'brullo a bare

'bruma nf mist

'bruno a brown; (occhi, capelli) dark

brusca'mente adv (di colpo) suddenly

bru'schetta nf toasted bread rubbed with garlic and sprinkled with olive oil

'brusco a sharp; (persona) brusque, abrupt; (improvviso) sudden

bru'sio nm buzzing

bru'tal|e a brutal. **~ità** nf inv brutality. **~iz'zare** vt brutalize. **'bruto** a & nm brute

brut'tezza nf ugliness

'brut|to a ugly; (tempo, tipo, situazione, affare) nasty; (cattivo) bad; **~ta copia** rough copy; **~to tiro** dirty trick. **~'tura** nf ugly thing

'buca nf hole; (avvallamento) hollow. **~ delle lettere** (a casa) letter-box

buca'neve nm inv snowdrop

bu'car|e vt make a hole in; (pungere) prick; punch (biglietti) ●vi have a puncture. **~si** vr prick oneself; (con droga) shoot up

bu'cato nm washing

'buccia nf peel, skin

bucherel'lare vt riddle

'buco nm hole

bu'dello nm (pl nf budella) bowel

budget nm inv budget

bu'dino nm pudding

'bue nm (pl buoi) ox; **carne di ~** beef

'bufalo nm buffalo

bu'fera nf storm; (di neve) blizzard

buf'fetto nm cuff

'buffo a funny; Theat comic ●nm funny thing. **~'nata** nf (scherzo) joke. **buf'fone** nm buffoon; **fare il buffone** play the fool

bu'gi|a nf lie; **~a pietosa** white lie. **~'ardo, -a** a lying ●nmf liar

bugi'gattolo nm cubby-hole

'buio a dark ●nm darkness; **al ~ in the dark**; **~ pesto** pitch dark

'bulbo nm bulb; (dell'occhio) eyeball

Bulga'ria nf Bulgaria. **'bulgaro, -a** a & nmf Bulgarian

buli'mia nf bulimia. **bu'limico** a bulimic

'bullo nm bully

bul'lone nm bolt

'bunker nm inv bunker

buona'fede nf good faith

buona'notte int good night

buona'sera int good evening

buon'giorno int good morning; (di pomeriggio) good afternoon

buon'grado: di ~ adv willingly

buongu'staio, -a *nmf* gourmet. buon'gusto *nm* good taste

bu'ono *a* good; ⟨momento⟩ right; dar ~ ⟨convalidare⟩ accept; alla buona easy-going; ⟨cena⟩ informal; buona notte/ sera good night/evening; buon compleanno/Natale! happy birthday/ merry Christmas!; ~ senso common sense; di buon'ora early; una buona volta once and for all; buona parte di the best part of; tre ore buone three good hours ● *nm* good; ⟨in film⟩ goody; ⟨tagliando⟩ voucher; ⟨titolo⟩ bond; con le buone gently; ~ sconto money-off coupon ● *nmf* buono, -a a nulla dead loss

buontem'pone, -a *nmf* happy-go-lucky person

buonu'more *nm* good temper

buonu'scita *nf* retirement bonus; ⟨di dirigente⟩ golden handshake

burat'tino *nm* puppet

'burbero *a* surly; ⟨nei modi⟩ rough

bu'rocra|te *nm* bureaucrat. buro'cra-tico *a* bureaucratic. ~'zia *nf* bureaucracy

bur'ra|sca *nf* storm. ~'scoso *a* stormy

'burro *nm* butter

bur'rone *nm* ravine

bu'scar|e *vt*, ~si *vr* catch; ~le *fam* get a hiding

bus'sare *vt* knock

'bussola *nf* compass; perdere la ~ lose one's bearings

'busta *nf* envelope; ⟨astuccio⟩ case. ~ paga pay packet. ~'rella *nf* bribe. bu'stina *nf* ⟨di tè⟩ tea bag; ⟨per medicine⟩ sachet

'busto *nm* bust; ⟨indumento⟩ girdle

but'tar|e *vt* throw; ~e giù ⟨demolire⟩ knock down; ⟨inghiottire⟩ gulp down; scribble down ⟨scritto⟩; *fam* put on ⟨pasta⟩; ⟨scoraggiare⟩ dishearten; ~e via throw away. ~si *vr* throw oneself; ⟨saltare⟩ jump

butte'rato *a* pock-marked

buz'zurro *nm fam* yokel

Cc

caba'ret *nm inv* cabaret

ca'bina *nf* Naut, Aeron cabin; ⟨balneare⟩ beach hut. ~ elettorale polling booth. ~ di pilotaggio cockpit. ~ telefonica telephone box. cabi'nato *nm* cabin cruiser

ca'cao *nm* cocoa

'cacca *nf fam* pooh

'caccia *nf* hunt; ⟨con fucile⟩ shooting; ⟨inseguimento⟩ chase; ⟨selvaggina⟩ game ● *nm inv* Aeron fighter; Naut destroyer

cacciabombardi'ere *nm* fighter-bomber

cacciagi'one *nf* game

cacci'a|re *vt* hunt; ⟨mandar via⟩ chase away; ⟨scacciare⟩ drive out; ⟨ficcare⟩ shove ● *vi* go hunting. ~rsi *vr* ⟨nascondersi⟩ hide; ⟨andare a finire⟩ get to; ~rsi nei guai get into trouble; alla ~'tora *a* Culin chasseur. ~'tore, ~'trice *nmf* hunter. ~'tore di frodo poacher

caccia'vite *nm inv* screwdriver

ca'chet *nm inv* Med capsule; ⟨colorante⟩ colour rinse; ⟨stile⟩ cachet

'cachi *nm inv* ⟨albero, frutta⟩ persimmon

'cacio *nm* ⟨formaggio⟩ cheese

'caco *nm fam* ⟨frutto⟩ persimmon

'cactus *nm inv* cactus

ca'da|vere *nm* corpse. ~'verico *a fig* deathly pale

ca'dente *a* falling; ⟨casa⟩ crumbling

ca'denza *nf* cadence; ⟨ritmo⟩ rhythm; Mus cadenza

ca'dere *vi* fall; ⟨capelli ecc⟩ fall out; ⟨capitombolare⟩ tumble; ⟨verso ecc.⟩ hang; far ~ ⟨di mano⟩ drop; ~ dal sonno feel very sleepy; lasciar ~ drop; ~ dalle nuvole *fig* be taken aback

ca'detto *nm* cadet

ca'duta *nf* fall; ⟨di capelli⟩ loss; *fig* downfall

caffè *nm inv* coffee; ⟨locale⟩ café. ~ corretto espresso coffee with a dash of liqueur. ~ lungo weak black coffee. ~ macchiato coffee with a dash of milk.

35 caffettiera | camaleonte

~ **ristretto** extra-strong espresso coffee. ~ **solubile** instant coffee. ~**ina** *nf* caffeine. ~ **latte** *nm inv* white coffee.

caffetti'era *nf* coffee-pot

cafo'naggine *nf* boorishness

cafo'nata *nf* boorishness

ca'fone, -a *nmf* boor

ca'gare *vi fam* crap

cagio'nare *vt* cause

cagio'nevole *a* delicate

cagli'are vi **~si** *vr* curdle

cagna *nf* bitch

ca'gnara *nf fam* din

ca'gnesco *a* **guardare qcno in ~** scowl at sb

cala *nf* creek

cala'brone *nm* hornet

cala'maio *nm* inkpot

cala'mari *nmpl* squid

cala'mita *nf* magnet

calamità *nf inv* calamity

ca'lare *vi* come down; *(vento:)* drop; *(diminuire)* fall; *(tramontare)* set ●*vt* *(abbassare)* lower; *(nei lavori a maglia)* decrease ●*nm (di luna)* waning. ~**si** *vr* lower oneself

calca *nf* throng

cal'cagno *nm* heel

cal'care[1] *nm* limestone

cal'care[2] *vt* tread; *(premere)* press [down]; ~ **la mano** exaggerate; ~ **le orme di qcno** *fig* follow in sb's footsteps

calce[1] *nf* lime

calce[2] **in ~** = at the foot of the page

calce'struzzo *nm* concrete

cal'cetto *nm* Sport five-a-side [football]

calci'are *vt* kick. ~**tore** *nm* footballer

cal'cina *nf* mortar

calci'naccio *nm (pezzo di intonaco)* flake of plaster

calcio[1] *nm* kick; Sport football; *(di arma da fuoco)* butt; **dare un ~ a** kick. ~ **d'angolo** corner [kick]

calcio[2] *nm (chimica)* calcium

calco *nm (con carta)* tracing; *(arte)* cast

calco'lare *vt* calculate; *(considerare)* consider. ~**tore** *a* calculating ●*nm* calculator; *(macchina elettronica)* computer

calcolo *nm* calculation; *Med* stone

cal'daia *nf* boiler

caldar'rosta *nf* roast chestnut

caldeggi'are *vt* support

caldo *a* warm; *(molto caldo)* hot ●*nm* heat; **avere ~** be warm/hot; **fa ~** it is warm/hot

calen'dario *nm* calendar

calibro *nm* calibre; *(strumento)* callipers *pl*; **di grosso ~** *(persona)* top *attrib*

calice *nm* goblet; Relig chalice

ca'ligine *nm* fog; *(industriale)* smog

calligra'fia *nf* handwriting; *(cinese)* calligraphy

cal'lista *nmf* chiropodist. **callo** *nm* corn; **fare il callo a** become hardened to. **cal'loso** *a* callous

calma *nf* calm. **cal'mante** *a* calming ●*nm* sedative. **cal'mare** *vt* calm [down]; *(lenire)* soothe. **cal'marsi** *vr* calm down; *(vento:)* drop; *(dolore:)* die down. **calmo** *a* calm

calo *nm* Comm fall; *(di volume)* shrinkage; *(di peso)* loss

calorosa'mente *adv (cordialmente)* warmly

ca'lore *nm* heat; *(moderato)* warmth; **in ~** *(animale)* on heat. **calo'roso** *a* warm

calo'ria *nf* calorie

ca'lorico *a* calorific

calo'rifero *nm* radiator

calpe'stare *vt* trample [down]; *fig* trample on *(diritti, sentimenti)*; **vietato ~ l'erba** keep off the grass

calpe'stio *nm (passi)* footsteps

ca'lunnia *nf* slander. ~**are** *vt* slander. ~**oso** *a* slanderous

ca'lura *nf* heat

cal'vario *nm* Calvary; *fig* trial

cal'vizie *nf* baldness. **calvo** *a* bald

calza *nf (da donna)* stocking; *(da uomo)* sock. ~**a'maglia** *nf* tights *pl*; *(per danza)* leotard

cal'zante *a fig* fitting

cal'zare *vt (indossare)* wear; *(mettersi)* put on ●*vi* fit

calza'scarpe *nm inv* shoehorn

calza'tura *nf* footwear

calzatu'ri'ficio *nm* shoe factory

cal'zetta *nf* **è una mezza ~** *fig* he's no use

calzet'tone *nm* knee-length woollen sock. **cal'zino** *nm* sock

calzo'laio *nm* shoemaker. ~**e'ria** *nf* *(negozio)* shoe shop

calzon'cini *nmpl* shorts. ~ **da bagno** swimming trunks

cal'zone *nm* Culin folded pizza with tomato and mozzarella or ricotta inside

cal'zoni *nmpl* trousers, pants *Am*

camale'onte *nm* chameleon

cambi'ale *nf* bill of exchange

cambia'mento *nm* change

cambi'ar|e *vt/i* change; move ⟨*casa*⟩; ⟨*fare cambio di*⟩ exchange; **~e rotta** *Naut* alter course. **~si** *vr* change. **'cambio** *nm* change; ⟨*Comm, scambio*⟩ exchange; *Mech* gear; **dare il cambio a** qcno relieve sb; **in cambio di** in exchange for

'camera *nf* room; ⟨*mobili*⟩ [bedroom] suite; *Phot* camera; **C~** *Pol, Comm* Chamber. **~ ardente** funeral parlour. **~ d'aria** inner tube. **C~ di Commercio** Chamber of Commerce. **C~ dei Deputati** *Pol* ≈ House of Commons. **~ doppia** double room. **~ da letto** bedroom. **~ matrimoniale** double room. **~ oscura** darkroom. **~ singola** single room

came'rata¹ *nf* ⟨*dormitorio*⟩ dormitory; *Mil* barrack room

came'ra|ta² *nmf* ⟨*amico*⟩ mate; *Pol* comrade. **~'tismo** *nm* comradeship

cameri'era *nf* maid; ⟨*di ristorante*⟩ waitress; ⟨*in albergo*⟩ chamber-maid; ⟨*di bordo*⟩ stewardess

cameri'ere *nm* manservant; ⟨*di ristorante*⟩ waiter; ⟨*di bordo*⟩ steward

came'rino *nm* dressing-room

'camice *nm* overall. **cami'cetta** *nf* blouse. **ca'micia** *nf* shirt; **uovo in camicia** poached egg. **camicia da notte** nightdress

cami'netto *nm* fireplace

ca'mino *nm* chimney; ⟨*focolare*⟩ fireplace

'camion *nm inv* lorry *Br*, truck

camion'cino *nm* van

camio'netta *nf* jeep

camio'nista *nm* lorry driver *Br*, truck driver

cam'mello *nm* camel; ⟨*tessuto*⟩ camelhair ● *a inv* ⟨*colore*⟩ camel

cam'meo *nm* cameo

cammi'na|re *vi* walk; ⟨*auto, orologio:*⟩ go. **~ta** *nf* walk; **fare una ~ta** go for a walk. **cam'mino** *nm* way; **essere in cammino** be on the way; **mettersi in cammino** set out

camo'milla *nf* camomile; ⟨*bevanda*⟩ camomile tea

ca'morra *nf* local mafia

ca'moscio *nm* chamois; ⟨*pelle*⟩ suede

cam'pagna *nf* country; ⟨*paesaggio*⟩ countryside; *Comm, Mil* campaign; **in ~** in the country. **~ elettorale** election campaign. **~ pubblicitaria** marketing campaign. **campa'gnolo, -a** *a* rustic ● *nm* countryman ● *nf* countrywoman

cam'pale *a* field *attrib*; **giornata ~** *fig* strenuous day

cam'pa|na *nf* bell; ⟨*di vetro*⟩ belljar. **~'nella** *nf* ⟨*di tenda*⟩ curtain ring. **~'nello** *nm* door-bell; ⟨*cicalino*⟩ buzzer

campa'nile *nm* belfry

campani'lismo *nm* parochialism

campani'lista *nmf* person with a parochial outlook

cam'panula *nf Bot* campanula

cam'pare *vi* live; ⟨*a stento*⟩ get by

cam'pato *a* **~ in aria** unfounded

campeggi'a|re *vi* camp; ⟨*spiccare*⟩ stand out. **~'tore, ~'trice** *nmf* camper. **cam'peggio** *nm* camping; ⟨*terreno*⟩ campsite

cam'pestre *a* rural

'camping *nm inv* campsite

campio'nari|o *nm* [set of] samples ● *a* samples; **fiera ~a** a trade fair

campio'nato *nm* championship

campiona'tura *nf* ⟨*di merce*⟩ range of samples

campi'on|e *nm* champion; *Comm* sample; ⟨*esemplare*⟩ specimen. **~'essa** *nf* ladies' champion

'campo *nm* field; ⟨*accampamento*⟩ camp. **~ da calcio** football pitch. **~ di concentramento** concentration camp. **~ da golf** golf course. **~ da tennis** tennis court

campo'santo *nm* cemetery

camuf'far|e *vt* disguise. **~si** *vr* disguise oneself

'Cana|da *nm* Canada. **~'dese** *a & nmf* Canadian

ca'naglia *nf* scoundrel; ⟨*plebaglia*⟩ rabble

ca'nal|e *nm* channel; ⟨*artificiale*⟩ canal. **~iz'zare** *vt* channel ⟨*acque*⟩. **~izzazi'one** *nf* channelling; ⟨*rete*⟩ pipes *pl*

'canapa *nf* hemp

cana'rino *nm* canary

cancel'la|re *vt* cross out; ⟨*con la gomma*⟩ rub out; *fig* wipe out; ⟨*annullare*⟩ cancel; *Comput* delete, erase. **~'tura** *nf* erasure. **~zi'one** *nf* cancellation; *Comput* deletion

cancelle'ria *nf* chancellery; ⟨*articoli per scrivere*⟩ stationery

cancelli'ere *nm* chancellor; ⟨*di tribunale*⟩ clerk

can'cello *nm* gate

cance'ro|geno *nm* carcinogen ● *a* carcinogenic. **~'so** *a* cancerous

can'crena *nf* gangrene

'cancro *nm* cancer. **C~** *Astr* Cancer

candeg'gi‚na nf bleach. **~'are** vt bleach. **can'deggio** nm bleaching

can'de‚la nf candle; Auto spark plug; **~'labro** nm candelabra. **~li'ere** nm candlestick

cande'lotto nm (di dinamite) stick

candida'mente adv candidly

candi'dar‚si vr stand as a candidate. **~to, -a** nmf candidate. **~'tura** nf Pol candidacy; (per lavoro) application

'candido a snow-white; (sincero) candid; (puro) pure

can'dito a candied

can'dore nm whiteness; fig innocence

'cane nm dog; (di arma da fuoco) cock; **un tempo da cani** foul weather. **~ da caccia** hunting dog

ca'nestro nm basket

cangi'ante a iridescent; **seta ~** shot silk

can'guro nm kangaroo

ca'nile nm kennel; (di allevamento) kennels pl. **~ municipale** dog pound

ca'nino a & nm canine

'canna nf reed; (da zucchero) cane; (di fucile) barrel; (bastone) stick; (di bicicletta) crossbar; (asta) rod; (fam: hascish) joint; **povero in ~** destitute. **~ da pesca** fishing-rod

can'nella nf cinnamon

can'neto nm bed of reeds

canni'ba‚le nm cannibal. **~'lismo** nm cannibalism

cannocchi'ale nm telescope

canno'nata nf cannon shot; **è una ~** fig it's brilliant

cannon'cino nm (dolce) cream horn

can'none nm cannon; fig ace

can'nuccia nf (drinking) straw; (di pipa) stem

ca'noa nf canoe

'canone nm canon; (affitto) rent; **equo ~** fair rents act

ca'noni‚co nm canon. **~z'zare** vt canonize. **~zzazi'one** nf canonization

ca'noro a melodious

ca'notta nf (estiva) vest top

canot'taggio nm canoeing; (voga) rowing

canotti'era nf singlet

canotti'ere nm oarsman

ca'notto nm [rubber] dinghy

cano'vaccio nm (trama) plot; (straccio) duster

can'tante nmf singer

can't'are vt/i sing. **~au'tore, ~a'trice** nmf singer-songwriter. **~icchi'are** vt sing softly; (a bocca chiusa) hum

canti'ere nm yard; Naut shipyard; (di edificio) construction site. **~ navale** naval dockyard

canti'lena nf singsong; (ninna-nanna) lullaby

can'tina nf cellar; (osteria) wine shop

'canto¹ nm singing; (canzone) song; Relig chant; (poesia) poem

'canto² nm (angolo) corner; (lato) side; **dal ~ mio** for my part; **d'altro ~** on the other hand

canto'nata nf **prendere una ~** fig be sadly mistaken

can'tone nm canton; (angolo) corner

can'tuccio nm nook

canzo'na‚re vt tease. **~'torio** a teasing. **~'tura** nf teasing

can'zo‚ne nf song. **~'netta** nf fam pop song. **~ni'ere** nm songbook

'caos nm chaos. **ca'otico** a chaotic

C.A.P. nm abbr (**Codice di Avviamento Postale**) post code, zip code Am

ca'pa‚ce a able; (esperto) skilled; (stadio, contenitore) big; **~e di** (disposto a) capable of. **~'ità** nf inv ability; (attitudine) skill; (capienza) capacity

capaci'tar‚si vr **~ di** (rendersi conto) understand; (accorgersi) realize

ca'panna nf hut

capan'nello nm **fare ~ intorno a qcno/qcsa** gather round sb/sth

capan'none nm shed; Aeron hangar

ca'parbio a obstinate

ca'parra nf deposit

capa'tina nf short visit; **fare una ~ in città/da qcno** pop into town/in on sb

ca'pel‚lo nm hair; **~li** pl (capigliatura) hair sg. **~'lone** nm hippie. **~'luto** a hairy

capez'zale nm bolster; fig bedside

ca'pezzolo nm nipple

capi'en‚te a capacious. **~za** nf capacity

capiglia'tura nf hair

ca'pire vt understand; **~ male** misunderstand; **si capisce!** naturally!; **sì, ho capito** yes, I see

capi'ta‚le a Jur capital; (principale) main ● nf (città) capital ● nm Comm capital. **~'lismo** nm capitalism. **~ lista** nmf capitalist. **~'listico** a capitalist

capitane'ria nf **~ di porto** port authorities pl

capi'tano nm captain

capi'tare vi (giungere per caso) come; (accadere) happen

capi'tello nm Archit capital

capito'la|re *vi* capitulate. **~zi'one** *nf* capitulation

ca'pitolo *nm* chapter

capi'tombolo *nm* headlong fall; **fare un ~** tumble down

capo *nm* head; *(chi comanda)* boss *fam*; *(di vestiario)* item; *Geog* cape; *(in tribù)* chief; *(parte estrema)* top; **a ~** *(in detta-to)* new paragraph; **da ~** over again; **in ~ a un mese** within a month; **gira-mento di ~** dizziness; **mal di ~** head-ache; **~ d'abbigliamento** item of clothing. **~ d'accusa** *Jur* charge, count. **~ di bestiame** head of cattle

capo'banda *nm* *Mus* bandmaster; *(di delinquenti)* ringleader

ca'poccia *nm (fam: testa)* nut

capocci'one, -a *nmf fam* brainbox

capo'danno *nm* New Year's Day

capofa'miglia *nm* head of the family

capo'fitto *nm* **a ~** headlong

capo'giro *nm* giddiness

capola'voro *nm* masterpiece

capo'linea *nm* terminus

capo'lino *nm* **fare ~** peep in

capolu'ogo *nm* main town

capo'rale *nm* lance-corporal

capo'squadra *nmf* *Sport* team cap-tain

capo'stipite *nmf (di famiglia)* pro-genitor

capo'tavola *nmf* head of the table

capo'treno *nm* guard

capouf'ficio *nmf* head clerk

capo'verso *nm* first line

capo'vol|gere *vt* overturn; *fig* re-verse. **~gersi** *vr* overturn; *(barca:)* capsize; *fig* be reversed. **~to** *pp* di **capovolgere ● a** upside-down

'cappa *nf* cloak; *(di camino)* cowl; *(di cucina)* hood

cap'pel|la *nf* chapel. **~ lano** *nm* chap-lain

cap'pello *nm* hat. **~ a cilindro** top hat

'cappero *nm* caper

'cappio *nm* noose

cap'pone *nm* capon

cap'potto *nm* [over]coat

cappuc'cino *nm (frate)* Capuchin; *(bevanda)* white coffee

cap'puccio *nm* hood; *(di penna stilo-grafica)* cap

'capra *nf* goat. **ca'pretto** *nm* kid

ca'priccio *nm* whim; *(bizzarria)* freak; **fare i capricci** have tantrums. **~ 'oso** *a* capricious; *(bambino)* naughty

Capri'corno *nm* *Astr* Capricorn

capri'ola *nf* somersault

capri'olo *nm* roe-deer

'capro *nm* [billy-]goat. **~ espiatorio** scapegoat. **ca'prone** *nm* [billy] goat

'capsula *nf* capsule; *(di proiettile)* cap; *(di dente)* crown

cap'tare *vt* *Radio, TV* pick up; catch *(attenzione)*

cara'bina *nf* carbine

carabini'ere *nm* carabiniere; **carabi-ni'eri** *pl* Italian police force *(which is a branch of the army)*

ca'raffa *nf* carafe

Ca'raibi *nmpl (zona)* Caribbean *sg*; *(isole)* Caribbean Islands; **il mar dei ~** the Caribbean [Sea]

cara'mella *nf* sweet

cara'mello *nm* caramel

ca'rato *nm* carat

ca'ratte|re *nm* character; *(caratteri-stica)* characteristic; *Typ* type; **di buon ~re** good-natured. **~ ristico, -a** *a* char-acteristic; *(pittoresco)* quaint ● *nf* char-acteristic. **~riz'zare** *vt* characterize

carbon'cino *nm (per disegno)* char-coal

car'bone *nm* coal

carboniz'zare *vt* burn to a cinder

carbu'rante *nm* fuel

carbura'tore *nm* carburettor

car'cassa *nf* carcass; *fig* old wreck

carce'ra|rio *a* prison *attrib.* **~to, -a** *nmf* prisoner. **~zi'one** *nf* imprison-ment. **~zione preventiva** preventive detention

'carcer|e *nm* prison; *(punizione)* im-prisonment. **~i'ere, -a** *nmf* gaoler

carci'ofo *nm* artichoke

car'diaco *a* cardiac

cardi'nale *a* & *nm* cardinal

'cardine *nm* hinge

cardio|chi'rurgo *nm* heart surgeon. **~ lo'gia** *nf* cardiology. **cardi'ologo** *nm* heart specialist. **~ 'tonico** *nm* heart stimulant

'cardo *nm* thistle

ca'rena *nf* *Naut* bottom

ca'ren|te *a* **~ di** lacking in. **~za** *nf* lack; *(scarsità)* scarcity

care'stia *nf* famine; *(mancanza)* dearth

ca'rezza *nf* caress; **fare una ~** a ca-ress

cari'a|rsi *vi* decay. **~to** *a* decayed

'carica *nf* office; *Mil, Electr* charge; *fig* drive. **cari'care** *vt* load; *Mil, Electr* charge; wind up *(orologio)*. **~ 'tore** *nm* *(per proiettile)* magazine

carica'tu|ra *nf* caricature. **~'rale** *a* grotesque. **~'rista** *nmf* caricaturist

'carico *a* loaded (**di** with); ⟨*colore*⟩ strong; ⟨*orologio*⟩ wound [up]; ⟨*batteria*⟩ charged ● *nm* load; ⟨*di nave*⟩ cargo; ⟨*il caricare*⟩ loading; **a ~ di** *Comm* to be charged to; ⟨*persona*⟩ dependent on

'carie *nf* [tooth] decay

ca'rino *a* pretty; ⟨*piacevole*⟩ agreeable

ca'risma *nm* charisma. **cari'smatico** *a* charismatic

carit'à *nf* charity; **per ~à!** ⟨*come rifiuto*⟩ God forbid!. **~a'tevole** *a* charitable

carnagi'one *nf* complexion

car'naio *nm fig* shambles

car'nale *a* carnal; **cugino ~** first cousin

'carne *nf* flesh; ⟨*alimento*⟩ meat; **~ di manzo/maiale/vitello** beef/pork/veal

car'nefi|ce *nm* executioner. **~'cina** *nf* slaughter

carne'vale *nm* carnival. **~'lesco** *a* carnival

car'nivoro *nm* carnivore ● *a* carnivorous

car'noso *a* fleshy

'caro, -a *a* dear; **cari saluti** kind regards ● *nmf fam* darling, dear; **i miei cari** my nearest and dearest

ca'rogna *nf* carcass; *fig* bastard

caro'sello *nm* merry-go-round

ca'rota *nf* carrot

caro'vana *nf* caravan; ⟨*di veicoli*⟩ convoy

caro'vita *nm* high cost of living

'carpa *nf* carp

carpenti'ere *nm* carpenter

car'pire *vt* seize; ⟨*con difficoltà*⟩ extort

car'pone, car'poni *adv* on all fours

car'rabile *a* suitable for vehicles; **passo ~** *vedi* **carraio**

car'raio *a* **passo** *nm* **~** entrance to driveway, garage etc where parking is forbidden

carreggi'ata *nf* roadway; **doppia ~** dual carriageway, divided highway *Am*

carrel'lata *nf TV* pan

car'rello *nm* trolley; ⟨*di macchina da scrivere*⟩ carriage; *Aeron* undercarriage; *Cinema, TV* dolly. **~ d'atterraggio** *Aeron* landing gear

car'retto *nm* cart

carri'e|ra *nf* career; **di gran ~ra** at full speed; **fare ~ra** get on. **~'rismo** *nm* careerism

carri'ola *nf* wheelbarrow

'carro *nm* cart. **~ armato** tank. **~**

attrezzi breakdown vehicle, wrecker *Am*. **~ funebre** hearse. **~ merci** truck

car'rozza *nf* carriage; *Rail* car, coach. **~ cuccette** sleeping car. **~ ristorante** restaurant car

carroz'zella *nf* ⟨*per bambini*⟩ pram; ⟨*per invalidi*⟩ wheelchair

carrozze'ria *nf* bodywork; ⟨*officina*⟩ bodyshop

carroz'zina *nf* pram; ⟨*pieghevole*⟩ push-chair, stroller *Am*

carroz'zone *nm* ⟨*di circo*⟩ caravan

'carta *nf* paper; ⟨*da gioco*⟩ card; ⟨*statuto*⟩ charter; *Geog* map. **~ d'argento** ≈ senior citizens' railcard. **~ assorbente** blotting-paper. **~ di credito** credit card. **~ geografica** map. **~ d'identità** identity card. **~ igienica** toilet-paper. **~ di imbarco** boarding card. **~ da lettere** writing-paper. **~ da parati** wallpaper. **~ stagnola** silver paper; *Culin* aluminium foil. **~ straccia** waste paper. **~ stradale** road map. **~ velina** tissue-paper. **~ verde** *Auto* green card. **~ vetrata** sandpaper

cartacar'bone *nf* carbon paper

car'taccia *nf* waste paper

carta'modello *nm* pattern

cartamo'neta *nf* paper money

carta'pesta *nf* papier mâché

carta'straccia *nf* waste paper

cartave'trare *vt* sand [down]

car'tel|la *nf* ⟨*per documenti ecc*⟩ briefcase; ⟨*di cartone*⟩ folder; ⟨*di scolaro*⟩ satchel. **~la clinica** medical record. **~'lina** document wallet, folder

cartel'lino *nm* label; ⟨*dei prezzi*⟩ price-tag; ⟨*di presenza*⟩ time-card; **timbrare il ~** clock in; ⟨*all'uscita*⟩ clock out

car'tel|lo *nm* sign; ⟨*pubblicitario*⟩ poster; ⟨*stradale*⟩ road sign; ⟨*di protesta*⟩ placard; *Comm* cartel. **~'lone** *nm* poster; *Theat* bill

carti'era *nf* paper-mill

carti'lagine *nf* cartilage

car'tina *nf* map

car'toccio *nm* paper bag; **al ~** *Culin* baked in foil

carto'|laio, -a *nmf* stationer. **~le'ria** *nf* stationer's [shop]. **~libre'ria** *nf* stationer's and book shop

carto'lina *nf* postcard. **~ postale** postcard

carto'mante *nmf* fortune-teller

carton'cino *nm* ⟨*materiale*⟩ card

car'tone *nm* cardboard; ⟨*arte*⟩ cartoon. **~ animato** [animated] cartoon

car'tuccia *nf* cartridge

'**casa** *nf* house; (*abitazione propria*) home; (*ditta*) firm; **amico di ~** family friend; **andare a ~** go home; **essere di ~** be like one of the family; **fatto in ~** home-made; **padrone di ~** (*di pensione ecc*) landlord; (*proprietario*) house owner. **~ di cura** nursing home. **~ po-polare** council house. **~ dello studen-te** hall of residence

ca'**sacca** *nf* military coat; (*giacca*) jacket

ca'**saccio** *adv* **a ~** at random

casa'**linga** *nf* housewife. **~o** *a* domestic; (*fatto in casa*) home-made; (*amante della casa*) home-loving; (*semplice*) homely

ca'**scante** *a* falling; (*floscio*) flabby

ca'**scare** *vi* fall [down]. **~ta** *nf* (*di acqua*) waterfall

ca'**schetto** *nm* [capelli a] **~** bob

ca'**scina** *nf* farm building

'**casco** *nm* crash-helmet; (*asciuga-ca-pelli*) [hair-]drier; **~ di banane** bunch of bananas

caseggi'**ato** *nm* block of flats; *Br*, apartment block

casei'**ficio** *nm* dairy

ca'**sella** *nf* pigeon-hole. **~ postale** post office box; *Comput* mailbox

casel'**lante** *nmf* (*per treni*) signalman

casel'**lario** *nm* **~ giudiziario** record of convictions; **avere il ~ giudiziario vergine** have no criminal record

ca'**sello** [autostra'**dale**] *nm* [mo-torway] toll booth

case'**reccio** *a* home-made

ca'**serma** *nf* barracks *pl*; (*dei carabi-nieri*) [police] station

casi'**nista** *nmf fam* muddler. ca'**sino** *nm fam* (*bordello*) brothel; (*fig: confu-sione*) racket; (*disordine*) mess; **un casi-no di** loads of

casi'**no** *nm inv* casino

ca'**sistica** *nf* (*classificazione*) case records *pl*

'**caso** *nm* chance; (*fatto, circostanza, Med, Gram*) case; **a ~** at random; **~ mai** if need be; **far ~ a** pay attention to; **non far ~** a take no account of; **per ~** by chance. **~** [giudiziario] [legal] case

caso'**lare** *nm* farmhouse

'**caspita** *int* good gracious!

'**cassa** *nf* till; *Comm* cash; (*luogo di pa-gamento*) cash desk; (*mobile*) chest; (*isti-tuto bancario*) bank. **~ automatica prelievi** cash dispenser, automatic teller. **~ da morto** coffin. **~ toracica** ribcage

cassa'**forte** *nf* safe

cassa'**panca** *nf* linen chest

casseru'**ola** *nf* saucepan

cas'**setta** *nf* case; (*per registratore*) cassette. **~ delle lettere** postbox, letterbox. **~ di sicurezza** strong-box

cas'**set**|**to** *nm* drawer. **~'tone** *nm* chest of drawers

cassi'**ere, -a** *nmf* cashier; (*di super-mercato*) checkout assistant, checkout operator; (*di banca*) teller

'**casta** *nf* caste

ca'**stagn**|**a** *nf* chestnut. **casta'gneto** *nm* chestnut grove. **~o** *nm* chestnut[-tree]

ca'**stano** *a* chestnut

ca'**stello** *nm* castle; (*impalcatura*) scaffold

casti'**gare** *vt* punish

casti'**gato** *a* (*casto*) chaste

ca'**stigo** *nm* punishment

casti'**tà** *nf* chastity. '**casto** *a* chaste

ca'**storo** *nm* beaver

ca'**strare** *vt* castrate

casu'**ale** *a* chance *attrib*. **~'mente** *adv* by chance

ca'**supola** *nf* little house

cata'**clisma** *nm fig* upheaval

cata'**comba** *nf* catacomb

cata'**fascio** *nm* **andare a ~** go to rack and ruin

cata'**litico** *a* **marmitta catalitica** *Auto* catalytic converter

cataliz'**za**|**re** *vt fig* heighten. **~'tore** *nm Auto* catalytic converter

catalo'**gare** *vt* catalogue. ca'**talogo** *nm* catalogue

cata'**marano** *nm* (*da diporto*) catama-ran

cata'**pecchia** *nf* hovel; *fam* dump

catapul'**ta**|**re** *vt* (*scaraventare fuori*) eject. **~si** *vr* (*precipitarsi*) dive

catarifran'**gente** *nm* reflector

ca'**tarro** *nm* catarrh

ca'**tasta** *nf* pile

ca'**tasto** *nm* land register

ca'**tastrofe** *nf* catastrophe. **cata-'strofico** *a* catastrophic

cate'**chismo** *nm* catechism

catego'**ria** *nf* category. **~ gorico** *a* categorical

ca'**tena** *nf* chain. **~ montuosa** moun-tain range. **catene** *pl* **da neve** tyre-chains. **cate'naccio** *nm* bolt

cate'**nella** *nf* (*collana*) chain. **~'nina** *nf* chain

cate'**ratta** *nf* cataract

ca'**terva** *nf* **una ~ di** heaps of

cati'nell|a nf basin; **piovere a ~e** bucket down

ca'tino nm basin

ca'torcio nm fam old wreck

ca'trame nm tar

'cattedra nf (tavolo di insegnante) desk; (di università) chair

catte'drale nf cathedral

catti'veria nf wickedness; (azione) wicked action

cattività nf captivity

cat'tivo a bad; ⟨bambino⟩ naughty

cattoli'cesimo nm Catholicism

cat'tolico, -a a & nmf [Roman] Catholic

cat'tu|ra nf capture. **~rare** vt capture

caucciù nm rubber

'causa nf cause; Jur lawsuit; **far ~ a qcno** sue sb. **cau'sare** vt cause

'caustico a caustic

cauta'mente adv cautiously

cau'tela nf caution

caute'lar|e vt protect. **~si** vr take precautions

cauteriz'z|are vt cauterize. **~azi'one** nf cauterization

'cauto a cautious

cauzi'one nf security; (per libertà provvisoria) bail

'cava nf quarry; fig mine

caval'ca|re vt ride; (stare a cavalcioni) sit astride. **~ta** nf ride; (corteo) cavalcade. **~'via** nm flyover

cavalci'oni adv **a ~** astride

cavali'ere nm rider; (titolo) knight; (accompagnatore) escort; (al ballo) partner

cavalle'resco a chivalrous. **~'ria** nf chivalry; Mil cavalry. **~'rizzo, -a** nm horseman ⟨nf horsewoman

caval'letta nf grasshopper

caval'letto nm trestle; (di macchina fotografica) tripod; (di pittore) easel

caval'lina nf (ginnastica) horse

ca'vallo nm horse; (misura di potenza) horsepower; (scacchi) knight; (dei pantaloni) crotch; **a ~** on horseback; **andare a ~** go horse-riding. **~ a dondolo** rocking-horse

caval'lone nm (ondata) roller

caval'luccio ma'rino nm sea horse

ca'var|e vt take out; (di dosso) take off; **~sela** get away with it; **se la cava bene** he's/she's doing all right

cava'tappi nm inv corkscrew

ca'verna nf cave. **~'noso** a ⟨voce⟩ deep

'cavia nf guinea-pig

cavi'ale nm caviar

ca'viglia nf ankle

cavil'lare vi quibble. **ca'villo** nm quibble

cavità nf inv cavity

'cavo a hollow ⟨nm cavity; (di metallo) cable; Naut rope

cavo'lata nf fam rubbish

cavo'letto nm **~ di Bruxelles** Brussels sprout

cavolfi'ore nm cauliflower

'cavolo nm cabbage; **~!** fam sugar!

caz'zo int vulg fuck!

caz'zott|o nm punch; **prendere qcno a ~i** beat sb up

cazzu'ola nf trowel

c/c abbr (**conto corrente**) c/a

CD-Rom nm inv CD-Rom

ce pron pers (a noi) (to) us ⟨adv there; **~ ne sono molti** there are many

'cece nm chick-pea

cecità nf blindness

ceco, -a a & nmf Czech; **la Repubblica Ceca** the Czech Republic

Cecoslo'vacc|hia nf Czechoslovakia. **c~o, -a** a & nmf Czechoslovak

'cedere vi (arrendersi) surrender; (concedere) yield; (sprofondare) subside ⟨vt give up; make over (proprietà ecc). **ce'devole** a ⟨terreno ecc⟩ soft; fig yielding. **cedi'mento** nm (di terreno) subsidence

cedola nf coupon

cedro nm (albero) cedar; (frutto) citron

C.E.E. nf abbr (**Comunità Economica Europea**) E[E]C

'ceffo nm (muso) snout; (pej: persona) mug

ceff'one nm slap

ce'lar|e vt conceal. **~si** vr hide

cele'brare vt celebrate. **~zi'one** nf celebration

'celebr|e a famous. **~ità** nf inv celebrity

'celere a swift

ce'leste a (divino) heavenly ⟨a & nm (colore) sky-blue

celi'bato nm celibacy

'celibe a single ⟨nm bachelor

'cella nf cell

'cellofan nm inv cellophane; Culin cling film

cellul|a nf cell. **~ fotoelettrica** electronic eye

cellu'lare nm (telefono) cellular phone ⟨a **furgone ~** police van; **telefono ~** cellular phone

cellu'lite nf cellulite
cellu'loide a celluloid
cellu'losa nf cellulose
'celta nm Celt. ~ico a Celtic
cemen'tare vt cement. **ce'mento** nm cement. **cemento armato** reinforced concrete
'cena nf dinner; (leggera) supper
ce'nacolo nm circle
ce'nare vi have dinner
'cencio nm rag; (per spolverare) duster. ~oso a in rags
'cenere nf ash; (di carbone ecc) cinders
ce'netta nf (cena semplice) informal dinner
'cenno nm sign; (col capo) nod; (con la mano) wave; (allusione) hint; (breve resoconto) mention
ce'none nm il ~ di Capodanno/ Natale special New Year's Eve/Christmas Eve dinner
censi'mento nm census
cen'sore nm censor. ~ura nf censorship. ~u'rare vt censor
centelli'nare vt sip
cente'n|ario, -a a & nmf centenarian ● nm (commemorazione) centenary. ~'nale a centennial
cen'tesimo a hundredth ● nm (di dollaro) cent; **non avere un ~** be penniless
cen'ti|grado a centigrade. ~metro nm centimetre
centi'naio nm hundred
'cento a & nm a or one hundred; **per ~** per cent
centome'trista nmf Sport one hundred metres runner
cento'mila nm a or one hundred thousand
cen'trale a central ● nf (di società ecc) head office. **~ atomica** atomic power station. **~ elettrica** power station. **~ nucleare** nuclear power station. **~ telefonica** [telephone] exchange
centra'lina nf Teleph switchboard. ~'nista nmf operator
centra'lino nm Teleph exchange; (di albergo ecc) switchboard
centra'li|smo nm centralism. ~z'zare vt centralize
cen'trare vt ~ qcsa hit sth in the centre; (fissare nel centro) centre; fig hit on the head (idea)
cen'trifu|ga nf spin-drier. ~ [asciugaverdure] shaker. ~'gare vt Techn centrifuge; (lavatrice:) spin
cen'trino nm doily

'centro nm centre. **~ [città]** city centre. **~ commerciale** shopping centre, mall. **~ sociale** community centre
'ceppo nm (di albero) stump; (da ardere) log; (fig: gruppo) stock
'cera nf wax; (aspetto) look. **~ per il pavimento** floor-polish
ce'ramica nf (arte) ceramics; (materia) pottery; (oggetto) piece of pottery
ce'rato a (tela) waxed
cerbi'atto nm fawn
'cerca nf **andare in ~ di** look for
cercaper'sone nm inv beeper
cer'care vt look for ● vi **~ di** try to
'cerchi|a nf circle. **~are** vt circle (parola). **~ato** a (occhi) black-ringed. **~'etto** nm (per capelli) hairband
'cerchi|o nm circle; (giocattolo) hoop. **~one** nm alloy wheel
cere'ale nm cereal
cere'brale a cerebral
'cereo a waxen
ce'retta nf depilatory wax
ceri'moni|a nf ceremony. **~ale** nm ceremonial. **~oso** a ceremonious
ce'rino nm [wax] match
cerni'era nf hinge; (di borsa) clasp. **~ lampo** zip[-fastener], zipper Am
cernita nf selection
'cero nm candle
ce'rone nm grease-paint
ce'rotto nm [sticking] plaster
certa'mente adv certainly
cer'tezza nf certainty
certifi'ca|re vt certify. **~to** nm certificate
'certo a certain; (notizia) definite; (indeterminativo) some; **sono ~ di riuscire** I am certain to succeed; **a una certa età** at a certain age; **certi giorni** some days; **un ~ signor Giardini** a Mr Giardini; **una certa Anna** somebody called Anna; **certa gente** pej some people; **ho certi dolori!** I'm in such pain!. **certi** pron pl some; (alcune persone) some people ● adv of course; **sapere per ~** know for certain, know for sure; **di ~** surely; **~ che si!** of course!
cer'vel|lo nm brain. **~'lone, -a** nmf hum genius. **~'lotico** a (macchinoso) over-elaborate
'cervo nm deer
ce'sareo a Med Caesarean
cesel'la|re vt chisel. **~to** a chiselled. **ce'sello** nm chisel
ce'soie nfpl shears
ce'spugli|o nm bush. **~oso** a (terreno) bushy

ces'sa|re *vi* stop, cease ● *vt* stop. ~**re** *nm* il fuoco ceasefire. ~**zi'one** *nf* cessation

cessi'one *nf* handover

'**cesso** *nm* sl (*gabinetto*) bog, john *Am*; (*fig: locale, luogo*) dump

'**cesta** *nf* [large] basket. **ce'stello** *nm* (*per lavatrice*) drum

cesti'nare *vt* throw away. **ce'stino** *nm* [small] basket; (*per la carta straccia*) waste-paper basket. '**cesto** *nm* basket

'**cetò** *nm* [social] class

'**cetra** *nf* lyre

cetrio'lino *nm* gherkin. **cetri'olo** *nm* cucumber

cfr *abbr* (**confronta**) cf.

che *pron rel* (*persona: soggetto*) who; (*persona: oggetto*) that, who, whom *fml*; (*cosa, animale*) that, which; **questa è la casa ~ ho comprato** this is the house [that] I've bought; **il ~ mi sorprende** which surprises me; **dal ~ deduco che...** from which I gather that...; **avere di ~ vivere** have enough to live on; **grazie! – non c'è di!** ~ thank you! – don't mention it!; **il giorno ~ ti ho visto** *fam* the day I saw you ● *a inter* what; (*esclamativo: con aggettivo*) how; (*con nome*) what a; ~ **macchina prendiamo, la tua o la mia?** which car are we taking, yours or mine?; ~ **bello!** how nice!; ~ **idea!** what an idea!; ~ **bella giornata!** what a lovely day! ● *pron inter* what; **a ~ pensi?** what are you thinking about? ● *conj* that; (*con comparazioni*) than; **credo ~ abbia ragione** I think [that] he is right; **era così commosso ~ non riusciva a parlare** he was so moved [that] he couldn't speak; **aspetto ~ telefoni** I'm waiting for him to phone; **è da un po'** ~ **non lo vedo** it's been a while since I saw him; **mi piace più Roma ~ Milano** I like Rome better than Milan; ~ **ti piaccia o no** whether you like it or not; ~ **io sappia** as far as I know

checché *pron indef* whatever

chemiotera'pia *nf* chemotherapy

chero'sene *nm* paraffin

cheru'bino *nm* cherub

cheti'chella: alla ~ *adv* silently

'**cheto** *a* quiet

chi *pron rel* whoever; (*coloro che*) people who; **ho trovato ~ ti può aiutare** I found somebody who can help you; **c'è** ~ **dice che...** some people say that...; **senti ~ parla!** listen to who's talking! ● *pron inter* (*soggetto*) who; (*oggetto*,

con preposizione) who, whom *fml*; (*possessivo*) **di ~** whose; ~ **sei?** who are you?; ~ **hai incontrato?** who did you meet?; **di ~ sono questi libri?** whose books are these?; **con ~ parli?** who are you talking to?; **a ~ lo dici!** tell me about it!

chi'acchie|ra *nf* chat; (*pettegolezzo*) gossip. ~**rare** *vi* chat; (*far pettegolezzi*) gossip. ~**rato** *a* **essere** ~**rato** (*persona*) be the subject of gossip; ~**re** *pl* chitchat; **far quattro** ~**re** have a chat. ~**rone, -a** *a* talkative ● *nmf* chatterer

chia'ma|re *vt* call; (*far venire*) send for; **come ti chiami?** what's your name?; **mi chiamo Roberto** my name is Robert; ~**re alle armi** call up. ~**rsi** *vr* be called. ~**ta** *nf* call; *Mil* call-up

chi'appa *nf fam* cheek

chiara'mente *adv* clearly

chia'rezza *nf* clarity; (*limpidezza*) clearness

chiarifi'ca|re *vt* clarify. ~**tore** *a* clarificatory. ~**zi'one** *nf* clarification

chiari'mento *nm* clarification

chia'rir|e *vt* make clear; (*spiegare*) clear up. ~**si** *vr* become clear

chi'aro *a* clear; (*luminoso*) bright; (*colore*) light. **chia'rore** *nm* glimmer

chiaroveg'gente *a* clear-sighted ● *nmf* clairvoyant

chi'as|so *nm* din. ~**'soso** *a* rowdy

chi'ave *nf* key; **chiudere a** ~**e** lock. ~**e inglese** monkey-wrench. ~**i'stello** *nm* latch

chiazza *nf* stain. ~**zare** *vt* stain

chic *a inv* chic

chicches'sia *pron* anybody

'**chicco** *nm* grain; (*di caffe*) bean; (*d'uva*) grape

chi'eder|e *vt* ask; (*per avere*) ask for; (*esigere*) demand. ~**si** *vr* wonder

chi'esa *nf* church

chi'esto *pp di* **chiedere**

'**chiglia** *nf* keel

'**chilo** *nm* kilo

chilo'grammo *nm* kilogram[me]

chilome'traggio *nm Auto* ≈ mileage

chilo'metrico *a* in kilometres

chi'lometro *nm* kilometre

chi'mera *nf fig* illusion

'**chimic|a** *nf* chemistry. ~**o, -a** *a* chemical ● *nmf* chemist

'**china** *nf* (*declivio*) slope; **inchiostro di ~** Indian ink

chi'nar|e *vt* lower. ~**si** *vr* stoop

chincaglie'rie *nfpl* knick-knacks

chinesitera'pia *nf* physiotherapy

chi'nino *nm* quinine

'chino *a* bent

chi'notto *nm* sparkling soft drink

chi'occia *nf* sitting hen

chi'occiola *nf* snail; **scala a ~** spiral staircase

chi'odo *nm* nail; ⟨*idea fissa*⟩ obsession. **~ di garofano** clove

chi'oma *nf* head of hair; ⟨*fogliame*⟩ foliage

chi'osco *nm* kiosk; ⟨*per giornali*⟩ news-stand

chi'ostro *nm* cloister

chiro'man|te *nmf* palmist. **~'zia** *nf* palmistry

chirur'gia *nf* surgery. **chi'rurgico** *a* surgical. **chi'rurgo** *nm* surgeon

chissà *adv* who knows; **~ quando arriverà** I wonder when he will arrive

chi'tar|ra *nf* guitar. **~'rista** *nmf* guitarist

chi'uder|e *vt* shut, close; ⟨*con la chiave*⟩ lock; ⟨*luce, acqua ecc*⟩; ⟨*per sempre*⟩ close down ⟨*negozio, fabbrica ecc*⟩; ⟨*recingere*⟩ enclose ● *vi* shut, close. **~si** *vr* shut; ⟨*tempo:*⟩ cloud over; ⟨*ferita:*⟩ heal over; *fig* withdraw into oneself

chi'unque *pron indef* anyone, anybody ● *pron rel* whoever

chi'usa *nf* enclosure; ⟨*di canale*⟩ lock; ⟨*conclusione*⟩ close

chi'u|so *pp di* **chiudere** ● *a* shut; ⟨*tempo*⟩ overcast; ⟨*persona*⟩ reserved. **~'sura** *nf* closing; ⟨*sistema*⟩ lock; ⟨*allacciatura*⟩ fastener. **~sura lampo** zip, zipper *Am*

ci *pron* ⟨*personale*⟩ us; ⟨*riflessivo*⟩ ourselves; ⟨*reciproco*⟩ each other; ⟨*a ciò, di ciò ecc*⟩ about it; **non ci disturbare** don't disturb us; **aspettateci** wait for us; **ci ha detto tutto** he told us everything; **ce lo manderanno** they'll send it to us; **ci consideriamo...** we consider ourselves...; **ci laviamo le mani** we wash our hands; **ci odiamo** we hate each other; **non ci penso mai** I never think about it; **pensaci!** think about it! ● *adv* ⟨*qui*⟩ here; ⟨*li*⟩ there; ⟨*moto per luogo*⟩ through it; **ci siamo** we are here; **ci siete?** are you there?; **ci siamo passati tutti** we all went through it; **c'è** there is; **ce ne sono molti** there are many; **ci vuole pazienza** it takes patience; **non ci vedo/sento** I can't see/hear

cia'bat|ta *nf* slipper. **~'tare** *vi* shuffle

ciabat'tino *nm* cobbler

ci'alda *nf* wafer

cial'trone *nm* ⟨*mascalzone*⟩ scoundrel

ciam'bella *nf Culin* ring-shaped cake; ⟨*salvagente*⟩ lifebelt; ⟨*gonfiabile*⟩ rubber ring

cianci'are *vi* gossip

cianfru'saglie *nfpl* knick-knacks

cia'notico *a* ⟨*colorito*⟩ puce

ci'ao *int fam* ⟨*all' arrivo*⟩ hello!, hi!; ⟨*alla partenza*⟩ bye-bye!, cheerio!

ciar'la|re *vi* chat. **~'tano** *nm* charlatan

cias'cuno *a* each ● *pron* everyone, everybody; ⟨*distributivo*⟩ each [one]; **per ~** each

ci'bar|e *vt* feed. **~ie** *nfpl* provisions. **~si** *vr* eat; **~si di** live on

ciber'netico *a* cybernetic

'cibo *nm* food

ci'cala *nf* cicada

cica'lino *nm* buzzer

cica'tri|ce *nf* scar. **~z'zante** *nm* ointment

cicatriz'zarsi *vr* heal [up]. **cicatrizzazi'one** *nf* healing

'cicca *nf* cigarette end; ⟨*fam: sigaretta*⟩ fag; ⟨*fam: gomma*⟩ [chewing] gum

cic'chetto *nm* ⟨*bicchierino*⟩ nip; ⟨*rimprovero*⟩ telling-off

cicci|a *nf fam* fat, flab. **~'one, -a** *nmf fam* fatty, fatso

cice'rone *nm* guide

ci'cla'mino *nm* cyclamen

ci'clis|mo *nm* cycling. **~ta** *nmf* cyclist

'ciclo *nm* cycle; ⟨*di malattia*⟩ course

ciclomo'tore *nm* moped

ci'clone *nm* cyclone

ci'cogna *nf* stork

cico'ria *nf* chicory

ci'eco, -a *a* blind ● *nm* blind man ● *nf* blind woman

ci'elo *nm* sky; *Relig* heaven; **santo ~!** good heavens!

'cifra *nf* figure; ⟨*somma*⟩ sum; ⟨*monogramma*⟩ monogram; ⟨*codice*⟩ code

ci'fra|re *vt* embroider with a monogram; ⟨*codificare*⟩ code. **~to** *a* monogrammed; coded

'ciglio *nm* ⟨*bordo*⟩ edge; ⟨*pl nf* **ciglia**: *delle palpebre*⟩ eyelash

'cigno *nm* swan

cigo'l|are *vt* squeak. **~io** *nm* squeak

'Cile *nm* Chile

ci'lecca *nf far* **~** miss

ci'leno, -a *a & nmf* Chilean

cili'egi|a *nf* cherry. **~o** *nm* cherry [tree]

cilin'drata nf cubic capacity, c.c.; **macchina di alta ~** highpowered car

ci'lindro nm cylinder; (cappello) top hat

'cima nf top; (fig: persona) genius; **da ~ a fondo** from top to bottom

ci'melio nm relic

cimen'tare vt put to the test. **~si** vr (provare) try one's hand

'cimice nf bug; (puntina) drawing pin, thumbtack Am

cimini'era nf chimney; Naut funnel

cimi'tero nm cemetery

ci'murro nm distemper

'Cina nf China

cin cin! int cheers!

cincischi'are vi fiddle

'cine nm fam cinema

cine'asta nmf film maker

'cinema nm inv cinema. **cine'presa** nf cine-camera

ci'nese a & nmf Chinese

cine'teca nf (raccolta) film collection

ci'netico a kinetic

'cingere vt (circondare) surround

'cinghia nf strap; (cintura) belt

cinghi'ale nm wild boar; **pelle di ~** pigskin

cinguet't|are vi twitter. **~io** nm twittering

'cinico a cynical

ci'niglia nf (tessuto) chenille

ci'nismo nm cynicism

ci'nofilo a (unità) dog-loving

cin'quanta a & nm fifty. **cinquan'tenne** a & nmf fifty-year-old. **cinquan'tesimo** a fiftieth. **cinquan'tina** nf **una cinquantina** about fifty

'cinque a & nm five

cinquecen'tesco a sixteenth-century

cinque'cento a five hundred ● nm **il C~** the sixteenth century

cinque'mila a & nm five thousand

'cinta nf (di pantaloni) belt; **muro di ~** [boundary] wall. **cin'tare** vt enclose

'cintola nf (di pantaloni) belt

cin'tura nf belt. **~ di salvataggio** lifebelt. **~ di sicurezza** Aeron, Auto seat-belt

cintu'rino nm **~ dell'orologio** watchstrap

ciò pron this; that; **~ che** what; **~ nondimeno** nevertheless

ci'occa nf lock

ciocco'la|ta nf chocolate; (bevanda) [hot] chocolate. **~ tino** nm chocolate.

~to nm chocolate. **~to al latte/ fondente** milk/plain chocolate

cioè adv that is

ciondo'l|are vi dangle. **ci'ondolo** nm pendant. **~oni** adv fig hanging about

ciono'nostante adv nonetheless

ci'otola nf bowl

ci'ottolo nm pebble

ci'polla nf onion; (bulbo) bulb

ci'presso nm cypress

'cipria nf [face] powder

Cipro nm Cyprus. **cipri'ota** a & nmf Cypriot

'circa adv & prep about

'circo nm circus

circo'la|re a circular ● nf circular; (di metropolitana) circle line ● vi circulate. **~torio** a Med circulatory. **~zi'one** nf circulation; (traffico) traffic

'circolo nm circle; (società) club

circon'ci|dere vt circumcise. **~si'one** nf circumcision

circon'dar|e vt surround. **~io** nm (amministrativo) administrative district. **~si** di vr surround oneself with

circonfe'renza nf circumference. **~ dei fianchi** hip measurement

circonvallazi'one nf ring road

circo'scritto a limited

circoscrizi'one nf area. **~ elettorale** constituency

circo'spetto a wary

circospezi'one nf **con ~** warily

circo'stante a surrounding

circo'stanza nf circumstance; (occasione) occasion

circu'ire vt (ingannare) trick

cir'cuito nm circuit

circumnavi'ga|re vt circumnavigate. **~zi'one** nf circumnavigation

'ciste nf inv cyst

'cisti nf inv cyst

ci'sterna nf cistern; (serbatoio) tank

ci'ta|re vt (riportare brani ecc) quote; (come esempio) cite; Jur summons. **~zi'one** nf quotation; Jur summons sg

citofo'nare vt buzz. **ci'tofono** nm entry phone; (in ufficio, su aereo ecc) intercom

ci'trullo nmf fam dimwit

città nf inv town; (grande) city

citta'della nf citadel

cittadi'nanza nf citizenship; (popolazione) citizens pl. **~dino, -a** nmf citizen; (abitante di città) city dweller

ciucci'are vt fam suck. **ci'uccio** nm fam dummy

ci'uco nm ass

ci'uffo nm tuft

ci'urma nf Naut crew

ci'vetta nf owl; (fig: donna) flirt; |auto| ~ unmarked police car. ~'tare vi flirt. ~te'ria nf coquettishness

'civico a civic

ci'vile a civil. ~iz'zare vt civilize. ~iz'zato a (paese) civilized. ~izzazi'one nf civilization. ~'mente adv civilly

civiltà nf inv civilization; (cortesia) civility

'clacson nm inv horn. clacso'nare vi beep the horn, hoot

cla'more nm clamour; fare ~re cause a sensation. ~rosa'mente adv (sbagliare) sensationally. ~'roso a noisy; (sbaglio) sensational

clan nm inv clan; fig clique

clandestina'mente adv secretly. ~ità nf secrecy

clande'stino a clandestine; movimento ~ underground movement; passeggero ~ stowaway

clari'netto nm clarinet

'classe nf class. ~ turistica tourist class

classi'cismo nm classicism. ~ta nmf classicist

'classico a classical; (tipico) classic ● nm classic

clas'sifica nf classification; Sport results pl. ~'care vt classify. ~'carsi vr be placed. ~ca'tore nm (cartella) folder. ~cazi'one nf classification

clas'sista nmf class-conscious person

'clausola nf clause

claustro'fobia nf claustrophobia. ~'fobico a claustrophobic

clau'sura nf Relig enclosed order

clavi'cembalo nm harpsichord

cla'vicola nf collar-bone

cle'mente a merciful; (tempo) mild. ~za nf mercy

cleri'cale a clerical. 'clero nm clergy

clic nm Comput click; fare ~ su click on

cli'ente nmf client; (di negozio) customer. ~'tela nf customers pl

'clima nm climate. cli'matico a climatic; stazione climatica health resort

'clinica nf clinic. clinico a clinical ● nm clinician

clo'aca nf sewer

'cloro nm chlorine. ~'formio nm chloroform

clou a inv momenti ~ highlights

coabi'tare vi live together. ~zi'one nf cohabitation

coagu'lare vt, ~rsi vr coagulate. ~zi'one nf coagulation

coalizi'one nf coalition. ~'zarsi vr unite

co'atto a Jur compulsory

'cobra nm inv cobra

coca'ina nf cocaine. cocai'nomane nmf cocaine addict

cocci'nella nf ladybird

'coccio nm earthenware; (frammento) fragment

cocciu'taggine nf stubbornness. ~'uto a stubborn

'cocco nm coconut palm; fam love; noce di ~ coconut

cocco'drillo nm crocodile

cocco'lare vt cuddle

co'cente a (sole) burning

'cocktail nm inv (ricevimento) cocktail party

co'comero nm watermelon

co'cuzzolo nm top; (di testa, cappello) crown

'coda nf tail; (di abito) train; (fila) queue; fare la ~ queue [up], stand in line Am. ~ di cavallo (acconciatura) ponytail. ~ dell'occhio corner of one's eye ~ di paglia guilty conscience

co'dardo, -a a cowardly ● nmf coward

'codice nm code. ~ di avviamento postale postal code, zip code Am. ~ a barre bar-code. ~ fiscale tax code. ~ della strada highway code

codifi'care vt codify

coe'rente a consistent. ~za nf consistency

coesi'one nf cohesion

coe'sistere vi coexist

coe'taneo, -a a & nmf contemporary

cofa'netto nm casket. 'cofano nm (forziere) chest; Auto bonnet, hood Am

co'gliere vt pick; (sorprendere) catch; (afferrare) seize; (colpire) hit

co'gnato, -a nmf brother-in-law; sister-in-law

cognizi'one nf knowledge

co'gnome nm surname

'coi = con + i

coinci'denza nf coincidence; (di treno ecc) connection

coin'cidere vi coincide

coinqui'lino nm flatmate

coin'volgere vt involve. ~gi'mento nm involvement. ~to a involved

'coito nm coitus

col = con + il

colà *adv* there

cola|'brodo *nm inv* strainer; **ridotto a un ~brodo** *fam* full of holes. **~'pasta** *nm inv* colander

co'la|re *vt* strain; *(versare lentamente)* drip ● *vi (gocciolare)* drip; *(perdere)* leak; **~re a picco** *Naut* sink. **~ta** *nf (di metallo)* casting; *(di lava)* flow

colazi'one *nf (del mattino)* breakfast; *(di mezzogiorno)* lunch; **prima ~** breakfast; **far ~** have breakfast/lunch. **~ al sacco** packed lunch

co'lei *pron f* the one

co'lera *nm* cholera

coleste'rolo *nm* cholesterol

colf *nf abbr* **(collaboratrice familiare)** home help

'colica *nf* colic

co'lino *nm* [tea] strainer

'colla *nf* glue; *(di farina)* paste. **~ di pesce** gelatine

collabo'ra|re *vi* collaborate. **~'tore, ~'trice** *nmf* collaborator. **~zi'one** *nf* collaboration

col'lana *nf* necklace; *(serie)* series

col'lant *nm* tights *pl*

col'lare *nm* collar

col'lasso *nm* collapse

collau'dare *vt* test. **col'laudo** *nm* test

'colle *nm* hill

col'lega *nmf* colleague

collega'mento *nm* connection; *Mil* liaison; *Radio ecc* link. **colle'gar|e** *vt* connect. **~si** *vr TV, Radio* link up

collegi'ale *nmf* boarder ● *a (responsabilità, decisione)* collective

col'legio *nm (convitto)* boarding-school. **~ elettorale** constituency

'collera *nf* anger; **andare in ~** get angry. **col'lerico** *a* irascible

col'letta *nf* collection

collet'tività *nf inv* community. **~'tivo** *a* collective; *(interesse)* general; **biglietto ~'tivo** group ticket

col'letto *nm* collar

collezio'na|re *vt* collect. **~'one** *nf* collection. **~o'nista** *nmf* collector

colli'mare *vi* coincide

col'lina *nf* hill. **~'noso** *a (terreno)* hilly

col'lirio *nm* eyewash

collisi'one *nf* collision

'collo *nm* neck; *(pacco)* package; **a ~ alto** high-necked. **~ del piede** instep

colloca'mento *nm* placing; *(impiego)* employment

collo'ca|re *vt* place. **~rsi** *vr* take one's place. **~zi'one** *nf* placing

colloqui'ale *a (termine)* colloquial. **col'loquio** *nm* conversation; *(udienza ecc)* interview; *(esame)* oral [exam]

collusi'one *nf* collusion

colluttazi'one *nf* scuffle

col'mare *vt* fill [to the brim]; bridge *(divario)*; **~ qcno di gentilezze** overwhelm sb with kindness. **'colmo** *a* full ● *nm* top; *fig* height; **al colmo della disperazione** in the depths of despair; **questo è il colmo!** *(con indignazione)* this is the last straw!; *(con stupore)* I don't believe it!

co'lomb|a *nf* dove. **~o** *nm* pigeon

co'loni|a[^1] *nf* colony; **~a [estiva]** *(per bambini)* holiday camp. **~'ale** *a* colonial

co'lonia[^2] *nf* [acqua di] **~** [eau de] Cologne

co'lonico *a (terreno, casa)* farm

coloniz'za|re *vt* colonize. **~'tore, ~'trice** *nmf* colonizer

co'lon|na *nf* column. **~ sonora** sound-track. **~ vertebrale** spine. **~'nato** *nm* colonnade

colon'nello *nm* colonel

co'lono *nm* tenant farmer

colo'rante *nm* colouring

colo'rare *vt* colour; colour in *(disegno)*

co'lore *nm* colour; **a colori** in colour; **di ~** coloured. **colo'rito** *a* coloured; *(viso)* rosy; *(racconto)* colourful ● *nm* complexion

co'loro *pron pl* the ones

colos'sale *a* colossal. **co'losso** *nm* colossus

'colpa *nf* fault; *(biasimo)* blame; *(colpevolezza)* guilt; *(peccato)* sin; **dare la ~ a** blame; **essere in ~** be at fault; **per ~ di** because of. **col'pevole** *a* guilty ● *nmf* culprit

col'pire *vt* hit, strike; **~ nel segno** hit the nail on the head

'colpo *nm* blow; *(di arma da fuoco)* shot; *(urto)* knock; *(emozione)* shock; *Med, Sport* stroke; *(furto)* raid; **di ~** suddenly; **far ~** make a strong impression; **far venire un ~ a qcno** *fig* give sb a fright; **perdere colpi** *(motore)* keep missing; **a ~ d'occhio** at a glance; **a ~ sicuro** for certain. **~ d'aria** chill. **~ basso** blow below the belt. **~ di scena** coup de théâtre. **~ di sole** sunstroke; **colpi** *pl* **di sole** *(su capelli)* highlights. **~ di stato** coup [d'état]. **~**

[^1]: co'lonia¹
[^2]: co'lonia²

di telefono ring; **dare un ~ di telefono a qn** give sb a ring. **~ di testa** [sudden] impulse. **~ di vento** gust of wind

col'poso *a* **omicidio ~** manslaughter

coltel'lata *nf* stab. **col'tello** *nm* knife

colti'va|re *vt* cultivate. **~'tore, ~'trice** *nmf* farmer. **~zi'one** *nf* farming; (*di piante*) growing

'colto *pp di* cogliere ●*a* cultured

'coltre *nf* blanket

col'tura *nf* cultivation

co'lui *pron inv m* the one

'coma *nm inv* coma; **in ~** in a coma

coman'damento *nm* commandment

coman'dante *nm* commander; *Naut, Aeron* captain

coman'dare *vt* command; *Mech* control ●*vi* be in charge. **co'mando** *nm* command; (*di macchina*) control

co'mare *nf* (*madrina*) godmother

combaci'are *vi* fit together; (*testimonianze:*) concur

combat'tente *a* fighting ●*nm* combatant. **ex ~** ex-serviceman

com'bat|tere *vt/i* fight. **~ti'mento** *nm* fight; *Mil* battle; **fuori ~timento** (*pugilato*) knocked out. **~'tuto** *a* (*gara*) hard fought

combi'na|re *vt/i* arrange; (*mettere insieme*) combine; (*fam: fare*) do; **cosa stai ~ndo?** what are you doing?. **~rsi** *vr* combine; (*mettersi d'accordo*) come to an agreement. **~zi'one** *nf* combination; (*caso*) coincidence; **per ~zione** by chance

com'briccola *nf* gang

combu'sti|bile *a* combustible ●*nm* fuel. **~'one** *nf* combustion

com'butta *nf* gang; **in ~** in league

'come *adv* like; (*in qualità di*) as; (*interrogativo, esclamativo*) how; **questo vestito è ~ il tuo** this dress is like yours; **~ stai?** how are you?; **~ va?** how are things?; **~ mai?** how come?; **~? what?; non sa ~ fare** he doesn't know what to do; **~ sta bene!** how well he looks!; **~ no!** that will be right!; **~ tu sai** as you know; **fa ~ vuoi** do as you like; **~ se as** if ●*conj* (*non appena*) as soon as

co'meta *nf* comet

'comico, -a *a* comic[al]; (*teatro*) comic ●*nm* funny side ●*nmf* (*attore*) comedian, comic actor ●*nf* (*a torte in faccia*) slapstick sketch

co'mignolo *nm* chimney-pot

cominci'are *vt/i* begin, start; **a ~ da oggi** from today; **per ~** to begin with

comi'tato *nm* committee

comi'tiva *nf* party, group

co'mizio *nm* meeting

com'mando *nm inv* commando

com'medi|a *nf* comedy; (*opera teatrale*) play; *fig* sham. **~a musicale** musical. **~'ante** *nmf* comedian; *fig pej* phoney. **~'ografo, -a** *nmf* playwright

commemo'ra|re *vt* commemorate. **~zi'one** *nf* commemoration

commen'sale *nmf* fellow diner

commen'tare *vt* comment on; (*annotare*) annotate. **~'ario** *nm* commentary. **~a'tore, ~a'trice** *nmf* commentator. **com'mento** *nm* comment

commerci'ale *a* commercial; (*relazioni, trattative*) trade; (*attività*) business. **centro ~le** shopping centre. **~'lista** *nmf* business consultant; (*contabile*) accountant. **~liz'zare** *vt* market. **~lizzazi'one** *nf* marketing

commerci'ante *nmf* trader, merchant; (*negoziante*) shopkeeper. **~ all'ingrosso** wholesaler

commerci'are *vi* **~ in** deal in

com'mercio *nm* commerce; (*internazionale*) trade; (*affari*) business; **in ~** (*prodotto*) on sale. **~ all'ingrosso** wholesale trade. **~ al minuto** retail trade

com'messo, -a *pp di* committere ●*nmf* shop assistant. **~ viaggiatore** commercial traveller ●*nf* (*ordine*) order

comme'stibile *a* edible. **commestibili** *nmpl* groceries

com'mettere *vt* commit; make (*sbaglio*)

commi'ato *nm* leave; **prendere ~ da** take leave of

commise'rar|e *vt* commiserate. **~si** *vr* feel sorry for oneself

commissari'ato *nm* (*di polizia*) police station

commis's'ario *nm* ≈ [police] superintendent; (*membro di commissione*) commissioner; *Sport* steward; *Comm* commission agent. **~ario d'esame** examiner. **~i'one** *nf* (*incarico*) errand; (*comitato ecc*) commission; (*Comm: di merce*) order; **~ioni** *pl* (*acquisti*) **fare ~ioni** go shopping. **~ione d'esame** board of examiners. **C~ione Europea** European Commission

commit'tente *nmf* purchaser

com'mo|sso *pp di* commuovere ●*a* moved. **~'vente** *a* moving

commozi'one *nf* emotion. **~ cerebrale** concussion

commu'over|e *vt* touch, move. **~si** *vr* be touched

commu'tare *vt* change; *Jur* commute

comò *nm inv* chest of drawers

comoda'mente *adv* comfortably

como'dino *nm* bedside table

comodità *nf inv* comfort; *(convenienza)* convenience

'comodo *a* comfortable; *(conveniente)* convenient; *(spazioso)* roomy; *(facile)* easy; **stia ~!** don't get up!; **far ~** be useful ● *nm* comfort; **fare il proprio ~** do as one pleases

compae'sano, -a *nmf* fellow countryman

com'pagine *nf (squadra)* team

compa'gnia *nf* company; *(gruppo)* party; **fare ~ a qcno** keep sb company; **essere di ~** be sociable. **~ aerea** airline

com'pagno, -a *nmf* companion, mate; *Comm, Sport* partner; *Pol* comrade. **~ di scuola** schoolmate

compa'rabile *a* comparable

compa'ra|re *vt* compare. **~ tivo** *a & nm* comparative. **~zi'one** *nf* comparison

com'pare *nm (padrino)* godfather; *(testimone di matrimonio)* witness

compa'rire *vi* appear; *(spiccare)* stand out; **~ in giudizio** appear in court

com'parso, -a *pp di* comparire ● *nf* appearance; *Cinema* extra; *Theat* walk-on

compartecipazi'one *nf* sharing; *(quota)* share

comparti'mento *nm* compartment; *(amministrativo)* department

compas'sato *a* calm and collected

compassi'o|ne *nf* compassion; **aver ~ per** feel pity for; **far ~** arouse pity. **~ nevole** *a* compassionate

com'passo *nm* [pair of] compasses *pl*

compa'tibil|e *a (conciliabile)* compatible; *(scusabile)* excusable. **~ità** *nf* compatibility. **~ 'mente** *adv* **~mente con i miei impegni** if my commitments allow

compa'tire *vt* pity; *(scusare)* make allowances for

compatri'ota *nmf* compatriot

compat'tezza *nf (di materia)* compactness. **com'patto** *a* compact; *(denso)* dense; *(solido)* solid; *fig* united

compene'trare *vt* pervade

compen'sa|re *vt* compensate; *(supplire)* make up for. **~si** *vr* balance each other out

compen'sato *nm (legno)* plywood

compensazi'one *nf* compensation

com'penso *nm* compensation; *(retribuzione)* remuneration; **in ~** *(in cambio)* in return; *(d'altra parte)* on the other hand; *(invece)* instead

'compera *nf* purchase; **far ~e** do some shopping

compe'rare *vt* buy

compe'ten|te *a* competent. **~za** *nf* competence; *(responsabilità)* responsibility

com'petere *vi* compete; **~ a** *(compito:)* be the responsibility of

competi|tività *nf* competitiveness. **~ 'tivo** *a (prezzo, carattere)* competitive. **~ 'tore, ~ 'trice** *nmf* competitor. **~zi'one** *nf* competition

compia'cen|te *a* obliging. **~za** *nf* obligingness

compia'c|ere *vt/i* please. **~ersi** *vr (congratularsi)* congratulate. **~ersi di** *(degnarsi)* condescend. **~i'mento** *nm* satisfaction. **~i'uto** *a (aria, sorriso)* smug

compi'an|gere *vt* pity; *(per lutto ecc)* sympathize with. **~to** *a* lamented ● *nm* grief

'compier|e *vt (concludere)* complete; commit *(delitto:)*; **~e gli anni** have one's birthday. **~si** *vr* end; *(avverarsi)* come true

compi'lare *vt* compile; fill in *(modulo:)*. **~zi'one** *nf* compilation

compi'mento *nm* **portare a ~** *qcsa* conclude sth

com'pire *vt* = compiere

compi'tare *vt* spell

com'pito¹ *a* polite

'compito² *nm* task; *Sch* homework

compi'uto *a* **avere 30 anni ~i** be over 30

comple'anno *nm* birthday

complemen'tare *a* complementary; *(secondario)* subsidiary

comple'mento *nm* complement; *Mil* draft. **~ oggetto** direct object

comples'sità *nf* complexity. **~siva-'mente** *adv* on the whole. **~sivo** *a* comprehensive; *(totale)* total. **com'plesso** *a* complex; *(difficile)* complicated ● *nm* complex; *(di cantanti ecc)* group; *(di circostanze, fattori)* combination; **in ~so** on the whole

completa'mente *adv* completely

comple'tare *vt* complete

com'pleto *a* complete; *(pieno)* full [up]; **essere al ~** *(teatro:)* be sold out;

la famiglia al ~ the whole family ● *nm* (*vestito*) suit; (*insieme di cose*) set

compli'ca|re *vt* complicate. **~rsi** *vr* become complicated. **~to** *a* complicated. **~zi'one** *nf* complication; **salvo ~zioni** all being well

'complic|e *nmf* accomplice ● *a* (*sguardo*) knowing. **~ità** *nf* complicity

complimen'tar|e *vt* compliment. **~si** *vr*~**si con** congratulate

compli'menti *nmpl* (*ossequi*) regards; (*congratulazioni*) congratulations; **far ~** stand on ceremony

compli'mento *nm* compliment

complot'tare *vi* plot.**com'plotto** *nm* plot

compo'nente *a* & *nm* component ● *nmf* member

compo'nibile *a* (*cucina*) fitted; (*mobili*) modular

componi'mento *nm* composition; (*letterario*) work

com'por|re *vt* compose; (*ordinare*) put in order; *Typ* set.**~si** *vr*~**si di** be made up of

comporta'mento *nm* behaviour

compor'tar|e *vt* involve; (*consentire*) allow.**~si** *vr* behave

composi'tore, -'trice *nmf* composer; *Typ* compositor.**~zi'one** *nf* composition

com'posta *nf* stewed fruit; (*concime*) compost

compo'stezza *nf* composure

com'posto *pp di* **comporre** ● *a* composed; (*costituito*) comprising; **stai ~!** sit properly! ● *nm Chem* compound

com'pra|re *vt* buy. **~'tore, ~'trice** *nmf* buyer

compra'vendita *nf* buying and selling

com'pren|dere *vt* understand; (*includere*) comprise. **~'sibile** *a* understandable. **~sibil'mente** *adv* understandably. **~si'one** *nf* understanding. **~'sivo** *a* understanding; (*che include*) inclusive. **com'preso** *pp di* **comprendere** ● *a* included;**tutto compreso** (*prezzo*) all-in

com'pressa *nf* compress; (*pastiglia*) tablet

compressi'one *nf* compression. **com'presso** *pp di* **comprimere** ● *a* compressed

com'primere *vt* press; (*reprimere*) repress

compro'messo *pp di* **compromet-**

tere ● *nm* compromise. **~t'tente** *a* compromising.**~'ttere** *vt* compromise

compropri'età *nf* multiple ownership

compro'vare *vt* prove

com'punto *a* contrite

compu'tare *vt* calculate

com'puter *nm* computer. **~iz'zare** *vt* computerize.**~iz'zato** *a* computerized

computiste'ria *nf* book-keeping. **'computo** *nm* calculation

comu'nale *a* municipal

co'mune *a* common; (*condiviso*) mutual; (*ordinario*) ordinary ● *nm* borough, council; (*amministrativo*) commune;**fuori del ~** out of the ordinary. **~'mente** *adv* commonly

comuni'ca|re *vt* communicate; pass on (*malattia*); *Relig* administer Communion to. **~rsi** *vr* receive Communion. **~'tiva** *nf* communicativeness. **~'tivo** *a* communicative. **~to** *nm* communiqué. **~zi'one** *nf* communication; *Teleph* [phone] call;**avere la ~zione** get through;**dare la ~zione a qcno** put sb through

comuni'one *nf* communion; *Relig* [Holy] Communion

comu'nismo *nm* communism.**~ta** *a* & *nmf* communist

comunità *nf inv* community. **C~ [Economica] Europea** European [Economic] Community

co'munque *conj* however ● *adv* anyhow

con *prep* with; (*mezzo*) by; **~ facilità** easily; **~ mia grande gioia** to my great delight; **è gentile ~ tutti** he is kind to everyone;**col treno** by train; **~ questo tempo** in this weather

co'nato *nm* **~ di vomito** retching

'conca *nf* basin; (*valle*) dell

concate'na|re *vt* link together. **~zi'one** *nf* connection

'concavo *a* concave

con'ced|ere *vt* grant; award (*premio*); (*ammettere*) admit. **~si** *vr* allow oneself (*pausa*)

concentra'mento *nm* concentration

concen'tra|re *vt*, **~rsi** *vr* concentrate. **~to** *a* concentrated ● *nm* **~to di pomodoro** tomato purée. **~zi'one** *nf* concentration

concepi'mento *nm* conception

conce'pire *vt* conceive (*bambino*); (*capire*) understand; (*figurarsi*) conceive of; devise (*piano ecc*)

con'cernere *vt* concern

concer'tar|e *vt Mus* harmonize; (*organizzare*) arrange. **~si** *vr* agree

concer'tista *nmf* concert performer. **con'certo** *nm* concert; (*composizione*) concerto

concessio'nario *nm* agent

concessi'one *nf* concession

con'cesso *pp di* **concedere**

con'cetto *nm* concept; (*opinione*) opinion

concezi'one *nf* conception; (*idea*) concept

con'chiglia *nf* [sea] shell

'concia *nf* tanning; (*di tabacco*) curing

conci'a|re *vt* tan; cure (*tabacco*); **~re qcno per le feste** give sb a good hiding. **~rsi** *vr* (*sporcarsi*) get dirty; (*vestirsi male*) dress badly. **~to a** (*pelle, cuoio*) tanned

concili'abile *a* compatible

concili'ante *a* conciliatory

concili'a|re *vt* reconcile; settle (*contravvenzione*); (*favorire*) induce. **~rsi** *vr* go together; (*mettersi d'accordo*) become reconciled. **~zi'one** *nf* reconciliation; *Jur* settlement

con'cilio *nm Relig* council; (*riunione*) assembly

conci'mare *vt* feed (*pianta*). **con'cime** *nm* manure; (*chimico*) fertilizer

concisi'one *nf* conciseness. **con'ciso** *a* concise

conci'tato *a* excited

concit'ta'dino, -a *nmf* fellow citizen

con'clud|ere *vt* conclude; (*finire con successo*) achieve. **~dersi** *vr* come to an end. **~si'one** *nf* conclusion; **in ~sione** (*insomma*) in short. **~'sivo** *a* conclusive. **~so** *pp di* **concludere**

concomi'tanza *nf* (*di circostanze, fatti*) combination

concor'da|nza *nf* agreement. **~re** *vt* agree; *Gram* make agree. **~to** *nm* agreement; *Jur, Comm* arrangement

con'corde *a* in agreement; (*unanime*) unanimous

concor'ren|te *a* concurrent; (*rivale*) competing ●*nmf Comm, Sport* competitor; (*candidato*) candidate. **~za** *nf* competition. **~zi'ale** *a* competitive

con'cor|rere *vi* (*contribuire*) concur; (*andare insieme*) go together; (*competere*) compete. **~so** *pp di* **concorrere** ●*nm* competition; **fuori ~so** not in the official competition. **~so di bellezza** beauty contest

concreta'mente *adv* concretely

concre|'tare *vt* (*concludere*) achieve.

~tiz'zare *vt* put into concrete form (*idea, progetto*)

con'creto *a* concrete; **in ~** in concrete terms

concussi'one *nf* extortion

con'danna *nf* sentence; **pronunziare una ~** pass a sentence. **condan'nare** *vt* condemn; *Jur* sentence. **condan'nato, -a** *nmf* convict

conden'sa|re *vt*, **~rsi** *vr* condense. **~zi'one** *nf* condensation

condi'mento *nm* seasoning; (*salsa*) dressing. **con'dire** *vt* flavour; dress (*insalata*)

condiscen'den|te *a* indulgent; *pej* condescending. **~za** *nf* indulgence; *pej* condescension

condi'videre *vt* share

condizio'na|le *a & nm* conditional ●*nf Jur* suspended sentence. **~'mento** *nm Psych* conditioning

condizio'na|re *vt* condition. **~to** *a* conditional. **~ tore** *nm* air conditioner

condizi'one *nf* condition; **a ~ che** on condition that

condogli'anze *nfpl* condolences; **fare le ~** a offer condolences to

condomini'ale *a* (*spese*) common. **condo'minio** *nm* joint ownership; (*edificio*) condominium

condo'nare *vt* remit. **con'dono** *nm* remission

con'dotta *nf* conduct, (*circoscrizione di medico*) district; (*di gara ecc*) management; (*tubazione*) piping

con'dotto *pp di* **condurre** ●*a* **medico ~** district doctor ●*nm* pipe; *Anat* duct

condu'cente *nm* driver

con'du|rre *vt* lead; drive (*veicoli*); (*accompagnare*) take; conduct (*gas, elettricità ecc*); (*gestire*) run. **~rsi** *vr* behave. **~ tore, ~ trice** *nmf TV* presenter; (*di veicolo*) driver ●*nm Electr* conductor. **~t'tura** *nf* duct

confabu'lare *vi* have a confab

confa'cente *a* suitable. **con'farsi** *vr* **confarsi a suit**

confederazi'one *nf* confederation

confe'renz|a *nf* (*discorso*) lecture; (*congresso*) conference. **~a stampa** news conference. **~i'ere, -a** *nmf* lecturer

confe'rire *vt* (*donare*) give ●*vi* confer

con'ferma *nf* confirmation. **confer'mare** *vt* confirm

confes's|are *vt*, **~arsi** *vr* confess.

~io'nale *a* & *nm* confessional. ~'i one *nf* confession. ~ore *nm* confessor

con'fetto *nm* sugared almond

confet'tura *nf* jam

confezio'na|re *vt* manufacture; make ⟨*abiti*⟩; package ⟨*merci*⟩. ~to *a* ⟨*vestiti*⟩ off-the-peg; ⟨*gelato*⟩ wrapped

confezi'one *nf* manufacture; ⟨*di abiti*⟩ tailoring; ⟨*di pacchi*⟩ packaging; **confezioni** *pl* clothes. ~ **regalo** gift pack

confic'ca|re *vt* thrust. ~si *vr* run into

confi'da|re *vi* ~are in trust ● *vt* confide. ~arsi *vr* ~arsi con confide in. ~ente *a* confident ● *nmf* confidant

confi'denz|a *nf* confidence; ⟨*familiarità*⟩ familiarity; **prendersi delle** ~ take liberties. ~i'ale *a* confidential; ⟨*rapporto, tono*⟩ familiar

configu'ra|re *vt* Comput configure. ~zi'one *nf* configuration

confi'nante *a* neighbouring

confi'na|re *vi* ⟨*relegare*⟩ confine ● *vi* ~re con border on. ~rsi *vr* withdraw. ~to *a* confined

con'fin|e *nm* border; ⟨*tra terreni*⟩ boundary. ~o *nm* political exile

con'fi|sca *nf* ⟨*di proprietà*⟩ forfeiture. ~'scare *vt* confiscate

con'flitt|o *nm* conflict. ~u'ale *a* adversarial

conflu'enza *nf* confluence; ⟨*di strade*⟩ junction

conflu'ire *vi* ⟨*fiumi:*⟩ flow together; ⟨*strade:*⟩ meet

con'fonder|e *vt* confuse; ⟨*turbare*⟩ confound; ⟨*imbarazzare*⟩ embarrass. ~si *vr* ⟨*mescolarsi*⟩ mingle; ⟨*turbarsi*⟩ become confused; *vr* ⟨*sbagliarsi*⟩ be mistaken

confor'ma|re *vt*, ~rsi *vr* conform. ~zi'one *nf* conformity (**a** with); ⟨*del terreno*⟩ composition

con'forme *a* according. ~ **mente** *adv* accordingly

confor'mi|smo *nm* conformity. ~sta *nmf* conformist. ~tà *nf* ⟨*a norma*⟩ conformity

confor'tante *a* comforting

confor't|are *vt* comfort. ~evole *a* ⟨*comodo*⟩ comfortable. con'forto *nm* comfort

confron'tare *vt* compare

con'fronto *nm* comparison; **in** ~ **a** by comparison with; **nei tuoi confronti** towards you; **senza** ~ far and away

confusi|o'nario *a* ⟨*persona*⟩ muddleheaded. ~'one *nf* confusion; ⟨*baccano*⟩

racket; ⟨*disordine*⟩ mess; ⟨*imbarazzo*⟩ embarrassment. con'fuso *pp di* con'fondere ● *a* confused; ⟨*indistinto*⟩ indistinct; ⟨*imbarazzato*⟩ embarrassed

confu'tare *vt* confute

conge'da|re *vt* dismiss; Mil discharge. ~si *vr* take one's leave

con'gedo *nm* leave; **essere in** ~ be on leave. ~ **malattia** sick leave. ~ **maternità** maternity leave

conge'gnare *vt* devise; ⟨*mettere insieme*⟩ assemble. con'gegno *nm* device

congela'mento *nm* freezing; Med frost-bite

conge'la|re *vt* freeze. ~to *a* ⟨*cibo*⟩ deep-frozen. ~'tore *nm* freezer

congeni'ale *a* congenial

con'genito *a* congenital

congesti|o'na|re *vt* congest. ~to *a* ⟨*traffico*⟩ congested; ⟨*viso*⟩ flushed. congesti'one *nf* congestion

conget'tura *nf* conjecture

congi'unger|e *vt* join; combine ⟨*sforzi*⟩. ~si *vr* join

congiunti'vite *nf* conjunctivitis

congiun'tivo *nm* subjunctive

congi'unto *pp di* congiungere ● *a* joined ● *nm* relative

congiun'tura *nf* joint; ⟨*circostanza*⟩ juncture; ⟨*situazione*⟩ situation. ~'rale *a* economic

congiunzi'one *nf* Gram conjunction

congi'u|ra *nf* conspiracy. ~'rare *vi* conspire

conglome'rato *nm* conglomerate; *fig* conglomeration; ⟨*da costruzione*⟩ concrete

congratu'la|rsi *vr* ~rsi con qcno per congratulate sb on. ~zi'oni *nfpl* congratulations

con'grega *nf* band

congre'ga|re *vt*, ~rsi *vr* congregate. ~zi'one *nf* congregation

con'gresso *nm* congress

'congruo *a* proper; ⟨*giusto*⟩ fair

conguagli'are *vt* balance. con-gu'aglio *nm* balance

coni'are *vt* coin

'conico *a* conical

co'nifera *nf* conifer

co'niglio *nm* rabbit

coniu'gale *a* marital; ⟨*vita*⟩ married

coniu'ga|re *vt* conjugate. ~rsi *vr* get married. ~zi'one *nf* conjugation

'coniuge *nmf* spouse

connazio'nale *nmf* compatriot

connessi'one *nf* connection. con-'nesso *pp di* connettere

con'nettere *vt* connect ● *vi* think rationally

conni'vente *a* conniving

conno'ta|re *vt* connote. **~to** *nm* distinguishing feature; **~ti** *pl* description

con'nubio *nm fig* union

'cono *nm* cone

cono'scen|te *nmf* acquaintance. **~za** *nf* knowledge; (*persona*) acquaintance; (*sensi*) consciousness; **perdere ~za** lose consciousness; **riprendere ~za** regain consciousness, come to

co'nosc|ere *vt* know; (*essere a conoscenza di*) be acquainted with; (*fare la conoscenza di*) meet. **~i tore**, **~i'trice** *nmf* connoisseur. **~i uto** *pp di* **conoscere** ● *a* well-known

con'quista *nf* conquest. **conqui sta re** *vt* conquer; *fig* win

consa'cra|re *vt* consecrate; ordain (*sacerdote*); (*dedicare*) dedicate. **~rsi** *vr* devote oneself. **~zi one** *nf* consecration

consangu'ineo, -a *nmf* blood-relation

consa'pevo|le *a* conscious. **~ lezza** *nf* consciousness. **~l mente** *adv* consciously

'conscio *a* conscious

consecu'tivo *a* consecutive; (*seguente*) next

con'segna *nf* delivery; (*merce*) consignment; (*custodia*) care; (*di prigioniero*) handover; (*Mil: ordine*) orders *pl*; (*Mil: punizione*) confinement; **pagamento alla ~** cash on delivery

conse'gnare *vt* deliver; (*affidare*) give in charge; *Mil* confine to barracks

consegu'en|te *a* consequent. **~za** *nf* consequence; **di ~za** (*perciò*) consequently

consegui'mento *nm* achievement

consegu'ire *vt* achieve ● *vi* follow

con'senso *nm* consent

consensu'ale *a* consensus-based

consen'tire *vi* consent ● *vt* allow

con'serto *a* **a braccia conserte** with one's arms folded

con'serva *nf* preserve; (*di frutta*) jam; (*di agrumi*) marmalade. **~ di pomodoro** tomato sauce

conser'var|e *vt* preserve; (*mantenere*) keep. **~si** *vr* keep; **~si in salute** keep well

conserva'tore, -'trice *nmf Pol* conservative

conserva'torio *nm* conservatory

conservazi'one *nf* preservation; **a lunga ~** long-life

conside'ra|re *vt* consider; (*stimare*) regard. **~to a** (*stimato*) esteemed. **~zi one** *nf* consideration; (*osservazione, riflessione*) remark

conside'revole *a* considerable

consigli'abile *a* advisable

consigli'are *vt* advise; (*raccomandare*) recommend. **~ arsi** *vr* **~arsi con qcno** ask sb's advice. **~ ere, -a** *nmf* adviser; (*membro di consiglio*) councillor

con'siglio *nm* advice; (*ente*) council. **~ d'amministrazione** board of directors. **C~ dei Ministri** Cabinet

consi'sten|te *a* substantial; (*spesso*) thick; (*fig: argomento*) valid. **~za** *nf* consistency; (*spessore*) thickness

con'sistere *vi* **~ in** consist of

consoci'ata *nf* (*azienda*) associate company

conso'lar|e¹ *vt* console; (*rallegrare*) cheer. **~si** *vr* console oneself

conso'lare² *a* consular. **~to** *nm* consulate

consolazi'one *nf* consolation; (*gioia*) joy

con'sole *nf inv* (*tastiera*) console

'console *nm* consul

consoli'dar|e *vt*, **~si** *vr* consolidate

conso'nante *nf* consonant

'consono *a* consistent

con'sorte *nmf* consort

con'sorzio *nm* consortium

con'stare *vi* **~ di** consist of; (*risultare*) appear; **a quanto mi consta** as far as I know; **mi consta che** it appears that

consta'tare *vt* ascertain. **~zi one** *nf* observation

consu'eto *a & nm* usual. **~tudi nario** *a* (*diritto*) common; (*persona*) set in one's ways. **~ tudine** *nf* habit; (*usanza*) custom

consu'len|te *nmf* consultant. **~za** *nf* consultancy

consul'tare *vt* consult. **~rsi con** consult with. **~zi one** *nf* consultation

consul'tivo *a* consultative. **~orio** *nm* clinic

consu'ma|re *vt* (*usare*) consume; wear out (*abito, scarpe*); consummate (*matrimonio*); commit (*delitto*). **~rsi** *vr* consume; (*abito, scarpe*:) wear out; (*struggersi*) pine

consu'mato *a* (*politico*) seasoned; (*scarpe, tappeto*) worn

consuma'tore, -'trice *nmf* consumer. **~zi one** *nf* (*bibita*) drink; (*spuntino*) snack

consu'mis|mo nm consumerism. ~ta nmf consumerist

con'sumo nm consumption; (di abito, scarpe) wear; (uso) use; **generi di ~** consumer goods. ~ **|di carburante|** [fuel] consumption

consun'tivo nm |bilancio| ~ final statement

conta'balle nmf fam storyteller

con'tabil|e a book-keeping ● nmf accountant. ~ità nf accounting; **tenere la ~ità** keep the accounts

contachi'lometri nm inv mileometer, odometer Am

conta'dino, -a nmf farm-worker; (medievale) peasant

contagi'|are vt infect. **con'tagio** nm infection. ~'oso a infectious

conta'gocce nm inv dropper

contami'na|re vt contaminate. ~zi'one nf contamination

con'tante nm cash; **pagare in contanti** pay cash

con'tare vt/i count; (tenere conto di) take into account; (proporsi) intend

conta'scatti nm inv Teleph time-unit counter

conta'tore nm meter

contat'tare vt contact. **con'tatto** nm contact

'**conte** nm count

conteggi'|are vt put on the bill ● vi calculate. **con'teggio** nm calculation. **conteggio alla rovescia** countdown

con'te|gno nm behaviour; (atteggiamento) attitude. ~'gnoso a dignified

contem'pla|re vt contemplate; (fissare) gaze at. ~zi'one nf contemplation

con'tempo nm **nel ~** in the meantime

contempo|ranea'mente adv at once. ~'raneo, -a a & nmf contemporary

conten'dente nmf competitor. **con'tendere** vi compete; (litigare) quarrel ● vt contend

conte'n|ere vt contain; (reprimere) repress. ~'ersi vr contain oneself. ~i'tore nm container

conten'tarsi vr ~ **di** be content with

conten'tezza nf joy

conten'tino nm placebo

con'tento a glad; (soddisfatto) contented

conte'nuto nm contents pl; (soggetto) content

contenzi'oso nm legal department

con'tes|a nf disagreement; Sport contest. ~o pp di **contendere** ● a contested

con'tessa nf countess

conte'sta|re vt contest; Jur notify. ~'tario a anti-establishment. ~'tore, ~'trice nmf protester. ~zi'one nf (disputa) dispute

con'testo nm context

con'tiguo a adjacent

continen'tale a continental. **conti'nente** nm continent

conti'nenza nf continence

contin'gen|te nm contingent; (quota) quota. ~za nf contingency

continua'mente adv (senza interruzione) continuously; (frequentemente) continually

continu'|are vt/i continue; (riprendere) resume. ~a'tivo a permanent. ~azi'one nf continuation. ~ità nf continuity

con'tinuo a continuous; (molto frequente) continual. **corrente ~a** direct current; **di ~o** continually

'**conto** nm calculation; (in banca, negozio) account; (di ristorante ecc) bill; (stima) consideration; **a conti fatti** all things considered; **far ~ di** (supporre) suppose; (proporsi) intend; **far ~ su** rely on; **in fin dei conti** when all is said and done; **per ~ di** on behalf of; **per ~ mio** (a mio parere) in my opinion; (da solo) on my own; **starsene per ~ proprio** be on one's own; **rendersi ~ di** qcsa realize sth; **sul ~ di** qcno (voci, informazioni) about sb; **tener ~ di** qcsa take sth into account; **tenere da ~ qcsa** look after sth; **fare i conti con qcno** fig sort sb out. ~ **corrente** current account, checking account Am. ~ **alla rovescia** countdown

con'torcer|e vt twist. ~si vr twist about

contor'nare vt surround

con'torno nm contour; Culin vegetables pl

contorsi'one nf contortion. **con'torto** pp di **contorcere** ● a twisted

contrabban'|dare vt smuggle. ~di'ere, -a nmf smuggler. **contrab'bando** nm contraband

contrab'basso nm double bass

contraccambi'are vt return. **contrac'cambio** nm return

contracce't'tivo nm contraceptive. ~zi'one nf contraception

contrac'colpo nm rebound; (di arma da fuoco) recoil; fig repercussion

con'trada *nf* (*rione*) district

contrad'detto *pp di* **contraddire**

contrad'di|re *vt* contradict. ~t'torio *a* contradictory. ~zi'one *nf* contradiction

contraddi'stin|guere *vt* differentiate. ~to *a* distinct

contra'ente *nmf* contracting party

contra'ereo *a* anti-aircraft

contraf'fa|re *vt* disguise; (*imitare*) imitate; (*falsificare*) forge. ~tto *a* forged. ~zi'one *nf* disguising; (*imitazione*) imitation; (*falsificazione*) forgery

con'tralto *nm* countertenor ● *nf* contralto

contrap'peso *nm* counterbalance

contrap'por|re *vt* counter; (*confrontare*) compare. ~si *vr* contrast; ~si a be opposed to

contraria'mente *adv* contrary (a to)

contrari|'are *vt* oppose; (*infastidire*) annoy. ~'arsi *vr* get annoyed. ~età *nf inv* adversity; (*ostacolo*) set-back

con'trario *a* contrary, opposite; (*direzione*) opposite; (*sfavorevole*) unfavourable ● *nm* contrary, opposite; **al ~** on the contrary

con'trarre *vt* contract

contras'se'gnare *vt* mark. **~-'segno** *nm* mark; [**in**] **~segno** (*spedizione*) cash on delivery, COD

contra'stante *a* contrasting

contra'stare *vt* oppose; (*contestare*) contest ● *vi* clash. **con'trasto** *nm* contrast; (*litigio*) dispute

contrattac'care *vt* counter-attack. **contrat'tacco** *nm* counter-attack

contrat'ta|re *vt/i* negotiate; (*mercanteggiare*) bargain. ~zi'one *nf* (*salariale*) bargaining

contrat'tempo *nm* hitch

con'tratt|o *pp di* **contrarre** ● *nm* contract. **~o a termine** fixed-term contract. **~u'ale** *a* contractual

contravve'n|ire *vi* contravene. ~zi'one *nf* contravention; (*multa*) fine

contrazi'one *nf* contraction; (*di prezzi*) reduction

contribu'ente *nmf* contributor; (*del fisco*) taxpayer

contribu'ire *vi* contribute. **contri'buto** *nm* contribution

'contro *prep* against; **~ di me** against me ● *nm* **il pro e il ~** the pros and cons *pl*

contro'battere *vt* counter

controbilanci'are *vt* counterbalance

controcor'rente *a* (*idee, persona*) non-conformist ● *adv* upriver; *fig* upstream

controffen'siva *nf* counter-offensive

controfi'gura *nf* stand-in

controfir'mare *vt* countersign

controindicazi'one *nf* Med contra-indication

control'la|re *vt* control; (*verificare*) check; (*collaudare*) test. ~rsi *vr* have self-control. ~to *a* controlled

con'trollo *nm* control; (*verifica*) check; *Med* check-up. **~lo delle nascite** birth control. **~lore** *nm* controller; (*sui treni ecc*) [ticket] inspector. **~lore di volo** air-traffic controller

contro'luce *nf* **in ~** against the light

contro'mano *adv* in the wrong direction

contromi'sura *nf* countermeasure

contropi'ede *nm* **prendere in ~** catch off guard

controprodu'cente *a* self-defeating

con'trordine *nm* counter order; **salvo ~i** unless I/you hear to the contrary

contro'senso *nm* contradiction in terms

controspio'naggio *nm* counterespionage

contro'vento *adv* against the wind

contro'ver|sia *nf* controversy; *Jur* dispute. ~o *a* controversial

contro'voglia *adv* unwillingly

contu'macia *nf* default; **in ~** in one's absence

contun'dente *a* (*corpo, arma*) blunt

contur'bante *a* perturbing

contusi'one *nf* bruise

convale'scen|te *a* convalescent. ~za *nf* convalescence; **essere in ~za** be convalescing

con'vali|da *nf* validation. ~'dare *vt* confirm; validate (*atto, biglietto*)

con'vegno *nm* meeting; (*congresso*) congress

conve'nevole *a* suitable; **~i** *pl* pleasantries

conveni'en|te *a* convenient; (*prezzo*) attractive; (*vantaggioso*) advantageous. ~za *nf* convenience; (*interesse*) advantage; (*di prezzo*) attractiveness

conve'nire *vi* (*riunirsi*) gather; (*concordare*) agree; (*ammettere*) admit; (*essere opportuno*) be convenient ● *vt* agree on; **ci conviene andare** it is better to go; **non mi conviene stancarmi** I'd better not tire myself out

con'vento nm (di suore) convent; (di frati) monastery

conve'nuto a fixed

convenzio|o'nale a conventional. ~'one nf convention

conver'gen|te a converging. ~za nf fig confluence

con'vergere vi converge

conver'sa|re vi converse. ~zi'one nf conversation

conversi'one nf conversion

con'verso pp di convergere

conver'tibile nf Auto convertible

conver'ti|re vt convert. ~rsi vr be converted. ~to, -a nmf convert

con'vesso a convex

convin'cente a convincing

con'vin|cere vt convince. ~to a convinced. ~zi'one nf conviction

con'vitto nm boarding school

convi'vente nm common-law husband ●nf common-law wife. ~za nf cohabitation. con'vivere vi live together

convivi'ale a convivial

convo'ca|re vt convene. ~zi'one nf convening

convogli'are vt convey; (navi:) convoy. con'voglio nm convoy; (ferroviario) train

convulsi'one nf convulsion. con'vulso a convulsive; (febbrile) feverish

coope'ra|re vi co-operate. ~ 'tiva nf co-operative. ~zi'one nf co-operation

coordina'mento nm co-ordination

coordi'na|re vt co-ordinate. ~ta nf Math coordinate. ~zi'one nf co-ordination

co'perchio nm lid; (copertura) cover

co'perta nf blanket; (copertura) cover; Naut deck

coper'tina nf cover; (di libro) dustjacket

co'perto pp di coprire ●a covered; (cielo) overcast ●nm (a tavola) place; (prezzo del coperto) cover charge; al ~ under cover

coper'tone nm tarpaulin; (gomma) tyre

coper'tura nf covering; Comm, Fin cover

'copia nf copy; **bella/brutta ~** fair/rough copy. **~ su carta** hardcopy. copi'are vt copy

copi'one nm script

copi'oso a plentiful

'coppa nf (calice) goblet; (per gelato ecc) dish; Sport cup. ~ [di] gelato ice-cream (served in a dish)

cop'petta nf (di ceramica, vetro) bowl; (di gelato) small tub

'coppia nf couple; (in carte) pair

co'prente a (cipria, vernice) covering

copri'capo nm headgear

coprifu'oco nm curfew

copri'letto nm bedspread

copripiu'mino nm duvet cover

co'pri|re vt cover; drown (suono); hold (carica). ~si vr (vestirsi) cover up; fig cover oneself; (cielo:) become overcast

coque sf alla ~ (uovo) soft-boiled

co'raggio nm courage; (sfacciataggine) nerve; **~o!** come on. **~'oso** a courageous

co'rale a choral

co'rallo nm coral

co'rano nm Koran

co'raz|za nf armour; (di animali) shell. ~'zata nf battleship. ~'zato a (nave) armour-clad

corbelle'ria nf nonsense; (sproposito) blunder

'corda nf cord; (spago, Mus) string; (fune) rope; (cavo) cable; **essere giù di ~** be depressed; **dare ~ a qcno** encourage sb. **corde pl vocali** vocal cords

cor'data nf roped party

cordi'al|e a cordial ●nm (bevanda) cordial; **saluti ~i** best wishes. ~ità nf cordiality

cor'doglio nm grief; (lutto) mourning

cor'done nm cord; (schieramento) cordon. **~ ombelicale** umbilical cord

core|ogra'fia nf choreography. ~'ografo, -a nmf choreographer

cori'andoli nmpl confetti sg

cori'andolo nm (spezia) coriander

cori'car|e vt put to bed. **~si** vr go to bed

co'rista nmf choir member

cor'nacchia nf crow

'corna vedi corno

corna'musa nf bagpipes pl

'cornea nf cornea

cor'nett|a nf Mus cornet; (del telefono) receiver. **~o** nm (brioche) croissant

cor'ni|ce nf frame. ~ci'one nm cornice

'corno nm (pl nf corna) horn; **fare le corna a qcno** be unfaithful to sb; **fare le corna** (per scongiuro) touch wood. cor'nuto a horned ●nm (fam: marito tradito) cuckold; (insulto) bastard

'coro nm chorus; Relig choir

co'rolla nf corolla

co'rona *nf* crown; (*di fiori*) wreath; (*rosario*) rosary. **~'mento** *nm* (*di impresa*) crowning. **coro'nare** *vt* crown; (*sogno*) fulfil

cor'petto *nm* bodice

'corpo *nm* body; (*Mil, diplomatico*) corps *inv*; **a ~ a ~** man to man; **andare di ~** move one's bowels. **~ di ballo** corps de ballet. **~ insegnante** teaching staff. **~ del reato** incriminating item

corpo'rale *a* corporal

corporati'vismo *nm* corporatism

corpora'tura *nf* build

corporazi'one *nf* corporation

cor'poreo *a* bodily

cor'poso *a* full-bodied

corpu'lento *a* stout

cor'puscolo *nm* corpuscle

corre'dare *vt* equip

corre'dino *nm* (*per neonato*) layette

cor'redo *nm* (*nuziale*) trousseau

cor'reggere *vt* correct; lace (*bevanda*)

corre'lare *vt* correlate

cor'rente *a* running; (*in vigore*) current; (*frequente*) everyday; (*inglese ecc*) fluent ●*nf* current; (*d'aria*) draught; **essere al ~** be up to date. **~'mente** *adv* (*parlare*) fluently

'correre *vi* run; (*affrettarsi*) hurry; *Sport* race; (*notizie:*) circulate; **~ dietro a** run after ●*vt* run; **~ un pericolo** run a risk; **lascia ~!** don't bother!

corret'ta'mente *adv* correctly. **cor'retto** *pp di* **correggere** ●*a* correct; (*caffè*) with a drop of alcohol. **~zi'one** *nf* correction. **~zione di bozze** proofreading

cor'rida *nf* bullfight

cor'ridoio *nm* corridor; *Aeron* aisle

corri'dore, -'trice *nmf* racer; (*a piedi*) runner

corri'era *nf* coach, bus

corri'ere *nm* courier; (*posta*) mail; (*spedizioniere*) carrier

corri'mano *nm* bannister

corrispet'tivo *nm* amount due

corrispon'dente *a* corresponding ●*nmf* correspondent. **~za** *nf* correspondence; **scuola/corsi per ~za** correspondence course; **vendite per ~za** mail-order [shopping]. **corri'spondere** *vi* correspond; (*stanza:*) communicate; **corrispondere a** (*contraccambiare*) return

corri'sposto *a* (*amore*) reciprocated

corrobo'rare *vt* strengthen; *fig* corroborate

cor'roder|e *vt*, **~si** *vr* corrode

cor'rompere *vt* corrupt; (*con denaro*) bribe

corrosi'one *nf* corrosion. **corro'sivo** *a* corrosive

cor'roso *pp di* **corrodere**

cor'rotto *pp di* **corrompere** ●*a* corrupt

corrucci'ar|si *vr* be vexed. **~to** *a* upset

corru'gare *vt* wrinkle; **~ la fronte** knit one's brows

corruzi'one *nf* corruption; (*con denaro*) bribery

'corsa *nf* running; (*rapida*) dash; *Sport* race; (*di treno ecc*) journey; **di ~** at a run; **fare una ~** run

cor'sia *nf* gangway; (*di ospedale*) ward; *Auto* lane; (*di supermercato*) aisle

cor'sivo *nm* italics *pl*

'corso *pp di* **correre** ●*nm* course; (*strada*) main street; *Comm* circulation; **lavori in ~** work in progress; **nel ~ di** during. **~ d'acqua** watercourse

'corte *nf* [court]yard; (*Jur, regale*) court; **fare la ~ a qcno** court sb. **~ d'appello** court of appeal

cor'teccia *nf* bark

corteggia'mento *nm* courtship

corteggi'a|re *vt* court. **~tore** *nm* admirer

cor'teo *nm* procession

cor'te|se *a* courteous. **~'sia** *nf* courtesy; **per ~sia** please

cortigi'ano, -a *nmf* courtier ●*nf* courtesan

cor'tile *nm* courtyard

cor'tina *nf* curtain; (*schermo*) screen

'corto *a* short; **per farla corta** in short; **essere a ~ di** be short of. **~ circuito** *nm* short [circuit]

corto'me'traggio *nm* Cinema short

cor'vino *a* jet-black

'corvo *nm* raven

'cosa *nf* thing; (*faccenda*) matter; *inter, rel* what; [*che*] **~** what; **nessuna ~** nothing; **ogni ~** everything; **per prima ~** first of all; **tante cose** so many things; (*augurio*) all the best

'cosca *nf* clan

'coscia *nf* thigh; *Culin* leg

cosci'en|te *a* conscious. **~za** *nf* conscience; (*consapevolezza*) consciousness

co'scri|tto *nm* conscript. **~zi'one** *nf* conscription

così *adv* so; (*in questo modo*) like this, like that; (*perciò*) therefore; **le cose stanno ~** that's how things stand; **fermo ~!** hold it; **proprio ~!** exactly!; **basta ~!** that will do!; **ah, è ~?** it's like that, is it?; **~ ~** so-so; **e ~ via** and so on; **per ~ dire** so to speak; **più di ~** any more; **una ~ cara ragazza!** such a nice girl!; **è stato ~ generoso da aiutarti** he was kind enough to help you ● *conj* (*allora*) so ● *a inv* (*tale*) like that, such; **una ragazza ~** a girl like that, such a girl

cosicché *conj* and so

cosid'detto *a* so-called

co'smesi *nf* cosmetics

co'smetico *a & nm* cosmetic

'cosmico *a* cosmic

'cosmo *nm* cosmos

cosmopo'lita *a* cosmopolitan

co'spargere *vt* sprinkle; (*disseminare*) scatter

co'spetto *nm* **al ~ di** in the presence of

co'spicuo *a* conspicuous; ⟨*somma ecc*⟩ considerable

cospi'ra|re *vi* conspire. **~'tore, ~'trice** *nmf* conspirator. **~zi'one** *nf* conspiracy

'costa *nf* coast, coastline; *Anat* rib

costà *adv* there

co'stan|te *a & nf* constant. **~za** *nf* constancy

co'stare *vi* cost; **quanto costa?** how much is it?

co'stata *nf* chop

costeggi'are *vt* (*per mare*) coast; (*per terra*) skirt

co'stei *pron vedi* **costui**

costellazi'one *nf* constellation

coster'na|to *a* dismayed. **~zi'one** *nf* consternation

costi'er|a *nf* stretch of coast. **~o** *a* coastal

costi'pa|to *a* constipated. **~zi'one** *nf* constipation; (*raffreddore*) bad cold

costitu'ir|e *vt* constitute; (*formare*) form; (*nominare*) appoint. **~si** *vr Jur* give oneself up

costituzio'nale *a* constitutional. **costituzi'one** *nf* constitution; (*fondazione*) setting up

'costo *nm* cost; **ad ogni ~** at all costs; **a nessun ~** on no account

'costola *nf* rib; (*di libro*) spine

costo'letta *nf* cutlet

co'storo *pron vedi* **costui**

co'stoso *a* costly

co'stretto *pp di* **costringere**

co'strin|gere *vt* compel; (*stringere*) constrict. **~t'ivo** *a* coercive. **~zi'one** *nf* constraint

costru'ire *vt* build, construct. **~t'tivo** *a* constructive. **~zi'one** *nf* building, construction

co'stui, co'stei, *pl* **co'storo** *prons* (*soggetto*) he, she, *pl* they; (*complemento*) him, her, *pl* them

co'stume *nm* (*usanza*) custom; (*condotta*) morals *pl*; (*indumento*) costume. **~ da bagno** swim-suit; (*da uomo*) swimming trunks

co'tenna *nf* pigskin; (*della pancetta*) rind

coto'letta *nf* cutlet

co'tone *nm* cotton. **~ idrofilo** cotton wool, absorbent cotton *Am*

'cotta *nf* (*fam: innamoramento*) crush

'cottimo *nm* **lavorare a ~** do piecework

'cotto *pp di* **cuocere** ● *a* done; (*infatuato*) in love; (*sbronzo*) drunk; **ben ~** ⟨*carne*⟩ well done

cotton fi'oc® *nm inv* cotton bud

cot'tura *nf* cooking

co'vare *vt* hatch; sicken for ⟨*malattia*⟩; harbour ⟨*odio*⟩ ● *vi* smoulder

'covo *nm* den

co'vone *nm* sheaf

'cozza *nf* mussel

coz'zare *vi* **~ contro** bump into. **'cozzo** *nm fig* clash

C.P. *abbr* (**Casella Postale**) PO Box

'crampo *nm* cramp

'cranio *nm* skull

cra'tere *nm* crater

cra'vatta *nf* tie; (*a farfalla*) bow-tie

cre'anza *nf* politeness; **mala ~** bad manners

cre'a|re *vt* create; (*causare*) cause. **~tività** *nf* creativity. **~'tivo** *a* creative. **~to** *nm* creation. **~'tore, ~'trice** *nmf* creator. **~zi'one** *nf* creation

crea'tura *nf* creature; (*bambino*) baby; **povera ~!** poor thing!

cre'den|te *nmf* believer. **~za** *nf* belief; *Comm* credit; (*mobile*) sideboard. **~zi'ali** *nfpl* credentials

'creder|e *vt* believe; (*pensare*) think ● *vi* **~e in** believe in; **credo di sì** I think so; **non ti credo** I don't believe you. **~si** *vr* think oneself to be; **si crede uno scrittore** he flatters himself he is a writer. **cre'dibile** *a* credible.

credibilità *nf* credibility

'credi|to *nm* credit; (*stima*) esteem;

comprare a ~to buy on credit.
~'tore, ~'trice nmf creditor

'credo nm inv credo

credu'lità nf credulity

'credu|lo a credulous. ~'lone, -a nmf simpleton

'crema nf cream; (di uova e latte) custard. ~ idratante moisturizer. ~ pasticciera egg custard. ~ solare suntan lotion

cre'ma|re vt cremate. ~'torio nm crematorium. ~zi'one nf cremation

crème cara'mel nf crème caramel

creme'ria nf dairy (also selling ice cream and cakes)

Crem'lino nm Kremlin

'crepa nf crack

cre'paccio nm cleft; (di ghiacciaio) crevasse

crepacu'ore nm heart-break

crepa'pelle adv a ~ fit to burst; ridere a ~ split one's sides with laughter

cre'pare vi crack; (fam: morire) kick the bucket; ~ dal ridere laugh fit to burst

crepa'tura nf crevice

crêpe nf inv pancake

crepi'tare vi crackle

cre'puscolo nm twilight

cre'scendo nm crescendo

cresc|ere vi grow; (aumentare) increase ●vt (allevare) bring up; (aumentare) raise. ~'ita nf growth; (aumento) increase. ~i'uto pp di crescere

cresi'ma nf confirmation. ~'mare vt confirm

crespo a (capelli) frizzy ●nm crêpe

'cresta nf crest; (cima) peak

'creta nf clay

'Creta nf Crete

cre'tino, -a a stupid ●nmf idiot

cric nm jack

'cricca nf gang

'cri'ceto nm hamster

crimi'nal|e a & nmf criminal. ~'ità nf crime. 'crimine nm crime

crimi'noso a criminal

crin|e nm horsehair. ~i'era nf mane

'cripta nf crypt

crisan'temo nm chrysanthemum

'crisi nf inv crisis; Med fit

cristal'lino nm crystalline

cristalliz'zar|e vt, ~si vr crystallize; (fig: parola, espressione:) become part of the language

cri'stallo nm crystal

Cristia'nesimo nm Christianity

cristi'ano, -a a & nmf Christian

'Cristo nm Christ; un povero c~ a poor beggar

cri'terio nm criterion; (buon senso) [common] sense

'criti|ca nf criticism; (recensione) review. criti'care vt criticize. ~coa critical ●nm critic. ~cone, -a nmf faultfinder

crivel'lare vt riddle (di with)

cri'vello nm sieve

croc'cante a crisp ●nm type of crunchy nut biscuit

croc'chetta nf croquette

'croce nf cross; a occhio e ~ roughly; fare testa e ~ spin a coin. C~ Rossa Red Cross

croce'via nm inv crossroads sg

croci'ata nf crusade

cro'cicchio nm crossroads sg

croci'era nf cruise; Archit crossing

croci'fi|ggere vt crucify. ~ssi'one nf crucifixion. ~sso pp di crocifiggere ●a crucified ●nm crucifix

crogio'larsi vr bask

crogi[u]'olo nm crucible; fig melting pot

crol'lare vi collapse; (prezzi:) slump. 'crollo nm collapse; (dei prezzi) slump

cro'mato a chromium-plated. 'cromo nm chrome. cromo'soma nm chromosome

'cronaca nf chronicle; (di giornale) news; TV, Radio commentary; fatto di ~ news item. ~ nera crime news

'cronico a chronic

cro'nista nmf reporter

crono'logico a chronological

crono'traggio nm timing

crono'trare vt time

cro'nometro nm chronometer

'crosta nf crust; (di formaggio) rind; (di ferita) scab; (quadro) daub

cro'staceo nm shellfish

cro'stata nf tart

cro'stino nm croûton

crucci'arsi vr worry. 'cruccio nm worry

cruci'ale a crucial

cruci'verba nm inv crossword [puzzle]

cru'del|e a cruel. ~tà nf inv cruelty

'crudo a raw; (rigido) harsh

cru'ento a bloody

cru'miro nm blackleg, scab

'crusca nf bran

cru'scotto nm dashboard

'Cuba nf Cuba

cu'betto nm ~ **di ghiaccio** ice cube

'**cubico** a cubic

cubi'tale a **a caratteri ~i** in enormous letters

'**cubo** nm cube

cuc'cagna nf abundance; (baldoria) merry-making; **paese della ~** land of plenty

cuc'cetta nf (su un treno) couchette; Naut berth

cucchia'ino nm teaspoon

cucchi'aio nm spoon; **al ~io** (dolce) creamy. **~i'ata** nf spoonful

'**cuccia** nf dog's bed; **fa la ~!** lie down!

cucciò'lata nf litter

cucciolo nm puppy

cu'cina nf kitchen; (il cucinare) cooking; (cibo) food; (apparecchio) cooker; **far da ~** cook; **libro di ~** cook[ery] book. **~ a gas** gas cooker

cuci'n|are vt cook. **~ino** nm kitchenette

cu'cire vt sew; **macchina per ~re** sewing-machine. **~to** nm sewing. **~'tura** nf seam

cucù nm inv cuckoo

cuculo nm cuckoo

'**cuffia** nf bonnet; (da bagno) bathing-cap; (ricevitore) headphones pl

cu'gino, -a nmf cousin

'**cui** pron rel (persona: con prep) who, whom fml; (cose, animali: con prep) which; (tra articolo e nome) whose; **la persona con ~ ho parlato** the person [who] I spoke to; **la ditta per ~ lavoro** the company I work for, the company for which I work; **l'amico il ~ libro è stato pubblicato** the friend whose book was published; **in ~** (dove) where; (quando) that; **per ~** (perciò) so; **la città in ~ vivo** the city I live in, the city where I live; **il giorno in ~ l'ho visto** the day [that] I saw him

culi'nari|a nf cookery. **~o** a culinary

'**culla** nf cradle. **cul'lare** vt rock

culmi'na|nte a culminating. **~re** vi culminate. **'culmine** nm peak

'**culo** nm vulg arse; (fortuna) luck

'**culto** nm cult; Relig religion; (adorazione) worship

cul'tu|ra nf culture. **~ra generale** general knowledge. **~'rale** a cultural

cultu'ris|mo nm body-building. **~ta** nmf body builder

cumula'tivo a cumulative; **biglietto ~** group ticket

'**cumulo** nm pile; (mucchio) heap; (nuvola) cumulus

'**cuneo** nm wedge

cu'netta nf gutter

cu'ocere vt/i cook; fire (ceramica)

cu'oco, -a nmf cook

cu'oio nm leather. **~ capelluto** scalp

cu'ore nm heart; **cuori** pl (carte) hearts; **nel profondo del ~** in one's heart of hearts; **di [buon] ~** (persona) kind-hearted; **nel ~ della notte** in the middle of the night; **stare a ~ a qcno** be very important to sb

cupi'digia nf greed

'**cupo** a gloomy; (suono) deep

'**cupola** nf dome

'**cura** nf care; (amministrazione) management; Med treatment; **a ~ di** edited by; **in ~** under treatment. **~ dimagrante** [slimming] diet. **cu'rante** a **medico curante** GP, doctor

cu'rar|e vt take care of; Med treat; (guarire) cure; edit (testo). **~si** vr take care of oneself; Med follow a treatment; **~si di** (badare a) mind

cu'rato nm parish priest

cura'tore, -'trice nmf trustee; (di testo) editor

curia nf curia

curi'os|are vi be curious; (mettere il naso) pry (in into); (nei negozi) look around. **~ità** nf inv curiosity. **curi'oso** a curious; (strano) odd

cur'sore nm Comput cursor

'**curva** nf curve; (stradale) bend. **~ a gomito** U-bend. **cur'vare** vt curve; (strada:) bend. **cur'varsi** vr bend. '**curvo** a curved; (piegato) bent

cusci'netto nm pad; Mech bearing

cu'scino nm cushion; (guanciale) pillow. **~ d'aria** air cushion

'**cuspide** nf spire

cu'stod|e nm caretaker. **~e giudiziario** official receiver. **~ia** nf care; Jur custody; (astuccio) case. **~ia cautelare** remand. **custo'dire** vt keep; (badare a) look after

cu'taneo a skin attrib

'**cute** nf skin

cu'ticola nf cuticle

Dd

da *prep* from; (*con verbo passivo*) by; (*moto a luogo*) to; (*moto per luogo*) through; (*stato in luogo*) at; (*temporale*) since; (*continuativo*) for; (*causale*) with; (*in qualità di*) as; (*con caratteristica*) with; (*come*) like; **da Roma a Milano** from Rome to Milan; **staccare un quadro dalla parete** take a picture off the wall; **i bambini dai 5 ai 10 anni** children between 5 and 10; **vedere qcsa da vicino/lontano** see sth from up close/from a distance; **scritto da** written by; **andare dal panettiere** go to the baker's; **passo da te più tardi** I'll come over to your place later; **passiamo da qui** let's go this way; **un appuntamento dal dentista** an appointment at the dentist's; **il treno passa da Venezia** the train goes through Venice; **dall'anno scorso** since last year; **vivo qui da due anni** I've been living here for two years; **da domani** from tomorrow; **piangere dal dolore** cry with pain; **ho molto da fare** I have a lot to do; **occhiali da sole** sunglasses; **qualcosa da mangiare** something to eat; **un uomo dai capelli scuri** a man with dark hair; **è un oggetto da poco** it's not worth much; **l'ho fatto da solo** I did it by myself; **si è fatto da sé** he is a self-made man; **non è da lui** it's not like him

dac'capo *adv* again; (*dall'inizio*) from the beginning

dacché *conj* since

'dado *nm* dice; *Culin* stock cube; *Techn* nut

daf'fare *nm* work

'dagli =**da** +**gli. 'dai** =**da** +**i**

'dai *int* come on!

'daino *nm* deer; (*pelle*) buckskin

dal =**da** +**il. 'dalla** =**da** +**la. 'dalle** = **da** +**le. 'dallo** =**da** +**lo**

'dalia *nf* dahlia

dal'tonico *a* colour-blind

'dama *nf* lady; (*nei balli*) partner; (*gioco*) draughts *sg*

dami'gella *nf* (*di sposa*) bridesmaid

damigi'ana *nf* demijohn

dam'meno *adv* **non essere ~** (**di qcno**) be no less good (than sb)

da'naro *nm* =denaro

dana'roso *a* (*fam: ricco*) loaded

da'nese *a* Danish ● *nmf* Dane ● *nm* (*lingua*) Danish

Dani'marca *nf* Denmark

dan'na|re *vt* damn; **far ~re qcno** drive sb mad. **~to** *a* damned. **~zi'one** *nf* damnation

danneggi'a'mento *nm* damage. **~'are** *vt* damage; (*nuocere*) harm

'danno *nm* damage; (*a persona*) harm. **dan'noso** *a* harmful

Da'nubio *nm* Danube

'danza *nf* dance; (*il danzare*) dancing. **dan'zare** *vi* dance

dapper'tutto *adv* everywhere

dap'poco *a* worthless

dap'prima *adv* at first

'dardo *nm* dart

'dar|e *vt* give; sit (*esame*); have (*festa*); **~e qcsa a qcno** give sb sth; **~e da mangiare a qcno** give sb something to eat; **~e il benvenuto a qcno** welcome sb; **~e la buonanotte a qcno** say good night to sb; **~e del tu/del lei a qcno** address sb as "tu"/"lei"; **~e del cretino a qcno** call sb an idiot; **~e qcsa per scontato** take sth for granted; **cosa danno alla TV stasera?** what's on TV tonight? ● *vi* **~e nell'occhio** be conspicuous; **~e alla testa** go to one's head; **~e su** (*finestra, casa:*) look on to; **~e sui** *o* **ai nervi a qcno** get on sb's nerves ● *nm* Comm debit. **~si** *vr* (*scambiarsi*) give each other; **~si da fare** get down to it; **si è dato tanto da fare!** he went to so much trouble!; **~si a** (*cominciare*) take up; **~si al bere** take to drink; **~si per** (*malato, assente*) pretend to be; **~si per vinto** give up; **può ~si** maybe

'darsena *nf* dock

'data *nf* date. **~ di emissione** date of issue. **~ di nascita** date of birth. **~ di scadenza** cut-off date

da'ta|re *vt* date; **a ~re da** as from. **~to** *a* dated

'**dato** *a* given; (*dedito*) addicted; ~ **che**
seeing that, given that ●*nm* datum. ~
di fatto well-established fact; **dati** *pl*
data. **da'tore** *nm* giver. **datore, datrice**
nmf **di lavoro** employer

'**dattero** *nm* date

dattilogra'f|are *vt/i* type. ~**ia** *nf* typ-
ing. **datti'lografo, -a** *nmf* typist

dattilo'scritto *a* (*copia*) typewritten

dat'torno *adv* **togliersi** ~ clear off

da'vanti *adv* before; (*dirimpetto*) opposite; (*di fronte*) in front ●*a inv* front
●*nm* front; ~ **a** *prep* before, in front of

davan'zale *nm* window sill

da'vanzo *adv* more than enough

dav'vero *adv* really; **per** ~ in earnest;
dici ~? honestly?

'**dazio** *nm* duty; (*ufficio*) customs *pl*

d.C. *abbr* (*dopo Cristo*) AD

'**dea** *nf* goddess

debel'lare *vt* defeat

debili'ta|nte *a* weakening. ~**re** *vt*
weaken. ~**rsi** *vr* become debilitated.
~**zi'one** *nf* debilitation

debita'mente *adv* duly

'**debi|to** *a* due; **a tempo** ~ in due
course ●*nm* debt. ~**tore**, ~**trice** *nmf*
debtor

'**debo|le** *a* weak; (*luce*) dim; (*suono*)
faint ●*nm* weak point; (*preferenza*)
weakness. ~**lezza** *nf* weakness

debor'dare *vi* overflow

debosci'ato *a* debauched

debut'ta|nte *nm* (*attore*) actor mak-
ing his début ●*nf* actress making her
début. ~**re** *vi* make one's début.
de'butto *nm* début

deca'den|te *a* decadent. ~**tismo** *nm*
decadence. ~**za** *nf* decline; *Jur* loss.
deca'dere *vi* lapse. **decadi'mento** *nm*
(*delle arti*) decline

decaffei'nato *a* decaffeinated ●*nm*
decaffeinated coffee, decaf *fam*

decan'tare *vt* (*lodare*) praise

decapi'ta|re *vt* decapitate; behead
(*condannato*). ~**zi'one** *nf* decapitation;
beheading

decappot'tabile *a* convertible

de'ce|dere *vi* (*morire*) die. ~**duto** *a*
deceased

decele'rare *vt* decelerate, slow down

decen'nale *a* ten-yearly. **de'cennio**
nm decade

de'cen|te *a* decent. ~**te'mente** *adv*
decently. ~**za** *nf* decency

decentra'mento *nm* decentraliza-
tion

de'cesso *nm* death; **atto di** ~ death
certificate

de'cider|e *vt* decide; settle (*questione*).
~**si** *vr* make up one's mind

deci'frare *vt* decipher; (*documenti ci-
frati*) decode

deci'male *a* decimal

deci'mare *vt* decimate

'**decimo** *a* tenth

de'cina *nf Math* ten; **una** ~ **di** (*circa
dieci*) about ten

decisa'mente *adv* definitely, decidedly

decisio'nale *a* decision-making

deci'si|one *nf* decision. ~**sivo** *a* deci-
sive. **de'ciso** *pp di* **decidere** ●*a* decided

decla'ma|re *vt/i* declaim. ~**torio** *a*
(*stile*) declamatory

declas'sare *vt* downgrade

decli'na|re *vt* decline; **~re ogni re-
sponsabilità** disclaim all responsibility ●*vi* go down; (*tramontare*) set.
~**zi'one** *nf Gram* declension. **de'clino**
nm decline; **in declino** (*popolarità:*) on
the decline

decodificazi'one *nf* decoding

decol'lare *vi* take off

décolle'té *nm inv* décolleté, low neckline

de'collo *nm* take-off

decolo'ra|nte *nm* bleach. ~**re** *vt*
bleach

decolorazi'one *nf* bleaching

decom'po|rre *vt*, ~**rsi** *vr* decompose.
~**sizi'one** *nf* decomposition

deconcen'trarsi *vr* become dis-
tracted

deconge'lare *vt* defrost

decongestio'nare *vt Med, fig* relieve congestion in

deco'ra|re *vt* decorate. ~'**tivo** *a* deco-
rative. ~**to** *a* (*ornato*) decorated.
~**tore**, ~**trice** *nmf* decorator.
~**zi'one** *nf* decoration

de'coro *nm* decorum

decorosa'mente *adv* decorously.
decoroso *a* dignified

decor'renza *nf* ~ **dal...** starting
from...

de'correre *vi* pass; **a** ~ **da** with effect
from. **de'corso** *pp di* **decorrere** ●*nm*
passing; *Med* course

de'crepito *a* decrepit

decre'scente *a* decreasing. **de'crescere** *vi* decrease; (*prezzi:*) go down;
(*acque:*) subside

decre'tare *vt* decree. **de'creto** *nm* decree. **decreto legge** *decree which has the force of law*

'dedalo *nm* maze

'dedica *nf* dedication

dedi'care *vt* dedicate. **~si** *vr* dedicate oneself

'dedi|to *a* **~ a** given to; *(assorto)* engrossed in; addicted to *(vizi)*. **~'one** *nf* dedication

de'dotto *pp di* **dedurre**

dedu'cibile *a* *(tassa)* allowable

de'du|rre *vt* deduce; *(sottrarre)* deduct. **~'tivo** *a* deductive. **~zi'one** *nf* deduction

defal'care *vt* deduct

defe'rire *vt* Jur remit

defezio'nare *vi* *(abbandonare)* defect. **~'one** *nf* defection

defici'en|te *a* *(mancante)* deficient; Med mentally deficient ● *nmf* mental defective; *pej* half-wit. **~za** *nf* deficiency; *(lacuna)* gap; Med mental deficiency

'defici|t *nm inv* deficit. **~'tario** *a* *(bilancio)* deficit *attrib*

defi'larsi *vr* *(scomparire)* slip away

défilé *nm inv* fashion show

defi'ni|re *vt* define; *(risolvere)* settle. **~tiva'mente** *adv* for good. **~'tivo** *a* definitive. **~to** *a* definite. **~zi'one** *nf* definition; *(soluzione)* settlement

deflazi'one *nf* deflation

deflet'tore *nm* Auto quarterlight

deflu'ire *vi* *(liquidi:)* flow away; *(persone:)* stream out

de'flusso *nm* *(di marea)* ebb

defor'ma|re *vt* deform *(arto)*; *fig* distort. **~si** *vr* lose its shape

defor'm|ato *a* warped. **~azi'one** *nf* *(di fatti)* distortion; **è una ~azione professionale** put it down to the job. **de'forme** *a* deformed. **~ità** *nf* deformity

defrau'dare *vt* defraud

de'funto, -a *a & nmf* deceased

degene'ra|re *vi* degenerate. **~to** *a* degenerate. **~zi'one** *nf* degeneration. **de'genere** *a* degenerate

de'gen|te *a* bedridden ● *nmf* patient. **~za** *nf* confinement

'degli = **di** + **gli**

deglu'tire *vt* swallow

de'gna|re *vt* **~e qcno di uno sguardo** deign to look at sb. **~si** *vr* deign, condescend

'degno *a* worthy; *(meritevole)* deserving

degrada'mento *nm* degradation

degra'dante *a* demeaning

degra'da|re *vt* degrade. **~rsi** *vr* lower oneself; *(città:)* fall into a state of disrepair. **~zi'one** *nf* degradation

de'grado *nm* damage; **~ ambientale** *nm* environmental damage

degu'sta|re *vt* taste. **~zi'one** *nf* tasting

'dei = **di** + **i**. **'del** = **di** + **il**

dela'tore, -'trice *nmf* [police] informer. **~zi'one** *nf* informing

'delega *nf* proxy

dele'ga|re *vt* delegate. **~to** *nm* delegate. **~zi'one** *nf* delegation

dele'terio *a* harmful

del'fino *nm* dolphin; *(stile di nuoto)* butterfly [stroke]

de'libera *nf* bylaw

delibe'ra|re *vt/i* deliberate; **~ su/in** rule on/in. **~to** *a* deliberate

delicata'mente *adv* delicately

delica'tezza *nf* delicacy; *(fragilità)* frailty; *(tatto)* tact

deli'cato *a* delicate; *(salute)* frail; *(suono, colore)* soft

delimi'tare *vt* delimit

deline'a|re *vt* outline. **~rsi** *vr* be outlined; *fig* take shape. **~to** *a* defined

delin'quen|te *nmf* delinquent. **~za** *nf* delinquency

deli'rante *a* Med delirious; *(assurdo)* insane

deli'rare *vi* be delirious. **de'lirio** *nm* delirium; *fig* frenzy

de'litt|o *nm* crime. **~u'oso** *a* criminal

de'lizi|a *nf* delight. **~'are** *vt* delight. **~'oso** *a* delightful; *(cibo)* delicious

'della = **di** + **la**. **'delle** = **di** + **le**. **'dello** = **di** + **lo**

'delta *nm inv* delta

delta'plano *nm* hang-glider; **fare ~** go hang-gliding

delucidazi'one *nf* clarification

delu'dente *a* disappointing

de'lu|dere *vt* disappoint. **~si'one** *nf* disappointment. **de'luso** *a* disappointed

dema'gogico *a* popularity-seeking, demagogic

demar'ca|re *vt* demarcate. **~zi'one** *nf* demarcation

de'men|te *a* demented. **~za** *nf* dementia. **~zi'ale** *a* *(assurdo)* zany

demilitariz'za|re *vt* demilitarize. **~zi'one** *nf* demilitarization

demistificazi'one *nf* debunking

demo'cra|tico *a* democratic. **~'zia** *nf* democracy

democristi'ano, **-a** *a* & *nmf* Christian Democrat

demogra'fia *nf* demography. **demo'grafico** *a* demographic

demo'li|re *vt* demolish. **~zi'one** *nf* demolition

'**demone** *nm* demon. **de'monio** *nm* demon

demoraliz'zar|e *vt* demoralize. **~si** *vr* become demoralized

de'mordere *vi* give up

demoti'vato *a* demotivated

de'nari *nmpl* (*nelle carte*) diamonds

de'naro *nm* money

deni'gra|re *vt* denigrate. **~'torio** *a* denigratory

denomi'na|re *vt* name. **~'tore** *nm* denominator. **~zi'one** *nf* denomination; **~zione di origine controllata** mark guaranteeing the quality of a wine

deno'tare *vt* denote

densità *nf inv* density. '**denso** *a* thick, dense

den'ta|le *a* dental. **~rio** *a* dental. **~ta** *nf* bite. **~'tura** *nf* teeth *pl*

'**dente** *nm* tooth; (*di forchetta*) prong; **al ~** *Culin* just slightly firm. **~ del giudizio** wisdom tooth. **~ di latte** milk tooth. **denti'era** *nf* dentures *pl*, false teeth *pl*

denti'fricio *nm* toothpaste

den'tista *nmf* dentist

'**dentro** *adv* in, inside; (*in casa*) indoors; **da ~** from within; **qui ~** in here ● *prep* in, inside; (*di tempo*) within, by ● *nm* inside

denuclearizzazi'one *nf* denuclearization

denu'dar|e *vt* bare. **~si** *vr* strip

de'nunci|a, **de'nunzia** *nf* denunciation; (*alla polizia*) reporting; (*dei redditi*) [income] tax return. **~'are** *vt* denounce; (*accusare*) report

denu'trito *a* underfed. **~zi'one** *nf* malnutrition

deodo'rante *a* & *nm* deodorant

dépendance *nf inv* outbuilding

depe'ri|bile *a* perishable. **~'mento** *nm* wasting away; (*di merci*) deterioration. **~re** *vi* waste away

depi'la|re *vt* depilate. **~rsi** *vr* shave (*gambe*); pluck (*sopracciglia*). **~'torio** *nm* depilatory

deplo'rabile *a* deplorable

deplo'r|are *vt* deplore; (*dolersi di*) grieve over. **~evole** *a* deplorable

de'porre *vt* put down; lay down (*armi*); lay (*uova*); (*togliere da una carica*) depose; (*testimoniare*) testify

depor'ta|re *vt* deport. **~to, -a** *nmf* deportee. **~zi'one** *nf* deportation

deposi'tar|e *vt* deposit; (*lasciare in custodia*) leave; (*in magazzino*) store. **~io, -a** *nmf* (*di segreto*) repository. **~si** *vr* settle

de'posi|to *nm* deposit; (*luogo*) warehouse; *Mil* depot. **~ bagagli** left-luggage office. **~zi'one** *nf* deposition; (*da una carica*) removal

depra'va|re *vt* deprave. **~to** *a* depraved. **~zi'one** *nf* depravity

depre'cabile *a* appalling. **~re** *vt* deprecate

depre'dare *vt* plunder

depressi'one *nf* depression. **de'presso** *pp di* **deprimere** ● *a* depressed

deprez'zar|e *vt* depreciate. **~si** *vr* depreciate

depri'mente *a* depressing

de'prim|ere *vt* depress. **~si** *vr* become depressed

depu'ra|re *vt* purify. **~'tore** *nm* purifier

depu'ta|re *vt* delegate. **~to, -a** *nmf* deputy, Member of Parliament

deragli a'mento *nm* derailment

deragli'are *vi* go off the lines; **far ~** derail

'**derby** *nm inv Sport* local Derby

deregolamentazi'one *nf* deregulation

dere'litto *a* derelict

dere'tano *nm* backside, bottom

de'ri|dere *vt* deride. **~si'one** *nf* derision. **~'sorio** *a* derisory

de'riva *nf* drift; **andare alla ~** drift

deri'va|re *vi* **~ re da** (*provenire*) derive from ● *vt* derive; (*sviare*) divert. **~zi'one** *nf* derivation; (*di fiume*) diversion

dermato lo'gia *nf* dermatology. **~'logico** *a* dermatological. **derma'to logo, -a** *nmf* dermatologist

'**deroga** *nf* dispensation. **dero'gare** *vi* **derogare a** depart from

der'ra|ta *nf* merchandise. **~e alimen'tari** foodstuffs

deru'bare *vt* rob

descrit'tivo *a* descriptive. **des'critto** *pp di* **descrivere**

des'cri|vere *vt* describe. **~'vibile** *a* describable. **~zi'one** *nf* description

de'serto *a* uninhabited ● *nm* desert

deside'rabile *a* desirable

deside'rare *vt* wish; (*volere*) want;

(intensamente) long for; *(bramare)* desire; **desidera?** what would you like?, can I help you?; **lasciare a ~** leave a lot to be desired

desi'de|rio nm wish; *(brama)* desire; *(intenso)* longing. **~'roso** a desirous; *(bramoso)* longing

desi'gnare vt designate; *(fissare)* fix

desi'nenza nf ending

de'sistere vi **~ da** desist from

desktop publishing nm inv desktop publishing

deso'lante a distressing

deso'la|re vt distress. **~to** a desolate; *(spiacente)* sorry. **~zi'one** nf desolation

'despota nm despot

de'sta|re vt waken; *fig* awaken. **~rsi** vr waken; *fig* awaken

desti'na|re vt destine; *(nominare)* appoint; *(assegnare)* assign; *(indirizzare)* address. **~'tario** nm *(di lettera, pacco)* addressee. **~zi'one** nf destination; *fig* purpose

de'stino nm destiny; *(fato)* fate

destitu'i|re vt dismiss. **~zi'one** nf dismissal

'desto a liter awake

'destra nf *(parte)* right; *(mano)* right hand; **prendere a ~** turn right

destreggi'ar|e vi, **~si** vr manoeuvre

de'strezza nf dexterity; *(abilità)* skill

'destro a right; *(abile)* skilful

detei'nato a tannin-free

dete'n|ere vt hold; *(polizia:)* detain. **~uto, -a** nmf prisoner. **~zi'one** nf detention

deter'gente a cleaning; *(crema)* cleansing ● nm detergent; *(per la pelle)* cleanser

deteriora'mento nm deterioration

deterio'rar|e vt cause to deteriorate. **~si** vr deteriorate

determi'nante a decisive

determi'na|re vt determine. **~rsi** vr **~rsi a** resolve to. **~'tezza** nf determination. **~'tivo** a Gram definite. **~to** a *(risoluto)* determined; *(particolare)* specific. **~zi'one** nf determination; *(decisione)* decision

deter'rente a & nm deterrent

deter'sivo nm detergent. **~ per i piatti** washing-up liquid

dete'stare vt detest, hate

deto'nare vi detonate

de'tra|rre vt deduct *(da from)*. **~zi'one** nf deduction

detri'mento nm detriment; **a ~ di** to the detriment of

de'trito nm debris

'**detta** nf **a ~ di** according to

dettagli'ante nmf Comm retailer

dettagli'a|re vt detail. **~ta'mente** adv in detail

det'taglio nm detail; **al ~** Comm retail

det'ta|re vt dictate; **~re legge** *fig* lay down the law. **~to** nm. **~ tura** nf dictation

'detto a said; *(chiamato)* called; *(soprannominato)* nicknamed; **~ fatto** no sooner said than done ● nm saying

detur'pare vt disfigure

deva'sta|re vt devastate. **~to** a devastated. **~zi'one** nf devastation; *fig* ravages pl

devi'a|re vi deviate ● vt divert. **~zi'one** nf deviation; *(stradale)* diversion

devitaliz'zare vt deaden *(dente)*

devo'lu|to pp di **devolvere** ● a devolved. **~zi'one** nf devolution

de'volvere vt devolve

de'vo|to a devout; *(affezionato)* devoted. **~zi'one** nf devotion

di prep of; *(partitivo)* some; *(scritto da)* by; *(parlare, pensare ecc)* about; *(con causa, mezzo)* with; *(con provenienza)* from; *(in comparazioni)* than; *(con infinito)* to; **la casa di mio padre/dei miei genitori** my father's house/my parents' house; **compra del pane** buy some bread; **hai del pane?** do you have any bread?; **un film di guerra** a war film; **piangere di dolore** cry with pain; **coperto di neve** covered with snow; **sono di Genova** I'm from Genoa; **uscire di casa** leave one's house; **più alto di te** taller than you; **è ora di partire** it's time to go; **crede di aver ragione** he thinks he's right; **dire di sì** say yes; **di domenica** on Sundays; **di sera** in the evening; **una pausa di un'ora** an hour's break; **un corso di due mesi** a two-month course

dia'be|te nm diabetes. **~ico, -a** a & nmf diabetic

dia'bolico a diabolical

dia'dema nm diadem; *(di donna)* tiara

di'afano a diaphanous

dia'framma nm diaphragm; *(divisione)* screen

di'agnos|i nf diagnosis. **~ti'care** vt diagnose

diago'nale a & nf diagonal

dia'gramma nm diagram

dia'let|tale a dialect. **dia'letto** nm dialect

dialo'gante a **unità ~** Comput interactive terminal

di'alogo *nm* dialogue
dia'mante *nm* diamond
di'ametro *nm* diameter
di'amine *int* che ~... what on earth...
diaposi'tiva *nf* slide
di'ario *nm* diary
diar'rea *nf* diarrhoea
di'avolo *nm* devil; va al ~ go to hell!;
che ~ fai? what the hell are you doing?
di'batt|ere *vt* debate. ~ersi *vr* strug-
gle. ~ito *nm* debate; (*meno formale*) discussion
dica'stero *nm* office
di'cembre *nm* December
dice'ria *nf* rumour
dichia'ra|re *vt* state; (*ufficialmente*)
declare. ~rsi *vr* si dichiara innocente he says he's innocent. ~to *nm*
statement; (*documento, di guerra*) declaration
dician'nove *a & nm* nineteen
dicias'sette *a & nm* seventeen
dici'otto *a & nm* eighteen
dici'tura *nf* wording
didasca'lia *nf* (*di film*) subtitle; (*di
illustrazione*) caption
di'dattic|a *nf* didactics *sg*. ~o *a* didac-
tic; (*televisione*) educational
di'dentro *adv* inside
didi'etro *adv* behind ● *nm hum* hind-
quarters *pl*
di'eci *a & nm* ten
die'cina = decina
'diesel *a & nf inv* diesel
di'esis *nm inv* sharp
di'eta *nf* diet; essere a ~ be on a diet.
die'tetico *a* diet. die'tista *nmf* dietician. die'tologo *nmf* dietician
di'etro *adv* behind ● *prep* behind;
(*dopo*) after ● *a* back; (*di zampe*) hind
● *nm* back; le stanze di ~ the back
rooms; le zampe di ~ the hind legs
dietro'front *nm inv* about-turn; *fig* U-
turn
di'fatti *adv* in fact
di'fen|dere *vt* defend. ~dersi *vr* de-
fend oneself. ~'siva *nf* stare sulla
~siva be on the defensive. ~'sivo *a* defensive. ~'sore *nm* defender; avvocato
~sore defence counsel
di'fes|a *nf* defence; prendere le ~e di
qcno come to sb's defence. ~o *pp di*
difendere
difet'ta|re *vi* be defective; ~are di
lack. ~ivo *a* defective
di'fet|to *nm* defect; (*morale*) fault, flaw;
(*mancanza*) lack; (*in tessuto, abito*) flaw;
essere in ~to be at fault; far ~to be

lacking. ~'toso *a* defective; (*abto*)
flawed
diffa'ma|re *vt* (*con parole*) slander;
(*per iscritto*) libel. ~'torio *a* slanderous;
(*per iscritto*) libellous. ~zi'one *nf* slander; (*scritta*) libel
diffe'ren|te *a* different. ~za *nf* differ-
ence; a ~za di unlike; non fare ~za
make no distinction (fra between).
~zi'ale *a & nm* differential
differenzi'ar|e *vt* differentiate. ~si
vr ~si da differ from
diffe'ri|re *vt* postpone ● *vi* be different.
~ta *nf* in ~ta *TV* prerecorded
diffi'cile *a* difficult; (*duro*) hard;
(*improbabile*) unlikely ● *nm* difficulty.
~'mente *adv* with difficulty
difficoltà *nf inv* difficulty
diffi'da *nf* warning
diffi'd|are *vi* ~are di distrust ● *vt*
warn. ~'ente *a* mistrustful. ~'enza *nf*
mistrust
dif'fond|ere *vt* spread; diffuse (*calore,
luce ecc*). ~si *vr* spread. diffusi'one *nf*
diffusion; (*di giornale*) circulation
dif'fu|so *pp di* diffondere ● *a* com-
mon; (*malattia*) widespread; (*luce*) diffuse. ~'sore *nm* (*per asciugacapelli*)
diffuser
difi'lato *adv* straight; (*subito*) straight-
away
'diga *nf* dam; (*argine*) dike
dige'ribile *a* digestible
dige'ri|re *vt* digest; *fam* stomach.
~'stione *nf* digestion. ~'stivo *a* digestive ● *nm* digestive; (*dopo cena*) liqueur
digi'tale *a* digital; (*delle dita*) finger
attrib ● *nf* (*fiore*) foxglove
digi'tare *vt* key in
digiu'nare *vi* fast
digi'uno *a* essere ~ have an empty
stomach ● *nm* fast; a ~ on an empty
stomach
dignità *nf inv* dignity. ~'tario *nm* dignitary. ~'toso *a* dignified
digressi'one *nf* digression
digri'gnare *vi* ~ i denti grind one's
teeth
dila'gare *vi* flood; *fig* spread
dilani'are *vt* tear to pieces
dilapi'dare *vt* squander
dila'ta|re *vt*, ~rsi *vr* dilate; (*metallo,
gas*) expand. ~zi'one *nf* dilation
dilazio'nabile *a* postponable
dilazio|'nare *vt* delay. ~'one *nf* delay
dilegu'ar|e *vt* disperse. ~si *vr* disap-
pear
di'lemma *nm* dilemma

dilet'tan|te *nmf* amateur. **~'tistico** *a* amateurish

dilet'tare *vt* delight

di'letto, -a *a* beloved ●*nm* (*piacere*) delight ●*nmf* (*persona*) beloved

dili'gen|te *a* diligent; (*lavoro*) accurate. **~za** *nf* diligence

dilu'ire *vt* dilute

dilun'gar|e *vt* prolong. **~si** *vr* **~si su** dwell on (*argomento*)

diluvi'are *vi* pour [down]. **di'luvio** *nm* downpour; *fig* flood

dima'gr|ante *a* slimming, diet. **~i'mento** *nm* loss of weight. **~ire** *vi* slim

dime'nar|e *vt* wave; wag (*coda*). **~si** *vr* be agitated

dimensi'one *nf* dimension; (*misura*) size

dimenti'canza *nf* forgetfulness; (*svista*) oversight

dimenti'car|e *vt*, **~si** *vr* **~ [di]** forget. **dimentico** *a* **dimentico di** (*che non ricorda*) forgetful of

di'messo *pp di* **dimettere** ●*a* humble; (*trasandato*) shabby; (*voce*) low

dimesti'chezza *nf* familiarity

di'metter|e *vt* dismiss; (*da ospedale ecc*) discharge. **~si** *vr* resign

dimez'zare *vt* halve

diminu'ire *vt/i* diminish; (*in maglia*) decrease. **~tivo** *a* & *nm* diminutive. **~zi'one** *nf* decrease; (*riduzione*) reduction

dimissi'oni *nfpl* resignation *sg*; **dare le ~** resign

di'mo|ra *nf* residence. **~'rare** *vi* reside

dimo'strante *nmf* demonstrator

dimo'stra|re *vt* demonstrate; (*provare*) prove; (*mostrare*) show. **~rsi** *vr* prove [to be]. **~'tivo** *a* demonstrative. **~zi'one** *nf* demonstration; *Math* proof

di'namico, -a *a* dynamic ●*nf* dynamics *sg*. **dina'mismo** *nm* dynamism

dinami'tardo *a* **attentato ~** bomb attack

dina'mite *nf* dynamite

'dinamo *nf inv* dynamo

di'nanzi *adv* in front ●*prep* **~ a** in front of

dina'stia *nf* dynasty

dini'ego *nm* denial

dinocco'lato *a* lanky

dino'sauro *nm* dinosaur

din'torni *nmpl* outskirts; **nei ~i di** in the vicinity of. **~o** *adv* around

'dio *nm* (*pl* **dei**) god; **D~** God

di'ocesi *nf inv* diocese

dipa'nare *vt* wind into a ball; *fig* unravel

diparti'mento *nm* department

dipen'den|te *a* depending ●*nmf* employee. **~za** *nf* dependence; (*edificio*) annexe

di'pendere *vi* **~ da** depend on; (*provenire*) derive from; **dipende** it depends

di'pinger|e *vt* paint; (*descrivere*) describe. **~si** *vr* (*truccarsi*) make up. **di'pinto** *pp di* **dispingere** ●*a* painted ●*nm* painting

di'ploma *nm* diploma. **~'marsi** *vr* graduate

diplo'matico *a* diplomatic ●*nm* diplomat; (*pasticcino*) millefeuille (*with alcohol*)

diplo'mato *nm* person with school qualification ●*a* qualified

diploma'zia *nf* diplomacy

di'porto *nm* **imbarcazione da ~** pleasure craft

dira'dar|e *vt* thin out; make less frequent (*visite*). **~si** *vr* thin out; (*nebbia*) clear

dira'ma|re *vt* issue ●*vi*, **~rsi** *vr* branch out; (*diffondersi*) spread. **~zi'one** *nf* (*di strada*) fork

'dire *vt* say; (*raccontare, riferire*) tell; **~ quello che si pensa** speak one's mind; **voler ~** mean; **volevo ben ~!** I wondered!; **~ di sì/no** say yes/no; **si dice che...** rumour has it that...; **come si dice "casa" in inglese?** what's the English for "casa"?; **questo nome mi dice qualcosa** the name rings a bell; **che ne dici di...?** how about...?; **non c'è che ~** there's no disputing that; **e ~ che...** to think that...; **a dir poco/tanto** at least/most ●*vi* **~ bene/male di** speak highly/ill of sb; **dica pure** (*in negozio*) how can I help you?; **dici sul serio?** are you serious?; **per modo di ~** in a manner of speaking

diretta'mente *adv* directly

diret'tissima *nf* **processare per ~** *Jur* try as speedily as possible

diret'tissimo *nm* fast train

diret'tiva *nf* directive

di'retto *pp di* **dirigere** ●*a* direct. **~ a** (*inteso*) meant for. **essere ~ a** be heading for. **in diretta** (*trasmissione*) live ●*nm* (*treno*) through train

diret'tore, -'trice *nmf* manager; manageress; (*di scuola*) headmaster; headmistress. **~tore d'orchestra** conductor

direzi'one *nf* direction; (*di società*)

management; *Sch* headmaster's/head-mistress's office (*primary school*)

diri'gen|te *a* ruling ● *nmf* executive; *Pol* leader. **~za** *nf* management. **~zi'ale** *a* management *attrib*, managerial

di'riger|e *vt* direct; conduct ⟨orchestra⟩; run ⟨impresa⟩. **~si** *vr* **~si verso** head for

dirim'petto *adv* opposite ● *prep* **~ a** facing

di'ritto¹, dritto *a* straight; (*destro*) right ● *adv* straight; **andare ~** go straight on ● *nm* right side; *Tennis* forehand; **fare un ~** (*a maglia*) knit one

di'ritto² *nm* right; *Jur* law. **~i d'autore** royalties

dirit'tura *nf* straight line; *fig* honesty. **~ d'arrivo** *Sport* home straight

diroc'cato *a* tumbledown

dirom'pente *a fig* explosive

dirot'ta|re *vt* reroute ⟨treno, aereo⟩; (*illegalmente*) hijack; divert ⟨traffico⟩ ● *vi* alter course. **~'tore, ~'trice** *nmf* hijacker

di'rotto *a* ⟨pioggia⟩ pouring; ⟨pianto⟩ uncontrollable; **piovere a ~** rain heavily

di'rupo *nm* precipice

dis'abile *nmf* disabled person

disabi'tato *a* uninhabited

disabitu'arsi *vr* **~ a** get out of the habit of

disac'cordo *nm* disagreement

disadat'tato, -a *a* maladjusted ● *nmf* misfit

disa'dorno *a* unadorned

disa'gevole *a* (*scomodo*) uncomfortable

disagi'ato *a* poor; ⟨vita⟩ hard

di'sagio *nm* discomfort; (*difficoltà*) inconvenience; (*imbarazzo*) embarrassment; **sentirsi a ~** feel uncomfortable; **disagi** *pl* (*privazioni*) hardships

disappro'va|re *vt* disapprove of. **~zi'one** *nf* disapproval

disap'punto *nm* disappointment

disar'mante *a* disarming

disar'mare *vt/i* disarm. **di'sarmo** *nm* disarmament

disa'strato, -a *a* devastated ● *nmf* disaster victim

di'sastro *nm* disaster; (*fam: grande confusione*) mess; (*fig: persona*) disaster area. **disa'stroso** *a* disastrous

disat'ten|to *a* inattentive. **~zi'one** *nf* inattention; (*svista*) oversight

disatti'vare *vt* de-activate

disa'vanzo *nm* deficit

disavven'tura *nf* misadventure

dis'brigo *nm* dispatch

dis'capito *nm* **a ~ di** to the detriment of

dis'carica *nf* scrap-yard

descen'den|te *a* descending ● *nmf* descendant. **~za** *nf* descent; (*discendenti*) descendants *pl*

di'scendere *vt/i* descend; (*dal treno*) get off; (*da cavallo*) dismount; (*sbarcare*) land. **~ da** (*trarre origine da*) be a descendant of

di'scepolo, -a *nmf* disciple

di'scernere *vt* discern

di'sces|a *nf* descent; (*pendio*) slope; **~a in picchiata** (*di aereo*) nosedive; **essere in ~a** ⟨strada⟩ go downhill. **~a libera** (*in sci*) downhill race. **disce'sista** *mf* (*sciatore*) downhill skier. **~o** *pp di* **discendere**

dis'chetto *nm Comput* diskette

dischi'uder|e *vt* open; (*svelare*) disclose. **~si** *vr* open up

disci'oglier|e *vt*, **~si** *vr* dissolve; ⟨neve⟩ thaw; (*fondersi*) melt. **disci'olto** *pp di* **disciogliere**

disci'pli|na *nf* discipline. **~'nare** *a* disciplinary ● *vt* discipline. **~'nato** *a* disciplined

'disco *nm* disc; *Comput* disk; *Sport* discus; *Mus* record; **~ernia del ~** slipped disc. **~ fisso** *Comput* hard disk. **~ volante** flying saucer

discogra'fia *nf* (*insieme di incisioni*) discography. **disco'grafico** *a* ⟨industria⟩ record, recording; **casa discografica** record company, recording company

'discolo *nmf* rascal ● *a* unruly

discol'par|e *vt* clear. **~si** *vr* clear oneself

disco'noscere *vt* disown ⟨figlio⟩

discontinuità *nf* (*nel lavoro*) irregularity. **discon'tinuo** *a* intermittent; ⟨fig: impegno, rendimento⟩ uneven

discor'dan|te *a* discordant. **~za** *nf* mismatch

discor'dare *vi* ⟨opinioni⟩ conflict. **dis'corde** *a* clashing. **dis'cordia** *nf* discord; (*dissenso*) dissension

dis'cor|rere *vi* talk ⟨di about⟩. **~'sivo** *a* colloquial. **dis'corso** *pp di* **discorrere** ● *nm* speech; (*conversazione*) talk

dis'costo *a* distant ● *adv* far away; **stare ~** stand apart

disco'te|ca *nf* disco; (*raccolta*) record library. **~'caro** *nmf pej* disco freak

discre'pan|te *a* contradictory. **~za** *nf* discrepancy

dis'cre|to *a* discreet; (*moderato*) moderate; (*abbastanza buono*) fairly good. **~zi'one** *nf* discretion; (*giudizio*) judgement; **a ~zione di** at the discretion of

discrimi'nante *a* extenuating

discrimi'na|re *vt* discriminate. **~ to-rio** *a* (*atteggiamento*) discriminatory. **~zi'one** *nf* discrimination

discussi'one *nf* discussion; (*alterco*) argument. **dis'cusso** *pp di* **discutere** ● *a* controversial

dis'cutere *vt* discuss; (*formale*) debate; (*litigare*) argue; **~ sul prezzo** bargain. **discu'tibile** *a* debatable; (*gusto*) questionable

disde'gnare *vt* disdain. **dis'degno** *nm* disdain

disdet't|a *nf* retraction; (*sfortuna*) bad luck; *Comm* cancellation. **~o** *pp di* **disdire**

disdi'cevole *a* unbecoming

dis'dire *vt* retract; (*annullare*) cancel

diseduca'tivo *a* boorish, uncouth

dise'gna|re *vt* draw; (*progettare*) design. **~tore**, **~trice** *nmf* designer. **di'segno** *nm* drawing; (*progetto, linea*) design

diser'bante *nm* herbicide, weed-killer ● *a* herbicidal, weed-killing

disere'da|re *vt* disinherit. **~to** *a* dispossessed ● *nmf* **~ti** the dispossessed

diser'|tare *vt/i* desert; **~tare la scuola** stay away from school. **~ tore** *nm* deserter. **~zi'one** *nf* desertion

disfaci'mento *nm* decay

dis'fa|re *vt* undo; strip (*letto*); (*smantellare*) take down; (*annientare*) defeat; **~re le valigie** unpack [one's bags]. **~rsi** *vr* fall to pieces; (*sciogliersi*) melt; **~rsi di** (*liberarsi di*) get rid of; **~rsi in lacrime** dissolve into tears. **~tta** *nf* defeat. **~to** *a fig* worn out

disfat'tis|mo *nm* defeatism. **~ta** *a & nmf* defeatist

disfunzi'one *nf* disorder

dis'gelo *nm* thaw

dis'grazi|a *nf* misfortune; (*incidente*) accident; (*sfavore*) disgrace. **~ata men-te** *adv* unfortunately. **~ato**, **-a** *a* unfortunate ● *nmf* wretch

disgre'ga|re *vt* break up. **~si** *vr* disintegrate

disgu'ido *nm* **~ postale** mistake in delivery

disgu'st|are *vt* disgust. **~arsi** *vr*

~arsi di be disgusted by. **dis'gusto** *nm* disgust. **~oso** *a* disgusting

disidra'ta|re *vt* dehydrate. **~to** *a* dehydrated

disil'lu|dere *vt* disenchant. **~si'one** *nf* disenchantment. **~so** *a* disillusioned

disimbal'lare *vt* unpack

disimpa'rare *vt* forget

disimpe'gna|re *vt* release; (*compiere*) fulfil; redeem (*oggetto dato in pegno*). **~si** *vr* disengage oneself; (*cavarsela*) manage. **disim'pegno** *nm* (*locale*) vestibule

disincan'tato *a* (*disilluso*) disillusioned

disinfe'sta|re *vt* disinfest. **~zi'one** *nf* disinfestation

disinfet'tante *a & nm* disinfectant

disinfet't|are *vt* disinfect. **~zi'one** *nf* disinfection

disinfor'mato *a* uninformed

disini'bito *a* uninhibited

disinne'scare *vt* defuse (*mina*). **disin'nesco** *nm* (*di bomba*) bomb disposal

disinse'rire *vt* disconnect

disinte'gra|re *vt*, **~rsi** *vr* disintegrate. **~zi'one** *nf* disintegration

disinteres'sarsi *vr* **~ di** take no interest in. **disinte'resse** *nm* indifference; (*oggettività*) disinterestedness

disintossi'ca|re *vt* detoxify. **~rsi** *vr* come off drugs. **~zi'one** *nf* giving up alcohol/drugs

disin'volto *a* natural. **disinvol'tura** *nf* confidence

disles'sia *nf* dyslexia. **dis'lessico** *a* dyslexic

disli'vello *nm* difference in height; *fig* inequality

dislo'care *vt Mil* post

dismenor'rea *nf* dysmenorrhoea

dismi'sura *nf* excess; **a ~** excessively

disobbedi'ente *a* disobedient

disobbe'dire *vt* disobey

disoccu'pa|to, **-a** *a* unemployed ● *nmf* unemployed person. **~zi'one** *nf* unemployment

disonestà *nf* dishonesty. **diso'nesto** *a* dishonest

disono'rare *vt* dishonour. **diso'nore** *nm* dishonour

di'sopra *adv* above ● *a* upper ● *nm* top

disordi'na|re *vt* disarrange. **~ta-mente** *adv* untidily. **~to** *a* untidy; (*sregolato*) immoderate. **di'sordine** *nm* disorder, untidiness; (*sregolatezza*) debauchery

disorganiz'za|re vt disorganize. **~to** a disorganized. **~zi'one** nf disorganization

disorienta'mento nm disorientation

disorien'ta|re vt disorientate. **~rsi** vr lose one's bearings. **~to** a fig bewildered

di'sotto adv below ●a lower ●nm bottom

dis'paccio nm dispatch

dispa'rato a disparate

'dispari a odd, uneven. **~tà** nf inv disparity

dis'parte adv in ~ apart; stare in ~ stand aside

dis'pendi|o nm (spreco) waste. **~'oso** a expensive

dis'pen|sa nf pantry; (distribuzione) distribution; (mobile) cupboard; Jur exemption; Relig dispensation; (pubblicazione periodica) number. **~'sare** vt distribute; (esentare) exonerate

dispe'ra|re vi despair (di of). **~rsi** vr despair. **~ta'mente** (piangere) desperately. **~to** a desperate. **~zi'one** nf despair

dis'per|dere vt, **~dersi** vr scatter, disperse. **~si'one** nf dispersion; (di truppe) dispersal. **~'sivo** a disorganized. **~so** pp di disperdere ●a scattered; (smarrito) lost ●nm missing soldier

dis'pet|to nm spite; a ~to di in spite of; fare un ~to a qcnospite sb. **~'toso** a spiteful

dispia'c|ere nm upset; (rammarico) regret; (dolore) sorrow; (preoccupazione) worry ●vi mi dispiace I'm sorry; non mi dispiace I don't dislike it; se non ti dispiace if you don't mind. **~'iuto** a upset; (dolente) sorry

dispo'nibil|e a available; (gentile) helpful. **~ità** nf availability; (gentilezza) helpfulness

dis'por|re vt arrange ●vi dispose; (stabilire) order; **~re di** have at one's disposal. **~si** vr (in fila) line up

disposi'tivo nm device

disposizi'one nf disposition; (ordine) order; (libera disponibilità) disposal. **dis'posto** pp di disporre ●a ready; (incline) disposed; essere ben disposto verso a favourably disposed towards

di'spotico a despotic. **dispo'tismo** nm despotism

dispregia'tivo a disparaging

disprez'zare vt despise. **dis'prezzo** nm contempt

'disputa nf dispute

dispu'tar|e vi dispute; (gareggiare) compete. **~si** vr **~si qcsa** contend for sth

dissacra'torio a debunking

dissangua'mento nm loss of blood

dissangu'a|re vt, **~rsi** vr bleed. **~rsi** vr fig become impoverished. **~to** a bloodless; fig impoverished

dissa'pore nm disagreement

dissec'car|e vt, **~si** vr dry up

dissemi'nare vt disseminate; (notizie) spread

dis'senso nm dissent; (disaccordo) disagreement

dissente'ria nf dysentery

dissen'tire vi disagree (da with)

dissertazi'one nf dissertation

disser'vizio nm poor service

disse'sta|re vt upset; Comm damage. **~to** a (strada) uneven. **dis'sesto** nm ruin

disse'tante a thirst-quenching

disse'tare vt ~ qcno quench sb's thirst

dissi'dente a & nmf dissident

dis'sidio nm disagreement

dis'simile a unlike, dissimilar

dissimu'lare vt conceal; (fingere) dissimulate

dissi'pa|re vt dissipate; (sperperare) squander. **~rsi** vr (nebbia:) clear; (dubbio:) disappear. **~to** a dissipated. **~zi'one** nf squandering

dissoci'ar|e vt, **~si** vr dissociate

disso'dare vt till

dis'solto pp di dissolvere

disso'luto a dissolute

dis'sol|vere vt, **~si** vr dissolve; (disperdere) dispel

disso'nanza nf dissonance

dissu'a|dere vt dissuade. **~si'one** nf dissuasion. **~'sivo** a dissuasive

distac'car|e vt detach; Sport leave behind. **~si** vr be detached. **di'stacco** nm detachment; (separazione) separation; Sport lead

di'stan|te a far away; (fig: person) detached ●adv far away. **~za** nf distance. **~zi'are** vt space out; Sport outdistance

di'stare vi be distant; quanto dista? how far is it?

di'sten|dere vt stretch out (parte del corpo); (spiegare) spread; (deporre) lay. **~dersi** vr stretch; (sdraiarsi) lie down; (rilassarsi) relax. **~si'one** nf stretching; (*rilassamento*) relaxation; *Pol* détente. ~ **sivo** *a* relaxing

di'steso, -a *pp di* **distendere** ● *nf* expanse

distil'l|are *vt/i* distil. ~**azi'one** *nf* distillation. ~**e'ria** *nf* distillery

di'stinguer|e *vt* distinguish. ~**si** *vr* distinguish oneself. **distin'guibile** *a* distinguishable

di'stinta *nf Comm* list. ~ **di pagamento** receipt. ~ **di versamento** paying-in slip

distinta'mente *adv* (*separatamente*) individually, separately; (*chiaramente*) clearly

distin'tivo *a* distinctive ● *nm* badge

di'stin|to, -a *pp di* **distinguere** ● *a* distinct; (*signorile*) distinguished; ~**ti saluti** Yours faithfully. ~**zi'one** *nf* distinction

di'stogliere *vt* ~ **da** (*allontanare*) remove from; (*dissuadere*) dissuade from. **di'stolto** *pp di* **distogliere**

di'storcere *vt* twist

distorsi'one *nf Med* sprain; (*alterazione*) distortion

di'stra|rre *vt* distract; (*divertire*) amuse. ~**rsi** *vr* get distracted; (*svagarsi*) amuse oneself; **non ti distrarre!** pay attention!. ~**rsi** *vr* (*deconcentrarsi*) be distracted. ~**tta'mente** *adv* absently. ~**tto** *pp di* **distrarre** ● *a* absent-minded; (*disattento*) inattentive. ~**zi'one** *nf* absent-mindedness; (*errore*) inattention; (*svago*) amusement

di'stretto *nm* district

distribu'ire *vt* distribute; (*disporre*) arrange; deal (*carte*). ~**'tore** *nm* distributor; (*di benzina*) petrol pump; (*automatico*) slot-machine. ~**zi'one** *nf* distribution

distri'car|e *vt* disentangle; ~**si** *vr fig* get out of it

di'stru|ggere *vt* destroy. ~**t'tivo** *a* destructive; (*critica*) negative. ~**tto** *pp di* **distruggere** ● *a* destroyed; **un uomo** ~**tto** a broken man. ~**zi'one** *nf* destruction

distur'bar|e *vt* disturb; (*sconvolgere*) upset. ~**si** *vr* trouble oneself. **di'sturbo** *nm* bother; (*indisposizione*) trouble; *Med* problem; *Radio, TV* interference; **disturbi** *pl Radio, TV* static. **disturbi di stomaco** stomach trouble

disubbidi'en|te *a* disobedient. ~**za** *nf* disobedience

disubbi'dire *vi* ~ **a** disobey

disugu'agli'anza *nf* disparity. ~**'ale** *a* unequal; (*irregolare*) irregular

disu'mano *a* inhuman

di'suso *nm* **cadere in** ~ fall into disuse

di'tale *nm* thimble

di'tata *nf* poke; (*impronta*) finger-mark

'dito *nm* (*pl nf* **dita**) finger; (*di vino, acqua*) finger. ~ **del piede** toe

'ditta *nf* firm

dit'tafono *nm* dictaphone

ditta'tor|e *nm* dictator. ~**i'ale** *a* dictatorial. **ditta'tura** *nf* dictatorship

dit'tongo *nm* diphthong

di'urno *a* daytime; **spettacolo** ~ matinée

'diva *nf* diva

diva'gare *vi* digress. ~**zi'one** *nf* digression

divam'pare *vi* burst into flames; *fig* spread like wildfire

di'vano *nm* settee, sofa. ~ **letto** sofa bed

divari'care *vt* open

di'vario *nm* discrepancy; **un** ~ **di opinioni** a difference of opinion

dive'n|ire *vi* = **diventare**. ~**uto** *pp di* **divenire**

diven'tare *vi* become; (*lentamente*) grow; (*rapidamente*) turn

di'verbio *nm* squabble

diver'gen|te *a* divergent. ~**za** *nf* divergence; ~**za di opinioni** difference of opinion. **di'vergere** *vi* diverge

diversa'mente *adv* (*altrimenti*) otherwise; (*in modo diverso*) differently

diversifi'car|e *vt* diversify. ~**rsi** *vr* differ, be different. ~**zi'one** *nf* diversification

diversi'one *nf* diversion. ~**sità** *nf inv* difference. ~**'sivo** *nm* diversion.

di'verso *a* different; **diversi** *pl* (*parecchi*) several ● *pron* several [people]

diver'tente *a* amusing. **diverti'mento** *nm* amusement

diver'tir|e *vt* amuse. ~**si** *vr* enjoy oneself

divi'dendo *nm* dividend

di'vider|e *vt* divide; (*condividere*) share. ~**si** *vr* (*separarsi*) separate

divi'eto *nm* prohibition; ~ **di sosta** no parking

divin'colarsi *vr* wriggle

divinità *nf inv* divinity. **di'vino** *a* divine

di'visa *nf* uniform; *Comm* currency

divisi'one *nf* division

di'vismo *nm* worship; *(atteggiamento)* superstar mentality

di'viso *pp di* **dividere**. **~'sore** *nm* divisor. **~'soria** *a* dividing; **muro ~sorio** partition wall

'divo, a *nmf* star

divo'rare *vt* devour. **~si** *vr* **~si da be** consumed with

divorzi'are *vi* divorce. **~to, -a** *nmf* divorcee. **di'vorzio** *nm* divorce

divul'gare *vt* divulge; *(rendere popolare)* popularize. **~rsi** *vr* spread. **~'tivo** *a* popular. **~zi'one** *nf* popularization

dizio'nario *nm* dictionary

dizi'one *nf* diction

do *nm* Mus *(chiave, nota)* C

'doccia *nf* shower; *(grondaia)* gutter; **fare la ~** have a shower

do'cente *a* teaching ●*nmf* teacher; *(di università)* lecturer. **~za** *nf* university teacher's qualification

'docile *a* docile

documen'tare *vt* document. **~si** *vr* gather information (**su** about)

documen'tario *a & nm* documentary

documen'tato *a* well-documented; *(persona)* well-informed. **~zi'one** *nf* documentation

docu'mento *nm* document

dodi'cesimo *a & nm* twelfth. **'dodici** *a & nm* twelve

do'gana *nf* customs *pl*; *(dazio)* duty. **doga'nale** *a* customs. **~i'ere** *nm* customs officer

'doglie *nfpl* labour pains

'dogma *nm* dogma. **dog'matico** *a* dogmatic. **~'tismo** *nm* dogmatism

'dolce *a* sweet; *(clima)* mild; *(voce, consonante)* soft; *(acqua)* fresh ●*nm (portata)* dessert; *(torta)* cake; **non mangio dolci** I don't eat sweet things. **~'mente** *adv* sweetly. **dol'cezza** *nf* sweetness; *(di clima)* mildness

dolce'vita *a inv (maglione)* rollneck

dolci'ario *a* confectionery

dolci'astro *a* sweetish

dolcifi'cante *nm* sweetener ●*a* sweetening

dolci'umi *nmpl* sweets

do'lente *a* painful; *(spiacente)* sorry

do'lere *vi* ache, hurt; *(dispiacere)* regret. **~rsi** *vr* regret; *(protestare)* complain; **~rsi di** be sorry for

do'llaro *nm* dollar

'dolo *nm* Jur malice; *(truffa)* fraud

Dolo'miti *nfpl* **le ~** the Dolomites

do'lore *nm* pain; *(morale)* sorrow. **dolo'roso** *a* painful

do'loso *a* malicious

do'manda *nf* question; *(richiesta)* request; *(scritta)* application; Comm demand; **fare una ~ (a qcno)** ask (sb) a question. **~ di impiego** job application

doman'dare *vt* ask; *(esigere)* demand; **~e qcsa a qcno** ask sb for sth. **~si** *vr* wonder

do'mani *adv* tomorrow; **~ sera** tomorrow evening ●*nm* **il ~** the future; **a ~** see you tomorrow

do'mare *vt* tame; *fig* control *(emozioni)*. **~tore** *nm* tamer

domat'tina *adv* tomorrow morning

do'menica *nf* Sunday. **~'cale** *a* Sunday *attrib*

do'mestico, -a *a* domestic ●*nm* servant ●*nf* maid

domicili'are *a* **arresti domiciliari** Jur house arrest

domicili'arsi *vr* settle

domi'cilio *nm* domicile; *(abitazione)* home; **recapitiamo a ~** we do home deliveries

domi'nare *vt* dominate; *(controllare)* control ●*vi* rule over; *(prevalere)* be dominant. **~rsi** *vr* control oneself. **~'tore, ~'trice** *nmf* ruler **~zi'one** *nf* domination

do'minio *nm* control; Pol dominion; *(ambito)* field; **di ~ pubblico** common knowledge

don *nm inv (ecclesiastico)* Father

do'nare *vt* give; donate *(sangue, organo)* ●*vi* **~re a** *(giovare esteticamente)* suit. **~'tore, ~'trice** *nmf* donor. **~zi'one** *nf* donation

dondo'lare *vt* swing; *(cullare)* rock ●*vi* sway. **~rsi** *vr* swing. **~io** *nm* rocking. **'dondolo** *nm* swing; **cavallo/sedia a dondolo** rocking-horse/chair

dongio'vanni *nm inv* Romeo

'donna *nf* woman. **~ di servizio** domestic help

don'naccia *nf pej* whore

donnai'olo *nm* philanderer

'donnola *nf* weasel

'dono *nm* gift

'dopo *prep* after; *(a partire da)* since ●*adv* after, afterwards; *(più tardi)* later; *(in seguito)* later on; **~ di me** after me

dopo'barba *nm inv* aftershave

dopo'cena *nm inv* evening

dopodiché *adv* after which

dopodo'mani *adv* the day after tomorrow

dopogu'erra *nm inv* post-war period

dopo'pranzo nm inv afternoon

dopo'sci a & nm inv après-ski

doposcu'ola nm inv after-school activities pl

dopo-'shampoo nm inv conditioner ●a inv conditioning

dopo'sole nm inv aftersun cream ●a inv aftersun

dopo'tutto adv after all

doppi'aggio nm dubbing

doppia'mente adv (in misura doppia) doubly

doppi'are vt Naut double; Sport lap; Cinema dub. **~'tore, ~'trice** nmf dubber

'doppio a & adv double. **~ 'clic** nm Comput double click. **~ 'fallo** nm Tennis double fault. **~ 'gioco** nm double-dealing. **~ 'mento** nm double chin. **~'senso** nm double entendre. **doppi vetri** nmpl double glazing ●nm double, twice the quantity; Tennis doubles pl. **~ 'misto** nm Tennis mixed doubles ●adv double

doppi'one nm duplicate

doppio'petto a double-breasted

dop'pista nmf Tennis doubles player

do'rare vt gild; Culin brown. **~to** a gilt; (color oro) golden. **~'tura** nf gilding

dormicchi'are vi doze

dormigli'one, -a nmf sleepyhead; fig lazy-bones

dor'mire vi sleep; (essere addormentato) be asleep; fig be asleep. **~ta** nf good sleep. **~'tina** nf nap. **~'torio** nm dormitory

dormi'veglia nm essere in ~ be half asleep

dor'sale a dorsal ●nf (di monte) ridge

'dorso nm back; (di libro) spine; (di monte) crest; (nel nuoto) backstroke

do'saggio nm dosage

do'sare vt dose; fig measure; **~ le parole** weigh one's words

dosa'tore nm measuring jug

'dose nf dose; **in buona ~** fig in good measure. **~ eccessiva** overdose

dossi'er nm inv (raccolta di dati, fascicolo) file

'dosso nm (dorso) back; **levarsi di ~ gli abiti** take off one's clothes

do'tare vt endow; (di accessori) equip. **~to a** (persona) gifted; (fornito) equipped. **~zi'one** nf (attrezzatura) equipment; **in ~zione** at one's disposal

'dote nf dowry; (qualità) gift

'dotto a learned ●nm scholar; Anat duct

dotto'rato nm doctorate. **dot'tore, ~'ressa** nmf doctor

dot'trina nf doctrine

'dove adv where; **di ~ sei?** where do you come from; **fin ~?** how far?; **per ~?** which way?

do'vere vi (obbligo) have to, must; **devo andare** I have to go, I must go; **devo venire anch'io?** do I have to come too?; **avresti dovuto dirmelo** you should have told me, you ought to have told me; **devo sedermi un attimo** I must sit down for a minute, I need to sit down for a minute; **dev'essere successo qualcosa** something must have happened; **come si deve** properly ●vt (essere debitore di, derivare) owe; **essere dovuto a** be due to ●nm duty; **per ~** out of duty. **dove'roso** a only right and proper

do'vunque adv (dappertutto) everywhere; (in qualsiasi luogo) anywhere ●conj wherever

do'vuto a due; (debito) proper

doz'zina nf dozen. **~'nale** a cheap

dra'gare vt dredge

'drago nm dragon

'dramma nm drama. **dram'matico** a dramatic. **~atiz'zare** vt dramatize. **~a'turgo** nm playwright. **dram'mone** nm (film) tear-jerker

drappeggi'are vt drape. **drap'peggio** nm drapery

drap'pello nm Mil squad; (gruppo) band

'drastico a drastic

dre'naggio nm drainage. **~re** vt drain

drib'blare vt (in calcio) dribble. **'dribbling** nm inv (in calcio) dribble

'dritta nf (mano destra) right hand; Naut starboard; (informazione) pointer, tip; **a ~ e a manca** (dappertutto) left, right and centre

'dritto a = diritto¹ ●nmf fam crafty so-and-so

driz'zare vt straighten; (rizzare) prick up. **~si** vr straighten [up]; (alzarsi) raise

'droga nf drug. **~'gare** vt drug. **~'garsi** vr take drugs. **~'gato, -a** nmf drug addict

droghe'ria nf grocery. **~i'ere, -a** nmf grocer

drome'dario nm dromedary

'dubbio a doubtful; (ambiguo) dubious ●nm doubt; (sospetto) suspicion; **met-**

tere in ~o doubt; essere fuori ~o be beyond doubt; essere in ~o be doubtful. ~'oso a doubtful

dubi'ta|re vi doubt; ~re di doubt; (diffidare) mistrust; dubito che venga I doubt whether he'll come. ~'tivo a (ambiguo) ambiguous

'duca, du'chessa nmf duke; duchess

'due a & nm two

due'cento a & nm two hundred

du'ello nm duel

due'mila a & nm two thousand

due'pezzi nm inv (bikini) bikini

du'etto nm duo; Mus duet

'duna nf dune

'dunque conj therefore; (allora) well [then]

'duo nm inv duo; Mus duet

du'omo nm cathedral

'duplex nm Teleph party line

dupli'ca|re vt duplicate. ~to nm duplicate. 'duplice a double; in duplice in duplicate

dura'mente adv (lavorare) hard; (rimproverare) harshly

du'rante prep during

du'r|are vi last; (cibo:) keep; (resistere) hold out. ~ata nf duration. ~a'turo, ~evole a lasting, enduring

du'rezza nf hardness; (di carne) toughness; (di voce, padre) harshness

'duro, -a a hard; (persona, carne) tough; (voce) harsh; (pane) stale; tieni ~! (resistere) hang in there! ● nmf (persona) tough person, toughie fam

du'rone nm hardened skin

'duttile a (materiale) ductile; (carattere) malleable

Ee

e, ed conj and

'ebano nm ebony

eb'bene conj well [then]

eb'brezza nf inebriation; (euforia) elation; guida in stato di ~ drink-driving. 'ebbro a inebriated; ebbro di gioia delirious with joy

'ebete a stupid

ebollizi'one nf boiling

e'braico a Hebrew ● nm (lingua) Hebrew. e'br|eo, -a a Jewish ● nmf Jew; Jewess

'Ebridi nfpl le ~ the Hebrides

eca'tombe nf fare un'~ wreak havoc

ecc abbr (eccetera) etc

ecce'den|te a (peso, bagaglio) excess. ~za nf excess; (d'avanzo) surplus; avere qcsa in ~za have an excess of sth; bagagli in ~za excess baggage. ~za di cassa surplus. ec'cedere vt exceed ● vi go too far; eccedere nel mangiare overeat; eccedere nel bere drink to excess

eccel'len|te a excellent. ~za nf excellence; (titolo) Excellency; per ~za par excellence. ec'cellere vi excel (in at)

eccentricità nf eccentricity. ec'centrico, -a a & nmf eccentric

eccessiva'mente adv excessively. ecces'sivo a excessive

ec'cesso nm excess; andare agli eccessi go to extremes; all'~ to excess. ~ di velocità speeding

ec'cetera adv et cetera

ec'cetto prep except; ~ che (a meno che) unless. eccettu'are vt except

eccezio'nal|e a exceptional. ~'mente adv exceptionally; (contrariamente alla regola) as an exception

eccezi'one nf exception; Jur objection; a ~ di with the exception of

ecci'ta'mento nm excitement. ecci'tante a exciting; (sostanza) stimulant ● nm stimulant

ecci'ta|re vt excite. ~rsi vr get excited. ~to a excited

eccitazi'one nf excitement

ecclesi'astico a ecclesiastical ● nm priest

'ecco adv (qui) here; (là) there; ~! exactly!; ~ fatto there we are; ~ la tua borsa here is your bag; ~ [li] mio figlio there is my son; ~mi here I am; ~ tutto that is all

ec'come adv & int and how!

echeggi'are vi echo

e'clissi nf inv eclipse

'eco *nmf* (*pl m* echi) echo

ecogra'fia *nf* scan

ecolo'gia *nf* ecology. eco'logico *a* ecological; ⟨*prodotto*⟩ environmentally friendly

e commerci'ale *nf* ampersand

econo'm|ia *nf* economy; ⟨*scienza*⟩ economics *sg*; fare ~ia economize (di on). eco'nomico *a* economic; ⟨*a buon prezzo*⟩ cheap. ~ista *nmf* economist. ~iz'zare *vt/i* economize; save ⟨*tempo, denaro*⟩. e'conomo, -a *a* thrifty ●*nmf* (*di collegio*) bursar

écru*a inv* raw

'Ecu*nm inv* ECU, ecu

ec'zema*nm* eczema

ed*conj vedi* e

'edera *nf* ivy

e'dicola *nf* [newspaper] kiosk

edifi'cabile*a* ⟨*area, terreno*⟩ classified as suitable for development

edifi'cante*a* edifying

edifi'care *vt* build; ⟨*indurre al bene*⟩ edify

edi'ficio*nm* building; *fig* structure

e'dile*a* building *attrib*

edi'lizi|a*nf* building trade. ~o*a* building *attrib*

edi|'tore, -'trice*a* publishing ●*nmf* publisher; ⟨*curatore*⟩ editor. ~to'ria *nf* publishing. ~tori'ale *a* publishing ●*nm* (*articolo*) editorial, leader

edizi'one *nf* edition; ⟨*di manifestazione*⟩ performance. ~ ridotta abridg[e]-ment. ~ della sera (*del telegiornale*) evening news

edu'ca|re *vt* educate; ⟨*allevare*⟩ bring up. ~'tivo *a* educational. ~to *a* polite. ~'tore, ~'trice*nmf* educator. ~zi'one *nf* education; ⟨*di bambini*⟩ upbringing; ⟨*buone maniere*⟩ [good] manners *pl*. ~zione fisica physical education

e'felide *nf* freckle

effemi'nato*a* effeminate

efferve'scente *a* effervescent; ⟨*frizzante*⟩ fizzy; ⟨*aspirina*⟩ soluble

effettiva'mente*adv* è troppo tardi – ~ it's too late – so it is

effet'tivo *a* actual; ⟨*efficace*⟩ effective; ⟨*personale*⟩ permanent; *Mil* regular ●*nm* (*somma totale*) sum total

ef'fett|o *nm* effect; ⟨*impressione*⟩ impression; in ~i in fact; a tutti gli ~i to all intents and purposes; ~i personali personal belongings. ~u'are *vt* effect; carry out ⟨*controllo, sondaggio*⟩. ~u'arsi *vr* take place

effi'cac|e *a* effective. ~ia *nf* effectiveness

effici'en|te *a* efficient. ~za *nf* efficiency

ef'fimero*a* ephemeral

effusi'one *nf* effusion

E'geo*nm* l'~ the Aegean [Sea]

E'gitto *nm* Egypt. egizi'ano, -a *a* & *nmf* Egyptian

'egli*pron* he; ~ stesso he himself

ego'centrico, -a*a* egocentric ●*nmf* egocentric person

ego'is|mo *nm* selfishness. ~ta *a* selfish ●*nmf* selfish person. ~tico *a* selfish

e'gregio*a* distinguished; E~ Signore Dear Sir

eguali'tario*a* & *nm* egalitarian

eiaculazi'one*nf* ejaculation

elabo'ra|re *vt* elaborate; process ⟨*dati*⟩. ~to a elaborate. ~zi'one *nf* elaboration; ⟨*di dati*⟩ processing. ~zio-ne [di] testi word processing

elar'gire*vt* lavish

elastici'tà *nf* elasticity. ~z'zato *a* ⟨*stoffa*⟩ elasticated. e'lastico*a* elastic; ⟨*tessuto*⟩ stretch; ⟨*orario, mente*⟩ flexible; ⟨*persona*⟩ easy-going ●*nm* elastic; ⟨*fascia*⟩ rubber band

ele'fante*nm* elephant

ele'gan|te *a* elegant. ~za*nf* elegance

e'leggere*vt* elect. eleg'gibile*a* eligible

elemen'tare*a* elementary; scuola ~ primary school

ele'mento *nm* element; elementi *pl* ⟨*fatti*⟩ data; ⟨*rudimenti*⟩ elements

ele'mosina*nf* charity; chiedere l'~ beg. elemosi'nare*vt/i* beg

elen'care*vt* list

e'lenco*nm* list. ~ abbonati telephone directory. ~ telefonico telephone directory

elet'tivo*a* ⟨*carica*⟩ elective. e'letto, -a *pp di* eleggere ●*a* chosen ●*nmf* (*nominato*) elected member; per pochi eletti for the chosen few

eletto'ra|le *a* electoral. ~to *nm* electorate

elet'|tore, -'trice*nmf* voter

elet'trauto*nm* garage for electrical repairs

elettri'cista*nm* electrician

elettri'cità*nf* electricity. e'lettrico *a* electric. ~z'zante *a* ⟨*notizia, gara*⟩ electrifying. ~z'zare *vt fig* electrify. ~z'zato *a fig* electrified

elettrocardio'gramma *nm* electrocardiogram

e'lettrodo *nm* electrode

elettrodo'mestico *nm* [electrical] household appliance

elet'trone *nm* electron

elet'tronico, -a *a* electronic ● *nf* electronics

ele'va|re *vt* raise; (*promuovere*) promote; (*erigere*) erect; (*fig: migliorare*) better; ~ **al quadrato/cubo** square/cube. ~**rsi** *vr* rise; (*edificio:*) stand. ~**to a** high. ~**zi'one** *nf* elevation

elezi'one *nf* election

'elica *nf Naut* screw, propeller; *Aeron* propeller; (*del ventilatore*) blade

eli'cottero *nm* helicopter

elimi'na|re *vt* eliminate. ~**'toria** *nf Sport* preliminary heat. ~**zi'one** *nf* elimination

é'lite *nf inv* élite. ~**'tista** *a* élitist

'ella *pron* she

ellepi *nm inv* LP

el'metto *nm* helmet

elogi'are *vt* praise. **e'logio** *nm* praise; (*discorso, scritto*) eulogy

elo'quen|te *a* eloquent; *fig* tell-tale. ~**za** *nf* eloquence

e'lu|dere *vt* elude; evade (*sorveglianza, controllo*). ~**'sivo** *a* elusive

el'vetico *a* Swiss

emaci'ato *a* emaciated

E-mail *nf* e-mail

ema'na|re *vt* give off; pass (*legge*) ● *vi* emanate. ~**zi'one** *nf* giving off; (*di legge*) enactment

emanci'pa|re *vt* emancipate. ~**rsi** *vr* become emancipated. ~**to** *a* emancipated. ~**zi'one** *nf* emancipation

emargi'na|to *nm* marginalized person. ~**zi'one** *nf* marginalization

ema'toma *nm* haematoma

em'bargo *nm* embargo

em'ble|ma *nm* emblem. ~**'matico** *a* emblematic

embo'lia *nf* embolism

embrio'nale *a Biol, fig* embryonic. **embri'one** *nm* embryo

emen|da'mento *nm* amendment. ~**'dare** *vt* amend

emer'gen|te *a* emergent. ~**za** *nf* emergency; **in caso di ~za** in an emergency

e'mergere *vi* emerge; (*sottomarino:*) surface; (*distinguersi*) stand out

e'merito *a* (*professore*) emeritus; **un ~ imbecille** a prize idiot

e'merso *pp di* emergere

e'messo *pp di* emettere

e'mettere *vt* emit; give out (*luce, suono*); let out (*grido*); (*mettere in circolazione*) issue

emi'crania *nf* migraine

emi'gra|re *vi* emigrate. ~**to, -a** *nmf* immigrant. ~**zi'one** *nf* emigration

emi'nen|te *a* eminent. ~**za** *nf* eminence

e'miro *nm* emir

emis'fero *nm* hemisphere

emis'sario *nm* emissary

emissi'one *nf* emission; (*di denaro*) issue; (*trasmissione*) broadcast

emit'tente *a* issuing; (*trasmittente*) broadcasting ● *nf Radio* transmitter

emorra'gia *nf* haemorrhage

emor'roidi *nfpl* piles

emotività *nf* emotional make-up. **emo'tivo** *a* emotional

emozio'nan|te *a* exciting; (*commovente*) moving. ~**re** *vt* excite; (*commuovere*) move. ~**rsi** *vr* become excited; (*commuoversi*) be moved. ~**to** *a* excited; (*commosso*) moved. **emozi'one** *nf* emotion; (*agitazione*) excitement

'empio *a* impious; (*spietato*) pitiless; (*malvagio*) wicked

em'pirico *a* empirical

em'porio *nm* emporium; (*negozio*) general store

emu'la|re *vt* emulate. ~**zi'one** *nf* emulation

emulsi'one *nf* emulsion

en'ciclica *nf* encyclical

enciclope'dia *nf* encyclopaedia

encomi'are *vt* commend. **en'comio** *nm* commendation

en'demico *a* endemic

endo've|na *nf* intravenous injection. ~**'noso** *a* intravenous; **per via ~nosa** intravenously

E.N.I.T. *nm abbr* (**Ente Nazionale Italiano per il Turismo**) Italian State Tourist Office

ener'getico *a* (*risorse, crisi*) energy *attrib*; (*alimento*) energy-giving

ener'gia *nf* energy. **e'nergico** *a* energetic; (*efficace*) strong

ener'gumeno *nm* Neanderthal

'enfasi *nf* emphasis

en'fati|co *a* emphatic. ~**z'zare** *vt* emphasize

e'nigma *nm* enigma. **enig'matico** *a* enigmatic. **enig'mistica** *nf* puzzles *pl*

en'nesimo *a Math* nth; *fam* umpteenth

e'norm|e *a* enormous. ~**e'mente** *adv*

massively. ~ità *nf inv* enormity; (*assurdità*) absurdity

eno'teca *nf* wine-tasting shop

'ente *nm* board; (*società*) company; (*filosofia*) being

entità *nf inv* (*filosofia*) entity; (*gravità*) seriousness; (*dimensione*) extent

entou'rage *nm inv* entourage

en'trambi *a & pron* both

en'tra|re *vi* go in, enter; ~re in go into; (*stare, trovar posto*) fit into; (*arruolarsi*) join; ~rci (*avere a che fare*) have to do with; **tu che c'entri?** what has it got to do with you? ~ta *nf* entry, entrance; ~te *pl Comm* takings; (*reddito*) income *sg*

'entro *prep* (*tempo*) within

entro'terra *nm inv* hinterland

entusias'mante *a* fascinating, exciting

entusias'mar|e *vt* arouse enthusiasm in. ~si *vr* be enthusiastic (**per** about)

entusi'as|mo *nm* enthusiasm. ~ta *a* enthusiastic ● *nmf* enthusiast. ~tico *a* enthusiastic

enume'ra|re *vt* enumerate. ~zi'one *nf* enumeration

enunci'a|re *vt* enunciate. ~zi'one *nf* enunciation

epa'tite *nf* hepatitis

'epico *a* epic

epide'mia *nf* epidemic

epi'dermide *nf* epidermis

Epifa'nia *nf* Epiphany

epi'gramma *nm* epigram

epiles'sia *nf* epilepsy. epi'lettico, -a *a & nmf* epileptic

e'pilogo *nm* epilogue

epi'sodi|co *a* episodic; **caso ~co** one-off case. ~o *nm* episode

e'piteto *nm* epithet

'epoca *nf* age; (*periodo*) period; **a quell'~** in those days; **auto d'~** vintage car

ep'pure *conj* [and] yet

epu'rare *vt* purge

equa'tore *nm* equator. equatori'ale *a* equatorial

equazi'one *nf* equation

e'questre *a* equestrian; **circo ~** circus

equi'latero *a* equilateral

equili'bra|re *vt* balance. ~to *a* (*persona*) well-balanced. equi'librio *nm* balance; (*buon senso*) common sense; (*di bilancia*) equilibrium

equili'brismo *nm* **fare ~** do a balancing act

e'quino *a* horse *attrib*

equi'nozio *nm* equinox

equipaggia'mento *nm* equipment

equipaggi'are *vt* equip; (*di persone*) man

equi'paggio *nm* crew; *Aeron* cabin crew

equipa'rare *vt* make equal

é'quipe *nf* team

equità *nf* equity

equitazi'one *nf* riding

equiva'len|te *a & nm* equivalent. ~za *nf* equivalence

equiva'lere *vi* ~ a be equivalent to

equivo'care *vi* misunderstand

e'quivoco *a* equivocal; (*sospetto*) suspicious; **un tipo ~** a shady character ● *nm* misunderstanding

'equo *a* fair, just

'era *nf* era

'erba *nf* grass; (*aromatica, medicinale*) herb. ~ cipollina chives *pl*. er'baccia *nf* weed. er'baceo *a* herbaceous

erbi'cida *nm* weed-killer

erbo'rista *nmf* herbalist. ~e'ria *nf* herbalist's shop

er'boso *a* grassy

er'culeo *a* (*forza*) herculean

e'red|e *nmf* heir; heiress. ~ità *nf inv* inheritance; *Biol* heredity. ~i'tare *vt* inherit. ~itarietà *nf* heredity. ~i'tario *a* hereditary

ere'mita *nm* hermit

ere'sia *nf* heresy. e'retico, -a *a* heretical ● *nmf* heretic

e're|tto *pp di* erigere ● *a* erect. ~zi'one *nf* erection; (*costruzione*) building

er'gastolo *nm* life sentence; (*luogo*) prison

'erica *nf* heather

e'rigere *vt* erect; (*fig: fondare*) found

eri'tema *vt* (*cutaneo*) inflammation; (*solare*) sunburn

ermel'lino *nm* ermine

ermetica'mente *adv* hermetically. er'metico *a* hermetic; (*a tenuta d'aria*) airtight

'ernia *nf* hernia

e'rodere *vi* erode

e'ro|e *nm* hero. ~ico *a* heroic. ~ismo *nm* heroism

ero'ga|re *vt* distribute; (*fornire*) supply. ~zi'one *nf* supply

ero'ina *nf* heroine; (*droga*) heroin

erosi'one *nf* erosion

erotico | esile

e'rotico a erotic. **ero'tismo** nm eroticism

er'rante a wandering. **er'rare** vi wander; (sbagliare) be mistaken

er'rato a (sbagliato) mistaken

'erre nf ~ **moscia** burr

erronea'mente adv mistakenly

er'rore nm error, mistake; (di stampa) misprint; **essere in** ~ be wrong

'erta nf **stare all'**~ be on the alert

eru'di|rsi vr get educated. ~**to** a learned

erut'tare vt (vulcano:) erupt ● vi (ruttare) belch. **eruzi'one** nf eruption; Med rash

esacer'bare vt exacerbate

esage'ra|re vt exaggerate ● vi exaggerate; (nel comportamento) go over the top; ~**re nel mangiare** eat too much. ~**ta'mente** adv excessively. ~**to** a exaggerated; (prezzo) exorbitant ● nm person who goes to extremes. ~**zi'one** nf exaggeration; **è costato un'**~**zione** it cost the earth

esa'lare vt/i exhale

esal'ta|re vt exalt; (entusiasmare) elate. ~**to** a (fanatico) fanatical ● nm fanatic. ~**zi'one** nf exaltation; (in discorso) fervour

e'same nm examination, exam; **dare un** ~ take an exam; **prendere in** ~ examine. ~ **del sangue** blood test. **esami** pl **di maturità** ≈ A-levels

esami'na|re vt examine. ~**tore**, ~**trice** nmf examiner

e'sangue a bloodless

e'sanime a lifeless

esaspe'rante a exasperating

esaspe'ra|re vt exasperate. ~**rsi** vr get exasperated. ~**zi'one** nf exasperation

esatta'mente adv exactly. ~**tezza** nf exactness; (precisione) precision; (di risposta, risultato) accuracy

e'satto pp di **esigere** ● a exact; (risposta, risultato) correct; (orologio) right; **hai l'ora esatta?** do you have the right time?; **sono le due esatte** it's two o'clock exactly

esat'tore nm collector

esau'dire vt grant; fulfil (speranze)

esauri'ente a exhaustive

esau'ri|re vt exhaust. ~**rsi** vr exhaust oneself; (merci ecc:) run out. ~**to** a exhausted; (merci) sold out; (libro) out of print; **fare il tutto** ~**to** (spettacolo:) play to a full house

'esca nf bait

escande'scenz|a nf outburst; **dare in** ~**e** lose one's temper

escla'ma|re vi exclaim. ~**tivo** a exclamatory. ~**zi'one** nf exclamation

es'clu|dere vt exclude; rule out (possibilità, ipotesi). ~**si'one** nf exclusion. ~**siva** nf exclusive right, sole right; **in** ~**siva** exclusive. ~**siva'mente** adv exclusively. ~**sivo** a exclusive. ~**so** pp di **escludere** ● a **non è** ~**so che ci sia** it's not out of the question that he'll be there

escogi'tare vt contrive

escre'mento nm excrement

escursi'one nf excursion; (scorreria) raid; (di temperatura) range

ese'crabile a abominable. ~**re** vt abhor

esecu'tivo a & nm executive. ~**tore**, ~**trice** nmf executor; Mus performer. ~**zi'one** nf execution; Mus performance

esegu'ire vt carry out; Jur execute; Mus perform

e'sempio nm example; **ad o per** ~ for example; **dare l'**~ **a qcno** set sb an example; **fare un** ~ give an example. **esem'plare** a exemplary ● nm specimen; (di libro) copy. **esemplifi'care** vt exemplify

esen'ta|re vt exempt. ~**rsi** vr free oneself. **e'sente** a exempt. **esente da imposta** duty-free. **esente da IVA** VAT-exempt

esen'tasse a duty-free

e'sequie nfpl funeral rites

eser'cente nmf shopkeeper

eserci'ta|re vt exercise; (addestrare) train; (fare uso di) exert; (professione) practise. ~**rsi** vr practise. ~**zi'one** nf exercise; Mil drill

e'sercito nm army

eser'cizio nm exercise; (pratica) practice; Comm financial year; (azienda) business; **essere fuori** ~ be out of practice

esi'bire vt show off; produce (documenti). ~**rsi** vr Theat perform; fig show off. ~**zi'one** nf production; Theat performance

esibizio'nismo nm showing off. ~**ta** nmf exhibitionist

esi'ge|nte a exacting; (pignolo) fastidious. ~**za** nf demand; (bisogno) need. **e'sigere** vt demand; (riscuotere) collect

e'siguo a meagre

esila'rante a exhilarating

'esile a slender; (voce) thin

esili'a|re vt exile. ~**rsi** vr go into exile. ~**to, -a** a exiled ● nmf exile. **e'silio** nm exile

e'simere vt release. ~**si** vr ~**si da** get out of

esi'sten|te a existing. ~**za** nf existence. ~**zi'ale** a existential. ~**zia'lismo** nm existentialism

e'sistere vi exist

esi'tante a hesitating; (voce) faltering

esi'ta|re vi hesitate. ~**zi'one** nf hesitation

'esito nm result; **avere buon ~** be a success

'esodo nm exodus

e'sofago nm oesophagus

esone'rare vt exempt. **e'sonero** nm exemption

esorbi'tante a exorbitant

esorciz'zare vt exorcize

esordi'ente nmf person making his/ her début. **e'sordio** nm opening; (di attore) début. **esor'dire** vi début

esor'tare vt (pregare) beg; (incitare) urge

eso'terico a esoteric

e'sotico a exotic

espa'drillas nfpl espadrilles

es'pan|dere vt expand. ~**dersi** vr expand; (diffondersi) extend. ~**si'one** nf expansion. ~**sivo** a expansive; (persona) friendly

espatri'are vi leave one's country. **es'patrio** nm expatriation

espedi'ent|e nm expedient; **vivere di ~i** live by one's wits

es'pellere vt expel

esperi'enza nf experience; **parlare per ~** speak from experience. ~ **mento** nm experiment

es'perto, -a a & nmf expert

espi'a|re vt atone for. ~**torio** a expiatory

espi'rare vt/i breathe out

espli'care vt carry on

esplicita'mente adv explicitly. **es'plicito** a explicit

es'plodere vi explode ● vt fire

esplo'ra|re vt explore. ~**'tore, ~'trice** nmf explorer; **giovane ~tore** boy scout. ~**zi'one** nf exploration

esplosi'one nf explosion. ~**sivo** a & nm explosive

espo'nente nm exponent

es'por|re vt expose; display (merci); (spiegare) expound; exhibit (quadri ecc). ~**si** vr (compromettersi) compromise

oneself; (al sole) expose oneself; (alle critiche) lay oneself open

espor'ta|re vt export. ~**'tore, ~ 'trice** nmf exporter. ~**zi'one** nf export

esposizi'one nf (mostra) exhibition; (in vetrina) display; (spiegazione ecc) position; (posizione, fotografia) exposure. **es'posto** pp di **esporre** ● a exposed; **esposto a** (rivolto) facing ● nm Jur ecc statement

espressa'mente adv expressly; **non l'ha detto ~** he didn't put it in so many words

espressi'one nf expression. ~**'sivo** a expressive

es'presso pp di **esprimere** ● a express ● nm (lettera) express letter; (treno) express train; (caffè) espresso; **per ~** (spedire) [by] express [post]

es'primer|e vt express. ~**si** vr express oneself

espropri'a|re vt dispossess. ~**zi'one** nf Jur expropriation. **es'proprio** nm expropriation

espulsi'one nf expulsion. **es'pulso** pp di **espellere**

es'senz|a nf essence. ~**i'ale** a essential ● nm important thing. ~**i'al'mente** a essentially

'essere vi be; **c'è** there is; **ci sono** there are; **che ora è? – sono le dieci** what time is it? – it's ten o'clock; **chi è? – sono io** who is it? – it's me; **ci sono!** (ho capito) I've got it!; **ci siamo!** (siamo arrivati) here we are at last!; **è stato detto che** it has been said that; **siamo in due** there are two of us; **questa camicia è da lavare** this shirt is to be washed; **non è da te** it's not like you; **~ di** (provenire da) be from; **~ per** (favorevole) be in favour of; **se fossi in te,...** if I were you,...; **sarà!** if you say so!; **come sarebbe a dire?** what are you getting at? ● v aux have; (in passivi) be; **siamo arrivati** we have arrived; **ci sono stato ieri** I was there yesterday; **sono nato a Torino** I was born in Turin; **è riconosciuto come...** he is recognized as... ● nm being. ~ **umano** human being. ~ **vivente** living creature

essic'cato a Culin desiccated

'esso, -a pron he, she; (cosa, animale) it

est nm east

'estasi nf ecstasy; **andare in ~ per** go into raptures over. ~ **are** vt enrapture

e'state nf summer

e'sten|dere vt extend. ~**dersi** vr

spread; (allungarsi) stretch. **~si**one nf extension; (ampiezza) expanse; Mus range. **~**'sivo a extensive

estenu'ante a exhausting

estenu'a|re vt wear out; deplete (risorse, casse). **~rsi** vr wear oneself out

esteri'or|e a & nm exterior. **~**'mente adv externally; (di persone) outwardly

esterna'mente adv on the outside

ester'nare vt express, show

e'sterno a external; per uso **~** for external use only ● nm (allievo) day-boy; Archit exterior; (scala) outside; (in film) location shot

'estero a foreign ● nm foreign countries pl; all'**~** abroad

esterre'fatto a horrified

e'steso pp di estendere ● a extensive; (diffuso) widespread; per **~** (scrivere) in full

e'stetic|a nf aesthetics sg. **~a**'mente adv aesthetically. **~o, -a** a aesthetic; (chirurgia, chirurgo) plastic. este'tista nf beautician

'estimo nm estimate

e'stin|guere vt extinguish. **~guersi** vr die out. **~to, -a** pp di estinguere ● nmf deceased. **~**'tore nm [fire] extinguisher. **~zi**one nf extinction; (di incendio) putting out

estir'pa|re vt uproot; extract (dente); fig eradicate (crimine, malattia). **~zi**one nf eradication; (di dente) extraction

e'stivo a summer

e'stor|cere vt extort. **~si**one nf extortion. **~to** pp di estorcere

estradizi'one nf extradition

e'straneo, -a a extraneous; (straniero) foreign ● nmf stranger

estrani'ar|e vt estrange. **~si** vr become estranged

e'stra|rre vt extract; (sorteggiare) draw. **~tto** pp di estrarre ● nm extract; (brano) excerpt; (documento) abstract. **~tto conto** statement [of account], bank statement. **~zi**one nf extraction; (a sorte) draw

estrema'mente adv extremely

estre'mis|mo nm extremism. **~ta** nmf extremist

estremità nf inv extremity; (di una corda) end ● nfpl Anat extremities

e'stremo, -a a extreme; (ultimo) last; misure estreme drastic measures; l'E**~** Oriente the Far East ● nm (limite) extreme. estremi pl (di documento) main points; (di reato) essential ele-

ments; essere agli estremi be at the end of one's tether

'estro nm (disposizione artistica) talent; (ispirazione) inspiration; (capriccio) whim. e'stroso a talented; (capriccioso) unpredictable

estro'mettere vt expel

estro'verso a extroverted ● nm extrovert

estu'ario nm estuary

esube'ran|te a exuberant. **~za** nf exuberance

'esule nm exile

esul'tante a exultant

esul'tare vi rejoice

esu'mare vt exhume

età nf inv age; raggiungere la maggiore **~** come of age; un uomo di mezz'**~** a middle-aged man

'etere nm ether. e'tereo a ethereal

eterna'mente adv eternally

eternità nf eternity; è un'**~** che non la vedo I haven't seen her for ages

e'terno a eternal; (questione, problema) age-old; in **~** fam for ever

etero'geneo a diverse, heterogeneous

eterosessu'ale nmf heterosexual

'etic|a nf ethics. **~o** a ethical

eti'chetta[1] nf label; (con il prezzo) price-tag

eti'chetta[2] nf (cerimoniale) etiquette

etichet'tare vt label

eti'lometro nm Breathalyzer[R]

etimolo'gia nf etymology

Eti'opia nf Ethiopia

'etnico a ethnic. etno'lo'gia nf ethnology

e'trusco a & nm Etruscan

'ettaro nm hectare

'etto, etto'grammo nm hundred grams, ≈ quarter pound

euca'lipto nm eucalyptus

eucari'stia nf Eucharist

eufe'mismo nm euphemism

eufo'ria nf elation; Med euphoria. eu'forico a elated; Med euphoric

Euro'city nm international Intercity

eurodepu'tato nm Euro MP, MEP

Eu'ropa nf Europe. euro'peo, -a a & nmf European

euta'na'sia nf euthanasia

evacu'a|re vt evacuate. **~zi**one nf evacuation

e'vadere vt evade; (sbrigare) deal with ● vi **~ da** escape from

evane'scente a vanishing

evan'gel|ico a evangelical. **evange'-lista** nm evangelist. **~o** nm = **vangelo**

evapo'ra|re vi evaporate. **~zi'one** nf evaporation

evasi'one nf escape; (fiscale) evasion; fig escapism. **eva'sivo** a evasive

e'vaso pp di evadere ● nm fugitive

eva'sore nm ~ **fiscale** tax evader

eveni'enza nf eventuality

e'vento nm event

eventu'al|e a possible. **~ità** nf inv eventuality

evi'den|te a evident; **è ~te che** it is obvious that. **~te'mente** adv evidently. **~za** nf evidence; **mettere in ~za** emphasize; **mettersi in ~za** make oneself conspicuous

evidenzi'a|re vt highlight. **~'tore** nm

(penna) highlighter

evi'tare vt avoid; (risparmiare) spare

evo'care vt evoke

evo'lu|to pp di **evolvere** ● a evolved; (progredito) progressive; (civiltà, nazione) advanced; **una donna evoluta** a modern woman. **~zi'one** nf evolution; (di ginnasta, aereo) circle

e'volver|e vt develop. **~si** vr evolve

ev'viva int hurray; **~ il Papa!** long live the Pope!; **gridare ~** cheer

ex+ pref ex+, former

'extra a inv extra; (qualità) first-class ● nm inv extra

extracomuni'tario a non-EC

extraconiu'gale a extramarital

extrater'restre nmf extra-terrestrial

Ff

---

fa[1] nm inv Mus (chiave, nota) F

fa[2] adv ago; **due mesi ~** two months ago

fabbi'sogno nm requirements pl, needs pl

'fabbrica nf factory

fabbri'cabile a (area, terreno) that can be built on

fabbri'cante nm manufacturer

fabbri'ca|re vt build; (produrre) manufacture; (fig: inventare) fabricate. **~to** nm building. **~zi'one** nf manufacturing; (costruzione) building

'fabbro nm blacksmith

fac'cend|a nf matter; **~e** pl (lavori domestici) housework sg. **~i'ere** nm wheeler-dealer

fac'chino nm porter

'facci|a nf face; (di foglio) side; **~a a ~a** face to face; **~a tosta** cheek; **voltar ~a** change sides; **di ~a** (palazzo) opposite; **alla ~a di** (fam: a dispetto di) in spite of. **~'ata** nf façade; (di foglio) side; (fig: esteriorità) outward appearance

fa'ceto a facetious; **tra il serio e il ~** half joking

fa'chiro nm fakir

'facil|e a easy; (affabile) easy-going; **essere ~e alle critiche** be quick to criticize; **essere ~e al riso** laugh a lot; **~e a farsi** easy to do; **è ~e che**

piova it's likely to rain. **~ità** nf inv ease; (disposizione) aptitude; **avere ~ità di parola** express oneself well

facili'ta|re vt facilitate. **~zi'one** nf facility; **~zioni** pl special terms

facil'mente adv (con facilità) easily; (probabilmente) probably

faci'lone a slapdash. **~'ria** nf slapdash attitude

facino'roso a violent

facoltà nf inv faculty; (potere) power. **~'tivo** a optional; **fermata ~tiva** request stop

facol'toso a wealthy

fac'simile nf facsimile

fac'totum nmf man/girl Friday, factotum

'faggio nm beech

fagi'ano nm pheasant

fagio'lino nm French bean

fagi'olo nm bean; **a ~** (arrivare, capitare) at the right time

fagoci'tare vt gobble up (società)

fa'gotto nm bundle; Mus bassoon

'faida nf feud

fai da te nm do-it-yourself, DIY

fal'cata nf stride

'falc|e nf scythe. **fal'cetto** nm sickle. **~i'are** vt cut; fig mow down. **~ia'trice** nf [lawn-]mower

'falco *nm* hawk
fal'cone *nm* falcon
'falda *nf* stratum; (*di neve*) flake; (*di cappello*) brim; (*pendio*) slope
fale'gname *nm* carpenter. ~'ria *nf* carpentry
'falla *nf* leak
fal'lace *a* deceptive
'fallico *a* phallic
fallimen'tare *a* disastrous; *Jur* bankruptcy. falli'mento *nm Fin* bankruptcy; *fig* failure
fal'li|re *vi Fin* go bankrupt; *fig* fail ● *vt* miss (*colpo*). ~to, -a *a* unsuccessful; *Fin* bankrupt ● *nmf* failure; *Fin* bankrupt
'fallo *nm* fault; (*errore*) mistake; *Sport* foul; (*imperfezione*) flaw; senza ~ without fail
falò *nm inv* bonfire
fal'sar|e *vt* alter; (*falsificare*) falsify. ~io, -a *nmf* forger; (*di documenti*) counterfeiter
falsifi'ca|re *vt* fake; (*contraffare*) forge. ~zi'one *nf* (*di documento*) falsification
falsità *nf* falseness
'falso *a* false; (*sbagliato*) wrong; (*opera d'arte ecc*) fake; (*gioielli, oro*) imitation ● *nm* forgery; giurare il ~ commit perjury
'fama *nf* fame; (*reputazione*) reputation
'fame *nf* hunger; aver ~ be hungry; fare la ~ barely scrape a living.
fa'melico *a* ravenous
famige'rato *a* infamous
fa'miglia *nf* family
famili'ar|e *a* family *attrib*; (*ben noto*) familiar; (*senza cerimonie*) informal ● *nmf* relative, relation. ~ità *nf* familiarity; (*informalità*) informality.
~iz'zarsi *vr* familiarize oneself
fa'moso *a* famous
fa'nale *nm* lamp; *Auto ecc* light. fanali *pl* posteriori *Auto* rear lights
fa'natico, -a *a* fanatical; essere ~ di calcio/cinema be a football/cinema fanatic ● *nmf* fanatic. fana'tismo *nm* fanaticism
fanci'ul|la *nf* young girl. ~'lezza *nf* childhood. ~lo *nm* young boy
fan'donia *nf* lie; fandonie! nonsense!
fan'fara *nf* fanfare; (*complesso*) brass band
fanfaro'nata *nf* brag. fanfa'rone, -a *nmf* braggart
fan'ghiglia *nf* mud. 'fango *nm* mud. fan'goso *a* muddy

fannul'lone, -a *nmf* idler
fantasci'enza *nf* science fiction
fanta'si|a *nf* fantasy; (*immaginazione*) imagination; (*capriccio*) fancy; (*di tessuto*) pattern. ~'oso *a* (*stilista, ragazzo*) imaginative; (*resoconto*) improbable
fan'tasma *nm* ghost
fantasti'c|are *vi* day-dream. ~he'ria *nf* day-dream. fan'tastico *a* fantastic; (*racconto*) fantasy
'fante *nm* infantryman; (*carte*) jack. ~'ria *nf* infantry
fan'tino *nm* jockey
fan'toccio *nm* puppet
fanto'matico *a* (*inafferrabile*) phantom *attrib*
fara'butto *nm* trickster
fara'ona *nf* (*uccello*) guinea-fowl
far'ci|re *vt* stuff; fill (*torta*). ~to *a* stuffed; (*dolce*) filled
far'dello *nm* bundle; *fig* burden
'fare *vt* do; make (*dolce, letto ecc*); (*recitare la parte di*) play; (*trascorrere*) spend; ~ una pausa un sogno have a break/a dream; ~ colpo su impress; ~ paura a frighten; ~ piacere a please; farla put an end to it; ~ l'insegnante be a teacher; ~ lo scemo play the idiot; ~ una settimana al mare spend a week at the seaside; 3 più 3 fa 6 3 and 3 makes 6; quanto fa? – fanno 10 000 lira how much is it? – it's 10,000 lire; far ~ qcsa a qcno get sb to do sth; (*costringere*) make sb do sth; ~ vedere show; fammi parlare let me speak; niente a che ~ con nothing to do with; non c'è niente da ~ (*per problema*) there is nothing we/you/etc. can do; fa caldo/buio it's warm/dark; non fa niente it doesn't matter; strada facendo on the way. farcela (*riuscire*) manage ● *vi* fai in modo di venire try and come; ~ da act as; ~ per make as if to; ~ presto be quick; non fa per me it's not for me ● *nm* way; sul far del giorno at daybreak. farsi *vr* (*diventare*) get; (*sl: drogarsi*) shoot up; farsi avanti come forward; farsi i fatti propri mind one's own business; farsi la barba shave; farsi la villa *fam* buy a villa; farsi il ragazzo *fam* find a boyfriend; farsi due risate have a laugh; farsi male hurt oneself; farsi strada (*aver successo*) make one's way in the world
fa'retto *nm* spot[light]
far'falla *nf* butterfly

farfal'lino nm (cravatta) bow tie
farfugli'are vt mutter
fa'rina nf flour. **fari'nacei** nmpl starchy food sg
fa'ringe nf pharynx
fari'noso a (neve) powdery; (mela) soft; (patata) floury
farma'ceutico a pharmaceutical. ~**cia** nf pharmacy; (negozio) chemist's [shop]. ~**cia di turno** duty chemist. ~**cista** nmf chemist. **farmaco** nm drug
faro nm Auto headlight; Aeron beacon; (costruzione) lighthouse
farsa nf farce
fasci|a nf band; (zona) area; (ufficiale) sash; (benda) bandage. ~**are** vt bandage; cling to (fianchi). ~**a'tura** nf dressing; (azione) bandaging
fa'scicolo nm file; (di rivista) issue; (libretto) booklet
fascino nm fascination
fascio nm bundle; (di fiori) bunch
fa'scis|mo nm fascism. ~**ta** nmf fascist
fase nf phase
fa'stidi|o nm nuisance; (scomodo) inconvenience; **dar** ~**o a qcno** bother sb; ~**i** pl (preoccupazioni) worries; (disturbi) troubles. ~**oso** a tiresome
fasto nm pomp. **fa'stoso** a sumptuous
fa'sullo a bogus
fata nf fairy
fa'tale a fatal; (inevitabile) fated
fata'l|ismo nm fatalism. ~**ista** nmf fatalist. ~**ità** nf inv fate; (caso sfortunato) misfortune. ~**mente** adv inevitably
fa'tica nf effort; (lavoro faticoso) hard work; (stanchezza) fatigue; **a** ~ with great difficulty; **è** ~ **sprecata** it's a waste of time; **fare** ~ **a fare qcsa** find it difficult to do sth; **fare** ~ **a finire qcsa** struggle to finish sth. **fati'caccia** nf pain
fati'ca|re vi toil; ~**re a** (stentare) find it difficult to. ~**ta** nf effort; (sfacchinata) grind. **fati'coso** a tiring; (difficile) difficult
fato nm fate
fat'taccio nm hum foul deed
fat'tezze nfpl features
fat'tibile a feasible
fatto pp di **fare** ● a done, made; ~ **a mano/in casa** handmade/home-made ● nm fact; (azione) action; (avvenimento) event; **bada ai fatti tuoi!** mind your own business; **sa il** ~ **suo** he knows his

business; **di** ~ in fact; **in** ~ **di** as regards
fat'to|re nm (causa, Math) factor; (di fattoria) farm manager. ~**ria** nf farm; (casa) farmhouse
fatto'rino nm messenger [boy]
fattucchi'era nf witch
fat'tur|a nf (stile) cut; (lavorazione) workmanship; Comm invoice
fattu'ra|re vt invoice; (adulterare) adulterate. ~**to** nm turnover, sales pl. ~**zi'one** nf invoicing, billing
fatuo a fatuous
fauna nf fauna
fau'tore nm supporter
fava nf broad bean
fa'vella nf speech
fa'villa nf spark
favo'la nf fable; (fiaba) story; (oggetto di pettegolezzi) laughing-stock; (meraviglia) dream. ~**loso** a fabulous
fa'vore nm favour; **essere a** ~ **di** be in favour of; **per** ~ please; **di** ~ (condizioni, trattamento) preferential. ~**ggia-'mento** nm Jur aiding and abetting. **favo'revole** a favourable. ~**vol'mente** adv favourably
favo'ri|re vt favour; (promuovere) promote; **vuol** ~**re?** (accettare) will you have some?; (entrare) will you come in?. ~**to, -a** a & nmf favourite
fax nm inv fax. **fa'xare** vt fax
fazi'one nf faction
faziosità nf bias. **fazi'oso** nm sectarian
fazzolet'tino nm ~ **[di carta]** [paper] tissue
fazzo'letto nm handkerchief; (da testa) headscarf
feb'braio nm February
febbre nf fever; **avere la** ~ have o run a temperature. ~ **da fieno** hay fever. **febbrici'tante** a fevered. **feb'brile** a feverish
feccia nf dregs pl
fecola nf potato flour
fecon'da|re vt fertilize. ~**tore** nm fertilizer. ~**zi'one** nf fertilization. ~**zione artificiale** artificial insemination. **fe'condo** a fertile
fede nf faith; (fiducia) trust; (anello) wedding-ring; **in buona/mala** ~ in good/bad faith; **prestar** ~ **a** believe; **tener** ~ **alla parola** keep one's word. **fe'dele** a faithful ● nmf believer; (seguace) follower. ~**l'mente** adv faithfully. ~**ltà** nf faithfulness; **alta** ~**ltà** high fidelity

'federa *nf* pillowcase
fede'ra|le *a* federal. ~ lismo *nm* federalism. ~zi'one *nf* federation
fe'dina *nf* avere la ~ penale sporca/pulita have a/no criminal record
'fegato *nm* liver; *fig* guts *pl*
'felce *nf* fern
fe'lic|e *a* happy; *(fortunato)* lucky. ~ità *nf* happiness
felici'ta|rsi *vr* ~rsi con congratulate. ~zi'oni *nfpl* congratulations
fe'lino *a* feline
'felpa *nf (indumento)* sweatshirt
fel'pato *a* brushed; *(passo)* stealthy
'feltro *nm* felt; *(cappello)* felt hat
'femmin|a *nf* female. femmi'nile *a* feminine; *(rivista, abbigliamento)* women's; *(sesso)* female ● *nm* feminine. ~ità *nf* femininity. femmi'nismo *nm* feminism
'femore *nm* femur
'fend|ere *vt* split. ~i'tura *nf* split; *(nella roccia)* crack
feni'cottero *nm* flamingo
fenome'nale *a* phenomenal. fe'nomeno *nm* phenomenon
'feretro *nm* coffin
feri'ale *a* weekday; giorno ~ weekday
'ferie *nfpl* holidays; *(di università, tribunale ecc)* vacation *sg*; andare in ~ go on holiday
feri'mento *nm* wounding
fe'ri|re *vt* wound; *(in incidente)* injure; *fig* hurt. ~rsi *vr* injure oneself. ~ta *nf* wound. ~to *a* wounded ● *nm* wounded person; *Mil* casualty
'ferma *nf Mil* period of service
ferma'capelli *nm inv* hairslide
ferma'carte *nm inv* paperweight
fermacra'vatta *nm inv* tiepin
fer'maglio *nm* clasp; *(spilla)* brooch; *(per capelli)* hair slide
ferma'mente *adv* firmly
fer'ma|re *vt* stop; *(fissare)* fix; *Jur* detain ● *vi* stop. ~rsi *vr* stop. ~ta *nf* stop. ~ta dell'autobus bus-stop. ~ta a richiesta request stop
fermen'ta|re *vi* ferme. ~zi'one *nf* fermentation. fer'mento *nm* ferment; *(lievito)* yeast
fer'mezza *nf* firmness
'fermo *a* still; *(veicolo)* stationary; *(stabile)* steady; *(orologio)* not working ● *nm Jur* detention; *Mech* catch; in stato di ~ in custody
fe'roc|e *a* ferocious; *(bestia)* wild; *(freddo, dolore)* unbearable. ~e'mente *adv* fiercely, ferociously. ~ia *nf* ferocity

fer'raglia *nf* scrap iron
ferra'gosto *nm* 15 August *(bank holiday in Italy)*; *(periodo)* August holidays *pl*
ferra'menta *nfpl* ironmongery *sg*; negozio di ~ ironmonger's
fer'ra|re *vt* shoe *(cavallo)*. ~to a ~to in *(preparato in)* well up in
'ferreo *a* iron
'ferro *nm* iron; *(attrezzo)* tool; *(di chirurgo)* instrument; bistecca ai ferri grilled steak; di ~ *(memoria)* excellent; *(alibi)* cast-iron; salute di ~ iron constitution. ~ battuto wrought iron. ~ da calza knitting needle. ~ di cavallo horseshoe. ~ da stiro iron
ferro'vecchio *nm* scrap merchant
ferro'vi|a *nf* railway. ~'ario *a* railway. ~'ere *nm* railwayman
ferti|le *a* fertile. ~ità *nf* fertility. ~iz'zante *nm* fertilizer
fer'vente *a* blazing; *fig* fervent
'fervere *vi (preparativi:)* be well under way
'fervid|o *a* fervent; ~i auguri best wishes
fer'vore *nm* fervour
fesse'ria *nf* nonsense
'fesso *pp di* fendere ● *a* cracked; *(fam: sciocco)* foolish ● *nm (fam: idiota)* fool; far ~ qcno *fam* con sb
fes'sura *nf* crack; *(per gettone ecc)* slot
'festa *nf* feast; *(giorno festivo)* holiday; *(compleanno)* birthday; *(ricevimento)* party; *(fig* joy; fare ~ a qcno welcome sb; essere in ~ be on holiday; far ~ celebrate. ~i'olo *a* festive
festeggia'mento *nm* celebration; *(manifestazione)* festivity
festeggi'are *vt* celebrate; *(accogliere festosamente)* give a hearty welcome to
fe'stino *nm* party
festi'vità *nfpl* festivities. fe'stivo *a* holiday; *(lieto)* festive. festivi *nmpl* public holidays
fe'stone *nm (nel cucito)* scallop. scollop
fe'stoso *a* merry
fe'tente *a* evil smelling; *fig* revolting ● *nmf fam* bastard
fe'ticcio *nm* fetish
'feto *nm* foetus
fe'tore *nm* stench
'fetta *nf* slice; a fette sliced. ~ biscottata *slices of crispy toast-like bread*
fet'tuccia *nf* tape; *(con nome)* name tape
feu'dale *a* feudal. 'feudo *nm* feud

FFSS abbr (**Ferrovie dello Stato**) Italian state railways

fi'aba nf fairy-tale. **fia'besco** a fairytale

fi'acc|a nf weariness; (indolenza) laziness; **battere la ~a** be sluggish. **fiac'care** vt weaken. **~o** a weak; (indolente) slack; (stanco) weary; (partita) dull

fi'accola nf torch. **~'lata** nf torchlight procession

fi'ala nf phial

fi'amma nf flame; Naut pennant; **in fiamme** aflame. **andare in fiamme** go up in flames. **~ ossidrica** blowtorch

fiam'mante a flaming; **nuovo ~nte** brand new. **~'ta** nf blaze

fiammeggi'are vi blaze

fiam'mifero nm match

fiam'mingo, -a a Flemish ● nmf Fleming ● nm (lingua) Flemish

fiancheggi'are vt border; fig support

fi'anco nm side; (di persona) hip; (di animale) flank; Mil wing; **al mio ~** by my side; **~ a ~** (lavorare) side by side

fi'asco nm flask; fig fiasco; **fare ~** be a fiasco

fia'tare vi breathe; (parlare) breathe a word

fi'ato nm breath; (vigore) stamina; **strumenti a ~** wind instruments; **senza ~** breathlessly; **tutto d'un ~** (bere, leggere) all in one go

'fibbia nf buckle

'fibra nf fibre; **fibre** pl (alimentari) roughage. **~ ottica** optical fibre

ficca'naso nmf nosey parker

fic'care vt thrust; drive (chiodo ecc); (fam: mettere) shove. **~si** vr thrust oneself; (nascondersi) hide; **~si nei guai** get oneself into trouble

fiche nf (gettone) chip

'fico nm (albero) fig-tree; (frutto) fig. **~ d'India** prickly pear

'fico, -a fam nmf cool sort ● a cool

fidanza'mento nm engagement

fidan'zar|si vr become engaged. **~to, -a** nmf fiancé; fiancee

fi'dar|si vr **~rsi di** trust. **~to** a trustworthy

'fido nm devoted follower; Comm credit

fi'duci|a nf confidence; **degno di ~a** trustworthy; **di ~a** (fornitore, banca) regular, usual; **persona di ~a** reliable person. **~'oso** a trusting

fi'ele nm bile; fig bitterness

fie'nile nm barn. **fi'eno** nm hay

fi'era nf fair

fie'rezza nf (dignità) pride. **fi'ero** a proud

fi'evole a faint; (luce) dim

'fifa nf fam jitters; **aver ~** have the jitters. **fi'fone, -a** nmf fam chicken

'figli|a nf daughter; **~a unica** only child. **~'astra** nf stepdaughter. **~'astro** nm stepson. **~o** nm son; (generico) child. **~o di papà** spoilt brat. **~o unico** only child

figli'occi|a nf goddaughter. **~o** nm godson

figli'ol|a nf girl. **~'lanza** nf offspring. **~lo** nm boy

'figo, -a vedi**fico, -a**

fi'gura nf figure; (aspetto esteriore) shape; (illustrazione) illustration; **far bella/brutta ~** make a good/bad impression; **mi hai fatto fare una brutta ~** you made me look a fool; **che ~!** how embarrassing!. **figu'raccia** nf bad impression

figu'ra|re vt represent; (simboleggiare) symbolize; (immaginare) imagine ● vi (far figura) cut a fine figure; (in lista) appear, figure. **~rsi** vr (immaginarsi) imagine; **~ti!** imagine that!; **posso? -[ma] ~ti!** may I? - of course!. **~'tivo** a figurative

figu'rina nf (da raccolta) ≈ cigarette card

figuri'nista nmf dress designer. **~'rino** nm fashion sketch. **~'rone** nm **fare un ~rone** make an excellent impression

'fila nf line; (di soldati ecc) file; (di oggetti) row; (coda) queue; **di ~** in succession; **fare la ~** queue [up], stand in line Am; **in ~ indiana** single file

fila'mento nm filament

filantro'pia nf philanthropy

fi'lare vt spin; Naut pay out ● vi (andarsene) run away; (liquido:) trickle; **fila!** scram!; **~ con** (fam: amoreggiare) go out with; **~ dritto** toe the line

filar'monica nf (orchestra) orchestra

fila'strocca nf rigmarole; (per bambini) nursery rhyme

filate'lia nf philately

fi'lato a spun; (ininterrotto) running; (continuato) uninterrupted; **di ~to** (subito) immediately ● nm yarn. **~'tura** nf spinning; (filanda) spinning mill

fil di 'ferro nm wire

fi'letto nm (bordo) border; (di vite) thread; Culin fillet

fili'ale a filial ● nf Comm branch

fili'grana nf filigree; (su carta) watermark

film nm inv film. ~ **giallo** thriller. ~ **a lungo metraggio** feature film

fil'ma|re vt film. ~**to** nm short film. **fil'mino** nm cine film

filo nm thread; (tessile) yarn; (metallico) wire; (di lama) edge; (venatura) grain; (di perle) string; (d'erba) blade; (di luce) ray; **con un ~ di voce** in a whisper; **per ~ e per segno** in detail; **fare il ~ a qcno** fancy sb; **perdere il ~** lose the thread. ~ **spinato** barbed wire

filobus nm inv trolleybus

filodiffusi'one nf reddiffusion

fi'lone nm vein; (di pane) long loaf

filoso'fia nf philosophy. **fi'losofo, -a** nmf philosopher

fil'trare vt filter. **filtro** nm filter

filza nf string

fin vedi **fine, fino¹**

fi'nal|e a final ● nm end ● nf Sport final. **fina'lista** nmf finalist. ~**ità** nf inv finality; (scopo) aim. ~**mente** adv at last; (in ultimo) finally

fi'nanz|a nf finance; ~**i'ario** a financial. ~**i'ere** nm financier; (guardia di finanza) customs officer. ~**ia'mento** nm funding

finanzi'a|re vt fund, finance. ~**'tore,** ~**'trice** nmf backer

finché conj until; (per tutto il tempo che) as long as

fine a fine; (sottile) thin; (udito, vista) keen; (raffinato) refined ● nf end; **alla ~ in the end**; **alla fin ~** after all; **in fin dei conti** when all's said and done; **te lo dico a fin di bene** I'm telling you for your own good; **senza ~** endless ● nm aim. ~ **settimana** weekend

fi'nestra nf window. **fine'strella** nf di aiuto Comput help window, help box. **fine'strino** nm Rail, Auto window

fi'nezza nf fineness; (sottigliezza) thinness; (raffinatezza) refinement

'fingere vt pretend; feign (affetto ecc). ~**si** v pretend to be

fini'menti nmpl finishing touches; (per cavallo) harness sg

fini'mondo nm end of the world; fig pandemonium

fi'ni|re vt/i finish, end; (smettere) stop; (diventare, andare a finire) end up; ~**scila!** stop it!. ~**to** a finished; (abile) accomplished. ~**'tura** nf finish

finlan'dese a Finnish ● nmf Finn ● nm (lingua) Finnish

Fin'landia nf Finland

'fino¹ prep ~ **a** till, until; (spazio) as far as; ~ **all'ultimo** to the last; **fin da** (tempo) since; (spazio) from; **fin qui** as far as here; **fin troppo** too much; ~ **a che punto** how far

'fino² a fine; (acuto) subtle; (puro) pure

fi'nocchio nm fennel; (fam: omosessuale) poof

fi'nora adv so far, up till now

'finta nf pretence, sham; Sport feint; **far ~ di** pretend to; **far ~ di niente** act as if nothing had happened; **per ~** (per scherzo) for a laugh

fint|o, -a pp di **fingere** ● a false; (artificiale) artificial; **fare il ~o tonto** act dumb

finzi'one nf pretence

fi'occo nm bow; (di neve) flake; (nappa) tassel; **coi fiocchi** fig excellent. ~ **di neve** snowflake

fi'ocina nf harpoon

fi'oco a weak; (luce) dim

fi'onda nf catapult

fio'raio, -a nmf florist

fiorda'liso nm cornflower

fi'ordo nm fiord

fi'ore nm flower; (parte scelta) cream; **fiori** pl (nelle carte) clubs; **a fior d'acqua** on the surface of the water; **fior di** (abbondanza) a lot of; **ha i nervi a fior di pelle** his nerves are on edge; **a fiori** flowery

fioren'tino a Florentine

fio'retto nm (scherma) foil; Relig act of mortification

fio'rire vi flower; (albero:) blossom; fig flourish

fio'rista nmf florist

fiori'tura nf (di albero) blossoming

fi'otto nm **scorrere a fiotti** pour out; **piove a fiotti** the rain is pouring down

Fi'renze nf Florence

'firma nf signature; (nome) name

fir'ma|re vt sign. ~**'tario, -a** nmf signatory. ~**to** a (abito, borsa) designer attrib

fisar'monica nf accordion

fi'scale a fiscal

fischi'are vi whistle ● vt whistle; (in segno di disapprovazione) boo

fischiet'tare vt whistle. ~**io** nm whistling

fischi'etto nm whistle. **'fischio** nm whistle

'fisco nm treasury; (tasse) taxation; **il ~** the taxman

'fisica nf physics

fisica'mente adv physically

'**fisico, -a** *a* physical ● *nmf* physicist ● *nm* physique

'**fisima** *nf* whim

fisio'lo'gia *nf* physiology. ~**logico** *a* physiological

fisiono'mia *nf* features, face; (*di paesaggio*) appearance

fisiotera'pi'a *nf* physiotherapy. ~**sta** *nmf* physiotherapist

fis'sa're *vt* fix, fasten; (*guardare fissamente*) stare at; arrange (*appuntamento, ora*). ~**rsi** *vr* (*stabilirsi*) settle; (*fissare lo sguardo*) stare; ~**rsi su** (*ostinarsi*) set one's mind on; ~**rsi di fare qcsa** become obsessed with doing sth. ~**to** *nm* (*persona*) person with an obsession. ~**zi'one** *nf* fixation; (*ossessione*) obsession

'**fisso** *a* fixed; **un lavoro ~** a regular job; **senza fissa dimora** of no fixed abode

'**fitta** *nf* sharp pain

fit'tizio *a* fictitious

'**fitto**[1] *a* thick; ~ **di** full of ● *nm* depth

fitto[2] *nm* (*affitto*) rent; **dare a ~** let; **prendere a ~** rent; (*noleggiare*) hire

fiu'mana *nf* swollen river; *fig* stream

fi'ume *nm* river; *fig* stream

fiu'tare *vt* smell. **fi'uto** *nm* [sense of] smell; *fig* nose

'**flaccido** *a* flabby

fla'cone *nm* bottle

fla'gello *nm* scourge

fla'grante *a* flagrant; **in ~** in the act

fla'nella *nf* flannel

'**flash** *nm inv Journ* newsflash

'**flauto** *nm* flute

'**flebile** *a* feeble

'**flemma** *nf* calm; *Med* phlegm. **flem'matico** *a* phlegmatic

fles'sibile *a* flexible. ~**ità** *nf* flexibility

flessi'one *nf* (*del busto in avanti*) forward bend

'**flesso** *pp di* **flettere**

flessu'oso *a* supple

'**flettere** *vt* bend

flir'tare *vi* flirt

F.lli *abbr* (**fratelli**) Bros

'**floppy disk** *nm inv* floppy disk

'**flora** *nf* flora

'**florido** *a* flourishing

'**floscio** *a* limp; (*flaccido*) flabby

'**flotta** *nf* fleet. **flot'tiglia** *nf* flotilla

flu'ente *a* fluent

flu'ido *nm* fluid

flu'ire *vi* flow

fluore'scente *a* fluorescent

flu'oro *nm* fluorine

'**flusso** *nm* flow; *Med* flux; (*del mare*) flood[-tide]; ~ **e riflusso** ebb and flow

fluttu'ante *a* fluctuating

fluttu'a're *vi* (*prezzi, moneta:*) fluctuate. ~**zi'one** *nf* fluctuation

fluvi'ale *a* river

fo'bia *nf* phobia

'**foca** *nf* seal

fo'caccia *nf* (*pane*) flat bread; (*dolce*) ≈ raisin bread

fo'cale *a* (*distanza, punto*) focal. **focaliz'zare** *vt* get into focus (*fotografia*); focus (*attenzione*); define (*problema*)

'**foce** *nf* mouth

foco'laio *nm Med* focus; *fig* centre

foco'lare *nm* hearth; (*caminetto*) fireplace; *Techn* furnace

fo'coso *a* fiery

foder'a're *vt* line; (*di libro*) dustjacket; (*di poltrona ecc*) loose cover. **fode'rare** *vt* line; cover (*libro*). ~**o** *nm* sheath

'**foga** *nf* impetuosity

foggi'a *nf* lining; (*maniera*) manner; (*forma*) shape. ~**are** *vt* mould

'**foglia** *nf* leaf; (*di metallo*) foil. ~**'ame** *nm* foliage

fogli'etto *nm* (*pezzetto di carta*) piece of paper

'**foglio** *nm* sheet; (*pagina*) leaf. ~ **elettronico** *Comput* spreadsheet. ~ **rosa** ≈ provisional driving licence

'**fogna** *nf* sewer. ~**'tura** *nf* sewerage

fo'lata *nf* gust

fol'clore *nm* folklore. ~**ristico** *a* folk; (*bizzarro*) weird

folgo'ra're *vi* (*splendere*) shine ● *vt* (*con un fulmine*) strike. ~**zi'one** *nf* (*da fulmine, elettrica*) electrocution; (*idea*) brainwave

'**folgore** *nf* thunderbolt

'**folla** *nf* crowd

'**folle** *a* mad; **in ~** *Auto* in neutral; **andare in ~** *Auto* coast

folle'mente *adv* madly

fol'lia *nf* madness; **alla ~** (*amare*) to distraction

'**folto** *a* thick

fomen'tare *vt* stir up

fond'ale *nm Theat* backcloth

fonda'men'ta *nfpl* foundations. ~ **tale** *a* fundamental. ~**to** *nm* (*di principio, teoria*) foundation

fon'da're *vt* establish; base (*ragionamento, accusa*). ~**to** *a* (*ragionamento*) well-founded. ~**zi'one** *nf* establishment; ~**zioni** *pl* (*di edificio*) foundations

fon'delli *nmpl* **prendere qcno per i ~** pull sb's leg

fon'dente *a* ⟨cioccolato⟩ dark

'fonder|e *vt/i* melt; ⟨colori:⟩ blend. **~si** *vr* melt; *Comm* merge. **fonde'ria** *nf* foundry

'fondi *nmpl* ⟨denaro⟩ funds; ⟨di caffè⟩ grounds

'fondo *a* deep; **è notte fonda** it's the middle of the night ●*nm* bottom; ⟨fine⟩ end; ⟨sfondo⟩ background; ⟨indole⟩ nature; ⟨somma di denaro⟩ fund; ⟨feccia⟩ dregs *pl*; **andare a ~** ⟨nave:⟩ sink; **da cima a ~** from beginning to end; **in ~** after all; **in ~ in ~** deep down; **fino in ~** right to the end; ⟨capire⟩ thoroughly. **~ d'investimento** investment trust

fondo'tinta *nm inv* foundation cream

fon'duta *nf* fondue made with cheese, milk and eggs

fo'netic|a *nf* phonetics *sg*. **~o** *a* phonetic

fon'tana *nf* fountain

'fonte *nf* spring; *fig* source ●*nm* font

fo'raggio *nm* forage

fo'rar|e *vt* pierce; punch ⟨biglietto⟩ ●*vi* puncture. **~si** *vr* ⟨gomma, pallone:⟩ go soft

'forbici *nfpl* scissors

forbi'cine *nfpl* ⟨per le unghie⟩ nail scissors

for'bito *a* erudite

'forca *nf* fork; ⟨patibolo⟩ gallows *pl*

for'cella *nf* fork; ⟨per capelli⟩ hairpin

for'chet|ta *nf* fork. **~tata** *nf* ⟨quantità⟩ forkful

for'cina *nf* hairpin

'forcipe *nm* forceps *pl*

for'cone *nm* pitchfork

fo'resta *nf* forest. **fore'stale** *a* forest *attrib*

foresti'ero, -a *a* foreign ●*nmf* foreigner

for'fait *nm inv* fixed price; **dare ~** ⟨abbandonare⟩ give up

'forfora *nf* dandruff

'forgi|a *nf* forge. **~are** *vt* forge

'forma *nf* form; ⟨sagoma⟩ shape; *Culin* mould; ⟨da calzolaio⟩ last; **essere in ~** be in good form; **a ~ di** in the shape of; **forme** *pl* ⟨del corpo⟩ figure *sg*; ⟨convenzioni⟩ appearances

formag'gino *nm* processed cheese. **for'maggio** *nm* cheese

for'mal|e *a* formal. **~ità** *nf inv* formality. **~iz'zarsi** *vr* stand on ceremony. **~'mente** *adv* formally

for'mar|e *vt* form. **~rsi** *vr* form;

⟨svilupparsi⟩ develop. **~to** *nm* size; ⟨di libro⟩ format; **~to tessera** ⟨fotografia⟩ passport-size

format'tare *vt* format

formazi'one *nf* formation; *Sport* line-up. **~ professionale** vocational training

for'mi|ca *nf* ant. **~caio** *nm* anthill

'formica® *nf* ⟨laminato plastico⟩ Formica®

formico'l|are *vi* ⟨braccio ecc.⟩ tingle; **~are di** be swarming with; **mi ~a la mano** I have pins and needles in my hand. **~io** *nm* swarming; ⟨di braccio ecc⟩ pins and needles *pl*

formi'dabile *a* ⟨tremendo⟩ formidable; ⟨eccezionale⟩ tremendous

for'mina *nf* mould

for'moso *a* shapely

'formula *nf* formula. **formu'lare** *vt* formulate; ⟨esprimere⟩ express

for'nace *nf* furnace; ⟨per laterizi⟩ kiln

for'naio *nm* baker; ⟨negozio⟩ bakery

for'nello *nm* stove; ⟨di pipa⟩ bowl

for'ni|re *vt* supply ⟨di with⟩. **~tore** *nm* supplier. **~tura** *nf* supply

'forno *nm* oven; ⟨panetteria⟩ bakery; **al ~** roast. **~ a microonde** microwave [oven]

'foro *nm* hole; ⟨romano⟩ forum; ⟨tribunale⟩ [law] court

'forse *adv* perhaps, maybe; **essere in ~** be in doubt

forsen'nato, -a *a* mad ●*nmf* madman; madwoman

'forte *a* strong; ⟨colore⟩ bright; ⟨suono⟩ loud; ⟨resistente⟩ tough; ⟨spesa⟩ considerable; ⟨dolore⟩ severe; ⟨pioggia⟩ heavy; ⟨a tennis, calcio⟩ good; ⟨fam: simpatico⟩ great; ⟨taglia⟩ large ●*adv* strongly; ⟨parlare⟩ loudly; ⟨velocemente⟩ fast; ⟨piovere⟩ heavily ●*nm* ⟨fortezza⟩ fort; ⟨specialità⟩ strong point

for'tezza *nf* fortress; ⟨forza morale⟩ fortitude

fortifi'care *vt* fortify

for'tino *nm* *Mil* blockhouse

for'tuito *a* fortuitous; **incontro ~** chance encounter

for'tuna *nf* fortune; ⟨successo⟩ success; ⟨buona sorte⟩ luck. **atterraggio di ~** forced landing; **aver ~** be lucky; **buona ~!** good luck!; **di ~** makeshift; **per ~** luckily. **fortu'nato** *a* lucky, fortunate; ⟨impresa⟩ successful. **~ta'mente** *adv* fortunately

fo'runcolo *nm* pimple; ⟨grosso⟩ boil

'forza *nf* strength; ⟨potenza⟩ power;

(*fisica*) force; **di** ~ by force; **a** ~ **di** by dint of; **con** ~ hard; ~**!** come on!; ~ **di volontà** will-power; **per** ~ against one's will; (*naturalmente*) of course; **farsi** ~ bear up; **mare** ~ 8 force 8 gale; **bella** ~**!** *fam* big deal!. ~ **di gravità** [force of] gravity. **le forze armate** the armed forces

for'zare *vt* force; (*scassare*) break open; (*sforzare*) strain. ~**to** *a* forced; (*sorriso*) strained ●*nm* convict

forzi'ere *nm* coffer

for'zuto *a* strong

fo'schia *nf* haze

fosco *a* dark

fo'sfato *nm* phosphate

fosforo *nm* phosphorus

fossa *nf* pit; (*tomba*) grave. ~ **biologica** cesspool. **fos'sato** *nm* (*di fortificazione*) moat

fos'setta *nf* dimple

fossile *nm* fossil

fosso *nm* ditch; *Mil* trench

foto *nf inv fam* photo; **fare delle** ~ take some photos

foto'cellula *nf* photocell

fotocomposizi'one *nf* filmsetting, photocomposition

foto'copia *nf* photocopy. ~**are** *vt* photocopy. ~**a'trice** *nf* photocopier

foto'finish *nm inv* photo finish

foto'genico *a* photogenic

fotogra'fare *vt* photograph. ~**fia** *nf* (*arte*) photography; (*immagine*) photograph; **fare** ~**fie** take photographs. **foto'grafico** *a* photographic; **macchina fotografica** camera. **fo'tografo, -a** *nmf* photographer

foto'gramma *nm* frame

fotomo'dello *nm* [photographer's] model

fotomon'taggio *nm* photomontage

foto'romanzo *nm* photo story

fottere *vt* (*fam: rubare*) nick; *vulg* fuck, screw. ~**sene** *vr vulg* not give a fuck

fot'tuto *a* (*fam: maledetto*) bloody

fou'lard *nm inv* scarf

fra *prep* (*in mezzo a due*) between; (*in un insieme*) among; (*tempo, distanza*) in; **detto** ~ **noi** between you and me; ~ **sé e sé** to oneself; ~ **l'altro** what's more; ~ **breve** soon; ~ **quindici giorni** in two weeks' time; ~ **tutti, siamo in venti** there are twenty of us altogether

fracas'sare *vt* smash. ~**si** *vr* shatter

fra'casso *nm* din; (*di cose che cadono*) crash

fra'dicio *a* (*bagnato*) soaked; (*guasto*) rotten; **ubriaco** ~ blind drunk

fragile *a* fragile; *fig* frail. ~**ità** *nf* fragility; *fig* frailty

fragola *nf* strawberry

fra'gore *nm* uproar; (*di cose rotte*) clatter; (*di tuono*) rumble. ~ **roso** *a* uproarious; (*tuono*) rumbling; (*suono*) clanging

fra'grante *a* fragrant. ~**za** *nf* fragrance

frain'tendere *vt* misunderstand. ~**ndersi** *vr* be at cross-purposes. ~**so** *pp di* fraintendere

frammen'tario *a* fragmentary. **fram'mento** *nm* fragment

frana *nf* landslide; (*fam: persona*) walking disaster area. **fra'nare** *vi* slide down

franca'mente *adv* frankly

fran'cese *a* French ●*nm* Frenchman; Frenchwoman ●*nm* (*lingua*) French

fran'chezza *nf* frankness

Francia *nf* France

franco[1] *a* frank; *Comm* free; **farla franca** get away with sth

franco[2] *nm* (*moneta*) franc

franco'bollo *nm* stamp

fran'gente *nm* (*onda*) breaker; (*scoglio*) reef; (*fig: momento difficile*) crisis; **in quel** ~ given the situation

frangia *nf* fringe

fra'noso *a* subject to landslides

fran'toio *nm* olive-press

frantu'mare *vt*, ~**si** *vr* shatter. **fran'tumi** *nmpl* splinters; **andare in frantumi** be smashed to smithereens

frappé *nm inv* milkshake

frap'porre *vt* interpose. ~**si** *vr* intervene

fra'sario *nm* vocabulary; (*libro*) phrase book

frase *nf* sentence; (*espressione*) phrase. ~ **fatta** cliché

frassino *nm* ash[-tree]

frastagli'are *vt* make jagged. ~**to** *a* jagged

frastor'nare *vt* daze. ~**to** *a* dazed

frastu'ono *nm* racket

frate *nm* friar; (*monaco*) monk

fratel'lanza *nf* brotherhood. ~**stro** *nm* half-brother

fra'telli *nmpl* (*fratello e sorella*) brother and sister. ~**o** *nm* brother

fraterniz'zare *vi* fraternize. **fra'terno** *a* brotherly

frat'taglie *nfpl* (*di pollo ecc*) giblets

frat'tanto *adv* in the meantime

frat'tempo *nm* nel ~ meanwhile, in the meantime

frat'tu|ra *nf* fracture. **~'rare** *vt*, **~'rarsi** *vr* break

fraudo'lento *a* fraudulent

frazi'one *nf* fraction; (*borgata*) hamlet

'freccia *nf* arrow; *Auto* indicator. **~'ata** *nf* (*osservazione pungente*) cutting remark

fredda'mente *adv* coldly

fred'dare *vt* cool; (*fig: con sguardo, battuta*) cut down; (*uccidere*) kill

fred'dezza *nf* coldness

'freddo *a & nm* cold; **aver** ~ be cold; **fa** ~ it's cold

freddo'loso *a* sensitive to cold, chilly

fred'dura *nf* pun

fre'ga|re *vt* rub; (*fam: truffare*) cheat; (*fam: rubare*) swipe. **~rsene** *fam* not give a damn; **chi se ne frega!** what the heck!. **~si** *vr* rub (*occhi*). **~ta** *nf* rub. **~'tura** *nf fam* (*truffa*) swindle; (*delusione*) letdown

'fregio *nm Archit* frieze; (*ornamento*) decoration

fre'mente *a* quivering

'frem|ere *vi* quiver. **~ito** *nm* quiver

fre'na|re *vt* brake; (*fig* restrain; hold back (*lacrime, impazienza*) ● *vi* brake. **~rsi** *vr* check oneself. **~ta** *nf* **fare una ~ta brusca** hit the brakes

frene'sia *nf* frenzy; (*desiderio smodato*) craze. **fre'netico** *a* frenzied

'freno *nm* brake; *fig* check; **togliere il** ~ release the brake; **usare il** ~ apply the brake; **tenere a** ~ restrain. **~ a mano** handbrake

frequen'tare *vt* frequent; attend (*scuola ecc*); mix with (*persone*)

fre'quen|te *a* frequent; **di** ~**te** frequently. **~za** *nf* frequency; (*assiduità*) attendance

fre'schezza *nf* freshness; (*di temperatura*) coolness

'fresco *a* fresh; (*temperatura*) cool; **stai** ~! you're for it! ● *nm* coolness; **far** ~ be cool; **mettere/tenere in** ~ put/ keep in a cool place

'fretta *nf* hurry, haste; **aver** ~ be in a hurry; **far** ~ **a qcno** hurry sb; **in** ~ **e furia** in a great hurry. **frettolosa'mente** *adv* hurriedly. **fretto'loso** *a* (*persona*) in a hurry; (*lavoro*) rushed, hurried

fri'abile *a* crumbly

'friggere *vt* fry; **vai a farti** ~! get lost! ● *vi* sizzle

friggi'trice *nf* chip pan

frigidità *nf* frigidity. **'frigido** *a* frigid

fri'gnare *vi* whine

'frigo *nm* fridge

frigo'bar *nm inv* minibar

frigo'rifero *a* refrigerating ● *nm* refrigerator

fringu'ello *nm* chaffinch

frit'tata *nf* omelette

frit'tella *nf* fritter; (*fam: macchia d'unto*) grease stain

'fritto *pp di* friggere ● *a* fried; **essere** ~ be done for ● *nm* fried food. ~ **misto** mixed fried fish/vegetables. **frit'tura** *nf* (*pietanza*) fried dish

frivo'lezza *nf* frivolity. **'frivolo** *a* frivolous

frizio'nare *vt* rub. **frizi'one** *nf* friction; *Mech* clutch; (*di pelle*) rub

friz'zante *a* fizzy; (*vino*) sparkling; (*aria*) bracing

'frizzo *nm* gibe

fro'dare *vt* defraud

'frode *nf* fraud. ~ **fiscale** tax evasion

'frollo *a* tender; (*selvaggina*) high; (*persona*) spineless; **pasta frolla** short[crust] pastry

'fronda *nf* [leafy] branch; *fig* rebellion. **fron'doso** *a* leafy

fron'tale *a* frontal; (*scontro*) head-on

'fronte *nf* forehead; (*di edificio*) front; **di** ~ opposite; **di** ~ **a** opposite, facing; (*a paragone*) compared with; **far** ~ **a** face ● *nm Mil, Pol* front. **~ggi'are** *vt* face

fronte'spizio *nm* title page

fronti'era *nf* frontier, border

fron'tone *nm* pediment

'fronzolo *nm* frill

'frotta *nf* swarm; (*di animali*) flock

frot'tola *nf* fib; **frottole** *pl* nonsense *sg*

fru'gale *a* frugal

fru'gare *vi* rummage ● *vt* search

frul'la|re *vt Culin* whisk ● *vi* (*ali:*) whirr. **~to** *nm* ~**to di frutta** fruit drink with milk and crushed ice. ~ **tore** *nm* [electric] mixer. **frul'lino** *nm* whisk

fru'mento *nm* wheat

frusci'are *vi* rustle

fru'scio *nm* rustle; (*radio, giradischi*) background noise; (*di acque*) murmur

'frusta *nf* whip; (*frullino*) whisk

fru'sta|re *vt* whip. **~ta** *nf* lash. **fru'stino** *nm* riding crop

fru'stra|re *vt* frustrate. **~to** *a* frustrated. **~zi'one** *nf* frustration

'frutt|a *nf* fruit; (*portata*) dessert. **frut'tare** *vi* bear fruit ● *vt* yield. **frut'teto** *nm* orchard. **~i'vendolo, -a** *nmf* greengrocer. ~o *nm anche fig* fruit; *Fin* yield; ~i di bosco fruits of the forest. ~i di mare seafood *sg*. ~u'oso *a* profitable

f.to *abbr* (firmato) signed

fu *a* (*defunto*) late; il ~ signor Rossi the late Mr Rossi

fuci'la|re *vt* shoot. ~ta *nf* shot

fu'cile *nm* rifle

fu'cina *nf* forge

'**fucsia** *nf* fuchsia

'**fuga** *nf* escape; (*perdita*) leak; *Mus* fugue; darsi alla ~ take to flight

fu'gace *a* fleeting

fug'gevole *a* short-lived

fuggi'asco, -a *nmf* fugitive

fuggi'fuggi *nm* stampede

fug'gi|re *vi* flee; (*innamorati:*) elope; *fig* fly. ~'tivo, -a *nmf* fugitive

'**fulcro** *nm* fulcrum

ful'gore *nm* splendour

fu'liggine *nf* soot

fulmi'nar|e *vt* strike by lightning; (*con sguardo*) look daggers at; (*con scarica elettrica*) electrocute. ~si *vr* burn out.

'**fulmine** *nm* lightning. **ful'mineo** *a* rapid

'**fulvo** *a* tawny

fumai'olo *nm* funnel; (*di casa*) chimney

fu'ma|re *vt/i* smoke; (*in ebollizione*) steam. ~'tore, ~'trice *nmf* smoker; non fumatori non-smoker, non-smoking

fu'metto *nm* comic strip; **fumetti** *pl* comics

'**fumo** *nm* smoke; (*vapore*) steam; *fig* hot air; andare in ~ vanish. **fu'moso** *a* (*ambiente*) smoky; (*discorso*) vague

fu'nambolo, -a *nmf* tightrope walker

'**fune** *nf* rope; (*cavo*) cable

'**funebre** *a* funeral; (*cupa*) gloomy

fune'rale *nm* funeral

fu'nereo *a* (*aria*) funereal

fu'nesto *a* sad

fungere *vi* ~ da act as

'**fungo** *nm* mushroom; *Bot, Med* fungus

funico'lare *nf* funicular [railway]

funi'via *nf* cableway

funzio'nal|e *a* functional. ~ità *nf* functionality

funziona'mento *nm* functioning

funzio'nare *vi* work, function; ~ da (*fungere da*) act as

funzio'nario *nm* official

funzi'one *nf* function; (*carica*) office; *Relig* service; entrare in ~ take up office

fu'oco *nm* fire; (*fisica, fotografia*) fo-

cus; far ~ fire; dar ~ a set fire to; prendere ~ catch fire. **fuochi** *pl* d'artificio fireworks. ~ di paglia nine-days' wonder

fuorché *prep* except

fu'ori *adv* out; (*all'esterno*) outside; (*all'aperto*) outdoors; andare di ~ (*traboccare*) spill over; essere ~ di sé be beside oneself; essere in ~ (*sporgere*) stick out; far ~ *fam* do in; ~ mano out of the way; ~ moda old-fashioned; ~ pasto between meals; ~ pericolo out of danger; ~ questione out of the question; ~ uso out of use ●*nm* outside

fuori'bordo *nm* speedboat (*with outboard motor*)

fuori'classe *nmf inv* champion

fuori'gi'oco *nm & adv* offside

fuori'legge *nmf* outlaw

fuori'serie *a* custom-made ●*nf* custom-built model

fuori'strada *nm* off-road vehicle

fuorvi'are *vt* lead astray ●*vi* go astray

furbacchi'one *nm* crafty old devil

furbe'ria *nf* cunning. **fur'bizia** *nf* cunning

'**furbo** *a* cunning; (*intelligente*) clever; (*astuto*) shrewd; bravo ~! nice one!; fare il ~ try to be clever

fu'rente *a* furious

fur'fante *nm* scoundrel

furgon'cino *nm* delivery van. **fur'gone** *nm* van

furi|a *nf* fury; (*fretta*) haste; a ~ a di by dint of. ~'bondo, ~'osa *a* furious

fu'rore *nm* fury; (*veemenza*) frenzy; far ~ be all the rage. ~ggi'are *vi* be a great success

furtiva'mente *adv* covertly. **fur'tivo** *a* furtive

'**furto** *nm* theft; (*con scasso*) burglary

'**fusa** *nfpl* fare le ~ purr

fu'scello *nm* (*di legno*) twig; (*di paglia*) straw; sei un ~ you're as light as a feather

fu'seaux *mpl* leggings

fu'sibile *nm* fuse

fusi'one *nf* fusion; *Comm* merger

'**fuso** *pp di* fondere ●*a* melted ●*nm* spindle. ~ orario time zone

fuso'liera *nf* fuselage

fu'stagno *nm* corduroy

fu'stino *nm* (*di detersivo*) box

'**fusto** *nm* stem; (*tronco*) trunk; (*di metallo*) drum; (*di legno*) barrel

'**futile** *a* futile

fu'turo *a & nm* future

Gg

gab'bar|e *vt* cheat. **~si** *vr* **~si di** make fun of

'gabbia *nf* cage; (*da imballaggio*) crate. **~ degli imputati** dock. **~ toracica** rib cage

gabbi'ano *nm* [sea]gull

gabi'netto *nm* (*di medico*) consulting room; *Pol* cabinet; (*toletta*) lavatory; (*laboratorio*) laboratory

'gaffe *nf inv* blunder

gagli'ardo *a* vigorous

gai'ezza *nf* gaiety. **'gaio** *a* cheerful

'gala *nf* gala

ga'lante *a* gallant. **~'ria** *nf* gallantry. **galantu'omo** *nm* (*pl* **galantuomini**) gentleman

ga'lassia *nf* galaxy

gala'teo *nm* [good] manners *pl*; (*trattato*) book of etiquette

gale'otto *nm* (*rematore*) galley-slave; (*condannato*) convict

ga'lera *nf* (*nave*) galley; *fam* prison

'galla *nf Bot* gall; **a ~** *adv* afloat; **venire a ~** surface

galleggi'ante *a* floating ● *nm* craft; (*boa*) float

galleggi'are *vi* float

galle'ria *nf* (*traforo*) tunnel; (*d'arte*) gallery; *Theat* circle; (*arcata*) arcade. **~ d'arte** art gallery

'Galles *nm* Wales. **gal'lese** *a* welsh ● *nm* Welshman; (*lingua*) Welsh ● *nf* Welshwoman

gal'letto *nm* cockerel; **fare il ~** show off

gal'lina *nf* hen

gal'lismo *nm* machismo

'gallo *nm* cock

gal'lone *nm* stripe; (*misura*) gallon

galop'pare *vi* gallop. **ga'loppo** *nm* gallop; **al galoppo** at a gallop

galvaniz'zare *vt* galvanize

'gamba *nf* leg; (*di lettera*) stem; **a quattro gambe** on all fours; **darsela a gambe** take to one's heels; **essere in ~** (*essere forte*) be strong; (*capace*) be smart

gamba'letto *nm* pop sock

gambe'retto *nm* shrimp. **'gambero** *nm* prawn; (*di fiume*) crayfish

'gambo *nm* stem; (*di pianta*) stalk

'gamma *nf Mus* scale; *fig* range

ga'nascia *nf* jaw; **ganasce** *pl* **del freno** brake shoes

'gancio *nm* hook

'ganghero *nm* **uscire dai gangheri** *fig* get into a temper

'gara *nf* competition; (*di velocità*) race; **fare a ~** compete. **~ d'appalto** call for tenders

ga'rage *nm inv* garage

ga'ran|te *nmf* guarantor. **~'tire** *vt* guarantee; (*rendersi garante*) vouch for; (*assicurare*) assure. **~'zia** *nf* guarantee; **in ~zia** under guarantee

gar'ba|re *vi* like; **non mi garba** I don't like it. **~to** *a* courteous

'garbo *nm* courtesy; (*grazia*) grace; **con ~** graciously

gareggi'are *vi* compete

garga'nella *nf* **a ~** from the bottle

garga'rismo *nm* gargle; **fare i gargarismi** gargle

ga'rofano *nm* carnation

gar'rire *vi* chirp

'garza *nf* gauze

gar'zone *nm* boy. **~ di stalla** stable-boy

gas *nm inv* gas; **dare ~** *Auto* accelerate; **a tutto ~** flat out. **~ lacrimogeno** tear gas. **~ di scarico** *pl* exhaust fumes

gas'dotto *nm* natural gas pipeline

ga'solio *nm* diesel oil

ga'sometro *nm* gasometer

gas'sa|re *vt* aerate; (*uccidere col gas*) gas. **~ato** *a* gassy. **~oso, -a** *a* gassy; (*bevanda*) fizzy ● *nf* lemonade

'gastrico *a* gastric. **ga'strite** *nf* gastritis

gastro'no|mia *nf* gastronomy. **~'nomico, -a** *a* gastronomic. **ga'stronomo, -a** *nmf* gourmet

'gatta *nf* **una ~ da pelare** a headache

gatta'buia *nf hum* clink

gat'tino, -a *nmf* kitten

'gatto, -a *nmf* cat. **~ delle nevi** snowmobile

gat'toni adv on all fours

ga'vetta nf mess tin; **fare la ~** rise through the ranks

gay a inv gay

'gazza nf magpie

gaz'zarra nf racket

gaz'zella nf gazelle; Auto police car

gaz'zetta nf gazette

gaz'zosa nf clear lemonade

'geco nm gecko

ge'la|re vt/i freeze. **~ta** nf frost

gela't|aio, -a nmf ice-cream seller; (negozio) ice-cream shop. **~e'ria** nf ice-cream parlour. **~i'era** nf ice-cream maker

gela'ti|na nf gelatine; (dolce) jelly. **~na di frutta** fruit jelly. **~'noso** a gelatinous

ge'lato a frozen ● nm ice-cream

'gelido a freezing

'gelo nm (freddo intenso) freezing cold; (brina) frost; fig chill

ge'lone nm chilblain

gelosa'mente adv jealously

gelo'sia nf jealousy. **ge'loso** a jealous

'gelso nm mulberry[-tree]

gelso'mino nm jasmine

gemel'laggio nm twinning

ge'mello, -a a & nmf twin; (di polsino) cuff-link; **Gemelli** pl Astr Gemini sg

'gem|ere vi groan; (tubare) coo. **~ito** nm groan

'gemma nf gem; Bot bud

'gene nm gene

genealo'gia nf genealogy

gene'ra|le[1] a general; **spese ~i** overheads

gene'rale[2] nm Mil general

generalità nf (qualità) generality, general nature; **~** pl (dati personali) particulars

generaliz'za|re vt generalize. **~zi'one** nf generalization. **general'mente** adv generally

gene'ra|re vt give birth to; (causare) breed; Techn generate. **~'tore** nm Techn generator. **~zi'one** nf generation

'genere nm kind; Biol genus; Gram gender; (letterario, artistico) genre; (prodotto) product; **il ~ umano** mankind; **in ~** generally. **generi** pl **alimentari** provisions

generica'mente adv generically. **ge'nerico** a generic; **medico generico** general practitioner

'genero nm son-in-law

generosità nf generosity. **gene'roso** a generous

'genesi nf genesis

ge'netico, -a a genetic ● nf genetics sg

gen'giva nf gum

geni'ale a ingenious; (congeniale) congenial

'genio nm genius; **andare a ~** to be to one's taste. **~ civile** civil engineering. **~** |militare| Engineers

geni'tale a genital. **genitali** nmpl genitals

geni'tore nm parent

gen'naio nm January

'Genova nf Genoa

gen'taglia nf rabble

'gente nf people pl

gen'til|e a kind; **G~e Signore** Dear Sir. **genti'lezza** nf kindness; **per gentilezza** (per favore) please. **~'mente** adv kindly. **~u'omo** (pl **~u'omini**) nm gentleman

genu'ino a genuine; (cibo, prodotto) natural

geogra'fia nf geography. **geo'grafico** a geographical. **ge'ografo** nm geographer

geolo'gia nf geology. **geo'logico** a geological. **ge'ologo, -a** nmf geologist

ge'ometra nmf surveyor

geome'tria nf geometry. **geo'metrico** a geometric[al]

ge'ranio nm geranium

gerar'chia nf hierarchy. **ge'rarchico** a hierarchic[al]

ge'rente nm manager ● nf manageress

'gergo nm slang; (di professione ecc) jargon

geria'tria nf geriatrics sg

Ger'mania nf Germany

'germe nm germ; (fig: principio) seed

germogli'are vi sprout. **ger'moglio** nm sprout

gero'glifico nm hieroglyph

'gesso nm chalk; (Med, scultura) plaster

gestazi'one nf gestation

gestico'lare vi gesticulate

gesti'one nf management

ge'stir|e vi manage. **~si** vr budget one's time and money

'gesto nm gesture; (azione pl nf **gesta**) deed

ge'store nm manager

Gesù nm Jesus. **~ bambino** baby Jesus

gesu'ita nm Jesuit

get'ta|re *vt* throw; (*scagliare*) fling; (*emettere*) spout; *Techn, fig* cast; **~re via** throw away. **~rsi** *vr* throw oneself; **~rsi in** (*fiume:*) flow into. **~ta** *nf* throw; *Techn* casting

get'tito *nm* ~ fiscale tax revenue

'getto *nm* throw; (*di liquidi, gas*) jet; a **~ continuo** in a continuous stream; **di ~** straight off

getto'nato *a* (*canzone*) popular. **get'tone** *nm* token; (*per giochi*) counter

ghettiz'zare *vt* ghettoize. **'ghetto** *nm* ghetto

ghe'pardo *nm* cheetah

ghiacci'aio *nm* glacier

ghiacci'a|re *vt/i* freeze. **~to** *a* frozen; (*freddissimo*) ice-cold

ghi'acci|o *nm* ice; *Auto* black ice. **~'olo** *nm* icicle; (*gelato*) ice lolly

ghi'aia *nf* gravel

ghi'anda *nf* acorn

ghi'andola *nf* gland

ghigliot'tina *nf* guillotine

ghi'gnare *vi* sneer. **'ghigno** *nm* sneer

ghi'ot|to *a* greedy, gluttonous; (*appetitoso*) appetizing. **~'tone, -a** *nmf* glutton. **~tone'ria** *nf* (*qualità*) gluttony; (*cibo*) tasty morsel

ghir'landa *nf* (*corona*) wreath; (*di fiori*) garland

'ghiro *nm* dormouse; **dormire come un ~** sleep like a log

'ghisa *nf* cast iron

già *adv* already; (*un tempo*) formerly; **~!** indeed!; **~ da ieri** since yesterday

gi'acca *nf* jacket. **~ a vento** windcheater

giacché *conj* since

giac'cone *nm* jacket

gia'cere *vi* lie

giaci'mento *nm* deposit. **~ di petrolio** oil deposit

gia'cinto *nm* hyacinth

gi'ada *nf* jade

giaggi'olo *nm* iris

giagu'aro *nm* jaguar

gial'lastro *a* yellowish

gi'allo *a & nm* yellow; (*libro*) ~ thriller

Giap'pone *nm* Japan. **giappo'nese** *a & nmf* Japanese

giardi'n|aggio *nm* gardening. **~i'ere, -a** *nmf* gardener ●*nf Auto* estate car; (*sottaceti*) pickles *pl*

giar'dino *nm* garden. **~ d'infanzia** kindergarten. **~ pensile** roof-garden. **~ zoologico** zoo

giarretti'era *nf* garter

giavel'lotto *nm* javelin

gi'gan|te *a* gigantic ●*nm* giant. **~'tesco** *a* gigantic

gigantogra'fia *nf* blow-up

'giglio *nm* lily

gilè *nm inv* waistcoat

gin *nm inv* gin

gineco'lo'gia *nf* gynaecology. **~'logico** *a* gynaecological. **gine'cologo, -a** *nmf* gynaecologist

gi'nepro *nm* juniper

gi'nestra *nf* broom

gingil'larsi *vr* fiddle; (*perder tempo*) potter. **gin'gillo** *nm* plaything; (*ninnolo*) knick-knack

gin'nasio *nm* (*scuola*) ≈ grammar school

gin'nast|a *nmf* gymnast. **~ica** *nf* gymnastics; (*esercizi*) exercises *pl*

ginocchi'ata *nf* **prendere una ~** bang one's knee

gi'nocchi|o *nm* (*pl nm* **ginocchi** *o nf* **ginocchia**) knee; **in ~o** on one's knees; **mettersi in ~o** kneel down; (*per supplicare*) go down on one's knees; **al ~o** (*gonna*) knee-length. **~'oni** *adv* kneeling

gio'ca|re *vt/i* play; (*giocherellare*) toy; (*d'azzardo*) gamble; (*puntare*) stake; (*ingannare*) trick. **~rsi la carriera** throw one's career away. **~'tore, ~'trice** *nmf* player; (*d'azzardo*) gambler

gio'cattolo *nm* toy

giocherel'l|are *vi* toy; (*nervosamente*) fiddle. **~one** *a* skittish

gi'oco *nm* game; (*di bambini, Techn*) play; (*d'azzardo*) gambling; (*scherzo*) joke; (*insieme di pezzi ecc*) set; **essere in ~** be at stake; **fare il doppio ~ con** qcno double-cross sb

giocoli'ere *nm* juggler

gio'coso *a* playful

gi'ogo *nm* yoke

gi'oia *nf* joy; (*gioiello*) jewel; (*appellativo*) sweetie

gioiell'e|ria *nf* jeweller's [shop]. **~i'ere, -a** *nmf* jeweller; (*negozio*) jeweller's. **gio'iello** *nm* jewel; **gioielli** *pl* jewellery

gioi'oso *a* joyous

gio'ire *vi* **~ per** rejoice at

Gior'dania *nf* Jordan

giorna'laio, -a *nmf* newsagent, newsdealer

gior'nale *nm* [news]paper; (*diario*) journal. **~ di bordo** logbook. **~ radio** news bulletin

giornali'ero *a* daily ● *nm* (*per sciare*) day pass

giorna'lino *nm* comic

giorna'lis·mo *nm* journalism. **~ta** *nmf* journalist

giornal'mente *adv* daily

gior'nata *nf* day; **in ~** today; **vivere alla ~** live from day to day

gi'orno *nm* day; **al ~** per day; **al ~ d'oggi** nowadays; **di ~** by day; **in pieno ~** in broad daylight; **un ~, si, un ~ no** every other day

gi'ostra *nf* merry-go-round

giova'mento *nm* **trarre ~ da** derive benefit from

gi'ova|ne *a* young; (*giovanile*) youthful ● *nm* youth, young man ● *nf* girl, young woman. **~'nile** *a* youthful. **~'notto** *nm* young man

gio'var|e *vi* **~e a** be useful to; (*far bene*) be good for. **~si** *vr* **~si di** avail oneself of

giovedì *nm inv* Thursday. **~ grasso** *last Thursday before Lent*

gioventù *nf* youth; (*i giovani*) young people *pl*

giovi'ale *a* jovial

giovi'nezza *nf* youth

gira'dischi *nm inv* record-player

gi'raffa *nf* giraffe; *Cinema* boom

gi'randola *nf* (*fuoco d'artificio*) Catherine wheel; (*giocattolo*) windmill; (*banderuola*) weathercock

gi'rar|e *vt* turn; (*andare intorno, visitare*) go round; *Comm* endorse; *Cinema* shoot ● *vi* turn; (*aerei, uccelli:*) circle; (*andare in giro*) wander; **far ~re le scatole a qcno** *fam* drive sb round the twist; **~re al largo** steer clear. **~rsi** *vr* turn [round]; **mi gira la testa** I feel dizzy. **~ta** *nf* turn; *Comm* endorsement; (*in macchina ecc*) ride; **fare una ~ta** (*a piedi*) go for a walk; (*in macchina*) go for a ride

girar'rosto *nm* spit

gira'sole *nm* sunflower

gira'volta *nf* spin; *fig* U-turn

gi'rello *nm* (*per bambini*) babywalker; *Culin* topside

gi'revole *a* revolving

gi'rino *nm* tadpole

'giro *nm* turn; (*circolo*) circle; (*percorso*) round; (*viaggio*) tour; (*passeggiata*) short walk; (*in macchina*) drive; (*in bicicletta*) ride; (*circolazione di denaro*) circulation; **nel ~ di un mese** within a month; **prendere in ~ qcno** pull sb's leg; **senza giri di parole** without beat-

ing about the bush; **a ~ di posta** by return mail. **~ d'affari** *Comm* turnover. **~ [della] manica** armhole. **giri** *pl* **al minuto** rpm. **~ turistico** sightseeing tour. **~ vita** waist measurement

giro'collo *nm* choker; **a ~** crewneck

gi'rone *nm* round

gironzo'lare *vi* wander about

giro'tondo *nm* ring-a-ring-o'-roses

girova'gare *vi* wander about. **gi'ro·vago** *nm* wanderer

'gita *nf* trip; **andare in ~** go on a trip. **~ scolastica** school trip. **gi'tante** *nmf* tripper

giù *adv* down; (*sotto*) below; (*dabbasso*) downstairs; **a testa in ~** (*a capofitto*) headlong; **essere ~** be down; (*di salute*) be run down; **~ di corda** down; **~ di lì, su per ~** more or less; **non andare ~ a qcno** stick in sb's craw

gi'ub·ba *nf* jacket; *Mil* tunic. **~'botto** *nm* bomber jacket, jerkin

giudi'care *vt* judge; (*ritenere*) consider

gi'udice *nm* judge. **~ conciliatore** justice of the peace. **~ di gara** umpire. **~ di linea** linesman

giu'dizi|o *nm* judg[e]ment; (*opinione*) opinion; (*senno*) wisdom; (*processo*) trial; (*sentenza*) sentence; **mettere ~o** become wise. **~'oso** *a* sensible

gi'ugno *nm* June

giu'menta *nf* mare

gi'unco *nm* reed

gi'ungere *vi* arrive; **~ a** (*riuscire*) succeed in ● *vt* (*unire*) join

gi'ungla *nf* jungle

gi'unta *nf* addition; *Mil* junta; **per ~** in addition. **~ comunale** district council

gi'unto *pp di* **giungere** ● *nm* *Mech* joint

giun'tura *nf* joint

giuo'care, giuo'co = **giocare, gioco**

giura'mento *nm* oath; **prestare ~** take the oath

giu'ra|re *vt/i* swear. **~to, -a** *a* sworn ● *nmf* juror

giu'ria *nf* jury

giu'ridico *a* legal

giurisdizi'one *nf* jurisdiction

giurispru'denza *nf* jurisprudence

giu'rista *nmf* jurist

giustifi'ca|re *vt* justify. **~zi'one** *nf* justification

giu'stizi|a *nf* justice. **~'are** *vt* execute. **~'ere** *nm* executioner

gi'usto *a* just, fair; (*adatto*) right;

(*esatto*) exact ● *nm* (*uomo retto*) just man; (*cosa giusta*) right ● *adv* exactly; ~ ora just now

glaci'ale *a* glacial

gla'diolo *nm* gladiolus

'glassa *nf* Culin icing

gli *def art mpl* (*before vowel and s + consonant, gn, ps, z*) the; *vedi* **il** ● *pron* (*a lui*) [to] him; (*a esso*) [to] it; (*a loro*) [to] them

glice'rina *nf* glycerine

'glicine *nm* wisteria

gli'e|lo, -a *pron* [to] him/her/them; (*forma di cortesia*) [to] you; ~ **chiedo** I'll ask him/her/them/you; **gliel'ho prestato** I've lent it to him/her/them/you. ~**ne** *pron* (*di ciò*) [of] it; ~**ne ho dato un po'** I gave him/her/them/you some

glo'bal|e *a* global; *fig* overall. ~'**mente** *adv* globally

'globo *nm* globe. ~ **oculare** eyeball. ~ **terrestre** globe

'globulo *nm* globule; *Med* corpuscle. ~ **rosso** red cell, red corpuscle

'glori|a *nf* glory. ~'**arsi** *vr* ~**arsi di** be proud of. ~'**oso** *a* glorious

glos'sario *nm* glossary

glu'cosio *nm* glucose

'gluteo *nm* buttock

'gnomo *nm* gnome

'gnorri *nm* **fare lo ~** play dumb

'gobb|a *nf* hump. ~**o, -a** *a* hunchbacked ● *nmf* hunchback

'goccia *nf* drop; (*di sudore*) bead; **è stata l'ultima ~a** it was the last straw. ~**o'lare** *vi* drip. ~**o'lio** *nm* dripping

go'der|e *vi* (*sessualmente*) come; ~**e di** enjoy. ~**sela** have a good time. ~**si** *vr* ~**si qcsa** enjoy sth

godi'mento *nm* enjoyment

goffa'mente *adv* awkwardly. **'goffo** *a* awkward

'gola *nf* throat; (*ingordigia*) gluttony; *Geog* gorge; (*di camino*) flue; **avere mal di ~** have a sore throat; **far ~ a qcno** tempt sb

golf *nm inv* jersey; *Sport* golf

'golfo *nm* gulf

golosità *nf inv* greediness; (*cibo*) tasty morsel. **go'loso** *a* greedy

'golpe *nm inv* coup

gomi'tata *nf* nudge

'gomito *nm* elbow; **alzare il ~** raise one's elbow

go'mitolo *nm* ball

'gomma *nf* rubber; (*colla, da mastica-*

re) gum; (*pneumatico*) tyre. ~ **da masticare** chewing gum

gommapi'uma *nf* foam rubber

gom'mista *nm* tyre specialist

gom'mone *nm* [rubber] dinghy

gom'moso *a* chewy

'gondol|a *nf* gondola. ~**i'ere** *nm* gondolier

gonfa'lone *nm* banner

gonfi'abile *a* inflatable

gonfi'ar|e *vi* swell ● *vt* blow up; pump up (*pneumatico*); (*esagerare*) exaggerate. ~**si** *vr* swell; (*acque*) rise. **'gonfio** *a* swollen; (*pneumatico*) inflated; **a gonfie vele** splendidly. **gonfi'ore** *nm* swelling

gongo'la|nte *a* overjoyed. ~**re** *vi* be overjoyed

'gonna *nf* skirt. ~ **pantalone** culottes *pl*

'gonzo *nm* simpleton

gorgheggi'are *vi* warble. **gor'gheggio** *nm* warble

'gorgo *nm* whirlpool

gorgogli'are *vi* gurgle

go'rilla *nm inv* gorilla; (*guardia del corpo*) bodyguard, minder

'gotico *a & nm* Gothic

gover'nante *nf* housekeeper

gover'na|re *vt* govern; (*dominare*) rule; (*dirigere*) manage; (*curare*) look after. ~'**tivo** *a* government. ~'**tore** *nm* governor

go'verno *nm* government; (*dominio*) rule; **al ~** in power

gracchi'are *vi* caw; (*fig: persona*) screech

graci'dare *vi* croak

'gracile *a* delicate

gra'dasso *nm* braggart

gradata'mente *adv* gradually

gradazi'one *nf* gradation. ~ **alcoolica** alcohol[ic] content

gra'devol|e *a* agreeable. ~'**mente** *adv* pleasantly, agreeably

gradi'mento *nm* liking; **indice di ~** *Radio, TV* popularity rating; **non è di mio ~** it's not to my liking

gradi'nata *nf* flight of steps; (*di stadio*) stand; (*di teatro*) tiers *pl*

gra'dino *nm* step

gra'di|re *vt* like; (*desiderare*) wish. ~**to** *a* pleasant; (*bene accetto*) welcome

'grado *nm* degree; (*rango*) rank; **di buon ~** willingly; **essere in ~ di fare qcsa** be in a position to do sth; (*essere capace a*) be able to do sth

gradu'ale *a* gradual

gradu'a|re *vt* graduate. ~**to** *a* graded;

(*provvisto di scala graduata*) graduated
●*nm Mil* noncommissioned officer.
~'toria *nf* list. ~zi'one *nf* graduation
'graffa *nf* clip; (*segno grafico*) brace
graf'fetta *nf* staple
graffi'a|re *vt* scratch. ~'tura *nf*
scratch
'graffio *nm* scratch
gra'fia *nf* [hand]writing; (*ortografia*)
spelling
'grafic|a *nf* graphics; ~a pubblici-
taria commercial art. ~a'mente *adv* in
graphics, graphically. ~o *a* graphic
●*nm* graph; (*persona*) graphic designer
gra'migna *nf* weed
gram'matic|a *nf* grammar. ~'cale *a*
grammatical
'grammo *nm* gram[me]
gran *a vedi* grande
'grana *nf* grain; (*formaggio*) parmesan; (*fam: seccatura*) trouble; (*fam: soldi*) readies *pl*
gra'naio *nm* barn
gra'nat|a *nf* Mil grenade; (*frutto*)
pomegranate. ~i'ere *nm* Mil grenadier
Gran Bre'tagna *nf* Great Britain
'granchio *nm* crab; (*fig: errore*) blunder; prendere un ~ make a blunder
grandango'lare *nm* wide-angle lens
'grande (*a volte gran*) *a* (*ampio*) large;
(*grosso*) big; (*alto*) tall; (*largo*) wide; (*fig:
senso morale*) great; (*grandioso*) grand;
(*adulto*) grown-up; ho una gran fame
I'm very hungry; fa un gran caldo it is
very hot; in ~ on a large scale; in gran
parte to a great extent; non è un gran
che it is nothing much; un gran ballo a
grand ball ●*nmf* (*persona adulta*)
grown-up; (*persona eminente*) great
man/woman. ~ggi'are *vi* ~ggiare su
tower over; (*darsi arie*) show off
gran'dezza *nf* greatness; (*ampiezza*)
largeness; (*larghezza*) width, breadth;
(*dimensione*) size; (*fasto*) grandeur;
(*prodigalità*) lavishness; a ~ naturale
life-size
grandi'nare *vi* hail; grandina it's
hailing. 'grandine *nf* hail
grandiosità *nf* grandeur. grandi'oso
a grand
gran'duca *nm* grand duke
gra'nello *nm* grain; (*di frutta*) pip
gra'nita *nf* crushed ice drink
gra'nito *nm* granite
'grano *nm* grain; (*frumento*) wheat
gran'turco *nm* maize
'granulo *nm* granule
'grappa *nf* grappa; (*morsa*) cramp

'grappolo *nm* bunch. ~ d'uva bunch
of grapes
gras'setto *nm* bold [type]
gras'sezza *nf* fatness; (*untuosità*)
greasiness
'gras|so *a* fat; (*cibo*) fatty; (*unto*)
greasy; (*terreno*) rich; (*grossolano*)
coarse ●*nm* fat; (*sostanza*) grease.
~'soccio *a* plump
'grata *nf* grating. gra'tella,
gra'ticola *nf Culin* grill
gra'tifica *nf* bonus. ~zi'one *nf* satisfaction
gratis *adv* free
grati'tudine *nf* gratitude. 'grato *a*
grateful; (*gradito*) pleasant
gratta'capo *nm* trouble
grattaci'elo *nm* skyscraper
grat'tar|e *vt* scratch; (*raschiare*)
scrape; (*grattugiare*) grate; (*fam: rubare*) pinch ●*vi* grate. ~si *vr* scratch oneself
grat'tugi|a *nf* grater. ~'are *vt* grate
gratuita'mente *adv* free [of charge].
gra'tuito *a* free [of charge];
(*ingiustificato*) gratuitous
gra'vare *vt* burden ●*vi* ~ su weigh on
'grave *a* (*pesante*) heavy; (*serio*) serious; (*difficile*) hard; (*voce, suono*) low;
(*fonetica*) grave; essere ~ (*gravemente
ammalato*) be seriously ill. ~'mente
adv seriously, gravely
gravi'danza *nf* pregnancy. 'gravido *a*
pregnant
gravità *nf* seriousness; *Phys* gravity
gravi'tare *vi* gravitate
gra'voso *a* onerous
'grazi|a *nf* grace; (*favore*) favour; *Jur*
pardon; entrare nelle ~e di qcno get
into sb's good books. ~'are *vt* pardon
'grazie *int* thank you!, thanks!; ~
mille! many thanks!, thanks a lot!
grazi'oso *a* charming; (*carino*) pretty
'Grec|ia *nf* Greece. g~o, -a *a & nmf*
Greek
'gregge *nm* flock
'greggio *a* raw ●*nm* (*petrolio*) crude
[oil]
grembi'ale, grembi'ule *nm* apron
'grembo *nm* lap; (*utero*) womb; *fig*
bosom
gre'mi|re *vt* pack. ~rsi *vr* become
crowded (di with). ~to *a* packed
'gretto *a* stingy; (*di vedute ristrette*)
narrow-minded
'grezzo *a* = greggio

gri'dare *vi* shout; (*di dolore*) scream; (*animale:*) cry ● *vt* shout

'grido *nm* (*pl m* gridi *o f* grida) shout, cry; (*di animale*) cry; l'ultimo ~ the latest fashion; scrittore di ~ celebrated writer

'grigio *a* & *nm* grey

'griglia *nf* grill; alla ~ grilled

gril'letto *nm* trigger

'grillo *nm* cricket; (*fig: capriccio*) whim

grimal'dello *nm* picklock

'grinfia *nf fig* clutch

grin'ta *nf* grit. ~'toso *a* determined

'grinza *nf* wrinkle; (*di stoffa*) crease

grip'pare *vi Mech* seize

gris'sino *nm* bread-stick

'gronda *nf* eaves *pl*

gron'daia *nf* gutter

gron'dare *vi* pour; (*essere bagnato fradicio*) be dripping

'groppa *nf* back

'groppo *nm* knot; avere un ~ alla gola have a lump in one's throat

gros'sezza *nf* size; (*spessore*) thickness

gros'sista *nmf* wholesaler

'grosso *a* big, large; (*spesso*) thick; (*grossolano*) coarse; (*grave*) serious ● *nm* big part; (*massa*) bulk; farla grossa do a stupid thing

grossola'nità *nf inv* (*qualità*) coarseness; (*di errore*) grossness; (*azione, parola*) coarse thing. ~'lano *a* coarse; (*errore*) gross

grosso'modo *adv* roughly

'grotta *nf* cave, grotto

grot'tesco *a* & *nm* grotesque

grovi'era *nmf* Gruyère

gro'viglio *nm* tangle; *fig* muddle

gru *nf inv* (*uccello, edilizia*) crane

'gruccia *nf* (*stampella*) crutch; (*per vestito*) hanger

gru'gnire *vi* grunt. ~'to *nm* grunt

'grugno *nm* snout

'grullo *a* silly

'grumo *nm* clot; (*di farina ecc*) lump. gru'moso *a* lumpy

'gruppo *nm* group; (*comitiva*) party. ~ sanguigno blood group

gruvi'era *nmf* Gruyère

'gruzzolo *nm* nest-egg

guada'gnare *vt* earn; gain (*tempo, forza ecc*). gua'dagno *nm* gain; (*profitto*) profit; (*entrate*) earnings *pl*

gu'ado *nm* ford; passare a ~ ford

gua'ina *nf* sheath; (*busto*) girdle

gu'aio *nm* trouble; che ~! that's just brilliant!; essere nei guai be in a fix;

guai a te se lo tocchi! don't you dare touch it!

gua'ire *vi* yelp. ~to *nm* yelp

gu'anci|a *nf* cheek. ~ ale *nm* pillow

gu'anto *nm* glove. guanti *pl* (da boxe) boxing gloves

guarda'coste *nm inv* coastguard

guarda'linee *nm inv Sport* linesman

guar'dar|e *vt* look at; (*osservare*) watch; (*badare a*) look after; (*dare su*) look out on ● *vi* look; (*essere orientato verso*) face. ~si *vr* look at oneself; ~si da beware of; (*astenersi*) refrain from

guarda'rob|a *nm inv* wardrobe; (*di locale pubblico*) cloakroom. ~i'ere, -a *nmf* cloakroom attendant

gu'ardia *nf* guard; (*poliziotto*) policeman; (*vigilanza*) watch; essere di ~ be on guard; (*medico:*) be on duty; fare la ~ a keep guard over; mettere in ~ qcno warn sb; stare in ~ be on one's guard. ~ carceraria prison warder. ~ del corpo bodyguard, minder. ~ di finanza ≈ Fraud Squad. ~ forestale forest ranger. ~ medica duty doctor

guardi'ano, -a *nmf* caretaker. ~ notturno night watchman

guar'dingo *a* cautious

guardi'ola *nf* gatekeeper's lodge

guarigi'one *nf* recovery

gua'rire *vt* cure ● *vi* recover; (*ferita:*) heal [up]

guarnigi'one *nf* garrison

guar'nir|e *vt* trim; *Culin* garnish. ~zi'one *nf* trimming; *Culin* garnish; *Mech* gasket

guasta'feste *nmf inv* spoilsport

gua'star|e *vt* spoil; (*rovinare*) ruin; break (*meccanismo*). ~si *vr* spoil; (*andare a male*) go bad; (*tempo:*) change for the worse; (*meccanismo:*) break down. gu'asto *a* broken; (*ascensore, telefono*) out of order; (*auto*) broken down; (*cibo, dente*) bad ● *nm* breakdown; (*danno*) damage

guazza'buglio *nm* muddle

guaz'zare *vi* wallow

gu'ercio *a* cross-eyed

gu'err|a *nf* war; (*tecnica bellica*) warfare. ~ fredda Cold War. ~ mondiale world war. ~afon'daio *nm* warmonger. ~eggi'are *vi* wage war. guer'resco *a* (*di guerra*) war; (*bellicoso*) warlike. ~i'ero *nm* warrior

guer'rigli|a *nf* guerrilla warfare. ~'ero, -a *nmf* guerrilla

'gufo *nm* owl

'guglia *nf* spire

gu'id|a *nf* guide; *(direzione)* guidance; *(comando)* leadership; *Auto* driving; *(tappeto)* runner; **~a a destra/sinistra** right-/left-hand drive. **~a telefonica** telephone directory. **~a turistica** tourist guide. **gui'dare** *vt* guide; *Auto* drive; steer *(nave).* **~a'tore, ~a'trice** *nmf* driver

guin'zaglio *nm* leash

guiz'zare *vi* dart; *(luce:)* flash. **gu'izzo** *nm* dart; *(di luce)* flash

'guscio *nm* shell

gu'stare *vt* taste ●*vi* like. **'gusto** *nm* taste; *(piacere)* liking; **mangiare di gusto** eat heartily; **prenderci gusto** come to enjoy it, develop a taste for it. **gu'stoso** *a* tasty; *fig* delightful

guttu'rale *a* guttural

....

Hh

....

habitué *nmf inv* regular [customer]

ham'burger *nm inv* hamburger

'handicap *nm inv* *Sport* handicap

handicap'pa|re *vt* handicap. **~to, -a** *nmf* disabled person ●*a* disabled

'harem *nm inv* harem

'hascisc *nm* hashish

henné *nm* henna

hi-fi *nm inv* hi-fi

'hippy *a* hippy

'hockey *nm* hockey. **~ su ghiaccio** ice hockey. **~ su prato** hockey

hollywoodi'ano *a* Hollywood *attrib*

ho'tel *nm inv* hotel

....

Ii

....

i *def art mpl* the; *vedi* **il**

i'ato *nm* hiatus

iber'na|re *vi* hibernate. **~zi'one** *nf* hibernation

i'bisco *nm* hibiscus

'ibrido *a & nm* hybrid

'iceberg *nm inv* iceberg

i'cona *nf* icon

Id'dio *nm* God

i'dea *nf* idea; *(opinione)* opinion; *(ideale)* ideal; *(indizio)* inkling; *(piccola quantità)* hint; *(intenzione)* intention; **cambiare ~** change one's mind; **neanche per ~!** not on your life!; **chiarirsi le idee** get one's ideas straight. **~ fissa** obsession

ide'a|le *a & nm* ideal. **~ lista** *nmf* idealist. **~ liz'zare** *vt* idealize

ide'a|re *vt* conceive. **~ tore, ~ trice** *nmf* originator

'idem *adv* the same

i'dentico *a* identical

identifi'cabile *a* identifiable

identifi'ca|re *vt* identify. **~zi'one** *nf* identification

identi'kit *nm inv* identikit®

identità *nf inv* identity

ideolo'gia *nf* ideology. **ideo'logico** *a* ideological

i'dilli|co *a* idyllic. **~o** *nm* idyll

idi'oma *nm* idiom. **idio'matico** *a* idiomatic

idi'ota *a* idiotic ●*nmf* idiot. **idio'zia** *nf* *(cosa stupida)* idiocy

idola'trare *vt* worship

idoleggi'are *vt* idolize. **'idolo** *nm* idol

idoneità *nf* suitability; *Mil* fitness; **esame di ~** qualifying examination. **i'doneo** *a* idoneo *a* suitable for; *Mil* fit for

i'drante *nm* hydrant

idra'ta|re *vt* hydrate; *(cosmetico:)* moisturize. **~nte** *a (crema, gel)* moisturizing. **~zi'one** *nf* moisturizing i'draulico *a* hydraulic ● *nm* plumber

'idrico *a* water *attrib*

idrocar'buro *nm* hydrocarbon

idroe'lettrico *a* hydroelectric

i'drofilo *a* *vedi* cotone

i'drogeno *nm* hydrogen

idromas'saggio *nm* (*sistema*) whirlpool bath

idrovo'lante *nm* seaplane

i'ella *nf* bad luck; portare ~ be bad luck. iel'lato *a* plagued by bad luck

i'ena *nf* hyena

i'eri *adv* yesterday; ~ l'altro, l'altro ~ the day before yesterday; ~ pomeriggio yesterday afternoon; il giornale di ~ yesterday's paper

ietta'tore, -'trice *nmf* jinx. ~ tura *nf* (*sfortuna*) bad luck

igi'en|e *nf* hygiene. ~ico *a* hygienic. igie'nista *nmf* hygienist

i'gnaro *a* unaware

i'gnobile *a* base; (*non onorevole*) dishonourable

igno'ran|te *a* ignorant ● *nmf* ignoramus. ~za *nf* ignorance

igno'rare *vt* (*non sapere*) be unaware of; (*trascurare*) ignore

i'gnoto *a* unknown

il *def art m* the; il latte fa bene milk is good for you; il signor Magnetti Mr Magnetti; il dottor Piazza Dr Piazza; ha il naso storto he has a bent nose; mettiti il cappello put your hat on; il lunedì on Mondays; il 1986 1986; 5 000 lire il chilo 5,000 lire the *o* a kilo

'ilar|e *a* merry. ~ità *nf* hilarity

illazi'one *nf* inference

illecita'mente *adv* illicitly. il'lecito *a* illicit

ille'gal|e *a* illegal. ~ità *nf* illegality. ~'mente *adv* illegally

illeg'gibile *a* illegible; (*libro*) unreadable

illegittimità *nf* illegitimacy. ille'gittimo *a* illegitimate

il'leso *a* unhurt

illette'rato, -a *a* & *nmf* illiterate

illi'bato *a* chaste

illimi'tato *a* unlimited

illivi'dire *vt* bruise ● *vi* (*per rabbia*) turn livid

il'logico *a* illogical

il'luder|e *vt* deceive. ~si *vr* deceive oneself

illumi'nar|e *vt* light [up]; *fig* enlighten; ~re a giorno floodlight. ~rsi *vr* light up. ~zi'one *nf* lighting; *fig* enlightenment

Illumi'nismo *nm* Enlightenment

illusi'one *nf* illusion; farsi illusioni delude oneself

illusio'nis|mo *nm* conjuring. ~ta *nmf* conjurer

il'lu|so, -a *pp di* illudere ● *a* deluded ● *nmf* day-dreamer. ~'sorio *a* illusory

illu'stra|re *vt* illustrate. ~'tivo *a* illustrative. ~ tore, ~ 'trice *nmf* illustrator. ~zi'one *nf* illustration

il'lustre *a* distinguished

imbacuc'ca|re *vt*, ~rsi *vr* wrap up. ~to *a* wrapped up

imbal'la|ggio *nm* packing. ~re *vt* pack; *Auto* race

imbalsa'ma|re *vt* embalm; stuff (*animale*). ~to *a* embalmed; (*animale*) stuffed

imbam'bolato *a* vacant

imbaraz'zante *a* embarrassing

imbaraz'za|re *vt* embarrass; (*ostacolare*) encumber. ~to *a* embarrassed

imba'razzo *nm* embarrassment; (*ostacolo*) hindrance; trarre qcno d'~ help sb out of a difficulty; avere l'~ della scelta be spoilt for choice. ~ di stomaco indigestion

imbarca'dero *nm* landing-stage

imbar'ca|re *vt* embark; (*fam: rimorchiare*) score. ~rsi *vr* embark, go on board. ~zi'one *nf* boat. ~zione di salvataggio lifeboat. im'barco *nm* embarkation, boarding; (*banchina*) landing-stage

imba'sti|re *vt* tack; *fig* sketch. ~ tura *nf* tacking, basting

im'battersi *vr* ~ in run into

imbat'tibile *a* unbeatable. ~uto *a* unbeaten

imbavagli'are *vt* gag

imbec'cata *nf* *Theat* prompt

imbe'cille *a* stupid ● *nmf* *Med* imbecile

imbel'lire *vt* embellish

im'berbe *a* beardless; *fig* inexperienced

imbestia'li|re *vi*, ~rsi *vr* fly into a rage. ~to *a* enraged

im'bever|e *vt* imbue (di with). ~si *vr* absorb

imbe'vibile *a* undrinkable. ~uto *a* ~uto di (*acqua*) soaked in; (*nozioni*) imbued with

imbian'c|are *vt* whiten ● *vi* turn white. ~hino *nm* house painter

imbizzar'ri|re *vi*, ~si *vr* become restless; (*arrabbiarsi*) become angry

imboc'ca|re *vt* feed; (*entrare*) enter;

fig prompt. ~'tura *nf* opening; (*ingresso*) entrance; (*Mus: di strumento*) mouthpiece. im'bocco *nm* entrance

imbo'scar|e *vt* hide. ~si *vr Mil* shirk military service

imbo'scata *nf* ambush

imbottigli'a|re *vt* bottle. ~rsi *vr* get snarled up in a traffic jam. ~to *a* (*vino, acqua*) bottled

imbot'ti|re *vt* stuff; pad (*giacca*); *Culin* fill. ~rsi *vr* ~rsi di (*fig: di pasticche*) stuff oneself with. ~ta *nf* quilt. ~to *a* (*spalle*) padded; (*cuscino*) stuffed; (*panino*) filled. ~'tura *nf* stuffing; (*di giacca*) padding; *Culin* filling

imbracci'are *vt* shoulder (*fucile*)

imbra'nato *a* clumsy

imbrat'tar|e *vt* mark. ~si *vr* dirty oneself

imbroc'car|e *vt* hit; ~la giusta hit the nail on the head

imbrogli'a|re *vt* muddle; (*raggirare*) cheat. ~rsi *vr* get tangled; (*confondersi*) get confused. im'broglio *nm* tangle; (*pasticcio*) mess; (*inganno*) trick. ~'one, ~a *nmf* cheat

imbronci'a|re *vi*, ~rsi *vr* sulk. ~to *a* sulky

imbru'nire *vi* get dark; all'~ at dusk

imbrut'tire *vt* make ugly ● *vi* become ugly

imbu'care *vt* post, mail; (*nel biliardo*) pot

imbur'rare *vt* butter

im'buto *nm* funnel

imi'ta|re *vt* imitate. ~'tore, ~'trice *nmf* imitator, impersonator. ~zi'one *nf* imitation

immaco'lato *a* immaculate, spotless

immagazzi'nare *vt* store

immagi'na|re *vt* imagine; (*supporre*) suppose; s'immagini! imagine that!. ~rio *a* imaginary. ~zi'one *nf* imagination. im'magine *nf* image; (*rappresentazione, idea*) picture

imman'cabil|e *a* unfailing. ~'mente *adv* without fail

im'mane *a* huge; (*orribile*) terrible

imma'nente *a* immanent

immangi'abile *a* inedible

immatrico'la|re *vt* register. ~rsi *vr* (*studente:*) matriculate. ~zi'one *nf* registration; (*di studente*) matriculation

immaturità *nf* immaturity. imma'turo *a* unripe; (*persona*) immature; (*precoce*) premature

immedesi'ma|rsi *vr* ~rsi in identify oneself with. ~zi'one *nf* identification

immedia'ta'mente *adv* immediately. ~'tezza *nf* immediacy. immedi'ato *a* immediate

immemo'rabile *a* immemorial

immens'a'mente *adv* enormously. ~ità *nf* immensity. im'menso *a* immense

immensu'rabile *a* immeasurable

im'merger|e *vt* immerse. ~si *vr* plunge; (*sommergibile:*) dive; ~si in immerse oneself in

immeri'tato *a* undeserved. ~evole *a* undeserving

immersi'one *nf* immersion; (*di sommergibile*) dive. im'merso *pp di* immergere

immi'gra|nte *a* & *nmf* immigrant. ~re *vi* immigrate. ~to, -a *nmf* immigrant. ~zi'one *nf* immigration

immi'nen|te *a* imminent. ~za *nf* imminence

immischi'ar|e *vt* involve. ~si *vr* ~si in meddle in

immis'sario *nm* tributary

immissi'one *nf* insertion

im'mobile *a* motionless

im'mobili *nmpl* real estate. ~'are *a* società ~are building society, savings and loan *Am*

immobili'tà *nf* immobility. ~z'zare *vt* immobilize; *Comm* tie up

immo'desto *a* immodest

immo'lare *vt* sacrifice

immondez'zaio *nm* rubbish tip. immon'dizia *nf* filth; (*spazzatura*) rubbish. im'mondo *a* filthy

immo'ral|e *a* immoral. ~ità *nf* immorality

immorta'lare *vt* immortalize. immor'tale *a* immortal

immoti'vato *a* (*gesto*) unjustified

im'mun|e *a* exempt; *Med* immune. ~ità *nf* immunity. ~iz'zare *vt* immunize. ~izzazi'one *nf* immunization

immunodefici'enza *nf* immunodeficiency

immuso'nir|si *vr* sulk. ~to *a* sulky

immu'tabile *a* unchangeable. ~to *a* unchanging

impacchet'tare *vt* wrap up

impacci'a|re *vt* hamper; (*disturbare*) inconvenience; (*imbarazzare*) embarrass. ~to *a* embarrassed; (*goffo*) awkward. im'paccio *nm* embarrassment; (*ostacolo*) hindrance; (*situazione difficile*) awkward situation

im'pacco *nm* compress

impadro'nirsi vr ~ **di** take possession of; (fig: imparare) master

impa'gabile a priceless

impagi'na|re vt paginate. ~**zi'one** nf pagination

impagli'are vt stuff ⟨animale⟩

impa'lato a fig stiff

impalca'tura nf scaffolding; fig structure

impalli'dire vi turn pale; (fig: perdere d'importanza) pale into insignificance

impa'nare vt Culin roll in breadcrumbs

impanta'narsi vr get bogged down

impape'rarsi vr, **impappi'narsi** vr falter, stammer

impa'rare vt learn

impareggi'abile a incomparable

imparen'ta|rsi vr ~ **con** become related to. ~**to** a related

'impari a unequal; ⟨dispari⟩ odd

impar'tire vt impart

imparzi'al|e a impartial. ~**ità** nf impartiality

impas'sibile a impassive

impa'sta|re vt Culin knead; blend ⟨colori⟩. ~**tura** nf kneading. **im'pasto** nm Culin dough; (miscuglio) mixture

impastic'carsi vr pop pills

im'patto nm impact

impau'ri|re vt frighten. ~**si** vr become frightened

im'pavido a fearless

impazi'en|te a impatient; ~**te di fare qcsa** eager to do sth. ~'**tirsi** vr lose patience. ~**za** nf impatience

impaz'zata nf **all'~** at breakneck speed

impaz'zire vi go mad; ⟨maionese:⟩ separate; **far ~ qcno** drive sb mad; ~ **per** be crazy about; **da ~** ⟨mal di testa⟩ blinding

impec'cabile a impeccable

impedi'mento nm hindrance; ⟨ostacolo⟩ obstacle

impe'dire vt ~ **di** prevent from; (impacciare) hinder; (ostruire) obstruct; ~ **a qcno di fare qcsa** prevent sb [from] doing sth

impe'gna|re vt (dare in pegno) pawn; (vincolare) bind; (prenotare) reserve; (assorbire) take up. ~**rsi** vr apply oneself; ~**rsi a fare qcsa** commit oneself to doing sth. ~'**tiva** nf referral. ~'**tivo** a binding; ⟨lavoro⟩ demanding. ~**ato** a engaged; Pol committed. **im'pegno** nm engagement; Comm commitment; (zelo) care

impel'lente a pressing

impene'trabile a impenetrable

impen'na|rsi vr ⟨cavallo:⟩ rear; fig bristle. ~**ta** nf ⟨di prezzi⟩ sharp rise; ⟨di cavallo⟩ rearing; ⟨di moto⟩ wheelie

impen'sabile a unthinkable. ~**to** a unexpected

impensie'ri|re vt, ~**si** vr worry

impe'rante a prevailing. ~**re** vi reign; ⟨tendenza:⟩ prevail, hold sway

impera'tivo a & nm imperative

impera'tore, -'trice nm emperor ●nf empress

impercet'tibile a imperceptible

imperdo'nabile a unforgivable

imper'fe|tto a & nm imperfect. ~**zi'one** nf imperfection

imperi'al|e a imperial. ~**lismo** nm imperialism. ~**lista** a imperialist. ~**listico** a imperialistic

imperi'oso a imperious; (impellente) urgent

impe'rizia nf lack of skill

imperme'abile a waterproof ●nm raincoat

imperni'ar|e vt pivot; (fondare) base. ~**si** vr ~**si su** be based on

im'pero nm empire; (potere) rule

imperscru'tabile a inscrutable

imperso'nale a impersonal

imperso'nare vt personify; (interpretare) act [the part of]

imper'territo a undaunted

imperti'nen|te a impertinent. ~**za** nf impertinence

impertur'ba|bile a imperturbable. ~**to** a unperturbed

imperver'sare vi rage

im'pervio a inaccessible

'impet|o nm impetus; (impulso) impulse; (slancio) transport. ~**u'oso** a impetuous; ⟨vento⟩ blustering

impet'tito a stiff

impian'tare vt install; set up ⟨azienda⟩

impi'anto nm plant; (sistema) system; (operazione) installation. ~ **radio** Auto car stereo system

impia'strare vt plaster; (sporcare) dirty. **impi'astro** nm poultice; (persona noiosa) bore; (pasticcione) cack-handed person

impic'car|e vt hang. ~**si** vr hang oneself

impicci'|arsi vr meddle. **im'piccio** nm hindrance; (seccatura) bother. ~'**one, -a** nmf nosey parker

impie'ga|re vt employ; (usare) use; spend ⟨tempo, denaro⟩; Fin invest;

l'autobus ha ~to un'ora it took the bus an hour. **~rsi** *vr* get [oneself] a job

impiega'tizio *a* clerical

impie'gato, -a *nmf* employee. **~ di banca** bank clerk. **impi'ego** *nm* employment; (*posto*) job; *Fin* investment

impieto'sir|e *vt* move to pity. **~si** *vr* be moved to pity

impie'trito *a* petrified

impigli'ar|e *vt* entangle. **~si** *vr* get entangled

impi'grir|e *vt* make lazy. **~si** *vr* get lazy

impla'cabile *a* implacable

impli'ca|re *vt* implicate; (*sottintendere*) imply. **~rsi** *vr* become involved. **~zi'one** *nf* implication

implicita'mente *adv* implicitly. **im'plicito** *a* implicit

implo'ra|re *vt* implore. **~zi'one** *nf* entreaty

impolve'ra|re *vt* cover with dust. **~rsi** *vr* get covered with dust. **~to** *a* dusty

imponde'rabile *a* imponderable; (*causa, evento*) unpredictable

impo'nen|te *a* imposing. **~za** *nf* impressiveness

impo'nibile *a* taxable ● *nm* taxable income

impopo'lar|e *a* unpopular. **~ità** *nf* unpopularity

im'por|re *vt* impose; (*ordinare*) order. **~si** *vr* assert oneself; (*aver successo*) be successful; **~si di** (*prefiggersi*) set oneself the task of

impor'tan|te *a* important ● *nm* important thing. **~za** *nf* importance

impor'ta|re *vt* *Comm*, *Comput* import; (*comportare*) cause ● *vi* matter; (*essere necessario*) be necessary. **non ~!** it doesn't matter!;**non me ne ~ niente!** I couldn't care less!. **~ tore, -'trice** *nmf* importer. **~zi'one** *nf* importation; (*merce importata*) import

im'porto *nm* amount

importu'nare *vt* pester. **impor'tuno** *a* troublesome; (*inopportuno*) untimely

imposizi'one *nf* imposition; (*imposta*) tax

imposses'sarsi *vr* **~ di** seize

impos'sibile *a* impossible ● *nm*fare **l'~e** do absolutely all one can. **~ità** *nf* impossibility

im'posta[1] *nf* tax; **~ sul reddito** income tax; **~ sul valore aggiunto** value added tax

im'posta[2] *nf* (*di finestra*) shutter

impo'sta|re *vt* (*progettare*) plan; (*basare*) base; *Mus* pitch; (*imbucare*) post, mail; set out (*domanda, problema*). **~zi'one** *nf* planning; (*di voce*) pitching

im'posto *pp di* **imporre**

impo'store, -a *nmf* impostor

impo'ten|te *a* powerless; *Med* impotent. **~za** *nf* powerlessness; *Med* impotence

impove'rir|e *vt* impoverish. **~si** *vr* become poor

imprati'cabile *a* impracticable; (*strada*) impassable

imprati'chir|e *vt* train. **~si** *vr*=**~si in** *o* a get practice in

impre'ca|re *vi* curse. **~zi'one** *nf* curse

impreci's|abile *a* indeterminable. **~ato** *a* indeterminate. **~i'one** *nf* inaccuracy.**impre'ciso** *a* inaccurate

impre'gna|re *vt* impregnate; (*imbevere*) soak; *fig* imbue. **~si** *vr* become impregnated with

imprendi'tor|e, -'trice *nmf* entrepreneur. **~i'ale** *a* entrepreneurial

imprepa'rato *a* unprepared

im'presa *nf* undertaking; (*gesta*) exploit; (*azienda*) firm

impre'sario *nm* impresario; (*appaltatore*) contractor

imprescin'dibile *a* inescapable

impressio'nabile *a* impressionable. **~nte** *a* impressive; (*spaventoso*) frightening

impressio'nare *vt* impress; (*spaventare*) frighten; expose (*foto*). **~o'narsi** *vr* be affected; (*spaventarsi*) be frightened. **~'one** *nf* impression; (*sensazione*) sensation; (*impronta*) mark; **far ~one a qcno** upset sb

impressio'nismo *nm* impressionism. **~ta** *nmf* impressionist

im'presso *pp di* **imprimere** ● *a* printed

impre'stare *vt* lend

impreve'dibile *a* unforeseeable; (*persona*) unpredictable

imprevi'dente *a* improvident

impre'visto *a* unforeseen ● *nm* unforeseen event; **salvo imprevisti** all being well

imprigiona'mento *nm* imprisonment. **~'nare** *vt* imprison

im'primere *vt* impress; (*stampare*) print; (*comunicare*) impart

impro'babile *a* unlikely, improbable. **~ità** *nf* improbability

improdut'tivo *a* unproductive

im'pronta nf impression; fig mark. ~ **digitale** fingerprint. ~ **del piede** footprint

impro'perio nm insult; **improperi** pl abuse sg

im'proprio a improper

improvvisa'mente adv suddenly

improvvi'sa|re vt/i improvise. ~**rsi** vr turn oneself into a. ~**ta** nf surprise. ~**to** a (discorso) unrehearsed. ~**zi'one** nf improvisation

improv'viso a sudden; **all'~** unexpectedly

impru'den|te a imprudent. ~**za** nf imprudence

impu'gna|re vt grasp; Jur contest. ~'**tura** nf grip; (manico) handle

impulsività nf impulsiveness. **impul'sivo** a impulsive

im'pulso nm impulse; **agire d'~** act on impulse

impune'mente adv with impunity. **impu'nito** a unpunished

impun'tarsi vr dig one's heels in

impun'tura nf stitching

impurità nf inv impurity. **im'puro** a impure

impu'tabile a attributable (a to)

impu'ta|re vt attribute; (accusare) charge. ~**to**, **-a** nmf accused. ~**zi'one** nf charge

imputri'dire vi rot

in prep in; (moto a luogo) to; (su) on; (entro) within; (mezzo) by; (con materiale) made of; **essere in casa/ufficio** be at home/at the office; **in mano/tasca** in one's hand/pocket; **andare in Francia/campagna** go to France/the country; **salire in treno** get on the train; **versa la birra nel bicchiere** pour the beer into the glass; **in alto** up there; **in giornata** within the day; **nel 1997** in 1997; **una borsa in pelle** a bag made of leather, a leather bag; **in macchina** (viaggiare, venire) by car; **in contanti** [in] cash; **in vacanza** on holiday; **di giorno in giorno** from day to day; **se fossi in te** if I were you; **siamo in sette** there are seven of us

inabbor'dabile a unapproachable

i'nabil|e a incapable; (fisicamente) unfit. ~**ità** nf incapacity

inabi'tabile a uninhabitable

inacces'sibile a inaccessible; (persona) unapproachable

inaccet'tabil|e a unacceptable. ~**ità** nf unacceptability

inacer'bi|re vt embitter; exacerbate (rapporto). ~**si** vr grow bitter

inaci'dir|e vt turn sour. ~**si** vr go sour; (persona:) become embittered

ina'datto a unsuitable

inadegu'ato a inadequate

inadempi'ente nmf defaulter. ~'**mento** nm non-fulfilment

inaffer'rabile a elusive

ina'la|re vt inhale. ~'**tore** nm inhaler. ~**zi'one** nf inhalation

inalbe'rar|e vt hoist. ~**si** vr (cavallo:) rear [up]; (adirarsi) lose one's temper

inalte'ra|bile a unchangeable; (colore) fast. ~**to** a unchanged

inami'da|re vt starch. ~**to** a starched

inammis'sibile a inadmissible

inamovi'bile a irremovable

inani'mato a inanimate; (senza vita) lifeless

inappa'ga|bile a unsatisfiable. ~**to** a unfulfilled

inappel'labile a final

inappe'tenza nf lack of appetite

inappli'cabile a inapplicable

inappun'tabile a faultless

inar'ca|re vt arch; raise (sopracciglia). ~**si** vr (legno:) warp; (ripiano:) sag; (linea:) curve

inari'dir|e vt parch; empty of feelings (persona). ~**si** vr dry up; (persona:) become empty of feelings

inarti'co'lato a inarticulate

inaspettata'mente adv unexpectedly. **inaspet'tato** a unexpected

inaspri'mento nm (di carattere) embitterment; (di conflitto) worsening

ina'sprir|e vt embitter. ~**si** vr become embittered

inattac'cabile a unassailable; (irreprensibile) irreproachable

inatten'dibile a unreliable. **inat'teso** a unexpected

inattività nf inactivity. **inat'tivo** a inactive

inattu'abile a impracticable

inau'dito a unheard of

inaugu'rale a inaugural; **viaggio ~** maiden voyage

inaugu'ra|re vt inaugurate; open (mostra); unveil (statua); christen (lavastoviglie). ~**zi'one** nf inauguration; (di mostra) opening; (di statua) unveiling

inavver't'enza nf inadvertence. ~**ita'mente** adv inadvertently

incagli'ar|e vi ground ● vt hinder. ~**si** vr run aground

incalco'labile *a* incalculable

incal'lirsi *vr* grow callous; ⟨*abituarsi*⟩ become hardened. **~to** *a* callous; ⟨*abituato*⟩ hardened

incal'zante *a* ⟨*ritmo*⟩ driving; ⟨*richiesta*⟩ urgent. **~re** *vt* pursue; *fig* press

incame'rare *vt* appropriate

incammi'nare *vt* get going; ⟨*fig: guidare*⟩ set off. **~si** *vr* set out

incana'lare *vt* canalize; *fig* channel. **~si** *vr* converge on

incande'scente *a* incandescent; ⟨*discussione*⟩ burning. **~za** *nf* incandescence

incan'tare *vt* enchant. **~rsi** *vr* stand spellbound; ⟨*incepparsi*⟩ jam. **~'tore,** **~'trice** *nm* enchanter ● *nf* enchantress

incan'tesimo *nm* spell

incan'tevole *a* enchanting

in'canto *nm* spell; *fig* delight; ⟨*asta*⟩ auction; **come per ~** as if by magic

incanu'tire *vt* turn white. **~to** *a* white

inca'pace *a* incapable. **~ità** *nf* incapability

incapo'nirsi *vr* be set

incap'pare *vi* **~ in** run into

incappucci'arsi *vr* wrap up

incapricci'arsi *vr* **~ di** take a fancy to

incapsu'lare *vt* seal; crown ⟨*dente*⟩

incarce'rare *vt* imprison. **~zi'one** *nf* imprisonment

incari'care *vt* charge. **~rsi** *vr* take upon oneself; **me ne incarico io** I will see to it. **~to, -a** *a* in charge ● *nmf* representative. **in'carico** *nm* charge; **per incarico di** on behalf of

incar'nare *vt* embody. **~rsi** *vr* become incarnate. **~zi'one** *nf* incarnation

incarta'mento *nm* documents *pl.* **incar'tare** *vt* wrap [in paper]

incasi'nato *a fam* ⟨*vita*⟩ screwed up; ⟨*stanza*⟩ messed up

incas'sare *vt* pack; *Mech* embed; box in ⟨*mobile, frigo*⟩; ⟨*riscuotere*⟩ cash; take ⟨*colpo*⟩. **~to** *a* set; ⟨*fiume*⟩ deeply embanked. **in'casso** *nm* collection; ⟨*introito*⟩ takings *pl*

incasto'nare *vt* set. **~'tura** *nf* setting. **~to** *a* embedded; ⟨*anello*⟩ inset ⟨**di** with⟩

inca'strare *vt* fit in; ⟨*fam: in situazione*⟩ corner. **~si** *vr* fit. **in'castro** *nm* joint; **a incastro** ⟨*pezzi*⟩ interlocking

incate'nare *vt* chain

incatra'mare *vt* tar

in'cattivire *vt* turn nasty

in'cauto *a* imprudent

inca'vare *vt* hollow out. **~to** *a* hollow. **~'tura** *nf* hollow. **in'cavo** *nm* hollow; ⟨*scanalatura*⟩ groove

incavo'larsi *vr fam* get shirty. **~to** *a fam* shirty

incendi'are *vt* set fire to; *fig* inflame. **~si** *vr* catch fire. **~io, -a** *a* incendiary; ⟨*fig: discorso*⟩ inflammatory; ⟨*fig: bellezza*⟩ sultry ● *nmf* arsonist. **in'cendio** *nm* fire. **incendio doloso** arson

incene'rire *vt* burn to ashes; ⟨*cremare*⟩ cremate. **~rsi** *vr* be burnt to ashes. **~'tore** *nm* incinerator

in'censo *nm* incense

incensu'rato *a* blameless; **essere ~** *Jur* have a clean record

incenti'vare *vt* motivate. **incen'tivo** *nm* incentive

incen'trarsi *vr* **~ su** centre on

incep'pare *vt* block; *fig* hamper. **~si** *vr* jam

ince'rata *nf* oilcloth

incerot'tato *a* with a plaster on

incer'tezza *nf* uncertainty. **in'certo** *a* uncertain ● *nm* uncertainty

inces'sante *a* unceasing. **~'mente** *adv* incessantly

in'cesto *nm* incest. **~u'oso** *a* incestuous

in'cetta *nf* buying up; **fare ~ di** stockpile

inchi'esta *nf* investigation

inchi'nare *vt*, **~si** *vr* bow. **in'chino** *nm* bow; ⟨*di donna*⟩ curtsy

inchio'dare *vt* nail; nail down ⟨*coperchio*⟩; **~ a letto** ⟨*malattia:*⟩ confine to bed

inchi'ostro *nm* ink

inciam'pare *vi* stumble; **~ in** ⟨*imbattersi*⟩ run into. **inci'ampo** *nm* hindrance

inciden'tale *a* incidental

inci'dente *nm* ⟨*episodio*⟩ incident; ⟨*infortunio*⟩ accident. **~za** *nf* incidence

in'cidere *vt* cut; ⟨*arte*⟩ engrave; ⟨*registrare*⟩ record ● *vi* **~ su** ⟨*gravare*⟩ weigh upon

in'cinta *a* pregnant

incipi'ente *a* incipient

incipri'are *vt* powder. **~si** *vr* powder one's face

in'circa *adv* **all'~** more or less

incisi'one *nf* incision; ⟨*arte*⟩ engraving; ⟨*acquaforte*⟩ etching; ⟨*registrazione*⟩ recording

inci'sivo *a* incisive ● *nm* ⟨*dente*⟩ incisor

in'ciso *nm per* ~ incidentally

incita'mento *nm* incitement. **inci'ta·re** *vt* incite

inci'vil|e *a* uncivilized; (*maleducato*) impolite. ~tà *nf* barbarism; (*maleducazione*) rudeness

incle'men|te *a* harsh. ~za *nf* harshness

incli'nabile *a* reclining

incli'na|re *vt* tilt ● *vi* ~re a be inclined to. ~rsi *vr* list. ~to *a* tilted; (*terreno*) sloping. ~zi'one *nf* slope, inclination. in'cline *a* inclined

in'clu|dere *vt* include; (*allegare*) enclose. ~si'one *nf* inclusion. ~'sivo *a* inclusive. ~so *pp* di **includere** ● *a* included; (*compreso*) inclusive; (*allegato*) enclosed

incoe'ren|te *a* (*contraddittorio*) inconsistent. ~za *nf* inconsistency

in'cognit|a *nf* unknown quantity. ~o *a* unknown ● *nm* in ~o incognito

incol'lar|e *vt* stick; (*con colla liquida*) glue. ~si *a* stick to; ~si a qcno stick close to sb

incolle'ri|rsi *vr* lose one's temper. ~to *a* enraged

incol'mabile *a* (*differenza*) unbridgeable; (*vuoto*) unfillable

incolon'nare *vt* line up

inco'lore *a* colourless

incol'pare *vt* blame

in'colto *a* uncultivated; (*persona*) uneducated

in'colume *a* unhurt

incom'ben|te *a* impending. ~za *nf* task

in'combere *vi* ~ su hang over; ~ a (*spettare*) be incumbent on

incominci'are *vt/i* begin, start

incomo'dar|e *vt* inconvenience. ~si *vr* trouble. in'comodo *a* uncomfortable; (*inopportuno*) inconvenient ● *nm* inconvenience

incompa'rabile *a* incomparable

incompa'tibil|e *a* incompatible. ~ità *nf* incompatibility

incompe'ten|te *a* incompetent. ~za *nf* incompetence

incompi'uto *a* unfinished

incom'pleto *a* incomplete

incompren'si|bile *a* incomprehensible. ~'one *nf* lack of understanding; (*malinteso*) misunderstanding. **incom·'preso** *a* misunderstood

inconce'pibile *a* inconceivable

inconcili'abile *a* irreconcilable

inconclu'dente *a* inconclusive; (*persona*) ineffectual

incondizio|nata'mente *adv* uncondi-tionally. ~'nato *a* unconditional

inconfes'sabile *a* unmentionable

inconfon'dibile *a* unmistakable

inconfu'tabile *a* irrefutable

incongru'ente *a* inconsistent

in'congruo *a* inadequate

inconsa'pevol|e *a* unaware; (*inconscio*) unconscious. ~'mente *adv* unwit-tingly

inconscia'mente *adv* unconsciously. in'conscio *a & nm* *Psych* un-conscious

inconsi'sten|te *a* insubstantial; (*notizia ecc*) unfounded. ~za *nf* (*di ragionamento, prove*) flimsiness

inconso'labile *a* inconsolable

inconsu'eto *a* unusual

incon'sulto *a* rash

incontami'nato *a* uncontaminated

inconte'nibile *a* irrepressible

inconten'tabile *a* insatiable; (*esigente*) hard to please

inconte'stabile *a* indisputable

inconti'nen|te *a* incontinent. ~za *nf* incontinence

incon'trar|e *vt* meet; encounter, meet with (*difficoltà*). ~si *vr* meet (con qcno sb)

incon'trario: all'~ *adv* the other way around; (*in modo sbagliato*) the wrong way around

incontra'sta|bile *a* incontrovertible. ~to *a* undisputed

in'contro *nm* meeting; *Sport* match. ~ al vertice summit meeting ● *prep* ~ a towards; andare ~ a qn go to meet sb; *fig* meet sb half way

inconveni'ente *nm* drawback

incoraggi|a'mento *nm* encourage-ment. ~'ante *a* encouraging. ~'are *vt* encourage

incornici'a|re *vt* frame. ~'tura *nf* framing

incoro'na|re *vt* crown. ~zi'one *nf* coronation

incorpo'rar|e *vt* incorporate; (*mescolare*) blend. ~si *vr* blend; (*territori:*) merge

incorreg'gibile *a* incorrigible

in'correre *vt* ~ in incur; ~ nel pericolo di... run the risk of...

incorrut'tibile *a* incorruptible

incosci'en|te *a* unconscious; (*irresponsabile*) reckless ● *nmf* irresponsible person. **~za** *nf* unconsciousness; recklessness

inco'stan|te *a* changeable; *(persona)* fickle. **~za** *nf* changeableness; *(di persona)* fickleness

incostituzio'nale *a* unconstitutional

incre'dibile *a* unbelievable, incredible

incredulità *nf* incredulity. **in'credulo** *a* incredulous

incremen'tare *vt* increase; *(intensificare)* step up. **incre'mento** *nm* increase. **incremento demografico** population growth

incresci'oso *a* regrettable

incre'spare *vt* ruffle; wrinkle *(tessuto)*; make frizzy *(capelli)*; **~e la fronte** frown. **~si** *vr (acqua:)* ripple; *(tessuto:)* wrinkle; *(capelli:)* go frizzy

incrimi'nare *vt* indict; *fig* incriminate. **~zi'one** *nf* indictment

incri'na|re *vt* crack; *fig* affect *(amicizia)*. **~rsi** *vr* crack; *(amicizia:)* be affected. **~'tura** *nf* crack

incroci'a|re *vt* cross ● *vi* Naut, Aeron cruise. **~rsi** *vr* cross. **~'tore** *nm* cruiser

in'crocio *nm* crossing; *(di strade)* crossroads *sg*

incrol'labile *a* indestructible

incro'sta|re *vt* encrust. **~zi'one** *nf* encrustation

incuba'trice *nf* incubator. **~zi'one** *nf* incubation

'incubo *nm* nightmare

in'cudine *nf* anvil

incu'rabile *a* incurable

incu'rante *a* careless

incurio'sir|e *vt* make curious. **~si** *vr* become curious

incursi'one *nf* raid. **~ aerea** air raid

incurva'mento *nm* bending

incur'va|re *vt*, **~rsi** *vr* bend. **~'tura** *nf* bending

in'cusso *pp di* **incutere**

incusto'dito *a* unguarded

in'cutere *vt* arouse; **~ spavento a qcno** strike fear into sb

'indaco *nm* indigo

indaffa'rato *a* busy

inda'gare *vt/i* investigate

in'dagine *nf* research; *(giudiziaria)* investigation. **~ di mercato** market survey

indebi'tar|e *vt*, **~si** *vr* get into debt

in'debito *a* undue

indeboli'mento *nm* weakening

indebo'lir|e *vt*, **~si** *vr* weaken

inde'cen|te *a* indecent. **~za** *nf* indecency; *(vergogna)* disgrace

indeci'frabile *a* indecipherable

indecisi'one *nf* indecision. **inde'ciso** *a* undecided

inde'fesso *a* tireless

indefi'ni|bile *a* indefinable. **~to** *a* indefinite

indefor'mabile *a* crushproof

in'degno *a* unworthy

inde'lebile *a* indelible

indeli'ca'tezza *nf* indelicacy; *(azione)* tactless act. **indeli'cato** *a* indiscreet; *(grossolano)* indelicate

indemoni'ato *a* possessed

in'denne *a* uninjured; *(da malattia)* unaffected. **~ità** *nf inv* allowance; *(per danni)* compensation. **~ità di trasferta** travel allowance. **~iz'zare** *vt* compensate. **inden'nizzo** *nm* compensation

indero'gabile *a* binding

indescri'vibile *a* indescribable

indeside'ra|bile *a* undesirable. **~to** *a (figlio, ospite)* unwanted

indetermi'na|bile *a* indeterminable. **~'tezza** *nf* vagueness. **~to** *a* indeterminate

'Indi|a *nf* India. **i~'ano, -a** *a & nm/f* Indian; **in fila i~ana** in single file

indiavo'lato *a* possessed; *(vivace)* wild

indi'ca|re *vt* show, indicate; *(col dito)* point at; *(far notare)* point out; *(consigliare)* advise. **~'tivo** *a* indicative ● *nm* Gram indicative. **~'tore** *nm* indicator; Techn gauge; *(prontuario)* directory. **~zi'one** *nf* indication; *(istruzione)* direction

'indice *nm (dito)* forefinger; *(lancetta)* pointer; *(di libro, statistica)* index; *(fig: segno)* sign

indi'cibile *a* inexpressible

indietreggi'are *vi* draw back; Mil retreat

indi'etro *adv* back, behind; **all'~** backwards; **avanti e ~** back and forth; **essere ~** be behind; *(mentalmente)* be backward; *(con pagamenti)* be in arrears; *(di orologio)* be slow; **fare marcia ~** reverse; **rimandare ~** send back; **rimanere ~** be left behind; **torna ~!** come back!

indi'feso *a* undefended; *(inerme)* helpless

indiffe'ren|te *a* indifferent; **mi è ~te** it is all the same to me. **~za** *nf* indifference

indigeno | inesattezza

108

in'digeno, -a *a* indigenous ● *nmf* native

indi'gen|te *a* needy. ~**za** *nf* poverty

indigesti'one *nf* indigestion. **indi'gesto** *a* indigestible

indi'gna|re *vt* make indignant. ~**rsi** *vr* be indignant. ~**to** *a* indignant. ~**zi'one** *nf* indignation

indimenti'cabile *a* unforgettable

indipen'den|te *a* independent. ~**temente** *adv* independently; ~**temente dal tempo** regardless of the weather, whatever the weather. ~**za** *nf* independence

in'dire *vt* announce

indiretta'mente *adv* indirectly. **indi'retto** *a* indirect

indiriz'zare *vt* address; *(mandare)* send; *(dirigere)* direct. ~**si** *vr* direct one's steps. **indi'rizzo** *nm* address; *(direzione)* direction

indisci'plina *nf* lack of discipline. ~**'nato** *a* undisciplined

indi'scre|to *a* indiscreet. ~**zi'one** *nf* indiscretion

indiscrimi'nata'mente *adv* indiscriminately. ~**'nato** *a* indiscriminate

indi'scusso *a* unquestioned

indiscu'tibile *a* unquestionable. ~**'mente** *adv* unquestionably

indispen'sabile *a* essential, indispensable

indispet'tir|e *vt* irritate. ~**si** *vr* get irritated

indi'spo|rre *vt* antagonize. ~**sto** *pp di* **indisporre** ● *a* indisposed. ~**sizi'one** *nf* indisposition

indisso'lubile *a* indissoluble

indissolubil'mente *adv* indissolubly

indistin'guibile *a* indiscernible

indistinta'mente *adv* without exception. **indi'stinto** *a* indistinct

indistrut'tibile *a* indestructible

indistur'bato *a* undisturbed

in'divia *nf* endive

individu'a|le *a* individual. ~**'lista** *nmf* individualist. ~**lità** *nf* individuality. ~**re** *vt* individualize; *(localizzare)* locate; *(riconoscere)* single out

indi'viduo *nm* individual

indivi'sibile *a* indivisible. **indi'viso** *a* undivided

indizi'a|re *vt* throw suspicion on. ~**to, -a** *a* suspected ● *nmf* suspect. **in'dizio** *nm* sign; *Jur* circumstantial evidence

'indole *nf* nature

indo'len|te *a* indolent. ~**za** *nf* indolence

indolenzi'mento *nm* stiffness

indolen'zir|si *vr* go stiff. ~**to** *a* stiff

indo'lore *a* painless

indo'mani *nm* l'~ the following day

Indo'nesia *nf* Indonesia

indo'rare *vt* gild

indos'sa|re *vt* wear; *(mettere addosso)* put on. ~**tore**, ~**'trice** *nmf* model

in'dotto *pp di* **indurre**

indottri'nare *vt* indoctrinate

indovi'n|are *vt* guess; *(predire)* foretell. ~**ato** *a* successful; *(scelta)* well-chosen. ~**ello** *nm* riddle. **indo'vino, -a** *nmf* fortune-teller

indubbia'mente *adv* undoubtedly. **in'dubbio** *a* undoubted

indugi'ar|e *vi*, ~**si** *vr* linger. **in'dugio** *nm* delay

indul'gen|te *a* indulgent. ~**za** *nf* indulgence

in'dul|gere *vi* ~**gere a** indulge in. ~**to** *pp di* **indulgere** ● *nm Jur* pardon

indu'mento *nm* garment; **indumenti** *pl* clothes

induri'mento *nm* hardening

indu'rir|e *vt*, ~**si** *vr* harden

in'durre *vt* induce

in'dustri|a *nf* industry. ~**'ale** *a* industrial ● *nm* industrialist

industrializ'za|re *vt* industrialize. ~**to** *a* industrialized. ~**zi'one** *nf* industrialization

industrial'mente *adv* industrially

industri'ar|si *vr* try one's hardest. ~**'oso** *a* industrious

induzi'one *nf* induction

inebe'tito *a* stunned

inebri'ante *a* intoxicating, exciting

inecce'pibile *a* unexceptionable

i'nedia *nf* starvation

i'nedito *a* unpublished

ineffi'cace *a* ineffective

ineffici'en|te *a* inefficient. ~**za** *nf* inefficiency

inegualgli'abile *a* incomparable

inegu'ale *a* unequal; *(superficie)* uneven

inelut'tabile *a* inescapable

ine'rente *a* ~ concerning

i'nerme *a* unarmed; *fig* defenceless

inerpi'carsi *vr* ~ **su** clamber up; *(pianta:)* climb up

i'ner|te *a* inactive; *Phys* inert. ~**zia** *nf* inactivity; *Phys* inertia

inesat'tezza *nf* inaccuracy. **ine'satto**

a inaccurate; (*erroneo*) incorrect; (*non riscosso*) uncollected

inesau'ribile *a* inexhaustible

inesi'sten|te *a* non-existent. **~za** *nf* non-existence

ineso'rabile *a* inexorable

inesperi'enza *nf* inexperience. **ine-'sperto** *a* inexperienced

inespli'cabile *a* inexplicable

ine'sploso *a* unexploded

inespri'mibile *a* inexpressible

inesti'mabile *a* inestimable

inetti'tudine *nf* ineptitude. **i'netto** *a* inept; **inetto** *a* unsuited to

ine'vaso *a* (*pratiche*) pending; (*corrispondenza*) unanswered

inevi'tabile *a* inevitable. **~'mente** *adv* inevitably

i'nezia *nf* trifle

infagot'tare *vt* wrap up. **~si** *vr* wrap [oneself] up

infal'libile *a* infallible

infa'mare *vt* defame. **~'torio** *a* defamatory

in'fam|e *a* infamous; (*fam: orrendo*) awful, shocking. **~ia** *nf* infamy

infan'garsi *vr* get muddy

infan'tile *a* (*letteratura, abbigliamento*) children's; (*ingenuità*) childlike; *pej* childish

in'fanzia *nf* childhood; (*bambini*) children *pl*; **prima ~** infancy

infar'cire *vi* pepper (*discorso*) (**di** with)

infari'na|re *vt* flour; **~re di** sprinkle with. **~'tura** *nf fig* smattering

in'farto *nm* coronary

infasti'dire *vt* irritate. **~si** *vr* get irritated

infati'cabile *a* untiring

in'fatti *conj* as a matter of fact; (*veramente*) indeed

infatu'a|rsi *vr* become infatuated (**di** with). **~to** *a* infatuated. **~zi'one** *nf* infatuation

in'fausto *a* ill-omened

infe'condo *a* infertile

infe'del|e *a* unfaithful. **~tà** *nf* unfaithfulness; **~** *pl* affairs

infe'lic|e *a* unhappy; (*inappropriato*) unfortunate; (*cattivo*) bad. **~ità** *nf* unhappiness

infel'tri|rsi *vr* get matted. **~to** *a* matted

inferi'or|e *a* (*più basso*) lower; (*qualità*) inferior ● *nmf* inferior. **~ità** *nf* inferiority

inferme'ria *nf* infirmary; (*di nave*) sick-bay

infermi'er|a *nf* nurse. **~e** *nm* [male] nurse

infermità *nf* sickness. **~ mentale** mental illness. **in'fermo, -a** *a* sick ● *nmf* invalid

infer'nale *a* infernal; (*spaventoso*) hellish

in'ferno *nm* hell; **va all'~!** go to hell!

infero'cirsi *vr* become fierce

inferri'ata *nf* grating

infervo'rar|e *vt* arouse enthusiasm in. **~si** *vr* get excited

infe'stare *vt* infest

infet'tare *vt* infect. **~arsi** *vr* become infected. **~ivo** *a* infectious. **in'fetto** *a* infected. **infezi'one** *nf* infection

infiac'chir|e *vt/i*, **~si** *vr* weaken

infiam'mabile *a* [in]flammable

infiam'ma|re *vt* set on fire; *Med, fig* inflame. **~rsi** *vr* catch fire; *Med* become inflamed. **~zi'one** *nf Med* inflammation

in'fido *a* treacherous

infie'rire *vi* (*imperversare*) rage; **~ su** attack furiously

in'figger|e *vt* drive. **~si** *vr* **~si in** penetrate

infi'lar|e *vt* thread; (*mettere*) insert; (*indossare*) put on. **~si** *vr* slip on (*vestito*); **~si in** (*introdursi*) slip into

infil'tra|rsi *vr* infiltrate. **~zi'one** *nf* infiltration; (*d'acqua*) seepage; (*Med: iniezione*) injection

infil'zare *vt* pierce; (*infilare*) string; (*conficcare*) stick

'infimo *a* lowest

in'fine *adv* finally; (*insomma*) in short

infinità *nf* infinity; **un'~ di** masses of. **~'mente** *adv* infinitely. **infi'nito** *a* infinite; *Gram* infinitive ● *nm* infinite; *Gram* infinitive; *Math* infinity; **all'infinito** endlessly

infinocchi'are *vt fam* hoodwink

infischi'arsi *vr* **~ di** not care about; **me ne infischio** *fam* I couldn't care less

in'fisso *pp di* **infiggere** ● *nm* fixture; (*di porta, finestra*) frame

infit'tir|e *vt/i*, **~si** *vr* thicken

inflazi'one *nf* inflation

infles'sibile *a* inflexible. **~ità** *nf* inflexibility

inflessi'one *nf* inflexion

in'flig|**gere** *vt* inflict. **~tto** *pp di* **infliggere**

influ'en|te a influential. **~za** nf influence; Med influenza

influen'za|bile a (mente, opinione) impressionable. **~re** vt influence. **~to** a (malato) with the flu

influ'ire vi **~ su** influence

in'flusso nm influence

info'carsi vr catch fire; (viso:) go red; (discussione:) become heated

info'gnarsi vr fam get into a mess

infol'tire vi/t thicken

infon'dato a unfounded

in'fondere vt instil

infor'care vt fork up; get on (bici); put on (occhiali)

infor'male a informal

infor'ma|re vt inform. **~rsi** vr inquire (di about). **~ 'tivo** a informative.

infor'matic|a nf computing, IT. **~o** a computer attrib

infor'ma|tivo a informative. **infor'mato** a informed; **male informa** ill-informed. **~ 'tore, ~ 'trice** nmf (di polizia) informer. **~zi'one** nf information (solo sg); **un'~zione** a piece of information

in'forme a shapeless

infor'nare vt put into the oven

infortu'narsi vr have an accident.

infor'tu|nio nm accident. **~nio sul lavoro** industrial accident. **~ 'nistica** nf study of industrial accidents

infos'sa|rsi vr sink; (guance, occhi:) become hollow. **~to** a sunken, hollow

infradici'a|re vt drench. **~si** vr get drenched; (diventare marcio) rot

infra'dito nm inv (scarpa) flip-flop

in'frang|ere vt break; (in mille pezzi) shatter. **~ersi** vr break. **~ 'gibile** a unbreakable

in'franto pp di infrangere ●a shattered; (fig: cuore) broken

infra'rosso a infra-red

infrastrut'tura nf infrastructure

infrazi'one nf offence

infredda'tura nf cold

infreddo'li|rsi vr feel cold. **~to** a cold

infruttu'oso a fruitless

infuo'ca|re vt make red-hot. **~to** a burning

infu'ori adv **all'~** outwards; **all'~ di** except

infuri'a|re vi rage. **~rsi** vr fly into a rage. **~to** a blustering

infusi'one nf infusion. **in'fuso** pp di infondere ●nm infusion

Ing. abbr ingegnere

ingabbi'are vt cage; (fig: mettere in prigione) jail

ingaggi'are vt engage; sign up (calciatori ecc); begin (lotta, battaglia). **in'gaggio** nm engagement; (di calciatore) signing [up]

ingan'nar|e vt deceive; (essere infedele a) be unfaithful to. **~si** vr deceive oneself; **se non m'inganno** if I am not mistaken

ingan'nevole a deceptive. **in'ganno** nm deceit; (frode) fraud

ingarbugli'a|re vt entangle; (confondere) confuse. **~rsi** vr get entangled; (confondersi) become confused. **~to** a confused

inge'gnarsi vr do one's best

inge'gnere nm engineer. **ingegne'ria** nf engineering

in'gegno nm brains pl; (genio) genius; (abilità) ingenuity. **~sa'mente** adv ingeniously

ingegnosità nf ingenuity. **inge'gnoso** a ingenious

ingelo'sir|e vt make jealous. **~si** vr become jealous

in'gente a huge

ingenua'mente adv artlessly. **~ità** nf ingenuousness. **in'genuo** a ingenuous; (credulone) naïve

inge'renza nf interference

inge'rire vt swallow

inges'sa|re vt put in plaster. **~ 'tura** nf plaster

Inghil'terra nf England

inghiot'tire vt swallow

in'ghippo nm trick

ingial'li|re vi, **~rsi** vr turn yellow. **~to** a yellowed

ingigan'tir|e vt magnify ●vi, **~si** vr grow to enormous proportions

inginocchi'a|rsi vr kneel [down]. **~to** a kneeling. **~ 'toio** nm prie-dieu

ingioiel'larsi vr put on one's jewels

ingiù adv down; **all'~** downwards; **a testa ~** head downwards

ingi'un|gere vt order. **~zi'one** nf injunction. **~zione di pagamento** final demand

ingi'uri|a nf insult; (torto) wrong; (danno) damage. **~ 'are** vt insult; (fare un torto a) wrong. **~ 'oso** a insulting

ingiusta'mente adv unjustly, unfairly. **ingiu'stizia** nf injustice. **ingi'usto** a unjust, unfair

in'glese a English ●nm Englishman; (lingua) English ●nf Englishwoman

ingoi'are vt swallow

ingol'far|e *vt* flood ⟨*motore*⟩. ~si *vr fig* get involved; ⟨*motore:*⟩ flood

ingom'bra|nte *a* cumbersome; essere d'~ be in the way

in'gombro *nm* encumbrance; essere d'~ be in the way

ingor'digia *nf* greed. in'gordo *a* greedy

ingor'gar|e *vt* block. ~si *vr* be blocked [up]. in'gorgo *nm* blockage; ⟨*del traffico*⟩ jam

ingoz'zar|e *vt* gobble up; ⟨*nutrire eccessivamente*⟩ stuff; fatten ⟨*animali*⟩. ~si *vr* stuff oneself ⟨di with⟩

ingra'na|ggio *nm* gear; *fig* mechanism. ~re *vt* engage ● *vi* be in gear

ingrandi'mento *nm* enlargement

ingran'di|re *vt* enlarge; ⟨*esagerare*⟩ magnify. ~rsi *vr* become larger; ⟨*aumentare*⟩ increase

ingras'sar|e *vt* fatten up; *Mech* grease ● *vi*, ~si *vr* put on weight

ingrati'tudine *nf* ingratitude. in'grato *a* ungrateful; ⟨*sgradevole*⟩ thankless

ingrazi'arsi *vr* ingratiate oneself with

ingredi'ente *nm* ingredient

in'gresso *nm* entrance; ⟨*accesso*⟩ admittance; ⟨*sala*⟩ hall; ~ gratuito, libero admission free; vietato l'~ no entry; no admittance

ingros'sar|e *vt* make big; ⟨*gonfiare*⟩ swell ● *vi*, ~si *vr* grow big; ⟨*gonfiare*⟩ swell

in'grosso *adv* all'~ wholesale; ⟨*pressappoco*⟩ roughly

ingua'ribile *a* incurable

'inguine *nm* groin

ingurgi'tare *vt* gulp down

ini'bi|re *vt* inhibit; ⟨*vietare*⟩ forbid. ~to *a* inhibited. ~zi'one *nf* inhibition; ⟨*divieto*⟩ prohibition

iniet'tar|e *vt* inject. ~si *vr* ~si di sangue ⟨*occhi:*⟩ become bloodshot. iniezi'one *nf* injection

inimi'carsi *vr* make an enemy of. inimi'cizia *nf* enmity

inimi'tabile *a* inimitable

ininter'rotta'mente *adv* continuously. ~'rotto *a* continuous

iniquità *nf* iniquity. i'niquo *a* iniquitous

inizi'al|e *a & nf* initial. ~ mente *adv* initially

inizi'are *vt* begin; ⟨*avviare*⟩ open; ~ qcno a qcsa initiate sb in sth ● *vi* begin

inizia'tiva *nf* initiative; prendere l'~ take the initiative

inizi'a|to, -a *a* initiated ● *nmf* initiate; gli ~ti the initiated. ~ tore, ~ trice *nmf* initiator. ~zi'one *nf* initiation

i'nizio *nm* beginning, start; dare ~ a start; avere ~ get under way

innaffi'a|re *vt* water. ~ toio *nm* watering-can

innal'zar|e *vt* raise; ⟨*erigere*⟩ erect. ~si *vr* rise

innamo'ra|rsi *vr* fall in love ⟨di with⟩. ~ta *nf* girl-friend. ~to *a* in love ● *nm* boy-friend

in'nanzi *adv* ⟨*stato in luogo*⟩ in front; ⟨*di tempo*⟩ ahead; ⟨*avanti*⟩ forward; ⟨*prima*⟩ before; d'ora ~ from now on ● *prep* ⟨*prima*⟩ before; ~ a in front of. ~ tutto *adv* first of all; ⟨*soprattutto*⟩ above all

in'nato *a* innate

innatu'rale *a* unnatural

inne'gabile *a* undeniable

innervo'sir|e *vt* make nervous. ~si *vr* get irritated

inne'scare *vt* prime. in'nesco *nm* primer

inne'stare *vt* graft; *Mech* engage; ⟨*inserire*⟩ insert. in'nesto *nm* graft; *Mech* clutch; *Electr* connection

inne'vato *a* covered in snow

'inno *nm* hymn. ~ nazionale national anthem

inno'cen|te *a* innocent ~te'mente *adv* innocently. ~za *nf* innocence.

in'nocuo *a* innocuous

inno'va|re *vt* make changes in. ~ tivo *a* innovative. ~ tore *a* a trail-blazing. ~zi'one *nf* innovation

innume'revole *a* innumerable

ino'doro *a* odourless

inoffen'sivo *a* harmless

inol'trar|e *vt* forward. ~si *vr* advance

inol'trato *a* late

i'noltre *adv* besides

inon'da|re *vt* flood. ~zi'one *nf* flood

inope'roso *a* idle

inoppor'tuno *a* untimely

inorgo'glir|e *vt* make proud. ~si *vr* become proud

inorri'di|re *vt* horrify ● *vi* be horrified

inospi'tale *a* inhospitable

inosser'vato *a* unobserved; ⟨*non rispettato*⟩ disregarded; passare ~ go unnoticed

inossi'dabile *a* stainless

'inox *a* inv ⟨*acciaio*⟩ stainless

inqua'dra|re *vt* frame; *fig* put in context ⟨*scrittore, problema*⟩. ~rsi *vr* fit into. ~'tura *nf* framing

inqualifi'cabile a unspeakable

inquie'tar|e vt worry. ~**si** get worried; (impazientirsi) get cross. **inquie'to** a restless; (preoccupato) worried. **inquie'tudine** nf anxiety

inqui'lino, -a nmf tenant

inquina'mento nm pollution

inqui'na|re vt pollute. ~**to** a polluted

inqui'rente a Jur (magistrato) examining; **commissione** ~ commission of enquiry

inqui'si|re vt/i investigate. ~**to** a under investigation. ~**tore**, ~**trice** a inquiring ●nmf inquisitor. ~**zi'one** nf inquisition

insa'bbiare vt shelve

insa'lata nf salad. ~**a belga** endive. ~**i'era** nf salad bowl

insa'lubre a unhealthy

insa'nabile a incurable

insangui'na|re vt cover with blood. ~**to** a bloody

insapo'rare vt soap

insa'po|re a tasteless. ~**rire** vt flavour

insa'puta nf all'~ di unknown to

insazi'abile a insatiable

insce'nare vt stage

inscin'dibile a inseparable

insedia'mento nm installation

insedi'ar|e vt install. ~**si** vr install oneself

in'segna nf sign; (bandiera) flag; (decorazione) decoration; (emblema) insignia pl; (stemma) symbol. ~ **luminose** neon sign

insegna'mento nm teaching. **inse'gnante** a teaching ●nmf teacher

inse'gnare vt/i teach; ~ **qcsa a qcno** teach sb sth

insegui'mento nm pursuit

insegu'i|re vt pursue. ~**tore**, ~**trice** nmf pursuer

inselvati'chir|e vt make wild ●vi. ~**si** vr grow wild

insemi'na|re vt inseminate. ~**zi'one** nf insemination. ~**zione artificiale** artificial insemination

insena'tura nf inlet

insen'sato a senseless; (folle) crazy

insen'sibil|e a insensitive; (braccio ecc) numb. ~**ità** nf insensitivity

insepa'rabile a inseparable

inseri'mento nm insertion

inse'rir|e vt insert; place (annuncio); Electr connect. ~**si** vr ~**si in** get into. **in'serto** nm file; (in un film ecc) insert

inservi'ente nmf attendant

inserzi'o|ne nf insertion; (avviso) advertisement. ~**nista** nmf advertiser

insetti'cida nm insecticide

in'setto nm insect

insicu'rezza nf insecurity. **insi'curo** a insecure

in'sidi|a nf trick; (tranello) snare. ~**are** vt/i lay a trap for. ~**'oso** a insidious

insi'eme adv together; (contemporaneamente) at the same time ●prep ~ **a** [together] with ●nm whole; (completo) outfit; Theat ensemble; Math set; **nell'~** as a whole; **tutto** ~ all together; (bere) at one go

in'signe a renowned

insignifi'cante a insignificant

insi'gnire vt decorate

insinda'cabile a final

insinu'ante a insinuating

insinu'a|re vt insinuate. ~**rsi** vr penetrate; ~**rsi in** fig creep into. ~**zi'one** nf insinuation

in'sipido a insipid

insi'sten|te a insistent. ~**te'mente** adv repeatedly. ~**za** nf insistence. **in'sistere** vi insist; (perseverare) persevere

insoddisfa'cente a unsatisfactory

insoddi'sfa|tto a unsatisfied; (scontento) dissatisfied. ~**zi'one** nf dissatisfaction

insoffe'ren|te a intolerant. ~**za** nf intolerance

insolazi'one nf sunstroke

inso'len|te a rude, insolent. ~**za** nf rudeness, insolence; (commento) insolent remark

in'solito a unusual

inso'lubile a insoluble

inso'luto a unsolved; (non pagato) unpaid

insol'venza nf insolvency

in'somma adv in short; ~! well really!; (così così) so so

in'sonne a sleepless. ~**ia** nf insomnia

insonno'lito a sleepy

insonoriz'zato a soundproofed

insoppor'tabile a unbearable

insor'genza nf onset

in'sorgere vi revolt, rise up; (sorgere) arise; (difficoltà) crop up

insormon'tabile a (ostacolo, difficoltà) insurmountable

in'sorto pp di **insorgere** ●a rebellious ●nm rebel

insospet'tabile a unsuspected

insospet'tire vt make suspicious • vi, ~si vr become suspicious

insoste'nibile a untenable; (insopportabile) unbearable

insostitu'ibile a irreplaceable

inspe'rabile a una sua vittoria è ~bile there is no hope of him winning. ~to a unhoped-for

inspie'gabile a inexplicable

inspi'rare vi breathe in

in'stabile a unstable; (tempo) changeable. ~ità nf instability; (di tempo) changeability

instal'lare vt install. ~rsi vr settle in. ~zi'one nf installation

instan'cabile a untiring

instau'rare vt found. ~rsi vr become established. ~zi'one nf foundation

instra'dare vt direct

insù adv all'~ upwards

insubordinazi'one nf insubordination

insuc'cesso nm failure

insudici'are vt dirty. ~si vr get dirty

insuffici'en|te a insufficient; (inadeguato) • nf Sch fail. ~za nf insufficiency; (inadeguatezza) inadequacy; Sch fail. ~za cardiaca heart failure. ~za di prove lack of evidence

insu'lare a insular

insu'lina nf insulin

in'sulso a insipid; (sciocco) silly

insul'tare vt insult. **in'sulto** nm insult

insupe'rabile a insuperable; (eccezionale) incomparable

insurrezi'one nf insurrection

insussi'stente a groundless

intac'care vt nick; (corrodere) corrode; draw on (un capitale); (danneggiare) damage

intagli'are vt carve. **in'taglio** nm carving

intan'gibile a untouchable

in'tanto adv meanwhile; (per ora) for the moment; (avversativo) but; ~ che while

intarsi'a|re vt inlay. ~to a ~to di inset with. **in'tarsio** nm inlay

inta'sa|re vt clog; block (traffico). ~rsi vr get blocked. ~to a blocked

inta'scare vt pocket

in'tatto a intact

intavo'lare vt start

inte'gra|le a whole; edizione ~le unabridged edition; pane ~le wholemeal bread. ~l'mente adv fully. ~nte a

integral. **'integro** a complete; (retto) upright

inte'gra|re vt integrate; (aggiungere) supplement. ~rsi vr integrate. ~'tivo a (corso) supplementary. ~zi'one nf integration

integrità nf integrity

intelaia'tura nf framework

intel'letto nm intellect

intellettu'al|e a & nmf intellectual. ~'mente adv intellectually

intelli'gen|te a intelligent. ~te'mente adv intelligently. ~za nf intelligence

intelli'gibile a intelligible. ~'mente adv intelligibly

intempe'ranza nf intemperance

intem'perie nfpl bad weather

inten'den|te nm superintendent. ~za nf ~za di finanza inland revenue office

in'tender|e vt (comprendere) understand; (udire) hear; (avere intenzione) intend; (significare) mean. ~sela con have an understanding with; ~si vr (capirsi) understand each other; ~si di (essere esperto) have a good knowledge of

intendi'mento nm understanding; (intenzione) intention. ~ 'tore, ~'trice nmf connoisseur

intene'rir|e vt soften; (commuovere) touch. ~si vr be touched

intensa'mente adv intensely

intensifi'car|e vt, ~si vr intensify

intensità nf inv intensity. **inten'sivo** a intensive. **in'tenso** a intense

inten'tare vt start up; ~ causa contro qcno bring o institute proceedings against sb

in'tento a engrossed (a in) • nm purpose

intenzio'nato a essere ~ a fare qcsa have the intention of doing sth

intenzio'nale a intentional. **intenzi'one** nf intention; senza ~ne unintentionally; avere ~ne di fare qcsa intend to do sth, have the intention of doing sth.

intera'gire vi interact

intera'mente adv completely, entirely

intera|t'tivo a interactive. ~zi'one nf interaction

interca'lare[1] nm stock phrase

interca'lare[2] vt insert

intercambi'abile a interchangeable

interca'pedine nf cavity

inter'ce|dere *vi* intercede. **~ssi'one** *nf* intercession

intercet'ta|re *vt* intercept; tap *(telefono)*. **~zi'one** *nf* interception. **~zione telefonica** telephone tapping

inter'city *nm inv* inter-city

intercontinen'tale *a* intercontinental

inter'correre *vi (tempo:)* elapse; *(esistere)* exist

interco'stale *a* intercostal

inter'detto *pp di* **interdire ●** *a* astonished; *(proibito)* forbidden; **rimanere ~** be taken aback

inter'di|re *vt* forbid; *Jur* deprive of civil rights. **~zi'one** *nf* prohibition

interessa'mento *nm* interest

interes'sante *a* interesting; **essere in stato ~** be pregnant

interes'sa|re *vt* interest; *(riguardare)* concern **●** *vi* **~re** a matter to. **~rsi** *vr* **~rsi** a take an interest in. **~rsi di** take care of. **~to, -a** *nmf* interested party **●** *a* interested; **essere ~to** *pej* have an interest

inte'resse *nm* interest; **fare qcsa per ~** do sth out of self-interest

inter'faccia *nf Comput* interface

interfe'renza *nf* interference

interfe'rire *vi* interfere

interiezi'one *nf* interjection

interi'ora *nfpl* entrails

interi'ore *a* interior

inter'ludio *nm* interlude

intermedi'ario, -a *a & nmf* intermediary

inter'medio *a* in-between

inter'mezzo *nm Theat, Mus* intermezzo

intermi'nabile *a* interminable

intermit'ten|te *a* intermittent; *(luce)* flashing. **~za** *nf* luce a **~za** flashing light

interna'mento *nm* internment; *(in manicomio)* committal

inter'nare *vt* intern; *(in manicomio)* commit [to a mental institution]

in'terno *a* internal; *Geog* inland; *(interiore)* inner; *(politica)* national; **alunno ~** boarder **●** *nm* interior; *(di condominio)* flat; *Teleph* extension; *Cinema* interior shot; **all'~** inside

internazio'nale *a* international

in'tero *a* whole, entire; *(intatto)* intact; *(completo)* complete; **per ~** in full

interpel'lare *vt* consult

inter'por|re *vt* place *(ostacolo)*. **~si** *vr* come between

interpre'ta|re *vt* interpret; *Mus* perform. **~zi'one** *nf* interpretation; *Mus* performance. **in'terprete** *nmf* interpreter; *Mus* performer

inter'ra|re *vt (seppellire)* bury; plant *(pianta, seme)*. **~to** *nm* basement

interro'ga|re *vt* question; *Sch* test; examine *(studenti)*. **~tiva'mente** *adv* questioningly. **~tivo** *a* interrogative; *(sguardo)* questioning; **punto ~tivo** question mark **●** *nm* question **~torio** *a & nm* questioning. **~zi'one** *nf* question; *Sch* oral [test]

inter'romper|e *vt* interrupt; *(sospendere)* stop; cut off *(collegamento)*. **~si** *vr* break off

interrut'tore *nm* switch

interruzi'one *nf* interruption; **senza ~** non-stop. **~ di gravidanza** termination of pregnancy

interse'care, **~carsi** *vr* intersect. **~zi'one** *nf* intersection

inter'stizio *nm* interstice

interur'ban|a *nf* long-distance call. **~o** *a* inter-city; **telefonata ~a** long-distance call

interval'lare *vt* space out. **inter'vallo** *nm* interval; *(spazio)* space; *Sch* break. **intervallo pubblicitario** commercial break

interve'nire *vi* intervene; *(Med: operare)* operate; **~** a take part in. **inter'vento** *nm* intervention; *(presenza)* presence; *(chirurgico)* operation; **pronto intervento** emergency services

inter'vista *nf* interview

intervi'sta|re *vt* interview. **~tore,** **~trice** *nmf* interviewer

in'tes|a *nf* understanding; **cenno d'~a** acknowledgement. **~o** *pp di* **intendere ●** *a* **resta ~o che...** needless to say,...; **~i!** agreed!; **~o** a meant to; **non darsi per ~o** refuse to understand

inte'sta|re *vt* head; write one's name and address at the top of *(lettera)*; *Comm* register. **~rsi** *vr* **~rsi** a fare **qcsa** take it into one's head to do sth. **~'tario, -a** *nmf* holder. **~zi'one** *nf* heading; *(su carta da lettere)* letterhead

intesti'nale *a* intestinal

inte'stino *a (lotte)* internal **●** *nm* intestine

intima'mente *adv (conoscere)* intimately

inti'ma|re *vt* order; **~re l'alt a qcno** order sb to stop. **~zi'one** *nf* order

intimida'torio *a* threatening. **~zi'one** *nf* intimidation

intimi'dire vt intimidate

intimità nf coziness. 'intimo a intimate; (interno) innermost; ⟨amico⟩ close. ~ nm (amico) close friend; (dell'animo) heart

intimo'ri|re vt frighten. ~rsi vr get frightened. ~to a frightened

in'tingere vt dip

in'tingolo nm sauce; ⟨pietanza⟩ stew

intiriz'zi|re vt numb. ~rsi vr grow numb. ~to a essere ~to (dal freddo) be perished

intito'la|re vt entitle; ⟨dedicare⟩ dedicate. ~ rsi vr be called

intolle'rabile a intolerable

intona'care vt plaster. in'tonaco nm plaster

into'na|re vt start to sing; tune ⟨strumento⟩; ⟨accordare⟩ match. ~rsi vr match. ~ to a ⟨persona⟩ able to sing in tune; ⟨colore⟩ matching

intonazi'one nf ⟨inflessione⟩ intonation; ⟨ironico⟩ tone

inton'ti|re vt daze; ⟨gas:⟩ make dizzy ● vi be dazed. ~ to a dazed

intop'pare vi ~ in run into

in'toppo nm obstacle

in'torno adv around ● prep ~ a around; ⟨circa⟩ about

intorpi'dire vt numb. ~rsi vr become numb. ~ to a torpid

intossi'ca|re vt poison. ~rsi vr be poisoned. ~zi'one nf poisoning

intralci'are vt hamper

in'tralcio nm hitch; essere d'~ be a hindrance (a to)

intrallaz'zare vi intrigue. intral'lazzo nm racket

intramon'tabile a timeless

intramusco'lare a intramuscular

intransi'gen|te a intransigent, uncompromising. ~za nf intransigence

intransi'tivo a intransitive

intrappo'lato a rimanere ~ be trapped

intrapren'den|te a enterprising. ~za nf initiative

intra'prendere vt undertake

intrat'tabile a very difficult

intratte'ne|re vt entertain. ~ersi vr linger. ~i mento nm entertainment

intrave'dere vt catch a glimpse of; ⟨presagire⟩ foresee

intrecci'are vt interweave; plait ⟨capelli, corda⟩. ~si vr intertwine; ⟨aggrovigliarsi⟩ become tangled; ~ e le mani clasp one's hands

in'treccio nm ⟨trama⟩ plot

in'trepido a intrepid

intri'cato a tangled

intri'gante a scheming; ⟨affascinante⟩ intriguing

intri'ga|re vt entangle; ⟨incuriosire⟩ intrigue ● vi intrigue, scheme. ~rsi vr meddle. in'trigo nm plot; intrighi pl intrigues

in'trinseco a intrinsic

in'triso a ~ di soaked in

intri'stirsi vr grow sad

intro'du|rre vt introduce; ⟨inserire⟩ insert; ~rre a (iniziare a) introduce to. ~rsi vr get in (in to). ~t'tivo a ⟨pagine, discorso⟩ introductory. ~zi'one nf introduction

intro'metter|e vt introduce. ~si vr interfere; ⟨interporsi⟩ intervene. intromissi'one nf intervention

intro'vabile a that can't be found; ⟨prodotto⟩ unobtainable

intro'verso, -a a introverted ● nmf introvert

intrufo'larsi vr sneak in

in'truglio nm concoction

intrusi'one nf intrusion. in'truso, -a nmf intruder

intu'ire vt perceive

intui'tiva'mente adv intuitively. ~ tivo a intuitive. in'tuito nm intuition. ~zi'one nf intuition

inuguagli'anza nf inequality

inu'mano a inhuman

inu'mare vt inter

inumi'dire vt dampen; moisten ⟨labbra⟩. ~ si vr become damp

i'nutile a useless; ⟨superfluo⟩ unnecessary. ~ità nf uselessness

inutiliz'zabile a unusable. ~ to a unused

inutil'mente adv fruitlessly

in'vadente a intrusive

in'vadere vt invade; ⟨affollare⟩ overrun

invali'd|are vt invalidate. ~ità nf disability; Jur invalidity. in'valido, -a a invalid; ⟨handicappato⟩ disabled ● nmf disabled person

in'vano adv in vain

invari'abile a invariable

invari'ato a unchanged

invasi'one nf invasion. in'vaso pp di invadere inva'sore a invading ● nm invader

invecchia'mento nm ⟨di vino⟩ maturation

invecchi'are vt/i age

in've|ce *adv* instead; *(anzi)* but; ~ di instead of

inve'ire *vi* ~ contro inveigh against

inven'dibile *a* unsaleable. ~uto *a* unsold

inven'tare *vt* invent

inventari'are *vt* make an inventory of. inven'tario *nm* inventory

inven'tivo, -a *a* inventive ● *nf* inventiveness. ~'tore, ~'trice *nmf* inventor. ~zi'one *nf* invention

inver'nale *a* wintry. in'verno *nm* winter

invero'simile *a* improbable

inversa'mente *adv* inversely; ~ proporzionale in inverse proportion

inversi'one *nf* inversion; *Mech* reversal. in'verso *a* inverse; *(opposto)* opposite ● *nm* opposite

inverte'brato *a & nm* invertebrate

inver'ti|re *vt* reverse; *(capovolgere)* turn upside down. ~to, -a *nmf* homosexual

investi'ga|re *vt* investigate. ~'tore *nm* investigator. ~zi'one *nf* investigation

investi'mento *nm* investment; *(incidente)* crash

inve'sti|re *vt* invest; *(urtare)* collide with; *(travolgere)* run over; ~re qcno di investi sb with. ~'tura *nf* investiture

invet'tiva *nf* invective

invi'a|re *vt* send. ~to, -a *nmf* envoy; *(di giornale)* correspondent

invidi|a *nf* envy. i'are *vt* envy. ~'oso *a* envious

invigo'ri|re *vt* invigorate. ~si *vr* become strong

invin'cibile *a* invincible

in'vio *nm* dispatch; *Comput* enter

invio'labile *a* inviolable

invipe'ri|rsi *vr* get nasty. ~to *a* furious

invi'sibil|e *a* invisible. ~ità *nf* invisibility

invi'tante *a* *(piatto, profumo)* enticing

invi'ta|re *vt* invite. ~to, -a *nmf* guest. in'vito *nm* invitation

invo'ca|re *vt* invoke; *(implorare)* beg. ~zi'one *nf* invocation

invogli'ar|e *vt* tempt; *(indurre)* induce. ~si *vr*~si di take a fancy to

involon|taria'mente *adv* involuntarily. ~'taria *a* involuntary

invol'tino *nm* Culin beef olive

in'volto *nm* parcel; *(fagotto)* bundle

in'volucro *nm* wrapping

invulne'rabile *a* invulnerable

inzacche'rare *vt* splash with mud

inzup'par|e *vt* soak; *(intingere)* dip. ~si *vr* get soaked

'io *pron* I; chi è? - [sono] io who is it? - [it's] me; l'ho fatto io [stesso] I did it myself ● *nm* l'~ the ego

i'odio *nm* iodine

I'onio *nm* lo ~ the Ionian [Sea]

i'osa: a ~ *adv* in abundance

iperat'tivo *a* hyperactive

iper'cato *nm* hypermarket

iper'metrope *a* long-sighted

ipersen'sibile *a* hypersensitive

ipertensi'one *nf* high blood pressure

ip'no|si *nf* hypnosis. ~tico *a* hypnotic. ~'tismo *nm* hypnotism. ~tiz'zare *vt* hypnotize

ipoca'lorico *a* low-calorie

ipocon'driaco, -a *a & nmf* hypochondriac

ipocri'sia *nf* hypocrisy. i'pocrita *a* hypocritical ● *nmf* hypocrite

ipo'teca *nf* mortgage. ~'care *vt* mortgage

i'potesi *nf inv* hypothesis; *(caso, eventualità)* eventuality. ipo'tetico *a* hypothetical. ipotiz'zare *vt* hypothesize

'ippico, -a *a* horse attrib ● *nf* riding

ippoca'stano *nm* horse-chestnut

ip'podromo *nm* racecourse

ippo'potamo *nm* hippopotamus

'ira *nf* anger. ~'scibile *a* irascible

i'rato *a* irate

'iride *nf Anat* iris; *(arcobaleno)* rainbow

Ir'landa *nf* Ireland. ~da del Nord Northern Ireland. i~'dese *a* Irish ● *nm* Irishman; *(lingua)* Irish ● *nf* Irishwoman

iro'nia *nf* irony. i'ronico *a* ironic[al]

irradi'a|re *vt/i* radiate. ~zi'one *nf* radiation

irraggiun'gibile *a* unattainable

irragio'nevole *a* unreasonable; *(speranza, timore)* irrational; *(assurdo)* absurd

irrazio'nal|e *a* irrational. ~ità *nf* irrationality. ~'mente *adv* irrationally

irre'al|e *a* unreal. ~'listico *a* unrealistic. ~liz'zabile *a* unattainable. ~ità *nf* unreality

irrecupe'rabile *a* irrecoverable

irrego'lar|e *a* irregular. ~ità *nf inv* irregularity

irremo'vibile *a fig* adamant

irrepa'rabile *a* irreparable

irrepe'ribile *a* not to be found; sarò ~ I won't be contactable

irrepren'sibile *a* irreproachable

irrepri'mibile *a* irrepressible

irre'qui'eto *a* restless

irresi'stibile *a* irresistible

irrespon'sabil|e *a* irresponsible. **~ità** *nf* irresponsibility

irrever'sibile *a* irreversible

irrevo'cabile *a* irrevocable

irricono'scibile *a* unrecognizable

irri'ga|re *vt* irrigate; *(fiume:)* flow through. **~zi'one** *nf* irrigation

irrigidi'mento *nm* stiffening

irrigi'dir|e *vt*, **~si** *vr* stiffen

irrile'vante *a* unimportant

irrimedi'abile *a* irreparable

irripe'tibile *a* unrepeatable

irri'sorio *a* derisive; *(differenza, particolare, somma)* insignificant

irri'tabile *a* irritable. **~nte** *a* aggravating

irri'ta|re *vt* irritate. **~rsi** *vr* get annoyed. **~to** *a* irritated; *(gola)* sore. **~zi'one** *nf* irritation

irrobu'stir|e *vt* fortify. **~si** *vr* get stronger

ir'rompere *vi* burst (in into)

irro'rare *vt* sprinkle

irru'ente *a* impetuous

irruzi'one *nf* fare **~** in burst into

i'scritto, -a *pp di* iscrivere ● *a* registered ● *nmf* member; **per ~** in writing

i'scriver|e *vt* register. **~si** *vr* **~si** a register at, enrol at *(scuola)*; join *(circolo ecc)*. **iscrizi'one** *nf* registration; *(epigrafe)* inscription

i'sla'mico *a* Islamic. **~'mismo** *nm* Islam

l'slan|da *nf* Iceland. **i~'dese** *a* Icelandic ● *nmf* Icelander

'isola *nf* island. **le isole britanniche** the British Isles. **~ pedonale** traffic island. **~ spartitraffico** traffic island. **iso'lano, -a** *a* insular ● *nmf* islander

iso'lante *a* insulating ● *nm* insulator

iso'la|re *vt* isolate; *Mech, Electr* insulate; *(acusticamente)* soundproof. **~to** *a* isolated ● *nm* *(di appartamenti)* block

ispes'sir|e *vt*, **~si** *vr* thicken

ispetto'rato *nm* inspectorate. **ispet-** **tore** *nm* inspector. **ispezio'nare** *vt* inspect. **ispezi'one** *nf* inspection

'ispido *a* bristly

ispi'ra|re *vt* inspire; suggest *(idea, soluzione)*. **~rsi** *vr* **~rsi** a be based on. **~to** a inspired. **~zi'one** *nf* inspiration; *(idea)* idea

Isra'el|e *nm* Israel. **i~i'ano, -a** *a* & *nmf* Israeli

is'sare *vt* hoist

istan'taneo, -a *a* instantaneous ● *nf* snapshot

i'stante *nm* instant; **all'~** instantly

i'stanza *nf* petition

i'sterico *a* hysterical. **iste'rismo** *nm* hysteria

isti'ga|re *vt* instigate; **~re qcno al male** incite sb to evil. **~ tore**, **~ trice** *nmf* instigator. **~zi'one** *nf* instigation

istin'tiva'mente *adv* instinctively. **~'tivo** *a* instinctive. **i'stinto** *nm* instinct; **d'istinto** instinctively

istitu'ire *vt* institute; *(fondare)* found; initiate *(manifestazione)*

isti'tu|to *nm* institute; *(universitario)* department; *Sch* secondary school. **~to di bellezza** beauty salon. **~ tore**, **~ trice** *nmf* *(insegnante)* tutor; *(fondatore)* founder

istituzio'nale *a* institutional. **istitu-** **zi'one** *nf* institution

'istmo *nm* isthmus

'istrice *nm* porcupine

istru'ire *vt* instruct; *(addestrare)* train; *(informare)* inform; *Jur* prepare. **~to** *a* educated

istrut'tivo *a* instructive. **~ore**, **~rice** *nmf* instructor; **giudice ~ore** examining magistrate. **~oria** *nf* *Jur* investigation. **istruzi'one** *nf* education; *(indicazione)* instruction

l'tali|a *nf* Italy. **i~'ano, -a** *a* & *nmf* Italian

itine'rario *nm* route, itinerary

itte'rizia *nf* jaundice

'ittico *a* fishing *attrib*

I.V.A. *nf abbr (imposta sul valore aggiunto)* VAT

Jj

jack nm inv jack
jazz nm jazz. **jaz'zista** nmf jazz player
jeep nf inv jeep
'jolly nm inv (carta da gioco) joker

Jugo'slav|ia nf Yugoslavia. **j~o, -a** a & nmf Yugoslav[ian]
ju'niores nmfpl Sport juniors

Kk

ka'jal nm inv kohl
kara'oke nm inv karaoke
ka'rate nm karate

kg abbr (chilogrammo) kg
km abbr (chilometro) km

Ll

l' def art mf (before vowel) the; vedi il
la def art f the; vedi il ●pron (oggetto, riferito a persona) her; (riferito a cosa, animale) it; (forma di cortesia) you ●nm inv Mus (chiave, nota) A
là adv there; **di là** (in quel luogo) in there; (da quella parte) that way; **eccolo là!** there he is!; **farsi più in là** (far largo) make way; **là dentro** in there; **là fuori** out there; [ma] **va là!** come off it!; **più in là** (nel tempo) later on; (nello spazio) further on
'labbro nm (pl nf Anat **labbra**) lip
labi'rinto nm labyrinth; (di sentieri ecc) maze
labora'torio nm laboratory; (di negozio, officina ecc) workshop
labori'oso a (operoso) industrious; (faticoso) laborious
labu'rista a Labour ●nmf member of the Labour Party

'lacca nf lacquer; (per capelli) hairspray, lacquer. **lac'care** vt lacquer
'laccio nm noose; (lazo) lasso; (trappola) snare; (stringa) lace
lace'rante a (grido) earsplitting
lace'ra|re vt tear; lacerate (carne). **~rsi** vr tear. **~zi'one** nf laceration. **'lacero** a torn; (cencioso) ragged
la'conico a laconic
'lacri|ma nf tear; (goccia) drop. **~'mare** vi weep. **~'mevole** a tear-jerking
lacri'mogeno a gas **~** tear gas
lacri'moso a tearful
la'cuna nf gap. **lacu'noso** a (preparazione, resoconto) incomplete
la'custre a lake attrib
lad'dove conj whereas
'ladro, -a nmf thief; **al ~!** stop thief! **~'cinio** nm theft. **la'druncolo** nm petty thief
'lager nm inv concentration camp

laggiù *adv* down there; (*lontano*) over there

lagna *nf* (*fam: persona*) moaning Minnie; (*film*) bore

la'gna|nza *nf* complaint. **~rsi** *vr* moan; (*protestare*) complain (**di** about). **la'gnoso** *a* (*persona*) moaning

lago *nm* lake

la'guna *nf* lagoon

'laico, -a *a* lay; (*vita*) secular ● *nm* layman ● *nf* laywoman

'lama *nf* blade ● *nm inv* (*animale*) llama

lambic'carsi *vr* ~ **il cervello** rack one's brains

lam'bire *vt* lap

lamé *nm inv* lamé

lamen'tar|e *vt* lament. **~si** *vr* moan. **~si di** (*lagnarsi*) complain about

lamen'te|la *nf* complaint. **~vole** *a* mournful; (*pietoso*) pitiful. **la'mento** *nm* moan

la'metta *nf* ~ [**da barba**] razor blade

lami'era *nf* sheet metal

'lamina *nf* foil. **~ d'oro** gold leaf

lami'na|re *vt* laminate. **~to** *a* laminated ● *nm* laminate; (*tessuto*) lamé

'lampa|da *nf* lamp. **~da abbronzante** sunlamp. **~da a pila** torch. **~dario** *nm* chandelier. **~dina** *nf* light bulb

lam'pante *a* clear

lampeggi'a|re *vi* flash. **~tore** *nm* Auto indicator

lampi'one *nm* street lamp

'lampo *nm* flash of lightning; (*luce*) flash; **lampi** *pl* lightning *sg*. **~ di genio** stroke of genius. **[cerniera] ~** zip [fastener], zipper *Am*

lam'pone *nm* raspberry

'lana *nf* wool; **di ~** woollen. **~ d'acciaio** steel wool. **~ vergine** new wool. **~ di vetro** glass wool

lan'cetta *nf* pointer; (*di orologio*) hand

'lancia *nf* (*arma*) spear, lance; Naut launch

lanci'ar|e *vt* throw; (*da un aereo*) drop; launch (*missile, prodotto*); give (*grido*); **~e uno sguardo a** glance at. **~si** *vr* fling oneself; (*intraprendere*) launch out

lanci'nante *a* piercing

'lancio *nm* throwing; (*da aereo*) drop; (*di missile, prodotto*) launch. **~ del disco** discus [throwing]. **~ del giavellotto** javelin [throwing]. **~ del peso** putting the shot

'landa *nf* heath

'languido *a* languid

lani'ero *a* wool

lani'ficio *nm* woollen mill

lan'terna *nf* lantern; (*faro*) lighthouse

la'nugine *nf* down

lapi'dare *vt* stone; *fig* demolish

lapi'dario *a* (*conciso*) terse

'lapide *nf* tombstone; (*commemorativa*) memorial tablet

'lapis *nm inv* pencil

'lapsus *nm inv* lapse, error

'lardo *nm* lard

larga'mente *adv* (*ampiamente*) widely

lar'ghezza *nf* width, breadth; *fig* liberality. **~ di vedute** broadmindedness

'largo *a* wide; (*ampio*) broad; (*abito*) loose; (*liberale*) liberal; (*abbondante*) generous; **stare alla larga** keep away; **~ di manica** generous; **essere ~ di spalle/vedute** be broad-shouldered/minded ● *nm* width; **andare al ~** Naut go out to sea; **fare ~** make room; **farsi ~** make one's way; **al ~ di** off the coast of

'larice *nm* larch

la'ringe *nf* larynx. **larin'gite** *nf* laryngitis

'larva *nf* larva; (*persona emaciata*) shadow

la'sagne *nfpl* lasagna *sg*

lasciapas'sare *nm inv* pass

lasci'ar|e *vt* leave; (*rinunciare*) give up; (*rimetterci*) lose; (*smettere di tenere*) let go [of]; (*concedere*) let; **~e di fare qcsa** stop doing sth; **lascia perdere!** forget it!; **lascialo venire, lascia che venga** let him come. **~si** *vr* (*reciproco*) leave each other, split up; **~si andare** let oneself go

'lascito *nm* legacy

'laser *a & nm inv* [**raggio**] **~** laser [beam]

lassa'tivo *a & nm* laxative

'lasso *nm* **~ di tempo** period of time

lassù *adv* up there

'lastra *nf* slab; (*di ghiaccio*) sheet; (*di metallo, Phot*) plate; (*radiografia*) X-ray [plate]

lastri'ca|re *vt* pave. **~to, 'lastrico** *nm* pavement; **sul lastrico** on one's beam-ends

la'tente *a* latent

late'rale *a* side *attrib*; Med, Techn ecc lateral; **via ~** side street

late'rizi *nmpl* bricks

lati'fondo *nm* large estate

la'tino *a & nm* Latin

lati'tante *a* in hiding ● *nmf* fugitive [from justice]

lati'tudine *nf* latitude

'lato a (ampio) broad; in senso ~ broadly speaking ● nm side; (aspetto) aspect; a ~ di beside; dal ~ mio (punto di vista) for my part; d'altro ~ fig on the other hand

la'traire vi bark. ~to nm barking

la'trina nf latrine

'latta nf tin, can

lat'taio nm milkman

lat'tante a breast-fed ● nmf suckling

'latt|e nm milk. ~e acido sour milk. ~e condensato condensed milk. ~e detergente cleansing milk. ~e in polvere powdered milk. ~e scremato skimmed milk. ~eo a milky. ~e'ria nf dairy. ~i'cini nmpl dairy products. ~i'era nf milk jug

lat'tina nf can

lat'tuga nf lettuce

'laure|a nf degree; prendere la ~a graduate. ~'ando, -a nmf final-year student

laure'a|rsi vr graduate. ~to, -a a & nmf graduate

'lauro nm laurel

'lauto a lavish; ~ guadagno handsome profit

'lava nf lava

la'vabile a washable

la'vabo nm wash-basin

la'vaggio nm washing. ~ automatico (per auto) carwash. ~ del cervello brainwashing. ~ a secco dry-cleaning

la'vagna nf slate; Sch blackboard

la'van|da nf wash; Bot lavender; fare una ~a gastrica have one's stomach pumped. ~'daia nf washerwoman. ~de'ria nf laundry. ~deria automatica launderette

lavan'dino nm sink; (hum: persona) bottomless pit

lavapi'atti nmf inv dishwasher

la'var|e vt wash; ~e i piatti wash up. ~si vr wash, have a wash; ~si i denti brush one's teeth; ~si le mani wash one's hands

lava'secco nmf inv dry-cleaner's

lavasto'viglie nf inv dishwasher

la'vata nf wash; darsi una ~ have a wash; ~ di capo fig scolding

lava'tivo, -a nmf idler

lava'trice nf washing-machine

lavo'rante nmf worker

lavo'ra|re vi work ● vt work; knead (pasta ecc); till (la terra); ~re a maglia knit. ~'tivo a working. ~to a (pietra, legno) carved; (cuoio) tooled; (metallo) wrought. ~ tore, ~'trice nmf worker

● a working. ~zi'one nf manufacture; (di terra) working; (artigianale) workmanship; (del terreno) cultivation.

lavo'rio nm intense activity

la'voro nm work; (faticoso, sociale) labour; (impiego) job; Theat play; mettersi al ~ set to work (su on). ~ a maglia knitting. ~ nero moonlighting. ~ straordinario overtime. ~ a tempo pieno full-time job. lavori pl di casa housework. lavori pl in corso roadworks. lavori pl forzati hard labour. lavori pl stradali roadworks

le def art fpl the; vedi il ● pron (oggetto) them; (a lei) her; (forma di cortesia) you

le'al|e a loyal. ~ mente adv loyally. ~tà nf loyalty

'lebbra nf leprosy

'lecca 'lecca nm inv lollipop

leccapi'edi nmf inv pej bootlicker

lec'ca|re vt lick; fig suck up to. ~rsi vr lick; (fig: agghindarsi) doll oneself up; da ~rsi i baffi mouth-watering. ~ta nf lick

leccor'nia nf delicacy

'lecito a lawful; (permesso) permissible

'ledere vt damage; Med injure

'lega nf league; (di metalli) alloy; far ~ con qcno take up with sb

le'gaccio nm string; (delle scarpe) shoelace

le'gal|e a legal ● nm lawyer. ~ità nf legality. ~iz'zare vt authenticate; (rendere legale) legalize. ~'mente adv legally

lega'mento nm Med ligament

le'gar|e vt tie; tie up (persona); tie together (due cose); (unire, rilegare) bind; alloy (metalli); (connettere) connect; ~sela al dito bear a grudge ● vi (far lega) get on well. ~si vr bind oneself; ~si a qcno become attached to sb

le'gato nm legacy; Relig legate

lega'tura nf tying; (di libro) binding

le'genda nf legend

'legge nf law; (parlamentare) act; a norma di ~ by law

leg'genda nf legend; (didascalia) caption. leggen'dario a legendary

'leggere vt/i read

legge'r|ezza nf lightness; (frivolezza) frivolity; (incostanza) fickleness. ~'mente adv slightly

leg'gero a light; (bevanda) weak; (lieve) slight; (frivolo) frivolous; (incostante) fickle; alla leggera frivolously

leg'gibile a ⟨scrittura⟩ legible; ⟨stile⟩ readable

leg'gio nm lectern; Mus music stand

legife'rare vi legislate

legio'nario nm legionary. **legi'one** nf legion

legisla'tivo a legislative. **~'tore** nm legislator. **~'tura** nf legislature. **~zi'one** nf legislation

legittimità nf legitimacy. **le'gittimo** a legitimate; ⟨giusto⟩ proper; **legittima difesa** self-defence

'legna nf firewood

le'gname nm timber

le'gnata nf blow with a stick

'legno nm wood; **di ~** wooden. **~ compensato** plywood. **le'gnoso** a woody

le'gume nm pod

'lei pron ⟨soggetto⟩ she; ⟨oggetto, con prep⟩ her; ⟨forma di cortesia⟩ you; **lo ha fatto ~ stessa** she did it herself

'lembo nm edge; ⟨di terra⟩ strip

'lemma nm headword

'lena nf vigour

le'nire vt soothe

lenta'mente adv slowly

'lente nf lens. **~ a contatto** contact lens. **~ d'ingrandimento** magnifying glass

len'tezza nf slowness

len'ticchia nf lentil

len'tiggine nf freckle

'lento a slow; ⟨allentato⟩ slack; ⟨abito⟩ loose

'lenza nf fishing-line

len'zuolo nm (pl f lenzuola) nm sheet

le'one nm lion; Astr Leo

leo'pardo nm leopard

'lepre nf hare

'lercio a filthy

'lesbica nf lesbian

lesi'nare vt grudge ● vi be stingy

lesio'nare vt damage. **lesi'one** nf lesion

'leso pp di ledere ● a injured

les'sare vt boil

'lessico nm vocabulary

'lesso a boiled ● nm boiled meat

'lesto a quick; ⟨mente⟩ sharp

le'tale a lethal

leta'maio nm dunghill; fig pigsty. **le'tame** nm dung

le'targico a lethargic. **~o** nm lethargy; ⟨di animali⟩ hibernation

le'tizia nf joy

'lettera nf letter; **alla ~** literally; **~ maiuscola** capital letter; **~ minuscola** small letter; **lettere** pl ⟨letteratura⟩

literature sg; Univ Arts; **dottore in lettere** BA, Bachelor of Arts

lette'rale a literal

lette'rario a literary

lette'rato a well-read

lettera'tura nf literature

let'tiga nf stretcher

let'tino nm cot; Med couch

'letto nm bed. **~ a castello** bunkbed. **~ a una piazza** single bed. **~ a due piazze** double bed. **~ matrimoniale** double bed

letto'rato nm ⟨corso⟩ ≈ tutorial

let'tore, -'trice nmf reader; Univ language assistant ● nm Comput disk drive. **~ di CD-ROM** CD-Rom drive

let'tura nf reading

leuce'mia nf leukaemia

'leva nf lever; Mil call-up; **far ~** lever. **~ del cambio** gear lever

le'vante nm East; ⟨vento⟩ east wind

le'va|re vt ⟨alzare⟩ raise; ⟨togliere⟩ take away; ⟨rimuovere⟩ take off; ⟨estrarre⟩ pull out; **~rsi di mezzo qcsa** get sth out of the way. **~rsi** vr rise; ⟨da letto⟩ get up; **~rsi di mezzo, ~rsi dai piedi** get out of the way. **~ta** nf rising; ⟨di posta⟩ collection

leva'taccia nf **fare una ~** get up at the crack of dawn

leva'toio a **ponte ~** drawbridge

levi'ga|re vt smooth; ⟨con carta vetro⟩ rub down. **~to** a ⟨superficie⟩ polished

levri'ero nm greyhound

lezi'one nf lesson; Univ lecture; ⟨rimprovero⟩ rebuke

lezi'oso a ⟨stile, modi⟩ affected

li pron mpl them

lì adv there; **fin lì** as far as there; **giù di lì** thereabouts; **per lì** there and then

Li'bano nm Lebanon

'libbra nf ⟨peso⟩ pound

li'beccio nm south-west wind

li'bellula nf dragon-fly

libe'rale a liberal; ⟨generoso⟩ generous ● nmf liberal

libe'ra|re vt free; release ⟨prigioniero⟩; vacate ⟨stanza⟩; ⟨salvare⟩ rescue. **~rsi** vr ⟨stanza:⟩ become vacant; Teleph become free; ⟨da impegno⟩ get out of it; **~rsi di** get rid of. **~ 'tore, ~'trice** a liberating ● nmf liberator. **~'torio** a liberating. **~zi'one** nf liberation; **la L~zione** ⟨ricorrenza⟩ Liberation Day

'liber|o a free; ⟨strada⟩ clear. **~o docente** qualified university lecturer. **~o professionista** self-employed person. **~tà** nf inv freedom; ⟨di prigioniero) release. ~tà provvisoria *Jur* bail; ~tà *pl* (*confidenze*) liberties

'liberty *nm & a inv* Art Nouveau

'Libi|a *nf* Libya. l~co, -a *a & nmf* Libyan

li'bidi|ne *nf* lust. ~'noso *a* lustful. li'bido *nf* libido

libra'io *nm* bookseller

libre'ria *nf* (*negozio*) bookshop; (*mobile*) bookcase; (*biblioteca*) library

li'bretto *nm* booklet; *Mus* libretto. ~ degli assegni cheque book. ~ di circolazione logbook. ~ d'istruzioni instruction booklet. ~ di risparmio bankbook. ~ universitario *book held by students which records details of their exam performances*

'libro *nm* book. ~ giallo thriller. ~ paga payroll

lice'ale *nmf* secondary-school student ● *a* secondary-school *attrib*

li'cenza *nf* licence; (*permesso*) permission; *Mil* leave; *Sch* school-leaving certificate; essere in ~ be on leave

licenzia'mento *nm* dismissal

licenzi'a|re *vt* dismiss, sack *fam*. ~rsi *vr* (*da un impiego*) resign; (*accomiatarsi*) take one's leave

li'ceo *nm* secondary school, high school. ~ classico *secondary school with an emphasis on humanities*. ~ scientifico *secondary school with an emphasis on sciences*

li'chene *nm* lichen

'lido *nm* beach

li'eto *a* glad; (*evento*) happy; molto ~! pleased to meet you!

li'eve *a* light; (*debole*) faint; (*trascurabile*) slight

lievi'tare *vi* rise ● *vt* leaven. li'evito *nm* yeast. lievito in polvere baking powder

'lifting *nm inv* face-lift

'ligio *a* essere ~ al dovere have a sense of duty

'lilla *nf Bot* lilac ● *nm* (*colore*) lilac

'lima *nf* file

limacci'oso *a* slimy

li'mare *vt* file

'limbo *nm* limbo

li'metta *nf* nail-file

limi'ta|re *nm* threshold ● *vt* limit. ~rsi *vr* ~rsi a fare qcsa restrict oneself to doing sth; ~rsi in qcsa cut down on sth. ~'tivo *a* limiting. ~to *a* limited. ~zi'one *nf* limitation

'limite *nm* limit; (*confine*) boundary. ~ di velocità speed limit

li'mitrofo *a* neighbouring

limo'nata *nf* (*bibita*) lemonade; (*succo*) lemon juice

li'mone *nm* lemon; (*albero*) lemon tree

'limpido *a* clear; (*occhi*) limpid

'lince *nf* lynx

linci'are *vt* lynch

'lindo *a* neat; (*pulito*) clean

'linea *nf* line; (*di autobus, aereo*) route; (*di metro*) line; (*di abito*) cut; (*di auto, mobile*) design; (*fisico*) figure; in ~ d'aria as the crow flies; è caduta la ~ I've been cut off; in ~ di massima as a rule; a grandi linee in outline; mantenere la ~ keep one's figure; in prima ~ in the front line; mettersi in ~ line up; nave di ~ liner; volo di ~ scheduled flight. ~ d'arrivo finishing line. ~ continua unbroken line

linea'menti *nmpl* features

line'are *a* linear; (*discorso*) to the point; (*ragionamento*) consistent

line'etta *nf* (*tratto lungo*) dash; (*d'unione*) hyphen

lin'gotto *nm* ingot

'lingu|a *nf* tongue; (*linguaggio*) language. ~'accia *nf* (*persona*) backbiter. ~'aggio *nm* language. ~'etta *nf* (*di scarpa*) tongue; (*di strumento*) reed; (*di busta*) flap

lingu'ist|a *nmf* linguist. ~ica *nf* linguistics *sg*. ~ico *a* linguistic

'lino *nm Bot* flax; (*tessuto*) linen

li'noleum *nm* linoleum

liofiliz'za|re *vt* freeze-dry. ~to *a* freeze-dried

liposuzi'one *nf* liposuction

lique'fa|re *vt*, ~si *vr* liquefy; (*sciogliersi*) melt

liqui'da|re *vt* liquidate; settle (*conto*); pay off (*debiti*); clear (*merce*); (*fam: uccidere*) get rid of. ~zi'one *nf* liquidation; (*di conti*) settling; (*di merce*) clearance sale

'liquido *a & nm* liquid

liqui'rizia *nf* liquorice

li'quore *nm* liqueur; liquori *pl* (*bevande alcoliche*) liquors

'lira *nf* lira; *Mus* lyre

'lirico, -a *a* lyrical; (*poesia*) lyric; (*cantante, musica*) opera *attrib* ● *nf* lyric poetry; *Mus* opera

'lisca *nf* fishbone; avere la ~ (*fam: nel parlare*) have a lisp

lisci'a|re *vt* smooth; (*accarezzare*) stroke. 'liscio *a* smooth; (*capelli*) straight; (*liquore*) neat; (*non gassato*) still; passarla liscia get away with it '**liso** *a* worn [out]

'**lista** *nf* list; (*striscia*) strip. ~ di attesa waiting list; in ~ di attesa Aeron stand-by. ~ elettorale electoral register. ~ di nozze wedding list. li'stare *vt* edge; *Comput* list

li'stino *nm* list. ~ prezzi price list

Lit. *abbr* (lire italiane) Italian lire

'**lite** *nf* quarrel; (*baruffa*) row; *Jur* lawsuit

liti'gare *vi* quarrel. li'tigio *nm* quarrel. litigi'oso *a* quarrelsome

lito'rale *a* coastal ●*nm* coast

'**litro** *nm* litre

li'turgico *a* liturgical

li'vella *nf* level. ~ a bolla d'aria spirit level

livel'lar|e *vt* level. ~si *vr* level out

li'vello *nm* level; passaggio a ~ level crossing; sotto/sul ~ del mare below/above sea level

'**livido** *a* livid; (*per il freddo*) blue; (*per una botta*) black and blue ●*nm* bruise

Li'vorno *nm* Leghorn

'**lizza** *nf* lists *pl*; essere in ~ per qcsa be in the running for sth

lo *def art m* (*before* s + consonant, gn, ps, z) the; *vedi* il ●*pron* (riferito a persona) him; (riferito a cosa) it; non lo so I don't know

'**lobo** *nm* lobe

lo'cal|e *a* local ●*nm* (stanza) room; (treno) local train; ~i *pl* (edifici) premises. ~e notturno night-club. ~ità *nf inv* locality

localiz'zare *vt* localize; (trovare) locate

lo'canda *nf* inn

locan'dina *nf* bill, poster

loca'tario, -a *nmf* tenant. ~'tore, ~'trice *nm* landlord ●*nf* landlady. ~zi'one *nf* tenancy

locomo'tiva *nf* locomotive. ~zi'one *nf* locomotion; mezzi di ~zione means of transport

'**loculo** *nm* burial niche

lo'custa *nf* locust

locuzi'one *nf* expression

lo'dare *vt* praise. '**lode** *nf* praise; laurea con lode first-class degree

'**loden** *nm inv* (cappotto) loden coat

lo'devole *a* praiseworthy

'**lodola** *nf* lark

'**loggia** *nf* loggia; (massonica) lodge

loggi'one *nm* gallery, the gods

'**logica** *nf* logic

logica'mente *adv* (in modo logico) logically; (ovviamente) of course

'**logico** *a* logical

lo'gistica *nf* logistics *sg*

logo'rante *a* (esperienza) wearing

logo'ra|re *vt* wear out; (sciupare) waste. ~rsi *vr* wear out; (persona:) wear oneself out. logo'rio *nm* wear and tear. '**logoro** *a* worn-out

lom'baggine *nf* lumbago

Lombar'dia *nf* Lombardy

lom'bata *nf* loin. '**lombo** *nm* Anat loin

lom'brico *nm* earthworm

'**Londra** *nf* London

lon'gevo *a* long-lived

longi'lineo *a* tall and slim

longi'tudine *nf* longitude

lontana'mente *adv* distantly; (vagamente) vaguely; neanche ~ not for a moment

lonta'nanza *nf* distance; (separazione) separation; in ~ in the distance

lon'tano *a* far; (distante) distant; (nel tempo) remote; (parente) distant; (vago) vague; (assente) absent; più ~ further ●*adv* far [away]; da ~ from a distance; tenersi ~ da keep away from

'**lontra** *nf* otter

lo'quace *a* talkative

'**lordo** *a* dirty; (somma, peso) gross

'**loro**[1] *pron pl* (soggetto) they; (oggetto) them; (forma di cortesia) you; sta a ~ it is up to them

'**loro**[2] (il ~m, la ~ f, i ~ mpl, le ~ fpl) *a* their; (forma di cortesia) your; un ~ amico a friend of theirs; (forma di cortesia) a friend of yours ●*pron* theirs; (forma di cortesia) yours; i ~ their folk

lo'sanga *nf* lozenge; a losanghe diamond-shaped

'**losco** *a* suspicious

'**loto** *nm* lotus

'**lott|a** *nf* fight, struggle; (contrasto) conflict; *Sport* wrestling. lot'tare *vi* fight, struggle; *Sport*, *fig* wrestle. ~a'tore *nm* wrestler

lotte'ria *nf* lottery

'**lotto** *nm* [national] lottery; (porzione) lot; (di terreno) plot

lozi'one *nf* lotion

lubrifi'can|te *a* lubricating ●*nm* lubricant. ~re *vt* lubricate

luc'chetto *nm* padlock

lucci'ca|nte *a* sparkling. ~re *vi* sparkle. lucci'chio *nm* sparkle

'**luccio** *nm* pike

'**lucciola** *nf* glow-worm

'**luce** *nf* light; far ~ su shed light on; dare alla ~ give birth to. ~ della luna moonlight. luci di posizione sidelights. ~ del sole sunlight

lu'cen|te a shining. **~'tezza** nf shine
lucer'nario nm skylight
lu'certola nf lizard
lucida'labbra nm inv lip gloss
luci'da|re vt polish. **~'trice** nf [floor-]polisher. **'lucido** a shiny; (pavimento, scarpe) polished; (chiaro) clear; (persona, mente) lucid; (occhi) watery ●nm shine. **lucido [da scarpe]** [shoe] polish
lucra'tivo a lucrative. **'lucro** nm lucre
'luglio nm July
'lugubre a gloomy
'lui pron (soggetto) he; (oggetto, con prep) him; **lo ha fatto ~ stesso** he did it himself
lu'maca nf (mollusco) snail; fig slowcoach
'lume nm lamp; (luce) light; **a ~ di candela** by candlelight
luminosità nf brightness. **lumi'noso** a luminous; (stanza, cielo ecc) bright
'luna nf moon; **chiaro di ~** moonlight; **avere la ~ storta** be in a bad mood. **~ di miele** honeymoon
luna park nm inv fairground
lu'nare a lunar
lu'nario nm almanac; **sbarcare il ~** make both ends meet
lu'natico a moody
lunedì nm inv Monday
lu'netta nf half-moon [shape]
lun'gaggine nf slowness
lun'ghezza nf length. **~ d'onda** wavelength
'lungi adv ero [ben] **~ dall'immaginare che...** I never dreamt for a moment that...

lungimi'rante a far-seeing
'lungo a long; (diluito) weak; (lento) slow; **saperla lunga** be shrewd ●nm length; **di gran lunga** by far; **andare per le lunghe** drag on ● prep (durante) throughout; (per la lunghezza di) along
lungofi'ume nm riverside
lungo'lago nm lakeside
lungo'mare nm sea front
lungome'traggio nm feature film
lu'notto nm rear window
lu'ogo nm place; (punto preciso) spot; (passo d'autore) passage; **aver ~** take place; **dar ~ a** give rise to; **del ~** (usanze) local. **~ comune** platitude. **~ pubblico** public place
luogote'nente nm Mil lieutenant
lu'petto nm Cub [Scout]
'lupo nm wolf
'luppolo nm hop
'lurido a filthy. **luri'dume** nm filth
lu'singa nf flattery
lusin'g|are vt flatter. **~arsi** vr flatter oneself; (illudersi) fool oneself. **~hi'ero** a flattering
lus'sa|re vt, **~rsi** vr dislocate. **~zi'one** nf dislocation
Lussem'burgo nm Luxembourg
'lusso nm luxury; **di ~** luxury attrib
lussu'oso a luxurious
lussureggi'ante a luxuriant
lus'suria nf lust
lu'strare vt polish
lu'strino nm sequin
'lustro a shiny ●nm sheen; fig prestige; (quinquennio) five-year period
'lutt|o nm mourning; **~o stretto** deep mourning. **~u'oso** a mournful

Mm

m abbr (metro) m
ma conj but; (eppure) yet; **ma!** (dubbio) I don't know; (indignazione) really!; **ma davvero?** really?; **ma sì** why not!; (certo che sì) of course!
'macabro a macabre
macché int of course not!
macche'roni nmpl macaroni sg
macche'ronico a (italiano) broken
'macchia¹ nf stain; (di diverso colore)

spot; (piccola) speck; **senza ~** spotless
'macchia² nf (boscaglia) scrub; **darsi alla ~** take to the woods
macchi'a|re vt, **~rsi** vr stain. **~to a** (caffè) with a dash of milk; **~to di** (sporco) stained with
'macchina nf machine; (motore) engine; (automobile) car. **~ da cucire** sewing machine. **~ da presa** cine cam-

era, movie camera. **~ da scrivere** typewriter

macchinal'mente *adv* mechanically

macchi'nare *vt* plot

macchi'nario *nm* machinery

macchi'netta *nf (per i denti)* brace

macchi'nista *nm Rail* engine-driver; *Naut* engineer; *Theat* stagehand

macchi'noso *a* complicated

mace'donia *nf* fruit salad

macel'laio *nm* butcher. **~re** *vt* slaughter. **macelle'ria** *nf* butcher's [shop]. **ma'cello** *nm* slaughterhouse; *fig* shambles *sg*; **andare al macello** *fig* go to the slaughter; **mandare al macello** *fig* send to his/her death

mace'rare *vt* macerate; *fig* distress. **~si** *vr* be consumed

ma'cerie *nfpl* rubble *sg*; *(rottami)* debris *sg*

ma'cigno *nm* boulder

maci'lento *a* emaciated

'macina *nf* millstone

macina'caffè *nm inv* coffee mill

macina'pepe *nm inv* pepper mill

maci'na|re *vt* mill. **~to** *a* ground ●*nm (carne)* mince. **maci'nino** *nm* mill; *(hum: macchina)* old banger

maciul'lare *vt (stritolare)* crush

macrobiotic|a *nf* **negozio di ~a** health-food shop. **~a** *a* macrobiotic

macro'scopico *a* macroscopic

macu'lato *a* spotted

'madido *a* **~ di** moist with

Ma'donna *nf* Our Lady

mador'nale *a* gross

'madre *nf* mother. **~ lingua** *a inv* **inglese ~lingua** English native speaker. **~'patria** *nf* native land. **~'perla** *nf* mother-of-pearl

ma'drina *nf* godmother

mae'stà *nf* majesty

maestosità *nf* majesty. **mae'stoso** *a* majestic

mae'strale *nm* northwest wind

mae'stranza *nf* workers *pl*

mae'stria *nf* mastery

ma'estro, -a *nmf* teacher ●*nm* master; *Mus* maestro. **~ di cerimonie** master of ceremonies ●*a (principale)* chief; *(di grande abilità)* skilful

'mafi|a *nf* Mafia. **~'oso** *a* of the Mafia ●*nm* member of the Mafia, Mafioso

'maga *nf* sorceress

ma'gagna *nf* fault

ma'gari *adv (forse)* maybe ●*int* I wish! ●*conj (per esprimere desiderio)* if only; *(anche se)* even if

magazzini'ere *nm* storesman, warehouseman. **magaz'zino** *nm* warehouse; *(emporio)* shop; **grande magazzino** department store

'maggio *nm* May

maggio'lino *nm* May bug

maggio'rana *nf* marjoram

maggio'ranza *nf* majority

maggio'rare *vt* increase

maggior'domo *nm* butler

maggi'ore *a (di dimensioni, numero)* bigger, larger; *(superlativo)* biggest, largest; *(di età)* older; *(superlativo)* oldest; *(di importanza, Mus)* major; *(superlativo)* greatest; **la maggior parte di** most; **la maggior parte del tempo** most of the time ●*pron (di dimensioni)* the bigger, the larger; *(superlativo)* the biggest, the largest; *(di età)* the older; *(superlativo)* the oldest; *(di importanza)* the major; *(superlativo)* the greatest ●*nm Mil* major; *Aeron* squadron leader. **maggio'renne** *a* of age ●*nmf* adult

maggiori'tario *a (sistema)* first-past-the-post *attrib*. **~'mente** *adv* [all] the more; *(più di tutto)* most

'Magi *nmpl* **i re ~** the Magi

ma'gia *nf* magic; *(trucco)* magic trick

magica'mente *adv* magically. **'magico** *a* magic

magi'stero *nm (insegnamento)* teaching; *(maestria)* skill; **facoltà di ~** arts faculty

magi'strale *a* masterly; **istituto ~e** teachers' training college

magi'stra|to *nm* magistrate. **~'tura** *nf* magistrature. **la ~'tura** the Bench

'magli|a *nf* stitch; *(lavoro ai ferri)* knitting; *(tessuto)* jersey; *(di rete)* mesh; *(di catena)* link; *(indumento)* vest; **fare la ~a** knit. **~a diritta** knit. **~a rosa** *(ciclismo)* ≈ yellow jersey. **~a rovescia** purl. **~'eria** *nf* knitwear. **~'etta** *nf* **~'etta [a maniche corte]** tee-shirt. **~'ficio** *nm* knitwear factory. **ma'glina** *nf (tessuto)* jersey

magli'one *nm* sweater

'magma *nm* magma

ma'gnanimo *a* magnanimous

ma'gnate *nm* magnate

ma'gnesi|a *nf* magnesia. **~o** *nm* magnesium

ma'gne|te *nm* magnet. **~tico** *a* magnetic. **~'tismo** *nm* magnetism

magne'tofono *nm* tape recorder

magnifica'mente *adv* magnificently. **~'cenza** *nf* magnificence;

(generosità) munificence. **ma'gnifico** *a* magnificent; *(generoso)* munificent

ma'gnolia *nf* magnolia

'mago *nm* magician

ma'gone *nm* avere il ~ be down; **mi è venuto il** ~ I've got a lump in my throat

'magra *nf* low water. **ma'grezza** *nf* thinness. ~**o** *a* thin; *(carne)* lean; *(scarso)* meagre

'mai *adv* never; *(inter, talvolta)* ever; **caso** ~ if anything; **caso** ~ **tornasse** in case he comes back; **come** ~? why?; **cosa** ~? what on earth?; ~ **più** never again; **più che** ~ more than ever; **quando** ~? whenever?; **quasi** ~ hardly ever

mai'ale *nm* pig; *(carne)* pork

mai'olica *nf* majolica

maio'nese *nf* mayonnaise

'mais *nm* maize

mai'uscol|a *nf* capital [letter]. ~**o** *a* capital

mal *vedi* **male**

'mala *nf* la ~ *sl* the underworld

mala'fede *nf* bad faith

malaf'fare *nm* **gente di** ~ shady characters *pl*

mala'lingua *nf* backbiter

mala'mente *adv* *(ridotto)* badly

malan'dato *a* in bad shape; *(di salute)* in poor health

ma'lanimo *nm* ill will

ma'lanno *nm* misfortune; *(malattia)* illness; **prendersi un** ~ catch something

mala'pena: a ~ *adv* hardly

ma'laria *nf* malaria

mala'ticcio *a* sickly

ma'lato, -a *a* ill, sick; *(pianta)* diseased ● *nmf* sick person. ~ **di mente** mentally ill person. **malat'tia** *nf* disease, illness; **ho preso due giorni di malattia** I had two days off sick. **malattia venerea** venereal disease

malaugu'rato *a* ill-omened. **malau'gurio** *nm* bad o ill omen

mala'vita *nf* underworld

mala'voglia *nf* unwillingness; **di** ~ unwillingly

malcapi'tato *a* wretched

malce'lato *a* ill-concealed

mal'concio *a* battered

malcon'tento *nm* discontent

malco'stume *nm* immorality

mal'destro *a* awkward; *(inesperto)* inexperienced

maldi'cen|te *a* slanderous. ~**za** *nf* slander

maldi'sposto *a* ill-disposed

'male *adv* badly; **funzionare** ~ not work properly; **star** ~ be ill; **star** ~ a qcno *(vestito ecc.)* not suit sb; **rimanerci** ~ be hurt; **non c'è** ~! not bad at all! ● *nm* evil; *(dolore)* pain; *(malattia)* illness; *(danno)* harm. **distinguere il bene dal** ~ know right from wrong; **andare a** ~ go off; **aver** ~ a have a pain in; **dove hai** ~? where does it hurt?; **far** ~ a qcno *(provocare dolore)* hurt sb; *(cibo.)* be bad for sb; **le cipolle mi fanno** ~ onions don't agree with me; **mi fa** ~ **la schiena** my back is hurting; **mal d'auto** car-sickness. **mal di denti** toothache. **mal di gola** sore throat. **mal di mare** sea-sickness; **avere il mal di mare** be sea-sick. **mal di pancia** stomach ache. **mal di testa** headache

male'detto *a* cursed; *(orribile)* awful

male'di|re *vt* curse. ~**zi'one** *nf* curse; ~**zione!** damn!

maledu|cata'mente *adv* rudely. ~**'cato** *a* ill-mannered. ~**cazi'one** *nf* rudeness

male'fatta *nf* misdeed

male'ficio *nm* witchcraft. **ma'lefico** *a* *(azione)* evil; *(nocivo)* harmful

maleodo'rante *a* foul-smelling

ma'lessere *nm* indisposition; *fig* uneasiness

ma'levolo *a* malevolent

malfa'mato *a* of ill repute

mal'fat|to *a* badly done; *(malformato)* ill-shaped. ~**tore** *nm* wrongdoer

mal'fermo *a* unsteady; *(salute)* poor

malfor'ma|to *a* misshapen. ~**zi'one** *nf* malformation

malgo'verno *nm* misgovernment

mal'grado *prep* in spite of ● *conj* although

ma'lia *nf* spell

mali'gn|are *vi* malign. ~**ità** *nf* malice; *Med* malignancy. **ma'ligno** *a* malicious; *(perfido)* evil; *Med* malignant

malinco'ni|a *nf* melancholy. ~**ca'mente** *adv* melancholically. **malin'conico** *a* melancholy

malincu'ore: a ~ *adv* unwillingly, reluctantly

malinfor'mato *a* misinformed

malintenzio'nato, -a *nmf* miscreant

malin'teso *a* mistaken ● *nm* misunderstanding

ma'lizi|a *nf* malice; *(astuzia)* cunning; *(espediente)* trick. ~**oso** *a* malicious; *(birichino)* mischievous

malle'abile *a* malleable

mal'loppo *nm* *fam* loot

malme'nare *vt* ill-treat

mal'messo *a* (*vestito male*) shabbily dressed; (*casa*) poorly furnished; (*fig: senza soldi*) hard up

malnu'tri|to *a* undernourished. **~zi'one** *nf* malnutrition

'**malo** *a* in ~ **modo** badly

ma'locchio *nm* evil eye

ma'lora *nf* ruin; **della ~** awful; **andare in ~** go to ruin

ma'lore *nm* illness; **essere colto da ~** be suddenly taken ill

malri'dotto *a* (*persona*) in a sorry state

mal'sano *a* unhealthy

'**malta** *nf* mortar

mal'tempo *nm* bad weather

'**malto** *nm* malt

maltrat|ta'mento *nm* ill-treatment. **~'tare** *vt* ill-treat

malu'more *nm* bad mood; **di ~** in a bad mood

mal'vagi|o *a* wicked. **~tà** *nf* wickedness

malversazi'one *nf* embezzlement

mal'visto *a* unpopular (**da** with)

malvi'vente *nm* criminal

malvolenti'eri *adv* unwillingly

malvo'lere *vt* **farsi ~** make oneself unpopular

'**mamma** *nf* mummy, mum; **~ mia!** good gracious!

mam'mella *nf* breast

mam'mifero *nm* mammal

'**mammola** *nf* violet

ma'nata *nf* handful; (*colpo*) slap

'**manca** *nf vedi* **manco**

manca'mento *nm* **avere un ~** faint

man'can|te *a* missing. **~za** *nf* lack; (*assenza*) absence; (*insufficienza*) shortage; (*fallo*) fault; (*imperfezione*) defect; **in ~za d'altro** failing all else; **sento la sua ~za** I miss him

man'care *vi* be lacking; (*essere assente*) be missing; (*venir meno*) fail; (*morire*) pass away; **~ di** be lacking in; **~ a** fail to keep (*promessa*); **mi manca casa** I miss home; **mi manchi** I miss you; **mi è mancato il tempo** I didn't have [the] time; **mi mancano 1000 lire** I'm 1,000 lire short; **quanto manca alla partenza?** how long before we leave?; **è mancata la corrente** there was a power failure; **sentirsi ~** feel faint; **sentirsi ~ il respiro** be unable to breathe [properly] ● *vt* miss (*bersaglio*); **è mancato poco che cadesse** he nearly fell

'**manche** *nf inv* heat

man'chevole *a* defective

'**mancia** *nf* tip

manci'ata *nf* handful

man'cino *a* left-handed

'**manco, -a** *a* left ● *nf* left hand ● *adv* (*nemmeno*) not even

man'dante *nmf* (*di delitto*) instigator

manda'rancio *nm* clementine

man'dare *vt* send; (*emettere*) give off; utter (*suono*); **~ a chiamare** send for; **~ avanti la casa** run the house; **~ giù** (*ingoiare*) swallow

manda'rino *nm Bot* mandarin

man'data *nf* consignment; (*di serratura*) turn; **chiudere a doppia ~** double lock

man'dato *nm* (*incarico*) mandate; *Jur* warrant; (*di pagamento*) money order. **~ di comparizione** [**in giudizio**] subpoena. **~ di perquisizione** search warrant

man'dibola *nf* jaw

mando'lino *nm* mandolin

'**mandor|la** *nf* almond; **a ~la** (*occhi*) almond-shaped. **~'lato** *nm* nut brittle (*type of nougat*). **~lo** *nm* almond[-tree]

'**mandria** *nf* herd

maneg'gevole *a* easy to handle. **maneggi'are** *vt* handle

ma'neggio *nm* handling; (*intrigo*) plot; (*scuola di equitazione*) riding school

ma'nesco *a* quick to hit out

ma'netta *nf* hand lever; **manette** *pl* handcuffs

man'forte *nm* **dare ~ a qcno** support sb

manga'nello *nm* truncheon

manga'nese *nm* manganese

mange'reccio *a* edible

mangia'dischi® *nm inv* type of portable record player

mangia'fumo *a inv* **candela** *nf* **~** air-purifying candle

mangia'nastri *nm inv* cassette player

mangi'a|re *vt/i* eat; (*consumare*) eat up; (*corrodere*) eat away; take (*scacchi, carte ecc*) ● *nm* eating; (*cibo*) food; (*pasto*) meal. **~rsi** *vr* **~rsi le parole** mumble; **~rsi le unghie** bite one's nails

mangi'ata *nf* big meal; **farsi una bella ~ di...** feast on...

mangia'toia *nf* manger

man'gime *nm* fodder

mangi'one, -a *nmf/am* glutton

mangiucchi'are *vt* nibble

'**mango** *nm* mango

ma'nia *nf* mania. **~ di grandezza** delusions of grandeur. **~co, -a** *a* maniacal ● *nmf* maniac

'manica *nf* sleeve; (*fam: gruppo*) band; **a maniche lunghe** long-sleeved; **essere in maniche di camicia** be in shirt sleeves; **essere di ~ larga** be free with one's money. **~ a vento** wind sock

'Manica *nf* la ~ the [English] Channel

manica'retto *nm* tasty dish

mani'chetta *nf* hose

mani'chino *nm* (*da sarto, vetrina*) dummy

'manico *nm* handle; *Mus* neck

mani'comio *nm* mental home; (*fam: confusione*) tip

mani'cotto *nm* muff; *Mech* sleeve

mani'cure *nf* manicure ● *nmf inv* (*persona*) manicurist

mani'e|ra *nf* manner; **in ~ra che** so that. **~'rato** *a* affected; (*stile*) mannered. **~'rismo** *nm* mannerism

manifat'tura *nf* manufacture; (*fabbrica*) factory

manife'stante *nmf* demonstrator

manife'sta|re *vt* show; (*esprimere*) express ● *vi* demonstrate. **~rsi** *vr* show oneself. **~zi'one** *nf* show; (*espressione*) expression; (*sintomo*) manifestation; (*dimostrazione pubblica*) demonstration

mani'festo *a* evident ● *nm* poster; (*dichiarazione pubblica*) manifesto

ma'niglia *nf* handle; (*sostegno, in autobus ecc*) strap

manipo'la|re *vt* handle; (*massaggiare*) massage; (*alterare*) adulterate; *fig* manipulate. **~'tore, ~'trice** *nmf* manipulator. **~zi'one** *nf* handling; (*massaggio*) massage; (*alterazione*) adulteration; *fig* manipulation

mani'scalco *nm* smith

man'naia *nf* (*scure*) axe; (*da macellaio*) cleaver

man'naro *a* **lupo** *nm* ~ werewolf

'mano *nf* hand; (*strato di vernice ecc*) coat; **alla ~** informal; **fuori ~** out of the way; **man ~** little by little; **man ~ che** as; **sotto ~** to hand

mano'dopera *nf* labour

ma'nometro *nm* gauge

mano'mettere *vt* tamper with; (*violare*) violate

ma'nopola *nf* (*di apparecchio*) knob; (*guanto*) mitten; (*su pullman*) handle

mano'scritto *a* handwritten ● *nm* manuscript

mano'vale *nm* labourer

mano'vella *nf* handle; *Techn* crank

ma'no|vra *nf* manoeuvre; *Rail* shunt-

ing; **fare le ~vre** manoeuvre. **~'vrabile** *a fig* easy to manipulate. **~'vrare** *vt* (*azionare*) operate; *fig* manipulate (*persona*) ● *vi* manoeuvre

manro'vescio *nm* slap

man'sarda *nf* attic

mansi'one *nf* task; (*dovere*) duty

mansu'eto *a* meek; (*animale*) docile

man'tell|a *nf* cape. **~o** *nm* cloak; (*soprabito, di animale*) coat; (*di neve*) mantle

mante'ner|e *vt* (*conservare*) keep; (*in buono stato, sostentare*) maintain. **~si** *vr* **~si in forma** keep fit. **manteni'mento** *nm* maintenance

'mantice *nm* bellows *pl*; (*di automobile*) hood

'manto *nm* cloak; (*coltre*) mantle

manto'vana *nf* pelmet

manu'al|e *a & nm* manual. **~e d'uso** user manual. **~'mente** *adv* manually

ma'nubrio *nm* handle; (*di bicicletta*) handlebars *pl*; (*per ginnastica*) dumbbell

manu'fatto *a* manufactured

manutenzi'one *nf* maintenance

'manzo *nm* steer; (*carne*) beef

'mappa *nf* map

mappa'mondo *nm* globe

mar *vedi* **mare**

ma'rasma *nm fig* decline

mara'to|na *nf* marathon. **~'neta** *nmf* marathon runner

'marca *nf* mark; *Comm* brand; (*fabbricazione*) make; (*scontrino*) ticket. **~ da bollo** revenue stamp

mar'ca|re *vt* mark; *Sport* score. **~'tamente** *adv* markedly. **~to** *a* (*tratto, accento*) strong, marked. **~'tore** *nm* (*nel calcio*) scorer

mar'chese, -a *nm* marquis ● *nf* marchioness

marchi'are *vt* brand

'marchio *nm* brand; (*caratteristica*) mark. **~ di fabbrica** trademark. **~ registrato** registered trademark

'marcia *nf* march; *Auto* gear; *Sport* walk; **mettere in ~** put into gear; **mettersi in ~** start off. **~ funebre** funeral march. **~ indietro** reverse gear; **fare ~ indietro** reverse; *fig* back-pedal. **~ nuziale** wedding march

marciapi'ede *nm* pavement; (*di stazione*) platform

marci'a|re *vi* march; (*funzionare*) go, work. **~'tore, ~'trice** *nmf* walker

'marcio *a* rotten ● *nm* rotten part; *fig* corruption. **mar'cire** *vi* go bad, rot '**marco** nm (moneta) mark

'**mare** nm sea; (luogo di mare) seaside; sul ~ (casa) at the seaside; (città) on the sea; **in alto** ~ on the high seas; **essere in alto** ~ fig not know which way to turn. ~ **Adriatico** Adriatic Sea. **mar Ionio** Ionian Sea. **mar Mediterraneo** Mediterranean. **mar Tirreno** Tyrrhenian Sea

ma'**rea** nf tide; **una** ~ **di** hundreds of; **alta/bassa** ~ high/low tide

mareggi'**ata** nf [sea] storm

mare'**moto** nm tidal wave, seaquake

maresci'**allo** nm (ufficiale) marshal; (sottufficiale) warrant-officer

marga'**rina** nf margarine

marghe'**rita** nf marguerite. **margheri'tina** nf daisy

margi'**nale** a marginal. ~'**mente** adv marginally

'**margine** nm margin; (orlo) brink; (bordo) border. ~ **di errore** margin of error. ~ **di sicurezza** safety margin

ma'**rina** nf navy; (costa) seashore; (quadro) seascape. ~ **mercantile** merchant navy. ~ **militare** navy

mari'**naio** nm sailor

mari'**nare** vt marinate; ~**re la scuola** play truant. ~**ta** nf marinade. ~**to** a Culin marinated

ma'**rino** a sea attrib, marine

mario'**netta** nf puppet

ma'**rito** nm husband

ma'**rittimo** a maritime

mar'**maglia** nf rabble

marmel'**lata** nf jam; (di agrumi) marmalade

'**marmitta** nf pot; Auto silencer. ~ **catalitica** catalytic converter

'**marmo** nm marble

mar'**mocchio** nm fam brat

mar'**moreo** a marble. ~**iz'zato** a marbled

mar'**motta** nf marmot

Ma'**rocco** nm Morocco

ma'**roso** nm breaker

mar'**rone** a brown ● nm brown; (castagna) chestnut; **marroni** pl **canditi** marrons glacés

mar'**sina** nf tails pl

mar'**supio** nm (borsa) bumbag

marte'**dì** nm inv Tuesday. ~ **grasso** Shrove Tuesday

martel'**lante** a (mal di testa) pounding

martel'**lare** vt hammer ● vi throb. ~**ta** nf hammer blow

martel'**letto** nm (di giudice) gavel

mar'**tello** nm hammer; (di battente) knocker. ~ **pneumatico** pneumatic drill

marti'**netto** nm Mech jack

mar'**tire** nmf martyr. **mar'tirio** nm martyrdom

'**martora** nf marten

martori'**are** vt torment

mar'**xismo** nm Marxism. ~**ta** a & nmf Marxist

marza'**pane** nm marzipan

marzi'**ale** a martial

marzi'**ano, -a** nmf Martian

'**marzo** nm March

mascal'**zone** nm rascal

ma'**scara** nm inv mascara

mascar'**pone** nm full-fat cream cheese often used for desserts

ma'**scella** nf jaw

'**maschera** nf mask; (costume) fancy dress; Cinema, Theat usher m, usherette f; (nella commedia dell'arte) stock character. ~**a antigas** gas mask. ~**a di bellezza** face pack. ~ **a ad ossigeno** oxygen mask. ~**a'mento** nm masking; Mil camouflage. **masche'rare** vt mask; fig camouflage. ~**arsi** vr put on a mask; ~**arsi da** dress up as. ~**ata** nf masquerade

maschi'**accio** nm (ragazza) tomboy

ma'**schile** a masculine; (sesso) male ● nm masculine [gender]. ~'**lista** a sexist. '**maschio** a male; (virile) manly ● nm male; (figlio) son. **masco'lino** a masculine

ma'**scotte** nf inv mascot

maso'**chismo** nm masochism. ~**ta** a & nmf masochist

'**massa** nf mass; Electr earth, ground Am; **comunicazioni di** ~ mass media

massa'**crante** a gruelling. ~**re** vt massacre. **mas'sacro** nm massacre; fig mess

massaggi'**are** vt massage. **mas'saggio** nm massage. ~'**tore**, ~'**trice** nm masseur ● nf masseuse

mas'**saia** nf housewife

masse'**rizie** nfpl household effects

mas'**siccio** a massive; (oro ecc) solid; (corporatura) heavy ● nm massif

'**massima** nf maxim; (temperatura) maximum. ~**o** a greatest; (quantità) maximum, greatest ● nm **il** ~**o** the maximum; **al** ~**o** at [the] most, as a maximum

'**masso** nm rock

mas'sone nm [Free]mason. **~'ria** Freemasonry

ma'stello nm wooden box for the grape or olive harvest

masti'care vt chew; (borbottare) mumble

'mastice nm mastic; (per vetri) putty

ma'stino nm mastiff

masto'dontico a gigantic

'mastro nm master; **libro ~** ledger

mastur'ba|rsi vr masturbate. **~zi'o-ne** nf masturbation

ma'tassa nf skein

mate'matic|a nf mathematics, maths. **~o, -a** a mathematical ● nmf mathematician

materas'sino nm **~ gonfiabile** air bed

mate'rasso nm mattress. **~ a molle** spring mattress

ma'teria nf matter; (materiale) material; (di studio) subject. **~ prima** raw material

materi'a|le a material; (grossolano) coarse ● nm material. **~'lismo** nm materialism. **~'lista** a materialistic ● nmf materialist. **~liz'zarsi** vr materialize. **~l'mente** adv physically

maternità nf motherhood; **ospedale di ~** maternity hospital

ma'terno a maternal; **lingua materna** mother tongue

ma'tita nf pencil

ma'trice nf matrix; (origini) roots pl; Comm counterfoil

ma'tricola nf (registro) register; Univ fresher

ma'trigna nf stepmother

matrimoni'ale a matrimonial; **vita ~** married life. **matri'monio** nm marriage; (cerimonia) wedding

ma'trona nf matron

'matta nf (nelle carte) joker

mattacchi'one, -a nmf rascal

matta'toio nm slaughterhouse

matte'rello nm rolling-pin

mat'ti|na nf morning; **la ~na** in the morning. **~'nata** nf morning; Theat matinée. **~ni'ero** a essere **~niero** be an early riser. **~no** nm morning

'matto, -a a mad, crazy; Med insane; (falso) false; (opaco) matt; **~ da legare** barking mad; **avere una voglia matta di** be dying for ● nmf madman; madwoman

mat'tone nm brick; (libro) bore

matto'nella nf tile

mattu'tino a morning attrib

matu'rare vt ripen. **maturità** nf maturity; Sch school-leaving certificate. **ma-'turo** a mature; (frutto) ripe

ma'tusa nm old fogey

mauso'leo nm mausoleum

maxi+ pref maxi+

'mazza nf club; (martello) hammer; (da baseball, cricket) bat. **~ da golf** golf-club. **maz'zata** nf blow

maz'zetta nf (di banconote) bundle

'mazzo nm bunch; (carte da gioco) pack

me pers pron me; **me lo ha dato** he gave it to me; **fai come me** do as I do; **è più veloce di me** he is faster than me o faster than I am

me'andro nm meander

M.E.C. nm abbr (Mercato Comune Europeo) EEC

mec'canica nf mechanics sg

meccanica'mente adv mechanically

mec'canico a mechanical ● nm mechanic. **mecca'nismo** nm mechanism

mèche nfpl [farsi] **fare le ~** have one's hair streaked

me'daglia nf medal. **~'one** nm medallion; (gioiello) locket

me'desimo a same

'media nf average; Sch average mark; Math mean; **essere nella ~a** be in the mid-range. **~'ano** a middle ● nm (calcio) half-back

medi'ante prep by

medi'a|re vt act as intermediary in. **~tore, ~'trice** nmf mediator; Comm middleman. **~zi'one** nf mediation

medica'mento nm medicine

medi'ca|re vt treat; dress (ferita). **~zi'one** nf medication; (di ferita) dressing

medi'c|ina nf medicine. **~ina legale** forensic medicine. **~i'nale** a medicinal ● nm medicine

'medico a medical ● nm doctor. **~ ge-nerico** general practitioner. **~ legale** forensic scientist. **~ di turno** duty doctor

medie'vale a medieval

'medio a average; (punto) middle; (statura) medium ● nm (dito) middle finger

medi'ocre a mediocre; (scadente) poor

medio'evo nm Middle Ages pl

medi'ta|re vt meditate; (progettare) plan; (considerare attentamente) think over ● vi meditate. **~zi'one** nf meditation

mediter'raneo a Mediterranean; **il [mar] M~** the Mediterranean [Sea]

131

me'dusa *nf* jellyfish

me'gafono *nm* megaphone

mega'lattico *a fam* gigantic

mega'lomane *nmf* megalomaniac

me'gera *nf* hag

'meglio *adv* better; tanto ~, ~ così so much the better ● *a* better; (superlativo) best ● *nmf* best ● *nf* avere la ~ su have the better of; fare qcsa alla [bell'e] ~ do sth as best one can ● *nm* fare del proprio ~ do one's best; fare qcsa il ~ possibile make an excellent job of sth; al ~ to the best of one's ability; per il ~ for the best

'mela *nf* apple. ~ cotogna quince

mela'grana *nf* pomegranate

mela'nina *nf* melanin

melan'zana *nf* aubergine, eggplant *Am*

me'lassa *nf* molasses *sg*

me'lenso *a* (persona, film) dull

mel'lifluo *a* (parole) honeyed; (voce) sugary

'melma *nf* slime. mel'moso *a* slimy

'melo *nm* apple[-tree]

melo'di|a *nf* melody. me'lodico *a* melodic. ~'oso *a* melodious

melo'dram|ma *nm* melodrama. ~'matico *a* melodramatic

melo'grano *nm* pomegranate tree

me'lone *nm* melon

mem'brana *nf* membrane

'membro *nm* member; (pl *nf* membra *Anat*) limb

memo'rabile *a* memorable

'memore *a* mindful; (riconoscente) grateful

me'mori|a *nf* memory; (oggetto ricordo) souvenir. imparare a ~a learn by heart. ~a permanente *Comput* non-volatile memory. ~a tampone *Comput* buffer. ~a volatile *Comput* volatile memory; memorie *pl* (biografiche) memoirs. ~'ale *nm* memorial. ~z'zare *vt* memorize; *Comput* save, store

mena'dito: a ~ *adv* perfectly

me'nare *vt* lead; (fam: picchiare) hit

mendi'ca|nte *nmf* beggar. ~re *vt/i* beg

menefre'ghista *a* devil-may-care

me'ningi *nfpl* spremersi le ~ rack one's brains

menin'gite *nf* meningitis

me'nisco *nm* meniscus

'meno *adv* less; (superlativo) least; (in operazioni, con temperatura) minus; far qcsa alla ~ peggio do sth as best one can; fare a ~ di qcsa do without sth; non posso fare a ~ di ridere I can't help laughing; ~ male! thank goodness!; sempre ~ less and less; venir ~ (svenire) faint; venir ~ a qcno (coraggio:) fail sb; sono le tre ~ un quarto it's a quarter to three; che tu venga o ~ whether you're coming or not; quanto ~ at least ● *nm* least; (con nomi plurali) fewer ● *nm* least; *Math* minus sign; il ~ possibile as little as possible; per lo ~ at least ● *prep* except [for] ● *conj* a ~ che unless

meno'ma|re *vt* (incidente:) maim. ~to *a* disabled

meno'pausa *nf* menopause

'mensa *nf* table; *Mil* mess; *Sch, Univ* refectory

men'sil|e *a* monthly ● *nm* (stipendio) [monthly] salary; (rivista) monthly. ~ità *nf inv* monthly salary. ~'mente *adv* monthly

'mensola *nf* bracket; (scaffale) shelf

'menta *nf* mint. ~ peperita peppermint

men'tal|e *a* mental. ~ità *nf inv* mentality

'mente *nf* mind; a ~ fredda in cold blood; venire in ~ a qcno occur to sb; mi è uscito di ~ it slipped my mind

men'tina *nf* mint

men'tire *vi* lie

'mento *nm* chin

'mentre *conj* (temporale) while; (invece) whereas

menù *nm inv* menu. ~ fisso set menu. ~ a tendina *Comput* pulldown menu

menzio'nare *vt* mention. menzi'one *nf* mention

men'zogna *nf* lie

mera'vigli|a *nf* wonder; a ~ marvellously; che ~! how wonderful!; con mia grande ~ much to my amazement; mi fa ~ che... I am surprised that...

meravigli'ar|e *vt* surprise. ~si *vr* ~si di be surprised at

meravigli'osa'mente *adv* marvellously. ~'oso *a* marvellous

mer'can|te *nm* merchant. ~teggi'are *vi* trade; (sul prezzo) bargain. ~'tile *a* mercantile. ~'zia *nf* merchandise, goods *pl* ● *nm* merchant ship

mer'cato *nm* market; *Fin* market [-place]. a buon ~ (comprare) cheap[ly]; (articolo) cheap. ~ dei cambi foreign exchange market. M~ Comune [Europeo] [European] Common Market. ~ coperto covered market. ~ libero free market. ~ nero black market

'merce nf goods pl
mercè nf alla ~ di at the mercy of
merce'nario a & nm mercenary
merce'ria nf haberdashery; (negozio) haberdasher's
mercoledì nm inv Wednesday. ~ delle Ceneri Ash Wednesday
mer'curio nm mercury
me'renda nf afternoon snack; far ~ have an afternoon snack
meridi'ana nf sundial
meridi'ano a midday ● nm meridian
meridio'nale a southern ● nmf southerner. meridi'one nm south
me'ringa nf meringue. ~'gata nf meringue pie
meri'tare vt deserve. meri'tevole a deserving
'meri|to nm merit; (valore) worth; in ~to a as to; per ~to di thanks to. ~'torio a meritorious
mer'letto nm lace
'merlo nm blackbird
mer'luzzo nm cod
'mero a mere
meschine'ria nf meanness. me'schi|no a wretched; (gretto) mean ● nm wretch
mesco|la'mento nm mixing. ~'lanza nf mixture
mesco'la|re vt mix; shuffle (carte); (confondere) mix up; blend (tè, tabacco ecc). ~rsi vr mix; (immischiarsi) meddle. ~ta nf (a carte) shuffle; Culin stir
'mese nm month
me'setto nm un ~ about a month
'messa¹ nf Mass
'messa² nf (il mettere) putting. ~ in moto Auto starting. ~ in piega (di capelli) set. ~ a punto adjustment. ~ in scena production. ~ a terra earthing, grounding Am
messag'gero nm messenger. mes'saggio nm message
mes'sale nm missal
'messe nf harvest
Mes'sia nm Messiah
messi'cano, -a a & nmf Mexican
'Messico nm Mexico
messin'scena nf staging; fig act
'messo pp di mettere ● nm messenger
mesti'ere nm trade; (lavoro) job; essere del ~ be an expert, know one's trade
'mesto a sad
'mestola nf (di cuoco) ladle
mestru'a|le a menstrual. ~zi'one nf menstruation. ~zi'oni pl period

'meta nf destination; fig aim
metà nf inv half; (centro) middle; a ~ strada half-way; fare a ~ con qcno go halves with sb
metabo'lismo nm metabolism
meta'done nm methadone
meta'fisico a metaphysical
me'tafora nf metaphor. meta'forico a metaphorical
me'talli|co a metallic. ~z'zato a (grigio) metallic
me'tall|o nm metal. ~ur'gia nf metallurgy
metalmec'canico a engineering ● nm engineering worker
meta'morfosi nf metamorphosis
me'tano nm methane. ~'dotto nm methane pipeline
meta'nolo nm methanol
me'teora nf meteor. meteo'rite nm meteorite
meteoro'lo'gia nf meteorology. ~'logico a meteorological
me'ticcio, -a nmf half-caste
meti'coloso a meticulous
me'tod|ico a methodical. 'metodo nm method. ~olo'gia nf methodology
me'traggio nm length (in metres)
'metrico, -a a metric; (in poesia) metrical ● nf metrics sg
'metro nm metre; (nastro) tape measure ● nf (fam: metropolitana) tube Br, subway
me'tronomo nm metronome
metro'notte nmf inv night security guard
me'tropoli nf inv metropolis. ~'tana nf subway, underground Br. ~'tano a metropolitan
'metter|e vt put; (indossare) put on; (fam: installare) put in; ~e al mondo bring into the world; ~e da parte set aside; ~e a posto tidy up; ~e fiducia inspire trust; ~e qcsa in chiaro make sth clear; ~e in mostra display; ~e a posto tidy up; ~e in vendita put up for sale; ~e su set up (casa, azienda); metter su famiglia start a family; ci ho messo un'ora it took me an hour; mettiamo che... let's suppose that... ~si vr (indossare) put on; (diventare) turn out; ~si a start to; ~si con qcno (fam: formare una coppia) start to go out with sb; ~si a letto go to bed; ~si a sedere sit down; ~si in viaggio set out
'mezza nf è la ~ it's half past twelve; sono le quattro e ~ it's half past four
mezza'luna nf half moon; (simbolo

islamico) crescent; *(coltello)* two-handled chopping knife; **a ~** half-moon shaped
mezza'manica *nf* **a ~** *(maglia)* short-sleeved
mez'zano *a* middle
mezza'notte *nf* midnight
mezz'asta: a ~ *adv* at half mast
'**mezzo** *a* half; **di mezza età** middle-aged; **~ bicchiere** half a glass; **una mezza idea** a vague idea; **siamo mezzi morti** we're half dead; **sono le quattro e ~** it's half past four. **mezz'ora** *nf* half an hour. **mezza pensione** *nf* half board. **mezza stagione** *nf* **una giacca di mezza stagione** a spring/autumn jacket ● *adv (a metà)* half ● *nm (metà)* half; *(centro)* middle; *(per raggiungere un fine)* means *sg*; **uno e ~** one and a half; **tre anni e ~** three and a half years; **in ~ a** in the middle of; **il giusto ~** the happy medium; **levare di ~** clear away; **per ~ di** by means of; **a ~ posta** by mail; **via di ~** *fig* halfway house; *(soluzione)* middle way. **mezzi** *pl (denaro)* means *pl*. **mezzi pl pubblici** public transport. **mezzi pl di trasporto** [means of] transport.
mezzo'busto: a ~ *a (foto, ritratto)* half-length
mezzo'fondo *nm* middle-distance running
mezzogi'orno *nm* midday; *(sud)* South. **il M~** Southern Italy. **~ in punto** high noon
mi *pers pron* me; *(refl)* myself; **mi ha dato un libro** he gave me a book; **mi lavo le mani** I wash my hands; **eccomi** here I am ● *nm Mus (chiave, nota)* E
miago'llare *vi* miaow. **~io** *nm* miaowing
'**mica**[1] *nf* mica
'**mica**[2] *adv fam (per caso)* by any chance; **hai ~ visto Paolo?** have you seen Paul, by any chance?; **non è ~ bello** it is not at all nice; **~ male** not bad
'**miccia** *nf* fuse
micidi'ale *a* deadly
'**micio** *nm* pussy-cat
'**microbo** *nm* microbe
micro'cosmo *nm* microcosm
micro'fiche *nf inv* microfiche
micro'film *nm inv* microfilm
mi'crofono *nm* microphone
microorga'nismo *nm* microorganism
microproces'sore *nm* microprocessor

micro'scopi|o *nm* microscope. **~co** *a* microscopic
micro'solco *nm* long-playing record
mi'dollo *nm (pl nf* **midolla**, *Anat)* marrow; **fino al ~** through and through. **~ osseo** bone marrow. **~ spinale** spinal cord
'**mie, mi'ei** *vedi* **mio**
mi'ele *nm* honey
mi'et|ere *vt* reap. **~trice** *nf Mech* harvester. **~'tura** *nf* harvest
migli'aio *nm (pl nf* **migliaia**) thousand. **a migliaia** in thousands
'**miglio** *nm Bot* millet; *(pl nf* **miglia**: *misura)* mile
miglia'mento *nm* improvement
miglio'rare *vt/i* improve
migli'ore *a* better; *(superlativo)* best ● *nmf* **il/la ~** the best
'**mignolo** *nm* little finger; *(del piede)* little toe
mi'gra|re *vi* migrate. **~zi'one** *nf* migration
'**mila** *vedi* **mille**
Mi'lano *nf* Milan
miliar'dario, -a *nm* millionaire; *(plurimiliardario)* billionaire ● *nf* millionairess; billionairess. **mili'ardo** *nm* billion
mili'are *a* **pietra** *nf* **~** milestone
milio'nario, -a *nm* millionaire ● *nf* millionairess
mili'one *nm* million
milio'nesimo *a* millionth
mili'tante *a & nmf* militant
mili'tare *vi* **~ in** be a member of *(partito ecc)* ● *a* military ● *nm* soldier; **fare il ~** do one's military service. **~ di leva** National Serviceman
'**milite** *nm* soldier. **mil'izia** *nf* militia
'**mille** *a & nm (pl* **mila**) *a o* one thousand; **due/tre mila** two/three thousand; **~ grazie!** thanks a lot!
mille'foglie *nm inv Culin* vanilla slice
mil'lennio *nm* millennium
millepi'edi *nm inv* centipede
mil'lesimo *a & nm* thousandth
milli'grammo *nm* milligram
mil'limetro *nm* millimetre
'**milza** *nf* spleen
mi'mare *vt* mimic *(persona)* ● *vi* mime
mi'metico *a* camouflage *attrib*
mimetiz'zar|e *vt* camouflage. **~si** *vr* camouflage oneself
'**mim|ica** *nf* mime. **~ico** *a* mimic. **~o** *nm* mime
mi'mosa *nf* mimosa
'**mina** *nf* mine; *(di matita)* lead

mi'naccia *nf* threat

minacci|'are *vt* threaten. ~'oso *a* threatening

mi'nare *vt* mine; *fig* undermine

mina'tor|e *nm* miner. ~io *a* threatening

mine'ra|le *a* & *nm* mineral. ~rio *a* mining *attrib*

mi'nestra *nf* soup. mine'strone *nm* vegetable soup; *(fam: insieme confuso)* hotchpotch

mingher'lino *a* skinny

mini+ *pref* mini+

minia'tura *nf* miniature. miniaturiz-'zato *a* miniaturized

mini'era *nf* mine

mini'golf *nm* miniature golf

mini'gonna *nf* miniskirt

minima'mente *adv* minimally

mini'market *nm inv* minimarket

minimiz'zare *vt* minimize

'minimo *a* least, slightest; *(il più basso)* lowest; *(salario, quantità ecc)* minimum ● *nm* minimum; girare a ~ *Auto* idle

mini'stero *nm* ministry; *(governo)* government

mi'nistro *nm* minister. M~ del Tesoro Finance Minister, Chancellor of the Exchequer *Br*

mino'ranza *nf* minority *attrib*

mino'rato, -a *a* disabled ● *nmf* disabled person

mi'nore *a (gruppo, numero)* smaller; *(superlativo)* smallest; *(distanza)* shorter; *(superlativo)* shortest; *(prezzo)* lower; *(superlativo)* lowest; *(di età)* younger; *(superlativo)* youngest; *(di importanza)* minor; *(superlativo)* least important ● *nmf* younger; *(superlativo)* youngest; *Jur* minor; il ~ dei mali the lesser of two evils; i minori di 14 anni children under 14. mino'renne *a* under age ● *nmf* minor

minori'tario *a* minority *attrib*

minu'etto *nm* minuet

mi'nuscolo, -a *a* tiny ● *nf* small letter

mi'nuta *nf* rough copy

mi'nuto[1] *a* minute; *(persona)* delicate; *(ricerca)* detailed; *(pioggia, neve)* fine; al ~ *Comm* retail

mi'nuto[2] *nm (di tempo)* minute; spac'care il ~ be dead on time

mi'nuzia *nf* trifle. ~'oso *a* detailed; *(persona)* meticulous

'mio (il mio *m*, la mia *f*, i miei *mpl*, le mie *fpl*) *a poss* my; questa macchina è mia this car is mine; ~ padre my father; un ~ amico a friend of mine ● *poss pron* mine; i miei *(genitori ecc)* my folks

'miope *a* short-sighted. mio'pia *nf* short-sightedness

'mira *nf* aim; *(bersaglio)* target; prendere la ~ take aim; prendere di ~ qcno *fig* have it in for sb

mi'racolo *nm* miracle. ~sa'mente *adv* miraculously. miraco'loso *a* miraculous

mi'raggio *nm* mirage

mi'rar|e *vi* [take] aim. ~si *vr (guardarsi)* look at oneself

mi'riade *nf* myriad

mi'rino *nm* sight; *Phot* view-finder

mir'tillo *nm* blueberry

mi'santropo, -a *nmf* misanthropist

mi'scela *nf* mixture; *(di caffè, tabacco)* blend. ~'tore *nm (di acqua)* mixer tap

miscel'lanea *nf* miscellany

'mischia *nf* scuffle; *(nel rugby)* scrum

mischi'ar|e *vt* mix; shuffle *(carte da gioco)*. ~si *vr* mix; *(immischiarsi)* interfere

misco'noscere *vt* not appreciate

mi'scuglio *nm* mixture; *fig* medley

mise'rabile *a* wretched

misera'mente *adv (finire)* miserably; *(vivere)* in abject poverty

mi'seria *nf* poverty; *(infelicità)* misery; guadagnare una ~ earn a pittance; porca ~! hell!; miserie *pl (disgrazie)* misfortunes

miseri'cordi|a *nf* mercy. ~'oso *a* merciful

'misero *a (miserabile)* wretched; *(povero)* poor; *(scarso)* paltry

mi'sfatto *nm* misdeed

mi'sogino *nm* misogynist

mis'saggio *nm* vision mixer

'missile *nm* missile

missio'nario, -a *nmf* missionary.

missi'one *nf* mission

misteri'osa'mente *adv* mysteriously. ~'oso *a* mysterious. mi'stero *nm* mystery

'mistic|a *nf* mysticism. ~'cismo *nm* mysticism. ~co *a* mystic[al] ● *nm* mystic

mistifi'ca|re *vt* distort *(verità)*. ~zi'one *nf (della verità)* distortion

'misto *a* mixed; ~ lana/cotone wool/cotton-mix; scuola mista mixed *o* co-educational school ● *nm* mixture

mi'sura *nf* measure; *(dimensione)* measurement; *(taglia)* size; *(limite)* limit; **su ~** ⟨abiti⟩ made to measure; ⟨mobile⟩ custom-made; **a ~** ⟨andare, calzare⟩ perfectly; **a ~ che** as. **~ di sicurezza** safety measure. **misu'rare** vt measure; try on ⟨indumenti⟩; ⟨limitare⟩ limit. **misu'rarsi** vr **misurarsi con** ⟨gareggiare⟩ compete with. **misu'rato** a measured. **misu'rino** nm measuring spoon

'**mite** a mild; ⟨prezzo⟩ moderate
'**mitico** a mythical
miti'gare vt mitigate. **~si** vr calm down; ⟨clima:⟩ become mild
mitiz'zare vt mythicize
'**mito** nm myth. **~lo'gia** nf mythology. **~'logico** a mythological
mi'tomane nmf compulsive liar
'**mitra** nf Relig mitre ● nm inv Mil machine-gun
mitragli'a|re vt machine-gun; **~re di domande** fire questions at. **~'trice** nf machine-gun
mit'tente nmf sender
mne'monico a mnemonic
mo' nm **a ~ di** by way of ⟨esempio, consolazione⟩
'**mobile**¹ a mobile; ⟨volubile⟩ fickle; ⟨che si può muovere⟩ movable; **beni mobili** personal estate; **squadra ~** flying squad
'**mobile**² nm piece of furniture; **mobili** pl furniture sg. **mo'bilia** nf furniture. **~li'ficio** nm furniture factory
mo'bilio nm furniture
mobilità nf mobility
mobili'ta|re vt mobilize. **~zi'one** nf mobilization
mocas'sino nm moccasin
mocci'oso, -a nmf brat
'**moccolo** nm ⟨di candela⟩ candle-end; ⟨moccio⟩ snot
'**moda** nf fashion; **di ~** in fashion; **alla ~** ⟨musica, vestiti⟩ up-to-date; **fuori ~** unfashionable
modalità nf inv formality; **~ d'uso** instruction
mo'della nf model. **model'lare** vt model
model'li|no nm model. **~sta** nmf designer
mo'dello nm model; ⟨stampo⟩ mould; ⟨di carta⟩ pattern; ⟨modulo⟩ form
'**modem** nm inv modem; **mandare per ~ modem**, send by modem
mode'ra|re vt moderate; ⟨diminuire⟩ reduce. **~rsi** vr control oneself. **~ta'mente** adv moderately **~'to** a moderate. **~'tore**, **~'trice** nmf ⟨in tavola rotonda⟩ moderator. **~zi'one** nf moderation
moder|na'mente adv ⟨in modo moderno⟩ in a modern style. **~iz'zare** vt modernize. **mo'derno** a modern
mo'destia nf modesty. **~o** a modest
'**modico** a reasonable
mo'difica nf modification
modifi'ca|re vt modify. **~zi'one** nf modification
mo'dista nf milliner
'**modo** nm way; ⟨garbo⟩ manners pl; ⟨occasione⟩ chance; Gram mood; **ad ogni ~** anyhow; **di ~ che** so that; **fare in ~ di** try to; **in che ~** ⟨inter⟩ how; **in qualche ~** somehow; **in questo ~** like this; **~ di dire** idiom; **per ~ di dire** so to speak
modu'la|re vt modulate. **~zi'one** nf modulation. **~zione di frequenza** frequency modulation. **~'tore nm ~tore di frequenza** frequency modulator
'**modulo** nm form; ⟨lunare, di comando⟩ module. **~ continuo** continuous paper
'**mogano** nm mahogany
'**mogio** a dejected
'**moglie** nf wife
'**mola** nf millstone; Mech grindstone
mo'lare nm molar
'**mole** nf mass; ⟨dimensione⟩ size
mo'lecola nf molecule
mole'stare vt bother; ⟨più forte⟩ molest. **mo'lestia** nf nuisance. **mo'lesto** a bothersome
'**molla** nf spring; **molle** pl tongs
mol'lare vt let go; ⟨fam: lasciare⟩ leave; fam give ⟨ceffone⟩; Naut cast off ● vi cease; **mollala!** fam stop that!
'**molle** a soft; ⟨bagnato⟩ wet
mol'letta nf ⟨per capelli⟩ hair-grip; ⟨per bucato⟩ clothes-peg; **mollette** pl ⟨per ghiaccio ecc⟩ tongs
mol'lezz|a nf softness; **~e** pl fig luxury
mol'lica nf crumb
mol'lusco nm mollusc
'**molo** nm pier; ⟨banchina⟩ dock
mol'teplic|e a manifold; ⟨numeroso⟩ numerous. **~ità** nf multiplicity
moltipli'ca|re vt, **~rsi** vr multiply. **~'tore** nm multiplier. **~'trice** nf calculating machine. **~zi'one** nf multiplication
molti'tudine nf multitude
'**molto** a a lot of; ⟨con negazione e interrogazione⟩ much, a lot of; ⟨con nomi plurali⟩ many, a lot of; **non ~ tempo** not much time, not a lot of time ● adv very;

(con verbi) a lot; *(con avverbi)* much; ~ **stupido** very stupid; **mangiare** ~ eat a lot; ~ **più veloce** much faster; **non mangiare** ~ not eat a lot, not eat much ● *pron* a lot; *(molto tempo)* a lot of time; *(con negazione e interrogazione)* much, a lot; *(plurale)* many; **non ne ho** ~ I don't have much, I don't have a lot; **non ne ho molti** I don't have many, I don't have a lot; **non ci metterò** ~ I won't be long; **fra non** ~ before long; **molti** *(persone)* a lot of people; **eravamo in molti** there were a lot of us

momentanea'mente *adv* momentarily; **è** ~ **assente** he's not here at the moment. **momen'taneo** *a* momentary

mo'mento *nm* moment; **a momenti** *(a volte)* sometimes; *(fra un momento)* in a moment; **dal** ~ **che** since; **per il** ~ for the time being; **da un** ~ **all'altro** *(cambiare idea ecc)* from one moment to the next; *(aspettare qcno ecc)* at any moment

'monaca *nf* nun. ~**o** *nm* monk

'Monaco *nm* Monaco ● *nf (di Baviera)* Munich

mo'narca *nm* monarch. **monar'chia** *nf* monarchy. ~**hico, -a** *a* monarchic ● *nmf* monarchist

mona'stero *nm (di monaci)* monastery; *(di monache)* convent. **mo'nastico** *a* monastic

monche'rino *nm* stump

'monco *a* maimed; *(fig: troncato)* truncated; ~ **di un braccio** one-armed

mon'dano *a* worldly; **vita mondana** social life

mondi'ale *a* world *attrib*; **di fama** ~ world-famous

'mondo *nm* world; **il bel** ~ fashionable society; **un** ~ *(molto)* a lot

mondovisi'one *nf* **in** ~ transmitted worldwide

mo'nello, -a *nmf* urchin

mo'neta *nf* coin; *(denaro)* money; *(denaro spicciolo)* [small] change. ~ **estera** foreign currency. ~ **legale** legal tender. ~ **unica** single currency. **mone'tario** *a* monetary

mongolfi'era *nf* hot air balloon

mo'nile *nm* jewel

'monito *nm* warning

moni'tore *nm* monitor

mo'nocolo *nm* monocle

monoco'lore *a Pol* one-party

mono'dose *a inv* individually packaged

monogra'fia *nf* monograph

mono'gramma *nm* monogram

mono'kini *nm inv* monokini

mono'lingue *a* monolingual

monolo'cale *nm* studio flat, studio apartment *Am*

mo'nologo *nm* monologue

mono'pattino *nm* [child's] scooter

mono'poli|o *nm* monopoly. ~**o di stato** state monopoly. ~**z'zare** *vt* monopolize

mono'sci *nm inv* monoski

monosil'labico *a* monosyllabic. **mono'sillabo** *nm* monosyllable

mono'tonia *nf* monotony. **mo'notono** *a* monotonous

mono'uso *a* disposable

monou'tente *a inv* single-user *attrib*

monsi'gnore *nm* monsignor

mon'sone *nm* monsoon

monta'carichi *nm inv* hoist

mon'taggio *nm Mech* assembly; *Cinema* editing; **catena di** ~ production line

mon'ta|gna *nf* mountain; *(zona)* mountains *pl*; **montagne** *pl* **russe** big dipper. ~**'gnoso** *a* mountainous. ~**'naro, -a** *nmf* highlander. ~**no** *a* mountain *attrib*

mon'tante *nm (di finestra, porta)* upright

mon'ta|re *vt/i* mount; get on *(veicolo)*; *(aumentare)* rise; *Mech* assemble; frame *(quadro)*; *Culin* whip; edit *(film)*; *(a cavallo)* ride; *fig* blow up; ~**rsi la testa** get big-headed. ~**to, -a** *nmf* poser. ~**'tura** *nf Mech* assembling; *(di occhiali)* frame; *(di gioiello)* mounting; *fig* exaggeration

'monte *nm anche fig* mountain; **a** ~ upstream; **andare a** ~ be ruined; **mandare a** ~ **qcsa** ruin sth. ~ **di pietà** pawnshop

monte'premi *nm inv* jackpot

mont'gomery *nm inv* duffle coat

mon'tone *nm* ram; **carne di** ~ mutton

montu'oso *a* mountainous

monumen'tale *a* monumental. **monu'mento** *nm* monument

mo'quette *nf (tappeto)* fitted carpet

'mora *nf (del gelso)* mulberry; *(del rovo)* blackberry

mo'ral|e *a* moral ● *nf* morals *pl*; *(di storia)* moral ● *nm* morale. **mora'lista** *nmf* moralist. ~**ità** *nf* morality; *(condotta)* morals *pl.* ~**iz'zare** *vt/i* moralize. ~**'mente** *adv* morally

morbi'dezza *nf* softness

'morbido *a* soft

mor'billo *nm* measles *sg*

'**morbo** *nm* disease. **~sità** *nf* (*qualità*) morbidity

mor'boso *a* morbid

mor'dace *a* cutting

mor'dente *a* biting. '**mordere** *vt* bite; (*corrodere*) bite into. **mordicchi'are** *vt* gnaw

mor'fina *nf* morphine. **morfi'nomane** *nmf* morphine addict

mori'bondo *a* dying; (*istituzione*) moribund

morige'rato *a* moderate

mo'rire *vi* die; *fig* die out; **fa un freddo da ~** it's freezing cold, it's perishing; **~ di noia** be bored to death; **c'era da ~ dal ridere** it was hilariously funny

mor'mone *nmf* Mormon

mormo'r|are *vt/i* murmur; (*brontolare*) mutter. **~io** *nm* murmuring; (*lamentela*) grumbling

'**moro** *a* dark ● *nm* Moor

mo'roso *a* in arrears

'**morsa** *nf* vice; *fig* grip

'**morse** *a* alfabeto **~** Morse code

mor'setto *nm* clamp

morsi'care *vt* bite. '**morso** *nm* bite; (*di cibo, briglia*) bit; **i morsi della fame** hunger pangs

morta'della *nf* mortadella (*type of salted pork*)

mor'taio *nm* mortar

mor'tal|e *a* mortal; (*simile a morte*) deadly; **di una noia ~e** deadly. **~ità** *nf* mortality. **~'mente** *adv* (*ferito*) fatally; (*offeso*) mortally

morta'retto *nm* firecracker

'**morte** *nf* death

mortifi'cante *a* mortifying

mortifi'ca|re *vt* mortify. **~rsi** *vr* be mortified. **~to** *a* mortified. **~zi'one** *nf* mortification

'**morto, -a** *pp di* **morire** ● *a* dead; **~ di freddo** frozen to death; **stanco ~** dead tired ● *nm* dead man ● *nf* dead woman

mor'torio *nm* funeral

mo'saico *nm* mosaic

'**Mosca** *nf* Moscow

'**mosca** *nf* fly; (*barba*) goatee. **~ cieca** blindman's buff

mo'scato *a* muscat; **noce moscata** nutmeg ● *nm* muscatel

msce'rino *nm* midge; (*fam: persona*) midget

mo'schea *nf* mosque

moschi'cida *a* fly *attrib*

'**moscio** *a* limp; **avere l'erre moscia** not be able to say one's r's properly

mo'scone *nm* bluebottle; (*barca*) pedalo

'**moss|a** *nf* movement; (*passo*) move. **~o** *pp di* **muovere** ● *a* (*mare*) rough; (*capelli*) wavy; (*fotografia*) blurred

mo'starda *nf* mustard

'**mostra** *nf* show; (*d'arte*) exhibition; **far ~ di** pretend; **in ~** on show; **mettersi in ~** make oneself conspicuous

mo'stra|re *vt* show; (*indicare*) point out; (*spiegare*) explain. **~rsi** *vr* show oneself; (*apparire*) appear

'**mostro** *nm* monster; (*fig: persona*) genius; **~ sacro** *fig* sacred cow

mostru|osa'mente *adv* tremendously. **~'oso** *a* monstrous; (*incredibile*) enormous

mo'tel *nm inv* motel

moti'va|re *vt* cause; *Jur* justify. **~to a** *a* (*persona*) motivated. **~zi'one** *nf* motivation; (*giustificazione*) justification

mo'tivo *nm* reason; (*movente*) motive; (*in musica, letteratura*) theme; (*disegno*) motif

'**moto** *nm* motion; (*esercizio*) exercise; (*gesto*) movement; (*sommossa*) rising ● *nf inv* (*motocicletta*) motor bike; **mettere in ~** start (*motore*)

moto'carro *nm* three-wheeler

motoci'cl|etta *nf* motor cycle. **~ismo** *nm* motorcycling. **~ista** *nmf* motor-cyclist

moto'cros|s *nm* motocross. **~'sista** *nmf* scrambler

moto'lancia *nf* motor launch

moto'nave *nf* motor vessel

mo'tore *a* motor ● *nm* motor, engine. **moto'retta** *nf* motor scooter. **moto'rino** *nm* moped. **motorino d'avviamento** starter

motoriz'za|to *a Mil* motorized. **~zi'one** *nf* (*ufficio*) vehicle licensing office

moto'scafo *nm* motorboat

motove'detta *nf* patrol vessel

'**motto** *nm* motto; (*facezia*) witticism; (*massima*) saying

mountain bike *nf inv* mountain bike

mouse *nm inv Comput* mouse

mo'vente *nm* motive

movimen'ta|re *vt* enliven. **~to** *a* lively. **movi'mento** *nm* movement; **essere sempre in movimento** be always on the go

mozi'one *nf* motion

mozzafi'ato *a inv* nail-biting

moz'zare *vt* cut off; dock (*coda*); **~ il fiato a** qcno take sb's breath away mozza'rella *nf* mozzarella, *mild, white cheese*

mozzi'cone *nm* (*di sigaretta*) stub

'mozzo *nm Mech* hub; *Naut* ship's boy ● *a* (*coda*) truncated; (*testa*) severed

'mucca *nf* cow. morbo della ~ pazza mad cow disease

'mucchio *nm* heap, pile; un ~ di *fig* lots of

'muco *nm* mucus

'muffa *nf* mould; fare la ~ go mouldy. muf'fire *vi* go mouldy

muf'fole *nfpl* mittens

mug'gi|re *vi* (*mucca:*) moo, low; (*toro:*) bellow. ~to *nm* moo; bellow; (*azione*) mooing; bellowing

mu'ghetto *nm* lily of the valley

mugo'lare *vi* whine; (*persona:*) moan. mugo'lio *nm* whining

mugu'gnare *vt fam* mumble

mulat'tiera *nf* mule track

mu'latto, -a *nmf* mulatto

muli'nello *nm* (*d'acqua*) whirl-pool; (*di vento*) eddy; (*giocattolo*) windmill

mu'lino *nm* mill. ~ a vento windmill

'mulo *nm* mule

'multa *nf* fine. mul'tare *vt* fine

multico'lore *a* multicoloured

multi'lingue *a* multilingual

multi'media *mpl* multimedia

multimedi'ale *a* multimedia *attrib*

multimiliar'dario, -a *nmf* multi-millionaire

multinazio'nale *nf* multinational

'multiplo *a & nm* multiple

multiproprietà *nf inv* time-share

multi'uso *a* (*utensile*) all-purpose

'mummia *nf* mummy

'mungere *vt* milk

mungi'tura *nf* milking

munici'pal|e *a* municipal. ~ità *nf inv* town council. muni'cipio *nm* town hall

mu'nifico *a* munificent

mu'nire *vt* fortify; ~ di (*provvedere*) supply with

munizi'oni *nfpl* ammunition *sg*

'munto *pp di* mungere

mu'over|e *vt* move; (*suscitare*) arouse.

~si *vr* move; muoviti! hurry up!, come on!

'mura *nfpl* (*cinta di città*) walls

mu'raglia *nf* wall

mu'rale *a* mural; (*pittura*) wall *attrib*

mur'a|re *vt* wall up. ~'tore *nm* bricklayer; (*con pietre*) mason; (*operaio edile*) builder. ~'tura *nf* (*di pietra*) masonry, stonework; (*di mattoni*) brickwork

mu'rena *nf* moray eel

'muro *nm* wall; (*di nebbia*) bank; a ~ (*armadio*) built-in. ~ portante load-bearing wall. ~ del suono sound barrier

'muschio *nm Bot* moss

musco'la|re *a* muscular. ~'tura *nf* muscles *pl.* 'muscolo *nm* muscle

mu'seo *nm* museum

museru'ola *nf* muzzle

'musi|ca *nf* music. ~cal *nm inv* musical. ~'cale *a* musical. ~'cista *nmf* musician.

'muso *nm* muzzle; (*pej: di persona*) mug; (*di aeroplano*) nose; fare il ~ sulk. mu'sone, -a *nmf* sulker

'mussola *nf* muslin

musul'mano, -a *nmf* Moslem

'muta *nf* (*cambio*) change; (*di penne*) moult; (*di cani*) pack; (*per immersione subacquea*) wetsuit

muta'mento *nm* change

mu'tan|de *nfpl* pants; (*da donna*) knickers. ~'doni *nmpl* (*da uomo*) long johns; (*da donna*) bloomers

mu'tare *vt* change

mu'tevole *a* changeable

muti'la|re *vt* mutilate. ~to, -a *nmf* disabled person. ~to di guerra disabled ex-serviceman. ~zi'one *nf* mutilation

mu'tismo *nm* dumbness; *fig* obstinate silence

'muto *a* dumb; (*silenzioso*) silent; (*fonetica*) mute

'mutu|a *nf* [cassa *nf*] ~ sickness benefit fund. ~'ato, -a *nmf* ≈ NHS patient

'mutuo[1] *a* mutual

'mutuo[2] *nm* loan; (*per la casa*) mortgage; fare un ~ take out a mortgage. ~ ipotecario mortgage

Nn

'nacchera nf castanet

'nafta nf naphtha; (per motori) diesel oil

'naia nf cobra; (sl: servizio militare) national service

'nailon nm nylon

'nanna nf (sl: infantile) byebyes; **andare a ~** go byebyes; **fare la ~** sleep

'nano, -a a & nmf dwarf

napole'tano, -a a & nmf Neapolitan

'Napoli nf Naples

'nappa nf tassel; (pelle) soft leather

narci'sis|mo nm narcissism. **~ta** a & nmf narcissist

nar'ciso nm narcissus

nar'cotico a & nm narcotic

na'rice nf nostril

nar'ra|re vt tell. **~'tivo, -a** a narrative • nf fiction. **~'tore, ~'trice** nmf narrator. **~zi'one** nf narration; (racconto) story

na'sale a nasal

'nasc|ere vi (venire al mondo) be born; (germogliare) sprout; (sorgere) rise; **~ere da** fig arise from. **~ita** nf birth. **~i'turo** nm unborn child

na'scondere vt hide. **~si** vr hide

nascon'di|glio nm hiding-place. **~no** nm hide-and-seek. **na'scosto** pp di nascondere • a hidden; **di nascosto** secretly

na'sello nm (pesce) hake

'naso nm nose

'nastro nm ribbon; (di registratore ecc) tape. **~ adesivo** adhesive tape. **~ isolante** insulating tape. **~ trasportatore** conveyor belt

na'tal|e a (paese) of one's birth. **N~e** nm Christmas; **~i** pl parentage. **~ità** nf [number of] births. **nata'lizio** a (del Natale) Christmas attrib; (di nascita) of one's birth

na'tante a floating • nm craft

'natica nf buttock

na'tio a native

Nativ|ità nf Nativity. **na'tivo, -a** a & nmf native

'nato pp di nascere • a born; **uno scrittore ~** a born writer; **nata Rossi** née Rossi

NATO nf Nato, NATO

na'tura nf nature; **pagare in ~** pay in kind. **~ morta** still life

natu'ra|le a natural; **al ~le** (alimento) plain, natural; **~le!** naturally, of course. **~'lezza** nf naturalness. **~liz'zare** vt naturalize. **~l'mente** adv (ovviamente) naturally, of course

natu'rista nmf naturalist

naufra'gare vi be wrecked; (persona:) be shipwrecked. **nau'fragio** nm shipwreck; fig wreck. **'naufrago, -a** nmf survivor

'nause|a nf nausea; **avere la ~a** feel sick. **~a'bondo** a nauseating. **~'ante** a nauseating. **~'are** vt nauseate

'nautic|a nf navigation. **~o** a nautical

na'vale a naval

na'vata nf (centrale) nave; (laterale) aisle

'nave nf ship. **~ cisterna** tanker. **~ da guerra** warship. **~ spaziale** spaceship

na'vetta nf shuttle

navi'cella nf: **~ spaziale** nose cone

navi'gabile a navigable

navi'ga|re vi sail; **~re in Internet** surf the Net. **~'tore, ~'trice** mf navigator. **~zi'one** nf navigation

na'viglio nm fleet; (canale) canal

nazio'na|le a national • nf Sport national team. **~'lismo** nm nationalism. **~ lista** nmf nationalist. **~lità** nf inv nationality. **~liz'zare** vt nationalize. **nazi'one** nf nation

na'zista a nmf Nazi

N.B. abbr (nota bene) N.B.

ne pers pron (di lui) about him; (di lei) about her; (di loro) about them; (di ciò) about it; (da ciò) from that; (di un insieme) of it; (di un gruppo) of them; **non ne conosco nessuno** I don't know any of them; **ne ho l'ave some; non ne ho più** I don't have any left • adv from there; **ne vengo ora** I've just come from there; **me ne vado** I'm off

né conj né... né... neither... nor...; **non**

ne ho il tempo né la voglia I don't have either the time or the inclination; **né tu né io vogliamo andare** neither you nor I want to go; **né l'uno né l'altro** neither (of them/us)

ne'anche *adv* (*neppure*) not even; (*senza neppure*) without even ● *conj* (*e neppure*) neither... nor; **non parlo inglese, e lui ~ lui** I don't speak English, neither does he *o* and he doesn't either

'nebbi|a *nf* mist; (*in città, su strada*) fog. **~'oso** *a* misty; foggy

necessaria'mente *adv* necessarily. **neces'sario** *a* necessary

necessità *nf inv* necessity; (*bisogno*) need

necessi'tare *vi* **~ di** need; (*essere necessario*) be necessary

necro'logio *nm* obituary

ne'cropoli *nf inv* necropolis

ne'fando *a* wicked

ne'fasto *a* ill-omened

ne'ga|re *vt* deny; (*rifiutare*) refuse; **essere ~to per qcsa** be no good at sth. **~'tivo, -a** *a* negative ● *nf* negative. **~zi'one** *nf* negation; (*diniego*) denial; *Gram* negative

ne'gletto *a* neglected

'negli = **in + gli**

negli'gen|te *a* negligent. **~za** *nf* negligence

negozi'abile *a* negotiable

negozi'ante *nmf* dealer; (*bottegaio*) shopkeeper

negozi'a|re *vt* negotiate ● *vi* **~re in** trade in. **~ti** *nmpl* negotiations

ne'gozio *nm* shop

'negro, -a *a* Negro, black ● *nmf* Negro, black; (*scrittore*) ghost writer

'nei = **in + i. nel** = **in + il. nella** = **in + la. 'nelle** = **in + le. 'nello** = **in + lo**

'nembo *nm* nimbus

ne'mico, -a *a* hostile ● *nmf* enemy

nem'meno *conj* not even

'nenia *nf* dirge; (*per bambini*) lullaby; (*piagnucolio*) wail

'neo *nm* mole; (*applicato*) beauty spot

neo+ *pref* neo+

neofa'scismo *nm* neofascism

neo'litico *a* Neolithic

neolo'gismo *nm* neologism

'neon *nm* neon

neo'nato, -a *a* newborn ● *nmf* newborn baby

neozelan'dese *a* New Zealand ● *nmf* New Zealander

nep'pure *conj* not even

'nerb|o *nm* (*forza*) strength; *fig* backbone. **~o'ruto** *a* brawny

ne'retto *nm* *Typ* bold [type]

'nero *a* black; (*fam: arrabbiato*) fuming ● *nm* black; **mettere ~ su bianco** put in writing

nerva'tura *nf* nerves *pl*; *Bot* veining; (*di libro*) band

'nervo *nm* nerve; *Bot* vein; **avere i nervi** be bad-tempered; **dare ai nervi a qcno** get on sb's nerves. **~'sismo** *nm* nerviness

ner'voso *a* nervous; (*irritabile*) bad-tempered; **avere il ~** be irritable; **esaurimento** *nm* **~** nervous breakdown

'nespol|a *nf* medlar. **~o** *nm* medlar[tree]

'nesso *nm* link

nes'suno *a* no, not... any; (*qualche*) any; **non ho nessun problema** I don't have any problems, I have no problems; **non lo trovo da nessuna parte** I can't find it anywhere; **in nessun modo** on no account; **nessuna notizia?** any news? ● *pron* nobody, no one, not... anybody, not... anyone; (*qualcuno*) anybody, anyone; **hai delle domande? – nessuna** do you have any questions? – none; **~ di voi** none of you; **~ dei due** (*di voi due*) neither of you; **non ho visto ~ dei tuoi amici** I haven't seen any of your friends; **c'è ~?** is anybody there?

'nettare[1] *nm* nectar

net'tare[2] *vt* clean

net'tezza *nf* cleanliness. **~ urbana** cleansing department

'netto *a* clean; (*chiaro*) clear; *Comm* net; **di ~** just like that

nettur'bino *nm* dustman

neu'tral|e *a & nm* neutral. **~ità** *nf* neutrality. **~iz'zare** *vt* neutralize.

'neutro *a* neutral; *Gram* neuter ● *nm* *Gram* neuter

neu'trone *nm* neutron

'neve *nf* snow

nevi'|care *vi* snow; **~ca** it is snowing. **~'cata** *nf* snowfall. **ne'vischio** *nm* sleet. **ne'voso** *a* snowy

nevral'gia *nf* neuralgia. **ne'vralgico** *a* neuralgic

ne'vro|si *nf inv* neurosis. **~tico** *a* neurotic

'nibbio *nm* kite

'nicchia *nf* niche

nicchi'are *vi* shilly-shally

'nichel *nm* nickel

nichi'lista *a & nmf* nihilist

nico'tina nf nicotine

nidi'ata nf brood. **'nido** nm nest; (giardino d'infanzia) crèche

ni'ente pron nothing, not... anything; (qualcosa) anything; **non ho fatto ~ di male** I didn't do anything wrong; **grazie! – di ~!** thank you! – don't mention it!; **non serve a ~** it is no use; **vuoi ~?** do you want anything?; **da ~** (poco importante) minor; (di poco valore) worthless ● a inv fam **non ho ~ fame** I'm not the slightest bit hungry ● adv **non fa ~** (non importa) it doesn't matter; **per ~** at all; (litigare) over nothing; **~ affatto!** no way! ● nm **un bel ~** absolutely nothing

nientedi'meno, niente'meno adv **~ che** no less than ● int fancy that!

'ninfa nf nymph

nin'fea nf water-lily

ninna'nanna nf lullaby

'ninnolo nm plaything; (fronzolo) knick-knack

ni'pote nm (di zii) nephew; (di nonni) grandson, grandchild ● nf (di zii) niece; (di nonni) granddaughter, grandchild

'nisba pron (sl: niente) zilch

'nitido a neat; (chiaro) clear

ni'trato nm nitrate

ni'trire vi neigh. **~to** nm (di cavallo) neigh

n° abbr (numero) No

no adv no; (con congiunzione) not; **dire di no** say no; **credo di no** I don't think so; **perché no?** why not?; **io no** not me; **ha detto così, no?** he said so, didn't he?; **fa freddo, no?** it's cold, isn't it?

'nobil|e a noble ● nm noble, nobleman ● nf noble, noblewoman. **~i'are** a noble. **~tà** nf nobility

'nocca nf knuckle

nocci'ol|a nf hazel-nut. **~o** nm (albero) hazel

'nocciolo nm stone; fig heart

'noce nf walnut ● nm (albero, legno) walnut. **~ moscata** nutmeg. **~'pesca** nf nectarine

no'civo a harmful

'nodo nm knot; fig lump; Comput node; **fare il ~ della cravatta** do up one's tie. **~ alla gola** lump in the throat. **no'do-so** a knotty. **'nodulo** nm nodule

'noi pers pron (soggetto) we; (oggetto, con prep) us; **chi è? – siamo ~** who is it? – it's us

'noia nf boredom; (fastidio) bother; (persona) bore; **dar ~** annoy

noi'altri pers pron we

noi'oso a boring; (fastidioso) tiresome

noleggi'are vt hire; (dare a noleggio) hire out; charter (nave, aereo). **no'leg-gio** nm hire; (di nave, aereo) charter. **'nolo** nm hire; Naut freight; **a nolo** for hire

'nomade a nomadic ● nmf nomad

'nome nm name; Gram noun; **a ~ di** in the name of; **di ~** by name; **farsi un ~** make a name for oneself. **~ di famiglia** surname. **~ da ragazza** maiden name.

no'mea nf reputation

nomencla'tura nf nomenclature

no'mignolo nm nickname

'nomina nf appointment. **nomi'nale** a nominal; Gram noun attrib

nomi'na|re vt name; (menzionare) mention; (eleggere) appoint. **~'tivo** a nominative; Comm registered ● nm nominative; (nome) name

non adv not; **~ ti amo** I do not o don't love you; **~ c'è di che** not at all

nonché conj (tanto meno) let alone; (e anche) as well as

noncu'ran|te a nonchalant; (negligente) indifferent. **~za** nf nonchalance; (negligenza) indifference

nondi'meno conj nevertheless

'nonna nf grandmother, grandma fam

'nonno nm grandfather, grandpa fam; **nonni** pl grandparents

non'nulla nm inv trifle

'nono a & nm ninth

nono'stante prep in spite of ● conj although

nontiscordardimé nm inv forget-me-not

nonvio'lento a nonviolent

nord nm north; **del ~** northern

nor'd-est nm northeast; **a ~** north-easterly

'nordico a northern

nordocciden'tale a northwestern

nordorien'tale a northeastern

nor'd-ovest nm northwest; **a ~** north-westerly

'norma nf rule; (istruzione) instruction; **a ~ di legge** according to law; **è buona ~** it's advisable

nor'mal|e a normal. **~ità** nf normality. **~iz'zare** vt normalize. **~'mente** adv normally

norve'gese a & nmf Norwegian. **Nor'vegia** nf Norway

nossi'gnore adv no way

nostal'gia nf (di casa, patria) homesickness; (del passato) nostalgia; **aver ~** be homesick; **aver ~ di qcno** miss sb.

no'stalgico, -a *a* nostalgic ● *nmf* reactionary

no'strano *a* local; (*fatto in casa*) homemade

'nostro (il nostro *m*, la nostra *f*, i nostri *mpl*, le nostre *fpl*) *poss a* our; quella macchina è nostra that car is ours; ~ padre our father; un ~ amico a friend of ours ● *poss pron* ours

'nota *nf* (*segno*) sign; (*comunicazione, commento, Mus*) note; (*conto*) bill; (*lista*) list; degno di ~ noteworthy; prendere ~ take note. note *pl* caratteristiche distinguishing marks

no'tabile *a & nm* notable

no'taio *nm* notary

no'ta|re *vt* (*segnare*) mark; (*annotare*) note down; (*osservare*) notice; far ~re qcsa point sth out; farsi ~re get oneself noticed. ~zi'one *nf* marking; (*annotazione*) notation

'notes *nm inv* notepad

no'tevole *a* (*degno di nota*) remarkable; (*grande*) considerable

no'tifica *nf* notification. notifi'care *vt* notify; *Comm* advise. ~zi'one *nf* notification

no'tizi|a *nf* una ~ a piece of news, some news; (*informazione*) a piece of information, some information; le ~e the news *sg*. ~'ario *nm* news *sg*

'noto *a* [well-]known; rendere ~ (*far sapere*) announce

notorietà *nf* fame; raggiungere la ~ become famous. no'torio *a* well-known; *pej* notorious

not'tambulo *nm* night-bird

not'tata *nf* night; far ~ stay up all night

'notte *nf* night; di ~ at night; ~ bianca sleepless night; peggio che andar di ~ worse than ever. ~tempo *adv* at night

not'turno *a* nocturnal; (*servizio ecc*) night

no'vanta *a & nm* ninety

novan'tenne *a & nmf* ninety-year-old. ~'esimo *a* ninetieth. ~'ina *nf* about ninety. 'nove *a & nm* nine. nove'cento *a & nm* nine hundred. il N~cento the twentieth century

no'vella *nf* short story

novel'lino, -a *a* inexperienced ● *nmf* novice, beginner. no'vello *a* new

no'vembre *nm* November

novità *nf inv* novelty; (*notizie*) news *sg*; l'ultima ~ (*moda*) the latest fashion

no'stalgico ... novizi'ato *nm Relig* novitiate; (*tirocinio*) apprenticeship

nozi'one *nf* notion; nozioni *pl* rudiments

'nozze *nfpl* marriage *sg*; (*cerimonia*) wedding *sg*. ~ d'argento silver wedding [anniversary]. ~ d'oro golden wedding [anniversary]

'nub|e *nf* cloud. ~e tossica toxic cloud. ~i'fragio *nm* cloudburst

'nubile *a* unmarried ● *nf* unmarried woman

'nuca *nf* nape

nucle'are *a* nuclear

'nucleo *nm* nucleus; (*unità*) unit

nu'dismo *nm* nudism. ~sta *nmf* nudist. ~tà *nf inv* nudity, nakedness

'nudo *a* naked; (*spoglio*) bare; a occhio ~ to the naked eye

'nugolo *nm* large number

'nulla *pron* = niente; da ~ worthless

nulla'osta *nm inv* permit

nulla'nente *nm* i nullatenenti the have-nots

nullità *nf inv* (*persona*) nonentity

'nullo *a Jur* null and void

nume'ra|bile *a* countable. ~le *a & nm* numeral

nume'ra|re *vt* number. ~zi'one *nf* numbering. nu'merico *a* numerical

'numero *nm* number; (*romano, arabo*) numeral; (*di scarpe ecc*) size; dare i numeri be off one's head. ~ cardinale cardinal [number]. ~ decimale decimal. ~ ordinale ordinal [number]. ~ di telefono phone number. nume'roso *a* numerous

'nunzio *nm* nuncio

nu'ocere *vi* a ~ a harm

nu'ora *nf* daughter-in-law

nuo'ta|re *vi* swim; *fig* wallow; ~re nell'oro be stinking rich, be rolling in it. nu'oto *nm* swimming. ~tore, ~trice *nmf* swimmer

nu'ov|a *nf* (*notizia*) news *sg*. ~a'mente *adv* again. ~o *a* new; di ~o again; rimettere a ~o give a new lease of life to

nutri'ente *a* nourishing. ~'mento *nm* nourishment

nu'tri|re *vt* nourish; harbour (*sentimenti*). ~rsi eat; ~rsi di fig live on. ~'tivo *a* nourishing. ~zi'one *nf* nutrition

'nuvola *nf* cloud. nuvo'loso *a* cloudy

nuzi'ale *a* nuptial; (*vestito, anello ecc*) wedding *attrib*

O *abbr* (ovest) W

o *conj* or; ~ **l'uno ~ l'altro** one or the other, either

'oasi *nf inv* oasis

obbedi'ente ecc = **ubbidiente** ecc

obbli'ga|re *vt* force, oblige. ~**rsi** *vr* ~**rsi a** undertake to. ~**to a** obliged. ~**'torio** *a* compulsory. ~**zi'one** *nf* obligation; *Comm* bond. **'obbligo** *nm* obligation; (*dovere*) duty; **avere obblighi verso** be under an obligation to; **d'obbligo** obligatory

obbligatoria'mente *adv* **fare qcsa ~** be obliged to do sth; **bisogna ~ farlo** you absolutely have to do it

ob'bro|brio *nm* disgrace. ~**brioso** *a* disgraceful

obe'lisco *nm* obelisk

obe'rare *vt* overburden

obesità *nf* obesity. **o'beso** *a* obese

obiet'tare *vt/i* object; ~ **su** object to

obietti|va'mente *adv* objectively. ~**vità** *nf* objectivity. **obiet'tivo** *a* objective ● *nm* objective; (*scopo*) object

obiet't|ore *nm* objector. ~**tore di coscienza** conscientious objector. ~**zi'one** *nf* objection

obi'torio *nm* mortuary

o'blio *nm* oblivion

o'bliquo *a* oblique; *fig* underhand

oblite'rare *vt* obliterate

oblò *nm inv* porthole

'oboe *nm* oboe

obso'leto *a* obsolete

'oca *nf* (*pl* **oche**) goose; (*donna*) silly girl

occasio'nal|e *a* occasional. ~**'mente** *adv* occasionally

occasi'one *nf* occasion; (*buon affare*) bargain; (*motivo*) cause; (*opportunità*) chance; **d'~** secondhand

occhi'aia *nf* eye socket; **occhiaie** *pl* shadows under the eyes

occhi'ali *nmpl* glasses, spectacles. ~ **da sole** sunglasses. ~ **da vista** glasses, spectacles

occhi'ata *nf* look; **dare un'~ a** have a look at

occhieggi'are *vt* ogle ● *vi* (*far capolino*) peep

occhi'ello *nm* buttonhole; (*asola*) eyelet

'occhio *nm* eye; ~! watch out!; **a quattr'occhi** in private; **tenere d'~ qcno** keep an eye on sb; **a ~ [e croce]** roughly; **chiudere un'~** turn a blind eye; **dare nell'~** attract attention; **pagare o spendere un ~ [della testa]** pay an arm and a leg; **saltare agli occhi** be blindingly obvious. ~ **nero** (*pesto*) black eye. ~ **di pernice** (*callo*) corn. ~**'lino** *nm* **fare l'~lino a qcno** wink at sb

occiden'tale *a* western ● *nmf* westerner. **occi'dente** *nm* west

oc'clu|dere *vt* obstruct. ~**si'one** *nf* occlusion

occor'ren|te *a* necessary ● *nm* the necessary. ~**za** *nf* need; **all'~za** if need be

oc'correre *vi* be necessary

occulta'mento *nm* ~ **di prove** concealment of evidence

occul't|are *vt* hide. ~**'ismo** *nm* occult. **oc'culto** *a* hidden; (*magico*) occult

occu'pante *nmf* occupier; (*abusivo*) squatter

occu'pa|re *vt* occupy; spend (*tempo*); take up (*spazio*); (*dar lavoro a*) employ. ~**rsi** *vr* occupy oneself; (*trovare lavoro*) find a job; ~**rsi di** (*badare*) look after. ~**to** *a* engaged; (*persona*) busy; (*posto*) taken. ~**zi'one** *nf* occupation; **trovarsi un'~zione** (*interesse*) find oneself something to do

o'ceano *nm* ocean. ~ **Atlantico** Atlantic [Ocean]. ~ **Pacifico** Pacific [Ocean]

'ocra *nf* ochre

ocu'lare *a* ocular; (*testimone, bagno*) eye *attrib*

ocula'tezza *nf* care. **ocu'lato** *a* (*scelta*) wise

ocu'lista *nmf* optician; (*per malattie*) ophthalmologist

od *conj* or

'ode *nf* ode

odi'are *vt* hate

odi'erno *a* of today; (*attuale*) present

'odi|o *nm* hatred; **avere in ~o** hate. **~oso** *a* hateful

odo'ra|re *vt* smell; (*profumare*) perfume ● *vi* **~re di** smell of. **~to** *nm* sense of smell. **o'dore** *nm* smell; (*profumo*) scent; **c'è odore di...** there's a smell of...; **sentire odore di** smell; **odori** *pl* Culin herbs. **odo'roso** *a* fragrant

of'fender|e *vt* offend; (*ferire*) injure. **~si** *vr* take offence

offen'siv|a *nf* Mil offensive. **~o** *a* offensive

offe'rente *nmf* offerer; (*in aste*) bidder

of'fert|a *nf* offer; (*donazione*) donation; Comm supply; (*nelle aste*) bid; **in ~a** special on special offer. **~o** *pp di* **offrire**

of'fes|a *nf* offence. **~o** *pp di* **offendere** ● *a* offended

offici'are *vt* officiate

offi'cina *nf* workshop; **~ [meccanica]** garage

of'frir|e *vt* offer. **~si** *vr* offer oneself; (*occasione*) present itself; **~si di fare qcsa** offer to do sth

offu'scar|e *vt* darken; fig dull (*memoria, bellezza*); blur (*vista*). **~si** *vr* darken; (*fig: memoria, bellezza*:) fade away; (*vista*:) become blurred

of'talmico *a* ophthalmic

oggettività *nf* objectivity. **ogget'tivo** *a* objective

og'getto *nm* object; (*argomento*) subject; **oggetti** *pl* **smarriti** lost property, lost and found Am

'oggi *adv & nm* today; (*al giorno d'oggi*) nowadays; **da ~ in poi** from today on; **~ a otto** a week today; **dall'~ al domani** overnight; **il giornale di ~** today's paper; **al giorno d'~** these days, nowadays. **~gi'orno** *adv* nowadays

'ogni *a inv* every; (*qualsiasi*) any; **~ tre giorni** every three days; **ad ~ costo** at any cost; **ad ~ modo** anyway; **~ cosa** everything; **~ tanto** now and then; **~ volta che** every time, whenever

o'gnuno *pron* everyone, everybody; **~ di voi** each of you

ohimè *int* oh dear!

'ola *nf inv* Mexican wave

O'land|a *nf* Holland. **o~'dese** *a* Dutch ● *nm* Dutchman; (*lingua*) Dutch ● *nf* Dutchwoman

ole'andro *nm* oleander

ole'at|o *a* oiled; **carta ~a** grease-proof paper

oleo'dotto *nm* oil pipeline. **ole'oso** *a* oily

ol'fatto *nm* sense of smell

oli'are *vt* oil

oli'era *nf* cruet

olim'piadi *nfpl* Olympic Games. **o'limpico** *a* Olympic. **olim'pionico** *a* (*primato, squadra*) Olympic

'olio *nm* oil; **sott'~** in oil; **colori a ~** oils; **quadro a ~** oil painting. **~ di mais** corn oil. **~ d'oliva** olive oil. **~ di semi** vegetable oil. **~ solare** sun-tan oil

o'liv|a *nf* olive. **oli'vastro** *a* olive. **oli'veto** *nm* olive grove. **~o** *nm* olive tree

'olmo *nm* elm

olo'gramma *nm* hologram

oltraggi'are *vt* offend. **ol'traggio** *nm* offence

ol'tranza *nf* **ad ~** to the bitter end

'oltre *adv* (*di luogo*) further; (*di tempo*) longer ● *prep* (*di luogo*) over; (*di tempo*) later than; (*più di*) more than; (*in aggiunta*) besides; **~ a** (*eccetto*) except, apart from; **per ~ due settimane** for more than two weeks; **una settimana e ~** a week and more. **~'mare** *adv* overseas. **~'modo** *adv* extremely

oltrepas'sare *vt* go beyond; (*eccedere*) exceed

o'maggio *nm* homage; (*dono*) gift; **in ~** con free with; **omaggi** *pl* (*saluti*) respects

ombeli'cale *a* umbilical; **cordone ~** umbilical cord. **ombe'lico** *nm* navel

'ombr|a *nf* (*zona*) shade; (*immagine oscura*) shadow; **all'~a** in the shade. **~eggi'are** *vt* shade

om'brello *nm* umbrella. **ombrel'lone** *nm* beach umbrella

om'bretto *nm* eye-shadow

om'broso *a* shady; (*cavallo*) skittish

ome'lette *nf inv* omelette

ome'lia *nf* Relig sermon

omeopa'tia *nf* homoeopathy. **omeo'patico** *a* homoeopathic ● *nm* homoeopath

omertà *nf* conspiracy of silence

o'messo *pp di* **omettere**

o'mettere *vt* omit

omi'cid|a *a* murderous ● *nmf* murderer. **~io** *nm* murder. **~io colposo** manslaughter

omissi'one *nf* omission

omogeneiz'zato *a* homogenized. **omo'geneo** *a* homogeneous

omolo'gare *vt* approve

o'monimo, -a *nmf* namesake ● *nm* (*parola*) homonym

omosessu'al|e *a* & *nmf* homosexual. ~ità *nf* homosexuality

On. *abbr* (*onorevole*) M.P.

'oncia *nf* ounce

'onda *nf* wave; andare in ~ *Radio* go on the air. a ondate in waves. onde *pl* corte short wave. onde *pl* lunghe long wave. onde *pl* medie medium wave. on'data *nf* wave

'onde *conj* so that ● *pron* whereby

ondeggi'are *vi* wave; ⟨*barca*:⟩ roll

ondula'torio *a* undulating. ~zi'one *nf* undulation; (*di capelli*) wave

'oner|e *nm* burden. ~'oso *a* onerous

onestà *nf* honesty; (*rettitudine*) integrity. o'nesto *a* honest; (*giusto*) just

'onice *nf* onyx

onnipo'tente *a* omnipotent

onnipre'sente *a* ubiquitous; *Rel* omnipresent

ono'mastico *nm* name-day

ono'ra|bile *a* honourable. ~re *vt* (*fare onore a*) be a credit to; honour ⟨*promessa*⟩. ~rio *a* honorary ● *nm* fee. ~rsi *vr* ~rsi di be proud of

o'nore *nm* honour; in ~ di ⟨*festa, ricevimento*⟩ in honour of; fare ~ a do justice to ⟨*pranzo*⟩; farsi ~ in excel in; fare gli onori di casa do the honours

ono'revole *a* honourable ● *nmf* Member of Parliament

onorifi'cenza *nf* honour; (*decorazione*) decoration. ono'rifico *a* honorary

'onta *nf* shame

O.N.U. *nf abbr* (**Organizzazione delle Nazioni Unite**) UN

o'paco *a* opaque; ⟨*colori ecc*⟩ dull; ⟨*fotografia, rossetto*⟩ matt

o'pale *nf* opal

'opera *nf* (*lavoro*) work; (*azione*) deed; *Mus* opera; (*teatro*) opera house; (*ente*) institution; mettere in ~ put into effect; mettersi all'~ get to work; opere *pl* pubbliche public works. ~ d'arte work of art. ~ lirica opera

ope'raio, -a *a* working ● *nmf* worker; ~ specializzato skilled worker

ope'ra|re *vt Med* operate on; farsi ~re have an operation ● *vi* operate; (*agire*) work. ~'tivo, ~'torio *a* operating *attrib*. ~'tore, ~'trice *nmf* operator; *TV* cameraman. ~tore turistico tour operator. ~zi'one *nf* operation; *Comm* transaction

ope'retta *nf* operetta

ope'roso *a* industrious

opini'one *nf* opinion; rimanere della propria ~ still feel the same way. ~ pubblica public opinion, vox pop

'oppio *nm* opium

oppo'nente *a* opposing ● *nmf* opponent

op'por|re *vt* oppose; (*obiettare*) object; ~re resistenza offer resistance. ~si *vr* ~si a oppose

opportu'ni|smo *nm* expediency. ~sta *nmf* opportunist. ~tà *nf inv* opportunity; (*l'essere opportuno*) timeliness. oppor'tuno *a* opportune; (*adeguato*) appropriate; ritenere opportuno fare qcsa think it appropriate to do sth; il momento opportuno the right moment

opposi'tore *nm* opposer. ~zi'one *nf* opposition; d'~zione ⟨*giornale, partito*⟩ opposition

op'posto *pp di* opporre ● *a* opposite; ⟨*opinioni*⟩ opposite ● *nm* opposite; all'~ on the contrary

oppres|si'one *nf* oppression. ~'sivo *a* oppressive. op'presso *pp di* opprimere ● *a* oppressed. ~'sore *nm* oppressor

oppri'mente *a* oppressive. op'prime-re *vt* oppress; (*gravare*) weigh down

op'pure *conj* otherwise, or [else]; lunedì ~ martedì Monday or Tuesday

op'tare *vi* ~ per opt for

o'puscolo *nm* booklet; (*pubblicitario*) brochure

opzio'nale *a* optional. opzi'one *nf* option

'ora¹ *nf* time; (*unità*) hour; di buon'~ early; che ~ è?, che ore sono? what time is it?; mezz'~ half an hour; a ore ⟨*lavorare, pagare*⟩ by the hour; 50 km all'~ 50 km an hour; a un'~ di macchina one hour by car; non vedo l'~ di vederti I can't wait to see you; fare le ore piccole stay up until the small hours. ~ d'arrivo arrival time. l'~ esatta *Teleph* speaking clock. ~ legale daylight saving time. ~ di punta, ore *pl* di punta peak time; (*per il traffico*) rush hour

'ora² *adv* now; (*tra poco*) presently; ~ come ~ è?, che ore sono? just now, at the moment; d'~ in poi from now on; per ~ for the time being, for now; è ~ di finirla! that's enough now! ● *conj* (*dunque*) now [then]; ~ che ci penso,... now that I come to think about it,...

o'racolo nm oracle

'orafo nm goldsmith

o'rale a & nm oral; per via ~ by mouth

ora'mai adv = ormai

o'rario a ⟨tariffa⟩ hourly; ⟨segnale⟩ time attrib; ⟨velocità⟩ per hour ● nm time; ⟨tabella dell'orario⟩ timetable, schedule Am; essere in ~ be on time; in senso ~ clockwise. ~ di chiusura closing time. ~ flessibile flexitime. ~ di sportello banking hours. ~ d'ufficio business hours. ~ di visita Med consulting hours

o'rata nf gilthead

ora'tore, -'trice nmf speaker

ora'torio, -a a oratorical ● nm Mus oratorio ● nmf oratory. orazi'one nf Relig prayer

'orbita nf orbit; Anat [eye-]socket

or'chestra nf orchestra; ⟨parte del teatro⟩ pit

orche'stra|le a orchestral ● nmf member of an/the orchestra. ~re vt orchestrate

orchi'dea nf orchid

'orco nm ogre

'orda nf horde

or'digno nm device; ⟨arnese⟩ tool. ~ esplosivo explosive device

ordi'nale a & nm ordinal

ordina'mento nm order; ⟨leggi⟩ rules pl.

ordi'nanza nf ⟨del sindaco⟩ bylaw; d'~ ⟨soldato⟩ on duty

ordi'nare vt ⟨sistemare⟩ arrange; ⟨comandare⟩ order; ⟨prescrivere⟩ prescribe; Relig ordain

ordi'nario a ordinary; ⟨grossolano⟩ common; ⟨professore⟩ with a permanent position; di ordinaria amministrazione routine ● nm ordinary; Univ professor

ordi'nato a ⟨in ordine⟩ tidy

ordinazi'one nf order; fare un'~ place an order

'ordine nm order; ⟨di avvocati, medici⟩ association; mettere in ~ put in order; tidy up ⟨appartamento ecc⟩; di prim'~ first-class; di terz'~e ⟨film, albergo⟩ third- rate; di ~ pratico/economico ⟨problema⟩ of a practical/economic nature; fino a nuovo ~ until further notice; parola d'~ password. ~ del giorno agenda. ordini sacri pl Holy Orders

or'dire vt ⟨tramare⟩ plot

orec'chino nm ear-ring

o'recchi|o nm ⟨pl nf orecchie⟩ ear; avere ~o have a good ear; mi è giunto all'~o che... I've heard that...; parlare all'~o a qcno whisper in sb's ear; suonare a ~o play by ear; ~'oni pl Med mumps sg

o'refice nm jeweller. ~'ria nf ⟨arte⟩ goldsmith's art; ⟨negozio⟩ goldsmith's [shop]

'orfano, -a a orphan ● nmf orphan. ~'trofio nm orphanage

orga'netto nm barrel-organ; ⟨a bocca⟩ mouth-organ; ⟨fisarmonica⟩ accordion

or'ganico a organic ● nm personnel

orga'nismo nm organism; ⟨corpo umano⟩ body

orga'nista nmf organist

organiz'za|re vt organize. ~rsi vr get organized. ~'tore, ~'trice nmf organizer. ~zi'one nf organization

'organo nm organ

or'gasmo nm orgasm; fig agitation

'orgia nf orgy

or'gogli|o nm pride. ~'oso a proud

orien'tale a eastern; ⟨cinese ecc⟩ oriental

orienta'mento nm orientation; perdere l'~ lose one's bearings; senso dell'~ sense of direction

orien'ta|re vt orientate. ~rsi vr find one's bearings; ⟨tendere⟩ tend

ori'ente nm east. l'Estremo O~ the Far East. il Medio O~ the Middle East

o'rigano nm oregano

origi'nale a original; ⟨eccentrico⟩ odd ● nm original. ~lità nf originality. ~re vt/i originate. ~rio a ⟨nativo⟩ native

o'rigine nf origin; in ~ originally; aver ~ da originate from; dare ~ a give rise to

origli'are vi eavesdrop

o'rina nf urine. ori'nale nm chamber-pot. ori'nare vi urinate

ori'undo a native

orizzon'tale a horizontal

orizzon'tare vt = orientare orizzon'te nm horizon

or'la|re vt hem. ~'tura nf hem. 'orlo nm edge; ⟨di vestito ecc⟩ hem

'orma nf track; ⟨di piede⟩ footprint; ⟨impronta⟩ mark

or'mai adv by now; ⟨passato⟩ by then; ⟨quasi⟩ almost

ormegg'iare vt moor. or'meggio nm mooring

ormo'nale a hormonal. or'mone nm hormone

ornamen'tale a ornamental. orna'mento nm ornament

or'na|re *vt* decorate. ~rsi *vr* deck oneself. ~to *a* (*stile*) ornate

ornitolo'gia *nf* ornithology

'oro *nm* gold; d'~ gold; *fig* golden; una persona d'~ a wonderful person

orologi'aio, -a *nmf* clockmaker, watchmaker

oro'logio *nm* (*portatile*) watch; (*da tavolo, muro ecc*) clock. ~ a pendolo grandfather clock. ~ da polso wristwatch. ~ a sveglia alarm clock

o'roscopo *nm* horoscope

or'rendo *a* awful, dreadful

or'ribile *a* horrible

orripi'lante *a* horrifying

or'rore *nm* horror; avere qcsa in ~ hate sth

orsacchi'otto *nm* teddy bear

'orso *nm* bear; (*persona scontrosa*) hermit. ~ bianco polar bear

or'taggio *nm* vegetable

or'tensia *nf* hydrangea

or'tica *nf* nettle. orti'caria *nf* nettle-rash

orticol'tura *nf* horticulture. 'orto *nm* vegetable plot

orto'dosso *a* orthodox

ortogo'nale *a* perpendicular

orto|gra'fia *nf* spelling. ~'grafico *a* spelling *attrib*

orto'lano *nm* market gardener; (*negozio*) greengrocer's

orto|pe'dia *nf* orthopaedics *sg*. ~'pedico *a* orthopaedic ● *nm* orthopaedist

orzai'olo *nm* sty

or'zata *nf* barley-water

osan'nato *a* praised to the skies

o'sare *vt/i* dare; (*avere audacia*) be daring

oscenità *nf inv* obscenity. o'sceno *a* obscene

oscil'la|re *vi* swing; (*prezzi ecc*) fluctuate; *Tech* oscillate; (*fig: essere indeciso*) vacillate. ~zi'one *nf* swinging; (*di prezzi*) fluctuation; *Tech* oscillation

oscura'mento *nm* darkening; (*fig: di vista, mente*) dimming; (*totale*) black-out

oscu'r|are *vt* darken; *fig* obscure. ~arsi *vr* get dark. ~ità *nf* darkness. o'scuro *a* dark; (*triste*) gloomy; (*incomprensibile*) obscure

ospe'dal|e *nm* hospital. ~i'ero *a* hospital *attrib*

ospi'ta|le *a* hospitable. ~lità *nf* hospitality. ~re *vt* give hospitality to. 'ospite *nm* (*chi ospita*) host; (*chi viene ospitato*) guest ● *nf* hostess; guest

o'spizio *nm* (*per vecchi*) [old people's] home

ossa'tura *nf* bone structure; (*di romanzo*) structure, framework. 'osseo *a* bone *attrib*

ossequi'are *vt* pay one's respects to. os'sequio *nm* homage; ossequi *pl* respects. ~'oso *a* obsequious

osser'vante *a* (*cattolico*) practising. ~za *nf* observance

osser'va|re *vt* observe; (*notare*) notice; keep (*ordine, silenzio*). ~'tore, ~'trice *nmf* observer. ~'torio *nm Astr* observatory; *Mil* observation post. ~zi'one *nf* observation; (*rimprovero*) reproach

ossessio'na|nte *a* haunting; (*persona*) nagging. ~re *vt* obsess; (*infastidire*) nag. ossessi'one *nf* obsession; (*assillo*) pain in the neck. osses'sivo *a* obsessive. os'sesso *a* obsessed

os'sia *conj* that is

ossi'dabile *a* liable to tarnish

ossi'dar|e *vt*, ~si *vr* oxidize

'ossido *nm* oxide. ~ di carbonio carbon monoxide

os'sidrico *a* fiamma ossidrica blow-lamp

ossige'nar|e *vt* oxygenate; (*decolorare*) bleach; *fig* put back on its feet (*azienda*). ~si *vr* ~si i capelli dye one's hair blonde. os'sigeno *nm* oxygen

'osso *nm* (*Anat: pl nf* ossa) bone; (*di frutto*) stone

osso'buco *nm* marrowbone

os'suto *a* bony

ostaco'lare *vt* hinder, obstruct. o'stacolo *nm* obstacle; *Sport* hurdle

o'staggio *nm* hostage; prendere in ~ take hostage

o'stello *nm* ~ della gioventù youth hostel

osten'ta|re *vt* show off; ~re indifferenza pretend to be indifferent. ~zi'one *nf* ostentation

oste'ria *nf* inn

o'stetrico, -a *a* obstetric ● *nmf* obstetrician

'ostia *nf* host; (*cialda*) wafer

'ostico *a* tough

o'stil|e *a* hostile. ~ità *nf inv* hostility

osti'na|rsi *vr* persist (a in). ~to *a* obstinate. ~zi'one *nf* obstinacy

ostra'cismo *nm* ostracism

'ostrica *nf* oyster

ostro'goto *nm* parlare ~ talk double Dutch

ostru'i|re *vt* obstruct. **~zi'one** *nf* obstruction

otorinolaringoi'atra *nmf* ear, nose and throat specialist

ottago'nale *a* octagonal. **ot'tagono** *nm* octagon

ot'tan|ta *a & nm* eighty. **~'tenne** *a & nmf* eighty-year-old. **~'tesimo** *a* eightieth. **~'tina** *nf* about eighty

ot'tav|a *nf* octave. **~o** *a & nm* eighth

otte'nere *vt* obtain; *(più comune)* get; *(conseguire)* achieve

'ottico, -a *a* optic[al] ● *nmf* optician ● *nf (scienza)* optics *sg*; *(di lenti ecc)* optics *pl*

otti'ma|le *a* optimum. **~'mente** *adv* very well

otti'mis|mo *nm* optimism. **~ta** *nmf* optimist. **~tico** *a* optimistic

'ottimo *a* very good ● *nm* optimum

'otto *a & nm* eight

ot'tobre *nm* October

otto'cento *a & nm* eight hundred; **l'O~** the nineteenth century

ot'tone *nm* brass

ottuage'nario, -a *a & nmf* octogenarian

ottu'ra|re *vt* block; fill *(dente)*. **~rsi** *vr* clog. **~'tore** *nm* Phot shutter. **~zi'one** *nf* stopping; *(di dente)* filling

ot'tuso *pp di* ottundere ● *a* obtuse

o'vaia *nf* ovary

o'vale *a & nm* oval

o'vat|ta *nf* cotton wool. **~'tato** *a (suono, passi)* muffled

ovazi'one *nf* ovation

over'dose *nf inv* overdose

'ovest *nm* west

o'vi|le *nm* sheep-fold. **~no** *a* sheep *attrib*

ovo'via *nf* two-seater cable car

ovulazi'one *nf* ovulation

o'vunque *adv* = dovunque

ov'vero *conj* or; *(cioè)* that is

ovvia'mente *adv* obviously

ovvi'are *vi* **~ a** qcsa counter sth. **'ovvio** *a* obvious

ozi'are *vi* laze about. **'ozio** *nm* idleness; **stare in ozio** idle about. **ozi'oso** *a* idle; *(questione)* pointless

o'zono *nm* ozone; **buco nell'~** hole in the ozone layer

Pp

pa'ca|re *vt* quieten. **~to** *a* quiet

pac'chetto *nm* packet; *(postale)* parcel, package; *(di sigarette)* pack, packet. **~ software** software package

'pacchia *nf (fam: situazione)* bed of roses

pacchia'nata *nf* **è una ~** it's so garish. **pacchi'ano** *a* garish

'pacco *nm* parcel; *(involto)* bundle. **~ regalo** gift-wrapped package

paccot'tiglia *nf (roba scadente)* junk, rubbish

'pace *nf* peace; **darsi ~** forget it; **fare ~ con** qcno make it up with sb; **lasciare in ~** qcno leave sb in peace

pachi'derma *nm (animale)* pachyderm

pachi'stano, -a *nmf & a* Pakistani

pacifi'ca|re *vt* reconcile; *(mettere pace)* pacify. **~zi'one** *nf* reconciliation

pa'cifico *a* pacific; *(calmo)* peaceful; **il P~** the Pacific

paci'fis|mo *nm* pacifism. **~ta** *nmf* pacifist

pacioc'cone, -a *nmf fam* chubby-chops

pa'dano *a* pianura *nf* padana Po Valley

pa'del|la *nf* frying-pan; *(per malati)* bedpan. **~'lata** *nf* **una ~lata di** a frying-panful of

padigli'one *nm* pavilion

'padre *nm* father; **~i** *pl (antenati)* forefathers. **pa'drino** *nm* godfather. **~e'nostro** *nm* **il ~enostro** the Lord's Prayer. **~e'terno** *nm* God Almighty

padro'nanza *nf* mastery. **~ di sé** self-control

pa'drone, -a *nmf* master; mistress; *(datore di lavoro)* boss; *(proprietario)* owner. **~ggi'are** *vt* master

pae'sag|gio *nm* scenery; *(pittura)* landscape. **~'gista** *nmf* landscape architect

pae'sano, -a *a* country ● *nmf* villager

pa'ese *nm* (*nazione*) country; (*territorio*) land; (*villaggio*) village; **il Bel P~** Italy; **va' a quel ~!** get lost!; **Paesi** *pl* **Bassi** Netherlands

paf'futo *a* plump

paga *nf* pay, wages *pl*

pa'gabile *a* payable

pa'gaia *nf* paddle

paga'mento *nm* payment; **a ~** (*parcheggio*) which you have to pay to use. **~ anticipato** *Comm* advance payment. **~ alla consegna** cash on delivery, COD

paga'nesimo *nm* paganism

pa'gano, -a *a & nmf* pagan

pa'gare *vt/i* pay; **~ da bere a qcno** buy sb a drink; **te la faccio ~** you'll pay for this

pa'gella *nf* [school] report

pagina *nf* page. **Pagine** *pl* **Gialle** Yellow Pages. **~ web** *Comput* web page

paglia *nf* straw

pagliac'cetto *nm* (*per bambini*) rompers *pl*

pagliac'ciata *nf* farce

pagli'accio *nm* clown

pagli'aio *nm* haystack

paglie'riccio *nm* straw mattress

pagli'etta *nf* (*cappello*) boater; (*per pentole*) steel wool

pagli'uzza *nf* wisp of straw; (*di metallo*) particle

pa'gnotta *nf* [round] loaf

pa'goda *nf* pagoda

pail'lette *nf inv* sequin

paio *nm* (*pl nf* **paia**) pair; **un ~** (*circa due*) a couple; **un ~ di** (*scarpe, forbici*) a pair of

Pakistan *nm* Pakistan

pala *nf* shovel; (*di remo, elica*) blade; (*di ruota*) paddle

pala'fitta *nf* pile-dwelling

pala'sport *nm inv* indoor sports arena

pa'late *nfpl* **a ~** (*fare soldi*) hand over fist

pa'lato *nm* palate

palaz'zetto *nm* **~ dello sport** indoor sports arena

palaz'zina *nf* villa

pa'lazzo *nm* palace; (*edificio*) building. **~ delle esposizioni** exhibition centre. **~ di giustizia** law courts *pl*, courthouse. **~ dello sport** indoor sports arena

palco *nm* (*pedana*) platform; *Theat* box. **~['scenico]** *nm* stage

pale'sar|e *vt* disclose. **~si** *vr* reveal oneself. **pa'lese** *a* evident

Pale'stina *nf* Palestine. **p~'nese** *nmf* Palestinian

pa'lestra *nf* gymnasium, gym; (*ginnastica*) gymnastics *pl*

pa'letta *nf* spade; (*per focolare*) shovel. **~ [della spazzatura]** dustpan

pa'letto *nm* peg

palio *nm* (*premio*) prize. **il P~** horse-race held at Siena

paliz'zata *nf* fence

palla *nf* ball; (*proiettile*) bullet; (*fam: bugia*) porkie; **che palle!** *vulg* this is a pain in the arse!. **~ di neve** snowball. **~ al piede** *fig* millstone round one's neck

palla'nestro *nf* basketball

palla'mano *nf* handball

pallanu'oto *nf* water polo

palla'volo *nf* volley-ball

palleggi'are *vi* (*calcio*) practise ball control; *Tennis* knock up

pallia'tivo *nm* palliative

pallido *a* pale; **non ne ho la più pallida idea** I don't have the faintest idea

pal'lina *nf* (*di vetro*) marble

pal'lino *nm* **avere il ~ del calcio** be crazy about football

pallon'cino *nm* balloon; (*lanterna*) Chinese lantern; (*fam: etilometro*) Breathalyzer[R]

pal'lone *nm* ball; (*calcio*) football; (*aerostato*) balloon

pal'lore *nm* pallor

pal'loso *a sl* boring

pal'lottola *nf* pellet; (*proiettile*) bullet

palm|a *nf Bot* palm. **~o** *nm Anat* palm; (*misura*) hand's-breadth; **restare con un ~o di naso** feel disappointed

palo *nm* pole; (*di sostegno*) stake; (*in calcio*) goalpost; **fare il ~** (*ladro*) keep a lookout. **~ della luce** lamppost

palom'baro *nm* diver

pal'pare *vt* feel

palpebra *nf* eyelid

palpi'ta|re *vi* throb; (*fremere*) quiver. **~zi'one** *nf* palpitation. **'palpito** *nm* throb; (*del cuore*) beat

pa'lude *nf* marsh, swamp

palu'doso *a* marshy

pa'lustre *a* marshy; (*piante, uccelli*) marsh *attrib*

pampino *nm* vine leaf

pana'cea *nf* panacea

panca *nf* bench; (*in chiesa*) pew

pancarrè *nm* sliced bread

pan'cetta *nf Culin* bacon; (*di una certa età*) paunch

pan'chetto *nm* [foot]stool

pan'china *nf* garden seat; (*in calcio*) bench

'pancia *nf* belly, tummy *fam*; **mal di ~** stomach-ache; **metter su ~** develop a paunch; **a ~ in giù** lying face down. **panci'era** *nf* corset

panci'olle: stare in ~ lounge about

panci'one *nm* (*persona*) pot belly

panci'otto *nm* waistcoat

pande'monio *nm* pandemonium

pan'doro *nm* kind of sponge cake eaten at Christmas

'pane *nm* bread; (*pagnotta*) loaf; (*di burro*) block. **~ a cassetta** sliced bread. **pan grattato** breadcrumbs *pl.* **~ di segale** rye bread. **pan di Spagna** sponge cake. **~ tostato** toast

panett|e'ria *nf* bakery; (*negozio*) baker's [shop]. **~i'ere, -a** *nmf* baker

panet'tone *nf* dome-shaped cake with sultanas and candied fruit eaten at Christmas

'panfilo *nm* yacht

pan'forte *nm* nougat-like spicy delicacy from Siena

'panico *nm* panic; **lasciarsi prendere dal ~** panic

pani'ere *nm* basket; (*cesta*) hamper

pani'ficio *nm* bakery; (*negozio*) baker's [shop]

pani'naro *nm sl* ≈ preppie

pa'nino *nm* [bread] roll. **~ imbottito** filled roll. **~ al prosciutto** ham roll. **~teca** *nf* sandwich bar

'panna *nf* cream. **~ da cucina** [single] cream. **~ montata** whipped cream

'panne *nf* *Mech* **in ~** broken down; **restare in ~** break down

pan'nello *nm* panel. **~ solare** solar panel

'panno *nm* cloth; **panni** *pl* (*abiti*) clothes; **mettersi nei panni di qcno** *fig* put oneself in sb's shoes

pan'nocchia *nf* (*di granoturco*) cob

panno'lino *nm* (*per bambini*) nappy; (*da donna*) sanitary towel

pano'ram|a *nm* panorama; *fig* overview. **~ico** *a* panoramic

pantacol'lant *nmpl* leggings

pantalon'cini *nmpl* **~** [corti] shorts

panta'loni *nmpl* trousers, pants *Am*

pan'tano *nm* bog

pan'tera *nf* panther; (*auto della polizia*) high-speed police car

pan'tofol|a *nf* slipper. **~'laio, -a** *nmf* *fig* stay-at-home

pan'zana *nf* fib

pao'nazzo *a* purple

'papa *nm* Pope

papà *nm inv* dad[dy]

pa'pale *a* papal

papa'lina *nf* skull-cap

papa'razzo *nm* paparazzo

pa'pato *nm* papacy

pa'pavero *nm* poppy

'paper|a *nf* (*errore*) slip of the tongue. **~o** *nm* gosling

papil'lon *nm inv* bow tie

pa'piro *nm* papyrus

'pappa *nf* (*per bambini*) pap

pappa'gallo *nm* parrot

pappa'molle *nmf* wimp

'para *nf* **suole** *nfpl* **di ~** crêpe soles

pa'rabola *nf* parable; (*curva*) parabola

para'bolico *a* parabolic

para'brezza *nm inv* windscreen, windshield *Am*

paracadu'tar|e *vt* parachute. **~si** *vr* parachute

paraca'du|te *nm inv* parachute. **~'tismo** *nm* parachuting. **~'tista** *nmf* parachutist

para'carro *nm* roadside post

paradi'siaco *a* heavenly

para'diso *nm* paradise. **~ terrestre** Eden, earthly paradise

parados'sale *a* paradoxical. **para-'dosso** *nm* paradox

para'fango *nm* mudguard

paraf'fina *nf* paraffin

parafra'sare *vt* paraphrase

para'fulmine *nm* lightning-conductor

pa'raggi *nmpl* neighbourhood *sg*

parago'na|bile *a* comparable (**a** to). **~re** *vt* compare. **para'gone** *nm* comparison; **a paragone di** in comparison with

pa'ragrafo *nm* paragraph

pa'ra|lisi *nf inv* paralysis. **~'litico, -a** *a* & *nmf* paralytic. **~'liz'zare** *vt* paralyse. **~liz'zato** *a* (*dalla paura*) transfixed

paral'lel|a *nf* parallel line. **~a'mente** *adv* in parallel. **~o** *a* & *nm* parallel; **~e** *pl* parallel bars. **~o'gramma** *nm* parallelogram

para'lume *nm* lampshade

para'medico *nm* paramedic

pa'rametro *nm* parameter

para'noi|a *nf* paranoia. **~co, -a** *a* & *nmf* paranoid

paranor'male *a* (*fenomeno, facoltà*) paranormal

para'occhi *nmpl* blinkers. **parao'rec-chie** *nm* earmuffs

para'petto *nm* parapet

para'piglia *nm* turmoil

para'plegico, -a *a & nmf* paraplegic

pa'rar|e *vt* (*addobbare*) adorn; (*riparare*) shield; save (*tiro, pallone*); ward off, parry (*schiaffo, pugno*) ● *vi* (*mirare*) lead up to. ~**si** *vr* (*abbigliarsi*) dress up; (*da pioggia, pugni*) protect oneself; ~**si dinanzi a qcno** appear in front of sb

para'sole *nm inv* parasol

paras'sita *a* parasitic ● *nm* parasite

parasta'tale *a* a government-controlled

pa'rata *nf* parade; (*in calcio*) save; (*in scherma, pugilato*) parry

para'urti *nm inv* Auto bumper, fender *Am*

para'vento *nm* screen

par'cella *nf* bill

parcheggi'a|re *vt* park. **par'cheggio** *nm* parking; (*posteggio*) carpark, parking lot *Am*. ~**tore,** ~**trice** *nmf* parking attendant. ~**tore abusivo** *person who illegally earns money by looking after parked cars*

par'chimetro *nm* parking-meter

'parco[1] *a* sparing; (*moderato*) moderate

'parco[2] *nm* park. ~ **di divertimenti** fun-fair. ~ **giochi** playground. ~ **naturale** wildlife park. ~ **nazionale** national park. ~ **regionale** [regional] wildlife park

pa'recchi *a* a good many ● *pron* several

pa'recchio *a* quite a lot of ● *pron* quite a lot ● *adv* rather; (*parecchio tempo*) quite a time

pareggi'are *vt* level; (*eguagliare*) equal; *Comm* balance ● *vi* draw

pa'reggio *nm Comm* balance; *Sport* draw

paren'tado *nm* relatives *pl*; (*vincolo di sangue*) relationship

pa'rente *nmf* relative. ~ **stretto** close relation

paren'tela *nf* relatives *pl*; (*vincolo di sangue*) relationship

pa'rentesi *nf inv* parenthesis; (*segno grafico*) bracket; (*fig: pausa*) break. ~ *pl* **graffe** curly brackets. ~ **quadre** square brackets. ~ **tonde** round brackets

pa'reo *nm* (*copricostume*) sarong; **a** ~ (*gonna*) wrap-around

pa'rere[1] *nm* opinion; **a mio** ~ in my opinion

pa'rere[2] *vi* seem; (*pensare*) think; **che te ne pare?** what do you think of it?; **pare di sì** it seems so

pa'rete *nf* wall; (*in alpinismo*) face. ~ **divisoria** partition wall

'pari *a inv* equal; (*numero*) even; **andare di** ~ **passo** keep pace; **essere** ~ be even *o* quits; **arrivare** ~ draw; ~ ~ (*copiare, ripetere*) word for word; **fare** ~ **o dispari** ≈ toss a coin ● *nmf inv* equal, peer; **ragazza alla** ~ au pair [girl]; **mettersi in** ~ **con qcsa** catch up with sth ● *nm* (*titolo nobiliare*) peer

Pa'rigi *nf* Paris

pa'riglia *nf* pair

pari'tà *nf* equality; *Tennis* deuce. ~'tario *a* parity *attrib*

parlamen'tare *a* parliamentary ● *nmf* Member of Parliament ● *vi* discuss. **parla'mento** *nm* Parliament. **il Parlamento europeo** the European Parliament

parlan'tina *nf* avere la ~ be a chatterbox

par'la|re *vt/i* speak, talk; (*confessare*) talk; ~ **bene/male di qcno** speak well/ ill of somebody; **non parliamone più** let's forget about it; **non se ne parla nemmeno!** don't even mention it!. ~**to** *a* (*lingua*) spoken. ~'torio *nm* parlour; (*in prigione*) visiting room

parlot'tare *vi* mutter. **parlot'tio** *nm* muttering

parmigi'ano *nm* Parmesan

paro'dia *nf* parody

pa'rola *nf* word; (*facoltà*) speech; **è una** ~! it is easier said than done!; **parole** *pl* (*di canzone*) words, lyrics; **rivolgere la** ~ **a** address; **dare a qcno la propria** ~ give sb one's word; **in parole povere** crudely speaking. **parole** *pl* **incrociate** crossword [puzzle] *sg.* ~ **d'onore** word of honour. ~ **d'ordine** password. **paro'laccia** *nf* swear-word

par'quet *nm inv* (*pavimento*) parquet flooring

par'rocchi|a *nf* parish. ~**ale** *a* parish *attrib*. ~**'ano, -a** *nmf* parishioner. **'parroco** *nm* parish priest

par'rucca *nf* wig

parrucchi'ere, -a *nmf* hairdresser

parruc'chino *nm* toupée, hairpiece

parsi'moni|a *nf* thrift. ~**'oso** *a* thrifty

'parso *pp di* parere

parte *nf* part; (*lato*) side; (*partito*) party; (*porzione*) share; **a** ~ apart from; **in** ~ in part; **la maggior** ~ **di** the majority of; **d'altra** ~ on the other hand; **da** ~ aside; (*in disparte*) to one side; **farsi da** ~ stand aside; **da** ~ **di** from;

(*per conto di*) on behalf of; **è gentile da ~ tua** it is kind of you; **fare una brutta ~ a qcno** behave badly towards sb; **da che ~ è...?** whereabouts is...?; **da una ~..., dall'altra...** on the one hand..., on the other hand...; **dall'altra ~** di on the other side of; **da nessuna ~** nowhere; **da tutte le parti** (*essere*) everywhere; **da questa ~** (*in questa direzione*) this way; **da un anno a questa ~** for about a year now; **essere dalla ~ di qcno** be on sb's side; **prendere le parti di qcno** take sb's side; **essere ~ in causa** be involved; **fare ~ di** (*appartenere a*) be a member of; **rendere ~ a** take part in. **~ civile** plaintiff

parteci'pante *nmf* participant

parteci'pa|re *vi* **~re a** participate in, take part in; (*condividere*) share in. **~zi'one** *nf* participation; (*annuncio*) announcement; *Fin* shareholding; (*presenza*) presence. **par'tecipe** *a* participating

parteggi'are *vi* **~ per** side with

par'tenza *nf* departure; *Sport* start; **in ~ per** leaving for

parti'cella *nf* particle

parti'cipio *nm* participle

partico'lar|e *a* particular; (*privato*) private ● *nm* detail, particular; **fin nei minimi ~i** down to the smallest detail. **~eggi'ato** *a* detailed. **~ità** *nf inv* particularity; (*dettaglio*) detail

partigi'ano, **-a** *a* & *nmf* partisan

par'tire *vi* leave; (*aver inizio*) start; **a ~ da** [beginning] from

par'tita *nf* game; (*incontro*) match; *Comm* lot; (*contabilità*) entry. **~ di calcio** football match. **~ a carte** game of cards

par'tito *nm* party; (*scelta*) choice; (*occasione di matrimonio*) match; **per ~ preso** out of sheer pig-headedness

'parto *nm* childbirth; **un ~ facile** an easy birth *o* labour; **dolori** *pl* **del ~** labour pains. **~ cesareo** Caesarian section. **~rire** *vt* give birth to

par'venza *nf* appearance

parzi'al|e *a* partial. **~ità** *nf* partiality. **~'mente** *adv* (*non completamente*) partially; **~mente scremato** semi-skimmed

pasco'lare *vt* graze. 'pascolo *nm* pasture

'Pasqua *nf* Easter. pa'squale *a* Easter *attrib*

'passa: **e ~** *adv* (*e oltre*) plus

pas'sabile *a* passable

pas'saggio *nm* passage; (*traversata*) crossing; *Sport* pass; (*su veicolo*) lift; **essere di ~** be passing through. **~ a livello** level crossing, grade crossing *Am*. **~ pedonale** pedestrian crossing

passamon'tagna *nm inv* balaclava

pas'sante *nmf* passer-by ● *nm* (*di cintura*) loop ● *a Tennis* passing

passa'porto *nm* passport

pas'sa|re *vi* pass; (*attraversare*) pass through; (*far visita*) call; (*andare*) go; (*essere approvato*) be passed; **~re alla storia** go down in history; **mi è ~to di mente** it slipped my mind; **~re per un genio/idiota** be taken for a genius/an idiot; **farsi ~re per qcno** pass oneself off as sb ● *vt* (*far scorrere*) pass over; (*sopportare*) go through; (*al telefono*) put through; *Culin* strain; **~re di moda** go out of fashion; **le passo il signor Rossi** I'll put you through to Mr Rossi; **~rsela** be well off; **come te la passi?** how are you doing?. **~ta** *nf* (*di vernice*) coat; (*spolverata*) dusting; (*occhiata*) look

passa'tempo *nm* pastime

pas'sato *a* past; (*anno*) last year; **sono le tre passate** it's past *o* after three o'clock ● *nm* past; *Culin* purée; *Gram* past tense. **~ prossimo** *Gram* present perfect. **~ remoto** *Gram* [simple] past. **~ di verdure** cream of vegetable soup

passaver'dure *nm inv* food mill

passeg'gero, **-a** *a* passing ● *nmf* passenger

passeggi'a|re *vi* walk, stroll. **~ta** *nf* walk, stroll; (*luogo*) public walk; (*in bicicletta*) ride; **fare una ~ta** go for a walk

passeg'gino *nm* pushchair, stroller *Am*

pas'seggio *nm* walk; (*luogo*) promenade; **andare a ~** go for a walk; **scarpe da ~** walking shoes

passe-partout *nm inv* master-key

passe'rella *nf* gangway; *Aeron* boarding bridge; (*per sfilate*) catwalk

'passero *nm* sparrow. passe'rotto *nm* (*passero*) sparrow

pas'sibile *a* **~ di** liable to

passio'nale *a* passionate. passi'one *nf* passion

pas'sivo *a* passive ● *nm* passive; *Comm* liabilities *pl*; **in ~** (*bilancio*) loss-making

'passo *nm* step; (*orma*) footprint; (*andatura*) pace; (*brano*) passage; (*valico*) pass; **a due passi da qui** a stone's throw away; **a ~ d'uomo** at walking pace; **di buon ~** at a spanking pace; **fare due passi** go for a stroll; **di pari ~** *fig* hand in hand. **~ carrabile, ~ carraio** driveway

'pasta *nf* (*impasto per pane ecc*) dough; (*per dolci, pasticcino*) pastry; (*pastasciutta*) pasta; (*massa molle*) paste; *fig* nature. **~ frolla** shortcrust pastry

pastasci'utta *nf* pasta

pa'stella *nf* batter

pa'stello *nm* pastel

pa'sticca *nf* pastille; (*fam: pastiglia*) pill

pasticce'ria *nf* cake shop, patisserie; (*pasticcini*) pastries *pl*; (*arte*) confectionery

pasticci'are *vi* make a mess ● *vt* make a mess of

pasticci'ere, -a *nmf* confectioner

pastic'cino *nm* little cake

pa'sticcio *nm* Culin pie; (*lavoro disordinato*) mess; **mettersi nei pasticci** get into trouble. **~'one, -a** *nmf* bungler ● *a* bungling

pasti'ficio *nm* pasta factory

pa'stiglia *nf* Med pill, tablet; (*di menta*) sweet. **~ dei freni** brake pad

'pasto *nm* meal

pasto'rale *a* pastoral. **pa'store** *nm* shepherd; *Relig* pastor. **pastore tedesco** German shepherd, Alsatian

pastoriz'za|re *vt* pasteurize. **~to** *a* pasteurized. **~zi'one** *nf* pasteurization

pa'stoso *a* doughy; *fig* mellow

pa'stura *nf* pasture; (*per pesci*) bait

pa'tacca *nf* (*macchia*) stain; (*fig: oggetto senza valore*) piece of junk

pa'tata *nf* potato. **patate** *pl* **fritte** chips *Br*, French fries. **pata'tine** *nfpl* [potato] crisps, chips *Am*

pata'trac *nm inv* (*crollo*) crash

pâté *nm inv* pâté

pa'tella *nf* limpet

pa'tema *nm* anxiety

pa'tente *nf* licence. **~ di guida** driving licence, driver's license *Am*

pater'na|le *nf* scolding. **~'lista** *nm* paternalist

paternità *nf* paternity. **pa'terno** *a* paternal; (*affetto ecc*) fatherly

pa'tetico *a* pathetic. **'pathos** *nm* pathos

pa'tibolo *nm* gallows *sg*

'patina *nf* patina; (*sulla lingua*) coating

pa'ti|re *vt/i* suffer. **~to, -a** *a* suffering

● *nmf* fanatic. **~to della musica** music lover

patolo'gia *nf* pathology. **pato'logico** *a* pathological

'patria *nf* native land

patri'arca *nm* patriarch

pa'trigno *nm* stepfather

patrimoni'ale *a* property *attrib*. **patri'monio** *nm* estate

patri'o|ta *nmf* patriot. **~tico** *a* patriotic. **~'tismo** *nm* patriotism

pa'trizio, -a *a & nmf* patrician

patro|ci'nare *vt* support. **~ cinio** *nm* support

patro'nato *nm* patronage. **pa'trono** *nm* Relig patron saint; *Jur* counsel

'patta¹ *nf* (*di tasca*) flap

'patta² *nf* (*pareggio*) draw

patteggia'mento *nm* bargaining. **~'are** *vt/i* negotiate

patti'naggio *nm* skating. **~ su ghiaccio** ice skating. **~ a rotelle** roller skating

patti'na|re *vi* skate; ⟨*auto:*⟩ skid. **~'tore, ~'trice** *nmf* skater. **pat'tino** *nm* skate; *Aeron* skid. **pattino da ghiaccio** iceskate. **pattino a rotelle** roller-skate

'patto *nm* deal; *Pol* pact; **a ~ che** on condition that

pat'tuglia *nf* patrol. **~ stradale** ≈ patrol car; police motorbike, highway patrol *Am*

pattu'ire *vt* negotiate

pattumi'era *nf* dustbin, trashcan *Am*

pa'ura *nf* fear; (*spavento*) fright; **aver ~** be afraid; **mettere ~ a** frighten. **pau'roso** *a* (*che fa paura*) frightening; (*che ha paura*) fearful; (*fam: enorme*) awesome

'pausa *nf* pause; (*nel lavoro*) break; **fare una ~** pause; (*nel lavoro*) have a break

pavimen'ta|re *vt* pave ⟨*strada*⟩. **~zi'one** *nf* (*operazione*) paving. **pavi'mento** *nm* floor

pa'vone *nm* peacock. **~ggi'arsi** *vr* strut

pazien'tare *vi* be patient

pazi'ente *a & nmf* patient. **~'mente** *adv* patiently. **pazi'enza** *nf* patience; **pazienza!** never mind!

'pazza *nf* madwoman. **~'mente** *adv* madly

paz'z|esco *a* foolish; (*esagerato*) crazy. **~ia** *nf* madness; (*azione*) [act of] folly. **'pazzo** *a* mad; *fig* crazy ● *nm* madman; **essere pazzo di/per** be crazy about; **pazzo di gioia** mad with joy; **da pazzi**

fam crackpot; **darsi alla pazza gioia** live it up. **paz'zoide** *a* whacky

'pecca *nf* fault; **senza ~** flawless. **peccami'noso** *a* sinful

pec'ca|re *vi* sin; **~re di** be guilty of *(ingratitudine)*. **~to** *nm* sin; **~to che...** it's a pity that...; **[che] ~to!** [what a] pity!. **~'tore, ~'trice** *nmf* sinner

'pece *nf* pitch

'peco|ra *nf* sheep. **~ra nera** black sheep. **~'raio** *nm* shepherd. **~'rella** *nf* **cielo a ~relle** sky full of fluffy white clouds. **~'rino** *nm (formaggio)* sheep's milk cheese

peculi'ar|e *a* **~ di** peculiar to. **~ità** *nf inv* peculiarity

pe'daggio *nm* toll

pedago'gia *nf* pedagogy. **peda'gogi- co** *a* pedagogical

peda'lare *vi* pedal. **pe'dale** *nm* pedal. **pedalò** *nm inv* pedalo

pe'dana *nf* footrest; *Sport* springboard

pe'dante *a* pedantic. **~'ria** *nf* ped- antry. **pedan'tesco** *a* pedantic

pe'data *nf (in calcio)* kick; *(impronta)* footprint

pede'rasta *nm* pederast

pe'destre *a* pedestrian

pedi'atra *nmf* paediatrician. **pedia- 'tria** *nf* paediatrics *sg*

pedi'cure *nmf inv* chiropodist, podia- trist *Am* • *nm (cura dei piedi)* pedicure

pedi'gree *nm inv* pedigree

pe'dina *nf (alla dama)* piece; *fig* pawn. **~'mento** *nm* shadowing. **pedi'nare** *vt* shadow

pe'dofilo, -a *nmf* paedophile

pedo'nale *a* pedestrian. **pe'done, -a** *nmf* pedestrian

peeling *nm inv* exfoliation treatment

'peggio *adv* worse; **~ per te!** too bad!; **~ di cosí** any worse; **la persona ~ vestita** the worst dressed person • *a* worse; **niente di ~** nothing worse • *nm* **il ~ è che...** the worst of it is that...; **pensare al ~** think the worst • *nf* **alla ~** at worst; **avere la ~** get the worst of it; **alla meno ~** as best I can

peggiora'mento *nm* worsening

peggio'ra|re *vt* make worse, worsen • *vi* get worse, worsen. **~'tivo** *a* pejora- tive

peggi'ore *a* worse; *(superlativo)* worst; **nella ~ delle ipotesi** if the worst comes to the worst • *nmf* **il/la ~** the worst

'pegno *nm* pledge; *(nei giochi di società)* forfeit; *fig* token

pelan'drone *nm* slob

pe'la|re *vt (spennare)* pluck; *(spellare)* skin; *(sbucciare)* peel; *(fam: spillare denaro)* fleece. **~rsi** *vr fam* lose one's hair. **~to a** bald. **~ti** *nmpl (pomodori)* peeled tomatoes

pel'lame *nm* skins *pl*

'pelle *nf* skin; *(cuoio)* leather; *(buccia)* peel; **avere la ~ d'oca** have goose-flesh

pellegri'naggio *nm* pilgrimage. **pelle'grino, -a** *nmf* pilgrim

pelle'rossa *nm* Red Indian, Redskin

pellette'ria *nf* leather goods *pl*

pelli'cano *nm* pelican

pellicce'ria *nf* furrier's [shop]. **pel'liccia** *nf* fur; *(indumento)* fur coat. **~'iaio, -a** *nmf* furrier

pel'licola *nf* Phot, Cinema film. **~ [trasparente]** cling film

'pelo *nm* hair; *(di animale)* coat; *(di lana)* pile; **per un ~** by the skin of one's teeth; **cavarsela per un ~** have a nar- row escape. **pe'loso** *a* hairy

'peltro *nm* pewter

pe'luche *nm inv* **giocattolo di ~** soft toy

pe'luria *nf* down

'pelvico *a* pelvic

'pena *nf (punizione)* punishment; *(sof- ferenza)* pain; *(dispiacere)* sorrow; *(di- sturbo)* trouble; **a mala ~** hardly; **mi fa ~** I pity him; **vale la ~ andare** it is worth [while] going. **~ di morte** death sentence

pe'nal|e *a* criminal; **diritto** *nm* **~e** criminal law. **~ità** *nf inv* penalty

penaliz'za|re *vt* penalize. **~zi'one** *nf (penalità)* penalty

pe'nare *vi* suffer; *(faticare)* find it diffi- cult

pen'daglio *nm* pendant

pen'dant *nm inv* **fare ~ [con]** match

pen'den|te *a* hanging; *Comm* out- standing • *nm (ciondolo)* pendant; **~ti** *pl* drop earrings. **~za** *nf* slope; *Comm* outstanding account

'pendere *vi* hang; *(superficie:)* slope; *(essere inclinato)* lean

pen'dio *nm* slope; **in ~** sloping

pendo'l|are *a* pendulum • *nmf* com- muter. **~ino** *nm (treno)* special, first class only, fast train

'pendolo *nm* pendulum

'pene *nm* penis

pene'trante *a* penetrating; *(freddo)* biting

pene'tra|re *vt/i* penetrate; *(trafiggere)* pierce • *vt (odore:)* get into • *vi (entrare* *furtivamente)* steal in. **~zi'one** *nf* penetration

penicil'lina *nf* penicillin

pe'nisola *nf* peninsula

peni'tente *a* & *nmf* penitent. **~za** *nf* penitence; *(punizione)* penance; *(in gioco)* forfeit. **~zi'ario** *nm* penitentiary

'penna *nf (da scrivere)* pen; *(di uccello)* feather. **~ a feltro** felt-tip[ped pen]. **~ a sfera** ball-point [pen]. **~ stilografica** fountain-pen

pen'nacchio *nm* plume

penna'rello *nm* felt-tip[ped pen]

pennel'la|re *vt* paint. **~ta** *nf* brushstroke. **pen'nello** *nm* brush; **a pennello** *(a perfezione)* perfectly

pen'nino *nm* nib

pen'none *nm (di bandiera)* flagpole

pen'nuto *a* feathered

pe'nombra *nf* half-light

pe'noso *a (fam: pessimo)* painful

pen'sa|re *vi* think; **penso di sì** I think so; **~re a** think of; remember to *(chiudere il gas ecc)*; **pensa ai fatti tuoi!** mind your own business!; **ci penso io** I'll take care of it; **~re di fare qcsa** think of doing sth; **~re tra sé e sé** think to oneself ● *vt* think. **~ta** *nf* idea

pensi'e|ro *nm* thought; *(mente)* mind; *(preoccupazione)* worry; **stare in ~ro per** be anxious about. **~'roso** *a* pensive

pen'si|le *a* hanging; **giardino ~le** roof-garden ● *nm (mobile)* wall unit. **~'lina** *nf (di fermata d'autobus)* bus shelter

pensio'nante *nmf* boarder; *(ospite pagante)* lodger

pensio'nato, -a *nmf* pensioner ● *nm (per anziani)* [old folks'] home; *(per studenti)* hostel. **pensi'one** *nf* pension; *(albergo)* boarding-house; *(vitto e alloggio)* board and lodging; **andare in pensione** retire; **mezza pensione** half board. **pensione completa** full board

pen'soso *a* pensive

pen'tagono *nm* pentagon

Pente'coste *nf* Whitsun

penti'mento *nm* repentance

pen'ti|rsi *vr* **~rsi di** repent of; *(rammaricarsi)* regret. **~'tismo** *nm* turning informant. **~to** *nm* Mafioso turned informant

'pentola *nf* saucepan; *(contenuto)* potful. **~ a pressione** pressure cooker

pe'nultimo *a* last but one

pe'nuria *nf* shortage

penzo'l|are *vi* dangle. **~oni** *adv* dangling

pe'pa|re *vt* pepper. **~to** *a* peppery

'pepe *nm* pepper; **grano di ~** peppercorn. **~ in grani** whole peppercorns. **~ macinato** ground pepper

pepero'n|ata *nf* peppers cooked in olive oil with onion, tomato and garlic. **~'cino** *nm* chilli pepper. **pe'rone** *nm* pepper. **peperone verde** green pepper

pe'pita *nf* nugget

per *prep* for; *(attraverso)* through; *(stato in luogo)* in, on; *(distributivo)* per; *(mezzo, entro)* by; *(causa)* with; *(in qualità di)* as; **~ strada** on the street; **~ la fine del mese** by the end of the month; **in fila ~ due** in double file; **l'ho sentito ~ telefono** I spoke to him on the phone; **~ iscritto** in writing; **~ caso** by chance; **ho aspettato ~ ore** I've been waiting for hours; **~ tempo** in time; **~ sempre** forever; **~ scherzo** as a joke; **gridare ~ il dolore** scream with pain; **vendere ~ 10 milioni** sell for 10 million; **uno ~ volta** one at a time; **uno ~ uno** one by one; **venti ~ cento** twenty per cent; **~ fare qcsa** [in order] to do sth; **stare ~ essere** be about to; **è troppo bello ~ essere vero** it's too good to be true

'pera *nf* pear; **farsi una ~** *(sl: di eroina)* shoot up

perbe'nismo *nm* prissiness. **~ta** *a inv* prissy

per'cento *adv* per cent. **percentu'ale** *nf* percentage

perce'pibile *a* perceivable; *(somma)* payable

perce'pire *vt* perceive; *(riscuotere)* cash

perce't'tibile *a* perceptible. **~zi'one** *nf* perception

perché *conj (in interrogazioni)* why; *(per il fatto che)* because; *(affinché)* so that; **~ non vieni?** why don't you come?; **dimmi ~** tell me why; **~ no/sì!** because!; **la ragione ~ l'ho fatto** the reason [that] I did it, the reason why I did it; **è troppo difficile ~ lo possa capire** it's too difficult for me to understand ● *nm inv* reason [why]; **senza un ~** without any reason

perciò *conj* so

per'correre *vt* cover *(distanza)*; *(viaggiare)* travel. **per'corso** *pp di* **percorre-re** ● *nm (tragitto)* course, route; *(distanza)* distance; *(viaggio)* journey

per'coss|a *nf* blow. **~o** *pp di* **percuotere percu'otere** *vt* strike

percussi'one *nf* percussion; **strumenti a ~ne** percussion instruments. **~'nista** *nmf* percussionist

per'dente *nmf* loser

'**perder|e** *vt* lose; (*sprecare*) waste; (*non prendere*) miss; (*fig: vizio*) ruin; ~**e tempo** waste time ● *vi* lose; (*recipiente:*) leak; **lascia ~e!** forget it!. ~**si** *vr* get lost; (*reciproco*) lose touch

perdifi'ato: **a ~** *adv* (*gridare*) at the top of one's voice

perdi'giorno *nmf inv* idler

'**perdita** *nf* loss; (*spreco*) waste; (*falla*) leak; **a ~ d'occhio** as far as the eye can see. **~ di tempo** waste of time. **perdi'tempo** *nm* waste of time

perdo'nare *vt* forgive; (*scusare*) excuse. **per'dono** *nm* forgiveness; *Jur* pardon

perdu'rare *vi* last; (*perseverare*) persist

perduta'mente *adv* hopelessly. **per'duto** *pp di* **perdere** ● *a* lost; (*rovinato*) ruined

pe'renne *a* everlasting; *Bot* perennial; **nevi perenni** perpetual snow. **~'mente** *adv* perpetually

peren'torio *a* peremptory

per'fetto *a* perfect ● *nm Gram* perfect [tense]

perfezio'nar|e *vt* perfect; (*migliorare*) improve. **~si** *vr* improve oneself; (*specializzarsi*) specialize

perfezi'one *nf* perfection; **alla ~ne** to perfection. **~'nismo** *nm* perfectionism. **~'nista** *nmf* perfectionist

per'fidia *nf* wickedness; (*atto*) wicked act. '**perfido** *a* treacherous; (*malvagio*) perverse

per'fino *adv* even

perfo'ra|re *vt* pierce; punch (*schede*); *Mech* drill. **~'tore**, **~'trice** *nmf* punch-card operator ● *nm* perforator. **~zi'one** *nf* perforation; (*di schede*) punching

per'formance *nf inv* performance

perga'mena *nf* parchment

perico'lante *a* precarious; (*azienda*) shaky

pe'ricolo *nm* danger; (*rischio*) risk; **mettere in ~lo** endanger. **~lo pubblico** danger to society. **~'loso** *a* dangerous

perife'ria *nf* periphery; (*di città*) outskirts *pl*; *fig* fringes *pl*

peri'feric|a *nf* peripheral; (*strada*) ring road. **~o** *a* (*quartiere*) outlying

peri'frasi *nf* circumlocution

pe'rimetro *nm* perimeter

peri'odico *nm* periodical ● *a* periodical; (*vento, mal di testa*, *Math*) recurring. **pe'riodo** *nm* period; *Gram* sentence. **periodo di prova** trial period

peripe'zie *nfpl* misadventures

pe'rire *vi* perish

peri'scopio *nm* periscope

pe'rito, **-a** *a* skilled ● *nmf* expert

perito'nite *nf* peritonitis

pe'rizia *nf* skill; (*valutazione*) survey

'**perla** *nf* pearl. **per'lina** *nf* bead

perlo'meno *adv* at least

perlu'stra|re *vt* patrol. **~zi'one** *nf* patrol; **andare in ~zione** go on patrol

perma'loso *a* touchy

perma'ne|nte *a* permanent ● *nf* perm; **farsi** [**fare**] **la ~nte** have a perm. **~nza** *nf* permanence; (*soggiorno*) stay; **in ~nza** permanently. **~re** *vi* remain

perme'are *vt* permeate

per'messo *pp di* **permettere** ● *nm* permission; (*autorizzazione*) permit; *Mil* leave; [**è**] **~?** (*posso entrare?*) may I come in?; (*posso passare?*) excuse me. **~ di lavoro** work permit

per'mettere *vt* allow, permit; **potersi ~ qcsa** (*finanziariamente*) be able to afford sth; **come si permette?** how dare you?. **permis'sivo** *a* permissive

permutazi'one *nf* exchange; *Math* permutation

per'nacchia *nf* (*sl: con la bocca*) raspberry *sl*

per'nic|e *nf* partridge. **~'oso** *a* pernicious

'**perno** *nm* pivot

pernot'tare *vi* stay overnight

'**pero** *nm* pear-tree

però *conj* but; (*tuttavia*) however

pero'rare *vt* plead

perpendico'lare *a & nf* perpendicular

perpe'trare *vt* perpetrate

perpetu'are *vt* perpetuate. **per'petuo** *a* perpetual

perplessità *nf inv* perplexity; (*dubbio*) doubt. **per'plesso** *a* perplexed

perqui'si|re *vt* search. **~zi'one** *nf* search. **~zione domiciliare** search of the premises

persecu'tore, **-'trice** *nmf* persecutor. **~zi'one** *nf* persecution

persegu'ire *vt* pursue

persegui'tare *vt* persecute

perseve'ra|nte *a* persevering. **~nza** *nf* perseverance. **~re** *vi* persevere

persi'ano, **-a** *a* Persian ● *nf* (*di finestra*) shutter. '**persico** *a* Persian

per'sino *adv* = **perfino**

persi'sten|te *a* persistent. **~za** *nf* persistence. **per'sistere** *vi* persist '**perso** *pp di* **perdere** ● *a* lost; **a tempo ~** in one's spare time

per'**sona** *nf* person; *(un tale)* somebody; **di ~, in ~** in person, personally; **per ~** per person, a head; **per interposta ~** through an intermediary; **persone** *pl* people

perso'**naggio** *nm (persona di riguardo)* personality; *Theat ecc* character

perso'**nale** *a* personal ● *nm* staff. **~e di terra** ground crew. **~ità** *nf inv* personality. **~iz'zare** *vt* customize *(auto ecc)*; personalize *(penna ecc)*

personifi'**care** *vt* personify. **~zi'one** *nf* personification

perspi'**cace** *a* shrewd. **~ia** *nf* shrewdness

persua'**dere** *vt* convince; impress *(critici)*; **~dere qcno a fare qcsa** persuade sb to do sth. **~si'one** *nf* persuasion. **~'sivo** *a* persuasive. **persu'aso** *pp di* **persuadere**

per'**tanto** *conj* therefore

'**pertica** *nf* pole

perti'**nente** *a* relevant

per'**tosse** *nf* whooping cough

pertur'**bare** *vt* perturb. **~rsi** *vr* be perturbed. **~zi'one** *nf* disturbance. **~zione atmosferica** atmospheric disturbance

per'**vadere** *vt* pervade. **~so** *pp di* **pervadere**

perven'**ire** *vi* reach; **far ~ qcsa a qcno** send sth to sb

perversi'**one** *nf* perversion. **~ità** *nf* perversity. **per'verso** *a* perverse

perver'**tire** *vt* pervert. **~to** *a* perverted ● *nm* pervert

per'**vinca** *nm (colore)* blue with a touch of purple

p. es. *abbr (per esempio)* e.g.

pesa *nf* weighing; *(bilancia)* weighing machine; *(per veicoli)* weighbridge

pe'**sante** *a* heavy; *(stomaco)* overfull ● *adv (vestirsi)* warmly. **~'mente** *adv (cadere)* heavily. **pesan'tezza** *nf* heaviness

pe'**sare** *vt/i* weigh; **~e su** *fig* lie heavy on; **~e le parole** weigh one's words. **~si** *vr* weigh oneself

'**pesca**[1] *nf (frutto)* peach

'**pesca**[2] *nf* fishing; **andare a ~** go fishing. **~ subacquea** underwater fishing. pe'**scare** *vt (andare a pesca di)* fish for; *(prendere)* catch; *(fig: trovare)* fish out. **~ tore** *nm* fisherman

'**pesce** *nm* fish. **~ d'aprile!** April Fool!. **~ grosso** *fig* big fish. **~ piccolo** *fig*

small fry. **~ rosso** goldfish. **~ spada** swordfish. **Pesci** *Astr* Pisces

pesce'**cane** *nm* shark

pesche'**reccio** *nm* fishing boat

pesche'**ria** *nf* fishmonger's [shop]. **~hi'era** *nf* fish-pond. **~i'vendolo** *nm* fishmonger

'**pesco** *nm* peach-tree

'**peso** *nm* weight; **essere di ~ per qcno** be a burden to sb; **di poco ~** *(senza importanza)* not very important; **non dare ~ a qcsa** not attach any importance to sth

pessi'**mismo** *nm* pessimism. **~ta** *nmf* pessimist ● *a* pessimistic. '**pessimo** *a* very bad

pe'**staggio** *nm* beating-up. pe'**stare** *vt* tread on; *(schiacciare)* crush; *(picchiare)* beat; crush *(aglio, prezzemolo)*

'**peste** *nf* plague; *(persona)* pest

pe'**stello** *nm* pestle

pesti'**cida** *nm* pesticide. pe'**stifero** *a (fastidioso)* pestilential

pesti'**lenza** *nf* pestilence; *(fetore)* stench. **~zi'ale** *a (odore aria)* noxious

'**pesto** *a* ground; **occhio ~** ~ **black eye** ● *nm* basil and garlic sauce

'**petalo** *nm* petal

pe'**tardo** *nm* banger

petizi'**one** *nf* petition; **fare una ~** draw up a petition

petroli'**era** *nf* [oil] tanker. **~ lifero** *a* oil-bearing. pe'**trolio** *nm* oil

pettego'**lare** *vi* gossip. **~ lezzo** *nm* piece of gossip; **far ~ lezzi** gossip

pet'**tegolo, -a** *a* gossipy ● *nmf* gossip

petti'**nare** *vt* comb. **~rsi** *vr* comb one's hair. **~ tura** *nf* combing; *(acconciatura)* hair-style. '**pettine** *nm* comb

'**petting** *nm* petting

petti'**nino** *nm (fermaglio)* comb

petti'**rosso** *nm* robin [redbreast]

'**petto** *nm* chest; *(seno)* breast; **a doppio ~** double-breasted

petto'**rale** *nm (in gare sportive)* number.. **~ rina** *nf (di salopette)* bib. **~ ruto** *a (donna)* full-breasted; *(uomo)* broad-chested

petu'**lante** *a* impertinent

'**pezza** *nf* cloth; *(toppa)* patch; *(rotolo di tessuto)* roll

pez'**zente** *nmf* tramp; *(avaro)* miser

'**pezzo** *nm* piece; *(parte)* part; **un bel ~ d'uomo** a fine figure of a man; **un ~** *(di tempo)* some time; *(di spazio)* a long way; **al ~** *(costare)* each; **essere a pezzi** *(stanco)* be shattered; **fare a pezzi** tear to shreds. **~ grosso** bigwig

pia'cente a attractive

pia'ce|re nm pleasure; (favore) favour; **a ~re** as much as one likes; **per ~re!** please!; **con ~re** with pleasure ● vi **la Scozia mi piace** I like Scotland; **mi piacciono i dolci** I like sweets; **faccio come mi pare e piace** I do as I please; **ti piace?** do you like it?; **lo spettacolo è piaciuto** the show was a success. **~vole** a pleasant

piaci'mento nm **a ~** as much as you like

pia'dina nf unleavened focaccia bread

pi'aga nf sore; fig scourge; (fig: persona noiosa) pain; (fig: ricordo doloroso) wound

piagni'steo nm whining

piagnuco'lare vi whimper

pi'alla nf plane. **pial'lare** vt plane

pi'ana nf (pianura) plane. **pianeg-gi'ante** a level

piane'rottolo nm landing

pia'neta nm planet

pi'angere vi cry; (disperatamente) weep ● vt (lamentare) lament; (per un lutto) mourn

pianifi'ca|re vt plan. **~zi'one** nf planning

pia'nista nmf Mus pianist

pi'ano a flat; (a livello) flush; (regolare) smooth; (facile) easy ● adv slowly; (con cautela) gently; **andarci ~** go carefully ● nm plain; (di edificio) floor; (livello) plane; (progetto) plan; Mus plane; **di primo ~** first-rate; **primo ~** Phot close-up; **in primo ~** in the foreground. **~ regolatore** town plan. **~ di studi** syllabus

piano'forte nm piano. **~ a coda** grand piano

piano'terra nm inv ground floor, first floor Am

pi'anta nf plant; (del piede) sole; (disegno) plan; **di sana ~** (totalmente) entirely; **in ~ stabile** permanently. **~ stradale** road map. **~gi'one** nf plantation

piantagrane nmf fam **è un/una ~** he's/she's bolshie

pian'tar|e vt plant; (conficcare) drive; (fam: abbandonare) dump; **piantala!** fam stop it!. **~si** vr plant oneself; (fam: lasciarsi) leave each other

pianter'reno nm ground floor, first floor Am

pi'anto pp di piangere ● nm crying; (disperato) weeping; (lacrime) tears pl

pian|to'nare vt guard. **~'tone** nm guard

pia'nura nf plain

pi'astra nf plate; (lastra) slab; Culin griddle. **~ elettronica** circuit board. **~ madre** Comput motherboard

pia'strella nf tile

pia'strina nf Mil identity disc; Med platelet; Comput chip

piatta'forma nf platform. **~ di lancio** launch pad

piat'tino nm saucer

pi'atto a flat ● nm plate; (da portata, vivanda) dish; (portata) course; (parte piatta) flat; (di giradischi) turntable; **piatti** pl Mus cymbals; **lavare i piatti** do the dishes, do the washing-up. **~ fondo** soup plate. **~ piano** [ordinary] plate

pi'azza nf square; Comm market; **letto a una ~** single bed; **letto a due piazze** double bed; **far ~ pulita** make a clean sweep. **~forte** nf stronghold. **piaz'zale** nm large square. **~'mento** nm (in classifica) placing

piaz'za|re vt place. **~rsi** vr Sport be placed; **~rsi secondo** come second. **~to** a (cavallo) placed; **ben ~to** (robusto) well built

piaz'zista nm salesman

piaz'zuola nf **~ di sosta** pull-in

pic'cante a hot; (pungente) sharp; (salace) spicy

pic'carsi vr (risentirsi) take offence; **~ di** (vantarsi di) claim to

'picche nfpl (in carte) spades

picchet'tare vt stake; (scioperanti:) picket. **pic'chetto** nm picket

picchi'a|re vt beat, hit ● vi (bussare) knock; Aeron nosedive; **~re in testa** (motore:) knock. **~ta** nf beating; Aeron nosedive; **scendere in ~ta** nosedive

picchiet'tare vt tap; (punteggiare) spot

picchiet'tio nm tapping

'picchio nm woodpecker

pic'cino a tiny; (gretto) mean; (di poca importanza) petty ● nm little one, child

picci'one nm pigeon

'picco nm peak; **a ~** vertically; **colare a ~** sink

'piccolo, -a a small, little; (di età) young; (di statura) short; (gretto) petty ● nmf child, little one; **da ~** as a child

pic'co|ne nm pickaxe. **~zza** nf ice axe

pic'nic nm inv picnic

pi'docchio nm louse

piè nm inv **a ~ di pagina** at the foot of the page; **saltare a ~ pari** skip

pi'ede nm foot; **a piedi** on foot; **andare a piedi** walk; **a piedi nudi** barefoot; **a ~ libero** free; **in piedi** standing; **alzarsi in piedi** stand up; **in punta di piedi** on tiptoe; **ai piedi di** ⟨montagna⟩ at the foot of; **prendere ~** fig gain ground; ⟨moda:⟩ catch on; **mettere in piedi** ⟨allestire⟩ set up; **togliti dai piedi!** get out of the way!. **~ di porco** ⟨strumento⟩ jemmy

pie'dino nm **fare ~ a** qcno fam play footsie with sb

piedi'stallo nm pedestal

pi'ega nf ⟨piegatura⟩ fold; ⟨di gonna⟩ pleat; ⟨di pantaloni⟩ crease; ⟨grinza⟩ wrinkle; ⟨andamento⟩ turn; **non fare una ~** ⟨ragionamento:⟩ be flawless

pie'ga|re vt fold; ⟨flettere⟩ bend ●vi bend. **~rsi** vr bend. **~rsi a** fig yield to. **~'tura** nf folding

pieghet'ta|re vt pleat. **~to** a pleated. **pie'ghevole** a pliable; ⟨tavolo⟩ folding ●nm leaflet

piemon'tese a Piedmontese

pi'en|a|n f ⟨di fiume⟩ flood; ⟨folla⟩ crowd. **~o** a full; ⟨massiccio⟩ solid; **in ~a estate** in the middle of summer; **a ~i voti** ⟨diplomarsi⟩ with A-grades, with first class honours ●nm ⟨colmo⟩ height; ⟨carico⟩ full load; **in ~o** ⟨completamente⟩ fully; **fare il ~o** ⟨di benzina⟩ fill up

pie'none nm **c'era il ~** the place was packed

pietà nf pity; ⟨misericordia⟩ mercy; **senza ~** ⟨persona⟩ pitiless; ⟨spietatamente⟩ pitilessly; **avere ~ di** qcno take pity on sb; **far ~** ⟨far pena⟩ be pitiful

pie'tanza nf dish

pie'toso a pitiful, merciful; ⟨fam: pessimo⟩ terrible

pi'etr|a nf stone. **~a dura** semi-precious stone. **pie'trame** nm stones pl. **~a preziosa** precious stone. **~a dello scandalo** cause of the scandal. **~ifi'care** vt petrify. **pie'trina** nf ⟨di accendino⟩ flint. **pie'troso** a stony

'piffero nm fife

pi'giama nm pyjamas pl

'pigia 'pigia nm inv crowd, crush. **pigi'are** vt press

pigi'one nf rent; **dare a ~** let, rent out; **prendere a ~** rent

pigli'are vt ⟨fam: afferrare⟩ catch. **'piglio** nm air

pig'mento nm pigment

pig'meo, -a a & nmf pygmy

'pigna nf cone

pi'gnolo a pedantic

pigo'lare vi chirp. **pigo'lio** nm chirping

pi'grizia nf laziness. **'pigro** a lazy; ⟨intelletto⟩ slow

'pila nf pile; Electr battery; ⟨fam: lampadina tascabile⟩ torch; ⟨vasca⟩ basin; **a pile** battery operated, battery powered

pi'lastro nm pillar

'pillola nf pill; **prendere la ~** be on the pill

pi'lone nm pylon; ⟨di ponte⟩ pier

pi'lota nmf pilot ●nm Auto driver. **pilo'tare** vt pilot; drive ⟨auto⟩

pinaco'teca nf art gallery

'Pinco Pallino nm so-and-so

pi'neta nf pine-wood

ping-'pong nm table tennis, ping-pong fam

'pingu|e a fat. **~'edine** nf fatness

pingu'ino nm penguin; ⟨gelato⟩ choc ice on a stick

'pinna nf fin; ⟨per nuotare⟩ flipper

'pino nm pine[-tree]. **pi'nolo** nm pine kernel. **~ marittimo** cluster pine

'pinta nf pint

'pinza nf pliers pl; Med forceps pl

pin'za|re vt ⟨con pinzatrice⟩ staple. **~'trice** nf stapler

pin'zette nfpl tweezers pl

pinzi'monio nm sauce for crudités

'pio a pious; ⟨benefico⟩ charitable

pi'oggia nf rain; ⟨fig: di piombe, insulti⟩ hail, shower; **sotto la ~** in the rain. **~ acida** acid rain

pi'olo nm ⟨di scala⟩ rung

piom'ba|re vi fall heavily; **~re su** fall upon ●vt fill ⟨dente⟩. **~'tura** nf ⟨di dente⟩ filling. **piom'bino** nm ⟨sigillo⟩ [lead] seal; ⟨da pesca⟩ sinker; ⟨in gonne⟩ weight

pi'ombo nm lead; ⟨sigillo⟩ [lead] seal; **a ~** plumb; **senza ~** ⟨benzina⟩ lead-free

pioni'ere, -a nmf pioneer

pi'oppo nm poplar

pio'vano a **acqua piovana** rainwater

pi'ov|ere vi rain; **~e** it's raining; **~iggi'nare** vi drizzle. **pio'voso** a rainy

'pipa nf pipe

pipì nf **fare [la] ~** pee, piddle; **andare a fare [la] ~** go for a pee

pipi'strello nm bat

pi'ramide nf pyramid

pi'ranha nm inv piranha

pi'rat|a nm pirate. **~a della strada** road-hog ●a inv pirate. **~e'ria** nf piracy

piro'etta nf pirouette

pi'rofil|a nf ⟨tegame⟩ oven-proof dish. **~o** a heat-resistant

pi'romane nmf pyromaniac

pi'roscafo *nm* steamer. ~ **di linea** liner

pisci'are *vi vulg* piss

pi'scina *nf* swimming pool. ~ **coperta** indoor swimming pool. ~ **scoperta** outdoor swimming pool

pi'sello *nm* pea; *(fam: pene)* willie

piso'lino *nm* nap; **fare un** ~ have a nap

'pista *nf* track; *Aeron* runway; *(orma)* footprint; *(sci)* slope, piste. ~ **d'atterraggio** airstrip. ~ **da ballo** dance floor. ~ **ciclabile** cycle track

pi'stacchio *nm* pistachio

pi'stola *nf* pistol; *(per spruzzare)* spray-gun. ~ **a spruzzo** paint spray

pi'stone *nm* piston

pi'tone *nm* python

pit'tore, -'trice *nmf* painter. ~'resco *a* picturesque. pit'torico *a* pictorial

pit'tura *nf* painting. ~'rare *vt* paint

più *adv* more; *(superlativo)* most; *Math* plus; ~ **importante** more important; **il** ~ **importante** the most important; ~ **caro** dearer; **il** ~ **caro** the dearest; **di** ~ more; **una coperta in** ~ an extra blanket; **non ho** ~ **soldi** I don't have any more money; **non vive** ~ **a Milano** he no longer lives in Milan, he doesn't live in Milan any longer; ~ **o meno** more or less; **il** ~ **lentamente possibile** as slow as possible; **per di** ~ what's more; **mai** ~**!** never again!; ~ **di** more than; **sempre** ~ more and more ● *a* more; *(superlativo)* most; ~ **tempo** more time; **la classe con** ~ **alunni** the class with most pupils; ~ **volte** several times ● *nm* most; *Math* plus sign; **il** ~ **è fatto** the worst is over; **parlare del** ~ **e del meno** make small talk; **i** ~ the majority

piucchepper'fetto *nm* pluperfect

pi'uma *nf* feather. piu'maggio *nm* plumage. piu'mino *nm (di cigni)* down; *(copriletto)* eiderdown; *(per cipria)* powder-puff; *(per spolverare)* feather duster; *(giacca)* down jacket. piu'mone® *nm* duvet, continental quilt

piut'tosto *adv* rather; *(invece)* instead

pi'vello *nm fam* greenhorn

'pizza *nf* pizza; *Cinema* reel.

pizzai'ola *nf* slices of beef in tomato sauce, oregano and anchovies

pizze'ria *nf* pizza restaurant, pizzeria

pizzi'ca|re *vt* pinch; *(pungere)* sting; *(di sapore)* taste sharp; *(fam: sorprendere)* catch; *Mus* pluck ● *vi* scratch; *(cibo:)* be spicy. 'pizzico *nm*, ~'otto *nm* pinch

'pizzo *nm* lace; *(di montagna)* peak

pla'ca|re *vt* placate; assuage *(fame, dolore)*. ~**si** *vr* calm down

'placca *nf* plate; *(commemorativa, dentale)* plaque; *Med* patch

plac'ca|re *vt* plate. ~**to a** ~**to d'argento** silver-plated. ~**to d'oro** gold-plated. ~'**tura** *nf* plating

pla'centa *nf* placenta

'placido *a* placid

plagi'are *vt* plagiarize; pressure *(persona)*. 'plagio *nm* plagiarism

plaid *nm inv* tartan rug

pla'nare *vi* glide

'plancia *nf Naut* bridge; *(passerella)* gangplank

plane'tario *a* planetary ● *nm* planetarium

pla'smare *vt* mould

'plastic|a *nf (arte)* plastic art; *Med* plastic surgery; *(materia)* plastic. ~**o** *a* plastic ● *nm* plastic model

'platano *nm* plane[-tree]

pla'tea *nf* stalls *pl*; *(pubblico)* audience

'platino *nm* platinum

pla'tonico *a* platonic

plau'sibil|e *a* plausible. ~**ità** *nf* plausibility

ple'baglia *nf pej* mob

pleni'lunio *nm* full moon

'plettro *nm* plectrum

pleu'rite *nf* pleurisy

'plico *nm* packet; **in** ~ **a parte** under separate cover

plissé *a inv* plissé; *(gonna)* accordeon-pleated

plo'tone *nm* platoon; *(di ciclisti)* group. ~ **d'esecuzione** firing-squad

'plumbeo *a* leaden

plu'ral|e *a & nm* plural; **al** ~**e** in the plural. ~**ità** *nf (maggioranza)* majority

pluridiscipli'nare *a* multi-disciplinary

plurien'nale *a* ~ **esperienza** many years' experience

pluripar'titico *a Pol* multi-party

plu'tonio *nm* plutonium

pluvi'ale *a* rain *attrib*

pneu'matico *a* pneumatic ● *nm* tyre

pneu'monia *nf* pneumonia

po' *vedi* poco

po'chette *nf inv* clutch bag

po'chino *nm* **un** ~ a little bit

'poco *a* little; *(tempo)* short; *(con nomi plurali)* few ● *pron* little; *(poco tempo)* a short time; *(plurale)* few ● *nm* little; **un po'** a little [bit]; **un po' di** a little, some; *(con nomi plurali)* a few; **a** ~ **a** ~ little

161   **podere | ponderare**

by little; **fra** ~ soon; **per** ~ (*a poco prezzo*) cheap; (*quasi*) nearly; ~ **fa** a little while ago; **sono arrivato da** ~ I have just arrived; **un bel po'** quite a lot; **un** ~ **di buono** a shady character ● *adv* (*con verbi*) not much; (*con avverbi*) not very; **parla** ~ he doesn't speak much; **lo conosco** ~ I don't know him very well; ~ **spesso** not very often

po'dere *nm* farm

pode'roso *a* powerful

'podio *nm* dais; *Mus* podium

po'dismo *nm* walking. ~**ta** *nmf* walker

po'ema *nm* poem. ~**sia** *nf* poetry; (*componimento*) poem. ~**ta** *nm* poet. ~**'tessa** *nf* poetess. ~**tico** *a* poetic

poggiapi'edi *nm inv* footrest

poggi'are *vt* lean; (*posare*) place ● *vi* ~**re su** to be based on. ~ **testa** *nm inv* head-rest

'poggio *nm* hillock

poggi'olo *nm* balcony

'poi *adv* (*dopo*) then; (*più tardi*) later [on]; (*finalmente*) finally. **d'ora in** ~ from now on; **questa** ~! well!

poiché *conj* since

pois *nm inv* **a** ~ polka-dot

'poker *nm* poker

po'lacco, -a *a* Polish ● *nmf* Pole ● *nm* (*lingua*) Polish

po'lar|e *a* polar. ~**iz'zare** *vt* polarize

'polca *nf* polka

po'lemi|ca *nf* controversy. ~**ca'mente** *adv* controversially. ~**co** *a* controversial. ~**z'zare** *vi* engage in controversy

po'lenta *nf* cornmeal porridge

poli'clinico *nm* general hospital

poli'estere *nm* polyester

poliga'mia *nf* polygamy. **po'ligamo** *a* polygamous

polio[mie'lite] *nf* polio[myelitis]

po'lipo *nm* polyp

polisti'rolo *nm* polystyrene

poli'tecnico *nm* polytechnic

po'litic|a *nf* politics *sg*; (*linea di condotta*) policy; **fare** ~**a** be in politics. ~**iz'zare** *vt* politicize. ~**o, -a** *a* political ● *nmf* politician

poliva'lente *a* catch-all

poli'zi|a *nf* police. ~**a giudiziaria** ≈ Criminal Investigation Department, CID. ~**a stradale** traffic police. ~**'esco** *a* police *attrib*; (*romanzo, film*) detective *attrib*. ~**'otto** *nm* policeman

po'lizza *nf* policy

pol'la|io *nm* chicken run; (*fam: luogo chiassoso*) mad house. ~**me** *nm* poultry.

~**'strello** *nm* spring chicken. ~**stro** *nm* cockerel

'pollice *nm* thumb; (*unità di misura*) inch

'polline *nm* pollen; **allergia al** ~ hay fever

polli'vendolo, -a *nmf* poulterer

'pollo *nm* chicken; (*fam: sempliciotto*) simpleton. ~ **arrosto** roast chicken

polmo'nare *a* pulmonary. **pol'mone** *nm* lung. **polmone d'acciaio** iron lung. ~ **nite** *nf* pneumonia

'polo *nm* pole; *Sport* polo; (*maglietta*) polo top. ~ **nord** North Pole. ~ **sud** South Pole

Po'lonia *nf* Poland

'polpa *nf* pulp

pol'paccio *nm* calf

polpa'strello *nm* fingertip

pol'pet|ta *nf* meatball. ~**tone** *nm* meat loaf

'polpo *nm* octopus

pol'poso *a* fleshy

pol'sino *nm* cuff

'polso *nm* pulse; *Anat* wrist; *fig* authority; **avere** ~ be strict

pol'tiglia *nf* mush

pol'trire *vi* lie around

pol'tron|a *nf* armchair; *Theat* seat in the stalls. ~**e** *a* lazy

'polve|re *nf* dust; (*sostanza polverizzata*) powder; **in** ~**re** powdered; **sapone in** ~**re** soap powder. ~**re da sparo** gun powder. ~**rina** *nf* (*medicina*) powder. ~**riz'zare** *vt* pulverize; (*nebulizzare*) atomize. ~**rone** *nm* cloud of dust. ~**roso** *a* dusty

po'mata *nf* ointment, cream

po'mello *nm* knob; (*guancia*) cheek

pomeri'diano *a* afternoon *attrib*; **alle tre pomeridiane** at three in the afternoon, at three p.m. **pome'riggio** *nm* afternoon

'pomice *nf* pumice

'pomo *nm* (*oggetto*) knob. ~ **d'Adamo** Adam's apple

pomo'doro *nm* tomato

'pompa *nf* pump; (*sfarzo*) pomp. **pompe** *pl* **funebri** (*funzione*) funeral. **pom'pare** *vt* pump; (*gonfiare d'aria*) pump up; (*fig: esagerare*) exaggerate; **pompare fuori** pump out

pom'pelmo *nm* grapefruit

pompi'ere *nm* fireman; **i pompieri** the fire brigade

pom'pon *nm inv* pompom

pom'poso *a* pompous

ponde'rare *vt* ponder

po'nente *nm* west

'ponte *nm* bridge; *Naut* deck; (*impalcatura*) scaffolding; fare il ~ *fig* make a long weekend of it

pon'tefice *nm* pontiff

pontifi'ca|re *vi* pontificate. ~to *nm* pontificate

ponti'ficio *a* papal

pon'tile *nm* jetty

popò *nm inv fam* pooh

popo'lano *a* of the [common] people

popo'la|re *a* popular; (*comune*) common ● *vt* populate. ~rsi *vr* get crowded. ~rità *nf* popularity. ~zi'one *nf* population. 'popolo *nm* people. popo'loso *a* populous

'poppa *nf Naut* stern; (*mammella*) breast; a ~ astern

pop'pa|re *vt* suck. ~ta *nf* (*pasto*) feed. ~'toio *nm* [feeding-]bottle

popu'lista *nmf* populist

por'cata *nf* load of rubbish; porcate *pl* (*fam: cibo*) junk food

porcel'lana *nf* porcelain, china

porcel'lino *nm* piglet. ~ d'India guinea-pig

porche'ria *nf* dirt; (*fig: cosa orrenda*) piece of filth; (*fam: robaccia*) rubbish

por'ci|le *nm* pigsty. ~no *a* pig *attrib* ● *nm* (*fungo*) edible mushroom. porco *nm* pig; (*carne*) pork

porco'spino *nm* porcupine

'porgere *vt* give; (*offrire*) offer; porgo distinti saluti (*in lettera*) I remain, yours sincerely

porno|gra'fia *nf* pornography. ~'grafico *a* pornographic

'poro *nm* pore. po'roso *a* porous

'porpora *nf* purple

'por|re *vt* put; (*collocare*) place; (*supporre*) suppose; ask (*domanda*); present (*candidatura*); poniamo il caso che... let us suppose that...; ~re fine o termine a put an end to. ~si *vr* put oneself; ~si a sedere sit down; ~si in cammino set out

'porro *nm Bot* leek; (*verruca*) wart

'porta *nf* door; *Sport* goal; (*di città*) gate; *Comput* port. ~ a ~ door-to-door; mettere alla ~ show sb the door. ~ di servizio tradesmen's entrance

portaba'gagli *nm inv* (*facchino*) porter; (*di treno ecc*) luggage rack; *Auto* boot, trunk *Am*; (*sul tetto di un'auto*) roof rack

portabot'tiglie *nm inv* bottle rack, wine rack

porta'cenere *nm inv* ashtray

portachi'avi *nm inv* keyring

porta'cipria *nm inv* compact

portadocu'menti *nm inv* document wallet

porta'erei *nf inv* aircraft carrier

portafi'nestra *nf* French window

porta'foglio *nm* wallet; (*per documenti*) portfolio; (*ministero*) ministry

portafor'tuna *nm inv* lucky charm ● *a inv* lucky

portagi'oie *nm inv* jewellery box

por'tale *nm* door

portama'tite *nm inv* pencil case

porta'mento *nm* carriage; (*condotta*) behaviour

porta'mina *nm inv* propelling pencil

portamo'nete *nm inv* purse

por'tante *a* bearing *attrib*

portaom'brelli *nm inv* umbrella stand

porta'pacchi *nm inv* roof rack; (*su bicicletta*) luggage rack

porta'penne *nm inv* pencil case

por'ta|re *vt* (*verso chi parla*) bring; (*lontano da chi parla*) take; (*sorreggere, Math*) carry; (*condurre*) lead; (*indossare*) wear; (*avere*) bear. ~rsi *vr* (*trasferirsi*) move; (*comportarsi*) behave; ~rsi bene/male gli anni look young/old for one's age

porta'viste *nm inv* magazine rack

porta'sci *nm inv* ski rack

portasiga'rette *nm inv* cigarette-case

porta'spilli *nm inv* pin-cushion

por'ta|ta *nf* (*di pranzo*) course; *Auto* carrying capacity; (*di arma*) range; (*fig: abilità*) capability; a ~ta di mano within reach; alla ~ta di tutti accessible to all; (*finanziariamente*) within everybody's reach. por'tatile *a* & *nm* portable. ~to *a* (*indumento*) worn; (*dotato*) gifted; essere ~to per qcsa have a gift for sth; essere ~to a (*tendere a*) be inclined to. ~'tore, ~'trice *nmf* bearer; al ~tore to the bearer. ~tore di handicap disabled person

portatovagli'olo *nm* napkin ring

portau'ovo *nm inv* egg-cup

porta'voce *nm inv* spokesman ● *nf inv* spokeswoman

por'tento *nm* marvel; (*persona dotata*) prodigy

'portico *nm* portico

porti'er|a *nf* door; (*tendaggio*) door curtain. ~e *nm* porter, doorman; *Sport* goalkeeper. ~e di notte night porter

porti'n|aio, -a *nmf* caretaker, concierge. ~e'ria nf concierge's room; (di ospedale) porter's lodge

'porto pp di porgere ● nm harbour; (complesso) port; (vino) port [wine]; (spesa di trasporto) carriage; andare in ~ succeed. ~ d'armi gun licence

Porto'gallo nm Portugal. p~hese a & nmf Portuguese

por'tone nm main door

portu'ale nm dockworker, docker

porzi'one nf portion

'posa|re vt put; (giù) put [down] ● vi (poggiare) rest; (per un ritratto) pose. ~rsi vr alight; (sostare) rest; Aeron land. ~ta nf piece of cutlery; ~te pl cutlery sg. ~to a sedate

po'scritto nm postscript

posi'tivo a positive

posizio'nare vt position

posizi'one nf position; farsi una ~ get ahead

posolo'gia nf dosage

po'spo|rre vt place after; (posticipare) postpone. ~sto pp di posporre

posse'd|ere vt possess, own. ~i'mento nm possession

posses'sivo a possessive. pos'sesso nm ownership; (bene) possession. ~'sore nm owner

pos'sibil|e a possible; il più presto ~e as soon as possible ● nm fare [tutto] il ~e do one's best. ~ità nf inv possibility; (occasione) chance ● nfpl (mezzi) means

possi'dente nmf land-owner

'posta nf post, mail; (ufficio postale) post office; (al gioco) stake; spese di ~ postage; per ~ by post, by mail; la ~ in gioco è... fig what's at stake is...; a bella ~ on purpose; Poste e Tele-comunicazioni pl [Italian] Post Office. ~ elettronica electronic mail, e-mail. ~ elettronica vocale voice-mail

posta'giro nm postal giro

po'stale a postal

postazi'one nf position

postda'tare vt postdate (assegno)

posteggi'a|re vt/i park. ~'tore, ~'trice nmf parking attendant. po'steggio nm car-park, parking lot Am; (di taxi) taxi-rank

'posteri nmpl descendants. ~'ore a rear; (nel tempo) later ● nm fam poste-rior, behind. ~tà nf posterity

po'sticcio a artificial; ⟨baffi, barba⟩ false ● nm hair-piece

postici'pare vt postpone

po'stilla nf note; Jur rider

po'stino nm postman, mailman Am

'posto pp di porre ● nm place; (spazio) room; (impiego) job; Mil post; (sedile) seat; a/fuori ~ in/out of place; prende-re ~ take up room; sul ~ on-site; esse-re a ~ ⟨casa, libri⟩ be tidy; mettere a ~ ⟨stanza⟩; fare ~ a make room for; al ~ di (invece di) in place of, instead of. ~ di blocco checkpoint. ~ di guida driving seat. ~ di lavoro workstation. ~ di polizia police station. posti pl in piedi standing room. posti pl a sedere seating

post-partum nm inv post-natal

'postumo a posthumous ● nm after-ef-fect

po'tabile a drinkable; acqua ~ drink-ing water

po'tare vt prune

po'tassio nm potassium

po'ten|te a powerful; (efficace) potent. ~za nf power; (efficacia) potency. ~zi'ale a & nm potential

po'tere nm power; al ~ in power ● vi can, be able to; posso entrare? can I come in?; (formale) may I come in?; posso fare qualche cosa? can I do something?; che tu possa essere felice! may you be happy!; non ne posso più (sono stanco) I can't go on; (sono stufo) I can't take any more; può darsi perhaps; può darsi che sia vero perhaps it's true; potrebbe aver ragione he could be right, he might be right; avresti potuto telefonare you could have phoned, you might have phoned; spero di poter venire I hope to be able to come; senza poter telefonare without being able to phone

potestà nf inv power

'pover|o, -a a poor; (semplice) plain ● nm poor man ● nf poor woman; i ~i the poor. ~tà nf poverty

'pozza nf pool. poz'zanghera nf pud-dle

'pozzo nm well; (minerario) pit. ~ petrolifero oil-well

PP.TT. abbr (Poste e Telegrafi) [Ital-ian] Post Office

prag'matico a pragmatic

prali'nato a ⟨mandorla, gelato⟩ pra-line-coated

pram'matica nf essere di ~ be cus-tomary

pran'zare vi dine; (a mezzogiorno) lunch. **'pranzo** nm dinner; (a mezzogiorno) lunch. **pranzo di nozze** wedding breakfast

'prassi nf standard procedure

prate'ria nf grassland

'prati|ca nf practice; (esperienza) experience; (documentazione) file; avere ~ca di qcsa be familiar with sth; far ~ca gain experience; fare le pratiche per gather the necessary papers for. ~'cabile a practicable; (strada) passable. ~ca'mente adv practically. ~'cante nmf apprentice; Relig [regular] church-goer

prati'care vt practise; (frequentare) associate with; (fare) make

praticità nf practicality. **'pratico** a practical; (esperto) experienced; essere pratico di qcsa know about sth

'prato nm meadow; (di giardino) lawn

pre'ambolo nm preamble

preannunci'are vt give advance notice of

preav'visare vt forewarn. **preav'viso** nm warning

pre'cario a precarious

precauzi'one nf precaution; (cautela) care

prece'den|te a previous ● nm precedent. ~te'mente adv previously. ~za nf precedence; (di veicoli) right of way; dare la ~za give way. **pre'cedere** vt precede

pre'cetto nm precept

precipi'ta|re vt ~re le cose precipitate events; ~re qcno nella disperazione cast sb into a state of despair ● vi fall headlong; (situazione, eventi:) come to a head. ~rsi vr (gettarsi) throw oneself; (affrettarsi) rush; ~rsi a fare qcsa rush to do sth. ~zi'one nf (fretta) haste; (atmosferica) precipitation. **precipi'toso** a hasty; (avventato) reckless; (caduta) headlong

preci'pizio nm precipice; a ~ headlong

precisa'mente adv precisely

preci'sa|re vt specify; (spiegare) clarify. ~zi'one nf clarification

precisi'one nf precision. **pre'ciso** a precise; (ore) sharp; (identico) identical

pre'clu|dere vt preclude. ~so pp di **precludere**

pre'coce a precocious; (prematuro) premature. ~ità nf precociousness

precon'cetto a preconceived ● nm prejudice

pre'correre vt ~ i tempi be ahead of one's time

precur'sore nm forerunner, precursor

'preda nf prey; (bottino) booty; essere in ~ al panico be panic-stricken; in ~ alle fiamme engulfed in flames. **pre'dare** vt plunder. ~'tore nm predator

predeces'sore nmf predecessor

pre'del|la nf platform. ~'lino nm step

predesti'na|re vt predestine. ~to a Relig predestined, preordained

predetermi'nato a predetermined, preordained

pre'detto pp di **predire**

'predica nf sermon; fig lecture

predi'ca|re vt preach. ~to nm predicate

predi'let|to, -a pp di **prediligere** ● a favourite ● nmf pet. ~zi'one nf predilection. **predi'ligere** vt prefer

pre'dire vt foretell

predi'spo|rre vt arrange. ~rsi vr ~rsi a prepare oneself for. ~sizi'one nf predisposition; (al disegno ecc) bent (a for). ~sto pp di **predisporre**

predizi'one nf prediction

predomi'na|nte a predominant. ~re vi predominate. **predo'minio** nm predominance

pre'done nm robber

prefabbri'cato a prefabricated ● nm prefabricated building

prefazi'one nf preface

prefe'renz|a nf preference; di ~a preferably. ~i'ale a preferential; corsia ~iale bus and taxi lane

prefe'ribil|e a preferable. ~'mente adv preferably

prefe'rire vt prefer. ~to, -a a & nmf favourite

pre'fet|to nm prefect. ~'tura nf prefecture

pre'figgersi vr be determined

pre'fisso pp di **prefiggere** ● nm prefix; Teleph [dialling] code

pre'gare vt/i pray; (supplicare) beg; farsi ~ need persuading

pre'gevole a valuable

preghi'era nf prayer; (richiesta) request

pregi'ato a esteemed; (prezioso) valuable. **'pregio** nm esteem; (valore) value; (di persona) good point; di pregio valuable

pregiudi'ca|re vt prejudice; (danneggiare) harm. ~to a prejudiced ● nm Jur previous offender

pregiu'dizio *nm* prejudice; (*danno*) detriment

'prego *int* (*non c'è di che*) don't mention it!; (*per favore*) please; ~? I beg your pardon?

pregu'stare *vt* look forward to

prei'storia *nf* prehistory. **prei'storico** *a* prehistoric

pre'lato *nm* prelate

prela'vaggio *nm* prewash

preleva'mento *nm* withdrawal. **pre-le'vare** *vt* withdraw (*denaro*); collect (*merci*); *Med* take. **preli'evo** *nm* (*di soldi*) withdrawal. **prelievo di sangue** blood sample

prelimi'nare *a* preliminary ● *nm* **preliminari** *pl* preliminaries

pre'ludio *nm* prelude

prema'man *nm inv* maternity dress ● *a* maternity *attrib*

prematrimoni'ale *a* premarital

prema'turo, -a *a* premature ● *nmf* premature baby

premedi'ta're *vt* premeditate. **~zi'one** *nf* premeditation

'premere *vt* press; *Comput* hit (*tasto*) ● *vi* ~ *a* (*importare*) matter to; **mi preme sapere** I need to know; ~ **su** press on; push (*pulsante*)

pre'messa *nf* introduction

pre'messo *pp di* premettere. **~sso che** bearing in mind that. **~ttere** *vt* put forward; (*mettere prima*) put before.

premi'are *vt* give a prize to; (*ricompensare*) reward. **~zi'one** *nf* prize giving

premi'nente *a* pre-eminent

'premio *nm* prize; (*ricompensa*) reward; *Comm* premium. ~ **di consolazione** booby prize

premoni'tore *a* (*sogno, segno*) premonitory. **~zi'one** *nf* premonition

premu'nire *vt* fortify. **~si** *vr* take protective measures; **~si di** provide oneself with; **~si contro** protect oneself against

pre'mura *nf* (*fretta*) hurry; (*cura*) care. **~'roso** *a* thoughtful

prena'tale *a* antenatal

'prendere *vt* take; (*afferrare*) seize; catch (*treno, malattia, ladro, pesce*); have (*cibo, bevanda*); (*far pagare*) charge; (*assumere*) take on; (*ottenere*) get; (*occupare*) take up; **~e informazioni** make inquiries; **~e a calci/pugni** kick/punch; **che ti prende?** what's got into you?; **quanto prende?** what do you charge?; **~e una persona per**

un'altra mistake one person for somebody else ● *vi* (*voltare*) turn; (*attecchire*) take root; (*rapprendersi*) set; **~e a destra/sinistra** turn right/left; **~e a fare qcsa** start doing sth. **~si** *vr* **~si a pugni** come to blows; **~si cura di** take care of (*ammalato*); **~sela** take it to heart

prendi'sole *nm* sundress

preno'ta're *vt* book, reserve. **~to** *a* booked, reserved **~zi'one** *nf* booking, reservation

'prensile *a* prehensile

preoccu'pante *a* alarming

preoccu'pa're *vt* worry. **~rsi** *vr* **~rsi** worry (*di* about); **~rsi di fare qcsa** take the trouble to do sth. **~to** *a* (*ansioso*) worried. **~zi'one** *nf* worry; (*apprensione*) concern

prepa'ra're *vt* prepare. **~rsi** *vr* get ready. **~'tivi** *nmpl* preparations. **~to** *nm* (*prodotto*) preparation. ~ **'torio** *a* preparatory. **~zi'one** *nf* preparation

prepensiona'mento *nm* early retirement

preponde'rante *a* predominant. **~za** *nf* prevalence

pre'porre *vt* place before

preposizi'one *nf* preposition

pre'posto *pp di* preporre ● *a* ~ *a* (*addetto a*) in charge of

prepo'tente *a* overbearing ● *nmf* bully. **~za** *nf* high-handedness

preroga'tiva *nf* prerogative

'presa *nf* taking; (*conquista*) capture; (*stretta*) hold; (*di cemento ecc*) setting; *Electr* socket; (*pizzico*) pinch; **essere alle prese con** be struggling *o* grappling with; **a ~ rapida** (*cemento, colla*) quick-setting; **fare ~ su** qcno influence sb. **~ d'aria** air vent. **~ in giro** leg-pull. **~ multipla** adaptor

pre'sagio *nm* omen. **presa'gire** *vt* foretell

'presbite *a* long-sighted

presbiteri'ano, -a *a & nmf* Presbyterian. **presbi'terio** *nm* presbytery

pre'scelto *a* selected

pre'scindere *vi* ~ **da** leave aside; **a ~ da** apart from

presco'lare *a* in età ~ preschool

pre'scritto *pp di* prescrivere

pre'scri'vere *vt* prescribe. **~zi'one** *nf* prescription; (*norma*) rule

preselezi'one *nf* **chiamare** qcno **in ~** call sb via the operator

presen'ta're *vt* present; (*far conoscere*) introduce; show (*documento*); (*inoltrare*) submit. **~rsi** *vr* present oneself;

(*farsi conoscere*) introduce oneself; (*a ufficio*) attend; (*alla polizia ecc*) report; (*come candidato*) stand, run; (*occasione:*) occur; ~**rsi bene/male** (*persona:*) make a good/bad impression; (*situazione:*) look good/bad. ~**'tore**, ~**'trice** *nmf* presenter; (*di notizie*) announcer. ~**zi'one** *nf* presentation; (*per conoscersi*) introduction

pre'sente *a* present; (*attuale*) current; (*questo*) this; **aver** ~ remember ● *nm* present; **i presenti** those present ● *nf* **allegato alla** ~ (*in lettera*) enclosed

presenti'mento *nm* foreboding

pre'senza *nf* presence; (*aspetto*) appearance; **in** ~ **di**, **alla** ~ **di** in the presence of; **di bella** ~ personable. ~ **di spirito** presence of mind

presenzi'are *vi* a attend

pre'sepe *nm*, **pre'sepio** *nm* crib

preser'va|re *vt* preserve; (*proteggere*) protect (**da** from). ~**'tivo** *nm* condom. ~**zi'one** *nf* preservation

'preside *nm* headmaster; *Univ* dean ● *nf* headmistress; *Univ* dean

presi'den|te *nm* chairman; *Pol* president ● *nf* chairwoman; *Pol* president. ~ **del consiglio** [**dei ministri**] Prime Minister. ~ **della repubblica** President of the Republic. ~**za** *nf* presidency; (*di assemblea*) chairmanship. ~**zi'ale** *a* presidential

presidi'are *vt* garrison. **pre'sidio** *nm* garrison

presi'edere *vt* preside over

'preso *pp di* **prendere**

'pressa *nf Mech* press

pres'sante *a* urgent

pressap'poco *adv* about

pres'sare *vt* press

pressi'one *nf* pressure; **far** ~ **su** put pressure on. ~ **del sangue** blood pressure

'presso *prep* near; (*a casa di*) with; (*negli indirizzi*) care of, c/o; (*lavorare*) for ● *pressi nmpl:* **nei pressi di...** in the neighbourhood o vicinity of...

pressoché *adv* almost

pressuriz'za|re *vt* pressurize. ~**to** *a* pressurized

prestabi'li|re *vt* arrange in advance. ~**to** *a* agreed

prestam'pato *a* printed ● *nm* (*modulo*) form

pre'stante *a* good-looking

pre'star|e *vt* lend; ~**e attenzione** pay attention; ~**e aiuto** lend a hand; **farsi**

~**e** borrow (**da** from). ~**si** *vr* (*frase:*) lend itself; (*persona:*) offer

prestazi'one *nf* performance; **prestazioni** *pl* (*servizi*) services

prestigia'tore, **-'trice** *nmf* conjurer

pre'stigi|o *nm* prestige; **gioco di** ~**o** conjuring trick. ~**oso** *nm* prestigious

'prestito *nm* loan; **dare in** ~ lend; **prendere in** ~ borrow

'presto *adv* soon; (*di buon'ora*) early; (*in fretta*) quickly; **a** ~ see you soon; **al più** ~ as soon as possible; ~ **o tardi** sooner or later; **far** ~ be quick

pre'sumere *vt* presume; (*credere*) think

presu'mibile *a* **è** ~ **che...** presumably,...

pre'sunto *a* (*colpevole*) presumed

presun|tu'oso *a* presumptuous ● *nmf* presumptuous person. ~**zi'one** *nf* presumption

presup'po|rre *vt* suppose; (*richiedere*) presuppose. ~**sizi'one** *nf* presupposition. ~**sto** *nm* essential requirement

'prete *nm* priest

preten'dente *nmf* pretender ● *nm* (*corteggiatore*) suitor

pre'ten|dere *vt* (*sostenere*) claim; (*esigere*) demand ● *vi* ~**dere** a claim to; ~**dere di** (*esigere*) demand to. ~**si'one** *nf* pretension. ~**zi'oso** *a* pretentious

pre'tes|a *nf* pretension; (*esigenza*) claim; **senza** ~**e** unpretentious. ~**o** *pp di* **pretendere**

pre'testo *nm* pretext

pre'tore *nm* magistrate

pretta'mente *adv* decidedly

pre'tura *nf* magistrate's court

preva'len|te *a* prevalent. ~**temente** *adv* mainly. ~**za** *nf* prevalence. ~**re** *vi* prevail

pre'valso *pp di* **prevalere**

preve'dere *vt* foresee; forecast (*tempo*); (*legge ecc:*) provide for

preve'nire *vt* precede; (*evitare*) prevent; (*avvertire*) forewarn

preven|ti'vare *vt* estimate; (*aspettarsi*) budget for. ~**'tivo** *a* preventive ● *nm Comm* estimate

preve'n|uto *a* forewarned; (*mal disposto*) prejudiced. ~**zi'one** *nf* prevention; (*preconcetto*) prejudice

pre'vidente *a* provident. ~**za** *nf* foresight. ~**za sociale** social security, welfare *Am.* ~**zi'ale** *a* provident

'previo *a* ~ **pagamento** on payment

previsi'one *nf* forecast; **in** ~ **di** in anticipation of

pre'visto *pp di* prevedere ●*a* foreseen ●*nm* più/meno/prima del ~ more/less/earlier than expected

prezi'oso *a* precious

prez'zemolo *nm* parsley

'prezzo *nm* price. ~ di fabbrica factory price. ~ all'ingrosso wholesale price. [a] metà ~ half price

prigi'on|e *nf* prison; (*pena*) imprisonment. prigio'nia *nf* imprisonment. ~i'ero, -a *a* imprisoned ●*nmf* prisoner

'prima *adv* before; (*più presto*) earlier; (*in primo luogo*) first; ~, finiamo questo let's finish this first; puoi venire ~? (*di giorni*) can't you come any sooner?; (*di ore*) can't you come any earlier?; ~ o poi sooner or later; quanto ~ as soon as possible ●*prep* ~ di before; ~ d'ora before now ●*conj* ~ che before ●*nf* first class; *Theat* first night; *Auto* first [gear]

pri'mario *a* primary; (*principale*) principal

pri'mat|e *nm* primate. ~o *nm* supremacy; *Sport* record

prima've|ra *nf* spring. ~rile *a* spring *attrib*

primeggi'are *vi* excel

primi'tivo *a* primitive; (*originario*) original

pri'mizie *nfpl* early produce *sg*

'primo *a* first; (*fondamentale*) principal; (*precedente di due*) former; (*iniziale*) early; (*migliore*) best ●*nm* first; primi *pl* (*i primi giorni*) the beginning; in un ~ tempo at first. prima copia master copy

primo'genito, -a *a* & *nmf* first-born

primordi'ale *a* primordial

'primula *nf* primrose

princi'pale *a* main ●*nm* head, boss *fam*

princi'pato *nm* principality. 'principe *nm* prince. principe ereditario crown prince. ~'pesco *a* princely. ~'pessa *nf* princess

principi'ante *nmf* beginner

prin'cipio *nm* beginning; (*concetto*) principle; (*causa*) cause; per ~ on principle

pri'ore *nm* prior

priori'tà *nf inv* priority. ~'tario *a* having priority

'prisma *nm* prism

pri'va|re *vt* deprive. ~rsi *vr* deprive oneself

privatizzazi'one *nf* privatization.

pri'vato, -a *a* private ●*nmf* private citizen

privazi'one *nf* deprivation

privilegi'are *vt* privilege; (*considerare più importante*) favour. privi'legio *nm* privilege

'privo *a* ~ di devoid of; (*mancante*) lacking in

pro *prep* for ●*nm* advantage; a che ~? what's the point?; il ~ e il contro the pros and cons

pro'babil|e *a* probable. ~ità *nf inv* probability. ~'mente *adv* probably

pro'ble|ma *nm* problem. ~'matico *a* problematic

pro'boscide *nf* trunk

procacci'ar|e *vt*, ~si *vr* obtain

pro'cace *a* (*ragazza*) provocative

pro'ced|ere *vi* proceed; (*iniziare*) start; ~ere contro *Jur* start legal proceedings against. ~i'mento *nm* process; *Jur* proceedings *pl*. proce'dura *nf* procedure

proces'sare *vt Jur* try

processi'one *nf* procession

pro'cesso *nm* process; *Jur* trial

proces'sore *nm Comput* processor

processu'ale *a* trial

pro'cinto *nm* essere in ~ di be about to

pro'clama *nm* proclamation

procla'ma|re *vt* proclaim. ~zi'one *nf* proclamation

procrasti'nare *vt liter* postpone

procreazi'one *nf* procreation

pro'cura *nf* power of attorney; per ~ by proxy

procu'ra|re *vt/i* procure; (*causare*) cause; (*cercare*) try. ~'tore *nm* attorney. P~tore Generale Attorney General. ~'tore legale lawyer. ~'tore della repubblica public prosecutor

'prode *a* brave. pro'dezza *nf* bravery

prodi'gar|e *vt* lavish. ~si *vr* do one's best

pro'digi|o *nm* prodigy. ~'oso *a* prodigious

pro'dotto *pp di* produrre ●*nm* product. prodotti agricoli farm produce *sg*. ~ derivato by-product. ~ interno lordo gross domestic product. ~ nazionale lordo gross national product

pro'du|rre *vt* produce. ~rsi *vr* (*attore:*) play; (*accadere*) happen. ~ttività *nf* productivity. ~t'tivo *a* productive. ~t'tore, ~t'trice *nmf* producer. ~zi'one *nf* production

profa'na|re vt desecrate. **~zi'one** nf desecration. **pro'fano** a profane

profe'rire vt utter

Prof.essa abbr (**Professoressa**) Prof.

profes'sare vt profess; practise (professione)

professio'nale a professional

professi'o|ne nf profession; **libera ~e** profession. **~'nismo** nm professionalism. **~'nista** nmf professional

profes'sor|e, -'essa nmf Sch teacher; Univ lecturer; (titolare di cattedra) professor

pro'fe|ta nm prophet. **~tico** a prophetic. **~tiz'zare** vt prophesy. **~'zia** nf prophecy

pro'ficuo a profitable

profi'lar|e vt outline; (ornare) border; Aeron streamline. **~si** vr stand out

profi'lattico a prophylactic ● nm condom

pro'filo nm profile; (breve studio) outline; **di ~** in profile

profit'tare vi **~ di** (avvantaggiarsi) profit by; (approfittare) take advantage of. **pro'fitto** nm profit; (vantaggio) advantage

profond|a'mente adv deeply, profoundly. **~ità** nf inv depth

pro'fondo a deep; fig profound; (cultura) great

'**profugo, -a** nmf refugee

profu'mar|e vt perfume. **~si** vr put on perfume

profumata'mente adv pagare **~** pay through the nose

profu'mato a (fiore) fragrant; (fazzoletto ecc) scented

profume'ria nf perfumery. **pro'fumo** nm perfume, scent

profusi'one nf profusion; **a ~** in profusion. **pro'fuso** pp di profondere ● a profuse

proget'tare vt plan. **~'tista** nmf designer. **pro'getto** nm plan; (di lavoro importante) project. **progetto di legge** bill

prog'nosi nf inv prognosis; **in ~ riservata** on the danger list

pro'gramma nm programme; Comput program. **~ scolastico** syllabus

program'ma|re vt programme; Comput program. **~'tore, ~'trice** nmf [computer] programmer. **~zi'one** nf programming

progre'dire vi [make] progress

progres'sione nf progression.

~'sivo a progressive. **pro'gresso** nm progress

proi'bi|re vt forbid. **~'tivo** a prohibitive. **~to** a forbidden. **~zi'one** nf prohibition

proiet'tare vt project; show (film). **~t'tore** nm projector; Auto headlight

proi'ettile nm bullet

proiezi'one nf projection

'prole nf offspring. **proletari'ato** nm proletariat. **prole'tario** a & nm proletarian

prolife'rare vi proliferate. **pro'lifico** a prolific

pro'lisso a verbose, prolix

'prologo nm prologue

pro'lunga nf Electr extension

prolun'gar|e vt prolong; (allungare) lengthen; extend (contratto, scadenza). **~si** vr continue; **~si su** (dilungarsi) dwell upon

prome'moria nm memo; (per se stessi) reminder, note; (formale) memorandum

pro'me|ssa nf promise. **~sso** pp di **promettere**. **~ttere** vt/i promise

promet'tente a promising

promi'nente a prominent

promiscuità nf promiscuity. **pro'miscuo** a promiscuous

promon'torio nm promontory

pro'mo|sso pp di**promuovere** ● a Sch who has gone up a year; Univ who has passed an exam. **~'tore, ~'trice** nmf promoter

promozio'nale a promotional. **promozi'one** nf promotion

promul'gare vt promulgate

promu'overe vt promote; Sch move up a class

proni'pote nm (di bisnonno) great-grandson; (di prozio) great-nephew ● nf (di bisnonno) great-granddaughter; (di prozio) great-niece

pro'nome nm pronoun

pronosti'care vt forecast, predict. **pro'nostico** nm forecast

pron'tezza nf readiness; (rapidità) quickness

'**pronto** a ready; (rapido) quick; **~!** Teleph hallo!; **tenersi ~** be ready (per for); **pronti, via!** (in gara) ready! steady! go!. **~ soccorso** first aid; (in ospedale) accident and emergency

prontu'ario nm handbook

pro'nuncia nf pronunciation

pronunci'a|re vt pronounce; (dire) utter; deliver (discorso). **~rsi** vr (su un *argomento*) give one's opinion. **~to** *a* (pronounced); (*prominente*) prominent

pro'nunzia ecc = **pronuncia** ecc

propa'ganda *nf* propaganda

propa'gare *vt* propagate. **~rsi** *vr* spread. **~zi'one** *nf* propagation

prope'deutico *a* introductory

pro'pen|dere *vi* **~dere per** be in favour of. **~si'one** *nf* inclination, propensity. **~so** *pp di* propendere ● *a* **essere ~so a fare qcsa** be inclined to do sth

propi'nare *vt* administer

pro'pizio *a* favourable

proponi'mento *nm* resolution

pro'por|re *vt* propose; (*suggerire*) suggest. **~si** *vr* set oneself (*obiettivo, meta*); **~si di** intend to

proporzio'na|le *a* proportional. **~re** *vt* proportion. **~to** *a* proportioned. **proporzi'one** *nf* proportion

pro'posito *nm* purpose; **a ~** by the way; **a ~ di** with regard to; **di ~** (*apposta*) on purpose; **capitare a ~**, **giungere a ~** come at just the right time

proposizi'one *nf* clause; (*frase*) sentence

pro'post|a *nf* proposal. **~o** *pp di* proporre

proprietà *nf inv* property; (*diritto*) ownership; (*correttezza*) propriety. **~ immobiliare** property. **~ privata** private property. **proprie'taria** *nf* owner; (*di casa affittata*) landlady. **proprie'tario** *nm* owner; (*di casa affittata*) landlord

'proprio *a* one's [own]; (*caratteristico*) typical; (*appropriato*) proper ● *adv* just; (*veramente*) really; **non ~** not really, not exactly; (*affatto*) not... at all ● *pron* one's own ● *nm* one's [own]; **lavorare in ~** be one's own boss; **mettersi in ~** set up on one's own

propul'si|one *nf* propulsion. **~sore** *nm* propeller

'proroga *nf* extension

proro'ga|bile *a* extendable. **~re** *vt* extend

pro'rompere *vi* burst out

'prosa *nf* prose. **pro'saico** *a* prosaic

pro'scio|gliere *vt* release; *Jur* acquit. **~lto** *pp di* prosciogliere

prosciu'gare *vt* dry up; (*bonificare*) reclaim. **~si** *vr* dry up

prosci'utto *nm* ham. **~ cotto** cooked ham. **~ crudo** type of dry-cured ham, Parma ham

pro'scri|tto, -a *pp di* proscrivere ● *nmf* exile

prosecuzi'one *nf* continuation

prosegui'mento *nm* continuation; **buon ~!** (*viaggio*) have a good journey!; (*festa*) enjoy the rest of the party!

prosegu'ire *vt* continue ● *vi* go on, continue

prospe'r|are *vi* prosper. **~ità** *nf* prosperity. **'prospero** *a* prosperous; (*favorevole*) favourable. **~oso** *a* flourishing; (*ragazza*) buxom

prospet'tare *vt* show. **~si** *vr* seem

prospet'tiva *nf* perspective; (*panorama*) view; *fig* prospect. **pro'spetto** *nm* (*vista*) view; (*facciata*) façade; (*tabella*) table

prospici'ente *a* facing

prossima'mente *adv* soon

prossimità *nf* proximity

'prossimo, -a *a* near; (*seguente*) next; (*molto vicino*) close; **l'anno ~** next year ● *nmf* neighbour

prosti'tu|ta *nf* prostitute. **~zi'one** *nf* prostitution

pro'stra|re *vt* prostrate. **~rsi** *vr* prostrate oneself. **~to** *a* prostrate

protago'nista *nmf* protagonist

pro'teggere *vt* protect; (*favorire*) favour

prote'ina *nf* protein

pro'tender|e *vt* stretch out. **~si** *vr* (*in avanti*) lean out. **pro'teso** *pp di* protendere

pro'te|sta *nf* protest; (*dichiarazione*) protestation. **~stante** *a & nmf* Protestant. **~stare** *vt/i* protest

protet'tivo *a* protective. **~tto** *pp di* proteggere. **~t'tore, ~t'trice** *nmf* protector; (*sostenitore*) patron ● *nm* (*di prostituta*) pimp. **~zi'one** *nf* protection

protocol'lare *a* (*visita*) protocol ● *vt* register

proto'collo *nm* protocol; (*registro*) register; **carta ~** official stamped paper

proto'tipo *nm* prototype

pro'tra|rre *vt* protract; (*differire*) postpone. **~rsi** *vr* go on, continue. **~tto** *pp di* protrarre

protube'ran|te *a* protuberant. **~za** *nf* protuberance

'prova *nf* test; (*dimostrazione*) proof; (*tentativo*) try; (*di abito*) fitting; *Sport* heat; *Theat* rehearsal; (*bozza*) proof; **fino a ~ contraria** until I'm told otherwise; **in ~** (*assumere*) for a trial period;

mettere alla ~ put to the test. **~ generale** dress rehearsal

pro'var|e *vt* test; *(dimostrare)* prove; *(tentare)* try; try on *(abiti ecc)*; *(sentire)* feel; *Theat* rehearse. **~si** *vr* try

proveni'enza *nf* origin. **prove'nire** *vi* **provenire da** come from

pro'vento *nm* proceeds *pl*

prove'nuto *pp di* **provenire**

pro'verbio *nm* proverb

pro'vetta *nf* test-tube; **bambino in ~** test-tube baby

pro'vetto *a* skilled

pro'vinci|a *nf* province; *(strada)* B road, secondary road. **~ale** *a* provincial; **strada ~ale** B road, secondary road

pro'vino *nm* specimen; *Cinema* screen test

provo'ca|nte *a* provocative. **~re** *vt* provoke; *(causare)* cause. **~tore, ~trice** *nmf* trouble-maker. **~torio** *a* provocative. **~zi'one** *nf* provocation

provve'd|ere *vi* **~ere** *a* provide for. **~i'mento** *nm* measure; *(previdenza)* precaution

provvi'denz|a *nf* providence. **~i'ale** *a* providential

provvigi'one *nf Comm* commission

provvi'sorio *a* provisional

prov'vista *nf* supply

pro'zio, -a *nm* great-uncle ● *nf* great-aunt

'prua *nf* prow

pru'den|te *a* prudent. **~za** *nf* prudence; **per ~za** as a precaution

'prudere *vi* itch

'prugn|a *nf* plum. **~a secca** prune. **~o** *nm* plum[-tree]

prurigi'noso *a* itchy. **pru'rito** *nm* itch

pseu'donimo *nm* pseudonym

psica'na|lisi *nf* psychoanalysis. **~'lista** *nmf* psychoanalyst. **~liz'zare** *vt* psychoanalyse

'psiche *nf* psyche

psichi'a|tra *nmf* psychiatrist. **~'tria** *nf* psychiatry. **~trico** *a* psychiatric

'psichico *a* mental

psico|lo'gia *nf* psychology. **~'logico** *a* psychological. **psi'cologo, -a** *nmf* psychologist

psico'patico, -a *a* psychopathic ● *nmf* psychopath

PT *abbr (Posta e Telecomunicazioni)* PO

pubbli'ca|re *vt* publish. **~zi'one** *nf* publication. **~zioni** *pl (di matrimonio)* banns

pubbli'cista *nmf Journ* correspondent

pubblicità *nf inv* publicity, advertising; *(annuncio)* advertisement, advert; **fare ~ a qcsa** advertise sth; **piccola ~** small advertisements. **pubblici'tario** *a* advertising

'pubblico *a* public; **scuola pubblica** state school ● *nm* public; *(spettatori)* audience; **grande ~** general public. **Pubblica Sicurezza** Police. **~ ufficia-le** civil servant

'pube *nm* pubis

pubertà *nf* puberty

pu'dico *a* modest. **pu'dore** *nm* modesty

pue'rile *a* children's; *pej* childish

pugi'lato *nm* boxing. **'pugile** *nm* boxer

pugna'la|re *vt* stab. **~ta** *nf* stab. **pu'gnale** *nm* dagger

'pugno *nm* fist; *(colpo)* punch; *(manciata)* fistful; *(fig: numero limitato)* handful; **dare un ~ a** punch

'pulce *nf* flea; *(microfono)* bug

pul'cino *nm* chick; *(nel calcio)* junior

pu'ledra *nf* filly

pu'ledro *nm* colt

pu'li|re *vt* clean. **~re a secco** dry-clean. **~to** *a* clean. **~tura** *nf* cleaning. **~'zia** *nf (il pulire)* cleaning; *(l'essere pulito)* cleanliness; **~zie** *pl* housework; **fare le ~zie** do the cleaning

'pullman *nm inv* bus, coach; *(urbano)* bus

pul'mino *nm* minibus

'pulpito *nm* pulpit

pul'sante *nm* button; *Electr* [push-]button. **~ di accensione** on/off switch

pul'sa|re *vi* pulsate. **~zi'one** *nf* pulsation

pul'viscolo *nm* dust

'puma *nm inv* puma

pun'gente *a* prickly; *(insetto)* stinging; *(odore ecc)* sharp

'punger|e *vt* prick; *(insetto)* sting. **~si** *vr* **~si un dito** prick one's finger

pungigli'one *nm* sting

pu'ni|re *vt* punish. **~'tivo** *a* punitive. **~zi'one** *nf* punishment; *Sport* free kick

'punta *nf* point; *(estremità)* tip; *(di monte)* peak; *(un po')* pinch; *Sport* forward; **doppie punte** *(di capelli)* split ends

pun'tare *vt* point; *(spingere con forza)* push; *(scommettere)* bet; *(fam: appuntare)* fasten ● *vi* **~ su** *fig* rely on; **~ verso** *(dirigersi)* head for; **~ a** aspire to

punta'spilli *nm inv* pincushion

pun'tata *nf (di una storia)* instalment;

(*televisiva*) episode; (*al gioco*) stake, bet; (*breve visita*) flying visit; **a puntate** serialized, in instalments; **fare una ~ a/ in** pop over to (*luogo*)

punteggia'tura *nf* punctuation

pun'teggio *nm* score

puntel'lare *vt* prop. **pun'tello** *nm* prop

pun'tiglio *nm* spite; (*ostinazione*) obstinacy. **~'oso** *a* punctilious, pernickety *pej*

pun'tina *nf* (*da disegno*) drawing pin, thumb tack *Am*; (*di giradischi*) stylus. **~o** *nm* dot; **a ~o** perfectly; (*cotto*) to a T

'punto *nm* point; (*in cucito*, *Med*) stitch; (*in punteggiatura*) full stop; **in che ~?** where, exactly?; **~ in bianco** all of a sudden; **due punti** colon; **in ~** sharp; **mettere a ~** put right; *fig* fine tune; tune up (*motore*); **essere sul ~ di fare qcsa** be about to do sth, be on the point of doing sth. **punti cardinali** points of the compass. **~ debole** blind spot. **~ esclamativo** exclamation mark. **~ interrogativo** question mark. **~ nero** *Med* blackhead. **~ di riferimento** landmark; (*per la qualità*) benchmark. **~ di vendita** point of sale. **~ e virgola** semicolon. **~ di vista** point of view

puntu'al|e *a* punctual. **~ità** *nf* punctuality. **~'mente** *adv* punctually, on time

pun'tura *nf* (*di insetto*) sting; (*di ago ecc*) prick; *Med* puncture; (*iniezione*) injection; (*fitta*) stabbing pain

punzecchi'are *vt* prick; *fig* tease

'pupa *nf* doll. **pu'pazzo** *nm* puppet. **pupazzo di neve** snowman

pup'illa *nf Anat* pupil

pu'pillo, -a *nmf* (*di professore*) favourite

purché *conj* provided

'pure *adv* too, also; (*concessivo*) **fate ~!** please do! ●*conj* (*tuttavia*) yet; (*anche se*) even if; **pur di** just to

purè *nm inv* purée. **~ di patate** mashed potatoes, creamed potatoes

pu'rezza *nf* purity

'purga *nf* purge. **pu'pustola** *nf* laxative. **pur'gare** *vt* purge

purga'torio *nm* purgatory

purifi'care *vt* purify

puri'tano, -a *a & nmf* Puritan

'puro *a* pure; (*vino ecc*) undiluted; **per ~ caso** by sheer chance, purely by chance

puro'sangue *a & nm* thoroughbred

pur'troppo *adv* unfortunately

pus *nm* pus. **'pustola** *nf* pimple

puti'ferio *nm* uproar

putre'far|e *vi*, **~si** *vr* putrefy

'putrido *a* putrid

put'tana *nf vulg* whore

'puzza *nf* = puzzo

puz'zare *vi* stink; **~ di bruciato** *fig* smell fishy

'puzzo *nm* stink, bad smell. **~la** *nf* polecat. **~'lente** *a* stinking

p.zza *abbr* (**piazza**) Sq.

Qq

qua *adv* here; **da un anno in ~** for the last year; **da quando in ~?** since when?; **di ~** this way; **di ~ di** on this side of; **~ dentro** in here; **~ sotto** under here; **~ vicino** near here; **~ e là** here and there

qua'derno *nm* exercise book; (*per appunti*) notebook

quadrango'lare *a* (*forma*) quadrangular. **qua'drangolo** *nm* quadrangle

qua'drante *nm* quadrant; (*di orologio*) dial

qua'dra|re *vt* square; (*contabilità*) balance ●*vi* fit in. **~to** *a* square;

(*equilibrato*) levelheaded ●*nm* square; (*pugilato*) ring; **al ~to** squared

quadret'tato *a* squared; (*carta*) graph *attrib*. **qua'dretto** *nm* square; (*piccolo quadro*) small picture; **a quadretti** (*tessuto*) check

quadricro'mia *nf* four-colour printing

quadrien'nale *a* (*che dura quattro anni*) four-year

quadri'foglio *nm* four-leaf clover

quadri'latero *nm* quadrilateral

quadri'mestre *nm* (*periodo*) four-month period

quadro | quanto

'quadro *nm* picture, painting; *(quadrato)* square; *(fig: scena)* sight; *(tabella)* table; *Theat* scene; *Comm* executive **quadri** *pl (carte)* diamonds; **a quadri** *(tessuto, giacca, motivo)* check. **quadri** *pl* **direttivi** senior management

qua'drupede *nm* quadruped

quaggiù *adv* down here

'quaglia *nf* quail

qualche *a (alcuni)* a few, some; *(un certo)* some; *(in interrogazioni)* any; **ho ~ problema** I have a few problems, **~ tempo fa** some time ago; **hai ~ libro italiano?** have you any Italian books?; **posso prendere ~ libro?** can I take some books?; **in ~ modo** somehow; **in ~ posto** somewhere; **~ volta** sometimes; **~ cosa** = **qualcosa**

qual'cos|a *pron* something; *(in interrogazioni)* anything; **~'altro** something else; **vuoi ~'altro?** would you like anything else?; **~a di strano** something strange; **vuoi ~a da mangiare?** would you like something to eat?

qual'cuno *pron* someone, somebody; *(in interrogazioni)* anyone, anybody; *(alcuni)* some; *(in interrogazioni)* any; **c'è ~?** is anybody in?; **qualcun altro** someone else, somebody else; **c'è qualcun altro che aspetta?** is anybody else waiting?; **ho letto ~ dei suoi libri** I've read some of his books; **conosci ~ dei suoi amici?** do you know any of his friends?

'quale *a* which; *(indeterminato)* what; *(come)* as, like; **~ macchina è la tua?** which car is yours?; **~ motivo avrà di parlare così?** what reason would he have to speak like that?; **~ onore!** what an honour!; **città quali Venezia** towns like Venice; **~ che sia la tua opinione** whatever you may think **●** *pron inter* which [one]; **~ preferisci?** which [one] do you prefer? **●** *pron rel* **il/la ~** *(persona)* who; *(animale, cosa)* that, which; *(oggetto: con prep)* whom; *(animale, cosa)* which; **ho incontrato tua madre, la ~ mi ha detto...** I met your mother, who told me...; **l'ufficio nel ~ lavoro** the office in which I work; **l'uomo con il ~ parlavo** the man to whom I was speaking **●** *adv (come)* as

qua'lifica *nf* qualification; *(titolo)* title

qualifi'ca|re *vt* qualify; *(definire)* define. **~rsi** *vr* be placed. **~tivo** *a* qualifying. **~to** *a* *(operaio)* semiskilled. **~zi'one** *nf* qualification

qualità *nf inv* quality; *(specie)* kind; **in ~ di** in one's capacity as. **~tiva'mente** *adv* qualitatively. **~ tivo** *a* qualitative

qua'lora *conj* in case

qual'siasi, qua'lunque *a* any; *(non importa quale)* whatever; *(ordinario)* ordinary; **dammi una penna ~** give me any pen [whatsoever]; **farei ~ cosa** I would do anything; **~ cosa io faccia** whatever I do; **~ persona** anyone; **in ~ caso** in any case; **uno ~** any one, whichever; **l'uomo qualunque** the man in the street; **vivo in una casa ~** I live in an ordinary house

qualunqu'ismo *nm* lack of political views

'quando *conj & adv* when; **da ~ ti ho visto** since I saw you; **da ~ esci con lui?** how long have you been going out with him?; **da ~ in qua?** since when?; **~... ~...** sometimes..., sometimes...

quantifi'care *vt* quantify

quantità *nf inv* quantity; **una ~ di** *(gran numero)* a great deal of. **~tiva'mente** *adv* quantitatively. **~ tivo** *nm* amount **●** *a* quantitative

'quanto *a inter* how much; *(con nomi plurali)* how many; *(in esclamazione)* what a lot of; *(tempo)* how long; **quanti anni hai?** how old are you? **●** *a rel* as much... as; *(tempo)* as long as; *(con nomi plurali)* as many... as; **prendi ~ denaro ti serve** take as much money as you need; **prendi quanti libri vuoi** take as many books as you like **●** *pron inter* how much; *(quanto tempo)* how long; *(plurale)* how many; **quanti ne abbiamo oggi?** what date is it today? **●** *pron rel* as much as; *(quanto tempo)* as long as; *(plurale)* as many as; **prendine ~/quanti ne vuoi** take as much/as many as you like; **stai ~ vuoi** stay as long as you like; **questo è ~** that's it **●** *adv inter* how much; *(quanto tempo)* how long; **~ sei alto?** how tall are you?; **~ hai aspettato?** how long did you wait for?; **~ costa?** how much is it?; **~ mi dispiace!** I'm so sorry!; **~ è bello!** how nice! **●** *adv rel* as much as; **lavoro ~ posso** I work as much as I can; **è tanto intelligente ~ bello** he's as intelligent as he's good-looking; **in ~** *(in qualità di)* as; *(poiché)* since; **~ a me** as far as I'm concerned; **per ~** however; **per ~ ne sappia** as far as I know; **per ~ mi riguarda** as far as I'm concerned; **per ~ mi sia simpatico** much as I like him; ~ **a** as for; ~ **prima** (*al più presto*) as soon as possible

quan'tunque *conj* although

qua'ranta *a & nm* forty

quaran'tena *nf* quarantine

quaran'tenn|e *a* forty-year-old. ~**io** *nm* period of forty years

quaran't|esimo *a* fortieth. ~**ina** *nf* una ~**ina** about forty

qua'resima *nf* Lent

quar'tetto *nm* quartet

quarti'ere *nm* district; *Mil* quarters *pl.* ~ **generale** headquarters

quarto *a* fourth ● *nm* fourth; (*quarta parte*) quarter; **le sette e un** ~ **a** quarter past seven. **quarti** *pl* **di finale** quarterfinals. ~ **d'ora** quarter of an hour. **quar'tultimo, -a** *nmf* fourth from the end, fourth last

quarzo *nm* quartz

quasi *adv* almost, nearly; ~ **mai** hardly ever ● *conj* (*come se*) as if; ~ ~ **sto a casa** I'm tempted to stay home

quassù *adv* up here

quatto *a* crouching; (*silenzioso*) silent; **starsene** ~ keep very quiet

quat'tordici *a & nm* fourteen

quat'trini *nmpl* money *sg*, dosh *sg fam*

quattro *a & nm* four; **dirne** ~ **a** qcno give sb a piece of one's mind; **farsi in** ~ (**per qcno/per fare qcsa**) go to a lot of trouble (for sb/to do sth); **in** ~ **e quattr'otto** in a flash. ~ **per** ~ *nm inv Auto* four-wheel drive [vehicle]

quat'trocchi: a ~ *adv* in private

quattro'cento *a & nm* four hundred; **il Q~** the fifteenth century

quattro'mila *a & nm* four thousand

quello *a* that (*pl* those); **quell'albero** that tree; **quegli alberi** those trees; **quel cane** that dog; **quei cani** those dogs ● *pron* that [one] (*pl* those [ones]); ~ **lì** that one over there; ~ **che** the one that; (*ciò che*) what; **quelli che** the ones that, those that; ~ **a destra** the one on the right

quercia *nf* oak

que'rela *nf* [legal] action

quere'lare *vt* bring an action against

que'sito *nm* question

questio'nario *nm* questionnaire

questi'one *nf* question; (*faccenda*)

matter; (*litigio*) quarrel; **in** ~ in doubt; **è fuori** ~ it's out of the question; **è** ~ **di vita o di morte** it's a matter of life and death

quest'o *a* this (*pl* these) ● *pron* this [one] (*pl* these [ones]); ~**o qui,** ~**o qua** this one here; ~**o è quello che ha detto** that's what he said; **per** ~**o** for this *or* that reason. **quest'oggi** today

que'store *nm* chief of police

que'stura *nf* police headquarters

qui *adv* here; **da** ~ **in poi** from now on; **fin** ~ (*di tempo*) up till now, until now; ~ **dentro** in here; ~ **sotto** under here; ~ **vicino** *adv* near here ● *nm* ~ **pro quo** misunderstanding

quie'scienza *nf* **trattamento di** ~ retirement package

quie'tanza *nf* receipt

quie'tar|e *vt* calm. ~**si** *vr* quieten down

qui'et|e *nf* quiet; **disturbo della** ~ **e pubblica** breach of the peace. ~**o** *a* quiet

quindi *adv* then ● *conj* therefore

quindi'ci *a & nm* fifteen. ~**cina** *nf* una ~**cina** about fifteen; **una** ~**cina di giorni** a fortnight *Br*, two weeks

quinquen'nale *a* (*che dura cinque anni*) five-year. **quin'quennio** *nm* [period of] five years

quin'tale *nm* a hundred kilograms

quinte *nfpl Theat* wings

quin'tetto *nm* quintet

quinto *a* fifth

quin'tuplo *a* quintuple

qui'squiglia *nf* **perdersi in quisquiglie** get bogged down in details

quota *nf* quota; (*rata*) instalment; (*altitudine*) height; *Aeron* altitude, height; (*ippica*) odds *pl*; **perdere** ~ lose altitude; **prendere** ~ gain altitude. ~ **di iscrizione** entry fee

quo'ta|re *vt Comm* quote. ~**to** *a* quoted; **essere** ~**to in Borsa** be quoted on the Stock Exchange. ~**zi'one** *nf* quotation

quotidi'ana'mente *adv* daily. ~**'ano** *a* daily; (*ordinario*) everyday ● *nm* daily [paper]

quozi'ente *nm* quotient. ~ **d'intelligenza** intelligence quotient, IQ

Rr

ra'barbaro *nm* rhubarb
'rabbia *nf* rage; (*ira*) anger; *Med* rabies
sg; che ~! what a nuisance!; mi fa ~ it
makes me angry
rab'bino *nm* rabbi
rabbiosa'mente *adv* furiously.
rabbi'oso *a* hot-tempered; *Med* rabid;
(*violento*) violent
rabbo'nir|e *vt* pacify. ~si *vr* calm
down
rabbrivi'dire *vi* shudder; (*di freddo*)
shiver
rabbui'arsi *vr* become dark
raccapez'zar|e *vt* put together. ~si
vr see one's way ahead
raccapricci'ante *a* horrifying
raccatta'palle *nm inv* ball boy ●*nf
inv* ball girl
raccat'tare *vt* pick up
rac'chetta *nf* racket. ~ da ping pong
table-tennis bat. ~ da sci ski stick, ski
pole. ~ da tennis tennis racket
'racchio *a fam* ugly
racchi'udere *vt* contain
rac'cogli|ere *vt* pick; (*da terra*) pick
up; (*mietere*) harvest; (*collezionare*) collect; (*radunare*) gather; win (*voti ecc*);
(*dare asilo a*) take in. ~ersi *vr* gather;
(*concentrarsi*) collect one's thoughts.
~'mento *nm* concentration. ~'tore,
~'trice *nmf* collector ●*nm* (*cartella*)
ring-binder
rac'colto, -a *pp di raccogliere* ●*a*
(*rannicchiato*) hunched; (*intimo*) cosy;
(*concentrato*) engrossed ●*nm* (*mieti-
tura*) harvest; (*di scritti*)
compilation; (*del grano ecc*) harvesting;
(*adunata*) gathering
raccoman'dabile *a* recommend-
able; poco ~ (*persona*) shady
raccoman'dar|e *vt* recommend;
(*affidare*) entrust. ~si *vr* (*implorare*)
beg. ~ta *nf* registered letter; ~ta con
ricevuta di ritorno recorded delivery.
~-espresso *nf* guaranteed next-day delivery of recorded items. ~zi'one *nf* rec-
ommendation
raccon'tare *vt* tell. rac'conto *nm*
story

raccorci'are *vt* shorten
raccor'dare *vt* join. rac'cordo *nm*
connection; (*stradale*) feeder. raccordo
anulare ring road. raccordo ferroviario siding
ra'chitico *a* rickety; (*poco sviluppato*)
stunted
racimo'lare *vt* scrape together
racket *nm inv* racket
radar *nm* radar
raddol'cir|e *vt* sweeten; *fig* soften. ~si
vr become milder; (*carattere*) mellow
raddoppi'are *vt* double. rad'doppio
nm doubling
raddriz'zare *vt* straighten
'rader|e *vt* shave; graze (*muro*); ~e al
suolo raze [to the ground]. ~si *vr* shave
radi'are *vt* strike off; ~ dall'albo
strike off
radia'tore *nm* radiator. ~zi'one *nf*
radiation
'radica *nf* briar
radi'cale *a* radical ●*nm Gram* root;
Pol radical
ra'dicchio *nm* chicory
ra'dice *nf* root; mettere [le] radici*fig*
put down roots. ~ quadrata square
root
'radio *nf inv* radio; via ~ by radio. ~ a
transistor transistor radio ●*nm Chem*
radium.
radioama'tore, -'trice *nmf* [radio]
ham
radioascolta'tore, -'trice *nmf* lis-
tener
radioat|tivi'tà *nf* radioactivity. ~'tivo
a radioactive
radio'cro|naca *nf* radio commen-
tary; fare la ~naca di commentate on.
~'nista *nmf* radio reporter
radiodiffusi'one *nf* broadcasting
radiogra'fare *vt* X-ray. ~'fia *nf* X-ray
[photograph]; (*radiologia*) radiography;
fare una ~fia (*paziente:*) have an X-
ray; (*dottore:*) take an X-ray
radio'fonico *a* radio attrib
radio'lina *nf* transistor
radi'ologo, -a *nmf* radiologist
radi'oso *a* radiant

radio'sveglia *nf* radio alarm
radio'taxi *nm inv* radio taxi
radiote'lefono *nm* radio-telephone; (*privato*) cordless [phone]
radiotelevi'sivo *a* broadcasting *attrib*
'rado *a* sparse; (*non frequente*) rare; **di ~ seldom**
radu'nar|e *vt*, **~si** *vr* gather [together]. **ra'duno** *nm* meeting; *Sport* rally
ra'dura *nf* clearing
'rafano *nm* horseradish
raffazzo'nato *a* (*discorso, lavoro*) botched
raf'fermo *a* stale
'raffica *nf* gust; (*di armi da fuoco*) burst; (*di domande*) barrage
raffigu'ra|re *vt* represent. **~zi'one** *nf* representation
raffi'na|re *vt* refine. **~ta'mente** *adv* elegantly. **~'tezza** *nf* refinement. **~to** *a* refined. **raffine'ria** *nf* refinery
rafforza'|mento *nm* reinforcement; (*di muscolatura*) strengthening. **~re** *vt* reinforce. **~'tivo** *nm* *Gram* intensifier
raffredda'mento *nm* (*processo*) cooling
raffred'd|are *vt* cool. **~arsi** *vr* get cold; (*prendere un raffreddore*) catch a cold. **~ore** *nm* cold. **~ore da fieno** hay fever
raf'fronto *nm* comparison
'rafia *nf* raffia
Rag. *abbr* ragioniere
ra'gaz|za *nf* girl; (*fidanzata*) girlfriend. **~za alla pari** au pair [girl]. **~'zata** *nf* prank. **~zo** *nm* boy; (*fidanzato*) boyfriend; **da ~zo** (*da giovane*) as a boy
ragge'lar|e *vt fig* freeze. **~si** *vr fig* turn to ice
raggi'ante *a* radiant; **~ di successo** flushed with success
raggi'era *nf* **a ~** with a pattern like spokes radiating from a centre
'raggio *nm* ray; *Math* radius; (*di ruota*) spoke; **~ d'azione** range. **~ laser** laser beam
raggi'rare *vt* trick. **rag'giro** *nm* trick
raggi'un|gere *vt* reach; (*conseguire*) achieve. **~'gibile** *a* (*luogo*) within reach
raggomito'lar|e *vt* wind. **~si** *vr* curl up
raggranel'lare *vt* scrape together
raggrin'zir|e *vt*, **~si** *vr* wrinkle
raggrup|pa'mento *nm* (*gruppo*)

group; (*azione*) grouping. **~'pare** *vt* group together
ragguagli'are *vt* compare; (*informare*) inform. **raggu'aglio** *nm* comparison; (*informazione*) information
ragguar'devole *a* considerable
'ragia *nf* resin; **acqua** *nf* **~** turpentine
ragiona'mento *nm* reasoning; (*discussione*) discussion. **ragio'nare** *vi* reason; (*discutere*) discuss
ragi'one *nf* reason; (*ciò che è giusto*) right; **a ~ o a torto** rightly or wrongly; **aver ~** be right; **perdere la ~** go out of one's mind; **a ragion veduta** after due consideration
ragione'ria *nf* accountancy
ragio'nevol|e *a* reasonable. **~'mente** *adv* reasonably
ragioni'ere, -a *nmf* accountant
ragli'are *vi* bray
ragna'tela *nf* cobweb. **'ragno** *nm* spider
ragù *nm inv* meat sauce
RAI *nf abbr* (**Radio Audizioni Italiane**) *Italian public broadcasting company*
ralle'gra|re *vt* gladden. **~rsi** *vr* rejoice; **~rsi con qcno** congratulate sb. **~'menti** *nmpl* congratulations
rallenta'mento *nm* slowing down
rallen'ta|re *vt/i* slow down; (*allentare*) slacken. **~rsi** *vr* slow down. **~'tore** *nm* (*su strada*) speed bump; **al ~tore** in slow motion
raman'zina *nf* reprimand
ra'marro *nm* type of lizard
ra'mato *a* (*capelli*) copper[-coloured]
'rame *nm* copper
ramifi'ca|re *vi*, **~rsi** *vr* branch out; (*strada:*) branch. **~zi'one** *nf* ramification
rammari'carsi *vr* **~ di** regret; (*lamentarsi*) complain (**di** about). **ram'marico** *nm* regret
rammen'dare *vt* darn. **ram'mendo** *nm* darning
rammen'tar|e *vt* remember; **~e qcsa a qcno** (*richiamare alla memoria*) remind sb of sth. **~si** *vr* remember
rammol'li|re *vt* soften. **~rsi** *vr* go soft. **~to, -a** *nmf* wimp
'ramo *nm* branch. **~'scello** *nm* twig
'rampa *nf* (*di scale*) flight. **~ d'accesso** slip road. **~ di lancio** launch[ing] pad
ram'pante *a* **giovane ~** yuppie
rampi'cante *a* climbing ●*nm Bot* creeper

ram'pollo *nm hum* brat; *(discendente)* descendant

ram'pone *nm* harpoon; *(per scarpe)* crampon

'rana *nf* frog; *(nel nuoto)* breaststroke; *uomo* ~ frogman

'rancido *a* rancid

ran'core *nm* resentment

ran'dagio *a* stray

'rango *nm* rank

rannicchi'arsi *vr* huddle up

rannuvola'mento *nm* clouding over. rannuvo'larsi *vr* cloud over

ra'nocchio *nm* frog

ranto'lare *vi* wheeze. 'rantolo *nm* wheeze; *(di moribondo)* death-rattle

'rapa *nf* turnip

ra'pace *a* rapacious; *(uccello)* predatory

ra'pare *vt* crop

'rapida *nf* rapids *pl.* ~'mente *adv* rapidly

rapidità *nf* speed

'rapido *a* swift ● *nm (treno)* express [train]

rapi'mento *nm (crimine)* kidnapping

ra'pina *nf* robbery; ~ a mano armata armed robbery. ~ in banca bank robbery. rapi'nare *vt* rob. ~'tore *nm* robber

ra'pire *vt* abduct; *(a scopo di riscatto)* kidnap; *(estasiare)* ravish. ~'tore, ~'trice *nmf* kidnapper

rappacifi'care *vt* pacify. ~rsi *vr* be reconciled, make it up. ~zi'one *nf* reconciliation

rappor'tare *vt* reproduce *(disegno)*; *(confrontare)* compare

rap'porto *nm* report; *(connessione)* relation; *(legame)* relationship; *Math, Techn* ratio; rapporti *pl* relationship; essere in buoni rapporti be on good terms. ~ di amicizia friendship. ~ di lavoro working relationship. rapporti *pl* sessuali sexual intercourse

rap'prendersi *vr* set; *(latte:)* curdle

rappre'saglia *nf* reprisal

rappresen'tan|te *nmf* representative. ~te di classe class representative. ~te di commercio sales representative, [sales] rep *fam.* ~za *nf* delegation; *Comm* agency; spese *nfpl* di ~za entertainment expenses; di ~za *(appartamento ecc)* company

rappresen'ta|re *vt* represent; *Theat* perform. ~'tivo *a* representative. ~zi'one *nf* representation; *(spettacolo)* performance

rap'preso *pp di* rapprendersi

rapso'dia *nf* rhapsody

'raptus *nm inv* fit of madness

rara'mente *adv* rarely, seldom

rare'fa|re *vt*, ~rsi *vr* rarefy. ~tto *a* rarefied

rarità *nf inv* rarity. 'raro *a* rare

ra'sar|e *vt* shave; trim *(siepe ecc)*. ~si *vr* shave

raschia'mento *nm Med* curettage

raschi'are *vt* scrape; *(togliere)* scrape off

rasen'tare *vt* go close to. ra'sente *prep* very close to

'raso *pp di* radere ● *a* smooth; *(colmo)* full to the brim; *(barba)* close-cropped; ~ terra close to the ground; un cucchiaio ~ a level spoonful ● *nm* satin

ra'soio *nm* razor

ras'segna *nf* review; *(mostra)* exhibition; *(musicale, cinematografica)* festival; passare in ~ review; *Mil* inspect

rasse'gna|re *vt* present. ~rsi *vr* resign oneself. ~to a *(persona, aria, tono)* resigned. ~zi'one *nf* resignation

rassere'nar|e *vt* clear; *fig* cheer up. ~si *vr* become clear; *fig* cheer up

rasset'tare *vt* tidy up; *(riparare)* mend

rassicu'ra|nte *a (persona, parole, presenza)* reassuring. ~re *vt* reassure. ~zi'one *nf* reassurance

rasso'dare *vt* harden; *fig* strengthen

rassomigli'a|nza *nf* resemblance. ~re *vi* ~re a resemble

rastrella'mento *nm (di fieno)* raking; *(perlustrazione)* combing. rastrel'lare *vt* rake; *(perlustrare)* comb

rastrelli'era *nf* rack; *(per biciclette)* bicycle rack; *(scolapiatti)* [plate] rack. ra'strello *nm* rake

'rata *nf* instalment; pagare a rate pay by instalments; comprare qcsa a rate buy sth on hire purchase, buy sth on the installment plan *Am.* rate'ale *a* by instalments; pagamento rateale payment by instalments

ra'tifica *nf Jur* ratification

ratifi'care *vt Jur* ratify

'ratto *nm* abduction; *(roditore)* rat

rattop'pare *vt* patch. rat'toppo *nm* patch

rattrap'pir|e *vt* make stiff. ~si *vr* become stiff

rattri'star|e vt sadden. ~si vr become sad

rau'cedine nf hoarseness. 'rauco a hoarse

rava'nello nm radish

ravi'oli nmpl ravioli sg

ravve'dersi vr mend one's ways

ravvicina'mento nm (tra persone) reconciliation; Pol rapprochement

ravvici'nar|e vt bring closer; (riconciliare) reconcile. ~si vr be reconciled

ravvi'sare vt recognize

ravvi'var|e vt revive; fig brighten up. ~si vr revive

'rayon nm rayon

razio'cinio nm rational thought; (buon senso) common sense

razio'nal|e a rational. ~ità nf (raziocinio) rationality; (di ambiente) functional nature. ~iz'zare vt rationalize (programmi, metodi, spazio). ~'mente adv (con raziocinio) rationally

razio'nare vt ration. razi'one nf ration

'razza nf race; (di cani ecc) breed; (genere) kind; che ~ di idiota! fam what an idiot!

raz'zia nf raid

razzi'ale a racial

raz'zis|mo nm racism. ~ta a & nmf racist

'razzo nm rocket. ~ da segnalazione flare

razzo'lare vi (polli:) scratch about

re nm inv king; Mus (chiave, nota) D

rea'gire vi react

re'ale a real; (di re) royal

rea'lis|mo nm realism. ~ta nmf realist; (fautore del re) royalist

realistica'mente adv realistically. rea'listico a realistic

realiz'zabile a (programma) feasible

realiz'zar|e vt (attuare) carry out, realize; Comm make; score (gol, canestro); (rendersi conto di) realize. ~rsi vr come true; (nel lavoro ecc) fulfil oneself. ~zi'one nf realization; (di sogno, persona) fulfilment. ~zione scenica production

rea'lizzo nm (vendita) proceeds pl; (riscossione) yield

real'mente adv really

realtà nf inv reality. ~ virtuale virtual reality

re'ato nm crime, criminal offence

reat'tivo a reactive

reat'tore nm reactor; Aeron jet [aircraft]

reazio'nario, -a a & nmf reactionary

reazi'one nf reaction. ~ a catena chain reaction

'rebus nm inv rebus; (enigma) puzzle

recapi'tare vt deliver. re'capito nm address; (consegna) delivery. recapito a domicilio home delivery. recapito telefonico contact telephone number

re'car|e vt bear; (produrre) cause. ~si vr go

re'cedere vi recede; fig give up

recensi'one nf review

recen'sire vt review. ~ore nm reviewer

re'cente a recent; di ~ recently. ~'mente adv recently

recessi'one nf recession

reces'sivo a Biol recessive. re'cesso nm recess

re'cidere vt cut off

reci'divo, -a a Med recurrent • nmf repeat offender

recin'tare vt close off. re'cinto nm enclosure; (per animali) pen; (per bambini) play-pen. ~zi'one nf (muro) wall; (rete) wire fence; (cancellata) railings pl

recipi'ente nm container

re'ciproco a reciprocal

re'ciso pp di recidere

'recita nf performance. reci'tare vt recite; Theat act; play (ruolo). ~zi'one nf recitation; Theat acting

recla'mare vi protest • vt claim

ré'clame nf inv advertising; (avviso pubblicitario) advertisement

re'clamo nm complaint; ufficio reclami complaints department

recli'nabile a reclining; sedile ~bile reclining seat. ~re vt tilt (sedile), lean (capo)

reclusi'one nf imprisonment. re'cluso, -a a secluded • nmf prisoner

'recluta nf recruit

reclu'ta'mento nm recruitment. ~'tare vt recruit

'record nm inv record • a inv (cifra) record attrib

recrimi'na|re vi recriminate. ~zi'one nf recrimination

recupe'rare vt recover. re'cupero nm recovery; corso di recupero additional classes; minuti di recupero Sport injury time

redargu'ire vt rebuke

re'datto pp di redigere

redat'tore, **-'trice** *nmf* editor; (*di testo*) writer. **redazi'one** *nf* (*ufficio*) editorial office; (*di testi*) editing

reddi'tizio *a* profitable

'reddito *nm* income. ~ **imponibile** taxable income

re'den|to *pp di* **redimere** ~**'tore** *nm* redeemer. ~**zi'one** *nf* redemption

re'digere *vt* write; draw up (*documento*)

re'dimer|e *vt* redeem. ~**si** *vr* redeem oneself

'redini *nfpl* reins

'reduce *a* ~ **da** back from ● *nmf* survivor

refe'rendum *nm inv* referendum

refe'renza *nf* reference

refet'torio *nm* refectory

refrat'tario *a* refractory; **essere** ~ **a** have no aptitude for

refrige'ra|re *vt* refrigerate. ~**zi'one** *nf* refrigeration

refur'tiva *nf* stolen goods *pl*

rega'lare *vt* give

re'gale *a* regal

re'galo *nm* present, gift

re'gata *nf* regatta

reg'gen|te *nmf* regent. ~**za** *nf* regency

'regger|e *vt* (*sorreggere*) bear; (*tenere in mano*) hold; (*dirigere*) run; (*governare*) govern; *Gram* take ● *vi* (*resistere*) hold out; (*durare*) last; *fig* stand. ~**si** *vr* stand

'reggia *nf* royal palace

reggi'calze *nm inv* suspender belt

reggi'mento *nm* regiment; (*fig: molte persone*) army

reggi'petto, **reggi'seno** *nm* bra

re'gia *nf Cinema* direction; *Theat* production

re'gime *nm* regime; (*dieta*) diet; *Mech* speed. ~ **militare** military regime

re'gina *nf* queen

'regio *a* royal

regio'na|le *a* regional. ~**'lismo** *nm* (*parola*) regionalism

regi'one *nf* region

re'gista *nmf Cinema* director; *Theat*, *TV* producer

regi'stra|re *vt* register; *Comm* enter; (*incidere su nastro*) tape, record; (*su disco*) record. ~**'tore** *nm* recorder; (*magnetofono*) tape-recorder. ~**tore di cassa** cash register. ~**zi'one** *nf* registration; *Comm* entry; (*di programma*) recording

re'gistro *nm* register; (*ufficio*) registry. ~ **di cassa** ledger

re'gnare *vi* reign

'regno *nm* kingdom; (*sovranità*) reign. **R~ Unito** United Kingdom

'regola *nf* rule; **essere in** ~ be in order; (*persona:*) have one's papers in order. **rego'labile** *a* (*meccanismo*) adjustable. ~**'mento** *nm* regulation; *Comm* settlement. ~**mento di conti** settling of scores

rego'lar|e *a* regular ● *vt* regulate; (*ridurre, moderare*) limit; (*sistemare*) settle. ~**si** *vr* (*agire*) act; (*moderarsi*) control oneself. ~**ità** *nf inv* regularity. ~**iz'zare** *vt* settle (*debito*)

rego'la|ta *nf* **darsi una** ~**ta** pull oneself together. ~**tore**, ~**'trice** *a* **piano** ~**tore** urban development plan

'regolo *nm* ruler

regre'dire *vi Biol*, *Psych* regress

regres|si'one *nf* regression. ~**'sivo** *a* regressive. **re'gresso** *nm* decline

reinseri'mento *nm* (*di persona*) reintegration

reinser'irsi *vr* (*in ambiente*) reintegrate

reinte'grare *vt* restore

relativa'mente *adv* relatively; ~ **a** as regards. **relatività** *nf* relativity. **rela'tivo** *a* relative

rela'tore, **-'trice** *nmf* (*in una conferenza*) speaker

re'lax *nm* relaxation

relazi'one *nf* relation[ship]; (*rapporto amoroso*) [love] affair; (*resoconto*) report; **pubbliche relazioni** *pl* public relations

rele'gare *vt* relegate

religi'o|ne *nf* religion. ~**so**, **-a** *a* religious ● *nm* monk ● *nf* nun

re'liqui|a *nf* relic. ~**'ario** *nm* reliquary

re'litto *nm* wreck

re'ma|re *vi* row. ~**tore**, ~**'trice** *nmf* rower

remini'scenza *nf* reminiscence

remissi'one *nf* remission; (*sottomissione*) submissiveness. **remis'sivo** *a* submissive

'remo *nm* oar

'remora *nf* **senza remore** without hesitation

re'moto *a* remote

remune'ra|re *vt* remunerate. ~**'tivo** *a* remunerative. ~**zi'one** *nf* remuneration

'render|e *vt* (*restituire*) return;

(*esprimere*) render; (*fruttare*) yield; (*far diventare*) make. **~si** *vr* become; **~si conto di qcsa** realize sth; **~si utile** make oneself useful

rendi'conto *nm* report

rendi'mento *nm* rendering; (*produzione*) yield

rendita *nf* income; (*dello Stato*) revenue; **vivere di ~** *fig* rest on one's laurels

'rene *nm* kidney. **~ artificiale** kidney machine

reni *nfpl* (*schiena*) back

reni'tente *a* **essere ~ a** (*consigli di qcno*) be unwilling to accept

'renna *nf* reindeer (*pl inv*); (*pelle*) buckskin

'Reno *nm* Rhine

'reo, -a *a* guilty ● *nmf* offender

re'parto *nm* department; *Mil* unit

repel'lente *a* repulsive

repen'taglio *nm* **mettere a ~** risk

repen'tino *a* sudden

reper'ibile *a* available; **non è ~** (*perduto*) it's not to be found

repe'rire *vt* trace (*fondi*)

re'perto *nm* **~ archeologico** find

reper'torio *nm* repertory; (*elenco*) index; **immagini** *pl* **di ~** archive footage

replica *nf* reply; (*obiezione*) objection; (*copia*) replica; *Theat* repeat performance. **repli'care** *vt* reply; *Theat* repeat

repor'tage *nm inv* report

repres|si'one *nf* repression. **~'sivo** *a* repressive. **re'presso** *pp di* **reprimere**

re'primere *vt* repress

re'pubbli|ca *nf* republic. **~'cano, -a** *a* & *nmf* republican

repu'tare *vt* consider

reputazi'one *nf* reputation

requi'si|re *vt* requisition. **~to** *nm* requirement

requi'sitoria *nf* (*arringa*) closing speech

requisizi'one *nf* requisition

'resa *nf* surrender; *Comm* rendering. **~ dei conti** rendering of accounts

'residence *nm inv* residential hotel

resi'den|te *a* & *nmf* resident. **~za** *nf* residence; (*soggiorno*) stay. **~zi'ale** *a* residential; **zona ~ziale** residential district

re'siduo *a* residual ● *nm* remainder

'resina *nf* resin

resi'sten|te *a* resistant; **~te all'acqua** water-resistant. **~za** *nf* resistance; (*fisica*) stamina; *Electr* resistor; **la R~za** the Resistance

re'sistere *vi* **~** [**a**] resist; (*a colpi, scosse*) stand up to; **~ alla pioggia/al vento** be rain-/wind-resistant

'reso *pp di* **rendere**

reso'conto *nm* report

respin'gente *nm* *Rail* buffer

re'spingere *vt* repel; (*rifiutare*) reject; (*bocciare*) fail. **~to** *pp di* **respingere**

respi'ra|re *vt/i* breathe. **~'tore** *nm* respirator. **~'tore** [**a tubo**] snorkel. **~'torio** *a* respiratory. **~zi'one** *nf* breathing; *Med* respiration. **~zi'one bocca a bocca** mouth-to-mouth rescuscitation, kiss of life. **re'spiro** *nm* breath; (*il respirare*) breathing; *fig* respite

respon'sabil|e *a* responsible (**di** for); *Jur* liable ● *nm* person responsible; **~ della produzione** production manager. **~ità** *nf inv* responsibility; *Jur* liability. **~ità civile** *Jur* civil liability. **~zi'one** *vt* give responsibility to (*dipendente*)

re'sponso *nm* response

'ressa *nf* crowd

re'stante *a* remaining ● *nm* remainder

re'stare *vi* = **rimanere**

restau'ra|re *vt* restore. **~'tore, ~'trice** *nmf* restorer. **~zi'one** *nf* restoration. **re'stauro** *nm* (*riparazione*) repair

re'stio *a* restive; **~ a** reluctant to

resti'tu|ire *vt* return; (*reintegrare*) restore. **~zi'one** *nf* return; *Jur* restitution

'resto *nm* remainder; (*saldo*) balance; (*denaro*) change; **resti** *pl* (*avanzi*) remains; **del ~** besides

re'string|ere *vt* contract; take in (*vestiti*); (*limitare*) restrict; shrink (*stoffa*). **~si** *vr* contract; (*farsi più vicini*) close up; (*stoffa:*) shrink. **restrin'gimento** *nm* (*di tessuto*) shrinkage

restrit'tivo *a* (*legge, clausola*) restrictive. **~zi'one** *nf* restriction

resurrezi'one *nf* resurrection

resusci'tare *vt/i* revive

re'tata *nf* round-up

'rete *nf* net; (*sistema*) network; (*televisiva*) channel; (*in calcio, hockey*) goal; *fig* trap; (*per la spesa*) string bag. **~ locale** *Comput* local [area] network, LAN. **~ stradale** road network. **~ televisiva** television channel

reti'cen|te *a* reticent. **~za** *nf* reticence

retico'lato *nm* grid; (*rete metallica*) wire netting. **re'ticolo** *nm* network 'retina nf retina

re'tina nf (per capelli) hair net

re'torico, -a a rhetorical; domanda retorica rhetorical question ● nf rhetoric

retribu'ire vt remunerate. ~zi'one nf remuneration

'retro adv behind; vedi ~ see over ● nm inv back. ~ di copertina outside back cover

retroat'tivo a retroactive

retro'cedere vi retreat ● vt Mil demote; Sport relegate. ~ssi'one nf Sport relegation

retroda'tare vt backdate

re'trogrado a retrograde; fig old-fashioned; Pol reactionary

retrogu'ardia nf Mil rearguard

retro'marcia nf reverse [gear]

retro'scena nm inv Theat backstage; fig background details pl

retrospet'tivo a retrospective

retro'stante a il palazzo ~ the building behind

retrovi'sore nm rear-view mirror

'retta[1] nf Math straight line; (di collegio, pensionato) fee

'retta[2] nf dar ~ a qcno take sb's advice

rettango'lare a rectangular. ret'tangolo a right-angled ● nm rectangle

ret'tifica nf rectification. ~'care vt rectify

'rettile nm reptile

retti'lineo a rectilinear; (retto) upright ● nm Sport back straight

retti'tudine nf rectitude

'retto pp di reggere ● a straight; fig upright; (giusto) correct; angolo ~ right angle

ret'tore nm Relig rector; Univ chancellor

reu'matico a rheumatic

reuma'tismi nmpl rheumatism

reve'rendo a reverend

rever'sibile a reversible

revisio'nare vt revise; Comm audit; Auto overhaul. revisi'one nf revision; Comm audit; Auto overhaul. revi'sore nm (di conti) auditor; (di bozze) proofreader; (di traduzioni) revisor

re'vival nm inv revival

'revoca nf repeal. revo'care vt repeal

riabili'tare vt rehabilitate. ~zi'one nf rehabilitation

riabitu'are vt reaccustom. ~si vr reaccustom oneself

riac'cender|e vt rekindle (fuoco). ~si vr (luce:) come back on

riacqui'stare vt buy back; regain (libertà, prestigio); recover (vista, udito)

riagganci'are vt replace (ricevitore); ~ la cornetta hang up ● vi hang up

riallac'ciare vt refasten; reconnect (corrente); renew (amicizia)

rial'zare vt raise ● vi rise. ri'alzo nm rise

riani'mar|e vt Med resuscitate; (ridare forza a) revive; (ridare coraggio a) cheer up. ~si vr regain consciousness; (riprendere forza) revive; (riprendere coraggio) cheer up

riaper'tura nf reopening

riapri'r|e vt, ~si vr reopen

ri'armo nm rearmament

rias'sumere vt (ricapitolare) resume

rias'suntivo a summarizing. rias'sunto pp di riassumere ● nm summary

ria'ver|e vt get back; regain (salute, vista). ~si vr recover

riavvicina'mento nm (tra persone) reconciliation

riavvici'nar|e vt reconcile (paesi, persone). ~si vr (riconciliarsi) be reconciled, make it up

riba'dire vt (confermare) reaffirm

ri'balta nf flap; Theat footlights pl; fig limelight

ribal'tabile a tip-up

ribal'tar|e vt/i, ~si vr tip over; Naut capsize

ribas'sare vt lower ● vi fall. ri'basso nm fall; (sconto) discount

ri'battere vt (a macchina) retype; (controbattere) deny ● vi answer back

ribel'l|arsi vr rebel. ri'belle a rebellious ● nmf rebel. ~'ione nf rebellion

'ribes nm inv (rosso) redcurrant; (nero) blackcurrant

ribol'lire vi (fermentare) ferment; fig seethe

ri'brezzo nm disgust; far ~ a disgust

rica'dere vi fall back; (nel peccato ecc) lapse; (pendere) hang [down]; ~ su (riversarsi) fall on. rica'duta nf relapse

rical'care vt trace

rical'citrante a recalcitrant

rica'ma|re vt embroider. ~to a embroidered

ri'cambi nmpl spare parts

ricambi'are vt return; reciprocate (sentimento); ~ qcsa a qcno repay sb for sth. ri'cambio nm replacement; Biol metabolism; **pezzo di ricambio** spare [part]

ri'camo *nm* embroidery

ricapito'la|re *vt* sum up. ~zi'one *nf* summary, recap *fam*

ri'carica *nf* (di sveglia) rewinding

ricari'care *vt* reload (macchina fotografica, fucile, camion); recharge (batteria); Comput reboot

ricat'ta|re *vt* blackmail. ~'tore, ~'trice *nmf* blackmailer. ri'catto *nm* blackmail

rica'va|re *vt* get; (ottenere) obtain; (dedurre) draw. ~to *nm* proceeds *pl*. ri'cavo *nm* proceeds *pl*

'ricca *a* rich woman. ~'mente *adv* lavishly

ric'chezza *nf* wealth; *fig* richness; **ricchezze** *pl* riches

'riccio *a* curly ● *nm* curl; (animale) hedgehog. ~ **di mare** sea-urchin. ~lo *nm* curl. ~'luto *a* curly. ricci'uto *a* (barba) curly

'ricco *a* rich ● *nm* rich man

ri'cerca *nf* search; (indagine) investigation; (scientifica) research; Sch project

ricer'ca|re *vt* search for; (fare ricerche su) research. ~ta *nf* wanted woman. ~'tezza *nf* refinement. ~to *a* sought-after; (raffinato) refined; (affettato) affected ● *nm* (polizia) wanted man

ricetrasmit'tente *nf* transceiver

ri'cetta *nf* Med prescription; Culin recipe

ricet'tacolo *nm* receptacle

ricet'tario *nm* (di cucina) recipe book

ricetta'tore, -'trice *nmf* fence, receiver of stolen goods. ~zi'one *nf* receiving [stolen goods]

rice'vente *a* (apparecchio, stazione) receiving ● *nmf* receiver

ri'cev|ere *vt* receive; (dare il benvenuto) welcome; (di albergo) accommodate. ~i'mento *nm* receiving; (accoglienza) welcome; (trattenimento) reception

ricevi'tor|e *nm* receiver. ~ia *nf* ~ia del lotto agency authorized to sell lottery tickets

rice'vuta *nf* receipt. ~ fiscale tax receipt

ricezi'one *nf* Radio, TV reception

richia'mare *vt* (al telefono) call back; (far tornare) recall; (rimproverare) rebuke; (attirare) draw; ~ alla mente call to mind. richi'amo *nm* recall; (attrazione) call

richi'edere *vt* ask for; (di nuovo) ask again for; ~ a qcno di fare qcsa ask o request sb to do sth. richi'esta *nf* request; Comm demand

ri'chiud|ere *vt* shut again, close again. ~si *vr* (ferita:) heal

rici'claggio *nm* recycling

rici'cla|re *vt* recycle. ~si *vr* retrain; (cambiare lavoro) change one's line of work

'ricino *nm* olio di ~ castor oil

ricogni'zi'one *nf* Mil reconnaissance

ri'colmo *a* full

ricominci'are *vt/i* start again

ricompa'rire *vi* reappear

ricom'pen|sa *nf* reward. ~'sare *vt* reward

ricom'por|re *vt* (riscrivere) rewrite; (ricostruire) reform; Typ reset. ~si *vr* regain one's composure

riconcili'a|re *vt* reconcile. ~rsi *vr* be reconciled. ~zi'one *nf* reconciliation

ricono'scen|te *a* grateful. ~za *nf* gratitude

rico'nosc|ere *vt* recognize; (ammettere) acknowledge. ~i'mento *nm* recognition; (ammissione) acknowledgement; (per la polizia) identification. ~i'uto *a* recognized

riconqui'stare *vt* Mil retake, reconquer

riconside'rare *vt* rethink

rico'prire *vt* recover; (rivestire) coat; (di insulti) shower (di with); hold (carica)

ricor'dar|e *vt* remember; (richiamare alla memoria) recall; (far ricordare) remind; (rassomigliare) look like. ~si *vr* ~si [di] remember. ri'cordo *nm* memory; (oggetto) memento; (di viaggio) souvenir; **ricordi** *pl* (memorie) memoirs

ricor'ren|te *a* recurrent. ~za *nf* recurrence; (anniversario) anniversary

ri'correre *vi* recur; (accadere) occur; (data:) fall; ~ a have recourse to; (rivolgersi a) turn to. ri'corso *pp di* ricorrere ● *nm* recourse; Jur appeal

ricostitu'ente *nm* tonic

ricostitu'ire *vt* re-establish

ricostru'ire *vt* reconstruct. ~zi'one *nf* reconstruction

ricove'ra|re *vt* give shelter to; ~re in ospedale admit to hospital, hospitalize. ~to, -a *nmf* hospital patient. ri'covero *nm* shelter; (ospizio) home

ricre'a|re *vt* re-create; (ristorare) restore. ~rsi *vr* amuse oneself. ~'tivo *a* recreational. ~zi'one nf recreation; Sch break

ri'credersi vr change one's mind

ricupe'rare vt recover; rehabilitate ⟨tossicodipendente⟩; ~ il tempo perduto make up for lost time. ri'cupero nm recovery; (di tossicodipendente) rehabilitation; (salvataggio) rescue; [minuti nmpl di] ricupero injury time

ri'curvo a bent

ridacchi'are vi giggle

ri'dare vt give back, return

ri'dente a (piacevole) pleasant

'ridere vi laugh; ~ di (deridere) laugh at

ri'detto pp di ridire

ridicoliz'zare vt ridicule. ri'dicolo a ridiculous

ridimensio'nare vt reshape; fig see in the right perspective

ri'dire vt repeat; (criticare) find fault with; trova sempre da ~ he's always finding fault

ridon'dante a redundant

ri'dotto pp di ridurre ● nm Theat foyer ● a reduced

ri'du|rre vt reduce. ~rsi vr diminish. ~rsi a be reduced to. ~t'tivo a reductive. ~zi'one nf reduction; (per cinema, teatro) adaptation

rieducazi'one nf (di malato) rehabilitation

riem'pi|re vt fill [up]; fill in ⟨moduli ecc⟩. ~rsi vr fill [up]. ~'tivo a filling ● nm filler

rien'tranza nf recess

rien'trare vi go/come back in; (tornare) return; (piegare indentro) recede; ~ in (far parte) fall within. ri'entro nm return; (di astronave) re-entry

riepilo'gare vt recapitulate. rie'pilogo nm roundup

riesami'nare vt reappraise

ri'essere vi ci risiamo! here we go again!

riesu'mare vt exhume

rievo'ca|re vt (commemorare) commemorate. ~zi'one nf (commemorazione) commemoration

rifaci'mento nm remake

ri'fa|re vt do again; (creare) make again; (riparare) repair; (imitare) imitate; make ⟨letto⟩. ~rsi vr (rimettersi) recover; (vendicarsi) get even; ~rsi una vita/carriera make a new life/career for oneself; ~rsi il trucco touch up

one's makeup; ~rsi di make up for. ~tto pp di rifare

riferi'mento nm reference

rife'ri|re vt report; ~e a attribute to ● vi make a report. ~si vr ~si a refer to

rifi'lare vt (tagliare a filo) trim; (fam: affibbiare) saddle

rifi'ni|re vt finish off. ~'tura nf finish

rifio'rire vi blossom again; fig flourish again

rifiu'tare vt refuse. rifi'uto nm refusal; rifiuti pl (immondizie) rubbish. rifiuti pl urbani urban waste

riflessi'one nf reflection; (osservazione) remark. rifles'sivo a thoughtful; Gram reflexive

ri'flesso pp di riflettere ● nm (luce) reflection; Med reflex; per ~ indirectly

ri'flett|ere vt reflect ● vi think. ~si vr be reflected

riflet'tore nm reflector; (proiettore) searchlight

ri'flusso nm ebb

rifocil'lar|e vt restore. ~si vr liter, hum take some refreshment

ri'fondere vt (rimborsare) refund

ri'forma nf reform; Relig reformation; Mil exemption on medical grounds

rifor'ma|re vt reform; (migliorare) reform; Mil declare unfit for military service. ~to a ⟨chiesa⟩ Reformed. ~'tore, ~'trice nmf reformer. ~'torio nm reformatory. rifor'mista a reformist

riforni'mento nm supply; (scorta) stock; (di combustibile) refuelling; stazione f di ~ petrol station

rifor'nir|e vt ~e di provide with. ~si vr restock, stock up (di with)

ri'fra|ngere vt refract. ~tto pp di rifrangere. ~zi'one nf refraction

rifug'gire vi ~ da fig shun

rifugi'a|rsi vr take refuge. ~to, -a nmf refugee

ri'fugio nm shelter; (nascondiglio) hideaway

'riga nf line; (fila) row; (striscia) stripe; (scriminatura) parting; (regolo) rule; a righe (stoffa) striped; (quaderno) ruled; mettersi in ~ line up

ri'gagnolo nm rivulet

ri'gare vt rule (foglio) ● vi ~ dritto behave well

rigatti'ere nm junk dealer

rigene'rare vt regenerate

riget'tare vt (gettare indietro) throw back; (respingere) reject; (vomitare) throw up. ri'getto nm rejection

ri'ghello nm ruler

rigid|a'mente adv rigidly. **~ità** nf rigidity; (di clima) severity; (severità) strictness. **'rigido** a rigid; (freddo) severe; (severo) strict

rigi'rar|e vt turn again; (ripercorrere) go round; fig twist (argomentazione) ● vi walk about. **~si** vr turn round; (nel letto) turn over. **ri'giro** nm (imbroglio) trick

'rigo nm line; Mus staff

ri'gogli|o nm bloom. **~'oso** a luxuriant

ri'gonfio a swollen

ri'gore nm rigours pl; **a ~** strictly speaking; **calcio di ~** penalty [kick]; **area di ~** penalty area; **essere di ~** be compulsory

rigo'rosa'mente adv (giudicare) severely. **~'roso** a (severo) strict; (scrupoloso) rigorous.

riguada'gnare vt regain (quota, velocità)

riguar'dar|e vt look at again; (considerare) regard; (concernere) concern; **per quanto riguarda** with regard to. **~si** vr take care of oneself. **rigu'ardo** nm care; (considerazione) consideration; **nei riguardi di** towards; **riguardo a** with regard to

ri'gurgito nm regurgitation

rilanci'are vt throw back (palla); (di nuovo) throw again; increase (offerta); revive (moda); relaunch (prodotto) ● vi (a carte) raise the stakes

rilasci'ar|e vt (concedere) grant; (liberare) release; issue (documento). **~si** vr relax. **ri'lascio** nm release; (di documento) issue

rilassa'mento nm (relax) relaxation

rilas'sa|re vt, **~rsi** vr relax. **~to** a (ambiente) relaxed

rile'ga|re vt bind (libro). **~to** a bound. **~'tura** nf binding

ri'leggere vt reread

ri'lento: a ~ adv slowly

rileva'mento nm survey; Comm buyout

rile'vante a considerable

rile'va|re vt (trarre) get; (mettere in evidenza) point out; (notare) notice; (topografia) survey; Comm take over; Mil relieve. **~zi'one** nf (statistica) survey

rili'evo nm relief; Geog elevation; (topografia) survey; (importanza) importance; (osservazione) remark; **mettere in ~** qcsa point sth out

rilut'tan|te a reluctant. **~za** nf reluctance

'rima nf rhyme; **far ~ con** qcsa rhyme with sth

riman'dare vt (posporre) postpone; (mandare indietro) send back; (mandare di nuovo) send again; (far ridare un esame) make resit an examination. **ri'mando** nm return; (in un libro) cross-reference

rima'nen|te a remaining ● nm remainder. **~za** nf remainder; **~ze** pl remnants

rima'nere vi stay, remain; (essere d'avanzo) be left; (venirsi a trovare) be; (restare stupito) be astonished; (restare d'accordo) agree

rimar'chevole a remarkable

ri'mare vt/i rhyme

rimargi'nar|e vt, **~si** vr heal

ri'masto pp di **rimanere**

rima'sugli nmpl (di cibo) leftovers

rimbal'zare vi rebound; (proiettile:) ricochet; **far ~** bounce. **rim'balzo** nm rebound; (di proiettile) ricochet

rimbam'bi|re vi be in one's dotage ● vt stun. **~to** a in one's dotage

rimboc'care vt turn up; roll up (maniche); tuck in (coperte)

rimbom'bare vi resound

rimbor'sare vt reimburse, repay. **rim'borso** nm reimbursement, repayment. **rimborso spese** reimbursement of expenses

rimedi'are vi **~ a** remedy; make up for (errore); (procurare) scrape up. **ri'medio** nm remedy

rimesco'lare vt mix [up]; shuffle (carte); (rivangare) rake up

ri'messa nf (locale per veicoli) garage; (per aerei) hangar; (per autobus) depot; (di denaro) remittance; (di merci) consignment

ri'messo pp di **rimettere**

ri'metter|e vt (a posto) put back; (restituire) return; (affidare) entrust; (perdonare) remit; (rimandare) put off; (vomitare) bring up; **~ci** (fam: perdere) lose [out]. **~si** vr (ristabilirsi) recover; (tempo:) clear up; **~si a** start again

'rimmel® nm inv mascara

rimoder'nare vt modernize

rimon'tare vt (risalire) go up; Mech reassemble ● vi remount; **~ a** (risalire) go back to

rimorchi'ar|e vt tow; fam pick up (ragazza). **~'tore** nm tug[boat].

ri'morchio nm tow; (veicolo) trailer

ri'morso nm remorse

rimo'stranza nf complaint

rimozi'one nf removal; (da un incarico) dismissal. ~ forzata illegally parked vehicles removed at owner's expense

rim'pasto nm Pol reshuffle

rimpatri'are vt/i repatriate. rim'patrio nm repatriation

rim'pian|gere vt regret. ~to pp di rimpiangere ●nm regret

rimpiaz'zare vt replace

rimpiccio'lire vi become smaller

rimpinz'ar|e vt ~e di stuff with. ~si vr stuff oneself

improve'rare vt reproach; ~ qcsa a qcno reproach sb for sth. rim'provero nm reproach

rimugi'nare vt rummage; fig ~ su brood over

rimune'ra|re vt remunerate. ~'tivo a remunerative. ~zi'one nf remuneration

ri'muovere vt remove

ri'nascere vi be reborn, be born again

rinascimen'tale a Renaissance. Rinasci'mento nm Renaissance

ri'nascita nf rebirth

rincal'zare vt (sostenere) support; (rimboccare) tuck in. rin'calzo nm support; rincalzi pl Mil reserves

rincantucci'arsi vr hide oneself away in a corner

rinca'rare vt increase the price of ●vi become more expensive. rin'caro nm price increase

rinca'sare vi return home

rinchi'uder|e vt shut up. ~si vr shut oneself up

rin'correre vt run after

rin'cors|a nf run-up. ~o pp di rincorrere

rin'cresc|ere vi mi rincresce di non... I'm sorry o I regret that I can't...; se non ti ~e if you don't mind. ~i'mento nm regret. ~i'uto pp di rincrescere

rincreti'nire vi be stupid

rincu'lare vi (arma:) recoil; (cavallo:) shy. rin'culo nm recoil

rincuo'rar|e vt encourage. ~si vr take heart

rinfacci'are vt ~ qcsa a qcno throw sth in sb's face

rinfor'zar|e vt strengthen; (rendere più saldo) reinforce. ~si vr become stronger. rin'forzo nm reinforcement; fig support

rinfran'care vt reassure

rinfre'scante a cooling

rinfre'scar|e vt cool; (rinnovare) freshen up ●vi get cooler. ~si vr freshen [oneself] up. rin'fresco nm light refreshment; (ricevimento) party

rin'fusa nf alla ~ at random

ringhi'are vi snarl

ringhi'era nf railing; (di scala) banisters pl

ringiova'nire vt rejuvenate ⟨pelle, persona⟩; ⟨vestito:⟩ make look younger ●vi become young again; (sembrare) look young again

ringrazia'mento nm thanks pl. ~'are vt thank

rinne'ga|re vt disown. ~to, -a nmf renegade

rinnova'mento nm renewal; (di edifici) renovation

rinno'var|e vt renew; renovate ⟨edifici⟩. ~si vr be renewed; (ripetersi) recur, happen again. rin'novo nm renewal

rinoce'ronte nm rhinoceros

rino'mato a renowned

rinsal'dare vt consolidate

rinsa'vire vi come to one's senses

rinsec'chi|re vi shrivel up. ~to a shrivelled up

rinta'narsi vr hide oneself away; ⟨animale:⟩ retreat into its den

rintoc'care vi ⟨campana:⟩ toll; ⟨orologio:⟩ strike. rin'tocco nm toll; (di orologio) stroke

rinton'ti|re vt anche fig stun. ~to a (stordito) dazed

rintracci'are vt trace

rintro'nare vt stun ● vi boom

ri'nuncia nf renunciation

rinunci'a|re vi ~re a renounce, give up. ~'tario a defeatist

ri'nunzia, rinunzi'are = rinuncia, rinunciare

rinveni'mento nm (di reperti) discovery; (di refurtiva) recovery. rinve'nire vt find ● vi (riprendere i sensi) come round; (ridiventare fresco) revive

rinvi'are vt put off; (mandare indietro) return; (in libro) refer; ~ a giudizio indict

rin'vio nm Sport goal kick; (in libro) cross-reference; (di appuntamento) postponement; (di merce) return

rio'nale a local. ri'one nm district

riordi'nare vt tidy [up]; (ordinare di

nuovo) reorder; (*riorganizzare*) reorganize

riorganiz'zare *vt* reorganize

ripa'gare *vt* repay

ripa'ra|re *vt* (*proteggere*) shelter, protect; (*aggiustare*) repair; (*porre rimedio*) remedy ●*vi* ~re a make up for. ~rsi *vr* take shelter. ~to a (*luogo*) sheltered. ~zi'one *nf* repair; *fig* reparation. ri'paro *nm* shelter; (*rimedio*) remedy

ripar'ti|re *vt* (*dividere*) divide ●*vi* leave again. ~zi'one *nf* division

ripas'sa|re *vt* recross; (*rivedere*) revise ●*vi* pass again. ~ta *nf* (*di vernice*) second coat. ri'passo *nm* (*di lezione*) revision

ripensa'mento *nm* second thoughts *pl*

ripen'sare *vi* (*cambiare idea*) change one's mind; ~ a think of; **ripensaci!** think again!

riper'correre *vt* (*con la memoria*) go back over

riper'cosso *pp di* **ripercuotere**

ripercu'oter|e *vt* strike again. ~si *vr* (*suono:*) reverberate; ~si su (*fig: avere conseguenze*) impact on. **ripercussi'one** *nf* repercussion

ripe'scare *vt* fish out (*oggetti*)

ripe'tente *nmf* student repeating a year

ri'pet|ere *vt* repeat. ~ersi *vr* (*evento:*) recur. ~izi'one *nf* repetition; (*di lezione*) revision; (*lezione privata*) private lesson. ~uta'mente *adv* repeatedly

ri'piano *nm* (*di scaffale*) shelf; (*terreno pianeggiante*) terrace

ri'picc|a *nf* fare qcsa per ~a do sth out of spite. ~o *nm* spite

'ripido *a* steep

ripie'gar|e *vt* refold; (*abbassare*) lower ●*vi* (*indietreggiare*) retreat. ~si *vr* bend; (*sedile:*) fold. **ripi'ego** *nm* expedient; (*via d'uscita*) way out

ripi'eno *a* full; *Culin* stuffed ●*nm* filling; *Culin* stuffing

ripopo'lar|e *vt* repopulate. ~si *vr* be repopulated

ri'porre *vt* put back; (*mettere da parte*) put away; (*collocare*) place; repeat (*domanda*)

ripor'tar|e *vt* (*restituire*) bring/take back; (*riferire*) report; (*subire*) suffer; *Math* carry; win (*vittoria*); transfer (*disegno*). ~si *vr* go back; (*riferirsi*) refer. **ri'porto** *nm* cane da riporto gun dog

ripo'sante *a* (*colore*) restful, soothing

ripo'sa|re *vi* rest ●*vt* put back. ~rsi *vr* rest. ~to a (*mente*) fresh. **ri'poso** *nm* rest; **andare a riposo** retire; **riposo!** *Mil* at ease!; **giorno di riposo** day off

ripo'stiglio *nm* cupboard

ri'posto *pp di* **riporre**

ri'prender|e *vt* take again; (*prendere indietro*) take back; (*riconquistare*) recapture; (*ricuperare*) recover; (*ricominciare*) resume; (*rimproverare*) reprimand; take in (*cucitura*); *Cinema* shoot. ~si *vr* recover; (*correggersi*) correct oneself

ri'presa *nf* resumption; (*ricupero*) recovery; *Theat* revival; *Cinema* shot; *Auto* acceleration; *Mus* repeat. ~ aerea bird's-eye view

ripresen'tar|e *vt* resubmit (*domanda, certificato*). ~si *vr* (*a ufficio*) go/come back again; (*come candidato*) stand o run again; (*occasione:*) arise again

ri'preso *pp di* **riprendere**

ripristi'nare *vt* restore

ripro'dotto *pp di* **riprodurre**

ripro'du|rre *vt*, ~rsi *vr* reproduce. ~t'tivo *a* reproductive. ~zi'one *nf* reproduction

ripro'mettersi *vr* (*intendere*) intend

ri'prova *nf* confirmation

ripudi'are *vt* repudiate

ripu'gnan|te *a* repugnant. ~za *nf* disgust. **ripu'gnare** *vi* ripugnare a disgust

ripu'li|re *vt* clean [up]; *fig* polish. ~ta *nf* darsi una ~ta have a wash and brushup

ripuls|i'one *nf* repulsion. ~'ivo *a* repulsive

ri'quadro *nm* square; (*pannello*) panel

ri'sacca *nf* undertow

ri'saia *nf* rice field, paddy field

risa'lire *vt* go back up ●*vi* ~ a (*nel tempo*) go back to; (*essere datato a*) date back to, go back to

risal'tare *vi* (*emergere*) stand out. **ri'salto** *nm* prominence; (*rilievo*) relief

risa'nare *vt* heal; (*bonificare*) reclaim

risa'puto *a* well-known

risarci'mento *nm* compensation. **risar'cire** *vt* indemnify

ri'sata *nf* laugh

riscalda'mento *nm* heating. ~ autonomo central heating (*for one apartment*)

riscal'dar|e *vt* heat; warm (*persona*). ~si *vr* warm up

riscat'tar|e *vt* ransom. ~si *vr* redeem

oneself. **ri'scatto** nm ransom; (morale) redemption

rischia'rar|e vt light up; brighten (colore). **~si** vr light up; (cielo:) clear up

rischi'are vt risk ●vi run the risk. **'rischio** nm risk. **~'oso** a risky

risciac'quare vt rinse. **risci'acquo** nm rinse

riscon'trare vt (confrontare) compare; (verificare) check; (rilevare) find. **ri'scontro** nm comparison; check; (Comm: risposta) reply

ri'scossa nf revolt; (riconquista) recovery

riscossi'one nf collection

ri'scosso pp di riscuotere

riscu'oter|e vt shake; (percepire) draw; (ottenere) gain; cash (assegno). **~si** vr rouse oneself

risen'ti|re vt hear again; (provare) feel ●vi **~re** di feel the effect of. **~rsi** vr (offendersi) take offence. **~to** a resentful

ri'serbo nm reserve; **mantenere il ~** remain tight-lipped

ri'serva nf reserve; (di caccia, pesca) preserve; Sport substitute, reserve. **~ di caccia** game reserve. **~ indiana** Indian reservation. **~ naturale** wildlife reserve

riser'va|re vt reserve; (prenotare) book; (per occasione) keep. **~rsi** vr (ripromettersi) plan for oneself (cambiamento). **~'tezza** nf reserve. **~to** a reserved

ri'siedere vi **~ a** reside in

'riso[1] pp di ridere ●nm (pl nf risa) laughter; (singolo) laugh. **~'lino** nm giggle

'riso[2] nm (cereale) rice

ri'solto pp di risolvere

risolu'tezza nf determination. **riso'luto** a resolute, determined. **~zi'one** nf resolution

ri'solver|e vt resolve; Math solve. **~si** vr (decidersi) decide; **~si in** turn into

riso'na|nza nf resonance; **aver ~nza** fig arouse great interest. **~re** vi resound; (rimbombare) echo

ri'sorgere vi rise again

risorgi'mento nm revival; (storico) Risorgimento

ri'sorsa nf resource; (espediente) resort

ri'sorto pp di risorgere

ri'sotto nm risotto

ri'sparmi nmpl (soldi) savings

risparmi'a|re vt save; (salvare) spare. **~'tore, ~'trice** nmf saver **ri'sparmio** nm saving

rispecchi'are vt reflect

rispet'tabil|e a respectable. **~ità** nf respectability

rispet'tare vt respect; **farsi ~** command respect

rispet'tivo a respective

ri'spetto nm respect; **~ a** as regards; (in paragone a) compared to

rispet|tosa'mente adv respectfully. **~'toso** a respectful

risplen'dente a shining. **ri'splendere** vi shine

rispon'den|te a **~te** a in keeping with. **~za** nf correspondence

ri'spondere vi answer; (rimbeccare) answer back; (obbedire) respond; **~ a** reply to; **~ di** (rendersi responsabile) answer for

ri'spost|a nf answer, reply; (reazione) response. **~o** pp di rispondere

'rissa nf brawl. **ris'soso** a pugnacious

ristabi'li|re vt re-establish. **~si** vr (in salute) recover

rista'gnare vi stagnate; (sangue:) coagulate. **ri'stagno** nm stagnation

ri'stampa nf reprint; (azione) reprinting. **ristam'pare** vt reprint

risto'rante nm restaurant

risto'ra|re vt refresh. **~rsi** vr liter take some refreshment; (riposarsi) take a rest. **~tore, ~'trice** nmf (proprietario di ristorante) restaurateur; (fornitore) caterer ●a refreshing. **ri'storo** nm refreshment; (sollievo) relief

ristret'tezza nf narrowness; (povertà) poverty; **vivere in ristrettezze** live in straitened circumstances

ri'stretto pp di restringere ●a narrow; (condensato) condensed; (limitato) restricted; **di idee ristrette** narrow-minded

ristruttu'rare vt restructure, reorganize (ditta); refurbish (casa)

risucchi'are vt suck in. **ri'succhio** nm whirlpool; (di corrente) undertow

risul'ta|re vi result; (riuscire) turn out. **~to** nm result

risuo'nare vi (grida, parola:) echo; Phys resonate

risurrezi'one nf resurrection

risusci'tare vt resuscitate; fig revive ●vi return to life

risvegli'ar|e vt reawaken (interesse). **~si** vr wake up; (natura:) awake; (desiderio:) be aroused. **ri'sveglio** nm waking up; (dell'interesse) revival; (del desiderio) arousal ri'svolto nm (di giacca) lapel; (di pantaloni) turn-up, cuff Am; (di manica) cuff; (di tasca) flap; (di libro) inside flap

ritagli'are vt cut out. ri'taglio nm cutting; (di stoffa) scrap

ritar'da|re vi be late; ⟨orologio:⟩ be slow ● vt delay; slow down ⟨progresso⟩; (differire) postpone. ~'tario, -a nmf late-comer. ~to a Psych retarded

ri'tardo nm delay; essere in ~ be late; ⟨volo:⟩ be delayed

ri'tegno nm reserve

rite'ner|e vt retain; deduct ⟨somma⟩; (credere) believe. ~uta nf (sul salario) deduction

riti'ra|re vt throw back ⟨palla⟩; (prelevare) withdraw; (riscuotere) draw; collect ⟨pacco⟩. ~rsi vr withdraw; ⟨stoffa:⟩ shrink; (da attività) retire; ⟨marea:⟩ recede. ~ta nf retreat; (WC) toilet. ri'tiro nm withdrawal; Relig retreat; (da attività) retirement. ritiro bagagli baggage reclaim

'ritmo nm rhythm

'rito nm rite; di ~ customary

ritoc'care vt (correggere) touch up. ri'tocco nm retouch

ritor'nare vi return; (andare/venire indietro) go/come back; (ricorrere) recur; (ridiventare) become again

ritor'nello nm refrain

ri'torno nm return

ritorsi'one nf retaliation

ri'trarre vt (ritirare) withdraw; (distogliere) turn away; (rappresentare) portray

ritrat'ta|re vt deal with again; retract ⟨dichiarazione⟩. ~zi'one nf withdrawal, retraction

ritrat'tista nmf portrait painter. ri'tratto pp di ritrarre ● nm portrait

ritro'sia nf shyness. ri'troso a backward; (timido) shy; a ritroso backwards; ritroso a reluctant to

ritrova'mento nm (azione) finding

ritro'va|re vt find [again]; regain ⟨salute⟩. ~rsi vr meet; (di nuovo) meet again; (capitare) find oneself; (raccapezzarsi) see one's way. ~to nm discovery. ri'trovo nm meeting-place; (notturno) night-club

'ritto a upright; (diritto) straight

ritu'ale a & nm ritual

riunifi'ca|re vt reunify. ~rsi vr be reunited. ~zi'one nf reunification

riuni'one nf meeting; (fra amici) reunion

riu'nir|e vt (unire) join together; (radunare) gather. ~si vr be reunited; (adunarsi) meet

riusc'i|re vi (aver successo) succeed; (in matematica ecc) be good (in at); (aver esito) turn out; le è riuscito simpatico she found him likeable. ~ta nf (esito) result; (successo) success

'riva nf (di mare, lago) shore; (di fiume) bank

ri'val|e nmf rival. ~ità nf inv rivalry

rivalutazi'one nf revaluation

rivan'gare vt dig up again

rive'de|re vt see again; revise ⟨lezione⟩; (verificare) check

rive'la|re vt reveal. ~rsi vr (dimostrarsi) turn out. ~'tore a revealing ●nm Techn detector. ~zi'one nf revelation

ri'vendere vt resell

rivendi'ca|re vt claim. ~zi'one nf claim

ri'vendi|ta nf (negozio) shop. ~'tore, ~'trice nmf retailer. ~'tore autorizzato authorized dealer

ri'verbero nm reverberation; (bagliore) glare

rive'renza nf reverence; (inchino) curtsy; (di uomo) bow

rive'rire vt respect; (ossequiare) pay one's respects to

river'sar|e vt pour. ~si vr ⟨fiume:⟩ flow

river'sibile a reversible

rivesti'mento nm covering

rive'stir|e vt (rifornire di abiti) clothe; (ricoprire) cover; (internamente) line; hold ⟨carica⟩. ~rsi vr get dressed again; (per una festa) dress up

rivi'era nf coast; la ~ ligure the Italian Riviera

ri'vincita nf Sport return match; (vendetta) revenge

rivis'suto pp di rivivere

ri'vista nf review; (pubblicazione) magazine; Theat revue; passare in ~ review

ri'vivere vi come to life again; (riprendere le forze) revive ● vt relive

ri'volger|e vt turn; (indirizzare) address; ~e da (distogliere) turn away from. ~si vr turn round; ~si a (indirizzarsi) turn to

ri'volta nf revolt

rivol'tante a disgusting

rivol'tar|e vt turn [over]; (mettendo l'interno verso l'esterno) turn inside out; (sconvolgere) upset. ~si vr (ribellarsi) revolt

rivol'tella nf revolver

ri'volto pp di **rivolgere**

rivoluzio'nar|e vt revolutionize. **~io, -a** a & nmf revolutionary. **rivoluzi'one** nf revolution; (fig: disordine) chaos

riz'zar|e vt raise; (innalzare) erect; prick up (orecchie). **~si** vr stand up; (capelli:) stand on end; (orecchie:) prick up

'roba nf stuff; (personale) belongings pl, stuff; (faccenda) thing; (sl: droga) drugs pl; **~ da matti!** absolute madness!. **~ da mangiare** food, things to eat

ro'baccia nf rubbish

ro'bot nm inv robot. **~iz'zato** a robotic

robu'stezza nf sturdiness, robustness; (forza) strength. **ro'busto** a sturdy, robust; (forte) strong

'rocca nf fortress. **~'forte** nf stronghold

roc'chetto nm reel

'roccia nf rock

ro'da|ggio nm running in. **~re** vt run in

'roder|e vt gnaw; (corrodere) corrode. **~si** vr **~si da** (logorarsi) be consumed with. **rodi'tore** nm rodent

rodo'dendro nm rhododendron

'rogna nf scabies sg; fig nuisance

ro'gnone nm Culin kidney

'rogo nm (supplizio) stake; (per cadaveri) pyre

'Roma nf Rome

Roma'nia nf Romania

ro'manico a Romanesque

ro'mano, -a a & nmf Roman

romanti'cismo nm romanticism. **ro'mantico** a romantic

ro'man|za nf romance. **~zato** a romanticized. **~zesco** a fictional; (stravagante) wild, unrealistic. **~zi'ere** nm novelist

ro'manzo a Romance **●** nm novel. **~ d'appendice** serial story. **~ giallo** thriller

'rombo nm rumble; Math rhombus; (pesce) turbot

'romper|e vt break; break off (relazione); **non ~e** [le scatole]! (fam: seccare) don't be a pain [in the neck]!. **~si** vr break; **~si una gamba** break one's leg

rompi'capo nm nuisance; (indovinello) puzzle

rompi'collo nm daredevil; **a ~** at breakneck speed

rompighi'accio nm ice-breaker

rompi'scatole nmf inv fam pain

'ronda nf rounds pl

ron'della nf washer

'rondine nf swallow

ron'done nm swift

ron'fare vi (russare) snore

ron'zare vi buzz; **~ attorno a qcno** fig hang about sb

ron'zino nm jade

ron'zio nm buzz

'rosa nf rose. **~ dei venti** wind rose **●** a & nm (colore) pink. **ro'saio** nm rosebush

ro'sario nm rosary

ro'sato a rosy **●** nm (vino) rosé

'roseo a pink

ro'seto nm rose garden

rosicchi'are vt nibble; (rodere) gnaw

rosma'rino nm rosemary

'roso pp di **rodere**

roso'lare vt brown

roso'lia nf German measles

ro'sone nm rosette; (apertura) rose-window

'rospo nm toad

ros'setto nm (per labbra) lipstick

'rosso a & nm red; **passare con il ~** jump a red light. **~ d'uovo** [egg] yolk. **ros'sore** nm redness; (della pelle) flush

rosticce'ria nf shop selling cooked meat and other prepared food

ro'tabile a **strada ~** carriageway

ro'taia nf rail; (solco) rut

ro'ta|re vt/i rotate. **~zi'one** nf rotation

rote'are vt/i roll

ro'tella nf small wheel; (di mobile) castor

roto'lar|e vt/i roll. **~si** vr roll [about]. **'rotolo** nm roll; **andare a rotoli** go to rack and ruin

rotondità nf (qualità) roundness; **~ pl** (curve femminili) curves. **ro'tondo, -a** a round **●** nf (spiazzo) terrace

ro'tore nm rotor

'rotta¹ nf Naut, Aeron course; **far ~ per** make course for; **fuori ~** off course

'rotta² nf **a ~ di collo** at breakneck speed; **essere in ~ con** be on bad terms with

rot'tame nm scrap; fig wreck

'rotto pp di **rompere** **●** a broken; (stracciato) torn

rot'tura nf break; **che ~ di scatole!** fam what a pain!

'rotula nf kneecap

rou'lette nf inv roulette

rou'lotte nf inv caravan, trailer Am

rou'tine nf inv routine; **di ~** (operazioni, controlli) routine

ro'vente a scorching

'rovere *nm* (*legno*) oak

rovesci'ar|e *vt* (*buttare a terra*) knock over; (*sottosopra*) turn upside down; (*rivoltare*) turn inside out; spill ⟨*liquido*⟩; overthrow ⟨*governo*⟩; reverse ⟨*situazione*⟩. ~si *vr* (*capovolgersi*) overturn; (*riversarsi*) pour. ro'vescio *a* (*contrario*) reverse; **alla rovescia** (*capovolto*) upside down; (*con l'interno all'esterno*) inside out ●*nm* reverse; (*nella maglia*) purl; (*di pioggia*) downpour; *Tennis* backhand

ro'vina *nf* ruin; (*crollo*) collapse

rovi'na|re *vt* ruin; (*guastare*) spoil ● *vi* crash. ~rsi *vr* be ruined. ~to *a* ⟨*oggetto*⟩ ruined. rovi'noso *a* ruinous

rovi'stare *vt* ransack

'rovo *nm* bramble

'rozzo *a* rough

R.R. *abbr* (*ricevuta di ritorno*) return receipt for registered mail

'ruba *nf* andare a ~ sell like hot cakes

ru'bare *vt* steal

rubi'netto *nm* tap, faucet *Am*

ru'bino *nm* ruby

ru'brica *nf* (*in giornale*) column; (*in programma televisivo*) TV report; (*quaderno con indice*) address book. ~ telefonica telephone and address book

'rude *a* rough

'rudere *nm* ruin

rudimen'tale *a* rudimentary. rudi'menti *nmpl* rudiments

ruffi'an|a *nf* procuress. ~o *nm* pimp; (*adulatore*) bootlicker

'ruga *nf* wrinkle

'ruggine *nf* rust; fare la ~ go rusty

rug'gi|re *vi* roar. ~to *nm* roar

rugi'ada *nf* dew

ru'goso *a* wrinkled

rul'lare *vi* roll; *Aeron* taxi

rul'lino *nm* film

rul'lio *nm* rolling; *Aeron* taxiing

'rullo *nm* roll; *Techn* roller

rum *nm inv* rum

ru'meno, -a *a* & *nmf* Romanian

rumi'nare *vt* ruminate

ru'mor|e *nm* noise; *fig* rumour. ~eggiare *vi* rumble. rumo'roso *a* noisy; (*sonoro*) loud

ru'olo *nm* roll; *Theat* role; di ~ on the staff

ru'ota *nf* wheel; andare a ~ libera free-wheel. ~ di scorta spare wheel

'rupe *nf* cliff

ru'rale *a* rural

ru'scello *nm* stream

'ruspa *nf* bulldozer

rus'sare *vi* snore

'Russ|ia *nf* Russia. r~o, -a *a* & *nmf* Russian; (*lingua*) Russian

'rustico *a* rural; ⟨*carattere*⟩ rough

rut'tare *vi* belch. 'rutto *nm* belch

ru'vido *a* coarse

ruzzo'l|are *vi* tumble down. ~one *nm* tumble; cadere ruzzoloni tumble down

Ss

'sabato *nm* Saturday

'sabbi|a *nf* sand. ~e *pl* mobili quicksand. ~'oso *a* sandy

sabo'ta|ggio *nm* sabotage. ~re *vt* sabotage. ~tore, ~trice *nmf* saboteur

'sacca *nf* bag. ~ da viaggio travelling-bag

sacca'rina *nf* saccharin

sac'cente *a* pretentious ●*nmf* know-all

saccheggi'a|re *vt* sack; *hum* raid ⟨*frigo*⟩. ~tore, ~trice *nmf* plunderer. sac'cheggio *nm* sack

sac'chetto *nm* bag

'sacco *nm* sack; *Anat* sac; mettere nel ~ *fig* swindle; un ~ (*moltissimo*) a lot; un ~ di (*gran quantità*) lots of. ~ a pelo sleeping-bag

sacer'do|te *nm* priest. ~zio *nm* priesthood

sacra'mento *nm* sacrament

sacrifi'ca|re *vt* sacrifice. ~rsi *vr* sacrifice oneself. ~to *a* (*non valorizzato*) wasted. sacri'ficio *nm* sacrifice

sacri'legio *nm* sacrilege. sa'crilego *a* sacrilegious

'sacro *a* sacred ●*nm Anat* sacrum

sacro'santo *a* sacrosanct

'**sadico, -a** a sadistic ●nmf sadist. sa'**dismo** nm sadism

sa'**etta** nf arrow

sa'**fari** nm inv safari

'**saga** nf saga

sa'**gace** a shrewd

sag'**gezza** nf wisdom

saggi'**are** vt test

'**saggio**[1] nm (scritto) essay; (prova) proof; (di metallo) assay; (campione) sample; (esempio) example

'**saggio**[2] a wise ●nm (persona) sage

sag'**gistica** nf non-fiction

Sagit'**tario** nm Astr Sagittarius

sa'**goma** nf shape; (profilo) outline; **che ~!** fam what a character!. sa-go'**mato** a shaped

'**sagra** nf festival

sagre'**stano** nm sacristan. ~'**stia** nf sacristy

'**sala** nf hall; (stanza) room; (salotto) living room. ~ **d'attesa** waiting room. ~ **da ballo** ballroom. ~ **d'imbarco** departure lounge. ~ **macchine** engine room. ~ **operatoria** operating theatre Br, operating room Am. ~ **parto** delivery room. ~ **da pranzo** dining room

sa'**lame** nm salami

sala'**moia** nf brine

sa'**lare** vt salt

sa'**lario** nm wages pl

sa'**lasso** nm **essere un ~** fig cost a fortune

sala'**tini** nmpl savouries (eaten with aperitifs)

sa'**lato** a salty; (costoso) dear

sal'**ciccia** nf = **salsiccia**

sal'**dar|e** vt weld; set (osso); pay off (debito); settle (conto); **~e a stagno** solder. **~si** vr (Med: osso:) knit

salda'**trice** nf welder; (a stagno) soldering iron

salda'**tura** nf weld; (azione) welding; (di osso) knitting

'**saldo** a firm; (resistente) strong ●nm (di conto) settlement; (svendita) sale; Comm balance

'**sale** nm salt; **restare di ~** be struck dumb [with astonishment]. ~ **fine** table salt. ~ **grosso** cooking salt. **sali** pl **e tabacchi** tobacconist's shop

'**salice** nm willow. ~ **piangente** weeping willow

sali'**ente** a outstanding; **i punti salienti di un discorso** the main points of a speech

sali'**era** nf salt-cellar

sa'**lina** nf salt-works sg

sa'**li|re** vi go/come up; (levarsi) rise; (su treno ecc) get on; (in macchina) get in ● vt go/come up (scale). **~ta** nf climb; (aumento) rise; **in ~ta** uphill

sa'**liva** nf saliva

'**salma** nf corpse

'**salmo** nm psalm

sal'**mone** nm & a inv salmon

sa'**lone** nm hall; (salotto) living room; (di parrucchiere) salon. ~ **di bellezza** beauty parlour

salo'**pette** nf inv dungarees pl

salot'**tino** nm bower

sa'**lotto** nm drawing room; (soggiorno) sitting room; (mobili) [three-piece] suite; **fare ~** chat

sal'**pare** vt/i sail; **~ l'ancora** weigh anchor

'**salsa** nf sauce. ~ **di pomodoro** tomato sauce

sal'**sedine** nf saltiness

sal'**siccia** nf sausage

salsi'**era** nf sauce-boat

sal'**ta|re** vi jump; (venir via) come off; (balzare) leap; (esplodere) blow up; **~r fuori** spring from nowhere; (oggetto cercato:) turn up; **è ~to fuori che...** it emerged that...; **~re fuori con...** come out with...; **~re in aria** blow up; **~re in mente** spring to mind ● vt jump [over]; skip (pasti, lezioni); Culin sauté. **~to** a Culin sautéed

saltel'**lare** vi hop; (di gioia) skip

saltim'**banco** nm acrobat

'**salto** nm jump; (balzo) leap; (dislivello) drop; (fig: omissione, lacuna) gap; **fare un ~ da** (visitare) drop in on; **in un ~** fig in a jiffy. ~ **in alto** high jump. ~ **con l'asta** pole-vault. ~ **in lungo** long jump. ~ **pagina** Comput page down

saltuaria'**mente** adv occasionally. saltu'**ario** a desultory; **lavoro saltuario** casual work

sa'**lubre** a healthy

salume'**ria** nf ≈ delicatessen. sa'**lumi** nmpl cold cuts

salu'**tare** vt greet; (congedandosi) say goodbye to; (portare i saluti a) give one's regards to; Mil salute ● a healthy

sa'**lute** nf health; **~!** (dopo uno starnuto) bless you!; (a un brindisi) cheers!

sa'**luto** nm greeting; (di addio) goodbye; Mil salute; **saluti** pl (ossequi) regards

'**salva** nf salvo; **sparare a salve** fire blanks

salvada'naio *nm* money box
salva'gente *nm* lifebelt; (*a giubbotto*) life-jacket; (*ciambella*) rubber ring; (*spartitraffico*) traffic island
salvaguar'dare *vt* safeguard.
salvagu'ardia *nf* safeguard
sal'var|e *vt* save; (*proteggere*) protect. **~si** *vr* save oneself
salva'slip *nm inv* panty-liner
salva'taggio *nm* rescue; *Naut* salvage; *Comput* saving; **battello di ~taggio** lifeboat. **~ tore, ~ trice** *nmf* saviour
sal'vezza *nf* safety; *Relig* salvation
'salvia *nf* sage
salvi'etta *nf* serviette
'salvo *a* safe ● *prep* except [for] ● *conj* **~ che** (*a meno che*) unless; (*eccetto che*) except that
samari'tano, -a *a & nmf* Samaritan
sam'buco *nm* elder
san *nm* S**~ Francesco** Saint Francis
sa'nare *vt* heal
sana'torio *nm* sanatorium
san'cire *vt* sanction
san'dalo *nm* sandal; *Bot* sandalwood
'sangue *nm* blood; **al ~e** (*carne*) rare; **farsi cattivo ~e per** worry about; **occhi iniettati di ~e** bloodshot eyes. **~e freddo** composure; **a ~e freddo** in cold blood. **~'igno** *a* blood
sangui'naccio *nm* Culin black pudding
sangui'nante *a* bleeding
sangui'nar|e *vi* bleed. **~io** *a* bloodthirsty
sangui'noso *a* bloody
sangui'suga *nf* leech
sanità *nf* soundness; (*salute*) health. **~ mentale** sanity, mental health
sani'tario *a* sanitary; **Servizio S~** National Health Service
'sano *a* sound; (*salutare*) healthy; **~ di mente** sane; **~ come un pesce** as fit as a fiddle
San Sil'vestro *nm* New Year's Eve
santifi'care *vt* sanctify
'santo *a* holy; (*con nome proprio*) saint ● *nm* saint. **san'tone** *nm* guru. **santu'ario** *nm* sanctuary
sanzi'one *nf* sanction
sa'pere *vt* know; (*essere capace di*) be able to; (*venire a sapere*) hear; **saperla lunga** know a thing or two ● *vi ~ di* know about; (*aver sapore di*) taste of; (*aver odore di*) smell of; **saperci fare** have the know-how ● *nm* knowledge

sapi'en|te *a* wise; (*esperto*) expert ● *nm* (*uomo colto*) sage. **~za** *nf* wisdom
sa'pone *nm* soap. **~ da bucato** washing soap. **sapo'netta** *nf* bar of soap
sa'pore *nm* taste. **saporita'mente** *adv* (*dormire*) soundly. **sapo'rito** *a* tasty
sapu'tello, -a *a & nm sl* know-all, know-it-all *Am*
saraci'nesca *nf* roller shutter
sar'cas|mo *nm* sarcasm. **~tico** *a* sarcastic
Sar'degna *nf* Sardinia
sar'dina *nf* sardine
'sardo, -a *a & nmf* Sardinian
sar'donico *a* sardonic
'sarto, -a *nm* tailor ● *nf* dressmaker. **~'ria** *nf* tailor's; dressmaker's; (*arte*) couture
sas'sata *nf* blow with a stone; **prendere a sassate** stone. **'sasso** *nm* stone; (*ciottolo*) pebble
sassofo'nista *nmf* saxophonist. **sas'sofono** *nm* saxophone
sas'soso *a* stony
'Satana *nm* Satan. **sa'tanico** *a* satanic
sa'tellite *a inv & nm* satellite
sati'nato *a* glossy
'satira *nf* satire. **sa'tirico** *a* satirical
satu'ra|re *vt* saturate. **~zi'one** *nf* saturation. **'saturo** *a* saturated; (*pieno*) full
'sauna *nf* sauna
savoi'ardo *nm* (*biscotto*) sponge finger
sazi'ar|e *vt* satiate. **~si** *vr ~si di* fig grow tired of
sazietà *nf* **mangiare a ~** eat one's fill. **'sazio** *a* satiated
sbaciucchi'ar|e *vt* smother with kisses. **~si** *vr* kiss and cuddle
sbada'ta|ggine *nf* carelessness; **è stata una ~ggine** it was careless. **~'mente** *adv* carelessly. **sba'dato** *a* careless
sbadigli'are *vi* yawn. **sba'diglio** *nm* yawn
sba'far|e *vt* sponge. **~ta** *nf sl* nosh
'sbafo *nm* sponging; **a ~** (*gratis*) without paying
sbagli'ar|e *vi* make a mistake; (*aver torto*) be wrong ● *vt* make a mistake in; **~e strada** go the wrong way; **~e numero** get the number wrong; *Teleph* dial a wrong number. **~si** *vr* make a mistake. **'sbaglio** *nm* mistake; **per sbaglio** by mistake
sbal'l|are *vt* unpack; *fam* screw up (*conti*) ● *vi fam* go crazy. **~ato** *a* (*squilibrato*) unbalanced. **'sballo** *nm*

fam scream; (*per droga*) trip; **da sballo** *sl* terrific

sballot'tare *vt* toss about

sbalor'di|re *vt* stun ● *vi* be stunned. ~**tivo** *a* amazing. ~**to** *a* stunned

sbal'zare *vt* throw; (*da una carica*) dismiss ● *vi* bounce; (*saltare*) leap. '**sbalzo** *nm* bounce; (*sussulto*) jolt; (*di temperatura*) sudden change; **a sbalzi** in spurts; **a sbalzo** (*lavoro a rilievo*) embossed

sban'care *vt* bankrupt; ~ **il banco** break the bank

sbanda'mento *nm* Auto skid; Naut list; *fig* going off the rails

sban'da|re *vi* Auto skid; Naut list. ~**rsi** *vr* (*disperdersi*) disperse. ~**ta** *nf* skid; Naut list; **prendere una ~ta per** get a crush on. ~**to**, **-a** *a* mixed-up ● *nmf* mixed-up person

sbandie'rare *vt* wave; *fig* display

sbarac'care *vt/i* clear up

sbaragli'are *vt* rout. **sba'raglio** *nm* rout; **mettere allo sbaraglio** rout

sbaraz'zare *vt* clear. ~**si** *vr* ~**si di** get rid of

sbaraz'zino, **-a** *a* mischievous ● *nmf* scamp

sbar'bar|e *vt*, ~**si** *vr* shave

sbar'care *vt/i* disembark; ~ **il lunario** make ends meet. '**sbarco** *nm* landing; (*di merci*) unloading

'**sbarra** *nf* bar; (*di passaggio a livello*) barrier. ~**mento** *nm* barricade. **sbar'rare** *vt* bar; (*ostruire*) block; cross (*assegno*); (*spalancare*) open wide

sbatacchi'are *vt/i sl* bang, slam

'**sbatter|e** *vt* bang; slam, bang (*porta*); (*urtare*) knock; Culin beat; flap (*ali*); shake (*tappeto*) ● *vi* bang; (*porta:*) slam, bang. ~**si** *vr sl* rush around; ~**sene di** qcsa not give a damn about sth. **sbat'tuto** *a* tossed; Culin beaten; *fig* run down

sba'va|re *vi* dribble; (*colore:*) smear. ~'**tura** *nf* smear; **senza** ~**ture** *fig* faultless

sbelli'carsi *vr* ~ **dalle risa** split one's sides [with laughter]

'**sberla** *nf* slap

sbia'di|re *vt/i*, ~**rsi** *vr* fade. ~**to** *a* faded; *fig* colourless

sbian'car|e *vt/i*, ~**si** *vr* whiten

sbi'eco *a* slanting; **di** ~ on the slant; (*guardare*) sidelong; **guardare qcno di** ~ look askance at sb; **tagliare di** ~ cut on the bias

sbigot'ti|re *vt* dismay ● *vi*, ~**rsi** *vr* be dismayed. ~**to** *a* dismayed

sbilanci'ar|e *vt* unbalance ● *vi* (*perdere l'equilibrio*) overbalance. ~**si** *vr* lose one's balance

sbirci'a|re *vt* cast sidelong glances at. ~**ta** *nf* furtive glance. ~'**tina** *nf* **dare una** ~**tina a** sneak a glance at

sbizzar'rirsi *vr* satisfy one's whims

sbloc'care *vt* unblock; Mech release; decontrol (*prezzi*)

sboc'care *vi* ~ **in** (*fiume:*) flow into; (*strada:*) lead to; (*folla:*) pour into

sboc'cato *a* foul-mouthed

sbocci'are *vi* blossom

'**sbocco** *nm* flowing; (*foce*) mouth; Comm outlet

sbolo'gnare *vt fam* get rid of

'**sbornia** *nf* **prendere una** ~ get drunk

sbor'sare *vt* pay out

sbot'tare *vi* burst out

sbotto'nar|e *vt* unbutton. ~**si** *vr* (*fam: confidarsi*) open up; ~**si la camicia** unbutton one's shirt

bra'carsi *vr* put on something more comfortable; ~ **dalle risate** *fam* kill oneself laughing

sbracci'a|rsi *vr* wave one's arms. ~**to** *a* bare-armed; (*abito*) sleeveless

sbrai'tare *vi* bawl

sbra'nare *vt* tear to pieces

sbricio'lar|e *vt*, ~**si** *vr* crumble

sbri'ga|re *vt* expedite; (*occuparsi di*) attend to. ~**rsi** *vr* be quick. ~'**tivo** *a* quick

sbrindel'la|re *vt* tear to shreds. ~**to** *a* in rags

sbro'dol|are *vt* stain. ~**one** *nm* messy eater, dribbler

'**sbronz|a** *nf* **prendersi una** ~**a** get tight. **sbron'zarsi** *vr* get tight. ~**o** *a* (*ubriaco*) tight

sbuf'fare *vi* snort; (*per impazienza*) fume. '**sbuffo** *nm* puff

'**scabbia** *nf* scabies *sg*

sca'broso *a* rough; *fig* difficult; (*scena*) indecent

scacci'are *vt* chase away

'**scacc|o** *nm* check; ~**hi** *pl* (*gioco*) chess; (*pezzi*) chessmen; **dare** ~**o matto** checkmate; **a** ~**hi** (*tessuto*) checked. ~**hi'era** *nf* chess-board

sca'dente *a* shoddy

sca'denza *nf* (*di contratto*) expiry; Comm maturity; (*di progetto*) deadline; **a breve/lunga** ~**nza** short-/long-term.

~re *vi* expire; ⟨*valore:*⟩ decline; ⟨*debito:*⟩ be due. **sca'duto** *a* ⟨*biglietto*⟩ out-of-date

sca'fandro *nm* diving suit; ⟨*di astronauta*⟩ spacesuit

scaf'fale *nm* shelf; ⟨*libreria*⟩ bookshelf

'**scafo** *nm* hull

scagion'are *vt* exonerate

'**scaglia** *nf* scale; ⟨*di sapone*⟩ flake; ⟨*scheggia*⟩ chip

scagli'ar|e *vt* fling. ~**si** *vr* fling oneself; ~**si contro** *fig* rail against

scagli'o'nare *vt* space out. ~**one** *nm* group; **a** ~**oni** in groups. ~**one di reddito** tax bracket

'**scala** *nf* staircase; ⟨*portatile*⟩ ladder; ⟨*Mus, misura, fig*⟩ scale; **scale** *pl* stairs. ~ **mobile** escalator; ⟨*dei salari*⟩ cost of living index

sca'la|re *vt* climb; layer ⟨*capelli*⟩; ⟨*detrarre*⟩ deduct. ~**ta** *nf* climb; ⟨*dell'Everest ecc*⟩ ascent; **fare delle** ~**te** go climbing. ~'**tore**, ~'**trice** *nmf* climber

scalca'gnato *a* down at heel

scalci'are *vi* kick

scalci'nato *a* shabby

scalda'bagno *nm* water heater

scalda'muscoli *nm inv* leg-warmer

scal'dar|e *vt* heat. ~**si** *vr* warm up; ⟨*eccitarsi*⟩ get excited

scal'fi|re *vt* scratch. ~**t'tura** *nf* scratch

scali'nata *nf* flight of steps. **sca'lino** *nm* step; ⟨*di scala a pioli*⟩ rung

scalma'narsi *vr* get worked up

'**scalo** *nm* slipway; *Aeron, Naut* port of call; **fare** ~ a call at; *Aeron* land at

sca'lo|gna *nf* bad luck. ~'**gnato** *a* unlucky

scalop'pina *nf* escalope

scal'pello *nm* chisel

scalpi'tare *vi* paw the ground; *fig* champ at the bit

'**scalpo** *nm* scalp

scal'pore *nm* noise; **far** ~ *fig* cause a sensation

scal'trezza *nf* shrewdness. **scal'trir-si** *vr* get shrewder. '**scaltro** *a* shrewd

scal'zare *vt* bare the roots of ⟨*albero*⟩; *fig* undermine; ⟨*da una carica*⟩ oust

'**scalzo** *a* & *adv* barefoot

scambi'|are *vt* exchange; ~**are qcno per qualcun altro** mistake sb for somebody else. ~'**evole** *a* reciprocal

'**scambio** *nm* exchange; *Comm* trade; **libero** ~ free trade

scamosci'ato *a* suede

scampa'gnata *nf* trip to the country

scampa'nato *a* ⟨*gonna*⟩ flared

scampanel'lata *nf* [loud] ring

scam'pare *vt* save; ⟨*evitare*⟩ escape; **scamparla bella** have a lucky escape. '**scampo** *nm* escape

'**scampolo** *nm* remnant

scanala'tura *nf* groove

scandagli'are *vt* sound

scanda'listico *a* sensational

scandaliz'zare *vt* scandalize. ~**iz'zarsi** *vr* be scandalized

'**scanda|lo** *nm* scandal. ~'**loso** *a* ⟨*somma ecc*⟩ scandalous; ⟨*fortuna*⟩ outrageous

Scandi'navia *nf* Scandinavia. **scan'dinavo, -a** *a* & *nmf* Scandinavian

scan'dire *vt* scan ⟨*verso*⟩; pronounce clearly ⟨*parole*⟩

scan'nare *vt* slaughter

scanneriz'zare *vt Comput* scan

scansafa'tiche *nmf inv* lazybones *sg*

scan'sar|e *vt* shift; ⟨*evitare*⟩ avoid. ~**si** *vr* get out of the way

scansi'one *nf Comput* scanning

'**scanso** *nm* **a** ~ **di** in order to avoid; **a** ~ **di equivoci** to avoid any misunderstanding

scanti'nato *nm* basement

scanto'nare *vi* turn the corner; ⟨*svignarsela*⟩ sneak off

scanzo'nato *a* easy-going

scapacci'one *nm* smack

scape'strato *a* dissolute

'**scapito** *nm* loss; **a** ~ **di** to the detriment of

'**scapola** *nf* shoulder-blade

'**scapolo** *nm* bachelor

scappa'mento *nm Auto* exhaust

scap'pa|re *vi* escape; ⟨*andarsene*⟩ dash [off]; ⟨*sfuggire*⟩ slip; **mi** ~ **da ridere!** I want to burst out laughing; **mi** ~ **la pipì** I'm bursting, I need a pee. ~**ta** *nf* short visit. ~'**tella** *nf* escapade; ⟨*infedeltà*⟩ fling. ~'**toia** *nf* way out

scappel'lotto *nm* cuff

scara'bocchio *nm* scribble

scara'faggio *nm* cockroach

scara'mantico *a* ⟨*gesto*⟩ to ward off the evil eye

scara'muccia *nf* skirmish

scarabocchi'are *vt* scribble

scaraven'tare *vt* hurl

scarce'rare *vt* release [from prison]

scardi'nare *vt* unhinge

'**scarica** *nf* discharge; ⟨*di arma da fuoco*⟩ volley; *fig* shower

scari'ca|re vt discharge; unload ⟨arma, merci⟩; fig unburden. **~rsi** vr ⟨fiume:⟩ flow; ⟨orologio, batteria:⟩ run down; fig unwind. **~'tore** nm loader; ⟨di porto⟩ docker. **'scarico** a unloaded; ⟨vuoto⟩ empty; ⟨orologio⟩ run-down; ⟨batteria⟩ flat; fig untroubled ● nm unloading; ⟨di rifiuti⟩ dumping; ⟨di acqua⟩ draining; ⟨di sostanze inquinanti⟩ discharge; ⟨luogo⟩ [rubbish] dump; Auto exhaust; ⟨idraulico⟩ drain; ⟨tubo⟩ waste pipe

scarlat'tina nf scarlet fever

scar'latto a scarlet

'scarno a thin; ⟨fig: stile⟩ bare

scia'ro|gna nf fam bad luck. **~ gnato** a fam unlucky

'scarpa nf shoe; ⟨fam: persona⟩ dead loss. **scarpe** pl **da ginnastica** trainers, gym shoes

scar'pata nf slope; ⟨burrone⟩ escarpment

scarpi'nare vi hike

scar'pone nm boot. **scarponi** pl **da sci** ski boot. **scarponi** pl **da trekking** walking boots

scarroz'zare vt/i drive around

scarseggi'are vi be scarce; **~ di** ⟨mancare⟩ be short of

scar'sezza nf scarcity, shortage. **scarsità** nf shortage. **'scarso** a scarce; ⟨manchevole⟩ short

scarta'mento nm Rail gauge. **~ ridotto** narrow gauge

scar'tare vt discard; unwrap ⟨pacco⟩; ⟨respingere⟩ reject ● vi ⟨deviare⟩ swerve. **'scarto** nm scrap; ⟨in carte⟩ discard; ⟨deviazione⟩ swerve; ⟨distacco⟩ gap

scar'toffie nfpl bumf, bumph

scas'sa|re vt force open. **~to** a fam clapped out

scassi'nare vt force open

scassina'tore, **-'trice** nmf burglar. **'scasso** nm ⟨furto⟩ house-breaking

scate'na|re vt fig stir up. **~rsi** vr break out; ⟨fig: temporale:⟩ break; ⟨fam: infiammarsi⟩ get excited. **~to** a crazy

'scatola nf box; ⟨di latta⟩ can, tin Br; **in ~** ⟨cibo⟩ canned, tinned Br; **rompere le scatole a qcno** fam get on sb's nerves

scat'tare vi go off; ⟨balzare⟩ spring up; ⟨adirarsi⟩ lose one's temper; take ⟨foto⟩. **'scatto** nm ⟨balzo⟩ spring; ⟨d'ira⟩ outburst; ⟨di telefono⟩ unit; ⟨dispositivo⟩ release; **a scatti** jerkily; **di scatto** suddenly

scatu'rire vi spring

scaval'care vt jump over ⟨muretto⟩; climb over ⟨muro⟩; ⟨fig: superare⟩ overtake

sca'vare vt dig ⟨buca⟩; dig up ⟨tesoro⟩; excavate ⟨città sepolta⟩. **'scavo** nm excavation

scazzot'tata nf fam punch-up

'scegliere vt choose, select

scelle'rato a wicked

'scel|ta nf choice; ⟨di articoli⟩ range; **...a ~a** ⟨in menù⟩ choice of...; **prendine uno a ~a** take your choice o pick; **di prima ~a** a top-grade, choice. **~o** pp di **scegliere** ● a select; ⟨merce ecc⟩ choice

sce'mare vt/i diminish

sce'menza nf silliness; ⟨azione⟩ silly thing to do/say. **'scemo** a silly

'scempio nm havoc; ⟨fig: di paesaggio⟩ ruination; **fare ~ di** play havoc with

'scena nf scene; ⟨palcoscenico⟩ stage; **entrare in ~** go/come on; fig enter the scene; **fare ~** put on an act; **fare una ~** make a scene; **andare in ~** Theat be staged, be put on. **sce'nario** nm scenery

sce'nata nf row, scene

'scendere vi go/come down; ⟨da treno, autobus⟩ get off; ⟨da macchina⟩ get out; ⟨strada:⟩ slope; ⟨notte, prezzi:⟩ fall ● vt go/come down ⟨scale⟩

sceneggi'a|re vt dramatize. **~to** nm television serial. **~tura** nf screenplay

'scenico a scenic

scervel'la|rsi vr rack one's brains. **~to** a brainless

'sceso pp di **scendere**

scetti'cismo nm scepticism. **'scettico**, **-a** a sceptical ● nmf sceptic

'scettro nm sceptre

'scheda nf card. **~ elettorale** ballotpaper. **~ di espansione** Comput expansion card. **~ perforata** punch card. **~ telefonica** phonecard. **sche'dare** vt file. **sche'dario** nm file; ⟨mobile⟩ filing cabinet

sche'dina nf pools coupon; **giocare la ~** do the pools

scheggi'a|re vt/i fragment; ⟨di legno⟩ splinter. **~'arsi** vr chip; ⟨legno:⟩ splinter

'scheletro nm skeleton

'schema nm diagram; ⟨abbozzo⟩ outline. **sche'matico** a schematic. **~tiz'zare** vt schematize

'scherma nf fencing

scher'mirsi vr protect oneself

'schermo nm screen; **grande ~** big screen

scher'nire vt mock. **'scherno** nm mockery

scher'zare *vi* joke; (*giocare*) play

'scherzo *nm* joke; (*trucco*) trick; (*effetto*) play; *Mus* scherzo; **fare uno ~ a qcno** play a joke on sb; **per ~** for fun; **stare allo ~** take a joke. **scher'zoso** *a* playful

schiaccia'noci *nm inv* nutcrackers *pl*

schiacci'ante *a* damning

schiacci'are *vt* crush; *Sport* smash; press (*pulsante*); crack (*noce*); **~ un pisolino** grab forty winks

schiaffeggi'are *vt* slap. **schi'affo** *nm* slap; **dare uno schiaffo a** slap

schiamaz'zare *vi* make a racket; (*galline:*) cackle

schian'tar|e *vt* break. **~si** *vr* crash ●*vi* **schianto dalla fatica** I'm wiped out. **'schianto** *nm* crash; *fam* knock-out; (*divertente*) scream

schia'rir|e *vt* clear; (*sbiadire*) fade ●*vi*, **~si** *vr* brighten up; **~si la gola** clear one's throat

schiavitù *nf* slavery. **schi'avo, -a** *nmf* slave

schi'ena *nf* back; **mal di ~** backache. **schie'nale** *nm* (*di sedia*) back

schi'er|a *nf* *Mil* rank; (*moltitudine*) crowd. **~a'mento** *nm* lining up

schie'rar|e *vt* draw up. **~si** *vr* draw up; **~si con** (*parteggiare*) side with

schiet'tezza *nf* frankness. **schi'etto** *a* frank; (*puro*) pure

schi'fezza *nf* **una ~** rubbish. **schi-fil'toso** *a* fussy. **schifo** *nm* disgust; **mi fa schifo** it makes me sick. **schi'foso** *a* disgusting; (*di cattiva qualità*) rubbishy

schioc'care *vt* crack; snap (*dita*). **schi'occo** *nm* (*di frusta*) crack; (*di bacio*) smack; (*di dita, lingua*) click

schi'oppo *nm* **ad un tiro di ~** a stone's throw away

schi'uder|e *vt*, **~si** *vr* open

schi'u|ma *nf* foam; (*di sapone*) lather; (*feccia*) scum. **~ma da barba** shaving foam. **~'mare** *vt* skim ●*vi* foam

schi'uso *pp di* **schiudere**

schi'var|e *vt* avoid. **'schivo** *a* bashful

schizo'frenico *a* schizophrenic

schiz'zare *vt* squirt; (*inzaccherare*) splash; (*abbozzare*) sketch ●*vi* spurt; **~ via** scurry away

schiz'zato, -a *a* & *nmf sl* loony

schizzi'noso *a* squeamish

'schizzo *nm* squirt; (*di fango*) splash; (*abbozzo*) sketch

sci *nm inv* ski; (*sport*) skiing. **~ d'acqua** water-skiing

'scia *nf* wake; (*di fumo ecc*) trail

sci'abola *nf* sabre

sciabor'dare *vt/i* lap

scia'callo *nm* jackal; *fig* profiteer

sciac'quar|e *vt* rinse. **~si** *vr* rinse oneself. **sci'acquo** *nm* mouthwash

scia'gu|ra *nf* disaster. **~'rato** *a* unfortunate; (*scellerato*) wicked

scialac'quare *vt* squander

scia'lare *vi* spend money like water

sci'albo *a* pale; *fig* dull

sci'alle *nm* shawl

scia'luppa *nf* dinghy. **~ di salvataggio** lifeboat

sci'ame *nm* swarm

sci'ampo *nm* shampoo

scian'cato *a* lame

sci'are *vi* ski

sci'arpa *nf* scarf

sci'atica *nf* *Med* sciatica

scia'tore, -'trice *nmf* skier

sci'atto *a* slovenly; (*stile*) careless. **sciat'tone, -a** *nmf* slovenly person

scienti'fico *a* scientific

sci'en|za *nf* science; (*sapere*) knowledge. **~i'ato, -a** *nmf* scientist

scimmi|a *nf* monkey. **~ot'tare** *vt* ape

scimpanzé *nm inv* chimpanzee, chimp

scimu'nito *a* idiotic

'scinder|e *vt*, **~si** *vr* split

scin'tilla *nf* spark. **scintil'lante** *a* sparkling. **scintil'lare** *vi* sparkle

scioc'cante *a* shocking. **~re** *vt* shock

scioc'chezza *nf* foolishness; (*assurdità*) nonsense. **sci'occo** *a* foolish

sci'oglier|e *vt* untie; undo, untie (*nodo*); (*liberare*) release; (*liquefare*) melt; dissolve (*contratto, qcsa nell'acqua*); loosen up (*muscoli*). **~si** *vr* release oneself; (*liquefarsi*) melt; (*contratto:*) be dissolved; (*pastiglia:*) dissolve

scioglilingua *nm inv* tongue-twister

scio'lina *nf* wax

sciol'tezza *nf* agility; (*disinvoltura*) ease

sci'olto *pp di* **sciogliere** ●*a* loose; (*agile*) agile; (*disinvolto*) easy; **versi sciolti** blank verse

sciope'ra|nte *nmf* striker. **~re** *vi* go on strike, strike. **sci'opero** *nm* strike. **sciopero a singhiozzo** on-off strike

sciori'nare *vt fig* show off

sci'pito *a* insipid

scip'par|e *vt fam* snatch. **~'tore, ~'trice** *nmf* bag snatcher. **'scippo** *nm* bag-snatching

sci'rocco nm sirocco

scirop'pato a ⟨frutta⟩ in syrup. **sci'roppo** nm syrup

'**scisma** nm schism

scissi'one nf division

'**scisso** pp di **scindere**

sciu'par|e vt spoil; ⟨sperperare⟩ waste. ~**si** vr get spoiled; ⟨deperire⟩ wear oneself out. **sciu'pio** nm waste

scivo'l|are vi slide; ⟨involontariamente⟩ slip. '**scivolo** nm slide; Techn chute. ~'**oso** a slippery

scle'rosi nf sclerosis

scoc'care vt shoot ● vi ⟨scintilla:⟩ shoot out; ⟨ora:⟩ strike

scocci'a|re vt ⟨dare noia a⟩ bother. ~**rsi** vr be bothered. ~'**to** a fam narked. ~'**tore**, ~'**trice** nmf bore. ~'**tura** nf nuisance

sco'della nf bowl

scodinzo'lare vi wag its tail

scogli'era nf cliff; ⟨a fior d'acqua⟩ reef. '**scoglio** nm rock; ⟨fig: ostacolo⟩ stumbling block

scoi'attolo nm squirrel

scola'pasta nm inv colander. ~**pi'atti** nm inv dish drainer

sco'lara nf schoolgirl

sco'lare vt drain; strain ⟨pasta, verdura⟩ ● vi drip

sco'la|ro nm schoolboy. ~'**resca** nf pupils pl. ~'**stico** a school attrib

scoli'osi nf curvature of the spine

scol'la|re vt cut away the neck of ⟨abito⟩; ⟨staccare⟩ unstick. ~'**to** a ⟨abito⟩ low-necked. ~'**tura** nf neckline

'**scolo** nm drainage

scolo'ri|re vt, ~**rsi** vr fade. ~'**to** a faded

scol'pire vt carve; ⟨imprimere⟩ engrave

scombi'nare vt upset

scombus'so|lare vt muddle up

scom'mess|a nf bet. ~'**o** pp di **scommettere scom'mettere** vt bet

scomo'dar|e vt, ~**si** vr trouble. **scomodità** nf discomfort. '**scomodo** a uncomfortable ● nm essere di sco- modo a qcno be a trouble to sb

scompa'rire vi disappear; ⟨morire⟩ pass on. **scom'parsa** nf disappearance; ⟨morte⟩ passing, death. **scom'parso, -a** pp di **scomparire** ● nmf departed

scomparti'mento nm compartment. **scom'parto** nf compartment

scom'penso nm imbalance

scompigli'are vt disarrange. **scom'piglio** nm confusion

scom'porre vt take to pieces; ⟨fig:

turbare⟩ upset. ~**rsi** vr get flustered, lose one's composure. ~'**sto** pp di **scomporre** ● a ⟨sguaiato⟩ unseemly; ⟨disordinato⟩ untidy

sco'munica nf excommunication. ~'**care** vt excommunicate

sconcer'ta|re vt disconcert; ⟨rendere perplesso⟩ bewilder. ~'**to** a disconcerted; bewildered

scon'cezza nf obscenity. '**sconcio** a ⟨osceno⟩ dirty ● nm è uno sconcio che... it's a disgrace that...

conclusio'nato a incoherent

scon'dito a unseasoned; ⟨insalata⟩ with no dressing

confes'sare vt disown

scon'figgere vt defeat

sconfi'nare vi cross the border; ⟨in proprietà privata⟩ trespass. ~'**to** a unlimited

scon'fitt|a nf defeat. ~'**o** pp di **sconfiggere**

scon'forto nm dejection

sconge'lare vt thaw out ⟨cibo⟩, defrost

scongiu'rare vt beseech; ⟨evitare⟩ avert. ~'**uro** nm fare gli scongiuri ≈ touch wood, knock on wood Am

scon'nesso pp disconnettere ● a fig incoherent. **scon'nettere** vt disconnect

sconosci'uto, -a a unknown ● nmf stranger

sconquas'sare vt smash; ⟨sconvolgere⟩ upset

sconside'rato a inconsiderate

sconsigli'a|bile a not advisable. ~**re** vt advise against

conso'lato a disconsolate

scon'ta|re vt discount; ⟨dedurre⟩ deduct; ⟨pagare⟩ pay off; serve ⟨pena⟩. ~'**to** a discount; ⟨ovvio⟩ expected; ~**to del 10%** with 10% discount; **dare qcsa per** ~'**to** take sth for granted

scon'tento a displeased ● nm discontent

'**sconto** nm discount; **fare uno** ~ give a discount

scon'trarsi vr clash; ⟨urtare⟩ collide

scon'trino nm ticket; ⟨di cassa⟩ receipt

'**scontro** nm clash; ⟨urto⟩ collision

scon'troso a unsociable

sconveni'ente a unprofitable; ⟨scorretto⟩ unseemly

sconvol'gente a mind-blowing

sconvol'ger|e vt upset; ⟨mettere in disordine⟩ disarrange. ~**gi'mento** nm upheaval. ~'**to** pp di **sconvolgere** ● a distraught

'scopa nf broom. sco'pare vt sweep; vulg shag, screw

scoperchi'are vt take the lid off ⟨pentola⟩; take the roof off ⟨casa⟩

sco'pert|a nf discovery. ~o pp di scoprire ● a uncovered; (senza riparo) exposed; (conto) overdrawn; (spoglio) bare

'scopo nm aim; allo ~ di in order to

scoppi|are vi burst; fig break out. scoppiet'tare vi crackle. 'scoppio nm burst; (di guerra) outbreak; (esplosione) explosion

sco'prire vt discover; (togliere la copertura a) uncover

scoraggi'ante a discouraging

scoraggi'a|re vt discourage. ~rsi vr lose heart

scor'butico a peevish

scorcia'toia nf short cut

'scorcio nm (di epoca) end; (di cielo) patch; (in arte) foreshortening; di ~ ⟨vedere⟩ from an angle. ~ panoramico panoramic view

scor'da|re vt, ~rsi vr forget. ~to a Mus out of tune

sco'reggi|a nf fam fart. ~'are vi fam fart

'scorgere vt make out; (notare) notice

'scoria nf waste; (di metallo, carbone) slag; scorie pl radioattive radioactive waste

scor'nato a fig hangdog. 'scorno nm humiliation

scorpacci'ata nf bellyful; fare una ~ di stuff oneself with

scorpi'one nm scorpion; Astr Scorpio

scorraz'zare vi run about

'scorrere vt (dare un'occhiata) glance through ● vi run; (scivolare) slide; (fluire) flow; Comput scroll. scor're-vole a porta scorrevole sliding door

scorre'ria nf raid

scorret'tezza nf (mancanza di educazione) bad manners pl. scor'retto a incorrect; (sconveniente) improper

scorri'banda nf raid; fig excursion

'scors|a nf glance. ~o pp di scorrere ● a last

scor'soio a nodo ~ noose

'scort|a nf escort; (provvista) supply. ~'tare vt escort

scor'te|se a discourteous. ~'sia nf discourtesy

scorti'ca|re vt skin. ~'tura nf graze

'scorto pp di scorgere

'scorza nf peel; (crosta) crust; (corteccia) bark

sco'sceso a steep

'scoss|a nf shake; Electr, fig shock; prendere la ~ get an electric shock. ~ elettrica electric shock. ~ sismica earth tremor

'scosso pp di scuotere ● a shaken; (sconvolto) upset

sco'stante a off-putting

sco'sta|re vt push away. ~rsi vr stand aside

scostu'mato a dissolute; (maledu-cato) ill-mannered

scot'tante a ⟨argomento⟩ dangerous

scot'ta|re vt scald ● vi burn; ⟨bevanda:⟩ be too hot; ⟨sole, pentola:⟩ be very hot. ~rsi vr burn oneself; (al sole) get sunburnt; fig get one's fingers burnt. ~'tura nf burn; (da liquido) scald; ~tura solare sunburn; fig painful experience

'scotto a overcooked

sco'vare vt (scoprire) discover

'Scoz|ia nf Scotland. s~'zese a Scot-tish ● nmf Scot

scredi'tare vt discredit

scre'mare vt skim

screpo'la|re vt, ~rsi vr crack. ~to a ⟨labbra⟩ chapped. ~'tura nf crack

screzi'ato a speckled

'screzio nm disagreement

scribac|chi'are vt scribble. ~'chino, -a nmf scribbler; (impiegato) pen-pusher

scricchio'l|are vi creak. ~io nm creaking

'scricciolo nm wren

'scrigno nm casket

scrimina'tura nf parting

'scrit|ta nf writing; (su muro) graffiti. ~to pp di scrivere ● a written ● nm writing; (lettera) letter. ~'toio nm writ-ing-desk. ~'tore, ~'trice nmf writer. ~'tura nf writing; Relig scripture

scrittu'rare vt engage

scriva'nia nf desk

'scrivere vt write; (descrivere) write about; ~ a macchina type

scroc|c'are vt ~are a sponge off. 'scrocco nm fam a scrocco fam with-out paying; vivere a scrocco sponge off other people. ~'one, -a nmf sponger

'scrofa nf sow

scrol'la|re vt shake; ~e le spalle shrug one's shoulders. ~si vr shake oneself; ~si qcsa di dosso shake sth off

scrosci'are vi roar; ⟨pioggia:⟩ pelt

down. **'scroscio** nm roar; (di pioggia) pelting; **uno scroscio di applausi** thunderous applause

scro'star|e vt scrape. **~si** vr peel off

'scrupo|lo nm scruple; (diligenza) care; **senza scrupoli** unscrupulous, without scruples. **~'loso** a scrupulous

scru'ta|re vt scan; (indagare) search. **~'tore** nm (alle elezioni) returning officer

scruti'nare vt scrutinize. **scru'tinio** nm (di voti alle elezioni) poll; Sch assessment of progress

scu'cire vt unstitch; **scuci i soldi!** fam cough up [the money]!

scude'ria nf stable

scu'detto nm Sport championship shield

'scudo nm shield

sculacci'|are vt spank. **~'ata** nf spanking. **~'one** nm spanking

sculet'tare vi wiggle one's hips

scul'to|re, -'trice nm sculptor • nf sculptress. **~'tura** nf sculpture

scu'ola nf school. **~ elementare** primary school. **~ guida** driving school. **~ materna** day nursery. **~ media** secondary school. **~ media [inferiore]** secondary school (10-13). **~ [media] superiore** secondary school (13-18). **~ dell'obbligo** compulsory education

scu'oter|e vt shake. **~si** vr (destarsi) rouse oneself; **~si di dosso** shake off

'scure nf axe

scu'reggia nf fam fart. **scureggi'are** vi fam fart

scu'rire vt/i darken

'scuro a dark • nm darkness; (imposta) shutter

scur'rile a scurrilous

'scusa nf excuse; (giustificazione) apology; **chiedere ~** apologize; **chiedo ~!** I'm sorry!

scu'sar|e vt excuse. **~si** vr si apologize (di for); **[mi] scusi!** excuse me!; (chiedendo perdono) [I'm] sorry!

sdebi'tarsi vr (disobbligarsi) repay a kindness

sde'gna|re vt despise. **~rsi** vr get angry. **~to** a indignant. **'sdegno** nm disdain. **sde'gnoso** a disdainful

sden'tato a toothless

sdolci'nato a sentimental, schmaltzy

sdoppi'are vt halve

sdrai'arsi vr lie down. **'sdraio** nm [sedia a] **sdraio** deckchair

sdrammatiz'zare vi provide some comic relief

sdruccio'l|are vi slither. **~evole** a slippery

se conj if; (interrogativo) whether, if; **se mai** (caso mai) if need be; **se mai telefonasse,...** should he call,..., if he calls,...; **se no** otherwise, or else; **se non altro** at least, if nothing else; **se pure** (sebbene) even though; (anche se) even if; **non so se sia vero** I don't know whether it's true, I don't know if it's true; **come se** as if; **se lo avessi saputo prima!** if only I had known before!; **e se andassimo fuori a cena?** how about going out for dinner? • nm inv if

sé pron oneself; (lui) himself; (lei) herself; (esso, essa) itself; (loro) themselves; **l'ha fatto da sé** he did it himself; **ha preso i soldi con sé** he took the money with him; **si sono tenuti le notizie per sé** they kept the news to themselves

seb'bene conj although

'secca nf shallows pl; **in ~** (nave) aground

sec'cante a annoying

sec'ca|re vt dry; (importunare) annoy • vi dry up. **~rsi** vr dry up; (irritarsi) get annoyed; (annoiarsi) get bored. **~'tore, -'trice** nmf nuisance. **~'tura** nf bother

secchi'ello nm pail

'secchio nm bucket. **~ della spazzatura** rubbish bin, trash can Am

'secco, -a a dry; (disseccato) dried; (magro) thin; (brusco) curt; (preciso) sharp; **restare a ~** be left penniless; **restarci ~** (fam: morire di colpo) be killed on the spot • nm (siccità) drought; **lavare a ~** dry-clean

secessi'one nf secession

seco'lare a age-old; (laico) secular. **'secolo** nm century; (epoca) age; **è un secolo che non lo vedo** fam I haven't seen him for ages o yonks

se'cond|a nf Sch, Rail second class; Auto second [gear]. **~o** a second • nm second; (secondo piatto) main course • prep according to; **~o me** in my opinion

secondo'genito, -a a & nm second-born

secrezi'one nf secretion

'sedano nm celery

seda'tivo a & nm sedative

'sede nf seat; (centro) centre; Relig see; Comm head office. **~ sociale** registered office

seden'tario a sedentary

199   **sedere | senno**

se'der|e *vi* sit. ~si *vr* sit down • *nm* (deretano) bottom

'sedia *nf* chair. ~ **a dondolo** rocking chair. ~ **a rotelle** wheelchair

sedi'cente *a* self-styled

'sedici *a* & *nm* sixteen

se'dile *nm* seat

sedizi'o|ne *nf* sedition. ~so *a* seditious

se'dotto *pp di* **sedurre**

sedu'cente *a* seductive; (allettante) enticing

se'durre *vt* seduce

se'duta *nf* session; (di posa) sitting. ~ **stante** *adv* here and now

seduzi'one *nf* seduction

'sega *nf* saw; *vulg* wank

'segala *nf* rye

se'gare *vt* saw

sega'tura *nf* sawdust

'seggio *nm* seat. ~ **elettorale** polling station

seg'gio|la *nf* chair. ~'lino *nm* seat; (da bambino) child's seat. ~'lone *nm* (per bambini) high chair

seggio'via *nf* chair lift

seghe'ria *nf* sawmill

se'ghetto *nm* hacksaw

seg'mento *nm* segment

segna'lar|e *vt* signal; (annunciare) announce; (indicare) point out. ~si *vr* distinguish oneself

se'gnal|e *nm* signal; (stradale) sign. ~le acustico beep. ~le orario time signal. ~'letica *nf* signals *pl*. ~'letica stradale road signs *pl*

segna'libro *nm* bookmark

se'gnar|e *vt* mark; (prendere nota) note; (indicare) indicate; Sport score. ~si *vr* cross oneself. 'segno *nm* sign; (traccia, limite) mark; (bersaglio) target; far segno (col capo) nod; (con la mano) beckon. segno zodiacale birth sign

segre'gare *vt* segregate. ~zi'one *nf* segregation

segre'tar|iato *nm* secretariat

segre'tario, -a *nmf* secretary. ~ comunale town clerk

segrete'ria *nf* (ufficio) [administrative] office; (segretariato) secretariat. ~ telefonica answering machine, answerphone

segre'tezza *nf* secrecy

se'greto *a* & *nm* secret; in ~ in secret

segu'ace *nmf* follower

segu'ente *a* following, next

se'gugio *nm* bloodhound

segu'ire *vt/i* follow; (continuare) continue

segui'tare *vt/i* continue

'seguito *nm* retinue; (sequela) series; (continuazione) continuation; di ~ in succession; in ~ later on; in ~ a following; al ~ in his/her wake; (a causa di) owing to; fare ~ a Comm follow up

'sei *a* & *nm* six. sei'cento *a* & *nm* six hundred; il Seicento the seventeenth century. sei'mila *a* & *nm* six thousand

sel'ciato *nm* paving

selet'tivo *a* selective. selezio'nare *vt* select. selezi'one *nf* selection

'sella *nf* saddle. sel'lare *vt* saddle

seltz *nm* soda water

'selva *nf* forest

selvag'gina *nf* game

sel'vaggio, -a *a* wild; (primitivo) savage • *nmf* savage

sel'vatico *a* wild

se'maforo *nm* traffic lights *pl*

se'mantica *nf* semantics *sg*

sem'brare *vi* seem; (assomigliare) look like; che te ne sembra? what do you think?; mi sembra che... I think...

'seme *nm* seed; (di mela) pip; (di carte) suit; (sperma) semen

se'mestre *nm* half-year

semi'cerchio *nm* semicircle

semifi'nale *nf* semifinal

semi'freddo *nm* ice cream and sponge dessert

'semina *nf* sowing

semi'nare *vt* sow; *fam* shake off (inseguitori)

semi'nario *nm* seminar; Relig seminary

seminter'rato *nm* basement

se'mitico *a* Semitic

sem'mai *conj* in case • *adv* è lui, ~, che... if anyone, it's him who...

'semola *nf* bran. semo'lino *nm* semolina

'sempli|ce *a* simple; in parole semplici in plain words. ~'cemente *adv* simply. ~ci'otto, -a *nmf* simpleton. ~'cistico *a* simplistic. ~ci'tà *nf* simplicity. ~fi'care *vt* simplify

'sempre *adv* always; (ancora) still; per ~ for ever

sempre'verde *a* & *nm* evergreen

se'nape *nf* mustard

se'nato *nm* senate. sena'tore *nm* senator

se'nil|e *a* senile. ~ità *nf* senility

'senno *nm* sense

'**seno** nm (petto) breast; Math sine; **in ~ a** in the bosom of

sen'sato a sensible

sensazi|o'nale a sensational. ~'one nf sensation

sen'sibil|e a sensitive; (percepibile) perceptible; (notevole) considerable. ~ità nf sensitivity. ~iz'zare vt make more aware (a of)

sensi'tivo, -a a sensory ●nmf sensitive person; (medium) medium

'**senso** nm sense; (significato) meaning; (direzione) direction; **far ~ a qcno** make sb shudder; **non ha ~** it doesn't make sense; **senza ~** meaningless; **perdere i sensi** lose consciousness. ~ **dell'umorismo** sense of humour. ~ **unico** (strada) one-way; ~ **vietato** no entry

sensu'al|e a sensual. ~ità nf sensuality

sen'tenz|a nf sentence; (massima) saying. ~i'are vi Jur pass judgment

senti'ero nm path

sentimen'tale a sentimental. senti'mento nm feeling

senti'nella nf sentry

sen'ti|re vt feel; (udire) hear; (ascoltare) listen to; (gustare) taste; (odorare) smell ●vi feel; (udire) hear; ~**re caldo/freddo** feel hot/cold. ~**rsi** vr feel; ~**rsi di fare qcsa** feel like doing sth; ~**rsi bene/feel well**; ~**rsi poco bene** feel unwell; ~**rsela di fare qcsa** feel up to doing sth. ~**to** a (sincero) sincere; **per ~ dire** by hearsay

sen'tore nm inkling

'**senza** prep without; ~ **correre** without running; **senz'altro** certainly; ~ **ombrello** without an umbrella

senza'tetto nm inv i ~ the homeless

sepa'ra|re vt separate. ~**rsi** vr separate; (amici:) part; ~**rsi da** be separated from. ~**ta'mente** adv separately. ~**zi'one** nf separation

se'pol|cro nm sepulchre. ~**to** pp di seppellire ~'**tura** nf burial

seppel'lire vt bury

'**seppia** nf cuttle fish; **nero di ~** sepia

sep'pure conj even if

se'quenza nf sequence

seque'strare vt (rapire) kidnap; Jur impound; (confiscare) confiscate. se'questro nm Jur impounding; (di persona) kidnap[ping]

'**sera** nf evening; **di ~** in the evening. se'rale a evening. se'rata nf evening; (ricevimento) party

ser'bare vt keep; harbour (odio); cherish (speranza)

serba'toio nm tank. ~ **d'acqua** water tank; (per una città) reservoir

'**serbo, -a** a & nmf Serbian ●nm (lingua) Serbian; **mettere in ~** put aside

sere'nata nf serenade

sereni'tà nf serenity. se'reno a serene; (cielo) clear

ser'gente nm sergeant

seria'mente adv seriously

'**serie** nf inv series; (complesso) set; Sport division; **fuori ~** custom-built; **produzione in ~** mass production; **di ~ B** second-rate

serie'tà nf seriousness. 'serio a serious; (degno di fiducia) reliable; **sul serio** seriously; (davvero) really

ser'mone nm sermon

'**serpe** nf liter viper. ~**ggi'are** vi meander; (diffondersi) spread

ser'pente nm snake. ~ **a sonagli** rattlesnake

'**serra** nf greenhouse; **effetto ~** greenhouse effect

ser'randa nf shutter

ser'ra|re vt shut; (stringere) tighten; (incalzare) press on. ~'**tura** nf lock

ser'vir|e vt serve; (al ristorante) wait on ●vi serve; (essere utile) be of use; **non serve** it's no good. ~**si** vr (di cibo) help oneself; ~**si da** buy from; ~**si di** use

servi'tù nf inv servitude; (personale di servizio) servants pl

servizi'evole a obliging

ser'vizio nm service; (da caffè ecc) set; (di cronaca, sportivo) report; **servizi** pl bathroom; **essere di ~** be on duty; **fare ~** (autobus ecc:) run; **fuori ~** (bus) not in service; (ascensore) out of order; ~ **compreso** service charge included. ~ **in camera** room service. ~ **civile** civilian duties done instead of national service. ~ **militare** military service. ~ **pubblico** utility company. ~ **al tavolo** waiter service

'**servo, -a** nmf servant

servo'sterzo nm power steering

ses'san|ta a & nm sixty. ~'**tina** nf una ~**tina** about sixty

sessi'one nf session

'**sesso** nm sex

sessu'al|e a sexual. ~ità nf sexuality

'**sesto**[1] a sixth

'**sesto**[2] nm (ordine) order

'**seta** nf silk

setacci'are vt sieve. se'taccio nm sieve

'sete *nf* thirst; avere ~ be thirsty

'setola *nf* bristle

'setta *nf* sect

set'tan|ta *a & nm* seventy. ~'tina *nf* una ~'tina about seventy

'sette *a & nm* seven. ~'cento *a & nm* seven hundred; il S~cento the eighteenth century

set'tembre *nm* September

settentrio'nale *a* northern ● *nmf* northerner. ~'one *nm* north

setti'ma|na *nf* week. ~'nale *a & nm* weekly

'settimo *a* seventh

set'tore *nm* sector

severità *nf* severity. se'vero *a* severe; *(rigoroso)* strict

se'vizi|a *nf* torture; se'vizie *pl* torture *sg*. ~'are *vt* torture

sezio'nare *vt* divide; *Med* dissect. sezi'one *nf* section; *(reparto)* department; *Med* dissection

sfaccen'dato *a* idle

sfacchi'na|re *vi* toil. ~ta *nf* drudgery

sfacci|a'taggine *nf* cheek, insolence. ~ato *a* cheeky, fresh *Am*

sfa'celo *nm* ruin; in ~ in ruins

sfal'darsi *vr* flake off

sfa'mar|e *vt* feed. ~si *vr* satisfy one's hunger, eat one's fill

'sfar|zo *nm* pomp. ~'zoso *a* sumptuous

sfa'sato *a fam* confused; *(motore)* which needs tuning

sfasci'a|re *vt* unbandage; *(fracassare)* smash. ~rsi *vr* fall to pieces. ~to *a* beat-up

sfa'tare *vt* explode

sfati'cato *a* lazy

sfavil'la|nte *a* sparkling. ~re *vi* sparkle

sfavo'revole *a* unfavourable

sfavo'rire *vt* disadvantage, put at a disadvantage

'sfer|a *nf* sphere. ~ico *a* spherical

sfer'rare *vt* unshoe *(cavallo)*; *(scagliare)* land

sfer'zare *vt* whip

sfian'carsi *vr* wear oneself out

sfi'bra|re *vt* exhaust. ~to *a* exhausted

'sfida *nf* challenge. sfi'dare *vt* challenge

sfi'duci|a *nf* mistrust. ~'ato *a* discouraged

'sfiga *nf vulg* bloody bad luck

sfigu'ra|re *vt* disfigure ● *vi (far cattiva figura)* look out of place

sfilacci'ar|e *vt*, ~si *vr* fray

sfi'la|re *vt* unthread; *(togliere di dosso)* take off ● *vi (truppe:)* march past; *(in parata)* parade. ~rsi *vr* come unthreaded; *(collant:)* ladder; take off *(pantaloni)*. ~ta *nf* parade; *(sfilza)* series. ~ta di moda fashion show

'sfilza *nf (di errori, domande)* string

'sfinge *nf* sphinx

sfi'nito *a* worn out

sfio'ra|re *vt* skim; touch on *(argomento)*

sfio'rire *vi* wither; *(bellezza:)* fade

'sfitto *a* vacant

'sfizio *nm* whim, fancy; togliersi uno ~ satisfy a whim

sfo'cato *a* out of focus

sfoci'are *vi* ~ in flow into

sfode'ra|re *vt* draw *(pistola, spada)*. ~to *a* unlined

sfo'gar|e *vt* vent. ~si *vr* give vent to one's feelings

sfoggi'are *vt/i* show off. 'sfoggio *nm* show, display; fare sfoggio di show off

'sfogli|a *nf* sheet of pastry; pasta ~ puff pastry

sfogli'are *vt* leaf through

'sfogo *nm* outlet; *fig* outburst; *Med* rash; dare ~ a blazing. ~re *vi* blaze

sfolgo'ra|nte *a* blazing. ~re *vi* blaze

sfol'la|re *vt* clear ● *vi Mil* be evacuated

sfol'tire *vt* thin [out]

sfon'dar|e *vt* break down ● *vi (aver successo)* make a name for oneself

'sfondo *nm* background

sfor'ma|re *vt* pull out of shape *(tasche)*. ~rsi *vr* lose its shape; *(persona:)* lose one's figure. ~to *nm* Culin flan

sfor'nito *a* ~ di *(negozio)* out of

sfor'tuna *nf* bad luck. ~ta'mente *adv* unfortunately. sfortu'nato *a* unlucky

sfor'zar|e *vt* force. ~si *vr* try hard. sforzo *nm* effort; *(tensione)* strain

sfottere *vt sl* tease

sfracel'larsi *vr* smash

sfrat'tare *vt* evict. 'sfratto *nm* eviction

sfrecci'are *vi* flash past

sfregi'a|re *vt* slash. ~to *a* scarred sfregio *nm* slash

sfre'na|rsi *vr* run wild. ~to *a* wild

sfron'tato *a* shameless

sfrutta'mento *nm* exploitation. sfrut'tare *vt* exploit

sfug'gente *a* elusive; *(mento)* receding

sfug'gi|re *vi* escape; ~re *a* escape [from]; mi sfugge it escapes me; mi è

sfuggito di mano I lost hold of it ● *vt* avoid. **~ta** *nf* di **~ta** in passing

sfu'ma|re *vi* (*svanire*) vanish; ⟨*colore:*⟩ shade off ● *vt* soften ⟨*colore*⟩. **~'tura** *nf* shade

sfuri'ata *nf* outburst [of anger]

sga'bello *nm* stool

sgabuz'zino *nm* cupboard

sgam'bato *a* ⟨*costume da bagno*⟩ high-cut

sgambet'tare *vi* kick one's legs; (*camminare*) trot. **sgam'betto** *nm* **fare lo sgambetto a** qcno trip sb up

sganasci'arsi *vr* **~ dalle risa** roar with laughter

sganci'ar|e *vt* unhook; Rail uncouple; drop ⟨*bombe*⟩; *fam* cough up ⟨*denaro*⟩. **~si** *vr* become unhooked; *fig* get away

sanghe'rato *a* ramshackle

sgar'bato *a* rude. **'sgarbo** *nm* discourtesy; **fare uno sgarbo** be rude

sgargi'ante *a* garish

sgar'rare *vi* be wrong; ⟨*da regola*⟩ stray from the straight and narrow. **'sgarro** *nm* mistake, slip

sgattaio'lare *vi* sneak away; **~ via** decamp

sghignaz'zare *vi* laugh scornfully, sneer

sgob'b|are *vi* slog; (*fam: studente:*) swot. **~one, -a** *nmf* slogger; (*fam: studente*) swot

sgocciol'are *vi* drip

sgo'larsi *vr* shout oneself hoarse

sgomb|e|'rare *vt* clear [out]. **'sgombro** *a* clear ● *nm* (*trasloco*) removal; (*pesce*) mackerel

sgomen'tar|e *vt* dismay. **~si** *vr* be dismayed. **sgo'mento** *nm* dismay

sgomi'nare *vt* defeat

sgom'mata *nf* screech of tyres

sgonfi'ar|e *vt* deflate. **~si** *vr* go down. **'sgonfio** *a* flat

'sgorbio *nm* scrawl; (*fig: vista sgradevole*) sight

sgor'gare *vi* gush [out] ● *vt* flush out, unblock ⟨*lavandino*⟩

sgoz'zare *vt* **~ qcno** cut sb's throat

sgra'd|evole *a* disagreeable. **~ito** *a* unwelcome

sgrammati'cato *a* ungrammatical

sgra'nare *vt* shell ⟨*piselli*⟩; open wide ⟨*occhi*⟩

sgran'chir|e *vt*, **~si** *vr* stretch

sgranocchi'are *vt* munch

sgras'sare *vt* remove the grease from

sgrazi'ato *a* ungainly

sgretol'ar|e *vt*, **~si** *vr* crumble

sgri'da|re *vt* scold. **~ta** *nf* scolding

sgros'sare *vt* rough-hew ⟨*marmo*⟩; *fig* polish

sgui'ato *a* coarse

sgual'cire *vt* crumple

sgual'drina *nf* slut

sgu'ardo *nm* look; (*breve*) glance

sguat'tero, -a *nmf* skivvy

sguaz'zare *vi* splash; (*nel fango*) wallow

sguinzagli'are *vt* unleash

sgusci'ar|e *vt* shell ● *vi* (*sfuggire*) slip away; **~ fuori** slip out

shake'rare *vt* shake

si *pron* (*riflessivo*) oneself; (*lui*) himself; (*lei*) herself; (*esso, essa*) itself; (*loro*) themselves; (*reciproco*) each other; (*tra più di due*) one another; (*impersonale*) you, one; **lavarsi** wash [oneself]; **si è lavata** she washed [herself]; **lavarsi le mani** wash one's hands; **si è lavata le mani** she washed her hands; **si è mangiato un pollo intero** he ate an entire chicken by himself; **incontrarsi** meet each other; **la gente si aiuta a vicenda** people help one another; **non si sa mai** you never know, one never knows; **queste cose si dimenticano facilmente** these things are easily forgotten ● *nm* (*chiave, nota*) B

si *adv* yes

'sia¹ *vedi* essere

'sia² *conj* **~...~...** (*entrambi*) both... and...; (*o l'uno o l'altro*) either...or...~ **che venga, ~ che non venga** whether he comes or not; **scegli ~ questo ~ quello** choose either this one or that one; **voglio ~ questo che quello** I want both this one and that one

sia'mese *a* Siamese

sibi'lare *vi* hiss. **'sibilo** *nm* hiss

si'cario *nm* hired killer

sicché *conj* (*perciò*) so [that]; (*allora*) then

siccità *nf* drought

sic'come *conj* as

Si'cili|a *nf* Sicily. **s~ano, -a** *a & nmf* Sicilian

si'cura *nf* safety catch; (*di portiera*) child-proof lock. **~'mente** *adv* definitely

sicu'rezza *nf* (*certezza*) certainty; (*salvezza*) safety; **uscita di ~** emergency exit

si'curo *a* (*non pericoloso*) safe; (*certo*) sure; ⟨*saldo*⟩ steady; Comm sound ● *adv* certainly ● *nm* safety; **al ~** safe; **andare sul ~** play [it] safe; **di ~** definitely; **di ~**, **sarà arrivato** he must have arrived

siderur'gia *nf* iron and steel industry. **side'rurgico** *a* iron and steel *attrib*

'**sidro** *nm* cider

si'epe *nf* hedge

si'ero *nm* serum

sieroposi'tivo, -a *a* HIV positive ● *nmf* person who is HIV positive

si'esta *nf* afternoon nap, siesta

si'fone *nm* siphon

Sig. *abbr* (signore) Mr

Sig.a *abbr* (signora) Mrs, Ms

siga'retta *nf* cigarette; **pantaloni a ~** drainpipes

'**sigaro** *nm* cigar

Sigg. *abbr* (signori) Messrs

sigil'lare *vt* seal. **si'gillo** *nm* seal

'**sigla** *nf* initials *pl*. **~ musicale** signature tune. **si'glare** *vt* initial

Sig.na *abbr* (signorina) Miss, Ms

signifi'ca|re *vt* mean. **~tivo** *a* significant. **~to** *nm* meaning

si'gnora *nf* lady; *(davanti a nome proprio)* Mrs; *(non sposata)* Miss; *(in lettere ufficiali)* Dear Madam; **il signor Venè e ~** Mr and Mrs Venè

si'gnore *nm* gentleman; *Relig* lord; *(davanti a nome proprio)* Mr; *(in lettere ufficiali)* Dear Sir. **signo'rile** *a* gentlemanly; *(di lusso)* luxury

signo'rina *nf* young lady; *(seguito da nome proprio)* Miss

silenzia'tore *nm* silencer

si'lenzio *nm* silence. **~oso** *a* silent

silhou'ette *nf* silhouette, outline

si'licio *nm* **piastrina di ~** silicon chip

sili'cone *nm* silicone

'**sillaba** *nf* syllable

silu'rare *vt* torpedo. **si'luro** *nm* torpedo

simboleggi'are *vt* symbolize

sim'bolico *a* symbolic[al]

'**simbolo** *nm* symbol

similarità *nf inv* similarity

'**simil|e** *a* similar; *(tale)* such; **~ e a** like ● *nm (il prossimo)* fellow man. **~'mente** *adv* similarly. **~'pelle** *nf* Leatherette®

simme'tria *nf* symmetry. **sim'metrico** *a* symmetric[al]

simpa'ti|a *nf* liking; *(compenetrazione)* sympathy; **prendere qcno in ~a** take a liking to sb. **sim'patico** *a* nice. **~iz'zante** *nmf* well-wisher. **~iz'zare** *vt* **~izzare con** take a liking to; **~izzare per qcsa/qcno** lean towards sth/sb

sim'posio *nm* symposium

simu'la|re *vt* simulate; feign *(amicizia, interesse)*. **~zi'one** *nf* simulation

simul'tane|a *nf* in **~a** simultaneously. **~o** *a* simultaneous

sina'goga *nf* synagogue

sincerità *nf* sincerity. **sin'cero** *a* sincere

'**sincope** *nf* syncopation; *Med* fainting fit

sincro'nia *nf* synchronization; **in ~** with synchronized timing

sincroniz'za|re *vt* synchronize. **~zi'one** *nf* synchronization

sinda'ca|le *a* [trade] union, [labor] union *Am*. **~'lista** *nmf* trade unionist, labor union member *Am*. **~re** *vt* inspect. **~to** *nm* [trade] union, [labor] union *Am*; *(associazione)* syndicate

'sindaco *nm* mayor

'**sindrome** *nf* syndrome

sinfo'nia *nf* symphony. **sin'fonico** *a* symphonic

singhioz'zare *vi (di pianto)* sob. **~'ozzo** *nm* hiccup; *(di pianto)* sob; **avere il ~ozzo** have the hiccups

singo'la|re *a* singular ● *nm* singular. **~'mente** *adv* individually; *(stranamente)* peculiarly

'**singolo** *a* single ● *nm* individual; *Tennis* singles *pl*

si'nistra *nf* left; **a ~** on the left; **girare a ~** turn to the left; **con la guida a ~** *(auto)* with left-hand drive

sini'strato *a* injured

si'nistr|o, -a *a* left[-hand]; *(avverso)* sinister ● *nm* accident ● *nf* left [hand]; *Pol* left [wing]

'**sino** *prep* = **fino**¹

si'nonimo *a* synonymous ● *nm* synonym

sin'tassi *nf* syntax. **~ttico** *a* syntactic[al]

'**sintesi** *nf* synthesis; *(riassunto)* summary

sin'tetico *a* synthetic; *(conciso)* summary. **~z'zare** *vt* summarize

sintetizza'tore *nm* synthesizer

sinto'matico *a* symptomatic. '**sintomo** *nm* symptom

sinto'nia *nf* tuning; **in ~** on the same wavelength

sinu'oso *a (strada)* winding

sinu'site *nf* sinusitis

si'pario *nm* curtain

si'rena *nf* siren

'**Siri|a** *nf* Syria. **s~'ano, -a** *a & nmf* Syrian

si'ringa *nf* syringe

'sismico *a* seismic

si'stema *nm* system. S~ Monetario Europeo European Monetary System. ~ operativo *Comput* operating system

siste'ma|re *vt* (*mettere*) put; tidy up (*casa, camera*); (*risolvere*) sort out; (*procurare lavoro a*) fix up with a job; (*trovare alloggio a*) find accommodation for; (*sposare*) marry off; (*fam: punire*) sort out. ~rsi *vr* settle down; (*trovare un lavoro*) find a job; (*trovare alloggio*) find accommodation; (*sposarsi*) marry. ~tico *a* systematic. ~zi'one *nf* arrangement; (*di questione*) settlement; (*lavoro*) job; (*alloggio*) accommodation; (*matrimonio*) marriage

'sito *nm* site. ~ web *Comput* web site

situ'are *vt* place

situazi'one *nf* situation

ski-'lift *nm* ski tow

slacci'are *vt* unfasten

slanci'a|rsi *vr* hurl oneself. ~to *a* slender. 'slancio *nm* impetus; (*impulso*) impulse

sla'vato *a* (*carnagione, capelli*) fair

'slavo *a* Slav[onic]

sle'al|e *a* disloyal. ~tà *nf* disloyalty

sle'gare *vt* untie

'slitta *nf* sledge, sleigh. ~'mento *nm* (*di macchina*) skid; (*fig: di riunione*) postponement

slit'ta|re *vi* *Auto* skid; (*riunione:*) be put off. ~ta *nf* skid

slit'tino *nm* toboggan

'slogan *nm* *inv* slogan

slo'ga|re *vt* dislocate. ~rsi *vr* ~rsi una caviglia sprain one's ankle. ~'tura *nf* dislocation

sloggi'are *vt* dislodge ● *vi* move out

Slo'vacchia *nf* Slovakia

Slo'venia *nf* Slovenia

smacchi'a|re *vt* clean. ~'tore *nm* stain remover

'smacco *nm* humiliating defeat

smagli'ante *a* dazzling

smagli'a|rsi *vr* (*calza:*) ladder *Br*, run. ~'tura *nf* ladder *Br*, run

smalizi'ato *a* cunning

smal'ta|re *vt* enamel; glaze (*ceramica*); varnish (*unghie*). ~to *a* enamelled

smalti'mento *nm* disposal; (*di merce*) selling off. ~ rifiuti waste disposal; (*di grassi*) burning off

smal'tire *vt* burn off; (*merce*) sell off; *fig* get through (*corrispondenza*); ~ la sbornia sober up

'smalto *nm* enamel; (*di ceramica*) glaze; (*per le unghie*) nail varnish

'smani|a *nf* fidgets *pl*; (*desiderio*) longing. ~'are *vi* have the fidgets; ~are per long for. ~'oso *a* restless

smantel'la|'mento *nm* dismantling. ~'lare *vt* dismantle

smarri'mento *nm* loss; (*psicologico*) bewilderment

smar'ri|re *vt* lose; (*temporaneamente*) mislay. ~rsi *vr* get lost; (*turbarsi*) be bewildered

smasche'ra|re *vt* unmask. ~si *vr* (*tradirsi*) give oneself away

SME *nm abbr* (Sistema Monetario Europeo) EMS

smemo'rato, -a *a* forgetful ● *nmf* scatterbrain

smen'ti|re *vt* deny. ~ta *nf* denial

sme'raldo *nm* & *a* emerald

smerci'are *vt* sell off

smerigli'ato *a* emery; vetro ~ frosted glass. sme'riglio *nm* emery

'smesso *pp di* smettere ● *a* (*abiti*) cast-off

'smett|ere *vt* stop; stop wearing (*abiti*); ~ila! stop it!

smidol'lato *a* spineless

sminu'ir|e *vt* diminish. ~si *vr* *fig* belittle oneself

sminuz'zare *vt* crumble; (*fig: analizzare*) analyse in detail

smista'mento *nm* clearing; (*postale*) sorting. smi'stare *vt* sort; *Mil* posto

smisu'rato *a* boundless; (*esorbitante*) excessive

smobili'ta|re *vt* demobilize. ~zi'one *nf* demobilization

smo'dato *a* immoderate

smog *nm* smog

smoking *nm* *inv* dinner jacket, tuxedo *Am*

smon'tabile *a* jointed

smon'tar|e *vt* take to pieces; (*scoraggiare*) dishearten ● *vi* (*da veicolo*) get off; (*da cavallo*) dismount; (*dal servizio*) go off duty. ~si *vr* lose heart

'smorfi|a *nf* grimace; (*moina*) simper; fare ~e make faces. ~'oso *a* affected

'smorto *a* pale; (*colore*) dull

smor'zare *vt* dim (*luce*); tone down (*colori*); deaden (*suoni*); quench (*sete*)

'smosso *pp di* smuovere

smotta'mento *nm* landslide

'smunto *a* emaciated

smu'over|e *vt* shift; (*commuovere*) move. ~si *vr* move; (*commuoversi*) be moved

smus'sar|e *vt* round off; (*fig: attenuare*) tone down. ~si *vr* go blunt

snatu'rato *a* inhuman
snel'lir|e *vt* slim down. ~**si** *vr* slim [down]. **'snello** *a* slim
sner'vante *a* enervating
sner'va|re *vt* enervate. ~**rsi** *vr* get exhausted
sni'dare *vt* drive out
snif'fare *vt* snort
snob'bare *vt* snub. **sno'bismo** *nm* snobbery
snoccio'lare *vt* stone; *fig* blurt out
sno'da|re *vt* untie; (*sciogliere*) loosen. ~**rsi** *vr* come untied; (*strada:*) wind. ~**to** *a* (*persona*) double-jointed; (*dita*) flexible
so'ave *a* gentle
sobbal'zare *vi* jerk; (*trasalire*) start. **sob'balzo** *nm* jerk; (*trasalimento*) start
sobbar'carsi *vr* ~ **a** undertake
sob'borgo *nm* suburb
sobil'lare *vt* stir up
'sobrio *a* sober
socchi'u|dere *vt* half-close. ~**so** *pp di* **socchiudere** ● *a* (*occhi*) half-closed; (*porta*) ajar
soc'combere *vi* succumb
soc'cor|rere *vt* assist. ~**so** *pp di* **soccorrere** ● *nm* assistance; **soccorsi** *pl* rescuers; (*dopo disastro*) relief workers. ~**so stradale** breakdown service
socialdemo'cra|tico, -a *a* Social Democratic ● *nmf* Social Democrat. ~**zia** *nf* Social Democracy
soci'ale *a* social
socia'li|smo *nm* Socialism. ~**sta** *a & nmf* Socialist. ~**z'zare** *vi* socialize
società *nf inv* society; *Comm* company. ~ **per azioni** plc. ~ **a responsabilità limitata** limited liability company
soci'evole *a* sociable
'socio, -a *nmf* member; *Comm* partner
sociolo'gia *nf* sociology. **socio'logico** *a* sociological
'soda *nf* soda
soddisfa'cente *a* satisfactory
soddi'sfa|re *vt/i* satisfy; meet (*richiesta*); make amends for (*offesa*). ~**tto** *pp di* **soddisfare** ● *a* satisfied. ~**zi'one** *nf* satisfaction
'sodo *a* hard; *fig* firm; (*uovo*) hard-boiled ● *adv* hard; **dormire** ~ sleep soundly ● **venire al** ~ get to the point
sofà *nm inv* sofa
soffe'ren|te *a* (*malato*) ill. ~**za** *nf* suffering
soffer'marsi *vr* pause; ~ **su** dwell on

sof'ferto *pp di* **soffrire**
soffi'a|re *vt* blow; reveal (*segreto*); (*rubare*) pinch *fam* ● *vi* blow. ~**ta** *nf fig sl* tip-off
'soffice *a* soft
'soffio *nm* puff; *Med* murmur
sof'fitt|a *nf* attic. ~**o** *nm* ceiling
soffoca'mento *nm* suffocation
soffo'ca|nte *a* suffocating. ~**re** *vt/i* suffocate; (*con cibo*) choke; *fig* stifle
sof'friggere *vt* fry lightly
sof'frire *vt/i* suffer; (*sopportare*) bear; ~ **di** suffer from
sof'fritto *pp di* **soffriggere**
sof'fuso *a* (*luce*) soft
sofisti'ca|re *vt* (*adulterare*) adulterate ● *vi* (*sottilizzare*) quibble. ~**to** *a* sophisticated
sogget'tiva'mente *adv* subjectively. ~**tivo** *a* subjective
sog'getto *nm* subject ● *a* subject; **essere** ~ **a** be subject to
soggezi'one *nf* subjection; (*rispetto*) awe
sogghi'gnare *vi* sneer. **sog'ghigno** *nm* sneer
soggio'gare *vt* subdue
soggior'nare *vi* stay. **soggi'orno** *nm* stay; (*stanza*) living room
soggi'ungere *vt* add
'soglia *nf* threshold
'sogliola *nf* sole
so'gna|re *vt/i* dream; ~**re a occhi aperti** daydream. ~**tore**, ~**trice** *nmf* dreamer. **'sogno** *nm* dream; **fare un sogno** have a dream; **neanche per sogno!** not at all!
'soia *nf* soya
sol *nm Mus* (*chiave, nota*) G
so'laio *nm* attic
sola'mente *adv* only
so'lar|e *a* (*energia, raggi*) solar; (*crema*) sun *attrib*. ~**ium** *nm inv* solarium
sol'care *vt* plough. **'solco** *nm* furrow; (*di ruota*) track; (*di nave*) wake; (*di disco*) groove
sol'dato *nm* soldier
'soldo *nm* **non ha un** ~ he hasn't got a penny to his name; **senza un** ~ penniless; **soldi** *pl* (*denaro*) money *sg*
'sole *nm* sun; (*luce del sole*) sun[light]; **al** ~ **in** the sun; **prendere il** ~ sunbathe
soleggi'ato *a* sunny
so'lenn|e *a* solemn. ~**ità** *nf* solemnity
so'lere *vi* be in the habit of; **come si suol dire** as they say
sol'fato *nm* sulphate

soli'dal|le *a* in agreement. **~rietà** *nf* solidarity

solidifi'car|e *vt/i*, **~si** *vr* solidify

solidità *nf* solidity; (*di colori*) fastness. **'solido** *a* solid; (*robusto*) sturdy; (*colore*) fast ●*nm* solid

soli'loquio *nm* soliloquy

so'lista *a* solo ●*nmf* soloist

solita'mente *adv* usually

soli'tario *a* solitary; (*isolato*) lonely ●*nm* (*brillante*) solitaire; (*gioco di carte*) patience, solitaire

'solito *a* usual; **essere ~ fare qcsa** be in the habit of doing sth ●*nm* usual; **di ~** usually

soli'tudine *nf* solitude

solleci'ta|re *vt* speed up; urge (*persona*). **~zi'one** *nf* (*richiesta*) request; (*preghiera*) entreaty

sol'leci|to *a* prompt ●*nm* reminder. **~'tudine** *nf* promptness; (*interessamento*) concern

solle'one *nm* noonday sun; (*periodo*) dog days of summer

solleti'care *vt* tickle. **sol'letico** *nm* tickling; **fare il solletico a qcno** tickle sb; **soffrire il solletico** be ticklish

solleva'mento *nm* ~ **pesi** weightlifting

solle'var|e *vt* lift; (*elevare*) raise; (*confortare*) comfort. **~si** *vr* rise; (*riaversi*) recover

solli'evo *nm* relief

'solo, -a *a* alone; (*isolato*) lonely; (*unico*) only; *Mus* solo; **da ~** by myself/ yourself/himself etc ●*nmf* **il ~, la sola** the only one ●*nm Mus* solo ●*adv* only

sol'stizio *nm* solstice

sol'tanto *adv* only

so'lubile *a* soluble; (*caffè*) instant

soluzi'one *nf* solution; *Comm* payment; **in unica ~** *Comm* as a lump sum

sol'vente *a & nm* solvent; **~ per unghie** nail polish remover

'soma *nf* **bestia da ~** beast of burden

so'maro *nm* ass; *Sch* dunce

so'matico *a* somatic

somigli'an|te *a* similar. **~za** *nf* resemblance

somigli'ar|e *vi* **~e a** resemble. **~si** *vr* be alike

'somma *nf* sum; *Math* addition

som'mare *vt* add; (*totalizzare*) add up

som'mario *a & nm* summary

som'mato *a* **tutto ~** all things considered

sommeli'er *nm inv* wine waiter

som'mer|gere *vt* submerge. **~'gibile** *nm* submarine. **~so** *pp di* **sommergere**

som'messo *a* soft

sommini'stra|re *vt* administer. **~zi'one** *nf* administration

sommità *nf inv* summit

'sommo *a* highest; *fig* supreme ●*nm* summit

som'mossa *nf* rising

sommozza'tore *nm* frogman

so'naglio *nm* bell

so'nata *nf* sonata; *fig fam* beating

'sonda *nf Mech* drill; (*spaziale, Med*) probe. **son'daggio** *nm* drilling; (*spaziale, Med*) probe; (*indagine*) survey. **sondaggio d'opinioni** opinion poll. **son'dare** *vt* sound; (*investigare*) probe

so'netto *nm* sonnet

sonnambu'lismo *nm* sleepwalking. **son'nambulo, -a** *nmf* sleepwalker

sonnecchi'are *vi* doze

son'nifero *nm* sleeping-pill

'sonno *nm* sleep; **aver ~** be sleepy. **~'lenza** *nf* sleepiness

so'noro *a* resonant; (*rumoroso*) loud; (*onde, scheda*) sound *attrib*

sontu'oso *a* sumptuous

sopo'rifero *a* soporific

sop'palco *nm* platform

soppe'rire *vi* **~ a qcsa** provide for sth

soppe'sare *vt* weigh up (*situazione*)

soppi'atto: di ~ *adv* furtively

soppor'tare *vt* support; (*tollerare*) stand; bear (*dolore*)

soppressi'one *nf* removal; (*di legge*) abolition; (*di diritti, pubblicazione*) suppression; (*annullamento*) cancellation.

sop'presso *pp di* **sopprimere**

sop'primere *vt* get rid of; abolish (*legge*); suppress (*diritti, pubblicazione*); (*annullare*) cancel

'sopra *adv* on top; (*più in alto*) higher [up]; (*al piano superiore*) upstairs; (*in testo*) above; **mettilo lì ~** put it up there; **di ~** upstairs; **dormirci ~** *fig* sleep on it; **pensarci ~** think about it; **vedi ~** see above ●*prep* ~ **[a]** on; (*senza contatto, oltre*) over; (*riguardo a*) about; **è ~ al tavolo, è ~ il tavolo** it's on the table; **il quadro è appeso ~ al camino** the picture is hanging over the fireplace; **il ponte passa ~ all'autostrada** the bridge crosses over the motorway; **è caduto ~ il tetto** it fell on the roof; **l'uno ~ l'altro** one on top of the other; (*senza contatto*) one above the other; **abita ~ di me** he lives upstairs from me; **i bambini ~ i dieci anni** children over ten; **20° ~ lo zero** 20° above zero; **~ il livello del mare** above sea level; **rifletti ~ quello che è successo** think about what happened; **non ha nessuno ~ di sé** he has nobody above him; **al di ~ di** over ● *nm* **il** [di] **~** the top

so'**prabito** *nm* overcoat

soprac'**ciglio** *nm* (*pl nf* **sopracciglia**) eyebrow

sopracco'**perta** *nf* (*di letto*) bedspread; (*di libro*) [dust-]jacket. **~'tina** *nf* book jacket

soprad'**detto** *a* above-mentioned

sopraele'**vata** *nf* elevated railway

sopraf'**fare** *vt* overwhelm. **~'tto** *pp di* **soprafare** **~zi**'**one** *nf* abuse of power

sopraf'**fino** *a* excellent; (*gusto, udito*) highly refined

sopraggi'**ungere** *vi* (*persona:*) turn up; (*accadere*) happen

soprallu'**ogo** *nm* inspection

sopram'**mobile** *nm* ornament

soprannatu'**rale** *a & nm* supernatural

sopran'**nome** *nm* nickname. **~'nare** *vt* nickname

so'**prano** *nmf* soprano

soprappensi'**ero** *adv* lost in thought

sopras'**salto** *nm* **di ~** with a start

soprasse'**dere** *vi* **~ a** postpone

soprat'**tutto** *adv* above all

sopravvalu'**tare** *vt* overvalue

soprav'**venire** *vi* turn up; (*accadere*) happen. **~'vento** *nm fig* upper hand

sopravvi'**suto** *pp di* **sopravvivere** **~'venza** *nf* survival. **soprav**'**vivere** *vi* survive; **sopravvivere a** outlive (*persona*)

soprinten'**dente** *nmf* supervisor; (*di museo ecc*) keeper. **~za** *nf* supervision; (*ente*) board

so'**pruso** *nm* abuse of power

soq'**quadro** *nm* **mettere a ~** turn upside down

sor'**betto** *nm* sorbet

sor'**bire** *vt* sip; *fig* put up with

'**sordido** *a* sordid; (*avaro*) stingy

sor'**dina** *nf* mute; **in ~** *fig* on the quiet

sordità *nf* deafness. **sordo, -a** *a* deaf; (*rumore, dolore*) dull ● *nmf* deaf person. **sordo**'**muto, -a** *a* deaf-and-dumb ● *nmf* deaf mute

so'**rella** *nf* sister. **~ 'lastra** *nf* stepsister

sor'**gente** *nf* spring; (*fonte*) source

'**sorgere** *vi* rise; *fig* arise

sormon'**tare** *vt* surmount

sorni'**one** *a* sly

sorpas'**sare** *vt* surpass; (*eccedere*) exceed; overtake, pass *Am* (*veicolo*). **~'to a** old-fashioned. **sor**'**passo** *nm* overtaking, passing *Am*

sorpren'**dente** *a* surprising; (*straordinario*) remarkable

sor'**prendere** *vt* surprise; (*cogliere in flagrante*) catch

sor'**pres|a** *nf* surprise; **di ~a** by surprise. **~o** *pp di* **sorprendere**

sor'**reggere** *vt* support; (*tenere*) hold up. **~ggersi** *vr* support oneself. **~tto** *pp di* **sorreggere**

sorri'**dente** *a* smiling

sor'**ridere** *vi* smile. **~so** *pp di* **sorridere** ● *nm* smile

sorseggi'**are** *vt* sip. '**sorso** *nm* sip; (*piccola quantità*) drop

'**sorta** *nf* sort; **di ~** whatever; **ogni ~ di** all sorts of

'**sorte** *nf* fate; (*caso imprevisto*) chance; **tirare a ~** draw lots. **~ggi**'**are** *vt* draw lots for. **sor**'**teggio** *nm* draw

sorti'**legio** *nm* witchcraft

sor'**ti|re** *vi* come out. **~ta** *nf Mil* sortie; (*battuta*) witticism

'**sorto** *pp di* **sorgere**

sorvegli'**an|te** *nmf* keeper; (*controllore*) overseer. **~za** *nf* watch; *Mil ecc* surveillance

sorvegli'**are** *vt* watch over; (*controllare*) oversee; (*polizia:*) watch, keep under surveillance

sorvo'**lare** *vt* fly over; *fig* skip

'**sosia** *nm inv* double

so'**spen|dere** *vt* hang; (*interrompere*) stop; (*privare di una carica*) suspend. **~si**'**one** *nf* suspension. **~'sorio** *nm Sport* jockstrap

so'**speso** *pp di* **sospendere** ● *a* (*impiegato, alunno*) suspended; **~ a** hanging from; **~ a un filo** *fig* hanging by a thread ● *nm* **in ~** pending; (*emozionato*) in suspense

sospet'**tare** *vt* suspect. **so**'**spetto** *a* suspicious ● *nm* suspicion; (*persona*) suspect. **~'toso** *a* suspicious

so'**spingere** *vt* drive. **~'to** *pp di* **sospingere**

sospi'**rare** *vi* sigh ● *vt* long for. **so**'**spiro** *nm* sigh

'**sosta** *nf* stop; (*pausa*) pause; **senza ~** non-stop; "**divieto di ~**" "no parking"

sostan'**tivo** *nm* noun

so'**stanz|a** *nf* substance; **~e** *pl*

(*patrimonio*) property *sg*; in ~ a to sum up. ~**i'oso** *a* substantial; (*cibo*) nourishing

so'**stare** *vi* stop; (*fare una pausa*) pause

so'**stegno** *nm* support

soste'**nere** *vt* support; (*sopportare*) bear; (*resistere*) withstand; (*affermare*) maintain; (*nutrire*) sustain; sit (*esame*); ~ **e le spese** meet the costs. ~**si** *vr* support oneself

soste**ni'tore**, -'**trice** *nmf* supporter

sostenta'**mento** *nm* maintenance

soste'**nuto** *a* (*stile*) formal; (*prezzi, velocità*) high

sostitu'**ire** *vt* substitute (a for), replace (con with). ~**si** *vr* ~ **si a** replace

sosti'**tuto**, -**a** *nmf* replacement, stand-in ● *nm* (*surrogato*) substitute. ~**zi'one** *nf* substitution

sotta'**ceto** *a* pickled; **sottaceti** *pl* pickles

sot'**tana** *nf* petticoat; (*di prete*) cassock

sotter'**fugio** *nm* subterfuge; **di** ~ secretly

sotter'**raneo** *a* underground ● *nm* cellar

sotter'**rare** *vt* bury

sottigli'**ezza** *nf* slimness; *fig* subtlety

sot'**tile** *a* thin; (*udito, odorato*) keen; (*osservazione, distinzione*) subtle. ~**iz-'zare** *vi* split hairs

sottin'**tendere** *vt* imply. ~**so** *pp di* **sottintendere** ● *nm* allusion; **senza** ~**si** openly ● *a* implied

'**sotto** *adv* below; (*più in basso*) lower [down]; (*al di sotto*) underneath; (*al piano di sotto*) downstairs; **è li** ~ **it's underneath;** ~ ~ **deep down;** (*di nascosto*) on the quiet; **di** ~ **downstairs; mettersi** ~ *fig* get down to it; **mettere** ~ (*fam: investire*) knock down; **fatti** ~! *fam* get stuck in! ● *prep* ~ **|a|** under; (*al di sotto di*) under[neath]; **abita** ~ **di me he lives downstairs from me; i bambini** ~ **i dieci anni** children under ten; **20°** ~ **zero** 20° below zero; ~ **il livello del mare** below sea level; ~ **la pioggia** in the rain; ~ **Elisabetta I** under Elizabeth I; ~ **calmante** under sedation; ~ **condizione che...** on condition that...; ~ **giuramento** under oath; ~ **sorveglianza** under surveillance; ~ **Natale/gli esami** around Christmas/ exam time; **al di** ~ **di** under; **andare a i 50 all'ora** do less than 50km an hour ● *nm* **il** |**di**| ~ **the bottom**

sotto'**banco** *adv* under the counter

sottobicchi'**ere** *nm* coaster

sotto'**bosco** *nm* undergrowth

sotto'**braccio** *adv* arm in arm

sotto'**fondo** *nm* background

sottoline'**are** *vt* underline; *fig* stress

sot'**tolio** *adv* in oil

sotto'**mano** *adv* within reach

sottoma'**rino** *a & nm* submarine

sotto'**messo** *pp di* **sottomettere** ● *a* (*remissivo*) submissive

sotto'**mettere** *vt* submit; subdue (*popolo*). ~**si** *vr* submit. **sottomissi'one** *nf* submission

sottopa'**gare** *vt* underpay

sottopas'**saggio** *nm* underpass; (*pedonale*) subway

sotto'**porre** *vt* submit; (*costringere*) subject. ~**si** *vr* submit oneself; ~ **si a** undergo. **sotto'posto** *pp di* **sottoporre**

sotto'**scala** *nm* cupboard under the stairs

sotto'**scritto** *pp di* **sottoscrivere** ● *nm* undersigned

sotto'**scrivere** *vt* sign; (*approvare*) sanction, subscribe to. ~**zi'one** *nf* (*petizione*) petition; (*approvazione*) sanction; (*raccolta di denaro*) appeal

sottosegre'**tario** *nm* undersecretary

sotto'**sopra** *adv* upside down

sotto'**stante** *a* **la strada** ~ **the road below**

sottosu'**olo** *nm* subsoil

sottosvi**lup'pato** *a* underdeveloped. ~**'luppo** *nm* underdevelopment

sotto'**terra** *adv* underground

sotto'**titolo** *nm* subtitle

sottovalu'**tare** *vt* underestimate

sotto'**veste** *nf* slip

sotto'**voce** *adv* in a low voice

sottovu'**oto** *a* vacuum-packed

sot'**trarre** *vt* remove; embezzle (*fondi*); *Math* subtract. ~**rsi** *vr* ~**rsi a** escape from; avoid (*responsabilità*). ~**tto** *pp di* **sottrarre.** ~**zi'one** *nf* removal; (*di fondi*) embezzlement; *Math* subtraction

sottuffici'**ale** *nm* non-commissioned officer; *Naut* petty officer

sou'**brette** *nf inv* showgirl

so'**vietico**, -**a** *a & a* Soviet

sovraccari'**care** *vt* overload. **sovrac'carico** *a* overloaded (**di** with) ● *nm* overload

sovraffati'**carsi** *vr* overexert oneself

sovrannatu'**rale** *a & nm* = **soprannaturale**

so'**vrano**, -**a** *a* sovereign; *fig* supreme ● *nmf* sovereign

sovrap'por|re vt superimpose. **~si** vr overlap. **sovrapposizi'one** nf superimposition

sovra'stare vt dominate; ⟨fig: pericolo:⟩ hang over

sovrinten'den|te, **~za** = **soprintendente**, **soprintendenza**

sovru'mano a superhuman

sovvenzi'one nf subsidy

sovver'sivo a subversive

'sozzo a filthy

S.p.A. abbr **(società per azioni)** plc

spac'ca|re vt split; chop ⟨legna⟩. **~rsi** vr split. **~tura** nf split

spacci'a|re vt deal in, push ⟨droga⟩; **~re qcsa per qcsa** pass sth off as sth; **essere ~to** be done for, be a goner. **~rsi** vr **~rsi per** pass oneself off as. **~'tore**, **~'trice** nmf ⟨di droga⟩ pusher; ⟨di denaro falso⟩ distributor of forged bank notes. **'spaccio** nm ⟨di droga⟩ dealer, pusher; ⟨negozio⟩ shop

'spacco nm split

spac'cone, **-a** nmf boaster

'spada nf sword. **~c'cino** nm swordsman

spadroneggi'are vi act the boss

spae'sato a disorientated

spa'ghetti nmpl spaghetti sg

spa'ghetto nm ⟨fam: spavento⟩ fright

'Spagna nf Spain

spa'gnolo, **-a** a Spanish ● nmf Spaniard ● nm ⟨lingua⟩ Spanish

'spago nm string; **dare ~ a qcno** encourage sb

spai'ato a odd

spalan'ca|re vt, **~rsi** vr open wide. **~to** a wide open

spa'lare vt shovel

'spall|a nf shoulder; ⟨di comico⟩ straight man; **~e** pl ⟨schiena⟩ back; **alle ~e di qcno** ⟨ridere⟩ behind sb's back. **~eggi'are** vt back up

spal'letta nf parapet

spalli'era nf back; ⟨di letto⟩ headboard; ⟨ginnastica⟩ wall bars pl

spal'lina nf strap; ⟨imbottitura⟩ shoulder pad

spal'mare vt spread

'spander|e vt spread; ⟨versare⟩ spill. **~si** vr spread

spappo'lare vt crush

spa'ra|re vt/i shoot; **~rle grosse** talk big. **~ta** nf fam tall story. **~'toria** nf shooting

sparecchi'are vt clear

spa'reggio nm Comm deficit; Sport play-off

'sparg|ere vt scatter; ⟨diffondere⟩ spread; shed ⟨lacrime, sangue⟩. **~ersi** vr spread. **~i'mento** nm scattering; ⟨di lacrime, sangue⟩ shedding; **~imento di sangue** bloodshed

spa'ri|re vi disappear; **~sci!** get lost!. **~zi'one** nf disappearance

spar'lare vi **~ di** run down

'sparo nm shot

sparpagli'are vt, **~si** vr scatter

'sparso pp di **spargere** ● a scattered; ⟨sciolto⟩ loose

spar'tire vt share out; ⟨separare⟩ separate

sparti'traffico nm inv traffic island; ⟨di autostrada⟩ central reservation, median strip Am

spartizi'one nf division

spa'ruto a gaunt; ⟨gruppo⟩ small; ⟨peli, capelli⟩ sparse

sparvi'ero nm sparrow-hawk

spasi'man|te nm hum admirer. **~re** vi suffer agonies

'spasimo nm spasm

spa'smodico a spasmodic

spas'sar|si vr amuse oneself; **~sela** have a good time

spassio'nato a ⟨osservatore⟩ dispassionate, impartial

'spasso nm fun; **essere uno ~** be hilarious; **andare a ~** go for a walk. **spas'soso** a hilarious

'spatola nf spatula

spau'racchio nm scarecrow; fig bugbear. **spau'rire** vt frighten

spa'valdo a defiant

spaventa'passeri nm inv scarecrow

spaven'ta|re vt frighten, scare. **~si** vr be frightened, be scared. **spa'vento** nm fright. **spaven'toso** a frightening; ⟨fam: enorme⟩ incredible

spazi'ale a spatial; ⟨cosmico⟩ space attrib

spazi'are vt space out ● vi range

spazien'tirsi vr lose [one's] patience

'spazio nm space. **~'oso** a spacious

spazzaca'mino nm chimney sweep

spaz'z|are vt sweep; **~are via** sweep away; ⟨fam: mangiare⟩ devour. **~a'tura** nf ⟨immondizia⟩ rubbish. **~ino** nm road sweeper; ⟨netturbino⟩ dustman

spazzo'la nf brush; ⟨di tergicristallo⟩ blade. **~ 'lare** vt brush. **~'lino** nm small brush. **~lino da denti** toothbrush. **~ 'lone** nm scrubbing brush

specchi'arsi vr look at oneself in a/ the mirror; ⟨riflettersi⟩ be mirrored; **~ in qcno** model oneself on sb

210

specchi'etto *nm* ~ retrovisore driving mirror, rearview mirror

'specchio *nm* mirror

speci'ale *a* special ● *nm* TV special [programme]. ~'lista *nmf* specialist. ~lità *nf inv* speciality, specialty *Am*

specializ'zare *vt*, ~rsi *vr* specialize. ~to *a* (operaio) skilled

special'mente *adv* especially

'specie *nf inv* (scientifico) species; (tipo) kind; fare ~ a surprise

specifi'care *vt* specify. **spe'cifico** *a* specific

specu'lare[1] *vi* speculate; ~ su (indagare) speculate on; *Fin* speculate in

specu'lare[2] *a* mirror *attrib*

specula'tore, -'trice *nmf* speculator. ~zi'one *nf* speculation

spe'di|re *vt* send. ~to *pp di* spedire ● *a* quick; (parlata) fluent. ~zi'one *nf* (di lettere ecc) dispatch; *Comm* consignment; (scientifica) expedition

'spegner|e *vt* put out; turn off (gas, luce); switch off (motore); slake (sete). ~si *vr* go out; (morire) pass away

spelacchi'ato *a* (tappeto) threadbare; (cane) mangy

spe'lar|e *vt* skin (coniglio). ~si *vr* (cane:) moult

speleolo'gia *nf* potholing, speleology

spel'lar|e *vt* skin; *fig* fleece. ~si *vr* peel off

spe'lonca *nf* cave; *fig* dingy hole

spendacci'one, -a *nmf* spendthrift

'spendere *vt* spend; ~ fiato waste one's breath

spen'nare *vt* pluck; *fam* fleece (cliente)

spennel'lare *vt* brush

spensie|ra'tezza *nf* lightheartedness. ~'rato *a* carefree

'spento *pp di* spegnere ● *a* off; (gas) out; (smorto) dull

spe'ranza *nf* hope; pieno di ~ hopeful; senza ~ hopeless

spe'rare *vt* hope for; (aspettarsi) expect ● *vi* ~ in trust in; spero di sì I hope so

'sper|dersi *vr* get lost. ~'duto *a* lost; (isolato) secluded

spergi'uro, -a *nmf* perjurer ● *nm* perjury

sperico'lato *a* swashbuckling

sperimen'tal|e *a* experimental. ~re *vt* experiment with; test (resistenza, capacità, teoria). ~zi'one *nf* experimentation

'sperma *nm* sperm

spe'rone *nm* spur

sperpe'rare *vt* squander. **'sperpero** *nm* waste

'spesa *nf* expense; (acquisto) purchase; andare a far ~e go shopping; fare la ~ do the shopping; fare le ~e di pay for. ~e *pl* bancarie bank charges. ~e a carico del destinatario carriage forward. ~e di spedizione shipping costs. **spe'sato** *a* all-expenses-paid. ~o *pp di* spendere

'spesso[1] *a* thick

'spesso[2] *adv* often

spes'sore *nm* thickness; (fig: consistenza) substance

spet'tabile *a* (Comm abbr Spett.) S~ ditta Rossi Messrs Rossi

spettaco'lare *a* spectacular. **spet'tacolo** *nm* spectacle; (rappresentazione) show. ~'loso *a* spectacular

spet'tare *vi* ~ a be up to; (diritto:) ~e di be due to

spetta'tore, -'trice *nmf* spectator; spettatori *pl* (di cinema etc) audience *sg*

spetto'lare *vi* gossip

spetti'nar|e *vt* ~e qcno ruffle sb's hair. ~si *vr* ruffle one's hair

spet'trale *a* ghostly. **'spettro** *nm* ghost; *Phys* spectrum

'spezie *nfpl* spices

spez'zar|e *vt*, ~si *vr* break

spezza'tino *nm* stew

spez'zato *nm* coordinated jacket and trousers

spezzet'tare *vt* break into small pieces

'spia *nf* spy; (della polizia) informer; (di porta) peep-hole; fare la ~ sneak. ~ [luminosa] light. ~ dell'olio oil [warning] light

spiacci'care *vt* squash

spia'ce|nte *a* sorry. ~vole *a* unpleasant

spi'aggia *nf* beach

spia'nare *vt* level; (rendere liscio) smooth; roll out (pasta); raze to the ground (edificio)

spi'ano *nm* a tutto ~ flat out

spian'tato *a fig* penniless

spi'are *vt* spy on; wait for (occasione ecc)

spiattel'lare *vt* blurt out; shove (oggetto)

spiaz'zare *vt* wrong-foot

spi'azzo *nm* (radura) clearing

spic'ca|re *vt* ~re un salto jump; ~re il volo take flight ● *vi* stand out. ~to *a* marked '**spicchio** *nm* (*di agrumi*) segment; (*di aglio*) clove

spicci'a|rsi *vr* hurry up. **~'tivo** *a* speedy

'**spicciolo** *a* (*comune*) banal; (*denaro, 10 000 lire*) in change. **spiccioli** *pl* change *sg*

'**spicco** *nm* relief; **fare ~** stand out

'**spider** *nmf inv* open-top sports car

spie'dino *nm* kebab. **spi'edo** *nm* spit; **allo spiedo** on a spit, spit-roasted

spie'ga|re *vt* explain; open out (*cartina*) unfurl (*vele*). **~rsi** *vr* explain oneself; (*vele, bandiere:*) unfurl. **~zi'one** *nf* explanation

spiegaz'zato *a* crumpled

spie'tato *a* ruthless

spiffe'rare *vt* blurt out ●*vi* (*vento:*) whistle. '**spiffero** *nm* (*corrente d'aria*) draught

'**spiga** *nf* spike; *Bot* ear

spigli'ato *a* self-possessed

'**spigolo** *nm* edge; (*angolo*) corner

spilla *nf* (*gioiello*) brooch. **~ di sicurezza** safety pin

spil'lare *vt* tap

'**spillo** *nm* pin. **~ di sicurezza** safety pin; (*in arma*) safety catch

spi'lorcio *a* stingy

spilun'gone, -a *nmf* beanpole

'**spina** *nf* thorn; (*di pesce*) bone; *Electr* plug. **~ dorsale** spine

spi'nale *a* spinal

spi'naci *nmpl* spinach *sg*

spi'nale *a* spinal

spi'nato *a* (*filo*) barbed; (*pianta*) thorny

spi'nello *nm fam* joint

'**spinger|e** *vt* push; *fig* drive. **~si** *vr* (*andare*) proceed

spi'noso *a* thorny

'**spint|a** *nf* push; (*violenta*) thrust; *fig* spur. **~o|pp di spingere**

spio'naggio *nm* espionage, spying

spio'vente *a* (*tetto*) sloping

spi'overe *vi liter* stop raining; (*ricadere*) fall; (*scorrere*) flow down

'**spira** *nf* coil

spi'raglio *nm* small opening; (*soffio d'aria*) breath of air; (*raggio di luce*) gleam of light

spi'rale *a* spiral ●*nf* spiral; (*negli orologi*) hairspring; (*anticoncezionale*) coil

spi'rare *vi* (*soffiare*) blow; (*morire*) pass away

spiri't|ato *a* possessed; (*espressione*) wild. **~ismo** *nm* spiritualism. '**spirito** *nm* spirit; (*arguzia*) wit; (*intelletto*)

mind; **fare dello spirito** be witty; **sotto spirito** ≈ in brandy. **~o'saggine** *nf* witticism. **spiri'toso** *a* witty

spiritu'ale *a* spiritual

splen'dente *a* shining

splen|dere *vi* shine. **~dido** *a* splendid. **~'dore** *nm* splendour

spode'stare *vt* dispossess; depose (*re*)

spoglia *nf* (*di animale*) skin; **spoglie** *pl* (*salma*) mortal remains; (*bottino*) spoils

spogli'a|re *vt* strip; (*svestire*) undress; (*fare lo spoglio di*) go through. **~rello** *nm* strip-tease. **~rsi** *vr* strip, undress. **~'toio** *nm* dressing room; *Sport* changing room; (*guardaroba*) cloakroom, checkroom *Am*. '**spoglio** *a* undressed; (*albero, muro*) bare ●*nm* (*scrutinio*) perusal

'**spola** *nf* shuttle; **fare la ~** shuttle

spol'pare *vt* take the flesh off; *fig* fleece

spolve'rare *vt* dust; *fam* devour (*cibo*)

'**sponda** *nf* (*di mare, lago*) shore; (*di fiume*) bank; (*bordo*) edge

sponsoriz'zare *vt* sponsor

spon'taneo *a* spontaneous

spopo'lar|e *vt* depopulate ●*vi* (*avere successo*) draw the crowds. **~si** *vr* become depopulated

sporadica'mente *adv* sporadically. **spo'radico** *a* sporadic

sporcacci'one, -a *nmf* dirty pig

spor'c|are *vt* dirty; (*macchiare*) soil. **~arsi** *vr* get dirty. **~izia** *nf* dirt. '**sporco** *a* dirty; **avere la coscienza sporca** have a guilty conscience ●*nm* dirt

spor'gen|te *a* jutting. **~za** *nf* projection

sporg|ere *vt* stretch out; **~e querela contro** take legal action against ●*vi* jut out. **~si** *vr* lean out

sport *nm inv* sport

sporta *nf* shopping basket

spor'tello *nm* door; (*di banca ecc*) window. **~ automatico** cash dispenser

spor'tivo, -a *a* sports *attrib*; (*persona*) sporty ●*nm* sportsman ●*nf* sportswoman

'**sporto** *pp di sporgere**

'**sposa** *nf* bride. **~ 'lizio** *nm* wedding

spo'sa|re *vt* marry; *fig* espouse. **~rsi** *vr* get married; (*vino:*) go (**con** with). **~to** *a* married. '**sposo** *nm* bridegroom; **sposi** *pl* (*novelli*) newlyweds

spossa'tezza *nf* exhaustion. **spos'sato** *a* exhausted, worn out

spo'sta|re *vt* move; (*differire*) postpone; (*cambiare*) change. **~rsi** *vr* move. **~to, -a** *a* ill-adjusted ●*nmf* (*disadattato*) misfit

'**spranga** *nf* bar. **spran'gare** *vt* bar

'**sprazzo** *nm* (*di colore*) splash; (*di luce*) flash; *fig* glimmer

spre'**care** *vt* waste. '**spreco** *nm* waste

spre'**g|evole** *a* despicable. **~ia'tivo** *a* pejorative. '**spregio** *nm* contempt

spregiudi'**cato** *a* unscrupulous

'**spremere** *vt* squeeze. **~si** *vr* **~si le meningi** rack one's brains

spremia'**grumi** *nm* lemon squeezer

spre'**muta** *nf* juice. **~ d'arancia** fresh orange [juice]

sprez'**zante** *a* contemptuous

sprigio'**nar|e** *vt* emit. **~si** *vr* burst out

spriz'**zare** *vt/i* spurt; be bursting with ‹*salute, gioia*›

sprofon'**dar|e** *vi* sink; (*crollare*) collapse. **~si** *vr* **~si in** sink into; *fig* be engrossed in

spro'**nare** *vt* spur on. '**sprone** *nm* spur; (*sartoria*) yoke

sproporzio'**nato** *a* disproportionate. **~'one** *nf* disproportion

spropositato** *a* full of blunders; (*enorme*) huge. **spro'posito** *nm* blunder; (*eccesso*) excessive amount; **a spro'posito** inopportunely

sprovve'**duto** *a* unprepared; **~ di** lacking in

sprov'**visto** *a* **~ di** out of; lacking in ‹*fantasia, pazienza*›; **alla sprovvista** unexpectedly

spruz'**za|re** *vt* sprinkle; (*vaporizzare*) spray; (*inzaccherare*) spatter. **~'tore** *nm* spray; '**spruzzo** *nm* spray; (*di fango*) splash

spudora'**tezza** *nf* shamelessness. **~'rato** *a* shameless

'**spugna** *nf* sponge; (*tessuto*) towelling. spu'**gnoso** *a* spongy

'**spuma** *nf* foam; (*schiuma*) froth; *Culin* mousse. spu'**mante** *nm* sparkling wine, spumante. spumeggi'**are** *vi* foam

spun'**ta|re** *vt* (*rompere la punta di*) break the point of; trim ‹*capelli*›; **~rla** *fig* win ●*vi* ‹*pianta:*› sprout; ‹*capelli:*› begin to grow; (*sorgere*) rise; (*apparire*) appear. **~rsi** *vr* get blunt. **~ta** *nf* trim

spun'**tino** *nm* snack

'**spunto** *nm* cue; *fig* starting point; **dare ~ a** give rise to

spur'**gar|e** *vt* purge. **~si** *vr* *Med* expectorate

spu'**tare** *vt/i* spit; **~ sentenze** pass judgment. '**sputo** *nm* spit

'**squadra** *nf* (*gruppo*) team, squad; (*di polizia ecc*) squad; (*da disegno*) square. squa'**drare** *vt* square; (*guardare*) look up and down

squa'dr|**iglia** *nf*, **~one** *nm* squadron

squagli'**ar|e** *vt*, **~si** *vr* melt; **~sela** (*fam: svignarsela*) steal out

squa'**lifi|ca** *nf* disqualification. **~'care** *vt* disqualify

'**squallido** *a* squalid. squal'**lore** *nm* squalor

'**squalo** *nm* shark

'**squama** *nf* scale; (*di pelle*) flake

squa'**m|are** *vt* scale. **~arsi** *vr* ‹*pelle:*› flake off. **~'moso** *a* scaly; ‹*pelle*› flaky

squarcia'**gola: a ~** *adv* at the top of one's voice

squarci'**are** *vt* rip. '**squarcio** *nm* rip; (*di ferita, in nave*) gash; (*di cielo*) patch

squar'**tare** *vt* quarter; dismember ‹*animale*›

squattri'**nato** *a* penniless

squili'**bra|re** *vt* unbalance. **~to, -a** *a* unbalanced ●*nmf* lunatic. squi'**librio** *nm* imbalance

squil'**la|nte** *a* shrill. **~re** *vi* ‹*campana:*› peal; ‹*tromba:*› blare; ‹*telefono:*› ring. '**squillo** *nm* blare; *Teleph* ring; (*ragazza*) call girl

squi'**sito** *a* exquisite

squit'**tire** *vi* ‹*pappagallo, fig:*› squawk; ‹*topo:*› squeak

sradi'**care** *vt* uproot; eradicate (*vizio, male*)

sragio'**nare** *vi* rave

srego'**la|tezza** *nf* dissipation. **~'lato** *a* inordinate; (*dissoluto*) dissolute

s.r.l. *abbr* (**società a responsabilità limitata**) Ltd

sroto'**lare** *vt* uncoil

SS *abbr* (**strada statale**) national road

'**stabile** *a* stable; (*permanente*) lasting; (*saldo*) steady; **compagnia ~** *Theat* repertory company ●*nm* (*edificio*) building

stabili'**mento** *nm* factory; (*industriale*) plant; (*edificio*) establishment. **~ balneare** lido

stabi'**lire** *vt* establish; (*decidere*) decide. **~rsi** *vr* settle. **~tà** *nf* stability

stabiliz'**za|re** *vt* stabilize. **~rsi** *vr* stabilize. **~'tore** *nm* stabilizer

stac'**car|e** *vt* detach; pronounce clearly (*parole*); (*separare*) separate; turn off (*corrente*); **~e gli occhi da** take one's eyes off ●*vi* (*fam: finire di lavorare*) knock off. **~si** *vr* come off;

~**si da** break away from ⟨*partito, famiglia*⟩

staccio'nata *nf* fence

'**stacco** *nm* gap

'**stadio** *nm* stadium

'**staffa** *nf* stirrup

staf'fetta *nf* dispatch rider

stagio'nale *a* seasonal

stagio'na|re *vt* season ⟨*legno*⟩; mature ⟨*formaggio*⟩. ~**to a** ⟨*legno*⟩ seasoned; ⟨*formaggio*⟩ matured

stagi'one *nf* season; **alta/bassa** ~ high/low season

stagli'arsi *vr* stand out

sta'gna|nte *a* stagnant. ~**re** *vt* ⟨*saldare*⟩ solder; ⟨*chiudere ermeticamente*⟩ seal ●*vi* ⟨*acqua:*⟩ stagnate. '**stagno a** ⟨*a tenuta d'acqua*⟩ watertight ●*nm* ⟨*acqua ferma*⟩ pond; ⟨*metallo*⟩ tin

sta'gnola *nf* tinfoil

stalag'mite *nf* stalagmite

stalat'tite *nf* stalactite

stall|a *nf* stable; ⟨*per buoi*⟩ cowshed. ~**i'ere** *nm* groom

stal'lone *nm* stallion

sta'mani, stamat'tina *adv* this morning

stam'becco *nm* ibex

stam'berga *nf* hovel

'**stampa** *nf* *Typ* printing; ⟨*giornali, giornalisti*⟩ press; ⟨*riproduzione*⟩ print

stam'pa|nte *nf* printer. ~**nte ad aghi** dot matrix printer. ~**nte laser** laser printer. ~**re** *vt* print. ~**'tello** *nm* block letters *pl*

stam'pella *nf* crutch

'**stampo** *nm* mould; **di vecchio** ~ ⟨*persona*⟩ of the old school

sta'nare *vt* drive out

stan'car|e *vt* tire; ⟨*annoiare*⟩ bore. ~**si** *vr* get tired

stan'chezza *nf* tiredness. '**stanco a** tired; **stanco di** ⟨*stufo*⟩ fed up with. **stanco morto** dead tired, knackered *fam*

'**standard** *a* & *nm inv* standard. ~**iz'zare** *vt* standardize

'**stan|ga** *nf* bar; ⟨*persona*⟩ beanpole. ~**'gata** *nf fig* blow; ⟨*fam: nel calcio*⟩ big kick; **prendere una** ~**gata** ⟨*fam: agli esami, economica*⟩ come a cropper. **stan'ghetta** *nf* ⟨*di occhiali*⟩ leg

sta'notte *nf* tonight; ⟨*la notte scorsa*⟩ last night

'**stante** *prep* on account of; **a sé** ~ separate

stan'tio *a* stale

stan'tuffo *nm* piston

'**stanza** *nf* room; ⟨*metrica*⟩ stanza

stanzi'are *vt* allocate

stap'pare *vt* uncork

'**stare** *vi* ⟨*rimanere*⟩ stay; ⟨*abitare*⟩ live; ⟨*con gerundio*⟩ be; **sto solo cinque minuti** I'll stay only five minutes; **sto in piazza Peyron** I live in Peyron Square; **sta dormendo** he's sleeping; ~ **a** ⟨*attenersi*⟩ keep to; ⟨*spettare*⟩ be up to; ~ **bene** ⟨*economicamente*⟩ be well off; ⟨*di salute*⟩ be well; ⟨*addirsi*⟩ suit; ~ **dietro a** ⟨*seguire*⟩ follow; ⟨*sorvegliare*⟩ keep an eye on; ⟨*corteggiare*⟩ run after; ~ **in piedi** stand; ~ **per** be about to; **ben ti sta!** it serves you right!; **come stai/ sta?** how are you?; **lasciar** ~ leave alone; **starci** ⟨*essere d'accordo*⟩ agree; **il 3 nel 12 ci sta 4 volte** 3 into 12 goes 4; **non sa** ~ **agli scherzi** he can't take a joke; ~ **su** ⟨*con la schiena*⟩ sit up straight; ~ **sulle proprie** keep oneself to oneself. **starsene** *vr* ⟨*rimanere*⟩ stay

starnu'tire *vi* sneeze. **star'nuto** *nm* sneeze

sta'sera *adv* this evening, tonight

sta'tale *a* state *attrib* ●*nmf* state employee ●*nf* ⟨*strada*⟩ main road, trunk road

'**statico** *a* static

sta'tista *nm* statesman

sta'tistic|a *nf* statistics *sg*. ~**o a** statistical

'**stato** *pp di* **essere, stare** ●*nm* state; ⟨*posizione sociale*⟩ position; *Jur* status. ~ **d'animo** frame of mind. ~ **civile** marital status. **S~ Maggiore** *Mil* General Staff. **Stati** *pl* **Uniti [d'America]** United States [of America]

'**statua** *nf* statue

statuni'tense *a* United States *attrib*, US *attrib* ●*nmf* citizen of the United States, US citizen

sta'tura *nf* height; **di alta** ~ tall; **di bassa** ~ short

sta'tuto *nm* statute

stazio'nario *a* stationary

stazi'one *nf* station; ⟨*città*⟩ resort. ~ **balneare** seaside resort. ~ **ferroviaria** railway station *Br*, train station. ~ **di servizio** petrol station *Br*, service station. ~ **termale** spa

'**stecca** *nf* stick; ⟨*di ombrello*⟩ rib; ⟨*da biliardo*⟩ cue; *Med* splint; ⟨*di sigarette*⟩ carton; ⟨*di reggiseno*⟩ stiffener

stec'cato *nm* fence

stec'chito *a* skinny; ⟨*rigido*⟩ stiff; ⟨*morto*⟩ stone cold dead

'**stella** *nf* star; **salire alle stel'e** ⟨*prezzi:*⟩ rise skyhigh. **~ alpina** edelweiss. **~ cadente** shooting star. **~ filante** streamer. **~ di mare** starfish

stel'la|re *a* star *attrib*; ⟨*grandezza*⟩ stellar. **~to** *a* starry

'**stelo** *nm* stem; **lampada** *nf* **a ~** standard lamp

'**stemma** *nm* coat of arms

stempi'ato *a* bald at the temples

sten'dardo *nm* standard

'**stender|e** *vt* spread out; ⟨*appendere*⟩ hang out; ⟨*distendere*⟩ stretch [out]; ⟨*scrivere*⟩ write down. **~si** *vr* stretch out

stendibianche'ria *nm* *inv*, **stendi'toio** *nm* clothes horse

stenodatti|logra'fia *nf* shorthand typing. **~'lografo, -a** *nmf* shorthand typist

stenogra'f|are *vt* take down in shorthand. **~ia** *nf* shorthand

sten'ta|re *vi* **~re a** find it hard to. **~to** *a* laboured. '**stento** *nm* ⟨*fatica*⟩ effort; **a stento** with difficulty; **stenti** *pl* hardships, privations

'**sterco** *nm* dung

'**stereo**['**fonico**] *a* stereo[phonic]

stereoti'pato *a* stereotyped; ⟨*sorriso*⟩ insincere. **stere'otipo** *nm* stereotype

'**steril|e** *a* sterile; ⟨*terreno*⟩ barren. **~ità** *nf* sterility. **~iz'zare** *vt* sterilize. **~izzazi'one** *nf* sterilization

ster'lina *nf* pound; **lira ~** [pound] sterling

stermi'nare *vt* exterminate

stermi'nato *a* immense

ster'minio *nm* extermination

'**sterno** *nm* breastbone

ster'zare *vi* steer. '**sterzo** *nm* steering

'**steso** *pp di* **stendere**

'**stesso** *a* same; **io ~** myself; **tu ~** yourself; **me ~** myself; **se ~** himself; **in quel momento ~** at that very moment; **dalla stessa regina** ⟨*in persona*⟩ by the Queen herself; **tuo fratello ~ dice che hai torto** even your brother says you're wrong; **coi miei stessi occhi** with my own eyes ●*pron* **lo ~** the same one; ⟨*la stessa cosa*⟩ the same; **fa lo ~** it's all the same; **ci vado lo ~** I'll go just the same

ste'sura *nf* drawing up; ⟨*documento*⟩ draft

stick *nm* **colla a ~** glue stick; **deodorante a ~** stick deodorant

'**stigma** *nm* stigma. **~te** *nfpl* stigmata

sti'lare *vt* draw up

'**stil|e** *nm* style. **~e libero** ⟨*nel nuoto*⟩ freestyle, crawl. **sti'lista** *nmf* stylist. **~iz'zato** *a* stylized

stil'lare *vi* ooze

stilo'grafic|a *nf* fountain pen. **~o** *a* **penna ~a** fountain pen

'**stima** *nf* esteem; ⟨*valutazione*⟩ estimate. **sti'mare** *vt* esteem; ⟨*valutare*⟩ estimate; ⟨*ritenere*⟩ consider

stimo'la|nte *a* stimulating ●*nm* stimulant. **~re** *vt* stimulate; ⟨*incitare*⟩ incite

'**stimolo** *nm* stimulus; ⟨*fitta*⟩ pang

'**stinco** *nm* shin

'**stinger|e** *vt/i* fade. **~si** *vr* fade. '**stinto** *pp di* **stingere**

sti'par|e *vt* cram. **~si** *vr* crowd together

stipendi'ato *a* salaried ● *nm* salaried worker. **sti'pendio** *nm* salary

sti'pite *nm* doorpost

stipu'la|re *vt* stipulate. **~zi'one** *nf* stipulation; ⟨*accordo*⟩ agreement

stira'mento *nm* sprain

sti'ra|re *vt* iron; ⟨*distendere*⟩ stretch. **~rsi** *vr* ⟨*distendersi*⟩ stretch; pull ⟨*muscolo*⟩. **~ 'tura** *nf* ironing. '**stiro ferro da stiro** iron

'**stirpe** *nf* stock

stiti'chezza *nf* constipation. '**stitico** *a* constipated

'**stiva** *nf* *Naut* hold

sti'vale *nm* boot. **stivali** *pl* **di gomma** Wellington boots, Wellingtons

'**stizza** *nf* anger

stiz'zi|re *vt* irritate. **~rsi** *vr* become irritated. **~to** *a* irritated. **stiz'zoso** *a* peevish

stocca'fisso *nm* stockfish

stoc'cata *nf* stab; ⟨*battuta pungente*⟩ gibe

'**stoffa** *nf* material; *fig* stuff

'**stola** *nf* stole

'**stolto** *a* foolish

stoma'chevole *a* revolting

'**stomaco** *nm* stomach; **mal di ~** stomach-ache

sto'na|re *vt/i* sing/play out of tune ●*vi* ⟨*non intonarsi*⟩ clash. **~to** *a* out of tune; ⟨*discordante*⟩ clashing; ⟨*confuso*⟩ bewildered. **~ 'tura** *nf* false note; ⟨*discordanza*⟩ clash

'**stoppia** *nf* stubble

stop'pino *nm* wick

stop'poso *a* tough

storcer|e *vt*, **~si** *vr* twist

stor'di|re *vt* stun; ⟨*intontire*⟩ daze. **~rsi** *vr* dull one's senses. **~to** *a* stunned; ⟨*intontito*⟩ dazed; ⟨*sventato*⟩ heedless

'storia nf history; (racconto, bugia) story; (pretesto) excuse; senza storie! no fuss!; fare [delle] storie make a fuss

'storico, -a a historical; (di importanza storica) historic ● nmf historian

stori'one nm sturgeon

'stormo nm flock

'storno nm starling

storpi'a|re vt cripple; mangle (parole). ~'tura nf deformation. 'storpio, -a a crippled ● nmf cripple

'stort|a nf (distorsione) sprain; prendere una ~a alla caviglia sprain one's ankle. ~o pp di storcere ● a crooked; (ritorto) twisted; (gambe) bandy; fig wrong

sto'viglie nfpl crockery sg

'strabico a cross-eyed; essere ~ be cross-eyed, have a squint

strabili'ante a astonishing

stra'bismo nm squint

straboc'care vi overflow

stra'carico a overloaded

stracci'a|re vt tear; (fam: vincere) thrash. ~'ato a torn; (persona) in rags; (prezzi) slashed; a un prezzo ~ato dirt cheap. 'straccio a torn ● nm rag; (strofinaccio) cloth ~'one nm tramp

stra'cotto a overdone; (fam: innamorato) head over heels ● nm stew

'strada nf road; (di città) street; (fig: cammino) way; essere fuori ~ be on the wrong track; fare ~ lead the way; farsi ~ make one's way. ~ maestra main road. ~ a senso unico one-way street. ~ senza uscita blind alley. stra'dale a road attrib

strafalci'one nm blunder

stra'fare vi overdo it, overdo things

stra'foro: di ~ adv on the sly

strafot'ten|te a arrogant. ~za nf arrogance

'strage nf slaughter

'stralcio nm (parte) extract

stralu'na|re vt ~re gli occhi open one's eyes wide. ~to a (occhi) staring; (persona) distraught

stramaz'zare vi fall heavily

strambe'ria nf oddity. 'strambo a strange

strampa'lato a odd

stra'nezza nf strangeness

strango'lare vt strangle

strani'ero, -a a foreign ● nmf foreigner

'strano a strange

straordi|naria'mente adv extraor-

dinarily. ~'nario a extraordinary; (notevole) remarkable; (edizione) special; lavoro ~nario overtime; treno ~nario special train

strapaz'zar|e vt ill-treat; scramble (uova). ~si vr tire oneself out. stra'pazzo nm strain; da strapazzo fig worthless

strapi'eno a overflowing

strapi'ombo nm projection; a ~ sheer

strap'par|e vt tear; (per distruggere) tear up; pull out (dente, capelli); (sradicare) pull up; (estorcere) wring. ~si vr get torn; (allontanarsi) tear oneself away. 'strappo nm tear; (strattone) jerk; (fam: passaggio) lift; fare uno strappo alla regola make an exception to the rule. ~ muscolare muscle strain

strapun'tino nm folding seat

strari'pare vi flood

strasci'care vt trail; shuffle (piedi); drawl (parole). 'strascico nm train; fig after-effect

strass nm inv rhinestone

strata'gemma nm stratagem

strate'gia nf strategy. stra'tegico a strategic

'strato nm layer; (di vernice ecc) coat, layer; (roccioso, sociale) stratum. ~'sfera nf stratosphere. ~'sferico a stratospheric; fig sky-high

stravac'ca|rsi vr fam slouch. ~to a fam slouching

strava'gan|te a extravagant; (eccentrico) eccentric. ~za nf extravagance; (eccentricità) eccentricity

stra'vecchio a ancient

strave'dere vt ~ per worship

stravizi'are vi indulge oneself. stra'vizio nm excess

stra'volg|ere vt twist; (turbare) upset. ~i'mento nm twisting. stra'volto a distraught; (fam: stanco) done in

strazi'a|nte a heartrending; (dolore) agonizing. ~re vt grate on (orecchie); break (cuore). 'strazio nm agony; essere uno strazio be agony; che strazio! fam it's awful!

'strega nf witch. stre'gare vt bewitch. stre'gone nm wizard

'stregua nf alla ~ di like

stre'ma|re vt exhaust. ~to a exhausted

'stremo nm ridotto allo ~ at the end of one's tether

'strenuo a strenuous

strepi'tare vi make a din. 'strepito

nm noise. ~**toso** *a* noisy; *fig* resounding

stres'sante *a* (*lavoro, situazione*) stressful. ~**to a** stressed [out]

'stretta *nf* grasp; (*dolore*) pang; **essere alle strette** be in dire straits; **mettere alle strette qcno** have sb's back up against the wall. ~ **di mano** handshake

stret'tezza *nf* narrowness; **stret'tezze** *pl* (*difficoltà finanziarie*) financial difficulties

'stretto *pp di* **stringere** ●*a* narrow; (*serrato*) tight; (*vicino*) close; (*dialetto*) broad; (*rigoroso*) strict; **lo ~to necessario** the bare minimum ●*nm* *Geog* strait. ~**toia** *nf* bottleneck; (*fam. difficoltà*) tight spot

stri'a|to *a* striped. ~**tura** *nf* streak

stri'dente *a* strident

'stridere *vi* squeak; *fig* clash. **stri'dore** *nm* screech

'stridulo *a* shrill

strigli'a|re *vt* groom. ~**ta** *nf* grooming; *fig* dressing down

stril'lare *vi/t* scream. **'strillo** *nm* scream

strimin'zito *a* skimpy; (*magro*) skinny

strimpel'lare *vt* strum

'stringa *nf* lace; *Comput* string. ~**gato** *a fig* terse

'stringer|e *vt* press; (*serrare*) squeeze; (*tenere stretto*) hold tight; take in (*abito*); (*comprimere*) be tight; (*restringere*) tighten; ~**e la mano a** shake hands with ●*vi* (*premere*) press. ~**si** *vr* (*accostarsi*) draw close (**a** to); (*avvicinarsi*) squeeze up

'striscia *nf* strip; (*riga*) stripe. **strisce** *pl* [**pedonali**] zebra crossing *sg*

strisci'a|re *vi* crawl; (*sfiorare*) graze ●*vt* drag (*piedi*). ~**si** *vr* ~**si a** rub against. **'striscio** *nm* graze; *Med* smear; **colpire di striscio** graze

strisci'one *nm* banner

strito'lare *vt* grind

striz'zare *vt* squeeze; (*torcere*) wring [out]; ~ **l'occhio** wink

'strofa *nf* strophe

strofi'naccio *nm* cloth; (*per spolverare*) duster. ~ **da cucina** tea towel

strofi'nare *vt* rub

strombaz'zare *vt* boast about ●*vi* hoot

strombaz'zata *nf* (*di clacson*) hoot

stron'care *vt* cut off; (*reprimere*) crush; (*criticare*) tear to shreds

'stronzo *nm* *vulg* shit

stropicci'are *vt* rub; crumple (*vestito*)

stroz'za|re *vt* strangle. ~**tura** *nf* strangling; (*di strada*) narrowing

strozzi'naggio *nm* loan-sharking

stroz'zino *nm pej* usurer; (*truffatore*) shark

strug'gente *a* all-consuming

'struggersi *vr* pine [away]

strumen'tale *a* instrumental

strumentaliz'zare *vt* make use of

strumentazi'one *nf* instrumentation

stru'mento *nm* instrument; (*arnese*) tool. ~ **a corda** string instrument. ~ **musicale** musical instrument

strusci'are *vt* rub

'strutto *nm* lard

strut'tura *nf* structure. **struttu'rale** *a* structural

struttu'rare *vt* structure

strutturazi'one *nf* structuring

'struzzo *nm* ostrich

stuc'care *vt* stucco

stuc'chevole *a* nauseating

'stucco *nm* stucco

stu'den|te, -'essa *nmf* student; (*di scuola*) schoolboy; schoolgirl. ~'**tesco** *a* student; (*di scolaro*) school *attrib*

studi'ar|e *vt* study. ~**si** *vr* ~**si di** try to

'studio *nm* studying; (*stanza, ricerca*) study; (*di artista, TV ecc*) studio; (*di professionista*) office. ~**oso, -a** studious ●*nmf* scholar

'stufa *nf* stove. ~ **elettrica** electric fire

stu'fare *vt* *Culin* stew; (*dare fastidio*) bore. ~**rsi** *vr* get bored. ~**to** *nm* stew

'stufo *a* bored; **essere** ~ **di** be fed up with

stu'oia *nf* mat

stupefa'cente *a* amazing ●*nm* drug

stu'pendo *a* stupendous

stupid'daggine *nf* (*azione*) stupid thing; (*cosa da poco*) nothing. ~**ata** *nf* stupid thing. ~**ità** *nf* stupidity. **'stupido** *a* stupid

stu'pir|e *vt* astonish ●*vi*, ~**si** *vr* be astonished. **stu'pore** *nm* amazement

stu'prare *vt* rape. ~**tore** *nm* rapist. **'stupro** *nm* rape

sturalavan'dini *nm inv* plunger

stu'rare *vt* uncork; unblock (*lavandino*)

stuzzica'denti *nm inv* toothpick

stuzzi'care *vt* prod [at]; pick (*denti*); poke (*fuoco*); (*molestare*) tease; whet (*appetito*)

stuzzi'chino *nm* *Culin* appetizer

217

su *prep* on; *(senza contatto)* over; *(riguardo a)* about; *(circa, intorno a)* about, around; **le chiavi sono sul tavolo** the keys are on the table; **il quadro è appeso sul camino** the picture is hanging over the fireplace; **un libro sull'antico Egitto** a book on *o* about Ancient Egypt; **costa sulle 50 000 lire** it costs about 50,000 lire; **decidere sul momento** decide at the time; **su commissione** on commission; **su due piedi** on the spot; **uno su dieci** one out of ten ● *adv* up; *(al piano di sopra)* upstairs; *(addosso)* on; **ho su il cappotto** I've got my coat on; **in su** *(guardare)* up; **dalla vita in su** from the waist up; **su!** come on!

su'bacqueo *a* underwater

subaffit'tare *vt* sublet. **subaf'fitto** *nm* sublet

subal'terno *a & nm* subordinate

sub'buglio *nm* turmoil

sub'conscio *a & nm* subconscious

subdola'mente *adv* deviously. **'subdolo** *a* devious, underhand

suben'trare *vi (circostanze:)* come up; **~ a** take the place of

su'bire *vt* undergo; *(patire)* suffer

subis'sare *vt fig* **~ di** overwhelm with

'subito *adv* at once; **~ dopo** straight after

su'blime *a* sublime

subodo'rare *vt* suspect

subordi'nato, -a *a & nmf* subordinate

subur'bano *a* suburban

suc'cederje *vi (accadere)* happen; **~e a** succeed; *(venire dopo)* follow; **~ al trono** succeed to the throne. **~si** *vr* happen one after the other

successi'one *nf* succession; **in ~** in succession

succes'siva'mente *adv* subsequently. **~'sivo** *a* successive

suc'cesso *pp di* **succedere** ● *nm* success; *(esito)* outcome; *(disco ecc)* hit. **~'sone** *nm* huge success

succes'sore *nm* successor

succhi'are *vt* suck [up]

suc'cinto *a (conciso)* concise; *(abito)* scanty

'succo *nm* juice; *fig* essence; **~ di frutta** fruit juice. **suc'coso** *a* juicy

suc'cube *nm* **essere ~ di qcno** be totally dominated by sb

succu'lento *a* succulent

succur'sale *nf* branch [office]

sud *nm* south; **del ~** southern

su'darje *vi* sweat, perspire; *(faticare)* sweat blood; **~re freddo** be in a cold sweat. **~ta** *nf anche fig* sweat. **~'ticcio** *a* sweaty. **~to** *a* sweaty; *(vittoria)* hard-won; *(pane)* hard-earned

sud'detto *a* above-mentioned

'suddito, -a *nmf* subject

suddi'viderje *vt* subdivide. **~si'one** *nf* subdivision

su'd-est *nm* southeast

'sudici|o *a* dirty, filthy. **~'ume** *nm* dirt, filth

sudorazi'one *nf* perspiring. **su'dore** *nm* sweat, perspiration; *fig* sweat

su'd-ovest *nm* southwest

suffici'en|te *a* sufficient; *(presuntuoso)* conceited ● *nm* bare essentials *pl*; *Sch* pass mark. **~za** *nf* sufficiency; *(presunzione)* conceit; *Sch* pass; **a ~za** enough

suf'fisso *nm* suffix

suf'fragio *nm* *(voto)* vote. **~ universale** universal suffrage

suggeri'mento *nm* suggestion

sugge'ri|re *vt* suggest; *Theat* prompt. **~tore, ~trice** *nmf Theat* prompter

suggestiona'bile *a* suggestible

suggestio'na|re *vt* influence. **~to a** influenced. **suggesti'one** *nf* influence

sugge'stivo *a* suggestive; *(musica ecc)* evocative

'sughero *nm* cork

'sugli = **su** + **gli**

'sugo *nm* *(di frutta)* juice; *(di carne)* gravy; *(salsa)* sauce; *(sostanza)* substance

'sui = **su** + **i**

sui'cid|a *a* suicidal ● *nmf* suicide. **suici'darsi** *vr* commit suicide. **~io** *nm* suicide

su'ino *a* **carne suina** pork ● *nm* swine

sul = **su** + **il**. **'sullo** = **su** + **lo**. **'sulla** = **su** + **la**. **'sulle** = **su** + **le**

sul'ta|na *nf* sultana. **~'nina** *a* **uva ~nina** sultana. **~no** *nm* sultan

'sunto *nm* summary

'suo, -a *poss a* **il ~**, **i suoi** his; *(di cosa, animale)* its; *(forma di cortesia)* your; **la sua, le sue** her; *(di cosa, animale)* its; *(forma di cortesia)* your; **questa macchina è sua** this car is his/hers; **~ padre** his/her/your father; **un ~ amico** a friend of his/hers/yours ● *poss pron* **il ~**, **i suoi** his; *(di cosa, animale)* its; *(forma di cortesia)* yours; **la sua, le sue** hers; *(di cosa animale)* its; *(forma di cortesia)* yours; **i suoi** his/her folk

su'ocera *nf* mother-in-law

su'ocero *nm* father-in-law

su'ola *nf* sole

su'olo *nm* ground; (*terreno*) soil

suo'na|re *vt/i Mus* play; ring (*campanello*); sound (*allarme, clacson*); (*orologio:*) strike. ~'tore, ~'trice *nmf* player.
suone'ria *nf* alarm. su'ono *nm* sound

su'ora *nf* nun; **Suor Maria** Sister Maria

superal'colico *nm* spirit ● *a* **bevande superalcoliche** spirits

supera'mento *nm* (*di timidezza*) overcoming; (*di esame*) success (*di in*)

supe'rare *vt* surpass; (*eccedere*) exceed; (*vincere*) overcome; overtake, pass *Am* (*veicolo*); pass (*esame*)

su'perb|ia *nf* haughtiness. ~o *a* haughty; (*magnifico*) superb

superdo'tato *a* highly gifted

superfici'al|e *a* superficial ● *nmf* superficial person. ~ità *nf* superficiality.
super'ficie *nf* surface; (*area*) area

su'perfluo *a* superfluous

superi'or|e *a* superior; (*di grado*) senior; (*più elevato*) higher; (*sovrastante*) upper; (*al di sopra*) above ● *nmf* superior. ~ità *nf* superiority

superla'tivo *a & nm* superlative

supermer'cato *nm* supermarket

super'sonico *a* supersonic

su'perstite *a* surviving ● *nmf* survivor

superstizi'o|ne *nf* superstition. ~so *a* superstitious

super'strada *nf* toll-free motorway

supervisi|'one *nf* supervision.
~'sore *nm* supervisor

su'pino *a* supine

suppel'lettili *nfpl* furnishings

suppergiù *adv* about

supplemen'tare *a* additional, supplementary

supple'mento *nm* supplement; ~ rapido express train supplement

sup'plen|te *a* temporary ● *nmf Sch* supply teacher. ~za *nf* temporary post

'suppli|ca *nf* plea; (*domanda*) petition. ~'care *vt* beg. ~'chevole *a* imploring

sup'plire *vt* replace ● *vi* ~ a (*compensare*) make up for

sup'plizio *nm* torture

sup'porre *vt* suppose

sup'porto *nm* support

supposizi'one *nf* supposition

sup'posta *nf* suppository

sup'posto *pp di* supporre

supre'mazia *nf* supremacy.
su'premo *a* supreme

sur'fare *vi* ~ **in Internet** surf the Net

surge'la|re *vt* deep-freeze. ~ti *nmpl* frozen food *sg*. ~to *a* frozen

surrea'lis|mo *nm* surrealism. ~ta *nmf* surrealist

surris'cal'dare *vt* overheat

surro'gato *nm* substitute

suscet'tibil|e *a* touchy. ~ità *nf* touchiness

susci'tare *vt* stir up; arouse (*ammirazione ecc*)

su'sin|a *nf* plum. ~o *nm* plumtree

su'spense *nf* suspense

sussegu'ente *a* subsequent. ~ irsi *vr* follow one after the other

sussidi'ar|e *vt* subsidize. ~io *a* subsidiary. sus'sidio *nm* subsidy; (*aiuto*) aid. **sussidio di disoccupazione** unemployment benefit

sussi'ego *nm* haughtiness

sussi'stenza *nf* subsistence. sus'sistere *vi* subsist; (*essere valido*) hold good

sussul'tare *vi* start. sus'sulto *nm* start

sussur'rare *vt* whisper. sus'surro *nm* whisper

su'tu|ra *nf* suture. ~'rare *vt* suture

sva'ga|re *vt* amuse. ~si *vr* amuse oneself. 'svago *nm* relaxation; (*divertimento*) amusement

svaligi'are *vt* rob; burgle (*casa*)

svalu'ta|re *vt* devalue; *fig* underestimate. ~rsi *vr* lose value. ~zi'one *nf* devaluation

svam'pito *a* absent-minded

sva'nire *vi* vanish

svantaggi|'ato *a* at a disadvantage; (*bambino, paese*) disadvantaged.
svan'taggio *nm* disadvantage; **essere in svantaggio** *Sport* be losing; **in svantaggio di tre punti** three points down. ~'oso *a* disadvantageous

svapo'rare *vi* evaporate

svari'ato *a* varied

sva'sato *a* flared

'svastica *nf* swastika

sve'dese *a & nm* (*lingua*) Swedish ● *nmf* Swede

'sveglia *nf* (*orologio*) alarm [clock]; ~! get up!; **mettere la** ~ set the alarm [clock]

svegli'ar|e *vt* wake up; *fig* awaken. ~si *vr* wake up. 'sveglio *a* awake; (*di mente*) quick-witted

sve'lare *vt* reveal

svel'tezza *nf* speed; *fig* quick-wittedness

svel'tir|e *vt* quicken. ~**si** *vr* ⟨*persona:*⟩ liven up. **'svelto** *a* quick; ⟨*slanciato*⟩ svelte; **alla svelta** quickly

'svend|ere *vt* undersell. ~**ita** *nf* [clearance] sale

sveni'mento *nm* fainting fit. **sve'nire** *vi* faint

sven'ta|re *vt* foil. ~**to** *a* thoughtless ●*nmf* thoughtless person

'sventola *nf* slap; **orecchie** *nfpl* **a** ~ protruding ears

svento'lare *vt/i* wave

sven'trare *vt* disembowel; *fig* demolish ⟨*edificio*⟩

sven'tura *nf* misfortune. **sventu'rato** *a* unfortunate

sve'nuto *pp di* **svenire**

svergo'gnato *a* shameless

sver'nare *vi* winter

sve'stir|e *vt* undress. ~**si** *vr* undress, get undressed

'Svezia *nf* Sweden

svezza'mento *nm* weaning. **svez'zare** *vt* wean

svi'ar|e *vt* divert; ⟨*corrompere*⟩ lead astray. ~**si** *vr fig* go astray

svico'lare *vi* turn down a side street; ⟨*fig: dalla questione ecc*⟩ evade the issue; ⟨*fig: da una persona*⟩ dodge out of the way

svi'gnarsela *vr* slip away

svi'lire *vt* debase

svilup'par|e *vt*, ~**si** *vr* develop. **svi'luppo** *nm* development; **paese in via di sviluppo** developing country

svinco'lar|e *vt* release; clear ⟨*merce*⟩. ~**si** *vr* free oneself. **'svincolo** *nm* clearance; ⟨*di autostrada*⟩ exit

svisce'ra|re *vt* gut; *fig* dissect. ~**to** *a* ⟨*amore*⟩ passionate; ⟨*ossequioso*⟩ obsequious

'svista *nf* oversight

svi'ta|re *vt* unscrew. ~**to** *a* ⟨*fam: matto*⟩ cracked, nutty

'Svizzer|a *nf* Switzerland. **s~o, -a** *a* & *nmf* Swiss

svogli|a'tezza *nf* half-heartedness. ~**'ato** *a* lazy

svolaz'za|nte *a* ⟨*capelli*⟩ wind-swept. ~**re** *vi* flutter

'svolger|e *vt* unwind; unwrap ⟨*pacco*⟩; ⟨*risolvere*⟩ solve; ⟨*portare a termine*⟩ carry out; ⟨*sviluppare*⟩ develop. ~**si** *vr* ⟨*accadere*⟩ take place. **svolgi'mento** *nm* course; ⟨*sviluppo*⟩ development

'svolta *nf* turning; *fig* turning-point. **svol'tare** *vi* turn

'svolto *pp di* **svolgere**

svuo'tare *vt* empty [out]

Tt

tabac'c|aio, -a *nmf* tobacconist. ~**he'ria** *nf* tobacconist's ⟨*which also sells stamps, postcards etc*⟩. **ta'bacco** *nm* tobacco

ta'bel|la *nf* table; ⟨*lista*⟩ list. ~**la dei prezzi** price list. ~**'lina** *nf Math* multiplication table. ~**'lone** *nm* wall chart. ~**'lone del canestro** backboard

taber'nacolo *nm* tabernacle

tabù *a & nm inv* taboo

tabu'lato *nm Comput* [data] printout

'tacca *nf* notch; **di mezza** ~ ⟨*attore, giornalista*⟩ second-rate

tac'cagno *a fam* stingy

tac'cheggio *nm* shoplifting

tac'chetto *nm Sport* stud

tac'chino *nm* turkey

tacci'are *vt* ~ **qcno di qcsa** accuse sb of sth

'tacco *nm* heel; **alzare i tacchi** take to one's heels; **scarpe senza** ~ flat shoes. **tacchi** *pl* **a spillo** stiletto heels

tac'cuino *nm* notebook

ta'cere *vi* be silent ●*vt* say nothing about; **mettere a** ~ **qcsa** ⟨*scandalo*⟩ hush sth up; **mettere a** ~ **qcno** silence sb

ta'chimetro *nm* speedometer

'tacito *a* silent; ⟨*inespresso*⟩ tacit. **taci'turno** *a* taciturn

ta'fano *nm* horsefly

taffe'ruglio *nm* scuffle

'taglia *nf* ⟨*riscatto*⟩ ransom; ⟨*ricompensa*⟩ reward; ⟨*statura*⟩ height; ⟨*misura*⟩ size. ~ **unica** one size

taglia'carte *nm inv* paperknife

taglia'erba *nm inv* lawn-mower

tagliafu'oco *a inv* porta ~ fire door; striscia ~ fire break

tagli'ando *nm* coupon; fare il ~ ≈ put one's car in for its MOT

tagli'ar|e *vt* cut; (*attraversare*) cut across; (*interrompere*) cut off; (*togliere*) cut out; carve (*carne*); mow (*erba*); farsi ~ i capelli have a haircut ● *vi* cut. ~si *vr* cut oneself; ~si i capelli have a haircut

taglia'telle *nfpl* tagliatelle *sg*, thin, flat strips of egg pasta

taglieggi'are *vt* extort money from

tagli'e|nte *a* sharp ● *nm* cutting edge. ~re *nm* chopping board

'taglio *nm* cut; (*il tagliare*) cutting; (*di stoffa*) length; (*parte tagliente*) edge; a doppio ~ double-edged. ~ cesareo Caesarean section

tagli'ola *nf* trap

tagli'one *nm* legge del ~ an eye for an eye and a tooth for a tooth

tagliuz'zare *vt* cut into small pieces

tail'leur *nm inv* [lady's] suit

talassotera'pia *nf* thalassotherapy

'talco *nm* talcum powder

'tale *a* such a; (*con nomi plurali*) such; c'è un ~ disordine there is such a mess; non accetto tali scuse I won't accept such excuses; il rumore era ~ che non si sentiva nulla there was so much noise you couldn't hear yourself think; il ~ giorno on such and such a day; quel tal signore that gentleman; ~ quale just like ● *pron* un ~ someone; quel ~ that man; il tal dei tali such and such a person

ta'lento *nm* talent

tali'smano *nm* talisman

tallo'nare *vt* be hot on the heels of

tallon'cino *nm* coupon

tal'lone *nm* heel

tal'mente *adv* so

ta'lora *adv* = talvolta

'talpa *nf* mole

tal'volta *adv* sometimes

tamburel'lare *vi* (*con le dita*) drum; (*pioggia:*) beat, drum. **tambu'rello** *nm* tambourine. **tambu'rino** *nm* drummer. **tam'buro** *nm* drum

Ta'migi *nm* Thames

tampona'mento *nm* Auto collision; (*di ferita*) dressing; (*di falla*) plugging. ~ a catena pile-up. **tampo'nare** *vt* (*urtare*) crash into; (*otturare*) plug. **tam'pone** *nm* swab; (*per timbri*) pad;

(*per mestruazioni*) tampon; (*per treni, Comput*) buffer

'tana *nf* den

'tanfo *nm* stench

'tanga *nm inv* tanga

tan'gen|te *a* tangent ● *nf* tangent; (*somma*) bribe. ~ **topoli** *nf* widespread corruption in Italy in the early 90s. ~zi'ale *nf* orbital road

tan'gibile *a* tangible

'tango *nm* tango

tan'tino: un ~ *adv* a little [bit]

'tanto *a* [so] much; (*con nomi plurali*) [so] many, [such] a lot of; ~ tempo [such] a long time; non ha tanta pazienza he doesn't have much patience; ~ tempo quanto ti serve as much time as you need; non è ~ intelligente quanto suo padre he's not as intelligent as his father; tanti amici quanti parenti as many friends as relatives ● *pron* much; (*plurale*) many; (*tanto tempo*) a long time; è un uomo come tanti he's just an ordinary man; tanti (*molte persone*) many people; non ci vuole così ~ it doesn't take that long; ~ quanto as much as; tanti quanti as many as ● *conj* (*comunque*) anyway, in any case ● *adv* (*così*) so; (*con verbi*) so much; ~ debole so weak; è ~ ingenuo da crederle he's naive enough to believe her; di ~ in ~ every now and then; ~ l'uno come l'altro both; ~ quanto as much as; tre volte ~ three times as much; una volta ~ once in a while; ~ meglio così! so much the better!; tant'è so much so; ~ per cambiare for a change

'tappa *nf* stop; (*parte di viaggio*) stage

tappa'buchi *nm inv* stopgap

tap'par|e *vt* plug; cork (*bottiglia*); ~e la bocca a qcno *fam* shut sb up. ~si *vr* ~si gli occhi cover one's eyes; ~si il naso hold one's nose; ~si le orecchie put one's fingers in one's ears

tappa'rella *nf fam* roller blind

tappe'tino *nm* mat; Comput mouse mat. ~ antiscivolo safety bathmat

tap'peto *nm* carpet; (*piccolo*) rug; andare al ~ (*pugilato:*) hit the canvas; mandare qcno al ~ knock sb down

tappez'z|are *vt* paper (*pareti*); (*rivestire*) cover. ~e'ria *nf* tapestry; (*di carta*) wallpaper; (*arte*) upholstery. ~i'ere *nm* upholsterer; (*imbianchino*) decorator

'tappo *nm* plug; (*di sughero*) cork; (*di*

metallo, per penna) top; (*fam: persona piccola*) dwarf. ~ **di sughero** cork

'**tara** *nf* (*difetto*) flaw; (*ereditaria*) hereditary defect; (*peso*) tare

ta'**rantola** *nf* tarantula

ta'**ra**|**re** *vt* calibrate (*strumento*). ~**to a** *Comm* discounted; *Techn* calibrated; *Med* with a hereditary defect; *fam* crazy

tarchi'**ato** *a* stocky

tar'**dare** *vi* be late ● *vt* delay

'**tard**|**i** *adv* late; **al più** ~**i** at the latest; **più** ~**i** later [on]; **sul** ~**i** late in the day; **far** ~**i** (*essere in ritardo*) be late; (*con gli amici*) stay up late; **a più** ~**i** see you later. tar'**divo** *a* late; (*bambino*) retarded. ~**o a** slow; (*tempo*) late

'**targ**|**a** *nf* plate; *Auto* numberplate. ~**a di circolazione** numberplate. tar'**gato** *a* **un'auto targata...** a car with the registration number.... ~'**hetta** *nf* (*su porta*) nameplate; (*sulla valigia*) name tag

ta'**rif**|**fa** *nf* rate, tariff. ~'**fario** *nm* price list

tar'**larsi** *vr* get wormeaten. '**tarlo** *nm* woodworm

'**tarma** *nf* moth. tar'**marsi** *vr* get motheaten

ta'**rocco** *nm* tarot; ta'**rocchi** *pl* tarot

tartagli'**are** *vi* stutter

'**tartaro** *a & nm* tartar

tarta'**ruga** *nf* tortoise; (*di mare*) turtle; (*per pettine ecc*) tortoiseshell

tartas'**sare** *vt* (*angariare*) harass

tar'**tina** *nf* canapé

tar'**tufo** *nm* truffle

'**tasca** *nf* pocket; (*in borsa*) compartment; **da** ~ pocket *attrib*; **avere le tasche piene di qcsa** *fam* have had a bellyful of sth. ~ **da pasticciere** icing bag

ta'**scabile** *a* pocket *attrib* ● *nm* paperback

tasca'**pane** *nm inv* haversack

ta'**schino** *nm* breast pocket

'**tassa** *nf* tax; (*discrizione ecc*) fee; (*doganale*) duty. ~ **di circolazione** road tax. ~ **d'iscrizione** registration fee

tas'**sametro** *nm* taximeter

tas'**sare** *vt* tax

tassa|**tiva**'**mente** *adv* without question. ~'**tivo** *a* peremptory

tassazi'**one** *nf* taxation

tas'**sello** *nm* wedge; (*di stoffa*) gusset

'**tassi** *nm inv* taxi. tas'**sista** *nmf* taxi driver

'**tasso**[1] *nm Bot* yew; (*animale*) badger

'**tasso**[2] *nm Comm* rate. ~ **di cambio** exchange rate. ~ **di interesse** interest rate

ta'**stare** *vt* feel; (*sondare*) sound; ~ **il terreno** *fig* test the water *or* ground, feel one's way

tasti'**e**|**ra** *nf* keyboard. ~'**rista** *nmf* keyboarder

'**tasto** *nm* key; (*tatto*) touch. ~ **delicato** *fig* touchy subject. ~ **funzione** *Comput* function key. ~ **tabulatore** tab key

ta'**stoni**: **a** ~ *adv* gropingly

'**tattica** *nf* tactics *pl*

'**tattico** *a* tactical

'**tatto** *nm* (*senso*) touch; (*accortezza*) tact; **aver** ~ be tactful

tatu'**a**|**ggio** *nm* tattoo. ~**re** *vt* tattoo

'**tavola** *nf* table; (*illustrazione*) plate; (*asse*) plank. ~ **calda** snackbar

tavo'**lato** *nm* boarding; (*pavimento*) wood floor

tavo'**letta** *nf* bar; (*medicinale*) tablet; **andare a** ~ *Auto* drive flat out

tavo'**lino** *nm* small table

'**tavolo** *nm* table. ~ **operatorio** *Med* operating table

tavo'**lozza** *nf* palette

'**tazza** *nf* cup; (*del water*) bowl. ~ **da caffè**/**tè** coffee-cup/teacup

taz'**zina** *nf* ~ **da caffè** espresso coffee cup

T.C.I. *abbr* (**Touring Club Italiano**) Italian Touring Club

te *pers pron* you; **te l'ho dato** I gave it to you

tè *nm inv* tea

tea'**trale** *a* theatrical

te'**atro** *nm* theatre. ~ **all'aperto** open-air theatre. ~ **di posa** *Cinema* set. ~ **tenda** *marquee for theatre performances*

'**tecnico, -a** *a* technical ● *nmf* technician ● *nf* technique

tec'**nigrafo** *nm* drawing board

tecno|**lo**'**gia** *nf* technology. ~'**logico** *a* technological

te'**desco, -a** *a & nmf* German

'**tedi**|**o** *nm* tedium. ~'**oso** *a* tedious

te'**game** *nm* saucepan

'**teglia** *nf* baking tin

'**tegola** *nf* tile; *fig* blow

tei'**era** *nf* teapot

tek *nm* teak

'**tela** *nf* cloth; (*per quadri, vele*) canvas; *Theat* curtain. ~ **cerata** oilcloth. ~ **di lino** linen

te'**laio** *nm* (*di bicicletta, finestra*) frame; *Auto* chassis; (*per tessere*) loom

tele'camera nf television camera

teleco|man'dato a remote-control-led, remote control attrib. ~'mando nm remote control

Telecom Italia nf Italian State telephone company

telecomunicazi'oni nfpl telecommunications

tele'cro|naca nf [television] commentary. ~'naca diretta live [television] coverage. ~'naca registrata recording. ~'nista nmf television commentator

tele'ferica nf cableway

telefo'na|re vt/i [tele]phone, ring. ~ta nf call. ~ta interurbana long-distance call

telefonica'mente adv by [tele]phone

tele'fonico a [tele]phone attrib.

telefo'nino nm mobile [phone]

telefo'nista nmf operator

te'lefono nm [tele]phone. ~ senza filo cordless [phone]. ~ a gettoni pay phone, coin-box. ~ interno internal telephone. ~ a schede cardphone

telegior'nale nm television news sg

telegra'fare vt telegraph. **tele'grafico** a telegraphic; ⟨risposta⟩ monosyllabic; **sii telegrafico** keep it brief

tele'gramma nm telegram

tele'matica nf data communications, telematics

teleno'vela nf soap opera

teleobiet'tivo nm telephoto lens

telepa'tia nf telepathy

telero'manzo nm television serial

tele'schermo nm television screen

tele'scopio nm telescope

teleselezi'one nf subscriber trunk dialling, STD; **chiamare in ~** dial direct

telespetta'tore, -'trice nmf viewer

tele'text® nm Teletext®

tele'video nm videophone

televisi'one nf television; **guardare la ~** watch television

televi'sivo a television attrib; **operatore ~** television cameraman; **apparecchio ~** television set

televi'sore nm television [set]

'tema nm theme; Sch essay. **te'matica** nf main theme

teme'rario a reckless

te'mere vt be afraid of, fear ●vi be afraid, fear

tem'paccio nm filthy weather

temperama'tite nm inv pencil-sharpener

tempera'mento nm temperament

tempe'ra|re vt temper; sharpen ⟨matita⟩. **~to** a temperate. **~'tura** nf temperature. **~tura ambiente** room temperature

tempe'rino nm penknife

tem'pesta nf storm. **~ di neve** snowstorm. **~ di sabbia** sandstorm

tempe'stiva'mente adv quickly. **~'stivo** a timely. **~'stoso** a stormy

'tempia nf Anat temple

'tempio nm Relig temple

tem'pismo nm timing

'tempo nm time; ⟨atmosferico⟩ weather; Mus tempo; Gram tense; ⟨di film⟩ part; ⟨di partita⟩ half; **a suo ~** in due course; **~ fa** some time ago; **un ~** once; **ha fatto il suo ~** it's superannuated. **~ reale** real time. **~ supplementare** Sport extra time, overtime Am. **~'rale** a temporal ●nm [thunder]storm. **~ranea'mente** adv temporarily. **~'raneo** a temporary. **~reggi'are** vi play for time

tem'prare vt temper

te'nace a tenacious. **~ia** nf tenacity

te'naglia nf pincers pl

'tenda nf curtain; ⟨per campeggio⟩ tent; ⟨tendone⟩ awning. **~ a ossigeno** oxygen tent

ten'denza nf tendency. **~ial'mente** adv by nature. **~i'oso** a tendentious

'tendere vt ⟨allargare⟩ stretch [out]; ⟨tirare⟩ tighten; ⟨porgere⟩ hold out; fig lay ⟨trappola⟩ ●vi **~ a** aim at; ⟨essere portato a⟩ tend to

'tendine nm tendon

ten'do|ne nm awning; ⟨di circo⟩ tent. **~poli** nf inv tent city

'tenebre nfpl darkness. **tene'broso** a gloomy

te'nente nm lieutenant

tenera'mente adv tenderly

te'ner|e vt hold; ⟨mantenere⟩ keep; ⟨gestire⟩ run; ⟨prendere⟩ take; ⟨seguire⟩ follow; ⟨considerare⟩ consider ●vi hold; **~ci a, ~e a** be keen on; **~e per** support ⟨squadra⟩. **~si|ur** hold on ⟨a to⟩; ⟨in una condizione⟩ keep oneself; ⟨seguire⟩ stick to; **~si indietro** stand back

tene'rezza nf tenderness. **'tenero** a tender

'tenia nf tapeworm

'tennis nm tennis. **~ da tavolo** table tennis. **ten'nista** nmf tennis player

te'nore nm standard; Mus tenor; **a ~ di**

legge by law. **~ di vita** standard of living

tensi'one *nf* tension; *Electr* voltage; **alta ~** high voltage

ten'tacolo *nm* tentacle

ten'ta|**re** *vt* attempt; (*sperimentare*) try; (*indurre in tentazione*) tempt. **~'tivo** *nm* attempt. **~zi'one** *nf* temptation

tenten|**na'mento** *nm* wavering. **~'nare** *vi* waver

'tenue *a* fine; (*debole*) weak; (*esiguo*) small; (*leggero*) slight

te'nuta *nf* (*capacità*) capacity; (*Sport: resistenza*) stamina; (*possedimento*) estate; (*divisa*) uniform; (*abbigliamento*) clothes *pl*; **a ~ d'aria** airtight. **~ di strada** road holding

teolo'gia *nf* theology. **teo'logico** *a* theological. **te'ologo** *nm* theologian

teo'rema *nm* theorem

teo'ria *nf* theory

teorica'mente *adv* theoretically. **te'orico** *a* theoretical

te'pore *nm* warmth

'teppa *nf* mob. **tep'pismo** *nm* hooliganism. **tep'pista** *nm* hooligan

tera'peutico *a* therapeutic. **tera'pia** *nf* therapy

tergicri'stallo *nm* windscreen wiper, windshield wiper *Am*

tergilu'notto *nm* rear windscreen wiper

tergiver'sare *vi* hesitate

'tergo *nm* **a ~** behind; **segue a ~** please turn over, PTO

ter'male *a* thermal; **stazione ~** spa. **'terme** *nfpl* thermal baths

'termico *a* thermal

termi'na|**le** *a & nm* terminal; **malato ~le** terminally ill person. **~re** *vt/i* finish, end. **'termine** *nm* (*limite*) limit; (*fine*) end; (*condizione, espressione*) term

terminolo'gia *nf* terminology

termite *nf* termite

termoco'perta *nf* electric blanket

ter'mometro *nm* thermometer

'termos *nm inv* thermos®

termosi'fone *nm* radiator; (*sistema*) central heating

ter'mostato *nm* thermostat

'terra *nf* earth; (*regione*) land; (*terreno*) ground; (*argilla*) clay; (*cosmetico*) dark face powder (*which gives the impression of a tan*); **a ~** (*sulla costa*) ashore; (*installazioni*) onshore; **per ~** on the ground; **sotto ~** underground. **~'cot-** ta *nf* terracotta; **vasellame di ~cotta** earthenware. **~'ferma** *nf* dry land. **~pi'eno** *nm* embankment

ter'razz|**a** *nf*, **~o** *nm* balcony

terremo'tato, -a *a* (*zona*) affected by an earthquake ● *nmf* earthquake victim. **terre'moto** *nm* earthquake

ter'reno *a* earthly ● *nm* ground; (*suolo*) soil; (*proprietà terriera*) land; **perdere/guadagnare ~** lose/gain ground. **~ di gioco** playing field

ter'restre *a* terrestrial; **esercito ~** land forces *pl*

ter'ribil|**e** *a* terrible. **~'mente** *adv* terribly

ter'riccio *nm* potting compost

terrifi'cante *a* terrifying

territori'ale *a* territorial. **terri'torio** *nm* territory

ter'rore *nm* terror

terro'ris|**mo** *nm* terrorism. **~ta** *nmf* terrorist

terroriz'zare *vt* terrorize

'terso *a* clear

ter'zetto *nm* trio

terzi'ario *a* tertiary

'terzo *a* third; **di terz'ordine** (*locale, servizio*) third-rate; **fare il ~ grado a qn** give sb the third degree; **la terza età** the third age ● *nm* third; **terzi** *pl Jur* third party *sg*. **ter'zultimo, -a** *a & nmf* third from last

'tesa *nf* brim

'teschio *nm* skull

'tesi *nf inv* thesis

'teso *pp di* **tendere** ● *a* taut; *fig* tense

tesor|**e'ria** *nf* treasury. **~i'ere** *nm* treasurer

te'soro *nm* treasure; (*tesoreria*) treasury

'tessera *nf* card; (*abbonamento all'autobus*) season ticket

'tessere *vt* weave; hatch (*complotto*)

tesse'rino *nm* travel card

'tessile *a* textile. **tessili** *nmpl* textiles; (*operai*) textile workers

tessi|**'tore, -'trice** *nmf* weaver. **~'tura** *nf* weaving

tes'suto *nm* fabric; *Anat* tissue

'testa *nf* head; (*cervello*) brain; **essere in ~ a** be ahead of; **in ~** *Sport* in the lead; **~ o croce?** heads or tails?; **fare o croce** have a toss-up to decide

testa-'coda *nm inv* **fare un ~** spin right round

testa'mento *nm* will; **T~** *Relig* Testament

testar'daggine *nf* stubbornness. **te'stardo** *a* stubborn

te'stata *nf* head; (*intestazione*) heading; (*colpo*) butt

'teste *nmf* witness

te'sticolo *nm* testicle

testi'mone *nmf* witness. **~ oculare** eye witness

testi'monial *nmf inv* celebrity who promotes a brand of cosmetics

testimoni'anza *nf* testimony; **falsa ~anza** *Jur* perjury. **~'are** *vt* testify to ● *vi* testify, give evidence

'testo *nm* text; **far ~** be an authority

te'stone, -a *nmf* blockhead

testu'ale *a* textual

'tetano *nm* tetanus

'tetro *a* gloomy

tetta'rella *nf* teat

'tetto *nm* roof. **~ apribile** (*di auto*) sunshine roof. **tet'toia** *nf* roofing. **tet'tuccio** *nm* tettuccio apribile sunroof

'Tevere *nm* Tiber

ti *pers pron* you; (*riflessivo*) yourself; **ti ha dato un libro** he gave you a book; **lavati le mani** wash your hands; **eccoti!** here you are!; **sbrigati! hurry up!**

ti'ara *nf* tiara

tic *nm inv* tic

ticchet't|are *vi* tick. **~io** *nm* ticking

'ticchio *nm* tic; (*ghiribizzo*) whim

'ticket *nm inv* (*per farmaco, esame*) *amount paid by National Health patients*

tiepida'mente *adv* halfheartedly. **ti'epido** *a anche fig* lukewarm

ti'fare *vi* **~ per** shout for. **'tifo** *nm Med* typhus; **fare il tifo per** *fig* be a fan of

tifoi'dea *nf* typhoid

ti'fone *nm* typhoon

ti'foso, -a *nmf* fan

'tiglio *nm* lime

ti'grato *a* **gatto ~** tabby [cat]

'tigre *nf* tiger

'tilde *nmf* tilde

tim'ballo *nm Culin* pie

tim'brare *vt* stamp; **~ il cartellino** clock in/out

'timbro *nm* stamp; (*di voce*) tone

timida'mente *adv* timidly, shyly. **timi'dezza** *nf* timidity, shyness. **'timido** *a* timid, shy

'timo *nm* thyme

ti'mon|e *nm* rudder. **~i'ere** *nm* helmsman

ti'more *nm* fear; (*soggezione*) awe. **timo'roso** *a* timorous

'timpano *nm* eardrum; *Mus* kettledrum

ti'nello *nm* dining room

'tinger|e *vt* dye; (*macchiare*) stain. **~si** *vi* (*viso, cielo:*) be tinged (**di** with); **~si i capelli** have one's hair dyed; (*da solo*) dye one's hair

'tino *nm*, **ti'nozza** *nf* tub

'tint|a *nf* dye; (*colore*) colour; **in ~a unita** plain. **~a'rella** *nf fam* suntan

tintin'nare *vi* tinkle

'tinto *pp di* tingere. **~'ria** *nf* (*negozio*) cleaner's. **tin'tura** *nf* dyeing; (*colorante*) dye.

'tipico *a* typical

'tipo *nm* type; (*fam: individuo*) chap, guy

tipogra'fia *nf* printery; (*arte*) typography. **tipo'grafico** *a* typographic[al]. **ti'pografo** *nm* printer

tip tap *nm* tap dancing

ti'raggio *nm* draught

tiramisù *nm inv* dessert made of coffee-soaked sponge, eggs, Marsala, cream and cocoa powder

tiran|neggi'are *vt* tyrannize. **~'nia** *nf* tyranny. **ti'ranno, -a** *a* tyrannical ● *nmf* tyrant

tirapi'edi *nm inv pej* hanger-on

ti'rar|e *vt* pull; (*gettare*) throw; kick (*palla*); (*sparare*) fire; (*tracciare*) draw; (*stampare*) print ● *vi* pull; (*vento:*) blow; (*abito:*) be tight; (*sparare*) fire; **~e avanti** get by; **~e su** (*crescere*) bring up; (*da terra*) pick up; **tirar su col naso** sniffle. **~si** *vr* **~si indietro** *fig* back out, pull out

tiras'segno *nm* target shooting; (*alla fiera*) rifle range

ti'rata *nf* (*strattone*) pull, tug; **in una ~** in one go

tira'tore *nm* shot. **~ scelto** marksman

tira'tura *nf* printing; (*di giornali*) circulation; (*di libri*) [print] run

tirchie'ria *nf* meanness. **'tirchio** *a* mean

tiri'tera *nf* spiel

'tiro *nm* (*traino*) draught; (*lancio*) throw; (*sparo*) shot; (*scherzo*) trick. **~ con l'arco** archery. **~ alla fune** tug-of-war. **~ a segno** rifle-range

tiro'cinio *nm* apprenticeship

ti'roide *nf* thyroid

Tir'reno *nm* **il [mar] ~** the Tyrrhenian Sea

ti'sana *nf* herb[al] tea

tito'lare a regular ●*nmf* principal; (*proprietario*) owner; (*calcio*) regular player

'titolo *nm* title; (*accademico*) qualification; *Comm* security; **a ~ di**as; **a ~ di favore** as a favour. **titoli** *pl* **di studio** qualifications

titu'ba|nte a hesitant. **~nza** *nf* hesitation. **~re** *vi* hesitate

tivù *nf inv fam* TV, telly

'tizio *nm* fellow

tiz'zone *nm* brand

toc'cante a touching

toc'care *vt* touch; touch on (*argomento*); (*tastare*) feel; (*riguardare*) concern ●*vi* **~ a** (*capitare*) happen to; **mi tocca aspettare** I'll have to wait; **tocca a te** it's your turn; (*da pagare da bere*) it's your round

tocca'sana *nm inv* cure-all

'tocco *nm* touch; (*di pennello, orologio*) stroke; (*di pane ecc*) chunk ●*a fam* crazy, touched

'toga *nf* toga; (*accademica, di magistrato*) gown

'toglier|e *vt* take off (*coperta*); take away (*bambino da scuola, sete, Math*); take out, remove (*dente*); **~e** **qcsa di mano a** qcno take sth away from sb; **~e** qcno dei guaiget sb out of trouble; **ciò non toglie che...** nevertheless... **~si** *vr* take off (*abito*); **~si la vita** take one's [own] life; **togliti dai piedi!** get out of here!

toilette *nf inv*, **to'letta** *nf* toilet; (*mobile*) dressing table

tolle'ra|nte a tolerant. **~nza** *nf* tolerance. **~re** *vt* tolerate

'tolto *pp di* **togliere**

to'maia *nf* upper

'tomba *nf* grave, tomb

tom'bino *nm* manhole cover

'tombola *nf* bingo; (*caduta*) tumble

'tomo *nm* tome

'tonaca *nf* habit

tonalità *nf inv Mus* tonality

'tondo a round ●*nm* circle

'tonfo *nm* thud; (*in acqua*) splash

'tonico a & *nm* tonic

tonifi'care *vt* brace

tonnel'la|ggio *nm* tonnage. **~ta** *nf* ton

'tonno *nm* tuna [fish]

'tono *nm* tone

ton'silla *nf* tonsil. **~lite** *nf* tonsillitis

'tonto a *fam* thick

top *nm inv* (*indumento*) sun-top

to'pazio *nm* topaz

'topless *nm inv* **in ~** topless

'topo *nm* mouse. **~ di biblioteca** *fig* bookworm

topogra'fia *nf* topography. **topo'grafico** a topographic[al]

to'ponimo *nm* place name

'toppa *nf* (*rattoppo*) patch; (*serratura*) keyhole

to'race *nm* chest. **to'racico** a thoracic; **gabbia toracica** rib cage

'torba *nf* peat

'torbido a cloudy; *fig* troubled

'torcer|e *vt* twist; wring [out] (*biancheria*). **~si** *vr* twist

'torchio *nm* press

'torcia *nf* torch

torci'collo *nm* stiff neck

'tordo *nm* thrush

to'rero *nm* bullfighter

To'rino *nf* Turin

tor'menta *nf* snowstorm

tormen'tare *vt* torment. **tor'mento** *nm* torment

torna'conto *nm* benefit

tor'nado *nm* tornado

tor'nante *nm* hairpin bend

tor'nare *vi* return, go/come back; (*ridiventare*) become again; (*conto*) add up; **~ a sorridere** become happy again

tor'neo *nm* tournament

'tornio *nm* lathe

'torno *nm* **togliersi di ~** get out of the way

'toro *nm* bull; *Astr* Taurus

tor'pedin|e *nf* torpedo. **~i'era** *nf* torpedo boat

tor'pore *nm* torpor

'torre *nf* tower; (*scacchi*) castle. **~ di controllo** control tower

torrefazi'one *nf* roasting

tor'ren|te *nm* torrent, mountain stream; (*fig: di lacrime*) flood. **~zi'ale** a torrential

tor'retta *nf* turret

'torrido a torrid

torri'one *nm* keep

tor'rone *nm* nougat

'torso *nm* torso; (*di mela, pera*) core; **a ~ nudo** bare-chested

'torsolo *nm* core

'torta *nf* cake; (*crostata*) tart

tortel'lini *nmpl* tortellini, *small packets of pasta stuffed with pork, ham, Parmesan and nutmeg*

torti'era *nf* baking tin

tor'tino *nm* pie

'**torto** pp di **torcere** ● a twisted ● nm wrong; (colpa) fault; **aver ~ be** wrong; a ~ wrongly

tor'tora nf turtle-dove

tortu'oso a winding; (ambiguo) tortuous

tor'tu|ra nf torture. ~**'rare** vt torture

'torvo a grim

to'sare vt shear

tosa'tura nf shearing

To'scana nf Tuscany

'tosse nf cough

'tossico a toxic ● nm poison. **tossi'comane** nmf drug addict, drug user

tos'sire vi cough

tosta'pane nm inv toaster

to'stare vt toast (pane); roast (caffè)

'tosto adv (subito) soon ● a fam cool

tot a inv **una cifra ~** such and such a figure ● nm **un ~** so much

to'tal|e a & nm total. ~**ità** nf entirety; **la ~ità dei presenti** all those present

totali'tario a totalitarian

totaliz'zare vt total; score (punti)

total'mente adv totally

'totano nm squid

toto'calcio nm ≈ [football] pools pl

tournée nf inv tour

to'vagli|a nf tablecloth. ~**'etta di ~etta [all'americana]** place mat. ~**'olo** nm napkin

'tozzo a squat ● nm ~ **di pane** stale piece of bread

tra =fra

trabal'lan|te a staggering; (sedia) rickety, wonky. ~**re** vi stagger; (veicolo:) jolt

tra'biccolo nm fam contraption; (auto) jalopy

trabocc'care vi overflow

trabocc'chetto nm trap

tracan'nare vt gulp down

'tracci|a nf track; (orma) footstep; (striscia) trail; (residuo) trace; fig sign. ~**'are** vt trace; sketch out (schema); draw (linea). ~**'ato** nm (schema) layout

tra'chea nf windpipe

tra'colla nf shoulder-strap; **borsa a ~** shoulder-bag

tra'collo nm collapse

tradi'mento nm betrayal; Pol treason

tra'di|re vt betray; be unfaithful to (moglie, marito). ~**'tore**, ~**'trice** nmf traitor

tradizio'na|le a traditional. ~**'lista** nmf traditionalist. ~**l'mente** adv traditionally. **tradizi'one** nf tradition

tra'dotto pp di **tradurre**

tra'du|rre vt translate. ~**t'tore**, ~**t'trice** nmf translator. ~**ttore elettronico** electronic phrasebook. ~**zi'one** nf translation

tra'ente nmf Comm drawer

trafe'lato a breathless

traffi'can|te nmf dealer. ~**nte di droga** [drug] pusher. ~**re** vi (affaccendarsi) busy oneself; ~**re in** pej traffic in. **'traffico** nm traffic; Comm trade

tra'figgere vt stab; (straziare) pierce

tra'fila nf fig rigmarole

trafo'rare vt bore, drill. **tra'foro** nm boring; (galleria) tunnel

trafu'gare vt steal

tra'gedia nf tragedy

tragh'et'tare vt ferry. **tra'ghetto** nm ferrying; (nave) ferry

tragica'mente adv tragically.

'tragico a tragic ● nm (autore) tragedian

tra'gitto nm journey; (per mare) crossing

tragu'ardo nm finishing post; (meta) goal

traiet'toria nf trajectory

trai'nare vt drag; (rimorchiare) tow

tralasci'are vt interrupt; (omettere) leave out

'tralcio nm Bot shoot

tra'liccio nm (graticcio) trellis

tram nm inv tram, streetcar Am

'trama nf weft; (di film ecc) plot

traman'dare vt hand down

tra'mare vt weave; (macchinare) plot

tram'busto nm turmoil, hullabaloo

trame'stio nm bustle

tramez'zino nm sandwich

tra'mezzo nm partition

'tramite prep through ● nm link; **fare da ~** act as go-between

tramon'tana nf north wind

tramon'tare vi set; (declinare) decline. **tra'monto** nm sunset; (declino) decline

tramor'tire vt stun ● vi faint

trampo'lino nm springboard; (per lo sci) ski-jump

'trampolo nm stilt

tramu'tare vt transform

'trancia nf shears pl; (fetta) slice

tra'nello nm trap

trangugi'are vt gulp down, gobble up

'tranne prep except

tranquilla'mente adv peacefully

tranquil'lante nm tranquillizer

tranquilli'tà nf calm; (di spirito) tranquillity. ~**z'zare** vt reassure.

tran'quillo *a* quiet; (*pacifico*) peaceful; (*coscienza*) easy

transat'lantico *a* transatlantic ●*nm* ocean liner

tran'satto *pp di* transigere ~**zi'one** *nf Comm* transaction

tran'senna *nf* (*barriera*) barrier

tran'sigere *vi* reach an agreement; (*cedere*) yield

transi'tabile *a* passable. ~**re** *vi* pass

transi'tivo *a* transitive

'transito *nm* transit; **diritto di** ~**to** right of way; **"divieto di** ~**to"** "no thoroughfare". ~**torio** *a* transitory. ~**zi'one** *nf* transition

tran'tran *nm fam* routine

tranvi'ere *nm* tram driver, streetcar driver *Am*

'trapano *nm* drill

trapas'sare *vt* go [right] through ●*vi* (*morire*) pass away

tra'passo *nm* passage

trape'lare *vi* (*liquido, fig:*) leak out

tra'pezio *nm* trapeze; *Math* trapezium

trapian'tare *vt* transplant. ~**'anto** *nm* transplant

'trappola *nf* trap

tra'punta *nf* quilt

'trarre *vt* draw; (*ricavare*) obtain; ~ **in inganno** deceive

trasa'lire *vi* start

trasan'dato *a* shabby

trasbor'dare *vt* transfer; *Naut* tran[s]ship ●*vi* change. **tra'sbordo** *nm* trans[s]hipment

tra'scendere *vt* transcend ●*vi* (*eccedere*) go too far

trasci'nare *vt* drag; (*fig: entusiasmo:*) carry away. ~**si** *vr* drag oneself

tra'scorrere *vt* spend ●*vi* pass

tra'scritto *pp di* trascrivere ~**vere** *vt* transcribe. ~**zi'one** *nf* transcription

trascu'rabile *a* negligible. ~**re** *vt* neglect; (*non tenere conto di*) disregard. ~**'tezza** *nf* negligence. ~**to** *a* negligent; (*curato male*) neglected; (*nel vestire*) slovenly

traseco'lato *a* amazed

trasferi'mento *nm* transfer; (*trasloco*) move

trasfe'rire *vt* transfer. ~**rsi** *vr* move

tra'sferta *nf* transfer; (*indennità*) subsistence allowance; *Sport* away match; **in** ~ (*impiegato*) on secondment; **giocare in** ~ play away

trasfigu'rare *vt* transfigure

trasfor'mare *vt* transform; (*in rugby*) convert. ~**'tore** *nm* transformer.

~**zi'one** *nf* transformation; (*in rugby*) conversion

trasfor'mista *nmf* (*artista*) quick-change artist

trasfusi'one *nf* transfusion

trasgre'dire *vt* disobey; *Jur* infringe

trasgredi'trice *nf* transgressor

trasgres'si'one *nf* infringement. ~**'sivo** *a* intended to shock. ~**'sore** *nm* transgressor

tra'slato *a* metaphorical

traslo'care *vt* move ●*vi*, ~**si** *vr* move house. **tra'sloco** *nm* removal

tra'smesso *pp di* trasmettere

tra'smett|ere *vt* pass on; *TV, Radio* broadcast; *Techn, Med* transmit. ~**i'tore** *nm* transmitter

trasmis'si|bile *a* transmissible. ~**'one** *nf* transmission; *TV, Radio* programme

trasmit'tente *nm* transmitter ●*nf* broadcasting station

traso'gna|re *vi* day-dream. ~**to** *a* dreamy

traspa'ren|te *a* transparent. ~**za** *nf* transparency; **in** ~**za** against the light. **traspa'rire** *vi* show [through]

traspi'ra|re *vi* perspire; *fig* transpire. ~**zi'one** *nf* perspiration

tra'sporre *vt* transpose

traspor'tare *vt* transport; **lasciarsi** ~ **da** get carried away by. **tra'sporto** *nm* transport; (*passione*) passion

trastul'lar|e *vt* amuse. ~**si** *vr* amuse oneself

trasu'dare *vt* ooze with ●*vi* sweat

trasver'sale *a* transverse

trasvo'la|re *vt* fly over ●*vi* ~**re su** *fig* skim over. ~**ta** *nf* crossing [by air]

'tratta *nf* (*traffico illegale*) trade; *Comm* draft

trat'tabile *a* or nearest offer, o.n.o.

tratta'mento *nm* treatment. ~ **di riguardo** special treatment

trat'ta|re *vt* treat; (*commerciare in*) deal in; (*negoziare*) negotiate ●*vi* ~**re di** deal with. ~**rsi** *vr* **di che si tratta?** what is it about?; **si tratta di...** it's about... ~**'tive** *nfpl* negotiations. ~**to** *nm* treaty; (*opera scritta*) treatise

tratteggi'are *vt* outline; (*descrivere*) sketch

tratte'ner|e *vt* (*far restare*) keep; hold (*respiro, in questura*); hold back (*lacrime, riso*); (*frenare*) restrain; (*da paga*) withhold; **sono stato trattenuto** (*ritardato*) I was ●got held up. ~**si** *vr* restrain oneself; (*fermarsi*) stay;

~**si su** (*indugiare*) dwell on. **trat-teni'mento** *nm* entertainment; (*rice-vimento*) party

tratte'nuta *nf* deduction

trat'tino *nm* dash; (*in parole composte*) hyphen

'**tratto** *pp di* trarre ● *nm* (*di spazio, tempo*) stretch; (*di penna*) stroke; (*linea*) line; (*brano*) passage; **tratti** *pl* (*lineamenti*) features; **a tratti** at inter-vals; **ad un** ~ suddenly

trat'tore *nm* tractor

tratto'ria *nf* restaurant

'**trauma** *nm* trauma. **trau'matico** *a* traumatic. ~**tiz'zare** *vt* traumatize

tra'vaglio *nm* labour; (*angoscia*) an-guish

trava'sare *vt* decant

'**trave** *nf* beam

tra'veggole *nfpl* **avere le** ~ be see-ing things

tra'versa *nf* crossbar; **è una** ~ **di Via Roma** it's off Via Roma, it crosses with Roma

traver'sa|re *vt* cross. ~**ta** *nf* crossing

traver'sie *nfpl* misfortunes

traver'sina *nf* Rail sleeper

tra'vers|o *a* crosswise ● *adv* **di** ~**o** crossways; **andare di** ~**o** (*cibo:*) go down the wrong way; **camminare di** ~**o** not walk in a straight line; **guardare qcno di** ~**o** look askance at sb. ~**one** *nm* (*in calcio*) cross

travesti'mento *nm* disguise

trave'sti|re *vt* disguise. ~**rsi** *vr* dis-guise oneself. ~**to** *a* disguised ● *nm* transvestite

travi'are *vt* lead astray

travi'sare *vt* distort

travol'gente *a* overwhelming

tra'vol|gere *vt* sweep away; (*sopraffare*) overwhelm. ~**to** *pp di* travolgere

trazi'one *nf* traction. ~ **anteriore/ posteriore** front-/rear-wheel drive

tre *a & nm* three

trebbi'are *vt* thresh

'**treccia** *nf* plait, braid

tre'cento *a & nm* three hundred; **il T**~ the fourteenth century

tredi'cesima *nf* extra month's salary paid as a Christmas bonus

'**tredici** *a & nm* thirteen

'**tregua** *nf* truce; *fig* respite

tre'mare *vi* tremble; (*di freddo*) shiver. **trema'rella** *nf fam* jitters *pl*

tremenda'mente *adv* terribly.

tre'mendo *a* terrible; **ho una fame tremenda** I'm terribly hungry

tremen'tina *nf* turpentine

tre'mila *a & nm* three thousand

'**tremito** *nm* tremble

tremo'lare *vi* shake; (*luce:*) flicker. **tre'more** *nm* trembling

tre'nino *nm* miniature railway

'**treno** *nm* train

'**tren|ta** *a & nm* thirty; ~**ta e lode** top marks. ~**tatrè giri** *nm inv* LP. ~**tenne** *a & nmf* thirty-year-old. ~**tesimo** *a & nm* thirtieth. ~**tina** *nf* **una** ~**tina di** about thirty

trepi'dare *vi* be anxious. '**trepido** *a* anxious

treppi'ede *nm* tripod

'**tresca** *nf* intrigue; (*amorosa*) affair

'**trespolo** *nm* perch

triango'lare *a* triangular. **tri'angolo** *nm* triangle

tri'bale *a* tribal

tribo'la|re *vi* (*soffrire*) suffer; (*fare fatica*) go through all kinds of trials and tribulations. ~**zi'one** *nf* tribulation

tribù *nf inv* tribe

tri'buna *nf* tribune; (*per uditori*) gal-lery; *Sport* stand. ~ **coperta** stand

tribu'nale *nm* court

tribu'tare *vt* bestow

tribu'tario *a* tax *attrib.* **tri'buto** *nm* tribute; (*tassa*) tax

tri'checo *nm* walrus

tri'ciclo *nm* tricycle

trico'lore *a* three-coloured ● *nm* (*bandiera*) tricolour

tri'dente *nm* trident

trien'nale *a* (*ogni tre anni*) three-yearly; (*lungo tre anni*) three-year. **tri'ennio** *nm* three-year period

tri'foglio *nm* clover

trifo'lato *a* sliced thinly and cooked with olive oil, parsley and garlic

'**triglia** *nf* mullet

trigonome'tria *nf* trigonometry

tril'lare *vi* trill

trilo'gia *nf* trilogy

tri'mestre *nm* quarter; *Sch* term

'**trina** *nf* lace

trin'ce|a *nf* trench. ~**rare** *vt* entrench

trincia'pollo *nm inv* poultry shears *pl*

trinci'are *vt* cut up

Trinità *nf* Trinity

'**trio** *nm* trio

trion'fa|le *a* triumphal. ~**nte** *a* triumphant. ~**re** *vi* triumph; ~**re su** triumph over. **tri'onfo** *nm* triumph

tripli'care *vt* triple. '**triplice** *a* triple;

in triplice [copia] in triplicate. **'triplo** *a* treble ● *nm* **il triplo (di)** three times as much (as)

'trippa *nf* tripe; (*fam: pancia*) belly

'triste *a* sad; (*luogo*) gloomy. **tri'stezza** *nf* sadness. **~o** *a* wicked; (*meschino*) miserable

trita'carne *nm inv* mincer. **~ghi'accio** *nm inv* ice-crusher

tri'tare *vt* mince. **'trito** *a* **trito e ritrito** well-worn, trite

'trittico *nm* triptych

tritu'rare *vt* chop finely

triumvi'rato *nm* triumvirate

tri'vella *nf* drill. **trivel'lare** *vt* drill

trivi'ale *a* vulgar

tro'feo *nm* trophy

'trogolo *nm* (*per maiali*) trough

'troia *nf* sow; *vulg* bitch; (*sessuale*) whore

'tromba *nf* trumpet; *Auto* horn; (*delle scale*) well. **~ d'aria** whirlwind

trom'bare *vt vulg* screw; (*fam: in esame*) fail

trom'betta *nm* toy trumpet. **~one** *nm* trombone

trom'bosi *nf* thrombosis

tron'care *vt* sever; truncate (*parola*)

'tronco *a* truncated; **licenziare in ~** fire on the spot ● *nm* trunk; (*di strada*) section. **tron'cone** *nm* stump

troneggi'are *vi* **~ su** tower over

'trono *nm* throne

tropi'cale *a* tropical. **'tropico** *nm* tropic

'troppo *a* too much; (*con nomi plurali*) too many ● *pron* too much; (*plurale*) too many; (*troppo tempo*) too long; **troppi** (*troppa gente*) too many people ● *adv* too; (*con verbi*) too much; **~ stanco** too tired; **ho mangiato ~** I ate too much; **hai fame? – non ~** are you hungry? – not very; **sentirsi di ~** feel unwanted

'trota *nf* trout

trot'tare *vi* trot. **trotterel'lare** *vi* trot along; (*bimbo:*) toddle

'trotto *nm* trot; **andare al ~** trot

'trottola *nf* [spinning] top; (*movimento*) spin

troupe *nf inv* **~ televisiva** camera crew

tro'vare *vt* find; (*scoprire*) find out; (*incontrare*) meet; (*ritenere*) think; **andare a ~re** go and see. **~rsi** *vr* find oneself; (*luogo:*) be; (*sentirsi*) feel. **~ta** *nf* bright idea. **~ta pubblicitaria** advertising gimmick

truc'care *vt* make up; (*falsificare*) fix

sl. **~rsi** *vr* make up. **~tore**, **~'trice** *nmf* make-up artist

'trucco *nm* (*cosmetico*) make-up; (*imbroglio*) trick

'truce *a* fierce; (*delitto*) appalling

truci'dare *vt* slay

'truciolo *nm* shaving

trucu'lento *a* truculent

'truffa *nf* fraud. **truf'fare** *vt* swindle. **~'tore**, **~'trice** *nmf* swindler

'truppa *nf* troops *pl*; (*gruppo*) group

tu *pers pron* you; **sei tu?** is that you?; **l'hai fatto tu?** did you do it yourself?; **a tu per tu** in private; **darsi del tu** *use the familiar tu*

'tuba *nf* Mus tuba; (*cappello*) top hat

tu'bare *vi* coo

tuba'tura, **tubazi'one** *nf* piping

tubazi'oni *nfpl* piping *sg*, pipes

tuberco'losi *nf* tuberculosis

tu'betto *nm* tube

tu'bino *nm* (*vestito*) shift

'tubo *nm* pipe; *Anat* canal; **non ho capito un ~** *fam* I understood zilch. **~ di scappamento** exhaust [pipe]

tubo'lare *a* tubular

tuf'fare *vt* plunge. **~rsi** *vr* dive. **~ tore**, **~'trice** *nmf* diver

'tuffo *nm* dive; (*bagno*) dip; **ho avuto un ~ al cuore** my heart missed a beat. **~ di testa** dive

'tufo *nm* tufa

tu'gurio *nm* hovel

tuli'pano *nm* tulip

'tulle *nm* tulle

tume'fatto *a* swollen. **~zi'one** *nf* swelling. **'tumido** *a* swollen

tu'more *nm* tumour

tumulazi'one *nf* burial

tu'multo *nm* turmoil; (*sommossa*) riot. **~u'oso** *a* uproarious

'tunica *nf* tunic

Tuni'sia *nf* Tunisia

'tunnel *nm inv* tunnel

'tuo (*il ~ m*, **la tua** *f*, **i ~i** *mpl*, **le tue** *fpl*) *poss a* your; **è tua questa macchina?** is this car yours?; **un ~ amico** a friend of yours; **~ padre** your father ● *poss pron* yours; **i tuoi** your folks

tuo'nare *vi* thunder. **tu'ono** *nm* thunder

tu'orlo *nm* yolk

tu'racciolo *nm* stopper; (*di sughero*) cork

tu'rare *vt* stop; cork (*bottiglia*). **~si** *vr* become blocked; **~si le orecchie** stick one's fingers in one's ears; **~si il naso** hold one's nose

turba'mento *nm* disturbance; (*sconvolgimento*) upsetting. ~ **della quiete pubblica** breach of the peace

tur'bante *nm* turban

tur'ba|re *vt* upset. ~**rsi** *vr* get upset. ~**to** *a* upset

tur'bina *nf* turbine

turbi'nare *vi* whirl. **'turbine** *nm* whirl. **turbine di vento** whirlwind

turbo'len|to *a* turbulent. ~**za** *nf* turbulence

turboreat'tore *nm* turbo-jet

tur'chese *a & nmf* turquoise

Tur'chia *nf* Turkey

tur'chino *a & nm* deep blue

'turco, -a *a* Turkish ●*nmf* Turk ●*nm* (*lingua*) Turkish; *fig* double Dutch; **fumare come un** ~ smoke like a chimney; **bestemmiare come un** ~ swear like a trooper

tu'rismo *nm* tourism. ~**ta** *nmf* tourist. ~**tico** *a* tourist *attrib*

'turno *nm* turn; **a** ~ in turn; **di** ~ on duty; **fare a** ~ take turns. ~ **di notte** night shift

'turpe *a* base. ~**i'loquio** *nm* foul language

'tuta *nf* overalls *pl*; *Sport* tracksuit. ~ **da ginnastica** tracksuit. ~ **da lavoro** overalls. ~ **mimetica** camouflage. ~ **spaziale** spacesuit. ~ **subacquea** wetsuit

tu'tela *nf Jur* guardianship; (*protezione*) protection. **tute'lare** *vt* protect

tu'tina *nf* sleepsuit; (*da danza*) leotard

tu'tore, -'trice *nmf* guardian

'tutta *nf* **mettercela** ~ **per fare qcsa** go flat out for sth

tutta'via *conj* nevertheless, still

'tutto *a* whole; (*con nomi plurali*) all; (*ogni*) every; **tutta la classe** the whole class, all the class; **tutti gli alunni** all the pupils; **a tutta velocità** at full speed; **ho aspettato** ~ **il giorno** I waited all day [long]; **in** ~ **il mondo** all over the world; **noi tutti** all of us; **era tutta contenta** she was delighted; **tutti e due** both; **tutti e tre** all three ●*pron* all; (*tutta la gente*) everything; (*tutte le cose*) everything, (*qualunque cosa*) anything; **l'ho mangiato** ~ I ate it all; **le ho lavate tutte** I washed them all; **raccontami** ~ tell me everything; **lo sanno tutti** everybody knows; **è capace di** ~ he's capable of anything; ~ **compreso** all in; **del** ~ quite; **in** ~ altogether ●*adv* completely; **tutt'a un tratto** all at once; **tutt'altro** not at all; **tutt'altro** *che* anything but ●*nm* whole; **tentare il** ~ **per** ~ go for broke. ~**'fare** *a inv & nmf* [impiegato] ~ general handyman; **donna** ~ general maid

tut'tora *adv* still

tutù *nm inv* tutu, ballet dress

tv *nf inv* TV

Uu

ubbidi'en|te *a* obedient. ~**za** *nf* obedience. **ubbi'dire** *vi* ~ (**a**) obey

ubi'cato *a* located. ~**zi'one** *nf* location

ubria'car|e *vt* get drunk. ~**si** *vr* get drunk; ~**si di** *fig* become intoxicated with

ubria'chezza *nf* drunkenness; **in stato di** ~ inebriated

ubri'aco, -a *a* drunk; ~ **fradicio** dead o blind drunk ●*nmf* drunk

ubria'cone *nm* drunkard

uccelli'era *nf* aviary. **uc'cello** *nm* bird; (*vulg: pene*) cock

uc'cider|e *vt* kill. ~**si** *vr* kill oneself

ucci'si'one *nf* killing. **uc'ciso** *pp di* **uccidere** ~**'sore** *nm* killer

u'dente *a* **i non udenti** the hearing impaired

u'dibile *a* audible

udi'enza *nf* audience; (*colloquio*) interview; *Jur* hearing

u'di|re *vt* hear. ~**tivo** *a* auditory. ~**to** *nm* hearing. ~**tore, -'trice** *nmf* listener; *Sch* unregistered student (*allowed to sit in on lectures*). ~**'torio** *nm* audience

'uffa *int* (*con impazienza*) come on!; (*con tono seccato*) damn!

uffici'al|e *a* official ●*nm* officer;

(*funzionario*) official; **pubblico** ~**e** public official. ~**e giudiziario** clerk of the court. ~**iz'zare** *vt* make official, officialize

uf'ficio *nm* office; (*dovere*) duty. ~ **di collocamento** employment office. ~ **informazioni** information office. ~ **del personale** personnel department. ~**sa'mente** *adv* unofficially. **uffici'oso** *a* unofficial

'**ufo**¹ *nm inv* UFO

'**ufo**²: **a** ~ *adv* without paying

uggi'oso *a* boring

uguagli'a|nza *nf* equality. ~**re** *vt* make equal; (*essere uguale*) equal; (*livellare*) level. ~**rsi** *vr* ~**rsi a** compare oneself to

ugu'al|e *a* equal; (*lo stesso*) the same; (*simile*) like. ~'**mente** *adv* equally; (*malgrado tutto*) all the same

'**ulcera** *nf* ulcer

uli'veto *nm* olive grove

ulteri'or|e *a* further. ~'**mente** *adv* further

ultima'mente *adv* lately

ulti'ma|re *vt* complete. ~**tum** *nm inv* ultimatum

ulti'missime *nfpl* *Journ* stop press, latest news *sg*

'**ultimo** *a* last; (*notizie ecc*) latest; (*più lontano*) farthest; *fig* ultimate ● *nm* last; **fino all'**~ to the last; **per** ~ at the end; **l'**~ **piano** the top floor

ultrà *nmf inv* *Sport* fanatical supporter

ultramo'derno *a* ultramodern

ultra'rapido *a* extra-fast

ultrasen'sibile *a* ultrasensitive

ultra's|onico *a* ultrasonic. ~**u'ono** *nm* ultrasound

ultrater'reno *a* (*vita*) after death

ultravio'letto *a* ultraviolet

ulu'la|re *vi* howl. ~**to** *nm* howling; **gli** ~**ti** the howls, the howling

umana'mente *adv* (*trattare*) humanely; ~ **impossibile** not humanly possible

uma'nesimo *nm* humanism

umani'tà *nf* humanity. ~**'tario** *a* humanitarian. **u'mano** *a* human; (*benevolo*) humane

umidifica'tore *nm* humidifier

umidità *nf* dampness; (*di clima*) humidity. '**umido** *a* damp; (*clima*) humid; (*mani, occhi*) moist ● *nm* dampness; **in umido** *Culin* stewed

'**umile** *a* humble

umili'a|nte *a* humiliating. ~**re** *vt* humiliate. ~**rsi** *vr* humble oneself.

~**zi'one** *nf* humiliation. **umiltà** *nf* humility. **umil'mente** *adv* humbly

u'more *nm* humour; (*stato d'animo*) mood; **di cattivo/buon** ~ in a bad/good mood

umo'ris|mo *nm* humour. ~**ta** *nmf* humorist. ~**tico** *a* humorous

un *indef art* a; (*davanti a vocale o h muta*) an; *vedi* **uno**

una *indef art* f a; *vedi* **un**

u'nanim|e *a* unanimous. ~**e'mente** *adv* unanimously. ~**ità** *nf* unanimity; **all'**~**ità** unanimously

unci'nato *a* hooked; (*parentesi*) angle

unci'netto *nm* crochet hook

un'cino *nm* hook

'**undici** *a* & *nm* eleven

'**unger|e** *vt* grease; (*sporcare*) get greasy; *Relig* anoint; (*blandire*) flatter. ~**si** *vr* (*con olio solare*) oil oneself; ~**si le mani** get one's hands greasy

unghe'rese *a* & *nmf* Hungarian. **Unghe'ria** *nf* Hungary; (*lingua*) Hungarian

'**unghi|a** *nf* nail; (*di animale*) claw. ~'**ata** *nf* (*graffio*) scratch

ungu'ento *nm* ointment

unica'mente *adv* only. '**unico** *a* only; (*singolo*) single; (*incomparabile*) unique

unifi'ca|re *vt* unify. ~**zi'one** *nf* unification

unifor'mar|e *vt* level. ~**si** *vr* conform (**a** to)

uni'form|e *a* & *nf* uniform. ~**ità** *nf* uniformity

unilate'rale *a* unilateral

uni'one *nf* union; (*armonia*) unity. **U**~ **Europea** European Union. **U**~ **Monetaria Europea** European Monetary Union. ~ **sindacale** trade union, labor union *Am*. **U**~ **Sovietica** Soviet Union

u'ni|re *vt* unite; (*collegare*) join; blend (*colori ecc*). ~**rsi** *vr* unite; (*collegarsi*) join

'**unisex** *a inv* unisex

uni'tà *nf inv* unity; *Math, Mil* unit; *Comput* drive. ~ **di misura** unit of measurement. ~**rio** *a* unitary

u'nito *a* united; (*tinta*) plain

univer'sal|e *a* universal. ~**iz'zare** *vt* universalize. ~'**mente** *adv* universally

università *nf inv* university. ~**rio**, **-a** *a* university *attrib* ● *nmf* (*insegnante*) university lecturer; (*studente*) undergraduate

uni'verso *nm* universe

uno, **-a** *indef art* (*before s + consonant*,

gn, ps, z) a ●*pron* one; **a ~ a ~** one by one; **l'~ e l'altro** both [of them]; **né l'~ né l'altro** neither [of them]; **~ di noi** one of us; **~ fa quello che può** you do what you can ●*a* a, one ●*nm* (*numerale*) one; (*un tale*) some man ●*nf* some woman

'**unto** *pp di* **ungere** ●*a* greasy ●*nm* grease. **~u'oso** *a* greasy. **unzi'one** *nf* **l'Estrema Unzione** Extreme Unction

u'omo *nm* (*pl* **uomini**) man. **~ d'affari** business man. **~ di fiducia** right-hand man. **~ di Stato** statesman

u'ovo *nm* (*pl nf* **uova**) egg. **~ in camicia** poached egg. **~ alla coque** boiled egg. **~ di Pasqua** Easter egg. **~ sodo** hard-boiled egg. **~ strapazzato** scrambled egg

ura'gano *nm* hurricane

u'ranio *nm* uranium

urba'n|esimo *nm* urbanization. **~ista** *nmf* town planner. **~istica** *nf* town planning. **~istico** *a* urban. **urbanizzazi'one** *nf* urbanization. **ur'bano** *a* urban; (*cortese*) urbane

ur'gen|te *a* urgent. **~te'mente** *adv* urgently. **~za** *nf* urgency; **in caso d'~za** in an emergency; **d'~za** (*misura, chiamata*) emergency

'**urgere** *vi* be urgent

u'rina *nf* urine. **uri'nare** *vi* urinate

ur'lare *vi* shout, yell; (*cane, vento:*) howl. '**urlo** *nm* (*pl nm* **urli**, *nf* **urla**) shout; (*di cane, vento*) howling

'**urna** *nf* urn; (*elettorale*) ballot box; **andare alle urne** go to the polls

urrà *int* hurrah!

U.R.S.S. *nf abbr* (**Unione delle Repubbliche Socialiste Sovietiche**) USSR

ur'tar|e *vt* knock against; (*scontrarsi*) bump into; *fig* irritate. **~si** *vr* collide; *fig* clash

'**urto** *nm* knock; (*scontro*) crash; (*contrasto*) conflict; *fig* clash; **d'~** (*misure, terapia*) shock

usa e getta *a inv* (*rasoio, siringa*) throw-away, disposable

u'sanza *nf* custom; (*moda*) fashion

u'sa|re *vt* use; (*impiegare*) employ; (*esercitare*) exercise; **~re fare qcsa** be in the habit of doing sth ●*vi* (*essere di moda*) be fashionable; **non si usa più it is out of fashion;** (*attrezzatura, espressione:*) it's not used any more. **~to** *a* used; (*non nuovo*) second-hand

U.S.A. *nmpl* US[A] *sg*

u'scente *a* (*presidente*) outgoing

usci'ere *nm* usher. '**uscio** *nm* door

u'sci|re *vi* come out; (*andare fuori*) go out; (*sfuggire*) get out; (*essere sorteggiato*) come up; (*giornale:*) come out; **~re da** *Comput* exit from, quit; **~re di strada** leave the road. **~ta** *nf* exit, way out; (*spesa*) outlay; (*di autostrada*) junction; (*battuta*) witty remark; **essere in libera ~ta** be off duty. **~ta di servizio** back door. **~ta di sicurezza** emergency exit

usi'gnolo *nm* nightingale

'**uso** *nm* use; (*abitudine*) custom; (*usanza*) usage; **fuori ~** out of use; **per ~ esterno** (*medicina*) for external use only

U.S.S.L. *nf abbr* (**Unità Socio-Sanitaria Locale**) local health centre

ustio'na|rsi *vr* burn oneself. **~to, -a** *nmf* burns case ●*a* burnt. **usti'one** *nf* burn

usu'ale *a* usual

usufru'ire *vi* **~ di** take advantage of

u'sura *nf* usury. **usu'raio** *nm* usurer

usur'pare *vt* usurp

u'tensile *nm* tool; *Culin* utensil; **cassetta degli utensili** tool box

u'tente *nmf* user. **~ finale** end user

u'tenza *nf* use; (*utenti*) users *pl*

ute'rino *a* uterine. '**utero** *nm* womb

'**util|e** *a* useful ●*nm* *Comm* profit. **~ità** *nf* usefulness, utility; *Comput* utility. **~i'taria** *nf* *Auto* small car. **~i'tario** *a* utilitarian

utiliz'za|re *vt* utilize. **~zi'one** *nf* utilization. **uti'lizzo** *nm* (*utilizzazione*) use

uto'pistico *a* Utopian

'**uva** *nf* grapes *pl*; **chicco d'~** grape. **~ passa** raisins *pl*. **~ sultanina** currants *pl*

va'cante a vacant
va'canza nf holiday; (posto vacante) vacancy. **essere in ~** be on holiday
'**vacca** nf cow. **~ da latte** dairy cow
vacci|'nare vt vaccinate. **~inazi'one** nf vaccination. **vac'cino** nm vaccine
vacil'la|nte a tottering; (oggetto) wobbly; (luce) flickering; fig wavering. **~re** vi totter; (oggetto:) wobble; (luce:) flicker; fig waver
'**vacuo** a (vano) vain; fig empty ● nm vacuum
vagabon'dare vi wander. **vaga'bondo, -a** a (cane) stray; **gente vagabonda** tramps pl ● nmf tramp
va'gare vi wander
vagheggi'are vt long for
va'gi|na nf vagina. **~'nale** a vaginal
va'gi|re vi whimper. **~to** nm whimper
'**vaglia** nm inv money order. **~ bancario** bank draft. **~ postale** postal order
vagli'are vt sift; fig weigh
'**vago** a vague
vagon'cino nm (di funivia) car
va'gone nm (per passeggeri) carriage; (per merci) wagon. **~ letto** sleeper. **~ ristorante** restaurant car
vai'olo nm smallpox
va'langa nf avalanche
va'lente a skilful
va'ler|e vi be worth; (contare) count; (regola:) apply (per to); (essere valido) be valid; **far ~ i propri diritti** assert one's rights; **farsi ~e** assert oneself; **non vale!** that's not fair!; **tanto vale che me ne vada** I might as well go ● vt **~re qcsa a qcno** (procurare) earn sb sth; **~ne la pena** be worth it; **vale la pena di vederlo** it's worth seeing; **~si di** avail oneself of
valeri'ana nf valerian
va'levole a valid
vali'care vt cross. '**valico** nm pass
validità nf validity; **con ~ illimitata** valid indefinitely
'**valido** a valid; (efficace) efficient; (contributo) valuable

valige'ria nf (fabbrica) leather factory; (negozio) leather goods shop
va'ligia nf suitcase; **fare le valigie** pack; fig pack one's bags. **~ diplomatica** diplomatic bag
val'lata nf valley. '**valle** nf valley; **a valle** downstream
val'lett|a nf TV assistant. **~o** nm valet; TV assistant
val'lone nm (valle) deep valley
va'lor|e nm value, worth; (merito) merit; (coraggio) valour; **~i** pl Comm securities; **di ~e** (oggetto) valuable; **oggetti** nmpl **di ~e** valuables; **senza ~e** worthless. **~iz'zare** vt (mettere in valore) use to advantage; (aumentare di valore) increase the value of; (migliorare l'aspetto di) enhance
valo'roso a courageous
'**valso** pp di **valere**
va'luta nf currency. **~ estera** foreign currency
valu'ta|re vt value; weigh up (situazione). **~rio** a (mercato, norme) currency. **~zi'one** nf valuation
'**valva** nf valve. '**valvola** nf valve; Electr fuse
'**valzer** nm inv waltz
vam'pata nf blaze; (di calore) blast; (al viso) flush
vam'piro nm vampire; fig blood-sucker
vana'mente adv (inutilmente) in vain
van'da|lico a atto **~lico** act of vandalism. **~'lismo** nm vandalism. '**vandalo** nm vandal
vaneggi'are vi rave
'**vanga** nf spade. **van'gare** vt dig
van'gelo nm Gospel; (fam: verità) gospel [truth]
vanifi'care vt nullify
va'niglia nf vanilla. **~ato** a (zucchero) vanilla attrib
vanil'lina nf vanillin
vanità nf vanity. **vani'toso** a vain
'**vano** a vain ● nm (stanza) room; (spazio vuoto) hollow
van'taggi|o nm advantage; Sport lead; Tennis advantage; **trarre ~o da qcsa**

derive benefit from sth. **~'oso** a advantageous

van't|are vt praise; (possedere) boast. **~arsi** vr boast. **~e'ria** nf boasting. **'vanto** nm boast

van'vera nf a **~** at random; **parlare a ~** talk nonsense

va'por|e nm steam; (di benzina, cascata) vapour; **a ~e** steam attrib; **al ~e** Culin steamed. **~e acqueo** steam, water vapour; **battello a ~e** steamboat. **vapo'retto** nm ferry. **~i'era** nf steam engine

vaporiz'zare vt vaporize. **~'tore** nm spray

vapo'roso a (vestito) filmy; **capelli vaporosi** big hair sg

va'rare vt launch

var'care vt cross. **'varco** nm passage; **aspettare al varco** lie in wait

vari'abil|e a changeable, variable ● nf variable. **~ità** nf changeableness, variability

vari'a|nte nf variant. **~re** vt/i vary; **~re di umore** change one's mood. **~zi'one** nf variation

va'rice nf varicose vein

vari'cella nf chickenpox

vari'coso a varicose

varie'gato a variegated

varietà nf inv variety ● nm inv variety show

'vario a varied; (al pl, parecchi) various; **vari** pl (molti) several; **varie ed eventuali** any other business

vario'pinto a multicoloured

'varo nm launch

va'saio nm potter

'vasca nf tub; (piscina) pool; (lunghezza) length. **~ da bagno** bath

va'scello nm vessel

va'schetta nf tub

vase'lina nf Vaseline®

vasel'lame nm china. **~ d'oro/d'argento** gold/silver plate

'vaso nm pot; (da fiori) vase; Anat vessel; (per cibi) jar. **~ da notte** chamber pot

vas'soio nm tray

vastità nf vastness. **'vasto** a vast; **di vaste vedute** broad-minded

Vati'cano nm Vatican

vattela'pesca adv fam God knows!

ve pers pron you; **ve l'ho dato** I gave it to you

vecchia nf old woman. **vecchi'aia** nf old age. **'vecchio** a old ● nmf old man; **i vecchi** old people

'vece nf **in ~ di** in place of; **fare le veci di qcno** take sb's place

ve'dente a **i non vedenti** the visually handicapped

ve'der|e vt/i see; **far ~e** show; **farsi ~e** show one's face; **non vedo l'ora di ...** I can't wait to... **~si** vr see oneself; (reciproco) see each other

ve'detta nf (luogo) lookout; Naut patrol vessel

vedovo, -a nm widower ● nf widow

ve'duta nf view

vee'mente a vehement

vege'ta|le a & nm vegetable. **~li'ano** a & nmf vegan. **~re** vi vegetate. **~ri'ano, -a** a & nmf vegetarian. **~zi'one** nf vegetation

'vegeto a vedi **vivo**

veg'gente nmf clairvoyant

veglia nf watch; **fare la ~** keep watch. **~ funebre** vigil

vegli|'are vi be awake; **~are su** watch over. **~'one** nm **~one di capodanno** New Year's Eve celebration

ve'icolo nm vehicle

'vela nf sail; Sport sailing; **far ~** set sail

ve'la|re vt veil; (fig: nascondere) hide. **~rsi** vr (vista:) mist over; (voce:) go husky. **~ta'mente** adv indirectly. **~to** a veiled; (occhi:) misty; (collant) sheer

'velcro® nm velcro®

veleggi'are vi sail

ve'leno nm poison. **vele'noso** a poisonous

veli'ero nm sailing ship

ve'lina nf |carta| **~** tissue paper; (copia) carbon copy

ve'lista nm yachtsman ● nf yachtswoman

ve'livolo nm aircraft

velleità nf inv foolish ambition. **~'tario** a unrealistic

'vello nm fleece

vellu'tato a velvety. **vel'luto** nm velvet. **velluto a coste** corduroy

'velo nm veil; (di zucchero, cipria) dusting; (tessuto) voile

ve'loc|e a fast. **~e'mente** adv quickly. **velo'cista** nmf Sport sprinter. **~ità** nf inv speed; (Auto: marcia) gear. **~ità di crociera** cruising speed. **~iz'zare** vt speed up

ve'lodromo nm cycle track

'vena nf vein; **essere in ~ di** be in the mood for

ve'nale a venal; (persona) mercenary, venal

ve'nato a grainy

vena'torio *a* hunting *attrib*

vena'tura *nf* (*di legno*) grain; (*di foglia, marmo*) vein

ven'demmi|a *nf* grape harvest. ~**are** *vt* harvest

'vender|e *vt* sell. ~**si** *vr* sell oneself; **vendesi** for sale

ven'detta *nf* revenge

vendi'ca|re *vt* avenge. ~**rsi** *vr* get one's revenge. ~**tivo** *a* vindictive

'vendi|ta *nf* sale; **in** ~**ta** on sale. ~**ta all'asta** sale by auction. ~**ta al dettaglio** retailing. ~**ta all'ingrosso** wholesaling. ~**ta al minuto** retailing. ~**ta porta a porta** door-to-door selling. ~**'tore**, ~**'trice** *nmf* seller. ~**tore ambulante** hawker, pedlar

vene'ra|bile, ~**ndo** *a* venerable

vene'rare *vt* revere

venerdi *nm inv* Friday. **V~ Santo** Good Friday

'Venere *nf* Venus. **ve'nereo** *a* venereal

Ve'nezi|a *nf* Venice. **v~'ano, -a** *a & nmf* Venetian ●*nf* (*persiana*) Venetian blind; *Culin* sweet bun

veni'ale *a* venial

ve'nire *vi* come; (*riuscire*) turn out; (*costare*) cost; (*in passivi*) be; ~ **a sapere** learn; ~ **in mente** occur; ~ **meno** (*svenire*) faint; ~ **meno a un contratto** go back on a contract; ~ **via** come away; (*staccarsi*) come off; **mi viene da piangere** I feel like crying; **vieni a prendermi** come and pick me up

ven'taglio *nm* fan

ven'tata *nf* gust [of wind]; *fig* breath

ven'te|nne *a & nmf* twenty-year-old. ~**simo** *a & nm* twentieth. **venti** *a & nm* twenty

venti'la|re *vt* air. ~**tore** *nm* fan. ~**zi'one** *nf* ventilation

ven'tina *nf* **una** ~ (*circa venti*) about twenty

ventiquat'trore *nf inv* (*valigia*) overnight case

'vento *nm* wind; **farsi** ~ fan oneself

ven'tosa *nf* sucker

ven'toso *a* windy

'ventre *nm* stomach. **ven'triloquo** *nm* ventriloquist

ven'tura *nf* fortune; **andare alla** ~ trust to luck

ven'turo *a* next

ve'nuta *nf* coming

vera'mente *adv* really

ve'randa *nf* veranda

ver'bal|e *a* verbal ●*nm* (*di riunione*) minutes *pl*. ~**'mente** *adv* verbally

'verbo *nm* verb. ~ **ausiliare** auxiliary [verb]

'verde *a* green ●*nm* green; (*vegetazione*) greenery; (*semaforo*) green light; **essere al** ~ be broke. ~ **oliva** olive green. ~ **pisello** pea green. ~**'rame** *nm* verdigris

ver'detto *nm* verdict

ver'dura *nf* vegetables *pl*; **una** ~ a vegetable

'verga *nf* rod

vergi'n|ale *a* virginal. **'vergine** *nf* virgin; *Astr* Virgo ●*a* virgin; (*cassetta*) blank. ~**ità** *nf* virginity

ver'gogna *nf* shame; (*timidezza*) shyness

vergo'gn|arsi *vr* feel ashamed; (*essere timido*) feel shy. ~**oso** *a* ashamed; (*timido*) shy; (*disonorevole*) shameful

ve'rifica *nf* check. **verifi'cabile** *a* verifiable

verifi'car|e *vt* check. ~**si** *vr* come true

ve'rismo *nm* realism

verit|à *nf* truth. ~**'iero** *a* truthful

'verme *nm* worm. ~ **solitario** tapeworm

ver'miglio *a & nm* vermilion

vermut *nm inv* vermouth

ver'nacolo *nm* vernacular

ver'nic|e *nf* paint; (*trasparente*) varnish; (*pelle*) patent leather; *fig* veneer; **"vernice fresca"** "wet paint". ~**i'are** *vt* paint; (*con vernice trasparente*) varnish. ~**ia'tura** *nf* painting; (*strato*) paintwork; *fig* veneer

'vero *a* true; (*autentico*) real; (*perfetto*) perfect; **è ~?** is that so?; ~ **e proprio** full-blown; **sei stanca, ~?** you're tired, aren't you? ●*nm* truth; (*realtà*) life

verosimigli'anza *nf* probability. **vero'simile** *a* probable

ver'ruca *nf* wart; (*sotto la pianta del piede*) verruca

versa'mento *nm* (*pagamento*) payment; (*in banca*) deposit

ver'sante *nm* slope

ver'sa|re *vt* pour; (*spargere*) shed; (*rovesciare*) spill; pay (*denaro*). ~**rsi** *vr* spill; (*sfociare*) flow

ver'satil|e *a* versatile. ~**ità** *nf* versatility

ver'setto *nm* verse

versi'one *nf* version; (*traduzione*) translation; **"~ integrale"** "unabridged version"; **"~ ridotta"** "abridged version"

'verso[1] *nm* verse; (*grido*) cry; (*gesto*) gesture; (*senso*) direction; (*modo*) manner; **fare il ~ a** qcno ape sb; **non c'è ~ di** there is no way of

'**verso**[2] *prep* towards; (*nei pressi di*) round about; **~ dove?** which way?

'**vertebra** *nf* vertebra

'**vertere** *vi* **~ su** focus on

verti'**cale** *a* vertical; (*in parole crociate*) down ● *nm* vertical ● *nf* handstand. **~mente** *adv* vertically

'**vertice** *nm* summit; *Math* vertex; **conferenza al ~** summit conference

ver'**tigine** *nf* dizziness; *Med* vertigo; **vertigini** *pl* giddy spells; **aver le vertigini** feel dizzy

vertigi'**nosa**'**mente** *adv* dizzily. **~'noso** *a* dizzy; (*velocità*) breakneck; (*prezzi*) sky-high; (*scollatura*) plunging

ve'**scica** *nf* bladder; (*sulla pelle*) blister

'**vescovo** *nm* bishop

'**vespa** *nf* wasp

vespasi'**ano** *nm* urinal

'**vespro** *nm* vespers *pl*

ves'**sillo** *nm* standard

ve'**staglia** *nf* dressing gown

vest|e *nf* dress; (*rivestimento*) covering; **in ~e di** in the capacity of; **in ~e ufficiale** in an official capacity. **~i'ario** *nm* clothing

ve'**stibolo** *nm* hall

ves'**tigio** *nm* (*pl nm* **vestigi**, *pl nf* **vestigia**) trace

ve'**sti|re** *vt* dress. **~rsi** *vr* get dressed. **~ti** *pl* clothes. **~to** *a* dressed ● *nm* (*da uomo*) suit; (*da donna*) dress

vete'**rano**, **-a** *a & nf* veteran

veteri'**naria** *nf* veterinary science

veteri'**nario** *a* veterinary ● *nm* veterinary surgeon

'**veto** *nm inv* veto

ve'**tra|io** *nm* glazier. **~ta** *nf* big window; (*in chiesa*) stained glass window; (*porta*) glass door. **~to** *a* glazed. **vetre'ria** *nf* glass works

ve'**trina** *nf* [shop-]window; (*mobile*) display cabinet. **~'nista** *nmf* window dresser

vetri'**olo** *nm* vitriol

'**vetro** *nm* glass; (*di finestra, porta*) pane. **~'resina** *nf* fibreglass

'**vetta** *nf* peak

vet'**tore** *nm* vector

vetto'**vaglie** *nfpl* provisions

vet'**tura** *nf* coach; (*ferroviaria*) carriage; *Auto* car. **vettu'rino** *nm* coachman

vezzeggi'**a|re** *vt* fondle. **~'tivo** *nm* pet name. '**vezzo** *nm* habit; (*attrattiva*) charm; **vezzi** *pl* (*moine*) affectation *sg*.

vez'**zoso** *a* charming; *pej* affected

vi *pers pron* you; (*riflessivo*) yourselves; (*reciproco*) each other; (*tra più persone*) one another; **vi ho dato un libro** I gave you a book; **lavatevi le mani** wash your hands; **eccovi** here you are! ● *adv* = **ci**

'**via**[1] *nf* street, road; *fig* way; *Anat* tract; **in ~ di** in the course of; **per ~ di** on account of; **~ ~ che** as; **per ~ aerea** by airmail

'**via**[2] *adv* away; (*fuori*) out; **andar ~** go away; **e così ~** and so on; **e ~ dicendo** and whatnot ● *int* **~!** go away!; *Sport* go!; (*andiamo*) come on! ● *nm* starting signal

viabilità *nf* road conditions *pl*; (*rete*) road network; (*norme*) road and traffic laws *pl*

via'**card** *nf inv* motorway card

via'**dotto** *nm* viaduct

viaggi'**a|re** *vi* travel. **~'tore**, **~'trice** *nmf* traveller

vi'**aggio** *nm* journey; (*breve*) trip; **buon ~!** safe journey!, have a good trip!; **fare un ~** go on a journey. **~ di nozze** honeymoon

vi'**ale** *nm* avenue; (*privato*) drive

via'**vai** *nm* coming and going

vi'**bra|nte** *a* vibrant. **~re** *vi* vibrate; (*fremere*) quiver. **~zi'one** *nf* vibration

vi'**cario** *nm* vicar

vice+ *pref* vice+

'**vice** *nmf* deputy. **~diret'tore** *nm* assistant manager

vi'**cenda** *nf* event; **a ~** (*fra due*) each other; (*a turno*) in turn[s]

vice'**versa** *adv* vice versa

vici'**na|nza** *nf* nearness; **~nze** *pl* (*paraggi*) neighbourhood. **~to** *nm* neighbourhood; (*vicini*) neighbours *pl*

vi'**cino**, **-a** *a* near; (*accanto*) next ● *adv* near, close. **~ a** *prep* near [to] ● *nmf* neighbour. **~ di casa** nextdoor neighbour

vicissi'**tudine** *nf* vicissitude

'**vicolo** *nm* alley

'**video** *nm* video. **~'camera** *nf* camcorder. **~cas'setta** *nf* video cassette

videoci'**tofono** *nm* video entry phone

video'**clip** *nm inv* video clip

videogi'**oco** *nm* video game

videoregistra'**tore** *nm* videorecorder

video'**teca** *nf* video library

video'**tel**® *nm* ≈ Videotex^℠

videotermi'**nale** *nm* visual display unit, VDU

vidi'**mare** *vt* authenticate

vie'**ta|re** *vt* forbid; **sosta ~ta** no parking; ~**to fumare** no smoking; ~**to ai minori di 18 anni** prohibited to children under the age of 18

vi'gente *a* in force. **'vigere** *vi* be in force

vigi'la|nte *a* vigilant. ~**nza** *nf* vigilance. ~**re** *vt* keep an eye on ● *vi* keep watch

'vigile *a* watchful ● *nm* ~ **[urbano]** policeman. ~ **del fuoco** fireman

vi'gilia *nf* eve

vigliacche'ria *nf* cowardice. **vi-gli'acco, -a** *a* cowardly ● *nmf* coward

'vigna *nf*, **vi'gneto** *nm* vineyard

vi'gnetta *nf* cartoon

vi'gore *nm* vigour; **entrare in ~** come into force. **vigo'roso** *a* vigorous

'vile *a* cowardly; (*abietto*) vile

'villa *nf* villa

vil'laggio *nm* village. ~ **turistico** holiday village

vil'lano *a* rude ● *nm* boor; (*contadino*) peasant

villeggi'a|nte *nmf* holiday-maker. ~**re** *vi* spend one's holidays. ~**tura** *nf* holiday[s] [*pl*], vacation *Am*

vil'l|etta *nf* small detached house. ~**ino** *nm* detached house

viltà *nf* cowardice

'vimine *nm* wicker

'vinc|ere *vt* win; (*sconfiggere*) beat; (*superare*) overcome. ~**ita** *nf* win; (*somma vinta*) winnings *pl*. ~**i'tore, ~i'trice** *nmf* winner

vinco'la|nte *a* binding. ~**re** *vt* bind; *Comm* tie up. **'vincolo** *nm* bond

vi'nicolo *a* wine *attrib*

vinil'pelle® *nm* Leatherette®

'vino *nm* wine. ~ **spumante** sparkling wine. ~ **da taglio** blending wine. ~ **da tavola** table wine

'vinto *pp di* **vincere**

vi'ola *nf Bot* violet; *Mus* viola. **vio'laceo** *a* purplish; (*labbra*) blue

vio'la|re *vt* violate. ~**zi'one** *nf* violation. ~**zione di domicilio** breaking and entering

violen'tare *vt* rape

violente'mente *adv* violently

vio'len|to *a* violent. ~**za** *nf* violence. ~**za carnale** rape

vio'letta *nf* violet

vio'letto *a & nm* (*colore*) violet

violi'nista *nmf* violinist. **vio'lino** *nm* violin. **violon'cello** *nm* cello

vi'ottolo *nm* path

'vipera *nf* viper

vi'ra|ggio *nm Phot* toning; *Naut, Aeron* turn. ~**re** *vi* turn; ~**re di bordo** veer

'virgol|a *nf* comma. ~**ette** *nfpl* inverted commas

vi'ril|e *a* virile; (*da uomo*) manly. ~**ità** *nf* virility; manliness

virtù *nf inv* virtue; **in ~ di** (*legge*) under. ~ **ale** *a* virtual. ~**oso** *a* virtuous ● *nm* virtuoso

viru'lento *a* virulent

'virus *nm inv* virus

visa'gista *nmf* beautician

visce'rale *a* visceral; (*odio*) deepseated; (*reazione*) gut

'viscere *nm* internal organ ● *nfpl* guts

'vischi|o *nm* mistletoe. ~**oso** *a* viscous; (*appiccicoso*) sticky

'viscido *a* slimy

vi'scont|e *nm* viscount. ~**essa** *nf* viscountess

vi'scoso *a* viscous

vi'sibile *a* visible

visi'bilio *nm* profusion; **andare in ~** go into ecstasies

visibilità *nf* visibility

visi'era *nf* (*di elmo*) visor; (*di berretto*) peak

visio'nare *vt* examine; *Cinema* screen. **visi'one** *nf* vision; **prima visione** *Cinema* first showing

'visit|a *nf* visit; (*breve*) call; *Med* examination; **fare ~a a** qcno pay sb a visit. ~**a di controllo** *Med* checkup. **visi'tare** *vt* visit; (*brevemente*) call on; *Med* examine; ~**a'tore, ~a'trice** *nmf* visitor

vi'sivo *a* visual

'viso *nm* face

vi'sone *nm* mink

'vispo *a* lively

vis'suto *pp di* **vivere** ● *a* experienced

'vist|a *nf* sight; (*veduta*) view; **a ~a d'occhio** (*crescere*) visibly; (*estendersi*) as far as the eye can see; **in ~a di** in view of; **perdere di ~a** qcno lose sight of sb; *fig* lose touch with sb. ~**o** *pp di* **vedere** ● *nm* visa. **vi'stoso** *a* showy; (*notevole*) considerable

visu'al|e *a* visual. ~**izza'tore** *nm Comput* display, VDU. ~**izzazi'one** *nf Comput* display

'vita *nf* life; (*durata della vita*) lifetime; *Anat* waist; **a ~** for life; **essere in fin di ~** be at death's door; **essere in ~** be alive

vi'tal|e *a* vital. ~**ità** *nf* vitality

vita'lizio *a* life *attrib* ● *nm* [life] annuity

vita'min|a *nf* vitamin. ~**iz'zato** *a* vitamin-enriched

'vite *nf Mech* screw; *Bot* vine

vi'tello *nm* calf; *Culin* veal; (*pelle*) calfskin

vi'ticcio *nm* tendril

viticol't|ore *nm* wine grower. ~**ura** *nf* wine growing

'vitreo *a* vitreous; ⟨*sguardo*⟩ glassy

'vittima *nf* victim

'vitto *nm* food; ⟨*pasti*⟩ board. ~ **e alloggio** board and lodging

vit'toria *nf* victory

vittori'ano *a* Victorian

vittori'oso *a* victorious

vi'uzza *nf* narrow lane

'viva *int* hurrah!; ~ **la Regina!** long live the Queen!

vi'vac|e *a* vivacious; ⟨*mente*⟩ lively; ⟨*colore*⟩ bright. ~**ità** *nf* vivacity; ⟨*di mente*⟩ liveliness; ⟨*di colore*⟩ brightness. ~**iz'zare** *vt* liven up

vi'vaio *nm* nursery; ⟨*per pesci*⟩ pond; *fig* breeding ground

viva'mente *adv* ⟨*ringraziare*⟩ warmly

vi'vanda *nf* food; ⟨*piatto*⟩ dish

vi'vente *a* living ●*nmpl* **i viventi** the living

'vivere *vi* live; ~ **di** live on ●*vt* ⟨*passare*⟩ go through ●*nm* life

'viveri *nmpl* provisions

'vivido *a* vivid

vivisezi'one *nf* vivisection

'vivo *a* alive; ⟨*vivente*⟩ living; ⟨*vivace*⟩ lively; ⟨*colore*⟩ bright; ~ **e vegeto** alive and kicking; **farsi** ~ keep in touch; ⟨*arrivare*⟩ turn up ●*nm* **colpire qcno sul** ~ cut sb to the quick; **dal** ~ ⟨*trasmissione*⟩ live; ⟨*disegnare*⟩ from life; **i vivi** the living

vizi|'are *vt* spoil ⟨*bambino ecc*⟩; ⟨*guastare*⟩ vitiate. ~**'ato** *a* spoilt; ⟨*aria*⟩ stale. **'vizio** *nm* vice; ⟨*cattiva abitudine*⟩ bad habit; ⟨*difetto*⟩ flaw. ~**'oso** *a* dissolute; ⟨*difettoso*⟩ faulty; **circolo** ~**oso** vicious circle

vocabo'lario *nm* dictionary; ⟨*lessico*⟩ vocabulary. **vo'cabolo** *nm* word

vo'cale *a* vocal ●*nf* vowel. **vo'calico** *a* ⟨*corde*⟩ vocal; ⟨*suono*⟩ vowel *attrib*

vocazi'one *nf* vocation

'voce *nf* voice; ⟨*diceria*⟩ rumour; ⟨*di bilancio, dizionario*⟩ entry

voci'are *vi* ⟨*spettegolare*⟩ gossip ●*nm* buzz of conversation

vocife'rare *vi* shout; **si vocifera che...** it is rumoured that...

'vog|a *nf* rowing; ⟨*lena*⟩ enthusiasm; ⟨*moda*⟩ vogue; **essere in ~a** be in fashion. **vo'gare** *vi* row. ~**a'tore** *nm* oarsman; ⟨*attrezzo*⟩ rowing machine

'vogli|a *nf* desire; ⟨*volontà*⟩ will; ⟨*della pelle*⟩ birthmark; **aver ~a di fare qcsa**

feel like doing sth. ~**'oso** *a* ⟨*occhi, persona*⟩ covetous

'voi *pers pron* you; **siete ~?** is that you?; **l'avete fatto ~?** did you do it yourself?. ~**'altri** *pers pron* you

vo'lano *nm* shuttlecock; *Mech* flywheel

vo'lante *a* flying; ⟨*foglio*⟩ loose ●*nm* steering-wheel

volan'tino *nm* leaflet

vo'la|re *vi* fly. ~**ta** *nf Sport* final sprint; **di** ~**ta** in a rush

vo'latile *a* ⟨*liquido*⟩ volatile ●*nm* bird

vo'lée *nf inv Tennis* volley

vo'lente *a* ~ **o nolente** whether you like it or not

volente'roso *a* willing

volenti'eri *adv* willingly; ~**!** with pleasure!

vo'lere *vt* want; ⟨*chiedere di*⟩ ask for; ⟨*aver bisogno di*⟩ need; **vuole che lo faccia io** he wants me to do it; **fai come vuoi** do as you like; **se tuo padre vuole, ti porto al cinema** if your father agrees, I'll take you to the cinema; **vorrei un caffè** I'd like a coffee; **la leggenda vuole che...** legend has it that...; **la vuoi smettere?** will you stop that!; **senza** ~ without meaning to; **voler bene/male a qcno** love/have something against sb; **voler dire** mean; **ci vuole il latte** we need milk; **ci vuole tempo/pazienza** it takes time/patience; **volerne a** have a grudge against; **vuoi...vuoi...** either...or... ●*nm* will; **voleri** *pl* wishes

vol'gar|e *a* vulgar; ⟨*popolare*⟩ common. ~**ità** *nf inv* vulgarity. ~**iz'zare** *vt* popularize. ~**'mente** *adv* ⟨*grossolanamente*⟩ vulgarly, coarsely; ⟨*comunemente*⟩ commonly

'volger|e *vt/i* turn. ~**si** *vr* turn [round]; ~**si a** ⟨*dedicarsi*⟩ take up

voli'era *nf* aviary

voli'tivo *a* strong-minded

'volo *nm* flight; **al** ~ ⟨*fare qcsa*⟩ quickly; ⟨*prendere qcsa*⟩ in mid-air; **alzarsi in** ~ ⟨*uccello*⟩ take off; **in** ~ airborne. ~ **di linea** scheduled flight. ~ **nazionale** domestic flight. ~ **a vela** gliding.

volontà *nf inv* will; ⟨*desiderio*⟩ wish; **a** ~ ⟨*mangiare*⟩ as much as you like. ~**ria'mente** *adv* voluntarily. **volon'tario** *a* voluntary ●*nm* volunteer

volonte'roso *a* willing

'volpe *nf* fox

volt *nm inv* volt

'volta *nf* time; ⟨*turno*⟩ turn; ⟨*curva*⟩ bend; *Archit* vault; **4 volte** 4 times 4; **a volte** sometimes; **c'era una ~...** once upon a time, there was...; **una ~** once; **due volte** twice; **tre/quattro volte** three/four times; **una ~ per tutte** once and for all; **uno per ~** one at a time; **uno alla ~** one at a time; **alla ~ di** in the direction of

volta'faccia *nm inv* volte-face

vol'taggio *nm* voltage

vol'ta|re *vt/i* turn; (*rigirare*) turn round; (*rivoltare*) turn over; **~re pagi-na** *fig* forget the past. **~rsi** *vr* turn [round]

volta'stomaco *nm* nausea; *fig* disgust

volteggi'are *vi* circle; (*ginnastica*) vault

'volto *pp di* **volgere** • *nm* face; **mi ha mostrato il suo vero ~** he revealed his true colours

vo'lubile *a* fickle

vo'lum|e *nm* volume. **~i'noso** *a* voluminous

voluta'mente *adv* deliberately

voluttu|osità *nf* voluptuousness. **~'oso** *a* voluptuous

vomi'tare *vt* vomit. **vomi'tevole** *a* nauseating. **'vomito** *nm* vomit.

'vongola *nf* clam

vo'race *a* voracious. **~'mente** *adv* voraciously

vo'ragine *nf* abyss

'vortice *nm* whirl; (*gorgo*) whirlpool; (*di vento*) whirlwind

'vostro (**il ~** *m*, **la vostra** *f*, **i vostri** *mpl*, **le vostre** *fpl*) *poss a* your; **è vostra questa macchina?** is this car yours?; **un ~ amico** a friend of yours; **~ padre** your father • *poss pron* yours; **i vostri** your folks

vo'ta|nte *nmf* voter. **~re** *vi* vote. **~zi'one** *nf* voting; *Sch* marks *pl*. **'voto** *nm* vote; *Sch* mark; *Relig* vow

vs. *abbr Comm* (**vostro**) yours

vul'canico *a* volcanic. **vul'cano** *nm* volcano

vulne'rabil|e *a* vulnerable. **~ità** *nf* vulnerability

vuo'tare *vt*, **vuo'tarsi** *vr* empty

vu'oto *a* empty; (*non occupato*) vacant; **~ di** (*sprovvisto*) devoid of • *nm* empty space; *Phys* vacuum; *fig* void; **assegno a ~** dud cheque; **sotto ~** (*prodotto*) vacuum-packed; **~ a perdere** no deposit. **~ d'aria** air pocket

WwXxYy

W *abbr* (**viva**) long live

'wafer *nm inv* (*biscotto*) wafer

walkie-'talkie *nm inv* walkie-talkie

water *nm inv* toilet, loo *fam*

watt *nm inv* watt

wat'tora *nm inv Phys* watt-hour

WC *nm* WC

'western *a inv* cowboy *attrib* • *nm Cinema* western

X, x *a raggi nmpl* X X-rays; **il giorno X** D-day

xenofo'bia *nf* xenophobia. **xe'nofo-bo, -a** *a* xenophobic • *nmf* xenophobe

xe'res *nm inv* sherry

xi'lofono *nm* xylophone

yacht *nm inv* yacht

yen *nm inv Fin* yen

'yeti *nm inv* yeti

'yoga *nm* yoga; (*praticante*) yogi

'yogurt *nm inv* yoghurt. **~i'era** *nf* yoghurt-maker

'yorkshire *nm inv* (*cane*) Yorkshire terrier

yo-yo *nm inv* yoyo®

Zz

za·ba[gl]i·one *nm* zabaglione (*dessert made from eggs, wine or marsala and sugar*)

zac·chera *nf* (*schizzo*) splash of mud

zaf·fata *nf* whiff; (*di fumo*) cloud

zaffe·rano *nm* saffron

zaf·firo *nm* sapphire

zaino *nm* rucksack

zampa *nf* leg; a quattro zampe (*animale*) four-legged; (*carponi*) on all fours. zampe *pl* di gallina crow's feet

zampil·la·nte *a* spurting. ~re *vi* spurt. zam·pillo *nm* spurt

zam·pogna *nf* bagpipe. zampo·gnaro *nm* piper

zanna *nf* fang; (*di elefante*) tusk

zan·zar·a *nf* mosquito. ~i·era *nf* (*velo*) mosquito net; (*su finestra*) insect screen

zappa *nf* hoe. zap·pare *vt* hoe

zattera *nf* raft

za·vorra *nf* ballast; *fig* dead wood

zazzera *nf* mop of hair

zebra *nf* zebra; zebre *pl* (*passaggio pedonale*) zebra crossing

zecca[1] *nf* mint; nuovo di ~ brand-new

zecca[2] *nf* (*parassita*) tick

zec·chino *nm* sequin; oro ~ pure gold

ze·lante *a* zealous. zelo *nm* zeal

zenit *nm* zenith

zenzero *nm* ginger

zeppa *nf* wedge

zeppo *a* packed full; pieno ~ di crammed o packed with

zer·bino *nm* doormat

zero *nm* zero, nought; (*in calcio*) nil; *Tennis* love; due a ~ (*in partite*) two nil; ricominciare da ~ *fig* start again from scratch

zeta *nf* zed, zee *Am*

zia *nf* aunt

zibel·lino *nm* sable

zigomo *nm* cheek-bone

zigri·nato *a* (*pelle*) grained; (*metallo*) milled

zig·zag *nm inv* zigzag

zim·bello *nm* decoy; (*oggetto di scherno*) laughing-stock

zinco *nm* zinc

zingaro, -a *nmf* gypsy

zio *nm* uncle

zi·tel·la *nf* spinster; *pej* old maid. ~lona *nf pej* old maid

zit·tire *vi* fall silent ●*vt* silence. zitto *a* silent; sta' zitto! keep quiet!

ziz·zania *nf* (*discordia*) discord; seminare ~ cause trouble

zoccolo *nm* clog; (*di cavallo*) hoof; (*di terra*) clump; (*di parete*) skirting board, baseboard *Am*; (*di colonna*) base

zodia·cale *a* of the zodiac. zo·diaco *nm* zodiac

zolfo *nm* sulphur

zolla *nf* clod; (*di zucchero*) lump

zol·letta *nf* sugar cube, sugar lump

zombi *nmf inv fig* zombi

zona *nf* zone; (*area*) area. ~ di depressione area of low pressure. ~ disco area for parking discs only. ~ pedonale pedestrian precinct. ~ verde green belt

zonzo *adv* andare a ~ stroll about

zoo *nm inv* zoo

zoolo·gia *nf* zoology. zoo·logico *a* zoological. zo·ologo, -a *nmf* zoologist

zoo sa·fari *nm inv* safari park

zoppi·ca·nte *a* limping; *fig* shaky. ~re *vi* limp; (*essere debole*) be shaky. zoppo, -a *a* lame ●*nmf* cripple

zoti·cone *nm* boor

zu·ava *nf* calzoni alla ~ plus-fours

zucca *nf* marrow; (*fam: testa*) head; (*fam: persona*) thickie

zucche·r·are *vt* sugar. ~i·era *nf* sugar bowl. ~i·ficio *nm* sugar refinery. zucche·rino *a* sugary ●*nm* sugar lump

zuc·chero *nm* sugar. ~ di canna cane sugar. ~ a velo icing sugar. zuc·che·roso *a fig* honeyed

zuc·chin·a *nf*, ~o *nm* courgette, zucchini *Am*

zuc·cone *nm* blockhead

zuffa *nf* scuffle

zufo·lare *vt/i* whistle

zu·mare *vi* zoom

zuppa *nf* soup. ~ inglese trifle

zup·petta *nf* fare ~ [con] dunk

zuppi·era *nf* soup tureen

zuppo *a* soaked

TEST YOURSELF WITH WORD GAMES

This section contains a number of word games which will help you to use your dictionary more effectively and to build up your knowledge of Italian vocabulary and usage in a fun and entertaining way. You will find answers to all puzzles and games at the end of the section.

1 X files

A freak power cut in the office has caused all the computers to go down. When they are re-booted, all the words on the screen have become mysteriously jumbled. Use the English to Italian side of the dictionary to help you decipher these Italian names of everyday office and computer equipment.

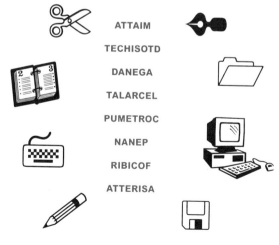

ATTAIM

TECHISOTD

DANEGA

TALARCEL

PUMETROC

NANEP

RIBICOF

ATTERISA

2 Crowded suitcase

You are at the airport on your way to visit your Welsh cousins in Patagonia when you are told that your suitcase is overweight. Luckily, you had packed a number of things that you did not need because you had forgotten that it was wintertime in the southern hemisphere. Decide which 5 items to jettison from your luggage.

occhiali da sole   calzettoni   sandali

pigiama   guanti   spazzolino da denti   maglietta

crema solare   maglione   cintura

costume da bagno   cappotto   riviste

pantaloncini   sciarpa

3 What are they like?

Here are two lists of adjectives you can use to describe people's characteristics. Each word in the second column is the opposite of one of the adjectives in the first column. Can you link them?

1.	grande	A.	intelligente
2.	biondo	B.	cattivo
3.	stupido	C.	grasso
4.	nervoso	D.	piccolo
5.	buono	E.	simpatico
6.	alto	F.	bruno
7.	paziente	G.	calmo
8.	antipatico	H.	basso
9.	educato	I.	impaziente
10.	magro	J.	maleducato

Example: 1.D. **grande** è il contrario di **piccolo**

4 Link-up

The Italian nouns on the left-hand side are all made up of two
separate words but they have been split apart. Try to link up the
two halves of each compound, then do the same for the English
compounds in the right-hand columns. Now you can match up the
Italian compounds with their English translations.

spaventa	capelli	nut	sport
macina	noci	pencil	gloss
taglia	labbra	pepper	screw
dopo	erba	hair	shave
guasta	matite	key	crackers
schiaccia	barba	spoil	crow
porta	tappi	lawn	sharpener
lucida	feste	after	ring
tempera	pepe	lip	mill
asciuga	chiavi	scare	dryer
cava	passeri	cork	mower

5 Body parts

Can you put the right number in the boxes next to the Italian words in the list?

- ☐ l'alluce
- ☐ la bocca
- ☐ il braccio
- ☐ la caviglia
- ☐ il collo
- ☐ la coscia
- ☐ il dito
- ☐ il fianco
- ☐ la fronte
- ☐ la gamba
- ☐ il ginocchio
- ☐ il gomito
- ☐ la mano
- ☐ il mento
- ☐ il naso
- ☐ l'occhio
- ☐ l'ombelico
- ☐ l'orecchio
- ☐ il piede
- ☐ il polpaccio
- ☐ il polso
- ☐ la spalla
- ☐ la testa
- ☐ lo zigomo

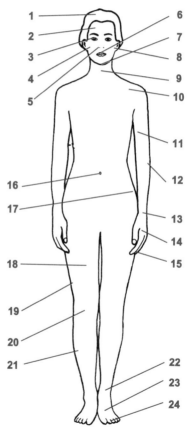

6 Mystery word

To fill in the grid, find the Italian words for all the musical instruments illustrated below. Once you have completed the grid, you'll discover the name of a famous Italian opera singer.

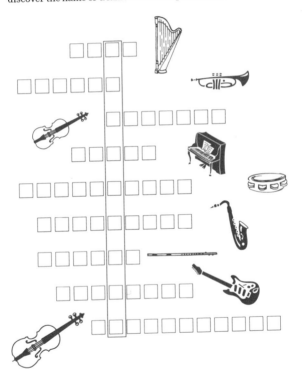

The opera singer is _ _ _ _ _ _ _ _ _

7 The odd one out

In each of the following series, all the words but one are related. Find the odd one out and explain why. If there are words you don't know, use your dictionary to find out what they mean.

example:

- ☐ penna
- ☐ diario
- ☐ libro
- ☐ quaderno
- ☑ spazzola

The odd one out is 'spazzola', because you wouldn't find it in a school-bag.

- ☐ auto
- ☐ aereo
- ☐ motore
- ☐ treno
- ☐ camion

- ☐ nuoto
- ☐ calcio
- ☐ pugilato
- ☐ equitazione
- ☐ ciclismo

- ☐ pentola
- ☐ padella
- ☐ caffettiera
- ☐ portacenere
- ☐ friggitrice

- ☐ correre
- ☐ saltare
- ☐ ballare
- ☐ sognare
- ☐ salire

- ☐ televisore
- ☐ registratore
- ☐ stereo
- ☐ videocassetta
- ☐ giradischi

- ☐ batteria
- ☐ chitarra
- ☐ violino
- ☐ arpa
- ☐ contrabbasso

8 Hidden words — false friends

Hidden in the grid are nine Italian words. First look at the list of false friends below – look up the translation of the Italian words listed, then using your own knowledge and the dictionary, find the translations of the English to search for in the grid.

O	S	E	P	O	G	D	I	C	B
I	S	O	G	L	I	O	L	A	Q
S	U	P	T	C	U	S	T	R	O
C	R	M	S	R	M	A	E	I	V
I	O	U	L	G	E	S	N	N	E
M	F	L	V	A	N	C	U	O	N
M	V	T	O	I	T	Q	T	L	D
I	I	A	T	M	A	R	A	F	I
A	P	S	V	U	B	O	C	H	T
F	D	A	T	I	Z	A	X	E	A

English   **Italian**

fine[1]	fine	....	....
sale	sale	....	....
mare	mare	....	....
sole[2]	sole	....	....
estate	estate	....	....
dove	dove	....	....
data	data	....	....
ape	ape	....	....
cute	cute	....	....

9 Curly words

One word is missing in each of the curly lists. Which day, month, capital city and number are missing?
Can you write out the four lists in the right order?

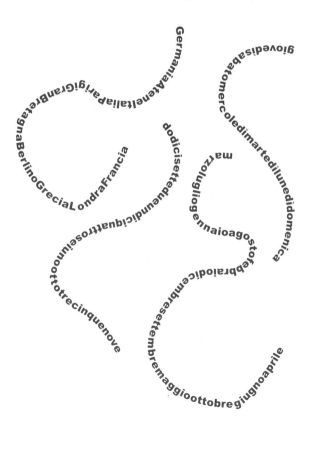

10 Amelia's shooting stars

Amelia is very good at predicting the future, but she is not very good at conjugating Italian verbs in the future tense. Help her to replace all the verbs in brackets with the correct future form.

Leone

23 luglio–22 agosto

(Essere) una settimana fortunata per i Leoni. Lavoro: Un superiore vi (affidare) un compito di grande responsabilità e ciò (potere) creare gelosie tra i colleghi, ma con un po' di diplomazia (risolvere) la situazione. Un viaggio (portare) spese impreviste. Amore: (Fare) incontri piacevoli e interessanti e con Venere che vi protegge nessuno (sapere) resistere al vostro fascino! Gli amici (avere) bisogno del vostro aiuto. Salute: Attenzione allo stress: fate dello sport o prendete una vacanza, (essere) più rilassati e anche l'umore (migliorare).

11 Recipe of the week

The printers have left out some important words in this recipe. Can you supply the missing words from the jumble below?

Ricetta della settimana

Soffriggete una .... piccola e uno spicchio d' .... in 5 cucchiai di ....

Dopo un paio di minuti aggiungete 2 .... sottolio e spappolatele con una ....

Poi, sempre a .... basso, aggiungete il .... sottolio spezzettato e una scatola di .... , ... e ....

Cuocete per una ventina di minuti, poi aggiungete il ....

Nel frattempo lessate 350 grammi di .... in abbondante acqua salata, scolatela al dente e servitela con la .... preparata e, se volete, con ....

prezzemolo   pasta   **acciughe**

cipolla   salsa   parmigiano   **pelati**

sale   **tonno**   olio d'oliva   **pepe**

aglio   **forchetta**   fuoco

12 My life's a mess

Sabrina has a busy schedule but she is a creature of habit and likes to stick to her daily routine. The order of her normal workday has been muddled up in the sentences below. Link up the matching halves of each sentence in the two columns and then try to put the complete sentences in sequence. Be careful, some can link up with more than one from the other column, so you'll have to do them all before you can be sure which go together best.

legge il giornale	per pranzo
torna a casa	come prima cosa
non beve mai caffè	prima delle nove
di solito porta fuori il cane	stanchissima
le piace fare un giro	durante il viaggio di ritorno
legge la corrispondenza	dopo cena
esce a mezzogiorno	durante una riunione
preferisce fare la doccia	di mattina
entra al lavoro	prima di tornare in ufficio
insiste a tenere le riunioni	prima di cena

13 Crossword

Across
1 chicken
4 dog
7 indefinite article (masculine)
8 veil
9 bag
12 ship
13 future of the verb meaning
   'to burn' (1st person singular)
15 to tie up
16 one
18 art
19 interrogative pronoun
20 beautiful (feminine)
21 you and me, us
22 beginning of the word
   meaning 'den'
23 three
24 heart

26 definite article (feminine)
27 age
Down
1 advertising
2 honour
3 fishbone
4 past historic of the verb
   meaning 'to have dinner'
   (3rd person singular)
5 wing
6 ninety
10 rust
11 aerobics
14 king
16 to yell
17 first and last letter of the
   word meaning 'smell'
18 high
25 beginning of the word
   meaning 'label'

Answers

1
matita
computer

dischetto
penna

agenda
forbici

cartella
tastiera

2
sandali
costume da bagno

maglietta
pantaloncini

crema solare

3
1.D. *grande* è il contrario di *piccolo*.
2.F. *biondo* è il contrario di *bruno*.
3.A. *stupido* è il contrario di *intelligente*.
4.G. *nervoso* è il contrario di *calmo*.
5.B. *buono* è il contrario di *cattivo*.
6.H. *alto* è il contrario di *basso*.
7.I. *paziente* è il contrario di *impaziente*.
8.E. *antipatico* è il contrario di *simpatico*.
9.J. *educato* è il contrario di *maleducato*.
10.C. *magro* è il contrario di *grasso*.

4
spaventapasseri	=	scarecrow
macinapepe	=	peppermill
tagliaerba	=	lawn-mower
dopobarba	=	aftershave
guastafeste	=	spoilsport
schiaccianoci	=	nutcrackers
portachiavi	=	keyring
lucidalabbra	=	lipgloss
temperamatite	=	pencil sharpener
asciugacapelli	=	hairdryer
cavatappi	=	corkscrew

5
1	la testa	10	la spalla	19	la gamba
2	la fronte	11	il braccio	20	il ginocchio
3	l'occhio	12	il gomito	21	il polpaccio
4	lo zigomo	13	il polso	22	la caviglia
5	il naso	14	la mano	23	il piede
6	la bocca	15	il dito	24	l'alluce
7	il mento	16	l'ombelico		
8	l'orecchio	17	il fianco		
9	il collo	18	la coscia		

6

```
      AR PA
   TROMB A
          VIOLINO
      PI ANO
TAMBU RELLO
    SASS OFONO
    FLAU TO
      CHI TARRA
         V IOLONCELLO
```

The opera singer's name is PAVAROTTI

7

motore – because it isn't a vehicle

portacenere – because it isn't used for cooking

videocassetta – because it isn't an electrical device

calcio – because it's the only team game in the list

sognare – because it's the only verb in the list which doesn't describe a
   movement

batteria – because it isn't a stringed instrument

8

end	summer	skin	giumenta	dati
salt	where		sogliola	scimmia
sea	date	multa	tenuta	carino
sun	bee	vendita	colomba	

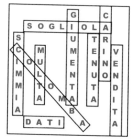

9

venerdì;   domenica, lunedì, martedì, mercoledì, giovedì, venerdì,
              sabato

novembre;   gennaio, febbraio, marzo, aprile, maggio, giugno, luglio,
              agosto, settembre, ottobre, novembre, dicembre

Roma;   Germania/Berlino, Francia/Parigi, Grecia/Atene, Gran
              Bretagna/Londra, Italia/Roma

dieci;   uno, due, tre, quattro, cinque, sei, sette, otto, nove, dieci,
              undici, dodici

10

sarà	affiderà	potrà	risolverete
porterà	farete	saprà	avranno
sarete	migliorerà		

11

Soffriggete una CIPOLLA piccola e uno spicchio d'AGLIO in 5 cucchiai di OLIO D'OLIVA

Dopo un paio di minuti aggiungete 2 ACCIUGHE sottolio e spappolatele con una FORCHETTA.

Poi, sempre a FUOCO basso, aggiungete il TONNO sottolio spezzettato e una scatola di PELATI, SALE e PEPE.

Cuocete per una ventina di minuti, poi aggiungete il PREZZEMOLO.

Nel frattempo lessate 350 grammi di PASTA in abbondante acqua salata, scolatela al dente e servitela con la SALSA preparata e, se volete, con PARMIGIANO.

12

entra al lavoro prima delle nove
legge la corrispondenza come prima cosa
insiste a tenere le riunioni di mattina
non beve mai caffè durante una riunione
esce a mezzogiorno per pranzo
le piace fare un giro prima di tornare in ufficio
legge il giornale durante il viaggio di ritorno
torna a casa stanchissima
preferisce fare la doccia prima di cena
di solito porta fuori il cane dopo cena

13

Aa

A /eɪ/ *n Mus* la *m inv*

a /ə/, *accentato* /eɪ/ *(davanti a una vocale an)* *indef art* un *m*, una *f*; *(before s + consonant, gn, ps and z)* uno; *(before feminine noun starting with a vowel)* un'; *(each)* a; **I am a lawyer** sono avvocato; **a tiger is a feline** la tigre è un felino; **a knife and fork** un coltello e una forchetta; **a Mr Smith is looking for you** un certo signor Smith ti sta cercando; **£2 a kilo/a head** due sterline al chilo/a testa

aback /ə'bæk/ *adv* **be taken** ~ essere preso in contropiede

abandon /ə'bændən/ *vt* abbandonare; *(give up)* rinunciare a ● *n* abbandono *m*. **~ed** *a* abbandonato

abashed /ə'bæʃt/ *a* imbarazzato

abate /ə'beɪt/ *vi* calmarsi

abattoir /'æbətwɑː(r)/ *n* mattatoio *m*

abbey /'æbɪ/ *n* abbazia *f*

abbreviat|e /ə'briːvɪeɪt/ *vt* abbreviare. **~ion** /-'eɪʃn/ *n* abbreviazione *f*

abdicat|e /'æbdɪkeɪt/ *vi* abdicare. ● *vt* rinunciare a. **~ion** /-'keɪʃn/ *n* abdicazione *f*

abdom|en /'æbdəmən/ *n* addome *m*. **~inal** /-'dɒmɪnl/ *a* addominale

abduct /əb'dʌkt/ *vt* rapire. **~ion** /-'ʌkʃn/ *n* rapimento *m*

aberration /æbə'reɪʃn/ *n* aberrazione *f*

abet /ə'bet/ *vt* (*pt/pp* abetted) aid and ~ *Jur* essere complice di

abeyance /ə'beɪəns/ *n* in ~ in sospeso; **fall into** ~ cadere in disuso

abhor /əb'hɔː(r)/ *vt* (*pt/pp* abhorred) aborrire. **~rence** /-'hɒrəns/ *n* orrore *m*

abid|e /ə'baɪd/ *vt* (*pt/pp* abided) *(tolerate)* sopportare ● **abide by** *vi* rispettare. **~ing** *a* perpetuo

ability /ə'bɪlətɪ/ *n* capacità *f inv*

abject /'æbdʒekt/ *a* *(poverty)* degradante; *(apology)* umile; *(coward)* abietto

ablaze /ə'bleɪz/ *a* in fiamme; **be** ~ **with light** risplendere di luci

able /'eɪbl/ *a* capace, abile; **be** ~ **to do sth** poter fare qcsa; **were you** ~ **to...?**

sei riuscito a...? **~-bodied** *a* robusto; *Mil* abile

ably /'eɪblɪ/ *adv* abilmente

abnormal /æb'nɔːml/ *a* anormale. **~ity** /-'mælətɪ/ *n* anormalità *f inv*. **~ly** *adv* in modo anormale

aboard /ə'bɔːd/ *adv & prep* a bordo

abol|ish /ə'bɒlɪʃ/ *vt* abolire. **~ition** /æbə'lɪʃn/ *n* abolizione *f*

abomina|ble /ə'bɒmɪnəbl/ *a* abominevole

Aborigine /æbə'rɪdʒənɪ/ *n* aborigeno, -a *mf* d'Australia

abort /ə'bɔːt/ *vt* fare abortire; *fig* annullare. **~ion** /-ɔːʃn/ *n* aborto *m*; **have an ~ion** abortire. **~ive** /-tɪv/ *a* *(attempt)* infruttuoso

abound /ə'baʊnd/ *vi* abbondare; ~ **in** abbondare di

about /ə'baʊt/ *adv* *(here and there)* [di] qua e [di] là; *(approximately)* circa; **be** ~ *(illness, tourists:)* essere in giro; **be up and** ~ essere alzato; **leave sth lying** ~ lasciare in giro qcsa ● *prep* *(concerning)* su; *(in the region of)* intorno a; *(here and there in)* per; **what is the book/the film** ~? di cosa parla il libro/il film?; **he wants to see you - what** ~? ti vuole vedere - a che proposito?; **talk/know** ~ parlare/sapere di; **I know nothing** ~ **it** non ne so niente; ~ **5** o'clock intorno alle 5; **travel** ~ **the world** viaggiare per il mondo; **be** ~ **to do sth** stare per fare qcsa; **how** ~ **going to the cinema?** e se andassimo al cinema?

about: **~-face** *n*, **~-turn** *n* dietro front *m inv*

above /ə'bʌv/ *adv & prep* sopra; ~ **all** soprattutto

above: **~-board** *a* onesto. **~-mentioned** *a* suddetto

abrasive /ə'breɪsɪv/ *a* abrasivo; *(remark)* caustico ● *n* abrasivo *m*

abreast /ə'brest/ *adv* fianco a fianco; **come** ~ **of** allinearsi con; **keep** ~ **of** tenersi al corrente di

abridged /ə'brɪdʒd/ *a* ridotto

abroad /ə'brɔːd/ *adv* all'estero

abrupt /əˈbrʌpt/ *a* brusco

abscess /ˈæbsɪs/ *n* ascesso *m*

abscond /əbˈskɒnd/ *vi* fuggire

absence /ˈæbsəns/ *n* assenza *f*; ⟨*lack*⟩ mancanza *f*

absent[1] /ˈæbsənt/ *a* assente

absent[2] /æbˈsent/ *vt* ~ oneself essere assente

absentee /æbsənˈtiː/ *n* assente *mf*

absent-minded /æbsəntˈmaɪndɪd/ *a* distratto

absolute /ˈæbsəluːt/ *a* assoluto; an ~ idiot un perfetto idiota. ~ly *adv* assolutamente; ⟨*fam: indicating agreement*⟩ esattamente

absolution /æbsəˈluːʃn/ *n* assoluzione *f*

absolve /əbˈzɒlv/ *vt* assolvere

absorb /əbˈsɔːb/ *vt* assorbire; ~ed in assorto in. ~ent /-ənt/ *a* assorbente

absorption /əbˈsɔːpʃn/ *n* assorbimento *m*; ⟨*in activity*⟩ concentrazione *f*

abstain /əbˈsteɪn/ *vi* astenersi ⟨from da⟩

abstemious /əbˈstiːmɪəs/ *a* moderato

abstention /əbˈstenʃn/ *n* Pol astensione *f*

abstinence /ˈæbstɪnəns/ *n* astinenza *f*

abstract /ˈæbstrækt/ *a* astratto ●*n* astratto *m*; ⟨*summary*⟩ estratto *m*

absurd /əbˈsɜːd/ *a* assurdo. ~ity *n* assurdità *f inv*

abundan|ce /əˈbʌndəns/ *n* abbondanza *f*. ~t *a* abbondante

abuse[1] /əˈbjuːz/ *vt* ⟨*misuse*⟩ abusare di; ⟨*insult*⟩ insultare; ⟨*ill-treat*⟩ maltrattare

abuse[2] /əˈbjuːs/ *n* abuso *m*; ⟨*verbal*⟩ insulti *mpl*; ⟨*ill-treatment*⟩ maltrattamento *m*. ~ive /-ɪv/ *a* offensivo

abut /əˈbʌt/ *vi* ⟨*pt/pp* abutted⟩ confinare ⟨onto con⟩

abysmal /əˈbɪzml/ *a fam* pessimo; ⟨*ignorance*⟩ abissale

abyss /əˈbɪs/ *n* abisso *m*

academic /ækəˈdemɪk/ *a* teorico; ⟨*qualifications, system*⟩ scolastico; be ~ ⟨*person:*⟩ avere predisposizione allo studio ●*n* docente *mf* universitario, -a

academy /əˈkædəmɪ/ *n* accademia *f*; ⟨*of music*⟩ conservatorio *m*

accede /əkˈsiːd/ *vi* ~ to accedere a ⟨*request*⟩; salire a ⟨*throne*⟩

accelerat|e /əkˈseləreɪt/ *vt/i* accelerare. ~ion /-ˈreɪʃn/ *n* accelerazione *f*. ~or *n* Auto acceleratore *m*

accent /ˈæksənt/ *n* accento *m*

accentuate /əkˈsentjʊeɪt/ *vt* accentuare

accept /əkˈsept/ *vt* accettare. ~able /-əbl/ *a* accettabile. ~ance *n* accettazione *f*

access /ˈækses/ *n* accesso *m*. ~ible /əkˈsesɪbl/ *a* accessibile

accession /əkˈseʃn/ *n* ⟨*to throne*⟩ ascesa *f* al trono

accessory /əkˈsesərɪ/ *n* accessorio *m*; Jur complice *mf*

accident /ˈæksɪdənt/ *n* incidente *m*; ⟨*chance*⟩ caso *m*; by ~ per caso; ⟨*unintentionally*⟩ senza volere; I'm sorry, it was an ~ mi dispiace, non l'ho fatto apposta. ~al /-ˈdentl/ *a* ⟨*meeting*⟩ casuale; ⟨*death*⟩ incidentale; ⟨*unintentional*⟩ involontario. ~ally *adv* per caso; ⟨*unintentionally*⟩ inavvertitamente

acclaim /əˈkleɪm/ *n* acclamazione *f* ●*vt* acclamare ⟨as come⟩

acclimatize /əˈklaɪmətaɪz/ *vt* become ~d acclimatarsi

accolade /ˈækəleɪd/ *n* riconoscimento *m*

accommodat|e /əˈkɒmədeɪt/ *vt* ospitare; ⟨*oblige*⟩ favorire. ~ing *a* accomodante. ~ion /-ˈdeɪʃn/ *n* ⟨*place to stay*⟩ sistemazione *f*

accompan|iment /əˈkʌmpənɪmənt/ *n* accompagnamento *m*. ~ist *n* Mus accompagnatore, -trice *mf*

accompany /əˈkʌmpənɪ/ *vt* ⟨*pt/pp* -ied⟩ accompagnare

accomplice /əˈkʌmplɪs/ *n* complice *mf*

accomplish /əˈkʌmplɪʃ/ *vt* ⟨*achieve*⟩ concludere; realizzare ⟨aim⟩. ~ed *a* dotato; ⟨*fact*⟩ compiuto. ~ment *n* realizzazione *f*; ⟨*achievement*⟩ risultato *m*; ⟨*talent*⟩ talento *m*

accord /əˈkɔːd/ *n* ⟨*treaty*⟩ accordo *m*; with one ~ tutti d'accordo; of his own ~ di sua spontanea volontà. ~ance *n* in ~ance with in conformità di *o* a

according /əˈkɔːdɪŋ/ *adv* ~ to secondo. ~ly *adv* di conseguenza

accordion /əˈkɔːdɪən/ *n* fisarmonica *f*

accost /əˈkɒst/ *vt* abbordare

account /əˈkaʊnt/ *n* conto *m*; ⟨*report*⟩ descrizione *f*; ⟨*of eye-witness*⟩ resoconto *m*; ~s *pl* Comm conti *mpl*; on ~ of a causa di; on no ~ per nessun motivo; on this ~ per questo motivo; on my ~ per causa mia; of no ~ di nessuna importanza; take into ~ tener conto di ●**account for** *vi* ⟨*explain*⟩ spiegare; ⟨*person:*⟩ render conto di; ⟨*constitute*⟩ costituire. ~ability *n* responsabilità *f inv*. ~able *a* responsabile ⟨for di⟩

accountant /əˈkaʊntənt/ n (book-keeper) contabile mf; (consultant) commercialista mf

accredited /əˈkredɪtɪd/ a accreditato

accrue /əˈkruː/ vi (interest:) maturare

accumulat|e /əˈkjuːmjʊlert/ vt accumulare ● vi accumularsi. ~**ion** /-ˈleɪʃn/ n accumulazione f

accura|cy /ˈækʊrəsɪ/ n precisione f. ~**te** /-rət/ a preciso. ~**tely** adv con precisione

accusation /ækjʊˈzeɪʃn/ n accusa f

accusative /əˈkjuːzətɪv/ a & n ~ |case| Gram accusativo m

accuse /əˈkjuːz/ vt accusare; ~ sb of doing sth accusare qcno di fare qcsa. ~**d** n the ~**d** l'accusato m, l'accusata f

accustom /əˈkʌstəm/ vt abituare (to a); grow or get ~**ed** to abituarsi a. ~**ed** a abituato

ace /eɪs/ n Cards asso m; (tennis) ace m inv

ache /eɪk/ n dolore m ● vi dolere, far male; ~ all over essere tutto indolenzito

achieve /əˈtʃiːv/ vt ottenere (success); realizzare (goal, ambition). ~**ment** n (feat) successo m

acid /ˈæsɪd/ a acido ● n acido m. ~**ity** /əˈsɪdɪtɪ/ n acidità f. ~ **rain** n pioggia f acida

acknowledge /əkˈnɒlɪdʒ/ vt riconoscere; rispondere a (greeting); far cenno di aver notato (sb's presence); ~ **receipt of** accusare ricevuta di. ~**ment** n riconoscimento m; send an ~**ment of a letter** confermare il ricevimento di una lettera

acne /ˈæknɪ/ n acne f

acorn /ˈeɪkɔːn/ n ghianda f

acoustic /əˈkuːstɪk/ a acustico. ~**s** npl acustica fsg

acquaint /əˈkweɪnt/ vt ~ sb with mettere qcno al corrente di; be ~**ed with** conoscere (person); essere a conoscenza di (fact). ~**ance** n (person) conoscente mf; make sb's ~**ance** fare la conoscenza di qcno

acquiesce /ækwɪˈes/ vi acconsentire (to, in a). ~**nce** n acquiescenza f

acquire /əˈkwaɪə(r)/ vt acquisire

acquisit|ion /ækwɪˈzɪʃn/ n acquisizione f. ~**ive** /əˈkwɪzɪtɪv/ a avido

acquit /əˈkwɪt/ vt (pt/pp acquitted) assolvere; ~ **oneself well** cavarsela bene. ~**tal** n assoluzione f

acre /ˈeɪkə(r)/ n acro m (= 4 047 m²)

acrid /ˈækrɪd/ a acre

acrimon|ious /ækrɪˈməʊnɪəs/ a aspro. ~**y** /ˈækrɪmənɪ/ n asprezza f

acrobat /ˈækrəbæt/ n acrobata mf. ~**ic** /-ˈbætɪk/ a acrobatico

across /əˈkrɒs/ adv dall'altra parte; (wide) in larghezza; (not lengthwise) attraverso; (in crossword) orizzontale; come ~ sth imbattersi in qcsa; go ~ attraversare ● prep (crosswise) di traverso su; (on the other side of) dall'altra parte di

act /ækt/ n atto m; (in variety show) numero m; put on an ~ fam fare scena ● vi agire; (behave) comportarsi; Theat recitare; (pretend) fingere; ~ as fare da ● vt recitare (role). ~**ing** a (deputy) provvisorio ● n Theat recitazione f; (profession) teatro m. ~**ing profession** n professione f dell'attore

action /ˈækʃn/ n azione f; Mil combattimento m; Jur azione f legale; out of ~ (machine:) fuori uso; take ~ agire. ~ **replay** n replay m inv

activ|e /ˈæktɪv/ a attivo. ~**ely** adv attivamente. ~**ity** /-ˈtɪvɪtɪ/ n attività f inv

act|or /ˈæktə(r)/ n attore m. ~**ress** n attrice f

actual /ˈæktʃʊəl/ a (real) reale. ~**ly** adv in realtà

acumen /ˈækjʊmən/ n acume m

acupuncture /ˈækjʊ-/ n agopuntura f

acute /əˈkjuːt/ a acuto; (shortage, hardship) estremo

ad /æd/ n fam pubblicità f inv; (in paper) inserzione f. annuncio m

AD abbr (Anno Domini) d.C.

adamant /ˈædəmənt/ a categorico (that sul fatto che)

adapt /əˈdæpt/ vt adattare (play) ● vi adattarsi. ~**ability** /-əˈbɪlətɪ/ n adattabilità f. ~**able** /-əbl/ a adattabile

adaptation /ædæpˈteɪʃn/ n Theat adattamento m

adapter, adaptor /əˈdæptə(r)/ n adattatore m; (two-way) presa f multipla

add /æd/ vt aggiungere; Math addizionare ● vi addizionare; ~ to (fig: increase) aggravare. **add up** vt addizionare (figures) ● vi addizionare; ~ **up to** ammontare a; it doesn't ~ **up** fig non quadra

adder /ˈædə(r)/ n vipera f

addict /ˈædɪkt/ n tossicodipendente mf; fig fanatico, -a mf

addict|ed /əˈdɪktɪd/ a assuefatto (to a); ~**ed to drugs** tossicodipendente; he's ~**ed to television** è videodipendente. ~**ion** /-ɪkʃn/ n dipendenza f; (to drugs) tossicodipendenza f. **~ive** /-ɪv/ a be ~ive dare assuefazione

addition /əˈdɪʃn/ n *Math* addizione f; *(thing added)* aggiunta f; **in ~** in aggiunta. **~al** a supplementare. **~ally** adv in più

additive /ˈædɪtɪv/ n additivo m

address /əˈdres/ n indirizzo m; *(speech)* discorso m; **form of ~** formula f di cortesia ● vt indirizzare; *(speak to)* rivolgersi a *(person)*; tenere un discorso a *(meeting)*. **~ee** /ædreˈsiː/ n destinatario, -a mf

adenoids /ˈædənɔɪdz/ npl adenoidi fpl

adept /ˈædept/ a & n esperto, -a mf *(at in)*

adequate /ˈædɪkwət/ a adeguato. **~ly** adv adeguatamente

adhere /ədˈhɪə(r)/ vi aderire; **~ to** attenersi a *(principles, rules)*

adhesive /ədˈhiːsɪv/ a adesivo ● n adesivo m

adjacent /əˈdʒeɪsənt/ a adiacente

adjective /ˈædʒɪktɪv/ n aggettivo m

adjoin /əˈdʒɔɪn/ vt essere adiacente a. **~ing** a adiacente

adjourn /əˈdʒɜːn/ vt/i aggiornare *(until a)*. **~ment** n aggiornamento m

adjudicate /əˈdʒuːdɪkeɪt/ vi decidere; *(in competition)* giudicare

adjust /əˈdʒʌst/ vt modificare; regolare *(focus, sound etc)* ● vi adattarsi. **~able** /-əbl/ a regolabile. **~ment** n adattamento m; *Techn* regolamento m

ad lib /ædˈlɪb/ a improvvisato ● adv a piacere ● vi *(pt/pp ad libbed)* fam improvvisare

administer /ədˈmɪnɪstə(r)/ vt amministrare; somministrare *(medicine)*

administrat|ion /ədmɪnɪˈstreɪʃn/ n amministrazione f; *Pol* governo m. **~or** /ədˈmɪnɪstreɪtə(r)/ n amministratore, -trice mf

admirable /ˈædmərəbl/ a ammirevole

admiral /ˈædmərəl/ n ammiraglio m

admiration /ædməˈreɪʃn/ n ammirazione f

admire /ədˈmaɪə(r)/ vt ammirare. **~r** n ammiratore, -trice mf

admissible /ədˈmɪsəbl/ a ammissibile

admission /ədˈmɪʃn/ n ammissione f; *(to hospital)* ricovero m; *(entry)* ingresso m

admit /ədˈmɪt/ vt *(pt/pp admitted)* *(let in)* far entrare; *(to hospital)* ricoverare; *(acknowledge)* ammettere ● vi **~ to sth** ammettere qcsa. **~tance** n ammissione

f; **'no ~tance'** 'vietato l'ingresso'. **~tedly** adv bisogna riconoscerlo

admonish /ədˈmɒnɪʃ/ vt ammonire

ado /əˈduː/ n **without more ~** senza ulteriori indugi

adolescen|ce /ædəˈlesns/ n adolescenza f. **~t** a & n adolescente mf

adopt /əˈdɒpt/ vt adottare; *Pol* scegliere *(candidate)*. **~ion** /-ɒpʃn/ n adozione f. **~ive** /-ɪv/ a adottivo

ador|able /əˈdɔːrəbl/ a adorabile. **~ation** /ædəˈreɪʃn/ n adorazione f

adore /əˈdɔː(r)/ vt adorare

adrenalin /əˈdrenəlɪn/ n adrenalina f

Adriatic /eɪdrɪˈætɪk/ a & n **the ~** [Sea] il mare Adriatico, l'Adriatico m

adrift /əˈdrɪft/ a alla deriva; **be ~** andare alla deriva; **come ~** staccarsi

adroit /əˈdrɔɪt/ a abile

adulation /ædjʊˈleɪʃn/ n adulazione f

adult /ˈædʌlt/ n adulto, -a mf

adulterate /əˈdʌltəreɪt/ vt adulterare *(wine)*

adultery /əˈdʌltəri/ n adulterio m

advance /ədˈvɑːns/ n avanzamento m; *Mil* avanzata f; *(payment)* anticipo m; **in ~** in anticipo ● vi avanzare; *(make progress)* fare progressi ● vt avanzare *(theory)*; promuovere *(cause)*; anticipare *(money)*. **~ booking** n prenotazione f [in anticipo]. **~d** a avanzato. **~ment** n promozione f

advantage /ədˈvɑːntɪdʒ/ n vantaggio m; **take ~ of** approfittare di. **~ous** /ædvənˈteɪdʒəs/ a vantaggioso

advent /ˈædvent/ n avvento m

adventur|e /ədˈventʃə(r)/ n avventura f. **~ous** /-rəs/ a avventuroso

adverb /ˈædvɜːb/ n avverbio m

adversary /ˈædvəsəri/ n avversario, -a mf

advers|e /ˈædvɜːs/ a avverso. **~ity** /ədˈvɜːsəti/ n avversità f

advert /ˈædvɜːt/ n fam = **advertisement**

advertise /ˈædvətaɪz/ vt reclamizzare; mettere un annuncio per *(job, flat)* ● vi fare pubblicità; *(for job, flat)* mettere un annuncio

advertisement /ədˈvɜːtɪsmənt/ n pubblicità f inv; *(in paper)* inserzione f, annuncio m

advertis|er /ˈædvətaɪzə(r)/ n *(in newspaper)* inserzionista mf. **~ing** n pubblicità f ● attrib pubblicitario

advice /ədˈvaɪs/ n consigli mpl; **piece of ~** consiglio m

advisable /ədˈvaɪzəbl/ a consigliabile

advis|e /əd'vaɪz/ vt consigliare; (inform) avvisare; **~e sb to do sth** consigliare a qcno di fare qcsa; **~e sb against sth** sconsigliare qcsa a qcno. **~er** n consulente mf. **~ory** a consultivo

advocate¹ /'ædvəkət/ n (supporter) fautore, -trice mf

advocate² /'ædvəkeɪt/ vt propugnare

aerial /'eərɪəl/ a aereo ● n antenna f

aerobics /eə'rəʊbɪks/ n aerobica fsg

aero|drome /'eərədrəʊm/ n aerodromo m. **~plane** n aeroplano m

aerosol /'eərəsɒl/ n bomboletta f spray

aesthetic /iːs'θetɪk/ a estetico

afar /ə'fɑː(r)/ adv **from ~** da lontano

affable /'æfəbl/ a affabile

affair /ə'feə(r)/ n affare m; (scandal) caso m; (sexual) relazione f

affect /ə'fekt/ vt influire su; (emotionally) colpire; (concern) riguardare. **~ation** /æfek'teɪʃn/ n affettazione f. **~ed** a affettato

affection /ə'fekʃn/ n affetto m. **~ate** /-ət/ a affettuoso

affiliated /ə'fɪlieɪtɪd/ a affiliato

affinity /ə'fɪnəti/ n affinità f inv

affirm /ə'fɜːm/ vt affermare; Jur dichiarare solennemente

affirmative /ə'fɜːmətɪv/ a affermativo ● n **in the ~** affermativamente

afflict /ə'flɪkt/ vt affliggere. **~ion** /-ɪkʃn/ n afflizione f

affluen|ce /'æfluəns/ n agiatezza f. **~t** a agiato

afford /ə'fɔːd/ vt **be able to ~ sth** potersi permettere qcsa. **~able** /-əbl/ a abbordabile

affray /ə'freɪ/ n rissa f

affront /ə'frʌnt/ n affronto m

afield /ə'fiːld/ adv **further ~** più lontano

afloat /ə'fləʊt/ a a galla

afoot /ə'fʊt/ a **there's something ~** si sta preparando qualcosa

aforesaid /ə'fɔːsed/ a Jur suddetto

afraid /ə'freɪd/ a **be ~** aver paura; **I'm ~ not** purtroppo no; **I'm ~ so** temo di sì; **I'm ~ I can't help you** mi dispiace, ma non posso essere d'aiuto

afresh /ə'freʃ/ adv da capo

Africa /'æfrɪkə/ n Africa f. **~n** a & n africano, -a mf

after /'ɑːftə(r)/ adv dopo; **the day ~** il giorno dopo; **be ~** cercare ● prep dopo; **~ all** dopotutto; **the day ~ tomorrow** dopodomani ● conj dopo che

after: **~-effect** n conseguenza f. **~math** /-mɑːθ/ n conseguenze fpl; **the**

~math of war il dopoguerra; **in the ~math** nel periodo successivo a. **~'noon** n pomeriggio m; **good ~noon!** buon giorno! **~sales service** n servizio m assistenza clienti. **~shave** n [lozione f] dopobarba m inv. **~thought** n added as an **~thought** aggiunto in un secondo momento; **~wards** adv in seguito

again /ə'gein/ adv di nuovo; [then] **~** (besides) inoltre; (on the other hand) d'altra parte; **~ and ~** continuamente

against /ə'geinst/ prep contro

age /eɪdʒ/ n età f inv; (era) era f; **~s** fam secoli; **what ~ are you?** quanti anni hai?; **be under ~** non avere l'età richiesta; **he's two years of ~** ha due anni ● vt/i (pres p ageing) invecchiare

aged¹ /eɪdʒd/ a **~ two** di due anni

aged² /'eɪdʒɪd/ a anziano ● npl **the ~** gli anziani

ageless /'eɪdʒlɪs/ a senza età

agency /'eɪdʒənsi/ n agenzia f; **have the ~ for** essere un concessionario di

agenda /ə'dʒendə/ n ordine m del giorno; **on the ~** all'ordine del giorno; fig in programma

agent /'eɪdʒənt/ n agente mf

aggravat|e /'ægrəveɪt/ vt aggravare; (annoy) esasperare. **~ion** /-'veɪʃn/ n aggravamento m; (annoyance) esasperazione f

aggregate /'ægrɪgət/ a totale ● n totale m; **on ~** nel complesso

aggress|ion /ə'greʃn/ n aggressione f. **~ive** /-sɪv/ a aggressivo. **~iveness** n aggressività f. **~or** n aggressore m

aggro /'ægrəʊ/ n fam aggressività f; (problems) grane fpl

aghast /ə'gɑːst/ a inorridito

agil|e /'ædʒaɪl/ a agile. **~ity** /ə'dʒɪləti/ n agilità f

agitat|e /'ædʒɪteɪt/ vt mettere in agitazione; (shake) agitare ● vi fig **~e for** creare delle agitazioni per. **~ed** a agitato. **~ion** /-'teɪʃn/ n agitazione f. **~or** n agitatore, -trice mf

agnostic /æg'nɒstɪk/ n agnostico, -a mf

ago /ə'gəʊ/ adv fa; **a long time/a month ~** molto tempo/un mese fa

agog /ə'gɒg/ a eccitato

agoni|ze /'ægənaɪz/ vi angosciarsi (over per). **~ing** a angosciante

agony /'ægəni/ n agonia f; (mental) angoscia f; **be in ~** avere dei dolori atroci

agree /ə'griː/ vt accordarsi su; **~ to do sth** accettare di fare qcsa; **~ that** essere d'accordo [sul fatto] che ● *vi* essere d'accordo; ⟨*figures:*⟩ concordare; ⟨*reach agreement*⟩ mettersi d'accordo; ⟨*get on*⟩ andare d'accordo; ⟨*consent*⟩ acconsentire (to a); it doesn't ~ with me mi fa male; ~ with sth ⟨*approve of*⟩ approvare qcsa

agreeable /əˈgriːəbl/ *a* gradevole; ⟨*willing*⟩ d'accordo

agreed /əˈgriːd/ *a* convenuto

agreement /əˈgriːmənt/ *n* accordo *m*; in ~ d'accordo

agricultur|al /ægrɪˈkʌltʃərəl/ *a* agricolo. ~e /ˈægrɪkʌltʃə(r)/ *n* agricoltura *f*

aground /əˈgraʊnd/ *adv* run ~ ⟨*ship:*⟩ arenarsi

ahead /əˈhed/ *adv* avanti; be ~ of essere davanti a; *fig* essere avanti rispetto a; draw ~ passare davanti (of a); get ~ ⟨*in life*⟩ riuscire; go ~! fai pure!; look ~ pensare all'avvenire; plan ~ fare progetti per l'avvenire

aid /eɪd/ *n* aiuto *m*; in ~ of a favore di ● *vt* aiutare

aide /eɪd/ *n* assistente *mf*

Aids /eɪdz/ *n* AIDS *m*

ail|ing /ˈeɪlɪŋ/ *a* malato. ~ment *n* disturbo *m*

aim /eɪm/ *n* mira *f*; *fig* scopo *m*; take ~ prendere la mira ● *vt* puntare ⟨*gun*⟩ (at contro) ● *vi* mirare; ~ to do sth aspirare a fare qcsa. ~less *a*, ~lessly *adv* senza scopo

air /eə(r)/ *n* aria *f*; be on the ~ ⟨*programme:*⟩ essere in onda; put on ~s darsi delle arie; by ~ in aereo; ⟨*airmail*⟩ per via aerea ● *vt* arieggiare; far conoscere ⟨*views*⟩

air: ~-bed *n* materassino *m* [gonfiabile]. ~-conditioned *a* con aria condizionata. ~-conditioning *n* aria *f* condizionata. ~craft *n* aereo *m*. ~craft carrier *n* portaerei *f inv*. ~fare *n* tariffa *f* aerea. ~field *n* campo d'aviazione. ~ force *n* aviazione *f*. ~ freshener *n* deodorante *m* per l'ambiente. ~gun *n* fucile *m* pneumatico. ~ hostess *n* hostess *f inv*. ~ letter *n* aerogramma *m*. ~line *n* compagnia *f* aerea. ~lock *n* bolla *f* d'aria. ~mail *n* posta *f* aerea. ~plane *n* Am aereo *m*. ~pocket *n* vuoto *m* d'aria. ~port *n* aeroporto *m*. ~-raid *n* incursione *f* aerea. ~-raid shelter *n* rifugio *m* antiaereo. ~ship *n* dirigibile *m*. ~tight *a* ermetico. ~ traffic *n* traffico *m* aereo. ~-traffic controller *n* controllore *m* di volo. ~worthy *a* idoneo al volo.

airy /ˈeərɪ/ *a* (-ier, -iest) arieggiato; ⟨*manner*⟩ noncurante

aisle /aɪl/ *n* corridoio *m*; (*in supermarket*) corsia *f*; (*in church*) navata *f*

ajar /əˈdʒɑː(r)/ *a* socchiuso

akin /əˈkɪn/ *a* ~ to simile a

alacrity /əˈlækrətɪ/ *n* alacrità *f inv*

alarm /əˈlɑːm/ *n* allarme *m*; set the ~ ⟨*of alarm clock*⟩ mettere la sveglia ● *vt* allarmare. ~ clock *n* sveglia *f*

alas /əˈlæs/ *int* ahimè

album /ˈælbəm/ *n* album *m inv*

alcohol /ˈælkəhɒl/ *n* alcol *m*. ~ic /-ˈhɒlɪk/ *a* alcolico ● *n* alcolizzato, -a *mf*. ~ism *n* alcolismo *m*

alcove /ˈælkəʊv/ *n* alcova *f*

alert /əˈlɜːt/ *a* sveglio; ⟨*watchful*⟩ vigile ● *n* segnale *m* d'allarme; be on the ~ stare allerta ● *vt* allertare

algae /ˈældʒiː/ *npl* alghe *fpl*

algebra /ˈældʒɪbrə/ *n* algebra *f*

Algeria /ælˈdʒɪərɪə/ *n* Algeria *f*. ~n *a* & *n* algerino, -a *mf*

alias /ˈeɪlɪəs/ *n* pseudonimo *m* ● *adv* alias

alibi /ˈælɪbaɪ/ *n* alibi *m inv*

alien /ˈeɪlɪən/ *a* straniero; *fig* estraneo ● *n* straniero, -a *mf*; ⟨*from space*⟩ alieno, -a *mf*

alienat|e /ˈeɪlɪəneɪt/ *vt* alienare. ~ion /-ˈneɪʃn/ *n* alienazione *f*

alight[1] /əˈlaɪt/ *vi* scendere; ⟨*bird:*⟩ posarsi

alight[2] *a* be ~ essere in fiamme; set ~ dar fuoco a

align /əˈlaɪn/ *vt* allineare. ~ment *n* allineamento *m*; out of ~ment non allineato

alike /əˈlaɪk/ *a* simile; be ~ rassomigliarsi ● *adv* in modo simile; look ~ rassomigliarsi; summer and winter ~ sia d'estate che d'inverno

alimony /ˈælɪmənɪ/ *n* alimenti *mpl*

alive /əˈlaɪv/ *a* vivo; ~ with brulicante di; ~ to sensibile a

alkali /ˈælkəlaɪ/ *n* alcali *m*

all /ɔːl/ *a* tutto; ~ the children, ~ children tutti i bambini; ~ day tutto il giorno; he refused ~ help ha rifiutato qualsiasi aiuto; for ~ that (*nevertheless*) ciononostante; in ~ sincerity in tutta sincerità; be ~ for essere favorevole a ● *pron* tutto; ~ of you/them tutti voi/loro; ~ of it tutto; ~ of the town tutta la città; in ~ in tutto; ~ in ~ tutto sommato; most of ~ più di ogni altra cosa; once and for ~ una volta per tutte ● *adv* completamente; ~ but quasi; ~ **at once** (*at the same time*) tutto in una volta; ~ **at once**, ~ **of a sudden** all'improvviso; ~ **too soon** troppo presto; ~ **the same** (*nevertheless*) ciononostante; ~ **the better** meglio ancora; **she's not** ~ **that good an actress** non è poi così brava come attrice; ~ **in** in tutto; ~ **in** (*fam*) esausto; **thirty/three** ~ (*in sport*) trenta/tre pari; ~ **over** (*finished*) tutto finito; (*everywhere*) dappertutto; **it's** ~ **right** (*I don't mind*) non fa niente; **I'm** ~ **right** (*not hurt*) non ho niente; ~ **right!** va bene!

allay /əˈleɪ/ *vt* placare ⟨*suspicions, anger*⟩

allegation /ælɪˈɡeɪʃn/ *n* accusa *f*

allege /əˈledʒ/ *vt* dichiarare. ~**dly** /-ɪdlɪ/ *adv* a quanto si dice

allegiance /əˈliːdʒəns/ *n* fedeltà *f*

allegor|ical /ælɪˈɡɒrɪkl/ *a* allegorico. ~**y** /ˈælɪɡərɪ/ *n* allegoria *f*

allerg|ic /əˈlɜːdʒɪk/ *a* allergico. ~**y** /ˈælədʒɪ/ *n* allergia *f*

alleviate /əˈliːvɪeɪt/ *vt* alleviare

alley /ˈælɪ/ *n* vicolo *m*; (*for bowling*) corsia *f*

alliance /əˈlaɪəns/ *n* alleanza *f*

allied /ˈælaɪd/ *a* alleato; (*fig: related*) connesso ⟨**to** a⟩

alligator /ˈælɪɡeɪtə(r)/ *n* alligatore *m*

allocat|e /ˈæləkeɪt/ *vt* assegnare; distribuire ⟨*resources*⟩. ~**ion** /-ˈkeɪʃn/ *n* assegnazione *f*; (*of resources*) distribuzione *f*

allot /əˈlɒt/ *vt* (*pt/pp* **allotted**) distribuire. ~**ment** *n* distribuzione *f*; (*share*) parte *f*; (*land*) piccolo lotto *m* di terreno

allow /əˈlaʊ/ *vt* permettere; (*grant*) accordare; (*reckon on*) contare; (*agree*) ammettere; ~ **for** tener conto di; ~ **sb to do sth** permettere a qcno di fare qcsa; **you are not** ~**ed to...** è vietato...

allowance /əˈlaʊəns/ *n* sussidio *m*; (*Am: pocket money*) paghetta *f*; (*for petrol etc*) indennità *f inv*; (*of luggage, duty free*) limite *m*; **make** ~**s for** essere indulgente verso ⟨*sb*⟩; tener conto di ⟨*sth*⟩

alloy /ˈælɔɪ/ *n* lega *f*

allude /əˈluːd/ *vi* alludere

allusion /əˈluːʒn/ *n* allusione *f*

ally[1] /ˈælaɪ/ *n* alleato, -a *mf*

ally[2] /əˈlaɪ/ *vt* (*pt/pp* **-ied**) alleare; ~ **oneself with** allearsi con

almighty /ɔːlˈmaɪtɪ/ *a* (*fam: big*) mega *inv* ● **the A~** l'Onnipotente *m*

almond /ˈɑːmənd/ *n* mandorla *f*; (*tree*) mandorlo *m*

almost /ˈɔːlməʊst/ *adv* quasi

alone /əˈləʊn/ *a* solo; **leave me** ~! lasciami in pace!; **let** ~ (*not to mention*) figurarsi ● *adv* da solo

along /əˈlɒŋ/ *prep* lungo ● *adv* ~ **with** assieme a; **all** ~ tutto il tempo; **come** ~! (*hurry up*) vieni qui!; **I'll be** ~ **in a minute** arrivo tra un attimo; **move** ~ spostarsi; **move** ~! circolare!

along'side *adv* lungo bordo ● *prep* lungo; **work** ~ **sb** lavorare fianco a fianco con qcno

aloof /əˈluːf/ *a* distante

aloud /əˈlaʊd/ *adv* ad alta voce

alphabet /ˈælfəbet/ *n* alfabeto *m*. ~**ical** /-ˈbetɪkl/ *a* alfabetico

alpine /ˈælpaɪn/ *a* alpino

Alps /ælps/ *npl* Alpi *fpl*

already /ɔːlˈredɪ/ *adv* già

Alsatian /ælˈseɪʃn/ *n* (*dog*) pastore *m* tedesco

also /ˈɔːlsəʊ/ *adv* anche; ~, **I need...** [e] inoltre, ho bisogno di...

altar /ˈɔːltə(r)/ *n* altare *m*

alter /ˈɔːltə(r)/ *vt* cambiare; aggiustare ⟨*clothes*⟩ ● *vi* cambiare. ~**ation** /-ˈreɪʃn/ *n* modifica *f*

alternate[1] /ˈɔːltəneɪt/ *vi* alternarsi ● *vt* alternare

alternate[2] /ɔːlˈtɜːnət/ *a* alterno; **on** ~ **days** a giorni alterni

'alternating current *n* corrente *f* alternata

alternative /ɔːlˈtɜːnətɪv/ *a* alternativo ● *n* alternativa *f*. ~**ly** *adv* alternativamente

although /ɔːlˈðəʊ/ *conj* benché, sebbene

altitude /ˈæltɪtjuːd/ *n* altitudine *f*

altogether /ɔːltəˈɡeðə(r)/ *adv* (*in all*) in tutto; (*completely*) completamente; **I'm not** ~ **sure** non sono del tutto sicuro

altruistic /æltruˈɪstɪk/ *a* altruistico

aluminium /æljʊˈmɪnɪəm/ *n*, *Am* **aluminum** /əˈluːmɪnəm/ *n* alluminio *m*

always /ˈɔːlweɪz/ *adv* sempre

am /æm/ *see* **be**

a.m. *abbr* (*ante meridiem*) del mattino

amalgamate /əˈmælɡəmeɪt/ *vt* fondere ● *vi* fondersi

amass /əˈmæs/ *vt* accumulare

amateur /ˈæmətə(r)/ *n* non professionista *mf*; *pej* dilettante *mf* ● *attrib* dilet-

amaze | angry

tante; ~ **dramatics** filodrammatica f. ~**ish** a dilettantesco

amaze /ə'meɪz/ vt stupire. ~**d** a stupito. ~**ment** n stupore m

amazing /ə'meɪzɪŋ/ a incredibile

ambassador /æm'bæsədə(r)/ n ambasciatore, -trice mf

amber /'æmbə(r)/ n ambra f ●a ⟨colour⟩ ambra inv

ambidextrous /æmbɪ'dekstrəs/ a ambidestro

ambience /'æmbɪəns/ n atmosfera f

ambiguity /æmbɪ'gjuːətɪ/ n ambiguità f inv. ~**ous** /-'bɪgjʊəs/ a ambiguo

ambition /æm'bɪʃn/ n ambizione f; ⟨aim⟩ aspirazione f. ~**ous** /-ʃəs/ a ambizioso

ambivalent /æm'bɪvələnt/ a ambivalente

amble /'æmbl/ vi camminare senza fretta

ambulance /'æmbjʊləns/ n ambulanza f

ambush /'æmbʊʃ/ n imboscata f ●vt tendere un'imboscata a

amenable /ə'miːnəbl/ a conciliante; ~ **to** sensibile a

amend /ə'mend/ vt modificare. ~**ment** n modifica f. ~**s** npl **make** ~**s** fare ammenda (**for** di, per)

amenities /ə'miːnətɪz/ npl comodità fpl

America /ə'merɪkə/ n America f. ~**n** a & n americano, -a mf

amiable /'eɪmɪəbl/ a amabile

amicable /'æmɪkəbl/ a amichevole

amiss /ə'mɪs/ a **there's something** ~ c'è qualcosa che non va ● adv **take sth** ~ prendersela [a male]; **it won't come** ~ non sarebbe sgradito

ammonia /ə'məʊnɪə/ n ammoniaca f

ammunition /æmjʊ'nɪʃn/ n munizioni fpl

amnesia /æm'niːzɪə/ n amnesia f

amnesty /'æmnəstɪ/ n amnistia f

among[st] /ə'mʌŋ[st]/ prep tra, fra

amoral /eɪ'mɒrəl/ a amorale

amorous /'æmərəs/ a amoroso

amount /ə'maʊnt/ n quantità f inv; ⟨sum of money⟩ importo m ● vi ~ **to** ammontare a; fig equivalere a

amp /æmp/ n ampère m inv

amphibian /æm'fɪbɪən/ n anfibio m. ~**ous** /-ɪəs/ a anfibio

amphitheatre /'æmfɪ-/ n anfiteatro m

ample /'æmpl/ a ⟨large⟩ grande; ⟨proportions⟩ ampio; ⟨enough⟩ largamente sufficiente

amplifier /'æmplɪfaɪə(r)/ n amplificatore m. ~**y** /-faɪ/ vt ⟨pt/pp -**ied**⟩ amplificare ⟨sound⟩

amputate /'æmpjʊteɪt/ vt amputare. ~**ion** /-'teɪʃn/ n amputazione f

amuse /ə'mjuːz/ vt divertire. ~**ment** n divertimento m. ~**ment arcade** n sala f giochi

amusing /ə'mjuːzɪŋ/ a divertente

an /ən/, accentato /æn/ see **a**

anaemia /ə'niːmɪə/ n anemia f. ~**ic** a anemico

anaesthetic /ænəs'θetɪk/ n anestesia f

anaesthetist /ə'niːsθɪtɪst/ n anestesista mf

analogue /'ænəlɒg/ a analogico

analogy /ə'nælədʒɪ/ n analogia f

analyse /'ænəlaɪz/ vt analizzare

analysis /ə'næləsɪs/ n analisi f inv

analyst /'ænəlɪst/ n analista mf

analytical /ænə'lɪtɪkl/ a analitico

anarchist /'ænəkɪst/ n anarchico, -a mf. ~**y** n anarchia f

anatomical /ænə'tɒmɪkl/ a anatomico. ~**ically** adv anatomicamente. ~**y** /ə'nætəmɪ/ n anatomia f

ancestor /'ænsestə(r)/ n antenato, -a mf. ~**ry** n antenati mpl

anchor /'æŋkə(r)/ n ancora f ● vi gettar l'ancora ● vt ancorare

anchovy /'æntʃəvɪ/ n acciuga f

ancient /'eɪnʃnt/ a antico; fam vecchio

ancillary /æn'sɪlərɪ/ a ausiliario

and /ænd/, accentato /ænd/ conj e; **two** ~ **two** due più due; **six hundred** ~ **two** seicentodue; **more** ~ **more** sempre più; **nice** ~ **warm** bello caldo; **try** ~ **come** cerca di venire; **go** ~ **get** vai a prendere

anecdote /'ænɪkdəʊt/ n aneddoto m

anew /ə'njuː/ adv di nuovo

angel /'eɪndʒl/ n angelo m. ~**ic** /æn'dʒelɪk/ a angelico

anger /'æŋgə(r)/ n rabbia f ● vt far arrabbiare

angle[1] /'æŋgl/ n angolo m; fig angolazione f; **at an** ~ storto

angle[2] vi pescare con la lenza; ~ **for** fig cercare di ottenere. ~**r** n pescatore, -trice mf

Anglican /'æŋglɪkən/ a & n anglicano, -a mf

Anglo-Saxon /æŋgləʊ'sæksn/ a & n anglo-sassone mf

angry /'æŋgrɪ/ a ⟨-ier, -iest⟩ arrabbiato; **get** ~**y** arrabbiarsi; ~**y with** or **at sb** arrabbiato con qcno; ~**y at** or

249

about sth arrabbiato per qcsa. ~ily
adv rabbiosamente

anguish /ˈæŋgwɪʃ/ *n* angoscia *f*

angular /ˈæŋgjʊlə(r)/ *a* angolare

animal /ˈænɪml/ *a & n* animale *m*

animate[1] /ˈænɪmət/ *a* animato

animate[2] /ˈænɪmeɪt/ *vt* animare. ~ed
a animato; ⟨person⟩ vivace. ~ion
/-ˈmeɪʃn/ *n* animazione *f*

animosity /ænɪˈmɒsətɪ/ *n* animosità *f*
inv

ankle /ˈæŋkl/ *n* caviglia *f*

annex /əˈneks/ *vt* annettere

annex[e] /ˈæneks/ *n* annesso *m*

annihilat|e /əˈnaɪəleɪt/ *vt* annientare.
~ion /-ˈleɪʃn/ *n* annientamento *m*

anniversary /ænɪˈvɜːsərɪ/ *n* anniversario *m*

announce /əˈnaʊns/ *vt* annunciare.
~ment *n* annuncio *m*. ~r *n* annunciatore, -trice *mf*

annoy /əˈnɔɪ/ *vt* dare fastidio a; **get**
~ed essere infastidito. ~ance *n* seccatura *f*; ⟨anger⟩ irritazione *f*. ~ing *a* fastidioso

annual /ˈænjʊəl/ *a* annuale; ⟨income⟩
annuo ● *n Bot* pianta *f* annua;
⟨children's book⟩ almanacco *m*

annuity /əˈnjuːətɪ/ *n* annualità *f inv*

annul /əˈnʌl/ *vt* (*pt/pp* annulled) annullare

anomaly /əˈnɒməlɪ/ *n* anomalia *f*

anonymous /əˈnɒnɪməs/ *a* anonimo

anorak /ˈænəræk/ *n* giacca *f* a vento

anorex|ia /ænəˈreksɪə/ *n* anoressia *f*.
~ic *a* anoressico

another /əˈnʌðə(r)/ *a & pron*; ~ [one]
un altro, un'altra; in ~ way diversamente; one ~ l'un l'altro

answer /ˈɑːnsə(r)/ *n* risposta *f*;
⟨solution⟩ soluzione *f* ● *vt* rispondere a
⟨person, question, letter⟩; esaudire
⟨prayer⟩; ~ the door aprire la porta; ~
the telephone rispondere al telefono
● *vi* rispondere; ~ back ribattere; ~
for rispondere di. ~able /-əbl/ *a* responsabile; be ~able to sb rispondere
a qcno. ~ing machine *n Teleph* segreteria *f* telefonica

ant /ænt/ *n* formica *f*

antagonis|m /ænˈtægənɪzm/ *n* antagonismo *m*. ~tic /-ˈnɪstɪk/ *a* antagonistico

antagonize /ænˈtægənaɪz/ *vt* provocare l'ostilità di

Antarctic /ænˈtɑːktɪk/ *n* Antartico *m*
● *a* antartico

antenatal /æntɪˈneɪtl/ *a* prenatale

antenna /ænˈtenə/ *n* antenna *f*

anthem /ˈænθəm/ *n* inno *m*

anthology /ænˈθɒlədʒɪ/ *n* antologia *f*

anthropology /ænθrəˈpɒlədʒɪ/ *n* antropologia *f*

anti-aircraft /æntɪ-/ *a* antiaereo

antibiotic /æntɪbaɪˈɒtɪk/ *n* antibiotico *m*

antibody /ˈæntɪbɒdɪ/ *n* anticorpo *m*

anticipat|e /ænˈtɪsɪpeɪt/ *vt* prevedere;
⟨forestall⟩ anticipare. ~ion /-ˈpeɪʃn/ *n*
anticipo *m*; ⟨excitement⟩ attesa *f*

antiˈ**climax** *n* delusione *f*

antiˈ**clockwise** *a & adv* in senso
antiorario

antics /ˈæntɪks/ *npl* gesti *mpl* buffi

antiˈ**cyclone** *n* anticiclone *m*

antidote /ˈæntɪdəʊt/ *n* antidoto *m*

antifreeze *n* antigelo *m*

antipathy /ænˈtɪpəθɪ/ *n* antipatia *f*

antiquated /ˈæntɪkweɪtɪd/ *a* antiquato

antique /ænˈtiːk/ *a* antico ● *n* antichità *f inv*. ~ dealer *n* antiquario, -a *mf*

antiquity /ænˈtɪkwətɪ/ *n* antichità *f*

anti-Semitic /æntɪsɪˈmɪtɪk/ *a* antisemita

antiˈ**septic** *a & n* antisettico *m*

antiˈ**social** *a* ⟨behaviour⟩ antisociale;
⟨person⟩ asociale

antiˈ**virus program** *n Comput* programma *m* di antivirus

antlers /ˈæntləz/ *npl* corna *fpl*

anus /ˈeɪnəs/ *n* ano *m*

anxiety /æŋˈzaɪətɪ/ *n* ansia *f*

anxious /ˈæŋkʃəs/ *a* ansioso. ~ly *adv*
con ansia

any /ˈenɪ/ *a* ⟨no matter which⟩ qualsiasi,
qualunque; have we ~ wine/
biscuits? abbiamo del vino/dei biscotti?; have we ~ jam/apples? abbiamo
della marmellata/delle mele?; ~
colour/number you like qualsiasi
colore/numero ti piaccia; we don't
have ~ wine/biscuits non abbiamo
vino/biscotti; I don't have ~ reason
to lie non ho nessun motivo per mentire; for ~ reason per qualsiasi ragione
● *pron* ⟨some⟩ ne; ⟨no matter which⟩ uno
qualsiasi; I don't want ~ [of it] non ne
voglio [nessuno]; there aren't ~ non
ce ne sono; have we ~? ne abbiamo?;
have you read ~ of her books? hai
letto qualcuno dei suoi libri? ● *adv* I
can't go ~ quicker non posso andare
più in fretta; is it ~ better? a un po'
meglio?; would you like ~ more? ne
vuoi ancora?; I can't eat ~ more non
posso mangiare più niente

'anybody *pron* chiunque; (*after negative*) nessuno; **I haven't seen ~** non ho visto nessuno

'anyhow *adv* ad ogni modo, comunque; (*badly*) non importa come

'anyone *pron* = anybody

'anything *pron* qualche cosa, qualcosa; (*no matter what*) qualsiasi cosa; (*after negative*) niente; **take/ buy ~ you like** prendi/compra quello che vuoi; **I don't remember ~** non mi ricordo niente; **he's ~ but stupid** è tutto, ma non stupido; **I'll do ~ but that** farò qualsiasi cosa, tranne quello

'anyway *adv* ad ogni modo, comunque

'anywhere *adv* dovunque; (*after negative*) da nessuna parte; **put it ~** mettilo dove vuoi; **I can't find it ~** non lo trovo da nessuna parte; **~ else** da qualch'altra parte; (*after negative*) da nessun'altra parte; **I don't want to go ~ else** non voglio andare da nessun'altra parte

apart /əˈpɑːt/ *adv* lontano; **live ~** vivere separati; **100 miles ~** lontani 100 miglia; **~ from** a parte; **you can't tell them ~** non si possono distinguere; **joking ~** scherzi a parte

apartment /əˈpɑːtmənt/ *n* (*Am: flat*) appartamento *m*; **in my ~** a casa mia

apathy /ˈæpəθɪ/ *n* apatia *f*

ape /eɪp/ *n* scimmia *f* ●*vt* scimmiottare

aperitif /əˈperətɪf/ *n* aperitivo *m*

aperture /ˈæpətʃə(r)/ *n* apertura *f*

apex /ˈeɪpeks/ *n* vertice *m*

apiece /əˈpiːs/ *adv* ciascuno

apologetic /əˌpɒləˈdʒetɪk/ *a* (*air, remark*) di scusa; **be ~** essere spiacente

apologize /əˈpɒlədʒaɪz/ *vi* scusarsi (**for** per)

apology /əˈpɒlədʒɪ/ *n* scusa *f*. *fig* **an ~ for a dinner** una sottospecie di cena

apostle /əˈpɒsl/ *n* apostolo *m*

apostrophe /əˈpɒstrəfɪ/ *n* apostrofo *m*

appal /əˈpɔːl/ *vt* (*pt/pp* **appalled**) sconvolgere. **~ling** a sconvolgente

apparatus /æpəˈreɪtəs/ *n* apparato *m*

apparent /əˈpærənt/ *a* evidente; (*seeming*) apparente. **~ly** *adv* apparentemente

apparition /æpəˈrɪʃn/ *n* apparizione *f*

appeal /əˈpiːl/ *n* appello *m*; (*attraction*) attrattiva *f* ●*vi* fare appello; **~ to** (*be attractive to*) attrarre. **~ing** a attraente

appear /əˈpɪə(r)/ *vi* apparire; (*seem*) sembrare; (*publication*) uscire; *Theat* esibirsi. **~ance** *n* apparizione *f*; (*look*)

aspetto *m*; **to all ~ances** a giudicare dalle apparenze; **keep up ~ances** salvare le apparenze

appease /əˈpiːz/ *vt* placare

appendicitis /əpendɪˈsaɪtɪs/ *n* appendicite *f*

appendix /əˈpendɪks/ *n* (*pl* **-ices** /-ɪsiːz/) (*of book*) appendice *f*; (*pl* **-es**) *Anat* appendice *f*

appetite /ˈæpɪtaɪt/ *n* appetito *m*

appetizer /ˈæpɪtaɪzə(r)/ *n* stuzzichino *m*. **~ing** a appetitoso

applaud /əˈplɔːd/ *vt/i* applaudire. **~se** *n* applauso *m*

apple /ˈæpl/ *n* mela *f*. **~-tree** *n* melo *m*

appliance /əˈplaɪəns/ *n* attrezzo *m*; [**electrical**] **~** elettrodomestico *m*

applicable /ˈæplɪkəbl/ *a* **be ~ to** essere valido per; **not ~** (*on form*) non applicabile

applicant /ˈæplɪkənt/ *n* candidato, -a *mf*

application /æplɪˈkeɪʃn/ *n* applicazione *f*; (*request*) domanda *f*; (*for job*) candidatura *f*; **~ form** *n* modulo *m* di domanda

applied /əˈplaɪd/ *a* applicato

apply /əˈplaɪ/ *vt* (*pt/pp* **-ied**) applicare; **~ oneself** applicarsi ●*vi* applicarsi; **~ to** (*ask*) rivolgersi a; (*law*) essere applicabile; **~ for** fare domanda per (*job etc*)

appoint /əˈpɔɪnt/ *vt* nominare; fissare (*time*). **~ment** *n* appuntamento *m*; (*to job*) nomina *f*; (*job*) posto *m*

appraisal /əˈpreɪz(ə)l/ *n* valutazione *f*

appreciable /əˈpriːʃəbl/ *a* sensibile

appreciate /əˈpriːʃɪeɪt/ *vt* apprezzare; (*understand*) comprendere ●*vi* (*increase in value*) aumentare di valore. **~ion** /-ˈeɪʃn/ *n* (*gratitude*) riconoscenza *f*; (*enjoyment*) apprezzamento *m*; (*understanding*) comprensione *f*; (*in value*) aumento *m*. **~ive** /-ətɪv/ a riconoscente

apprehend /æprɪˈhend/ *vt* arrestare

apprehens|ion /æprɪˈhenʃn/ *n* arresto *m*; (*fear*) apprensione *f*. **~ive** /-sɪv/ a apprensivo

apprentice /əˈprentɪs/ *n* apprendista *mf*. **~ship** *n* apprendistato *m*

approach /əˈprəʊtʃ/ *n* avvicinamento *m*; (*to problem*) approccio *m*; (*access*) accesso *m*; **make ~es to** fare degli approcci con ●*vi* avvicinarsi ●*vt* avvicinarsi a; (*with request*) rivolgersi a; affrontare (*problem*). **~able** /-əbl/ a accessibile

appropriate¹ /ə'prəʊprɪət/ *a* appropriato

appropriate² /ə'prəʊprɪeɪt/ *vt* appropriarsi di

approval /ə'pruːvl/ *n* approvazione *f*; **on ~** in prova

approv|e /ə'pruːv/ *vt* approvare ● *vi* **~ e of** approvare (*sth*); avere una buona opinione di (*sb*). **~ing** (*smile, nod*) d'approvazione

approximate /ə'prɒksɪmət/ *a* approssimativo. **~ly** *adv* approssimativamente

approximation /əprɒksɪ'meɪʃn/ *n* approssimazione *f*

apricot /'eɪprɪkɒt/ *n* albicocca *f*

April /'eɪprəl/ *n* aprile *m*; **~ Fool's Day** il primo d'aprile

apron /'eɪprən/ *n* grembiule *m*

apt /æpt/ *a* appropriato; **be ~ to do** *sth* avere tendenza a fare qcsa

aptitude /'æptɪtjuːd/ *n* disposizione *f*. **~ test** *n* test *m inv* attitudinale

aqualung /'ækwəlʌŋ/ *n* autorespiratore *m*

aquarium /ə'kweərɪəm/ *n* acquario *m*

Aquarius /ə'kweərɪəs/ *n Astr* Acquario *m*

aquatic /ə'kwætɪk/ *a* acquatico

Arab /'ærəb/ *a & n* arabo, -a *mf*. **~ian** /ə'reɪbɪən/ *a* arabo

Arabic /'ærəbɪk/ *a* arabo; **~ numerals** numeri *mpl* arabici ●*n* arabo *m*

arable /'ærəbl/ *a* coltivabile

arbitrary /'ɑːbɪtrərɪ/ *a* arbitrario

arbitrat|e /'ɑːbɪtreɪt/ *vi* arbitrare. **~ion** /-'treɪʃn/ *n* arbitraggio *m*

arc /ɑːk/ *n* arco *m*

arcade /ɑː'keɪd/ *n* portico *m*; (*shops*) galleria *f*

arch /ɑːtʃ/ *n* arco *m*; (*of foot*) dorso *m* del piede

archaeological /ɑːkɪə'lɒdʒɪkl/ *a* archeologico

archaeolog|ist /ɑːkɪ'ɒlədʒɪst/ *n* archeologo, -a *mf*. **~y** *n* archeologia *f*

archaic /ɑː'keɪɪk/ *a* arcaico

arch'bishop /ɑːtʃ-/ *n* arcivescovo *m*

arch-'enemy *n* acerrimo nemico *m*

architect /'ɑːkɪtekt/ *n* architetto *m*. **~ural** /ɑːkɪ'tektʃərəl/ *a* architettonico

architecture /'ɑːkɪtektʃə(r)/ *n* architettura *f*

archives /'ɑːkaɪvz/ *npl* archivi *mpl*

archiving /'ɑːkaɪvɪŋ/ *n Comput* archiviazione *f*

archway /'ɑːtʃweɪ/ *n* arco *m*

Arctic /'ɑːktɪk/ *a* artico ● *n* **the ~** l'Artico

ardent /'ɑːdənt/ *a* ardente

arduous /'ɑːdjʊəs/ *a* arduo

are /ɑː(r)/ *see* **be**

area /'eərɪə/ *n* area *f*; (*region*) zona *f*; (*fig: field*) campo *m*. **~ code** *n* prefisso *m* [telefonico]

arena /ə'riːnə/ *n* arena *f*

aren't /ɑːnt/ = **are not** *see* **be**

Argentina /ɑːdʒən'tiːnə/ *n* Argentina *f*

Argentinian /-'tɪnɪən/ *a & n* argentino, -a *mf*

argue /'ɑːgjuː/ *vi* litigare (**about** su); (*debate*) dibattere; **don't ~!** non discutere! ● *vt* (*debate*) dibattere; (*reason*) **~ that** sostenere che

argument /'ɑːgjʊmənt/ *n* argomento *m*; (*reasoning*) ragionamento *m*; **have an ~** litigare. **~ative** /-'mentətɪv/ *a* polemico

aria /'ɑːrɪə/ *n* aria *f*

arid /'ærɪd/ *a* arido

Aries /'eəriːz/ *n Astr* Ariete *m*

arise /ə'raɪz/ *vi* (*pt* **arose**, *pp* **arisen**) (*opportunity, need, problem:*) presentarsi; (*result*) derivare

aristocracy /ærɪ'stɒkrəsɪ/ *n* aristocrazia *f*

aristocrat /'ærɪstəkræt/ *n* aristocratico, -a *mf*. **~ic** /-'krætɪk/ *a* aristocratico

arithmetic /ə'rɪθmətɪk/ *n* aritmetica *f*

arm /ɑːm/ *n* braccio *m*; (*of chair*) bracciolo *m*; **~s** *pl* (*weapons*) armi *fpl*; **~ in ~** a braccetto; **up in ~s** *fam* furioso (**about** per) ● *vt* armare

armaments /'ɑːməmənts/ *npl* armamenti *mpl*

armchair *n* poltrona *f*

armed /ɑːmd/ *a* armato; **~ forces** forze *fpl* armate; **~ robbery** rapina *f* a mano armata

armistice /'ɑːmɪstɪs/ *n* armistizio *m*

armour /'ɑːmə(r)/ *n* armatura *f*. **~ed** *a* (*vehicle*) blindato

armpit *n* ascella *f*

army /'ɑːmɪ/ *n* esercito *m*; **join the ~** arruolarsi

aroma /ə'rəʊmə/ *n* aroma *f*. **~tic** /ærə'mætɪk/ *a* aromatico

arose /ə'rəʊz/ *see* **arise**

around /ə'raʊnd/ *adv* intorno; **all ~** tutt'intorno; **I'm not from ~ here** non sono di qui; **he's not ~** non c'è ● *prep* intorno a; in giro per (*room, shops, world*)

arouse /ə'raʊz/ *vt* svegliare; (*sexually*) eccitare

arrange /ə'reɪndʒ/ vt sistemare ⟨furniture, books⟩; organizzare ⟨meeting⟩; fissare ⟨date, time⟩; ~ **to do sth** combinare di fare qcsa. **~ment** n ⟨of furniture⟩ sistemazione f; Mus arrangiamento m; ⟨agreement⟩ accordo; ⟨of flowers⟩ composizione f; **make ~ments** prendere disposizioni

arrears /ə'rɪəz/ npl arretrati mpl; **be in ~** essere in arretrato; **paid in ~** pagato a lavoro eseguito

arrest /ə'rest/ n arresto m; **under ~** in stato d'arresto ●vt arrestare

arrival /ə'raɪvl/ n arrivo m; **new ~s** pl nuovi arrivati mpl

arrive /ə'raɪv/ vi arrivare; **~ at** fig raggiungere

arrogan|ce /'ærəgəns/ n arroganza f. **~t** a arrogante

arrow /'ærəʊ/ n freccia f

arse /ɑ:s/ n vulg culo m

arsenic /'ɑ:sənɪk/ n arsenico m

arson /'ɑ:sn/ n incendio m doloso. **~ist** /-sənɪst/ n incendiario, -a mf

art /ɑ:t/ n arte f; **~s and crafts** pl artigianato m; **the A~s** pl l'arte f; **A~s degree** Univ laurea f in Lettere

artery /'ɑ:tərɪ/ n arteria f

artful /'ɑ:tfl/ a scaltro

'**art gallery** n galleria f d'arte

arthritis /ɑ:'θraɪtɪs/ n artrite f

artichoke /'ɑ:tɪtʃəʊk/ n carciofo m

article /'ɑ:tɪkl/ n articolo m; **~ of clothing** capo m d'abbigliamento

articulate¹ /ɑ:'tɪkjʊlət/ a ⟨speech⟩ chiaro; **be ~** esprimersi bene

articulate² /ɑ:'tɪkjʊleɪt/ vt scandire ⟨words⟩. **~d lorry** n autotreno m

artifice /'ɑ:tɪfɪs/ n artificio m

artificial /ɑ:tɪ'fɪʃl/ a artificiale. **~ly** adv artificialmente; ⟨smile⟩ artificiosamente

artillery /ɑ:'tɪlərɪ/ n artiglieria f

artist /'ɑ:tɪst/ n artista mf

artiste /ɑ:'ti:st/ n Theat artista mf

artistic /ɑ:'tɪstɪk/ a artistico

as /æz/ conj come; ⟨since⟩ siccome; ⟨while⟩ mentre; **as he grew older** diventando vecchio; **as you get to know her** conoscendola meglio; **young as she is** per quanto sia giovane ●prep come; **as a friend** come amico; **as a child** da bambino; **as a foreigner** in quanto straniero; **disguised as** travestito da ●adv **as well as** ⟨also⟩ anche; **as soon as I get home** [non] appena arrivo a casa; **as quick as you** veloce quanto te; **as quick as you can** più

veloce che puoi; **as far as** ⟨distance⟩ fino a; **as far as I'm concerned** per quanto mi riguarda; **as long as** finché; ⟨provided that⟩ purché

asbestos /æz'bestɒs/ n amianto m

ascend /ə'send/ vi salire ●vt salire a ⟨throne⟩

Ascension /ə'senʃn/ n Relig Ascensione f

ascent /ə'sent/ n ascesa f

ascertain /æsə'teɪn/ vt accertare

ascribe /ə'skraɪb/ vt attribuire

ash¹ /æʃ/ n ⟨tree⟩ frassino m

ash² n cenere f

ashamed /ə'ʃeɪmd/ a **be/feel ~** vergognarsi

ashore /ə'ʃɔ:(r)/ adv a terra; **go ~** sbarcare

ash: ~tray n portacenere m. **A~ Wednesday** n mercoledì m inv delle Ceneri

Asia /'eɪʒə/ n Asia f. **~n** a & n asiatico, -a mf. **~tic** /eɪʒɪ'ætɪk/ a asiatico

aside /ə'saɪd/ adv **take sb ~** prendere qcno a parte; **put sth ~** mettere qcsa da parte; **~ from** you Am a parte te

ask /ɑ:sk/ vt fare ⟨question⟩; ⟨invite⟩ invitare; **~ sb sth** domandare o chiedere qcsa a qcno; **~ sb to do sth** domandare o chiedere a qcno di fare qcsa ●vi **~ about sth** informarsi su qcsa; **~ after** chiedere [notizie] di; **~ for** chiedere ⟨sth⟩; chiedere di ⟨sb⟩; **~ for trouble** fam andare in cerca di guai. **ask in** vt **~ sb in** invitare qcno ad entrare. **ask out** vt **~ sb out** chiedere a qcno di uscire

askance /ə'skɑ:ns/ adv **look ~ at sb/sth** guardare qcno/qcsa di traverso

askew /ə'skju:/ a & adv di traverso

asleep /ə'sli:p/ a **be ~** dormire; **fall ~** addormentarsi

asparagus /ə'spærəgəs/ n asparagi mpl

aspect /'æspekt/ n aspetto m

aspersions /ə'spɜ:ʃnz/ npl **cast ~ on** diffamare

asphalt /'æsfælt/ n asfalto m

asphyxia /əs'fɪksɪə/ n asfissia f. **~te** /əs'fɪksɪeɪt/ vt asfissiare. **~tion** /-'eɪʃn/ n asfissia f

aspirations /æspə'reɪʃnz/ npl aspirazioni fpl

aspire /ə'spaɪə(r)/ vi **~ to** aspirare a

ass /æs/ n asino m

assailant /ə'seɪlənt/ n assalitore, -trice mf

assassin /ə'sæsɪn/ n assassino, -a mf.

~ate *vt* assassinare. **~ation**/-'neɪʃn/ *n* assassinio *m*

assault /ə'sɔːlt/ *n Mil* assalto *m*; *Jur* aggressione *f* ●*vt* aggredire

assemble /ə'sembl/ *vi* radunarsi ●*vt* radunare; *Techn* montare

assembly /ə'semblɪ/ *n* assemblea *f*; *Sch* assemblea *f* giornaliera di alunni e professori di una scuola; *Techn* montaggio *m*. **~ line** *n* catena *f* di montaggio

assent /ə'sent/ *n* assenso *m* ●*vi* acconsentire

assert /ə'sɜːt/ *vt* asserire; far valere ‹one's rights›; **~ oneself** farsi valere. **~ion** /-ʃn/ *n* asserzione *f*. **~ive** /-tɪv/ *a* **be ~ive** farsi valere

assess /ə'ses/ *vt* valutare; (for tax purposes) stabilire l'imponibile di. **~ment** *n* valutazione *f*; (of tax) accertamento *m*

asset /'æset/ *n* (advantage) vantaggio *m*; (person) elemento *m* prezioso. **~s** *pl* beni *mpl*; (on balance sheet) attivo *msg*

assign /ə'saɪn/ *vt* assegnare. **~ment** *n* (task) incarico *m*

assimilate /ə'sɪmɪleɪt/ *vt* assimilare; integrare ‹person›

assist /ə'sɪst/ *vt/i* assistere; **~ sb to do sth** assistere qcno nel fare qcsa. **~ance** *n* assistenza *f*. **~ant** *a* **~ant manager** vicedirettore, -trice *mf* ●*n* assistente *mf*; (in shop) commesso, -a *mf*

associat|e¹ /ə'səʊʃɪeɪt/ *vt* associare (with a); **be ~ed with sth** (involved in) essere coinvolto in qcsa ●*vi* **~e with** frequentare. **~ion** /-'eɪʃn/ *n* associazione *f*. **A~ion Football** *n* [gioco *m* del] calcio *m*

associate² /ə'səʊʃɪət/ *a* associato ●*n* collega *mf*; (member) socio, -a *mf*

assort|ed /ə'sɔːtɪd/ *a* assortito. **~ment** *n* assortimento *m*

assum|e /ə'sjuːm/ *vt* presumere; assumere ‹control›; **~e office** entrare in carica; **~ing that you're right,...** ammettendo che tu abbia ragione,...

assumption /ə'sʌmpʃn/ *n* supposizione *f*; **on the ~ that** partendo dal presupposto che; **the A~** *Relig* l'Assunzione *f*

assurance /ə'ʃʊərəns/ *n* assicurazione *f*; (confidence) sicurezza *f*

assure /ə'ʃʊə(r)/ *vt* assicurare. **~d** *a* sicuro

asterisk /'æstərɪsk/ *n* asterisco *m*

astern /ə'stɜːn/ *adv* a poppa

asthma /'æsmə/ *n* asma *f*. **~tic** /-'mætɪk/ *a* asmatico

astonish /ə'stɒnɪʃ/ *vt* stupire. **~ing** *a* stupefacente. **~ment** *n* stupore *m*

astound /ə'staʊnd/ *vt* stupire

astray /ə'streɪ/ *adv* **go ~** smarrirsi; (morally) uscire dalla retta via; **lead ~** traviare

astride /ə'straɪd/ *adv* [a] cavalcioni ●*prep* a cavalcioni di

astrolog|er /ə'strɒlədʒə(r)/ *n* astrologo, -a *mf*. **~y** *n* astrologia *f*

astronaut /'æstrənɔːt/ *n* astronauta *mf*

astronom|er /ə'strɒnəmə(r)/ *n* astronomo, -a *mf*. **~ical** /æstrə'nɒmɪkl/ *a* astronomico. **~y** *n* astronomia *f*

astute /ə'stjuːt/ *a* astuto

asylum /ə'saɪləm/ *n* [political] **~** asilo *m* politico; [lunatic] **~** manicomio *m*

at /ət/, accentato /æt/ *prep* **a**; **at the station** alla stazione/al mercato; **at the office/the bank** in ufficio/banca; **at the beginning** all'inizio; **at John's** da John; **at the hairdresser's** dal parrucchiere; **at home** a casa; **at work** al lavoro; **at school** a scuola; **at a party/wedding** a una festa/un matrimonio; **at 1 o'clock** all'una; **at 50 km an hour** ai 50 all'ora; **at Christmas/Easter** a Natale/Pasqua; **at times** talvolta; **two at a time** due alla volta; **good at languages** bravo nelle lingue; **at sb's request** su richiesta di qcno; **are you at all worried?** sei preoccupato?

ate /et/ *see* **eat**

atheist /'eɪθɪɪst/ *n* ateo, -a *mf*

athlet|e /'æθliːt/ *n* atleta *mf*. **~ic** /-'letɪk/ *a* atletico. **~ics** /-'letɪks/ *n* atletica *fsg*

Atlantic /ət'læntɪk/ *a & n* **the ~ [Ocean]** l'[Oceano *m*] Atlantico *m*

atlas /'ætləs/ *n* atlante *m*

atmospher|e /'ætməsfɪə(r)/ *n* atmosfera *f*. **~ic** /-'ferɪk/ *a* atmosferico

atom /'ætəm/ *n* atomo *m*. **~ bomb** *n* bomba *f* atomica

atomic /ə'tɒmɪk/ *a* atomico

atone /ə'təʊn/ *vi* **~ for** pagare per. **~ment** *n* espiazione *f*

atrocious /ə'trəʊʃəs/ *a* atroce; (fam: meal, weather) abominevole

atrocity /ə'trɒsətɪ/ *n* atrocità *f inv*

attach /ə'tætʃ/ *vt* attaccare; attribuire ‹importance›; **be ~ed to** *fig* essere attaccato a

attaché /ə'tæʃeɪ/ *n* addetto *m*. **~ case** *n* ventiquattrore *f inv*

attachment /əˈtætʃmənt/ n (affection) attaccamento m; (accessory) accessorio m

attack /əˈtæk/ n attacco m; (physical) aggressione f ● vt attaccare; (physically) aggredire. **~er** n assalitore, ·trice mf; (critic) detrattore, ·trice mf

attain /əˈteɪn/ vt realizzare (ambition); raggiungere (success, age, goal)

attempt /əˈtempt/ n tentativo m ● vt tentare

attend /əˈtend/ vt essere presente a; (go regularly to) frequentare; (doctor:) avere in cura ● vi essere presente; (pay attention) prestare attenzione. **attend to** vt occuparsi di; (in shop) servire. **~ance** n presenza f. **~ant** n guardiano, ·a mf

attention /əˈtenʃn/ n attenzione f. **~!** Mil attenti!; **pay ~** prestare attenzione; **need ~** aver bisogno di attenzioni; (skin, hair, plant:) dover essere curato; (car, tyres:) dover essere riparato; **for the ~ of** all'attenzione di

attentive /əˈtentɪv/ a (pupil, audience) attento

attest /əˈtest/ vt/i attestare

attic /ˈætɪk/ n soffitta f

attitude /ˈætɪtjuːd/ n atteggiamento m

attorney /əˈtɜːnɪ/ n (Am: lawyer) avvocato m; **power of ~** delega f

attract /əˈtrækt/ vt attirare. **~ion** /-ækʃn/ n attrazione f; (feature) attrattiva f. **~ive** /-tɪv/ a (person) attraente; (proposal, price) allettante

attribute¹ /ˈætrɪbjuːt/ n attributo m

attribut|e² /əˈtrɪbjuːt/ vt attribuire

attrition /əˈtrɪʃn/ n **war of ~** guerra f di logoramento

aubergine /ˈəʊbəʒiːn/ n melanzana f

auburn /ˈɔːbən/ a castano ramato

auction /ˈɔːkʃn/ n asta f ● vt vendere all'asta. **~eer** /-ʃəˈnɪə(r)/ n banditore m

audaci|ous /ɔːˈdeɪʃəs/ a sfacciato; (daring) audace. **~ty** /-ˈdæsətɪ/ n sfacciataggine f; (daring) audacia f

audible /ˈɔːdəbl/ a udibile

audience /ˈɔːdɪəns/ n Theat pubblico m; TV telespettatori mpl; Radio ascoltatori mpl; (meeting) udienza f

audio /ˈɔːdɪəʊ/: **~tape** n audiocassetta f. **~ typist** n dattilografo, ·a mf (che trascrive registrazioni). **~visual** a audiovisivo

audit /ˈɔːdɪt/ n verifica f del bilancio ● vt verificare

audition /ɔːˈdɪʃn/ n audizione f ● vi fare un'audizione

auditor /ˈɔːdɪtə(r)/ n revisore m di conti

auditorium /ɔːdɪˈtɔːrɪəm/ n sala f

augment /ɔːɡˈment/ vt aumentare

augur /ˈɔːɡə(r)/ vi **~ well/ill** essere di buon/cattivo augurio

August /ˈɔːɡəst/ n agosto m

aunt /ɑːnt/ n zia f

au pair /əʊˈpeə(r)/ n **~ [girl]** ragazza f alla pari

aura /ˈɔːrə/ n aura f

auspices /ˈɔːspɪsɪz/ npl **under the ~** sotto l'egida di

auspicious /ɔːˈspɪʃəs/ a di buon augurio

auster|e /ɒˈstɪə(r)/ a austero. **~ity** /-ˈterətɪ/ n austerità f

Australia /ɒˈstreɪlɪə/ n Australia f. **~n** a & n australiano, ·a mf

Austria /ˈɒstrɪə/ n Austria f. **~n** a & n austriaco, ·a mf

authentic /ɔːˈθentɪk/ a autentico. **~ate** vt autenticare. **~ity** /-ˈtɪsətɪ/ n autenticità f

author /ˈɔːθə(r)/ n autore m

authoritarian /ɔːθɒrɪˈteərɪən/ a autoritario

authoritative /ɔːˈθɒrɪtətɪv/ a autorevole; (manner) autoritario

authority /ɔːˈθɒrətɪ/ n autorità f; (permission) autorizzazione f; **be in ~ over** avere autorità su

authorization /ɔːθəraɪˈzeɪʃn/ n autorizzazione f

authorize /ˈɔːθəraɪz/ vt autorizzare

autobi|ography /ɔːtə-/ n autobiografia f

autocratic /ɔːtəˈkrætɪk/ a autocratico

autograph /ˈɔːtəɡrɑːf/ n autografo m

automate /ˈɔːtəmeɪt/ vt automatizzare

automatic /ɔːtəˈmætɪk/ a automatico ● n (car) macchina f col cambio automatico; (washing machine) lavatrice f automatica. **~ally** adv automaticamente

automation /ɔːtəˈmeɪʃn/ n automazione f

automobile /ˈɔːtəməbiːl/ n automobile f

autonom|ous /ɔːˈtɒnəməs/ a autonomo. **~y** n autonomia f

autopsy /ˈɔːtɒpsɪ/ n autopsia f

autumn /ˈɔːtəm/ n autunno m. **~al** /-ˈtʌmnl/ a autunnale

auxiliary /ɔːɡˈzɪlɪərɪ/ a ausiliario ● n ausiliare m

avail /əˈveɪl/ n **to no ~** invano ● vi **~ oneself of** approfittare di

available /ə'veɪləbl/ a disponibile; ⟨book, record etc⟩ in vendita

avalanche /'ævəlɑːnʃ/ n valanga f

avarice /'ævərɪs/ n avidità f

avenge /ə'vendʒ/ vt vendicare

avenue /'ævənjuː/ n viale m; fig strada f

average /'ævərɪdʒ/ a medio; ⟨mediocre⟩ mediocre ●n media f; **on** ~ in media ●vt ⟨sales, attendance etc⟩ raggiungere una media di. **average out at** vt risultare in media

averse /ə'vɜːs/ a **not be ~e to sth** non essere contro qcsa. **~ion** /-ɜːʃn/ n avversione f (**to** per)

avert /ə'vɜːt/ vt evitare ⟨crisis⟩; distogliere ⟨eyes⟩

aviary /'eɪvɪərɪ/ n uccelliera f

aviation /eɪvɪ'eɪʃn/ n aviazione f

avid /'ævɪd/ a avido (**for** di); ⟨reader⟩ appassionato

avocado /ævə'kɑːdəʊ/ n avocado m

avoid /ə'vɔɪd/ vt evitare. **~able** /-əbl/ a evitabile

await /ə'weɪt/ vt attendere

awake /ə'weɪk/ a sveglio; **wide ~** completamente sveglio ●vi (pt **awoke**, pp **awoken**) svegliarsi

awaken /ə'weɪkn/ vt svegliare. **~ing** n risveglio m

award /ə'wɔːd/ n premio m; ⟨medal⟩ riconoscimento m; ⟨of prize⟩ assegnazione f ●vt assegnare; ⟨hand over⟩ consegnare

aware /ə'weə(r)/ a **be ~ of** ⟨sense⟩ percepire; ⟨know⟩ essere conscio di; **become ~ of** accorgersi di; ⟨learn⟩ venire a sapere di; **be ~ that** rendersi conto che. **~ness** n percezione f; ⟨knowledge⟩ consapevolezza f

awash /ə'wɒʃ/ a inondato (**with** di)

away /ə'weɪ/ adv via; **go/stay ~** andare/stare via; **he's ~ from his desk/the office** non è alla sua scrivania/in ufficio; **far** ~ lontano; **four kilometres** ~ a quattro chilometri; **play ~** Sport giocare fuori casa. **~ game** n partita f fuori casa

awe /ɔː/ n soggezione f

awful /ɔːfl/ a terribile. **~ly** adv /'ɔːf(ə)lɪ/ terribilmente; ⟨pretty⟩ estremamente

awhile /ə'waɪl/ adv per un po'

awkward /'ɔːkwəd/ a ⟨movement⟩ goffo; ⟨moment, situation⟩ imbarazzante; ⟨time⟩ scomodo. **~ly** adv ⟨move⟩ goffamente; ⟨say⟩ con imbarazzo

awning /'ɔːnɪŋ/ n tendone m

awoke(n) /ə'wəʊk(ən)/ see **awake**

awry /ə'raɪ/ adv storto

axe /æks/ n scure f ●vt (pres p **axing**) fare dei tagli a ⟨budget⟩; sopprimere ⟨jobs⟩; annullare ⟨project⟩

axis /'æksɪs/ n (pl **axes** /-siːz/) asse m

axle /'æksl/ n Techn asse m

ay[e] /aɪ/ adv sì ●n sì m invar

Bb

B /biː/ n Mus si m inv

BA n abbr **Bachelor of Arts**

babble /'bæbl/ vi farfugliare; ⟨stream⟩ gorgogliare

baby /'beɪbɪ/ n bambino. -a mf; ⟨fam: darling⟩ tesoro m

baby: ~ **carriage** n Am carrozzina f. **~ish** a bambinesco. **~-sit** vi fare da baby-sitter. **~-sitter** n baby-sitter mf

bachelor /'bætʃələ(r)/ n scapolo m; **B~ of Arts/Science** laureato, -a mf in lettere/in scienze

back /bæk/ n schiena f; ⟨of horse, hand⟩ dorso m; ⟨of chair⟩ schienale m; ⟨of house, cheque, page⟩ retro m; ⟨in football⟩ difesa f; **at the ~** in fondo; **in the ~** Auto dietro; ~ **to front** ⟨sweater⟩ il davanti di dietro; **at the ~ of beyond** in un posto sperduto ●a posteriore; ⟨taxes, payments⟩ arretrato ●adv indietro; ⟨returned⟩ di ritorno; **turn/move ~** tornare/spostarsi indietro; **put it ~ here/there** rimettilo qui/là; ~ **at home** di ritorno a casa; **I'll be ~ in five minutes** torno fra cinque minuti; **I'm just ~** sono appena tornato; **when do you want the book ~?** quando rivuoi il libro?; **pay ~** ripagare ⟨sb⟩; restituire ⟨money⟩; ~ **in power** di nuovo al potere ●vt ⟨support⟩ sostenere; ⟨with money⟩

finanziare; puntare su ‹horse›; ‹cover the back of› rivestire il retro di● vi Auto fare retromarcia. **back down** vi battere in ritirata. **back in** vi Auto entrare in retromarcia; ‹person:› entrare camminando all'indietro. **back out** vi Auto uscire in retromarcia; ‹person:› uscire camminando all'indietro; fig tirarsi indietro (**of** da). **back up** vt sostenere; confermare ‹person's alibi›; Comput fare una copia di salvataggio di;**be ~ed up** ‹traffic:› essere congestionato ● vi Auto fare retromarcia

back: ~**ache** n mal m di schiena. ~**bencher** n parlamentare mf ordinario, -a.~**biting** n maldicenza f.~**bone** n spina f dorsale. ~**chat** n risposta f impertinente. ~**date** vt retrodatare ‹cheque›;~**dated** to valido a partire da. ~ '**door** n porta f di servizio

backer /'bækə(r)/ n sostenitore, -trice mf; ‹with money› finanziatore, -trice mf

back: ~ '**fire** vi Auto avere un ritorno di fiamma; ‹fig: plan› fallire. ~**ground** n sfondo m; ‹environment› ambiente m. ~**hand** n ‹tennis› rovescio m.~'**handed** a ‹compliment› implicito. ~'**hander** n ‹fam: bribe› bustarella f

backing /'bækɪŋ/ n ‹support› supporto m; ‹material› riserva f; Mus accompagnamento m; ~ **group** gruppo m d'accompagnamento

back: ~**lash** n fig reazione f opposta. ~**log** n ~**log of work** lavoro m arretrato.~ '**seat** n sedile m posteriore. ~**side** n fam fondoschiena m inv. ~**slash** n Typ barra f retroversa. ~**stage** a & adv dietro le quinte. ~**stroke** n dorso m. ~'**up** n rinforzi mpl; Comput riserva f. ~'**up copy** n Comput copia f di riserva

backward /'bækwəd/ a ‹step› indietro; ‹child› lento nell'apprendimento; ‹country› arretrato ● adv ~**s** (also Am: ~) indietro; ‹fall, walk› all'indietro;~**s and forwards** avanti e indietro

back: ~**water** n fig luogo m allo scarto. ~ '**yard** n cortile f

bacon /'beɪkn/ n ≈ pancetta f

bacteria /bæk'tɪərɪə/ npl batteri mpl

bad /bæd/ a ‹worse, worst› cattivo; ‹weather, habit, news, accident› brutto; ‹apple etc› marcio;**the light is** ~ non c'è una buona luce;**use** ~ **language** dire delle parolacce; **feel** ~ sentirsi male; ‹feel guilty› sentirsi in colpa;**have a** ~ **back** avere dei problemi alla schiena. **smoking is** ~ **for you** fumare fa male;

go ~ andare a male;**that's just too** ~! pazienza!;**not** ~ niente male

bade /bæd/ see**bid**

badge /bædʒ/ n distintivo m

badger /'bædʒə(r)/ n tasso m ● vt tormentare

badly /'bædlɪ/ adv male; ‹hurt› gravemente; ~ **off** povero; ~ **behaved** maleducato;**need** ~ aver estremamente bisogno di

bad-'mannered a maleducato

badminton /'bædmɪntən/ n badminton m

bad-'tempered a irascibile

baffle /'bæfl/ vt confondere

bag /bæg/ n borsa f; ‹of paper› sacchetto m; **old** ~ sl megera f; ~**s under the eyes** occhiaie fpl;~**s of** fam un sacco di

baggage /'bægɪdʒ/ n bagagli mpl

baggy /'bægɪ/ a ‹clothes› ampio

'**bagpipes** npl cornamusa fsg

Bahamas /bə'hɑːməz/ npl**the** ~ le Bahamas

bail /beɪl/ n cauzione f;**on** ~ su cauzione ● **bail out** vt Naut aggottare; ~ **sb out** Jur pagare la cauzione per qcno ● vi Aeron paracadutarsi

bait /beɪt/ n esca f● vt innescare; ‹fig: torment› tormentare

bake /beɪk/ vt cuocere al forno; ‹make› fare● vi cuocersi al forno

baker /'beɪkə(r)/ n fornaio, -a mf, panettiere, -a mf.~**'s** [**shop**] panetteria f.~**y** n panificio m, forno m

baking /'beɪkɪŋ/ n cottura f al forno. ~-**powder** n lievito m in polvere. ~-**tin** n teglia f

balance /'bæləns/ n equilibrio m; Comm bilancio m; ‹outstanding sum› saldo m; ‹bank› ~ saldo m; **be or hang in the** ~ fig essere in sospeso● vt bilanciare; equilibrare ‹budget›; Comm fare il bilancio di ‹books› ● vi bilanciarsi; Comm essere in pareggio. ~**d** a ‹equilibrato. ~ **sheet** n bilancio m [d'esercizio]

balcony /'bælkənɪ/ n balcone m

bald /bɔːld/ a ‹person› calvo; ‹tyre› liscio; ‹statement› nudo e crudo;**go** ~ perdere i capelli

bald|ing /'bɔːldɪŋ/ a**be** ~**ing** stare perdendo i capelli. ~**ness** n calvizie f

bale /beɪl/ n balla f

baleful /'beɪlfl/ a malvagio; ‹sad› triste

balk /bɔːlk/ vt ostacolare ● vi ~ **at** ‹horse:› impennarsi davanti a; fig tirarsi indietro davanti a

Balkans /'bɔːlknz/ npl Balcani mpl

ball¹ /bɔːl/ n palla f; (football) pallone m; (of yarn) gomitolo m; **on the ~** fam sveglio

ball² n (dance) ballo m

ballad /'bæləd/ n ballata f

ballast /'bæləst/ n zavorra f

ball-bearing n cuscinetto m a sfera

ballerina /bælə'riːnə/ n ballerina f [classica]

ballet /'bæleɪ/ n balletto m; (art form) danza f; **~ dancer** n ballerino, -a mf [classico, -a]

ballistic /bə'lɪstɪk/ a balistico. **~s** n balistica fsg

balloon /bə'luːn/ n pallone m; Aeron mongolfiera f

ballot /'bælət/ n votazione f. **~-box** n urna f. **~-paper** n scheda f di votazione

ball: **~-point** ['pen] n penna f a sfera. **~room** n sala f da ballo

balm /bɑːm/ n balsamo m

balmy /'bɑːmɪ/ a (-ier, -iest) mite; (fam: crazy) strampalato

Baltic /'bɔːltɪk/ a & n **the ~** [Sea] il [mar] Baltico

bamboo /bæm'buː/ n bambù m inv

bamboozle /bæm'buːzl/ vt (fam: mystify) confondere

ban /bæn/ n proibizione f ● vt (pt/pp banned) proibire; **~ from** espellere da (club); **she was ~ned from driving** le hanno ritirato la patente

banal /bə'nɑːl/ a banale. **~ity** /-'nælətɪ/ n banalità f inv

banana /bə'nɑːnə/ n banana f

band /bænd/ n banda f; (stripe) nastro m; (Mus: pop group) complesso m; (Mus: brass ~) banda f; Mil fanfara f ● **band together** vi riunirsi

bandage /'bændɪdʒ/ n benda f ● vt fasciare (limb)

b. & b. abbr bed and breakfast

bandit /'bændɪt/ n bandito m

band: **~stand** n palco m coperto [dell'orchestra]. **~wagon** n jump on the **~wagon** fig seguire la corrente

bandy¹ /'bændɪ/ vt (pt/pp -ied) scambiarsi (words). **bandy about** vt far circolare

bandy² a (-ier, -iest) **be ~** avere le gambe storte

bang /bæŋ/ n (noise) fragore m; (of gun, firework) scoppio m; (blow) colpo m ● adv **~ in the middle of** fam proprio nel mezzo di; **go ~** (gun:) sparare; (balloon:) esplodere ● int bum! ● vt battere (fist); battere su (table); sbattere

banger /'bæŋə(r)/ n (firework) petardo m; (fam: sausage) salsiccia f; **old ~** (fam: car) macinino m

bangle /'bæŋgl/ n braccialetto m

banish /'bænɪʃ/ vt bandire

banisters /'bænɪstəz/ npl ringhiera fsg

bank¹ /bæŋk/ n (of river) sponda f; (slope) scarpata f ● vi Aeron inclinarsi in virata

bank² n banca f ● vt depositare in banca ● vi **~ with** avere un conto [bancario] presso. **bank on** vt contare su

bank account n conto m in banca

bank card n carta f assegno.

banker /'bæŋkə(r)/ n banchiere m

bank: **~ holiday** n giorno m festivo. **~ing** n bancario m. **~ manager** n direttore, -trice mf di banca. **~note** n banconota f

bankrupt /'bæŋkrʌpt/ a fallito; **go ~** fallire ● n persona f che ha fatto fallimento ● vt far fallire. **~cy** n bancarotta f

banner /'bænə(r)/ n stendardo m; (of demonstrators) striscione m

banns /bænz/ npl Relig pubblicazioni fpl [di matrimonio]

banquet /'bæŋkwɪt/ n banchetto m

banter /'bæntə(r)/ n battute fpl di spirito

baptism /'bæptɪzm/ n battesimo m

Baptist /'bæptɪst/ a & n battista mf

baptize /bæp'taɪz/ vt battezzare

bar /bɑː(r)/ n sbarra f; Jur ordine m degli avvocati; (of chocolate) tavoletta f; (café) bar m inv; (counter) banco m; Mus battuta f; (fig: obstacle) ostacolo m; **~ of soap/gold** saponetta f/lingotto m; **behind ~s** fam dietro le sbarre ● vt (pt/pp barred) sbarrare (way); sprangare (door); escludere (person) ● prep tranne; **~ none** in assoluto

barbarian /bɑː'beərɪən/ n barbaro, -a mf

barbaric /bɑː'bærɪk/ a barbarico. **~ity** n barbarie f inv. **~ous** /'bɑːbərəs/ a barbaro

barbecue /'bɑːbɪkjuː/ n barbecue m inv; (party) grigliata f, barbecue m inv ● vt arrostire sul barbecue

barbed /bɑːbd/ a **~ wire** filo m spinato

barber /'bɑːbə(r)/ n barbiere m

barbiturate /bɑː'bɪtjʊrət/ n barbiturico m

bar code n codice m a barre

bare /beə(r)/ a nudo; (tree, room) spo-

bareback | **bay**

glio; ⟨*floor*⟩ senza moquette ●*vt* scoprire; mostrare ⟨*teeth*⟩

bare: ~**back** *adv* senza sella. ~**faced** *a* sfacciato. ~**foot** *adv* scalzo. ~**headed** *a* a capo scoperto

barely /'beəlɪ/ *adv* appena

bargain /'bɑ:gɪn/ *n* ⟨*agreement*⟩ patto *m*; ⟨*good buy*⟩ affare *m*; **into the** ~ per di più ●*vi* contrattare; ⟨*haggle*⟩ trattare. **bargain for** *vt* ⟨*expect*⟩ aspettarsi

barge /bɑ:dʒ/ *n* barcone *m* ● **barge in** *vi fam* ⟨*to room*⟩ piombare dentro; ⟨*into conversation*⟩ interrompere bruscamente. ~ **into** *vt* piombare dentro a ⟨*room*⟩; venire addosso a ⟨*person*⟩

baritone /'bærɪtəʊn/ *n* baritono *m*

bark[1] /bɑːk/ *n* ⟨*of tree*⟩ corteccia *f*

bark[2] *n* abbaiamento *m* ● *vi* abbaiare

barley /'bɑːlɪ/ *n* orzo *m*

bar: ~**maid** *n* barista *f*. ~**man** *n* barista *m*

barmy /'bɑːmɪ/ *a fam* strampalato

barn /bɑːn/ *n* granaio *m*

barometer /bə'rɒmɪtə(r)/ *n* barometro *m*

baron /'bærn/ *n* barone *m*. ~**ess** *n* baronessa *f*

baroque /bə'rɒk/ *a & n* barocco *m*

barracks /'bærəks/ *npl* caserma *fsg*

barrage /'bærɑːʒ/ *n Mil* sbarramento *m*; ⟨*fig: of criticism*⟩ sfilza *f*

barrel /'bærl/ *n* barile *m*, botte *f*; ⟨*of gun*⟩ canna *f*. ~**-organ** *n* organetto *m* [a cilindro]

barren /'bærən/ *a* sterile; ⟨*landscape*⟩ brullo

barricade /bærɪ'keɪd/ *n* barricata *f* ●*vt* barricare

barrier /'bærɪə(r)/ *n* barriera *f*; *Rail* cancello *m*; *fig* ostacolo *m*

barring /'bɑːrɪŋ/ *prep* ~ **accidents** tranne imprevisti

barrister /'bærɪstə(r)/ *n* avvocato *m*

barrow /'bærəʊ/ *n* carretto *m*; ⟨*wheel-*⟩ carriola *f*

barter /'bɑːtə(r)/ *vi* barattare (**for** con)

base /beɪs/ *n* base *f* ● *a* vile ● *vt* basare; **be** ~**d on** basarsi su

base: ~**ball** *n* baseball *m*. ~**less** *a* infondato. ~**ment** *n* seminterrato *m*. ~**ment flat** *n* appartamento *m* nel seminterrato

bash /bæʃ/ *n* colpo *m* [violento] ● *vt* colpire [violentemente]; ⟨*dent*⟩ ammaccare; ~**ed in** ammaccato

bashful /'bæʃfl/ *a* timido

basic /'beɪsɪk/ *a* di base; ⟨*condition, requirement*⟩ basilare; ⟨*living conditions*⟩ povero; **my Italian is pretty** ~ il mio italiano è abbastanza rudimentale; **the** ~**s** ⟨*of language, science*⟩ i rudimenti; ⟨*essentials*⟩ l'essenziale *m*. ~**ally** *adv* fondamentalmente

basil /'bæzɪl/ *n* basilico *m*

basilica /bə'zɪlɪkə/ *n* basilica *f*

basin /'beɪsn/ *n* bacinella *f*; ⟨*wash-hand* ~⟩ lavabo *m*; ⟨*for food*⟩ recipiente *m*; *Geog* bacino *m*

basis /'beɪsɪs/ *n* (*pl* -**ses** /-siːz/) base *f*

bask /bɑːsk/ *vi* crogiolarsi

basket /'bɑːskɪt/ *n* cestino *m*. ~**ball** *n* pallacanestro *f*

Basle /bɑːl/ *n* Basilea *f*

bass /beɪs/ *a* basso; ~ **voice** voce *f* di basso ● *n* basso *m*

bastard /'bɑːstəd/ *n* ⟨*illegitimate child*⟩ bastardo, -a *mf*; *sl* figlio *m* di puttana

bastion /'bæstɪən/ *n* bastione *m*

bat[1] /bæt/ *n* mazza *f*; ⟨*for table tennis*⟩ racchetta *f*; **off one's own** ~ *fam* tutto da solo ● *vt* (*pt/pp* **batted**) battere; **she didn't** ~ **an eyelid** *fig* non ha battuto ciglio

bat[2] *n Zool* pipistrello *m*

batch /bætʃ/ *n* gruppo *m*; ⟨*of goods*⟩ partita *f*; ⟨*of bread*⟩ infornata *f*

bated /'beɪtɪd/ *a* **with** ~ **breath** col fiato sospeso

bath /bɑːθ/ *n* (*pl* ~**s** /bɑːðz/) bagno *m*; ⟨*tub*⟩ vasca *f* da bagno; ~**s** *pl* piscina *f*; **have a** ~ fare un bagno ● *vt* fare il bagno a

bathe /beɪð/ *n* bagno *m* ● *vi* fare il bagno ● *vt* lavare ⟨*wound*⟩. ~**r** *n* bagnante *mf*

bathing /'beɪðɪŋ/ *n* bagni *mpl*. ~**cap** *n* cuffia *f*. ~**-costume** *n* costume *m* da bagno

bath: ~**-mat** *n* tappetino *m* da bagno. ~**robe** *n* accappatoio *m*. ~**room** *n* bagno *m*. ~**-towel** *n* asciugamano *m* da bagno

baton /'bætn/ *n Mus* bacchetta *f*

battalion /bə'tælɪən/ *n* battaglione *m*

batter /'bætə(r)/ *n Culin* pastella *f*. ~**ed** *a* ⟨*car*⟩ malandato; ⟨*wife, baby*⟩ maltrattato

battery /'bætərɪ/ *n* batteria *f*; ⟨*of torch, radio*⟩ pila *f*

battle /'bætl/ *n* battaglia *f*; *fig* lotta *f* ● *vi fig* lottare

battle: ~**field** *n* campo *m* di battaglia. ~**ship** *n* corazzata *f*

bawdy /'bɔːdɪ/ *a* (**-ier, -iest**) piccante

bawl /bɔːl/ *vt/i* urlare

bay[1] /beɪ/ *n Geog* baia *f*

bay[2] *n* **keep at** ~ tenere a bada

bay[3] *n Bot* alloro *m*. **~-leaf** *n* foglia *f* d'alloro

bayonet /'beɪənɪt/ *n* baionetta *f*

bay 'window *n* bay window *f inv* (*grande finestra sporgente*)

bazaar /bə'zɑ:(r)/ *n* bazar *m inv*

BC *abbr* (before Christ) a.C.

be /bi:/ *vi* (*pres* am, are, is, are; *pt* was, were; *pp* been) essere;**he is a teacher** è un'insegnante, fa l'insegnante;**what do you want to be?** cosa vuoi fare?; **be quiet!** sta' zitto!; **I am cold/hot** ho freddo/caldo;**it's cold/hot, isn't it?** fa freddo/caldo, vero?; **how are you?** come stai?;**I am well** sto bene;**there is** c'è;**there are** ci sono;**I have been to Venice** sono stato a Venezia;**has the postman been?** è passato il postino?; **you're coming too, aren't you?** vieni anche tu, no?;**it's yours, is it?** è tuo, vero?;**was John there? - yes, he was** c'era John? - sì;**John wasn't there - yes he was!** John non c'era - sì che c'era!;**three and three are six** tre più tre fanno sei;**he is five** ha cinque anni; **that will be £10, please** fanno 10 sterline, per favore;**how much is it?** quanto costa?;**that's £5 you owe me** mi devi 5 sterline ● *v aux* I am coming/reading sto venendo/leggendo;**I'm staying** (*not leaving*) resto;**I am being lazy** sono pigro;**I was thinking of you** stavo pensando a te;**you are not to tell him** non devi dirglielo;**you are to do that immediately** devi farlo subito ● *passive* essere;**I have been robbed** sono stato derubato

beach /bi:tʃ/ *n* spiaggia *f*. **~wear** *n* abbigliamento *m* da spiaggia

bead /bi:d/ *n* perlina *f*

beak /bi:k/ *n* becco *m*

beaker /'bi:kə(r)/ *n* coppa *f*

beam /bi:m/ *n* trave *f*; (*of light*) raggio *m* ● *vi* irradiare; (*person:*) essere raggiante. **~ing** *a* raggiante

bean /bi:n/ *n* fagiolo *m*; (*of coffee*) chicco *m*

bear[1] /beə(r)/ *n* orso *m*

bear[2] *v* (*pt* bore, *pp* borne) ● *vt* (*endure*) sopportare; mettere al mondo (*child*); (*carry*) portare; **~ in mind** tenere presente ● *vi* **~ left/right** andare a sinistra/a destra. **bear with** *vt* aver pazienza con. **~able** /-əbl/ *a* sopportabile

beard /bɪəd/ *n* barba *f*. **~ed** *a* barbuto

bearer /'beərə(r)/ *n* portatore, -trice *mf*; (*of passport*) titolare *mf*

bearing /'beərɪŋ/ *n* portamento *m*;

Techn cuscinetto *m* [a sfera]; **have a ~ on** avere attinenza con; **get one's ~s** orientarsi

beast /bi:st/ *n* bestia *f*; (*fam: person*) animale *m*

beat /bi:t/ *n* battito *m*; (*rhythm*) battuta *f*; (*of policeman*) giro *m* d'ispezione ● *v* (*pt* beat, *pp* beaten) ● *vt* battere; picchiare (*person*);**~ it!** *fam* darsela a gambe!;**it ~s me why...** *fam* non capisco proprio perché...**beat up** *vt* picchiare

beaten /'bi:tn/ *a* off the **~en track** fuori mano. **~ing** *n* bastonata *f*; get a **~ing** (*with fists*) essere preso a pugni; (*team, player:*) prendere una batosta

beautician /bju:'tɪʃn/ *n* estetista *f*

beauti|ful /'bju:tɪfl/ *a* bello. **~fully** *adv* splendidamente

beauty /'bju:tɪ/ *n* bellezza *f*. **~ parlour** *n* istituto *m* di bellezza. **~ spot** *n* neo *m*; (*place*) luogo *m* pittoresco

beaver /'bi:və(r)/ *n* castoro *m*

became /br'keɪm/ *see* become

because /br'kɒz/ *conj* perché; **~ you didn't tell me, I...** poiché non me lo hai detto,... ● *adv* **~ of** a causa di

beck /bek/ *n* at the **~ and call of** a completa disposizione di.

beckon /'bekn/ *vt/i* **~ [to]** chiamare con un cenno

become /br'kʌm/ *v* (*pt* became, *pp* become) ● *vt* diventare ● *vi* diventare; **what has ~ of her?** che ne è di lei? **~ing** *a* (*clothes*) bello

bed /bed/ *n* letto *m*; (*of sea, lake*) fondo *m*; (*layer*) strato *m*; (*of flowers*) aiuola *f*; **in ~** a letto; **go to ~** andare a letto; **~ and breakfast** pensione *f* familiare in cui il prezzo della camera comprende la prima colazione. **~clothes** *npl* lenzuola e coperte *fpl*. **~ding** *n* biancheria *f* per il letto, materasso e guanciali

bedlam /'bedləm/ *n* baraonda *f*

bedraggled /br'drægld/ *a* inzaccherato

bed: **~ridden** *a* costretto a letto. **~room** *n* camera *f* da letto

bedside *n* at his **~** al suo capezzale. **~ lamp** *n* abat-jour *m inv*. **~ table** *n* comodino *m*

bed: **~sit** *n*, **~sitter** *n*, **~sitting-room** *n* = camera *f* ammobiliata fornita di cucina. **~spread** *n* copriletto *m*. **~time** *n* l'ora *f* di andare a letto

bee /bi:/ *n* ape *f*

beech /bi:tʃ/ *n* faggio *m*

beef /bi:f/ *n* manzo *m*. **~burger** *n* hamburger *m inv*

bee: ~hive*n* alveare *m*. ~-line*n* make a ~line for*fam* precipitarsi verso

been/bi:n/ *see* be

beer/bɪə(r)/ *n* birra *f*

beetle /'bi:tl/ *n* scarafaggio *m*

beetroot /'bi:tru:t/ *n* barbabietola *f*

before /brfɔ:(r)/ *prep* prima di; **the day ~ yesterday** ieri l'altro; ~ **long** fra poco ●*adv* prima; **never ~ have I seen...** non ho mai visto prima...; ~ **that** prima; ~ **going** prima di andare ●*conj* (*time*) prima che; ~ **you go**prima che tu vada. ~**hand**adv in anticipo

befriend /brfrend/ *vt* trattare da amico

beg /beg/ *v* (*pt/pp* begged) ●*vi* mendicare ●*vt* pregare; chiedere (*favour, forgiveness*)

began /brgæn/ *see* begin

beggar /'begə(r)/ *n* mendicante *mf*; **poor ~!** povero cristo!

begin /brgɪn/ *vt/i* (*pt* began,*pp* begun, *pres p* beginning) cominciare. ~**ner***n* principiante *mf*. ~**ning***n* principio *m*

begonia /brgəʊnɪə/ *n* begonia *f*

begrudge /brgrʌdʒ/ *vt* (*envy*) essere invidioso di; dare malvolentieri (*money*)

begun /brgʌn/ *see* begin

behalf /brhɑ:f/ *n* **on ~ of**a nome di; **on my ~**a nome mio

behave /brheɪv/ *vi* comportarsi; ~ [oneself]comportarsi bene

behaviour /brheɪvjə(r)/ *n* comportamento *m*; (*of prisoner, soldier*) condotta *f*

behead /brhed/ *vt* decapitare

behind /brhaɪnd/ *prep* dietro; **be ~ sth** *fig* stare dietro qcsa ●*adv* dietro, indietro; (*late*) in ritardo; **a long way ~**molto indietro ●*n fam* didietro *m*. ~**hand** *adv* indietro

beholden /brhəʊldn/ *a* obbligato (to verso)

beige /beɪʒ/ *a & n* beige *m inv*

being /'bi:ɪŋ/ *n* essere *m*; **come into ~** nascere

belated /brleɪtɪd/ *a* tardivo

belch /beltʃ/ *vi* ruttare ●*vt* ~ [out] eruttare (*smoke*)

belfry /'belfrɪ/ *n* campanile *m*

Belgian /'beldʒən/ *a & n* belga *mf*

Belgium /'beldʒəm/ *n* Belgio *m*

belief /brli:f/ *n* fede *f*; (*opinion*) convinzione *f*

believable /brli:vəbl/ *a* credibile

believe /brli:v/ *vt/i* credere. ~**r***n Relig* credente *mf*; **be a great ~r in**credere fermamente in

belittle /brlɪtl/ *vt* sminuire (*person, achievements*)

bell /bel/ *n* campana *f*; (*on door*) campanello *m*

belligerent/brlɪdʒərənt/ *a* belligerante, (*aggressive*) bellicoso

bellow /'beləʊ/ *vi* gridare a squarciagola; (*animal:*) muggire

bellows /'beləʊz/ *npl* (*for fire*) soffietto *msg*

belly /'belɪ/ *n* pancia *f*

belong /brlɒŋ/ *vi* appartenere (to a); (*be member*) essere socio (to di). ~**ings** *npl* cose *fpl*

beloved /brlʌvɪd/ *a & n* amato, -a *mf*

below /brləʊ/ *prep* sotto; (*with numbers*) al di sotto di ●*adv* sotto, di sotto; *Naut* sotto coperta; **see** ~guardare qui di seguito

belt /belt/ *n* cintura *f*; (*area*) zona *f*; *Techn* cinghia *f* ●*vi* ~ **along** (*fam: rush*) filare velocemente ●*vt* (*fam: hit*) picchiare

bemused /brmju:zd/ *a* confuso

bench /bentʃ/ *n* panchina *f*; (*work~*) piano *m* da lavoro; **the B ~** *Jur* la magistratura

bend /bend/ *n* curva *f*; (*of river*) ansa *f* ●*v* (*pt/pp* bent) ●*vt* piegare ●*vi* piegarsi; (*road:*) curvare; ~ [down]chinarsi. **bend over***vi* inchinarsi

beneath /brni:θ/ *prep* sotto, al di sotto di; **he thinks it's ~ him***fig* pensa che sia sotto al suo livello ●*adv* giù

benediction /benrdɪkʃn/ *n Relig* benedizione *f*

benefactor /'benɪfæktə(r)/ *n* benefattore, -trice *mf*

beneficial /benrfɪʃl/ *a* benefico

beneficiary /benrfɪʃərɪ/ *n* beneficiario, -a *mf*

benefit /'benɪfɪt/ *n* vantaggio *m*; (*allowance*) indennità *f inv* ●*v* (*pt/pp* -fited,*pres p* -fiting) ●*vt* giovare a ●*vi* trarre vantaggio (from da)

benevolen|ce /brnevələns/ *n* benevolenza *f*. ~**t***a* benevolo

benign /brnaɪn/ *a* benevolo; *Med* benigno

bent /bent/ *see* bend ●*a* (*person*) ricurvo; (*distorted*) curvato; (*fam: dishonest*) corrotto; **be ~ on doing sth** essere ben deciso a fare qcsa ●*n* predisposizione *f*

be|queath /brkwi:ð/ *vt* lasciare in eredità. ~**quest**/·'kwest/ *n* lascito *m*

bereave|d /brri:vd/ *n* **the ~**d*pl* i familiari del defunto. ~**ment***n* lutto *m*

bereft /brɪˈreft/ *a* ~ **of** privo di

beret /ˈbereɪ/ *n* berretto *m*

berry /ˈberɪ/ *n* bacca *f*

berserk /bəˈsɜːk/ *a* **go** ~ diventare una belva

berth /bɜːθ/ *n* (*bed*) cuccetta *f*; (*anchorage*) ormeggio *m* • *vt* ormeggiare

beseech /brɪˈsiːtʃ/ *vt* (*pt/pp* **beseeched** *or* **besought**) supplicare

beside /brɪˈsaɪd/ *prep* accanto a; ~ **oneself** fuori di sé

besides /brɪˈsaɪdz/ *prep* oltre a • *adv* inoltre

besiege /brɪˈsiːdʒ/ *vt* assediare

besought /brɪˈsɔːt/ *see* **beseech**

best /best/ *a* migliore; **the ~ part of a year** la maggior parte dell'anno; ~ **before** *Comm* preferibilmente prima di • *n* **the** ~ il meglio; (*person*) il/la migliore; **at** ~ tutt'al più; **all the ~!** tanti auguri!; **do one's** ~ fare del proprio meglio; **to the ~ of my knowledge** per quel che ne so; **make the** ~ **of it** cogliere il lato buono della cosa • *adv* meglio, nel modo migliore; **as** ~ **I could** meglio che potevo. ~**man** *n* testimone *m*

bestow /brɪˈstəʊ/ *vt* conferire (**on** a)

best'seller *n* bestseller *m inv*

bet /bet/ *n* scommessa *f* • *vt/i* (*pt/pp* **bet** *or* **betted**) scommettere

betray /brɪˈtreɪ/ *vt* tradire. ~**al** *n* tradimento *m*

better /ˈbetə(r)/ *a* migliore, meglio; **get** ~ migliorare; (*after illness*) rimettersi • *adv* meglio; ~ **off** meglio; (*wealthier*) più ricco; **all the** ~ tanto meglio; **the sooner the** ~ prima è, meglio è; **I've thought** ~ **of it** ci ho ripensato; **you'd** ~ **stay** faresti meglio a restare; **I'd** ~ **not** è meglio che non lo faccia • *vt* migliorare; ~ **oneself** migliorare le proprie condizioni

'betting shop *n* ricevitoria *f* (*dell'allibratore*)

between /brɪˈtwiːn/ *prep* fra, tra; ~ **you and me** detto fra di noi; ~ **us** (*together*) tra me e te • *adv* [**in**] ~ in mezzo; (*time*) frattempo

beverage /ˈbevərɪdʒ/ *n* bevanda *f*

beware /brɪˈweə(r)/ *vi* guardarsi (**of** da); ~ **of the dog!** attenti al cane!

bewilder /brɪˈwɪldə(r)/ *vt* disorientare; ~**ed** perplesso. ~**ment** *n* perplessità *f*

beyond /brɪˈjɒnd/ *prep* oltre; ~ **reach** irraggiungibile; ~ **doubt** senza alcun dubbio; ~ **belief** da non credere; **it's** ~ **me** *fam* non riesco proprio a capire • *adv* più in là

bias /ˈbaɪəs/ *n* (*preference*) preferenza *f*; *pej* pregiudizio *m* • *vt* (*pt/pp* **biased**) (*influence*) influenzare. ~**ed** *a* parziale

bib /bɪb/ *n* bavaglino *m*

Bible /ˈbaɪbl/ *n* Bibbia *f*

biblical /ˈbɪblɪkl/ *a* biblico

bicarbonate /baɪˈkɑːbənɪt/ *n* ~ **of soda** bicarbonato *m* di sodio

biceps /ˈbaɪseps/ *n* bicipite *m*

bicker /ˈbɪkə(r)/ *vi* litigare

bicycle /ˈbaɪsɪkl/ *n* bicicletta *f* • *vi* andare in bicicletta

bid¹ /bɪd/ *n* offerta *f*; (*attempt*) tentativo *m* • *vt/i* (*pt/pp* **bid**, *pres p* **bidding**) offrire; (*in cards*) dichiarare

bid² *vt* (*pt* **bade** *or* **bid**, *pp* **bidden** *or* **bid**, *pres p* **bidding**) *liter* (*command*) comandare; ~ **sb welcome** dare il benvenuto a qcno

bidder /ˈbɪdə(r)/ *n* offerente *mf*

bide /baɪd/ *vt* ~ **one's time** aspettare il momento buono

biennial /baɪˈenɪəl/ *a* biennale

bifocals /baɪˈfəʊklz/ *npl* occhiali *mpl* bifocali

big /bɪg/ *a* (**bigger**, **biggest**) grande; (*brother*, *sister*) più grande; (*fam: generous*) generoso • *adv* **talk** ~ *fam* sparare grosse

bigam|ist /ˈbɪgəmɪst/ *n* bigamo, -a *mf*. ~**y** *n* bigamia *f*

'big-head *n fam* gasato, -a *mf*

big-'hearted *a fam* generoso

bigot /ˈbɪgət/ *n* fanatico, -a *mf*. ~**ed** *a* di mentalità ristretta

bigwig *n fam* pezzo *m* grosso

bike /baɪk/ *n fam* bici *f inv*

bikini /bɪˈkiːnɪ/ *n* bikini *m inv*

bile /baɪl/ *n* bile *f*

bilingual /baɪˈlɪŋgwəl/ *a* bilingue

bill¹ /bɪl/ *n* fattura *f*; (*in restaurant etc*) conto *m*; (*poster*) manifesto *m*; *Pol* progetto *m* di legge; (*Am: note*) biglietto *m* di banca • *vt* fatturare

bill² *n* (*beak*) becco *m*

'billfold *n Am* portafoglio *m*

billiards /ˈbɪljədz/ *n* biliardo *m*

billion /ˈbɪljən/ *n* (*thousand million*) miliardo *m*; (*old-fashioned Br: million million*) mille miliardi *mpl*

billy-goat /ˈbɪlɪ-/ *n* caprone *m*

bin /bɪn/ *n* bidone *m*

bind /baɪnd/ *vt* (*pt/pp* **bound**) legare (**to** a); (*bandage*) fasciare; *Jur* obbligare. ~**ing** *a* (*promise*, *contract*) vincolante • *n* (*of book*) rilegatura *f*; (*on ski*) attacco *m* (*di sicurezza*)

binge /bɪndʒ/ *n fam* **have a** ~ fare baldoria; (eat a lot) abbuffarsi ● vi abbuffarsi (**on** di)

binoculars /bɪ'nɒkjʊləz/ npl [**pair of**] ~ binocolo msg

bio'chemist /baɪəʊ-/ n biochimico, -a mf. ~**ry** n biochimica f

biodegradable /-dɪ'greɪdəbl/ a biodegradabile

biograph|er /baɪ'ɒɡrəfə(r)/ n biografo, -a mf. ~**y** n biografia f

biological /baɪə'lɒdʒɪkl/ a biologico

biolog|ist /baɪ'ɒlədʒɪst/ n biologo, -a mf. ~**y** n biologia f

birch /bɜːtʃ/ n (tree) betulla f

bird /bɜːd/ n uccello m; (fam: girl) ragazza f

Biro® /'baɪrəʊ/ n biro f inv

birth /bɜːθ/ n nascita f

birth: ~ **certificate** n certificato m di nascita. ~-**control** n controllo m delle nascite. ~**day** n compleanno m. ~**mark** n voglia f. ~-**rate** n natalità f

biscuit /'bɪskɪt/ n biscotto m

bisect /baɪ'sekt/ vt dividere in due [parti]

bishop /'bɪʃəp/ n vescovo m; (in chess) alfiere m

bit[1] /bɪt/ n pezzo m; (smaller) pezzetto m; (for horse) morso m; Comput bit m inv; **a** ~ **of** un pezzo di (cheese, paper); un po' di (time, rain, silence); ~ **by** ~ poco a poco; **do one's** ~ fare la propria parte

bit[2] see **bite**

bitch /bɪtʃ/ n cagna f; sl stronza f. ~**y** a velenoso

bit|e /baɪt/ n (insect m; (insect:) puntura f; (mouthful) boccone m ● vt (pt bit, pp bitten) mordere; (insect:) pungere; ~**e one's nails** mangiarsi le unghie ● vi mordere; (insect:) pungere. ~**ing** a (wind, criticism) pungente; (remark) mordace

bitter /'bɪtə(r)/ a amaro ● n Br birra f amara. ~**ly** adv amaramente; **it's** ~**ly cold** c'è un freddo pungente. ~**ness** n amarezza f

bitty /'bɪtɪ/ a Br fam frammentario

bizarre /bɪ'zɑː(r)/ a bizzarro

blab /blæb/ vi (pt/pp **blabbed**) spifferare

black /blæk/ a nero; **be** ~ **and blue** essere pieno di lividi ● n negro, -a mf ● vt boicottare (goods). **black out** vt cancellare ● vi (lose consciousness) perdere coscienza

black: ~**berry** n mora f. ~**bird** n merlo m. ~**board** n Sch lavagna f. ~**currant** n ribes m inv nero; ~ **eye** n occhio m nero.

~ **ice** n ghiaccio m (sulla strada). ~**leg** n Br crumiro m. ~**list** vt mettere sulla lista nera. ~**mail** n ricatto m ● vt ricattare. ~**mailer** n ricattatore, -trice mf. ~ **market** n mercato m nero. ~-**out** n blackout m inv; **have a** ~-**out** Med perdere coscienza. ~**smith** n fabbro m

bladder /'blædə(r)/ n Anat vescica f

blade /bleɪd/ n lama f; (of grass) filo m

blame /bleɪm/ n colpa f ● vt dare la colpa a; ~ **sb for doing sth** dare la colpa a qcno per aver fatto qcsa; **no one is to** ~ non è colpa di nessuno. ~**less** a innocente

blanch /blɑːntʃ/ vi sbiancare ● vt Culin sbollentare

blancmange /blə'mɒnʒ/ n biancomangiare m inv

bland /blænd/ a (food) insipido; (person) insulso

blank /blæŋk/ a bianco; (look) vuoto ● n spazio m vuoto; (cartridge) a salve. ~ '**cheque** n assegno m in bianco

blanket /'blæŋkɪt/ n coperta f

blank 'verse n versi mpl sciolti

blare /bleə(r)/ vi suonare a tutto volume. **blare out** vt far risuonare ● vi (music, radio:) strillare

blasé /'blɑːzeɪ/ a vissuto, blasé inv

blaspheme /blæs'fiːm/ vi bestemmiare

blasphem|ous /'blæsfəməs/ a blasfemo. ~**y** n bestemmia f

blast /blɑːst/ n (gust) raffica f; (sound) scoppio m ● vt (with explosive) far saltare ● int sl maledizione!. ~**ed** a sl maledetto

blast: ~-**furnace** n altoforno m. ~-**off** n (of missile) lancio m

blatant /'bleɪtənt/ a sfacciato

blaze /bleɪz/ n incendio m; **a** ~ **of colour** un'esplosione f di colori ● vi ardere

blazer /'bleɪzə(r)/ n blazer m inv

bleach /bliːtʃ/ n decolorante m; (for cleaning) candeggina f ● vt sbiancare; ossigenare (hair)

bleak /bliːk/ a desolato; (fig: prospects, future) tetro

bleary-eyed /blɪərɪ'aɪd/ a **look** ~ avere gli occhi assonnati

bleat /bliːt/ vi belare ● n belato m

bleed /bliːd/ v (pt/pp **bled**) ● vi sanguinare ● vt spurgare (brakes, radiator)

bleep /bliːp/ n bip m ● vi suonare ● vt chiamare (col cercapersone) (doctor). ~**er** n cercapersone m inv

blemish /'blemɪʃ/ n macchia f

blend /blend/ *n (of tea, coffee, whisky)* miscela *f*; *(of colours)* insieme *m* ●*vt* mescolare ●*vi (colours, sounds:)* fondersi (**with** con). ~**er***n Culin* frullatore *m*

bless /bles/ *vt* benedire. ~**ed** /blesɪd/ *a also sl* benedetto. ~**ing***n* benedizione *f*

blew /blu:/ *see* **blow²**

blight /blaɪt/ *n Bot* ruggine *f* ●*vt* far avvizzire *(plants)*

blind¹ /blaɪnd/ *a cieco;* ~ **man | woman** cieco/cieca ●*npl* **the** ~ i ciechi *mpl*; ●*vt* accecare

blind² *n* [**roller**] ~ avvolgibile *m*; [**Venetian**] ~ veneziana *f*

blind: ~ **alley***n* vicolo *m* cieco. ~**fold** **be** ~**fold** avere gli occhi bendati ●*n* benda *f* ●*vt* bendare gli occhi a. ~**ly***adv* ciecamente. ~**ness***n* cecità *f*

blink /blɪŋk/ *vi* sbattere le palpebre; *(light:)* tremolare

blinkered /blɪŋkəd/ *adj* fig **be** ~ avere i paraocchi

blinkers /blɪŋkəz/ *npl* paraocchi *mpl*

bliss /blɪs/ *n Rel* beatitudine *f*; *(happiness)* felicità *f*. ~**ful** *a* beato; *(single one)* fiore *m* ●*vi* sbocciare

blister /blɪstə(r)/ *n Med* vescica *f*; *(in paint)* bolla *f* ●*vi (paint:)* formare una bolla/delle bolle

blitz /blɪts/ *n* bombardamento *m* aereo; **have a** ~ **on sth***fig* darci sotto con qcsa

blizzard /blɪzəd/ *n* tormenta *f*

bloated /bləʊtɪd/ *a* gonfio

blob /blɒb/ *n* goccia *f*

bloc /blɒk/ *n Pol* blocco *m*

block /blɒk/ *n* blocco *m*; *(building)* isolato *m*; *(building)* cubo *m (per giochi di costruzione);* ~ **of flats** palazzo *m* ●*vt* bloccare. **block up***vt* bloccare

blockade /blɒˈkeɪd/ *n* blocco *m* ●*vt* bloccare

blockage /blɒkɪdʒ/ *n* ostruzione *f*

block: ~**head** *n fam* testone, -a *mf.* ~**letters** *npl* stampatello *m*

bloke /bləʊk/ *n fam* tizio *m*

blonde /blɒnd/ *a* biondo ●*n* bionda *f*

blood /blʌd/ *n* sangue *m*

blood: ~ **bath** *n* bagno *m* di sangue. ~ **count** *n* esame *m* emocromocitometrico. ~ **donor** *n* donatore *m* di sangue. ~ **group** *n* gruppo *m* sanguigno. ~**hound***n* segugio *m*. ~-**poisoning** *n* setticemia *f*. ~ **pressure** *n* pressione *f* del sangue. ~**shed** *n* spargimento *m* di sangue. ~**shot** *a* iniettato di sangue. ~ **sports** *npl* sport *mpl* cruenti. ~-**stained** *a* macchiato di sangue. ~**stream***n* sangue *m*. ~ **test***n* analisi *f*

del sangue. ~**thirsty** *a* assetato di sangue. ~ **transfusion** *n* trasfusione *f* del sangue

bloody /blʌdɪ/ *a* (-**ier**, -**iest**) insanguinato; *sl* maledetto ●*adv sl* ~ **easy**/**difficult** facile/difficile da matti. ~-**minded***a* scorbutico

bloom /blu:m/ *n* fiore *m*; **in** ~ *(flower:)* sbocciato; *(tree:)* in fiore ●*vi* fiorire; *fig* essere in forma smagliante

bloomer /blu:mə(r)/ *n fam* papera *f*. ~**ing** *a fam* maledetto. ~**ers** *npl* mutandoni *mpl (da donna)*

blossom /blɒsəm/ *n* fiori *mpl (d'albero);* *(single one)* fiore *m* ●*vi* sbocciare

blot /blɒt/ *n also fig* macchia *f*. ● **blot out** *vt (pt/pp* **blotted)** *fig* cancellare

blotch /blɒtʃ/ *n* macchia *f*. ~**y** *a* chiazzato

blotting-paper *n* carta *f* assorbente

blouse /blaʊz/ *n* camicetta *f*

blow¹ /bləʊ/ *n* colpo *m*

blow² *v (pt* **blew,** *pp* **blown)** ●*vi (wind:)* soffiare; *(fuse:)* saltare ●*vt (fam:* squander*)* sperperare; ~ **one's nose** soffiarsi il naso. **blow away** *vt* far volar via *(papers)* ●*vi (papers:)* volare via. **blow down** *vt* abbattere ●*vi* abbattersi al suolo. **blow out** *vt (extinguish)* spegnere. **blow over** *vi (storm:)* passare; *(fuss, trouble:)* dissiparsi. **blow up** *vt (inflate)* gonfiare; *(enlarge)* ingrandire *(photograph);* *(by explosion)* far esplodere ●*vi* esplodere

blow: ~-**dry** *vt* asciugare col fon. ~-**lamp** *n* fiamma *f* ossidrica

blown /bləʊn/ *see* **blow²**

blowtorch *n* fiamma *f* ossidrica

blowy /bləʊɪ/ *a* ventoso

blue /blu:/ *a (pale)* celeste; *(navy)* blu *inv; (royal)* azzurro; ~ **with cold** livido per il freddo ●*n* blu *m inv;* **have the** ~**s** essere giù [di tono]; **out of the** ~ inaspettatamente

blue: ~**bell** *n* giacinto *m* di bosco. ~**berry** *n* mirtillo *m*. ~**bottle** *n* moscone *m*. ~ **film** *n* film *m inv* a luci rosse. ~**print***n fig* riferimento *m*

bluff /blʌf/ *n* bluff *m inv* ●*vi* bluffare

blunder /blʌndə(r)/ *n* gaffe *f inv* ●*vi* fare una/delle gaffe

blunt /blʌnt/ *a* spuntato; *(person)* reciso. ~**ly***adv* schiettamente

blur /blɜ:(r)/ *n* **it's all a** ~ *fig* è tutto un insieme confuso ●*vt (pt/pp* **blurred)** rendere confuso *(vision, photo)* sfocato

blurb /blɜ:b/ *n* soffietto *m* editoriale

blurt /blɜːt/ *vt* ~ **out** spifferare

blush /blʌʃ/ *n* rossore *m* • *vi* arrossire

blusher /ˈblʌʃə(r)/ *n* fard *m*

bluster /ˈblʌstə(r)/ *n* sbruffonata *f.* ~**y** *a* ⟨*wind*⟩ furioso; ⟨*day, weather*⟩ molto ventoso

boar /bɔː(r)/ *n* cinghiale *m*

board /bɔːd/ *n* tavola *f*; ⟨*for notices*⟩ tabellone *m*; ⟨*committee*⟩ assemblea *f*; ⟨*of directors*⟩ consiglio *m*; **full** ~ *Br* pensione *f* completa; **half** ~ *Br* mezza pensione *f*; ~ **and lodging** vitto e alloggio *m*; **go by the** ~ *fam* andare a monte *• vi* Naut, Aeron salire a bordo di *• vi* ⟨*passengers:*⟩ salire a bordo. **board up** *vt* sbarrare con delle assi. **board with** *vt* stare a pensione da.

boarder /ˈbɔːdə(r)/ *n* pensionante *mf*; Sch convittore, -trice *mf*

board: ~**game** *n* gioco *m* da tavolo. ~**ing-house** *n* pensione *f*. ~**ing-school** *n* collegio *m*

boast /bəʊst/ *vi* vantarsi (**about** di). ~**ful** *a* vanaglorioso

boat /bəʊt/ *n* barca *f*; ⟨*ship*⟩ nave *f*. ~**er** *n* ⟨*hat*⟩ paglietta *f*

bob /bɒb/ *n* ⟨*hairstyle*⟩ caschetto *m* • *vi* (*pt/pp* **bobbed**) (*also* ~ **up and down**) andare su e giù

'bob-sleigh *n* bob *m* *inv*

bode /bəʊd/ *vi* ~ **well/ill** essere di buono/cattivo augurio

bodily /ˈbɒdɪlɪ/ *a* fisico • *adv* ⟨*forcibly*⟩ fisicamente

body /ˈbɒdɪ/ *n* corpo *m*; ⟨*organization*⟩ ente *m*; ⟨*amount: of poems etc*⟩ quantità *f*. ~**guard** *n* guardia *f* del corpo. ~**work** *n* Auto carrozzeria *f*

bog /bɒg/ *n* palude *f* • *vt* (*pt/pp* **bogged**) **get** ~**ged down** impantanarsi

boggle /ˈbɒgl/ *vi* **the mind** ~**s** non posso neanche immaginarlo

bogus /ˈbəʊgəs/ *a* falso

boil[1] /bɔɪl/ *n* Med foruncolo *m*

boil² *n* **bring/come to the** ~ portare/arrivare ad ebollizione • *vt* [far] bollire • *vi* bollire; ⟨*fig: with anger*⟩ ribollire; **the water** *or* **kettle's** ~**s** l'acqua bolle. **boil down to** *vt fig* ridursi a. **boil over** *vi* straboccare (*bollendo*). **boil up** *vt* far bollire

boiler /ˈbɔɪlə(r)/ *n* caldaia *f*. ~**suit** *n* tuta *f*

'boiling point *n* punto *m* di ebollizione

boisterous /ˈbɔɪstərəs/ *a* chiassoso

bold /bəʊld/ *a* audace • *n* Typ neretto *m*. ~**ness** *n* audacia *f*

bollard /ˈbɒləd/ *n* colonnina *m* di sbarramento al traffico

bolster /ˈbəʊlstə(r)/ *n* cuscino *m* ⟨*lungo e rotondo*⟩ • *vt* ~ [**up**] sostenere

bolt /bəʊlt/ *n* ⟨*for door*⟩ catenaccio *m*; ⟨*for fixing*⟩ bullone *m* • *vt* fissare (con i bulloni) (**to** a); chiudere col chiavistello ⟨*door*⟩; ingurgitare ⟨*food*⟩ • *vi* svignarsela; ⟨*horse:*⟩ scappar via • *adv* ~ **upright** diritto come un fuso

bomb /bɒm/ *n* bomba *f* • *vt* bombardare

bombard /bɒmˈbɑːd/ *vt also fig* bombardare

bombastic /bɒmˈbæstɪk/ *a* ampolloso

bomb|er /ˈbɒmə(r)/ *n* Aeron bombardiere *m*; ⟨*person*⟩ dinamitardo *m*. ~**er jacket** *n* giubbotto *m*, bomber *m* *inv*. ~**shell** *n* ⟨*fig: news*⟩ bomba *f*

bond /bɒnd/ *n* Comm obbligazione *f* • *vt* ⟨*glue:*⟩ attaccare

bondage /ˈbɒndɪdʒ/ *n* schiavitù *f*

bone /bəʊn/ *n* osso *m*; ⟨*of fish*⟩ spina *f* • *vt* disossare ⟨*meat*⟩; togliere le spine da ⟨*fish*⟩. ~**'dry** *a* secco

bonfire /ˈbɒn-/ *n* falò *m* *inv*. ~ **night** *festa* celebrata la notte del 5 novembre con fuochi d'artificio e falò

bonnet /ˈbɒnɪt/ *n* cuffia *f*; ⟨*of car*⟩ cofano *m*

bonus /ˈbəʊnəs/ *n* ⟨*individual*⟩ gratifica *f*; ⟨*production* ~⟩ premio *m*; ⟨*life insurance*⟩ dividendo *m*; **a** ~ *fig* qualcosa in più

bony /ˈbəʊnɪ/ *a* (**-ier, -iest**) ossuto; ⟨*fish*⟩ pieno di spine

boo /buː/ *int* ⟨*to surprise or frighten*⟩ bu! • *vt/i* fischiare

boob /buːb/ *n* ⟨*fam: mistake*⟩ gaffe *f* *inv*; ⟨*breast*⟩ tetta *f* • *vi fam* fare una gaffe

book /bʊk/ *n* libro *m*; ⟨*of tickets*⟩ blocchetto *m*; **keep the** ~**s** Comm tenere la contabilità; **be in sb's bad/good** ~**s** essere nel libro nero/nelle grazie di qcno • *vt* ⟨*reserve*⟩ prenotare; ⟨*offence*⟩ multare • *vi* ⟨*reserve*⟩ prenotare

book: ~**case** *n* libreria *f*. ~**ends** *npl* reggilibri *mpl*. ~**ing-office** *n* biglietteria *f*. ~**keeping** *n* contabilità *f*. ~**let** *n* opuscolo *m*. ~**maker** *n* allibratore *m*. ~**mark** *n* segnalibro *m*. ~**seller** *n* libraio, -a *mf*. ~**shop** *n* libreria *f*. ~**worm** *n* topo *m* di biblioteca

boom /buːm/ *n* Comm boom *m* *inv*; ⟨*upturn*⟩ impennata *f*; ⟨*of thunder, gun*⟩ rimbombo *m* • *vi* ⟨*thunder, gun:*⟩ rimbombare; *fig* prosperare

boon /buːn/ *n* benedizione *f*

boor /bʊə(r)/ n zoticone m. **~ish** a maleducato

boost /buːst/ n spinta f ● vt stimolare ⟨sales⟩; sollevare ⟨morale⟩; far crescere ⟨hopes⟩. **~er** n Med dose f supplementare

boot /buːt/ n stivale m; (up to ankle) stivaletto m; (football) scarpetta f; (climbing) scarpone m; Auto portabagagli m inv ● vt Comput inizializzare

booth /buːð/ n (Teleph, voting) cabina f; (at market) bancarella f

'boot-up n Comput boot m inv

booty /'buːtɪ/ n bottino m

booze /buːz/ fam n alcolici mpl. **~-up** n bella bevuta f

border /'bɔːdə(r)/ n bordo m; (frontier) frontiera f; (in garden) bordura f ● vi **~ on** confinare con; fig essere ai confini di ⟨madness⟩. **~line** n linea f di demarcazione; **~line case** caso m dubbio

bore¹ /bɔː(r)/ see **bear²**

bore² vt Techn forare

bor|e³ n (of gun) calibro m; (person) seccatore, -trice mf; (thing) seccatura f ● vt annoiare. **~edom** n noia f. **be ~ed (to tears or to death)** annoiarsi (da morire). **~ing** a noioso

born /bɔːn/ pp **be ~** nascere; **I was ~ in 1966** sono nato nel 1966 ● a nato; **a ~ liar/actor** un bugiardo/ attore nato

borne /bɔːn/ see **bear²**

borough /'bʌrə/ n municipalità f inv

borrow /'bɒrəʊ/ vt prendere a prestito (**from** da); **can I ~ your pen?** mi presti la tua penna?

bosom /'bʊzm/ n seno m

boss /bɒs/ n direttore, -trice mf ● vt (also **~ about**) comandare a bacchetta. **~y** a autoritario

botanical /bə'tænɪkl/ a botanico

botan|ist /'bɒtənɪst/ n botanico, -a mf. **~y** n botanica f

botch /bɒtʃ/ vt fare un pasticcio con

both /bəʊθ/ a & pron tutti e due, entrambi ● adv **~ men and women** entrambi uomini e donne; **~** ⟨**of**⟩ **the children** tutti e due i bambini; **they are ~ dead** sono morti entrambi; **~ of them** tutti e due

bother /'bɒðə(r)/ n preoccupazione f; (minor trouble) fastidio m; **it's no ~** non c'è problema ● int fam che seccatura! ● vt (annoy) dare fastidio a; (disturb) disturbare ● vi preoccuparsi ⟨**about** di⟩; **don't ~** lascia perdere

bottle /'bɒtl/ n bottiglia f; (baby's) bibe-

ron m inv ● vt imbottigliare. **bottle up** vt fig reprimere

bottle: ~ bank n contenitore m per la raccolta del vetro. **~-neck** n fig ingorgo m. **~-opener** n apribottiglie m inv

bottom /'bɒtm/ a ultimo; **the ~ shelf** l'ultimo scaffale in basso ● n (of container) fondo m; (of river) fondale m; (of hill) piedi mpl; (buttocks) sedere m; **at the ~ of the page** in fondo alla pagina; **get to the ~ of** fig vedere cosa c'è sotto. **~less** a senza fondo

bough /baʊ/ n ramoscello m

bought /bɔːt/ see **buy**

boulder /'bəʊldə(r)/ n masso m

bounce /baʊns/ vi rimbalzare; ⟨fam: cheque:⟩ essere respinto ● vt far rimbalzare ⟨ball⟩

bouncer /'baʊnsə(r)/ n fam buttafuori m inv

bound¹ /baʊnd/ n balzo m ● vi balzare

bound² see **bind** ● a **~ for** ⟨ship⟩ diretto a; **be ~ to do** ⟨likely⟩ dovere fare per forza; ⟨obliged⟩ essere costretto a fare

boundary /'baʊndərɪ/ n limite m

'boundless a illimitato

bounds /baʊndz/ npl fig limiti mpl; **out of ~** fuori dai limiti

bouquet /bʊ'keɪ/ n mazzo m di fiori; (of wine) bouquet m

bourgeois /'bʊəʒwɑː/ a pej borghese

bout /baʊt/ n Med attacco m; Sport incontro m

bow¹ /bəʊ/ n (weapon) arco m; Mus archetto m; (knot) nodo m

bow² /baʊ/ n inchino m ● vi inchinarsi ● vt piegare ⟨head⟩

bow³ /baʊ/ n Naut prua f

bowel /baʊəl/ n intestino m; **~s** pl intestini mpl

bowl¹ /bəʊl/ n (for soup, cereal) scodella f; (of pipe) fornello m

bowl² n (ball) boccia f ● vt lanciare ● vi Cricket servire; (in bowls) lanciare. **bowl over** vt buttar giù; (fig: leave speechless) lasciar senza parole

bow-legged /bəʊ'legd/ a dalle gambe storte

bowler¹ /'bəʊlə(r)/ n Cricket lanciatore m; Bowls giocatore m di bocce

bowler² n **~ [hat]** bombetta f

bowling /'bəʊlɪŋ/ n gioco m delle bocce. **~-alley** n pista f da bowling

bowls /bəʊlz/ n gioco m delle bocce

bow-'tie /bəʊ-/ n cravatta f a farfalla

box¹ /bɒks/ n scatola f; Theat palco m

box² vi Sport fare il pugile ● vt **~ sb's ears** dare uno scappaccione a qcno

box|er /'bɒksə(r)/ n pugile m. **~ing** n pugilato m. **B~ing Day** n [giorno m di] Santo Stefano

box: **~-office** n Theat botteghino m. **~-room** n Br sgabuzzino m

boy /bɔɪ/ n ragazzo m; (younger) bambino m

boycott /'bɔɪkɒt/ n boicottaggio m ● vt boicottare

boy: **~friend** n ragazzo m. **~ish** a da ragazzino

bra /brɑː/ n reggiseno m

brace /breɪs/ n sostegno m; (dental) apparecchio m; **~s** npl bretelle fpl ● vt **~ oneself** fig farsi forza (**for** per affrontare)

bracelet /'breɪslɪt/ n braccialetto m

bracing /'breɪsɪŋ/ a tonificante

bracken /'brækn/ n felce f

bracket /'brækɪt/ n mensola f; (group) categoria f; Typ parentesi f inv ● vt mettere fra parentesi

brag /bræg/ vi (pt/pp **bragged**) vantarsi (**about**di)

braid /breɪd/ n (edging) passamano m

braille /breɪl/ n braille m

brain /breɪn/ n cervello m; **~s** pl fig testa fsg

brain: **~child** n invenzione f personale. **~ dead** a Med celebralmente morto; fig fam senza cervello. **~less** a senza cervello. **~wash** vt fare il lavaggio del cervello a. **~wave** n lampo m di genio

brainy /'breɪnɪ/ a (**-ier, -iest**) intelligente

braise /breɪz/ vt brasare

brake /breɪk/ n freno m ● vi frenare. **~-light** n stop m inv

bramble /'bræmbl/ n rovo m; (fruit) mora f

bran /bræn/ n crusca f

branch /brɑːntʃ/ n also fig ramo m; Comm succursale f ● vi (road:) biforcarsi. **branch off** vi biforcarsi. **branch out** vi **~ out into** allargare le proprie attività nel ramo di

brand /brænd/ n marca f; (on animal) marchio m ● vt marcare (animal); fig tacciare (**as** di)

brandish /'brændɪʃ/ vt brandire

brand-new a nuovo fiammante

brandy /'brændɪ/ n brandy m inv

brash /bræʃ/ a sfrontato

brass /brɑːs/ n ottone m; **the ~** Mus gli ottoni mpl; **top ~** fam pezzi mpl grossi. **~ band** n banda f (di soli ottoni)

brassiere /'bræzɪə(r)/ n fml, Am reggipetto m

brat /bræt/ n pej marmocchio, -a mf

bravado /brə'vɑːdəʊ/ n bravata f

brave /breɪv/ a coraggioso ● vt affrontare. **~ry** /-ərɪ/ n coraggio m

brawl /brɔːl/ n rissa f ● vi azzuffarsi

brawn /brɔːn/ n Culin soppressata f

brawny /'brɔːnɪ/ a muscoloso

brazen /'breɪzn/ a sfrontato

brazier /'breɪzɪə(r)/ n braciere m

Brazil /brə'zɪl/ n Brasile m. **~ian** a & n brasiliano, -a mf. **~ nut** n noce f del Brasile

breach /briːtʃ/ n (of law) violazione f; (gap) breccia f; (fig: in party) frattura f; **~ of contract** inadempienza f di contratto; **~ of the peace** violazione f della quiete pubblica ● vt recedere (contract)

bread /bred/ n pane m; **a slice of ~ and butter** una fetta di pane imburrato

bread: **~ bin** n cassetta f portapane inv. **~crumbs** npl briciole fpl; Culin pangrattato m. **~line** n **be on the ~line** essere povero in canna

breadth /bredθ/ n larghezza f

'bread-winner n quello, -a mf che porta i soldi a casa

break /breɪk/ n rottura f; (interval) intervallo m; (interruption) interruzione f; (fam: chance) opportunità f inv ● v (pt **broke**, pp **broken**) ● vt rompere; **~ one's arm** rompersi un braccio ● vi rompersi; (day:) spuntare; (storm:) scoppiare; (news:) diffondersi; (boy's voice:) cambiare. **break away** vi scappare; fig chiudere (**from** con). **break down** vi (machine, car:) guastarsi; (emotionally) cedere ● vt sfondare (door); ripartire (figures). **break into** vt introdursi (con la forza) in; forzare (car). **break off** vt rompere (engagement) ● vi (part of whole:) rompersi. **break out** vi (fight, war:) scoppiare. **break up** vt far cessare (fight); disperdere (crowd) ● vi (crowd:) disperdersi; (couple:) separarsi; Sch iniziare le vacanze

'break|able /'breɪkəbl/ a fragile. **~age** /-ɪdʒ/ n rottura f. **~down** n (of car, machine) guasto m; Med esaurimento m nervoso; (of figures) analisi f inv. **~er** n (wave) frangente m

breakfast /'brekfəst/ n [prima] colazione f

break: **~through** n scoperta f. **~water** n frangiflutti m inv

breast /brest/ n seno m. **~-feed** vt allattare [al seno]. **~-stroke** n nuoto m a rana

breath /breθ/ n respiro m, fiato m; **out of ~** senza fiato

breathalyse /'breθəlaɪz/ vt sottoporre alla prova [etilica] del palloncino. **~r®** n Br alcoltest m inv

breathe /briːð/ vt/i respirare. **breathe in** vi inspirare ● vt respirare ⟨scent, air⟩. **breathe out** vt/i espirare

breath|er /'briːðə(r)/ n pausa f. **~ing** n respirazione f

breath /breθ/ n: **~less** a senza fiato. **~-taking** a mozzafiato. **~ test** n prova [etilica] f del palloncino

bred /bred/ see **breed**

breed /briːd/ n razza f ● v (pt/pp **bred**) ● vt allevare; ⟨give rise to⟩ generare ● vi riprodursi. **~er** n allevatore, -trice mf. **~ing** n allevamento m; fig educazione f

breez|e /briːz/ n brezza f. **~y** a ventoso

brew /bruː/ n infuso m ● vt mettere in infusione ⟨tea⟩; produrre ⟨beer⟩ ● vi fig ⟨trouble:⟩ essere nell'aria. **~er** n birraio m. **~ery** n fabbrica f di birra

bribe /braɪb/ n ⟨money⟩ bustarella f; ⟨large sum of money⟩ tangente f ● vt corrompere. **~ry** /-ərɪ/ n corruzione f

brick /brɪk/ n mattone m. **~layer** n muratore m ● **brick up** vt murare

bridal /'braɪdl/ a nuziale

bride /braɪd/ n sposa f. **~groom** n sposo m. **~smaid** n damigella f d'onore

bridge¹ /brɪdʒ/ n ponte m; ⟨of nose⟩ setto m nasale; ⟨of spectacles⟩ ponticello m ● vt fig colmare ⟨gap⟩

bridge² n Cards bridge m

bridle /'braɪdl/ n briglia f

brief¹ /briːf/ a breve

brief² n istruzioni fpl; ⟨Jur: case⟩ causa f ● vt dare istruzioni a; Jur affidare la causa a. **~case** n cartella f

brief|ing /'briːfɪŋ/ n briefing m inv. **~ly** adv brevemente. **~ly,...** in breve,.... **~ness** n brevità f

briefs /briːfs/ npl slip m inv

brigad|e /brɪ'geɪd/ n brigata f. **~ier** /-ə'dɪə(r)/ n generale m di brigata

bright /braɪt/ a ⟨metal, idea⟩ brillante; ⟨day, room, future⟩ luminoso; ⟨clever⟩ intelligente. **~ red** rosso m acceso

bright|en /'braɪtn/ v **~en [up]** ● vt ravvivare; rallegrare ⟨person⟩ ● vi ⟨weather:⟩ schiarirsi; ⟨face:⟩ illuminarsi; ⟨person:⟩ rallegrarsi. **~ly** adv ⟨shine⟩ intensamente; ⟨smile⟩ allegramente. **~ness** n luminosità f; ⟨intelligence⟩ intelligenza f

brilliance /'brɪljəns/ n luminosità f; ⟨of person⟩ genialità f

brilliant /'brɪljənt/ a ⟨very good⟩ eccezionale; ⟨very intelligent⟩ brillante; ⟨sunshine⟩ splendente

brim /brɪm/ n bordo m; ⟨of hat⟩ tesa f ● **brim over** vi (pt/pp **brimmed**) traboccare

brine /braɪn/ n salamoia f

bring /brɪŋ/ vt (pt/pp **brought**) portare ⟨person, object⟩. **bring about** vt causare. **bring along** vt portare [con sé]. **bring back** vt restituire ⟨sth borrowed⟩; reintrodurre ⟨hanging⟩; fare ritornare in mente ⟨memories⟩. **bring down** vt portare giù; fare cadere ⟨government⟩; fare abbassare ⟨price⟩. **bring off** vt **~ sth off** riuscire a fare qcsa. **bring on** vt ⟨cause⟩ provocare. **bring out** vt ⟨emphasize⟩ mettere in evidenza; pubblicare ⟨book⟩. **bring round** vt portare; ⟨persuade⟩ convincere; far rinvenire ⟨unconscious person⟩. **bring up** vt ⟨vomit⟩ rimettere; allevare ⟨children⟩; tirare fuori ⟨question, subject⟩

brink /brɪŋk/ n orlo m

brisk /brɪsk/ a svelto; ⟨person⟩ sbrigativo; ⟨trade, business⟩ redditizio; ⟨walk⟩ a passo spedito

brist|le /'brɪsl/ n setola f ● vi **~ling with** pieno di. **~ly** a ⟨chin⟩ ispido

Brit|ain /'brɪtn/ n Gran Bretagna f. **~ish** a britannico; ⟨ambassador⟩ della Gran Bretagna ● npl the **~ish** il popolo britannico. **~on** n cittadino, -a britannico, -a mf

brittle /'brɪtl/ a fragile

broach /brəʊtʃ/ vt toccare ⟨subject⟩

broad /brɔːd/ a ampio; ⟨hint⟩ chiaro; ⟨accent⟩ marcato. **two metres ~** largo due metri; **in ~ daylight** in pieno giorno. **~ beans** npl fave fpl

broadcast n trasmissione f ● vt/i (pt/pp -**cast**) trasmettere. **~er** n giornalista mf radiotelevisivo, -a. **~ing** n diffusione f radiotelevisiva; **be in ~ing** lavorare per la televisione/radio

broaden /'brɔːdn/ vt allargare ● vi allargarsi

broadly /'brɔːdlɪ/ adv largamente; **~ [speaking]** generalmente

broad'minded a di larghe vedute

broccoli /'brɒkəlɪ/ n inv broccoli mpl

brochure /'brəʊʃə(r)/ n opuscolo m; ⟨travel ~⟩ dépliant m inv

broke /brəʊk/ see **break** ● a fam al verde

broken /'brəʊkn/ see **break** ● a rotto;

⟨*fig: marriage*⟩ fallito. **~ English** inglese *m* stentato. **~-hearted** *a* affranto

broker /'brəʊkə(r)/ *n* broker *m inv*

brolly /'brɒlɪ/ *n fam* ombrello *m*

bronchitis /brɒŋ'kaɪtɪs/ *n* bronchite *f*

bronze /brɒnz/ *n* bronzo *m* ●*attrib* di bronzo

brooch /brəʊtʃ/ *n* spilla *f*

brood /bru:d/ *n* covata *f*; ⟨*hum: children*⟩ prole *f* ●*vi fig* rimuginare

brook /brʊk/ *n* ruscello *m*

broom /bru:m/ *n* scopa *f*. **~ stick** *n* manico *m* di scopa

broth /brɒθ/ *n* brodo *m*

brothel /'brɒθl/ *n* bordello *m*

brother /'brʌðə(r)/ *n* fratello *m*

brother: **~-in-law** (*pl* **~s-in-law**) cognato *m*. **~ly** *a* fraterno

brought /brɔːt/ *see* **bring**

brow /braʊ/ *n* fronte *f*; ⟨*of hill*⟩ cima *f*

browbeat *vt* (*pt* **-beat**, *pp* **-beaten**) intimidire

brown /braʊn/ *a* marrone; castano ⟨*hair*⟩ ●*n* marrone *m* ●*vt* rosolare ⟨*meat*⟩ ●*vi* ⟨*meat:*⟩ rosolarsi. **~ paper** *n* carta *f* da pacchi

Brownie /'braʊnɪ/ *n* coccinella *f* ⟨*negli scout*⟩

browse /braʊz/ *vi* ⟨*read*⟩ leggicchiare; ⟨*in shop*⟩ curiosare

bruise /bru:z/ *n* livido *m*; ⟨*on fruit*⟩ ammaccatura *f* ●*vt* ammaccare ⟨*fruit*⟩; **~ one's arm** farsi un livido sul braccio. **~d** *a* contuso

brunette /bru:'net/ *n* bruna *f*

brunt /brʌnt/ *n* **bear the ~ of sth** subire maggiormente qcsa

brush /brʌʃ/ *n* spazzola *f*; ⟨*with long handle*⟩ spazzolone *m*; ⟨*for paint*⟩ pennello *m*; ⟨*bushes*⟩ boscaglia *f*; ⟨*fig: conflict*⟩ breve scontro *m* ●*vt* spazzolare ⟨*hair*⟩; lavarsi ⟨*teeth*⟩; scopare ⟨*stairs, floor*⟩. **brush against** *vt* sfiorare. **brush aside** *vt fig* ignorare. **brush off** *vt* spazzolare; ⟨*with hands*⟩ togliere; ignorare ⟨*criticism*⟩. **brush up** *vt/i fig* **~ up** [**on**] rinfrescare

brusque /brʊsk/ *a* brusco

Brussels /'brʌslz/ *n* Bruxelles *f*. **~ sprouts** *npl* cavoletti *mpl* di Bruxelles

brutal /'bru:tl/ *a* brutale. **~ity** /-'tælɪtɪ/ *n* brutalità *f inv*

brute /bru:t/ *n* bruto *m*. **~ force** *n* forza *f* bruta

BSc *n abbr* Bachelor of Science

BSE *n abbr* (**bovine spongiform encephalitis**) encefalite *f* bovina spongiforme

bubble /'bʌbl/ *n* bolla *f*; ⟨*in drink*⟩ bollicina *f*

buck[1] /bʌk/ *n* maschio *m* del cervo; ⟨*rabbit*⟩ maschio *m* del coniglio ●*vi* ⟨*horse:*⟩ saltare a quattro zampe. **buck up** *vi fam* tirarsi su; ⟨*hurry*⟩ sbrigarsi

buck[2] *n Am fam* dollaro *m*

buck[3] *n* **pass the ~** scaricare la responsabilità

bucket /'bʌkɪt/ *n* secchio *m*

buckle /'bʌkl/ *n* fibbia *f* ●*vt* allacciare ●*vi* ⟨*shelf:*⟩ piegarsi; ⟨*wheel:*⟩ storcersi

bud /bʌd/ *n* bocciolo *m*

Buddhis|m /'bʊdɪzm/ *n* buddismo *m*. **~t** *a & n* buddista *mf*

buddy /'bʌdɪ/ *n fam* amico, -a *mf*

budge /bʌdʒ/ *vt* spostare ●*vi* spostarsi

budgerigar /'bʌdʒərɪgɑ:(r)/ *n* cocorita *f*

budget /'bʌdʒɪt/ *n* bilancio *m*; ⟨*allotted to specific activity*⟩ budget *m inv* ●*vi* (*pt/pp* **budgeted**) prevedere le spese; **~ for sth** includere qcsa nelle spese previste

buff /bʌf/ *a* ⟨*colour*⟩ [color] camoscio ●*n fam* fanatico, -a *mf*

buffalo /'bʌfələʊ/ *n* (*inv or pl* **-es**) bufalo *m*

buffer /'bʌfə(r)/ *n* Rail respingente *m*; **old ~** *fam* vecchio bacucco *m*. **~ zone** *n* zona *f* cuscinetto

buffet[1] /'bʊfeɪ/ *n* buffet *m inv*

buffet[2] /'bʌfɪt/ *vt* (*pt/pp* **buffeted**) sferzare

buffoon /bə'fu:n/ *n* buffone, -a *mf*

bug /bʌg/ *n* ⟨*insect*⟩ insetto *m*; Comput bug *m inv*; ⟨*fam: device*⟩ cimice *f* ●*vt* (*pt/pp* **bugged**) *fam* installare delle microspie in ⟨*room*⟩; mettere sotto controllo ⟨*telephone*⟩; ⟨*fam: annoy*⟩ scocciare

buggy /'bʌgɪ/ *n* [**baby**] **~** passeggino *m*

bugle /'bju:gl/ *n* tromba *f*

build /bɪld/ *n* ⟨*of person*⟩ corporatura *f* ●*vt/i* (*pt/pp* **built**) costruire. **build on** *vt* aggiungere ⟨*extra storey*⟩; sviluppare ⟨*previous work*⟩. **build up** *vt* **~ up one's strength** rimettersi in forza ●*vi* ⟨*pressure, traffic:*⟩ aumentare; ⟨*excitement, tension:*⟩ crescere

builder /'bɪldə(r)/ *n* ⟨*company*⟩ costruttore *m*; ⟨*worker*⟩ muratore *m*

building /'bɪldɪŋ/ *n* edificio *m*. **~ site** *n* cantiere *m* [di costruzione]. **~ society** *n* istituto *m* di credito immobiliare

build-up *n* ⟨*of gas etc*⟩ accumulo *m*; *fig* battage *m inv* pubblicitario

built /bɪlt/ *see* **build**. **~-in** *a* ⟨*unit*⟩ a

269

bulb | bus

muro; ⟨fig: feature⟩ incorporato. **~-up area** n Auto centro m abitato

bulb /bʌlb/ n bulbo m; ⟨Electr⟩ lampadina f

bulge /bʌldʒ/ n rigonfiamento m ● vi esser gonfio ⟨with di⟩; ⟨stomach, wall:⟩ sporgere; ⟨eyes, with surprise:⟩ uscire dalle orbite. **~ing** a gonfio; ⟨eyes⟩ sporgente

bulk /bʌlk/ n volume m; ⟨greater part⟩ grosso m; **in ~** in grande quantità; ⟨loose⟩ sfuso. **~y** a voluminoso

bull /bʊl/ n toro m

bulldog n bulldog m inv

bulldozer /bʊldəʊzə(r)/ n bull-dozer m inv

bullet /bʊlɪt/ n pallottola f

bulletin /bʊlɪtɪn/ n bollettino m. **~ board** n Comput bacheca f elettronica

bullet-proof a antiproiettile inv; ⟨vehicle⟩ blindato

bullfight n corrida f. **~er** n torero m

bullion /bʊljən/ n **gold ~** oro m in lingotti

bullock /bʊlək/ n manzo m

bull: **~ring** n arena f. **~'s-eye** n centro m del bersaglio; **score a ~'s-eye** fare centro

bully /bʊlɪ/ n prepotente mf ● vt fare il/la prepotente con. **~ing** n prepotenze fpl

bum[1] /bʌm/ n sl sedere m

bum[2] n Am fam vagabondo, -a m f ● **bum around** vi fam vagabondare

bumble-bee /bʌmbl-/ n calabrone m

bump /bʌmp/ n botta f; ⟨swelling⟩ bozzo m, gonfiore m; ⟨in road⟩ protuberanza f ● vt sbattere. **bump into** vt sbattere contro; ⟨meet⟩ imbattersi in. **bump off** vt fam far fuori

bumper /bʌmpə(r)/ n Auto paraurti m inv ● a abbondante

bumpkin /bʌmpkɪn/ n **country ~** zoticone, -a mf

bumptious /bʌmpʃəs/ a presuntuoso

bumpy /bʌmpɪ/ a ⟨road⟩ accidentato; ⟨flight⟩ turbolento

bun /bʌn/ n focaccina f ⟨dolce⟩; ⟨hair⟩ chignon m inv

bunch /bʌntʃ/ n ⟨of flowers, keys⟩ mazzo m; ⟨of bananas⟩ casco m; ⟨of people⟩ gruppo m; **~ of grapes** grappolo m d'uva

bundle /bʌndl/ n fascio m; ⟨of money⟩ mazzetta f; **a ~ of nerves** fam un fascio di nervi ● vt **~ [up]** affastellare

bung /bʌŋ/ vt fam ⟨throw⟩ buttare. **bung up** vt ⟨block⟩ otturare

bungalow /bʌŋgələʊ/ n bungalow m inv

bungle /bʌŋgl/ vt fare un pasticcio di

bunion /bʌnjən/ n Med callo m all'alluce

bunk /bʌŋk/ n cuccetta f. **~-beds** npl letti mpl a castello

bunny /bʌnɪ/ n fam coniglietto m

buoy /bɔɪ/ n boa f

buoyan|cy /bɔɪənsɪ/ n galleggiabilità f. **~t** a ⟨boat⟩ galleggiante; ⟨water⟩ che aiuta a galleggiare

burden /bɜːdn/ n carico m ● vt caricare. **~some** /-səm/ a gravoso

bureau /bjʊərəʊ/ n (pl -x /-əʊz/ or ~s) ⟨desk⟩ scrivania f; ⟨office⟩ ufficio m

bureaucracy /bjʊəˈrɒkrəsɪ/ n burocrazia f

bureaucrat /bjʊərəkræt/ n burocrate mf. **~ic** /-ˈkrætɪk/ a burocratico

burger /bɜːgə(r)/ n hamburger m inv

burglar /bɜːglə(r)/ n svaligiatore, -trice mf. **~ alarm** n antifurto m inv

burglar|ize /bɜːgləraɪz/ vt Am svaligiare. **~y** n furto m con scasso

burgle /bɜːgl/ vt svaligiare

Burgundy /bɜːgəndɪ/ n Borgogna f

burial /berɪəl/ n sepoltura f. **~ ground** n cimitero m

burlesque /bɜːˈlesk/ n parodia f

burly /bɜːlɪ/ a (-ier, -iest) corpulento

Burma /bɜːmə/ n Birmania f. **~ese** /-ˈmiːz/ a & n birmano, -a mf

burn /bɜːn/ n bruciatura f ● v (pt/pp burnt or burned) ● vt bruciare ● vi bruciare. **burn down** vt/i bruciare. **burn out** vi fig esaurirsi. **~er** ⟨on stove⟩ bruciatore m

burnish /bɜːnɪʃ/ vt lucidare

burnt /bɜːnt/ see burn

burp /bɜːp/ n fam rutto m ● vi fam ruttare

burrow /bʌrəʊ/ n tana f ● vt scavare ⟨hole⟩

bursar /bɜːsə(r)/ n economo, -a mf. **~y** n borsa f di studio

burst /bɜːst/ n ⟨of gunfire, energy, laughter⟩ scoppio m; ⟨of speed⟩ scatto m ● v (pt/pp burst) ● vt far scoppiare ● vi scoppiare; **~ into tears** scoppiare in lacrime; **she ~ into the room** ha fatto irruzione nella stanza. **burst out** vi **~ out laughing/crying** scoppiare a ridere/piangere

bury /berɪ/ vt (pt/pp -ied) seppellire; ⟨hide⟩ nascondere

bus /bʌs/ n autobus m inv, pullman m

bush | byword

inv; (*long distance*) pullman *m inv*, corriera *f*

bush /bʊʃ/ *n* cespuglio *m*; (*land*) boscaglia *f*. **~y** *a* (**-ier, -iest**) folto

busily /ˈbɪzɪlɪ/ *adv* con grande impegno

business /ˈbɪznɪs/ *n* affare *m*; *Comm* affari *mpl*; (*establishment*) attività *f* di commercio; **on ~** per affari; **he has no ~ to** non ha alcun diritto di; **mind one's own ~** farsi gli affari propri; **that's none of your ~** non sono affari tuoi. **~-like** *a* efficiente. **~man** *n* uomo *m* d'affari. **~woman** *n* donna *f* d'affari

busker /ˈbʌskə(r)/ *n* suonatore, -trice *mf* ambulante

bus station *n* stazione *f* degli autobus

bus-stop *n* fermata *f* d'autobus

bust¹ /bʌst/ *n* busto *m*; (*chest*) petto *m*

bust² *a fam* rotto; **go ~** fallire ● *v* (*pt/pp* **busted** *or* **bust**) *fam* ● *vt* far scoppiare ● *vi* scoppiare

bustl|e /ˈbʌsl/ *n* (*activity*) trambusto *m* ● **bustle about** *vi* affannarsi. **~ing** *a* animato

bust-up *n fam* lite *f*

busy /ˈbɪzɪ/ *a* (**-ier, -iest**) occupato; (*day, time*) intenso; (*street*) affollato; (*with traffic*) pieno di traffico; **be ~ doing** essere occupato a fare ● *vt* **~ oneself** darsi da fare

busybody *n* ficcanaso *mf inv*

but /bʌt/, *atono* /bət/ *conj* ma ● *prep* eccetto, tranne; **nobody ~ you** nessuno tranne te; **~ for** (*without*) se non fosse stato per; **the last ~ one** il penultimo; **the next ~ one** il secondo ● *adv* (*only*) soltanto; **there were ~ two** ce n'erano soltanto due

butcher /ˈbʊtʃə(r)/ *n* macellaio *m*; **~'s** [**shop**] macelleria *f* ● *vt* macellare; *fig* massacrare

butler /ˈbʌtlə(r)/ *n* maggiordomo *m*

butt /bʌt/ *n* (*of gun*) calcio *m*; (*of cigarette*) mozzicone *m*; (*for water*) barile *m*; (*fig: target*) bersaglio *m* ● *vt* dare una testata a; (*goat:*) dare una cornata a. **butt in** *vi* interrompere

butter /ˈbʌtə(r)/ *n* burro *m* ● *vt* imburrare. **butter up** *vt fam* arruffianarsi

butter: **~cup** *n* ranuncolo *m*. **~fingers** *nsg fam* **be a ~fingers** avere le mani di pasta frolla. **~fly** *n* farfalla *f*

buttocks /ˈbʌtəks/ *npl* natiche *fpl*

button /ˈbʌtn/ *n* bottone *m* ● *vt* ~ [**up**] abbottonare ● *vi* ~ [**up**] abbottonarsi. **~hole** *n* occhiello *m*, asola *f*

buttress /ˈbʌtrɪs/ *n* contrafforte *m*

buxom /ˈbʌksəm/ *a* formosa

buy /baɪ/ *n* good/bad ~ buon/cattivo acquisto *m* ● *vt* (*pt/pp* **bought**) comprare; ~ **sb a drink** pagare da bere a qcno; **I'll ~ this one** (*drink*) questo, lo offro io. **~er** *n* compratore, -trice *mf*

buzz /bʌz/ *n* ronzio *m*; **give sb a ~** *fam* (*on phone*) dare un colpo di telefono a qcno; (*excite*) mettere in fermento qcno ● *vi* ronzare ● *vt* ~ **sb** chiamare qcno col cicalino. **buzz off** *vi fam* levarsi di torno

buzzer /ˈbʌzə(r)/ *n* cicalino *m*

by /baɪ/ *prep* (*near, next to*) vicino a; (*at the latest*) per; **by Mozart** di Mozart; **he was run over by a bus** è stato investito da un autobus; **by oneself** da solo; **by the sea** al mare; **by sea** via mare; **by car/bus** in macchina/autobus; **by day/ night** di giorno/notte; **by the hour/ metre** a ore/metri; **six metres by four** sei metri per quattro; **he won by six metres** ha vinto di sei metri; **I missed the train by a minute** ho perso il treno per un minuto; **I'll be home by six** sarò a casa per le sei; **by this time next week** a quest'ora tra una settimana; **he rushed by me** mi è passato accanto di corsa ● *adv* **she'll be here by and by** sarà qui fra poco; **by and large** in complesso

bye[-bye] /baɪ('baɪ)/ *int fam* ciao

by: **~-election** *n* elezione *f* straordinaria indetta per coprire una carica rimasta vacante in Parlamento. **~gone** *a* passato. **~-law** *n* legge *f* locale. **~pass** *n* circonvallazione *f*; *Med* by-pass *m inv* ● *vt* evitare. **~-product** *n* sottoprodotto *m*. **~stander** *n* spettatore, -trice *mf*. **~word** *n* **be a ~word for** essere sinonimo di

Cc

cab /kæb/ n taxi m inv; (of lorry, train) cabina f

cabaret /'kæbəreɪ/ n cabaret m inv

cabbage /'kæbɪdʒ/ n cavolo m

cabin /'kæbɪn/ n (of plane, ship) cabina f; (hut) capanna f

cabinet /'kæbɪnɪt/ n armadietto m; [display] ~ vetrina f; C~ Pol consiglio m dei ministri. **~-maker** n ebanista mf

cable /'keɪbl/ n cavo m. ~ **railway** n funicolare f. ~ **television** n televisione f via cavo

cache /kæʃ/ n nascondiglio m; ~ of **arms** deposito m segreto di armi

cackle /'kækl/ vi ridacchiare

cactus /'kæktəs/ n (pl **-ti** /-taɪ/ or **-tuses**) cactus m inv

caddie /'kædɪ/ n portabastoni m inv

caddy /'kædɪ/ n [tea-]~ barattolo m del tè

cadet /kə'det/ n cadetto m

cadge /kædʒ/ vt/i fam scroccare

Caesarean /sɪ'zeərɪən/ n parto m cesareo

café /'kæfeɪ/ n caffè m inv

cafeteria /kæfə'tɪərɪə/ n tavola f calda

caffeine /'kæfi:n/ n caffeina f

cage /keɪdʒ/ n gabbia f

cagey /'keɪdʒɪ/ a fam riservato (**about** su)

cajole /kə'dʒəʊl/ vt persuadere con le lusinghe

cake /keɪk/ n torta f; (small) pasticcino m. ~d a incrostato (**with** di)

calamity /kə'læmɪtɪ/ n calamità f inv

calcium /'kælsɪəm/ n calcio m

calculat|e /'kælkjʊleɪt/ vt calcolare. **~ing** a fig calcolatore. **~ion** /-'leɪʃn/ n calcolo m. **~or** n calcolatrice f

calendar /'kælɪndə(r)/ n calendario m

calf¹ /kɑ:f/ n (pl **calves**) vitello m

calf² n (pl **calves**) Anat polpaccio m

calibre /'kælɪbə(r)/ n calibro m

call /kɔ:l/ n grido m; Teleph telefonata f; (visit) visita f; **be on** ~ (doctor:) essere di guardia ● vt chiamare; indire (strike); **be** ~**ed** chiamarsi ● vi chiamare; ~ [**in** or **round**] passare. **call back** vt/i richiamare. **call for** vt (ask

for) chiedere; (require) richiedere; (fetch) passare a prendere. **call off** vt richiamare (dog); disdire (meeting); revocare (strike). **call on** vt chiamare; (appeal to) fare un appello a; (visit) visitare. **call out** vt chiamare ad alta voce (names) ● vi chiamare ad alta voce. **call together** vt riunire. **call up** vt Mil chiamare alle armi; Teleph chiamare

call: ~**-box** n cabina f telefonica. **~er** n visitatore, -trice mf; Teleph persona f che telefona. **~ing** n vocazione f

callous /'kæləs/ a insensibile

call-up n Mil chiamata f alle armi

calm /kɑ:m/ a calmo ● n calma f. **calm down** vt calmare ● vi calmarsi. **~ly** adv con calma

calorie /'kælərɪ/ n caloria f

calves /kɑ:vz/ npl see **calf¹** & ²

camber /'kæmbə(r)/ n curvatura f

Cambodia /kæm'bəʊdɪə/ n Cambogia f. **~n** a & n cambogiano, -a mf

camcorder /'kæmkɔ:də(r)/ n videocamera f

came /keɪm/ see **come**

camel /'kæml/ n cammello m

camera /'kæmərə/ n macchina f fotografica; TV telecamera f. **~man** n operatore m [televisivo], cameraman m inv

camouflage /'kæməflɑ:ʒ/ n mimetizzazione f ● vt mimetizzare

camp /kæmp/ n campeggio f; Mil campo m ● vi campeggiare; Mil accamparsi

campaign /kæm'peɪn/ n campagna f ● vi fare una campagna

camp: ~**-bed** n letto m da campo. **~er** n campeggiatore, -trice mf; Auto camper m inv. **~ing** n campeggio m. **~site** n campeggio m

campus /'kæmpəs/ n (pl **-puses**) Univ città f universitaria, campus m inv

can¹ /kæn/ n (for petrol) latta f; (tin) scatola f; ~ **of beer** lattina f di birra ● vt mettere in scatola

can² /kæn/, atono /kən/ v aux (pres **can**; pt **could**) (be able to) potere; (know how to) sapere; **I cannot** or **can't go** non posso andare; **he could not** or **couldn't go** non poteva andare; **she**

can't swim non sa nuotare; **I ~ smell something burning** sento odor di bruciato

Canad|a /'kænədə/ n Canada m. **~ian** /kə'neɪdɪən/ a & n canadese mf

canal /kə'næl/ n canale m

Canaries /kə'neərɪz/ npl Canarie fpl

canary /kə'neərɪ/ n canarino m

cancel /'kænsl/ v (pt/pp **cancelled**) ● vt disdire ⟨meeting, newspaper⟩; revocare ⟨contract, order⟩; annullare ⟨reservation, appointment, stamp⟩. **~lation** /-ə'leɪʃn/ n (of meeting, contract) revoca f; (in hotel, restaurant, for flight) cancellazione f

cancer /'kænsə(r)/ n cancro m; **C~** Astr Cancro m. **~ous** /-rəs/ a canceroso

candelabra /kændə'lɑːbrə/ n candelabro m

candid /'kændɪd/ a franco

candidate /'kændɪdət/ n candidato, -a mf

candle /'kændl/ n candela f. **~stick** n portacandele m inv

candour /'kændə(r)/ n franchezza f

candy /'kændɪ/ n Am caramella f; a **[piece of] ~** una caramella. **~floss** /-flɒs/ n zucchero m filato

cane /keɪn/ n (stick) bastone m; Sch bacchetta f ● vt prendere a bacchettate ⟨pupil⟩

canine /'keɪnaɪn/ a canino. **~ tooth** n canino m

canister /'kænɪstə(r)/ n barattolo m (di metallo)

cannabis /'kænəbɪs/ n cannabis f

canned /kænd/ a in scatola; **~ music** fam musica f registrata

cannibal /'kænəbl/ n cannibale mf. **~ism** n cannibalismo m

cannon /'kænən/ n inv cannone m. **~-ball** n palla f di cannone

cannot /'kænɒt/ see can²

canny /'kænɪ/ a astuto

canoe /kə'nuː/ n canoa f ● vi andare in canoa

'can-opener n apriscatole m inv

canopy /'kænəpɪ/ n baldacchino f; (of parachute) calotta f

can't /kɑːnt/ = **cannot** see can²

cantankerous /kæn'tæŋkərəs/ a stizzoso

canteen /kæn'tiːn/ n mensa f; **~ of cutlery** servizio m di posate

canter /'kæntə(r)/ vi andare a piccolo galoppo

canvas /'kænvəs/ n tela f; (painting) dipinto m su tela

canvass /'kænvəs/ vi Pol fare propaganda elettorale. **~ing** n sollecitazione f di voti

canyon /'kænjən/ n canyon m inv

cap /kæp/ n berretto m; (nurse's) cuffia f; (top, lid) tappo m ● vt (pt/pp**capped**) (fig: do better than) superare

capability /keɪpə'bɪlətɪ/ n capacità f

capab|le /'keɪpəbl/ a capace; (skilful) abile; **be ~e of doing sth** essere capace di fare qcsa. **~y** adv con abilità

capacity /kə'pæsətɪ/ n capacità f; (function) qualità f; **in my ~ as** in qualità di

cape¹ /keɪp/ n (cloak) cappa f

cape² n Geog capo m

caper¹ /'keɪpə(r)/ vi saltellare ● n fam birichinata f

caper² n Culin cappero m

capital /'kæpɪtl/ n (town) capitale f; (money) capitale m; (letter) lettera f maiuscola. **~ city** n capitale f

capital|ism /'kæpɪtəlɪzm/ n capitalismo m. **~ist** /-ɪst/ a & n capitalista mf. **~ize** /-aɪz/ vi **~ize on** fig trarre vantaggio da. **~ 'letter** n lettera f maiuscola. **~ 'punishment** n pena f capitale

capitulat|e /kə'pɪtjʊleɪt/ vi capitolare. **~ion** /-'leɪʃn/ n capitolazione f

capricious /kə'prɪʃəs/ a capriccioso

Capricorn /'kæprɪkɔːn/ n Astr Capricorno m

capsize /kæp'saɪz/ vi capovolgersi ● vt capovolgere

capsule /'kæpsjʊl/ n capsula f

captain /'kæptɪn/ n capitano m ● vt comandare ⟨team⟩

caption /'kæpʃn/ n intestazione f; (of illustration) didascalia f

captivate /'kæptɪveɪt/ vt incantare

captiv|e /'kæptɪv/ a prigioniero; **hold/take ~e** tenere/fare prigioniero ● n prigioniero, -a mf. **~ity** /-'tɪvɪtɪ/ n prigionia f; (animals) cattività f

capture /'kæptʃə(r)/ n cattura f ● vt catturare; attirare ⟨attention⟩

car /kɑː(r)/ n macchina f; **by ~** in macchina

carafe /kə'ræf/ n caraffa f

caramel /'kærəmel/ n (sweet) caramella f al mou; Culin caramello m

carat /'kærət/ n carato m

caravan /'kærəvæn/ n roulotte f inv; (horse-drawn) carovana f

carbohydrate /kɑːbə'haɪdreɪt/ n carboidrato m

carbon /'kɑːbən/ n carbonio m

carbon: ~ copy n copia f in carta car-

bone; ⟨fig: person⟩ ritratto m. ~
di'oxide n anidride f carbonica. ~
paper n carta f carbone
carburettor /ˌkaːbjʊˈretə(r)/ n carbu-
ratore m
carcass /ˈkaːkəs/ n carcassa f
card /kaːd/ n ⟨for birthday, Christmas
etc⟩ biglietto m di auguri; ⟨playing ~⟩
carta f [da gioco]; ⟨membership ~⟩ tessera f; ⟨business ~⟩ biglietto m da visita;
⟨credit ~⟩ carta f di credito; Comput
scheda f
'cardboard n cartone m. ~ 'box n scatola f di cartone; ⟨large⟩ scatolone m
'card-game n gioco m di carte
cardiac /ˈkaːdɪæk/ a cardiaco
cardigan /ˈkaːdɪɡən/ n cardigan m inv
cardinal /ˈkaːdɪnl/ a cardinale; ~
number numero m cardinale. ● n Relig
cardinale m
card 'index n schedario m
care /keə(r)/ n cura f; ⟨caution⟩ attenzione f; ⟨worry⟩ preoccupazione f. ~ of
⟨on letter abbr c/o⟩ presso; take ~ ⟨be
cautious⟩ fare attenzione; bye, take ~
ciao, stammi bene; take ~ of
occuparsi di; be taken into ~ essere
preso in custodia da un ente
assistenziale ● vi ~ about interessarsi
di; ~ for ⟨feel affection for⟩ volere bene
a; ⟨look after⟩ aver cura di; I don't ~ for
chocolate non mi piace il cioccolato; I
don't ~ non me ne importa; who ~s?
chi se ne frega?
career /kəˈrɪə(r)/ n carriera f;
⟨profession⟩ professione f ● vi andare a
tutta velocità
care: ~free a spensierato. ~ful a attento; ⟨driver⟩ prudente. ~fully adv con
attenzione. ~less a irresponsabile; ⟨in
work⟩ trascurato; ⟨work⟩ fatto con poca
cura; ⟨driver⟩ distratto. ~lessly adv
negligentemente. ~lessness n trascuratezza f. ~r n persona f che accudisce a
un anziano o a un malato
caress /kəˈres/ n carezza f ● vt accarezzare
'caretaker n custode mf; ⟨in school⟩ bidello m
'car ferry n traghetto m ⟨per il trasporto di auto⟩
cargo /ˈkaːɡəʊ/ n ⟨pl -es⟩ carico m
Caribbean /ˌkærɪˈbiːən/ n the ~ ⟨sea⟩
il Mar dei Caraibi ● a caraibico
caricature /ˈkærɪkətjʊə(r)/ n carica-
tura f
caring /ˈkeərɪŋ/ a ⟨parent⟩ premuroso;

⟨attitude⟩ altruista; the ~ professions
le attività assistenziali
carnage /ˈkaːnɪdʒ/ n carneficina f
carnal /ˈkaːnl/ a carnale
carnation /kaːˈneɪʃn/ n garofano m
carnival /ˈkaːnɪvl/ n carnevale m
carnivorous /kaːˈnɪvərəs/ a carnivo-
ro
carol /ˈkærəl/ n [Christmas] ~ canzone f natalizia
carp¹ /kaːp/ n inv carpa f
carp² vi ~ at trovare da ridire su
'car park n parcheggio m
carpent|er /ˈkaːpɪntə(r)/ n falegname
m. ~ry n falegnameria f
carpet /ˈkaːpɪt/ n tappeto m; ⟨wall-to-
wall⟩ moquette f inv ● vt mettere la
moquette in ⟨room⟩
'car phone n telefono m in macchina
carriage /ˈkærɪdʒ/ n carrozza f; ⟨of
goods⟩ trasporto m; ⟨cost⟩ spese fpl di
trasporto; ⟨bearing⟩ portamento m;
~way n strada f carrozzabile; north-
bound ~way carreggiata f nord
carrier /ˈkærɪə(r)/ n ⟨company⟩ impresa f di trasporti; Aeron compagnia f di
trasporto aereo; ⟨of disease⟩ portatore
m. ~ [bag] n borsa f [per la spesa]
carrot /ˈkærət/ n carota f
carr|y /ˈkærɪ/ v ⟨pt/pp -ied⟩ ● vt porta-
re; ⟨transport⟩ trasportare; get carried
away fam lasciarsi prender la mano
● vi ⟨sound:⟩ trasmettersi. carry off vt
portare via; vincere ⟨prize⟩. carry on vi
continuare; ⟨fam: make scene⟩ fare delle
storie; ~ with sth continuare qcsa;
~ on with sb fam intendersela con
qcno ● vt mantenere ⟨business⟩. carry
out vt portare fuori; eseguire
⟨instructions, task⟩; mettere in atto
⟨threat⟩; effettuare ⟨experiment, survey⟩
'carry-cot n porte-enfant m inv
cart /kaːt/ n carretto m ● vt ⟨fam:
carry⟩ portare
cartilage /ˈkaːtɪlɪdʒ/ n Anat cartilagine f
carton /ˈkaːtn/ n scatola f di cartone;
⟨for drink⟩ cartone m; ⟨of cream, yo-
ghurt⟩ vasetto m; ⟨of cigarettes⟩ stecca f
cartoon /kaːˈtuːn/ n vignetta f; ⟨strip⟩
vignette fpl; ⟨film⟩ cartone m animato;
⟨in art⟩ bozzetto m. ~ist n vignettista
mf; ⟨for films⟩ disegnatore, -trice mf di
cartoni animati
cartridge /ˈkaːtrɪdʒ/ n cartuccia f; ⟨for
film⟩ bobina f; ⟨of record player⟩ testi-
na f
carve /kaːv/ vt scolpire; tagliare ⟨meat⟩

carving /'kɑːvɪŋ/ n scultura f. **~-knife** n trinciante m

'**car wash** n autolavaggio m inv

case¹ /keɪs/ n caso m; **in any ~** in ogni caso; **in that ~** in questo caso; **just in ~** per sicurezza; **in ~ he comes** nel caso in cui venisse

case² n (container) scatola f; (crate) cassa f; (for spectacles) astuccio m; (suitcase) valigia f; (for display) vetrina f

cash /kæʃ/ n denaro m contante; (fam: money) contanti mpl; **pay [in] ~** pagare in contanti; **~ on delivery** pagamento alla consegna ● vt incassare (cheque). **~ desk** n cassa f

cashier /kæ'ʃɪə(r)/ n cassiere, -a mf

'**cash register** n registratore m di cassa

casino /kə'siːnəʊ/ n casinò m inv

casket /'kɑːskɪt/ n scrigno m; (Am: coffin) bara f

casserole /'kæsərəʊl/ n casseruola f; (stew) stufato m

cassette /kə'set/ n cassetta f. **~ recorder** n registratore m (a cassette)

cast /kɑːst/ n (mould) forma f; Theat cast m inv; (plaster) ~ Med ingessatura f ● vt (pt/pp **cast**) dare (vote); Theat assegnare le parti di (play); fondere (metal); (throw) gettare; **~ an actor as** dare ad un attore il ruolo di: **~ a glance at** lanciare uno sguardo a. **cast off** vi Naut sganciare gli ormeggi ● vt (in knitting) diminuire. **cast on** vt (in knitting) avviare

castaway /'kɑːstəweɪ/ n naufrago, -a mf

caste /kɑːst/ n casta f

caster /'kɑːstə(r)/ n (wheel) rotella f. **~ sugar** n zucchero m raffinato

cast iron n ghisa f

cast-iron a di ghisa; fig solido

castle /'kɑːsl/ n castello m; (in chess) torre f

'**cast-offs** npl abiti mpl smessi

castor /'kɑːstə(r)/ n (wheel) rotella f. **~ oil** n olio m di ricino. **~ sugar** n zucchero m raffinato

castrat|e /kæ'streɪt/ vt castrare. **~ion** /-eɪʃn/ n castrazione f

casual /'kæʒʊəl/ a (chance) casuale; (remark) senza importanza; (glance) di sfuggita; (attitude, approach) disinvolto; (chat) informale; (clothes) casual inv; (work) saltuario; **~ wear** abbigliamento m casual. **~ly** adv (dress) casual; (meet) casualmente

casualty /'kæʒʊəltɪ/ n (injured person) ferito m; (killed) vittima f. **~ [department]** n pronto soccorso m

cat /kæt/ n gatto m; pej arpia f

catalogue /'kætəlɒg/ n catalogo m ● vt catalogare

catalyst /'kætəlɪst/ n Chem & fig catalizzatore m

catalytic /kætə'lɪtɪk/ a **~ converter** Auto marmitta f catalitica

catapult /'kætəpʌlt/ n catapulta f; (child's) fionda f ● vt fig catapultare

cataract /'kætərækt/ n Med cataratta f

catarrh /kə'tɑː(r)/ n catarro m

catastroph|e /kə'tæstrəfɪ/ n catastrofe f. **~ic** /kætə'strɒfɪk/ a catastrofico

catch /kætʃ/ n (of fish) pesca f; (fastener) fermaglio m; (on door) fermo m; (on window) gancio m; (fam: snag) tranello m ● v (pt/pp **caught**) ● vt acchiappare (ball); (grab) afferrare; prendere (illness, fugitive, train); **~ a cold** prendersi un raffreddore; **~ sight of** scorgere; **I caught him stealing** l'ho sorpreso mentre rubava; **~ one's finger in the door** chiudersi il dito nella porta; **~ sb's eye** or **attention** attirare l'attenzione di qcno ● vi (fire:) prendere; (get stuck) impigliarsi. **catch on** vi fam (understand) afferrare; (become popular) diventare popolare. **catch up** vt raggiungere ● vi recuperare; (runner:) riguadagnare terreno; **~ up with** raggiungere (sb); mettersi in pari con (work)

catching /'kætʃɪŋ/ a contagioso

catch: ~-phrase n tormentone m. **~word** n slogan m inv

catchy /'kætʃɪ/ a (-ier, -iest) orecchiabile

categor|ical /kætɪ'gɒrɪkl/ a categorico. **~y** /'kætɪgərɪ/ n categoria f

cater /'keɪtə(r)/ vi **~ for** provvedere a (needs); fig venire incontro alle esigenze di. **~ing** n (trade) ristorazione f; (food) rinfresco m

caterpillar /'kætəpɪlə(r)/ n bruco m

cathedral /kə'θiːdrl/ n cattedrale f

Catholic /'kæθəlɪk/ a & n cattolico, -a mf. **~ism** /kə'θɒlɪsɪzm/ n cattolicesimo m

cat's eyes npl catarifrangente msg (inserito nell'asfalto)

cattle /'kætl/ npl bestiame msg

catty /'kætɪ/ a (-ier, -iest) dispettoso

catwalk /'kætwɔːk/ n passerella f

caught /kɔːt/ see **catch**

cauliflower /'kɒlɪ-/ n cavolfiore m

cause /kɔːz/ n causa f ● vt causare; **~ sb to do sth** far fare qcsa a qcno

'causeway n strada f sopraelevata

caustic /'kɔːstɪk/ a caustico

caution /'kɔːʃn/ n cautela f; (warning) ammonizione f ● vt mettere in guardia; Jur ammonire

cautious /'kɔːʃəs/ a cauto

cavalry /'kævəlrɪ/ n cavalleria f

cave /keɪv/ n caverna f ● **cave in** vi ⟨roof:⟩ crollare; ⟨fig: give in⟩ capitolare

cavern /'kævən/ n caverna f

caviare /'kævɪɑː(r)/ n caviale m

caving /'keɪvɪŋ/ n speleologia f

cavity /'kævətɪ/ n cavità f inv; (in tooth) carie f inv

cavort /kə'vɔːt/ vi saltellare

CD n CD m inv. ~ **player** n lettore m [di] compact

CD-Rom /siːdɪ'rɒm/ n CD-Rom m inv. ~ **drive** n lettore m [di] CD-Rom

cease /siːs/ n **without** ~ incessantemente ● vt/i cessare. **~-fire** n cessate il fuoco m inv. **~less** a incessante

cedar /'siːdə(r)/ n cedro m

cede /siːd/ vt cedere

ceiling /'siːlɪŋ/ n soffitto m; fig tetto m [massimo]

celebrate /'selɪbreɪt/ vt festeggiare ⟨birthday, victory⟩ ● vi far festa. **~ed** a celebre (**for** per). **~ion** /-'breɪʃn/ n celebrazione f

celebrity /sɪ'lebrətɪ/ n celebrità f inv

celery /'selərɪ/ n sedano m

celiba|cy /'selɪbəsɪ/ n celibato m. **~te** a ⟨man⟩ celibe; ⟨woman⟩ nubile

cell /sel/ n cella f; Biol cellula f

cellar /'selə(r)/ n scantinato m; (for wine) cantina f

cellist /'tʃelɪst/ n violoncellista mf

cello /'tʃeləʊ/ n violoncello m

Cellophane® /'seləfeɪn/ n cellofan m inv

cellular phone /seljʊlə'fəʊn/ n [telefono m] cellulare m

celluloid /'seljʊlɔɪd/ n celluloide f

Celsius /'selsɪəs/ a Celsius

Celt /kelt/ n celta mf. **~ic** a celtico

cement /sɪ'ment/ n cemento m; (adhesive) mastice m ● vt cementare; fig consolidare

cemetery /'semətrɪ/ n cimitero m

censor /'sensə(r)/ n censore m ● vt censurare. **~ship** n censura f

censure /'senʃə(r)/ vt biasimare

census /'sensəs/ n censimento m

cent /sent/ n (coin) centesimo m

centenary /sen'tiːnərɪ/ n, Am **centennial** /sen'tenɪəl/ n centenario m

center /'sentə(r)/ n Am = **centre**

centi|grade /'sentɪ-/ a centigrado. **~metre** n centimetro m. **~pede** /-piːd/ n centopiedi m inv

central /'sentrəl/ a centrale. ~ **heating** n riscaldamento m autonomo. **~ize** vt centralizzare. **~ly** adv al centro; **~ly heated** con riscaldamento autonomo. ~ **reservation** n Auto banchina f spartitraffico

centre /'sentə(r)/ n centro m ● v ⟨pt/pp **centred**⟩ ● vt centrare ● vi ~ **on** fig incentrarsi su. **~-forward** n centravanti m inv

centrifugal /sentrɪ'fjuːgl/ a ~ **force** forza f centrifuga

century /'sentʃərɪ/ n secolo m

ceramic /sɪ'ræmɪk/ a ceramico. **~s** n ⟨art⟩ ceramica fsg; ⟨objects⟩ ceramiche fpl

cereal /'sɪərɪəl/ n cereale m

cerebral /'serɪbrl/ a cerebrale

ceremon|ial /serɪ'məʊnɪəl/ a da cerimonia ● n cerimoniale m. **~ious** /-ɪəs/ a cerimonioso

ceremony /'serɪmənɪ/ n cerimonia f

certain /'sɜːtn/ a certo; **for** ~ di sicuro; **make** ~ accertarsi; **he is** ~ **to win** è certo di vincere; **it's not** ~ **whether he'll come** non è sicuro che venga. **~ly** adv certamente; **~ly not!** no di certo! **~ty** n certezza f; **it's a ~ty** è una cosa certa

certificate /sə'tɪfɪkət/ n certificato m

certify /'sɜːtɪfaɪ/ vt ⟨pt/pp **-ied**⟩ certificare; ⟨declare insane⟩ dichiarare malato di mente

cessation /se'seɪʃn/ n cessazione f

cesspool /'ses-/ n pozzo m nero

cf abbr ⟨compare⟩ cf, cfr

chafe /tʃeɪf/ vt irritare

chain /tʃeɪn/ n catena f ● vt incatenare ⟨prisoner⟩; attaccare con la catena ⟨dog⟩ ⟨to a⟩. **chain up** vt legare alla catena ⟨dog⟩

chain: ~ **re'action** n reazione f a catena. **~-smoke** vi fumare una sigaretta dopo l'altra. **~-smoker** n fumatore, trice mf accanito, -a. ~ **store** n negozio m appartenente a una catena

chair /tʃeə(r)/ n sedia f; Univ cattedra f ● vt presiedere. **~-lift** n seggiovia f. **~man** n presidente m

chalet /'ʃæleɪ/ n chalet m inv; (in holiday camp) bungalow m inv

chalice /'tʃælɪs/ n Relig calice m

chalk /tʃɔːk/ n gesso m. **~y** a gessoso

challenge /'tʃælɪndʒ/ n sfida f; Mil intimazione f ● vt sfidare; Mil intimare il chi va là a; *fig* mettere in dubbio ⟨*statement*⟩. **~er** *n* sfidante *mf*. **~ing** *a* ⟨*job*⟩ impegnativo

chamber /ˈtʃeɪmbə(r)/ *n* **C~ of Commerce** camera *f* di commercio

chamber: ~maid *n* cameriera *f* d'albergo]. **~ music** *n* musica *f* da camera

chamois¹ /ˈʃæmwɑː/ *n inv* ⟨*animal*⟩ camoscio *m*

chamois² /ˈʃæmɪ/ *n* ~[-leather] [pelle *f* di] camoscio *m*

champagne /ʃæmˈpeɪn/ *n* champagne *m inv*

champion /ˈtʃæmpɪən/ *n Sport* campione *m*; ⟨*of cause*⟩ difensore, difenditrice *mf* ● *vt* ⟨*defend*⟩ difendere; ⟨*fight for*⟩ lottare per. **~ship** *n Sport* campionato *m*

chance /tʃɑːns/ *n* caso *m*; ⟨*possibility*⟩ possibilità *f inv*; ⟨*opportunity*⟩ occasione *f*; **by ~** per caso; **take a ~** provarci; **give sb a second ~** dare un'altra possibilità a qcno ● *attrib* fortuito ● *vt* **I'll ~ it** *fam* corro il rischio

chancellor /ˈtʃɑːnsələ(r)/ *n* cancelliere *m*; *Univ* rettore *m*; **C~ of the Exchequer** *n* ministro *m* del tesoro

chancy /ˈtʃɑːnsɪ/ *a* rischioso

chandelier /ʃændəˈlɪə(r)/ *n* lampadario *m*

change /tʃeɪndʒ/ *n* cambiamento *m*; ⟨*money*⟩ resto *m*; ⟨*small coins*⟩ spiccioli *mpl*; **for a ~** tanto per cambiare; **a ~ of clothes** un cambio di vestiti; **the ~** [of life] la menopausa ● *vt* cambiare; ⟨*substitute*⟩ scambiare (**for** con); **~ one's clothes** cambiarsi [i vestiti]; **~ trains** cambiare treno ● *vi* cambiare; ⟨*~ clothes*⟩ cambiarsi; **all ~!** stazione terminale!

changeable /ˈtʃeɪndʒəbl/ *a* mutevole; ⟨*weather*⟩ variabile

'changing-room *n* camerino *m*; ⟨*for sports*⟩ spogliatoio *m*

channel /ˈtʃænl/ *n* canale *m*; **the [English] C~** la Manica; **the C~ Islands** le Isole del Canale ● *vt* ⟨*pt/pp* **channelled**⟩ **~ one's energies into sth** convogliare le proprie energie in qcsa

chant /tʃɑːnt/ *n* cantilena *f*; ⟨*of demonstrators*⟩ slogan *m inv* di protesta ● *vt* cantare; ⟨*demonstrators:*⟩ gridare

chao|s /ˈkeɪɒs/ *n* caos *m*. **~tic** /-ˈɒtɪk/ *a* caotico

chap /tʃæp/ *n fam* tipo *m*

chapel /ˈtʃæpl/ *n* cappella *f*

chaperon /ˈʃæpərəʊn/ *n* chaperon *f inv* ● *vt* fare da chaperon a ⟨*sb*⟩

chaplain /ˈtʃæplɪn/ *n* cappellano *m*

chapped /tʃæpt/ *a* ⟨*skin, lips*⟩ screpolato

chapter /ˈtʃæptə(r)/ *n* capitolo *m*

char¹ /tʃɑː(r)/ *n fam* donna *f* delle pulizie

char² *vt* ⟨*pt/pp* **charred**⟩ ⟨*burn*⟩ carbonizzare

character /ˈkærɪktə(r)/ *n* carattere *m*; ⟨*in novel, play*⟩ personaggio *m*; **quite a ~** *fam* un tipo particolare

characteristic /kærɪktəˈrɪstɪk/ *a* caratteristico ● *n* caratteristica *f*. **~ally** *adv* tipicamente

characterize /ˈkærɪktəraɪz/ *vt* caratterizzare

charade /ʃəˈrɑːd/ *n* farsa *f*

charcoal /ˈtʃɑː-/ *n* carbonella *f*

charge /tʃɑːdʒ/ *n* ⟨*cost*⟩ prezzo *m*; *Electr, Mil* carica *f*; *Jur* accusa *f*; **free of ~** gratuito; **be in ~** essere responsabile ⟨*of* di⟩; **take ~** assumersi la responsabilità; **take ~ of** occuparsi di ● *vt* far pagare ⟨*fee*⟩; far pagare a ⟨*person*⟩; *Electr, Mil* caricare; *Jur* accusare (**with** di); **~ sb for sth** far pagare qcsa a qcno; **~ it to my account** lo addebiti sul mio conto ● *vi* ⟨*attack*⟩ caricare

chariot /ˈtʃærɪət/ *n* cocchio *m*

charisma /kəˈrɪzmə/ *n* carisma *m*. **~tic** /kærɪzˈmætɪk/ *a* carismatico

charitable /ˈtʃærɪtəbl/ *a* caritatevole; ⟨*kind*⟩ indulgente

charity /ˈtʃærətɪ/ *n* carità *f*; ⟨*organization*⟩ associazione *f* di beneficenza; **concert given for ~** concerto *m* di beneficenza; **live on ~** vivere di elemosina

charm /tʃɑːm/ *n* fascino *m*; ⟨*object*⟩ ciondolo *m* ● *vt* affascinare. **~ing** *a* affascinante

chart /tʃɑːt/ *n* carta *f* nautica; ⟨*table*⟩ tabella *f*

charter /ˈtʃɑːtə(r)/ *n* **~ [flight]** [volo *m*] charter *m inv* ● *vt* noleggiare. **~ed accountant** *n* commercialista *mf*

charwoman /ˈtʃɑː-/ *n* donna *f* delle pulizie

chase /tʃeɪs/ *n* inseguimento *m* ● *vt* inseguire. **chase away** or **off** *vt* cacciare via

chasm /ˈkæz(ə)m/ *n* abisso *m*

chassis /ˈʃæsɪ/ *n* ⟨*pl* **chassis** /-sɪz/⟩ telaio *m*

chaste /tʃeɪst/ *a* casto

chastity /ˈtʃæstətɪ/ *n* castità *f*

chat /tʃæt/ n chiacchierata f; **have a ~ with** fare quattro chiacchere con ● vi (pt/pp **chatted**) chiacchierare. **~ show** n talk show m inv

chatter /'tʃætə(r)/ n chiacchiere fpl ● vi chiacchierare; ⟨teeth:⟩ battere. **~box** n fam chiacchierone, -a mf

chatty /'tʃætɪ/ a (-ier, -iest) chiacchierone; ⟨style⟩ familiare

chauffeur /'ʃəʊfə(r)/ n autista mf

chauvin|ism /'ʃəʊvɪnɪzm/ n sciovinismo m. **~ist** n sciovinista mf. **male ~ist** n fam maschilista m

cheap /tʃiːp/ a a buon mercato; ⟨rate⟩ economico; ⟨vulgar⟩ grossolano; (of poor quality) scadente ● adv a buon mercato. **~ly** adv a buon mercato

cheat /tʃiːt/ n imbroglione, -a mf; (at cards) baro m ● vt imbrogliare; **~ sb out of sth** sottrarre qcsa a qcno con l'inganno ● vi imbrogliare; (at cards) barare. **cheat on** vt fam tradire ⟨wife⟩

check[1] /tʃek/ a ⟨pattern⟩ a quadri ● n disegno m a quadri

check[2] n verifica f; (of tickets) controllo m; (in chess) scacco m; (Am: bill) conto m; (Am: cheque) assegno m; (Am: tick) segnetto m; **keep a ~ on** controllare; **keep in ~** tenere sotto controllo ● vt verificare; controllare ⟨tickets⟩; ⟨restrain⟩ contenere; ⟨stop⟩ bloccare ● vi controllare; **~ on sth** controllare qcsa. **check in** vi registrarsi all'arrivo (in albergo); Aeron fare il check-in ● vt registrare all'arrivo (in albergo). **check out** vi (of hotel) saldare il conto ● vt ⟨fam: investigate⟩ controllare. **check up** vi accertarsi; **~ up on** prendere informazioni su

check|ed /tʃekt/ a a quadri. **~ers** n Am dama f

check: **~-in** n (in airport: place) banco m accettazione, check-in m inv; **~-in time** check-in m inv. **~ mark** n Am segnetto m. **~mate** int scacco matto! **~-out** n (in supermarket) cassa f. **~room** n Am deposito m bagagli. **~-up** n Med visita f di controllo, check-up m inv

cheek /tʃiːk/ n guancia f; ⟨impudence⟩ sfacciataggine f. **~y** a sfacciato

cheep /tʃiːp/ vi pigolare

cheer /tʃɪə(r)/ n evviva m inv; **three ~s** tre urrà; **~s!** salute!; ⟨goodbye⟩ arrivederci!; ⟨thanks⟩ grazie! ● vt/i acclamare. **cheer up** vt tirare su [di morale] ● vi tirarsi su [di morale]; **~ up!** su con

la vita!. **~ful** a allegro. **~fulness** n allegria f. **~ing** n acclamazione f

cheerio /tʃɪərɪ'əʊ/ int fam arrivederci

'cheerless a triste, tetro

cheese /tʃiːz/ n formaggio m. **~cake** n dolce m al formaggio

chef /ʃef/ n cuoco, -a mf, chef mf inv

chemical /'kemɪkl/ a chimico ● n prodotto m chimico

chemist /'kemɪst/ n ⟨pharmacist⟩ farmacista mf; ⟨scientist⟩ chimico, -a mf; **~'s [shop]** farmacia f. **~ry** n chimica f

cheque /tʃek/ n assegno m. **~-book** n libretto m degli assegni. **~ card** n carta f assegni

cherish /'tʃerɪʃ/ vt curare teneramente; ⟨love⟩ avere caro; nutrire ⟨hope⟩

cherry /'tʃerɪ/ n ciliegia f; ⟨tree⟩ ciliegio m

cherub /'tʃerəb/ n cherubino m

chess /tʃes/ n scacchi mpl

chess: **~board** n scacchiera f. **~-man** n pezzo m degli scacchi. **~player** n scacchista mf

chest /tʃest/ n petto m; ⟨box⟩ cassapanca f

chestnut /'tʃesnʌt/ n castagna f; ⟨tree⟩ castagno m

chest of 'drawers n cassettone m

chew /tʃuː/ vt masticare. **~ing-gum** n gomma f da masticare

chic /ʃiːk/ a chic inv

chick /tʃɪk/ n pulcino m; ⟨fam: girl⟩ ragazza f

chicken /'tʃɪkn/ n pollo m ● attrib ⟨soup, casserole⟩ di pollo ● a fam fifone ● **chicken out** vi fam **he ~ed out** gli è venuta fifa. **~pox** n varicella f

chicory /'tʃɪkərɪ/ n cicoria f

chief /tʃiːf/ a principale ● n capo m. **~ly** adv principalmente

chilblain /'tʃɪlbleɪn/ n gelone m

child /tʃaɪld/ n (pl **~ren**) bambino, -a mf; ⟨son/daughter⟩ figlio, -a mf

child: **~birth** n parto m. **~hood** n infanzia f. **~ish** a infantile. **~ishness** n puerilità f. **~less** a senza figli. **~like** a ingenuo. **~-minder** n baby-sitter mf inv

children /'tʃɪldrən/ see child

Chile /'tʃɪlɪ/ n Cile m. **~an** a & n cileno, -a mf

chill /tʃɪl/ n freddo m; ⟨illness⟩ infreddatura f ● vt raffreddare

chilli /'tʃɪlɪ/ n (pl **-es**) **~ [pepper]** peperoncino m

chilly /'tʃɪlɪ/ a freddo

chime /tʃaɪm/ vi suonare

chimney /'tʃɪmnɪ/ n camino m. **~-pot**

n comignolo *m*. **~-sweep** *n* spazzacamino *m*

chimpanzee /tʃɪmpænˈziː/ *n* scimpanzé *m inv*

chin /tʃɪn/ *n* mento *m*

china /ˈtʃaɪnə/ *n* porcellana *f*

Chin|a *n* Cina *f*. **~ese** /-ˈniːz/ *a & n* cinese *mf*: (*language*) cinese *m*; **the ~ese** *pl* i cinesi

chink[1] /tʃɪŋk/ *n* (*slit*) fessura *f*

chink[2] *n* (*noise*) tintinnio *m*

chip /tʃɪp/ *n* (*fragment*) scheggia *f*. (*in china, paintwork*) scheggiatura *f*; *Comput* chip *m inv*; (*in gambling*) fiche *f inv*; **~s** *pl Br Culin* patatine *fpl* fritte; *Am Culin* patatine *fpl* ● *vt* (*pt/pp* **chipped**) (*damage*) scheggiare. **chip in** *vi fam* intromettersi; (*with money*) contribuire. **~ped** *a* (*damaged*) scheggiato

chiropod|ist /kɪˈrɒpədɪst/ *n* podiatra *mf inv*. **~y** *n* podiatria *f*

chirp /tʃɜːp/ *vi* cinguettare; (*cricket:*) fare cri cri. **~y** *a fam* pimpante

chisel /ˈtʃɪzl/ *n* scalpello *m*

chival|rous /ˈʃɪvlrəs/ *a* cavalleresco. **~ry** *n* cavalleria *f*

chives /tʃaɪvz/ *npl* erba *f* cipollina

chlorine /ˈklɔːriːn/ *n* cloro *m*

chloroform /ˈklɒrəfɔːm/ *n* cloroformio *m*

chock-a-block /tʃɒkəˈblɒk/, **chock-full** /tʃɒkˈfʊl/ *a* pieno zeppo

chocolate /ˈtʃɒkələt/ *n* cioccolato *m*; (*drink*) cioccolata *f*; **a ~** un cioccolatino

choice /tʃɔɪs/ *n* scelta *f* ● *a* scelto

choir /ˈkwaɪə(r)/ *n* coro *m*. **~boy** *n* corista *m*

choke /tʃəʊk/ *n* Auto aria *f* ● *vt/i* soffocare

cholera /ˈkɒlərə/ *n* colera *m*

cholesterol /kəˈlestərɒl/ *n* colesterolo *m*

choose /tʃuːz/ *vt/i* (*pt* **chose**, *pp* **chosen**) scegliere; **as you ~** come vuoi

choos|ey /ˈtʃuːzɪ/ *a fam* difficile

chop /tʃɒp/ *n* (*blow*) colpo *m* (*d'ascia*); *Culin* costata *f* ● *vt* (*pt/pp* **chopped**) tagliare. **chop down** *vt* abbattere (*tree*). **chop off** *vt* spaccare

chopp|er /ˈtʃɒpə(r)/ *n* accetta *f*; *fam* elicottero *m*. **~y** *a* increspato

chopsticks *npl* bastoncini *mpl* cinesi

choral /ˈkɔːrəl/ *a* corale

chord /kɔːd/ *n* Mus corda *f*

chore /tʃɔː(r)/ *n* corvé *f inv*; [**household**] **~s** faccende *fpl* domestiche

choreograph|er /kɒrɪˈɒɡrəfə(r)/ *n* coreografo, -a *mf*. **~y** /-ɪ/ *n* coreografia *f*

chortle /ˈtʃɔːtl/ *vi* ridacchiare

chorus /ˈkɔːrəs/ *n* coro *m*; (*of song*) ritornello *m*

chose, chosen /tʃəʊz, ˈtʃəʊzn/ *see* **choose**

Christ /kraɪst/ *n* Cristo *m*

christen /ˈkrɪsn/ *vt* battezzare. **~ing** *n* battesimo *m*

Christian /ˈkrɪstʃən/ *a & n* cristiano, -a *mf*. **~ity** /-stɪˈænətɪ/ *n* cristianesimo *m*. **~ name** *n* nome *m* di battesimo

Christmas /ˈkrɪsməs/ *n* Natale *m* ● *attrib* di Natale. **~ card** *n* biglietto *m* d'auguri di Natale. **~ Day** *n* il giorno di Natale. **~ Eve** *n* la vigilia di Natale. **~ present** *n* regalo *m* di Natale. **~ pudding** *n* dolce *m* natalizio a base di frutta candita e liquore. **~ tree** *n* albero *m* di Natale

chrome /krəʊm/ *n*, **chromium** /ˈkrəʊmɪəm/ *n* cromo *m*

chromosome /ˈkrəʊməsəʊm/ *n* cromosoma *m*

chronic /ˈkrɒnɪk/ *a* cronico

chronicle /ˈkrɒnɪkl/ *n* cronaca *f*

chronological /krɒnəˈlɒdʒɪkl/ *a* cronologico. **~ly** *adv* (*ordered*) in ordine cronologico

chrysanthemum /krɪˈsænθəməm/ *n* crisantemo *m*

chubby /ˈtʃʌbɪ/ *a* (-**ier**, -**iest**) paffuto

chuck /tʃʌk/ *vt fam* buttare. **chuck out** *vt fam* buttare via (*object*); buttare fuori (*person*)

chuckle /ˈtʃʌkl/ *vi* ridacchiare

chug /tʃʌɡ/ *vi* (*pt/pp* **chugged**) **the train ~ged out of the station** il treno è uscito dalla stazione sbuffando

chum /tʃʌm/ *n* amico, -a *mf*. **~my** *a fam* **be ~my with** essere amico di

chunk /tʃʌŋk/ *n* grosso pezzo *m*

church /tʃɜːtʃ/ *n* chiesa *f*. **~yard** *n* cimitero *m*

churlish /ˈtʃɜːlɪʃ/ *a* sgarbato

churn /tʃɜːn/ *vt* **churn out** sfornare

chute /ʃuːt/ *n* scivolo *m*; (*for rubbish*) canale *m* di scarico

CID *n abbr* (**Criminal Investigation Department**) polizia *f* giudiziaria

cider /ˈsaɪdə(r)/ *n* sidro *m*

cigar /sɪˈɡɑː(r)/ *n* sigaro *m*

cigarette /sɪɡəˈret/ *n* sigaretta *f*

cine-camera /ˈsɪnɪ-/ *n* cinepresa *f*

cinema /ˈsɪnɪmə/ *n* cinema *m inv*

cinnamon /ˈsɪnəmən/ *n* cannella *f*

circle /ˈsɜːkl/ *n* cerchio *m*; *Theat* galleria *f*; **in a ~** in cerchio ●*vt* girare intorno a; cerchiare (*mistake*) ●*vi* descrivere dei cerchi

circuit /'sɜːkɪt/ *n* circuito *m*; (*lap*) giro *m*; **~ board** *n* circuito *m* stampato. **~ous** /sə'kjuːɪtəs/ *a* **~ous route** percorso *m* lungo e indiretto

circular /'sɜːkjʊlə(r)/ *a* circolare ●*n* circolare *f*

circulat|e /'sɜːkjʊleɪt/ *vt* far circolare ●*vi* circolare. **~ion** /-'leɪʃn/ *n* circolazione *f*; (*of newspaper*) tiratura *f*

circumcis|e /'sɜːkəmsaɪz/ *vt* circoncidere. **~ion** /-'sɪʒn/ *n* circoncisione *f*

circumference /fə'kʌmfərəns/ *n* conconferenza *f*

circumstance /'sɜːkəmstəns/ *n* circostanza *f*; **~s** *pl* (*financial*) condizioni *fpl* finanziarie

circus /'sɜːkəs/ *n* circo *m*

CIS *n abbr* (**Commonwealth of Independent States**) CSI *f*

cistern /'sɪstən/ *n* (*tank*) cisterna *f*; (*of WC*) serbatoio *m*

cite /saɪt/ *vt* citare

citizen /'sɪtɪzn/ *n* cittadino, -a *mf*; (*of town*) abitante *mf*. **~ship** *n* cittadinanza *f*

citrus /'sɪtrəs/ *n* **|fruit|** agrume *m*

city /'sɪtɪ/ *n* città *f inv*; **the C~** la City (*di Londra*)

civic /'sɪvɪk/ *a* civico

civil /'sɪvl/ *a* civile

civilian /sɪ'vɪljən/ *a* civile; **in ~ clothes** in borghese ●*n* civile *mf*

civiliz|ation /sɪvɪlaɪ'zeɪʃn/ *n* civiltà *f inv*. **~e** /'sɪvɪlaɪz/ *vt* civilizzare

civil: ~ servant *n* impiegato, -a *mf* statale. **C~ Service** *n* pubblica amministrazione *f*

clad /klæd/ *a* vestito (**in** di)

claim /kleɪm/ *n* richiesta *f*; (*right*) diritto *m*; (*assertion*) dichiarazione *f*; **lay ~ to sth** rivendicare qcsa ●*vt* richiedere; reclamare (*lost property*); rivendicare (*ownership*); **~ that** sostenere che. **~ant** *n* richiedente *mf*

clairvoyant /kleə'vɔɪənt/ *n* chiaroveggente *f*

clam /klæm/ *n Culin* vongola *f* ● **clam up** *vi* (*pt/pp* **clammed**) zittirsi

clamber /'klæmbə(r)/ *vi* arrampicarsi

clammy /'klæmɪ/ *a* (**-ier, -iest**) appiccicaticcio

clamour /'klæmə(r)/ *n* (*protest*) rimostranza *f* ●*vi* **~ for** chiedere a gran voce

clamp /klæmp/ *n* morsa *f* ●*vt*

ammorsare; *Auto* mettere i ceppi bloccaruote a. **clamp down** *vi fam* essere duro; **~ down on** reprimere

clan /klæn/ *n* clan *m inv*

clandestine /klæn'destɪn/ *a* clandestino

clang /klæŋ/ *n* suono *m* metallico. **~er** *n fam* gaffe *f inv*

clank /klæŋk/ *n* rumore *m* metallico

clap /klæp/ *n* **give sb a ~** applaudire qcno; **~ of thunder** tuono *m* ●*vt/i* (*pt/pp* **clapped**) applaudire; **~ one's hands** applaudire. **~ping** *n* applausi *mpl*

clari|fication /klærɪfɪ'keɪʃn/ *n* chiarimento *m*. **~fy** /'klærɪfaɪ/ *vt/i* (*pt/pp* **-ied**) chiarire

clarinet /klærɪ'net/ *n* clarinetto *m*

clarity /'klærətɪ/ *n* chiarezza *f*

clash /klæʃ/ *n* scontro *m*; (*noise*) fragore *m* ●*vi* scontrarsi; (*colours:*) stonare; (*events:*) coincidere

clasp /klɑːsp/ *n* chiusura *f* ●*vt* agganciare; (*hold*) stringere

class /klɑːs/ *n* classe *f*; (*lesson*) corso *m* ●*vt* classificare

classic /'klæsɪk/ *a* classico ●*n* classico *m*; **~s** *pl Univ* lettere *fpl* classiche. **~al** *a* classico

classi|fication /klæsɪfɪ'keɪʃn/ *n* classificazione *f*. **~fy** /'klæsɪfaɪ/ *vt* (*pt/pp* **-ied**) classificare

classroom *n* aula *f*

classy /'klɑːsɪ/ *a* (**-ier, -iest**) *fam* d'alta classe

clatter /'klætə(r)/ *n* fracasso *m* ●*vi* far fracasso

clause /klɔːz/ *n* clausola *f*; *Gram* proposizione *f*

claustrophob|ia /klɔːstrə'fəʊbɪə/ *n* claustrofobia *f*

claw /klɔː/ *n* artiglio *m*; (*of crab, lobster & Techn*) tenaglia *f* ●*vt* (*cat:*) graffiare

clay /kleɪ/ *n* argilla *f*

clean /kliːn/ *a* pulito, lindo ●*adv* completamente ●*vt* pulire (*shoes, windows*); **~ one's teeth** lavarsi i denti; **have a coat ~ed** portare un cappotto in lavanderia. **clean up** *vt* pulire ●*vi* far pulizia

cleaner /'kliːnə(r)/ *n* uomo *m*/donna *f* delle pulizie; (*substance*) detersivo *m*; **|dry|** **~'s** lavanderia *f*, tintoria *f*

cleanliness /'klenlɪnɪs/ *n* pulizia *f*

cleanse /klenz/ *vt* pulire. **~r** *n* detergente *m*

clean-shaven *a* sbarbato

cleansing cream /'klenz-/ n latte m detergente

clear /klɪə(r)/ a chiaro; ⟨conscience⟩ pulito; ⟨road⟩ libero; ⟨profit, advantage, majority⟩ netto; ⟨sky⟩ sereno; ⟨water⟩ limpido; ⟨glass⟩ trasparente; **make sth ~** mettere qcsa in chiaro; **have I made myself ~?** mi sono fatto capire? **five ~ days** cinque giorni buoni ● adv **stand ~ of** allontanarsi da; **keep ~ of** tenersi alla larga da ● vt sgombrare ⟨room, street⟩; sparecchiare ⟨table⟩; ⟨acquit⟩ scagionare; ⟨authorize⟩ autorizzare; scavalcare senza toccare ⟨fence, wall⟩; guadagnare ⟨sum of money⟩; passare ⟨Customs⟩; **~ one's throat** schiarirsi la gola ● vi ⟨face, sky⟩ rasserenarsi; ⟨fog⟩ dissiparsi. **clear away** vt mettere via. **clear off** vi fam filar via. **clear out** vt sgombrare ● vi fam filar via. **clear up** vt ⟨tidy⟩ mettere a posto; chiarire ⟨mystery⟩ ● vi ⟨weather⟩ schiarirsi

clearance /'klɪərəns/ n ⟨space⟩ spazio m libero; ⟨authorization⟩ autorizzazione f; ⟨Customs⟩ sdoganamento m. **~ sale** n liquidazione f

clear|ing /'klɪərɪŋ/ n radura f. **~ly** adv chiaramente. **~ way** n Auto strada f con divieto di sosta

cleavage /'kli:vɪdʒ/ n ⟨woman's⟩ décolleté m inv

cleft /kleft/ n fenditura f

clench /klentʃ/ vt serrare

clergy /'klɜ:dʒi/ npl clero m. **~man** n ecclesiastico m

cleric /'klerɪk/ n ecclesiastico m. **~al** a impiegatizio; Relig clericale

clerk /klɑ:k/, Am /klɜ:k/ n impiegato, -a mf; ⟨Am: shop assistant⟩ commesso, -a mf

clever /'klevə(r)/ a intelligente; ⟨skilful⟩ abile

cliché /'kli:ʃeɪ/ n cliché m inv

click /klɪk/ vi scattare ● n Comput click m. **click on** vt Comput cliccare su

client /'klaɪənt/ n cliente mf

clientele /kli:ɒn'tel/ n clientela f

cliff /klɪf/ n scogliera f

climat|e /'klaɪmət/ n clima f. **~ic** /-'mætɪk/ a climatico

climax /'klaɪmæks/ n punto m culminante

climb /klaɪm/ n salita f ● vt scalare ⟨mountain⟩; arrampicarsi su ⟨ladder, tree⟩ ● vi arrampicarsi; ⟨rise⟩ salire; ⟨road⟩ salire. **climb down** vi scendere; ⟨from ladder, tree⟩ scendere; fig tornare sui propri passi

climber /'klaɪmə(r)/ n alpinista mf; ⟨plant⟩ rampicante m

clinch /klɪntʃ/ vt fam concludere ⟨deal⟩ ● n ⟨in boxing⟩ clinch m inv

cling /klɪŋ/ vi ⟨pt/pp clung⟩ aggrapparsi; ⟨stick⟩ aderire. **~ film** n pellicola f trasparente

clinic /'klɪnɪk/ n ambulatorio m. **~al** a clinico

clink /klɪŋk/ n tintinnio m; ⟨fam: prison⟩ galera f ● vi tintinnare

clip¹ /klɪp/ n fermaglio m; ⟨jewellery⟩ spilla f ● vt ⟨pt/pp clipped⟩ attaccare

clip² n ⟨extract⟩ taglio m ● vt obliterare ⟨ticket⟩. **~board** n fermabloc m inv. **~pers** npl ⟨for hair⟩ rasoio m; ⟨for hedge⟩ tosasiepi m inv; ⟨for nails⟩ tronchesina f. **~ping** n ⟨from newspaper⟩ ritaglio m

clique /kli:k/ n cricca f

cloak /kləʊk/ n mantello m. **~room** n guardaroba m inv; ⟨toilet⟩ bagno m

clock /klɒk/ n orologio m; ⟨fam: speedometer⟩ tachimetro m ● **clock in** vi attaccare. **clock out** vi staccare

clock: **~ tower** n torre f dell'orologio. **~wise** a & adv in senso orario. **~work** n meccanismo m

clod /klɒd/ n zolla f

clog /klɒg/ n zoccolo m ● vt ⟨pt/pp clogged⟩ ~ [up] intasare ⟨drain⟩; inceppare ⟨mechanism⟩ ● vi ⟨drain⟩ intasarsi

cloister /'klɔɪstə(r)/ n chiostro m

clone /kləʊn/ n clone m

close¹ /kləʊs/ a vicino; ⟨friend⟩ intimo; ⟨weather⟩ afoso; **have a ~ shave** fam scamparla bella; **be ~ to sb** essere unito a qcno ● adv vicino; **~ by** vicino; **it's ~ on five o'clock** sono quasi le cinque

close² /kləʊz/ n fine f ● vt chiudere ● vi chiudersi; ⟨shop⟩ chiudere. **close down** vt chiudere ● vi ⟨TV station⟩ interrompere la trasmissione; ⟨factory⟩ chiudere

closely /'kləʊsli/ adv da vicino; ⟨watch, listen⟩ attentamente

closet /'klɒzɪt/ n Am armadio m

close-up /'kləʊs-/ n primo piano m

closure /'kləʊʒə(r)/ n chiusura f

clot /klɒt/ n grumo m; ⟨fam: idiot⟩ tonto, -a mf ● vi ⟨pt/pp clotted⟩ ⟨blood⟩ coagularsi

cloth /klɒθ/ n ⟨fabric⟩ tessuto m; ⟨duster etc⟩ straccio m

clothe /kləʊð/ vt vestire

clothes /kləʊðz/ npl vestiti mpl, abiti

mpl. ~-**brush** *n* spazzola *f* per abiti.
~-**line** *n* corda *f* stendibiancheria
clothing /'kləʊðɪŋ/ *n* abbigliamento *m*
cloud /klaud/ *n* nuvola *f* ● **cloud over**
vi rannuvolarsi. ~**burst** *n* acquazzone *m*
cloudy /'klaudɪ/ *a* (-ier, -iest) nuvoloso; ⟨*liquid*⟩ torbido
clout /klaut/ *n fam* colpo *m*; ⟨*influence*⟩
impatto *m* (**with** su) ● *vt fam* colpire
clove /kləʊv/ *n* chiodo *m* di garofano; ~
of garlic spicchio *m* d'aglio
clover /'kləʊvə(r)/ *n* trifoglio *m*
clown /klaun/ *n* pagliaccio *m* ● *vi* ~
⟨**about**⟩ fare il pagliaccio
club /klʌb/ *n* club *m inv*; ⟨*weapon*⟩ clava
f; *Sport* mazza *f*; ~**s** *pl* ⟨*Cards*⟩ fiori *mpl*
● *v* (*pt/pp* **clubbed**) ● *vt* bastonare.
club together *vi* unirsi
cluck /klʌk/ *vi* chiocciare
clue /klu:/ *n* indizio *m*; ⟨*in crossword*⟩
definizione *f*; **I haven't a** ~ *fam* non ne
ho idea
clump /klʌmp/ *n* gruppo *m*
clumsiness /'klʌmzɪnɪs/ *n* goffaggine *f*
clumsy /'klʌmzɪ/ *a* (-ier, -iest) maldestro; ⟨*tool*⟩ scomodo; ⟨*remark*⟩ senza tatto
clung /klʌŋ/ *see* **cling**
cluster /'klʌstə(r)/ *n* gruppo *m* ● *vi*
raggrupparsi (**round** intorno a)
clutch /klʌtʃ/ *n* stretta *f*; *Auto* frizione
f; **be in sb's** ~**es** essere in balia di qcno
● *vt* stringere; ⟨*grab*⟩ afferrare ● *vi* ~
at afferrare
clutter /'klʌtə(r)/ *n* caos *m* ● *vt* ~ [**up**]
ingombrare
c/o *abbr* ⟨**care of**⟩ c/o, presso
coach /kəʊtʃ/ *n* pullman *m inv*; *Rail*
vagone *m*; ⟨*horse-drawn*⟩ carrozza *f*;
Sport allenatore, -trice *mf* ● *vt* fare
esercitare; *Sport* allenare
coagulate /kəʊ'æɡjʊleɪt/ *vi* coagularsi
coal /kəʊl/ *n* carbone *m*
coalition /kəʊə'lɪʃn/ *n* coalizione *f*
'**coal-mine** *n* miniera *f* di carbone
coarse /kɔːs/ *a* grossolano; ⟨*joke*⟩ spinto
coast /kəʊst/ *n* costa *f* ● *vi* ⟨*freewheel*⟩
scendere a ruota libera; *Auto* scendere
in folle. ~**al** *a* costiero. ~**er** *n* ⟨*mat*⟩
sottobicchiere *m inv*
coast: ~**guard** *n* guardia *f* costiera.
~**line** *n* litorale *m*
coat /kəʊt/ *n* cappotto *m*; ⟨*of animal*⟩
manto *m*; ⟨*of paint*⟩ mano *f*; ~ **of arms**

stemma *f* ● *vt* coprire; ⟨*with paint*⟩ ricoprire. ~-**hanger** *n* gruccia *f*. ~-**hook** *n*
gancio *m* [appendiabiti]
coating /'kəʊtɪŋ/ *n* rivestimento *m*; ⟨*of
paint*⟩ stato *m*
coax /kəʊks/ *vt* convincere con le moine
cob /kɒb/ *n* ⟨*of corn*⟩ pannocchia *f*
cobble /'kɒbl/ *vt* ~ **together** raffazzonare. ~**r** *n* ciabattino *m*
'**cobblestones** *npl* ciottolato *msg*
cobweb /'kɒb-/ *n* ragnatela *f*
cocaine /kə'keɪn/ *n* cocaina *f*
cock /kɒk/ *n* gallo *m*; ⟨*any male bird*⟩
maschio *m* ● *vt* sollevare il grilletto di
⟨*gun*⟩. ~ **its ears** ⟨*animal*:⟩ drizzare le
orecchie
cockerel /'kɒkərəl/ *n* galletto *m*
cock-'eyed *a fam* storto; ⟨*absurd*⟩ assurdo
cockle /'kɒkl/ *n* cardio *m*
cockney /'kɒknɪ/ *n* ⟨*dialect*⟩ dialetto *m*
londinese; ⟨*person*⟩ abitante *mf* dell'est
di Londra
cock: ~**pit** *n Aeron* cabina *f*. ~**roach**
/-rəʊtʃ/ *n* scarafaggio *m*. ~**tail** *n* cocktail *m inv*. ~-**up** *n sl* **make a** ~-**up** fare
un casino ⟨*of* di⟩
cocky /'kɒkɪ/ *a* (-ier, -iest) *fam* presuntuoso
cocoa /'kəʊkəʊ/ *n* cacao *m*
coconut /'kəʊkənʌt/ *n* noce *f* di cocco
cocoon /kə'kuːn/ *n* bozzolo *m*
cod /kɒd/ *n inv* merluzzo *m*
COD *abbr* ⟨**cash on delivery**⟩ pagamento *m* alla consegna
code /kəʊd/ *n* codice *m*. ~**d** *a* codificato
coedu'cational /kəʊ-/ *a* misto
coerc|e /kəʊ'ɜːs/ *vt* costringere. ~**ion**
/-'ɜːʃn/ *n* coercizione *f*
coe'xist *vi* coesistere. ~**ence** *n*
coesistenza *f*
coffee /'kɒfɪ/ *n* caffè *m inv*
coffee: ~-**grinder** *n* macinacaffè *m
inv*. ~-**pot** *n* caffettiera *f*. ~-**table** *n* tavolino *m*
coffin /'kɒfɪn/ *n* bara *f*
cog /kɒg/ *n Techn* dente *m* ⟨*di ruota*⟩
cogent /'kəʊdʒənt/ *a* convincere
cog-wheel *n* ruota *f* dentata
cohabit /kəʊ'hæbɪt/ *vi Jur* convivere
coherent /kəʊ'hɪərənt/ *a* coerente;
⟨*when speaking*⟩ logico
coil /kɔɪl/ *n* rotolo *m*; *Electr* bobina *f*;
~**s** *pl* spire *fpl* ● *vt* ~ [**up**] avvolgere
coin /kɔɪn/ *n* moneta *f* ● *vt* coniare
⟨*word*⟩
coincide /kəʊɪn'saɪd/ *vi* coincidere

coinciden|ce /kəʊˈɪnsɪdəns/ *n* coincidenza *f.* ~**tal** /-ˈdentl/ *a* casuale. ~**tally** *adv* casualmente

coke /kəʊk/ *n* [carbone *m*] coke *m*

Coke® *n* Coca[-cola]® *f*

cold /kəʊld/ *a* freddo; **I'm** ~ ho freddo ● *n* freddo *m; Med* raffreddore *m*

cold: ~-**blooded** *a* spietato. ~-**hearted** *a* insensibile. ~**ly** *adv* fig freddamente. ~ **meat** *n* salumi *mpl.* ~**ness** *n* freddezza *f*

coleslaw /ˈkəʊlslɔː/ *n* insalata *f* di cavolo crudo, cipolle e carote in maionese

colic /ˈkɒlɪk/ *n* colica *f*

collaborat|e /kəˈlæbəreɪt/ *vi* collaborare; ~**e on sth** collaborare in qcsa. ~**ion** /-ˈreɪʃn/ *n* collaborazione *f;* (with enemy) collaborazionismo *m.* ~**or** *n* collaboratore, -trice *mf;* (with enemy) collaborazionista *mf*

collaps|e /kəˈlæps/ *n* crollo *m* ● *vi* (person:) svenire; (roof, building:) crollare. ~**ible** *a* pieghevole

collar /ˈkɒlə(r)/ *n* colletto *m;* (for animal) collare *m.* ~-**bone** *n* clavicola *f*

colleague /ˈkɒliːg/ *n* collega *mf*

collect /kəˈlekt/ *vt* andare a prendere (person); ritirare (parcel, tickets); riscuotere (taxes); raccogliere (rubbish); (as hobby) collezionare ● *vi* riunirsi ● *adv* **call** ~ *Am* telefonare a carico del destinatario. ~**ed** /-ɪd/ *a* controllato

collection /kəˈlekʃn/ *n* collezione *f;* (in church) questua *f;* (of rubbish) raccolta *f;* (of post) levata *f*

collective /kəˈlektɪv/ *a* collettivo

collector /kəˈlektə(r)/ *n* (of stamps etc) collezionista *mf*

college /ˈkɒlɪdʒ/ *n* istituto *m* parauniversitario; **C~ of...** Scuola *f* di...

collide /kəˈlaɪd/ *vi* scontrarsi

colliery /ˈkɒlɪərɪ/ *n* miniera *f* di carbone

collision /kəˈlɪʒn/ *n* scontro *m*

colloquial /kəˈləʊkwɪəl/ *a* colloquiale. ~**ism** *n* espressione *f* colloquiale

cologne /kəˈləʊn/ *n* colonia *f*

colon /ˈkəʊlən/ *n* due punti *mpl; Anat* colon *m inv*

colonel /ˈkɜːnl/ *n* colonnello *m*

colonial /kəˈləʊnɪəl/ *a* coloniale

coloniz|e /ˈkɒlənaɪz/ *vt* colonizzare. ~**y** *n* colonia *f*

colossal /kəˈlɒsl/ *a* colossale

colour /ˈkʌlə(r)/ *n* colore *m;* (complexion) colorito *m;* ~**s** *pl* (flag) bandiera *fsg;* **off** ~ *fam* giù di tono ● *vt*

colorare; ~ [**in**] colorare ● *vi* (blush) arrossire

colour: ~ **bar** *n* discriminazione *f* razziale. ~-**blind** *a* daltonico. ~**ed** *a* colorato; (person) di colore ● *n* (person) persona *f* di colore, di dai colori resistenti. ~ **film** *n* film *m inv* a colori. ~**ful** *a* pieno di colore. ~**less** *a* incolore. ~ **television** *n* televisione *f* a colori

colt /kəʊlt/ *n* puledro *m*

column /ˈkɒləm/ *n* colonna *f.* ~**ist** /-nɪst/ *n* giornalista *mf* che cura una rubrica

coma /ˈkəʊmə/ *n* coma *m inv*

comb /kəʊm/ *n* pettine *m;* (for wearing) pettinino *m* ● *vt* pettinare; (fig: search) setacciare; ~ **one's hair** pettinarsi i capelli

combat /ˈkɒmbæt/ *n* combattimento *m* ● *vt* (pt/pp combated) combattere

combination /kɒmbɪˈneɪʃn/ *n* combinazione *f*

combine[1] /kəmˈbaɪn/ *vt* unire; ~ **a job with being a mother** conciliare il lavoro con il ruolo di madre ● *vi* (chemical elements:) combinarsi

combine[2] /ˈkɒmbaɪn/ *n Comm* associazione *f.* ~ [**harvester**] *n* mietitrebbia *f*

combustion /kəmˈbʌstʃn/ *n* combustione *f*

come /kʌm/ *vi* (pt came, pp come) venire; **where do you** ~ **from?** da dove vieni?; ~ **to** (reach) arrivare a; **that** ~**s to £10** fanno 10 sterline; ~ **into money** ricevere dei soldi; ~ **true/open** verificarsi/aprirsi; ~ **first** arrivare primo; fig venire prima di tutto; ~ **in two sizes** esistere in due misure; **the years to** ~ gli anni a venire; **how** ~? fam come mai? **come about** *vi* succedere. **come across** *vi* ~ **across** as being dare l'impressione di essere ● *vt* (find) imbattersi in. **come along** *vi* venire; (job, opportunity:) venire; (progress) andare bene. **come apart** *vi* smontarsi; (break) rompersi. **come away** *vi* venir via; (button, fastener:) staccarsi. **come back** *vi* ritornare. **come by** *vi* passare ● *vt* (obtain) avere. **come down** *vi* scendere; ~ **down to** (reach) arrivare a. **come in** *vi* entrare; (in race) arrivare; (tide:) salire. **come in for** *vt* ~ **in for criticism** essere criticato. **come off** *vi* staccarsi; (take place) esserci; (succeed) riuscire. **come on** *vi* (make progress) migliorare; ~ **on!** (hurry) dai!; (indicating disbelief) ma va là!. **come out** vi venir fuori; ⟨book, sun:⟩ uscire; ⟨stain:⟩ andar via. **come over** vi venire. **come round** vi venire; ⟨after fainting⟩ riaversi; ⟨change one's mind⟩ farsi convincere. **come to** vi ⟨after fainting⟩ riaversi. **come up** vi salire; ⟨sun:⟩ sorgere; ⟨plant:⟩ crescere; **something came up** (I was prevented) ho avuto un imprevisto. **come up with** vt tirar fuori

'**come-back** n ritorno m
comedian /kə'miːdɪən/ n comico m
'**come-down** n passo m indietro
comedy /'kɒmədɪ/ n commedia f
comet /'kɒmɪt/ n cometa f
come-uppance /kʌm'ʌpəns/ n **get one's ~** fam avere quel che si merita
comfort /'kʌmfət/ n benessere m; ⟨consolation⟩ conforto m ● vt confortare
comfortable /'kʌmfətəbl/ a comodo; **be ~e** ⟨person:⟩ stare comodo; ⟨fig: in situation⟩ essere a proprio agio; ⟨financially⟩ star bene. **~y** adv comodamente
'**comfort station** n Am bagno m pubblico
comfy /'kʌmfɪ/ a fam comodo
comic /'kɒmɪk/ a comico ● n comico, -a mf; ⟨periodical⟩ fumetto m. **~al** a comico. **~ strip** n striscia f di fumetti
coming /'kʌmɪŋ/ n venuta f; **~s and goings** viavai m
comma /'kɒmə/ n virgola f
command /kə'mɑːnd/ n comando m; ⟨order⟩ ordine m; ⟨mastery⟩ padronanza f ● vt ordinare; comandare ⟨army⟩
commandeer /kɒmən'dɪə(r)/ vt requisire
command|er /kə'mɑːndə(r)/ n comandante m. **~ing** ⟨view⟩ imponente; ⟨lead⟩ dominante. **~ing officer** n comandante m. **~ment** n comandamento m
commemorat|e /kə'meməreɪt/ vt commemorare. **~ion** /-'reɪʃn/ n commemorazione f. **~ive** /-ətɪv/ a commemorativo
commence /kə'mens/ vt/i cominciare. **~ment** n inizio m
commend /kə'mend/ vt complimentarsi con ⟨on per⟩; ⟨recommend⟩ raccomandare ⟨to a⟩. **~able** /-əbl/ a lodevole
commensurate /kə'menʃərət/ a proporzionato ⟨with a⟩
comment /'kɒment/ n commento m ● vi fare commenti ⟨on su⟩
commentary /'kɒməntrɪ/ n commento m; [**running**] **~** ⟨on radio, TV⟩ cronaca f diretta
commentat|e /'kɒmənteɪt/ vt **~e on**

TV, Radio fare la cronaca di. **~or** n cronista mf
commerce /'kɒmɜːs/ n commercio m
commercial /kə'mɜːʃl/ a commerciale ● n TV pubblicità f inv. **~ize** vt commercializzare
commiserate /kə'mɪzəreɪt/ vi esprimere il proprio rincrescimento ⟨with a⟩
commission /kə'mɪʃn/ n commissione f; **receive one's ~** Mil essere promosso ufficiale; **out of ~** fuori uso ● vt commissionare
commissionaire /kəmɪʃə'neə(r)/ n portiere m
commissioner /kə'mɪʃənə(r)/ n commissario m
commit /kə'mɪt/ vt ⟨pt/pp committed⟩ commettere; ⟨to prison, hospital⟩ affidare ⟨to a⟩; impegnare ⟨funds⟩; **~ oneself** impegnarsi. **~ment** n impegno m; ⟨involvement⟩ compromissione f. **~ted** a impegnato
committee /kə'mɪtɪ/ n comitato m
commodity /kə'mɒdətɪ/ n prodotto m
common /'kɒmən/ a comune; ⟨vulgar⟩ volgare ● n prato m pubblico; **have in ~** avere in comune; **House of C~s** Camera f dei Comuni. **~er** n persona f non nobile
common: **~ law** n diritto m consuetudinario. **~ly** adv comunemente. **C~ Market** n Mercato m Comune. **~place** a banale. **~-room** n sala f dei professori/degli studenti. **~ 'sense** n buon senso m
commotion /kə'məʊʃn/ n confusione f
communal /'kɒmjʊnl/ a comune
communicate /kə'mjuːnɪkeɪt/ vt/i comunicare
communication /kəmjuːnɪ'keɪʃn/ n comunicazione f; ⟨of disease⟩ trasmissione f; **be in ~ with sb** essere in contatto con qcno; **~s** pl ⟨technology⟩ telecomunicazioni fpl. **~ cord** n fermata f d'emergenza
communicative /kə'mjuːnɪkətɪv/ a comunicativo
Communion /kə'mjuːnɪən/ n [**Holy**] **~** comunione f
communiqué /kə'mjuːnɪkeɪ/ n comunicato m stampa
Communis|m /'kɒmjʊnɪzm/ n comunismo m. **~t** /-ɪst/ a & n comunista mf
community /kə'mjuːnətɪ/ n comunità f. **~ centre** n centro m sociale
commute /kə'mjuːt/ vi fare il pendolare ● vt Jur commutare. **~r** n pendolare mf

compact¹ /kəm'pækt/ *a* compatto

compact² /'kɒmpækt/ *n* portacipria *m inv*. ~ **disc** *n* compact disc *m inv*

companion /kəm'pænjən/ *n* compagno, -a *mf*. ~**ship** *n* compagnia *f*

company /'kʌmpənɪ/ *n* compagnia *f*; (*guests*) ospiti *mpl*. ~ **car** *n* macchina *f* della ditta

comparable /'kɒmpərəbl/ *a* paragonabile

comparative /kəm'pærətɪv/ *a* comparativo; (*relative*) relativo ● *n* Gram comparativo *m*. ~**ly** *adv* relativamente

compare /kəm'peə(r)/ *vt* paragonare (**with/to** *a*) ● *vi* essere paragonato

comparison /kəm'pærɪsn/ *n* paragone *m*

compartment /kəm'ɑːtmənt/ *n* compartimento *m*; Rail scompartimento *m*

compass /'kʌmpəs/ *n* bussola *f*. ~**es** *npl*, **pair of** ~**es** compasso *msg*

compassion /kəm'pæʃn/ *n* compassione *f*. ~**ate** /-ʃənət/ *a* compassionevole

compatible /kəm'pætəbl/ *a* compatibile

compatriot /kəm'pætrɪət/ *n* compatriota *mf*

compel /kəm'pel/ *vt* (*pt/pp* **compelled**) costringere. ~**ling** *a* (*reason*) inconfutabile

compensat|**e** /'kɒmpənseɪt/ *vt* risarcire ● *vi* ~**e for** *fig* compensare di. ~**ion** /-'seɪʃn/ *n* risarcimento *m*; (*fig: comfort*) consolazione *f*

compère /'kɒmpeə(r)/ *n* presentatore, -trice *mf*

compete /kəm'piːt/ *vi* competere; (*take part*) gareggiare

competen|**ce** /'kɒmpɪtəns/ *n* competenza *f*. ~**t** *a* competente

competition /kɒmpə'tɪʃn/ *n* concorrenza *f*; (*contest*) gara *f*

competitive /kəm'petɪtɪv/ *a* competitivo; ~ **prices** prezzi *mpl* concorrenziali

competitor /kəm'petɪtə(r)/ *n* concorrente *mf*

complacen|**cy** /kəm'pleɪsənsɪ/ *n* compiacimento *m*. ~**t** *a* compiaciuto

complain /kəm'pleɪn/ *vi* lamentarsi (**about** *di*); (*formally*) reclamare; ~ **of** *Med* accusare. ~**t** *n* lamentela *f*, (*formal*) reclamo *m*; *Med* disturbo *m*

complement¹ /'kɒmplɪmənt/ *n* complemento *m*

complement² /'kɒmplɪment/ *vt* complementare; ~ **each other** complementarsi a vicenda. ~**ary** /-'mentərɪ/ *a* complementare

complete /kəm'pliːt/ *a* completo; (*utter*) finito ● *vt* completare; compilare (*form*). ~**ly** *adv* completamente

completion /kəm'pliːʃn/ *n* fine *f*

complex /'kɒmpleks/ *a* complesso ● *n* complesso *m*

complexion /kəm'plekʃn/ *n* carnagione *f*

complexity /kəm'pleksətɪ/ *n* complessità *f inv*

compliance /kəm'plaɪəns/ *n* accettazione *f*; (*with rules*) osservanza *f*; **in** ~ **with** in osservanza a (*law*); conformemente a (*request*)

complicat|**e** /'kɒmplɪkeɪt/ *vt* complicare. ~**ed** *a* complicato. ~**ion** /-'keɪʃn/ *n* complicazione *f*

compliment /'kɒmplɪmənt/ *n* complimento *m*; ~**s** *pl* omaggi *mpl* ● *vt* complimentare. ~**ary** /-'mentərɪ/ *a* complimentoso; (*given free*) in omaggio

comply /kəm'plaɪ/ *vi* (*pt/pp* -**ied**) ~ **with** conformarsi a

component /kəm'pəʊnənt/ *a* & *n* ~ (**part**) componente *m*

compose /kəm'pəʊz/ *vt* comporre; ~ **oneself** ricomporsi; **be** ~**d of** essere composto da. ~**d** *a* (*calm*) composto. ~**r** *n* compositore, -trice *mf*

composition /kɒmpə'zɪʃn/ *n* composizione *f*; (*essay*) tema *m*

compost /'kɒmpɒst/ *n* composta *f*

composure /kəm'pəʊʒə(r)/ *n* calma *f*

compound /'kɒmpaʊnd/ *a* composto. ~ **fracture** *n* frattura *f* esposta. ~ **interest** *n* interesse *m* composto ● *n* Chem composto *m*; Gram parola *f* composta; (*enclosure*) recinto *m*

comprehend /kɒmprɪ'hend/ *vt* comprendere. ~**sible** /-'hensəbl/ *a* comprensibile. ~**sion** /-'henʃn/ *n* comprensione *f*

comprehensive /kɒmprɪ'hensɪv/ *a* & *n* comprensivo; ~ **[school]** *scuola f media* in cui gli allievi hanno capacità d'apprendimento *diverse*. ~ **insurance** *n* Auto polizza *f* casco

compress¹ /'kɒmpres/ *n* compressa *f*

compress² /kəm'pres/ *vt* comprimere; ~**ed air** aria *f* compressa

comprise /kəm'praɪz/ *vt* comprendere; (*form*) costituire

compromise /'kɒmprəmaɪz/ *n* compromesso *m* ● *vt* compromettere ● *vi* fare un compromesso

285

compuls|ion /kəm'pʌlʃn/ n desiderio m irresistibile. **~ive** /-sɪv/ a Psych patologico. **~ive eating** voglia f ossessiva di mangiare. **~ory** /-sərɪ/ a obbligatorio

comput|er /kəm'pjuːtə(r)/ n computer m inv. **~erize** vt computerizzare. **~ing** n informatica f

comrade /'kɒmreɪd/ n camerata m; Pol compagno, -a mf. **~ship** n cameratismo m

con[1] /kɒn/ see **pro**

con[2] n fam fregatura f ●vt (pt/pp conned) fam fregare

concave /'kɒnkeɪv/ a concavo

conceal /kən'siːl/ vt nascondere

concede /kən'siːd/ vt (admit) ammettere; (give up) rinunciare a; lasciar fare ⟨goal⟩

conceit /kən'siːt/ n presunzione f. **~ed** a presuntuoso

conceivable /kən'siːvəbl/ a concepibile

conceive /kən'siːv/ vt Biol concepire ●vi aver figli. **conceive of** vt fig concepire

concentrat|e /'kɒnsəntreɪt/ vt concentrare ●vi concentrarsi. **~ion** /-'treɪʃn/ n concentrazione f. **~ion camp** n campo m di concentramento

concept /'kɒnsept/ n concetto m. **~ion** /kən'sepʃn/ n concezione f; (idea) idea f

concern /kən'sɜːn/ n preoccupazione f; Comm attività f inv ●vt (be about, affect) riguardare; (worry) preoccupare; **be ~ed about** essere preoccupato per; **~ oneself with** preoccuparsi di; **as far as I am ~ed** per quanto mi riguarda. **~ing** prep riguardo a

concert /'kɒnsət/ n concerto m. **~ed** /kən'sɜːtɪd/ a collettivo

concertina /kɒnsə'tiːnə/ n piccola fisarmonica f

'concertmaster n Am primo violino m

concerto /kən'tʃeətəʊ/ n concerto m

concession /kən'seʃn/ n concessione f; (reduction) sconto m. **~ary** a (reduced) scontato

conciliation /kənsɪlɪ'eɪʃn/ n conciliazione f

concise /kən'saɪs/ a conciso

conclu|de /kən'kluːd/ vt concludere ●vi concludersi. **~ding** a finale

conclusion /kən'kluːʒn/ n conclusione f; **in ~** per concludere

conclusive /kən'kluːsɪv/ a definitivo. **~ly** adv in modo definitivo

concoct /kən'kɒkt/ vt confezionare; fig inventare. **~ion** /-ɒkʃn/ n mistura f; (drink) intruglio m

concourse /'kɒnkɔːs/ n atrio m

concrete /'kɒnkriːt/ a concreto ●n calcestruzzo m

concur /kən'kɜː(r)/ vi (pt/pp concurred) essere d'accordo

concurrently /kən'kʌrəntlɪ/ adv contemporaneamente

concussion /kən'kʌʃn/ n commozione f cerebrale

condemn /kən'dem/ vt condannare; dichiarare inagibile ⟨building⟩. **~ation** /kɒndem'neɪʃn/ n condanna f

condensation /kɒnden'seɪʃn/ n condensazione f

condense /kən'dens/ vt condensare; Phys condensare ●vi condensarsi. **~d milk** n latte m condensato

condescend /kɒndɪ'send/ vi degnarsi. **~ing** a condiscendente

condition /kən'dɪʃn/ n condizione f; **on ~ that** a condizione che ●vt Psych condizionare. **~al** a ⟨acceptance⟩ condizionato; Gram condizionale ●n Gram condizionale m. **~er** n balsamo m; (for fabrics) ammorbidente m

condolences /kən'dəʊlənsɪz/ npl condoglianze fpl

condom /'kɒndɒm/ n preservativo m

condo[minium] /'kɒndə('mɪnɪəm)/ n Am condominio m

condone /kən'dəʊn/ vt passare sopra a

conducive /kən'djuːsɪv/ a **be ~ to** contribuire a

conduct[1] /'kɒndʌkt/ n condotta f

conduct[2] /kən'dʌkt/ vt condurre; dirigere ⟨orchestra⟩. **~or** n direttore m d'orchestra; (of bus) bigliettaio m; Phys conduttore m. **~ress** n bigliettaia f

cone /kəʊn/ n cono m; Bot pigna f; Auto birillo m ●**cone off** vt **be ~d off** Auto essere chiuso da birilli

confectioner /kən'fekʃənə(r)/ n pasticciere, -a mf. **~y** n pasticceria f

confederation /kənfedə'reɪʃn/ n federazione f

confer /kən'fɜː(r)/ v (pt/pp conferred) ●vt conferire (ona) ●vi (discuss) conferire

conference /'kɒnfərəns/ n conferenza f

confess /kən'fes/ vt confessare ●vi confessare; Relig confessarsi. **~ion** /-eʃn/ n confessione f. **~ional** /-eʃənəl/ n confessionale m. **~or** n confessore m

confetti /kən'fetɪ/ n coriandoli mpl

confide /kənˈfaɪd/ vt confidare. **confide in** vt ~ **in sb** fidarsi di qcno

confidence /ˈkɒnfɪdəns/ n (trust) fiducia f; (self-assurance) sicurezza f di sé; (secret) confidenza f; **in** ~ **in** confidenza. ~ **trick** n truffa f

confident /ˈkɒnfɪdənt/ a fiducioso; (self-assured) sicuro di sé. ~**ly** adv con aria fiduciosa

confidential /kɒnfɪˈdenʃl/ a confidenziale

confine /kənˈfaɪn/ vt rinchiudere; (limit) limitare; **be** ~**d to bed** essere confinato a letto. ~**d** a (space) limitato. ~**ment** n detenzione f; Med parto m

confines /ˈkɒnfaɪnz/ npl confini mpl

confirm /kənˈfɜːm/ vt confermare; Relig cresimare. ~**ation** /kɒnfəˈmeɪʃn/ n conferma f; Relig cresima f. ~**ed** a incallito; ~**ed bachelor** scapolo m impenitente

confiscat|e /ˈkɒnfɪskeɪt/ vt confiscare. ~**ion** /-ˈkeɪʃn/ n confisca f

conflict¹ /ˈkɒnflɪkt/ n conflitto m

conflict² /kənˈflɪkt/ vi essere in contraddizione. ~**ing** a contraddittorio

conform /kənˈfɔːm/ vi (person:) conformarsi; (thing:) essere conforme (**to** a). ~**ist** n conformista mf

confounded /kənˈfaʊndɪd/ a fam maledetto

confront /kənˈfrʌnt/ vt affrontare; **the problems** ~**ing us** i problemi che dobbiamo affrontare. ~**ation** /kɒnfrʌnˈteɪʃn/ n confronto m

confus|e /kənˈfjuːz/ vt confondere. ~**ing** a che confonde. ~**ion** /-ˈjuːʒn/ n confusione f

congeal /kənˈdʒiːl/ vi (blood:) coagularsi

congenial /kənˈdʒiːnɪəl/ a congeniale

congenital /kənˈdʒenɪtl/ a congenito

congest|ed /kənˈdʒestɪd/ a congestionato. ~**ion** /-estʃn/ n congestione f

congratulat|e /kənˈɡrætjʊleɪt/ vt congratularsi con (**on** per). ~**ions** /-ˈeɪʃnz/ npl congratulazioni fpl

congregat|e /ˈkɒŋɡrɪɡeɪt/ vi radunarsi. ~**ion** /-ˈɡeɪʃn/ n Relig assemblea f

congress /ˈkɒŋɡres/ n congresso m. ~**man** n Am Pol membro m del congresso

conical /ˈkɒnɪkl/ a conico

conifer /ˈkɒnɪfə(r)/ n conifera f

conjecture /kənˈdʒektʃə(r)/ n congettura f

conjugal /ˈkɒndʒʊɡl/ a coniugale

conjugat|e /ˈkɒndʒʊɡeɪt/ vt coniugare. ~**ion** /-ˈɡeɪʃn/ n coniugazione f

conjunction /kənˈdʒʌŋkʃn/ n congiunzione f; **in** ~ **with** insieme a

conjunctivitis /kəndʒʌŋktɪˈvaɪtɪs/ n congiuntivite f

conjur|e /ˈkʌndʒə(r)/ vi ~**ing tricks** npl giochi mpl di prestigio. ~**or** n prestigiatore, -trice mf. **conjure up** vt evocare (image); tirar fuori dal nulla (meal)

conk /kɒŋk/ vi ~ **out** fam (machine:) guastarsi; (person:) crollare

con-man n fam truffatore m

connect /kəˈnekt/ vt collegare; **be** ~**ed with** avere legami con; (be related to) essere imparentato con; **be well** ~**ed** avere conoscenze influenti ● vi essere collegato (**with** a); (train:) fare coincidenza

connection /kəˈnekʃn/ n (between ideas) nesso m; (in travel) coincidenza f; Electr collegamento m; **in** ~ **with** con riferimento a. ~**s** pl (people) conoscenze fpl

connoisseur /kɒnəˈsɜː(r)/ n intenditore, -trice mf

conquer /ˈkɒŋkə(r)/ vt conquistare; fig superare (fear). ~**or** n conquistatore m

conquest /ˈkɒŋkwest/ n conquista f

conscience /ˈkɒnʃəns/ n coscienza f

conscientious /kɒnʃɪˈenʃəs/ a coscienzoso. ~ **objector** n obiettore m di coscienza

conscious /ˈkɒnʃəs/ a conscio; (decision) meditato; |fully| ~ cosciente; **be/become** ~ **of sth** rendersi conto di qcsa. ~**ly** adv consapevolmente. ~**ness** n consapevolezza f; Med conoscenza f

conscript¹ /ˈkɒnskrɪpt/ n coscritto m

conscript² /kənˈskrɪpt/ vt Mil chiamare alle armi. ~**ion** /-ɪpʃn/ n coscrizione f, leva f

consecrat|e /ˈkɒnsɪkreɪt/ vt consacrare. ~**ion** /-ˈkreɪʃn/ n consacrazione f

consecutive /kənˈsekjʊtɪv/ a consecutivo

consensus /kənˈsensəs/ n consenso m

consent /kənˈsent/ n consenso m ● vi acconsentire

consequen|ce /ˈkɒnsɪkwəns/ n conseguenza f; (importance) importanza f. ~**t** a conseguente. ~**tly** adv di conseguenza

conservation /kɒnsəˈveɪʃn/ n conservazione f. ~**ist** n fautore, -trice mf della tutela ambientale

conservative /kənˈsɜːvətɪv/ a conservativo; (estimate) ottimistico. **C**~

287

Pol *a* conservatore. ● *n* conservatore, -trice *mf*

conservatory /kənˈsɜːvətrɪ/ *n* spazio *m* chiuso da vetrate adiacente alla casa

conserve /kənˈsɜːv/ *vt* conservare

consider /kənˈsɪdə(r)/ *vt* considerare; **~ doing sth** considerare la possibilità di fare qcsa. **~able** /-əbl/ *a* considerevole. **~ably** *adv* considerevolmente

considerate /kənˈsɪdərət/ *a* pieno di riguardo. **~ately** *adv* con riguardo. **~ation** /-ˈreɪʃn/ *n* considerazione *f*; *(thoughtfulness)* attenzione *f*; *(respect)* riguardo *m*; *(payment)* compenso *m*; **take into ~ation** prendere in considerazione. **~ing** *prep* considerando

consign /kənˈsaɪn/ *vt* affidare. **~ment** *n* consegna *f*

consist /kənˈsɪst/ *vi* **~ of** consistere di

consisten|cy /kənˈsɪstənsɪ/ *n* coerenza *f*; *(density)* consistenza *f*. **~t** *a* coerente; *(loyalty)* costante. **~tly** *adv* coerentemente; *(late, loyal)* costantemente

consolation /kɒnsəˈleɪʃn/ *n* consolazione *f*. **~ prize** *n* premio *m* di consolazione

console /kənˈsəʊl/ *vt* consolare

consolidate /kənˈsɒlɪdeɪt/ *vt* consolidare

consonant /ˈkɒnsənənt/ *n* consonante *f*

consort /kənˈsɔːt/ *vi* **~ with** frequentare

consortium /kənˈsɔːtɪəm/ *n* consorzio *m*

conspicuous /kənˈspɪkjʊəs/ *a* facilmente distinguibile

conspiracy /kənˈspɪrəsɪ/ *n* cospirazione *f*

conspire /kənˈspaɪə(r)/ *vi* cospirare

constable /ˈkʌnstəbl/ *n* agente *m* [di polizia]

constant /ˈkɒnstənt/ *a* costante. **~ly** *adv* costantemente

constellation /kɒnstəˈleɪʃn/ *n* costellazione *f*

consternation /kɒnstəˈneɪʃn/ *n* costernazione *f*

constipat|ed /ˈkɒnstɪpeɪtɪd/ *a* stitico. **~ion** /-ˈpeɪʃn/ *n* stitichezza *f*

constituency /kənˈstɪtjʊənsɪ/ *n* area *f* elettorale di un deputato nel Regno Unito

constituent /kənˈstɪtjʊənt/ *n* costituente *m*; *Pol* elettore, -trice *mf*

constitut|e /ˈkɒnstɪtjuːt/ *vt* costituire. **~ion** /-ˈtjuːʃn/ *n* costituzione *f*. **~ional** /-ˈtjuːʃənl/ *a* costituzionale

constrain /kənˈstreɪn/ *vt* costringere.

~t *n* costrizione *f*; *(restriction)* restrizione *f*; *(strained manner)* disagio *m*

construct /kənˈstrʌkt/ *vt* costruire. **~ion** /-ˈʌkʃn/ *n* costruzione *f*; **under ~ion** in costruzione. **~ive** /-ɪv/ *a* costruttivo

construe /kənˈstruː/ *vt* interpretare

consul /ˈkɒnsl/ *n* console *m*. **~ar** /ˈkɒnsjʊlə(r)/ *a* consolare. **~ate** /ˈkɒnsjʊlət/ *n* consolato *m*

consult /kənˈsʌlt/ *vt* consultare. **~ant** *n* consulente *mf*; *Med* specialista *mf*. **~ation** /kɒnslˈteɪʃn/ *n* consultazione *f*; *Med* consulto *m*

consume /kənˈsjuːm/ *vt* consumare. **~r** *n* consumatore, -trice *mf*. **~r goods** *npl* beni *mpl* di consumo. **~er organization** *n* organizzazione *f* per la tutela dei consumatori

consumerism /kənˈsjuːmərɪzm/ *n* consumismo *m*

consummate /ˈkɒnsəmeɪt/ *vt* consumare

consumption /kənˈsʌmpʃn/ *n* consumo *m*

contact /ˈkɒntækt/ *n* contatto *m*; *(person)* conoscenza *f* ● *vt* mettersi in contatto con. **~ lenses** *npl* lenti *fpl* a contatto

contagious /kənˈteɪdʒəs/ *a* contagioso

contain /kənˈteɪn/ *vt* contenere; **~ oneself** controllarsi. **~er** *n* recipiente *m*; *(for transport)* container *m inv*

contaminat|e /kənˈtæmɪneɪt/ *vt* contaminare. **~ion** /-ˈneɪʃn/ *n* contaminazione *f*

contemplat|e /ˈkɒntəmpleɪt/ *vt* contemplare; *(consider)* considerare; **~e doing sth** considerare di fare qcsa. **~ion** /-ˈpleɪʃn/ *n* contemplazione *f*

contemporary /kənˈtempərərɪ/ *a & n* contemporaneo, -a *mf*

contempt /kənˈtempt/ *n* disprezzo *m*; **beneath ~** più che vergognoso; **~ of court** oltraggio *m* alla Corte. **~ible** /-əbl/ *a* spregevole. **~uous** /-tjʊəs/ *a* sprezzante

contend /kənˈtend/ *vi* **~ with** occuparsi di. ● *vt (assert)* sostenere. **~er** *n* concorrente *mf*

content[1] /ˈkɒntent/ *n* contenuto *m*

content[2] /kənˈtent/ *a* soddisfatto ● *vt* **~ oneself** accontentarsi *(with* di). **~ed** *a* soddisfatto. **~edly** *adv* con aria soddisfatta

contention /kənˈtenʃn/ *n (assertion)* opinione *f*

contentment /kən'tentmənt/ n soddisfazione f

contents /'kɒntents/ npl contenuto m

contest[1] /'kɒntest/ n gara f

contest[2] /kən'test/ vt contestare ⟨statement⟩; impugnare ⟨will⟩; Pol ⟨candidates⟩ contendersi; ⟨one candidate⟩ aspirare a. ~**ant** n concorrente mf

context /'kɒntekst/ n contesto m

continent /'kɒntinənt/ n continente m; **the C~** l'Europa f continentale

continental /kɒntɪ'nentl/ a continentale. ~ **breakfast** n prima colazione f a base di pane, burro, marmellata, croissant, ecc. ~ **quilt** n piumone m

contingency /kən'tɪndʒənsɪ/ n eventualità f inv

continual /kən'tɪnjʊəl/ a continuo

continuation /kəntɪnjʊ'eɪʃn/ n continuazione f

continue /kən'tɪnjuː/ vt continuare; ~ **doing** or **to do sth** continuare a fare qcsa; **to be ~d** continua ● vi continuare. ~**d** a continuo

continuity /kɒntɪ'njuːətɪ/ n continuità f

continuous /kən'tɪnjʊəs/ a continuo

contort /kən'tɔːt/ vt contorcere. ~**ion** /-ʃ/n contorsione f. ~**ionist** n contorsionista mf

contour /'kɒntʊə/ n contorno m; ⟨line⟩ curva f di livello

contraband /'kɒntrəbænd/ n contrabbando m

contracep|tion /kɒntrə'sepʃn/ n contraccezione f. ~**tive** /-tɪv/ n contraccettivo m

contract[1] /'kɒntrækt/ n contratto m

contract[2] /kən'trækt/ vi ⟨get smaller⟩ contrarsi ● vt contrarre ⟨illness⟩. ~**ion** /-ækʃn/ n contrazione f. ~**or** n imprenditore, -trice mf

contradict /kɒntrə'dɪkt/ vt contraddire. ~**ion** /-ɪkʃn/ n contraddizione f. ~**ory** a contraddittorio

contra-flow /'kɒntrəfləʊ/ n utilizzazione f di una corsia nei due sensi di marcia durante lavori stradali

contralto /kən'træltəʊ/ n contralto m

contraption /kən'træpʃn/ n fam aggeggio m

contrary[1] /'kɒntrərɪ/ a contrario ● adv ~ **to** contrariamente a ● n contrario m; **on the** ~ al contrario

contrary[2] /kən'treərɪ/ a disobbediente

contrast[1] /'kɒntrɑːst/ n contrasto m

contrast[2] /kən'trɑːst/ vt confrontare ● vi contrastare. ~**ing** a contrastante

contraven|e /kɒntrə'viːn/ vt trasgredire. ~**tion** /-'venʃn/ n trasgressione f

contribut|e /kən'trɪbjuːt/ vt/i contribuire. ~**ion** /kɒntrɪ'bjuːʃn/ n contribuzione f; ⟨what is contributed⟩ contributo m. ~**or** n contributore, -trice mf

contrive /kən'traɪv/ vt escogitare; ~ **to do sth** riuscire a fare qcsa

control /kən'trəʊl/ n controllo m; ~**s** pl ⟨of car, plane⟩ comandi mpl; **get out of** ~ sfuggire al controllo ● vt (pt/pp **controlled**) controllare; ~ **oneself** controllarsi

controvers|ial /kɒntrə'vɜːʃl/ a controverso. ~**y** /'kɒntrəvɜːsɪ/ n controversia f

conurbation /kɒnɜː'beɪʃn/ n conurbazione f

convalesce /kɒnvə'les/ vi essere in convalescenza

convalescent /kɒnvə'lesənt/ a convalescente. ~ **home** n convalescenziario m

convector /kən'vektə(r)/ n ~ [**heater**] convettore m

convene /kən'viːn/ vt convocare ● vi riunirsi

convenience /kən'viːnɪəns/ n convenienza f; [**public**] ~ gabinetti mpl pubblici; **with all modern** ~**s** con tutti i comfort

convenient /kən'viːnɪənt/ a comodo; **be** ~ **for sb** andar bene per qcno; **if it is** ~ [**for you**] se ti va bene. ~**ly** adv comodamente; ~**ly located** in una posizione comoda

convent /'kɒnvənt/ n convento m

convention /kən'venʃn/ n convenzione f; ⟨assembly⟩ convegno m. ~**al** a convenzionale

converge /kən'vɜːdʒ/ vi convergere

conversant /kən'vɜːsənt/ a ~ **with** pratico di

conversation /kɒnvə'seɪʃn/ n conversazione f. ~**al** a di conversazione. ~**alist** n conversatore, -trice mf

converse[1] /kən'vɜːs/ vi conversare

converse[2] /'kɒnvɜːs/ n inverso m. ~**ly** adv viceversa

conversion /kən'vɜːʃn/ n conversione f

convert[1] /'kɒnvɜːt/ n convertito, -a mf

convert[2] /kən'vɜːt/ vt convertire ⟨into in⟩; sconsacrare ⟨church⟩. ~**ible** /-əbl/ a convertibile ● n Auto macchina f decappottabile

convex /'kɒnveks/ a convesso

convey /kən'veɪ/ vt portare; trasmettere ⟨idea, message⟩. ~or belt n nastro m trasportatore

convict[1] /ˈkɒnvɪkt/ n condannato, -a mf

convict[2] /kənˈvɪkt/ vt giudicare colpevole. ~ion /-ɪkʃn/ n condanna f; ⟨belief⟩ convinzione f; **previous** ~ion precedente m penale

convinc|e /kənˈvɪns/ vt convincere. ~ing a convincente

convivial /kənˈvɪvɪəl/ a conviviale

convoluted /ˈkɒnvəluːtɪd/ a contorto

convoy /ˈkɒnvɔɪ/ n convoglio m

convuls|e /kənˈvʌls/ vt sconvolgere; **be ~ed with laughter** contorcersi dalle risa. ~ion /-ʌlʃn/ n convulsione f

coo /kuː/ vi tubare

cook /kʊk/ n cuoco, -a mf ● vt cucinare; **is it ~ed?** è cotto?; ~ **the books** fam truccare i libri contabili ● vi ⟨food:⟩ cuocere; ⟨person:⟩ cucinare. ~**book** n libro m di cucina

cooker /ˈkʊkə(r)/ n cucina f; ⟨apple⟩ mela f da cuocere. ~**y** n cucina f. ~**y book** n libro m di cucina

cookie /ˈkʊkɪ/ n Am biscotto m

cool /kuːl/ a fresco; ⟨calm⟩ calmo; ⟨unfriendly⟩ freddo ● n fresco m ● vt rinfrescare ● vi rinfrescarsi. ~**box** n borsa f termica. ~**ness** n freddezza f

coop /kuːp/ n stia f ● vt ~ **up** rinchiudere

co-operat|e /kəʊˈɒpəreɪt/ vi cooperare. ~**ion** /-ˈreɪʃn/ n cooperazione f

co-operative /kəʊˈɒpərətɪv/ a cooperativo ● n cooperativa f

co-opt /kəʊˈɒpt/ vt eleggere

co-ordinat|e /kəʊˈɔːdɪneɪt/ vt coordinare. ~**ion** /-ˈneɪʃn/ n coordinazione f

cop /kɒp/ n fam poliziotto m

cope /kəʊp/ vi fam farcela; **can she ~ by herself?** ce la fa da sola?; ~ **with** farcela con

copious /ˈkəʊpɪəs/ a abbondante

copper[1] /ˈkɒpə(r)/ n rame m; ~**s** pl monete fpl da uno o due pence ● attrib di rame

copper[2] n fam poliziotto m

coppice /ˈkɒpɪs/ n, **copse** /kɒps/ n boschetto m

copulat|e /ˈkɒpjʊleɪt/ vi accoppiarsi. ~**ion** /-ˈleɪʃn/ n copulazione f

copy /ˈkɒpɪ/ n copia f ● vt ⟨pt/pp -ied⟩ copiare

copy: ~**right** n diritti mpl d'autore. ~**writer** n copywriter mf inv

coral /ˈkɒrəl/ n corallo m

cord /kɔːd/ n corda f; ⟨thinner⟩ cordon-

cino m; ⟨fabric⟩ velluto m a coste; ~**s** pl pantaloni mpl di velluto a coste

cordial /ˈkɔːdɪəl/ a cordiale ● n analcolico m

cordon /ˈkɔːdn/ n cordone m ⟨di persone⟩ ● **cordon off** vt mettere un cordone ⟨di persone⟩ intorno a

corduroy /ˈkɔːdərɔɪ/ n velluto m a coste

core /kɔː(r)/ n ⟨of apple, pear⟩ torsolo m; ⟨fig: of organization⟩ cuore m; ⟨of problem, theory⟩ nocciolo m

cork /kɔːk/ n sughero m; ⟨for bottle⟩ turacciolo m. ~**screw** n cavatappi m inv

corn[1] /kɔːn/ n grano m; ⟨Am: maize⟩ granturco m

corn[2] n Med callo m

cornea /ˈkɔːnɪə/ n cornea f

corned beef /kɔːndˈbiːf/ n manzo m sotto sale

corner /ˈkɔːnə(r)/ n angolo m; ⟨football⟩ calcio m d'angolo, corner m inv ● vt fig bloccare; Comm accaparrarsi ⟨market⟩

cornet /ˈkɔːnɪt/ n Mus cornetta f; ⟨for ice-cream⟩ cono m

corn: ~**flour** n, Am ~**starch** n farina f di granturco

corny /ˈkɔːnɪ/ a ⟨-ier, -est⟩ ⟨fam: joke, film⟩ scontato; ⟨person⟩ banale; ⟨sentimental⟩ sdolcinato

coronary /ˈkɒrənərɪ/ a coronario ● n ~ **[thrombosis]** trombosi f coronarica

coronation /kɒrəˈneɪʃn/ n incoronazione f

coroner /ˈkɒrənə(r)/ n coroner m inv ⟨nel diritto britannico, ufficiale incaricato delle indagini su morti sospette⟩

corporal[1] /ˈkɔːpərəl/ n Mil caporale m

corporal[2] a corporale; ~ **punishment** punizione f corporale

corporate /ˈkɔːpərət/ a ⟨decision, policy, image⟩ aziendale; ~ **life** la vita in un'azienda

corporation /kɔːpəˈreɪʃn/ n ente m; ⟨of town⟩ consiglio m comunale

corps /kɔː(r)/ n ⟨pl corps /kɔːz/⟩ corpo m

corpse /kɔːps/ n cadavere m

corpulent /ˈkɔːpjʊlənt/ a corpulento

corpuscle /ˈkɔːpʌsl/ n globulo m

correct /kəˈrekt/ a corretto; **be** ~ ⟨person:⟩ aver ragione; ~! esatto! ● vt correggere. ~**ion** /-ekʃn/ n correzione f. ~**ly** adv correttamente

correlation /kɒrəˈleɪʃn/ n correlazione f

correspond /kɒrɪˈspɒnd/ vi corrispondere ⟨to a⟩; ⟨two things:⟩ corrispondere; (write) scriversi. ~ence n corrispondenza f. ~ent n corrispondente mf. ~ing a corrispondente. ~ingly adv in modo corrispondente

corridor /'kɒrɪdɔː(r)/ n corridoio m

corroborate /kə'rɒbəreɪt/ vt corroborare

corro|de /kə'rəʊd/ vt corrodere ● vi corrodersi. ~sion /-'rəʊʒn/ n corrosione f

corrugated /'kɒrəgeɪtɪd/ a ondulato. ~ iron n lamiera f ondulata

corrupt /kə'rʌpt/ a corrotto ● vt corrompere. ~ion /-ʌpʃn/ n corruzione f

corset /'kɔːsɪt/ n & -s pl busto m

Corsica /'kɔːsɪkə/ n Corsica f. ~n a & n corso, -a mf

cortège /kɔː'teɪʒ/ n |funeral| ~ corteo m funebre

cosh /kɒʃ/ n rundello m

cosmetic /kɒz'metɪk/ a cosmetico ● n ~s pl cosmetici mpl

cosmic /'kɒzmɪk/ a cosmico

cosmonaut /'kɒzmənɔːt/ n cosmonauta mf

cosmopolitan /kɒzmə'pɒlɪtən/ a cosmopolita

cosmos /'kɒzmɒs/ n cosmo m

cosset /'kɒsɪt/ vt coccolare

cost /kɒst/ n costo m; ~s pl Jur spese fpl processuali; **at all** ~**s** a tutti i costi; **I learnt to my** ~ ho imparato a mie spese ● vt (pt/pp cost) costare; **it** ~ **me £20** mi è costato 20 sterline ● vt (pt/pp costed) ~ |out| stabilire il prezzo di

costly /'kɒstlɪ/ a (-ier, -iest) costoso

cost: ~ **of living** n costo m della vita. ~ **price** n prezzo m di costo

costume /'kɒstjuːm/ n costume m. ~ **jewellery** n bigiotteria f

cosy /'kəʊzɪ/ a (-ier, -iest) (pub, chat) intimo; **it's nice and** ~ **in here** si sta bene qui

cot /kɒt/ n lettino m; (Am: camp-bed) branda f

cottage /'kɒtɪdʒ/ n casetta f. ~ **cheese** n fiocchi mpl di latte

cotton /'kɒtn/ n cotone m ● attrib di cotone ● **cotton on** vi fam capire

cotton 'wool n cotone m idrofilo

couch /kaʊtʃ/ n divano m. ~ **potato** n pantofolaio, -a f

couchette /kuː'ʃet/ n cuccetta f

cough /kɒf/ n tosse f ● vi tossire. **cough up** vt/i sputare; (fam: pay) sborsare

cough mixture n sciroppo m per la tosse

could /kʊd/, atono /kəd/ v aux (see also

can²) ~ **I have a glass of water?** potrei avere un bicchier d'acqua?; **I** ~**n't do it even if I wanted to** non potrei farlo nemmeno se lo volessi; **I** ~**n't care less** non potrebbe importarmene di meno; **he** ~**n't have done it without help** non avrebbe potuto farlo senza aiuto; **you** ~ **have phoned** avresti potuto telefonare

council /'kaʊnsl/ n consiglio m. ~ **house** n casa f popolare

councillor /'kaʊnsələ(r)/ n consigliere, -a f

council tax n imposta f locale sugli immobili

counsel /'kaʊnsl/ n consigli mpl; Jur avvocato m ● vt (pt/pp counselled) consigliare a (person). ~**lor** n consigliere, -a f

count¹ /kaʊnt/ n (nobleman) conte m

count² n conto m; **keep** ~ tenere il conto ● vt/i contare. **count on** vt contare su

countdown /'kaʊntdaʊn/ n conto m alla rovescia

countenance /'kaʊntənəns/ n espressione f ● vt approvare

counter¹ /'kaʊntə(r)/ n banco m; (in games) gettone m

counter² adv ~ **to** contro, in contrasto a; **go** ~ **to sth** andare contro qcsa ● vt/i opporre (measure, effect); parare (blow)

counter'act vt neutralizzare

counter-attack n contrattacco m

counter-'espionage n controspionaggio m

counterfeit /-fɪt/ a contraffatto ● n contraffazione f ● vt contraffare

counterfoil n matrice f

counterpart n equivalente mf

counter-pro'ductive a controproduttivo

countersign vt controfirmare

countess /'kaʊntɪs/ n contessa f

countless /'kaʊntlɪs/ a innumerevole

country /'kʌntrɪ/ n nazione f, paese m; (native land) patria f; (countryside) campagna f; **in the** ~ in campagna; **go to the** ~ andare in campagna; Pol indire le elezioni politiche. ~**man** n uomo m di campagna; (fellow ~man) compatriota m. ~**side** n campagna f

county /'kaʊntɪ/ n contea f (unità amministrativa britannica)

coup /kuː/ n Pol colpo m di stato

couple /'kʌpl/ n coppia f; **a** ~ **of** un paio di

coupon /'kuːpɒn/ n tagliando m; (for discount) buono m sconto

courage /'kʌrɪdʒ/ n coraggio m. **~ous** /kə'reɪdʒəs/ a coraggioso

courgette /kʊə'ʒet/ n zucchino m

courier /'kʊrɪə(r)/ n corriere m; (for tourists) guida f

course /kɔːs/ n Sch corso m: Naut rotta f; Culin portata f; (for golf) campo m: **~ of treatment** Med serie f inv di cure; **of ~** naturalmente; **in the ~ of** durante; **in due ~** a tempo debito

court /kɔːt/ n tribunale m; Sport campo m; **take sb to ~** citare qcno in giudizio ● vt fare la corte a ⟨woman⟩; sfidare ⟨danger⟩. **~ing couples** coppiette fpl

courteous /'kɜːtɪəs/ a cortese

courtesy /'kɜːtəsɪ/ n cortesia f

court: ~ 'martial n (pl **~s martial**) corte f marziale ● **~-martial** vt (pt **~-martialled**) portare davanti alla corte marziale; **~yard** n cortile m

cousin /'kʌzn/ n cugino, -a mf

cove /kəʊv/ n insenatura f

cover /'kʌvə(r)/ n copertura f; (of cushion, to protect sth) fodera f; (of book, magazine) copertina f; **take ~** mettersi al riparo; **under separate ~** a parte ● vt coprire: foderare ⟨cushion⟩: Journ fare un servizio su. **cover up** vt coprire: fig soffocare ⟨scandal⟩

coverage /'kʌvərɪdʒ/ n Journ **it got a lot of ~** i media gli hanno dedicato molto spazio

cover: ~ charge n coperto m. **~ing** n copertura f; (for floor) rivestimento m; **~ing letter** lettera f d'accompagnamento. **~-up** n messa f a tacere

covet /'kʌvɪt/ vt bramare

cow /kaʊ/ n vacca f, mucca f

coward /'kaʊəd/ n vigliacco, -a mf. **~ice** /-ɪs/ n vigliaccheria f. **~ly** a da vigliacco

'cowboy n cowboy m inv, buffone m fam

cower /'kaʊə(r)/ vi acquattarsi

'cowshed n stalla f

cox /kɒks/ n, **coxswain** /'kɒksn/ n timoniere, -a mf

coy /kɔɪ/ a falsamente timido; ⟨flirtatiously⟩ civettuolo; **be ~ about sth** essere evasivo su qcsa

crab /kræb/ n granchio m

crack /kræk/ n (in wall) crepa f; (in china, glass, bone) incrinatura f; (noise) scoppio m; (fam: joke) battuta f; **have a ~** (try) fare un tentativo ● a (fam: best) di prim'ordine ● vt incrinare ⟨china, glass⟩: schiacciare ⟨nut⟩: decifrare ⟨code⟩; fam risolvere ⟨problem⟩. **~ a joke** fam fare una battuta ● vi ⟨china,

glass⟩ incrinarsi; ⟨whip⟩ schioccare.
crack down vi fam prendere seri provvedimenti. **crack down on** vt fam prendere seri provvedimenti contro

cracked /krækt/ a ⟨plaster⟩ crepato; ⟨skin⟩ screpolato; ⟨rib⟩ incrinato; (fam: crazy) svitato

cracker /'krækə(r)/ n (biscuit) cracker m inv; (firework) petardo m; **|Christmas| ~** tubo m di cartone colorato contenente una sorpresa

crackers /'krækəz/ a fam matto

crackle /'krækl/ vi crepitare

cradle /'kreɪdl/ n culla f

craft[1] /krɑːft/ n inv ⟨boat⟩ imbarcazione f

craft[2] n mestiere m; (technique) arte f. **~sman** n artigiano m

crafty /'krɑːftɪ/ a (-ier, -iest) astuto

crag /kræg/ n rupe f. **~gy** a scosceso; ⟨face⟩ dai lineamenti marcati

cram /kræm/ v (pt/pp crammed) ● vt stipare (**into** in) ● vi (for exams) sgobbare

cramp /kræmp/ n crampo m. **~ed** a ⟨room⟩ stretto; ⟨handwriting⟩ appiccicato

crampon /'kræmpən/ n rampone m

cranberry /'krænbərɪ/ n Culin mirtillo m rosso

crane /kreɪn/ n (at docks, bird) gru f inv ● vt **~ one's neck** allungare il collo

crank[1] /kræŋk/ n tipo, -a mf strampalato, -a

crank[2] n Techn manovella f. **~shaft** n albero m a gomiti

cranky /'kræŋkɪ/ a strampalato; (Am: irritable) irritabile

cranny /'krænɪ/ n fessura f

crash /kræʃ/ n (noise) fragore m; Auto, Aeron incidente m; Comm crollo m ● vi schiantarsi (**into** contro); ⟨plane⟩ precipitare ● vt schiantare ⟨car⟩

crash: ~ course n corso m intensivo. **~-helmet** n casco m. **~-landing** n atterraggio m di fortuna

crate /kreɪt/ n (for packing) cassa f

crater /'kreɪtə(r)/ n cratere m

crav|**e** /kreɪv/ vt morire dalla voglia di. **~ing** n voglia f smodata

crawl /krɔːl/ n (swimming) stile m libero; **do the ~** nuotare a stile libero; **at a ~** a passo di lumaca ● vi andare carponi; **~ with** brulicare di. **~er lane** n Auto corsia f riservata al traffico lento

crayon /'kreɪən/ n pastello m a cera; (pencil) matita f colorata

craze /kreɪz/ n mania f

crazy | **cross**

crazy /'kreɪzɪ/ *a* (-ier, -iest) matto; **be ~ about** andar matto per

creak /kriːk/ *n* scricchiolio *m* •*vi* scricchiolare

cream /kriːm/ *n* crema *f*; (fresh) panna *f* •*a* (colour) [bianco] panna *inv* •*vt* Culin sbattere. **~ 'cheese** *n* formaggio *m* cremoso. **~y** *a* cremoso

crease /kriːs/ *n* piega *f* •*vt* stropicciare •*vi* stropicciarsi. **~-resistant** *a* che non si stropiccia

creat|e /kriːˈeɪt/ *vt* creare. **~ion** /-ˈeɪʃn/ *n* creazione *f*. **~ive** /-tɪv/ *a* creativo. **~or** *n* creatore, -trice *mf*

creature /ˈkriːtʃə(r)/ *n* creatura *f*

crèche /kreʃ/ *n* asilo *m* nido

credentials /krɪˈdenʃlz/ *npl* credenziali *fpl*

credibility /kredəˈbɪlətɪ/ *n* credibilità *f*

credible /ˈkredəbl/ *a* credibile

credit /ˈkredɪt/ *n* credito *m*; (honour) merito *m*; **take the ~ for** prendersi il merito di •*vt* (pt/pp credited) accreditare; **~ sb with sth** Comm accreditare qcsa a qcno; *fig* attribuire qcsa a qcno. **~able** /-əbl/ *a* lodevole

credit: **~ card** *n* carta *f* di credito. **~or** *n* creditore, -trice *mf*

creed /kriːd/ *n* credo *m inv*

creek /kriːk/ *n* insenatura *f*; (Am: stream) torrente *m*

creep /kriːp/ *vi* (pt/pp crept) muoversi furtivamente •*n* fam tipo *m* viscido. **~er** *n* pianta *f* rampicante. **~y** *a* che fa venire i brividi

cremat|e /krɪˈmeɪt/ *vt* cremare. **~ion** /-ˈeɪʃn/ *n* cremazione *f*

crematorium /kreməˈtɔːrɪəm/ *n* crematorio *m*

crêpe /kreɪp/ *n* (fabric) crespo *m*

crept /krept/ *see* **creep**

crescent /ˈkresənt/ *n* mezzaluna *f*

cress /kres/ *n* crescione *m*

crest /krest/ *n* cresta *f*; (coat of arms) cimiero *m*

Crete /kriːt/ *n* Creta *f*

crevasse /krɪˈvæs/ *n* crepaccio *m*

crevice /ˈkrevɪs/ *n* crepa *f*

crew /kruː/ *n* equipaggio *m*; (gang) équipe *f inv*. **~ cut** *n* capelli *mpl* a spazzola. **~ neck** *n* girocollo *m*

crib[1] /krɪb/ *n* (for baby) culla *f*

crib[2] *vt/i* (pt/pp cribbed) fam copiare

crick /krɪk/ *n* **~ in the neck** torcicollo *m*

cricket[1] /ˈkrɪkɪt/ *n* (insect) grillo *m*

cricket[2] *n* cricket *m*. **~er** *n* giocatore *m* di cricket

crime /kraɪm/ *n* crimine *m*; (criminality) criminalità *f*

criminal /ˈkrɪmɪnl/ *a* criminale; (law, court) penale •*n* criminale *mf*

crimson /ˈkrɪmzn/ *a* cremisi *inv*

cringe /krɪndʒ/ *vi* (cower) acquattarsi; (at bad joke etc) fare una smorfia

crinkle /ˈkrɪŋkl/ *vt* spiegazzare •*vi* spiegazzarsi

cripple /ˈkrɪpl/ *n* storpio, -a *mf* •*vt* storpiare; *fig* danneggiare. **~d** *a* (person) storpio; (ship) danneggiato

crisis /ˈkraɪsɪs/ *n* (pl -ses /-siːz/) crisi *f inv*

crisp /krɪsp/ *a* croccante; (air) frizzante; (style) incisivo. **~bread** *n* crostini *mpl* di pane. **~s** *npl* patatine *fpl*

criterion /kraɪˈtɪərɪən/ *n* (pl -ria /-rɪə/) criterio *m*

critic /ˈkrɪtɪk/ *n* critico, -a *mf*. **~al** *a* critico. **~ally** *adv* in modo critico; **~ally ill** gravemente malato

criticism /ˈkrɪtɪsɪzm/ *n* critica *f*; **he doesn't like ~** non ama le critiche

criticize /ˈkrɪtɪsaɪz/ *vt* criticare

croak /krəʊk/ *vi* gracchiare; (frog:) gracidare

crochet /ˈkrəʊʃeɪ/ *n* lavoro *m* all'uncinetto •*vt* fare all'uncinetto. **~-hook** *n* uncinetto *m*

crock /krɒk/ *n* fam **old ~** (person) rudere *m*; (car) macinino *m*

crockery /ˈkrɒkərɪ/ *n* terrecotte *fpl*

crocodile /ˈkrɒkədaɪl/ *n* coccodrillo *m*. **~ tears** lacrime *fpl* di coccodrillo

crocus /ˈkrəʊkəs/ *n* (pl -es) croco *m*

crony /ˈkrəʊnɪ/ *n* compare *m*

crook /krʊk/ *n* (fam: criminal) truffatore, -trice *mf*

crooked /ˈkrʊkɪd/ *a* storto; (limb) storpiato; (fam: dishonest) disonesto

crop /krɒp/ *n* raccolto *m*; *fig* quantità *f inv* •*v* (pt/pp cropped) •*vt* coltivare. **crop up** *vi* fam presentarsi

croquet /ˈkrəʊkeɪ/ *n* croquet *m*

croquette /krəʊˈket/ *n* crocchetta *f*

cross /krɒs/ *a* (annoyed) arrabbiato; **talk at ~ purposes** fraintendersi •*n* croce *f*; Bot, Zool incrocio *m* •*vt* sbarrare (cheque); incrociare (road, animals); **~ oneself** farsi il segno della croce; **~ one's arms** incrociare le braccia; **~ one's legs** accavallare le gambe; **keep one's fingers ~ed for sb** tenere le dita incrociate per qcno; **it ~ed my mind** mi è venuto in mente •*vi* (go across) attraversare; (lines:) incrociarsi. **cross out** *vt* depennare

cross: ~**bar** n (of goal) traversa f; (on bicycle) canna f. ~'**country** n Sport corsa f campestre. ~**ex'amine** vt sottoporre a controinterrogatorio. ~-**exami'nation** n controinterrogatorio m. ~**eyed** a/a strabico. ~**fire** n fuoco m incrociato. ~**ing** n (for pedestrians) passaggio m pedonale; (sea journey) traversata f. ~-'**reference** n rimando m. ~**roads** n incrocio m. ~-'**section** n sezione f; (of community) campione m. ~**wise** adv in diagonale. ~**word** n ~**word** [**puzzle**] parole fpl crociate

crotchet /'krɒtʃɪt/ n Mus semiminima f

crotchety /'krɒtʃɪtɪ/ a irritabile

crouch /krautʃ/ vi accovacciarsi

crow /krəʊ/ n corvo m; **as the** ~ **flies** in linea d'aria ● vi cantare. ~**bar** n piede m di porco

crowd /kraʊd/ n folla f ● vt affollare ● vi affollarsi. ~**ed** /'kraʊdɪd/ a affollato

crown /kraʊn/ n corona f ● vt incoronare; incapsulare ⟨tooth⟩

crucial /'kru:ʃl/ a cruciale

crucifix /'kru:sɪfɪks/ n crocifisso m

cruci|fixion /kru:sɪ'fɪkʃn/ n crocifissione f. ~**fy** /'kru:sɪfaɪ/ vt (pt/pp -**ied**) crocifiggere

crude /kru:d/ a ⟨oil⟩ greggio; ⟨language⟩ crudo; ⟨person⟩ rozzo

cruel /'kru:əl/ a (**crueller, cruellest**) crudele (**to** verso). ~**ly** adv con crudeltà. ~**ty** n crudeltà f

cruis|e /kru:z/ n crociera f ● vi fare una crociera; ⟨car:⟩ andare a velocità di crociera. ~**er** n Mil incrociatore m; ⟨motor boat⟩ motoscafo m. ~**ing speed** n velocità m inv di crociera

crumb /krʌm/ n briciola f

crumb|le /'krʌmbl/ vt sbriciolare ● vi sbriciolarsi; ⟨building, society:⟩ sgretolarsi. ~**ly** a friabile

crumple /'krʌmpl/ vt spiegazzare ● vi spiegazzarsi

crunch /krʌntʃ/ n fam **when it comes to the** ~ quando si viene al dunque ● vt sgranocchiare ● vi ⟨snow:⟩ scricchiolare

crusade /kru:'seɪd/ n crociata f. ~**r** n crociato m

crush /krʌʃ/ n ⟨crowd⟩ calca f; **have a** ~ **on sb** essersi preso una cotta per qcno ● vt schiacciare; sgualcire ⟨clothes⟩

crust /krʌst/ n crosta f

crutch /krʌtʃ/ n gruccia f; Anat inforcatura f

crux /krʌks/ n fig punto m cruciale

cry /kraɪ/ n grido m; **have a** ~ farsi un pianto; **a far** ~ **from** fig tutta un'altra cosa rispetto a ● vi (pt/pp **cried**) ⟨weep⟩ piangere; ⟨call⟩ gridare

crypt /krɪpt/ n cripta f. ~**ic** a criptico

crystal /'krɪstl/ n cristallo m; ⟨glassware⟩ cristalli mpl. ~**lize** vi ⟨become clear⟩ concretizzarsi

cub /kʌb/ n ⟨animal⟩ cucciolo m; **C~** [**Scout**] lupetto m

Cuba /'kju:bə/ n Cuba f

cubby-hole /'kʌbɪ-/ n ⟨compartment⟩ scomparto m; ⟨room⟩ ripostiglio m

cub|e /kju:b/ n cubo m. ~**ic** a cubico

cubicle /'kju:bɪkl/ n cabina f

cuckoo /'kʊku:/ n cuculo m. ~ **clock** n orologio m a cucù

cucumber /'kju:kʌmbə(r)/ n cetriolo m

cuddl|e /'kʌdl/ vt coccolare ● vi ~**e up to** starsene accoccolato insieme a ● n **have a** ~**e** ⟨child:⟩ farsi coccolare; ⟨lovers:⟩ abbracciarsi. ~**y** a tenerone; ⟨wanting cuddles⟩ coccolone. ~**y** '**toy** n peluche m inv

cudgel /'kʌdʒl/ n randello m

cue¹ /kju:/ n segnale m; Theat battuta f d'entrata

cue² n (in billiards) stecca f. ~ **ball** n pallino m

cuff /kʌf/ n polsino m; (Am: turn-up) orlo m; ⟨blow⟩ scapaccione m; **off the** ~ improvvisando ● vt dare una pacca a. ~-**link** n gemello m

cul-de-sac /'kʌldəsæk/ n vicolo m cieco

culinary /'kʌlɪnərɪ/ a culinario

cull /kʌl/ vt scegliere ⟨flowers⟩; ⟨kill⟩ selezionare e uccidere

culminat|e /'kʌlmɪneɪt/ vi culminare. ~**ion** /-'neɪʃn/ n culmine m

culottes /kju:'lɒts/ npl gonna fsg pantalone

culprit /'kʌlprɪt/ n colpevole mf

cult /kʌlt/ n culto m

cultivate /'kʌltɪveɪt/ vt coltivarsi; fig coltivarsi ⟨person⟩

cultural /'kʌltʃərəl/ a culturale

culture /'kʌltʃə(r)/ n cultura f. ~**d** a colto

cumbersome /'kʌmbəsəm/ a ingombrante

cumulative /'kju:mjʊlətɪv/ a cumulativo

cunning /'kʌnɪŋ/ a astuto ● n astuzia f

cup /kʌp/ n tazza f; (prize, of bra) coppa f

cupboard /'kʌbəd/ n armadio m. ~ **love** n fam amore m interessato

Cup 'Final n finale f di coppa

Cupid /'kju:pɪd/ n Cupido m

curable /'kjʊərəbl/ a curabile

curate /'kjʊərət/ n curato m

curator /kjʊə'reɪtə(r)/ n direttore, ·trice mf (di museo)

curb /kɜ:b/ vt tenere a freno

curdle /'kɜ:dl/ vi coagularsi

cure /kjʊə(r)/ n cura f ● vt curare; (salt) mettere sotto sale; (smoke) affumicare

curfew /'kɜ:fju:/ n coprifuoco m

curio /'kjʊərɪəʊ/ n curiosità f inv

curiosity /kjʊərɪ'ɒsətɪ/ n curiosità f

curious /'kjʊərɪəs/ a curioso. ~ly adv curiosamente

curl /kɜ:l/ n ricciolo m ● vt arricciare ● vi arricciarsi. **curl up** vi raggomitolarsi

curler /'kɜ:lə(r)/ n bigodino m

curly /'kɜ:lɪ/ a (·ier, ·iest) riccio

currant /'kʌrənt/ n (dried) uvetta f

currency /'kʌrənsɪ/ n valuta f; (of word) ricorrenza f; **foreign ~** valuta f estera

current /'kʌrənt/ a corrente ● n corrente f. **~ affairs** or **events** npl attualità fsg. **~ly** adv attualmente

curriculum /kə'rɪkjʊləm/ n programma m di studi. **~ vitae** /'vi:taɪ/ n curriculum vitae m inv

curry /'kʌrɪ/ n curry m inv; (meal) piatto m cucinato nel curry ● vt (pt/pp -ied) **~ favour with sb** cercare d'ingraziarsi qcno

curse /kɜ:s/ n maledizione f; (oath) imprecazione f ● vt maledire ● vi imprecare

cursor /'kɜ:sə(r)/ n cursore m

cursory /'kɜ:sərɪ/ a sbrigativo

curt /kɜ:t/ a brusco

curtail /kɜ:'teɪl/ vt ridurre

curtain /'kɜ:tn/ n tenda f. Theat sipario m

curtsy /'kɜ:tsɪ/ n inchino m ● vi (pt/pp -ied) fare l'inchino

curve /kɜ:v/ n curva f ● vi curvare; **~ to the right/left** curvare a destra/sinistra. **~d** a curvo

cushion /'kʊʃn/ n cuscino m ● vt attutire; (protect) proteggere

cushy /'kʊʃɪ/ a (-ier, -iest) fam facile

custard /'kʌstəd/ n (liquid) crema f pasticciera

custodian /kʌ'stəʊdɪən/ n custode mf

custody /'kʌstədɪ/ n (of child) custodia f; (imprisoning) detenzione f preventiva

custom /'kʌstəm/ n usanza f; Jur consuetudine f; Comm clientela f. **~ary** a (habitual) abituale; **it's ~ to...** è consuetudine.... **~er** n cliente mf

customs /'kʌstəmz/ npl dogana f. **~ officer** n doganiere m

cut /kʌt/ n (with knife etc. of clothes) taglio m; (reduction) riduzione f; (in public spending) taglio m ● vt/i (pt/pp **cut**, pres p **cutting**) tagliare; (reduce) ridurre; **~ one's finger** tagliarsi il dito; **~ sb's hair** tagliare i capelli a qcno ● vi (with cards) alzare. **cut back** vt tagliare (hair); potare (hedge); (reduce) ridurre. **cut down** vt abbattere (tree); (reduce) ridurre. **cut off** vt tagliar via; (disconnect) interrompere; fig isolare; **I was ~ off** Teleph la linea è caduta. **cut out** vt ritagliare; (delete) eliminare; **be ~ out for** fam essere tagliato per; **it out!** fam dacci un taglio!. **cut up** vt (slice) tagliare a pezzi

cut-back n riduzione f; (in government spending) taglio m

cute /kju:t/ a fam (in appearance) carino; (clever) acuto

cuticle /'kju:tɪkl/ n cuticola f

cutlery /'kʌtlərɪ/ n posate fpl

cutlet /'kʌtlɪt/ n cotoletta f

cut-price a a prezzo ridotto; (shop) che fa prezzi ridotti

cut-throat a spietato

cutting /'kʌtɪŋ/ a (remark) tagliente ● n (from newspaper) ritaglio m; (of plant) talea f

CV n abbr curriculum vitae

cyanide /'saɪənaɪd/ n cianuro m

cybernetics /saɪbə'netɪks/ n cibernetica f

cycle /'saɪkl/ n ciclo m; (bicycle) bicicletta f, bici f inv fam ● vi andare in bicicletta. **~ing** n ciclismo m. **~ist** n ciclista mf

cyclone /'saɪkləʊn/ n ciclone m

cylinder /'sɪlɪndə(r)/ n cilindro m. **~rical** /·'lɪndrɪkl/ a cilindrico

cymbals /'sɪmblz/ npl Mus piatti mpl

cynic /'sɪnɪk/ n cinico, ·a mf. **~al** a cinico. **~ism** /·sɪzm/ n cinismo m

cypress /'saɪprəs/ n cipresso m

Cypriot /'sɪprɪət/ n cipriota mf

Cyprus /'saɪprəs/ n Cipro m

cyst /sɪst/ n ciste f. **~itis** /·'staɪtɪs/ n cistite f

Czech /tʃek/ a ceco; **~ Republic** Repubblica f Ceca ● n ceco, ·a mf

Czechoslovak /tʃekə'sləʊvæk/ a cecoslovacco. **~ia** /·'vækɪə/ n Cecoslovacchia f

Dd

dab /dæb/ n colpetto m; **a ~ of** un pochino di • vt (pt/pp **dabbed**) toccare leggermente ‹eyes›. **dab on** vt mettere un po' di ‹paint etc›

dabble /'dæbl/ vi **~ in sth** fig occuparsi di qcsa a tempo perso

dachshund /'dækshund/ n bassotto m

dad|dy /'dæd[ɪ]/ n fam papà m inv, babbo m

daddy-long-legs n zanzarone m [dei boschi]; ‹Am: spider› ragno m

daffodil /'dæfədɪl/ n giunchiglia f

daft /dɑ:ft/ a sciocco

dagger /'dægə(r)/ n stiletto m

dahlia /'deɪlɪə/ n dalia f

daily /'deɪlɪ/ a giornaliero • adv giornalmente • n ‹newspaper› quotidiano m; ‹fam: cleaner› donna f delle pulizie

dainty /'deɪntɪ/ a (-ier, -iest) grazioso; ‹movement› delicato

dairy /'deərɪ/ n caseificio m; ‹shop› latteria f. **~ cow** n mucca f da latte. **~ products** npl latticini mpl

dais /'deɪɪs/ n pedana f

daisy /'deɪzɪ/ n margheritina f; ‹larger› margherita f

dale /deɪl/ n liter valle f

dam /dæm/ n diga f • vt (pt/pp **dammed**) costruire una diga su

damag|e /'dæmɪdʒ/ n danno m (to a); **~es** pl Jur risarcimento msg • vt danneggiare; fig nuocere a. **~ing** a dannoso

dame /deɪm/ n liter dama f; Am sl donna f

damn /dæm/ a fam maledetto • adv ‹lucky, late› maledettamente • n **I don't care** or **give a ~** fam non me ne frega un accidente • vt dannare. **~ation** /-'neɪʃn/ n dannazione f • int fam accidenti!

damp /dæmp/ a umido • n umidità f • vt = **dampen**

damp|en /'dæmpən/ vt inumidire; fig raffreddare ‹enthusiasm›. **~ness** n umidità f

dance /dɑ:ns/ n ballo m • vt/i ballare. **~-hall** n sala f da ballo. **~ music** n musica f da ballo

dancer /'dɑ:nsə(r)/ n ballerino, -a mf

dandelion /'dændɪlaɪən/ n dente m di leone

dandruff /'dændrʌf/ n forfora f

Dane /deɪn/ n danese mf; **Great ~** danese m

danger /'deɪndʒə(r)/ n pericolo m; **in/out of ~** in/fuori pericolo. **~ous** /-rəs/ a pericoloso. **~ously** adv pericolosamente; **~ously ill** in pericolo di vita

dangle /'dæŋgl/ vi penzolare • vt far penzolare

Danish /'deɪnɪʃ/ a & n danese. **~ pastry** n dolce m a base di pasta sfoglia contenente pasta di mandorle, mele ecc

dank /dæŋk/ a umido e freddo

Danube /'dænju:b/ n Danubio m

dare /deə(r)/ vt/i osare; ‹challenge› sfidare (to a); **~ |to| do sth** osare fare qcsa; **I ~ say!** molto probabilmente! • n sfida f. **~devil** n spericolato, -a mf

daring /'deərɪŋ/ a audace • n audacia f

dark /dɑ:k/ a buio; **~ blue/brown** blu/marrone scuro; **it's getting ~** sta cominciando a fare buio; **~ horse** fig ‹in race, contest› vincitore m imprevisto; ‹not much known about› misterioso m; **keep sth ~** fig tenere qcsa nascosto • n **after ~** col buio; **in the ~** al buio; **keep sb in the ~** fig tenere qcno all'oscuro

dark|en /'dɑ:kn/ vt oscurare • vi oscurarsi. **~ness** n buio m

dark-room n camera f oscura

darling /'dɑ:lɪŋ/ a adorabile; **my ~ Joan** carissima Joan • n tesoro m

darn /dɑ:n/ vt rammendare. **~ing-needle** n ago m da rammendo

dart /dɑ:t/ n dardo m; ‹in sewing› pince f inv; **~s** sg ‹game› freccette fpl • vi lanciarsi

dartboard /'dɑ:tbɔ:d/ n bersaglio m [per freccette]

dash /dæʃ/ n Typ trattino m; ‹in Morse› linea f; **a ~ of milk** un goccio di latte; **make a ~ for** lanciarsi verso • vt **I must ~** devo scappare • vt far svanire ‹hopes›. **dash off** vi scappar via • vt (*write quickly*) buttare giù. **dash out** *vi* uscire di corsa

'**dashboard** *n* cruscotto *m*

dashing /'dæʃɪŋ/ *a* (*bold*) ardito; (*in appearance*) affascinante

data /'deɪtə/ *npl & sg* dati *mpl*. ~**base** *n* base [di] dati *f*, database *m inv*. ~**comms** /'kɒmz/ *n* telematica *f*. ~ **processing** *n* elaborazione *f* [di] dati

date¹ /deɪt/ *n* (*fruit*) dattero *m*

date² *n* data *f*; (*meeting*) appuntamento *m*; **to** ~ fino ad oggi; **out of** ~ (*not fashionable*) fuori moda; (*expired*) scaduto; ⟨*information*⟩ non aggiornato; **make a** ~ **with sb** dare un appuntamento a qcno; **be up to** ~ essere aggiornato ●*vt/i* datare; (*go out with*) uscire con. **date back to** *vi* risalire a

dated /'deɪtɪd/ *a* fuori moda; ⟨*language*⟩ antiquato

'**date-line** *n* linea *f* [del cambiamento] di data

daub /dɔːb/ *vt* imbrattare ⟨*walls*⟩

daughter /'dɔːtə(r)/ *n* figlia *f*. ~**-in-law** *n* (*pl* ~**s-in-law**) nuora *f*

daunt /dɔːnt/ *vt* scoraggiare; **nothing** ~**ed** per niente scoraggiato. ~**less** *a* intrepido

dawdle /'dɔːdl/ *vi* bighellonare; (*over work*) cincischiarsi

dawn /dɔːn/ *n* alba *f*; **at** ~ all'alba ●*vi* albeggiare; **it** ~**ed on me** *fig* mi è apparso chiaro

day /deɪ/ *n* giorno *m*; (*whole day*) giornata *f*; (*period*) epoca *f*; **these** ~**s** oggigiorno; **in those** ~**s** a quei tempi; **it's had its** ~ *fam* ha fatto il suo tempo

day: ~ **break** *n* **at** ~**break** allo spuntar del giorno. ~**-dream** *n* sogno *m* ad occhi aperti ●*vi* sognare ad occhi aperti. ~**light** *n* luce *f* del giorno. ~ **re'turn** *n* (*ticket*) biglietto *m* di andata e ritorno con validità giornaliera. ~**time** *n* giorno *m*; **in the** ~**time** di giorno

daze /deɪz/ *n* **in a** ~ stordito; *fig* sbalordito. ~**d** *a* stordito; *fig* sbalordito

dazzle /'dæzl/ *vt* abbagliare

deacon /'diːkn/ *n* diacono *m*

dead /ded/ *a* morto; (*numb*) intorpidito; ~ **body** morto *m*; ~ **centre** pieno centro *m* ●*adv* ~ **tired** stanco morto; ~ **slow/easy** lentissimo/facilissimo; **you're** ~ **right** hai perfettamente ragione; **stop** ~ fermarsi di colpo; **be** ~ **on time** essere in perfetto orario ●*n* **the** ~ *pl* i morti; **in the** ~ **of night** nel cuore della notte

deaden /'dedn/ *vt* attutire ⟨*sound*⟩; calmare ⟨*pain*⟩

dead: ~ '**end** *n* vicolo *m* cieco. ~ 'heat *n* **it was a** ~ **heat** è finita a pari merito. ~**line** *n* scadenza *f*. ~**lock** *fig* giungere a un punto morto

deadly /'dedlɪ/ *a* (**-ier, -iest**) mortale; (*fam: dreary*) barboso; ~ **sins** peccati *mpl* capitali

deadpan /'dedpæn/ *a* impassibile; ⟨*humour*⟩ all'inglese

deaf /def/ *a* sordo; ~ **and dumb** sordomuto. ~**-aid** *n* apparecchio *m* acustico

deaf|en /'defn/ *vt* assordare; (*permanently*) render sordo. ~**ening** *a* assordante. ~**ness** *n* sordità *f*

deal /diːl/ *n* (*agreement*) patto *m*; (*in business*) accordo *m*; **whose** ~? (*in cards*) a chi tocca dare le carte?; **a good or great** ~ molto; **get a raw** ~ *fam* ricevere un trattamento ingiusto ●*vt* (*pt/pp* **dealt**) (*in cards*) dare; ~ **sb a blow** dare un colpo a qcno. **deal in** *vt* trattare in. **deal out** *vt* ⟨*hand out*⟩ distribuire. **deal with** *vt* ⟨*handle*⟩ occuparsi di; trattare con ⟨*company*⟩; (*be about*) trattare di; **that's been** ~**t with** è stato risolto

deal|er /'diːlə(r)/ *n* commerciante *mf*; (*in drugs*) spacciatore, -trice *mf*. ~**ings** *npl* **have** ~**ings with** avere a che fare con

dean /diːn/ *n* decano *m*; *Univ* ≈ preside *mf* di facoltà

dear /dɪə(r)/ *a* caro; (*in letter*) Caro; (*formal*) Gentile ●*n* caro, -a *mf* ●*int* **oh** ~! Dio mio!. ~**ly** *adv* ⟨*love*⟩ profondamente; (*pay*) profumatamente

dearth /dɜːθ/ *n* penuria *f*

death /deθ/ *n* morte *f*. ~ **certificate** *n* certificato *m* di morte. ~ **duty** *n* tassa *f* di successione

deathly /'deθlɪ/ *a* ~ **silence** silenzio *m* di tomba ●*adv* ~ **pale** di un pallore cadaverico

death: ~ **penalty** *n* pena *f* di morte. ~**-trap** *n* trappola *f* mortale

debar /dɪ'bɑː(r)/ *vt* (*pt/pp* **debarred**) escludere

debase /dɪ'beɪs/ *vt* degradare

debatable /dɪ'beɪtəbl/ *a* discutibile

debate /dɪ'beɪt/ *n* dibattito *m* ●*vt* discutere; (*in formal debate*) dibattere ●*vi* ~ **whether to...** considerare se...

debauchery /dɪ'bɔːtʃərɪ/ *n* dissolutezza *f*

debility /dɪ'bɪlɪtɪ/ *n* debilitazione *f*

debit /'debɪt/ n debito m • vt (pt/pp **debited**) Comm addebitare (sum)

debris /'debriː/ n macerie fpl

debt /det/ n debito m; **be in ~** avere dei debiti. **~or** n debitore, -trice mf

début /'deɪbuː/ n debutto m

decade /'dekeɪd/ n decennio m

decaden|ce /'dekədəns/ n decadenza f. **~t** a decadente

decaffeinated /diː'kæfɪneɪtɪd/ a decaffeinato

decant /dɪ'kænt/ vt travasare. **~er** n caraffa f (di cristallo)

decapitate /dɪ'kæpɪtet/ vt decapitare

decay /dɪ'keɪ/ n (also fig) decadenza f; (rot) decomposizione f; (of tooth) carie f inv • vi imputridire; (rot) decomporsi; ‹tooth:› cariarsi

deceased /dɪ'siːst/ a defunto • n the **~d** il defunto; la defunta

deceit /dɪ'siːt/ n inganno m. **~ful** a falso

deceive /dɪ'siːv/ vt ingannare

December /dɪ'sembə(r)/ n dicembre m

decency /'diːsənsɪ/ n decenza f

decent /'diːsənt/ a decente; (respectable) rispettabile; **very ~ of you** molto gentile da parte tua. **~ly** adv decentemente; (kindly) gentilmente

decentralize /diː'sentrəlaɪz/ vt decentrare

decept|ion /dɪ'sepʃn/ n inganno m. **~ive** /-tɪv/ a ingannevole. **~ively** adv ingannevolmente; **it looks ~ively easy** sembra facile, ma non lo è

decibel /'desɪbel/ n decibel m inv

decide /dɪ'saɪd/ vt decidere • vi decidere (on di)

decided /dɪ'saɪdɪd/ a risoluto. **~ly** adv risolutamente; (without doubt) senza dubbio

deciduous /dɪ'sɪdjʊəs/ a a foglie decidue

decimal /'desɪml/ a decimale • n numero m decimale. **~ 'point** n virgola f

decimate /'desɪmet/ vt decimare

decipher /dɪ'saɪfə(r)/ vt decifrare

decision /dɪ'sɪʒn/ n decisione f

decisive /dɪ'saɪsɪv/ a decisivo

deck[1] /dek/ vt abbigliare

deck[2] n Naut ponte m; **on ~** in coperta; **top ~** (of bus) piano m di sopra; **~ of cards** mazzo m. **~-chair** n [sedia f a] sdraio f inv

declaration /deklə'reɪʃn/ n dichiarazione f

declare /dɪ'kleə(r)/ vt dichiarare; **anything to ~?** niente da dichiarare?

declension /dɪ'klenʃn/ n declinazione f

decline /dɪ'klaɪn/ n declino m • vt also Gram declinare • vi (decrease) diminuire; (health:) deperire; (say no) rifiutare

decode /diː'kəʊd/ vt decifrare; Comput decodificare

decompose /diːkəm'pəʊz/ vi decomporsi

décor /'deɪkɔː(r)/ n decorazione f; (including furniture) arredamento m

decorat|e /'dekəret/ vt decorare; (paint) pitturare; (wallpaper) tappezzare. **~ion** /-'reɪʃn/ n decorazione f. **~ive** /-rətɪv/ a decorativo. **~or** n painter **and ~or** imbianchino m

decorum /dɪ'kɔːrəm/ n decoro m

decoy[1] /'diːkɔɪ/ n esca f

decoy[2] /dɪ'kɔɪ/ vt adescare

decrease[1] /'diːkriːs/ n diminuzione f

decrease[2] /dɪ'kriːs/ vt/i diminuire

decree /dɪ'kriː/ n decreto m • vt (pt/pp **decreed**) decretare

decrepit /dɪ'krepɪt/ a decrepito

dedicat|e /'dedɪket/ vt dedicare. **~ed** a (person) scrupoloso. **~ion** /-'keɪʃn/ n dedizione f; (in book) dedica f

deduce /dɪ'djuːs/ vt dedurre (from da)

deduct /dɪ'dʌkt/ vt dedurre

deduction /dɪ'dʌkʃn/ n deduzione f

deed /diːd/ n azione f; Jur atto m di proprietà

deem /diːm/ vt ritenere

deep /diːp/ a profondo; **go off the ~ end** fam arrabbiarsi

deepen /'diːpn/ vt approfondire; scavare più profondamente (trench) • vi approfondirsi; (fig: mystery:) infittirsi

deep-'freeze n congelatore m

deeply /'diːplɪ/ adv profondamente

deer /dɪə(r)/ n inv cervo m

deface /dɪ'feɪs/ vt sfigurare (picture); deturpare (monument)

defamat|ion /defə'meɪʃn/ n diffamazione f. **~ory** /dɪ'fæmətərɪ/ a diffamatorio

default /dɪ'fɔːlt/ n (Jur: non-payment) morosità f; (failure to appear) contumacia f; **win by ~** Sport vincere per abbandono dell'avversario; **in ~ of** per mancanza di • a ~ **drive** Comput lettore m di default • vi (not pay) venire meno a un pagamento

defeat /dɪ'fiːt/ n sconfitta f • vt sconfiggere; (frustrate) vanificare (attempts); **that ~s the object** questo fa fallire l'obiettivo

defect[1] /dɪ'fekt/ vi Pol fare defezione

defect | demarcation

defect² /'di:fekt/ n difetto m. **~ive**
/dɪ'fektɪv/ a difettoso

defence /dɪ'fens/ n difesa f. **~less** a
indifeso

defend /dɪ'fend/ vt difendere; ⟨justify⟩
giustificare. **~ant** n Jur imputato, -a mf

defensive /dɪ'fensɪv/ a difensivo • n
difensiva f; **on the ~** sulla difensiva

defer /dɪ'fɜ:(r)/ v (pt/pp **deferred**)
⟨postpone⟩ rinviare • vi ~ **to sb** rimettersi a qcno

deferen|ce /'defərəns/ n deferenza f.
~tial /-'renʃl/ a deferente

defian|ce /dɪ'faɪəns/ n sfida f; **in ~ce
of** sfidando. **~t** a ⟨person⟩ ribelle;
⟨gesture, attitude⟩ di sfida. **~tly** adv con
aria di sfida

deficien|cy /dɪ'fɪʃənsɪ/ n insufficienza
f. **~t** a insufficiente; **be ~t in** mancare
di

deficit /'defɪsɪt/ n deficit m inv

defile /dɪ'faɪl/ vt fig contaminare

define /dɪ'faɪn/ vt definire

definite /'defɪnɪt/ a definito; ⟨certain⟩
⟨answer, yes⟩ definitivo; ⟨improvement,
difference⟩ netto; **he was ~** about it è
stato chiaro in proposito. **~ly** adv sicuramente

definition /defɪ'nɪʃn/ n definizione f

definitive /dɪ'fɪnətɪv/ a definitivo

deflate /dɪ'fleɪt/ vt sgonfiare. **~ion**
/-eɪʃn/ n Comm deflazione f

deflect /dɪ'flekt/ vt deflettere

deform|ed /dɪ'fɔ:md/ a deforme. **~ity**
n deformità f inv

defraud /dɪ'frɔ:d/ vt defraudare

defrost /di:'frɒst/ vt sbrinare ⟨fridge⟩;
scongelare ⟨food⟩

deft /deft/ a abile

defunct /dɪ'fʌŋkt/ a morto e sepolto;
⟨law⟩ caduto in disuso

defuse /di:'fju:z/ vt disinnescare; calmare ⟨situation⟩

defy /dɪ'faɪ/ vt (pt/pp **-ied**) ⟨challenge⟩
sfidare; resistere a ⟨attempt⟩; ⟨not obey⟩
disobbedire a

degenerate¹ /dɪ'dʒenəreɪt/ vi degenerare; ~ **into** fig degenerare in

degenerate² /dɪ'dʒenərət/ a degenerato

degrading /dɪ'greɪdɪŋ/ a degradante

degree /dɪ'gri:/ n grado m; Univ laurea
f; **20 ~s** 20 gradi; **not to the same ~**
non allo stesso livello

dehydrate /di:'haɪdreɪt/ vt disidratare. **~d** /-ɪd/ a disidratato

de-ice /di:'aɪs/ vt togliere il ghiaccio da

deign /deɪn/ vi ~ **to do sth** degnarsi di
fare qcsa

deity /'di:ɪtɪ/ n divinità f inv

dejected /dɪ'dʒektɪd/ a demoralizzato

delay /dɪ'leɪ/ n ritardo m; **without ~**
senza indugio • vt ritardare; **be ~ed**
⟨person⟩ essere trattenuto; ⟨train,
aircraft⟩ essere in ritardo • vi indugiare

delegate¹ /'delɪgət/ n delegato, -a mf

delegate² /'delɪgeɪt/ vt delegare.
~ion /-'geɪʃn/ n delegazione f

delet|e /dɪ'li:t/ vt cancellare. **~ion**
/-i:ʃn/ n cancellatura f

deliberate¹ /dɪ'lɪbərət/ a deliberato;
⟨slow⟩ posato. **~ly** adv deliberatamente;
⟨slowly⟩ in modo posato

deliberate² /dɪ'lɪbəreɪt/ vt/i deliberare. **~ion** /-'reɪʃn/ n deliberazione f

delicacy /'delɪkəsɪ/ n delicatezza f;
⟨food⟩ prelibatezza f

delicate /'delɪkət/ a delicato

delicatessen /delɪkə'tesn/ n negozio
m di specialità gastronomiche

delicious /dɪ'lɪʃəs/ a delizioso

delight /dɪ'laɪt/ n piacere m • vt deliziare • vi ~ **in** dilettarsi con. **~ed** a lieto. **~ful** a delizioso

delinquen|cy /dɪ'lɪŋkwənsɪ/ n delinquenza f. **~t** a delinquente • n delinquente mf

deli|rious /dɪ'lɪrɪəs/ a **be ~rious** delirare; ⟨fig: very happy⟩ essere pazzo di
gioia. **~rium** /-rɪəm/ n delirio m

deliver /dɪ'lɪvə(r)/ vt consegnare; recapitare ⟨post, newspaper⟩; tenere
⟨speech⟩; dare ⟨message⟩; tirare ⟨blow⟩;
⟨set free⟩ liberare; ~ **a baby** far nascere
un bambino. **~ance** n liberazione f. **~y**
n consegna f; ⟨of post⟩ distribuzione f;
Med parto m; **cash on ~y** pagamento
m alla consegna

delude /dɪ'lu:d/ vt ingannare; ~ **oneself** illudersi

deluge /'delju:dʒ/ n diluvio m • vt ⟨fig:
with requests etc⟩ inondare

delusion /dɪ'lu:ʒn/ n illusione f

de luxe /dɪ'lʌks/ a di lusso

delve /delv/ vi ~ **into** ⟨into pocket etc⟩
frugare in; ⟨into notes, the past⟩ fare ricerche in

demand /dɪ'mɑ:nd/ n richiesta f;
Comm domanda f; **in ~** richiesto; **on ~**
a richiesta • vt esigere (**of/from** da).
~ing a esigente

demarcation /di:mɑ:'keɪʃn/ n demarcazione f

299

demean | depth

demean /dɪˈmiːn/ vt ~ oneself abbassarsi (**to** a)

demeanour /dɪˈmiːnə(r)/ n comportamento m

demented /dɪˈmentɪd/ a demente

demise /dɪˈmaɪz/ n decesso m

demister /diːˈmɪstə(r)/ n Auto sbrinatore m

demo /ˈdeməʊ/ n (pl ~s) fam manifestazione f; ~ **disk** Comput demodisk m inv

democracy /dɪˈmɒkrəsɪ/ n democrazia f

democrat /ˈdeməkræt/ n democratico, -a mf. ~**ic** /-ˈkrætɪk/ a democratico

demolish /dɪˈmɒlɪʃ/ vt demolire. ~**lition** /deməˈlɪʃn/ n demolizione f

demon /ˈdiːmən/ n demonio m

demonstrat|e /ˈdemənstreɪt/ vt dimostrare; fare una dimostrazione sull'uso di (appliance) ● vi Pol manifestare. ~**ion** /-ˈstreɪʃn/ n dimostrazione f; Pol manifestazione f

demonstrative /dɪˈmɒnstrətɪv/ a Gram dimostrativo; **be** ~ essere espansivo

demonstrator /ˈdemənstreɪtə(r)/ n Pol manifestante mf; (for product) dimostratore, -trice mf

demoralize /dɪˈmɒrəlaɪz/ vt demoralizzare

demote /dɪˈməʊt/ vt retrocedere di grado; Mil degradare

demure /dɪˈmjʊə(r)/ a schivo

den /den/ n tana f; (room) rifugio m

denial /dɪˈnaɪəl/ n smentita f

denim /ˈdenɪm/ n [tessuto m] jeans m; ~**s** pl [blue]jeans mpl

Denmark /ˈdenmɑːk/ n Danimarca f

denomination /dɪnɒmɪˈneɪʃn/ n Relig confessione f; (money) valore f

denounce /dɪˈnaʊns/ vt denunciare

dens|e /dens/ a denso; (crowd, forest) fitto; (stupid) ottuso. ~**ely** adv (populated) densamente; ~**ely wooded** fittamente ricoperto di alberi. ~**ity** n densità f inv; (of forest) fittezza f

dent /dent/ n ammaccatura f ● vt ammaccare; ~**ed** a ammaccato

dental /ˈdentl/ a dei denti; (treatment) dentistico; (hygiene) dentale. ~ **surgeon** n odontoiatra mf; medico m dentista

dentist /ˈdentɪst/ n dentista mf. ~**ry** n odontoiatria f

dentures /ˈdentʃəz/ npl dentiera fsg

denunciation /dɪnʌnsɪˈeɪʃn/ n denuncia f

deny /dɪˈnaɪ/ vt (pt/pp -ied) negare; (officially) smentire; ~ **sb sth** negare qcsa a qcno

deodorant /diːˈəʊdərənt/ n deodorante m

depart /dɪˈpɑːt/ vi (plane, train:) partire; (liter: person) andare via; (deviate) allontanarsi (**from** da)

department /dɪˈpɑːtmənt/ n reparto m; Pol ministero m; (of company) sezione f; Univ dipartimento m. ~ **store** n grande magazzino m

departure /dɪˈpɑːtʃə(r)/ n partenza f; (from rule) allontanamento m; **new** ~ svolta f

depend /dɪˈpend/ vi dipendere (**on** da); (rely) contare (**on** su); **it all** ~**s** dipende; ~**ing on what he says** a seconda di quello che dice. ~**able** /-əbl/ a fidato. ~**ant** n persona f a carico. ~**ence** n dipendenza f. ~**ent** a dipendente (**on** da)

depict /dɪˈpɪkt/ vt (in writing) dipingere; (with picture) rappresentare

depilatory /dɪˈpɪlətərɪ/ n (cream) crema f depilatoria

deplete /dɪˈpliːt/ vt ridurre; **totally** ~**d** completamente esaurito

deplor|able /dɪˈplɔːrəbl/ a deplorevole. ~**e** vt deplorare

deploy /dɪˈplɔɪ/ vt Mil spiegare ● vi schierarsi

deport /dɪˈpɔːt/ vt deportare. ~**ation** /diːpɔːˈteɪʃn/ n deportazione f

depose /dɪˈpəʊz/ vt deporre

deposit /dɪˈpɒzɪt/ n deposito m; (against damage) cauzione f; (first instalment) acconto m ● vt (pt/pp deposited) depositare. ~ **account** n libretto m di risparmio; (without instant access) conto m vincolato

depot /ˈdepəʊ/ n deposito m; Am Rail stazione f ferroviaria

deprav|e /dɪˈpreɪv/ vt depravare. ~**ed** a depravato. ~**ity** /-ˈprævətɪ/ n depravazione f

depreciat|e /dɪˈpriːʃɪeɪt/ vi deprezzarsi. ~**ion** /-ˈeɪʃn/ n deprezzamento m

depress /dɪˈpres/ vt deprimere; (press down) premere. ~**ed** a depresso; ~**ed area** zona f depressa. ~**ing** a deprimente. ~**ion** /-eʃn/ n depressione f

deprivation /deprɪˈveɪʃn/ n privazione f

deprive /dɪˈpraɪv/ vt ~ **sb of sth** privare qcno di qcsa. ~**d** a (area, childhood) disagiato

depth /depθ/ n profondità f inv; **in** ~ (study, analyse) in modo approfondito;

in the ~s of winter in pieno inverno; be out of one's ~ (in water) non toccare il fondo; fig sentirsi in alto mare

deputation /depju'teɪʃn/ n deputazione f

deputize /'depjʊtaɪz/ vi ~ **for** fare le veci di

deputy /'depjʊti/ n vice mf; (temporary) sostituto, -a mf; ●attrib ~ **leader** vicesegretario, -a mf; ~ **chairman** vicepresidente m

derail /dɪ'reɪl/ vt be ~**ed** (train:) essere deragliato. ~**ment** n deragliamento m

deranged /dɪ'reɪndʒd/ a squilibrato

derelict /'derəlɪkt/ a abbandonato

deri|de /dɪ'raɪd/ vt deridere. ~**sion** /-'rɪʒn/ n derisione f

derisory /dɪ'raɪsəri/ a (laughter) derisorio; (offer) irrisorio

derivation /derɪ'veɪʃn/ n derivazione f

derivative /dɪ'rɪvətɪv/ a derivato ●n derivato m

derive /dɪ'raɪv/ vt (obtain) derivare; be ~**d from** (word:) derivare da

dermatologist /dɜːmə'tɒlədʒɪst/ n dermatologo, -a mf

derogatory /dɪ'rɒgətrɪ/ a (comments) peggiorativo

descend /dɪ'send/ vi scendere ●vt scendere da; be ~**ed from** discendere da. ~**ant** n discendente mf

descent /dɪ'sent/ n discesa f; (lineage) origine f

describe /dɪ'skraɪb/ vt descrivere

descrip|tion /dɪ'skrɪpʃn/ n descrizione f; they had no help of any ~**tion** non hanno avuto proprio nessun aiuto. ~**tive** /-tɪv/ a descrittivo; (vivid) vivido

desecrat|e /'desɪkreɪt/ vt profanare. ~**ion** /-'kreɪʃn/ n profanazione f

desert[1] /'dezət/ n deserto m ●a deserto; ~ **island** isola f deserta

desert[2] /dɪ'zɜːt/ vt abbandonare ●vi disertare. ~**ed** a deserto. ~**er** n Mil disertore m. ~**ion** /-'zɜːʃn/ n Mil diserzione f; (of family) abbandono m

deserts /dɪ'zɜːts/ npl get one's just ~ ottenere ciò che ci si merita

deserv|e /dɪ'zɜːv/ vt meritare. ~**ing** a meritevole; ~**ing cause** opera f meritoria

design /dɪ'zaɪn/ n progettazione f; (fashion ~, appearance) design m inv; (pattern) modello m; (aim) proposito m ●vt progettare; disegnare (clothes, furniture, model); be ~**ed for** essere fatto per

designat|e /'dezɪgneɪt/ vt designare. ~**ion** /-'neɪʃn/ n designazione f

designer /dɪ'zaɪnə(r)/ n progettista mf; (of clothes) stilista mf; (Theat: of set) scenografo, -a mf

desirable /dɪ'zaɪərəbl/ a desiderabile

desire /dɪ'zaɪə(r)/ n desiderio m ●vt desiderare

desk /desk/ n scrivania f; (in school) banco m; (in hotel) reception f inv; (cash ~) cassa f. ~**top 'publishing** n desktop publishing m, editoria f da tavolo

desolat|e /'desələt/ a desolato. ~**ion** /-'leɪʃn/ n desolazione f

despair /dɪ'speə(r)/ n disperazione f; in ~ disperato; (say) per disperazione ●vi I ~ **of that boy** quel ragazzo mi fa disperare

desperat|e /'despərət/ a disperato; be ~**e** (criminal:) essere un disperato; be ~**e for sth** morire dalla voglia di. ~**ely** adv disperatamente; he said ~**ely** ha detto, disperato. ~**ion** /-'reɪʃn/ n disperazione f; in ~**ion** per disperazione

despicable /dɪ'spɪkəbl/ a disprezzevole

despise /dɪ'spaɪz/ vt disprezzare

despite /dɪ'spaɪt/ prep malgrado

despondent /dɪ'spɒndənt/ a abbattuto

despot /'despɒt/ n despota m

dessert /dɪ'zɜːt/ n dolce m. ~ **spoon** n cucchiaio m da dolce

destination /destɪ'neɪʃn/ n destinazione f

destine /'destɪn/ vt destinare; be ~**d for sth** essere destinato a qcsa

destiny /'destɪni/ n destino m

destitute /'destɪtjuːt/ a bisognoso

destroy /dɪ'strɔɪ/ vt distruggere. ~**er** n Naut cacciatorpediniere m

destruc|tion /dɪ'strʌkʃn/ n distruzione f. ~**tive** /-tɪv/ a distruttivo; (fig: criticism) negativo

detach /dɪ'tætʃ/ vt staccare. ~**able** /-əbl/ a separabile. ~**ed** a fig distaccato; ~**ed house** villetta f

detachment /dɪ'tætʃmənt/ n distacco m; Mil distaccamento m

detail /dɪ'teɪl/ n particolare m, dettaglio m; in ~ particolareggiatamente ●vt esporre con tutti i particolari; Mil assegnare. ~**ed** a particolareggiato, dettagliato

detain /dɪ'teɪn/ vt (police:) trattenere; (delay) far ritardare. ~**ee** /diːteɪ'niː/ n detenuto, -a mf

detect /dɪ'tekt/ vt individuare;

(perceive) percepire. **~ion**/-ek∫n/ *n* scoperta *f*

detective /dɪ'tektɪv/ *n* investigatore, -trice *mf*. **~ story** *n* racconto *m* poliziesco

detector /dɪ'tektə(r)/ *n (for metal)* metal detector *m inv*

detention /dɪ'ten∫n/ *n* detenzione *f*; *Sch* punizione *f*

deter /dɪ'tɜ:(r)/ *vt (pt/pp* **deterred)** impedire; **~ sb from doing sth** impedire a qcno di fare qcsa

detergent /dɪ'tɜ:dʒənt/ *n* detersivo *m*

deteriorat|e /dɪ'tɪərɪəreɪt/ *vi* deteriorarsi. **~ion**/-'reɪ∫n/ *n* deterioramento *m*

determination /dɪtɜ:mɪ'neɪ∫n/ *n* determinazione *f*

determine /dɪ'tɜ:mɪn/ *vt (ascertain)* determinare; **~ to** *(resolve)* decidere di. **~d** *a* deciso

deterrent /dɪ'terənt/ *n* deterrente *m*

detest /dɪ'test/ *vt* detestare. **~able** /-əbl/ *a* detestabile

detonat|e /'detəneɪt/ *vt* far detonare ●*vi* detonare. **~or** *n* detonatore *m*

detour /'di:tʊə(r)/ *n* deviazione *f*

detract /dɪ'trækt/ *vi* **~ from** sminuire *(merit)*; rovinare *(pleasure, beauty)*

detriment /'detrɪmənt/ *n* **to the ~ of** a danno di. **~al** /-'mentl/ *a* dannoso

deuce /dju:s/ *n Tennis* deuce *m inv*

de'valuation /di:vælju'eɪ∫n/ *n* svalutazione *f*

de'value *vt* svalutare *(currency)*

devastat|e /'devəsteɪt/ *vt* devastare. **~ed** *a fam* sconvolto. **~ing** *a* devastante; *(news)* sconvolgente. **~ion** /-'steɪ∫n/ *n* devastazione *f*

develop /dɪ'veləp/ *vt* sviluppare; contrarre *(illness)*; *(add to value of)* valorizzare *(area)* ●*vi* svilupparsi; **~ into** divenire. **~er** *n* |*property*| **~er** imprenditore, -trice *mf* edile

de'veloping country *n* paese *m* in via di sviluppo

development /dɪ'veləpmənt/ *n* sviluppo *m*; *(of vaccine etc)* messa *f* a punto

deviant /'di:vɪənt/ *a* deviato

deviat|e /'di:vɪeɪt/ *vi* deviare. **~ion** /-'eɪ∫n/ *n* deviazione *f*

device /dɪ'vaɪs/ *n* dispositivo *m*

devil /'devl/ *n* diavolo *m*

devious /'di:vɪəs/ *a (person)* subdolo; *(route)* tortuoso

devise /dɪ'vaɪz/ *vt* escogitare

devoid /dɪ'vɔɪd/ *a* **~ of** privo di

devolution /di:və'lu:∫n/ *n (of power)* decentramento *m*

devot|e /dɪ'vəʊt/ *vt* dedicare. **~ed** *a (daughter etc)* affezionato; **be ~ed to sth** consacrarsi a qcsa. **~ee** /devə'ti:/ *n* appassionato, -a *mf*

devotion /dɪ'vəʊ∫n/ *n* dedizione *f*; **~s** *pl Relig* devozione *fsg*

devour /dɪ'vaʊə(r)/ *vt* divorare

devout /dɪ'vaʊt/ *a* devoto

dew /dju:/ *n* rugiada *f*

dexterity /dek'sterətɪ/ *n* destrezza *f*

diabet|es /daɪə'bi:ti:z/ *n* diabete *m*. **~ic** /-'betɪk/ *a* diabetico ●*n* diabetico, -a *mf*

diabolical /daɪə'bɒlɪkl/ *a* diabolico

diagnose /daɪəg'nəʊz/ *vt* diagnosticare

diagnosis /daɪəg'nəʊsɪs/ *n (pl* **-oses** /-si:z/*)* diagnosi *f inv*

diagonal /daɪ'ægənl/ *a* diagonale ●*n* diagonale *f*

diagram /'daɪəgræm/ *n* diagramma *m*

dial /'daɪəl/ *n (of clock, machine)* quadrante *m*; *Teleph* disco *m* combinatore ●*v (pt/pp* **dialled)** ●*vi Teleph* fare il numero; **~ direct** chiamare in teleselezione ●*vt* fare *(number)*

dialect /'daɪəlekt/ *n* dialetto *m*

dialling: ~ code *n* prefisso *m*. **~ tone** *n* segnale *m* di linea libera

dialogue /'daɪəlɒg/ *n* dialogo *m*

'dial tone *n Am Teleph* segnale *m* di linea libera

diameter /daɪ'æmɪtə(r)/ *n* diametro *m*

diametrically /daɪə'metrɪklɪ/ *adv* **~ opposed** diametralmente opposto

diamond /'daɪəmənd/ *n* diamante *m*, brillante *m*; *(shape)* losanga *f*; **~s** *pl (in cards)* quadri *mpl*

diaper /'daɪəpə(r)/ *n Am* pannolino *m*

diaphragm /'daɪəfræm/ *n* diaframma *m*

diarrhoea /daɪə'ri:ə/ *n* diarrea *f*

diary /'daɪərɪ/ *n (for appointments)* agenda *f*; *(for writing in)* diario *m*

dice /daɪs/ *n inv* dadi *mpl* ●*vt Culin* tagliare a dadini

dicey /'daɪsɪ/ *a fam* rischioso

dictat|e /dɪk'teɪt/ *vt/i* dettare. **~ion** /-'eɪ∫n/ *n* dettato *m*

dictator /dɪk'teɪtə(r)/ *n* dittatore *m*. **~ial** /-tə'tɔ:rɪəl/ *a* dittatoriale. **~ship** *n* dittatura *f*

dictionary /'dɪk∫ənrɪ/ *n* dizionario *m*

did /dɪd/ *see* **do**

didactic /dɪ'dæktɪk/ *a* didattico

diddle /'dɪdl/ *vt fam* gabbare

didn't /'dɪdnt/ = **did not**

die /daɪ/ *vi (pres p* **dying)** morire *(of* di); **be dying to do sth** *fam* morire

diesel | **directly**

dalla voglia di fare qcsa. **die down** *vi* calmarsi; *(fire, flames:)* spegnersi. **die out** *vi* estinguersi; *(custom:)* morire

diesel /ˈdiːzl/ *n* diesel *m*

diet /ˈdaɪət/ *n* regime *m* alimentare; *(restricted)* dieta *f*; **be on a ~** essere a dieta ● *vi* essere a dieta

differ /ˈdɪfə(r)/ *vi* differire; *(disagree)* non essere d'accordo

difference /ˈdɪfrəns/ *n* differenza *f*; *(disagreement)* divergenza *f*

different /ˈdɪfrənt/ *a* diverso, differente; *(various)* diversi; **be ~ from** essere diverso da

differential /dɪfəˈrenʃl/ *a* differenziale ● *n* differenziale *m*

differentiate /dɪfəˈrenʃieɪt/ *vt* distinguere **(between** fra); *(discriminate)* discriminare **(between** fra); *(make differ)* differenziare

differently /ˈdɪfrəntlɪ/ *adv* in modo diverso; **~ from** diversamente da

difficult /ˈdɪfɪkəlt/ *a* difficile. **~y** *n* difficoltà *f inv*; **with ~y** con difficoltà

diffuse[1] /dɪˈfjuːs/ *a* diffuso; *(wordy)* prolisso

diffuse[2] /dɪˈfjuːz/ *vt* Phys diffondere

dig /dɪg/ *n* *(poke)* spinta *f*; *(remark)* frecciata *f*; Archaeol scavo *m*; **~s** *pl fam* camera *fsg* ammobiliata ● *vt/i* *(pt/pp* **dug,** *pres p* **digging)** scavare *(hole)*; vangare *(garden)*; *(thrust)* conficcare; **~ sb in the ribs** dare una gomitata a qcno. **dig out** *vt fig* tirar fuori. **dig up** *vt* scavare *(garden, street, object)*; sradicare *(tree, plant)*; *(fig: find)* scovare

digest[1] /ˈdaɪdʒest/ *n* compendio *m*

digest[2] /daɪˈdʒest/ *vt* digerire. **~ible** *a* digeribile. **~ion** /-estʃn/ *n* digestione *f*

digger /ˈdɪgə(r)/ *n* Techn scavatrice *f*

digit /ˈdɪdʒɪt/ *n* cifra *f*; *(finger)* dito *m*

digital /ˈdɪdʒɪtl/ *a* digitale; **~ clock** orologio *m* digitale

dignified /ˈdɪgnɪfaɪd/ *a* dignitoso

dignitary /ˈdɪgnɪtərɪ/ *n* dignitario *m*

dignity /ˈdɪgnɪtɪ/ *n* dignità *f*

digress /daɪˈgres/ *vi* divagare. **~ion** /-eʃn/ *n* digressione *f*

dike /daɪk/ *n* diga *f*

dilapidated /dɪˈlæpɪdeɪtɪd/ *a* cadente

dilate /daɪˈleɪt/ *vi* dilatarsi

dilemma /dɪˈlemə/ *n* dilemma *m*

dilettante /dɪlɪˈtæntɪ/ *n* dilettante *mf*

dilly-dally /ˈdɪlɪdælɪ/ *vi* *(pt/pp* -ied) *fam* tentennare

dilute /daɪˈluːt/ *vt* diluire

dim /dɪm/ *a* **(dimmer, dimmest)** debole *(light)*; *(dark)* scuro; *(prospect,*

chance) scarso; *(indistinct)* impreciso; *(fam: stupid)* tonto ● *vt/i* *(pt/pp* **dimmed)** affievolire. **~ly** *adv* *(see, remember)* indistintamente; *(shine)* debolmente

dime /daɪm/ *n Am* moneta *f* da dieci centesimi

dimension /daɪˈmenʃn/ *n* dimensione *f*

diminish /dɪˈmɪnɪʃ/ *vt/i* diminuire

diminutive /dɪˈmɪnjʊtɪv/ *a* minuscolo ● *n* diminutivo *m*

dimple /ˈdɪmpl/ *n* fossetta *f*

din /dɪn/ *n* baccano *m*

dine /daɪn/ *vi* pranzare. **~r** *n* *(Am: restaurant)* tavola *f* calda; **the last ~r in the restaurant** l'ultimo cliente nel ristorante

dinghy /ˈdɪŋgɪ/ *n* dinghy *m*; *(inflatable)* canotto *m* pneumatico

dingy /ˈdɪndʒɪ/ *a* (-ier, -iest) squallido e tetro

dining /ˈdaɪnɪŋ/: **~-car** *n* carrozza *f* ristorante. **~-room** *n* sala *f* da pranzo. **.~-table** *n* tavolo *m* da pranzo

dinner /ˈdɪnə(r)/ *n* cena *f*; *(at midday)* pranzo *m*. **~-jacket** *n* smoking *m inv*

dinosaur /ˈdaɪnəsɔː(r)/ *n* dinosauro *m*

dint /dɪnt/ *n* **by ~ of** a forza di

diocese /ˈdaɪəsɪs/ *n* diocesi *f inv*

dip /dɪp/ *n* *(in ground)* inclinazione *f*; Culin salsina *f*; **go for a ~** andare a fare una nuotata ● *v* *(pt/pp* **dipped)** ● *vt* *(in liquid)* immergere; abbassare *(head, headlights)* ● *vi* *(land:)* formare un avvallamento. **dip into** *vt* scorrere *(book)*

diphtheria /dɪfˈθɪərɪə/ *n* difterite *f*

diphthong /ˈdɪfθɒŋ/ *n* dittongo *m*

diploma /dɪˈpləʊmə/ *n* diploma *m*

diplomacy /dɪˈpləʊməsɪ/ *n* diplomazia *f*

diplomat /ˈdɪpləmæt/ *n* diplomatico, -a *mf*. **~ic** /-ˈmætɪk/ *a* diplomatico. **~ically** *adv* con diplomazia

dip-stick *n* Auto astina *f* dell'olio

dire /ˈdaɪə(r)/ *a* *(situation, consequences)* terribile

direct /dɪˈrekt/ *a* diretto ● *adv* direttamente ● *vt* *(aim)* rivolgere *(attention, criticism)*; *(control)* dirigere; fare la regia di *(film, play)*; **~ sb** *(show the way)* indicare la strada a qcno; **~ sb to do sth** ordinare a qcno di fare qcsa. **~ current** *n* corrente *m* continua

direction /dɪˈrekʃn/ *n* direzione *f*; *(of play, film)* regia *f*; **~s** *pl* indicazioni *fpl*

directly /dɪˈrektlɪ/ *adv* direttamente; *(at once)* immediatamente ● *conj* [non] appena

director /dɪˈrɛktə(r)/ n Comm direttore, -trice mf; (of play, film) regista mf

directory /dɪˈrɛktərɪ/ n elenco m; Teleph elenco m [telefonico]; (of streets) stradario m

dirt /dɜːt/ n sporco m; ~ cheap fam a [un] prezzo stracciato

dirty /ˈdɜːtɪ/ a (-ier, -iest) sporco; ~ trick brutto scherzo m; ~ word parolaccia f ● vt (pt/pp -ied) sporcare

disa'bility /dɪs-/ n infermità f inv. ~abled /dɪˈseɪbld/ a invalido

disad'vantage n svantaggio m; at a ~tage in una posizione di svantaggio. ~taged a svantaggiato. ~'tageous a svantaggioso

disa'gree vi non essere d'accordo; ~ with ⟨food:⟩ far male a

disa'greeable a sgradevole

disa'greement n disaccordo m; (quarrel) dissidio m

disal'low vt annullare ⟨goal⟩

disap'pear vi scomparire. ~ance n scomparsa f

disap'point vt deludere; I'm ~ed sono deluso. ~ing a deludente. ~ment n delusione f

disap'proval n disapprovazione f

disap'prove vi disapprovare; ~ of sb/sth disapprovare qcno/qcsa

dis'arm vt disarmare ● vi Mil disarmarsi. ~ament n disarmo m. ~ing a ⟨frankness etc⟩ disarmante

disar'ray n in ~ in disordine

disast|er /dɪˈzɑːstə(r)/ n disastro m. ~rous /-rəs/ a disastroso

dis'band vt sciogliere; smobilitare ⟨troops⟩ ● vi sciogliersi; ⟨regiment:⟩ essere smobilitato

disbe'lief n incredulità f; in ~ con incredulità

disc /dɪsk/ n disco m; (CD) compact disc m inv

discard /dɪˈskɑːd/ vt scartare; (throw away) eliminare; scaricare ⟨boyfriend⟩

discern /dɪˈsɜːn/ vt discernere. ~ible a discernibile. ~ing a perspicace

discharge[1] n Electr scarica f; (dismissal) licenziamento m; Mil congedo m; (Med: of blood) emissione f; (of cargo) scarico m

dis'charge[2] vt scaricare ⟨battery, cargo⟩; (dismiss) licenziare; Mil congedare; Jur assolvere ⟨accused⟩; dimettere ⟨patient⟩ ● vi Electr scaricarsi

disciple /dɪˈsaɪpl/ n discepolo m

disciplinary /ˈdɪsɪplɪnərɪ/ a disciplinare

discipline /ˈdɪsɪplɪn/ n disciplina f ● vt disciplinare; (punish) punire

'disc jockey n disc jockey m inv

dis'claim vt disconoscere. ~er n rifiuto m

dis'close vt svelare. ~ure n rivelazione f

disco /ˈdɪskəʊ/ n discoteca f

dis'colour vt scolorire ● vi scolorirsi

dis'comfort n scomodità f, fig disagio m

disconcert /dɪskənˈsɜːt/ vt sconcertare

discon'nect vt disconnettere

disconsolate /dɪsˈkɒnsələt/ a sconsolato

discon'tent n scontentezza f. ~ed a scontento

discon'tinue vt cessare, smettere; Comm sospendere la produzione di; ~d line fine f serie

'discord n discordia f; Mus dissonanza f. ~ant /dɪˈskɔːdənt/ a ~ant note nota f discordante

discothèque /ˈdɪskətek/ n discoteca f

'discount[1] n sconto m ‚

dis'count[2] vt (not believe) non credere a; (leave out of consideration) non tener conto di

dis'courage vt scoraggiare; (dissuade) dissuadere

'discourse n discorso m

dis'courteous a scortese

discover /dɪˈskʌvə(r)/ vt scoprire. ~y n scoperta f

dis'credit n discredito m ● vt (pt/pp discredited) screditare

discreet /dɪˈskriːt/ a discreto

discrepancy /dɪˈskrepənsɪ/ n discrepanza f

discretion /dɪˈskreʃn/ n discrezione f

discriminat|e /dɪˈskrɪmɪneɪt/ vi discriminare (against contro); ~e between distinguere tra. ~ing a esigente. ~ion /-ˈneɪʃn/ n discriminazione f; (quality) discernimento m

discus /ˈdɪskəs/ n disco m

discuss /dɪˈskʌs/ vt discutere; (examine critically) esaminare. ~ion /-ʌʃn/ n discussione f

disdain /dɪsˈdeɪn/ n sdegno m ● vt sdegnare. ~ful a sdegnoso

disease /dɪˈziːz/ n malattia f. ~d a malato

disem'bark vi sbarcare

disen'chant vt disincantare. ~ment n disincanto m

disen'gage vt disimpegnare; disinnestare ⟨clutch⟩

disen'tangle *vt* districare

dis'favour *n* sfavore *m*

dis'figure *vt* deformare

dis'grace *n* vergogna *f*; **I am in ~** sono caduto in disgrazia; **it's a ~** è una vergogna ● *vt* disonorare. **~ful** *a* vergognoso

disgruntled /dɪs'grʌntld/ *a* malcontento

disguise /dɪs'gaɪz/ *n* travestimento *m*; **in ~** travestito ● *vt* contraffare ⟨voice⟩; dissimulare ⟨emotions⟩; **~d as** travestito da

disgust /dɪs'gʌst/ *n* disgusto *m*; **in ~** con aria disgustata ● *vt* disgustare. **~ing** *a* disgustoso

dish /dɪʃ/ *n* piatto *m*; **do the ~es** lavare i piatti ● **dish out** *vt* ⟨serve⟩ servire; ⟨distribute⟩ distribuire. **dish up** *vt* servire

'dishcloth *n* strofinaccio *m*

dis'hearten *vt* scoraggiare

dishevelled /dɪ'ʃevld/ *a* scompigliato

dis'honest *a* disonesto. **~y** *n* disonestà *f*

dis'honour *n* disonore *m* ● *vt* disonorare ⟨family⟩; non onorare ⟨cheque⟩. **~able** *a* disonorevole. **~ably** *adv* in modo disonorevole

'dishwasher *n* lavapiatti *f inv*

disil'lusion *vt* disilludere. **~ment** *n* disillusione *f*

disin'fect *vt* disinfettare. **~ant** *n* disinfettante *m*

disin'herit *vt* diseredare

dis'integrate *vi* disintegrarsi

dis'interested *a* disinteressato

dis'jointed *a* sconnesso

disk /dɪsk/ *n* Comput disco *m*; ⟨diskette⟩ dischetto *m*

dis'like *n* avversione *f*; **your likes and ~s** i tuoi gusti ● *vt* **I ~ him/it** non mi piace; **I don't ~ him/it** non mi dispiace

dislocate /'dɪsləkeɪt/ *vt* slogare; **~ one's shoulder** slogarsi una spalla

dis'lodge *vt* sloggiare

dis'loyal *a* sleale. **~ty** *n* slealtà *f*

dismal /'dɪzml/ *a* ⟨person⟩ abbacchiato; ⟨news, weather⟩ deprimente; ⟨performance⟩ mediocre

dismantle /dɪs'mæntl/ *vt* smontare ⟨tent, machine⟩; *fig* smantellare

dis'may *n* sgomento *m*. **~ed** *a* sgomento

dis'miss *vt* licenziare ⟨employee⟩; ⟨reject⟩ scartare ⟨idea, suggestion⟩. **~al** *n* licenziamento *m*

dis'mount *vi* smontare

diso'bedien|ce *n* disubbidienza *f*. **~t** *a* disubbidiente

diso'bey *vt* disubbidire a ⟨rule⟩ ● *vi* disubbidire

dis'order *n* disordine *m*; Med disturbo *m*. **~ly** *a* disordinato; ⟨crowd⟩ turbolento; **~ly conduct** turbamento *m* della quiete pubblica

dis'organized *a* disorganizzato

dis'orientate *vt* disorientare

dis'own *vt* disconoscere

disparaging /dɪ'spærɪdʒɪŋ/ *a* sprezzante

disparity /dɪ'spærətɪ/ *n* disparità *f inv*

dispassionate /dɪ'spæʃənət/ *a* spassionato

dispatch /dɪ'spætʃ/ *n* Comm spedizione *f*; ⟨Mil, report⟩ dispaccio *m*; **with ~** con prontezza ● *vt* spedire; ⟨kill⟩ spedire al creatore

dispel /dɪ'spel/ *vt* (*pt/pp* dispelled) dissipare

dispensable /dɪ'spensəbl/ *a* dispensabile

dispensary /dɪ'spensərɪ/ *n* farmacia *f*

dispense /dɪ'spens/ *vt* distribuire; **~ with** fare a meno di; **dispensing chemist** farmacista *mf*; ⟨shop⟩ farmacia *f*. **~r** *n* ⟨device⟩ distributore *m*

dispers|al /dɪ'spɜ:sl/ *n* disperzione *f*. **~e** /dɪ'spɜ:s/ *vt* disperdere ● *vi* disperdersi

dispirited /dɪ'spɪrɪtɪd/ *a* scoraggiato

dis'place *vt* spostare; **~d person** profugo, -a *mf*

display /dɪ'spleɪ/ *n* mostra *f*; Comm esposizione *f*; ⟨of feelings⟩ manifestazione *f*; *pej* ostentazione *f*; Comput display *m inv* ● *vt* mostrare; esporre ⟨goods⟩; manifestare ⟨feelings⟩; Comput visualizzare

dis'please *vt* non piacere a; **be ~d with** essere scontento di

dis'pleasure *n* malcontento *m*

disposable /dɪ'spəʊzəbl/ *a* ⟨throwaway⟩ usa e getta; ⟨income⟩ disponibile

disposal /dɪ'spəʊzl/ *n* ⟨getting rid of⟩ eliminazione *f*; **be at sb's ~** essere a disposizione di qcno

dispose /dɪ'spəʊz/ *vi* **~ of** ⟨get rid of⟩ disfarsi di; **be well ~d** essere ben disposto ⟨to verso⟩

disposition /dɪspə'zɪʃn/ *n* disposizione *f*; ⟨nature⟩ indole *f*

disproportionate /dɪsprə'pɔ:ʃənət/ *a* sproporzionato

dis'prove *vt* confutare

dispute /dɪ'spju:t/ *n* disputa *f*;

(*industrial*) contestazione f ● vt contestare ⟨*statement*⟩

disqualifi'cation n squalifica f; (*from driving*) ritiro m della patente

dis'qualify vt (pt/pp -ied) escludere; *Sport* squalificare; ~ **sb from driving** ritirare la patente a qcno

disquieting /dɪs'kwaɪətɪŋ/ a allarmante

disre'gard n mancanza f di considerazione ● vt ignorare

disre'pair n **fall into** ~ deteriorarsi; **in a state of** ~ in cattivo stato

dis'reputable a malfamato

disre'pute n discredito m; **bring sb into** ~ rovinare la reputazione a qcno

disre'spect n mancanza f di rispetto. ~**ful** a irrispettoso

disrupt /dɪs'rʌpt/ vt creare scompiglio in; sconvolgere ⟨*plans*⟩. ~**ion** /-'ʌpʃn/ n scompiglio m; (*of plans*) sconvolgimento m. ~**ive** /-tɪv/ a ⟨*person, behaviour*⟩ indisciplinato

dissatis'faction n malcontento m

dis'satisfied a scontento

dissect /dɪ'sekt/ vt sezionare. ~**ion** /-ekʃn/ n dissezione f

dissent /dɪ'sent/ n dissenso m ● vi dissentire

dissertation /dɪsə'teɪʃn/ n tesi f inv

dis'service n **do sb/oneself a** ~ rendere un cattivo servizio a qcno/se stesso

dissident /'dɪsɪdənt/ n dissidente mf

dis'similar a dissimile (**to** da)

dissociate /dɪ'səʊʃɪeɪt/ vt dissociare; ~ **oneself from** dissociarsi da

dissolute /'dɪsəluːt/ a dissoluto

dissolution /dɪsə'luːʃn/ n scioglimento m

dissolve /dɪ'zɒlv/ vt dissolvere ● vi dissolversi

dissuade /dɪ'sweɪd/ vt dissuadere

distance /'dɪstəns/ n distanza f; **it's a short** ~ **from here to the station** la stazione non è lontana da qui; **in the** ~ in lontananza; **from a** ~ da lontano

distant /'dɪstənt/ a distante; ⟨*relative*⟩ lontano

dis'taste n avversione f. ~**ful** a spiacevole

distil /dɪ'stɪl/ vt (pt/pp distilled) distillare. ~**lation** /-'leɪʃn/ n distillazione f. ~**lery** /-ərɪ/ n distilleria f

distinct /dɪ'stɪŋkt/ a chiaro; (*different*) distinto. ~**ion** /-ɪŋkʃn/ n distinzione f; *Sch* massimo m dei voti. ~**ive** /-tɪv/ a caratteristico. ~**ly** adv chiaramente

distinguish /dɪ'stɪŋgwɪʃ/ vt/i distin-

guere; ~ **oneself** distinguersi. ~**ed** a rinomato; ⟨*appearance*⟩ distinto; ⟨*career*⟩ brillante

distort /dɪ'stɔːt/ vt distorcere. ~**ion** /-'ɔːʃn/ n distorsione f

distract /dɪ'strækt/ vt distrarre. ~**ed** /-ɪd/ a assente; (*fam: worried*) preoccupato. ~**ing** a che distoglie. ~**ion** /-'ækʃn/ n distrazione f; (*despair*) disperazione f, **drive sb to** ~ portare qcno alla disperazione

distraught /dɪ'strɔːt/ a sconvolto

distress /dɪ'stres/ n angoscia f; (*pain*) sofferenza f; (*danger*) difficoltà f ● vt sconvolgere; (*sadden*) affliggere. ~**ing** a penoso; (*shocking*) sconvolgente. ~ **signal** n segnale m di richiesta di soccorso

distribut|e /dɪ'strɪbjuːt/ vt distribuire. ~**ion** /-'bjuːʃn/ n distribuzione f. ~**or** n distributore m

district /'dɪstrɪkt/ n regione f; *Admin* distretto m. ~ **nurse** n infermiere, -a mf che fa visite a domicilio

dis'trust n sfiducia f ● vt non fidarsi di. ~**ful** a diffidente

disturb /dɪ'stɜːb/ vt disturbare; (*emotionally*) turbare; spostare ⟨*papers*⟩. ~**ance** n disturbo m; ~**ances** (pl: *rioting etc*) disordini mpl. ~**ed** a turbato; [*mentally*] ~**ed** malato di mente. ~**ing** a inquietante

dis'used a non utilizzato

ditch /dɪtʃ/ n fosso m ● vt (*fam: abandon*) abbandonare ⟨*plan, car*⟩; piantare ⟨*lover*⟩

dither /'dɪðə(r)/ vi titubare

divan /dɪ'væn/ n divano m

dive /daɪv/ n tuffo m; *Aeron* picchiata f; (*fam: place*) bettola f ● vi tuffarsi; (*when in water*) immergersi; *Aeron* scendere in picchiata; (*fam: rush*) precipitarsi

diver /'daɪvə(r)/ n (*from board*) tuffatore, -trice mf; (*scuba*) sommozzatore, -trice mf; (*deep sea*) palombaro m

diverge /daɪ'vɜːdʒ/ vi divergere. ~**gent** /-ənt/ a divergente

diverse /daɪ'vɜːs/ a vario

diversify /daɪ'vɜːsɪfaɪ/ vt/i (pt/pp -ied) diversificare

diversion /daɪ'vɜːʃn/ n deviazione f; (*distraction*) diversivo m

diversity /daɪ'vɜːsətɪ/ n varietà f

divert /daɪ'vɜːt/ vt deviare ⟨*traffic*⟩; distogliere ⟨*attention*⟩

divest /daɪ'vest/ vt privare (**of** di)

divide /dɪ'vaɪd/ *vt* dividere (by per); **six ~d by two** sei diviso due ●*vi* dividersi

dividend /'dɪvɪdend/ *n* dividendo *m*; **pay ~s** *fig* ripagare

divine /dɪ'vaɪn/ *a* divino

diving /'daɪvɪŋ/ *n* (from board) tuffi *mpl*; (scuba) immersione *f*. **~-board** *n* trampolino *m*. **~ mask** *n* maschera *f* [subacquea]. **~-suit** *n* muta *f*; (deep sea) scafandro *m*

divinity /dɪ'vɪnətɪ/ *n* divinità *f inv*; (subject) teologia *f*; (at school) religione *f*

divisible /dɪ'vɪzɪbl/ *a* divisibile (by per)

division /dɪ'vɪʒn/ *n* divisione *f*; (in sports league) serie *f*

divorce /dɪ'vɔːs/ *n* divorzio *m* ●*vt* divorziare da. **~d** *a* divorziato; **get ~d** divorziare

divorcee /dɪvɔː'siː/ *n* divorziato, -a *mf*

divulge /daɪ'vʌldʒ/ *vt* rendere pubblico

DIY *n abbr* do-it-yourself

dizziness /'dɪzɪnɪs/ *n* giramenti *mpl* di testa

dizzy /'dɪzɪ/ *a* (-ier, -iest) vertiginoso; **I feel ~** mi gira la testa

do /duː/ *n* (pl **dos** or **do's**) *fam* festa *f* ●*v* (3 *sg pres tense* **does**; *pt* **did**; *pp* **done**) ●*vt* fare; (fam: cheat) fregare; **be done** *Culin* essere cotto; **well done** bravo; *Culin* ben cotto; **do the flowers** sistemare i fiori; **do the washing up** lavare i piatti; **do one's hair** farsi i capelli ●*vi* (be suitable) andare; (be enough) bastare; **this will do** questo va bene; **that will do!** basta così!; **do well/badly** cavarsela bene/male; **how is he doing?** come sta? ●*v aux* **do you speak Italian?** parli italiano?; **you don't like him, do you?** non ti piace, vero?; (expressing astonishment) **non dirmi che ti piace!**; **yes, I do** sì; (emphatic) invece sì; **no, I don't** no; **I don't smoke** non fumo; **don't you/doesn't he?** vero?; **so do I** anch'io; **come in, John** entra, John; **how do you do?** piacere. **do away with** *vt* abolire (rule). **do for** *vt* *fam* rovinato. **do in** *vt* (fam: kill) uccidere; farsi male (back); **done in** *fam* esausto. **do up** *vt* (fasten) abbottonare; (renovate) rimettere a nuovo; (wrap) avvolgere. **do with** *vt* **I could do with a spanner** mi ci vorrebbe una chiave inglese. **do without** *vt* fare a meno di

docile /'dəʊsaɪl/ *a* docile

dock[1] /dɒk/ *n* *Jur* banco *m* degli imputati

dock[2] *n* *Naut* bacino *m* ●*vi* entrare in porto; (spaceship:) congiungersi. **~er** *n* portuale *m*. **~s** *npl* porto *m*. **~yard** *n* cantiere *m* navale

doctor /'dɒktə(r)/ *n* dottore *m*, dottoressa *f* ●*vt* alterare (drink); castrare (cat). **~ate** /-ət/ *n* dottorato *m*

doctrine /'dɒktrɪn/ *n* dottrina *f*

document /'dɒkjʊmənt/ *n* documento *m*. **~ary** /-'mentərɪ/ *a* documentario ●*n* documentario *m*

doddery /'dɒdərɪ/ *a* *fam* barcollante

dodge /dɒdʒ/ *n* *fam* trucco *m* ●*vt* schivare (blow); evitare (person) ●*vi* scansarsi; **~ out of the way** scansarsi

dodgems /'dɒdʒəmz/ *npl* auto-scontro *msg*

dodgy /'dɒdʒɪ/ *a* (-ier, -iest) (fam: dubious) sospetto

doe /dəʊ/ *n* femmina *f* (di daino, renna, lepre); (rabbit) coniglia *f*

does /dʌz/ *see* **do**

doesn't /'dʌznt/ = **does not**

dog /dɒg/ *n* cane *m* ●*vt* (pt/pp **dogged**) (illness, bad luck:) perseguitare

dog: **~-biscuit** *n* biscotto *m* per cani. **~-collar** *n* collare *m* (per cani); *Relig* *fam* collare *m* del prete. **~-eared** *a* con le orecchie

dogged /'dɒgɪd/ *a* ostinato

'**dog house** *n* **in the ~** *fam* in disgrazia

dogma /'dɒgmə/ *n* dogma *m*. **~tic** /-'mætɪk/ *a* dogmatico

'**dogsbody** *n* *fam* tirapiedi *mf inv*

doily /'dɔɪlɪ/ *n* centrino *m*

do-it-yourself /duːɪtjə'self/ *n* fai da te *m*, bricolage *m*. **~ shop** *n* negozio *m* di bricolage

doldrums /'dɒldrəmz/ *npl* **be in the ~** essere giù di corda; (business:) essere in fase di stasi

dole /dəʊl/ *n* sussidio *m* di disoccupazione; **be on the ~** essere disoccupato ●**dole out** *vt* distribuire

doleful /'dəʊlfl/ *a* triste

doll /dɒl/ *n* bambola *f* ●**doll oneself up** *vt* *fam* mettersi in ghingheri

dollar /'dɒlə(r)/ *n* dollaro *m*

dollop /'dɒləp/ *n* *fam* cucchiaiata *f*

dolphin /'dɒlfɪn/ *n* delfino *m*

dome /dəʊm/ *n* cupola *f*

domestic /də'mestɪk/ *a* domestico; *Pol* interno; *Comm* nazionale. **~ animal** *n* animale *m* domestico

domesticated /də'mestɪkeɪtɪd/ *a* (animal) addomesticato

domestic: ~ **flight** n volo m nazionale. ~ **'servant** n domestico, -a mf

dominant /'dɒmɪnənt/ a dominante

dominat|e /'dɒmɪneɪt/ vt/i dominare. ~**ion** /-'neɪʃn/ n dominio m

domineering /dɒmɪ'nɪərɪŋ/ a autoritario

dominion /də'mɪnjən/ n Br Pol dominion m inv

domino /'dɒmɪnəʊ/ n (pl -es) tessera f del domino; ~**es** sg (game) domino m

don[1] /dɒn/ vt (pt/pp donned) liter indossare

don[2] n docente mf universitario, -a

donat|e /dəʊ'neɪt/ vt donare. ~**ion** /-ʃn/ n donazione f

done /dʌn/ see **do**

donkey /'dɒŋkɪ/ n asino m; ~**'s years** fam secoli mpl. ~**-work** n sgobbata f

donor /'dəʊnə(r)/ n donatore, -trice mf

don't /dəʊnt/ = **do not**

doodle /'duːdl/ vi scarabocchiare

doom /duːm/ n fato m; (ruin) rovina f ● vt be ~**ed** [to failure] essere destinato al fallimento; ~**ed** (ship) destinato ad affondare

door /dɔː(r)/ n porta f; (of car) portiera f; out of ~s all'aperto

door: ~**man** n portiere m. ~**mat** n zerbino m. ~**step** n gradino m della porta. ~**way** n vano m della porta

dope /dəʊp/ n fam (drug) droga f leggera; (information) indiscrezioni fpl; (idiot) idiota mf ● vt drogare; Sport dopare

dopey /'dəʊpɪ/ a fam addormentato

dormant /'dɔːmənt/ a latente; (volcano) inattivo

dormer /'dɔːmə(r)/ n ~ [window] abbaino m

dormitory /'dɔːmɪtərɪ/ n dormitorio m

dormouse /'dɔː-/ n ghiro m

dosage /'dəʊsɪdʒ/ n dosaggio m

dose /dəʊs/ n dose f

doss /dɒs/ vi sl accamparsi. ~**er** n barbone, -a mf. ~**house** n dormitorio m pubblico

dot /dɒt/ n punto m; at 8 o'clock on the ~ alle 8 in punto

dote /dəʊt/ vi ~ on stravedere per

dotted /'dɒtɪd/ a ~ line linea f punteggiata; be ~ with essere punteggiato di

dotty /'dɒtɪ/ a (-ier, -iest) fam tocco; (idea) folle

double /'dʌbl/ a doppio ● adv cost ~ costare il doppio; see ~ vedere doppio; ~ the amount la quantità doppia ● n doppio m; (person) sosia m inv; ~**s** pl

Tennis doppio m; at the ~ di corsa ● vt raddoppiare; (fold) piegare in due ● vi raddoppiare. **double back** vi (go back) fare dietro front. **double up** vi (bend over) piegarsi in due (with per); (share) dividere una stanza

double: ~**-bass** n contrabbasso m. ~ **bed** n letto m matrimoniale. ~**-breasted** a a doppio petto. ~ **chin** n doppio mento m. ~**-cross** vt ingannare. ~**-decker** n autobus m inv a due piani. ~ **Dutch** n fam ostrogoto m. ~ **glazing** n doppiovetro m. ~ **room** n camera f doppia

doubly /'dʌblɪ/ adv doppiamente

doubt /daʊt/ n dubbio m ● vt dubitare di. ~**ful** a dubbio; (having doubts) in dubbio. ~**fully** adv con aria dubbiosa. ~**less** adv indubbiamente

dough /dəʊ/ n pasta f; (for bread) impasto m; (fam: money) quattrini mpl. ~**nut** n bombolone m, krapfen m inv

douse /daʊs/ vt spegnere

dove /dʌv/ n colomba f. ~**tail** n Techn incastro m a coda di rondine

dowdy /'daʊdɪ/ a (-ier, -iest) trasandato

down[1] /daʊn/ n (feathers) piumino m

down[2] /daʊn/ adv giù; come ~ scendere; ~ there laggiù; sales are ~ le vendite sono diminuite; £50 ~ 50 sterline d'acconto; ~ 10% ridotto del 10%; ~ with...! abbasso...! ● prep walk ~ the road camminare per strada; ~ the stairs giù per le scale; fall ~ the stairs cadere giù dalle scale; get that ~ you! fam butta giù!; be ~ the pub fam essere al pub ● vt bere tutto d'un fiato (drink)

down: ~**-and-'out** n spiantato, -a mf. ~**cast** a abbattuto. ~**fall** n caduta f; (of person) rovina f. ~**grade** vt (in seniority) degradare. ~**-hearted** a scoraggiato. ~**hill** adv in discesa; go ~**hill** fig essere in declino. ~ **payment** n deposito m. ~**pour** n acquazzone m. ~**right** a (absolute) totale; (lie) bell'e buono; (idiot) perfetto ● adv (completely) completamente. ~**stairs** adv al piano di sotto ● a /'-'-/ del piano di sotto. ~**stream** adv a valle. ~**-to-'earth** a (person) con i piedi per terra. ~**town** adv Am in centro. ~**trodden** a oppresso. ~**ward[s]** a verso il basso; (slope) in discesa ● adv verso il basso

dowry /'daʊrɪ/ n dote f

doze /dəʊz/ n sonnellino m ● vi sonnec-

chiare. **doze off** vi assopirsi
dozen /'dʌzn/ n dozzina f; **~s of
books** libri a dozzine
Dr abbr **doctor**
drab /dræb/ a spento
draft[1] /drɑːft/ n abbozzo m; Comm cambiale f; Am Mil leva f ●vt abbozzare;
Am Mil arruolare
draft[2] n Am = **draught**
drag /dræg/ n fam scocciatura f; **in ~
fam (man)** travestito da donna ●vt
(pt/pp **dragged**) trascinare; dragare
(river). **drag on** vi (time, meeting:) trascinarsi
dragon /'drægən/ n drago m. **~-fly** n libellula f
drain /dreɪn/ n tubo m di scarico; (grid)
tombino m; **the ~s** pl le fognature; **be a
~ on sb's finances** prosciugare le finanze di qcno ●vt drenare (land,
wound); scolare (liquid, vegetables);
svuotare (tank, glass, person) ●vi **~
[away]** andar via
drain|age /'dreɪnɪdʒ/ n (system) drenaggio m; (of land) scolo m. **~ing
board** n scolapiatti m inv. **~-pipe** n
tubo m di scarico
drake /dreɪk/ n maschio m dell'anatra
drama /'drɑːmə/ n arte f drammatica;
(play) opera f teatrale; (event) dramma f sg
dramatic /drə'mætɪk/ a drammatico
dramat|ist /'dræmətɪst/ n drammaturgo, -a mf. **~ize** vt adattare per il teatro;
fig drammatizzare
drank /dræŋk/ see **drink**
drape /dreɪp/ n Am tenda f ●vt appoggiare (over su)
drastic /'dræstɪk/ a drastico; **~ally**
adv drasticamente
draught /drɑːft/ n corrente f [d'aria];
~s sg (game) [gioco m della] dama f sg
draught: ~ beer n birra f alla spina.
~sman n disegnatore, -trice mf
draughty /'drɑːftɪ/ a pieno di correnti
d'aria; **it's ~** c'è corrente
draw /drɔː/ n (in attraction) attrazione f;
Sport pareggio m; (in lottery) sorteggio
m ●v (pt **drew**, pp **drawn**) ●vt tirare;
(attract) attirare; disegnare (picture);
tracciare (line); ritirare (money); **~
lots** tirare a sorte ●vi (tea:) essere in
infusione; Sport pareggiare; **~ near** avvicinarsi. **draw back** vt tirare indietro;
ritirare (hand); tirare (curtains) ●vi
(recoil) tirarsi indietro. **draw in** vt ritirare (claws etc) ●vi (train:) arrivare;
(days:) accorciarsi. **draw out** vt (pull
out) tirar fuori; ritirare (money) ●vi

(train:) partire; (days:) allungarsi.
draw up vt redigere (document); accostare (chair); **~ oneself up to one's
full height** farsi grande ●vi (stop) fermarsi
draw: ~back n inconveniente m.
~bridge n ponte m levatoio
drawer /drɔː(r)/ n cassetto m
drawing /'drɔːɪŋ/ n disegno m
drawing: ~-board n tavolo m da disegno; fig **go back to the ~-board** ricominciare da capo. **~-pin** n puntina f.
~-room n salotto m
drawl /drɔːl/ n pronuncia f strascicata
drawn /drɔːn/ see **draw**
dread /dred/ n terrore m ●vt aver il
terrore di
dreadful /'dredfʊl/ a terribile. **~ly** adv
terribilmente
dream /driːm/ n sogno m ●attrib di sogno ●vt/i (pt/pp **dreamt** /dremt/ or
dreamed) sognare (about/of di)
dreary /'drɪərɪ/ a (-ier, -iest) tetro;
(boring) monotono
dredge /dredʒ/ vt/i dragare
dregs /dregz/ npl feccia f sg
drench /drentʃ/ vt get **~ed** inzupparsi; **~ed** zuppo
dress /dres/ n (woman's) vestito m;
(clothing) abbigliamento m ●vt vestire;
(decorate) adornare; Culin condire; Med
fasciare; **~ oneself, get ~ed** vestirsi
●vi vestirsi. **dress up** vi mettersi elegante; (in disguise) travestirsi (as da)
dress: ~ circle n Theat prima galleria
f. **~er** n (furniture) credenza f; (Am:
dressing-table) toilette f inv
dressing /'dresɪŋ/ n Culin condimento
m; Med fasciatura f
dressing: ~-gown n vestaglia f.
~-room n (in gym) spogliatoio m; Theat
camerino m. **~-table** n toilette f inv
dress: ~maker n sarta f. **~ rehearsal**
n prova f generale
dressy /'dresɪ/ a (-ier, -iest) elegante
drew /druː/ see **draw**
dribble /'drɪbl/ vi gocciolare; (baby:)
sbavare; Sport dribblare
dribs and drabs /drɪbzən'dræbz/ npl
in ~ alla spicciolata
dried /draɪd/ a (food) essiccato
drier /'draɪə(r)/ n asciugabiancheria m
inv
drift /drɪft/ n movimento m lento; (of
snow) cumulo m; (meaning) senso m
●vi (off course) andare alla deriva;
(snow:) accumularsi; (fig: person:) pro-

cedere senza meta. **drift apart** *vi* ⟨*people:*⟩ allontanarsi l'uno dall'altro

drill /drɪl/ *n* trapano *m*; *Mil* esercitazione *f* ● *vt* trapanare; *Mil* fare esercitare ● *vi Mil* esercitarsi; ~ **for oil** trivellare in cerca di petrolio

drily /'draɪlɪ/ *adv* seccamente

drink /drɪŋk/ *n* bevanda *f*; ⟨*alcoholic*⟩ bicchierino *m*; **have a** ~ bere qualcosa; **a** ~ **of water** un po' d'acqua ● *vt/i* (*pt* **drank**, *pp* **drunk**) bere. **drink up** *vt* finire ● *vi* finire il bicchiere

drink|able /'drɪŋkəbl/ *a* potabile. ~**er** *n* bevitore, -trice *mf*

'drinking-water *n* acqua *f* potabile

drip /drɪp/ *n* gocciolamento *m*; ⟨*drop*⟩ goccia *f*; *Med* flebo *f* *inv*; ⟨*fam: person*⟩ mollaccione, -a *mf* ● *vi* (*pt/pp* **dripped**) gocciolare. ~-**dry** *a* che non si stira. ~**ping** *n* (*from meat*) grasso *m* d'arrosto ● *a* ~**ping** [**wet**] fradicio

drive /draɪv/ *n* (*in car*) giro *m*; ⟨*entrance*⟩ viale *m*; ⟨*energy*⟩ grinta *f*; *Psych* pulsione *f*; ⟨*organized effort*⟩ operazione *f*; *Techn* motore *m*; *Comput* lettore *m* ● *v* (*pt* **drove**, *pp* **driven**) ● *vt* portare ⟨*person by car*⟩; guidare ⟨*car*⟩; ⟨*Sport: hit*⟩ mandare; *Techn* far funzionare; ~ **sb mad** far diventare matto qcno ● *vi* guidare. **drive at** *vt* **what are you driving at?** dove vuoi arrivare? **drive away** *vt* portare via in macchina; ⟨*chase*⟩ cacciare ● *vi* andare via in macchina. **drive in** *vt* piantare ⟨*nail*⟩ ● *vi* arrivare [in macchina]. **drive off** *vt* portare via in macchina; ⟨*chase*⟩ cacciare ● *vi* andare via in macchina. **drive on** *vi* proseguire (*in macchina*). **drive up** *vi* arrivare (*in macchina*)

drivel /'drɪvl/ *n fam* sciocchezze *fpl*

driven /'drɪvn/ *see* **drive**

driver /'draɪvə(r)/ *n* guidatore, -trice *mf*; ⟨*of train*⟩ conducente *mf*

driving /'draɪvɪŋ/ *a* ⟨*rain*⟩ violento; ⟨*force*⟩ motore ● *n* guida *f*

driving: ~ **lesson** *n* lezione *f* di guida. ~ **licence** *n* patente *f* di guida. ~ **school** *n* scuola *f* guida. ~ **test** *n* esame *m* di guida

drizzle /'drɪzl/ *n* pioggerella *f* ● *vi* piovigginare

drone /drəʊn/ *n* ⟨*bee*⟩ fuco *m*; ⟨*sound*⟩ ronzio *m*

droop /druːp/ *vi* abbassarsi; ⟨*flowers:*⟩ afflosciarsi

drop /drɒp/ *n* ⟨*of liquid*⟩ goccia *f*; ⟨*fall*⟩ caduta *f*; (*in price, temperature*) calo *m* ● *v* (*pt/pp* **dropped**) ● *vt* far cadere;

sganciare ⟨*bomb*⟩; ⟨*omit*⟩ omettere; ⟨*give up*⟩ abbandonare ● *vi* cadere; ⟨*price, temperature, wind:*⟩ calare; ⟨*ground:*⟩ essere in pendenza. **drop in** *vi* passare. **drop off** *vt* depositare ⟨*person*⟩ ● *vi* cadere; ⟨*fall asleep*⟩ assopirsi. **drop out** *vi* cadere; ⟨*of race, society*⟩ ritirarsi; ~ **out of school** lasciare la scuola

'drop-out *n* persona *f* contro il sistema sociale

droppings /'drɒpɪŋz/ *npl* sterco *m*

drought /draʊt/ *n* siccità *f*

drove /drəʊv/ *see* **drive**

droves /drəʊvz/ *npl* **in** ~ in massa

drown /draʊn/ *vi* annegare ● *vt* annegare; coprire ⟨*noise*⟩; **he was** ~**ed** è annegato

drowsy /'draʊzɪ/ *a* sonnolento

drudgery /'drʌdʒərɪ/ *n* lavoro *m* pesante e noioso

drug /drʌg/ *n* droga *f*; *Med* farmaco *m*; **take** ~**s** drogarsi ● *vt* (*pt/pp* **drugged**) drogare

drug: ~ **addict** *n* tossicomane, -a *mf*. ~ **dealer** *n* spacciatore, -trice *mf* [di droga]. ~**gist** *n Am* farmacista *mf*. ~**store** *n Am* negozio *m* di generi vari, inclusi medicinali, che funge anche da bar; ⟨*dispensing*⟩ farmacia *f*

drum /drʌm/ *n* tamburo *m*; ⟨*for oil*⟩ bidone *m*; ~**s** (*pl: in pop-group*) batteria *f* ● *v* (*pt/pp* **drummed**) ● *vi* suonare il tamburo; (*in pop-group*) suonare la batteria ● *vt* ~ **sth into sb** *fam* ripetere qcsa a qcno cento volte. ~**mer** *n* percussionista *mf*; (*in pop-group*) batterista *mf*. ~**stick** *n* bacchetta *f*; ⟨*of chicken, turkey*⟩ coscia *f*

drunk /drʌŋk/ *see* **drink** ● *a* ubriaco; **get** ~ ubriacarsi ● *n* ubriaco, -a *mf*

drunk|ard /'drʌŋkəd/ *n* ubriacone, -a *mf*. ~**en** *a* ubriaco; ~**en driving** guida *f* in stato di ebbrezza

dry /draɪ/ *a* (**drier, driest**) asciutto; ⟨*climate, country*⟩ secco ● *vt/i* (*pt/pp* **dried**) asciugare; ~ **one's eyes** asciugarsi le lacrime. **dry up** *vi* seccarsi; ⟨*fig: source:*⟩ prosciugarsi; (*fam: be quiet*) stare zitto; (*do dishes*) asciugare i piatti

dry: ~-**'clean** *vt* pulire a secco. ~-**'cleaner's** *n* ⟨*shop*⟩ tintoria *f*. ~**ness** *n* secchezza *f*

DTP *n abbr* (**desktop publishing**) desktop publishing *m*

dual /'djuːəl/ *a* doppio

dual: ~ **'carriageway** *n* strada *f* a due carreggiate. ~-**'purpose** *a* a doppio uso

dub | **dyslexia**

dub /dʌb/ vt (pt/pp **dubbed**) doppiare ⟨film⟩; ⟨name⟩ soprannominare

dubious /ˈdjuːbɪəs/ a dubbio; **be ~ about** avere dei dubbi riguardo

duchess /ˈdʌtʃɪs/ n duchessa f

duck /dʌk/ n anatra f ● vt (in water) immergere; **~ one's head** abbassare la testa ● vi abbassarsi. **~ling** n anatroccolo m

duct /dʌkt/ n condotto m; Anat dotto m

dud /dʌd/ fam a Mil disattivato; ⟨coin⟩ falso; ⟨cheque⟩ a vuoto ● n (banknote) banconota f falsa

due /djuː/ a dovuto; **be ~** ⟨train:⟩ essere previsto; **the baby is ~ next week** il bambino dovrebbe nascere la settimana prossima; **~ to** (owing to) a causa di; **be ~ to** (causally) essere dovuto a; **I'm ~ to...** dovrei...; **in ~ course** a tempo debito ● adv **~ north** direttamente a nord

duel /ˈdjuːəl/ n duello m

dues /djuːz/ npl quota f [di iscrizione]

duet /djuːˈet/ n duetto m

dug /dʌɡ/ see **dig**

duke /djuːk/ n duca m

dull /dʌl/ a (overcast, not bright) cupo; (not shiny) opaco; ⟨sound⟩ soffocato; (boring) monotono; (stupid) ottuso ● vt intorpidire ⟨mind⟩; attenuare ⟨pain⟩

duly /ˈdjuːlɪ/ adv debitamente

dumb /dʌm/ a muto; (fam: stupid) ottuso. **~founded** /dʌmˈfaʊndɪd/ a sbigottito

dummy /ˈdʌmɪ/ n (tailor's) manichino m; (for baby) succhiotto m; (model) riproduzione f

dump /dʌmp/ n (for refuse) scarico m; (fam: town) mortorio m; **be down in the ~s** fam essere depresso ● vt scaricare; (fam: put down) lasciare; (fam: get rid of) liberarsi di

dumpling /ˈdʌmplɪŋ/ n gnocco m

dunce /dʌns/ n zuccone, -a mf

dune /djuːn/ n duna f

dung /dʌŋ/ n sterco m

dungarees /dʌŋɡəˈriːz/ npl tuta fsg

dungeon /ˈdʌndʒən/ n prigione f sotterranea

duo /ˈdjuːəʊ/ n duo m inv; Mus duetto m

duplicate¹ /ˈdjuːplɪkət/ a doppio ● n duplicato m; ⟨document⟩ copia f; **in ~** in duplicato

duplicat|e² /ˈdjuːplɪkeɪt/ vt fare un duplicato di; ⟨research:⟩ essere una ripetizione di ⟨work⟩

durable /ˈdjʊərəbl/ a resistente; durevole ⟨basis, institution⟩

duration /djʊəˈreɪʃn/ n durata f

duress /djʊəˈres/ n costrizione f; **under ~** sotto minaccia

during /ˈdjʊərɪŋ/ prep durante

dusk /dʌsk/ n crepuscolo m

dust /dʌst/ n polvere f ● vt spolverare; (sprinkle) cospargere ⟨cake⟩ (with di) ● vi spolverare

dust: ~bin n pattumiera f. **~-cart** n camion m della nettezza urbana. **~er** n strofinaccio m. **~-jacket** n sopraccoperta f. **~man** n spazzino m. **~pan** n paletta f per la spazzatura

dusty /ˈdʌstɪ/ a (-ier, -iest) polveroso

Dutch /dʌtʃ/ a olandese; **go ~** fam fare alla romana ● n (language) olandese m; **the ~** pl gli olandesi. **~man** n olandese m

dutiable /ˈdjuːtɪəbl/ a soggetto a imposta

dutiful /ˈdjuːtɪfl/ a rispettoso

duty /ˈdjuːtɪ/ n dovere m; (task) compito m; (tax) dogana f; **be on ~** essere di servizio. **~-free** a esente da dogana

duvet /ˈduːveɪ/ n piumone m

dwarf /dwɔːf/ n (pl **-s** or **dwarves**) nano, -a mf ● vt rimpicciolire

dwell /dwel/ vi (pt/pp **dwelt**) liter dimorare. **dwell on** vt fig soffermarsi su. **~ing** n abitazione f

dwindle /ˈdwɪndl/ vi diminuire

dye /daɪ/ n tintura f ● vt (pres p **dyeing**) tingere

dying /ˈdaɪɪŋ/ see **die²**

dynamic /daɪˈnæmɪk/ a dinamico

dynamite /ˈdaɪnəmaɪt/ n dinamite f

dynamo /ˈdaɪnəməʊ/ n dinamo f inv

dynasty /ˈdɪnəstɪ/ n dinastia f

dysentery /ˈdɪsəntrɪ/ n dissenteria f

dyslex|ia /dɪsˈleksɪə/ n dislessia f. **~ic** a dislessico

Ee

each /iːtʃ/ *a* ogni ● *pron* ognuno; **£1 ~** una sterlina ciascuno; **they love/hate ~ other** si amano/odiano; **we lend ~ other money** ci prestiamo i soldi

eager /ˈiːɡə(r)/ *a* ansioso (**to do di** fare); avido di sapere. **~ly** *adv* (*wait*) ansiosamente; (*offer*) premurosamente. **~ness** *n* premura *f*

eagle /ˈiːɡl/ *n* aquila *f*

ear¹ /ɪə(r)/ *n* (*of corn*) spiga *f*

ear² *n* orecchio *m*. **~ache** *n* mal *m* d'orecchi. **~-drum** *n* timpano *m*

earl /ɜːl/ *n* conte *m*

early /ˈɜːlɪ/ *a* (**-ier, -iest**) (*before expected time*) in anticipo; (*spring*) prematuro; (*reply*) pronto; (*works, writings*) primo; **be here ~!** sii puntuale!; **you're ~!** sei in anticipo!; **~ morning walk** passeggiata *f* mattutina; **in the ~ morning** la mattina presto; **in the ~ spring** all'inizio della primavera; **~ retirement** prepensionamento *m* ● *adv* presto; (*ahead of time*) in anticipo; **~ in the morning** la mattina presto

earmark *vt* riservare (**for** a)

earn /ɜːn/ *vt* guadagnare; (*deserve*) meritare

earnest /ˈɜːnɪst/ *a* serio ● *n* **in ~** sul serio. **~ly** *adv* con aria seria

earnings /ˈɜːnɪŋz/ *npl* guadagni *mpl*; (*salary*) stipendio *m*

ear: ~phones *npl* cuffia *fsg*. **~-ring** *n* orecchino *m*. **~shot** *within* **~shot** a portata d'orecchio; **he is out of ~shot** non può sentire

earth /ɜːθ/ *n* terra *f* **where on ~?** dove/che diavolo? ● *vt Electr* mettere a terra

earthenware /ˈɜːθən-/ *n* terraglia *f*

earthly /ˈɜːθlɪ/ *a* terrestre; **be no ~ use** *fam* essere perfettamente inutile

earthquake *n* terremoto *m*

earthy /ˈɜːθɪ/ *a* terroso; (*coarse*) grossolano

earwig /ˈɪəwɪɡ/ *n* forbicina *f*

ease /iːz/ *n* **at ~** a proprio agio; **at ~!** *Mil* riposo!; **ill at ~** a disagio; **with ~** con facilità ● *vt* calmare (*pain*); alleviare (*tension, shortage*); (*slow down*) rallentare; (*loosen*) allentare ● *vi* (*pain, situation, wind:*) calmarsi

easel /ˈiːzl/ *n* cavalletto *m*

easily /ˈiːzɪlɪ/ *adv* con facilità; **~ the best** certamente il meglio

east /iːst/ *n* est *m*; **to the ~ of** a est di ● *a* dell'est ● *adv* verso est

Easter /ˈiːstə(r)/ *n* Pasqua *f*. **~ egg** *n* uovo *m* di Pasqua

east|erly /ˈiːstəlɪ/ *a* da levante. **~ern** *a* orientale. **~ward(s)** /-wəd(z)/ *adv* verso est

easy /ˈiːzɪ/ *a* (**-ier, -iest**) facile; **take it or things ~** prendersela con calma; **take it ~!** (*don't get excited*) calma!; **go ~ with** andarci piano con

easy: ~ chair *n* poltrona *f*. **~ going** *a* conciliante; **too ~going** troppo accomodante

eat /iːt/ *vt/i* (*pt* **ate**, *pp* **eaten**) mangiare. **eat into** *vt* intaccare. **eat up** *vt* mangiare tutto (*food*); *fig* inghiottire (*profits*)

eat|able /ˈiːtəbl/ *a* mangiabile. **~er** *n* (*apple*) mela *f* da tavola; **be a big ~er** (*person:*) essere una buona forchetta

eau-de-Cologne /əʊdəkəˈləʊn/ *n* acqua *f* di Colonia

eaves /iːvz/ *npl* cornicione *msg*. **~drop** *vi* (*pt/pp* **~dropped**) origliare; **~drop on** ascoltare di nascosto

ebb /eb/ *n* (*tide*) riflusso *m*; **at a low ~** *fig* a terra ● *vi* rifluire; *fig* declinare

ebony /ˈebənɪ/ *n* ebano *m*

EC *n abbr* (**European Community**) CE *f*

eccentric /ɪkˈsentrɪk/ *a & n* eccentrico, -a *mf*

ecclesiastical /ɪkliːzɪˈæstɪk/ *a* ecclesiastico

echo /ˈekəʊ/ *n* (*pl* **-es**) eco *f or m* ● *v* (*pt/pp* **echoed**, *pres p* **echoing**) ● *vt* echeggiare; ripetere (*words*) ● *vi* risuonare (**with** di)

eclipse /ɪˈklɪps/ *n Astr* eclissi *f inv* ● *vt* *fig* eclissare

ecolog|ical /iːkəˈlɒdʒɪkl/ *a* ecologico. **~y** /ɪˈkɒlədʒɪ/ *n* ecologia *f*

economic /iːkəˈnɒmɪk/ *a* economico.

312

~al a economico. ~ally adv economicamente; (thriftily) in economia. ~s n economia f

economist /ɪˈkɒnəmɪst/ n economista mf

economize /ɪˈkɒnəmaɪz/ vi economizzare (on su)

economy /ɪˈkɒnəmɪ/ n economia f

ecstasy /ˈekstəsɪ/ n estasi f inv; (drug) ecstasy f

ecstatic /ɪkˈstætɪk/ a estatico

ecu /ˈeɪkjuː/ n ecu m inv

eczema /ˈeksɪmə/ n eczema m

edge /edʒ/ n bordo m; (of knife) filo m; (of road) ciglio m; **on** ~ con i nervi tesi; **have the** ~ **on** fam avere un vantaggio su ● vt bordare. **edge forward** vi avanzare lentamente

edgeways /ˈedʒweɪz/ adv di fianco; **I couldn't get a word in** ~ non ho potuto infilare neanche mezza parola nel discorso

edging /ˈedʒɪŋ/ n bordo m

edgy /ˈedʒɪ/ a nervoso

edible /ˈedɪbl/ a commestibile; **this pizza's not** ~ questa pizza è immangiabile

edict /ˈiːdɪkt/ n editto m

edify /ˈedɪfaɪ/ vt (pt/pp -ied) edificare. ~ing a edificante

edit /ˈedɪt/ vt (pt/pp edited) far la revisione di (text); curare l'edizione di (anthology, dictionary); dirigere (newspaper); montare (film); editare (tape); ~ed by (book) a cura di

edition /ɪˈdɪʃn/ n edizione f

editor /ˈedɪtə(r)/ n (of anthology, dictionary) curatore, -trice mf; (of newspaper) redattore, -trice mf; (of film) responsabile mf del montaggio

editorial /edɪˈtɔːrɪəl/ a redazionale ● n Journ editoriale m

educate /ˈedjʊkeɪt/ vt istruire; educare (public, mind); **be** ~**d at Eton** essere educato a Eton. ~**d** a istruito

education /edjʊˈkeɪʃn/ n istruzione f; (culture) cultura f, educazione f. ~**al** a istruttivo; (visit) educativo; (publishing) didattico

eel /iːl/ n anguilla f

eerie /ˈɪərɪ/ a (-ier, -iest) inquietante

effect /ɪˈfekt/ n effetto m; **in** ~ in effetti; **take** ~ (law:) entrare in vigore; (medicine:) fare effetto ● vt effettuare

effective /ɪˈfektɪv/ a efficace; (striking) che colpisce; (actual) di fatto; ~ **from** in vigore a partire da. ~**ly** adv

efficacemente; (actually) di fatto. ~**ness** n efficacia f

effeminate /ɪˈfemɪnət/ a effeminato

effervescent /efəˈvesnt/ a effervescente

efficiency /ɪˈfɪʃənsɪ/ n efficienza f; (of machine) rendimento m

efficient /ɪˈfɪʃənt/ a efficiente. ~**ly** adv efficientemente

effort /ˈefət/ n sforzo m; **make an** ~ sforzarsi. ~**less** a facile. ~**lessly** adv con facilità

effrontery /ɪˈfrʌntərɪ/ n sfrontatezza f

effusive /ɪˈfjuːsɪv/ a espansivo; (speech) caloroso

e.g. abbr (exempli gratia) per es.

egalitarian /ɪɡælɪˈteərɪən/ a egalitario

egg[1] /eg/ vt ~ **on** fam incitare

egg[2] n uovo m. ~**-cup** n portauovo m inv. ~**shell** n guscio m d'uovo. ~**-timer** n clessidra f per misurare il tempo di cottura delle uova

ego /ˈiːɡəʊ/ n ego m. ~**centric** /-ˈsentrɪk/ a egocentrico. ~**ism** n egoismo m. ~**ist** n egoista mf. ~**tism** n egotismo m. ~**tist** n egotista mf

Egypt /ˈiːdʒɪpt/ n Egitto m. ~**ian** /ɪˈdʒɪpʃn/ a & n egiziano, -a mf

eiderdown /ˈaɪdə-/ n (quilt) piumino m

eight /eɪt/ a otto ● n otto m. ~**teen** a & n diciotto m. ~**teenth** a & n diciottesimo, -a mf

eighth /eɪtθ/ a ottavo ● n ottavo m

eightieth /ˈeɪtɪɪθ/ a & n ottantesimo, -a mf

eighty /ˈeɪtɪ/ a & n ottanta m

either /ˈaɪðə(r)/ a & pron ~ [**of them**] l'uno o l'altro; **I don't like** ~ [**of them**] non mi piace né l'uno né l'altro; **on** ~ **side** da tutte e due le parti ● adv **I don't like John** ~ nemmeno io; **I don't like John or his brother** ~ non mi piace John e nemmeno suo fratello ● conj ~ **John or his brother will be there** ci saranno o John o suo fratello; **I don't like** ~ **John or his brother** non mi piacciono né John né suo fratello; ~ **you go to bed or** [**else**]... o vai a letto o [altrimenti]..

eject /ɪˈdʒekt/ vt eiettare (pilot); espellere (tape, drunk)

eke /iːk/ vt ~ **out** far bastare; (increase) arrotondare; ~ **out a living** arrangiarsi

elaborate[1] /ɪˈlæbərət/ a elaborato

elaborate[2] /ɪˈlæbəreɪt/ vi entrare nei particolari (on di)

elapse /ɪˈlæps/ vi trascorrere

elastic /ɪˈlæstɪk/ a elastico ● n elastico m. ~ '**band** n elastico m

elasticity /ɪlæs'tɪsətɪ/ n elasticità f

elated /ɪ'leɪtɪd/ a esultante

elbow /'elbəʊ/ n gomito m

elder[1] /'eldə(r)/ n (tree) sambuco m

elder[2] a maggiore • n the ~ il/la maggiore. **~erly** a anziano. **~est** a maggiore • n the ~est il/la maggiore

elect /ɪ'lekt/ a the president ~ il futuro presidente • vt eleggere; **~ to do sth** decidere di fare qcsa. **~ion** /-ekʃn/ n elezione f

elector /ɪ'lektə(r)/ n elettore, -trice mf. **~al** a elettorale; **~al roll** liste fpl elettorali. **~ate** /-rət/ n elettorato m

electric /ɪ'lektrɪk/ a elettrico

electrical /ɪ'lektrɪkl/ a elettrico; **~ engineering** elettrotecnica f

electric: ~ **blanket** n termocoperta f. ~ **fire** n stufa f elettrica

electrician /ɪlek'trɪʃn/ n elettricista m

electricity /ɪlek'trɪsətɪ/ n elettricità f

electrify /ɪ'lektrɪfaɪ/ vt (pt/pp -ied) elettrificare; fig elettrizzare. **~ing** a fig elettrizzante

electrocute /ɪ'lektrəkjuːt/ vt fulminare; (execute) giustiziare sulla sedia elettrica

electrode /ɪ'lektrəʊd/ n elettrodo m

electron /ɪ'lektrɒn/ n elettrone m

electronic /ɪlek'trɒnɪk/ a elettronico. ~ **mail** n posta f elettronica. **~s** n elettronica f

elegance /'elɪɡəns/ n eleganza f

elegant /'elɪɡənt/ a elegante

elegy /'elɪdʒɪ/ n elegia f

element /'elɪmənt/ n elemento m. **~ary** /-'mentərɪ/ a elementare

elephant /'elɪfənt/ n elefante m

elevat|e /'elɪveɪt/ vt elevare. **~ion** /-'veɪʃn/ n elevazione f; (height) altitudine f; (angle) alzo m

elevator /'elɪveɪtə(r)/ n Am ascensore m

eleven /ɪ'levn/ a undici • n undici m. **~th** a & n undicesimo, -a mf; **at the ~th hour** fam all'ultimo momento

elf /elf/ n (pl **elves**) elfo m

elicit /ɪ'lɪsɪt/ vt ottenere

eligible /'elɪdʒəbl/ a eleggibile; ~ **young man** buon partito; **be ~ for** aver diritto a

eliminate /ɪ'lɪmɪneɪt/ vt eliminare

élite /eɪ'liːt/ n fior fiore m

ellip|se /ɪ'lɪps/ n ellisse f. **~tical** a ellittico

elm /elm/ n olmo m

elocution /elə'kjuːʃn/ n elocuzione f

elope /ɪ'ləʊp/ vi fuggire [per sposarsi]

eloquen|ce /'eləkwəns/ n eloquenza f. **~t** a eloquente. **~tly** adv con eloquenza

else /els/ adv altro; **who ~?** e chi altro?; **he did of course, who ~?** l'ha fatto lui e chi, se no?; **nothing ~** nient'altro; **or ~** altrimenti; **someone ~** qualcun altro; **somewhere ~** da qualche altra parte; **anyone ~** chiunque altro; (as question) nessun'altro?; **anything ~** qualunque altra cosa; (as question) altro?. **~where** adv altrove

elucidate /ɪ'luːsɪdeɪt/ vt delucidare

elude /ɪ'luːd/ vt eludere; (avoid) evitare; **the name ~s me** il nome mi sfugge

elusive /ɪ'luːsɪv/ a elusivo

emaciated /ɪ'meɪsɪeɪtɪd/ a emaciato

e-mail /'iːmeɪl/ n posta f elettronica • vt spedire via posta elettronica

emanate /'eməneɪt/ vi emanare

emancipat|ed /ɪ'mænsɪpeɪtɪd/ a emancipato. **~ion** /-'peɪʃn/ n emancipazione f; (of slaves) liberazione f

embankment /ɪm'bæŋkmənt/ n argine m; Rail massicciata f

embargo /em'bɑːɡəʊ/ n (pl -es) embargo m

embark /ɪm'bɑːk/ vi imbarcarsi; ~ **on** intraprendere. **~ation** /embɑː'keɪʃn/ n imbarco m

embarrass /ɪm'bærəs/ vt imbarazzare. **~ed** a imbarazzato. **~ing** a imbarazzante. **~ment** n imbarazzo m

embassy /'embəsɪ/ n ambasciata f

embedded /ɪm'bedɪd/ a (in concrete) cementato; (traditions, feelings) radicato

embellish /ɪm'belɪʃ/ vt abbellire

embers /'embəz/ npl braci fpl

embezzle /ɪm'bezl/ vt appropriarsi indebitamente di. **~ment** n appropriazione f indebita

embitter /ɪm'bɪtə(r)/ vt amareggiare

emblem /'embləm/ n emblema m

embody /ɪm'bɒdɪ/ vt (pt/pp -ied) incorporare; ~ **what is best in...** rappresentare quanto c'è di meglio di...

emboss /ɪm'bɒs/ vt sbalzare (metal); stampare in rilievo (paper). **~ed** a in rilievo

embrace /ɪm'breɪs/ n abbraccio m • vt abbracciare • vi abbracciarsi

embroider /ɪm'brɔɪdə(r)/ vt ricamare (design); fig abbellire. **~y** n ricamo m

embryo /'embrɪəʊ/ n embrione m

emerald /'emərəld/ n smeraldo m

emer|ge /ɪ'mɜːdʒ/ vi emergere; (come into being: nation) nascere; (sun,

flowers⟩ spuntare fuori. **~gence** /-əns/
n emergere *m*; ⟨*of new country*⟩ nascita *f*

emergency /ɪˈmɜːdʒənsɪ/ *n* emergenza *f*; **in an ~** in caso di emergenza. **~ exit** *n* uscita *f* di sicurezza

emery /ˈemərɪ/: **~ board** *n* limetta *f* [per le unghie]

emigrant /ˈemɪɡrənt/ *n* emigrante *mf*

emigrat|e /ˈemɪɡreɪt/ *vi* emigrare. **~ion** /-ˈgreɪʃn/ *n* emigrazione *f*

eminent /ˈemɪnənt/ *a* eminente. **~ly** *adv* eminentemente

emission /ɪˈmɪʃn/ *n* emissione *f*; ⟨*of fumes*⟩ esalazione *f*

emit /ɪˈmɪt/ *vt* ⟨*pt/pp* emitted⟩ emettere; esalare ⟨*fumes*⟩

emotion /ɪˈməʊʃn/ *n* emozione *f*. **~al** *a* denso di emozione; ⟨*person, reaction*⟩ emotivo; **become ~al** avere una reazione emotiva

emotive /ɪˈməʊtɪv/ *a* emotivo

empathize /ˈempəθaɪz/ *vi* **~ with sb** immedesimarsi nei problemi di qcno

emperor /ˈempərə(r)/ *n* imperatore *m*

emphasis /ˈemfəsɪs/ *n* enfasi *f*; **put the ~ on sth** accentuare qcsa

emphasize /ˈemfəsaɪz/ *vt* accentuare ⟨*word, syllable*⟩; sottolineare ⟨*need*⟩

emphatic /ɪmˈfætɪk/ *a* categorico

empire /ˈempaɪə(r)/ *n* impero *m*

empirical /ɪmˈpɪrɪkl/ *a* empirico

employ /emˈplɔɪ/ *vt* impiegare; *fig* usare ⟨*tact*⟩. **~ee** /emplɔˈiː/ *n* impiegato, -a *mf*. **~er** *n* datore *m* di lavoro. **~ment** *n* occupazione *f*; ⟨*work*⟩ lavoro *m*. **~ment agency** *n* ufficio *m* di collocamento

empower /ɪmˈpaʊə(r)/ *vt* autorizzare; ⟨*enable*⟩ mettere in grado

empress /ˈempris/ *n* imperatrice *f*

empties /ˈemptɪz/ *npl* vuoti *mpl*

emptiness /ˈemptɪnɪs/ *n* vuoto *m*

empty /ˈemptɪ/ *a* vuoto; ⟨*promise, threat*⟩ vano ●*v* ⟨*pt/pp* -ied⟩ ●*vt* vuotare ⟨*container*⟩ ●*vi* vuotarsi

emulate /ˈemjʊleɪt/ *vt* emulare

emulsion /ɪˈmʌlʃn/ *n* emulsione *f*

enable /ɪˈneɪbl/ *vt* **~ sb to** mettere qcno in grado di

enact /ɪˈnækt/ *vt Theat* rappresentare; decretare ⟨*law*⟩

enamel /ɪˈnæml/ *n* smalto *m* ●*vt* ⟨*pt/pp* enamelled⟩ smaltare

enchant /ɪnˈtʃɑːnt/ *vt* incantare. **~ing** *a* incantevole. **~ment** *n* incanto *m*

encircle /ɪnˈsɜːkl/ *vt* circondare

enclave /ˈenkleɪv/ *n* enclave *f inv*; *fig* territorio *m*

enclos|e /ɪnˈkləʊz/ *vt* circondare ⟨*land*⟩; ⟨*in letter*⟩ allegare ⟨*with a*⟩. **~ed** *a* ⟨*space*⟩ chiuso; ⟨*in letter*⟩ allegato. **~ure** /-ʒə(r)/ *n* ⟨*at zoo*⟩ recinto *m*; ⟨*in letter*⟩ allegato *m*

encompass /ɪnˈkʌmpəs/ *vt* ⟨*include*⟩ comprendere

encore /ˈɒŋkɔː(r)/ *n & int* bis *m inv*

encounter /ɪnˈkaʊntə(r)/ *n* incontro *m*; ⟨*battle*⟩ scontro *m* ●*vt* incontrare

encourag|e /ɪnˈkʌrɪdʒ/ *vt* incoraggiare; promuovere ⟨*the arts, independence*⟩. **~ement** *n* incoraggiamento *m*; ⟨*of the arts*⟩ promozione *f*. **~ing** *a* incoraggiante; ⟨*smile*⟩ di incoraggiamento

encroach /ɪnˈkrəʊtʃ/ *vt* **~ on** invadere ⟨*land, privacy*⟩; abusare di ⟨*time*⟩; interferire con ⟨*rights*⟩

encumb|er /ɪnˈkʌmbə(r)/ *vt* **~ered with** essere carico di ⟨*children, suitcases*⟩; ingombro di ⟨*furniture*⟩. **~rance** /-rəns/ *n* peso *m*

encyclop[a]edia /ɪnsaɪkləˈpiːdɪə/ *n* enciclopedia *f*. **~ic** *a* enciclopedico

end /end/ *n* fine *f*; ⟨*of box, table, piece of string*⟩ estremità *f*; ⟨*of town, room*⟩ parte *f*; ⟨*purpose*⟩ fine *m*; **in the ~** alla fine; **at the ~ of May** alla fine di maggio; **at the ~ of the street/garden** in fondo alla strada/al giardino; **on ~** ⟨*upright*⟩ in piedi; **for days on ~** per giorni e giorni; **for six days on ~** per sei giorni di fila; **put an ~ to sth** mettere fine a qcsa; **make ~s meet** *fam* sbarcare il lunario; **no ~ of** *fam* un sacco di ●*vt/i* finire. **end up** *vi* finire; **~ up doing sth** finire col fare qcsa

endanger /ɪnˈdeɪndʒə(r)/ *vt* rischiare ⟨*one's life*⟩; mettere a repentaglio ⟨*sb else, success of sth*⟩

endear|ing /ɪnˈdɪərɪŋ/ *a* accattivante. **~ment** *n* term of **~ment** vezzeggiativo *m*

endeavour /ɪnˈdevə(r)/ *n* tentativo *m* ●*vi* sforzarsi ⟨**to** di⟩

ending /ˈendɪŋ/ *n* fine *f*; *Gram* desinenza *f*

endive /ˈendaɪv/ *n* indivia *f*

endless /ˈendlɪs/ *a* interminabile; ⟨*patience*⟩ infinito. **~ly** *adv* continuamente; ⟨*patient*⟩ infinitamente

endorse /enˈdɔːs/ *vt* girare ⟨*cheque*⟩; ⟨*sports personality:*⟩ fare pubblicità a ⟨*product*⟩; approvare ⟨*plan*⟩. **~ment** *n* ⟨*of cheque*⟩ girata *f*; ⟨*of plan*⟩ conferma *f*; ⟨*on driving licence*⟩ registrazione *f* su patente di un'infrazione

endow /ɪnˈdaʊ/ *vt* dotare

endur|able /ɪnˈdjʊərəbl/ *a* sopportabile. ~**ance** /-rəns/ *n* resistenza *f*; **it is beyond ~ance** è insopportabile

endur|e /ɪn'djʊə(r)/ *vt* sopportare ● *vi* durare. ~**ing** *a* duraturo

'**end user** *n* utente *m* finale

enemy /'enəmɪ/ *n* nemico, -a *mf* ● *attrib* nemico

energetic /enə'dʒetɪk/ *a* energico

energy /'enədʒɪ/ *n* energia *f*

enforce /ɪn'fɔːs/ *vt* far rispettare ⟨*law*⟩. ~**d** *a* forzato

engage /ɪn'geɪdʒ/ *vt* assumere ⟨*staff*⟩; *Theat* ingaggiare; *Auto* ingranare ⟨*gear*⟩ ● *vi Techn* ingranare; ~ **in** impegnarsi in. ~**d** *a* (*in use, busy*) occupato; ⟨*person*⟩ impegnato; (*to be married*) fidanzato; **get ~d** fidanzarsi (**to** con); ~**d tone** *Teleph* segnale *m* di occupato. ~**ment** *n* fidanzamento *m*; ⟨*appointment*⟩ appuntamento *m*; *Mil* combattimento *m*; ~**ment ring** anello *m* di fidanzamento

engaging /ɪn'geɪdʒɪŋ/ *a* attraente

engender /ɪn'dʒendə(r)/ *vt fig* generare

engine /'endʒɪn/ *n* motore *m*; *Rail* locomotrice *f*. ~-**driver** *n* macchinista *m*

engineer /endʒɪ'nɪə(r)/ *n* ingegnere *m*; ⟨*service, installation*⟩ tecnico *m*; *Naut, Am Rail* macchinista *m* ● *vt fig* architettare. ~**ing** *n* ingegneria *f*

England /'ɪŋglənd/ *n* Inghilterra *f*

English /'ɪŋglɪʃ/ *a* inglese; **the ~ Channel** la Manica ● *n* ⟨*language*⟩ inglese *m*; **the ~** *pl* gli inglesi. ~**man** *n* inglese *m*. ~**woman** *n* inglese *f*

engrav|e /ɪn'greɪv/ *vt* incidere. ~**ing** *n* incisione *f*

engross /ɪn'grəʊs/ *vt* ~**ed in** assorto in

engulf /ɪn'gʌlf/ *vt* ⟨*fire, waves*⟩ inghiottire

enhance /ɪn'hɑːns/ *vt* accrescere ⟨*beauty, reputation*⟩; migliorare ⟨*performance*⟩

enigma /ɪ'nɪgmə/ *n* enigma *m*. ~**tic** /enɪg'mætɪk/ *a* enigmatico

enjoy /ɪn'dʒɔɪ/ *vt* godere di ⟨*good health*⟩; ~ **oneself** divertirsi; **I ~ cooking/painting** mi piace cucinare/dipingere; ~ **your meal** buon appetito. ~**able** /-əbl/ *a* piacevole. ~**ment** *n* piacere *m*

enlarge /ɪn'lɑːdʒ/ *vt* ingrandire ● *vi* ~ **upon** dilungarsi su. ~**ment** *n* ingrandimento *m*

enlighten /ɪn'laɪtn/ *vt* illuminare.

~**ed** *a* progressista. ~**ment** *n* **The E~ment** l'Illuminismo *m*

enlist /ɪn'lɪst/ *vt Mil* reclutare; ~ **sb's help** farsi aiutare da qcno ● *vi Mil* arruolarsi

enliven /ɪn'laɪvn/ *vt* animare

enmity /'enmɪtɪ/ *n* inimicizia *f*

enormity /ɪ'nɔːmɪtɪ/ *n* enormità *f*

enormous /ɪ'nɔːməs/ *a* enorme. ~**ly** *adv* estremamente; ⟨*grateful*⟩ infinitamente

enough /ɪ'nʌf/ *a & n* abbastanza; **I didn't bring ~ clothes** non ho portato abbastanza vestiti; **have you had ~?** ⟨*to eat/drink*⟩ hai mangiato/bevuto abbastanza?; **I've had ~!** fam ne ho abbastanza!; **is that ~?** basta?; **that's ~!** basta così!; **£50 isn't ~** 50 sterline non sono sufficienti ● *adv* abbastanza; **you're not working fast ~** non lavori abbastanza in fretta; **funnily ~** stranamente

enquir|e /ɪn'kwaɪə(r)/ *vi* domandare; ~**e about** chiedere informazioni su. ~**y** *n* domanda *f*; ⟨*investigation*⟩ inchiesta *f*

enrage /ɪn'reɪdʒ/ *vt* fare arrabbiare

enrich /ɪn'rɪtʃ/ *vt* arricchire; ⟨*improve*⟩ migliorare ⟨*vocabulary*⟩

enrol /ɪn'rəʊl/ *vi* (*pt/pp* -**rolled**) (*for exam, in club*) iscriversi (**for, in** a). ~**ment** *n* iscrizione *f*

ensemble /ɒn'sɒmbl/ *n* ⟨*clothing & Mus*⟩ complesso *m*

enslave /ɪn'sleɪv/ *vt* render schiavo

ensu|e /ɪn'sjuː/ *vi* seguire; **the ~ing discussion** la discussione che ne è seguita

ensure /ɪn'ʃʊə(r)/ *vt* assicurare; ~ **that** ⟨*person*⟩ assicurarsi che; ⟨*measure*⟩ garantire che

entail /ɪn'teɪl/ *vt* comportare; **what does it ~?** in che cosa consiste?

entangle /ɪn'tæŋgl/ *vt* **get ~d in** rimanere impigliato in; *fig* rimanere coinvolto in

enter /'entə(r)/ *vt* entrare in; iscrivere ⟨*horse, runner in race*⟩; cominciare ⟨*university*⟩; partecipare a ⟨*competition*⟩; *Comput* immettere ⟨*data*⟩; ⟨*write down*⟩ scrivere ● *vi* entrare; *Theat* entrare in scena; (*register as competitor*) iscriversi; (*take part*) partecipare (**in** a)

enterpris|e /'entəpraɪz/ *n* impresa *f*; ⟨*quality*⟩ iniziativa *f*. ~**ing** *a* intraprendente

entertain /entə'teɪn/ *vt* intrattenere;

(invite) ricevere; nutrire *(ideas, hopes)*; prendere in considerazione *(possibility)* ● *vi* intrattenersi; *(have guests)* ricevere. ~er *n* artista *mf*. ~ing *a (person)* di gradevole compagnia; *(evening, film, play)* divertente. ~ment *n (amusement)* intrattenimento *m*

enthral /ɪn'θrɔːl/ *vt (pt/pp* **enthralled)** be ~led essere affascinato *(by da)*

enthusias|m /ɪn'θjuːzıæzm/ *n* entusiasmo *m*. ~t *n* entusiasta *mf*. ~tic /-'æstɪk/ *a* entusiastico

entice /ɪn'taɪs/ *vt* attirare. ~ment *n (incentive)* incentivo *m*

entire /ɪn'taɪə(r)/ *a* intero. ~ly *adv* del tutto; **I'm not ~ly satisfied** non sono completamente soddisfatto. ~ty /-rəti/ *n* in sts ~ty nell'insieme

entitled /ɪn'taɪtld/ *a (book)* intitolato; be ~ to sth aver diritto a qcsa

entitlement /ɪn'taɪtlmənt/ *n* diritto *m*

entity /'entəti/ *n* entità *f*

entrance[1] /'entrəns/ *n* entrata *f*; Theat entrata *f* in scena; *(right to enter)* ammissione *f*; 'no ~' 'ingresso vietato'. ~ examination *n* esame *m* di ammissione. ~ fee *n* how much is the ~ fee? quanto costa il biglietto di ingresso?

entrance[2] /ɪn'trɑːns/ *vt* estasiare

entrant /'entrənt/ *n* concorrente *mf*

entreat /ɪn'triːt/ *vt* supplicare

entrenched /ɪn'trentʃt/ *a (ideas, views)* radicato

entrust /ɪn'trʌst/ *vt* ~ sb with sth, ~ sth to sb affidare qcsa a qcno

entry /'entri/ *n* ingresso *m*; *(way in)* entrata *f*; *(in directory etc)* voce *f*; *(in appointment diary)* appuntamento *m*; no ~ ingresso vietato; *Auto* accesso vietato. ~ form *n* modulo *m* di ammissione. ~ visa *n* visto *m* di ingresso

enumerate /ɪ'njuːməreɪt/ *vt* enumerare

enunciate /ɪ'nʌnsɪeɪt/ *vt* enunciare

envelop /ɪn'veləp/ *vt (pt/pp* **enveloped)** avviluppare

envelope /'envələʊp/ *n* busta *f*

enviable /'envɪəbl/ *a* invidiabile

envious /'envɪəs/ *a* invidioso. ~ly *adv* con invidia

environment /ɪn'vaɪrənmənt/ *n* ambiente *m*

environmental /ɪnvaɪrən'mentl/ *a* ambientale. ~ist *n* ambientalista *mf*. ~ly *adv* ~ly friendly che rispetta l'ambiente

envisage /ɪn'vɪzɪdʒ/ *vt* prevedere

envoy /'envɔɪ/ *n* inviato, -a *mf*

envy /'envɪ/ *n* invidia *f* ● *vt (pt/pp* -ied) ~ sb sth invidiare qcno per qcsa

enzyme /'enzaɪm/ *n* enzima *m*

epic /'epɪk/ *a* epico ● *n* epopea *f*

epidemic /epɪ'demɪk/ *n* epidemia *f*

epilep|sy /'epɪlepsɪ/ *n* epilessia *f*. ~tic /-'leptɪk/ *a & n* epilettico, -a *mf*

epilogue /'epɪlɒg/ *n* epilogo *m*

episode /'epɪsəʊd/ *n* episodio *m*

epitaph /'epɪtɑːf/ *n* epitaffio *m*

epithet /'epɪθet/ *n* epiteto *m*

epitom|e /ɪ'pɪtəmɪ/ *n* epitome *f*. ~ize *vt* essere il classico esempio di

epoch /'iːpɒk/ *n* epoca *f*

equal /'iːkwl/ *a (parts, amounts)* uguale; **of ~ height** della stessa altezza; be ~ to the task essere a l'altezza del compito ● *n* pari *m inv* ● *vt (pt/pp* **equalled)** *(be same in quantity as)* essere pari a; *(rival)* uguagliare; **5 plus 5 ~s 10** 5 più 5 [è] uguale a 10. ~ity /ɪ'kwɒlətɪ/ *n* uguaglianza *f*

equalize /'iːkwəlaɪz/ *vi* Sport pareggiare. ~r *n* Sport pareggio *m*

equally /'iːkwəlɪ/ *adv (divide)* in parti uguali; ~ intelligent della stessa intelligenza; ~,... allo stesso tempo...

equanimity /ekwə'nɪmətɪ/ *n* equanimità *f*

equat|e /ɪ'kweɪt/ *vt* ~e sth with sth equiparare qcsa a qcsa. ~ion /-eɪʒn/ *n* Math equazione *f*

equator /ɪ'kweɪtə(r)/ *n* equatore *m*

equestrian /ɪ'kwestrɪən/ *a* equestre

equilibrium /iːkwɪ'lɪbrɪəm/ *n* equilibrio *m*

equinox /'iːkwɪnɒks/ *n* equinozio *m*

equip /ɪ'kwɪp/ *vt (pt/pp* **equipped)** equipaggiare; attrezzare *(kitchen, office)*. ~ment *n* attrezzatura *f*

equitable /'ekwɪtəbl/ *a* giusto

equity /'ekwɪtɪ/ *n (justness)* equità *f*; Comm azioni *fpl*

equivalent /ɪ'kwɪvələnt/ *a* equivalente; be ~ to equivalere a ● *n* equivalente *m*

equivocal /ɪ'kwɪvəkl/ *a* equivoco

era /'ɪərə/ *n* età *f*; *(geological)* era *f*

eradicate /ɪ'rædɪkeɪt/ *vt* eradicare

erase /ɪ'reɪz/ *vt* cancellare. ~r *n* gomma *f* [da cancellare]; *(for blackboard)* cancellino *m*

erect /ɪ'rekt/ *a* eretto ● *vt* erigere. ~ion /-ekʃn/ *n* erezione *f*

ero|de /ɪ'rəʊd/ *vt (water:)* erodere; *(acid:)* corrodere. ~sion /-əʊʒn/ *n* erosione *f*; *(by acid)* corrosione *f*

erotic /ɪ'rɒtɪk/ *a* erotico. ~ism /-tɪsɪzm/ *n* erotismo *m*

err /ɜ:(r)/ *vi* errare; *(sin)* peccare

errand /'erənd/ *n* commissione *f*

erratic /ɪ'rætɪk/ *a* irregolare; *(person, moods)* imprevedibile; *(exchange rate)* incostante

erroneous /ɪ'rəʊnɪəs/ *a* erroneo

error /'erə(r)/ *n* errore *m*; **in ~** per errore

erudit|e /'erʊdaɪt/ *a* erudito. **~ion** /-'dɪʃn/ *n* erudizione *f*

erupt /ɪ'rʌpt/ *vi* eruttare; *(spots:)* spuntare; *(fig: in anger)* dare in escandescenze. **~ion** /-ʌpʃn/ *n* eruzione *f*; *fig* scoppio *m*

escalat|e /'eskəleɪt/ *vi* intensificarsi ●*vt* intensificare. **~ion** /-'leɪʃn/ *n* escalation *f* *inv.* **~or** *n* scala *f* mobile

escapade /'eskəpeɪd/ *n* scappatella *f*

escape /ɪ'skeɪp/ *n* fuga *f*; *(from prison)* evasione *f*; **have a narrow ~** cavarsela per un pelo ●*vi* *(prisoner:)* evadere (**from** da); sfuggire (**from sb** alla sorveglianza di qcno); *(animal:)* scappare; *(gas:)* fuoriuscire ●*vt* ~ **notice** passare inosservato; **the name ~s me** mi sfugge il nome

escapism /ɪ'skeɪpɪzm/ *n* evasione *f* [dalla realtà]

escort[1] /'eskɔ:t/ *n* *(of person)* accompagnatore, -trice *mf*; *Mil etc* scorta *f*

escort[2] /ɪ'skɔ:t/ *vt* accompagnare; *Mil etc* scortare

Eskimo /'eskɪməʊ/ *n* esquimese *mf*

esoteric /esə'terɪk/ *a* esoterico

especial /ɪ'speʃl/ *a* speciale. **~ly** *adv* specialmente; *(kind)* particolarmente

espionage /'espɪənɑːʒ/ *n* spionaggio *m*

essay /'eseɪ/ *n* saggio *m*; *Sch* tema *f*

essence /'esns/ *n* essenza *f*; **in ~** in sostanza

essential /ɪ'senʃl/ *a* essenziale ●*n* **the ~s** *pl* l'essenziale *m*. **~ly** *adv* essenzialmente

establish /ɪ'stæblɪʃ/ *vt* stabilire *(contact, lead)*; fondare *(firm)*; *(prove)* accertare; ~ **oneself as** affermarsi come. **~ment** *n* *(firm)* azienda *f*; **the E~ment** l'ordine *m* costituito

estate /ɪ'steɪt/ *n* tenuta *f*; *(possessions)* patrimonio *m*; *(housing)* quartiere *m* residenziale. ~ **agent** *n* agente *m* immobiliare. ~ **car** *n* giardiniera *f*

esteem /ɪ'stiːm/ *n* stima *f* ●*vt* stimare; *(consider)* giudicare

estimate[1] /'estɪmət/ *n* valutazione *f*; *Comm* preventivo *m*; **at a rough ~** a occhio e croce

estimat|e[2] /'estɪmeɪt/ *vt* stimare. **~ion** /-'meɪʃn/ *n* *(esteem)* stima *f*; **in my ~ion** *(judgement)* a mio giudizio

estuary /'estjʊərɪ/ *n* estuario *m*

etc /et'setərə/ *abbr* (**et cetera**) ecc

etching /'etʃɪŋ/ *n* acquaforte *f*

eternal /ɪ'tɜ:nl/ *a* eterno

eternity /ɪ'tɜ:nətɪ/ *n* eternità *f*

ethic /'eθɪk/ *n* etica *f*. ~ **al** *a* etico. **~s** *n* etica *f*

Ethiopia /i:θɪ'əʊpɪə/ *n* Etiopia *f*

ethnic /'eθnɪk/ *a* etnico

etiquette /'etɪket/ *n* etichetta *f*

EU *n* *abbr* (**European Union**) UE *f*

eucalyptus /ju:kə'lɪptəs/ *n* eucalipto *m*

eulogy /'ju:lədʒɪ/ *n* elogio *m*

euphemis|m /'ju:fəmɪzm/ *n* eufemismo *m*. **~tic** /-'mɪstɪk/ *a* eufemistico

euphoria /ju:'fɔ:rɪə/ *n* euforia *f*

Euro+ /'jʊərəʊ-/ *pref* **~cheque** *n* eurochèque *m* *inv.* **~dollar** *n* eurodollaro *m*

Europe /'jʊərəp/ *n* Europa *f*

European /jʊərə'pɪən/ *a* europeo; ~ **Community** Comunità *f* Europea; ~ **Union** Unione *f* Europea ●*n* europeo, -a *mf*

evacuat|e /ɪ'vækjʊeɪt/ *vt* evacuare *(building, area)*. **~ion** /-'eɪʃn/ *n* evacuazione *f*

evade /ɪ'veɪd/ *vt* evadere *(taxes)*; evitare *(the enemy, authorities)*; ~ **the issue** evitare l'argomento

evaluate /ɪ'væljʊeɪt/ *vt* valutare

evangel|ical /i:væn'dʒelɪkl/ *a* evangelico. **~list** /ɪ'vændʒəlɪst/ *n* evangelista *m*

evaporat|e /ɪ'væpəreɪt/ *vi* evaporare; *fig* svanire. **~ion** /-'reɪʃn/ *n* evaporazione *f*

evasion /ɪ'veɪʒn/ *n* evasione *f*

evasive /ɪ'veɪsɪv/ *a* evasivo

eve /iːv/ *n* *liter* vigilia *f*

even /'iːvn/ *a* *(level)* piatto; *(same, equal)* uguale; *(regular)* regolare; *(number)* pari; **get ~ with** vendicarsi di; **now we're ~** adesso siamo pari ●*adv* anche, ancora; ~ **if** anche se; **~ so** con tutto ciò; **not ~** nemmeno; ~ **bigger/hotter** ancora più grande/caldo ●*vt* ~ **the score** *Sport* pareggiare. **even out** *vi* livellarsi. **even up** *vt* livellare

evening /'iːvnɪŋ/ *n* sera *f*; *(whole evening)* serata *f*; **this ~** stasera; **in the ~** la sera. ~ **class** *n* corso *m* serale. ~ **dress** *n* *(man's)* abito *m* scuro; *(woman's)* abito *m* da sera

evenly /'iːvnlɪ/ *adv* *(distributed)* uniformemente; ⟨*breathe*⟩ regolarmente; ⟨*divided*⟩ in uguali parti

event /ɪ'vent/ *n* avvenimento *m*; ⟨*function*⟩ manifestazione *f*; *Sport* gara *f*; **in the ~ of** nell'eventualità di; **in the ~ful** *a* movimentato

eventual /ɪ'ventjʊəl/ *a* **the ~ winner was...** alla fine il vincitore è stato.... **~ity** /'æləti/ *n* eventualità *f*. **~ly** *adv* alla fine; **~ly!** finalmente!

ever /'evə(r)/ *adv* mai; **I haven't ~...** non ho mai...; **for ~** per sempre; **hardly ~** quasi mai; **~ since** da quando; ⟨*since that time*⟩ da allora; **~ so** fam veramente

'evergreen *n* sempreverde *m*

ever'lasting *a* eterno

every /'evrɪ/ *a* ogni; **~ one** ciascuno; **~ other day** un giorno si un giorno no

every: **~body** *pron* tutti *pl*. **~ day** *a* quotidiano, di ogni giorno. **~one** *pron* tutti *pl*; **~one else** tutti gli altri. **~thing** *pron* tutto; **~thing else** tutto il resto. **~where** *adv* dappertutto; ⟨*wherever*⟩ dovunque

evict /ɪ'vɪkt/ *vt* sfrattare. **~ion** /-ɪkʃn/ *n* sfratto *m*

eviden|ce /'evɪdəns/ *n* evidenza *f*; *Jur* testimonianza *f*; **give ~ce** testimoniare. **~t** *a* evidente. **~tly** *adv* evidentemente

evil /'i:vl/ *a* cattivo ●*n* male *m*

evocative /ɪ'vɒkətɪv/ *a* evocativo; **be ~ of** evocare

evoke /ɪ'vəʊk/ *vt* evocare

evolution /i:və'lu:ʃn/ *n* evoluzione *f*

evolve /ɪ'vɒlv/ *vt* evolvere ●*vi* evolversi

ewe /ju:/ *n* pecora *f*

exacerbate /ɪg'zæsəbeɪt/ *vt* esacerbare ⟨*situation*⟩

exact /ɪg'zækt/ *a* esatto ●*vt* esigere. **~ing** *a* esigente. **~itude** /-ɪtju:d/ *n* esattezza *f*. **~ly** *adv* esattamente; **not ~ly** non proprio. **~ness** *n* precisione *f*

exaggerate /ɪg'zædʒəreɪt/ *vt/i* esagerare. **~ion** /-'reɪʃn/ *n* esagerazione *f*

exam /ɪg'zæm/ *n* esame *m*

examination /ɪgzæmɪ'neɪʃn/ *n* esame *m*; ⟨*of patient*⟩ visita *f*

examine /ɪg'zæmɪn/ *vt* esaminare; visitare ⟨*patient*⟩. **~r** *n Sch* esaminatore, -trice *mf*

example /ɪg'zɑ:mpl/ *n* esempio *m*; **for ~** per esempio; **make an ~ of sb** punire qcno per dare un esempio; **be an ~ to sb** dare il buon esempio a qcno

exasperat|e /ɪg'zæspəreɪt/ *vt* esasperare. **~ion** /-'reɪʃn/ *n* esasperazione *f*

excavat|e /'ekskəveɪt/ *vt* scavare; *Archaeol* fare gli scavi di. **~ion** /-'veɪʃn/ *n* scavo *m*

exceed /ɪk'si:d/ *vt* eccedere. **~ingly** *adv* estremamente

excel /ɪk'sel/ *v* (*pt/pp* **excelled**) ●*vi* eccellere ●*vt* **~ oneself** superare se stessi

excellen|ce /'eksələns/ *n* eccellenza *f*. **E~cy** *n* ⟨*title*⟩ Eccellenza *f*. **~t** *a* eccellente

except /ɪk'sept/ *prep* eccetto, tranne; **~ for** eccetto, tranne; **~ that...** eccetto che... ●*vt* eccettuare. **~ing** *prep* eccetto, tranne

exception /ɪk'sepʃn/ *n* eccezione *f*; **take ~ to** fare obiezioni a. **~al** *a* eccezionale. **~ally** *adv* eccezionalmente

excerpt /'eksɜ:pt/ *n* estratto *m*

excess /ɪk'ses/ *n* eccesso *m*; **in ~ of** oltre. **~ baggage** *n* bagaglio *m* in eccedenza. **~ fare** *n* supplemento *m*

excessive /ɪk'sesɪv/ *a* eccessivo. **~ly** *adv* eccessivamente

exchange /ɪks'tʃeɪndʒ/ *n* scambio *m*; *Teleph* centrale *f*; *Comm* cambio *m*; [**stock**] ~ borsa *f* valori; **in ~ for** in cambio (**for** di) ●*vt* scambiare (**for** con); cambiare ⟨*money*⟩. **~ rate** *n* tasso *m* di cambio

exchequer /ɪks'tʃekə(r)/ *n Pol* tesoro *m*

excise[1] /'eksaɪz/ *n* dazio *m*; **~ duty** dazio *m*

excise[2] /ek'saɪz/ *vt* recidere

excitable /ɪk'saɪtəbl/ *a* eccitabile

excit|e /ɪk'saɪt/ *vt* eccitare. **~ed** *a* eccitato; **get ~ed** eccitarsi. **~edly** *adv* tutto eccitato. **~ement** *n* eccitazione *f*. **~ing** *a* eccitante; ⟨*story, film*⟩ appassionante; ⟨*holiday*⟩ entusiasmante

exclaim /ɪk'skleɪm/ *vt/i* esclamare

exclamation /eksklə'meɪʃn/ *n* esclamazione *f*. **~ mark** *n*, *Am* **~ point** *n* punto *m* esclamativo

exclude /ɪk'sklu:d/ *vt* escludere. **~ding** *pron* escluso. **~sion** /-ʒn/ *n* esclusione *f*

exclusive /ɪk'sklu:sɪv/ *a* ⟨*rights, club*⟩ esclusivo; ⟨*interview*⟩ in esclusiva; **~ of...** ...escluso. **~ly** *adv* esclusivamente

excommunicate /ekskə'mju:nɪkeɪt/ *vt* scomunicare

excrement /'ekskrɪmənt/ *n* escremento *m*

excruciating /ɪk'skru:ʃɪeɪtɪŋ/ *a* atroce ⟨*pain*⟩; ⟨*fam: very bad*⟩ spaventoso

excursion /ɪkˈskɜ:ʃn/ n escursione f
excusable /ɪkˈskju:zəbl/ a perdonabile
excuse¹ /ɪkˈskju:s/ n scusa f
excuse² /ɪkˈskju:z/ vt scusare; ~ **from** esonerare da; ~ **me!** (to get attention) scusi!; (to get past) permesso!, scusi!; (indignant) come ha detto?
ex-di'rectory a **be** ~ non figurare sull'elenco telefonico
execute /ˈeksɪkju:t/ vt eseguire; (put to death) giustiziare; attuare (plan)
execution /eksɪˈkju:ʃn/ n esecuzione f; (of plan) attuazione f. ~**er** n boia m inv
executive /ɪgˈzekjʊtɪv/ a esecutivo ● n dirigente mf; Pol esecutivo m
executor /ɪgˈzekjʊtə(r)/ n Jur esecutore, -trice mf
exemplary /ɪgˈzemplərɪ/ a esemplare
exemplify /ɪgˈzemplɪfaɪ/ vt (pt/pp -ied) esemplificare
exempt /ɪgˈzempt/ a esente ● vt esentare (from da). ~**ion** /-empʃn/ n esenzione f
exercise /ˈeksəsaɪz/ n esercizio m; Mil esercitazione f; **physical** ~**s** ginnastica f; **take** ~ fare del moto ● vt esercitare (muscles, horse); portare a spasso (dog); mettere in pratica (skills) ● vi esercitarsi. ~ **book** n quaderno m
exert /ɪgˈzɜ:t/ vt esercitare; ~ **oneself** sforzarsi. ~**ion** /-ɜ:ʃn/ n sforzo m
exhale /eksˈheɪl/ vt/i esalare
exhaust /ɪgˈzɔ:st/ n Auto scappamento m; (pipe) tubo m di scappamento; ~ **fumes** fumi mpl di scarico ● vt esaurire. ~**ed** a esausto. ~**ing** a estenuante; (climate, person) sfibrante. ~**ion** /-ɔ:stʃn/ n esaurimento m. ~**ive** /-ɪv/ a fig esauriente
exhibit /ɪgˈzɪbɪt/ n oggetto m esposto; Jur reperto m ● vt esporre; fig dimostrare
exhibition /eksɪˈbɪʃn/ n mostra f; (of strength, skill) dimostrazione f. ~**ist** n esibizionista mf
exhibitor /ɪgˈzɪbɪtə(r)/ n espositore, -trice mf
exhilarat|ed /ɪgˈzɪləreɪtɪd/ a rallegrato. ~**ing** a stimolante; (mountain air) tonificante. ~**ion** /-ˈreɪʃn/ n allegria f
exhort /ɪgˈzɔ:t/ vt esortare
exhume /ɪgˈzju:m/ vt esumare
exile /ˈeksaɪl/ n esilio m; (person) esule mf ● vt esiliare
exist /ɪgˈzɪst/ vi esistere. ~**ence** /-əns/

n esistenza f; **in** ~ esistente; **be in** ~**ence** esistere. ~**ing** a attuale
.**exit** /ˈeksɪt/ n uscita f; Theat uscita f di scena ● vi Theat uscire di scena; Comput uscire
exonerate /ɪgˈzɒnəreɪt/ vt esonerare
exorbitant /ɪgˈzɔ:bɪtənt/ a esorbitante
exorcize /ˈeksɔ:saɪz/ vt esorcizzare
exotic /ɪgˈzɒtɪk/ a esotico
expand /ɪkˈspænd/ vt espandere ● vi espandersi; Comm svilupparsi; (metal:) dilatarsi; ~ **on** (fig: explain better) approfondire
expans|e /ɪkˈspæns/ n estensione f. ~**ion** /-ænʃn/ n espansione f; Comm sviluppo m; (of metal) dilatazione f. ~**ive** /-ɪv/ a espansivo
expatriate /eksˈpætrɪət/ a espatriato, -a mf
expect /ɪkˈspekt/ vt aspettare (letter, baby); (suppose) pensare; (demand) esigere; **I** ~ **so** penso di sì; **be** ~**ing** essere in stato interessante
expectan|cy /ɪkˈspektənsɪ/ n aspettativa f. ~**t** a in attesa; ~**t mother** donna f incinta. ~**tly** adv con impazienza
expectation /ekspekˈteɪʃn/ n aspettativa f, speranza f
expedient /ɪkˈspi:dɪənt/ a conveniente ● n espediente m
expedition /ekspɪˈdɪʃn/ n spedizione f. ~**ary** a Mil di spedizione
expel /ɪkˈspel/ vt (pt/pp **expelled**) espellere
expend /ɪkˈspend/ vt consumare. ~**able** /-əbl/ a sacrificabile
expenditure /ɪkˈspendɪtʃə(r)/ n spesa f
expense /ɪkˈspens/ n spesa f; **business** ~**s** pl spese fpl; **at my** ~ a mie spese; **at the** ~ **of** fig a spese di
expensive /ɪkˈspensɪv/ a caro, costoso. ~**ly** adv costosamente
experience /ɪkˈspɪərɪəns/ n esperienza f ● vt provare (sensation); avere (problem). ~**d** a esperto
experiment /ɪkˈsperɪmənt/ n esperimento ● /-ment/ vi sperimentare. ~**al** /-ˈmentl/ a sperimentale
expert /ˈekspɜ:t/ a & n esperto, -a mf. ~**ly** adv abilmente
expertise /ekspɜ:ˈti:z/ n competenza f
expire /ɪkˈspaɪə(r)/ vi scadere
expiry /ɪkˈspaɪərɪ/ n scadenza f. ~ **date** n data f di scadenza
explain /ɪkˈspleɪn/ vt spiegare
explana|tion /ekspləˈneɪʃn/ n spiegazione f. ~**tory** /ɪkˈsplænətərɪ/ a esplicativo

expletive /ɪkˈspliːtɪv/ n imprecazione f

explicit /ɪkˈsplɪsɪt/ a esplicito. ~ly adv esplicitamente

explode /ɪkˈspləʊd/ vi esplodere ● vt fare esplodere

exploit¹ /ˈeksplɔɪt/ n impresa f

exploit² /ɪkˈsplɔɪt/ vt sfruttare. ~ation /eksplɔɪˈteɪʃn/ n sfruttamento m

explora|tion /eksplaˈreɪʃn/ n esplorazione f. ~tory /ɪkˈsplɒrətərɪ/ a esploratorio

explore /ɪkˈsplɔː(r)/ vt esplorare; fig studiare ‹implications›. ~r n esploratore, -trice mf

explos|ion /ɪkˈspləʊʒn/ n esplosione f. ~ive /-sɪv/ a & n esplosivo m

exponent /ɪkˈspəʊnənt/ n esponente mf

export /ˈekspɔːt/ n esportazione f ● vt /-ˈspɔːt/ esportare. ~er n esportatore, -trice mf

expos|e /ɪkˈspəʊz/ vt esporre; ‹reveal› svelare; smascherare ‹traitor etc›. ~ure /-ʒə(r)/ n esposizione f; Med esposizione f prolungata al freddo/caldo; (of crimes) smascheramento m; 24 ~ures Phot 24 pose

expound /ɪkˈspaʊnd/ vt esporre

express /ɪkˈspres/ a espresso ● adv ‹send› per espresso ● n (train) espresso m ● vt esprimere; ~ oneself esprimersi. ~ion /-ʃn/ n espressione f. ~ive /-ɪv/ a espressivo. ~ly adv espressamente

expulsion /ɪkˈspʌlʃn/ n espulsione f

exquisite /ek'skwɪzɪt/ a squisito

ex-'serviceman n ex-combattente m

extend /ɪkˈstend/ vt prolungare ‹visit, road›; prorogare ‹visa, contract›; ampliare ‹building, knowledge›; (stretch out) allungare; tendere ‹hand› ● vi ‹garden, knowledge:› estendersi

extension /ɪkˈstenʃn/ n prolungamento m; (of visa, contract) proroga f; (of treaty) ampliamento m; (part of building) annesso m; (length of cable) prolunga f; Teleph interno m; ~ 226 interno 226

extensive /ɪkˈstensɪv/ a ampio, vasto. ~ly adv ampiamente

extent /ɪkˈstent/ n (scope) portata f; to a certain ~ fino a un certo punto; to such an ~ that... fino al punto che...

extenuating /ɪkˈstenjʊeɪtɪŋ/ a ~ circumstances attenuanti fpl

exterior /ɪkˈstɪərɪə(r)/ a & n esterno m

exterminat|e /ɪkˈstɜːmɪneɪt/ vt sterminare. ~ion /-ˈneɪʃn/ n sterminio m

external /ɪkˈstɜːnl/ a esterno; for ~ use only Med per uso esterno. ~ly adv esternamente

extinct /ɪkˈstɪŋkt/ a estinto. ~ion /-ɪŋkʃn/ n estinzione f

extinguish /ɪkˈstɪŋgwɪʃ/ vt estinguere. ~er n estintore m

extort /ɪkˈstɔːt/ vt estorcere. ~ion /-ɔːʃn/ n estorsione f

extortionate /ɪkˈstɔːʃənət/ a esorbitante

extra /ˈekstrə/ a in più; ‹train› straordinario; an ~ £10 10 sterline extra, 10 sterline in più ● adv in più; (especially) più; pay ~ pagare in più, pagare extra; ~ strong/busy fortissimo/occupatissimo ● n Theat comparsa f; ~s pl extra mpl

extract¹ /ˈekstrækt/ n estratto m

extract² /ɪkˈstrækt/ vt estrarre ‹tooth, oil›; strappare ‹secret›; ricavare ‹truth›. ~or /fan/ n aspiratore m

extradit|e /ˈekstrədaɪt/ Jur vt estradare. ~ion /-ˈdɪʃn/ n estradizione f

extra'marital a extraconiugale

extraordinar|y /ɪkˈstrɔːdɪnərɪ/ a straordinario. ~ily /-ɪlɪ/ adv straordinariamente

extravagan|ce /ɪkˈstrævəgəns/ n (with money) prodigalità f; (of behaviour) stravaganza f. ~t a spendaccione; (bizarre) stravagante; ‹claim› esagerato

extrem|e /ɪkˈstriːm/ a estremo ● n estremo m; in the ~e al massimo. ~ely adv estremamente. ~ist n estremista mf

extremity /ɪkˈstremətɪ/ n (end) estremità f inv

extricate /ˈekstrɪkeɪt/ vt districare

extrovert /ˈekstrəvɜːt/ n estroverso, -a m

exuberant /ɪgˈzjuːbərənt/ a esuberante

exude /ɪgˈzjuːd/ vt also fig trasudare

exult /ɪgˈzʌlt/ vi esultare

eye /aɪ/ n occhio m; (of needle) cruna f; keep an ~ on tener d'occhio; see ~ to ~ aver le stesse idee ● vt (pt/pp eyed, pres eye[e]ing) guardare

eye: ~ball n bulbo m oculare. ~ brow n sopracciglio m (pl sopracciglia f). ~lash n ciglio m (pl ciglia f). ~lid n palpebra f. ~-opener n rivelazione f. ~-shadow n ombretto m. ~sight n vista f. ~sore n fam pugno m nell'occhio. ~witness n testimone mf oculare

fable /'feɪbl/ n favola f

fabric /'fæbrɪk/ n also fig tessuto m

fabrication /fæbrɪ'keɪʃn/ n invenzione f; (manufacture) fabbricazione f

fabulous /'fæbjʊləs/ a fam favoloso

façade /fə'sɑːd/ n (of building, person) facciata f

face /feɪs/ n faccia f, viso m; (grimace) smorfia f; (surface) faccia f; (of clock) quadrante m; **pull** ~**s** far boccacce; **in the** ~ **of** di fronte a; **on the** ~ **of it** in apparenza ● vt essere di fronte a; (confront) affrontare; ~ **north** ⟨house:⟩ dare a nord; ~ **the fact that** arrendersi al fatto che. **face up to** vt accettare (facts); affrontare (person)

face: ~**flannel** n guanto m di spugna. ~**less** a anonimo. ~**-lift** n plastica f facciale

facet /'fæsɪt/ n sfaccettatura f; fig aspetto m

facetious /fə'siːʃəs/ a spiritoso. ~ **remarks** spiritosaggini mpl

'**face value** n (of money) valore m nominale; **take sb/sth at** ~ fermarsi alle apparenze

facial /'feɪʃl/ a facciale ● n trattamento m di bellezza al viso

facile /'fæsaɪl/ a semplicistico

facilitate /fə'sɪlɪteɪt/ vt rendere possibile; (make easier) facilitare

facility /fə'sɪlətɪ/ n facilità f; ~**ies** pl (of area, in hotel etc) attrezzature fpl

facing /'feɪsɪŋ/ prep ~ **the sea** ⟨house⟩ che dà sul mare; **the person** ~ **me** la persona di fronte a me

facsimile /fæk'sɪmɪlɪ/ n facsimile m

fact /fækt/ n fatto m; **in** ~ infatti

faction /'fækʃn/ n fazione f

factor /'fæktə(r)/ n fattore m

factory /'fæktərɪ/ n fabbrica f

factual /'fæktʃʊəl/ a **be** ~ attenersi ai fatti. ~**ly** adv (inaccurate) dal punto di vista dei fatti

faculty /'fækltɪ/ n facoltà f inv

fad /fæd/ n capriccio m

fade /feɪd/ vi sbiadire; (sound, light:) affievolirsi; (flower:) appassire. **fade in** vt cominciare in dissolvenza (picture).

fade out vt finire in dissolvenza (picture)

fag /fæg/ n (chore) fatica f; (fam: cigarette) sigaretta f; (Am sl: homosexual) frocio m. ~ **end** n fam cicca f

fagged /fægd/ a ~ **out** fam stanco morto

Fahrenheit /'færənhaɪt/ a Fahrenheit

fail /feɪl/ n **without** ~ senz'altro ● vi (attempt:) fallire; (eyesight, memory:) indebolirsi; (engine, machine:) guastarsi; (marriage:) andare a rotoli; (in exam) essere bocciato; ~ **to do sth** non fare qcsa; **I tried but I** ~**ed** ho provato ma non ci sono riuscito ● vt non superare (exam); bocciare (candidate); (disappoint) deludere; **words** ~ **me** mi mancano le parole

failing /'feɪlɪŋ/ n difetto m ● prep ~ **that** altrimenti

failure /'feɪljə(r)/ n fallimento m; (mechanical) guasto m; (person) incapace mf

faint /feɪnt/ a leggero; (memory) vago; **feel** ~ sentirsi mancare ● n svenimento m ● vi svenire

faint: ~**-hearted** a timido. ~**ly** adv (slightly) leggermente. ~**ness** n (physical) debolezza f

fair[1] /feə(r)/ n fiera f

fair[2] a (hair, person) biondo; (skin) chiaro; (weather) bello; (just) giusto; (quite good) discreto; Sch abbastanza bene; **a** ~ **amount** abbastanza ● adv **play** ~ fare un gioco pulito. ~**ly** adv con giustizia; (rather) discretamente, abbastanza. ~**ness** n giustizia f. ~ **play** n fair play m inv

fairy /'feərɪ/ n fata f; ~ **story**, ~**-tale** n fiaba f

faith /feɪθ/ n fede f; (trust) fiducia f; **in good/bad** ~ in buona/mala fede

faithful /'feɪθfl/ a fedele. ~**ly** adv fedelmente; **yours** ~**ly** distinti saluti. ~**ness** n fedeltà f

faith-healer n guaritore, -trice mf

fake /feɪk/ a falso ● n falsificazione f;

falcon | fasten

(person) impostore m ●vt falsificare; (pretend) fingere

falcon /'fɔːlkən/ n falcone m

fall /fɔːl/ n caduta f; (in prices) ribasso m; (Am: autumn) autunno m; **have a ~** fare una caduta ●vi (pt **fell**, pp **fallen**) cadere; (night:) scendere; **~ in love** innamorarsi. **fall about** vi (with laughter) morire dal ridere. **fall back on** vt ritornare su. **fall for** vt fam innamorarsi di (person); cascarci (sth, trick). **fall down** vi cadere; (building:) crollare. **fall in** vi caderci dentro; (collapse) crollare; Mil mettersi in riga; **~ in with** concordare con (suggestion, plan). **fall off** vi cadere; (diminish) diminuire. **fall out** vi (quarrel) litigare; **his hair is ~ing out** perde i capelli. **fall over** vi cadere. **fall through** vi (plan:) andare a monte

fallacy /'fæləsɪ/ n errore m

fallible /'fæləbl/ a fallibile

'fall-out n pioggia f radioattiva

false /fɔːls/ a falso; **~ bottom** doppio fondo m; **~ start** Sport falsa partenza f. **~hood** n menzogna f. **~ness** n falsità f

false 'teeth npl dentiera f

falsify /'fɔːlsɪfaɪ/ vt (pt/pp -**ied**) falsificare

falter /'fɔːltə(r)/ vi vacillare; (making speech) esitare

fame /feɪm/ n fama f

familiar /fə'mɪljə(r)/ a familiare; **be ~ with** (know) conoscere. **~ity** /-lɪ'ærɪtɪ/ n familiarità f. **~ize** vt familiarizzare; **~ize oneself with** familiarizzarsi con

family /'fæməlɪ/ n famiglia f

family: **~ al'lowance** n assegni mpl familiari. **~ 'doctor** n medico m di famiglia. **~ 'life** n vita f familiare. **~ 'planning** n pianificazione f familiare. **~ 'tree** n albero m genealogico

famine /'fæmɪn/ n carestia f

famished /'fæmɪʃt/ a **be ~** fam avere una fame da lupo

famous /'feɪməs/ a famoso

fan¹ /fæn/ n ventilatore m; (handheld) ventaglio m ●vt (pt/pp **fanned**) far vento a; **~ oneself** sventagliarsi; fig **~ the flames** soffiare sul fuoco. **fan out** vi spiegarsi a ventaglio

fan² n (admirer) ammiratore, -trice mf; Sport tifoso m; (of Verdi etc) appassionato, -a mf

fanatic /fə'nætɪk/ n fanatico, -a mf. **~al** a fanatico. **~ism** /-sɪzm/ n fanatismo m

'fan belt n cinghia f per ventilatore

fanciful /'fænsɪfl/ a fantasioso

fancy /'fænsɪ/ n fantasia f; **I've taken a real ~ to him** mi è molto simpatico; **as the ~ takes you** come ti pare ●a [a] fantasia ●vt (pt/pp -**ied**) (believe) credere; (fam: want) aver voglia di; **he fancies you** fam gli piaci; **~ that!** ma guarda un po'! **~ 'dress** n costume m (per maschera)

fanfare /'fænfeə(r)/ n fanfara f

fang /fæŋ/ n zanna f; (of snake) dente m

fan: **~ heater** n termoventilatore m. **~light** n lunetta f

fantasize /'fæntəsaɪz/ vi fantasticare. **~tic** /-'tæstɪk/ a fantastico. **~y** n fantasia f

far /fɑː(r)/ adv lontano; (much) molto; **by ~** di gran lunga; **~ away** lontano; **as ~ as the church** fino alla chiesa; **how ~ is it from here?** quanto dista da qui?; **as ~ as I know** per quanto io sappia ●a (end, side) altro; **the F~ East** l'Estremo Oriente m

farcic /fɑːs/ n farsa f. **~ical** a ridicolo

fare /feə(r)/ n tariffa f; (food) vitto m. **~-dodger** /-dɒdʒə(r)/ n passeggero, -a mf senza biglietto

farewell /feə'wel/ int liter addio! ●n addio m

far-'fetched a improbabile

farm /fɑːm/ n fattoria f ●vi fare l'agricoltore ●vt coltivare (land). **~er** n agricoltore m

farm: **~house** n casa f colonica. **~ing** n agricoltura f. **~yard** n aia f

far: **~-reaching** a di larga portata. **~-'sighted** a fig prudente; (Am: long-sighted) presbite

fart /fɑːt/ fam n scoreggia f ●vi scoreggiare

farther /'fɑːðə(r)/ adv più lontano ●a **at the ~ end** all'altra estremità di

fascinate /'fæsɪneɪt/ vt affascinare. **~ing** a affascinante. **~ion** /-'neɪʃn/ n fascino m

fascism /'fæʃɪzm/ n fascismo m. **~t** n fascista mf ●a fascista

fashion /'fæʃn/ n moda f; (manner) maniera f ●vt modellare. **~able** /-əbl/ a di moda; **be ~able** essere alla moda. **~ably** adv alla moda

fast¹ /fɑːst/ a veloce; (colour) indelebile; **be ~** (clock:) andare avanti ●adv velocemente; (firmly) saldamente; **~er!** più in fretta!; **be ~ asleep** dormire profondamente

fast² n digiuno m ●vi digiunare

fasten /'fɑːsn/ vt allacciare; chiudere (window); (stop flapping) mettere un fermo a ● *vi* allacciarsi. **~er** *n*, **~ing** *n* chiusura *f*

fastidious /fəˈstɪdɪəs/ *a* esigente

fat /fæt/ *a* (**fatter, fattest**) ⟨*person, cheque*⟩ grasso ● *n* grasso *m*

fatal /ˈfeɪtl/ *a* mortale; ⟨*error*⟩ fatale. **~ism** /-təlɪzm/ *n* fatalismo *m*. **~ist** /-təlɪst/ *n* fatalista *mf*. **~ity** /fəˈtælətɪ/ *n* morte *f*. **~ly** *adv* mortalmente

fate /feɪt/ *n* destino *m*. **~ful** *a* fatidico

'fat-head *n* fam zuccone, -a *mf*

father /ˈfɑːðə(r)/ *n* padre *m*; **F~ Christmas** Babbo *m* Natale ● *vt* generare ⟨*child*⟩

father: **~hood** *n* paternità *f*. **~-in-law** *n* (*pl* **~s-in-law**) suocero *m*. **~ly** *a* paterno

fathom /ˈfæðəm/ *n* Naut braccio *m* ● *vt* ~ [**out**] comprendere

fatigue /fəˈtiːg/ *n* fatica *f*

fatten /ˈfætn/ *vt* ingrassare ⟨*animal*⟩. **~ing** *a* **cream is ~ing** la panna fa ingrassare

fatty /ˈfætɪ/ *a* grasso ● *n* fam ciccione, -a *mf*

fatuous /ˈfætjʊəs/ *a* fatuo

faucet /ˈfɔːsɪt/ *n* Am rubinetto *m*

fault /fɔːlt/ *n* difetto *m*; Geol faglia *f*; Tennis fallo *m*; **be at ~** avere torto; **find ~ with** trovare da ridire su; **it's your ~** è colpa tua ● *vt* criticare. **~less** *a* impeccabile

faulty /ˈfɔːltɪ/ *a* difettoso

fauna /ˈfɔːnə/ *n* fauna *f*

favour /ˈfeɪvə(r)/ *n* favore *m*; **be in ~ of sth** essere a favore di qcsa; **do sb a ~** fare un piacere a qcno ● *vt* ⟨*prefer*⟩ preferire. **~able** /-əbl/ *a* favorevole

favourit|e /ˈfeɪv(ə)rɪt/ *a* preferito ● *n* preferito, -a *mf*; Sport favorito, -a *mf*. **~ism** *n* favoritismo *m*

fawn /fɔːn/ *a* fulvo ● *n* ⟨*animal*⟩ cerbiatto *m*

fax /fæks/ *n* ⟨*document, machine*⟩ fax *m inv*; **by ~** per fax ● *vt* faxare. **~ machine** *n* fax *m inv*. **~-modem** *n* modem-fax *m inv*, fax-modem *m inv*

fear /fɪə(r)/ *n* paura *f*; **no ~!** *fam* vai tranquillo! ● *vt* temere ● *vi* ~ **for sth** temere per qcsa

fear|ful /ˈfɪəfl/ *a* pauroso; ⟨*awful*⟩ terribile. **~less** *a* impavido. **~some** /-səm/ *a* spaventoso

feas|ibility /fiːzɪˈbɪlɪtɪ/ *n* praticabilità *f*. **~ible** *a* fattibile; ⟨*possible*⟩ probabile

feast /fiːst/ *n* festa *f*; ⟨*banquet*⟩ banchetto *m* ● *vi* banchettare; ~ **on** godersi

feat /fiːt/ *n* impresa *f*

feather /ˈfeðə(r)/ *n* piuma *f*

feature /ˈfiːtʃə(r)/ *n* ⟨*quality*⟩ caratteristica *f*; Journ articolo *m*; **~s** (*pl: of face*) lineamenti *mpl* ● *vt* ⟨*film:*⟩ avere come protagonista ● *vi* (*on a list etc*) comparire. **~ film** *n* lungometraggio *m*

February /ˈfebrʊərɪ/ *n* febbraio *m*

fed /fed/ *see* **feed** ● *a* **be ~ up** *fam* essere stufo (**with** di)

federal /ˈfed(ə)rəl/ *a* federale

federation /fedəˈreɪʃn/ *n* federazione *f*

fee /fiː/ *n* tariffa *f*; (*lawyer's, doctor's*) onorario *m*; (*for membership, school*) quota *f*

feeble /ˈfiːbl/ *a* debole; ⟨*excuse*⟩ fiacco

feed /fiːd/ *n* mangiare *m*; (*for baby*) pappa *f* ● *v* (*pt/pp* **fed**) ● *vt* dar da mangiare a ⟨*animal*⟩; (*support*) mantenere; ~ **sth into sth** inserire qcsa in qcsa ● *vi* mangiare

'feedback *n* controreazione *f*; (*of information*) reazione *f*, feedback *m*

feel /fiːl/ *v* (*pt/pp* **felt**) ● *vt* sentire; (*experience*) provare; (*think*) pensare; (*touch: searching*) tastare; (*touch: for texture*) toccare ● *vi* ~ **soft/hard** essere duro/morbido al tatto; ~ **hot/hungry** aver caldo/fame; ~ **ill** sentirsi male; **I don't ~ like it** non ne ho voglia; **how do you ~ about it?** (*opinion*) che te ne pare?; **it doesn't ~ right** non mi sembra giusto. **~er** *n* (*of animal*) antenna *f*; **put out ~ers** *fig* tastare il terreno. **~ing** *n* sentimento *m*; (*awareness*) sensazione *f*

feet /fiːt/ *see* **foot**

feign /feɪn/ *vt* simulare

feline /ˈfiːlaɪn/ *a* felino

fell¹ /fel/ *vt* (*knock down*) abbattere

fell² *see* **fall**

fellow /ˈfeləʊ/ *n* (*of society*) socio *m*; (*fam: man*) tipo *m*

fellow: **~-countryman** *n* compatriota *m*. **~-men** *npl* prossimi *mpl*. **~ship** *n* cameratismo *m*; (*group*) associazione *f*; Univ incarico *m* di ricercatore, -trice

felony /ˈfelənɪ/ *n* delitto *m*

felt¹ /felt/ *see* **feel**

felt² *n* feltro *m*. **~[-tipped] 'pen** /[-tɪpt]/ *n* pennarello *m*

female /ˈfiːmeɪl/ *a* femminile; **the ~ antelope** l'antilope femmina ● *n* femmina *f*

feminine /ˈfemɪnɪn/ *a* femminile ● *n* Gram femminile *m*. **~inity** /-ˈnɪnətɪ/ *n* femminilità *f*. **~ist** *a* & *n* femminista *mf*

fenc|e /fens/ *n* recinto *m*; (*fam: person*)

ricettatore *m* ● *vi Sport* tirar di scherma. **fence** *in vt* chiudere in un recinto. ~**er** *n* schermidore *m*. ~**ing** *n* steccato *m*; *Sport* scherma *f*

fend /fend/ *vi* ~ **for oneself** badare a se stesso. **fend off** *vt* parare; difendersi da ⟨*criticisms*⟩

fender /'fendə(r)/ *n* parafuoco *m inv*; (*Am: on car*) parafango *m*

fennel /'fenl/ *n* finocchio *m*

ferment[1] /'fɜ:ment/ *n* fermento *m*

ferment[2] /fə'ment/ *vi* fermentare ● *vt* far fermentare. ~**ation** /fɜ:men'teɪʃn/ *n* fermentazione *f*

fern /fɜ:n/ *n* felce *f*

feroc|ious /fə'rəʊʃəs/ *a* feroce. ~**ity** /-'rɒsətɪ/ *n* ferocia *f*

ferret /'ferɪt/ *n* furetto *m* ● **ferret out** *vt* scovare

ferry /'ferɪ/ *n* traghetto *m* ● *vt* traghettare

fertil|e /'fɜ:taɪl/ *a* fertile. ~**ity** /fɜ:'tɪlətɪ/ *n* fertilità *f*

fertilize /'fɜ:tɪlaɪz/ *vt* fertilizzare ⟨*land*, *ovum*⟩. ~ *r n* fertilizzante *m*

fervent /'fɜ:vənt/ *a* fervente

fervour /'fɜ:və(r)/ *n* fervore *m*

fester /'festə(r)/ *vi* suppurare

festival /'festɪvl/ *n Mus, Theat* festival *m*; *Relig* festa *f*

festive /'festɪv/ *a* festivo; ~**e season** periodo *m* delle feste natalizie. ~**ities** /fe'strvatɪz/ *npl* festeggiamenti *mpl*

festoon /fe'stu:n/ *vt* ~ **with** ornare di

fetch /fetʃ/ *vt* andare/venire a prendere; (*be sold for*) raggiungere (il prezzo di)

fetching /'fetʃɪŋ/ *a* attraente

fête /feɪt/ *n* festa *f* ● *vt* festeggiare

fetish /'fetɪʃ/ *n* feticcio *m*

fetter /'fetə(r)/ *vt* incatenare

fettle /'fetl/ *n* **in fine** ~ in buona forma

feud /fju:d/ *n* faida *f*

feudal /'fju:dl/ *a* feudale

fever /'fi:və(r)/ *n* febbre *f*. ~**ish** *a* febbricitante; *fig* febbrile

few /fju:/ *a* pochi; **every** ~ **days** ogni due o tre giorni; **a** ~ **people** alcuni; ~ **reservations** meno prenotazioni; **the** ~**est number** il numero più basso ● *pron* pochi; ~ **of us** pochi di noi; **a** ~ alcuni; **quite a** ~ parecchi; ~**er than last year** meno dell'anno scorso

fiancé /fɪ'ɒnseɪ/ *n* fidanzato *m*. ~**e** *n* fidanzata *f*

fiasco /fɪ'æskəʊ/ *n* fiasco *m*

fib /fɪb/ *n* storia *f*; **tell a** ~ raccontare una storia

fibre /'faɪbə(r)/ *n* fibra *f*. ~**glass** *n* fibra *f* di vetro

fickle /'fɪkl/ *a* incostante

fiction /'fɪkʃn/ *n* ⟨*works of*⟩ ~ narrativa *f*; (*fabrication*) finzione *f*. ~**al** *a* immaginario

fictitious /fɪk'tɪʃəs/ *a* fittizio

fiddle /'fɪdl/ *n fam* violino *m*; (*cheating*) imbroglio *m* ● *vi* gingillarsi (**with** con) ● *vt fam* truccare ⟨*accounts*⟩

fiddly /'fɪdlɪ/ *a* intricato

fidelity /fɪ'delətɪ/ *vi* fedeltà *f*

fidget /'fɪdʒɪt/ *vi* agitarsi. ~**y** *a* agitato

field /fi:ld/ *n* campo *m*

field: ~ **events** *npl* atletica *fsg* leggera. ~**-glasses** *npl* binocolo *msg*. F~ 'Marshal *n* feldmaresciallo *m*. ~**work** *n* ricerche *fpl* sul terreno

fiend /fi:nd/ *n* demonio *m*

fierce /fɪəs/ *a* feroce. ~**ness** *n* ferocia *f*

fiery /'faɪərɪ/ *a* (*-ier*, *-iest*) focoso

fifteen /fɪf'ti:n/ *a & n* quindici *m*. ~**th** *a & n* quindicesimo, -a *mf*

fifth /fɪfθ/ *a & n* quinto, -a *mf*

fiftieth /'fɪftɪθ/ *a & n* cinquantesimo, -a *mf*

fifty /'fɪftɪ/ *a & n* cinquanta *m*

fig /fɪg/ *n* fico *m*

fight /faɪt/ *n* lotta *f*; (*brawl*) zuffa *f*; (*argument*) litigio *m*; (*boxing*) incontro *m* ● *v* (*pt/pp fought*) ● *vt also fig* combattere ● *vi* combattere; (*brawl*) azzuffarsi; (*argue*) litigare. ~**er** *n* combattente *mf*; *Aeron* caccia *m inv*. ~**ing** *n* combattimento *m*

figment /'fɪgmənt/ *n* **it's a** ~ **of your imagination** questo è tutta una tua invenzione

figurative /'fɪgjərətɪv/ *a* ⟨*sense*⟩ figurato; ⟨*art*⟩ figurativo

figure /'fɪgə(r)/ *n* (*digit*) cifra *f*; (*carving*, *sculpture*, *illustration*, *form*) figura *f*; (*body shape*) linea *f*; ~ **of speech** modo *m* di dire ● *vi* (*appear*) figurare ● *vt* (*Am: think*) pensare. **figure out** *vt* dedurre; capire ⟨*person*⟩

figure: ~**-head** *n* figura *f* simbolica. ~ **skating** *n* pattinaggio *m* artistico

file[1] /faɪl/ *n* scheda *f*; (*set of documents*) incartamento *m*; (*folder*) cartellina *f*; *Comput* file *m inv* ● *vt* archiviare ⟨*documents*⟩

file[2] *n* (*line*) fila *f*; **in single** ~ in fila

file[3] *n Techn* lima *f* ● *vt* limare

filing cabinet /'faɪlɪŋkæbɪnət/ *n* schedario *m*, classificatore *m*

filings /'faɪlɪŋz/ *npl* limatura *fsg*

fill /fɪl/ *n* **eat one's** ~ mangiare a

325 **fillet | fish finger**

sazietà ● *vt* riempire; otturare ⟨*tooth*⟩ ● *vi* riempirsi. **fill in** *vt* compilare ⟨*form*⟩. **fill out** *vt* compilare ⟨*form*⟩. **fill up** *vi* ⟨*room, tank:*⟩ riempirsi; *Auto* far il pieno ● *vt* riempire

fillet /'fɪlɪt/ *n* filetto *m* ● *vt* ⟨*pt/pp* **filleted**⟩ disossare

filling /'fɪlɪŋ/ *n* Culin ripieno *m*; ⟨*of tooth*⟩ piombatura *f*. **~ station** *n* stazione *f* di rifornimento

filly /'fɪlɪ/ *n* puledra *f*

film /fɪlm/ *n* Cinema film *m inv*; Phot pellicola *f*; ⟨*cling*⟩ ~ pellicola *f* per alimenti ● *vt/i* filmare. **~ star** star *f inv*, divo, -a *mf*

filter /'fɪltə(r)/ *n* filtro *m* ● *vt* filtrare. **filter through** *vi* ⟨*news:*⟩ trapelare. **~ tip** *n* filtro *m*; ⟨*cigarette*⟩ sigaretta *f* col filtro

filth /fɪlθ/ *n* sudiciume *m*. **~y** *a* (-ier, -iest) sudicio; ⟨*language*⟩ sconcio

fin /fɪn/ *n* pinna *f*

final /'faɪnl/ *a* finale; ⟨*conclusive*⟩ decisivo ● *n* Sport finale *f*; **~s** *pl* Univ esami *mpl* finali

finale /fɪ'nɑːlɪ/ *n* finale *m*

final|ist /'faɪnəlɪst/ *n* finalista *mf*. **~ity** /-'nælətɪ/ *n* finalità *f*

final|ize /'faɪnəlaɪz/ *vt* mettere a punto ⟨*text*⟩; definire ⟨*agreement*⟩. **~ly** *adv* ⟨*at last*⟩ finalmente; ⟨*at the end*⟩ alla fine; ⟨*to conclude*⟩ per finire

finance /'faɪnæns/ *n* finanza *f* ● *vt* finanziare

financial /faɪ'nænʃl/ *a* finanziario

finch /fɪntʃ/ *n* fringuello *m*

find /faɪnd/ *n* scoperta *f* ● *vt* ⟨*pt/pp* **found**⟩ trovare; ⟨*establish*⟩ scoprire; **~ sb guilty** Jur dichiarare qcno colpevole. **find out** *vt* scoprire ● *vi* ⟨*enquire*⟩ informarsi

findings /'faɪndɪŋz/ *npl* conclusioni *fpl*

fine[1] /faɪn/ *n* ⟨*penalty*⟩ multa *f* ● *vt* multare

fine[2] *a* bello; ⟨*slender*⟩ fine; **he's ~** ⟨*in health*⟩ sta bene; **~ arts** belle arti *fpl* ● *adv* bene; **that's cutting it ~** non ci lascia molto tempo ● *int* [va] bene. **~ly** *adv* ⟨*cut*⟩ finemente

finery /'faɪnərɪ/ *n* splendore *m*

finesse /fɪ'nes/ *n* finezza *f*

finger /'fɪŋɡə(r)/ *n* dito *m* ⟨*pl* dita *f*⟩ ● *vt* tastare

finger: **~-mark** *n* ditata *f*. **~-nail** *n* unghia *f*. **~print** *n* impronta *f* digitale. **~tip** *n* punta *f* del dito; **have sth at one's ~tips** sapere qcsa a menadito;

⟨*close at hand*⟩ avere qcsa a portata di mano

finicky /'fɪnɪkɪ/ *a* ⟨*person*⟩ pignolo; ⟨*task*⟩ intricato

finish /'fɪnɪʃ/ *n* fine *f*; ⟨*finishing line*⟩ traguardo *m*; ⟨*of product*⟩ finitura *f*; **have a good ~** ⟨*runner:*⟩ avere un buon finale ● *vt* finire; **~ reading** finire di leggere ● *vi* finire

finite /'faɪnaɪt/ *a* limitato

Finland /'fɪnlənd/ *n* Finlandia *f*

Finn /fɪn/ *n* finlandese *mf*. **~ish** *a* finlandese ● *n* ⟨*language*⟩ finnico *m*

fiord /fjɔːd/ *n* fiordo *m*

fir /fɜː(r)/ *n* abete *m*

fire /'faɪə(r)/ *n* fuoco *m*; ⟨*forest, house*⟩ incendio *m*; **be on ~** bruciare; **catch ~** prendere fuoco; **set ~ to** dar fuoco a; **under ~** sotto il fuoco ● *vt* cuocere ⟨*pottery*⟩; sparare ⟨*shot*⟩; tirare ⟨*gun*⟩; ⟨*fam: dismiss*⟩ buttar fuori ● *vi* sparare ⟨*at*⟩

fire: **~ alarm** *n* allarme *m* antincendio. **~arm** *n* arma *f* da fuoco. **~ brigade** *n* vigili *mpl* del fuoco. **~-engine** *n* autopompa *f*. **~-escape** *n* uscita *f* di sicurezza. **~ extinguisher** *n* estintore *m*. **~man** *n* pompiere *m*, vigile *m* del fuoco. **~place** *n* caminetto *m*. **~side** *n* by or at the **~side** accanto al fuoco. **~ station** *n* caserma *f* dei pompieri. **~wood** *n* legna *f* da ardere). **~work** *n* fuoco *m* d'artificio; **~works** *pl* ⟨*display*⟩ fuochi *mpl* d'artificio

'firing squad *n* plotone *m* d'esecuzione

firm[1] /fɜːm/ *n* ditta *f*, azienda *f*

firm[2] *a* fermo; ⟨*soil*⟩ compatto; ⟨*stable, fixed*⟩ solido; ⟨*resolute*⟩ risoluto. **~ly** *adv* ⟨*hold*⟩ stretto; ⟨*say*⟩ con fermezza

first /fɜːst/ *a & a* primo, -a *mf*; **at ~** all'inizio; **who's ~?** chi è il primo?; **from the ~** [fin] dall'inizio ● *adv* ⟨*arrive, leave*⟩ per primo; ⟨*beforehand*⟩ prima; ⟨*in listing*⟩ prima di tutto, innanzitutto

first: **~ aid** *n* pronto soccorso *m*. **~-'aid kit** *n* cassetta *f* di pronto soccorso. **~-class** *a* di prim'ordine; Rail di prima classe ● *adv* ⟨*travel*⟩ in prima classe. **~ floor** *n* primo piano *m*; ⟨*Am: ground floor*⟩ pianterreno *m*. **~ly** *adv* in primo luogo. **~ name** *n* nome *m* di battesimo. **~-rate** *a* ottimo

fish /fɪʃ/ *n* pesce *m* ● *vt/i* pescare. **fish out** *vt* tirar fuori

fish: **~bone** *n* lisca *f*. **~erman** *n* pescatore *m*. **~-farm** *n* vivaio *m*. **~ 'finger** *n* bastoncino *m* di pesce

fishing /'fɪʃɪŋ/ n pesca f. ~ **boat** n peschereccio m. ~**rod** n canna f da pesca

fish: ~**monger** /-mʌŋɡə(r)/ n pescivendolo m. ~**slice** n paletta f per fritti. ~**y** a (fam: suspicious) sospetto

fission /'fɪʃn/ n Phys fissione f

fist /fɪst/ n pugno m

fit¹ /fɪt/ n (attack) attacco m; (of rage) accesso m; (of generosity) slancio m

fit² a (fitter, fittest) (suitable) adatto; (healthy) in buona salute; Sport in forma; **be** ~ **to do sth** essere in grado di fare qcsa; ~ **to eat** buono da mangiare; **keep** ~ tenersi in forma

fit³ n (of clothes) taglio m; **it's a good** ~ (coat etc:) ti/le sta bene ● v (pt/pp fitted) ● vi (be the right size) andare bene; **it won't** ~ (no room) non ci sta ● vt (fix) applicare (to a); (install) installare; **it doesn't** ~ **me** (coat etc:) non mi va bene; ~ **with** fornire di. **fit in** vi (person:) adattarsi; **it won't** ~ **in** (no room) non ci sta ● vt (in schedule, vehicle) trovare un buco per

fit|ful /fɪtfl/ a irregolare. ~**fully** adv (sleep) a sprazzi. ~**ments** npl (in house) impianti mpl fissi. ~**ness** n (suitability) capacità f; [physical] ~**ness** forma f, fitness m

fitted: ~ **carpet** n moquette f inv. ~ **cupboard** n armadio m a muro; (smaller) armadietto m a muro. ~ **kitchen** n cucina f componibile. ~ **sheet** n lenzuolo m con angoli

fitter /'fɪtə(r)/ n installatore, -trice m/f

fitting /fɪtɪŋ/ a appropriato ● n (of clothes) prova f; Techn montaggio m; ~**s** pl accessori mpl. ~ **room** n camerino m

five /faɪv/ n & a cinque m. ~**r** n fam biglietto m da cinque sterline

fix /fɪks/ n (sl: drugs) pera f; **be in a** ~ fam essere nei guai ● vt fissare; (repair) aggiustare; preparare (meal). **fix up** vt fissare (meeting)

fixation /fɪk'seɪʃn/ n fissazione f

fixed /fɪkst/ a fisso

fixture /'fɪkstʃə(r)/ n Sport incontro m; ~**s and fittings** impianti mpl fissi

fizz /fɪz/ vi frizzare

fizzle /'fɪzl/ vi ~ **out** finire in nulla

fizzy /'fɪzɪ/ a gassoso. ~ **drink** n bibita f gassata

flabbergasted /'flæbəɡɑːstɪd/ a **be** ~ rimanere a bocca aperta

flabby /'flæbɪ/ a floscio

flag¹ /flæɡ/ n bandiera f ● **flag down** vt (pt/pp flagged) far segno di fermarsi a (taxi)

flag² vi (pt/pp flagged) cedere

flag-pole n asta f della bandiera

flagrant /'fleɪɡrənt/ a flagrante

flagship n Naut nave f ammiraglia; fig fiore m all'occhiello

flagstone n pietra f da lastricare

flair /fleə(r)/ n (skill) talento m; (style) stile m

flake /fleɪk/ n fiocco m ● vi |off| cadere in fiocchi

flaky /'fleɪkɪ/ a a scaglie. ~ **pastry** n pasta f sfoglia

flamboyant /flæm'bɔɪənt/ a (personality) brillante; (tie) sgargiante

flame /fleɪm/ n fiamma f

flammable /'flæməbl/ a infiammabile

flan /flæn/ n |fruit| ~ crostata f

flank /flæŋk/ n fianco m ● vt fiancheggiare

flannel /'flæn(ə)l/ n flanella f; (for washing) guanto m di spugna; ~**s** (trousers) pantaloni mpl di flanella

flannelette /flænə'let/ n flanella f di cotone

flap /flæp/ n (of pocket, envelope) risvolto m; (of table) ribalta f; **in a** ~ fam in grande agitazione ● v (pt/pp flapped) ● vi sbattere; fam agitarsi ● vt ~ **its wings** battere le ali

flare /fleə(r)/ n fiammata f; (device) razzo m ● **flare up** vi (rash:) venire fuori; (fire:) fare una fiammata; (person, situation:) esplodere. ~**d** a (garment) svasato

flash /flæʃ/ n lampo m; **in a** ~ fam in un attimo ● vi lampeggiare; ~ **past** passare come un bolide ● vt lanciare (smile); ~ **one's head-lights** lampeggiare; ~ **a torch at** puntare una torcia su

flash: ~**back** n scena f retrospettiva. ~**bulb** n Phot flash m inv. ~**er** n Auto lampeggiatore m. ~**light** n Phot flash m inv; (Am: torch) torcia f [elettrica]. ~**y** a vistoso

flask /flɑːsk/ n fiasco m; (vacuum ~) termos m inv

flat /flæt/ a (flatter, flattest) piatto; (refusal) reciso; (beer) sgassato; (battery) scarico; (tyre) a terra; **A** ~ Mus la bemolle ● n appartamento m; Mus bemolle m; (puncture) gomma f a terra m

flat: ~ **feet** npl piedi mpl piatti. ~**-fish** n pesce m piatto. ~**ly** adv (refuse) categoricamente. ~ **rate** n tariffa f unica

flatten /'flætn/ vt appiattire

flatter /'flætə(r)/ vt adulare. ~**ing** a (comments) lusinghiero; (colour, dress) che fa sembrare più bello. **~y** *n* adulazione *f*

flat 'tyre *n* gomma *f* a terra

flaunt /flɔːnt/ *vt* ostentare

flautist /'flɔːtɪst/ *n* flautista *mf*

flavour /'fleɪvə(r)/ *n* sapore *m* ● *vt* condire: **chocolate ~ed** al sapore di cioccolato. **~ing** *n* condimento *m*

flaw /flɔː/ *n* difetto *m*. **~less** *a* perfetto

flax /flæks/ *n* lino *m*. **~en** *a* ⟨hair⟩ biondo platino

flea /fliː/ *n* pulce *f*. **~ market** *n* mercato *m* delle pulci

fleck /flek/ *n* macchiolina *f*

fled /fled/ *see* **flee**

flee /fliː/ *vt/i* ⟨*pt/pp* **fled**⟩ fuggire (**from** da)

fleece /fliːs/ *n* pelliccia *f* ● *vt fam* spennare. **~y** *a* ⟨lining⟩ felpato

fleet /fliːt/ *n* flotta *f*; ⟨of cars⟩ parco *m*

fleeting /'fliːtɪŋ/ *a* **catch a ~ glance of sth** intravedere qcsa: **for a ~ moment** per un attimo

flesh /fleʃ/ *n* carne *f*: **in the ~** in persona. **~y** *a* carnoso

flew /fluː/ *see* **fly²**

flex¹ /fleks/ *vt* flettere ⟨muscle⟩

flex² *n* Electr filo *m*

flexibility /fleksɪ'bɪlətɪ/ *n* flessibilità *f*. **~le** *a* flessibile

flexitime /'fleksɪ-/ *n* orario *m* flessibile

flick /flɪk/ *vt* dare un buffetto a: **~ sth off sth** togliere qcsa da qcsa con un colpetto. **flick through** *vt* sfogliare

flicker /'flɪkə(r)/ *vi* tremolare

flier /'flaɪə(r)/ *n* = **flyer**

flight¹ /flaɪt/ *n* ⟨fleeing⟩ fuga *f*. **take ~** darsi alla fuga

flight² *n* ⟨flying⟩ volo *m*: **~ of stairs** rampa *f*

flight: ~ path *n* traiettoria *f* di volo. **~ recorder** *n* registratore *m* di volo

flighty /'flaɪtɪ/ *a* (**-ier, -iest**) frivolo

flimsy /'flɪmzɪ/ *a* (**-ier, -iest**) ⟨material⟩ leggero; ⟨shelves⟩ poco robusto; ⟨excuse⟩ debole

flinch /flɪntʃ/ *vi* ⟨wince⟩ sussultare; ⟨draw back⟩ ritirarsi; **~ from a task** *fig* sottrarsi a un compito

fling /flɪŋ/ *n* **have a ~** ⟨fam: affair⟩ aver un'avventura ● *vt* ⟨*pt/pp* **flung**⟩ gettare

flint /flɪnt/ *n* pietra *f* focaia; ⟨for lighter⟩ pietrina *f*

flip /flɪp/ *v* ⟨*pt/pp* **flipped**⟩ ● *vt* dare un colpetto a; buttare in aria ⟨coin⟩ ● *vi fam* uscire dai gangheri; ⟨go mad⟩ impazzire. **flip through** *vt* sfogliare

flippant /'flɪpənt/ *a* irriverente

flipper /'flɪpə(r)/ *n* pinna *f*

flirt /flɜːt/ *vi* civetta *f* ● *vi* flirtare

flirtation /flɜː'teɪʃn/ *n* flirt *m inv*. **~ious** /-ʃəs/ *a* civettuolo

flit /flɪt/ *vi* ⟨*pt/pp* **flitted**⟩ volteggiare

float /fləʊt/ *n* galleggiante *m*; ⟨in procession⟩ carro *m*; ⟨money⟩ riserva *f* di cassa ● *vi* galleggiare; Fin fluttuare

flock /flɒk/ *n* gregge *m*; ⟨of birds⟩ stormo *m* ● *vi* affollarsi

flog /flɒg/ *vt* ⟨*pt/pp* **flogged**⟩ bastonare; ⟨fam: sell⟩ vendere

flood /flʌd/ *n* alluvione *f*; ⟨of river⟩ straripamento *m*; ⟨fig: of letters, tears⟩ diluvio *m*; **be in ~** ⟨river:⟩ essere straripato ● *vt* allagare ● *vi* ⟨river:⟩ straripare

floodlight *n* riflettore *m* ● *vt* ⟨*pt/pp* **floodlit**⟩ illuminare con riflettori

floor /flɔː(r)/ *n* pavimento *m*; ⟨storey⟩ piano *m*; ⟨for dancing⟩ pista *f* ● *vt* ⟨baffle⟩ confondere; ⟨knock down⟩ stendere ⟨person⟩

floor: ~ board *n* asse *f* del pavimento. **~-polish** *n* cera *f* per il pavimento. **~ show** *n* spettacolo *m* di varietà

flop /flɒp/ *n fam* ⟨failure⟩ tonfo *m*; Theat fiasco *m* ● *vi* ⟨*pt/pp* **flopped**⟩ ⟨fam: fail⟩ far fiasco. **flop down** *vi* accasciarsi

floppy /'flɒpɪ/ *a* floscio. **~ disk** *n* floppy disk *m inv*. **~ |disk| drive** *n* lettore di floppy *m*

flora /'flɔːrə/ *n* flora *f*

floral /'flɔːrəl/ *a* floreale

Florence /'flɒrəns/ *n* Firenze *f*

florid /'flɒrɪd/ *a* ⟨complexion⟩ florido; ⟨style⟩ troppo ricercato

florist /'flɒrɪst/ *n* fioraio, -a *mf*

flounce /flaʊns/ *n* balza *f* ● *vi* **~ out** uscire con aria melodrammatica

flounder¹ /'flaʊndə(r)/ *vi* dibattersi; ⟨speaker:⟩ impappinarsi

flounder² *n* ⟨fish⟩ passera *f* di mare

flour /'flaʊə(r)/ *n* farina *f*

flourish /'flʌrɪʃ/ *n* gesto *m* drammatico; ⟨scroll⟩ ghirigoro *m* ● *vi* prosperare ● *vt* brandire

floury /'flaʊərɪ/ *a* farinoso

flout /flaʊt/ *vt* fregarsene di ⟨rules⟩

flow /fləʊ/ *n* flusso *m* ● *vi* scorrere; ⟨hang loosely⟩ ricadere

flower /'flaʊə(r)/ *n* fiore *m* ● *vi* fiorire

flower: ~-bed *n* aiuola *f*. **~ed** *a* a fiori. **~pot** *n* vaso *m* [per i fiori]. **~y** *a* fiorito

flown /fləʊn/ *see* **fly²**

flu /fluː/ *n* influenza *f*

fluctuat|e /'flʌktjʊeɪt/ vi fluttuare. **~ion** /-'eɪʃn/ n fluttuazione f

fluent /'flu:ənt/ a spedito; **speak ~ Italian** parlare correntemente l'italiano. **~ly** adv speditamente

fluff /flʌf/ n peluria f. **~y** a (-ier, -iest) vaporoso; (toy) di peluche

fluid /'flu:ɪd/ a fluido ● n fluido m

fluke /flu:k/ n colpo m di fortuna

flung /flʌŋ/ see **fling**

flunk /flʌŋk/ vt Am fam essere bocciato in

fluorescent /floə'resnt/ a fluorescente

fluoride /'floəraɪd/ n fluoruro m

flurry /'flʌrɪ/ n (snow) raffica f; fig agitazione f

flush /flʌʃ/ n (blush) [vampata f di] rossore m ● vi arrossire ● vt lavare con un getto d'acqua; **~ the toilet** tirare l'acqua ● a a livello (**with** di); (fam: affluent) a soldi

flustered /'flʌstəd/ a in agitazione; **get ~** mettersi in agitazione

flute /flu:t/ n flauto m

flutter /'flʌtə(r)/ n battito m ● vi svolazzare

flux /flʌks/ n **in a state of ~** in uno stato di flusso

fly¹ /flaɪ/ n (pl flies) mosca f

fly² v (pt flew, pp flown) ● vi volare; (go by plane) andare in aereo; (flag:) sventolare; (rush) precipitarsi; **~ open** spalancarsi ● vt pilotare (plane); trasportare [in aereo] (troops, supplies); volare con (Alitalia etc)

fly³ n & **flies** pl (on trousers) patta f

flyer /'flaɪə(r)/ n aviatore m; (leaflet) volantino m

flying /'flaɪɪŋ/: **~ 'buttress** n arco m rampante. **~ 'colours: with ~ colours** a pieni voti. **~ 'saucer** n disco m volante. **~ 'start: get off to a ~ start** fare un'ottima partenza. **~ 'visit** n visita f lampo

fly: ~ leaf n risguardo m. **~over** n cavalcavia m inv

foal /fəʊl/ n puledro m

foam /fəʊm/ n schiuma f; (synthetic) gommapiuma® f ● vi spumare; **~ at the mouth** far la bava alla bocca. **~ 'rubber** n gommapiuma® f

fob /fɒb/ vt (pt/pp fobbed) **~ sth off** affibbiare qcsa (**on sb** a qcno); **~ sb off** liquidare qcno

focal /'fəʊkl/ a focale

focus /'fəʊkəs/ n fuoco m; **in ~** a fuoco; **out of ~** sfocato ● v (pt/pp focused or

focussed) ● vt fig concentrare (**on** su) ● vi Phot **~ on** mettere a fuoco; fig concentrarsi (**on** su)

fodder /'fɒdə/ n foraggio m

foe /fəʊ/ n nemico, -a mf

foetus /'fi:təs/ n (pl -tuses) feto m

fog /fɒg/ n nebbia f

fogey /'fəʊgɪ/ n old **~** persona f antiquata

foggy /'fɒgɪ/ a (foggier, foggiest) nebbioso; **it's ~** c'è nebbia

'fog-horn n sirena f da nebbia

foil¹ /fɔɪl/ n lamina f di metallo

foil² vt (thwart) frustrare

foil³ n (sword) fioretto m

foist /fɔɪst/ vt appioppare (**on sb** a qcno)

fold¹ /fəʊld/ n (for sheep) ovile m

fold² n piega f ● vt piegare; **~ one's arms** incrociare le braccia ● vi piegarsi; (fail) crollare. **fold up** vt ripiegare (chair) ● vi essere pieghevole; (fam: business:) collassare

fold|er /'fəʊldə(r)/ n cartella f. **~ing** a pieghevole

foliage /'fəʊlɪɪdʒ/ n fogliame m

folk /fəʊk/ npl gente f; **my ~s** (family) i miei; **hello there ~s** ciao a tutti

folk: ~-dance n danza f popolare. **~lore** n folclore m. **~-song** n canto m popolare

follow /'fɒləʊ/ vt/i seguire; **it doesn't ~** non è necessariamente così; **~ suit** fig fare lo stesso; **as ~s** come segue. **follow up** vt fare seguito a (letter)

follow|er /'fɒləʊə(r)/ n seguace mf. **~ing** a seguente ● n seguito m; (supporters) seguaci mpl ● prep in seguito a

folly /'fɒlɪ/ n follia f

fond /fɒnd/ a affezionato m; (hope) vivo; **be ~ of** essere appassionato di (music); **I'm ~ of...** (food, person) mi piace moltissimo...

fondle /'fɒndl/ vt coccolare

fondness /'fɒndnɪs/ n affetto m; (for things) amore m

font /fɒnt/ n fonte f battesimale; Typ carattere m di stampa

food /fu:d/ n cibo m; (for animals, groceries) mangiare m; **let's buy some ~** compriamo qualcosa da mangiare

food: ~ mixer n frullatore m. **~ poisoning** n intossicazione f alimentare. **~ processor** n tritatutto m inv elettrico

fool¹ /fu:l/ n sciocco, -a mf; **she's no ~** non è una stupida; **make a ~ of**

oneself rendersi ridicolo ● *vt* prendere in giro ● *vi* ~ **around** giocare; ⟨*husband, wife:*⟩ avere l'amante

fool² *n Culin* crema *f*

'fool|hardy *a* temerario. ~**ish** *a* stolto. ~**ishly** *adv* sciocamente. ~**ishness** *n* sciocchezza *f*. ~**proof** *a* facilissimo

foot /fʊt/ *n* (*pl* **feet**) piede *m*; ⟨*of animal*⟩ zampa *f*; (*measure*) piede *m* (= 30,48 *cm*); on ~ a piedi; on one's feet in piedi; **put one's ~ in it** *fam* fare una gaffe

foot: ~**-and-'mouth disease** *n* afta *f* epizootica. ~**ball** *n* calcio *m*; (*ball*) pallone *m*. ~**baller** *n* giocatore *m* di calcio. ~**ball pools** *npl* ≈ totocalcio *m*. ~**-brake** *n* freno *m* a pedale. ~**-bridge** *n* passerella *f*. ~**hills** *npl* colline *fpl* pedemontane. ~**hold** *n* punto *m* d'appoggio. ~**ing** *n* **lose one's** ~**ing** perdere l'appiglio; **on an equal** ~**ing** in condizioni di parità. ~**man** *n* valletto *m*. ~**note** *n* nota *f* a piè di pagina. ~**path** *n* sentiero *m*. ~**print** *n* orma *f*. ~**step** *n* passo *m*; **follow in sb's** ~**steps** *fig* seguire l'esempio di qcno. ~**stool** *n* sgabellino *m*. ~**wear** *n* calzature *fpl*

for /fə(r)/, *accentato* /fɔː(r)/ *prep* per; ~ **this reason** per questa ragione; **I have lived here** ~ **ten years** vivo qui da dieci anni; ~ **supper** per cena; ~ **all that** nonostante questo; **what** ~? a che scopo?; **send** ~ **a doctor** chiamare un dottore; **fight** ~ **a cause** lottare per una causa; **go** ~ **a walk** andare a fare una passeggiata; **there's no need** ~ **you to go** non c'è bisogno che tu vada; **it's not** ~ **me to say** non sta a me dirlo; **now you're** ~ **it** ora sei nei pasticci ● *conj* poiché, perché

forage /'fɒrɪdʒ/ *n* foraggio *m* ● *vi* ~ **for** cercare

forbade /fə'bæd/ *see* **forbid**

forbear|ance /fɔː'beərəns/ *n* pazienza *f*. ~**ing** *a* tollerante

forbid /fə'bɪd/ *vt* (*pt* **forbade**, *pp* **forbidden**) proibire. ~**ding** *a* ⟨*prospect*⟩ che spaventa; ⟨*stern*⟩ severo

force /fɔːs/ *n* in forza *f*; **in** ~ in vigore; (*in large numbers*) in massa; **come into** ~ entrare in vigore; **the** ⟨*armed*⟩ ~**s** *pl* le forze armate ● *vt* forzare; ~ **sth on sb** ⟨*decision*⟩ imporre qcsa a qcno; ⟨*drink*⟩ costringere qcno a fare qcsa

forced /fɔːst/ *a* forzato

force: ~**-feed** *vt* (*pt*/*pp* **-fed**) nutrire a forza. ~**ful** *a* energico. ~**fully** *adv* ⟨*say, argue*⟩ con forza

forceps /'fɔːseps/ *npl* forcipe *m*

forcible /'fɔːsɪbl/ *a* forzato

ford /fɔːd/ *n* guado *m* ● *vt* guadare

fore /fɔː(r)/ *n* **to the** ~ in vista; **come to the** ~ salire alla ribalta

fore: ~**arm** *n* avambraccio *m*. ~**boding** /-'bəʊdɪŋ/ *n* presentimento *m*. ~**cast** *n* previsione *f* ● *vt* (*pt*/*pp* ~**cast**) prevedere. ~**court** *n* cortile *m* anteriore. ~**fathers** *npl* antenati *mpl*. ~**finger** *n* [dito *m*] indice *m*. ~**front** *n* **be in the** ~**front** essere all'avanguardia. ~**gone** *a* **be a** ~**gone conclusion** essere una cosa scontata. ~**ground** *n* primo piano *m*. ~**head** /'fɔːhed, 'fɒrɪd/ *n* fronte *f*. ~**hand** *n Tennis* diritto *m*

foreign /'fɒrən/ *a* straniero; ⟨*trade*⟩ estero; (*not belonging*) estraneo; **he is** ~ è uno straniero. ~ **currency** *n* valuta *f* estera. ~**er** *n* straniero, -a *mf*. ~ **language** *n* lingua *f* straniera

Foreign: ~ **Office** *n* ministero *m* degli [affari] esteri. ~ '**Secretary** *n* ministro *m* degli esteri

fore: ~**man** *n* caporeparto *m*. ~**most** *a* principale ● *adv* **first and** ~**most** in primo luogo. ~**name** *n* nome *m* di battesimo

forensic /fə'rensɪk/ *a* ~ **medicine** medicina *f* legale

'forerunner *n* precursore *m*

fore'see *vt* (*pt* **-saw**, *pp* **-seen**) prevedere. ~**able** /-əbl/ *a* **in the** ~**able future** in futuro per quanto si possa prevedere

'foresight *n* previdenza *f*

forest /'fɒrɪst/ *n* foresta *f*. ~**er** *n* guardia *f* forestale

fore'stall *vt* prevenire

forestry /'fɒrɪstrɪ/ *n* silvicoltura *f*

'foretaste *n* pregustazione *f*

fore'tell *vt* (*pt*/*pp* **-told**) predire

forever /fə'revə(r)/ *adv* per sempre; **he's** ~ **complaining** si lamenta sempre

fore'warn *vt* avvertire

foreword /'fɔːwɜːd/ *n* prefazione *f*

forfeit /'fɔːfɪt/ *n* (*in game*) pegno *m*; *Jur* penalità *f* ● *vt* perdere

forgave /fə'geɪv/ *see* **forgive**

forge¹ /fɔːdʒ/ *vi* ~ **ahead** ⟨*runner:*⟩ lasciarsi indietro gli altri; *fig* farsi strada

forge² *n* fucina *f* ● *vt* fucinare; (*counterfeit*) contraffare. ~**r** *n* contraffattore *m*. ~**ry** *n* contraffazione *f*

forget /fə'get/ *vt*/*i* (*pt* **-got**, *pp* **-gotten**, *pres p* **-getting**) dimenticare; dimenticarsi di ⟨*language, skill*⟩. ~**table** /-əbl/

a ⟨*day, film*⟩ da dimenticare. **~ful** *a* smemorato. **~fulness** *n* smemoratezza *f.* **~me-not** *n* non-ti-scordar-dimé *m inv*

forgive /fə'gɪv/ *vt* (*pt* -**gave**, *pp* -**given**) **~ sb for sth** perdonare qcno per qcsa. **~ness** *n* perdono *m*

forgo /fɔː'gəʊ/ *vt* (*pt* -**went**, *pp* -**gone**) rinunciare a

forgot(ten) /fə'gɒt(n)/ *see* **forget**

fork /fɔːk/ *n* forchetta *f*; (*for digging*) forca *f*; (*in road*) bivio *m* ● *vi* ⟨*road:*⟩ biforcarsi; **~ right** prendere a destra. **fork out** *vt fam* sborsare

fork-lift 'truck *n* elevatore *m*

forlorn /fə'lɔːn/ *a* ⟨*look*⟩ perduto; ⟨*place*⟩ derelitto; **~ hope** speranza *f* vana

form /fɔːm/ *n* forma *f*; (*document*) modulo *m*; *Sch* classe *f* ● *vt* formare; (*opinion*) ● *vi* formarsi

formal /'fɔːml/ *a* formale. **~ity** /-'mælətɪ/ *n* formalità *f inv*. **~ly** *adv* in modo formale; (*officially*) ufficialmente

format /'fɔːmæt/ *n* formato *m* ● *vt* formattare ⟨*disk, page*⟩

formation /fɔː'meɪʃn/ *n* formazione *f*

formative /'fɔːmətɪv/ *a* **~ years** anni *mpl* formativi

former /'fɔːmə(r)/ *a* precedente; ⟨*PM, colleague*⟩ ex: **the ~, the latter** il primo, l'ultimo. **~ly** *adv* precedentemente; (*in olden times*) in altri tempi

formidable /'fɔːmɪdəbl/ *a* formidabile

formula /'fɔːmjʊlə/ *n* (*pl* -**ae** /-liː/ *or* -**s**) formula *f*

formulate /'fɔːmjʊleɪt/ *vt* formulare

forsake /fə'seɪk/ *vt* (*pt* -**sook** /-sʊk/, *pp* -**saken**) abbandonare

fort /fɔːt/ *n Mil* forte *m*

forte /'fɔːteɪ/ *n* [pezzo *m*] forte *m*

forth /fɔːθ/ *adv* **back and ~** avanti e indietro; **and so ~** e così via

forth: ~'coming *a* prossimo; (*communicative*) comunicativo; **no response was ~** non arrivava nessuna risposta. **~right** *a* schietto. **~'with** *adv* immediatamente

fortieth /'fɔːtɪɪθ/ *a & n* quarantesimo, -a *mf*

fortification /fɔːtɪfɪ'keɪʃn/ *n* fortificazione *f*

fortify /'fɔːtɪfaɪ/ *vt* (*pt/pp* -**ied**) fortificare; *fig* rendere forte

fortnight /'fɔːt-/ *Br n* quindicina *f*. **~ly** *a* bimensile ● *adv* ogni due settimane

fortress /'fɔːtrɪs/ *n* fortezza *f*

fortuitous /fɔː'tjuːɪtəs/ *a* fortuito

fortunate /'fɔːtʃənət/ *a* fortunato;

that's ~! meno male!. **~ly** *adv* fortunatamente

fortune /'fɔːtʃuːn/ *n* fortuna *f*. **~-teller** *n* indovino, -a *mf*

forty /'fɔːtɪ/ *a & n* quaranta *m*

forum /'fɔːrəm/ *n* foro *m*

forward /'fɔːwəd/ *adv* avanti; (*towards the front*) in avanti ● *a* in avanti: (*presumptuous*) sfacciato ● *n Sport* attaccante *m* ● *vt* inoltrare ⟨*letter*⟩; spedire ⟨*goods*⟩. **~s** *adv* avanti

fossil /'fɒsl/ *n* fossile *m*. **~ized** *a* fossile; (*ideas*) fossilizzato

foster /'fɒstə(r)/ *vt* allevare ⟨*child*⟩. **~-child** *n* figlio, -a *mf* in affidamento. **~-mother** *n* madre *f* affidataria

fought /fɔːt/ *see* **fight**

foul /faʊl/ *a* ⟨*smell, taste*⟩ cattivo; ⟨*air*⟩ viziato; ⟨*language*⟩ osceno; ⟨*mood, weather*⟩ orrendo; **~ play** *Jur* delitto *m* ● *n Sport* fallo *m* ● *vt* inquinare ⟨*water*⟩; *Sport* commettere un fallo contro; ⟨*nets, rope:*⟩ impigliarsi in. **~-smelling** *a* puzzo

found[1] /faʊnd/ *see* **find**

found[2] *vt* fondare

foundation /faʊn'deɪʃn/ *n* (*basis*) fondamento *m*; (*charitable*) fondazione *f*. **~s** *pl* (*of building*) fondamenta *fpl*: **lay the ~-stone** porre la prima pietra

founder[1] /'faʊndə(r)/ *n* fondatore, -trice *mf*

founder[2] *vi* ⟨*ship:*⟩ affondare

foundry /'faʊndrɪ/ *n* fonderia *f*

fountain /'faʊntɪn/ *n* fontana *f*. **~-pen** *n* penna *f* stilografica

four /fɔː(r)/ *a & n* quattro *m*

four: ~-poster *n* letto *m* a baldacchino. **~some** /'fɔːsəm/ *n* quartetto *m*. **~ teen** *a & n* quattordici *m*. **~'teenth** *a & n* quattordicesimo, -a *mf*

fourth /fɔːθ/ *a & n* quarto, -a *mf*

fowl /faʊl/ *n* pollame *m*

fox /fɒks/ *n* volpe *f* ● *vt* (*puzzle*) ingannare

foyer /'fɔɪeɪ/ *n Theat* ridotto *m*; (*in hotel*) salone *m* d'ingresso

fraction /'frækʃn/ *n* frazione *f*

fracture /'fræktʃə(r)/ *n* frattura *f* ● *vt* fratturare ● *vi* fratturarsi

fragile /'frædʒaɪl/ *a* fragile

fragment /'frægmənt/ *n* frammento *m*. **~ary** *a* frammentario

fragran|ce /'freɪgrəns/ *n* fragranza *f*. **~t** *a* fragrante

frail /freɪl/ *a* gracile

frame /freɪm/ *n* (*of picture, door, window*) cornice *f*; (*of spectacles*) montatura *f; Anat* ossatura *f; (structure, of bike)* telaio *m;* ~ **of mind** stato *m* d'animo ● *vt* incorniciare *(picture); fig* formulare; *(sl: incriminate)* montare. ~**work** *n* struttura *f*

franc /fræŋk/ *n* franco *m*

France /frɑːns/ *n* Francia *f*

franchise /ˈfræntʃaɪz/ *n Pol* diritto *m* di voto; *Comm* franchigia *f*

frank[1] /fræŋk/ *vt* affrancare *(letter)*

frank[2] *a* franco. ~**ly** *adv* francamente

frankfurter /ˈfræŋkfɜːtə(r)/ *n* würstel *m inv*

frantic /ˈfræntɪk/ *a* frenetico; **be** ~ **with worry** essere agitatissimo. ~**ally** *adv* freneticamente

fraternal /frəˈtɜːnl/ *a* fraterno

fraud /frɔːd/ *n* frode *f; (person)* impostore *m.* ~**ulent** /-jʊlənt/ *a* fraudolento

fraught /frɔːt/ *a* ~ **with** pieno di

fray[1] /freɪ/ *n* mischia *f*

fray[2] *vi* sfilacciarsi

frayed /freɪd/ *a (cuffs)* sfilacciato; *(nerves)* a pezzi

freak /friːk/ *n* fenomeno *m; (person)* scherzo *m* di natura; *(fam: weird person)* tipo *m* strambo ● *a* anormale. ~**ish** *a* strambo

freckle /ˈfrekl/ *n* lentiggine *f.* ~**d** *a* lentigginoso

free /friː/ *a* (**freer**, **freest**) libero; *(ticket, copy)* gratuito; *(lavish)* generoso; ~ **of charge** gratuito; **set** ~ liberare ● *vt (pt/pp freed)* liberare

free: ~**dom** *n* libertà *f.* ~**hand** *adv* a mano libera. ~**hold** *n* proprietà *f* [fondiaria] assoluta. ~ **'kick** *n* calcio *m* di punizione. ~**lance** *a & adv* indipendente. ~**ly** *adv* liberamente; *(generously)* generosamente; **I** ~**ly admit that...** devo ammettere che.... **F~mason** *n* massone *m.* ~**range** *a* ~**range egg** uovo *m* di gallina ruspante. ~**'sample** *n* campione *m* gratuito. ~**style** *n* stile *m* libero. ~**way** *n Am* autostrada *f.* ~**'wheel** *vi (car:) (in neutral)* andare in folle; *(with engine switched off)* andare a motore spento; *(bicycle:)* andare a ruota libera

freez|e /friːz/ *vt (pt froze, pp frozen)* gelare; bloccare *(wages)* ● *vi (water:)* gelare; **it's ~ing** si gela; **my hands are** ~**ing** ho le mani congelate

freez|er /ˈfriːzə(r)/ *n* freezer *m inv,* congelatore *m.* ~**ing** *a* gelido ● *n* **below** ~**ing** sotto zero

freight /freɪt/ *n* carico *m.* ~**er** *n* nave *f* da carico. ~ **'train** *n Am* treno *m* merci

French /frentʃ/ *a* francese ● *n (language)* francese *m;* **the** ~ *pl* i francesi *mpl*

French: ~ **'beans** *npl* fagiolini *mpl* [verdi]. ~ **'bread** *n* filone *m (di pane).* ~ **'fries** *npl* patate *fpl* fritte. ~**man** *n* francese *m.* ~ **'window** *n* porta-finestra *f.* ~**woman** *n* francese *f*

frenzied /ˈfrenzɪd/ *a* frenetico

frenzy /ˈfrenzɪ/ *n* frenesia *f*

frequency /ˈfriːkwənsɪ/ *n* frequenza *f*

frequent[1] /ˈfriːkwənt/ *a* frequente. ~**ly** *adv* frequentemente

frequent[2] /frɪˈkwent/ *vt* frequentare

fresco /ˈfreskəʊ/ *n* affresco *m*

fresh /freʃ/ *a* a fresco; *(new)* nuovo; *(Am: cheeky)* sfacciato. ~**ly** *adv* di recente

freshen /ˈfreʃn/ *vi (wind:)* rinfrescare. **freshen up** *vt* dare una rinfrescata a ● *vi* rinfrescarsi

freshness /ˈfreʃnɪs/ *n* freschezza *f*

'freshwater *a* di acqua dolce

fret /fret/ *vi (pt/pp fretted)* inquietarsi. ~**ful** *a* irritabile

'fretsaw *n* seghetto *m* da traforo

friar /ˈfraɪə(r)/ *n* frate *m*

friction /ˈfrɪkʃn/ *n* frizione *f*

Friday /ˈfraɪdeɪ/ *n* venerdì *m inv*

fridge /frɪdʒ/ *n* frigo *m*

fried /fraɪd/ *see* **fry** ● *a* fritto; ~ **egg** uovo *m* fritto

friend /frend/ *n* amico, -a *mf.* ~**ly** *a* (**-ier**, **-iest**) *(relations, meeting, match)* amichevole; *(neighbourhood, smile)* piacevole; *(software)* di facile uso; **be** ~**ly with** essere amico di. ~**ship** *n* amicizia *f*

frieze /friːz/ *n* fregio *m*

fright /fraɪt/ *n* paura *f;* **take** ~ spaventarsi

frighten /ˈfraɪtn/ *vt* spaventare. ~**ed** *a* spaventato; **be** ~**ed** aver paura **(of** di). ~**ing** *a* spaventoso

frightful /ˈfraɪtfʊl/ *a* terribile

frigid /ˈfrɪdʒɪd/ *a* frigido. ~**ity** /-ˈdʒɪdətɪ/ *n* freddezza *f; Psych* frigidità *f*

frill /frɪl/ *n* volant *m inv.* ~**y** *a (dress)* con tanti volant

fringe /frɪndʒ/ *n* frangia *f; (of hair)* frangetta *f, (fig: edge)* margine *m.* ~ **benefits** *npl* benefici *mpl* supplementari

frisk /frɪsk/ *vt (search)* perquisire

frisky /ˈfrɪskɪ/ *a* (**-ier**, **-iest**) vispo

fritter /ˈfrɪtə(r)/ *n* frittella *f* ● **fritter away** *vt* sprecare

frivol|ity /frɪˈvɒlətɪ/ *n* frivolezza *f.* ~**ous** /ˈfrɪvələs/ *a* frivolo

frizzy /'frɪzɪ/ a crespo

fro /frəʊ/ see **to**

frock /frɒk/ n abito m

frog /frɒg/ n rana f. ~**man** n uomo m rana

frolic /'frɒlɪk/ vi (pt/pp **frolicked**) ⟨lambs:⟩ sgambettare; ⟨people:⟩ folleggiare

from /frɒm/ prep da; ~ **Monday** da lunedì; ~ **that day** da quel giorno; **he's** ~ **London** è di Londra; **this is a letter** ~ **my brother** questa è una lettera di mio fratello; **documents** ~ **the 16th century** documenti del XVI secolo; **made** ~ fatto con; **she felt ill** ~ **fatigue** si sentiva male dalla stanchezza; ~ **now on** d'ora in poi

front /frʌnt/ n parte f anteriore; ⟨fig: organization etc⟩ facciata f, ⟨of garment⟩ davanti m; ⟨sea~⟩ lungomare m; Mil, Pol, Meteorol fronte m; **in** ~ **of** davanti a; **in or at the** ~ davanti; **to the** ~ ● a davanti; ⟨page, row, wheel⟩ anteriore

frontal /'frʌntl/ a frontale

front: ~ '**door** n porta f d'entrata. ~ 'garden n giardino m d'avanti

frontier /frʌntɪə(r)/ n frontiera f

front-wheel 'drive n trazione f anteriore

frost /frɒst/ n gelo m; ⟨hoar~⟩ brina f. ~**bite** n congelamento m. ~**bitten** a congelato

frost|ed /'frɒstɪd/ a ~**ed glass** vetro m smerigliato. ~**ily** adv gelidamente. ~**ing** n Am Culin glassa f. ~**y** a also fig gelido

froth /frɒθ/ n schiuma f ● vi far schiuma. ~**y** a schiumoso

frown /fraʊn/ n cipiglio m ● vi aggrottare le sopracciglia. **frown on** vt disapprovare

froze /frəʊz/ see **freeze**

frozen /'frəʊzn/ see **freeze** ● a ⟨corpse, hand⟩ congelato; ⟨wastes⟩ gelido; Culin surgelato; **I'm** ~ sono gelato. ~ **food** n surgelati mpl

frugal /'fru:gl/ a frugale

fruit /fru:t/ n frutto m; ⟨collectively⟩ frutta f; **eat more** ~ mangia più frutta. ~ **cake** n dolce m con frutta candita

fruit|erer /'fru:tərə(r)/ n fruttivendolo, -a mf. ~**ful** a fig fruttuoso

fruition /fru:'ɪʃn/ n **come to** ~ dare dei frutti

fruit: ~ **juice** n succo m di frutta. ~**less** a infruttuoso. ~ **machine** n

macchinetta f mangiasoldi. ~ 'salad n macedonia f ⟨di frutta⟩

frumpy /'frʌmpɪ/ a sciatto

frustrat|e /frʌ'streɪt/ vt frustrare; rovinare ⟨plans⟩. ~**ing** a frustrante. ~**ion** /-eɪʃn/ n frustrazione f

fry¹ /fraɪ/ vt/i (pt/pp **fried**) friggere

fry² /fraɪ/ n inv **small** ~ fig pesce m piccolo

frying pan n padella f

fuck /fʌk/ vulg vt/i scopare ● int cazzo. ~**ing** a del cazzo

fuddy-duddy /'fʌdɪdʌdɪ/ n fam matusa mf inv

fudge /fʌdʒ/ n caramella f a base di zucchero, burro e latte

fuel /'fju:əl/ n carburante m; fig nutrimento m ● vt fig alimentare

fugitive /'fju:dʒɪtɪv/ n fuggiasco, -a f

fugue /fju:g/ n Mus fuga f

fulfil /fʊl'fɪl/ vt (pt/pp -**filled**) soddisfare ⟨conditions, need⟩; realizzare ⟨dream, desire⟩; ~ **oneself** realizzarsi. ~**ling** a soddisfacente. ~**ment** n **sense of** ~**ment** senso m di appagamento

full /fʊl/ a pieno ⟨of di⟩; ⟨detailed⟩ esauriente; ⟨bus, hotel⟩ completo; ⟨skirt⟩ ampio; **at** ~ **speed** a tutta velocità; **in** ~ **swing** in pieno fervore ● n **in** ~ per intero

full: ~ '**moon** n luna f piena. ~-**scale** a ⟨model⟩ in scala reale; ⟨alert⟩ di massima gravità. ~ '**stop** n punto m. ~-'**time** a & adv a tempo pieno

fully /'fʊlɪ/ adv completamente; ⟨in detail⟩ dettagliatamente; ~ **booked** ⟨hotel, restaurant⟩ tutto prenotato

fumble /'fʌmbl/ vi ~ **in** rovistare in; ~ **with** armeggiare con; ~ **for one's keys** rovistare alla ricerca delle chiavi

fume /fju:m/ vi ⟨be angry⟩ essere furioso

fumes /'fju:mz/ npl fumi mpl; ⟨from car⟩ gas mpl di scarico

fumigate /'fju:mɪgeɪt/ vt suffumicare

fun /fʌn/ n divertimento m; **for** ~ per ridere; **make** ~ **of** prendere in giro; **have** ~ divertirsi

function /'fʌŋkʃn/ n funzione f; ⟨event⟩ cerimonia f ● vi funzionare; ~ **as** ⟨serve as⟩ funzionare da. ~**al** a funzionale

fund /fʌnd/ n fondo m; fig pozzo m; ~**s** pl fondi mpl ● vt finanziare

fundamental /fʌndə'mentl/ a fondamentale

funeral /'fju:nərəl/ n funerale m

funeral: ~ **directors** n impresa f di pompe funebri. ~ **home** Am, ~

parlour n camera f ardente. ~ **march** n marcia f funebre. ~ **service** n rito m funebre

'funfair n luna park m inv

fungus /'fʌŋɡəs/ n (pl -gi /-ɡaɪ/) fungo m

funicular /fju:'nɪkjʊlə(r)/ n funicolare f

funnel /'fʌnl/ n imbuto m; (on ship) ciminiera f

funnily /'fʌnɪlɪ/ adv comicamente; (oddly) stranamente; ~ **enough** strano a dirsi

funny /'fʌnɪ/ a (-ier, -iest) buffo; (odd) strano. ~ **business** n affare m losco

fur /fɜ:(r)/ n pelo m; (for clothing) pelliccia f; (in kettle) deposito m. ~ **'coat** n pelliccia f

furious /'fjʊərɪəs/ a furioso

furnace /'fɜ:nɪs/ n fornace f

furnish /'fɜ:nɪʃ/ vt ammobiliare ⟨flat⟩; fornire ⟨supplies⟩. ~**ed** a ~**ed room** stanza f ammobiliata. ~**ings** npl mobili mpl

furniture /'fɜ:nɪtʃə(r)/ n mobili mpl

furred /fɜ:d/ a ⟨tongue⟩ impastato

furrow /'fʌrəʊ/ n solco m

furry /'fɜ:rɪ/ a ⟨animal⟩ peloso; ⟨toy⟩ di peluche

further /'fɜ:ðə(r)/ a (additional) ulteriore; at the ~ **end** all'altra estremità; **until** ~ **notice** fino a nuovo avviso ● adv più lontano; ~**,...** inoltre,...; ~ **off** più lontano ● vt promuovere

further: ~ **edu'cation** n ≈ formazione f parauniversitaria. ~**'more** adv per di più

furthest /'fɜ:ðɪst/ a più lontano ● adv più lontano

furtive /'fɜ:tɪv/ a furtivo

fury /'fjʊərɪ/ n furore m

fuse[1] /fju:z/ n (of bomb) detonatore m; (cord) miccia f

fuse[2] n Electr fusibile m ● vt fondere; Electr far saltare ● vi fondersi; Electr saltare; **the lights have** ~**d** sono saltate le luci. ~**-box** n scatola f dei fusibili

fuselage /'fju:zəlɑ:ʒ/ n Aeron fusoliera f

fusion /'fju:ʒn/ n fusione f

fuss /fʌs/ n storie fpl; **make a** ~ fare storie; **make a** ~ **of** colmare di attenzioni ● vi fare storie

fussy /'fʌsɪ/ a (-ier, -iest) ⟨person⟩ difficile da accontentare; ⟨clothes etc⟩ pieno di fronzoli

fusty /'fʌstɪ/ a che odora di stantio; ⟨smell⟩ di stantio

futile /'fju:taɪl/ a inutile. ~**ity** /-'tɪlətɪ/ n futilità f

future /'fju:tʃə(r)/ a & n futuro; **in** ~ in futuro. ~ **perfect** futuro m anteriore

futuristic /fju:tʃə'rɪstɪk/ a futuristico

fuzz /fʌz/ n **the** ~ (sl: police) la pula

fuzzy /'fʌzɪ/ a (-ier, -iest) ⟨hair⟩ crespo; ⟨photo⟩ sfuocato

Gg

gab /ɡæb/ n fam **have the gift of the** ~ avere la parlantina

gabble /'ɡæb(ə)l/ vi parlare troppo in fretta

gad /ɡæd/ vi (pt/pp gadded) ~ **about** andarsene in giro

gadget /'ɡædʒɪt/ n aggeggio m

Gaelic /'ɡeɪlɪk/ a & n gaelico m

gaffe /ɡæf/ n gaffe f inv

gag /ɡæɡ/ n bavaglio m; (joke) battuta f ● vt (pt/pp gagged) imbavagliare

gaily /'ɡeɪlɪ/ adv allegramente

gain /ɡeɪn/ n guadagno m; (increase) aumento m ● vt acquisire; ~ **weight** aumentare di peso; ~ **access** accedere ● vi ⟨clock:⟩ andare avanti. ~**ful** a ~**ful employment** lavoro m remunerativo

gait /ɡeɪt/ n andatura f

gala /'ɡɑ:lə/ n gala f; **swimming** ~ manifestazione f di nuoto ● attrib di gala

galaxy /'ɡæləksɪ/ n galassia f

gale /ɡeɪl/ n bufera f

gall /ɡɔ:l/ n (impudence) impudenza f

gallant /'ɡælənt/ a coraggioso; (chivalrous) galante. ~**ry** n coraggio m

'gall-bladder n cistifellea f

gallery /'ɡælərɪ/ n galleria f

galley /'ɡælɪ/ n (ship's kitchen) cambusa f; ~ [**proof**] bozza f in colonna

gallivant /'ɡælɪvænt/ vi fam andare in giro

gallon /'gælən/ n gallone m (= 4,5 l; Am = 3,7 l)

gallop /'gæləp/ n galoppo m ●vi galoppare

gallows /'gæləʊz/ n forca f

'gallstone n calcolo m biliare

galore /gə'lɔ:(r)/ adv a bizzeffe

galvanize /'gælvənaɪz/ vt Techn galvanizzare; fig stimolare (**into** a)

gambit /'gæmbɪt/ n prima mossa f

gamble /'gæmbl/ n (risk) azzardo m ●vi giocare; (on Stock Exchange) speculare; ~ **on** (rely) contare su. ~**r** n giocatore, -trice mf [d'azzardo]. ~**ing** n gioco m [d'azzardo]

game /geɪm/ n gioco m; (match) partita f; (animals, birds) selvaggina f; ~**s** Sch ≈ ginnastica f ●a (brave) coraggioso; **are you ~?** ti va?; **be ~ for** essere pronto per. ~**keeper** n guardacaccia m inv

gammon /'gæmən/ n coscia f di maiale

gamut /'gæmət/ n fig gamma f

gander /'gændə(r)/ n oca f maschio

gang /gæŋ/ n banda f; (of workmen) squadra f ● **gang up** vi far comunella (**on** contro)

gangling /'gæŋglɪŋ/ a spilungone

gangrene /'gæŋgri:n/ n cancrena f

gangster /'gæŋstə(r)/ n gangster m inv

gangway /'gæŋweɪ/ n passaggio m; Naut, Aeron passerella f

gaol /dʒeɪl/ n carcere m ●vt incarcerare. ~**er** n carceriere m

gap /gæp/ n spazio m; (in ages, between teeth) scarto m; (in memory) vuoto m; (in story) punto m oscuro

gaple /geɪp/ vi stare a bocca aperta; (be wide open) spalancarsi; ~**e** at guardare a bocca aperta. ~**ing** a aperto

garage /'gærɑ:ʒ/ n garage m inv; (for repairs) meccanico m; (for petrol) stazione f di servizio

garbage /'gɑ:bɪdʒ/ n immondizia f; (nonsense) idiozie fpl. **can** n Am bidone m dell'immondizia

garbled /'gɑ:bld/ a confuso

garden /'gɑ:dn/ n giardino m; [public] ~**s** pl giardini mpl pubblici ● **centre** n negozio m di piante e articoli da giardinaggio. ~**er** n giardiniere, -a mf. ~**ing** n giardinaggio m

gargle /'gɑ:gl/ n gargarismo m ●vi fare gargarismi

gargoyle /'gɑ:gɔɪl/ n gargouille f inv

garish /'geərɪʃ/ a sgargiante

garland /'gɑ:lənd/ n ghirlanda f

garlic /'gɑ:lɪk/ n aglio m. ~ **bread** n pane m condito con aglio

garment /'gɑ:mənt/ n indumento m

garnish /'gɑ:nɪʃ/ n guarnizione f ●vt guarnire

garrison /'gærɪsn/ n guarnigione f

garter /'gɑ:tə(r)/ n giarrettiera f; (Am: on man's sock) reggicalze m inv da uomo

gas /gæs/ n gas m inv; (Am fam: petrol) benzina f ●v (pt/pp **gassed**) ●vt asfissiare ●vi fam blaterare. ~ **cooker** n cucina a gas. ~ **'fire** n stufa f a gas

gash /gæʃ/ n taglio m ●vt tagliare

gasket /'gæskɪt/ n Techn guarnizione f

gas: ~ **mask** n maschera f antigas. ~**-meter** n contatore m del gas

gasoline /'gæsəli:n/ n Am benzina f

gasp /gɑ:sp/ vi avere il fiato mozzato

gas station n Am distributore m di benzina

gastric /'gæstrɪk/ a gastrico. ~ **'flu** n influenza f gastro-intestinale. ~ **'ulcer** n ulcera f gastrica

gastronomy /gæ'strɒnəmɪ/ n gastronomia f

gate /geɪt/ n cancello m; (at airport) uscita f

gâteau /'gætəʊ/ n torta f

gate: ~**crash** vt entrare senza invito a. ~**crasher** n intruso, -a mf. ~**way** n ingresso m

gather /'gæðə(r)/ vt raccogliere; (conclude) dedurre; (in sewing) arricciare; ~ **speed** acquistare velocità; ~ **together** radunare (people, belongings); (obtain gradually) acquistare ●vi (people) radunarsi. ~**ing** n **family** ~**ing** ritrovo m di famiglia

gaudy /'gɔ:dɪ/ a (-ier, -iest) pacchiano

gauge /geɪdʒ/ n calibro m; Rail scartamento m; (device) indicatore m ●vt misurare; fig stimare

gaunt /gɔ:nt/ a (thin) smunto

gauze /gɔ:z/ n garza f

gave /geɪv/ see **give**

gawky /'gɔ:kɪ/ a (-ier, -iest) sgraziato

gawp /gɔ:p/ vi [at] fam guardare con aria da ebete

gay /geɪ/ a gaio; (homosexual) omosessuale; (bar, club) gay

gaze /geɪz/ n sguardo m fisso ●vi guardare; ~ **at** fissare

GB abbr (**Great Britain**) GB

gear /gɪə(r)/ n equipaggiamento m; Techn ingranaggio m; Auto marcia f; **in** ~ con la marcia innestata; **change** ~ cambiare marcia ●vt finalizzare (**to** a)

gear: ~**box** n Auto scatola f del

cambio. ~**-lever** n. Am ~**-shift** n leva f del cambio

geese /giːs/ see goose

geezer /'giːzə(r)/ n sl tipo m

gel /dʒel/ n gel m inv

gelatine /'dʒelətɪn/ n gelatina f

gelignite /'dʒelɪgnaɪt/ n gelatina f esplosiva

gem /dʒem/ n gemma f

Gemini /'dʒemɪnaɪ/ n Astr Gemelli mpl

gender /'dʒendə(r)/ n Gram genere m

gene /dʒiːn/ n gene m

genealogy /dʒiːnɪˈælədʒɪ/ n genealogia f

general /'dʒenrəl/ a generale ● n generale m; in ~ in generale. ~ **election** n elezioni fpl politiche

generaliz|ation /dʒenrəlaɪˈzeɪʃn/ n generalizzazione f. ~**e** /'dʒenrəlaɪz/ vi generalizzare

generally /'dʒenrəlɪ/ adv generalmente

general prac'titioner n medico m generico

generate /'dʒenəreɪt/ vt generare

generation /dʒenəˈreɪʃn/ n generazione f

generator /'dʒenəreɪtə(r)/ n generatore m

generic /dʒɪˈnerɪk/ a ~ **term** termine m generico

generosity /dʒenəˈrɒsɪtɪ/ n generosità f

generous /'dʒenərəs/ a generoso. ~**ly** adv generosamente

genetic /dʒɪˈnetɪk/ a genetico. ~ **engineering** n ingegneria f genetica. ~**s** n genetica f sg

Geneva /dʒɪˈniːvə/ n Ginevra f

genial /'dʒiːnɪəl/ a gioviale

genitals /'dʒenɪtlz/ npl genitali mpl

genitive /'dʒenɪtɪv/ a & n ~ [case] genitivo m

genius /'dʒiːnɪəs/ n (pl -uses) genio m

genocide /'dʒenəsaɪd/ n genocidio m

genre /'ʒɔ̃rə/ n genere m [letterario]

gent /dʒent/ n fam signore m; **the** ~**s** sg il bagno per uomini

genteel /dʒenˈtiːl/ a raffinato

gentle /'dʒentl/ a delicato; (breeze, tap, slope) leggero

gentleman /'dʒentlmən/ n signore m; (well-mannered) gentiluomo m

gent|leness /'dʒentlnɪs/ n delicatezza f. ~**ly** adv delicatamente

genuine /'dʒenjʊɪn/ a genuino. ~**ly** adv (sorry) sinceramente

geograph|ical /dʒɪəˈgræfɪkl/ a geografico. ~**y** /dʒɪˈɒgrəfɪ/ n geografia f

geological /dʒɪəˈlɒdʒɪkl/ a geologico

geolog|ist /dʒɪˈɒlədʒɪst/ n geologo, -a mf. ~**y** n geologia f

geometric|al] /dʒɪəˈmetrɪk(l)/ a geometrico. ~**y** /dʒɪˈɒmətrɪ/ n geometria f

geranium /dʒəˈreɪnɪəm/ n geranio m

geriatric /dʒerɪˈætrɪk/ a geriatrico; ~ **ward** n reparto m geriatria. ~**s** n geriatria f

germ /dʒɜːm/ n germe m; ~**s** pl microbi mpl

German /'dʒɜːmən/ n & a tedesco, -a mf; (language) tedesco m

Germanic /dʒɜːˈmænɪk/ a germanico

German: ~ **measles** n rosolia f. ~ **shepherd** n pastore m tedesco

Germany /'dʒɜːmənɪ/ n Germania f

germinate /'dʒɜːmɪneɪt/ vi germogliare

gesticulate /dʒeˈstɪkjʊleɪt/ vi gesticolare

gesture /'dʒestʃə(r)/ n gesto m

get /get/ v (pt/pp got, pp Am also gotten, prcs p getting) ● vt (receive) ricevere; (obtain) ottenere; trovare (job); (buy, catch, fetch) prendere; (transport, deliver to airport etc) portare; (reach on telephone) trovare; (fam: understand) comprendere; preparare (meal); ~ **sb to do sth** far fare qcsa a qcno ● vi (become) ~ **tired/bored/angry** stancarsi/annoiarsi/arrabbiarsi; **I'm** ~**ting hungry** mi sta venendo fame; ~ **dressed/married** vestirsi/sposarsi; ~ **sth ready** preparare qcsa; ~ **nowhere** non concludere nulla; **this is** ~**ting us nowhere** questo non ci è di nessun aiuto; ~ **to** (reach) arrivare a. **get at** vt (criticize) criticare; **I see what you're** ~**ting at** ho capito cosa vuoi dire; **what are you** ~**ting at?** dove vuoi andare a parare? **get away** vi (leave) andarsene; (escape) scappare. **get back** vi tornare ● vt (recover) riavere; ~ **one's own back** rifarsi. **get by** vi passare; (manage) cavarsela. **get down** vi scendere; ~ **down to work** mettersi al lavoro ● vt (depress) buttare giù. **get in** vi entrare ● vt mettere dentro (washing); far venire (plumber). **get off** vi scendere; (from work) andarsene; Jur essere assolto; ~ **off the bus/one's bike** scendere dal pullman/dalla bici ● vt (remove) togliere. **get on** vi salire; (be on good terms) andare d'accordo; (make progress) andare avanti; (in life) riuscire; ~ **on the bus/one's bike** salire sul pullman/sulla bici; **how are you**

~ting on? come va?. **get out** *vi* uscire; *(of car)* scendere; ~ out! fuori!; ~ **out of** *(avoid doing)* evitare ● *vt* togliere *(cork, stain)*. **get over** *vi* andare al di là ● *vt fig* riprendersi da *(illness)*. **get round** *vt* aggirare *(rule)*; rigirare *(person)* ● *vi* I never ~ round to it non mi sono mai deciso a farlo. **get through** *vi* *(on telephone)* prendere la linea. **get up** *vi* alzarsi; *(climb)* salire; ~ **up a hill** salire su una collina

get: ~away *n* fuga *f*. ~**up** *n* tenuta *f*

geyser /ˈgiːzə(r)/ *n* scaldabagno *m*; *Geol* geyser *m inv*

ghastly /ˈgɑːstlɪ/ *a* (-ier, -iest) terribile; **feel** ~ sentirsi da cani

gherkin /ˈgɜːkɪn/ *n* cetriolino *m*

ghetto /ˈgetəʊ/ *n* ghetto *m*

ghost /ɡəʊst/ *n* fantasma *m*. ~**ly** *a* spettrale

ghoulish /ˈɡuːlɪʃ/ *a* macabro

giant /ˈdʒaɪənt/ *n* gigante *m* ● *a* gigante

gibberish /ˈdʒɪbərɪʃ/ *n* stupidaggini *fpl*

gibe /dʒaɪb/ *n* malignità *f inv*

giblets /ˈdʒɪblɪts/ *npl* frattaglie *fpl*

giddiness /ˈɡɪdɪnɪs/ *n* vertigini *fpl*

giddy /ˈɡɪdɪ/ *a* (-ier, -iest) vertiginoso; **feel** ~ avere le vertigini

gift /ɡɪft/ *n* dono *m*; *(to charity)* donazione *f*. ~**ed** /-ɪd/ *a* dotato. ~**wrap** *vt* impacchettare in carta da regalo

gig /ɡɪɡ/ *n Mus fam* concerto *m*

gigantic /dʒaɪˈɡæntɪk/ *a* gigantesco

giggle /ˈɡɪɡl/ *n* risatina *f* ● *vi* ridacchiare

gild /ɡɪld/ *vt* dorare

gills /ɡɪlz/ *npl* branchia *fsg*

gilt /ɡɪlt/ *a* dorato ● *n* doratura *f*. ~**-edged stock** *n* investimento *m* sicuro

gimmick /ˈɡɪmɪk/ *n* trovata *f*

gin /dʒɪn/ *n* gin *m inv*

ginger /ˈdʒɪndʒə(r)/ *a* rosso fuoco *inv*; *(cat)* rosso ● *n* zenzero *m*. ~ **ale** *n*, ~ **beer** *n* bibita *f* allo zenzero. ~**bread** *n* panpepato *m*

gingerly /ˈdʒɪndʒəlɪ/ *adv* con precauzione

gipsy /ˈdʒɪpsɪ/ *n* = gypsy

giraffe /dʒɪˈrɑːf/ *n* giraffa *f*

girder /ˈɡɜːdə(r)/ *n Techn* trave *f*

girl /ɡɜːl/ *n* ragazza *f*; *(female child)* femmina *f*. ~**friend** *n* amica *f*; *(of boy)* ragazza *f*. ~**ish** *a* da ragazza

giro /ˈdʒaɪrəʊ/ *n* bancogiro *m*; *(cheque)* sussidio *m* di disoccupazione

girth /ɡɜːθ/ *n* circonferenza *f*

gist /dʒɪst/ *n* **the** ~ la sostanza

give /ɡɪv/ *n* elasticità *f* ● *v* (*pt* gave, *pp* given) ● *vt* dare; *(as present)* regalare *(to* a); fare *(lecture, present, shriek)*; donare *(blood)*; ~ **birth** partorire ● *vi* *(to charity)* fare le donazioni; *(yield)* cedere. **give away** *vt* dar via; *(betray)* tradire; *(distribute)* assegnare; ~ **away the bride** portare la sposa all'altare. **give back** *vt* restituire. **give in** *vt* consegnare ● *vi* *(yield)* arrendersi. **give off** *vt* emanare. **give over** *vi* ~ **over!** piantala!. **give up** *vt* rinunciare a; ~ **oneself up** arrendersi ● *vi* rinunciare. **give way** *vi* cedere; *Auto* dare la precedenza; *(collapse)* crollare

given /ˈɡɪvn/ *see* **give** ● *a* ~ **name** nome *m* di battesimo

glacier /ˈɡlæsɪə(r)/ *n* ghiacciaio *m*

glad /ɡlæd/ *a* contento (**of** di). ~**den** /ˈɡlædn/ *vt* rallegrare

glade /ɡleɪd/ *n* radura *f*

gladly /ˈɡlædlɪ/ *adv* volentieri

glamor|ize /ˈɡlæməraɪz/ *vt* rendere affascinante. ~**ous** *a* affascinante

glamour /ˈɡlæmə(r)/ *n* fascino *m*

glance /ɡlɑːns/ *n* sguardo *m* ● *vi* ~ **at** dare un'occhiata a. **glance up** *vi* alzare gli occhi

gland /ɡlænd/ *n* glandola *f*

glandular /ˈɡlændjʊlə(r)/ *a* ghiandolare. ~ **fever** *n* mononucleosi *f*

glare /ɡleə(r)/ *n* bagliore *m*; *(look)* occhiataccia *f* ● *vi* ~ **at** dare un'occhiataccia a

glaring /ˈɡleərɪŋ/ *a* sfolgorante; *(mistake)* madornale

glass /ɡlɑːs/ *n* vetro *m*; *(for drinking)* bicchiere *m*; ~**es** *pl* *(spectacles)* occhiali *mpl*. ~**y** *a* vitreo

glaze /ɡleɪz/ *n* smalto *m* ● *vt* mettere i vetri a *(door, window)*; smaltare *(pottery)*; *Culin* spennellare. ~**d** *a* *(eyes)* vitreo

glazier /ˈɡleɪzɪə(r)/ *n* vetraio *m*

gleam /ɡliːm/ *n* luccichio *m* ● *vi* luccicare

glean /ɡliːn/ *vt* racimolare *(information)*

glee /ɡliː/ *n* gioia *f*. ~**ful** *a* gioioso

glen /ɡlen/ *n* vallone *m*

glib /ɡlɪb/ *a pej* insincero

glid|e /ɡlaɪd/ *vi* scorrere; *(through the air)* planare. ~**er** *n* aliante *m*

glimmer /ˈɡlɪmə(r)/ *n* barlume *m* ● *vi* emettere un barlume

glimpse /ɡlɪmps/ *n* occhiata *f*; **catch a** ~ **of** intravedere ● *vt* intravedere

glint /glɪnt/ *n* luccichio *m* ● *vi* luccicare

glisten /ˈglɪsn/ *vi* luccicare

glitter /ˈglɪtə(r)/ *vi* brillare

gloat /gləʊt/ *vi* gongolare (**over** su)

global /ˈgləʊbl/ *a* mondiale

globe /gləʊb/ *n* globo *m*; (*map*) mappamondo *m*

gloom /gluːm/ *n* oscurità *f*; (*sadness*) tristezza *f*. **~ily** *adv* (*sadly*) con aria cupa

gloomy /ˈgluːmɪ/ *a* (**-ier, -iest**) cupo

glorif|y /ˈglɔːrɪfaɪ/ *vt* (*pt/pp* **-ied**) glorificare; **a ~ied waitress** niente più che una cameriera

glorious /ˈglɔːrɪəs/ *a* splendido; (*deed, hero*) glorioso

glory /ˈglɔːrɪ/ *n* gloria *f*; (*splendour*) splendore *m*; (*cause for pride*) vanto *m* ● *vi* (*pt/pp* **-ied**) **~ in** vantarsi di

gloss /glɒs/ *n* lucentezza *f*. **~ paint** *n* vernice *f* lucida ● **gloss over** *vt* sorvolare su

glossary /ˈglɒsərɪ/ *n* glossario *m*

glossy /ˈglɒsɪ/ *a* (**-ier, -iest**) lucido; **~ [magazine]** rivista *f* femminile

glove /glʌv/ *n* guanto *m*. **~ compartment** *n* Auto cruscotto *m*

glow /gləʊ/ *n* splendore *m*; (*in cheeks*) rossore *m*; (*of candle*) luce *f* soffusa ● *vi* risplendere; (*candle:*) brillare; (*person:*) avvampare. **~ing** *a* ardente; (*account*) entusiastico

'glow-worm *n* lucciola *f*

glucose /ˈgluːkəʊs/ *n* glucosio *m*

glue /gluː/ *n* colla *f* ● *vt* (*pres p* **gluing**) incollare

glum /glʌm/ *a* (**glummer, glummest**) tetro

glut /glʌt/ *n* eccesso *m*

glutton /ˈglʌtən/ *n* ghiottone, -a *mf*. **~ous** /-əs/ *a* ghiotto. **~y** *n* ghiottoneria *f*

gnarled /nɑːld/ *a* nodoso

gnash /næʃ/ *vt* **~ one's teeth** digrignare i denti

gnat /næt/ *n* moscerino *m*

gnaw /nɔː/ *vt* rosicchiare

gnome /nəʊm/ *n* gnomo *m*

go /gəʊ/ *n* (*pl* **goes**) energia *f*; (*attempt*) tentativo *m*; **on the go** in movimento; **at one go** in una sola volta; **it's your go** tocca a te; **make a go of it** riuscire ● *vi* (*pt* **went**, *pp* **gone**) andare; (*leave*) andar via; (*vanish*) sparire; (*become*) diventare; (*be sold*) vendersi; **go and see** andare a vedere; **go swimming/shopping** andare a nuotare/fare spese; **where's the time gone?** come ha fatto il tempo a volare così?; **it's all gone** è fi-nito; **be going to** stare per fare; **I'm not going to** non ne ho nessuna intenzione; **to go** (*Am: hamburgers etc*) da asporto; **a coffee to go** un caffè da portar via. **go about** *vi* andare in giro. **go away** *vi* andarsene. **go back** *vi* ritornare. **go by** *vi* passare. **go down** *vi* scendere; (*sun:*) tramontare; (*ship:*) affondare; (*swelling:*) diminuire. **go for** *vt* andare a prendere; (*choose*) optare per; (*fam: attack*) aggredire; **he's not the kind I go for** non è il genere che mi attira. **go in** *vi* entrare. **go in for** *vt* partecipare a (*competition*); darsi a (*tennis*). **go off** *vi* andarsene; (*alarm:*) scattare; (*gun, bomb:*) esplodere; (*food, milk:*) andare a male; **go off well** riuscire. **go on** *vi* andare avanti; **what's going on?** cosa succede? **go on at** *vt fam* scocciare. **go out** *vi* uscire; (*light, fire:*) spegnersi. **go over** *vi* andare ● *vt* (*check*) controllare. **go round** *vi* andare in giro; (*visit*) andare; (*turn*) girare; **is there enough to go round?** ce n'è abbastanza per tutti? **go through** *vi* (*bill, proposal:*) passare ● *vt* (*suffer*) subire; (*check*) controllare; (*read*) leggere. **go under** *vi* passare sotto; (*ship, swimmer:*) andare sott'acqua; (*fail*) fallire. **go up** *vi* salire; (*Theat: curtain:*) aprirsi. **go with** *vt* accompagnare. **go without** *vt* fare a meno di (*supper, sleep*) ● *vi* fare senza

goad /gəʊd/ *vt* spingere (**into** a); (*taunt*) spronare

'go-ahead *a* (*person, company*) intraprendente ● *n* okay *m*

goal /gəʊl/ *n* porta *f*; (*point scored*) gol *m inv*; (*in life*) obiettivo *m*; **score a ~** segnare. **~ie** *fam*, **~keeper** *n* portiere *m*. **~-post** *n* palo *m*

goat /gəʊt/ *n* capra *f*

gobble /ˈgɒbl/ *vt* **~ [down, up]** trangugiare

'go-between *n* intermediario, -a *mf*

God, god /gɒd/ *n* Dio *m*, dio *m*

god: **~child** *n* figlioccio, -a *mf*. **~-daughter** *n* figlioccia *f*. **~dess** *n* dea *f*. **~father** *n* padrino *m*. **~-fearing** *a* timorato di Dio. **~-forsaken** *a* dimenticato da Dio. **~mother** *n* madrina *f*. **~parents** *npl* padrino *m* e madrina *f*. **~send** *n* manna *f*. **~son** *n* figlioccio *m*

'go-getter /ˈgəʊgetə(r)/ *n* ambizioso, -a *mf*

goggle /ˈgɒgl/ *vi fam* **~ at** fissare con gli occhi sgranati. **~s** *npl* occhiali *mpl*;

going | **graft**

going (of swimmer) occhialini mpl [da piscina]; (of worker) occhiali mpl protettivi

going /'gəʊɪŋ/ a (price, rate) corrente; ~ **concern** azienda f florida ● n it's **hard** ~ è una faticaccia; while the ~ is good finché si può. ~s-**on** npl avvenimenti mpl

gold /gəʊld/ n oro m ● a d'oro

golden /'gəʊldn/ a dorato. ~ **handshake** n buonuscita f (al termine di un rapporto di lavoro). ~ **mean** n giusto mezzo m. ~ **wedding** n nozze fpl d'oro

gold: ~**fish** n inv pesce m rosso. ~-**mine** n miniera f d'oro. ~-**plated** a placcato d'oro. ~**smith** n orefice m

golf /gɒlf/ n golf m

golf: ~-**club** n circolo m di golf; (implement) mazza f da golf. ~-**course** n campo m da golf. ~**er** n giocatore, -trice mf di golf

gondola /'gɒndələ/ n gondola f. ~**lier** /-'lɪə(r)/ n gondoliere m

gone /gɒn/ see**go**

gong /gɒŋ/ n gong m inv

good /gʊd/ a (better, best) buono; (child, footballer, singer) bravo; (holiday, film) bello; ~ at bravo in; a ~ **deal of anger** molta rabbia; as ~ as (almost) quasi; ~ **morning,** ~ **afternoon** buon giorno; ~ **evening** buona sera; ~ **night** buonanotte; have a ~ **time** divertirsi ● n bene m; for ~ per sempre; do ~ far del bene; do sb ~ far bene a qcno; it's no ~ è inutile; be up to no ~ combinare qualcosa

goodbye /gʊd'baɪ/ int arrivederci

good: ~-**for-nothing** n buono, -a mf a nulla. G~ **Friday** n Venerdì m Santo

good: ~-**looking** a bello. ~-**natured** a be ~-natured avere un buon carattere

goodness /'gʊdnɪs/ n bontà f; my ~! santo cielo!; thank ~! grazie al cielo!

goods /gʊdz/ npl prodotti mpl. ~ **train** n treno m merci

good will n buona volontà f; Comm avviamento m

goody /'gʊdɪ/ n (fam: person) buono m. ~-**goody** n santarellino, -a mf

gooey /'gu:ɪ/ a fam appiccicaticcio; fig sdolcinato

goof /gu:f/ vi fam cannare

goose /gu:s/ n (pl geese) oca f

gooseberry /'gʊzbərɪ/ n uva f spina

goose /gu:s/: ~-**flesh** n, ~-**pimples** npl pelle fsg d'oca

gore[1] /gɔ:(r)/ n sangue m

gore[2] vt incornare

gorge /gɔ:dʒ/ n Geog gola f ● vt ~ **oneself** ingozzarsi

gorgeous /'gɔ:dʒəs/ a stupendo

gorilla /gə'rɪlə/ n gorilla m inv

gormless /'gɔ:mlɪs/ a fam stupido

gorse /gɔ:s/ n ginestrone m

gory /'gɔ:rɪ/ a (-ier, -iest) cruento

gosh /gɒʃ/ int fam caspita

gospel /'gɒspl/ n vangelo m. ~ **truth** n sacrosanta verità f

gossip /'gɒsɪp/ n pettegolezzi mpl; (person) pettegolo, -a mf ● vi pettegolare. ~y a pettegolo

got /gɒt/ see**get** ● have ~ avere; have ~ to **do sth** dover fare qcsa

Gothic /'gɒθɪk/ a gotico

gotten /'gɒtn/ Am see**get**

gouge /gaʊdʒ/ vt ~ **out** cavare

gourmet /'gʊəmeɪ/ n buongustaio, -a mf

gout /gaʊt/ n gotta f

govern /'gʌv(ə)n/ vt/i governare; (determine) determinare

government /'gʌvnmənt/ n governo m. ~**al** /-'mentl/ a governativo

governor /'gʌvənə(r)/ n governatore m; (of school) membro m de consiglio di istituto; (of prison) direttore, -trice mf; (fam: boss) capo m

gown /gaʊn/ n vestito m; Univ, Jur toga f

GP n abbr general practitioner

grab /græb/ vt (pt/pp grabbed) ~ [hold of] afferrare

grace /greɪs/ n grazia f; (before meal) benedicite m inv; with good ~ volentieri; three days' ~ tre giorni di proroga. ~**ful** a aggraziato. ~**fully** adv con grazia

gracious /'greɪʃəs/ a cortese; (elegant) lussuoso

grade /greɪd/ n livello m; Comm qualità f; Sch voto m; (Am Sch: class) classe f; Am = **gradient** ● vt Comm classificare; Sch dare il voto a. ~ **crossing** n Am passaggio m a livello

gradient /'greɪdɪənt/ n pendenza f

gradual /'grædʒʊəl/ a graduale. ~**ly** adv gradualmente

graduate[1] /'grædʒʊət/ n laureato, -a mf

graduate[2] /'grædʒʊeɪt/ vi Univ laurearsi

graduation /grædʒʊ'eɪʃn/ n laurea f

graffiti /grə'fi:tɪ/ npl graffiti mpl

graft /grɑ:ft/ n (Bot, Med) innesto m; (Med: organ) trapianto m; (fam: hard work) duro lavoro m; (fam: corruption) corruzione f ● vt innestare; trapiantare ⟨*organ*⟩

grain /greɪn/ n ⟨*of sand, salt*⟩ granello m; ⟨*of rice*⟩ chicco m; ⟨*cereals*⟩ cereali mpl; ⟨*in wood*⟩ venatura f; **it goes against the ~** fig è contro la mia/sua natura

gram /græm/ n grammo m

grammar /'græmə(r)/ n grammatica f. **~ school** n ≈ liceo m

grammatical /grə'mætɪkl/ a grammaticale

granary /'grænərɪ/ n granaio m

grand /grænd/ a grandioso; *fam* eccellente

grandad /'grændæd/ n *fam* nonno m

grandchild n nipote mf

granddaughter n nipote f

grandeur /'grændʒə(r)/ n grandiosità f

grandfather n nonno m. **~ clock** n pendolo m ⟨*che poggia a terra*⟩

grandiose /'grændɪəʊs/ a grandioso

grand: **~mother** n nonna f. **~parents** npl nonni mpl. **~ pi·ano** n pianoforte m a coda. **~son** n nipote m. **~stand** n tribuna f

granite /'grænɪt/ n granito m

granny /'grænɪ/ n *fam* nonna f

grant /grɑːnt/ n ⟨*money*⟩ sussidio m; *Univ* borsa f di studio ● vt accordare; ⟨*admit*⟩ ammettere; **take sth for ~ed** dare per scontato qcsa

granulated /'grænjʊleɪtɪd/ a **~ sugar** zucchero m semolato

granule /'grænjuːl/ n granello m

grape /greɪp/ n acino m; **~s** pl uva fsg

grapefruit /'greɪp-/ n inv pompelmo m

graph /grɑːf/ n grafico m

graphic /'græfɪk/ a grafico; ⟨*vivid*⟩ vivido. **~s** n grafica f

graph paper n carta f millimetrata

grapple /'græpl/ vi **~ with** also fig essere alle prese con

grasp /grɑːsp/ n stretta f; ⟨*understanding*⟩ comprensione f ● vt afferrare. **~ing** a avido

grass /grɑːs/ n erba f; **at the ~ roots** alla base. **~hopper** n cavalletta f. **~land** n prateria f

grassy /'grɑːsɪ/ a erboso

grate¹ /greɪt/ n grata f

grate² vt *Culin* grattugiare ● vi stridere

grateful /'greɪtfl/ a grato. **~ly** adv con gratitudine

grater /'greɪtə(r)/ n *Culin* grattugia f

gratify /'grætɪfaɪ/ vt (pt/pp -ied) appagare. **~ied** a appagato. **~ying** a appagante

grating /'greɪtɪŋ/ n grata f

gratis /'grɑːtɪs/ adv gratis

gratitude /'grætɪtjuːd/ n gratitudine f

gratuitous /grə'tjuːɪtəs/ a gratuito

gratuity /grə'tjuːɪtɪ/ n gratifica f

grave¹ /greɪv/ a grave

grave² n tomba f

gravel /'grævl/ n ghiaia f

grave: **~stone** n lapide f. **~yard** n cimitero m

gravitate /'grævɪteɪt/ vi gravitare

gravity /'grævɪtɪ/ n gravità f

gravy /'greɪvɪ/ n sugo m della carne

gray /greɪ/ n Am = **grey**

graze¹ /greɪz/ vi ⟨*animal:*⟩ pascolare

graze² n escoriazione f ● vt ⟨*touch lightly*⟩ sfiorare; ⟨*scrape*⟩ escoriare; sbucciarsi ⟨*knee*⟩

grease /griːs/ n grasso m ● vt ungere. **~-proof** **paper** n carta f oleata

greasy /'griːsɪ/ a (-ier, -iest) untuoso; ⟨*hair, skin*⟩ grasso

great /greɪt/ a grande; ⟨*fam: marvellous*⟩ eccezionale

great: **~-·aunt** n prozia f. **G~** ·Britain n Gran Bretagna f. **~-·grandchildren** npl pronipoti mpl. **~-·grandfather** n bisnonno m. **~-·grandmother** n bisnonna f

great|ly /'greɪtlɪ/ adv enormemente. **~ness** n grandezza f

great-·uncle n prozio m

Greece /griːs/ n Grecia f

greed /griːd/ n avidità f; ⟨*for food*⟩ ingordigia f

greedily /'griːdɪlɪ/ adv avidamente; ⟨*eat*⟩ con ingordigia

greedy /'griːdɪ/ a (-ier, -iest) avido; ⟨*for food*⟩ ingordo

Greek /griːk/ a & n greco, -a mf; ⟨*language*⟩ greco m

green /griːn/ a verde; ⟨*fig: inexperienced*⟩ immaturo ● n verde m; **~s** pl verdura f; **the G~s** pl Pol i verdi. **~ belt** n zona f verde intorno a una città. **~ card** n Auto carta f verde

greenery /'griːnərɪ/ n verde m

green fingers npl have **~ ~** avere il police verde

greenfly n afide m

green: **~grocer** n fruttivendolo, -a mf. **~house** n serra f. **~house effect** n effetto m serra. **~ light** n *fam* verde m

greet /griːt/ vt salutare; ⟨*welcome*⟩ accogliere. **~ing** n saluto m; ⟨*welcome*⟩ ac-

coglienza f. **~ings card** n biglietto m
d'auguri

gregarious /grɪ'geərɪəs/ a gregario; ⟨person⟩ socievole

grenade /grɪ'neɪd/ n granata f

grew /gru:/ see **grow**

grey /greɪ/ a grigio; ⟨hair⟩ bianco ● n grigio m. **~hound** n levriero m

grid /grɪd/ n griglia f; ⟨on map⟩ reticolato m; Electr rete f

grief /gri:f/ n dolore m; **come to ~** ⟨plans:⟩ naufragare

grievance /'gri:vəns/ n lamentela f

grieve /gri:v/ vt addolorare ● vi essere addolorato

grill /grɪl/ n graticola f, ⟨for grilling⟩ griglia f; **mixed ~** grigliata f mista ● vt/i cuocere alla griglia; ⟨interrogate⟩ sottoporre al terzo grado

grille /grɪl/ n grata f

grim /grɪm/ a (**grimmer, grimmest**) arcigno; ⟨determination⟩ accanito

grimace /grɪ'meɪs/ n smorfia f ● vi fare una smorfia

grime /graɪm/ n sudiciume m

grimy /'graɪmɪ/ a (**-ier, -iest**) sudicio

grin /grɪn/ n sorriso m ● vi (pt/pp **grinned**) fare un gran sorriso

grind /graɪnd/ n (fam: hard work) sfacchinata f ● vt (pt/pp **ground**) macinare; affilare ⟨knife⟩; (Am: mince) tritare; **~ one's teeth** digrignare i denti

grip /grɪp/ n presa f; fig controllo m; ⟨bag⟩ borsone m; **get a ~ of oneself** controllarsi ● vt (pt/pp **gripped**) afferrare; ⟨tyres:⟩ far presa su; tenere avvinto ⟨attention⟩

gripe /graɪp/ vi (fam: grumble) lagnarsi

gripping /'grɪpɪŋ/ a avvincente

grisly /'grɪzlɪ/ a (**-ier, -iest**) raccapricciante

gristle /'grɪsl/ n cartilagine f

grit /grɪt/ n graniglia f; ⟨for roads⟩ sabbia f; ⟨courage⟩ coraggio m ● vt (pt/pp **gritted**) spargere sabbia su ⟨road⟩; **~ one's teeth** serrare i denti

grizzle /'grɪzl/ vi piagnucolare

groan /grəʊn/ n gemito m ● vi gemere

grocer /'grəʊsə(r)/ n droghiere, -a mf; **~'s [shop]** drogheria f. **~ies** npl generi mpl alimentari

groggy /'grɒgɪ/ a (**-ier, -iest**) stordito; ⟨unsteady⟩ barcollante

groin /grɔɪn/ n Anat inguine m

groom /gru:m/ n sposo m; ⟨for horse⟩ stalliere m ● vt strigliare ⟨horse⟩; fig preparare; **well-~ed** ben curato

groove /gru:v/ n scanalatura f

grope /grəʊp/ vi brancolare; **~ for** cercare a tastoni

gross /grəʊs/ a obeso; ⟨coarse⟩ volgare; ⟨glaring⟩ grossolano; ⟨salary, weight⟩ lordo ● n inv grossa f. **~ly** adv ⟨very⟩ enormemente

grotesque /grəʊ'tesk/ a grottesco

grotto /'grɒtəʊ/ n (pl **-es**) grotta f

grotty /'grɒtɪ/ a (**-ier, -iest**) ⟨fam: flat, street⟩ squallido

ground[1] /graʊnd/ see **grind**

ground[2] n terra f; Sport terreno m; ⟨reason⟩ ragione f; **~s** pl ⟨park⟩ giardini mpl; ⟨of coffee⟩ fondi mpl ● vi ⟨ship:⟩ arenarsi ● vt bloccare a terra ⟨aircraft⟩; Am Electr mettere a terra

ground: ~ floor n pianterreno m. **~ing** n base f. **~less** a infondato. **~sheet** n telone m impermeabile. **~work** n lavoro m di preparazione

group /gru:p/ n gruppo m ● vt raggruppare ● vi raggrupparsi

grouse[1] /graʊs/ n inv gallo m cedrone

grouse[2] n fam brontolare

grovel /'grɒvl/ vi (pt/pp **grovelled**) strisciare. **~ling** a leccapiedi inv

grow /grəʊ/ v (pt **grew**, pp **grown**) ● vi crescere; ⟨become⟩ diventare; ⟨unemployment, fear:⟩ aumentare; ⟨town:⟩ ingrandirsi ● vt coltivare; **~ one's hair** farsi crescere i capelli. **grow up** vi crescere; ⟨town:⟩ svilupparsi

growl /graʊl/ n grugnito m ● vi ringhiare

grown /grəʊn/ see **grow** ● a adulto. **~-up** a & n adulto, -a mf

growth /grəʊθ/ n crescita f; ⟨increase⟩ aumento m; Med tumore m

grub /grʌb/ n larva f; ⟨fam: food⟩ mangiare m

grubby /'grʌbɪ/ a (**-ier, -iest**) sporco

grudg|e /grʌdʒ/ n rancore m; **bear sb a ~e** portare rancore a qcno ● vt dare a malincuore. **~ing** a reluttante. **~ingly** adv a malincuore

gruelling /'gru:əlɪŋ/ a estenuante

gruesome /'gru:səm/ a macabro

gruff /grʌf/ a burbero

grumble /'grʌmbl/ vi brontolare (at contro)

grumpy /'grʌmpɪ/ a (**-ier, -iest**) scorbutico

grunt /grʌnt/ n grugnito m ● vi fare un grugnito

guarantee /gærən'ti:/ n garanzia f ● vt garantire. **~or** n garante mf

guard /gɑ:d/ n guardia f; ⟨security⟩ guardiano m; ⟨on train⟩ capotreno m;

Techn schermo *m* protettivo; **be on ~** essere di guardia ● *vt* sorvegliare; (*protect*) proteggere. **guard against** *vt* guardarsi da. **~-dog** *n* cane *m* da guardia

guarded /'gɑːdɪd/ *a* guardingo

guardian /'gɑːdɪən/ *n* (*of minor*) tutore, -trice *mf*

guerrilla /gə'rɪlə/ *n* guerrigliero, -a *mf*. **~ warfare** *n* guerriglia *f*

guess /ges/ *n* supposizione *f* ● *vt* indovinare ● *vi* indovinare; (*Am: suppose*) supporre. **~work** *n* supposizione *f*

guest /gest/ *n* ospite *mf*; (*in hotel*) cliente *mf*. **~-house** *n* pensione *f*

guffaw /gʌ'fɔː/ *n* sghignazzata *f* ● *vi* sghignazzare

guidance /'gaɪdəns/ *n* guida *f*; (*advice*) consigli *mpl*

guide /gaɪd/ *n* guida *f*; [Girl] G~ giovane esploratrice *f* ● *vt* guidare. **~book** *n* guida *f* turistica

guided /'gaɪdɪd/ *a* ~ **missile** missile *m* teleguidato; **~ tour** giro *m* guidato

guide: ~-dog *n* cane *m* per ciechi. **~lines** *npl* direttive *fpl*

guild /gɪld/ *n* corporazione *f*

guile /gaɪl/ *n* astuzia *f*

guillotine /'gɪlətiːn/ *n* ghigliottina *f*; (*for paper*) taglierina *f*

guilt /gɪlt/ *n* colpa *f*. **~ily** *adv* con aria colpevole

guilty /'gɪltɪ/ *a* (**-ier, -iest**) colpevole; **have a ~ conscience** avere la coscienza sporca

guinea-pig /'gɪnɪ-/ *n* porcellino *m* d'India; (*in experiments*) cavia *f*

guise /gaɪz/ *n* **in the ~ of** sotto le spoglie di

guitar /gɪ'tɑː(r)/ *n* chitarra *f*. **~ist** *n* chitarrista *mf*

gulf /gʌlf/ *n* *Geog* golfo *m*; *fig* abisso *m*

gull /gʌl/ *n* gabbiano *m*

gullet /'gʌlɪt/ *n* esofago *m*; (*throat*) gola *f*

gullible /'gʌlɪbl/ *a* credulone

gully /'gʌlɪ/ *n* burrone *m*; (*drain*) canale *m* di scolo

gulp /gʌlp/ *n* azione *f* di deglutire; (*of food*) boccone *m*; (*of liquid*) sorso *m* ● *vi*

deglutire. **gulp down** *vt* tranguaiare (*food*); scolarsi (*liquid*)

gum¹ /gʌm/ *n Anat* gengiva *f*

gum² *n* gomma *f*; (*chewing-gum*) gomma *f* da masticare, chewing-gum *m inv* ● *vt* (*pt/pp* **gummed**) ingommare (**to a**)

gummed /gʌmd/ *see* **gum²** ● *a* (*label*) adesivo

gumption /'gʌmpʃn/ *n fam* buon senso *m*

gun /gʌn/ *n* pistola *f*; (*rifle*) fucile *m*; (*cannon*) cannone *m* ● **gun down** *vt* (*pt/pp* **gunned**) freddare

gun: ~fire *n* spari *mpl*; (*of cannon*) colpi *mpl* [di cannone]. **~man** uomo *m* armato

gun: ~powder *n* polvere *f* da sparo. **~shot** *n* colpo *m* [di pistola]

gurgle /'gɜːgl/ *vi* gorgogliare; (*baby:*) fare degli urletti

gush /gʌʃ/ *vi* sgorgare; (*enthuse*) parlare con troppo entusiasmo (**over** di). **gush out** *vi* sgorgare. **~ing** *a* eccessivamente entusiastico

gust /gʌst/ *n* (*of wind*) raffica *f*

gusto /'gʌstəʊ/ *n* **with ~** con trasporto

gusty /'gʌstɪ/ *a* ventoso

gut /gʌt/ *n* intestino *m*; **~s** *pl* pancia *f*; (*fam: courage*) fegato *m* ● *vt* (*pt/pp* **gutted**) *Culin* svuotare delle interiora; **~ted by fire** sventrato da un incendio

gutter /'gʌtə(r)/ *n* canale *m* di scolo; (*on roof*) grondaia *f*; *fig* bassifondi *mpl*

guttural /'gʌtərəl/ *a* gutturale

guy /gaɪ/ *n fam* tipo *m*, tizio *m*

guzzle /'gʌzl/ *vt* ingozzarsi con (*food*); **he's ~d the lot** si è sbafato tutto

gym /dʒɪm/ *n fam* palestra *f*; (*gymnastics*) ginnastica *f*

gymnasium /dʒɪm'neɪzɪəm/ *n* palestra *f*

gymnast /'dʒɪmnæst/ *n* ginnasta *mf*. **~ics** /-'næstɪks/ *n* ginnastica *f*

gym: ~ shoes *npl* scarpe *fpl* da ginnastica. **~-slip** *n Sch* ≈ grembiule *m* (*da bambina*)

gynaecolog|ist /gaɪnɪ'kɒlədʒɪst/ *n* ginecologo, -a *mf*. **~y** *n* ginecologia *f*

gypsy /'dʒɪpsɪ/ *n* zingaro, -a *mf*

gyrate /dʒaɪ'reɪt/ *vi* roteare

Hh

haberdashery /ˈhæbəˈdæʃərɪ/ n merceria f; Am negozio m d'abbigliamento da uomo

habit /ˈhæbɪt/ n abitudine f; (Relig: costume) tonaca f; **be in the ~ of doing sth** avere l'abitudine di fare qcsa

habitable /ˈhæbɪtəbl/ a abitabile

habitat /ˈhæbɪtæt/ n habitat m inv

habitation /hæbɪˈteɪʃn/ n **unfit for human ~** inagibile

habitual /həˈbɪtjʊəl/ a abituale; ⟨smoker, liar⟩ inveterato. **~ly** adv regolarmente

hack¹ /hæk/ n (writer) scribacchino, -a mf

hack² vt tagliare; **~ to pieces** tagliare a pezzi

hackneyed /ˈhæknɪd/ a trito [e ritrito]

hacksaw n seghetto m

had /hæd/ see **have**

haddock /ˈhædək/ n inv eglefino m

haemorrhage /ˈhemərɪdʒ/ n emorragia f

haemorrhoids /ˈhemərɔɪdz/ npl emorroidi fpl

hag /hæg/ n **old ~** vecchia befana f

haggard /ˈhægəd/ a sfatto

haggle /ˈhægl/ vi contrattare (**over** per)

hail¹ /heɪl/ vt salutare; far segno a ⟨taxi⟩ ● vi **~ from** provenire da

hail² n grandine f ● vi grandinare. **~stone** n chicco m di grandine. **~storm** n grandinata f

hair /heə(r)/ n capelli mpl; (on body, of animal) pelo m

hair: **~brush** n spazzola f per capelli. **~cut** n taglio m di capelli; **have a ~cut** farsi tagliare i capelli. **~do** n fam pettinatura f. **~dresser** n parrucchiere, -a mf. **~dryer** n fon m inv; (with hood) casco m [asciugacapelli]. **~grip** n molletta f. **~pin** n forcina f. **~pin bend** n tornante m, curva f a gomito. **~raising** a terrificante. **~style** n acconciatura f

hairy /ˈheərɪ/ a (-ier, -iest) peloso; (fam: frightening) spaventoso

hale /heɪl/ a **~ and hearty** in piena forma

half /hɑːf/ n (pl **halves**) metà f inv; **cut in ~** tagliare a metà; **one and a ~** uno e mezzo; **~ a dozen** mezza dozzina; **~ an hour** mezz'ora ● a mezzo; [at] **~ price** [a] metà prezzo ● adv a metà; **~ past two** le due e mezza

half: **~ board** n mezza pensione f. **~hearted** a esitante. **~hourly** a & adv ogni mezz'ora. **~ mast** n at **~ mast** a mezz'asta. **~ measures** npl mezze misure fpl. **~open** a socchiuso. **~term** n vacanza f di metà trimestre. **~time** n Sport intervallo m. **~way** a the **~way mark/stage** il livello intermedio ● adv a metà strada; **get ~way** fig arrivare a metà. **~wit** n idiota mf

hall /hɔːl/ n (entrance) ingresso m; (room) sala f; (mansion) residenza f di campagna; **~ of residence** Univ casa f dello studente

hallmark n marchio m di garanzia; fig marchio m

hallo /həˈləʊ/ int ciao!; (on telephone) pronto!; **say ~ to** salutare

Hallowe'en /hæləʊˈiːn/ n vigilia f d'Ognissanti e notte delle streghe, celebrata soprattutto dai bambini

hallucination /həluːsɪˈneɪʃn/ n allucinazione f

halo /ˈheɪləʊ/ n (pl **-es**) aureola f; Astr alone m

halt /hɔːlt/ n alt m inv; **come to a ~** fermarsi; ⟨traffic:⟩ bloccarsi ● vi fermarsi; **~!** alt! ● vt fermare. **~ing** a esitante

halve /hɑːv/ vt dividere a metà; (reduce) dimezzare

ham /hæm/ n prosciutto m; Theat attore, -trice mf da strapazzo

hamburger /ˈhæmbɜːgə(r)/ n hamburger m inv

hamlet /ˈhæmlɪt/ n paesino m

hammer /ˈhæmə(r)/ n martello m ● vt martellare ● vi **~ at/on** picchiare a

hammock /ˈhæmək/ n amaca f

hamper¹ /ˈhæmpə(r)/ n cesto m; [gift] **~** cestino m

hamper² *vt* ostacolare

hamster /'hæmstə(r)/ *n* criceto *m*

hand /hænd/ *n* mano *f*; *(of clock)* lancetta *f*; *(writing)* scrittura *f*; *(worker)* manovale *m*; **at ~, to ~** a portata di mano; **on the one ~** da un lato; **on the other ~** d'altra parte; **out of ~** incontrollabile; *(summarily)* su due piedi; **give sb a ~** dare una mano a qcno ● *vt* porgere. **hand down** *vt* tramandare. **hand in** *vt* consegnare. **hand out** *vt* distribuire. **hand over** *vt* passare; *(to police)* consegnare

hand: ~bag *n* borsa *f* *(da signora)*. **~book** *n* manuale *m*. **~brake** *n* freno *m* a mano. **~cuffs** *npl* manette *fpl*. **~ful** *n* manciata *f*; **be |quite| a ~ful** *fam* essere difficile da tenere a bada

handicap /'hændıkæp/ *n* handicap *m inv*. **~ped** *a* **mentally physically ~ped** mentalmente/fisicamente handicappato

handi|craft /'hændıkrɑːft/ *n* artigianato *m*. **~work** *n* opera *f*

handkerchief /'hæŋkətʃıf/ *n* (*pl* ~s & -chieves) fazzoletto *m*

handle /'hændl/ *n* manico *m*; *(of door)* maniglia *f*; **fly off the ~** *fam* perdere le staffe ● *vt* maneggiare; occuparsi di *(problem, customer)*; prendere *(difficult person)*; trattare *(subject)*. **~bars** *npl* manubrio *m*

hand: ~luggage *n* bagaglio *m* a mano. **~made** *a* fatto a mano. **~out** *n* *(at lecture)* foglio *m* informativo; *(fam: money)* elemosina *f*. **~rail** *n* corrimano *m*. **~shake** *n* stretta *f* di mano

handsome /'hænsəm/ *a* bello; *(fig: generous)* generoso

hand: ~stand *n* verticale *f*. **~writing** *n* calligrafia *f*. **~written** *a* scritto a mano

handy /'hændı/ *a* (-ier, -iest) utile; *(person)* abile; **have keep ~** avere/tenere a portata di mano. **~man** *n* tuttofare *m inv*

hang /hæŋ/ *vt* *(pt/pp* hung) appendere *(picture)*; *(pt/pp* hanged) impiccare *(criminal)*; **~ oneself** impiccarsi ● *vi* *(pt/pp* hung) pendere; *(hair:)* scendere ● *n* **get the ~ of it** *fam* afferrare. **hang about** *vi* gironzolare. **hang on** *vi* tenersi stretto; *(fam: wait)* aspettare; *Teleph* restare in linea. **hang on to** *vt* tenersi stretto a; *(keep)* tenere. **hang out** *vi* spuntare; **where does he usually ~ out?** *fam* dove bazzica di solito? ● *vt* stendere *(washing)*. **hang up** *vt* appen-

dere; *Teleph* riattaccare ● *vi* essere appeso; *Teleph* riattaccare

hangar /'hæŋə(r)/ *n* hangar *m inv*

hanger /'hæŋə(r)/ *n* gruccia *f*. **~-on** *n* leccapiedi *mf*

hang: ~-glider *n* deltaplano *m*. **~-gliding** *n* deltaplano *m*. **~man** *n* boia *m*. **~over** *n* *fam* postumi *mpl* da sbornia. **~-up** *n* *fam* complesso *m*

hanker /'hæŋkə(r)/ *vi* **~ after sth** smaniare per qcsa

hanky /'hæŋkı/ *n* *fam* fazzoletto *m*

hanky-panky /hæŋkı'pæŋkı/ *n* *fam* qualcosa *m* di losco

haphazard /hæp'hæzəd/ *a* a casaccio

happen /'hæpn/ *vi* capitare, succedere; **as it ~s** per caso; **I ~ed to meet him** mi è capitato di incontrarlo; **what has ~ed to him?** cosa gli è capitato?; *(become of)* che fine ha fatto? **~ing** *n* avvenimento *m*

happi|ly /'hæpılı/ *adv* felicemente; *(fortunately)* fortunatamente. **~ness** *n* felicità *f*

happy /'hæpı/ *a* (-ier, -iest) contento, felice. **~-go-lucky** *a* spensierato

harass /'hærəs/ *vt* perseguitare. **~ed** *a* stressato. **~ment** *n* persecuzione *f*; **sexual ~ment** molestie *fpl* sessuali

harbour /'hɑːbə(r)/ *n* porto *m* ● *vt* dare asilo a; nutrire *(grudge)*

hard /hɑːd/ *a* duro; *(question, problem)* difficile; **~ of hearing** duro d'orecchi; **be ~ on sb** *(person:)* essere duro con qcno ● *adv* *(work)* duramente; *(pull, hit, rain, snow)* forte; **~ hit by unemployment** duramente colpito dalla disoccupazione; **take sth ~** non accettare qcsa; **think ~!** pensaci bene!; **try ~** mettercela tutta; **try ~er** metterci più impegno; **~ done by** *fam* trattato ingiustamente

hard: ~back *n* edizione *f* rilegata. **~boiled** *a* *(egg)* sodo. **~ copy** *n* copia *f* stampata. **~ disk** *n* hard disk *m inv*, disco *m* rigido

harden /'hɑːdn/ *vi* indurirsi

hard: ~-headed *a* *(businessman)* dal sangue freddo. **~-hearted** *a* dal cuore duro. **~ line** *n* linea *f* dura; **~ lines!** che sfortuna!. **~-line** *a* duro. **~-liner** *n* fautore, -trice *mf* della linea dura. **~ luck** *n* sfortuna *f*

hard|ly /'hɑːdlı/ *adv* appena; **~ly ever** quasi mai. **~ness** *n* durezza *f*. **~ship** *n* avversità *f inv*

hard: ~ shoulder *n* *Auto* corsia *f* d'emergenza. **~ up** *a* *fam* a corto di soldì; ~ **up for sth** a corto di qcsa. **~ware** *n* ferramenta *fpl*; *Comput* hardware *m inv*. **~·'wearing** *a* be **~-wearing** essere un gran lavoratore

hardy /'hɑ:dɪ/ *a* (**-ier, -iest**) dal fisico resistente; ⟨*plant*⟩ che sopporta il gelo

hare /heə(r)/ *n* lepre *f*. **~-brained** *a fam* ⟨*scheme*⟩ da scervellati

hark /hɑ:k/ *vi* ~ **back to** *fig* ritornare su

harm /hɑ:m/ *n* male *m*; ⟨*damage*⟩ danni *mpl*; **out of** ~'**s way** in un posto sicuro; **it won't do any** ~ non farà certo male ● *vt* far male a; ⟨*damage*⟩ danneggiare. **~ful** *a* dannoso. **~less** *a* innocuo

harmonica /hɑ:'mɒnɪkə/ *n* armonica *f* [a bocca]

harmonious /hɑ:'məʊnɪəs/ *a* armonioso. **~ly** *adv* in armonia

harmon|ize /'hɑ:mənaɪz/ *vi fig* armonizzare. **~y** *n* armonia *f*

harness /'hɑ:nɪs/ *n* finimenti *mpl*; ⟨*of parachute*⟩ imbracatura *f* ● *vt* bardare ⟨*horse*⟩; sfruttare ⟨*resources*⟩

harp /hɑ:p/ *n* arpa *f* ● **harp on** *vi fam* insistere ⟨**about** su⟩. **~ist** *n* arpista *mf*

harpoon /hɑ:'pu:n/ *n* arpione *m*

harpsichord /'hɑ:psɪkɔ:d/ *n* clavicembalo *m*

harrowing /'hærəʊɪŋ/ *a* straziante

harsh /hɑ:ʃ/ *a* duro; ⟨*light*⟩ abbagliante. **~ness** *n* durezza *f*

harvest /'hɑ:vɪst/ *n* raccolta *f*; ⟨*of grapes*⟩ vendemmia *f*; ⟨*crop*⟩ raccolto *m* ● *vt* raccogliere

has /hæz/ *see* **have**

hash /hæʃ/ *n* **make a** ~ **of** *fam* fare un casino con

hashish /'hæʃɪʃ/ *n* hascish *m*

hassle /'hæsl/ *n fam* rottura *f* ● *vt* rompere le scatole a

haste /heɪst/ *n* fretta *f*

hast|y /'heɪstɪ/ *a* (**-ier, -iest**) frettoloso; ⟨*decision*⟩ affrettato. **~ily** *adv* frettolosamente

hat /hæt/ *n* cappello *m*

hatch[1] /hætʃ/ *n* ⟨*for food*⟩ sportello *m* passavivande; *Naut* boccaporto *m*

hatch[2] *vi* ~ [**out**] rompere il guscio; ⟨*egg:*⟩ schiudersi ● *vt* covare; tramare ⟨*plot*⟩

hatchback *n* tre/cinque porte *m inv*; ⟨*door*⟩ porta *f* del bagagliaio

hatchet /'hætʃɪt/ *n* ascia *f*

hate /heɪt/ *n* odio *m* ● *vt* odiare. **~ful** *a* odioso

hatred /'heɪtrɪd/ *n* odio *m*

haught|y /'hɔ:tɪ/ *a* (**-ier, -iest**) altezzoso. **~ily** *adv* altezzosamente

haul /hɔ:l/ *n* ⟨*fish*⟩ pescata *f*; ⟨*loot*⟩ bottino *m*; ⟨*pull*⟩ tirata *f* ● *vt* tirare; trasportare ⟨*goods*⟩ ● *vi* ~ **on** tirare. **~age** /-ɪdʒ/ *n* trasporto *m*. **~ier** /-ɪə(r)/ *n* autotrasportatore *m*

haunt /hɔ:nt/ *n* ritrovo *m* ● *vt* frequentare; ⟨*linger in the mind*⟩ perseguitare; **this house is ~ed** questa casa è abitata da fantasmi

have /hæv/ *vt* (*3 sg pres tense* **has**; *pt/pp* **had**) avere; fare ⟨*breakfast, bath, walk etc*⟩; ~ **a drink** bere qualcosa; ~ **lunch/dinner** pranzare/cenare; ~ **a rest** riposarsi; **I had my hair cut** mi sono tagliata i capelli; **we had the house painted** abbiamo fatto tinteggiare la casa; **I had it made** l'ho fatto fare; ~ **to do sth** dover fare qcsa; ~ **him telephone me tomorrow** digli di telefonarmi domani; **he has** *or* **he's got two houses** ha due case; **you've got the money, ~n't you?** hai i soldi, no? ● *v aux* avere; (*with verbs of motion & some others*) essere; **I ~ seen him** l'ho visto; **he has never been there** non ci è mai stato. **have on** *vt* (*be wearing*) portare; (*dupe*) prendere in giro; **I've got something on tonight** ho un impegno stasera. **have out** *vt* ~ **it out with sb** chiarire le cose con qcno ● *npl* **the ~s and the ~-nots** i ricchi e i poveri

haven /'heɪvn/ *n fig* rifugio *m*

haversack /'hævə-/ *n* zaino *m*

havoc /'hævək/ *n* strage *f*; **play ~ with** *fig* scombussolare

haw /hɔ:/ *see* **hum**

hawk /hɔ:k/ *n* falco *m*

hay /heɪ/ *n* fieno *m*. ~ **fever** *n* raffreddore *m* da fieno. **~stack** *n* pagliaio *m*

haywire *a fam* **go ~** dare i numeri; ⟨*plans:*⟩ andare all'aria

hazard /'hæzəd/ *n* (*risk*) rischio *m* ● *vt* rischiare; ~ **a guess** azzardare un'ipotesi. **~ous** /-əs/ *a* rischioso. ~ [**warning**] **lights** *npl Auto* luci *fpl* d'emergenza

haze /heɪz/ *n* foschia *f*

hazel /'heɪz(ə)l/ *n* nocciolo *m*; ⟨*colour*⟩ [color *m*] nocciola *m*. **~-nut** *n* nocciola *f*

hazy /'heɪzɪ/ *a* (**-ier, -iest**) nebbioso; ⟨*fig: person*⟩ confuso; ⟨*memories*⟩ vago

he /hi:/ *pron* lui; **he's tired** è stanco; **I'm going but he's not** io vengo, ma lui no

head /hed/ *n* testa *f*; ⟨*of firm*⟩ capo *m*;

(of primary school) direttore, -trice *mf*; *(of secondary school)* preside *mf*; *(on beer)* schiuma *f*; **be off one's** ~ essere fuori di testa; **have a good** ~ **for business** avere il senso degli affari; **have a good** ~ **for heights** non soffrire di vertigini; **10 pounds a** ~ 10 sterline a testa; **20** ~ **of cattle** 20 capi di bestiame; ~ **first** a capofitto; ~ **over heels in love** innamorato pazzo; ~**s or tails?** testa o croce? ●*vt* essere a capo di; essere in testa a *(list)*; colpire di testa *(ball)* ●*vi* ~ **for** dirigersi verso.

head: ~**ache** *n* mal *m* di testa. ~**-dress** *n* acconciatura *f.* ~**er** /'hedə(r)/ *n* rinvio *m* di testa; *(dive)* tuffo *m* di testa. ~**hunter** *n* cacciatore, -trice *mf* di teste. ~**ing** *n* *(in list etc)* titolo *m*. ~**lamp** *n* Auto fanale *m*. ~**land** *n* promontorio *m*. ~**light** *n* Auto fanale *m*. ~**line** *n* titolo *m*. ~**long** *a & adv* a capofitto. ~'**master** *n* *(of primary school)* direttore *m*; *(of secondary school)* preside *m*. ~'**mistress** *n* *(of primary school)* direttrice *f*; *(of secondary school)* preside *f*. ~ **office** *n* sede *f* centrale. ~**-on** *a* frontale ●*adv* frontalmente. ~**phones** *npl* cuffie *fpl*. ~**quarters** *npl* sede *fsg*; Mil quartier *m* generale *msg*. ~**-rest** *n* poggiatesta *m inv*. ~**room** *n* sottotetto *m*; *(of bridge)* altezza *f* libera di passaggio. ~**scarf** *n* foulard *m inv*, fazzoletto *m*. ~**strong** *a* testardo. ~'**waiter** *n* capocameriere *m*. ~**way** *n* progresso *m*. ~**wind** *n* vento *m* di prua

heady /'hedɪ/ *a* che dà alla testa

heal /hi:l/ *vt/i* guarire

health /helθ/ *n* salute *f*

health: ~ **farm** *n* centro *m* di rimessa in forma. ~ **foods** *npl* alimenti *mpl* macrobiotici. ~**-food shop** *n* negozio *m* di macrobiotica. ~ **insurance** *n* assicurazione *f* contro malattie

healthy /'helθɪ/ *a* (-ier, -iest) sano. ~**ily** *adv* in modo sano

heap /hi:p/ *n* mucchio *m*; ~**s of** *fam* un sacco di ●*vt* ~ [**up**] ammucchiare; ~**ed teaspoon** un cucchiaino abbondante

hear /hɪə(r)/ *vt/i* (*pt/pp* heard) sentire; ~, ~! bravo! ~ **from** *vi* aver notizie di. **hear of** *vi* sentir parlare di; **he would not** ~ **of it** non ne ha voluto sentir parlare

hearing /'hɪərɪŋ/ *n* udito *m*; Jur udienza *f*. ~**-aid** *n* apparecchio *m* acustico

'**hearsay** *n* **from** ~ per sentito dire

hearse /hɜ:s/ *n* carro *m* funebre

heart /hɑ:t/ *n* cuore *m*; ~**s** *pl* *(in cards)* cuori *mpl*; **by** ~ a memoria

heart: ~**ache** *n* pena *f.* ~ **attack** *n* infarto *m*. ~**beat** *n* battito *m* cardiaco. ~**break** *n* afflizione *f.* ~**breaking** *a* straziante. ~**broken** *a* **be** ~**-broken** avere il cuore spezzato. ~**burn** *n* mal *m* di stomaco. ~**en** *vt* rincuorare. ~**felt** *a* di cuore

hearth /hɑ:θ/ *n* focolare *m*

heart|**ily** /'hɑ:tɪlɪ/ *adv* di cuore; *(eat)* con appetito; **be** ~**ily sick of sth** non poterne più di qcsa. ~**less** *a* spietato. ~**-searching** *n* esame *m* di coscienza. ~**-to-** ~ *n* conversazione *f* a cuore aperto ●*a* a cuore aperto. ~**y** *a* caloroso; *(meal)* copioso; *(person)* gioviale

heat /hi:t/ *n* calore *m*; Sport prova *f* eliminatoria ●*vt* scaldare ●*vi* scaldarsi. ~**ed** *a* *(swimming pool)* riscaldato; *(discussion)* animato. ~**er** *n* *(for room)* stufa *f*; *(for water)* boiler *m inv*; Auto riscaldamento *m*

heath /hi:θ/ *n* brughiera *f*

heathen /'hi:ðn/ *a & n* pagano, -a *mf*

heather /'heðə(r)/ *n* erica *f*

heating /'hi:tɪŋ/ *n* riscaldamento *m*

heat: ~**stroke** *n* colpo *m* di sole. ~ **wave** *n* ondata *f* di calore

heave /hi:v/ *vt* tirare; *(lift)* tirare su; *(fam: throw)* gettare; emettere *(sigh)* ●*vi* tirare

heaven /'hev(ə)n/ *n* paradiso *m*; ~ **help you if...** Dio ti scampi se...; **H**~**s!** santo cielo!. ~**ly** *a* celeste; *fam* delizioso

heavy /'hevɪ/ *a* (-ier, -iest) pesante; *(traffic)* intenso; *(rain, cold)* forte; **be a** ~**y smoker/drinker** essere un gran fumatore/bevitore. ~**ily** *adv* pesantemente; *(smoke, drink etc)* molto. ~**yweight** *n* peso *m* massimo

Hebrew /'hi:bru:/ *a* ebreo

heckle /hekl/ *vt* interrompere di continuo. ~**r** *n* disturbatore, -trice *mf*

hectic /'hektɪk/ *a* frenetico

hedge /hedʒ/ *n* siepe *f* ●*vi fig* essere evasivo. ~**hog** *n* riccio *m*

heed /hi:d/ *n* **pay** ~ **to** prestare ascolto a ●*vt* prestare ascolto a. ~**less** *a* noncurante

heel[1] /hi:l/ *n* tallone *m*; *(of shoe)* tacco *m*; **take to one's** ~**s** *fam* darsela a gambe

heel[2] *vi* ~ **over** Naut inclinarsi

hefty /'heftɪ/ *a* (-ier, -iest) massiccio

heifer /'hefə(r)/ *n* giovenca *f*

height /haɪt/ n altezza f; (of plane) altitudine f; (of season, fame) culmine m. **~en** vt fig accrescere

heir /eə(r)/ n erede mf. **~ess** n ereditiera f. **~loom** n cimelio m di famiglia

held /held/ see hold²

helicopter /ˈhelɪkɒptə(r)/ n elicottero m

hell /hel/ n inferno m; go to ~! sl va' al diavolo! ● int porca miseria!

hello /həˈləʊ/ int & n = hallo

helm /helm/ n timone m; at the ~ fig al timone

helmet /ˈhelmɪt/ n casco m

help /help/ n aiuto m; (employee) aiuto m domestico; that's no ~ non è d'aiuto ● vt aiutare; ~ oneself to sth servirsi di qcsa; ~ yourself (at table) serviti pure; I could not ~ laughing non ho potuto trattenermi dal ridere; it cannot be ~ed non c'è niente da fare; I can't ~ it non ci posso far niente ● vi aiutare

help er /ˈhelpə(r)/ n aiutante mf. **~ful** a ⟨person⟩ di aiuto; ⟨advice⟩ utile. **~ing** n porzione f. **~less** a (unable to manage) incapace; (powerless) impotente

helter-skelter /heltəˈskeltə(r)/ adv in fretta e furia ● n scivolo m a spirale nei luna park

hem /hem/ n orlo m ● vt (pt/pp hemmed) orlare. **hem in** vt intrappolare

hemisphere /ˈhemɪ·/ n emisfero m

hemp /hemp/ n canapa f

hen /hen/ n gallina f; (any female bird) femmina f

hence /hens/ adv (for this reason) quindi. **~ forth** adv d'ora innanzi

henchman /ˈhentʃmən/ n pej tirapiedi m

hen: **~-party** n fam festa f di addio al celibato per sole donne. **~pecked** a tiranneggiato dalla moglie

her /hɜː(r)/ poss a il suo m, la sua f, i suoi mpl, le sue fpl; ~ mother sua madre/suo padre ● pers pron (direct object) la; (indirect object) le; (after prep) lei; I know ~ la conosco; give ~ the money dalle i soldi; give it to ~ daglielo; I came with ~ sono venuto con lei; it's ~ è lei; I've seen ~ l'ho vista; I've seen ~, but not him l'ho visto lei, ma non lui

herald /ˈherəld/ vt annunciare

herb /hɜːb/ n erba f

herbal /ˈhɜːb(ə)l/ a alle erbe; ~ tea tisana f

herbs /hɜːbz/ npl (for cooking) aromi mpl ⟨da cucina⟩; ⟨medicinal⟩ erbe fpl

herd /hɜːd/ n gregge m ● vt ⟨tend⟩ sorvegliare; ⟨drive⟩ far muovere; fig ammassare

here /hɪə(r)/ adv qui, qua; in ~ qui dentro; come/bring ~ vieni/porta qui; ~ is..., ~ are... ecco...; ~ you are! ecco qua!. **~ after** adv in futuro. **~ by** adv con la presente

heredit ary /həˈredɪtəri/ a ereditario. **~y** n eredità f

here sy /ˈherəsɪ/ n eresia f. **~tic** n eretico, -a mf

here with adv Comm con la presente

heritage /ˈherɪtɪdʒ/ n eredità f

hermetic /hɜːˈmetɪk/ a ermetico. **~ally** adv ermeticamente

hermit /ˈhɜːmɪt/ n eremita mf

hernia /ˈhɜːnɪə/ n ernia f

hero /ˈhɪərəʊ/ n (pl -es) eroe m

heroic /hɪˈrəʊɪk/ a eroico

heroin /ˈherəʊɪn/ n eroina f (droga)

hero ine /ˈherəʊɪn/ n eroina f. **~ism** n eroismo m

heron /ˈherən/ n airone m

herring /ˈherɪŋ/ n aringa f

hers /hɜːz/ poss pron il suo m, la sua f, i suoi mpl, le sue fpl; a friend of ~ un suo amico; friends of ~ dei suoi amici; that is ~ quello è suo; (as opposed to mine) quello è il suo

her self pers pron (reflexive) si; (emphatic) lei stessa; (after prep) sé, se stessa; she poured ~ a drink si è versata da bere; she told me so ~ me lo ha detto lei stessa; she's proud of ~ è fiera di sé; by ~ da sola

hesitant /ˈhezɪtənt/ a esitante. **~ly** adv con esitazione

hesitat e /ˈhezɪteɪt/ vi esitare. **~ion** /-ˈteɪʃn/ n esitazione f

het /het/ a ~ up fam agitato

hetero sexual /hetərəʊ-/ a eterosessuale

hexagon /ˈheksəgən/ n esagono m. **~al** /hekˈsægənl/ a esagonale

hey /heɪ/ int ehi

heyday /ˈheɪ-/ n tempi mpl d'oro

hi /haɪ/ int ciao!

hiatus /haɪˈeɪtəs/ n (pl -tuses) iato m

hibernat e /ˈhaɪbəneɪt/ vi andare in letargo. **~ion** /-ˈneɪʃn/ n letargo m

hiccup /ˈhɪkʌp/ n singhiozzo m; (fam: hitch) intoppo m ● vi fare un singhiozzo

hid /hɪd/, **hidden** /ˈhɪdn/ see hide²

hide¹ /haɪd/ n (leather) pelle f (di animale)

hide² *vt* (*pt* **hid**, *pp* **hidden**) nascondere
● *vi* nascondersi. ~-**and- seek** *n* play
~-**and-seek** giocare a nascondino

hideous /'hɪdɪəs/ *a* orribile

'**hide-out** *n* nascondiglio *m*

hiding¹ /'haɪdɪŋ/ *n* (*fam: beating*) bastonata *f*; (*defeat*) batosta *f*

hiding² *n* go into ~ sparire dalla circolazione

hierarchy /'haɪərɑːkɪ/ *n* gerarchia *f*

hieroglyphics /haɪərə'glɪfɪks/ *npl* ge-
roglifici *mpl*

hi-fi /'haɪfaɪ/ *n fam* stereo *m*, hi-fi *m inv*
● *a fam* ad alta fedeltà

higgledy-piggledy /ˌhɪɡldɪ'pɪɡldɪ/
adv alla rinfusa

high /haɪ/ *a* alto; (*meat*) che comincia
ad andare a male; (*wind*) forte; (*on
drugs*) fatto; **it's ~ time we did
something about it** è ora di fare qualcosa in proposito ● *adv* in alto; ~ **and
low** in lungo e in largo ● *n* massimo *m*;
(*temperature*) massima *f*; **be on a ~**
fam essere fatto

high: ~**brow** *a* & *n* intellettuale *mf*. ~
chair *n* seggiolone *m*. ~**er education** *n*
formazione *f* universitaria. ~ -**handed**
a dispotico. ~ -**heeled** *a* coi tacchi alti.
~ **heels** *npl* tacchi *mpl* alti. ~ **jump** *n*
salto *m* in alto

highlight /'haɪlaɪt/ *n fig* momento *m*
clou; ~**s** *pl* (*in hair*) mèche *fpl* ● *vt*
(*emphasize*) evidenziare. ~**er** *n*
(*marker*) evidenziatore *m*

highly /'haɪlɪ/ *adv* molto; **speak ~ of**
lodare; **think ~ of** avere un'alta opinione di. ~ -**strung** *a* nervoso

Highness /'haɪnɪs/ *n* altezza *f*; **Your ~**
Sua Altezza

high: ~ -**rise** *a* (*building*) molto alto ● *n*
edificio *m* molto alto. ~ **school** *n* scuola *f* superiore. ~ **season** *n* alta stagione *f*. ~ **street** *n* strada *f* principale. ~
tea *n* pasto *m* pomeridiano servito
insieme al tè. ~ **tide** *n* alta marea *f*.
~**way code** *n* codice *m* stradale

hijack /'haɪdʒæk/ *vt* dirottare ● *n* di-
rottamento *m*. ~**er** *n* dirottatore, -trice
mf

hike /haɪk/ *n* escursione *f* a piedi ● *vi*
fare un'escursione a piedi. ~**r** *n* escursionista *m*

hilarious /hɪ'leərɪəs/ *a* esilarante

hill /hɪl/ *n* collina *f*; (*mound*) collinetta *f*;
(*slope*) altura *f*

hill: ~**side** *n* pendio *m*. ~**y** *a* collinoso

hilt /hɪlt/ *n* impugnatura *f*; **to the ~**

(*fam: support*) fino in fondo;
(*mortgaged*) fino al collo

him /hɪm/ *pers pron* (*direct object*) lo;
(*indirect object*) gli; (*with prep*) lui; **I
know ~** lo conosco; **give ~ the money**
dagli i soldi; **give it to ~** daglielo; **I
spoke to ~** gli ho parlato; **it's ~** è lui;
she loves ~ lo ama; **she loves ~, not
you** ama lui, non te. ~ **self** *pers pron*
(*reflexive*) si; (*emphatic*) lui stesso;
(*after prep*) sè, se stesso; **he poured ~
a drink** si è versato da bere; **he told me
so** ~ **self** me lo ha detto lui stesso; **he's
proud of** ~ **self** è fiero di sé; **by** ~ **self**
da solo

hind /haɪnd/ *a* posteriore

hind|er /'hɪndə(r)/ *vt* intralciare.
~**rance** /-rəns/ *n* intralcio *m*

hindsight /'haɪnd-/ *n* **with ~** con il
senno del poi

Hindu /'hɪnduː/ *n* indù *mf inv* ● *a* indù.
~**ism** *n* induismo *m*

hinge /hɪndʒ/ *n* cardine *m* ● *vi* ~ **on** *fig*
dipendere da

hint /hɪnt/ *n* (*clue*) accenno *m*; (*advice*)
suggerimento *m*; (*indirect suggestion*)
allusione *f*; (*trace*) tocco *m* ● *vt* ~
that... far capire che... ● *vi* ~ **at** alludere a

hip /hɪp/ *n* fianco *m*

hippie /'hɪpɪ/ *n* hippy *mf inv*

hippo /'hɪpəʊ/ *n* ippopotamo *m*

hip 'pocket *n* tasca *f* posteriore

hippopotamus /hɪpə'pɒtəməs/ *n* (*pl*
-**muses** *or* -**mi** /-maɪ/) ippopotamo *m*

hire /'haɪə(r)/ *vt* affittare; assumere
(*person*); ~ [**out**] affittare ● *n* noleggio
m; '**for ~**' 'affittasi'. ~ **car** *n* macchina
f a noleggio. ~ **purchase** *n* acquisto *m*
rateale

his /hɪz/ *poss a* il suo *m*, la sua *f*, i suoi
mpl, le sue *fpl*: ~ **mother/father** sua
madre/suo padre ● *poss pron* il suo *m*,
la sua *f*, i suoi *mpl*, le sue *fpl*; **a friend
of** ~ un suo amico; **friends of** ~ dei
suoi amici; **that is** ~ questo è suo; (*as
opposed to mine*) questo è il suo

hiss /hɪs/ *n* sibilo *m*; (*of disapproval*) fischio *m* ● *vt* fischiare ● *vi* sibilare; (*in
disapproval*) fischiare

historian /hɪ'stɔːrɪən/ *n* storico, -a *mf*

historic /hɪ'stɒrɪk/ *a* storico. ~**al** *a* storico. ~**ally** *adv* storicamente

history /'hɪstərɪ/ *n* storia *f*; **make ~**
passare alla storia

hit /hɪt/ *n* (*blow*) colpo *m*; (*fam: success*)
successo *m*; **score a direct ~** (*missile*)
colpire in pieno ● *vt/i* (*pt/pp* **hit**, *pres p*

hitting) colpire; **~ one's head on the table** battere la testa contro il tavolo; **the car ~ the wall** la macchina ha sbattuto contro il muro; **the roof** *fam* perdere le staffe. **hit off** *vt* **~ it off** andare d'accordo. **hit on** *vt fig* trovare

hitch /hɪtʃ/ *n* intoppo *m*; **technical ~** problema *m* tecnico ● *vt* attaccare; **~ a lift** chiedere un passaggio. **hitch up** *vt* tirarsi su (*trousers*). **~-hike** *vi* fare l'autostop. **~-hiker** *n* autostoppista *mf*

hit-or-'miss *a* **on a very ~ basis** all'improvvisata

hither /'hɪðə(r)/ *adv* **~ and thither** di qua e di là. **~'to** *adv* finora

hive /haɪv/ *n* alveare *m*; **~ of industry** fucina *f* di lavoro ● **hive off** *vt Comm* separare

hoard /hɔːd/ *n* provvista *f*; (*of money*) gruzzolo *m* ● *vt* accumulare

hoarding /'hɔːdɪŋ/ *n* palizzata *f*; (*with advertisements*) tabellone *m* per manifesti pubblicitari

hoarse /hɔːs/ *a* rauco. **~ly** *adv* con voce rauca. **~ness** *n* raucedine *f*

hoax /həʊks/ *n* scherzo *m*; (*false alarm*) falso allarme *m*. **~er** *n* burlone, -a *mf*

hob /hɒb/ *n* piano *m* di cottura

hobble /'hɒbl/ *vi* zoppicare

hobby /'hɒbɪ/ *n* hobby *m inv*. **~-horse** *n* fig fissazione *f*

hockey /'hɒkɪ/ *n* hockey *m*

hoe /həʊ/ *n* zappa *f*

hog /hɒg/ *n* maiale *m* ● *vt* (*pt/pp* hogged) *fam* monopolizzare

hoist /hɔɪst/ *n* montacarichi *m inv*; (*fam: push*) spinta *f* in su ● *vt* sollevare; innalzare (*flag*); levare (*anchor*)

hold[1] /həʊld/ *n Naut, Aeron* stiva *f*

hold[2] *n* presa *f*; (*fig: influence*) ascendente *m*; **get ~ of** trovare; procurarsi (*information*) ● *v* (*pt/pp* held) ● *vt* tenere; (*container:*) contenere; essere titolare di (*licence, passport*); trattenere (*breath, suspect*); mantenere vivo (*interest*); (*civil servant etc:*) occupare (*position*); (*retain*) mantenere; **~ sb's hand** tenere qcno per mano; **~ one's tongue** tenere la bocca chiusa; **~ sb responsible** considerare qcno responsabile; **~ that** (*believe*) ritenere che ● *vi* tenere; (*weather, luck:*) durare; (*offer:*) essere valido; *Teleph* restare in linea; **I don't ~ with the idea that** *fam* non sono d'accordo sul fatto che. **hold back** *vt* rallentare ● *vi* esitare. **hold down** *vt* tenere a bada (*sb*). **hold on** *vi* (*wait*) attendere; *Teleph* restare in linea. **hold**

on to *vt* aggrapparsi a; (*keep*) tenersi. **hold out** *vt* porgere (*hand*); *fig* offrire (*possibility*) ● *vi* (*resist*) resistere. **hold up** *vt* tenere su; (*delay*) rallentare; (*rob*) assalire; **~ one's head up** *fig* tenere la testa alta

'hold: ~-all *n* borsone *m*. **~er** *n* titolare *mf*; (*of record*) detentore, -trice *mf*; (*container*) astuccio *m*. **~ing** *n* (*land*) terreno *m* in affitto; *Comm* azioni *fpl*. **~-up** *n* ritardo *m*; (*attack*) rapina *f* a mano armata

hole /həʊl/ *n* buco *m*

holiday /'hɒlɪdeɪ/ *n* vacanza *f*; (*public*) giorno *m* festivo; (*day off*) giorno *m* di ferie; **go on ~** andare in vacanza ● *vi* andare in vacanza. **~-maker** *n* vacanziere *mf*

holiness /'həʊlɪnɪs/ *n* santità *f*, **Your H~** Sua Santità

Holland /'hɒlənd/ *n* Olanda *f*

hollow /'hɒləʊ/ *a* cavo; (*promise*) a vuoto; (*voice*) assente; (*cheeks*) infossato ● *n* cavità *f inv*; (*in ground*) affossamento *m*

holly /'hɒlɪ/ *n* agrifoglio *m*

holocaust /'hɒləkɔːst/ *n* olocausto *m*

hologram /'hɒləgræm/ *n* ologramma *m*

holster /'həʊlstə(r)/ *n* fondina *f*

holy /'həʊlɪ/ *a* (-ier, -est) santo; (*water*) benedetto. **H~ Ghost** *or* **Spirit** *n* Spirito *m* Santo. **H~ Scriptures** *npl* sacre scritture *fpl*. **H~ Week** *n* settimana *f* santa

homage /'hɒmɪdʒ/ *n* omaggio *m*; **pay ~ to** rendere omaggio a

home /həʊm/ *n* casa *f*; (*for children*) istituto *m*; (*for old people*) casa *f* di riposo; (*native land*) patria *f* ● *adv* **at ~** a casa; (*football*) in casa; **feel at ~** sentirsi a casa propria; **come/go ~** venire/andare a casa; **drive a nail ~** piantare un chiodo a fondo ● *a* domestico; (*movie, video*) casalingo; (*team*) ospitante; *Pol* nazionale

home: ~ ad'dress *n* indirizzo *m* di casa. **~ com'puter** *n* computer *m* inv da casa. **H~ Counties** *npl* contee *fpl* intorno a Londra. **~ game** *n* gioco *m* in casa. **~ help** *n* aiuto *m* domestico (*per persone non autosufficienti*). **~land** *n* patria *f*. **~less** *a* senza tetto

home: ~-'made *a* fatto in casa. **H~ Office** *n Br* ministero *m* degli interni. **H~ 'Secretary** *n Br* ministro *m* degli

interni. ~**sick** *a* **be** ~**sick** avere nostalgia (*for* di). ~**sickness** *n* nostalgia
f di casa. ~ '**town** *n* città *f inv* natia.
~**ward** *a* di ritorno ●*adv* verso casa.
~**work** *n Sch* compiti *mpl*
homicide /'hɒmɪsaɪd/ *n* (*crime*) omicidio *m*
homoeopath|ic /ˌhəʊmɪə'pæθɪk/ *a*
omeopatico. ~**y**/-'ɒpəθɪ/ *n* omeopatia *f*
homogeneous /ˌhɒmə'dʒiːnɪəs/ *a*
omogeneo
homo'sexual *a & n* omosessuale *mf*
honest /'ɒnɪst/ *a* onesto; (*frank*) sincero. ~**ly** *adv* onestamente; (*frankly*) sinceramente; ~**ly!** ma insomma!. ~**y** *n*
onestà *f*; (*frankness*) sincerità *f*
honey /'hʌnɪ/ *n* miele *m*; (*fam: darling*)
tesoro *m*
honey: ~**comb** *n* favo *m*. ~**moon** *n*
luna *f* di miele. ~**suckle** *n* caprifoglio *m*
honk /hɒŋk/ *vi Aut* clacsonare
honorary /'ɒnərərɪ/ *a* onorario
honour /'ɒnə(r)/ *n* onore *m* ●*vt* onorare. ~**able** /-əbl/ *a* onorevole. ~**ably** *adv*
con onore. ~**s degree** *n* = diploma *m*
di laurea
hood /hʊd/ *n* cappuccio *m*; (*of pram*)
tettuccio *m*; (*over cooker*) cappa *f*; *Am*
Auto cofano *m*
hoodlum /'hu:dləm/ *n* teppista *m*
'**hoodwink** *vt fam* infinocchiare
hoof /hu:f/ *n* (*pl* ~**s** *or* **hooves**) zoccolo *m*
hook /hʊk/ *n* gancio *m*; (*for fishing*)
amo *m*; **off the** ~ *Teleph* staccato; *fig*
fuori pericolo ●*vt* agganciare ●*vi* ag-
ganciarsi
hook|ed /hʊkt/ *a* (*nose*) adunco; ~**ed**
on (*fam: drugs*) dedito a; **be** ~**ed on**
skiing essere un fanatico dello sci. ~**er**
n Am sl battona *f*
hookey /'hʊkɪ/ *n* **play** ~ *Am fam* marinare la scuola
hooligan /'hu:lɪgən/ *n* teppista *mf*.
~**ism** *n* teppismo *m*
hoop /hu:p/ *n* cerchio *m*
hooray /hʊ'reɪ/ *int & n* = **hurrah**
hoot /hu:t/ *n* colpo *m* di clacson; (*of
siren*) ululato *m*; (*of owl*) grido *m* ●*vi*
(*owl:*) gridare; (*car:*) clacsonare; (*siren:*)
ululare; (*jeer*) fischiare. ~**er** *n* (*of
factory*) sirena *f*; *Auto* clacson *m inv*
hoover® /'hu:və(r)/ *n* aspirapolvere *m
inv* ●*vt* passare l'aspirapolvere su
(*carpet*); passare l'aspirapolvere in
(*room*)
hop /hɒp/ *n* saltello *m* ●*vi* (*pt/pp*

hopped) saltellare; ~ **it!** *fam* tela!. **hop**
in *vi fam* saltar su
hope /həʊp/ *n* speranza *f* ●*vi* sperare
(**for** in); **I** ~ **so**/**not** spero di sì/no ●*vt*
~ **that** sperare che
hope|ful /'həʊpfl/ *a* pieno di speranza;
(*promising*) promettente; **be** ~**ful that**
avere buone speranze che. ~**fully** *adv*
con speranza; (*it is hoped*) se tutto va
bene. ~**less** *a* senza speranze; (*useless*)
impossibile; (*incompetent*) incapace.
~**lessly** *adv* disperatamente; (*ineffi-
cient, lost*) completamente. ~**lessness**
n disperazione *f*
horde /hɔ:d/ *n* orda *f*
horizon /hə'raɪzn/ *n* orizzonte *m*
horizontal /hɒrɪ'zɒntl/ *a* orizzontale
hormone /'hɔ:məʊn/ *n* ormone *m*
horn /hɔ:n/ *n* corno *m*; *Auto* clacson *m
inv*
horny /'hɔ:nɪ/ *a* calloso; *fam* arrapato
horoscope /'hɒrəskəʊp/ *n* oroscopo *m*
horrib|le /'hɒrɪbl/ *a* orribile. ~**y** *adv*
spaventosamente
horrid /'hɒrɪd/ *a* orrendo
horrific /hə'rɪfɪk/ *a* raccapricciante;
(*fam: accident, prices, story*) terrificante
horrify /'hɒrɪfaɪ/ *vt* (*pt/pp* -**ied**) far
inorridire; **I was horrified** ero sconvolto. ~**ing** *a* terrificante
horror /'hɒrə(r)/ *n* orrore *m*. ~ **film** *n*
film *m* dell'orrore
hors-d'œuvre /ɔ:'dɜ:vr/ *n* antipasto *m*
horse /hɔ:s/ *n* cavallo *m*
horse: ~**back** *n* **on** ~**back** a cavallo.
~**man** *n* cavaliere *m*. ~**play** *n* gioco *m*
pesante. ~**power** *n* cavallo *m* [vapore].
~-**racing** *n* corse *fpl* di cavalli. ~**shoe**
n ferro *m* di cavallo
horti'cultural /hɔ:tɪ-/ *a* di orticoltura
'**horticulture** *n* orticoltura *f*
hose /həʊz/ *n* (*pipe*) manichetta *f*
●**hose down** *vt* lavare con la
manichetta
hospice /'hɒspɪs/ *n* (*for the terminally
ill*) ospedale *m* per i malati in fase terminale
hospitab|le /hɒ'spɪtəbl/ *a* ospitale. ~**y**
adv con ospitalità
hospital /'hɒspɪtl/ *n* ospedale *m*
hospitality /hɒspɪ'tælətɪ/ *n* ospitalità *f*
host[1] /həʊst/ *n* **a** ~ **of** una moltitudine
di
host[2] *n* ospite *m*
host[3] *n Relig* ostia *f*
hostage /'hɒstɪdʒ/ *n* ostaggio *m*; **hold**
sb ~ tenere qcno in ostaggio
hostel /'hɒstl/ *n* ostello *m*

hostess /'həʊstɪs/ n padrona f di casa; *Aeron* hostess f inv

hostile /'hɒstaɪl/ a ostile

hostilit|y /hɒ'stɪlətɪ/ n ostilità f; ~**ies** pl ostilità fpl

hot /hɒt/ a (hotter, hottest) caldo; (spicy) piccante; **I am or feel** ~ ho caldo; **it is** ~ fa caldo

'**hotbed** n fig focolaio m

hotchpotch /'hɒtʃpɒtʃ/ n miscuglio m

'**hot-dog** n hot dog m inv

hotel /həʊ'tel/ n albergo m. ~**ier** /-ɪə(r)/ n albergatore, -trice mf

hot: ~**head** n persona f impetuosa. ~**house** n serra f. ~**ly** adv fig accanitamente. ~**plate** n piastra f riscaldante ● **tap** n rubinetto m dell'acqua calda. ~-**tempered** a irascibile. ~-**water bottle** n borsa f dell'acqua calda

hound /haʊnd/ n cane m da caccia ● vt fig perseguire

hour /'aʊə(r)/ n ora f. ~**ly** a ad ogni ora; (pay, rate) a ora ● adv ogni ora

house[1] /haʊs/ n casa f; *Pol* camera f; *Theat* sala f; **at my** ~ a casa mia, da me

house[2] /haʊz/ vt alloggiare (person)

house /haʊs/: ~**boat** n casa f galleggiante. ~**breaking** n furto m con scasso. ~**hold** n casa f, famiglia f. ~**holder** n capo m di famiglia. ~**keeper** n governante f di casa. ~**keeping** n governo m della casa; (money) soldi mpl per le spese di casa. ~-**plant** n pianta f da appartamento. ~-**trained** a che non sporca in casa. ~-**warming** |**party**| n festa f di inaugurazione della nuova casa. ~**wife** n casalinga f. ~**work** n lavoro m domestico

housing /'haʊzɪŋ/ n alloggio m. ~ **estate** n zona f residenziale

hovel /'hɒvl/ n tugurio m

hover /'hɒvə(r)/ vi librarsi; (linger) indugiare. ~**craft** n hovercraft m inv

how /haʊ/ adv come; ~ **are you?** come stai?; ~ **about a coffee/going on holiday?** che ne diresti di un caffè/di andare in vacanza?; ~ **do you do?** molto lieto!; ~ **old are you?** quanti anni hai?; ~ **long** quanto tempo; ~ **many** quanti; ~ **much** quanto; ~ **often** ogni quanto; **and** ~! eccome!; ~ **odd!** che strano!

how'ever adv (nevertheless) comunque; ~ **small** per quanto piccolo

howl /haʊl/ n ululato m ● vi ululare; (cry, with laughter) singhiozzare. ~**er** n fam strafalcione m

HP n abbr hire purchase; n abbr (horse power) C.V.

hub /hʌb/ n mozzo m; fig centro m

hubbub /'hʌbʌb/ n baccano m

'**hub-cap** n coprimozzo m

huddle /'hʌdl/ vi ~ **together** rannicchiarsi

hue[1] /hju:/ n colore m

hue[2] n ~ **and cry** clamore m

huff /hʌf/ n **be in/go into a** ~ fare il broncio

hug /hʌg/ n abbraccio m ● vt (pt/pp hugged) abbracciare; (keep close to) tenersi vicino a

huge /hju:dʒ/ a enorme

hulking /'hʌlkɪŋ/ a fam grosso

hull /hʌl/ n Naut scafo m

hullo /hə'ləʊ/ int = hallo

hum /hʌm/ n ronzio m ● v (pt/pp hummed) ● vt canticchiare ● vi (motor:) ronzare; fig fervere (di attività); ~ **and haw** esitare

human /'hju:mən/ a umano ● n essere m umano. ~ **being** n essere m umano

humane /hju:'meɪn/ a umano

humanitarian /hju:mænɪ'teərɪən/ a & n umanitario, -a mf

humanit|y /hju:'mænətɪ/ n umanità f; ~**ies** pl Univ dottrine fpl umanistiche

humble /'hʌmbl/ a umile ● vt umiliare

humdrum a noioso

humid /'hju:mɪd/ a umido. ~**ifier** /-ɪdɪfaɪə(r)/ n umidificatore m. ~**ity** /-'mɪdətɪ/ n umidità f

humiliat|e /hju:'mɪlɪeɪt/ vt umiliare. ~**ion** /-'eɪʃn/ n umiliazione f

humility /hju:'mɪlətɪ/ n umiltà f

humorous /'hju:mərəs/ a umoristico. ~**ly** adv con spirito

humour /'hju:mə(r)/ n umorismo m; (mood) umore m; **have a sense of** ~ avere il senso dell'umorismo ● vt compiacere

hump /hʌmp/ n protuberanza f; (of camel, hunchback) gobba f

hunch /hʌntʃ/ n (idea) intuizione f

'**hunch|back** n gobbo, -a mf. ~**ed** a ~**ed up** incurvato

hundred /'hʌndrəd/ a **one/a** ~ cento ● n cento m; ~**s of** centinaia di. ~**th** a centesimo ● n centesimo m. ~**weight** n cinquanta chili m

hung /hʌŋ/ see hang

Hungarian /hʌŋ'geərɪən/ a & n ungherese mf; (language) ungherese m

Hungary /'hʌŋgərɪ/ n Ungheria f

hunger /'hʌŋgə(r)/ n fame f. **~-strike** n sciopero m della fame m

hungr|y /'hʌŋgrɪ/ a (-ier, -iest) affamato; **be ~y** aver fame. **~ily** adv con appetito

hunk /hʌŋk/ n [grosso] pezzo m

hunt /hʌnt/ n caccia f● vt andare a caccia di ⟨animal⟩; dare la caccia a ⟨criminal⟩ ● vi andare a caccia; **~ for** cercare. **~er** n cacciatore m. **~ing** n caccia f

hurdle /'hɜ:dl/ n Sport & fig ostacolo m. **~r** n ostacolista mf

hurl /hɜ:l/ vt scagliare

hurrah /hʊ'rɑ:/, **hurray** /hʊ'reɪ/ int urrà! ● n urrà m

hurricane /'hʌrɪkən/ n uragano m

hurried /'hʌrɪd/ a affrettato; ⟨job⟩ fatto in fretta. **~ly** adv in fretta

hurry /'hʌrɪ/ n fretta f; **be in a ~** aver fretta ● vi (pt/pp -ied) affrettarsi. **hurry up** vi sbrigarsi ● vt fare sbrigare ⟨person⟩; accelerare ⟨things⟩

hurt /hɜ:t/ v (pt/pp **hurt**) ● vt far male a; ⟨offend⟩ ferire ● vi far male; **my leg ~s** mi fa male la gamba. **~ful** a fig offensivo

hurtle /'hɜ:tl/ vi **~ along** andare a tutta velocità

husband /'hʌzbənd/ n marito m

hush /hʌʃ/ n silenzio m ● **hush up** vt mettere a tacere. **~ed** a ⟨voice⟩ sommesso. **~-hush** a fam segretissimo

husky /'hʌskɪ/ a (-ier, -iest) ⟨voice⟩ rauco

hustle /'hʌsl/ vt affrettare ● n attività f incessante; **~ and bustle** trambusto m

hut /hʌt/ n capanna f

hybrid /'haɪbrɪd/ a ibrido ● n ibrido m

hydrant /'haɪdrənt/ n [fire] ~ idrante m

hydraulic /haɪ'drɔ:lɪk/ a idraulico

hydro'electric /haɪdrəʊ-/ a idroelettrico

hydrofoil /'haɪdrə-/ n aliscafo m

hydrogen /'haɪdrədʒən/ n idrogeno m

hyena /haɪ'i:nə/ n iena f

hygien|e /'haɪdʒi:n/ n igiene f. **~ic** /haɪ'dʒi:nɪk/ a igienico

hymn /hɪm/ n inno m. **~-book** n libro m dei canti

hypermarket /'haɪpəmɑ:kɪt/ n ipermercato m

hyphen /'haɪfn/ n lineetta f. **~ate** vt unire con lineetta

hypno|sis /hɪp'nəʊsɪs/ n ipnosi f. **~tic** /-'nɒtɪk/ a ipnotico

hypno|tism /'hɪpnətɪzm/ n ipnotismo m. **~tist** /-tɪst/ n ipnotizzatore, -trice mf. **~tize** vt ipnotizzare

hypochondriac /haɪpə'kɒndrɪæk/ a ⟨ipocondriaco ● n ipocondriaco, -a mf

hypocrisy /hɪ'pɒkrəsɪ/ n ipocrisia f

hypocrit|e /'hɪpəkrɪt/ n ipocrita mf. **~ical** /-'krɪtɪkl/ a ipocrita

hypodermic /haɪpə'dɜ:mɪk/ a & n ~ [syringe] siringa f ipodermica

hypothe|sis /haɪ'pɒθəsɪs/ n ipotesi f inv. **~tical** /-ə'θetɪkl/ a ipotetico. **~tically** adv in teoria; ⟨speak⟩ per ipotesi

hyster|ia /hɪ'stɪərɪə/ n isterismo m. **~ical** /-'sterɪkl/ a isterico. **~ically** adv istericamente; **~ically funny** da morir dal ridere. **~ics** /hɪ'sterɪks/ npl attacco m isterico

---

I i

I /aɪ/ pron io; **I'm tired** sono stanco; **he's going, but I'm not** lui va, ma io no

ice /aɪs/ n ghiaccio m ● vt glassare ⟨cake⟩. **ice over/up** vi ghiacciarsi

ice: ~ **age** n era f glaciale. **~-axe** n piccozza f per il ghiaccio. **~berg** /-bɜ:g/ n iceberg m inv. **~box** n Am frigorifero m. **~-'cream** n gelato m. **~-'cream parlour** n gelateria f. **~-cube** n cubetto m di ghiaccio. ~ **hockey** n hockey m su ghiaccio

Iceland /'aɪslənd/ n Islanda f. **~er** n islandese mf; **~ic** /-'lændɪk/ a & n islandese m

ice: ~ **'lolly** n ghiacciolo m. ~ **rink** n pista f di pattinaggio. ~ **skater** pattinatore, -trice mf sul ghiaccio. ~ **skating** pattinaggio m sul ghiaccio

icicle /'aɪsɪkl/ n ghiacciolo m

icily /'aɪsɪlɪ/ adv gelidamente

icing /'aɪsɪŋ/ n glassa f. ~ **sugar** n zucchero m a velo

icon /ˈaɪkɒn/ n icona f

icy /ˈaɪsɪ/ a (-ier, -iest) ghiacciato; fig gelido

idea /aɪˈdɪə/ n idea f; **I've no ~!** non ne ho idea!

ideal /aɪˈdɪəl/ a ideale ● n ideale m. **~ism** n idealismo m. **~ist** n idealista mf. **~istic** /-ˈlɪstɪk/ a idealistico. **~ize** vt idealizzare. **~ly** adv idealmente

identical /aɪˈdentɪkl/ a identico

identi|fication /aɪdentɪfɪˈkeɪʃn/ n identificazione f; (proof of identity) documento m di riconoscimento. **~fy** /aɪˈdentɪfaɪ/ vt (pt/pp -ied) identificare

identikit® /aɪˈdentɪkɪt/ n identikit m inv

identity /aɪˈdentətɪ/ n identità f inv. **~ card** n carta f d'identità

ideolog|ical /aɪdɪəˈlɒdʒɪkl/ a ideologico. **~y** /aɪdɪˈɒlədʒɪ/ n ideologia f

idiom /ˈɪdɪəm/ n idioma f. **~atic** /-ˈmætɪk/ a idiomatico

idiosyncrasy /ɪdɪəˈsɪŋkrəsɪ/ n idiosincrasia f

idiot /ˈɪdɪət/ n idiota mf. **~ic** /-ˈɒtɪk/ a idiota

idl|e /ˈaɪd(ə)l/ a (lazy) pigro, ozioso; (empty) vano; (machine) fermo ● vi oziare; (engine:) girare a vuoto. **~eness** n ozio m. **~y** adv oziosamente

idol /ˈaɪdl/ n idolo m. **~ize** /ˈaɪdəlaɪz/ vt idolatrare

idyllic /ɪˈdɪlɪk/ a idillico

i.e. abbr (id est) cioè

if /ɪf/ conj se; **as if** come se

ignite /ɪgˈnaɪt/ vt dar fuoco a ● vi prender fuoco

ignition /ɪgˈnɪʃn/ n Auto accensione f. **~ key** n chiave f d'accensione

ignoramus /ɪgnəˈreɪməs/ n ignorante mf

ignoran|ce /ˈɪgnərəns/ n ignoranza f. **~t** a (lacking knowledge) ignaro; (rude) ignorante

ignore /ɪgˈnɔː(r)/ vt ignorare

ill /ɪl/ a ammalato; **feel ~ at ease** sentirsi a disagio ● adv male ● n male m. **~-advised** a avventato. **~-bred** a maleducato

illegal /ɪˈliːgl/ a illegale

illegible /ɪˈledʒɪbl/ a illeggibile

illegitima|cy /ɪlɪˈdʒɪtɪməsɪ/ n illegittimità f. **~te** /-mət/ a illegittimo

illicit /ɪˈlɪsɪt/ a illecito

illitera|cy /ɪˈlɪtərəsɪ/ n analfabetismo m. **~te** /-rət/ a & n analfabeta mf

illness /ˈɪlnɪs/ n malattia f

illogical /ɪˈlɒdʒɪkl/ a illogico

ill-treat /ɪlˈtriːt/ vt maltrattare. **~ment** n maltrattamento m

illuminat|e /ɪˈluːmɪnət/ vt illuminare. **~ing** a chiarificatore. **~ion** /-ˈneɪʃn/ n illuminazione f

illusion /ɪˈluːʒn/ n illusione f; **be under the ~ that** avere l'illusione che

illusory /ɪˈluːsərɪ/ a illusorio

illustrat|e /ˈɪləstreɪt/ vt illustrare. **~ion** /-ˈstreɪʃn/ n illustrazione f. **~or** n illustratore, -trice mf

illustrious /ɪˈlʌstrɪəs/ a illustre

ill 'will n malanimo m

image /ˈɪmɪdʒ/ n immagine f; (exact likeness) ritratto m

imagin|able /ɪˈmædʒɪnəbl/ a immaginabile. **~ary** /-ərɪ/ a immaginario

imaginat|ion /ɪmædʒɪˈneɪʃn/ n immaginazione f, fantasia f; **it's your ~ion** è solo una tua idea. **~ive** /ɪˈmædʒɪnətɪv/ a fantasioso. **~ively** adv con fantasia or immaginazione

imagine /ɪˈmædʒɪn/ vt immaginare; (wrongly) inventare

im'balance n squilibrio m

imbecile /ˈɪmbəsiːl/ n imbecille mf

imbibe /ɪmˈbaɪb/ vt ingerire

imbue /ɪmˈbjuː/ vt **~d with** impregnato di

imitat|e /ˈɪmɪteɪt/ vt imitare. **~ion** /-ˈteɪʃn/ n imitazione f. **~or** n imitatore, -trice mf

immaculate /ɪˈmækjʊlət/ a immacolato. **~ly** adv immacolatamente

imma'terial a (unimportant) irrilevante

imma'ture a immaturo

immediate /ɪˈmiːdɪət/ a immediato; (relative) stretto; **in the ~ vicinity** nelle immediate vicinanze. **~ly** adv immediatamente; **~ly next to** subito accanto a ● conj (non) appena

immemorial /ɪmɪˈmɔːrɪəl/ a **from time ~** da tempo immemorabile

immense /ɪˈmens/ a immenso

immers|e /ɪˈmɜːs/ vt immergere; **be ~ed in** fig essere immerso in. **~ion** /-ɜːʃn/ n immersione f. **~ion heater** n scaldabagno m elettrico

immigrant /ˈɪmɪgrənt/ n immigrante mf

immigrat|e /ˈɪmɪgreɪt/ vi immigrare. **~ion** /-ˈgreɪʃn/ n immigrazione f

imminent /ˈɪmɪnənt/ a imminente

immobil|e /ɪˈməʊbaɪl/ a immobile. **~ize** /-bɪlaɪz/ vt immobilizzare

immoderate /ɪˈmɒdərət/ a smodato

immodest /ɪˈmɒdɪst/ a immodesto

immoral /ɪ'mɒrəl/ a immorale. **~ity** /ɪmə'rælətɪ/ n immoralità f

immortal /ɪ'mɔːtl/ a immortale. **~ity** /-'tælətɪ/ n immortalità f. **~ize** vt immortalare

immovable /ɪ'muːvəbl/ a fig irremovibile

immune /ɪ'mjuːn/ a immune (**to/from** da). **~ system** n sistema m immunitario

immunity /ɪ'mjuːnətɪ/ n immunità f

immunize /ɪ'mjunaɪz/ vt immunizzare

imp /ɪmp/ n diavoletto m

impact /'ɪmpækt/ n impatto m

impair /ɪm'peə(r)/ vt danneggiare

impale /ɪm'peɪl/ vt impalare

impart /ɪm'pɑːt/ vt impartire

im'parti|al a imparziale. **~ality** n imparzialità f

im'passable a impraticabile

impasse /æm'pɑːs/ n fig impasse f inv

impassioned /ɪm'pæʃnd/ a appassionato

im'passive a impassibile

im'patien|ce n impazienza f. **~t** a impaziente. **~tly** adv impazientemente

impeccabl|e /ɪm'pekəbl/ a impeccabile. **~y** adv in modo impeccabile

impede /ɪm'piːd/ vt impedire

impediment /ɪm'pedɪmənt/ n impedimento m; (in speech) difetto m

impel /ɪm'pel/ vt (pt/pp impelled) costringere; **feel ~led** to sentire l'obbligo di

impending /ɪm'pendɪŋ/ a imminente

impenetrable /ɪm'penɪtrəbl/ a impenetrabile

imperative /ɪm'perətɪv/ a imperativo ●n Gram imperativo m.

imper'ceptible a impercettibile

im'perfect a imperfetto; (faulty) difettoso ●n Gram imperfetto m. **~ion** /-'fekʃn/ n imperfezione f

imperial /ɪm'pɪərɪəl/ a imperiale. **~ism** n imperialismo m. **~ist** n imperialista mf

imperious /ɪm'pɪərɪəs/ a imperioso

im'personal a impersonale

impersonat|e /ɪm'pɜːsəneɪt/ vt impersonare. **~or** n imitatore, -trice mf

impertinen|ce /ɪm'pɜːtɪnəns/ n impertinenza f. **~t** a impertinente

imperturbable /ɪmpə'tɜːbəbl/ a imperturbabile

impervious /ɪm'pɜːvɪəs/ a **~ to** fig indifferente a

impetuous /ɪm'petjuəs/ a impetuoso. **~ly** adv impetuosamente

impetus /'ɪmpɪtəs/ n impeto m

implacable /ɪm'plækəbl/ a implacabile

im'plant¹ vt trapiantare; fig inculcare
'implant² n trapianto m

implement¹ /'ɪmplɪmənt/ n attrezzo m

implement² /'ɪmplɪment/ vt mettere in atto

implicat|e /'ɪmplɪkeɪt/ vt implicare. **~ion** /-'keɪʃn/ n implicazione f; **by ~ion** implicitamente

implicit /ɪm'plɪsɪt/ a implicito; (absolute) assoluto

implore /ɪm'plɔː(r)/ vt implorare

imply /ɪm'plaɪ/ vt (pt/pp -ied) implicare; **what are you ~ing?** che cosa vorresti insinuare?

impo'lite a sgarbato

import¹ /'ɪmpɔːt/ n Comm importazione f

import² /ɪm'pɔːt/ vt importare

importan|ce /ɪm'pɔːtəns/ n importanza f. **~t** a importante

importer /ɪm'pɔːtə(r)/ n importatore, -trice mf

impos|e /ɪm'pəʊz/ vt imporre (**on** a) ●vi imporsi; **~e on** abusare di. **~ing** a imponente. **~ition** /ɪmpə'zɪʃn/ n imposizione f

impossi'bility n impossibilità f

im'possibl|e a impossibile

impostor /ɪm'pɒstə(r)/ n impostore, -trice mf

impoten|ce /'ɪmpətəns/ n impotenza f. **~t** a impotente

impound /ɪm'paʊnd/ vt confiscare

impoverished /ɪm'pɒvərɪʃt/ a impoverito

im'practicable a impraticabile

im'practical a non pratico

impre'cise a impreciso

impregnable /ɪm'pregnəbl/ a imprendibile

impregnate /'ɪmpregneɪt/ vt impregnare (**with** di); Biol fecondare

im'press vt imprimere; fig colpire (positivamente); **~ sth [up]on sb** fare capire qcsa a qcno

impression /ɪm'preʃn/ n impressione f; (imitation) imitazione f. **~able** a (child, mind) influenzabile. **~ism** n impressionismo m. **~ist** n imitatore, -trice mf; (artist) impressionista mf

impressive /ɪm'presɪv/ a imponente

'imprint¹ n impressione f

im'print² vt imprimere; **~ed on my mind** impresso nella mia memoria

im'prison vt incarcerare. **~ment** n reclusione f

im'probable a improbabile

impromptu /ɪmˈprɒmptju:/ a improvvisato

im'proper a ⟨use⟩ improprio; ⟨behaviour⟩ scorretto. **~ly** adv scorrettamente

impro'priety n scorrettezza f

improve /ɪmˈpru:v/ vt/i migliorare. **improve |up|on** vt perfezionare. **~ment** /-mənt/ n miglioramento m

improvis|e /ˈɪmprəvaɪz/ vt/i improvvisare

im'prudent a imprudente

impuden|ce /ˈɪmpjʊdəns/ n sfrontatezza f. **~t** a sfrontato

impuls|e /ˈɪmpʌls/ n impulso m; on |an| **~e** impulsivamente. **~ive** /-ˈpʌlsɪv/ a impulsivo

impunity /ɪmˈpju:nətɪ/ n with **~** impunemente

im'pur|e a impuro; **~ity** n impurità f inv; **~ities** pl impurità fpl

impute /ɪmˈpju:t/ vt imputare (**to** a)

in /ɪn/ prep in; ⟨with names of towns⟩ a; **in the garden** in giardino; **in the street** in or per strada; **in bed/hospital** a letto/all'ospedale; **in the world** nel mondo; **in the rain** sotto la pioggia; **in the sun** al sole; **in this heat** con questo caldo; **in summer/winter** in estate/inverno; **in 1995** nel 1995; **in the evening** la sera; **he's arriving in two hours' time** arriva fra due ore; **deaf in one ear** sordo da un orecchio; **in the army** nell'esercito; **in English/Italian** in inglese/italiano; **in ink/pencil** a penna/matita; **in red** ⟨dressed, circled⟩ di rosso; **the man in the raincoat** l'uomo con l'impermeabile; **in a soft/loud voice** a voce bassa/alta; **one in ten people** una persona su dieci; **in doing this, he…** nel far questo,…; **in itself** in sé; **in that** in quanto ● adv ⟨at home⟩ a casa; ⟨indoors⟩ dentro; **he's not in yet** non è ancora arrivato; **in there/here** lì/qui dentro; **ten in all** dieci in tutto; **day in, day out** giorno dopo giorno; **have it in for sb** fam avercela con qcno; **send him in** fallo entrare; **come in** entrare; **bring in the washing** portare dentro i panni ● a ⟨fam: in fashion⟩ di moda ● n the **ins and outs** i dettagli

ina'bility n incapacità f

inac'cessible a inaccessibile

in'accura|cy n inesattezza f. **~te** a inesatto

in'ac|tive a inattivo. **~ tivity** n inattività f

in'adequate a inadeguato. **~ly** adv inadeguatamente

inad'missible a inammissibile

inadvertently /ɪnədˈvɜ:təntlɪ/ adv inavvertitamente

inad'visable a sconsigliabile

inane /ɪˈneɪn/ a stupido

in'animate a esanime

in'applicable a inapplicabile

inap'propriate a inadatto

inar'ticulate a inarticolato

inat'tentive a disattento

in'audib|le a impercettibile

inaugural /ɪˈnɔ:gjʊrəl/ a inaugurale

inaugurat|e /ɪˈnɔ:gjʊreɪt/ vt inaugurare. **~ion** /-ˈreɪʃn/ n inaugurazione f

inau'spicious a infausto

inborn /ˈɪnbɔ:n/ a innato

inbred /ɪnˈbred/ a congenito

incalculable /ɪnˈkælkjʊləbl/ a incalcolabile

in'capable a incapace

incapacitate /ɪnkəˈpæsɪteɪt/ vt rendere incapace

incarnate /ɪnˈkɑ:nət/ a **the devil ~e** il diavolo in carne e ossa

incendiary /ɪnˈsendɪərɪ/ a incendiario

incense¹ /ˈɪnsens/ n incenso m

incense² /ɪnˈsens/ vt esasperare

incentive /ɪnˈsentɪv/ n incentivo m

incessant /ɪnˈsesənt/ a incessante

incest /ˈɪnsest/ n incesto m

inch /ɪntʃ/ n pollice m (= 2.54 cm) ● vi **~ forward** avanzare gradatamente

inciden|ce /ˈɪnsɪdəns/ n incidenza f. **~t** n incidente m

incidental /ɪnsɪˈdentl/ a incidentale; **~ expenses** spese fpl accessorie. **~ly** adv incidentalmente; ⟨by the way⟩ a proposito

incinerat|e /ɪnˈsɪnəreɪt/ vt incenerire. **~or** n inceneritore m

incision /ɪnˈsɪʒn/ n incisione f

incisive /ɪnˈsaɪsɪv/ a incisivo

incisor /ɪnˈsaɪzə(r)/ n incisivo m

incite /ɪnˈsaɪt/ vt incitare. **~ment** n incitamento m

inclination /ɪnklɪˈneɪʃn/ n inclinazione f

incline¹ /ɪnˈklaɪn/ vt inclinare; **be ~d to do sth** essere propenso a fare qcsa

incline² /ˈɪnklaɪn/ n pendio m

include /ɪnˈklu:d/ vt includere. **~ding** prep incluso. **~sion** /-u:ʒn/ n inclusione f

inclusive /ɪnˈkluːsɪv/ *a* incluso; ~ **of** comprendente; **be** = **of** comprendere ● *adv* incluso

incognito /ɪnkɒɡˈniːtəʊ/ *adv* incognito

inco'herent *a* incoerente; (*because drunk etc*) incomprensibile

income /ˈɪnkʌm/ *n* reddito *m*. ~ **tax** *n* imposta *f* sul reddito

'incoming *a* in arrivo. ~ **tide** *n* marea *f* montante

in'comparable *a* incomparabile

incompati'bility *n* incompatibilità *f*

incom'patible *a* incompatibile

incom'peten|ce *n* incompetenza *f*. ~ **t** *a* incompetente

incom'plete *a* incompleto

incompre'hensible *a* incomprensibile

incon'ceivable *a* inconcepibile

incon'clusive *a* inconcludente

incongruous /ɪnˈkɒŋɡruəs/ *a* contrastante

inconsequential /ɪnkɒnsɪˈkwenʃl/ *a* senza importanza

incon'siderate *a* trascurabile

incon'sistency *n* incoerenza *f*

incon'sistent *a* incoerente; **be** = **with** non essere coerente con. ~**ly** *adv* in modo incoerente

inconsolable /ɪnkənˈsəʊləbl/ *a* inconsolabile

incon'spicuous *a* non appariscente. ~**ly** *adv* modestamente

incontinen|ce /ɪnˈkɒntɪnəns/ *n* incontinenza *f*. ~**t** *a* incontinente

incon'venien|ce *n* scomodità *f*; (*drawback*) inconveniente *m*; **put sb to** ~ **ce** dare disturbo a qcno. ~**t** *a* scomodo; (*time, place*) inopportuno. ~**tly** *adv* in modo inopportuno

incorporate /ɪnˈkɔːpəreɪt/ *vt* incorporare; (*contain*) comprendere

incor'rect *a* incorretto. ~**ly** *adv* scorrettamente

incorrigible /ɪnˈkɒrɪdʒəbl/ *a* incorreggibile

incorruptible /ɪnkəˈrʌptəbl/ *a* incorruttibile

increase[1] /ˈɪnkriːs/ *n* aumento *m*; **on the** ~ in aumento

increas|e[2] /ɪnˈkriːs/ *vt/i* aumentare. ~**ing** *a* (*impatience etc*) crescente; (*numbers*) in aumento. ~**ingly** *adv* sempre più

in'credible *a* incredibile

incredulous /ɪnˈkredjʊləs/ *a* incredulo

increment /ˈɪnkrɪmənt/ *n* incremento *m*

incriminate /ɪnˈkrɪmɪneɪt/ *vt* Jur incriminare

incubat|e /ˈɪnkjʊbeɪt/ *vt* incubare. ~**ion** /-ˈbeɪʃn/ *n* incubazione *f*. ~**ion period** *n* Med periodo *m* di incubazione. ~**or** *n* (*for baby*) incubatrice *f*

incumbent /ɪnˈkʌmbənt/ *a* **be** = **on sb** incombere a qcno

incur /ɪnˈkɜː(r)/ *vt* (*pt/pp* **incurred**) incorrere; contrarre (*debts*)

in'curable *a* incurabile

incursion /ɪnˈkɜːʃn/ *n* incursione *f*

indebted /ɪnˈdetɪd/ *a* obbligato (**to** verso)

in'decent *a* indecente

inde'cision *n* indecisione *f*

inde'cisive *a* indeciso. ~**ness** *n* indecisione *f*

indeed /ɪnˈdiːd/ *adv* (*in fact*) difatti; **yes** ~**!** sì, certamente!; ~ **I am/do** veramente!; **very much** ~ moltissimo; **thank you very much** ~ grazie infinite; ~**?** davvero?

indefatigable /ɪndɪˈfætɪɡəbl/ *a* instancabile

inde'finable *a* indefinibile

in'definite *a* indefinito. ~**ly** *adv* indefinitamente; (*postpone*) a tempo indeterminato

indelible /ɪnˈdelɪbl/ *a* indelebile

indemnity /ɪnˈdemnɪti/ *n* indennità *f inv*

indent[1] /ˈɪndent/ *n* Typ rientranza *f* dal margine

indent[2] /ɪnˈdent/ *vt* Typ fare rientrare dal margine. ~**ation** /-ˈteɪʃn/ *n* (*notch*) intaccatura *f*

inde'penden|ce *n* indipendenza *f*. ~**t** *a* indipendente. ~**tly** *adv* indipendentemente

indescribable /ɪndɪˈskraɪbəbl/ *a* indescrivibile

indestructible /ɪndɪˈstrʌktəbl/ *a* indistruttibile

indeterminate /ɪndɪˈtɜːmɪnət/ *a* indeterminato

index /ˈɪndeks/ *n* indice *m*

index: ~ **card** *n* scheda *f*. ~ **finger** *n* dito *m* indice. ~**-linked** *a* (*pension*) legato al costo della vita

India /ˈɪndɪə/ *n* India *f*. ~**n** *a* indiano; (*American*) indiano [d'America] ● *n* indiano, -a *mf*; (*American*) indiano, -a *mf* [d'America], pellerossa *mf inv*

indicat|e /ˈɪndɪkeɪt/ *vt* indicare;

(register) segnare ●vi Auto mettere la freccia. ~ion /-'keɪʃn/ n indicazione f
indicative /ɪn'dɪkətɪv/ a be ~ of essere indicativo di ●n Gram indicativo m
indicator /'ɪndɪkeɪtə(r)/ n Auto freccia f
indict /ɪn'daɪt/ vt accusare. ~ment n accusa f
in'differen|ce n indifferenza f. ~t a indifferente; (not good) mediocre
indigenous /ɪn'dɪdʒɪnəs/ a indigeno
indi'gest|ible a indigesto. ~ion n indigestione f
indignant /ɪn'dɪgnənt/ a indignato. ~ntly adv con indignazione. ~tion /-'neɪʃn/ n indignazione f
in'dignity n umiliazione f
indi'rect a indiretto. ~ly adv indirettamente
indi'screet a indiscreto
indis'cretion n indiscrezione f
indiscriminate /ɪndɪ'skrɪmɪnət/ a indiscriminato. ~ly adv senza distinzione
indi'spensable a indispensabile
indisposed /ɪndɪ'spəʊzd/ a indisposto
indisputable /ɪndɪ'spjuːtəbl/ a indisputabile
indi'stinct a indistinto
indistinguishable /ɪndɪ'stɪŋgwɪʃəbl/ a indistinguibile
individual /ɪndɪ'vɪdjʊəl/ a individuale ●n individuo m. ~ity /-'ælətɪ/ n individualità f
indi'visible a indivisibile
indoctrinate /ɪn'dɒktrɪneɪt/ vt indottrinare
indomitable /ɪn'dɒmɪtəbl/ a indomito
indoor /'ɪndɔː(r)/ a interno; (shoes) per casa; (plant) da appartamento; (swimming pool etc) coperto. ~s /-'dɔːz/ adv dentro
induce /ɪn'djuːs/ vt indurre (to a); (produce) causare. ~ment n (incentive) incentivo m
indulge /ɪn'dʌldʒ/ vt soddisfare; viziare (child) ●vi ~ in concedersi. ~nce /-əns/ n lusso m; (leniency) indulgenza f. ~nt a indulgente
industrial /ɪn'dʌstrɪəl/ a industriale; take ~ action scioperare. ~ist n industriale mf. ~ized a industrializzato
industri|ous /ɪn'dʌstrɪəs/ a industrioso. ~y /'ɪndəstrɪ/ n industria f; (zeal) operosità f
inebriated /ɪ'niːbrɪeɪtɪd/ a ebbro
in'edible a immangiabile
inef'fective a inefficace

ineffectual /ɪnɪ'fektʃʊəl/ a inutile; (person) inconcludente
inef'ficien|cy n inefficienza f. ~t a inefficiente
in'eligible a inadatto
inept /ɪ'nept/ a inetto
ine'quality n ineguaglianza f
inert /ɪ'nɜːt/ a inerte. ~ia /ɪ'nɜːʃə/ n inerzia f
inescapable /ɪnɪ'skeɪpəbl/ a inevitabile
inestimable /ɪn'estɪməbl/ a inestimabile
inevitabl|e /ɪn'evɪtəbl/ a inevitabile. ~y adv inevitabilmente
ine'xact a inesatto
inex'cusable a imperdonabile
inexhaustible /ɪnɪg'zɔːstəbl/ a inesauribile
inexorable /ɪn'eksərəbl/ a inesorabile
inex'pensive a poco costoso
inex'perience n inesperienza f. ~d a inesperto
inexplicable /ɪnɪk'splɪkəbl/ a inesplicabile
in'fallible a infallibile
infam|ous /'ɪnfəməs/ a infame; (person) famigerato. ~y n infamia f
infan|cy /'ɪnfənsɪ/ n infanzia f; in its ~cy fig agli inizi. ~t n bambino, -a mf piccolo, -a. ~tile a infantile
infantry /'ɪnfəntrɪ/ n fanteria f
infatuat|ed /ɪn'fætʃʊeɪtɪd/ a infatuato (with di). ~ion n infatuazione f
infect /ɪn'fekt/ vt infettare; become ~ed (wound:) infettarsi. ~ion /-'fekʃn/ n infezione f. ~ious /-'fekʃəs/ a infettivo
infer /ɪn'fɜː(r)/ vt (pt/pp inferred) dedurre (from da); (imply) implicare. ~ence /'ɪnfərəns/ n deduzione f
inferior /ɪn'fɪərɪə(r)/ a inferiore; (goods) scadente; (in rank) subalterno ●n inferiore mf; (in rank) subalterno, -a mf
inferiority /ɪnfɪərɪ'ɒrətɪ/ n inferiorità f. ~ complex n complesso m di inferiorità
infern|al /ɪn'fɜːnl/ a infernale. ~o n inferno m
in'fertile a sterile. ~'tility n sterilità f
infest /ɪn'fest/ vt be ~ed with essere infestato di
infi'delity n infedeltà f
infighting /'ɪnfaɪtɪŋ/ n fig lotta f per il potere
infiltrate /'ɪnfɪltreɪt/ vt infiltrare; Pol infiltrarsi in
infinite /'ɪnfɪnət/ a infinito

infinitive /ɪnˈfɪnətɪv/ n Gram infinito m

infinity /ɪnˈfɪnəti/ n infinità f

infirm /ɪnˈfɜ:m/ a debole. **~ary** n infermeria f. **~ity** n debolezza f

inflame /ɪnˈfleɪm/ vt infiammare; **become ~d** infiammarsi

in'flammable a infiammabile

inflammation /ɪnfləˈmeɪʃn/ n infiammazione f

inflammatory /ɪnˈflæmətrɪ/ a incendiario

inflatable /ɪnˈfleɪtəbl/ a gonfiabile

inflat|e /ɪnˈfleɪt/ vt gonfiare. **~ion** /-eɪʃn/ n inflazione f. **~ionary** /-eɪʃənərɪ/ a inflazionario

in'flexible a inflessibile

inflexion /ɪnˈflekʃn/ n inflessione f

inflict /ɪnˈflɪkt/ vt infliggere (**on** a)

influen|ce /ˈɪnfluəns/ n influenza f ● vt influenzare. **~tial** /-ˈenʃl/ a influente

influenza /ɪnfluˈenzə/ n influenza f

influx /ˈɪnflʌks/ n affluenza f

inform /ɪnˈfɔ:m/ vt informare; **keep sb ~ed** tenere qcno al corrente ● vi ~ **against** denunziare

in'for|mal a informale; ⟨agreement⟩ ufficioso. **~mally** adv in modo informale. **~mality** n informalità f inv

informant /ɪnˈfɔ:mənt/ n informatore, -trice mf

informat|ion /ɪnfəˈmeɪʃn/ n informazioni fpl; **a piece of ~** un'informazione. **~ion highway** n autostrada f telematica. **~ion technology** n informatica f. **~ive** /ɪnˈfɔ:mətɪv/ a informativo; ⟨film, book⟩ istruttivo

informer /ɪnˈfɔ:mə(r)/ n informatore, -trice mf; Pol delatore, -trice mf

infra-'red /ɪnfrə-/ a infrarosso

infrastructure /ˈɪnfrəstrʌktʃə(r)/ n infrastruttura f

infringe /ɪnˈfrɪndʒ/ vt ~ **on** usurpare. **~ment** n violazione f

infuriat|e /ɪnˈfjʊərɪeɪt/ vt infuriare. **~ing** a esasperante

infusion /ɪnˈfju:ʒn/ n ⟨drink⟩ infusione f; ⟨of capital, new blood⟩ afflusso m

ingenious /ɪnˈdʒi:nɪəs/ a ingegnoso

ingenuity /ɪndʒɪˈnju:ətɪ/ n ingegnosità f

ingenuous /ɪnˈdʒenjʊəs/ a ingenuo

ingot /ˈɪŋɡət/ n lingotto m

ingrained /ɪnˈɡreɪnd/ a ⟨in person⟩ radicato; ⟨dirt⟩ incrostato

ingratiate /ɪnˈɡreɪʃɪeɪt/ vt ~ **oneself with sb** ingraziarsi qcno

in'gratitude n ingratitudine f

ingredient /ɪnˈɡri:dɪənt/ n ingrediente m

ingrowing /ˈɪnɡrəʊɪŋ/ a ⟨nail⟩ incarnito

inhabit /ɪnˈhæbɪt/ vt abitare. **~ant** n abitante mf

inhale /ɪnˈheɪl/ vt aspirare; Med inalare ● vi inspirare; (when smoking) aspirare. **~r** n ⟨device⟩ inalatore m

inherent /ɪnˈhɪərənt/ a inerente

inherit /ɪnˈherɪt/ vt ereditare. **~ance** /-əns/ n eredità f inv

inhibit /ɪnˈhɪbɪt/ vt inibire. **~ed** a inibito. **~ion** /-ˈbɪʃn/ n inibizione f

inho'spitable a inospitale

in'human a disumano

initial /ɪˈnɪʃl/ a iniziale ● n iniziale f ● vt (pt/pp **initialled**) siglare. **~ly** adv all'inizio

initiat|e /ɪˈnɪʃɪeɪt/ vt iniziare. **~ion** /-ˈeɪʃn/ n iniziazione f

initiative /ɪˈnɪʃətɪv/ n iniziativa f

inject /ɪnˈdʒekt/ vt iniettare. **~ion** /-ekʃn/ n iniezione f

injur|e /ˈɪndʒə(r)/ vt ferire; (wrong) nuocere. **~y** n ferita f; (wrong) torto m

in'justice n ingiustizia f; **do sb an ~** giudicare qcno in modo sbagliato

ink /ɪŋk/ n inchiostro m

inkling /ˈɪŋklɪŋ/ n sentore m

inlaid /ɪnˈleɪd/ a intarsiato

inland /ˈɪnlənd/ a interno ● adv all'interno. **I~ Revenue** n fisco m

in-laws /ˈɪnlɔ:z/ npl fam parenti mpl acquisiti

inlay /ˈɪnleɪ/ n intarsio m

inlet /ˈɪnlet/ n insenatura f; Techn entrata f

inmate /ˈɪnmeɪt/ n ⟨of hospital⟩ degente mf; ⟨of prison⟩ carcerato, -a mf

inn /ɪn/ n locanda f

innate /ɪˈneɪt/ a innato

inner /ˈɪnə(r)/ a interno. **~most** a il più profondo. **~ tube** n camera f d'aria

'innkeeper n locandiere, -a mf

innocen|ce /ˈɪnəsəns/ n innocenza f. **~t** a innocente

innocuous /ɪˈnɒkjʊəs/ a innocuo

innovat|e /ˈɪnəveɪt/ vi innovare. **~ion** /-ˈveɪʃn/ n innovazione f. **~ive** /ˈɪnəvətɪv/ a innovativo. **~or** /ˈɪnəveɪtə(r)/ n innovatore, -trice mf

innuendo /ɪnjʊˈendəʊ/ n (pl **-es**) insinuazione f

innumerable /ɪˈnju:mərəbl/ a innumerevole

inoculat|e /ɪˈnɒkjʊleɪt/ vt vaccinare. **~ion** /-ˈleɪʃn/ n vaccinazione f

inof'fensive *a* inoffensivo

in'operable *a* inoperabile

in'opportune *a* inopportuno

inordinate /ɪˈnɔːdɪnət/ *a* smodato

inor'ganic *a* inorganico

'in-patient *n* degente *mf*

input /ˈɪnpʊt/ *n* input *m inv*, ingresso *m*

inquest /ˈɪnkwest/ *n* inchiesta *f*

inquire /ɪnˈkwaɪə(r)/ *vi* informarsi ⟨about⟩su⟩; ~e into far indagini su ● *vt* domandare. **~y** *n* domanda *f*. ⟨investigation⟩ inchiesta *f*

inquisitive /ɪnˈkwɪzətɪv/ *a* curioso

inroad /ˈɪnrəʊd/ *n* make ~s into intaccare ⟨savings⟩; cominciare a risolvere ⟨problem⟩

in'sane *a* pazzo; *fig* insensato

in'sanitary *a* malsano

in'sanity *n* pazzia *f*

insatiable /ɪnˈseɪʃəbl/ *a* insaziabile

inscribe /ɪnˈskraɪb/ *vt* iscrivere. **~ption** /ˈskrɪpʃn/ *n* iscrizione *f*

inscrutable /ɪnˈskruːtəbl/ *a* impenetrabile

insect /ˈɪnsekt/ *n* insetto *m*. **~icide** /ˈsektɪsaɪd/ *n* insetticida *m*

inse'cure *a* malsicuro; ⟨fig: person⟩ insicuro. **~ity** *n* mancanza *f* di sicurezza

insemination /ɪnsemɪˈneɪʃn/ *n* inseminazione *f*

in'sensitive *a* insensibile

in'separable *a* inseparabile

insert[1] /ˈɪnsɜːt/ *n* inserto *m*

insert[2] /ɪnˈsɜːt/ *vt* inserire. **~ion** /ˈɜːʃn/ *n* inserzione *f*

inside /ɪnˈsaɪd/ *n* interno *m*. **~s** *npl fam* pancia *f* ● *attrib Aut* **~ lane** *n* corsia *f* interna ● *adv* dentro; **~ out** a rovescio; ⟨thoroughly⟩ a fondo ● *prep* dentro; ⟨of time⟩ entro

insidious /ɪnˈsɪdɪəs/ *a* insidioso

insight /ˈɪnsaɪt/ *n* intuito *m* ⟨into per⟩; **an ~ into** un quadro di

insignia /ɪnˈsɪɡnɪə/ *npl* insegne *fpl*

insig'nificant *a* insignificante

insin'cere *a* poco sincero. **~ity** /ˈserɪtɪ/ *n* mancanza *f* di sincerità

insinuate /ɪnˈsɪnjʊeɪt/ *vt* insinuare. **~ion** /ˈeɪʃn/ *n* insinuazione *f*

insipid /ɪnˈsɪpɪd/ *a* insipido

insist /ɪnˈsɪst/ *vi* insistere (on per) ● *vt* **~ that** insistere che. **~ence** *n* insistenza *f*. **~ent** *a* insistente

insole *n* soletta *f*

insolence /ˈɪnsələns/ *n* insolenza *f*. **~t** *a* insolente

in'soluble *a* insolubile

in'solvency *n* insolvenza *f*. **~t** *a* insolvente

insomnia /ɪnˈsɒmnɪə/ *n* insonnia *f*

inspect /ɪnˈspekt/ *vt* ispezionare; controllare ⟨ticket⟩. **~ion** /ˈekʃn/ *n* ispezione *f*; ⟨of ticket⟩ controllo *m*. **~or** *n* ispettore, -trice *mf*; ⟨of tickets⟩ controllore *m*

inspiration /ɪnspəˈreɪʃn/ *n* ispirazione *f*

inspire /ɪnˈspaɪə(r)/ *vt* ispirare

insta'bility *n* instabilità *f*

install /ɪnˈstɔːl/ *vt* installare. **~ation** /ˈstəˈleɪʃn/ *n* installazione *f*

instalment /ɪnˈstɔːlmənt/ *n Comm* rata *f*; ⟨of serial⟩ puntata *f*; ⟨of publication⟩ fascicolo *m*

instance /ˈɪnstəns/ *n* ⟨case⟩ caso *m*; ⟨example⟩ esempio *m*; **in the first ~** in primo luogo; **for ~** per esempio

instant /ˈɪnstənt/ *a* immediato; *Culin* espresso ● *n* istante *m*. **~aneous** /ˈteɪnɪəs/ *a* istantaneo

instant 'coffee *n* caffè *m inv* solubile

instantly /ˈɪnstəntlɪ/ *adv* immediatamente

instead /ɪnˈsted/ *adv* invece; **~ of doing** anziché fare; **~ of me** al mio posto; **~ of going** invece di andare

'instep *n* collo *m* del piede

instigate /ˈɪnstɪɡeɪt/ *vt* istigare. **~ion** /ˈɡeɪʃn/ *n* istigazione *f*; **at his ~ion** dietro suo suggerimento. **~or** *n* istigatore, -trice *mf*

instil /ɪnˈstɪl/ *vt* (*pt/pp* **instilled**) inculcare (**into** in)

instinct /ˈɪnstɪŋkt/ *n* istinto *m*. **~ive** /ɪnˈstɪŋktɪv/ *a* istintivo

institute /ˈɪnstɪtjuːt/ *n* istituto *m* ● *vt* istituire ⟨scheme⟩; iniziare ⟨search⟩; intentare ⟨legal action⟩. **~ion** /ˈtjuːʃn/ *n* istituzione *f*; ⟨home for elderly⟩ istituto *m* per anziani; ⟨for mentally ill⟩ istituto *m* per malati di mente

instruct /ɪnˈstrʌkt/ *vt* istruire; ⟨order⟩ ordinare. **~ion** /ˈʌkʃn/ *n* istruzione *f*; **~s** (*pl:* **orders**) ordini *mpl*. **~ive** /ˈɪv/ *a* istruttivo. **~or** *n* istruttore, -trice *mf*

instrument /ˈɪnstrʊmənt/ *n* strumento *m*. **~al** /ˈmentl/ *a* strumentale; **be ~al in** contribuire a. **~alist** *n* strumentista *mf*

insu'bordinate *a* insubordinato. **~nation** /ˈneɪʃn/ *n* insubordinazione *f*

in'sufferable *a* insopportabile

insuf'ficient *a* insufficiente

insular /ˈɪnsjʊlə(r)/ *a fig* gretto

insulate /ˈɪnsjʊleɪt/ *vt* isolare. **~ing**

tape *n* nastro *m* isolante. **~ion** /-'leɪʃn/ *n* isolamento *m*
insulin /'ɪnsjʊlɪn/ *n* insulina *f*
insult¹ /'ɪnsʌlt/ *n* insulto *m*
insult² /ɪn'sʌlt/ *vt* insultare
insuperable /ɪn'su:pərəbl/ *a* insuperabile
insur|ance /ɪn'ʃʊərəns/ *n* assicurazione *f*. **~e** *vt* assicurare
insurrection /ɪnsə'rekʃn/ *n* insurrezione *f*
intact /ɪn'tækt/ *a* intatto
intake *n* immissione *f*; (*of food*) consumo *m*
in'tangible *a* intangibile
integral /'ɪntɪɡrəl/ *a* integrale
integra|te /'ɪntɪɡreɪt/ *vt* integrare ● *vi* integrarsi. **~ion** /-'ɡreɪʃn/ *n* integrazione *f*
integrity /ɪn'teɡrəti/ *n* integrità *f*
intellect /'ɪntəlekt/ *n* intelletto *m*. **~ual** /-'lektjʊəl/ *a & n* intellettuale *mf*
intelligen|ce /ɪn'telɪdʒəns/ *n* intelligenza *f*; *Mil* informazioni *fpl*. **~t** *a* intelligente
intelligentsia /ɪntelɪ'dʒentsɪə/ *n* intellighenzia *f*
intelligible /ɪn'telɪdʒəbl/ *a* intelligibile
intend /ɪn'tend/ *vt* destinare; (*have in mind*) aver intenzione di; **be ~ed for** essere destinato a. **~ed** *a* (*effect*) voluto ● *n* **my ~ed** *fam* il mio/la mia fidanzato, -a
intense /ɪn'tens/ *a* intenso; (*person*) dai sentimenti intensi. **~ly** *adv* intensamente; (*very*) estremamente
intensi|fication /ɪntensɪfɪ'keɪʃn/ *n* intensificazione *f*. **~fy** /-'tensɪfaɪ/ *v* (*pt/pp* **-ied**) ● *vt* intensificare ● *vi* intensificarsi
intensity /ɪn'tensəti/ *n* intensità *f*
intensive /ɪn'tensɪv/ *a* intensivo. **~ care** (*for people in coma*) rianimazione *f*; **~ care** [**unit**] terapia *f* intensiva
intent /ɪn'tent/ *a* intento; **~ on** (*absorbed in*) preso da; **be ~ on doing sth** essere intento a fare qcsa ● *n* intenzione *f*; **to all ~s and purposes** a tutti gli effetti. **~ly** *adv* attentamente
intention /ɪn'tenʃn/ *n* intenzione *f*. **~al** *a* intenzionale. **~ally** *adv* intenzionalmente
inter'acti|on *n* cooperazione *f*. **~ve** *a* interattivo
intercede /ɪntə'si:d/ *vi* intercedere (**on behalf of** a favore di)
intercept /ɪntə'sept/ *vt* intercettare

'interchange *n* scambio *m*; *Auto* raccordo *m* [autostradale]
inter'changeable *a* interscambiabile
intercom /'ɪntəkɒm/ *n* citofono *m*
intercourse *n* (*sexual*) rapporti *mpl* [sessuali]
interest /'ɪntrəst/ *n* interesse *m*; **have an ~** in *Comm* essere cointeressato in; **be of ~** essere interessante; **~ rate** *n* tasso *m* di interesse ● *vt* interessare. **~ed** *a* interessato. **~ing** *a* interessante
interface /'ɪntəfeɪs/ *n* interfaccia *f* ● *vt* interfacciare ● *vi* interfacciarsi
interfere /ɪntə'fɪə(r)/ *vi* interferire; **~ with** interferire con. **~nce** /-əns/ *n* interferenza *f*
interim /'ɪntərɪm/ *a* temporaneo; **~ payment** acconto *m* ● *n* **in the ~** nel frattempo
interior /ɪn'tɪərɪə(r)/ *a* interiore ● *n* interno *m*. **~ designer** *n* arredatore, -trice *mf*
interject /ɪntə'dʒekt/ *vt* intervenire. **~ion** /-ekʃn/ *n Gram* interiezione *f*; (*remark*) intervento *m*
interloper /'ɪntələʊpə(r)/ *n* intruso, -a *mf*
interlude /'ɪntəlu:d/ *n* intervallo *m*
inter'marry *vi* sposarsi tra parenti; (*different groups*) contrarre matrimoni misti
intermediary /ɪntə'mi:dɪərɪ/ *n* intermediario, -a *mf*
intermediate /ɪntə'mi:dɪət/ *a* intermedio
interminable /ɪn'tɜ:mɪnəbl/ *a* interminabile
intermission /ɪntə'mɪʃn/ *n* intervallo *m*
intermittent /ɪntə'mɪtənt/ *a* intermittente
intern /ɪn'tɜ:n/ *vt* internare
internal /ɪn'tɜ:nl/ *a* interno. **~ly** *adv* internamente; (*deal with*) all'interno
inter'national *a* internazionale ● *n* (*game*) incontro *m* internazionale; (*player*) competitore, -trice *mf* in gare internazionali. **~ly** *adv* internazionalmente
Internet /'ɪntənet/ *n* Internet *m*
internist /ɪn'tɜ:nɪst/ *n Am* internista *mf*
internment /ɪn'tɜ:nmənt/ *n* internamento *m*
'interplay *n* azione *f* reciproca
interpret /ɪn'tɜ:prɪt/ *vt* interpretare

● *vi* fare l'interprete. **~ation** /-'teɪʃn/ *n* interpretazione *f*. **~er** *n* interprete *mf*
interre'lated *a* ⟨facts⟩ in correlazione
interrogat|e /ɪn'terəgeɪt/ *vt* interrogare. **~ion** /-'geɪʃn/ *n* interrogazione *f*; (by police) interrogatorio *m*
interrogative /ɪntə'rɒgətɪv/ *a* & *n* ~ [**pronoun**] interrogativo *m*
interrupt /ɪntə'rʌpt/ *vt/i* interrompere. **~ion** /-'rʌpʃn/ *n* interruzione *f*
intersect /ɪntə'sekt/ *vi* intersecarsi ● *vt* intersecare. **~ion** /-'ekʃn/ *n* intersezione *f*; (of street) incrocio *m*
interspersed /ɪntə'spɜːst/ *a* ~ **with** inframmezzato di
inter'twine *vi* attorcigliarsi
interval /'ɪntəvl/ *n* intervallo *m*; **bright ~s** *pl* schiarite *fpl*
interven|e /ɪntə'viːn/ *vi* intervenire. **~tion** /-'venʃn/ *n* intervento *m*
interview /'ɪntəvjuː/ *n* Journ intervista *f*; (for job) colloquio *m* [di lavoro] ● *vt* intervistare. **~er** *n* intervistatore, -trice *mf*
intestin|e /ɪn'testɪn/ *n* intestino *m*. **~al** *a* intestinale
intimacy /'ɪntɪməsɪ/ *n* intimità *f*
intimate¹ /'ɪntɪmət/ *a* intimo. **~ly** *adv* intimamente
intimate² /'ɪntɪmeɪt/ *vt* far capire; (imply) suggerire
intimidat|e /ɪn'tɪmɪdeɪt/ *vt* intimidire. **~ion** /-'deɪʃn/ *n* intimidazione *f*
into /'ɪntə/, *di fronte a una vocale* /'ɪntʊ/ *prep* dentro, in; **go ~ the house** andare dentro [casa] in casa; **be ~** (fam: like) essere appassionato di; **I'm not ~ that** questo non mi piace; **7 ~ 21 goes 3** il 7 nel 21 ci sta 3 volte; **translate ~ French** tradurre in francese; **get ~ trouble** mettersi nei guai
in'tolerable *a* intollerabile
in'toleran|ce *n* intolleranza *f*. **~t** *a* intollerante
intonation /ɪntə'neɪʃn/ *n* intonazione *f*
intoxicat|ed /ɪn'tɒksɪkeɪtɪd/ *a* inebriato. **~ion** /-'keɪʃn/ *n* ebbrezza *f*
intractable /ɪn'træktəbl/ *a* intrattabile; ⟨problem⟩ insolubile
intransigent /ɪn'trænzɪdʒənt/ *a* intransigente
in'transitive *a* intransitivo
intravenous /ɪntrə'viːnəs/ *a* endovenoso. **~ly** *adv* per via endovenosa
intrepid /ɪn'trepɪd/ *a* intrepido
intricate /'ɪntrɪkət/ *a* complesso
intrigu|e /ɪn'triːg/ *n* intrigo *m* ● *vt* intrigare. ● *vi* tramare. **~ing** *a* intrigante

intrinsic /ɪn'trɪnsɪk/ *a* intrinseco
introduce /ɪntrə'djuːs/ *vt* presentare; (bring in, insert) introdurre
introduct|ion /ɪntrə'dʌkʃn/ *n* introduzione *f*; (to person) presentazione *f*; (to book) prefazione *f*. **~ory** /-'tərɪ/ *a* introduttivo
introspective /ɪntrə'spektɪv/ *a* introspettivo
introvert /'ɪntrəvɜːt/ *n* introverso, -a *mf*
intru|de /ɪn'truːd/ *vi* intromettersi. **~der** *n* intruso, -a *mf*. **~sion** /-'uːʒn/ *n* intrusione *f*
intuit|ion /ɪntjʊ'ɪʃn/ *n* intuito *m*. **~ive** /-'tjuːɪtɪv/ *a* intuitivo
inundate /'ɪnəndeɪt/ *vt* fig inondare (with di)
invade /ɪn'veɪd/ *vt* invadere. **~r** *n* invasore *m*
invalid¹ /'ɪnvəlɪd/ *n* invalido, -a *mf*
invalid² /ɪn'vælɪd/ *a* non valido. **~ate** *vt* invalidare
in'valuable *a* prezioso; (priceless) inestimabile
in'variab|le *a* invariabile. **~y** *adv* invariabilmente
invasion /ɪn'veɪʒn/ *n* invasione *f*
invective /ɪn'vektɪv/ *n* invettiva *f*
invent /ɪn'vent/ *vt* inventare. **~ion** /-enʃn/ *n* invenzione *f*. **~ive** /-tɪv/ *a* inventivo. **~or** *n* inventore, -trice *mf*
inventory /'ɪnvəntrɪ/ *n* inventario *m*
inverse /ɪn'vɜːs/ *a* inverso ● *n* inverso *m*
invert /ɪn'vɜːt/ *vt* invertire; **in ~ed commas** tra virgolette
invest /ɪn'vest/ *vt* investire ● *vi* fare investimenti; **~ in** (fam: buy) comprarsi
investigat|e /ɪn'vestɪgeɪt/ *vt* investigare. **~ion** /-'geɪʃn/ *n* investigazione *f*
invest|ment /ɪn'vestmənt/ *n* investimento *m*. **~or** *n* investitore, -trice *mf*
inveterate /ɪn'vetərət/ *a* inveterato
invidious /ɪn'vɪdɪəs/ *a* ingiusto; (position) antipatico
invigilat|e /ɪn'vɪdʒɪleɪt/ *vi* Sch sorvegliare lo svolgimento di un esame. **~or** *n* persona *f* che sorveglia lo svolgimento di un esame
invigorate /ɪn'vɪgəreɪt/ *vt* rinvigorire
invigorating /ɪn'vɪgəreɪtɪŋ/ *a* tonificante
invincible /ɪn'vɪnsəbl/ *a* invincibile
inviolable /ɪn'vaɪələbl/ *a* inviolabile
in'visible *a* invisibile
invitation /ɪnvɪ'teɪʃn/ *n* invito *m*
invit|e /ɪn'vaɪt/ *vt* invitare; (attract) attirare. **~ing** *a* invitante

invoice /ˈɪnvɔɪs/ n fattura f ● vt ~ **sb**
emettere una fattura a qcno
invoke /ɪnˈvəʊk/ vt invocare
in'voluntary a involontario
involve /ɪnˈvɒlv/ vt comportare; ⟨affect,
include⟩ coinvolgere; ⟨entail⟩ implicare;
get ~d with sb legarsi a qcno;
⟨romantically⟩ legarsi sentimentalmen-
te a qcno. **~d** a complesso. **~ment** n
coinvolgimento m
in'vulnerable a invulnerabile;
⟨position⟩ inattaccabile
inward /ˈɪnwəd/ a interno; ⟨thoughts
etc⟩ interiore; **~ investment** Comm investimento m di capitali stranieri. **~ly**
adv interiormente. **~[s]** adv verso l'interno
iodine /ˈaɪədiːn/ n iodio m
iota /aɪˈəʊtə/ n briciolo m
IOU n abbr (**I owe you**) pagherò m inv
IQ n abbr (**intelligence quotient**) Q.I.
IRA n abbr (**Irish Republican Army**)
I.R.A. f
Iran /ɪˈrɑːn/ n Iran m. **~ian** /ɪˈreɪnɪən/ a
& n iraniano, -a mf
Iraq /ɪˈrɑːk/ n Iraq m. **~i** /ɪˈrɑːkɪ/ a & n
iracheno, -a mf
irascible /ɪˈræsəbl/ a irascibile
irate /aɪˈreɪt/ a adirato
Ireland /ˈaɪələnd/ n Irlanda f
iris /ˈaɪrɪs/ n Anat iride f; Bot iris f inv
Irish /ˈaɪrɪʃ/ a irlandese ● npl **the ~** gli
irlandesi. **~man** n irlandese m.
~ woman n irlandese f
iron /ˈaɪən/ a di ferro. **I~ Curtain** n cortina f di ferro ● n ferro m; ⟨appliance⟩
ferro m [da stiro] ● vt/i stirare. **iron out**
vt eliminare stirando; fig appianare
ironic[al] /aɪˈrɒnɪk[l]/ a ironico
ironing /ˈaɪənɪŋ/ n stirare m; ⟨articles⟩
roba f da stirare; **do the ~** stirare.
~-board n asse f da stiro
ironmonger /-mʌŋɡə(r)/ n **~'s**
[shop] negozio m di ferramenta
irony /ˈaɪrənɪ/ n ironia f
irradiate /ɪˈreɪdɪeɪt/ vt irradiare
irrational /ɪˈræʃənl/ a irrazionale
irreconcilable /ɪˈrekənsaɪləbl/ a
irreconciliabile
irrefutable /ɪrɪˈfjuːtəbl/ a irrefutabile
irregular /ɪˈreɡjʊlə(r)/ a irregolare.
~ity /-ˈlærətɪ/ n irregolarità f inv
irrelevant /ɪˈreləvənt/ a non pertinente
irreparabl|e /ɪˈrepərəbl/ a irreparabi-
le. **~y** adv irreparabilmente
irreplaceable /ɪrɪˈpleɪsəbl/ a inso-
stituibile

irrepressible /ɪrɪˈpresəbl/ a irrefre-
nabile; ⟨person⟩ incontenibile
irresistible /ɪrɪˈzɪstəbl/ a irresistibile
irresolute /ɪˈrezəluːt/ a irresoluto
irrespective /ɪrɪˈspektɪv/ a ~ **of** senza riguardo per
irresponsible /ɪrɪˈspɒnsɪbl/ a irresponsabile
irreverent /ɪˈrevərənt/ a irriverente
irreversible /ɪrɪˈvɜːsəbl/ a irrever-
sibile
irrevocabl|e /ɪˈrevəkəbl/ a irrevoca-
bile. **~y** adv irrevocabilmente
irrigat|e /ˈɪrɪɡeɪt/ vt irrigare. **~ion**
/-ˈɡeɪʃn/ n irrigazione f
irritability /ɪrɪtəˈbɪlətɪ/ n irritabilità f
irritable /ˈɪrɪtəbl/ a irritabile
irritant /ˈɪrɪtənt/ n sostanza f irritante
irritat|e /ˈɪrɪteɪt/ vt irritare. **~ing** a ir-
ritante. **~ion** /-ˈteɪʃn/ n irritazione f
is /ɪz/ see **be**
Islam /ˈɪzlɑːm/ n Islam m. **~ic** /-ˈlæmɪk/
a islamico
island /ˈaɪlənd/ n isola f; ⟨in road⟩ isola
f spartitraffico. **~er** n isolano, -a mf
isle /aɪl/ n liter isola f
isolat|e /ˈaɪsəleɪt/ vt isolare. **~ed** a iso-
lato. **~ion** /-ˈleɪʃn/ n isolamento m
Israel /ˈɪzreɪl/ n Israele m. **~i** /ɪzˈreɪlɪ/ a
& n israeliano, -a mf
issue /ˈɪʃuː/ n ⟨outcome⟩ risultato m; ⟨of
magazine⟩ numero m; ⟨of stamps etc⟩
emissione f; ⟨offspring⟩ figli mpl;
⟨matter, question⟩ questione f; **at ~** in
questione; **take ~ with sb** prendere
posizione contro qcno ● vt distribuire
⟨supplies⟩; rilasciare ⟨passport⟩; emettere ⟨stamps, order⟩; pubblicare ⟨book⟩;
be ~d with sth ricevere qcsa ● vi ~
from uscire da
isthmus /ˈɪsməs/ n (pl -muses) istmo m
it /ɪt/ pron ⟨direct object⟩ lo m, la f;
⟨indirect object⟩ gli m, le f; **it's broken** è
rotto/rotta; **will it be enough?** baste-
rà?; **it's hot** fa caldo; **it's raining** piove;
it's me sono io; **who is it?** chi è?; **it's
two o'clock** sono le due; **I doubt it** ne
dubito; **take it with you** prendilo con
te; **give it a wipe** dagli una pulita
Italian /ɪˈtæljən/ a & n italiano, -a mf;
⟨language⟩ italiano m
italic /ɪˈtælɪk/ a in corsivo. **~s** npl corsivo msg
Italy /ˈɪtəlɪ/ n Italia f
itch /ɪtʃ/ n prurito m ● vi avere prurito,
prudere; **be ~ing to fam** avere una voglia matta di. **~y** a che prude; **my foot
is ~y** ho prurito al piede

item /ˈaɪtəm/ n articolo m; (on agenda, programme) punto m; (on invoice) voce f. ~ [of news] notizia f. ~ize vt dettagliare (bill)

itinerant /aɪˈtɪnərənt/ a itinerante

itinerary /aɪˈtɪnərərɪ/ n itinerario m

its /ɪts/ poss pron suo m, sua f, suoi mpl, sue fpl; ~ **mother cage** sua madre/la sua gabbia

it's = it is, it has

itself /ɪtˈself/ pron (reflexive) si; (emphatic) essa stessa; **the baby looked at ~ in the mirror** il bambino si è guardato nello specchio; **by ~** da solo; **the machine in ~ is simple** la macchina di per sé è semplice

ITV n abbr (**Independent Television**) stazione f televisiva privata britannica

ivory /ˈaɪvərɪ/ n avorio m

ivy /ˈaɪvɪ/ n edera f

Jj

jab /dʒæb/ n colpo m secco; (fam: injection) puntura f ● vt (pt/pp **jabbed**) punzecchiare

jabber /ˈdʒæbə(r)/ vi borbottare

jack /dʒæk/ n Auto cric m inv; (in cards) fante m, jack m inv ● **jack up** vt Auto sollevare [con il cric]

jackdaw /ˈdʒækdɔː/ n taccola f

jacket /ˈdʒækɪt/ n giacca f; (of book) sopraccoperta f. ~ **po'tato** n patata f cotta al forno con la buccia

jackpot n premio m (di una lotteria); **win the ~** vincere alla lotteria; **hit the ~** fig fare un colpo grosso

jade /dʒeɪd/ n giada f ● attrib di giada

jaded /ˈdʒeɪdɪd/ a spossato

jagged /ˈdʒægɪd/ a dentellato

jail /dʒeɪl/ = **gaol**

jalopy /dʒəˈlɒpɪ/ n fam vecchia carretta f

jam¹ /dʒæm/ n marmellata f

jam² n Auto ingorgo m; (fam: difficulty) guaio m ● v (pt/pp **jammed**) ● vt (cram) pigiare; disturbare (broadcast); inceppare (mechanism, drawer etc); be **~med** (roads:) essere congestionato ● vi (mechanism:) incepparsi; (window, drawer:) incastrarsi

Jamaica /dʒəˈmeɪkə/ n Giamaica f. ~n a & n giamaicano, -a mf

jam-'packed a fam pieno zeppo

jangle /ˈdʒæŋgl/ vt far squillare ● vi squillare

janitor /ˈdʒænɪtə(r)/ n (caretaker) custode m; (in school) bidello, -a mf

January /ˈdʒænjʊərɪ/ n gennaio m

Japan /dʒəˈpæn/ n Giappone m. ~**ese** /dʒæpəˈniːz/ a & n giapponese mf; (language) giapponese m

jar¹ /dʒɑː(r)/ n (glass) barattolo m

jar² vi (pt/pp **jarred**) (sound:) stridere

jargon /ˈdʒɑːgən/ n gergo m

jaundice /ˈdʒɔːndɪs/ n itterizia f. ~**d** a fig inacidito

jaunt /dʒɔːnt/ n gita f

jaunty /ˈdʒɔːntɪ/ a (-ier, -iest) sbarazzino

javelin /ˈdʒævlɪn/ n giavellotto m

jaw /dʒɔː/ n mascella f; (bone) mandibola f

jay-walker /ˈdʒeɪwɔːkə(r)/ n pedone m indisciplinato

jazz /dʒæz/ n jazz m ● **jazz up** vt ravvivare. ~**y** a vistoso

jealous /ˈdʒeləs/ a geloso. ~**y** n gelosia f

jeans /dʒiːnz/ npl [blue] jeans mpl

jeep /dʒiːp/ n jeep f inv

jeer /dʒɪə(r)/ n scherno m ● vi schernire; ~ **at** prendersi gioco di ● vt (boo) fischiare

jell /dʒel/ vi concretarsi

jelly /ˈdʒelɪ/ n gelatina f. ~**fish** n medusa f

jeopar|dize /ˈdʒepədaɪz/ vt mettere in pericolo. ~**dy** /-dɪ/ n in ~**dy** in pericolo

jerk /dʒɜːk/ n scatto m, scossa f ● vt scattare ● vi sobbalzare; (limb, muscle:) muoversi a scatti. ~**ily** adv a scatti. ~**y** a traballante

jersey /ˈdʒɜːzɪ/ n maglia f; Sport maglietta f; (fabric) jersey m

jest /dʒest/ n scherzo m; **in ~** per scherzo ● vi scherzare

Jesus /ˈdʒiːzəs/ n Gesù m

jet¹ /dʒet/ n (stone) giaietto m

jet² n (of water) getto m; (nozzle) becco m; (plane) aviogetto m, jet m inv

jet: ~·'black *a* nero ebano. ~lag *n* scombussolamento *m* da fuso orario. ~-pro'pelled *a* a reazione

jettison /'dʒetɪsn/ *vt* gettare a mare; *fig* abbandonare

jetty /'dʒetɪ/ *n* molo *m*

Jew /dʒuː/ *n* ebreo *m*

jewel /'dʒuːəl/ *n* gioiello *m*. ~ler *n* gioielliere *m*; ⟨shop⟩ gioielleria *f*. ~lery *n* gioielli *mpl*

Jew|ess /'dʒuːɪs/ *n* ebrea *f*. ~ish *a* ebreo

jiffy /'dʒɪfɪ/ *n fam* in a ~ in un batter d'occhio

jigsaw /'dʒɪgsɔː/ *n* ~ ⟨puzzle⟩ puzzle *m inv*

jilt /dʒɪlt/ *vt* piantare

jingle /'dʒɪŋgl/ *n* ⟨rhyme⟩ canzoncina *f* pubblicitaria ●*vi* tintinnare

jinx /dʒɪŋks/ *n* ⟨person⟩ iettatore, -trice *mf*; it's got a ~ on it è iellato

jitter|s /'dʒɪtəz/ *npl fam* have the ~s aver una gran fifa. ~y *a fam* in preda alla fifa

job /dʒɒb/ *n* lavoro *m*; this is going to be quite a ~ *fam* [questa] non sarà un'impresa facile; it's a good ~ that… meno male che… ~ centre *n* ufficio *m* statale di collocamento. ~less *a* senza lavoro

jockey /'dʒɒkɪ/ *n* fantino *m*

jocular /'dʒɒkjʊlə/ *a* scherzoso

jog /dʒɒg/ *n* colpetto *m*; at a ~ in un balzo; *Sport* go for a ~ andare a fare jogging ●*v* (*pt/pp* jogged) ●*vt* ⟨hit⟩ urtare; ~ sb's memory farlo ritornare in mente a qcno ●*vi Sport* fare jogging. ~ging *n* jogging *m*

john /dʒɒn/ *n* (*Am fam: toilet*) gabinetto *m*

join /dʒɔɪn/ *n* giuntura *f* ●*vt* raggiungere, unire; raggiungere ⟨person⟩; ⟨become member of⟩ iscriversi a; entrare in ⟨firm⟩ ●*vi* ⟨roads:⟩ congiungersi. join in *vi* partecipare. join up *vi Mil* arruolarsi ●*vt* unire

joiner /'dʒɔɪnə(r)/ *n* falegname *m*

joint /dʒɔɪnt/ *a* comune ●*n* articolazione *f*; ⟨in wood, brickwork⟩ giuntura *f*; *Culin* arrosto *m*; ⟨fam: bar⟩ bettola *f*; ⟨sl:drug⟩ spinello *m*. ~ly *adv* unitamente

joist /dʒɔɪst/ *n* travetto *m*

jok|e /dʒəʊk/ *n* ⟨trick⟩ scherzo *m*; ⟨funny story⟩ barzelletta *f* ●*vi* scherzare. ~er *n* burlone, -a *mf*; ⟨in cards⟩ jolly *m inv*. ~ing *n* ~ing apart scherzi a parte. ~ingly *adv* per scherzo

jolly /'dʒɒlɪ/ *a* (-ier, -iest) allegro ●*adv fam* molto

jolt /dʒəʊlt/ *n* scossa *f*, sobbalzo *m* ●*vt* far sobbalzare ●*vi* sobbalzare

Jordan /'dʒɔːdn/ *n* Giordania *f*; ⟨river⟩ Giordano *m*. ~ian /-'deɪnɪən/ *a & n* giordano, -a *mf*

jostle /'dʒɒsl/ *vt* spingere

jot /dʒɒt/ *n* nulla *f* ●*vt* jot down (*pt/pp* jotted) annotare. ~ter *n* taccuino *m*; ⟨with a spine⟩ quaderno *m*

journal /'dʒɜːnl/ *n* giornale *m*; ⟨diary⟩ diario *m*. ~ese /-ə'liːz/ *n* gergo *m* giornalistico. ~ism *n* giornalismo *m*. ~ist *n* giornalista *mf*

journey /'dʒɜːnɪ/ *n* viaggio *m*

jovial /'dʒəʊvɪəl/ *a* gioviale

joy /dʒɔɪ/ *n* gioia *f*. ~ful *a* gioioso. ~ride *n fam* giro *m* con una macchina rubata. ~stick *n* *Comput* joystick *m inv*

jubil|ant /'dʒuːbɪlənt/ *a* giubilante. ~ation /-'leɪʃn/ *n* giubilo *m*

jubilee /'dʒuːbɪlɪ/ *n* giubileo *m*

judder /'dʒʌdə(r)/ *vi* vibrare violentemente

judge /dʒʌdʒ/ *n* giudice *m* ●*vt* giudicare; ⟨estimate⟩ valutare; ⟨consider⟩ ritenere ●*vi* giudicare (by da). ~ment *n* giudizio *m*; *Jur* sentenza *f*

judic|ial /dʒuː'dɪʃl/ *a* giudiziario. ~iary /-'ʃərɪ/ *n* magistratura *f*. ~ious /-'ʃəs/ *a* giudizioso

judo /'dʒuːdəʊ/ *n* judo *m*

jug /dʒʌg/ *n* brocca *f*; ⟨small⟩ bricco *m*

juggernaut /'dʒʌgənɔːt/ *n fam* grosso autotreno *m*

juggle /'dʒʌgl/ *vi* fare giochi di destrezza. ~r *n* giocoliere, -a *mf*

juice /dʒuːs/ *n* succo *m*

juicy /'dʒuːsɪ/ *a* (-ier, -iest) succoso; ⟨fam: story⟩ piccante

juke-box /'dʒuːk-/ *n* juke-box *m inv*

July /dʒʊ'laɪ/ *n* luglio *m*

jumble /'dʒʌmbl/ *n* accozzaglia *f* ●*vt* ~ ⟨up⟩ mischiare. ~ sale *n* vendita *f* di beneficenza

jumbo /'dʒʌmbəʊ/ *n* ~ ⟨jet⟩ jumbo jet *m inv*

jump /dʒʌmp/ *n* salto *m*; ⟨in prices⟩ balzo *m*; ⟨in horse racing⟩ ostacolo *m* ●*vi* saltare; ⟨with fright⟩ sussultare; ⟨prices:⟩ salire rapidamente; ~ to conclusions saltare alle conclusioni ●*vt* saltare; ~ the gun *fig* precipitarsi; ~ the queue non rispettare la fila. jump at *vt fig* accettare con entusiasmo ⟨offer⟩. jump up *vi* rizzarsi in piedi

jumper /ˈdʒʌmpə(r)/ n (sweater) golf m inv

jumpy /ˈdʒʌmpɪ/ a nervoso

junction /ˈdʒʌŋkʃn/ n (of roads) incrocio m; (of motorway) uscita f; Rail nodo m ferroviario

juncture /ˈdʒʌŋktʃə(r)/ n at this ~ a questo punto

June /dʒuːn/ n giugno m

jungle /ˈdʒʌŋgl/ n giungla f

junior /ˈdʒuːnɪə(r)/ a giovane; (in rank) subalterno; Sport junior inv ● npl the ~s Sch i più giovani. ~ school n scuola f elementare

junk /dʒʌŋk/ n cianfrusaglie fpl. ~ food n fam cibo m poco sano, porcherie fpl. ~ mail posta f spazzatura

junkie /ˈdʒʌŋkɪ/ n sl tossico, -a mf

'junk-shop n negozio m di rigattiere

jurisdiction /dʒʊərɪsˈdɪkʃn/ n giurisdizione f

juror /ˈdʒʊərə(r)/ n giurato, -a mf

jury /ˈdʒʊərɪ/ n giuria f; Jur giuria f [popolare]

just /dʒʌst/ a giusto ● adv (barely) appena; (simply) solo; (exactly) esattamente; ~ as tall altrettanto alto; ~ as I was leaving proprio quando stavo andando via; I've ~ seen her l'ho appena vista; it's ~ as well meno male; ~ at that moment proprio in quel momento; ~ listen! ascolta!; I'm ~ going sto andando proprio ora

justice /ˈdʒʌstɪs/ n giustizia f; do ~ to rendere giustizia a; J~ of the Peace giudice m conciliatore

justifiabl|e /ˈdʒʌstɪfaɪəbl/ a giustificabile

justi|fication /dʒʌstɪfɪˈkeɪʃn/ n giustificazione f. ~fy /ˈdʒʌstɪfaɪ/ vt (pt/pp -ied) giustificare

justly /ˈdʒʌstlɪ/ adv giustamente

jut /dʒʌt/ vi (pt/pp jutted) ~ out sporgere

juvenile /ˈdʒuːvənaɪl/ a giovanile; (childish) infantile; (for the young) per i giovani ● n giovane mf. ~ delinquency n delinquenza f giovanile

juxtapose /dʒʌkstəˈpəʊz/ vt giustapporre

Kk

kangaroo /kæŋgəˈruː/ n canguro m

karate /kəˈrɑːtɪ/ n karate m

kebab /kɪˈbæb/ n Culin spiedino m di carne

keel /kiːl/ n chiglia f ● keel over vi capovolgersi

keen /kiːn/ a (intense) acuto; (interest) vivo; (eager) entusiastico; (competition) feroce; (wind, knife) tagliente; ~ on entusiasta di; she's ~ on him le piace molto; be ~ to do sth avere voglia di fare qcsa. ~ness n entusiasmo m

keep /kiːp/ n (maintenance) mantenimento m; (of castle) maschio m; for ~s per sempre ● v (pt/pp kept) ● vt tenere; (not throw away) conservare; (detain) trattenere; mantenere (family, promise); avere (shop); allevare (animals); rispettare (law, rules); ~ sth hot tenere qcsa in caldo; ~ sb from doing sth impedire a qcno di fare qcsa; ~ sb waiting far aspettare qcno; ~ sth to oneself tenere qcsa per sé; ~ sth from sb tenere nascosto qcsa a qcno ● vi (remain) rimanere; (food:) conservarsi; ~ calm rimanere calmo; ~ left/right tenere la sinistra/destra; ~ [on] doing sth continuare a fare qcsa. **keep back** vt trattenere (person); ~ sth back from sb tenere nascosto qcsa a qcno ● vi tenersi indietro. **keep in with** vt mantenersi in buoni rapporti con. **keep on** vi fam assillare (at sb qcno). **keep up** vi stare al passo ● vt (continue) continuare

keep|er /ˈkiːpə(r)/ n custode mf. ~-fit n ginnastica f. ~ing n custodia f; be in ~ing with essere in armonia con. ~sake n ricordo m

keg /keg/ n barilotto m

kennel /ˈkenl/ n canile m; ~s pl (boarding) canile m; (breeding) allevamento m di cani

Kenya /ˈkenjə/ n Kenia m. ~n a & n keniota mf

kept /kept/ *see* **keep**

kerb /kɜːb/ *n* bordo *m* del marciapiede

kernel /ˈkɜːnl/ *n* nocciolo *m*

kerosene /ˈkerəsiːn/ *n Am* cherosene *m*

ketchup /ˈketʃʌp/ *n* ketchup *m*

kettle /ˈket(ə)l/ *n* bollitore *m*; **put the ~ on** mettere l'acqua a bollire

key /kiː/ *n also Mus* chiave *f*; (*of piano, typewriter*) tasto *m* ●*vt* ~ [**in**] digitare ⟨*character*⟩; **could you ~ this?** puoi battere questo?

key: **~board** *n Comput, Mus* tastiera *f*. **~boarder** *n* tastierista *mf*. **~ed-up** *a* (*anxious*) estremamente agitato; (*ready to act*) psicologicamente preparato. **~hole** *n* buco *m* della serratura. **~-ring** *n* portachiavi *m inv*

khaki /ˈkɑːkɪ/ *a* cachi *inv* ●*n* cachi *m*

kick /kɪk/ *n* calcio *m*; (*fam: thrill*) piacere *m*; **for ~s** *fam* per spasso ●*vt* dar calci a; **~ the bucket** *fam* crepare ●*vi* ⟨*animal*⟩ scalciare; ⟨*person*⟩ dare calci.
kick off *vi Sport* dare il calcio d'inizio; *fam* iniziare. **kick up** *vt* **~ up a row** fare una scenata

ˈkickback *n* (*fam: percentage*) tangente *f*

ˈkick-off *n Sport* calcio *m* d'inizio

kid /kɪd/ *n* capretto *m*; (*fam: child*) ragazzino, -a *mf* ●*v* (*pt/pp* **kidded**) ●*vt fam* prendere in giro ●*vi fam* scherzare

kidnap /ˈkɪdnæp/ *vt* (*pt/pp* **-napped**) rapire, sequestrare. **~per** *n* sequestratore, -trice *mf*, rapitore, -trice *mf*. **~ping** *n* rapimento *m*, sequestro *m* [di persona]

kidney /ˈkɪdnɪ/ *n* rene *m*; *Culin* rognone *m*. **~ machine** *n* rene *m* artificiale

kill /kɪl/ *vt* uccidere; *fig* metter fine a; ammazzare ⟨*time*⟩. **~er** *n* assassino, -a *mf*. **~ing** *n* uccisione *f*; (*murder*) omicidio *m*; **make a ~ing** *fig* fare un colpo grosso

ˈkilljoy *n* guastafeste *mf inv*

kiln /kɪln/ *n* fornace *f*

kilo /ˈkiːləʊ/ *n* chilo *m*

kilo /ˈkɪlə/: **~byte** *n* kilobyte *m inv*. **~gram** *n* chilogrammo *m*. **~metre** /kɪˈlɒmɪtə(r)/ *n* chilometro *m*. **~watt** *n* chilowatt *m inv*

kilt /kɪlt/ *n* kilt *m inv* (*gonnellino degli scozzesi*)

kin /kɪn/ *n* congiunti *mpl*; **next of ~** parente *m* stretto; **parenti** *mpl* stretti

kind[1] /kaɪnd/ *n* genere *m*, specie *f*; (*brand, type*) tipo *m*; **~ of** *fam* alquanto; **two of a ~** due della stessa specie

kind[2] *a* gentile, buono; **~ to animals**

amante degli animali; **~ regards** cordiali saluti

kindergarten /ˈkɪndəɡɑːtn/ *n* asilo *m* infantile

kindle /ˈkɪndl/ *vt* accendere

kind|ly /ˈkaɪndlɪ/ *a* (**-ier**, **-iest**) benevolo ●*adv* gentilmente, con gentilezza; (*if you please*) per favore. **~ness** *n* gentilezza *f*

kindred /ˈkɪndrɪd/ *a* **she's a ~ spirit** è la mia/sua/tua anima gemella

kinetic /kɪˈnetɪk/ *a* cinetico

king /kɪŋ/ *n* re *m inv*. **~dom** *n* regno *m*

king: **~fisher** *n* martin *m inv* pescatore. **~-sized** *a* ⟨*cigarette*⟩ king-size *inv*, lungo; ⟨*bed*⟩ matrimoniale grande

kink /kɪŋk/ *n* attarciagliamento *m*. **~y** *a* *fam* bizzarro

kiosk /ˈkiːɒsk/ *n* chiosco *m*; *Teleph* cabina *f* telefonica

kip /kɪp/ *n fam* pisolino *m*; **have a ~** schiacciare un pisolino ●*vi* (*pt/pp* **kipped**) *fam* dormire

kipper /ˈkɪpə(r)/ *n* aringa *f* affumicata

kiss /kɪs/ *n* bacio *m*; **~ of life** respirazione *f* bocca a bocca ●*vt* baciare ●*vi* baciarsi

kit /kɪt/ *n* equipaggiamento *m*, kit *m inv*; (*tools*) attrezzi *mpl*; (*construction ~*) pezzi *mpl* da montare, kit *m inv* ●**kit out** *vt* (*pt/pp* **kitted**) equipaggiare. **~bag** *n* sacco *m* a spalla

kitchen /ˈkɪtʃɪn/ *n* cucina *f* ●*attrib* di cucina. **~ette** /kɪtʃɪˈnet/ *n* cucinino *m*

kitchen: **~ garden** *n* orto *m*. **~ roll** *or* **towel** Scottex® *m inv*. **~ sink** *n* lavello *m*

kite /kaɪt/ *n* aquilone *m*

kitten /ˈkɪtn/ *n* gattino *m*

kitty /ˈkɪtɪ/ *n* (*money*) cassa *f* comune

kleptomaniac /kleptəˈmeɪnɪæk/ *n* cleptomane *mf*

knack /næk/ *n* tecnica *f*; **have the ~ for doing sth** avere la capacità di fare qcsa

knead /niːd/ *vt* impastare

knee /niː/ *n* ginocchio *m*. **~cap** *n* rotula *f*

kneel /niːl/ *vi* (*pt/pp* **knelt**) **~ [down]** inginocchiarsi; **be ~ing** essere inginocchiato

knelt /nelt/ *see* **kneel**

knew /njuː/ *see* **know**

knickers /ˈnɪkəz/ *npl* mutandine *fpl*

knick-knacks /ˈnɪknæks/ *npl* ninnoli *mpl*

knife /naɪf/ *n* (*pl* **knives**) coltello *m* ●*vt fam* accoltellare

knight /naɪt/ n cavaliere m; (in chess) cavallo m ● vt nominare cavaliere
knit /nɪt/ vt/i (pt/pp **knitted**) lavorare a maglia; ~ **one, purl one** un diritto, un rovescio. ~**ting** n lavorare m a maglia; (product) lavoro a maglia. ~**ting-needle** n ferro m da calza. ~**wear** n maglieria f
knives /naɪvz/ see **knife**
knob /nɒb/ n pomello m; (of stick) pomo m; (of butter) noce f. ~**bly** a nodoso; (bony) spigoloso
knock /nɒk/ n colpo m; **there was a ~ at the door** hanno bussato alla porta ● vt bussare a ⟨door⟩; (fam: criticize) denigrare; ~ **a hole in sth** fare un buco in qcsa; ~ **one's head** battere la testa (**on** contro) ● vi (at door) bussare. **knock about** vt malmenare ● vi fam girovagare. **knock down** vt far cadere; (with fist) stendere con un pugno; (in car) investire; (demolish) abbattere; (fam: reduce) ribassare ⟨price⟩. **knock off** vt (fam: steal) fregare; (fam: complete quickly) fare alla bell'e meglio ● vi (fam: cease work) staccare. **knock out** vt eliminare; (make unconscious) mettere K.O.; (fam: anaesthetize) addormentare. **knock over** vt rovesciare; (in car) investire

knock: ~**-down** a ~**-down price** prezzo m stracciato. ~**er** n battente m. ~**-kneed** /-'niːd/ a con gambe storte. ~**-out** n (in boxing) knock-out m inv
knot /nɒt/ n nodo m ● vt (pt/pp **knotted**) annodare
knotty /'nɒtɪ/ a (-ier, -iest) fam spinoso
know /nəʊ/ v (pt **knew**, pp **known**) ● vt sapere; conoscere ⟨person, place⟩; (recognize) riconoscere; **get to ~ sb** conoscere qcno; ~ **how to swim** sapere nuotare ● vi sapere; **did you ~ about this?** lo sapevi? ● n **in the ~** fam al corrente
know: ~**-all** n fam sapientone, -a mf. ~**-how** n abilità f. ~**ing** a d'intesa. ~**ingly** adv (intentionally) consapevolmente; (smile etc) con un'aria d'intesa
knowledge /'nɒlɪdʒ/ n conoscenza f. ~**able** /-əbl/ a ben informato
known /nəʊn/ see **know** ● a noto
knuckle /'nʌkl/ n nocca f ● **knuckle down** vi darci sotto (**to** con). **knuckle under** vi sottomettersi
Koran /kəˈrɑːn/ n Corano m
Korea /kəˈrɪə/ n Corea f. ~**n** a & n coreano, -a mf
kosher /ˈkəʊʃə(r)/ a kasher inv
kowtow /kaʊˈtaʊ/ vi piegarsi
kudos /ˈkjuːdɒs/ n fam gloria f

Ll

lab /læb/ n fam laboratorio m
label /ˈleɪbl/ n etichetta f ● vt (pt/pp **labelled**) mettere un'etichetta a; fig etichettare ⟨person⟩
laboratory /ləˈbɒrətrɪ/ n laboratorio m
laborious /ləˈbɔːrɪəs/ a laborioso
labour /ˈleɪbə(r)/ n lavoro m; (workers) manodopera f; Med doglie fpl; **be in ~** avere le doglie; **L~** Pol partito m laburista ● attrib Pol laburista ● vi lavorare ● vt ~ **the point** fig ribadire il concetto. ~**er** n manovale m
labour-saving a che fa risparmiare lavoro e fatica
labyrinth /ˈlæbərɪnθ/ n labirinto m
lace /leɪs/ n pizzo m; (of shoe) laccio m ● attrib di pizzo ● vt allacciare ⟨shoes⟩; correggere ⟨drink⟩

lacerate /ˈlæsəreɪt/ vt lacerare
lack /læk/ n mancanza f ● vt mancare di; **I ~ the time** mi manca il tempo ● vi **be ~ing** mancare; **be ~ing in sth** mancare di qcsa
lackadaisical /lækəˈdeɪzɪkl/ a senza entusiasmo
laconic /ləˈkɒnɪk/ a laconico
lacquer /ˈlækə(r)/ n lacca f
lad /læd/ n ragazzo m
ladder /ˈlædə(r)/ n scala f; (in tights) sfilatura f
laden /ˈleɪdn/ a carico (**with** di)
ladle /ˈleɪdl/ n mestolo m ● vt ~ [**out**] versare (col mestolo)
lady /ˈleɪdɪ/ n signora f; (title) Lady f; **ladies** [**room**] bagno m per donne

lady: ~**bird** n. Am ~**bug** n coccinella f. ~**like** a signorile

lag[1] /læg/ vi (pt/pp **lagged**) ~ **behind** restare indietro

lag[2] vt (pt/pp **lagged**) isolare ⟨pipes⟩

lager /ˈlɑːgə(r)/ n birra f chiara

lagoon /ləˈguːn/ n laguna f

laid /leɪd/ see **lay**[3]

lain /leɪn/ see **lie**[2]

lair /leə(r)/ n tana f

lake /leɪk/ n lago m

lamb /læm/ n agnello m

lame /leɪm/ a zoppo; fig ⟨argument⟩ zoppicante; ⟨excuse⟩ traballante

lament /ləˈment/ n lamento m ● vt lamentare ● vi lamentarsi

lamentable /ˈlæməntəbl/ a deplorevole

laminated /ˈlæmɪneɪtɪd/ a laminato

lamp /læmp/ n lampada f, (in street) lampione m. ~**post** n lampione m. ~**shade** n paralume m

lance /lɑːns/ n lancia f ● vt Med incidere. ~-**corporal** n appuntato m

land /lænd/ n terreno m; (country) paese m; (as opposed to sea) terra f; **plot of** ~ pezzo m di terreno ● vt Naut sbarcare; ⟨fam: obtain⟩ assicurarsi; **be** ~**ed with sth** fam ritrovarsi fra capo e collo qcsa ● vi Aeron atterrare; ⟨fall⟩ cadere. **land up** vi fam finire

landing /ˈlændɪŋ/ n Naut sbarco m; Aeron atterraggio m; (top of stairs) pianerottolo m. ~-**stage** n pontile m da sbarco. ~ **strip** n pista f d'atterraggio

land: ~**lady** n proprietaria f; (of flat) padrona f di casa. ~-**locked** a privo di sbocco sul mare. ~**lord** n proprietario m; (of flat) padrone m di casa. ~**mark** n punto m di riferimento; fig pietra f miliare. ~**owner** n proprietario, -a mf terriero, -a. ~**scape** /-skeɪp/ n paesaggio m. ~**slide** n frana f; Pol valanga f di voti

lane /leɪn/ n sentiero m; Auto, Sport corsia f

language /ˈlæŋgwɪdʒ/ n lingua f; (speech, style) linguaggio m. ~ **laboratory** n laboratorio m linguistico

languid /ˈlæŋgwɪd/ a languido

languish /ˈlæŋgwɪʃ/ vi languire

lank /læŋk/ a ⟨hair⟩ diritto

lanky /ˈlæŋkɪ/ a (-**ier**, -**iest**) allampanato

lantern /ˈlæntən/ n lanterna f

lap[1] /læp/ n grembo m

lap[2] n (of journey) tappa f; Sport giro m ● v (pt/pp **lapped**) ● vi ⟨water:⟩ ~ **against** lambire ● vt Sport doppiare

lap[3] vt (pt/pp **lapped**) ~ **up** bere avidamente; bersi completamente ⟨lies⟩; credere ciecamente a ⟨praise⟩

lapel /ləˈpel/ n bavero m

lapse /læps/ n sbaglio m; (moral) sbandamento m [morale]; (of time) intervallo m ● vi (expire) scadere; (morally) scivolare; ~ **into** cadere in

laptop /ˈlæptɒp/ n |**computer**| computer m inv portabile, laptop m inv

larceny /ˈlɑːsənɪ/ n furto m

lard /lɑːd/ n strutto m

larder /ˈlɑːdə(r)/ n dispensa f

large /lɑːdʒ/ a grande; ⟨number, amount⟩ grande, grosso; **by and** ~ in complesso; **at** ~ in libertà; (in general) ampiamente, ~**ly** adv ampiamente; ~**ly because of** in gran parte a causa di

lark[1] /lɑːk/ n (bird) allodola f

lark[2] n (joke) burla f ● **lark about** vi giocherellare

larva /ˈlɑːvə/ n (pl -**vae** /-viː/) larva f

laryngitis /lærɪnˈdʒaɪtɪs/ n laringite f

larynx /ˈlærɪŋks/ n laringe f

lascivious /ləˈsɪvɪəs/ a lascivo

laser /ˈleɪzə(r)/ n laser m inv. ~ |**printer**| n stampante f laser

lash /læʃ/ n frustata f; (eyelash) ciglio m ● vt (whip) frustare; (tie) legare fermamente. **lash out** vi attaccare; (spend) sperperare (**on** in)

lashings /ˈlæʃɪŋz/ npl ~ **of** fam una marea di

lass /læs/ n ragazzina f

lasso /ləˈsuː/ n lazo m

last[1] /lɑːst/ a (final) ultimo; (recent) scorso; ~ **year** l'anno scorso; ~ **night** ieri sera; **at** ~ alla fine; **at** ~! finalmente!; **that's the** ~ **straw** fam questa è l'ultima goccia ● n ultimo, -a mf; **the** ~ **but one** il penultimo ● adv per ultimo; (last time) l'ultima volta ● vi durare. ~**ing** a durevole. ~**ly** adv infine

late /leɪt/ a (delayed) in ritardo; (at a late hour) tardo; (deceased) defunto; **it's** ~ (at night) è tardi; **in** ~ **November** alla fine di Novembre ● adv tardi; **stay up** ~ stare alzati fino a tardi. ~**comer** n ritardatario, -a mf; (to political party etc) nuovo, -a arrivato, -a mf. ~**ly** adv recentemente. ~**ness** n ora f tarda; (delay) ritardo m

latent /ˈleɪtnt/ a latente

later /ˈleɪtə(r)/ a ⟨train⟩ che parte più tardi; (edition) più recente ● adv più tardi; ~ **on** più tardi, dopo

lateral /'lætərəl/ a laterale

latest /'leɪtɪst/ a ultimo; (most recent) più recente; **the ~** [news] le ultime notizie ● n six o'clock at the **~** alle sei al più tardi

lathe /leɪð/ n tornio m

lather /'lɑːðə(r)/ n schiuma f ● vt insaponare ● vi far schiuma

Latin /'lætɪn/ a latino ● n latino m. ~ A'merica n America f Latina. ~ A'merican a & n latino-americano, -a mf

latitude /'lætɪtjuːd/ n Geog latitudine f; fig libertà f d'azione

latter /'lætə(r)/ a ultimo ● n the **~** quest'ultimo. **~ly** adv ultimamente

lattice /'lætɪs/ n traliccio m

Latvia /'lætvɪə/ n Lettonia f. **~n** a & n lettone mf

laudable /'lɔːdəbl/ a lodevole

laugh /lɑːf/ n risata f ● vi ridere (at/about di); ~ at sb (mock) prendere in giro qcno. **~able** /-əbl/ a ridicolo. **~ing-stock** n zimbello m

laughter /'lɑːftə(r)/ n risata f

launch[1] /lɔːntʃ/ n (boat) lancia f

launch[2] n lancio m; (of ship) varo m ● vt lanciare (rocket, product); varare (ship); sferrare (attack)

launder /'lɔːndə(r)/ vt lavare e stirare; ~ money fig riciclare denaro sporco. **~ette** /-'dret/ n lavanderia f automatica

laundry /'lɔːndrɪ/ n lavanderia f; (clothes) bucato m

laurel /'lɒrəl/ n lauro m; rest on one's **~s** fig dormire sugli allori

lava /'lɑːvə/ n lava f

lavatory /'lævətrɪ/ n gabinetto m

lavender /'lævəndə(r)/ n lavanda f

lavish /'lævɪʃ/ a copioso; (wasteful) prodigo; on a **~** scale su vasta scala ● vt ~ sth on sb ricoprire qcno di qcsa. **~ly** adv copiosamente

law /lɔː/ n legge f; study **~** studiare giurisprudenza, studiare legge; ~ and order ordine m pubblico

law: ~-abiding a che rispetta la legge. **~court** n tribunale m. **~ful** a legittimo. **~less** a senza legge. ~ school n facoltà f di giurisprudenza

lawn /lɔːn/ n prato m [all'inglese]. **~-mower** n tosaerba m inv

'**law suit** n causa f

lawyer /'lɔːjə(r)/ n avvocato m

lax /læks/ a negligente; (morals etc) lassista

laxative /'læksətɪv/ n lassativo m

laxity /'læksətɪ/ n lassismo m

lay[1] /leɪ/ a laico; fig profano

lay[2] see lie[2]

lay[3] vt (pt/pp laid) porre, mettere; apparecchiare (table) ● vi (hen:) fare le uova. **lay down** vt posare; stabilire (rules, conditions). **lay off** vt licenziare (workers) ● vi (fam: stop) ~ off! smettila! **lay out** vt (display, set forth) esporre; (plan) pianificare (garden); (spend) sborsare; Typ impaginare

lay: ~about n fannullone, -a mf. **~-by** n piazzola f di sosta

layer /'leɪə(r)/ n strato m

lay: ~man n profano m. **~out** n disposizione f; Typ impaginazione f, layout m inv

laze /leɪz/ vi ~ [about] oziare

laziness /'leɪzɪnɪs/ n pigrizia f

lazy /'leɪzɪ/ a (-ier, -iest) pigro. **~-bones** n poltrone, -a mf

lb abbr (pound) libbra

lead[1] /led/ n piombo m; (of pencil) mina f

lead[2] /liːd/ n guida f; (leash) guinzaglio m; (flex) filo m; (clue) indizio m; Theat parte f principale; (distance ahead) distanza f (over su); in the ~ in testa ● v (pt/pp led) ● vt condurre; dirigere (expedition, party etc); (induce) indurre; ~ the way mettersi in testa ● vi (be in front) condurre; (in race, competition) essere in testa; (at cards) giocare (per primo). **lead away** vt portar via. **lead to** vt portare a. **lead up to** vt precludere; what's this **~ing** up to? dove porta questo?

leaded /'ledɪd/ a con piombo

leader /'liːdə(r)/ n capo m; (of orchestra) primo violino m; (in newspaper) articolo m di fondo. **~ship** n direzione f, leadership f inv; show **~ship** mostrare capacità di comando

lead-'free a senza piombo

leading /'liːdɪŋ/ a principale; ~ lady/man attrice f/attore m principale; ~ question domanda f tendenziosa

leaf /liːf/ n (pl leaves) foglia f; (of table) asse f ● leaf through vt sfogliare. **~let** n dépliant m inv; (advertising) dépliant m inv pubblicitario; (political) manifestino m

league /liːg/ n lega f, Sport campionato m; be in **~** with essere in combutta con

leak /liːk/ n (hole) fessura f; Naut falla f; (of gas & fig) fuga f ● vi colare; (ship:) fare acqua; (liquid, gas:) fuoriuscire ● vt ~ sth to sb fig far trapelare qcsa a qcno. **~y** a che perde; Naut che fa acqua

lean¹ /liːn/ a magro

lean² v (pt/pp **leaned** or **leant** /lent/) • vt appoggiare (**against/on** contro/su) • vi appoggiarsi (**against/on** contro/su); (not be straight) pendere; be ~**ing against** essere appoggiato contro; ~ **on sb** (depend on) appoggiarsi a qcno; (fam: exert pressure on) stare alle calcagne di qcno. **lean back** vi sporgersi indietro. **lean forward** vi piegarsi in avanti. **lean out** vi sporgersi. **lean over** vi piegarsi

leaning /ˈliːnɪŋ/ a pendente; **the L~ Tower of Pisa** la torre di Pisa, la torre pendente • n tendenza f

leap /liːp/ n salto m • vi (pt/pp **leapt** /lept/ or **leaped**) saltare; **he leapt at it** fam l'ha preso al volo. **~-frog** n cavallina f. **~ year** n anno m bisestile

learn /lɜːn/ v (pt/pp **learnt** or **learned**) • vt imparare; ~ **to swim** imparare a nuotare; **I have ~ed that...** (heard) sono venuto a sapere che... • vi imparare

learn|ed /ˈlɜːnɪd/ a colto. **~er** n also Auto principiante mf. **~ing** n cultura f

lease /liːs/ n contratto m d'affitto; (rental) affitto m • vt affittare

leash /liːʃ/ n guinzaglio m

least /liːst/ a più piccolo; (amount) minore; **you've got ~ luggage** hai meno bagagli di tutti • n **the ~** il meno; **at ~** almeno; **not in the ~** niente affatto • adv meno; **the ~ expensive wine** il vino meno caro

leather /ˈleðə(r)/ n pelle f, (of soles) cuoio m • attrib di pelle/cuoio. **~y** a (meat, skin) duro

leave /liːv/ n (holiday) congedo m; Mil licenza f; **on ~** in congedo/licenza • v (pt/pp **left**) • vt lasciare; uscire da (house, office); (forget) dimenticare; **there is nothing left** non è rimasto niente • vi andare via; (train, bus:) partire. **leave behind** vt lasciare; (forget) dimenticare. **leave out** vt omettere; (not put away) lasciare fuori

leaves /liːvz/ see **leaf**

Leban|on /ˈlebənən/ n Libano m **~ese** /-ˈniːz/ a & n libanese mf

lecherous /ˈletʃərəs/ a lascivo

lectern /ˈlektɜːn/ n leggio m

lecture /ˈlektʃə(r)/ n conferenza f; Univ lezione f; (reproof) ramanzina f • vi fare una conferenza (**on** su); Univ insegnare (**on sth** qcsa) • vt ~ **sb** rimproverare qcno. **~r** n conferenziere, -a mf; Univ docente mf universitario, -a

led /led/ see **lead**²

ledge /ledʒ/ n cornice f; (of window) davanzale m

ledger /ˈledʒə(r)/ n libro m mastro

leech /liːtʃ/ n sanguisuga f

leek /liːk/ n porro m

leer /lɪə(r)/ n sguardo m libidinoso • vi ~ [**at**] guardare in modo libidinoso

leeway /ˈliːweɪ/ n fig libertà f di azione

left¹ /left/ see **leave**

left² a sinistro • adv a sinistra • n also Pol sinistra f; **on the ~** a sinistra

left: **~-handed** a mancino. **~-luggage [office]** n deposito m bagagli. **~overs** npl rimasugli mpl. **~-'wing** a Pol di sinistra

leg /leg/ n gamba f; (of animal) zampa f; (of journey) tappa f; Culin (of chicken) coscia f; (of lamb) cosciotto m

legacy /ˈlegəsɪ/ n lascito m

legal /ˈliːgl/ a legale; **take ~ action** intentare un'azione legale. **~ly** adv legalmente

legality /lɪˈgælətɪ/ n legalità f

legalize /ˈliːgəlaɪz/ vt legalizzare

legend /ˈledʒənd/ n leggenda f. **~ary** a leggendario

legib|le /ˈledʒəbl/ a leggibile. **~ly** adv in modo leggibile

legislat|e /ˈledʒɪsleɪt/ vi legiferare. **~ion** /-ˈleɪʃn/ n legislazione f

legislat|ive /ˈledʒɪslətɪv/ a legislativo. **~ure** /-leɪtʃə(r)/ n legislatura f

legitimate /lɪˈdʒɪtɪmət/ a legittimo; (excuse) valido

leisure /ˈleʒə(r)/ n tempo m libero; **at your ~** con comodo. **~ly** a senza fretta

lemon /ˈlemən/ n limone m. **~ade** /-ˈneɪd/ n limonata f

lend /lend/ vt (pt/pp **lent**) prestare; ~ **a hand** fig dare una mano. **~ing library** n biblioteca f per il prestito

length /leŋθ/ n lunghezza f; (piece) pezzo m; (of wallpaper) parte f; (of visit) durata f; **at ~** a lungo; (at last) alla fine

length|en /ˈleŋθən/ vt allungare • vi allungarsi. **~ways** adv per lungo

lengthy /ˈleŋθɪ/ a (-ier, -iest) lungo

lenien|ce /ˈliːnɪəns/ n indulgenza f. **~t** a indulgente

lens /lenz/ n lente f; Phot obiettivo m; (of eye) cristallino m

Lent /lent/ n Quaresima f

lent see **lend**

lentil /ˈlentl/ n Bot lenticchia f

Leo /ˈliːəʊ/ n Astr Leone m

leopard /ˈlepəd/ n leopardo m

leotard /ˈliːətɑːd/ n body m inv

leprosy /'leprəsɪ/ n lebbra f
lesbian /'lezbɪən/ a lesbico ● n lesbica f
less /les/ a meno di; ~ **and** ~ sempre meno ● adv & prep meno ● n meno m
lessen /'lesn/ vt/i diminuire
lesser /'lesə(r)/ a minore
lesson /'lesn/ n lezione f
lest /lest/ conj liter per timore che
let /let/ vt (pt/pp let, pres p letting) lasciare, permettere; (rent) affittare; ~ **alone** (not to mention) tanto meno; 'to ~ 'affittasi'; ~ **us go** andiamo; ~ **sb do sth** lasciare fare qcsa a qcno, permettere a qcno di fare qcsa:; ~ **me know** fammi sapere; **just** ~ **him try!** che ci provi solamente!; ~ **oneself in for sth** fam impelagarsi in qcsa. **let down** vt sciogliersi (hair); abbassare (blinds); (lengthen) allungare; (disappoint) deludere; **don't** ~ **me down** conto su di te. **let in** vt far entrare. **let off** vt far partire; (not punish) perdonare; ~ **sb off doing sth** abbonare qcsa a qcno. **let out** vt far uscire; (make larger) allargare; emettere (scream, groan). **let through** vt far passare. **let up** vi fam diminuire
'let-down n delusione f
lethal /'liːθl/ a letale
letharg|ic /lɪ'θɑːdʒɪk/ a apatico. ~**y** /'leθədʒɪ/ n apatia f
letter /'letə(r)/ n lettera f. ~**-box** n buca f per le lettere. ~**-head** n carta f intestata. ~**ing** n caratteri mpl
lettuce /'letɪs/ n lattuga f
'let-up n fam pausa f
leukaemia /luːˈkiːmɪə/ n leucemia f
level /'levl/ a piano; (in height, competition) allo stesso livello; (spoonful) raso; **draw** ~ **with sb** affiancare qcno ● n livello m; **on the** ~ fam giusto ● vt (pt/pp levelled) livellare; (aim) puntare (at su)
level: ~ **'crossing** n passaggio m a livello. ~**-headed** a posato
lever /'liːvə(r)/ n leva f **lever up** vt sollevare (con una leva). ~**age** /-rɪdʒ/ n azione f di una leva; fig influenza f
levy /'levɪ/ vt (pt/pp levied) imporre (tax)
lewd /ljuːd/ a osceno
liab|ility /laɪə'bɪlətɪ/ n responsabilità f; (fam: burden) peso m; ~**ies** pl debiti mpl
liable /'laɪəbl/ a responsabile (for di); **be** ~ **to** (rain, break etc) rischiare di; (tend to) tendere a
liaise /lɪ'eɪz/ vi fam essere in contatto

liaison /lɪ'eɪzɒn/ n contatti mpl; Mil collegamento m; (affair) relazione f
liar /'laɪə(r)/ n bugiardo, -a mf
libel /'laɪbl/ n diffamazione f ● vt (pt/pp libelled) diffamare. ~**lous** a diffamatorio
liberal /'lɪb(ə)rəl/ a (tolerant) di larghe vedute; (generous) generoso. **L~** a Pol liberale ● n liberale mf
liberat|e /'lɪbəreɪt/ vt liberare. ~**ed** a (woman) emancipata. ~**ion** /-'reɪʃn/ n liberazione f; (of women) emancipazione f. ~**or** n liberatore, -trice mf
liberty /'lɪbətɪ/ n libertà f; **take the** ~ **of doing sth** prendersi la libertà di fare qcsa; **be at** ~ **to do sth** essere libero di fare qcsa
Libra /'liːbrə/ n Astr Bilancia f
librarian /laɪ'breərɪən/ n bibliotecario, -a mf
library /'laɪbrərɪ/ n biblioteca f
Libya /'lɪbɪə/ n Libia f. ~**n** a & n libico, -a mf
lice /laɪs/ see louse
licence /'laɪsns/ n licenza f; (for TV) canone m televisivo; (for driving) patente f; (freedom) sregolatezza f. ~**-plate** n targa f
license /'laɪsns/ vt autorizzare; **be** ~**d** (car:) avere il bollo; (restaurant:) essere autorizzato alla vendita di alcolici
licentious /laɪ'senʃəs/ a licenzioso
lick /lɪk/ n leccata f; **a** ~ **of paint** una passata leggera di pittura ● vt leccare; (fam: defeat) battere; leccarsi (lips)
lid /lɪd/ n coperchio m; (of eye) palpebra f
lie¹ /laɪ/ n bugia f; **tell a** ~ mentire ● vi (pt/pp lied, pres p lying) mentire
lie² vi (pt lay, pp lain, pres p lying) (person:) sdraiarsi; (object:) stare; (remain) rimanere; **leave sth lying about** or **around** lasciare qcsa in giro. **lie down** vi sdraiarsi
'lie: ~**-down** n **have a** ~**-down** fare un riposino. ~**-in** n fam **have a** ~**-in** restare a letto fino a tardi
lieu /ljuː/ n **in** ~ **of** in luogo di
lieutenant /lef'tenənt/ n tenente m
life /laɪf/ n (pl lives) vita f
life: ~**-belt** n salvagente m. ~**-boat** n lancia f di salvataggio; (on ship) scialuppa f di salvataggio. ~**-buoy** n salvagente m. ~**-guard** n bagnino m. ~ **insurance** n assicurazione f sulla vita. ~**-jacket** n giubbotto m di salvataggio. ~**less** a inanimato. ~**like** a realistico. ~**long** a di tutta la vita. ~**-size|d** a in grandezza naturale. ~**time** n vita f; the

chance of a ~time un'occasione unica

lift /lɪft/ n ascensore m; *Auto* passaggio
m • vt sollevare; revocare ⟨restrictions⟩;
⟨fam: steal⟩ rubare • vi ⟨fog:⟩ alzarsi.
lift up vt sollevare
'lift-off n decollo m (di razzo)
ligament /'lɪgəmənt/ n Anat legamen-
to m
light¹ /laɪt/ a (not dark) luminoso; ~
green verde chiaro • n luce f; (lamp)
lampada f; **in the ~ of** fig alla luce di;
have you got a ~? ha da accendere?;
come to ~ essere rivelato • vt (pt/pp
lit or lighted) accendere; ⟨illuminate⟩
illuminare. **light up** vi ⟨face:⟩ illumi-
narsi
light² a (not heavy) leggero • adv
travel ~ viaggiare con poco bagaglio
'light-bulb n lampadina f
lighten¹ /'laɪtn/ vt illuminare
lighten² vt alleggerire ⟨load⟩
lighter /'laɪtə(r)/ n accendino m
light: ~-**fingered** a svelto di mano.
~-**headed** a sventato. ~-**hearted** a
spensierato. ~**house** n faro m. ~**ing** n
illuminazione f. ~**ly** adv leggermente;
⟨accuse⟩ con leggerezza; ⟨without
concern⟩ senza dare importanza alla
cosa; **get off ~ly** cavarsela a buon mercato. ~**ness** n leggerezza f
lightning /'laɪtnɪŋ/ n lampo m, fulmine
m. ~-**conductor** n parafulmine m
light: ~**weight** a leggero • n (in
boxing) peso m leggero. ~ **year** n anno
m luce
like¹ /laɪk/ a simile • prep come; ~ **this/
that** così; **what's he ~?** com'è? • conj
⟨fam: as⟩ come; ⟨Am: as if⟩ come se
like² vt piacere, gradire; **I should** or
would ~ vorrei, gradirei; **I ~ him** mi
piace; **I ~ this car** mi piace questa
macchina; **I ~ dancing** mi piace ballare; **I ~ that!** fam questa mi è piaciuta!
• n ~**s and dislikes** pl gusti mpl
like|able /'laɪkəbl/ a simpatico.
~**lihood** /-lɪhʊd/ n probabilità f. ~**ly** a
(-ier, -iest) probabile • adv probabilmente; **not ~ly!** fam neanche per sogno!
like-'minded a con gusti affini
liken /'laɪkən/ vt paragonare ⟨to a⟩
like|ness /'laɪknɪs/ n somiglianza f.
~**wise** adv lo stesso
liking /'laɪkɪŋ/ n gusto m; **is it to your
~?** è di suo gusto?; **take a ~ to sb**
prendere qcno in simpatia
lilac /'laɪlək/ n lillà m • a color lillà

lily /'lɪlɪ/ n giglio m. ~ **of the valley** n
mughetto m
limb /lɪm/ n arto m
limber /'lɪmbə(r)/ vi ~ **up** sciogliersi i
muscoli
lime¹ /laɪm/ n (fruit) cedro m; (tree) tiglio m
lime² n calce f. '~**light** n **be in the
~-light** essere molto in vista. '~**stone** n
calcare m
limit /'lɪmɪt/ n limite m; **that's the ~!**
fam questo è troppo! • vt limitare ⟨to a⟩.
~**ation** /-'teɪʃn/ n limite m. ~**ed** a ristretto; ~**ed company** società f inv a
responsabilità limitata
limousine /'lɪməziːn/ n limousine f
inv
limp¹ /lɪmp/ n andatura f zoppicante;
have a ~ zoppicare • vi zoppicare
limp² a floscio
line¹ /laɪn/ n linea f; (length of rope,
cord) filo m; (of writing) riga f; (of
poem) verso m; (row) fila f; (wrinkle)
ruga f; (of business) settore m; ⟨Am:
queue⟩ coda f; **in ~ with** in conformità
con • vt segnare; fiancheggiare ⟨street⟩.
line up vi allinearsi • vt allineare
line² vt foderare ⟨garment⟩
linear /'lɪnɪə(r)/ a lineare
lined¹ /laɪnd/ a ⟨face⟩ rugoso; ⟨paper⟩ a
righe
lined² a ⟨garment⟩ foderato
linen /'lɪnɪn/ n lino m; (articles) biancheria f • attrib di lino
liner /'laɪnə(r)/ n nave f di linea
linesman n Sport guardalinee m inv
linger /'lɪŋgə(r)/ vi indugiare
lingerie /'lɒ̃ʒərɪ/ n biancheria f intima
(da donna)
linguist /'lɪŋgwɪst/ n linguista mf
linguistic /lɪŋ'gwɪstɪk/ a linguistico.
~**s** n linguistica fsg
lining /'laɪnɪŋ/ n (of garment) fodera f;
(of brakes) guarnizione f
link /lɪŋk/ n (of chain) anello m; fig legame m • vt collegare. **link up** vi unirsi
⟨with a⟩; TV collegarsi
lino /'laɪnəʊ/ n, **linoleum** /lɪ'nəʊlɪəm/
n linoleum m
lint /lɪnt/ n garza f
lion /'laɪən/ n leone m. ~**ess** n leonessa f
lip /lɪp/ n labbro m (pl labbra f); (edge)
bordo m
lip: ~-**read** vi leggere le labbra;
~-**reading** n lettura f delle labbra.
~-**service** n **pay ~-service to** approvare soltanto a parole. ~**salve** n burro
m [di] cacao. ~**stick** n rossetto m

liqueur /lɪˈkjʊə(r)/ n liquore m

liquid /ˈlɪkwɪd/ n liquido m ● a liquido

liquidat|e /ˈlɪkwɪdeɪt/ vt liquidare. ~ion /-ˈdeɪʃn/ n liquidazione f; **go into ~ion** Comm andare in liquidazione

liquidize /ˈlɪkwɪdaɪz/ vt rendere liquido. ~r n Culin frullatore m

liquor /ˈlɪkə(r)/ n bevanda f alcolica

liquorice /ˈlɪkərɪs/ n liquirizia f

liquor store n Am negozio m di alcolici

lisp /lɪsp/ n pronuncia f con la lisca ● vi parlare con la lisca

list[1] /lɪst/ n lista f ● vt elencare

list[2] vi ⟨ship.⟩ inclinarsi

listen /ˈlɪsn/ vi ascoltare; **~ to** ascoltare. **~er** n ascoltatore, -trice mf

listings /ˈlɪstɪŋz/ npl TV programma m tv

listless /ˈlɪstlɪs/ a svogliato

lit /lɪt/ see light[1]

literacy /ˈlɪtərəsɪ/ n alfabetizzazione f

literal /ˈlɪtərəl/ a letterale. **~ly** adv letteralmente

literary /ˈlɪtərərɪ/ a letterario

literate /ˈlɪtərət/ a **be ~** saper leggere e scrivere

literature /ˈlɪtrətʃə(r)/ n letteratura f

Lithuania /lɪθjʊˈeɪnɪə/ n Lituania f. **~n** a & n lituano, -a mf

litigation /lɪtɪˈɡeɪʃn/ n causa f [giudiziaria]

litre /ˈliːtə(r)/ n litro m

litter /ˈlɪtə(r)/ n immondizie fpl; Zool figliata f ● vt **be ~ed** with essere ingombrato di. **~-bin** n bidone m della spazzatura

little /ˈlɪtl/ a piccolo; ⟨not much⟩ poco ● adv & n poco m; **a ~** un po'; **a ~ water** un po' d'acqua; **a ~ better** un po' meglio; **~ by ~** a poco a poco

liturgy /ˈlɪtədʒɪ/ n liturgia f

live[1] /laɪv/ a vivo; ⟨ammunition⟩ carico; **~ broadcast** trasmissione f in diretta; **be ~** Electr essere sotto tensione; **~ wire** n fig persona f dinamica ● adv ⟨broadcast⟩ in diretta

live[2] /lɪv/ vi vivere; ⟨reside⟩ abitare; **~ with** convivere con. **live down** vt far dimenticare. **live off** vt vivere alle spalle di. **live on** vt vivere di ● vi sopravvivere. **live up** vt **~ it up** far la bella vita. **live up to** vt essere all'altezza di

liveli|hood /ˈlaɪvlɪhʊd/ n mezzi mpl di sostentamento. **~ness** n vivacità f

lively /ˈlaɪvlɪ/ a (-ier, -iest) vivace

liven /ˈlaɪvn/ vt **~ up** vivacizzare ● vi vivacizzarsi

liver /ˈlɪvə(r)/ n fegato m

lives /laɪvz/ see life

livestock /ˈlaɪv-/ n bestiame m

livid /ˈlɪvɪd/ a fam livido

living /ˈlɪvɪŋ/ a vivo ● n **earn one's ~** guadagnarsi da vivere; **the ~** pl i vivi. **~-room** n soggiorno m

lizard /ˈlɪzəd/ n lucertola f

load /ləʊd/ n carico m; **~s of** fam un sacco di ● vt caricare. **~ed** a carico; ⟨fam: rich⟩ ricchissimo

loaf[1] /ləʊf/ n (pl loaves) pagnotta f

loaf[2] vi oziare

loan /ləʊn/ n prestito m; **on ~** in prestito ● vt prestare

loath /ləʊθ/ a **be ~ to do sth** essere restio a fare qcsa

loath|e /ləʊð/ vt detestare. **~ing** n disgusto m. **~some** a disgustoso

loaves /ləʊvz/ see loaf

lobby /ˈlɒbɪ/ n atrio m; Pol gruppo m di pressione, lobby m inv

lobster /ˈlɒbstə(r)/ n aragosta f

local /ˈləʊkl/ a locale; **I'm not ~** non sono del posto ● n abitante mf del luogo; ⟨fam: public house⟩ pub m inv locale. **~ au'thority** n autorità f locale. **~ call** n Teleph telefonata f urbana. **~ government** n autorità f inv locale

locality /ləʊˈkælətɪ/ n zona f

localized /ˈləʊkəlaɪzd/ a localizzato

locally /ˈləʊkəlɪ/ adv localmente; ⟨live, work⟩ nei paraggi

local network n Comput rete f locale

locat|e /ləʊˈkeɪt/ vt situare; trovare ⟨person⟩; **be ~ed** essere situato. **~ion** /-ˈkeɪʃn/ n posizione f; **filmed on ~ion** girato in esterni

lock[1] /lɒk/ n (of hair) ciocca f

lock[2] n (on door) serratura f; (on canal) chiusa f ● vt chiudere a chiave; bloccare ⟨wheels⟩ ● vi chiudersi. **lock in** vt chiudere dentro. **lock out** vt chiudere fuori. **lock up** vt (in prison) mettere dentro ● vi chiudere

locker /ˈlɒkə(r)/ n armadietto m

locket /ˈlɒkɪt/ n medaglione m

lock: **~-out** n serrata f. **~smith** n fabbro m

locomotive /ləʊkəˈməʊtɪv/ n locomotiva f

locum /ˈləʊkəm/ n sostituto, -a mf

locust /ˈləʊkəst/ n locusta f

lodge /lɒdʒ/ n (porter's) portineria f; (masonic) loggia f ● vt presentare ⟨claim, complaint⟩; ⟨with bank, solicitor⟩ depositare; **be ~d** essersi conficcato

● *vi* essere a pensione (**with** da); (*become fixed*) conficcarsi. ~ r *n* inquilino, -a *mf*

lodgings /'lɒdʒɪŋz/ *npl* camere *fpl* in affitto

loft /lɒft/ *n* soffitta *f*

lofty /'lɒftɪ/ *a* (**-ier**, **-iest**) alto; (*haughty*) altezzoso

log /lɒg/ *n* ceppo *m*; *Auto* libretto *m* di circolazione; *Naut* giornale *m* di bordo ● *vt* (*pt/pp* **logged**) registrare. **log on** *to vt Comput* connettersi a

logarithm /'lɒgərɪðm/ *n* logaritmo *m*

'log-book *n Naut* giornale *m* di bordo; *Auto* libretto *m* di circolazione

loggerheads /'lɒgə-/ *npl* **be at** ~ *fam* essere in totale disaccordo

logic /'lɒdʒɪk/ *n* logica *f*. ~ **al** *a* logico. ~ **ally** *adv* logicamente

logistics /lə'dʒɪstɪks/ *npl* logistica *f*

logo /'ləʊgəʊ/ *n* logo *m inv*

loin /lɔɪn/ *n Culin* lombata *f*

loiter /'lɔɪtə(r)/ *vi* gironzolare

lollipop /'lɒlɪpɒp/ *n* lecca-lecca *m inv*. ~ **y** *n* lecca-lecca *m inv*; (*fam: money*) quattrini *mpl*

London /'lʌndən/ *n* Londra *f* ● *attrib* londinese, di Londra. ~ **er** *n* londinese *mf*

lone /ləʊn/ *a* solitario. ~ **liness** *n* solitudine *f*

lonely /'ləʊnlɪ/ *a* (**-ier**, **-iest**) solitario; ⟨*person*⟩ solo

lone|r /'ləʊnə(r)/ *n* persona *f* solitaria. ~ **some** *a* solo

long[1] /lɒŋ/ *a* lungo; **a** ~ **time** molto tempo; **a** ~ **way** distante; **in the** ~ **run** a lungo andare; (*in the end*) alla fin fine ● *adv* a lungo, lungamente; **how** ~ **is it?** quanto è lungo?; (*in time*) quanto dura?; **all day** ~ tutto il giorno; **not** ~ **ago** non molto tempo fa; **before** ~ fra breve; **he's no** ~ **er here** non è più qui; **as** *or* **so** ~ **as** finché; (*provided that*) purché; **so** ~! *fam* ciao!; **will you be** ~? [ti] ci vuole molto?

long[2] *vi* ~ **for** desiderare ardentemente

long-'distance *a* a grande distanza; *Sport* di fondo; (*call*) interurbano

'longhand *n* **in** ~ in scrittura ordinaria

longing /'lɒŋɪŋ/ *a* desideroso ● brama *f*. ~ **ly** *adv* con desiderio

longitude /'lɒŋgɪtjuːd/ *n Geog* longitudine *f*

long: ~ **jump** *n* salto *m* in lungo. ~ **-life 'milk** *n* latte *m* a lunga conservazione. ~ **-lived** /-lɪvd/ *a* longevo. ~ **-range** *a Mil, Aeron* a lunga portata; ⟨*forecast*⟩ a

lungo termine. ~ **-sighted** *a* presbite. ~ **-sleeved** *a* a maniche lunghe. ~ **-suffering** *a* infinitamente paziente. ~ **-term** *a* a lunga scadenza. ~ **wave** *n* onde *fpl* lunghe. ~ **-winded** /-'wɪndɪd/ *a* prolisso

loo /luː/ *n fam* gabinetto *m*

look /lʊk/ *n* occhiata *f*; (*appearance*) aspetto *m*; [**good**] ~ **s** *pl* bellezza *f*; **have a** ~ **at** dare un'occhiata a ● *vi* guardare; (*seem*) sembrare; ~ **here!** mi ascolti bene!; ~ **at** guardare; ~ **for** cercare; ~ **like** (*resemble*) assomigliare a. **look after** *vt* badare a. **look down** *vi* guardare in basso; ~ **down on sb** *fig* guardare dall'alto in basso qcno. **look forward to** *vt* essere impaziente di. **look in on** *vt* passare da. **look into** *vt* (*examine*) esaminare. **look on to** *vt* ⟨*room:*⟩ dare su. **look out** *vi* guardare fuori; (*take care*) fare attenzione; ~ **out!** attento! **look round** *vi* girarsi; (*in shop, town etc*) dare un'occhiata. **look through** *vt* dare un'occhiata a ⟨*script, notes*⟩. **look up** *vi* guardare in alto; ~ **up to sb** *fig* rispettare qcno ● *vt* cercare [nel dizionario] ⟨*word*⟩; (*visit*) andare a trovare

'look-out /'lʊkaʊt/ *n* guardia *f*; (*prospect*) prospettiva *f*; **be on the** ~ **for** tenere gli occhi aperti per

loom /luːm/ *vi* apparire; *fig* profilarsi

loony /'luːnɪ/ *a* & *n fam* matto, -a *mf*. ~ **bin** *n* manicomio *m*

loop /luːp/ *n* cappio *m*; (*on garment*) passante *m*. ~ **hole** *n* (*in the law*) scappatoia *f*

loose /luːs/ *a* libero; ⟨*knot*⟩ allentato; ⟨*page*⟩ staccato; ⟨*clothes*⟩ largo; ⟨*morals*⟩ dissoluto; (*inexact*) vago; **be at a** ~ **end** non sapere cosa fare; **come** ~ ⟨*knot:*⟩ sciogliersi; **set** ~ liberare. ~ **change** *n* spiccioli *mpl*. ~ **ly** *adv* scorrevolmente; ⟨*defined*⟩ vagamente

loosen /'luːsn/ *vt* sciogliere

loot /luːt/ *n* bottino *m* ● *vt/i* depredare. ~ **er** *n* predatore, -trice *mf*. ~ **ing** *n* saccheggio *m*

lop /lɒp/ ~ **off** *vt* (*pt/pp* **lopped**) potare

lop'sided *a* sbilenco

lord /lɔːd/ *n* signore *m*; (*title*) Lord *m*; **House of L~s** Camera *f* dei Lords; **the L~'s Prayer** il Padrenostro; **good L~!** Dio mio!

lore /lɔː/ *n* tradizioni *fpl*

lorry /'lɒrɪ/ *n* camion *m inv*; ~ **driver** camionista *mf*

lose /luːz/ *v* (*pt/pp* **lost**) ● *vt* perdere

● *vi* perdere; ⟨*clock:*⟩ essere indietro; **get lost** perdersi; **get lost!** *fam* va a quel paese! **~r** *n* perdente *mf*

loss /lɒs/ *n* perdita *f*; **~es** *pl Comm* perdite *fpl*; **be at a ~** essere perplesso; **be at a ~ for words** non trovare le parole

lost /lɒst/ *see* **lose** ● *a* perduto. ~ 'property office *n* ufficio *m* oggetti smarriti

lot¹ /lɒt/ ⟨*at auction*⟩ lotto *m*; **draw ~s** tirare a sorte

lot² *n* **the ~** il tutto; **a ~ of**, **~s of** molto/i; **the ~ of you** tutti voi; **it has changed a ~** è cambiato molto

lotion /'ləʊʃn/ *n* lozione *f*

lottery /'lɒtəri/ *n* lotteria *f*. **~ ticket** *n* biglietto *m* della lotteria

loud /laʊd/ *a* sonoro, alto; ⟨*colours*⟩ sgargiante ● *adv* forte; **out ~** ad alta voce. **~ 'hailer** *n* megafono *m*. **~ly** *adv* forte. **~'speaker** *n* altoparlante *m*

lounge /laʊndʒ/ *n* salotto *m*; ⟨*in hotel*⟩ salone *m* ● *vi* poltrire. **~ suit** *n* vestito *m* da uomo, completo *m* da uomo

louse /laʊs/ *n* ⟨*pl* **lice**⟩ pidocchio *m*

lousy /'laʊzɪ/ *a* (-ier, -iest) *fam* schifoso

lout /laʊt/ *n* zoticone *m*. **~ish** *a* rozzo

lovable /'lʌvəbl/ *a* adorabile

love /lʌv/ *n* amore *m*; *Tennis* zero *m*; **in ~** innamorato (**with** di) ● *vt* amare ⟨*person, country*⟩; **I ~ watching tennis** mi piace molto guardare il tennis. **~-affair** *n* relazione *f* [sentimentale]. **~ letter** *n* lettera *f* d'amore

lovely /'lʌvlɪ/ *a* (-ier, -iest) bello; ⟨*in looks*⟩ bello, attraente; ⟨*in character*⟩ piacevole; ⟨*meal*⟩ delizioso; **have a ~ time** divertirsi molto

lover /'lʌvə(r)/ *n* amante *mf*

love: **~ song** *n* canzone *f* d'amore. **~ story** *n* storia *f* d'amore

loving /'lʌvɪŋ/ *a* affettuoso

low /ləʊ/ *a* basso; ⟨*depressed*⟩ giù *inv* ● *adv* basso; **feel ~** sentirsi giù ● *n* minimo *m*; *Meteorol* depressione *f*; **at an all-time ~** ⟨*prices etc*⟩ al livello minimo

low: **~-brow** *a* di scarsa cultura. **~-cut** *a* ⟨*dress*⟩ scollato

lower /'ləʊə(r)/ *a & adv see* **low** ● *vt* abbassare; **~ oneself** abbassarsi

low: **~-'fat** *a* magro. **~-'grade** *a* di qualità inferiore. **~-key** *fig* moderato. **~lands** /-ləndz/ *npl* pianure *fpl*. **~ 'tide** *n* bassa marea *f*

loyal /'lɔɪəl/ *a* leale. **~ty** *n* lealtà *f*

lozenge /'lɒzɪndʒ/ *n* losanga *f*; ⟨*tablet*⟩ pastiglia *f*

LP *n abbr* **long-playing record**

Ltd *abbr* (**Limited**) s.r.l.

lubricant /'luːbrɪkənt/ *n* lubrificante *m*

lubricat|e /'luːbrɪkeɪt/ *vt* lubrificare. **~ion** /-'keɪʃn/ *n* lubrificazione *f*

lucid /'luːsɪd/ *a* ⟨*explanation*⟩ chiaro; ⟨*sane*⟩ lucido. **~ity** /-'sɪdətɪ/ *n* lucidità *f*; ⟨*of explanation*⟩ chiarezza *f*

luck /lʌk/ *n* fortuna *f*; **bad ~** sfortuna *f*; **good ~!** buona fortuna! **~ily** *adv* fortunatamente

lucky /'lʌkɪ/ *a* (-ier, -iest) fortunato; **be ~** essere fortunato; ⟨*thing:*⟩ portare fortuna. **~ 'charm** *n* portafortuna *m inv*

lucrative /'luːkrətɪv/ *a* lucrativo

ludicrous /'luːdɪkrəs/ *a* ridicolo. **~ly** *adv* ⟨*expensive, complex*⟩ eccessivamente

lug /lʌg/ *vt* (*pt/pp* **lugged**) *fam* trascinare

luggage /'lʌgɪdʒ/ *n* bagaglio *m*; **~-rack** *n* portabagagli *m inv*. **~ trolley** *n* carrello *m* portabagagli. **~-van** *n* bagagliaio *m*

lukewarm /'luːk-/ *a* tiepido; *fig* poco entusiasta

lull /lʌl/ *n* pausa *f* ● *vt* **~ to sleep** cullare

lullaby /'lʌləbaɪ/ *n* ninnananna *f*

lumbago /lʌm'beɪgəʊ/ *n* lombaggine *f*

lumber /'lʌmbə(r)/ *n* cianfrusaglie *fpl*; ⟨*Am: timber*⟩ legname *m* ● *vt fam* **~ sb with sth** affibbiare qcsa a qcno. **~ jack** *n* tagliaboschi *m inv*

luminous /'luːmɪnəs/ *a* luminoso

lump¹ /lʌmp/ *n* ⟨*of sugar*⟩ zolletta *f*; ⟨*swelling*⟩ gonfiore *m*; ⟨*in breast*⟩ nodulo *m*; ⟨*in sauce*⟩ grumo *m* ● *vt* **~ together** ammucchiare

lump² *vt* **~ it** *fam* **you'll just have to ~ it** che ti piaccia o no è così

lump sum *n* somma *f* globale

lumpy /'lʌmpɪ/ *a* (-ier, -iest) grumoso

lunacy /'luːnəsɪ/ *n* follia *f*

lunar /'luːnə(r)/ *a* lunare

lunatic /'luːnətɪk/ *n* pazzo, -a *mf*

lunch /lʌntʃ/ *n* pranzo *m* ● *vi* pranzare

luncheon /'lʌntʃn/ *n* ⟨*formal*⟩ pranzo *m*. **~ meat** *n* carne *f* in scatola. **~ voucher** *n* buono *m* pasto

lunch: **~-hour** *n* intervallo *m* per il pranzo. **~-time** *n* ora *f* di pranzo

lung /lʌŋ/ *n* polmone *m*. **~ cancer** *n* cancro *m* al polmone

lunge /lʌndʒ/ *vi* lanciarsi (**at** su)

lurch¹ /lɜːtʃ/ *n* **leave in the ~** *fam* lasciare nei guai

lurch² *vi* barcollare

lure /lʊə(r)/ *n* esca *f*; *fig* lusinga *f* ● *vt* adescare

lurid /'lʊərɪd/ a (gaudy) sgargiante; (sensational) sensazionalistico

lurk /lɜːk/ vi appostarsi

luscious /'lʌʃəs/ a saporito; fig sexy inv

lush /lʌʃ/ a lussureggiante

lust /lʌst/ n lussuria f ● vi ~ after desiderare [fortemente]. ~ful a lussurioso

lusty /'lʌstɪ/ a (-ier, -iest) vigoroso

lute /luːt/ n liuto m

luxuriant /lʌg'ʒʊərɪənt/ a lussureggiante

luxurious /lʌg'ʒʊərɪəs/ a lussuoso

luxury /'lʌkʃərɪ/ n lusso m ● attrib di lusso

lying /'laɪɪŋ/ see lie¹ & ² ● n mentire m

lymph gland /'lɪmf/ n linfoghiandola f

lynch /lɪntʃ/ vt linciare

lynx /lɪŋks/ n lince f

lyric /'lɪrɪk/ a lirico. ~al a lirico; (fam: enthusiastic) entusiasta. ~s npl parole fpl

Mm

mac /mæk/ n fam impermeabile m

macabre /mə'kɑːbr/ a macabro

macaroni /mækə'rəʊnɪ/ n maccheroni mpl

mace¹ /meɪs/ n (staff) mazza f

mace² n (spice) macis m o f

machinations /mækɪ'neɪʃnz/ npl macchinazioni fpl

machine /mə'ʃiːn/ n macchina f ● vt (sew) cucire a macchina; Techn lavorare a macchina. ~-gun n mitragliatrice f

machinery /mə'ʃiːnərɪ/ n macchinario m

machinist /mə'ʃiːnɪst/ n macchinista mf, (on sewing machine) lavorante mf adetto, -a alla macchina da cucire

machismo /mə'tʃɪzməʊ/ n machismo m

macho /'mætʃəʊ/ a macho inv

mackerel /'mækr(ə)l/ n inv sgombro m

mackintosh /'mækɪntoʃ/ n impermeabile m

mad /mæd/ a (madder, maddest) pazzo, matto; (fam: angry) furioso (at con); like ~ fam come un pazzo; be ~ about sb sth (fam: keen on) andare matto per qcno/qcsa

madam /'mædəm/ n signora f

madden /'mædən/ vt (make angry) far diventare matto

made /meɪd/ see make. ~ to measure [fatto] su misura

Madeira cake /mə'dɪərə/ n dolce m di pan di Spagna

mad|ly /'mædlɪ/ adv fam follemente; ~ly in love innamorato follemente. ~man n pazzo m. ~ness n pazzia f

madonna /mə'donə/ n madonna f

magazine /mægə'ziːn/ n rivista f; Mil, Phot magazzino m

maggot /'mægət/ n verme m

Magi /'meɪdʒaɪ/ npl the ~ i Re Magi

magic /'mædʒɪk/ n magia f; (tricks) giochi mpl di prestigio ● a magico; (trick) di prestigio. ~al a magico

magician /mə'dʒɪʃn/ n mago, -a mf; (entertainer) prestigiatore, -trice mf

magistrate /'mædʒɪstreɪt/ n magistrato m

magnanim|ity /mægnə'nɪmətɪ/ n magnanimità f. ~ous /-'nænɪməs/ a magnanimo

magnet /'mægnɪt/ n magnete m, calamita f. ~ic /-'netɪk/ a magnetico. ~ism n magnetismo m

magnification /mægnɪfɪ'keɪʃn/ n ingrandimento m

magnificen|ce /mæg'nɪfɪsəns/ n magnificenza f. ~t a magnifico

magnify /'mægnɪfaɪ/ vt (pt/pp -ied) ingrandire; (exaggerate) ingigantire. ~ing glass n lente f d'ingrandimento

magnitude /'mægnɪtjuːd/ n grandezza f; (importance) importanza f

magpie /'mægpaɪ/ n gazza f

mahogany /mə'hogənɪ/ n mogano m ● a di mogano

maid /meɪd/ n cameriera f; old ~ pej zitella f

maiden /'meɪdn/ n liter fanciulla f ● a (speech, voyage) inaugurale. ~ aunt n zia f zitella. ~ name n nome m da ragazza

mail /meɪl/ n posta f ● vt impostare

mail: ~-bag n sacco m postale. ~box n

Am cassetta *f* delle lettere; (*e-mail*) casella *f* di posta elettronica. **~ing list** *n* elenco *m* d'indirizzi per un mailing. **~man** *n Am* postino *m*. **~ order** *n* vendita *f* per corrispondenza. **~order firm** *n* ditta *f* di vendita per corrispondenza

mailshot /ˈmeɪlʃɒt/ *n* mailing *m inv*

maim /meɪm/ *vt* menomare

main[1] /meɪn/ *n* (*water, gas, electricity*) conduttura *f* principale

main[2] *a* principale; **the ~ thing is to...** la cosa essenziale è di... ● *n* **in the ~** in complesso

main: ~land /-lənd/ *n* continente *m*. **~ly** *adv* principalmente. **~stay** *n fig* pilastro *m*. **~ street** *n* via *f* principale

maintain /meɪnˈteɪn/ *vt* mantenere; (*keep in repair*) curare la manutenzione di; (*claim*) sostenere

maintenance /ˈmeɪntənəns/ *n* mantenimento *m*; (*care*) manutenzione *f*; (*allowance*) alimenti *mpl*

maisonette /meɪzəˈnet/ *n* appartamento *m* a due piani

majestic /məˈdʒestɪk/ *a* maestoso

majesty /ˈmædʒəstɪ/ *n* maestà *f inv*; **His/Her M~** Sua Maestà

major /ˈmeɪdʒə(r)/ *a* maggiore; **~ road** strada *f* con diritto di precedenza ● *n Mil, Mus* maggiore *m* ● *vi Am* **~ in** specializzarsi in

Majorca /məˈjɔːkə/ *n* Maiorca *f*

majority /məˈdʒɒrətɪ/ *n* maggioranza *f*; **be in the ~** avere la maggioranza

make /meɪk/ *n* (*brand*) marca *f* ● *v* (*pt/pp* **made**) ● *vt* fare; (*earn*) guadagnare; rendere (*happy, clear*); prendere (*decision*); **~ sb laugh** far ridere qcno; **~ sb do sth** far fare qcsa a qcno; **~ it** (*to party, top of hill etc*) farcela; **what time do you ~ it?** che ore fai? ● *vi* **~ as if to** fare per. **make do** *vi* arrangiarsi. **make for** *vt* dirigersi verso. **make off** *vi* fuggire. **make out** *vt* (*distinguish*) distinguere; (*write out*) rilasciare (*cheque*); compilare (*list*); (*claim*) far credere. **make over** *vt* cedere. **make up** *vt* (*constitute*) comporre; (*complete*) completare; (*invent*) inventare; (*apply cosmetics to*) truccare; fare (*parcel*); **~ up one's mind** decidersi; **~ it up** (*after quarrel*) riconciliarsi ● *vi* (*after quarrel*) fare la pace; **~ up for** compensare; **~ up for lost time** recuperare il tempo perso

make-believe *n* finzione *f*

maker /ˈmeɪkə(r)/ *n* fabbricante *mf*; **M~** *Relig* Creatore *m*

make: ~ shift *a* di fortuna ● *n* espediente *m*. **~-up** *n* trucco *m*; (*character*) natura *f*

making /ˈmeɪkɪŋ/ *n* **have the ~s of** aver la stoffa di

maladjust|ed /mælæˈdʒʌstɪd/ *a* disadattato

malaise /məˈleɪz/ *n fig* malessere *m*

malaria /məˈleərɪə/ *n* malaria *f*

Malaysia /məˈleɪzɪə/ *n* Malesia *f*

male /meɪl/ *a* maschile ● *n* maschio *m*. **~ nurse** *n* infermiere *m*

malevolen|ce /məˈlevələns/ *n* malevolenza *f*. **~t** *a* malevolo

malfunction /mælˈfʌŋkʃn/ *n* funzionamento *m* imperfetto ● *vi* funzionare male

malice /ˈmælɪs/ *n* malignità *f*; **bear sb ~** voler del male a qcno

malicious /məˈlɪʃəs/ *a* maligno

malign /məˈlaɪn/ *vt* malignare su

malignan|cy /məˈlɪgnənsɪ/ *n* malignità *f*. **~t** *a* maligno

malinger /məˈlɪŋɡə(r)/ *vi* fingersi malato. **~er** *n* scansafatiche *mf inv*

malleable /ˈmælɪəbl/ *a* malleabile

mallet /ˈmælɪt/ *n* martello *m* di legno

malnu'trition /mæl-/ *n* malnutrizione *f*

mal'practice *n* negligenza *f*

malt /mɔːlt/ *n* malto *m*

Malta /ˈmɔːltə/ *n* Malta *f*. **~ese** /-iːz/ *a* & *n* maltese *mf*

mal'treat /mæl-/ *vt* maltrattare. **~ment** *n* maltrattamento *m*

mammal /ˈmæml/ *n* mammifero *m*

mammoth /ˈmæməθ/ *a* mastodontico ● *n* mammut *m inv*

man /mæn/ *n* (*pl* **men**) uomo *m*; (*chess, draughts*) pedina *f* ● *vt* (*pt/pp* **manned**) equipaggiare; essere di servizio a (*counter, telephones*)

manage /ˈmænɪdʒ/ *vt* dirigere; gestire (*shop, affairs*); (*cope with*) farcela; **~ to do sth** riuscire a fare qcsa ● *vi* riuscire; (*cope*) farcela (**on** con). **~able** /-əbl/ *a* (*hair*) docile; (*size*) maneggevole. **~ment** /-mənt/ *n* gestione *f*; **the ~ment** la direzione

manager /ˈmænɪdʒə(r)/ *n* direttore *m*; (*of shop, bar*) gestore *m*; *Sport* manager *m inv*. **~ess** /-ˈres/ *n* direttrice *f*. **~ial** /-ˈdʒɪərɪəl/ *a* **~ial staff** personale *m* direttivo

managing /ˈmænɪdʒɪŋ/ *a* **~ director** direttore, -trice *mf* generale

mandarin /ˈmændərɪn/ *n* ~ [orange] mandarino *m*

mandat|e /'mændeɪt/ n mandato m. **~ory** /-dtrɪ/ a obbligatorio

mane /meɪn/ n criniera f

mangle /'mæŋgl/ vt (damage) maciullare

mango /'mæŋgəʊ/ n (pl -es) mango m

mangy /'meɪndʒɪ/ a (dog) rognoso

man: **~ handle** vt malmenare. **~hole** n botola f. **~hole cover** n tombino m. **~hood** n età f adulta; (quality) virilità f. **~-hour** n ora f lavorativa. **~-hunt** n caccia f all'uomo

man|ia /'meɪnɪə/ n mania f. **~iac** /-ɪæk/ n maniaco, -a mf

manicure /'mænɪkjʊə(r)/ n manicure f inv ● vt fare la manicure a

manifest /'mænɪfest/ a manifesto ● vt **~ itself** manifestarsi. **~ly** adv palesemente

manifesto /mænɪ'festəʊ/ n manifesto m

manifold /'mænɪfəʊld/ a molteplice

manipulat|e /mə'nɪpjuleɪt/ vt manipolare. **~ion** /-'leɪʃn/ n manipolazione f

man'kind n genere m umano

manly /'mænlɪ/ a virile

'man-made a artificiale. **~ fibre** n fibra f sintetica

manner /'mænə(r)/ n maniera f; **in this ~** in questo modo; **have no ~s** avere dei pessimi modi; **good/bad ~s** buone/cattive maniere fpl. **~ism** n affettazione f

manœuvre /mə'nu:və(r)/ n manovra f ● vt fare manovra con (vehicle); manovrare (person)

manor /'mænə(r)/ n maniero m

'manpower n manodopera f

mansion /'mænʃn/ n palazzo m

'manslaughter n omicidio m colposo

mantelpiece /'mæntl-/ n mensola f di caminetto

manual /'mænjʊəl/ a manuale ● n manuale m

manufacture /mænjʊ'fæktʃə(r)/ vt fabbricare ● n manifattura f. **~r** n fabbricante m

manure /mə'njʊə(r)/ n concime m

manuscript /'mænjʊskrɪpt/ n manoscritto m

many /'menɪ/ a & pron molti; **there are as ~ boys as girls** ci sono tanti ragazzi quante ragazze; **as ~ as 500** ben 500; **as ~ as that** così tanti; **as ~** altrettanti; **very ~, a good/great ~** moltissimi; **~ a time** molte volte

map /mæp/ n carta f geografica; (of town) mappa f ● **map out** vt (pt/pp **mapped**) fig programmare

maple /'meɪpl/ n acero m

mar /mɑ:(r)/ vt (pt/pp **marred**) rovinare

marathon /'mærəθən/ n maratona f

marble /'mɑ:bl/ n marmo m; (for game) pallina f ● attrib di marmo

March /mɑ:tʃ/ n marzo m

march n marcia f; (protest) dimostrazione f ● vi marciare ● vt far marciare; **~ sb off** scortare qcno fuori

mare /meə(r)/ n giumenta f

margarine /mɑ:dʒə'ri:n/ n margarina f

margin /'mɑ:dʒɪn/ n margine m. **~al** a marginale. **~ally** adv marginalmente

marigold /'mærɪgəʊld/ n calendula f

marijuana /mærʊ'wɑ:nə/ n marijuana f

marina /mə'ri:nə/ n porticciolo m

marinade /mærɪ'neɪd/ n marinata f ● vt marinare

marine /mə'ri:n/ a marino ● n (sailor) soldato m di fanteria marina

marionette /mærɪə'net/ n marionetta f

marital /'mærɪtl/ a coniugale. **~ status** stato m civile

maritime /'mærɪtaɪm/ a marittimo

mark¹ /mɑ:k/ n (currency) marco m

mark² n (stain) macchia f; (sign, indication) segno m; Sch voto m ● vt segnare; (stain) macchiare; Sch correggere; Sport marcare; **~ time** Mil segnare il passo; fig non far progressi; **~ my words** ricordati quello che dico. **mark out** vt delimitare; fig designare

marked /mɑ:kt/ a marcato. **~ly** /-kɪdlɪ/ adv notevolmente

marker /'mɑ:kə(r)/ n (for highlighting) evidenziatore m; Sport marcatore m; (of exam) esaminatore, -trice mf

market /'mɑ:kɪt/ n mercato m ● vt vendere al mercato; (launch) commercializzare; **on the ~** sul mercato. **~ing** n marketing m. **~ re'search** n ricerca f di mercato

marksman /'mɑ:ksmən/ n tiratore m scelto

marmalade /'mɑ:məleɪd/ n marmellata f d'arance

maroon /mə'ru:n/ a marrone rossastro

marooned /mə'ru:nd/ a abbandonato

marquee /mɑ:'ki:/ n tendone m

marquis /'mɑ:kwɪs/ n marchese m

marriage /'mærɪdʒ/ n matrimonio m

married /'mærɪd/ a sposato; (life) coniugale

marrow /'mærəʊ/ n Anat midollo m; (vegetable) zucca f

marr|y /'mærɪ/ vt (pt/pp -ied) sposare; **get ~ied** sposarsi ●vi sposarsi

marsh /mɑːʃ/ n palude f

marshal /'mɑːʃl/ n (steward) cerimoniere m ●vt (pt/pp **marshalled**) fig organizzare (arguments)

marshy /'mɑːʃɪ/ a paludoso

marsupial /mɑːˈsuːpɪəl/ n marsupiale m

martial /'mɑːʃl/ a marziale

martyr /'mɑːtə(r)/ n martire mf ●vt martirizzare. **~dom** /-dəm/ n martirio m. **~ed** a fam da martire

marvel /'mɑːvl/ n meraviglia f ●vi (pt/pp **marvelled**) meravigliarsi (at di). **~lous** /-vələs/ a meraviglioso

Marxis|m /'mɑːksɪzm/ n marxismo m. **~t** a & n marxista mf

marzipan /'mɑːzɪpæn/ n marzapane m

mascara /mæˈskɑːrə/ n mascara m inv

mascot /'mæskət/ n mascotte f inv

masculin|e /'mæskjʊlɪn/ a maschile ●n Gram maschile m. **~ity** /-'lɪnətɪ/ n mascolinità f

mash /mæʃ/ vt impastare. **~ed potatoes** npl purè m inv di patate

mask /mɑːsk/ n maschera f ●vt mascherare

masochis|m /'mæsəkɪzm/ n masochismo m. **~t** /-ɪst/ n masochista mf

mason /'meɪsn/ n muratore m

Mason n massone m. **~ic** /məˈsɒnɪk/ a massonico

masonry /'meɪsnrɪ/ n massoneria f

masquerade /mæskəˈreɪd/ n fig mascherata f ●vi **as** (pose) farsi passare per

mass[1] /mæs/ n Relig messa f

mass[2] n massa f; **es of** fam un sacco di ●vi ammassarsi

massacre /'mæsəkə(r)/ n massacro m ●vt massacrare

massage /'mæsɑːʒ/ n massaggio m ●vt massaggiare; fig manipolare (statistics)

masseu|r /mæˈsɜː(r)/ n massaggiatore m. **~se** /-ˈsɜːz/ n massaggiatrice f

massive /'mæsɪv/ a enorme

mass: **~ media** npl mezzi mpl di comunicazione di massa, mass media mpl. **~-pro'duce** vt produrre in serie. **~-pro'duction** n produzione f in serie

mast /mɑːst/ n Naut albero m; (for radio) antenna f

master /'mɑːstə(r)/ n maestro m, padrone m; (teacher) professore m; (of ship) capitano m; **M~** (boy) signorino m

master: **~-key** n passe-partout m inv. **~ly** a magistrale. **~-mind** n cervello m ●vt ideare e dirigere. **~piece** n capolavoro m. **~-stroke** n colpo m da maestro. **~y** n (of subject) padronanza f

masturbat|e /'mæstəbeɪt/ vi masturbarsi. **~ion** /-'beɪʃn/ n masturbazione f

mat /mæt/ n stuoia f; (on table) sottopiatto m

match[1] /mætʃ/ n Sport partita f; (equal) uguale mf; (marriage) matrimonio m; (person to marry) partito m; **be a good ~** (colours:) intonarsi bene; **be no ~ for** non essere dello stesso livello di ●vt (equal) uguagliare; (be like) andare bene con ●vi intonarsi

match[2] n fiammifero m. **~box** n scatola f di fiammiferi

matching /'mætʃɪŋ/ a intonato

mate[1] /meɪt/ n compagno, -a mf; (assistant) aiuto m; Naut secondo m; (fam: friend) amico, -a mf ●vi accoppiarsi ●vt accoppiare

mate[2] n (in chess) scacco m matto

material /məˈtɪərɪəl/ n materiale m; (fabric) stoffa f; **raw ~s** pl materie fpl prime ●a materiale

material|ism /məˈtɪərɪəlɪzm/ n materialismo m. **~istic** /-'lɪstɪk/ a materialistico. **~ize** /-laɪz/ vi materializzarsi

maternal /məˈtɜːnl/ a materno

maternity /məˈtɜːnətɪ/ n maternità f. **~ clothes** npl abiti mpl pre-maman. **~ ward** n maternità f inv

matey /'meɪtɪ/ a fam amichevole

mathematic|al /mæθəˈmætɪkl/ a matematico. **~ian** /-məˈtɪʃn/ n matematico, -a mf

mathematics /mæθəˈmætɪks/ n matematica fsg

maths /mæθs/ n fam matematica fsg

matinée /'mætɪneɪ/ n Theat matinée f inv

mating /'meɪtɪŋ/ n accoppiamento m; **~ season** stagione f degli amori

matriculat|e /məˈtrɪkjʊleɪt/ vi immatricolarsi. **~ion** /-'leɪʃn/ n immatricolazione f

matrix /'meɪtrɪks/ n (pl **matrices** /-sɪːz/) n matrice f

matted /'mætɪd/ a **~ hair** capelli mpl tutti appiccicati tra loro

matter /'mætə(r)/ n (affair) faccenda f; (question) questione f; (pus) pus m; (phys: substance) materia f; **as a ~ of fact** a dire la verità, **what is the ~?** che cosa c'è? ●vi importare; **~ to sb**

essere importante per qcno; **it doesn't ~** non importa. **~-of-fact** *a* pratico

mattress /'mætrɪs/ *n* materasso *m*

matur|e /mə'tʃʊə(r)/ *a* maturo; *Comm* in scadenza ● *vi* maturare ● *vt* far maturare. **~ity** *n* maturità *f*; *Fin* maturazione *f*

maul /mɔːl/ *vt* malmenare

Maundy /'mɔːndɪ/ *n* **~ Thursday** giovedi *m* santo

mauve /məʊv/ *a* malva

maxim /'mæksɪm/ *n* massima *f*

maximum /'mæksɪməm/ *a* massimo; **ten minutes ~** dieci minuti al massimo ● *n* (*pl* **-ima**) massimo *m*

May /meɪ/ *n* maggio *m*

may /meɪ/ *v aux* (*solo al presente*) potere; **~ I come in?** posso entrare?; **if I say so** se mi posso permettere; **~ you both be very happy** siate felici; **I ~ as well stay** potrei anche rimanere; **it ~ be true** potrebbe esser vero; **she ~ be old, but...** sarà anche vecchia, ma...

maybe /'meɪbɪ/ *adv* forse, può darsi

May Day *n* il primo maggio

mayonnaise /meɪə'neɪz/ *n* maionese *f*

mayor /'meə(r)/ *n* sindaco *m*. **~ess** *n* sindaco *m*; (*wife of mayor*) moglie *f* del sindaco

maze /meɪz/ *n* labirinto *m*

me /miː/ *pron* (*object*) mi; (*with preposition*) me; **she called me** mi ha chiamato; **she called me, not you** ha chiamato me, non te; **give me the money** dammi i soldi; **give it to me** dammelo; **he gave it to me** me lo ha dato; **it's ~** sono io

meadow /'medəʊ/ *n* prato *m*

meagre /'miːgə(r)/ *a* scarso

meal[1] /miːl/ *n* pasto *m*

meal[2] *n* (*grain*) farina *f*

mealy-mouthed /miːlɪ'maʊðd/ *a* ambiguo

mean[1] /miːn/ *a* avaro; (*unkind*) meschino

mean[2] *a* medio ● *n* (*average*) media *f*; **Greenwich ~ time** ora *f* media di Greenwich

mean[3] *vt* (*pt/pp* **meant**) voler dire; (*signify*) significare; (*intend*) intendere; **I ~ it** lo dico seriamente; **~ well** avere buone intenzioni; **be ~t for** (*present:*) essere destinato a; (*remark:*) essere riferito a

meander /mɪ'ændə(r)/ *vi* vagare

meaning /'miːnɪŋ/ *n* significato *m*. **~ful** *a* significativo. **~less** *a* senza senso

means /miːnz/ *n* mezzo *m*; **~ of transport** mezzo *m* di trasporto; **by ~ of** per mezzo di; **by all ~!** certamente!; **by no ~** niente affatto ● *npl* (*resources*) mezzi *mpl*

meant /ment/ *see* **mean**[3]

meantime *n* **in the ~** nel frattempo ● *adv* intanto

meanwhile *adv* intanto

measles /'miːzlz/ *nsg* morbillo *m*

measly /'miːzlɪ/ *a fam* misero

measurable /'meʒərəbl/ *a* misurabile

measure /'meʒə(r)/ *n* misura *f* ● *vt/i* misurare. **measure up to** *vt fig* essere all'altezza di. **~d** *a* misurato. **~ment** /-mənt/ *n* misura *f*

meat /miːt/ *n* carne *f*. **~ ball** *n Culin* polpetta *f* di carne. **~ loaf** *n* polpettone *m*

mechan|ic /mɪ'kænɪk/ *n* meccanico *m*. **~ical** *a* meccanico; **~ical engineering** ingegneria *f* meccanica. **~ically** *adv* meccanicamente. **~ics** *n* meccanica *f* ● *npl* meccanismo *msg*

mechan|ism /'mekənɪzm/ *n* meccanismo *m*. **~ize** *vt* meccanizzare

medal /medl/ *n* medaglia *f*

medallion /mɪ'dæljən/ *n* medaglione *m*

medallist /'medəlɪst/ *n* vincitore, -trice *mf* di una medaglia

meddle /medl/ *vi* immischiarsi (**in** di); (*tinker*) armeggiare (**with** con)

media /'miːdɪə/ *npl* **the ~** i mass media. **~ studies** *npl* scienze *fpl* della comunicazione

median /'miːdɪən/ *a* **~ strip** *Am* banchina *f* spartitraffico

mediat|e /'miːdɪeɪt/ *vi* fare da mediatore. **~ion** /-'eɪʃn/ *n* mediazione *f*. **~or** *n* mediatore, -trice *mf*

medical /'medɪkl/ *a* medico ● *n* visita *f* medica. **~ insurance** *n* assicurazione *f* sanitaria. **~ student** *n* studente, -essa *mf* di medicina

medicat|ed /'medɪkeɪtɪd/ *a* medicato. **~ion** /-'keɪʃn/ *n* (*drugs*) medicinali *mpl*

medicinal /mɪ'dɪsɪnl/ *a* medicinale

medicine /'medsən/ *n* medicina *f*

medieval /medɪ'iːvl/ *a* medievale

mediocr|e /miːdɪ'əʊkə(r)/ *a* mediocre. **~ity** /-'ɒkrətɪ/ *n* mediocrità *f*

meditat|e /'medɪteɪt/ *vi* meditare (**on** su). **~ion** /-'teɪʃn/ *n* meditazione *f*

Mediterranean /medɪtə'reɪnɪən/ *n* **the ~** [**Sea**] il [mare] Mediterraneo ● *a* mediterraneo

medium /'miːdɪəm/ *a* medio; *Culin* di media cottura ● *n* (*pl* **media**) mezzo *m*; (*pl* **-s**) (*person*) medium *mf inv*

medium: ~**-sized** a di taglia media. ~ **wave** n onde fpl medie

medley /'medlɪ/ n miscuglio m; Mus miscellanea f

meek /miːk/ a mite, mansueto. ~**ly** adv docilmente

meet /miːt/ v (pt/pp met) ●vt incontrare; (at station, airport) andare incontro a; (for first time) far la conoscenza di; pagare (bill); soddisfare (requirements) ●vi incontrarsi; (committee:) riunirsi; ~ **with** incontrare (problem); incontrarsi con (person) ●n raduno m (sportivo)

meeting /'miːtɪŋ/ n riunione f, meeting m inv; (large) assemblea f; (by chance) incontro m

megabyte /'megəbaɪt/ n megabyte m

megalomania /megələ'meɪnɪə/ n megalomania f

megaphone /'megəfəʊn/ n megafono m

melancholy /'melənkəlɪ/ a malinconico ●n malinconia f

mellow /'meləʊ/ a (wine) generoso; (sound, colour) caldo; (person) dolce ●vi (person:) addolcirsi

melodic /mɪ'lɒdɪk/ a melodico

melodrama /'melə-/ n melodramma m. ~**tic** /-drə'mætɪk/ a melodrammatico

melody /'melədɪ/ n melodia f

melon /'melən/ n melone m

melt /melt/ vt sciogliere ●vi sciogliersi. **melt down** vt fondere. ~**ing-pot** n fig crogiuolo m

member /'membə(r)/ n membro m; ~ **countries** paesi mpl membri; M~ **of Parliament** deputato, -a mf; M~ **of the European Parliament** eurodeputato, -a mf. ~**ship** n iscrizione f; (members) soci mpl

membrane /'membreɪn/ n membrana f

memo /'meməʊ/ n promemoria m inv

memoirs /'memwɑːz/ npl ricordi mpl

memorable /'memərəbl/ a memorabile

memorandum /memə'rændəm/ n promemoria m inv

memorial /mɪ'mɔːrɪəl/ n monumento m. ~ **service** n funzione f commemorativa

memorize /'meməraɪz/ vt memorizzare

memory /'memərɪ/ n also Comput memoria f; (thing remembered) ricordo m; **from** ~ a memoria; **in** ~ **of** in ricordo di

men /men/ see man

menace /'menəs/ n minaccia f; (nuisance) piaga f ●vt minacciare. ~**ing** a minaccioso

mend /mend/ vt riparare; (darn) rammendare ●n **on the** ~ in via di guarigione

menfolk n uomini mpl

menial /'miːnɪəl/ a umile

meningitis /menɪn'dʒaɪtɪs/ n meningite f

menopause /'menə-/ n menopausa f

menstruate /'menstrʊeɪt/ vi mestruare. ~**ion** /-'eɪʃn/ n mestruazione f

mental /'mentl/ a mentale; (fam: mad) pazzo. ~ a'**rithmetic** n calcolo m mentale. ~ **illness** n malattia f mentale

mentality /men'tælətɪ/ n mentalità f inv. ~**ly** adv mentalmente; ~**ly ill** malato di mente

mention /'menʃn/ n menzione f ●vt menzionare; **don't** ~ **it** non c'è di che

menu /'menjuː/ n menu m inv

MEP n abbr Member of the European Parliament

mercenary /'mɜːsɪnərɪ/ a mercenario ●n mercenario m

merchandise /'mɜːtʃəndaɪz/ n merce f

merchant /'mɜːtʃənt/ n commerciante mf. ~ **bank** n banca f d'affari. ~ '**navy** n marina f mercantile

merciful /'mɜːsɪfl/ a misericordioso. ~**fully** adv fam grazie a Dio. ~**less** a spietato

mercury /'mɜːkjʊrɪ/ n mercurio m

mercy /'mɜːsɪ/ n misericordia f; **be at sb's** ~ essere alla mercé di qcno, essere in balia di qcno

mere /mɪə(r)/ a solo. ~**ly** adv solamente

merest /'mɪərɪst/ a minimo

merge /mɜːdʒ/ vi fondersi

merger /'mɜːdʒə(r)/ n fusione f

meringue /mə'ræŋ/ n meringa f

merit /'merɪt/ n merito m; (advantage) qualità f inv ●vt meritare

mermaid /'mɜːmeɪd/ n sirena f

merrily /'merɪlɪ/ adv allegramente. ~**ment** /-mənt/ n baldoria f

merry /'merɪ/ a (-ier, -iest) allegro; ~ **Christmas!** Buon Natale!

merry: ~-**go-round** n giostra f. ~-**making** n festa f

mesh /meʃ/ n maglia f

mesmerize /'mezməraɪz/ vt ipnotizzare. ~**d** a fig ipnotizzato

mess /mes/ n disordine m, casino m fam; (trouble) guaio m; (something spilt) sporco m; Mil mensa f; **make a** ~ **of**

(*botch*) fare un pasticcio di ● **mess about** *vi* perder tempo; ~ **about with** armeggiare con ● *vt* prendere in giro (*person*). **mess up** *vt* mettere in disordine, incasinare *fam*; (*botch*) mandare all'aria

message /'mesɪdʒ/ *n* messaggio *m*

messenger /'mesɪndʒə(r)/ *n* messaggero *m*

Messiah /mɪ'saɪə/ *n* Messia *m*

Messrs /'mesəz/ *npl* (*on letter*) ~ Smith Spett. ditta Smith

messy /'mesɪ/ *a* (-ier, -iest) disordinato; (*in dress*) sciatto

met /met/ *see* meet

metal /'metl/ *n* metallo *m* ● *a* di metallo. ~**lic** /mɪ'tælɪk/ *a* metallico

metamorphosis /metə'mɔ:fəsɪs/ *n* (*pl* -**phoses** /-si:z/) metamorfosi *f inv*

metaphor /'metəfə(r)/ *n* metafora *f*. ~**ical** /-'forɪkl/ *a* metaforico

meteor /'mi:tɪə(r)/ *n* meteora *f*. ~**ic** /-'orɪk/ *a* fulmineo

meteorological /mi:tɪərə'lodʒɪkl/ *a* meteorologico

meteorolog|ist /mi:tɪə'rolədʒɪst/ *n* meteorologo, -a *mf*. ~**y** *n* meteorologia *f*

meter[1] /'mi:tə(r)/ *n* contatore *m*

meter[2] *n Am* = metre

method /'meθəd/ *n* metodo *m*

methodical /mɪ'θodɪkl/ *a* metodico. ~**ly** *adv* metodicamente

Methodist /'meθədɪst/ *n* metodista *mf*

meths /meθs/ *n fam* alcol *m* denaturato

methylated /'meθɪleɪtɪd/ *a* ~ **spirit**[s] alcol *m* denaturato

meticulous /mɪ'tɪkjʊləs/ *a* meticoloso. ~**ly** *adv* meticolosamente

metre /'mi:tə(r)/ *n* metro *m*

metric /'metrɪk/ *a* metrico

metropolis /mɪ'trɒpəlɪs/ *n* metropoli *f inv*

metropolitan /metrə'polɪtən/ *a* metropolitano

mew /mju:/ *n* miao *m* ● *vi* miagolare

Mexican /'meksɪkən/ *a* & *n* messicano, -a *mf*. '**Mexico** *n* Messico *m*

miaow /mɪ'aʊ/ *n* miao *m* ● *vi* miagolare

mice /maɪs/ *see* mouse

mickey /'mɪkɪ/ *n* **take the** ~ **out of** prendere in giro

microbe /'maɪkrəʊb/ *n* microbo *m*

micro /'maɪkrəʊ/: ~**chip** *n* microchip *m inv*. ~**computer** *n* microcomputer *m inv*. ~**film** *n* microfilm *m inv*. ~**phone** *n* microfono *m*. ~**processor** *n* microprocessore *m*. ~**scope** *n* microscopio *m*. ~**scopic** /-'skɒpɪk/ *a* microscopico

~**wave** *n* microonda *f*; (*oven*) forno *m* a microonde

mid /mɪd/ *a* ~ **May** metà maggio; **in** ~ **air** a mezz'aria

midday /mɪd'deɪ/ *n* mezzogiorno *m*

middle /'mɪdl/ *a* di centro; **the M~ Ages** il medioevo; **the** ~ **class**[es] la classe media; **the M~ East** il Medio Oriente ● *n* mezzo *m*; **in the** ~ **of** (*room, floor etc*) in mezzo a; **in the** ~ **of the night** nel pieno della notte, a notte piena

middle: ~-**aged** *a* di mezza età. ~-**class** *a* borghese. ~**man** *n Comm* intermediario *m*

middling /'mɪdlɪŋ/ *a* discreto

midge /mɪdʒ/ *n* moscerino *m*

midget /'mɪdʒɪt/ *n* nano, -a *mf*

Midlands /'mɪdləndz/ *npl* **the** ~ l'Inghilterra *fsg* centrale

'**midnight** *n* mezzanotte *f*

midriff /'mɪdrɪf/ *n* diaframma *m*

midst /mɪdst/ *n* **in the** ~ **of** in mezzo a; **in our** ~ fra di noi, in mezzo a noi

mid: ~**summer** *n* mezza estate *f*. ~**way** *adv* a metà strada. ~**wife** *n* ostetrica *f*. ~**wifery** /-wɪfrɪ/ *n* ostetricia *f*. ~**winter** *n* pieno inverno *m*

might[1] /maɪt/ *v aux* **I** ~ **potrei**; **will you come? - I** ~ **potrei**? - può darsi; **it** ~ **be true** potrebbe essere vero; **I** ~ **as well stay** potrei anche restare; **you** ~ **have drowned** avresti potuto affogare; **you** ~ **have said so!** avresti potuto dirlo!

might[2] *n* potere *m*

mighty /'maɪtɪ/ *a* (-ier, -iest) potente ● *adv fam* molto

migraine /'mi:greɪn/ *n* emicrania *f*

migrant /'maɪgrənt/ *a* migratore ● *n* (*bird*) migratore, -trice *mf*; (*person: for work*) emigrante *mf*

migrat|e /maɪ'greɪt/ *vi* migrare. ~**ion** /-'greɪʃn/ *n* migrazione *f*

mike /maɪk/ *n fam* microfono *m*

Milan /mɪ'læn/ *n* Milano *f*

mild /maɪld/ *a* (*weather*) mite; (*person*) dolce; (*flavour*) delicato; (*illness*) leggero

mildew /'mɪldju:/ *n* muffa *f*

mild|ly /'maɪldlɪ/ *adv* moderatamente; (*say*) dolcemente; **to put it** ~**ly** a dir poco, senza esagerazione. ~**ness** *n* (*of person, words*) dolcezza *f*; (*of weather*) mitezza *f*

mile /maɪl/ *n* miglio *m* (= 1,6 km); ~**s nicer** *fam* molto più bello

mile|age /-ɪdʒ/ n chilometraggio m. **~stone** n pietra f miliare

militant /'mɪlɪtənt/ a & n militante mf

military /'mɪlɪtrɪ/ a militare. **~ service** n servizio m militare

militate /'mɪlɪteɪt/ vi ~ **against** opporsi a

militia /mɪˈlɪʃə/ n milizia f

milk /mɪlk/ n latte m ● vt mungere

milk: **~man** n lattaio m. **~ shake** n frappé m

milky /'mɪlkɪ/ a (-ier, -iest) latteo; ‹tea etc› con molto latte. M~ **Way** n Astr Via f Lattea

mill /mɪl/ n mulino m; ‹factory› fabbrica f; ‹for coffee etc› macinino m ● vt macinare ‹grain›. **mill about, mill around** vi brulicare

millennium /mɪˈlenɪəm/ n millennio m

miller /'mɪlə(r)/ n mugnaio m

milli|gram /'mɪlɪ-/ n milligrammo m. **~metre** n millimetro m

million /'mɪljən/ a & n milione m; a ~ **pounds** un milione di sterline. **~aire** /-'neə(r)/ n miliardario, -a mf

millstone n fig peso m

mime /maɪm/ n mimo m ● vt mimare

mimic /'mɪmɪk/ n imitatore, -trice mf ● vt (pt/pp mimicked) imitare. **~ry** n mimetismo m

mimosa /mɪˈməʊzə/ n mimosa f

mince /mɪns/ n carne f tritata ● vt Culin tritare; **not** ~ **one's words** parlare senza mezzi termini

mince: **~meat** n miscuglio m di frutta secca; **make** ~**meat of** fig demolire. **~'pie** n pasticcino m a base di frutta secca

mincer /'mɪnsə(r)/ n tritacarne m inv

mind /maɪnd/ n mente f; ‹sanity› ragione f; **to my** ~ a mio parere; **give sb a piece of one's** ~ dire chiaro e tondo a qcno quello che si pensa; **make up one's** ~ decidersi; **have sth in** ~ avere qcosa in mente; **bear sth in** ~ tenere presente qcsa; **have something on one's** ~ essere preoccupato; **have a good** ~ **to** avere una gran voglia di; **I have changed my** ~ ho cambiato idea; **in two** ~**s** indeciso; **are you out of your** ~? sei diventato matto? ● vt ‹look after› occuparsi di; **I don't** ~ **the noise** il rumore non mi dà fastidio; **I don't** ~ **what we do** non mi importa quello che facciamo; ~ **the step!** attenzione al gradino! ● vi **I don't** ~ non mi importa; **never** ~! non importa!; **do**

you ~ **if...?** ti dispiace se...? **mind out** vi ~ **out!** [fai] attenzione!

minder /'maɪndə(r)/ n (Br: bodyguard) gorilla m inv; ‹for child› baby-sitter mf inv

mind|ful a ~**ful of** attento a. **~less** a noncurante

mine[1] /maɪn/ poss pron il mio m, la mia f, i miei mpl, le mie fpl; **a friend of** ~ un mio amico; **friends of** ~ dei miei amici; **that is** ~ questo è mio; (as opposed to yours) questo è il mio

mine[2] n miniera f, ‹explosive› mina f ● vt estrarre; Mil minare. **~ detector** n rivelatore m di mine. **~field** n campo m minato

miner /'maɪnə(r)/ n minatore m

mineral /'mɪnərəl/ n minerale m ● a minerale. **~ water** n acqua f minerale

minesweeper /'maɪn-/ n dragamine m inv

mingle /'mɪŋgl/ vi ~ **with** mescolarsi a

mini /'mɪnɪ/ n ‹skirt› mini f

miniature /'mɪnɪtʃə(r)/ a in miniatura ● n miniatura f

mini|bus /'mɪnɪ-/ n minibus m inv, pulmino m. **~cab** n taxi m inv

minim /'mɪnɪm/ n Mus minima f

minim|al /'mɪnɪməl/ a minimo. **~ize** vt minimizzare. **~um** n (pl -ima) minimo m ● a minimo; **ten minutes** ~**um** minimo dieci minuti

mining /'maɪnɪŋ/ n estrazione f ● a estrattivo

miniskirt /'mɪnɪ-/ n minigonna f

minist|er /'mɪnɪstə(r)/ n ministro m; Relig pastore m. **~erial** /-'stɪərɪəl/ a ministeriale

ministry /'mɪnɪstrɪ/ n Pol ministero m; **the** ~ Relig il ministero sacerdotale

mink /mɪŋk/ n visone m

minor /'maɪnə(r)/ a minore ● n minorenne mf

minority /maɪˈnɒrətɪ/ n minoranza f; (age) minore età f

minor road n strada f secondaria

mint[1] /mɪnt/ n fam patrimonio m ● a in ~ **condition** in condizione perfetta

mint[2] n (herb) menta f

minus /'maɪnəs/ prep meno; ‹fam: without› senza ● n ~ [sign] meno m

minute[1] /'mɪnɪt/ n minuto m; **in a** ~ (shortly) in un minuto; ~**s** pl (of meeting) verbale msg

minute[2] /maɪˈnjuːt/ a minuto; (precise) minuzioso

mirac|le /'mɪrəkl/ n miracolo m. **~ulous** /-'rækjʊləs/ a miracoloso

mirage /'mıra:ʒ/ n miraggio m

mirror /'mırə(r)/ n specchio m ● vt rispecchiare

mirth /mɜ:θ/ n ilarità f

misad'venture /mɪs-/ n disavventura f

misanthropist /mɪ'zænθrəpɪst/ n misantropo, -a f

misappre'hension n malinteso m; **be under a ~** avere frainteso

misbe'have vi comportarsi male

mis'calcu|late vt/i calcolare male. **~'lation** n calcolo m sbagliato

'miscarriage n aborto m spontaneo; **~ of justice** errore m giudiziario. **mis'carry** vi abortire

miscellaneous /mɪsə'leınıəs/ a assortito

mischief /'mıstʃıf/ n malefatta f; (harm) danno m

mischievous /'mıstʃıvəs/ a (naughty) birichino; (malicious) dannoso

miscon'ception n concetto m erroneo

mis'conduct n cattiva condotta f

misde'meanour n reato m

miser /'maızə(r)/ n avaro m

miserab|le /'mızrəbl/ a (unhappy) infelice; (wretched) miserabile; (fig: weather) deprimente. **~y** adv (live, fail) miseramente; (say) tristemente

miserly /'maızəlı/ a avaro; (amount) ridicolo

misery /'mızərı/ n miseria f; (fam: person) piagnone, -a mf

mis'fire vi (gun:) far cilecca; (plan etc:) non riuscire

'misfit n disadattato, -a mf

mis'fortune n sfortuna f

mis'givings npl dubbi mpl

mis'guided a fuorviato

mishap /'mıshæp/ n disavventura f

misin'terpret vt fraintendere

mis'judge vt giudicar male; (estimate wrongly) valutare male

mis'lay vt (pt/pp -laid) smarrire

mis'lead vt (pt/pp -led) fuorviare. **~ing** a fuorviante

mis'manage vt amministrare male. **~ment** n cattiva amministrazione f

misnomer /mɪs'nəʊmə(r)/ n termine m improprio

'misprint n errore m di stampa

mis'quote vt citare erroneamente

misrepre'sent vt rappresentare male

miss /mɪs/ n colpo m mancato ● vt (fail to hit or find) mancare; (feel the loss of) sentire la mancanza di; **I ~ed that part** (failed to

notice) mi è sfuggita quella parte ● vi but he ~ed (failed to hit) ma l'ha mancato. **miss out** vt saltare, omettere

Miss n (pl -es) signorina f

misshapen /mɪs'ʃeıpən/ a malformato

missile /'mısaıl/ n missile m

missing /'mısıŋ/ a mancante; (person) scomparso; Mil disperso; **be ~** essere introvabile

mission /'mıʃn/ n missione f

missionary /'mıʃənrı/ n missionario, -a mf

mis'spell vt (pt/pp -spelled, -spelt) sbagliare l'ortografia di

mist /mıst/ n (fog) foschia f ● mist up vi appannarsi, annebbiarsi

mistake /mɪ'steık/ n sbaglio m; **by ~** per sbaglio ● vt (pt mistook, pp mistaken) sbagliare (road, house); fraintendere (meaning, words); **~ for** prendere per

mistaken /mɪ'steıkən/ a sbagliato; **be ~** sbagliarsi; **~ identity** errore m di persona. **~ly** adv erroneamente

mistletoe /'mısltəʊ/ n vischio m

mistress /'mıstrıs/ n padrona f; (teacher) maestra f; (lover) amante f

mis'trust n sfiducia f ● vt non aver fiducia in

misty /'mıstı/ a (-ier, -iest) nebbioso

misunder'stand vt (pt/pp -stood) fraintendere. **~ing** n malinteso m

misuse¹ /mɪs'ju:z/ vt usare male

misuse² /mɪs'ju:s/ n cattivo uso m

mite /maıt/ n (child) piccino, -a mf

mitigat|e /'mıtıgeıt/ vt attenuare. **~ing** a attenuante

mitten /'mıtn/ n manopola f, muffola f

mix /mıks/ n (combination) mescolanza f; Culin miscuglio m; (ready-made) preparato m ● vt mischiare ● vi mischiarsi; (person:) inserirsi; **~ with** (associate with) frequentare. **mix up** vt mescolare (papers); (confuse, mistake for) confondere

mixed /mıkst/ a misto; **~ up** (person) confuso

mixer /'mıksə(r)/ n Culin frullatore m, mixer m inv; **he's a good ~** è un tipo socievole

mixture /'mıkstʃə(r)/ n mescolanza f; (medicine) sciroppo m; Culin miscela f

'mix-up n (confusion) confusione f; (mistake) pasticcio m

moan /məʊn/ n lamento m ● vi lamentarsi; (complain) lagnarsi

moat /məʊt/ n fossato m

mob /mɒb/ n folla f; (rabble) gentaglia f; (fam: gang) banda f • vt (pt/pp **mobbed**) assalire

mobile /ˈməʊbaɪl/ a mobile • n composizione f mobile. ~ 'home n casa f roulotte. ~ [phone] n [telefono m] cellulare m

mobility /məˈbɪlətɪ/ n mobilità f

mock /mɒk/ a finto • vt canzonare. ~ery n derisione f

'mock-up n modello m in scala

mode /məʊd/ n modo m; Comput modalità f

model /ˈmɒdl/ n modello m; [fashion] ~ indossatore, -trice mf, modello, -a f • a (yacht, plane) in miniatura; (pupil, husband) esemplare, modello • v (pt/pp **modelled**) • vt indossare (clothes) • vi fare l'indossatore, -trice mf, (for artist) posare

modem /ˈməʊdem/ n modem m inv

moderate[1] /ˈmɒdəreɪt/ vt moderare • vi moderarsi

moderate[2] /ˈmɒdərət/ a moderato • n Pol moderato, -a mf. ~ly adv (drink, speak etc) moderatamente; (good, bad etc) relativamente

moderation /mɒdəˈreɪʃn/ n moderazione f; in ~ con moderazione

modern /ˈmɒdn/ a moderno. ~ize vt modernizzare

modest /ˈmɒdɪst/ a modesto. ~y n modestia f

modicum /ˈmɒdɪkəm/ n a ~ of un po' di

modif|ication /mɒdɪfɪˈkeɪʃn/ n modificazione f. ~y /ˈmɒdɪfaɪ/ vt (pt/pp -fied) modificare

module /ˈmɒdjuːl/ n modulo m

moist /mɔɪst/ a umido

moisten /ˈmɔɪsn/ vt inumidire

moistur|e /ˈmɔɪstʃə(r)/ n umidità f. ~izer n [crema f] idratante m

molar /ˈməʊlə(r)/ n molare m

molasses /məˈlæsɪz/ n Am melassa f

mole[1] /məʊl/ n (on face etc) neo m

mole[2] n Zool talpa f

molecule /ˈmɒlɪkjuːl/ n molecola f

molest /məˈlest/ vt molestare

mollycoddle /ˈmɒlɪkɒdl/ vt tenere nella bambagia

molten /ˈməʊltən/ a fuso

mom /mɒm/ n Am fam mamma f

moment /ˈməʊmənt/ n momento m; at the ~ in questo momento. ~arily adv momentaneamente. ~ary a momentaneo

momentous /məˈmentəs/ a molto importante

momentum /məˈmentəm/ n impeto m

monarch /ˈmɒnək/ n monarca m. ~y n monarchia f

monast|ery /ˈmɒnəstrɪ/ n monastero m. ~ic /məˈnæstɪk/ a monastico

Monday /ˈmʌndeɪ/ n lunedì m inv

monetary /ˈmʌnɪtrɪ/ a monetario

money /ˈmʌnɪ/ n denaro m

money: ~-box n salvadanaio m. ~-lender n usuraio m

mongrel /ˈmʌŋɡrəl/ n bastardo m

monitor /ˈmɒnɪtə(r)/ n Techn monitor m inv • vt controllare

monk /mʌŋk/ n monaco m

monkey /ˈmʌŋkɪ/ n scimmia f. ~-nut n nocciolina f americana. ~-wrench n chiave f inglese a rullino

mono /ˈmɒnəʊ/ n mono m

monogram /ˈmɒnəɡræm/ n monogramma m

monologue /ˈmɒnəlɒɡ/ n monologo m

monopol|ize /məˈnɒpəlaɪz/ vt monopolizzare. ~y n monopolio m

monosyllabic /mɒnəsɪˈlæbɪk/ a monosillabico

monotone /ˈmɒnətəʊn/ n speak in a ~ parlare con tono monotono

monoton|ous /məˈnɒtənəs/ a monotono. ~y n monotonia f

monsoon /mɒnˈsuːn/ n monsone m

monster /ˈmɒnstə(r)/ n mostro m

monstrosity /mɒnˈstrɒsətɪ/ n mostruosità f

monstrous /ˈmɒnstrəs/ a mostruoso

month /mʌnθ/ n mese m. ~ly a mensile • adv mensilmente • n (periodical) mensile m

monument /ˈmɒnjʊmənt/ n monumento m. ~al /-ˈmentl/ a fig monumentale

moo /muː/ n muggito m • vi (pt/pp **mooed**) muggire

mooch /muːtʃ/ vi ~ about fam gironzolare (the house per casa)

mood /muːd/ n umore m; be in a good/bad ~ essere di buon/cattivo umore; be in the ~ for essere in vena di

moody /ˈmuːdɪ/ a (-ier, -iest) (variable) lunatico; (bad-tempered) di malumore

moon /muːn/ n luna f; over the ~ fam al settimo cielo

moon: ~light n chiaro m di luna • vi fam lavorare in nero. ~lit a illuminato dalla luna

moor[1] /mʊə(r)/ n brughiera f

moor[2] *vt Naut* ormeggiare

moose /muːs/ *n* (*pl* **moose**) alce *m*

moot /muːt/ *a* it's a ~ **point** è un punto controverso

mop /mɒp/ *n* mocio® *m* ; ~ **of hair** zazzera *f* ● *vt* (*pt*/*pp* **mopped**) lavare con il mocio. **mop up** *vt* (*dry*) asciugare con lo straccio; (*clean*) pulire con lo straccio

mope /məʊp/ *vi* essere depresso

moped /'məʊped/ *n* ciclomotore *m*

moral /'mɒrəl/ *a* morale ● *n* morale *f*. ~**ly** *adv* moralmente. ~**s** *pl* moralità *f*

morale /mə'rɑːl/ *n* morale *m*

morality /mə'rælətɪ/ *n* moralità *f*

morbid /'mɔːbɪd/ *a* morboso

more /mɔː(r)/ *a* più; **a few** ~ **books** un po' più di libri; **some** ~ **tea?** ancora un po' di tè?; **there's no** ~ **bread** non c'è più pane; **there are no** ~ **apples** non ci sono più mele; **one** ~ **word and...** ancora una parola e... ● *pron* di più; **would you like some** ~? ne vuoi ancora?; **no** ~, **thank you** non ne voglio più, grazie ● *adv* più; ~ **interesting** più interessante; ~ [**and** ~] **quickly** [sempre] più veloce; ~ **than** più di; **I don't love him any** ~ no lo amo più; **once** ~ ancora una volta; ~ **or less** più o meno; **the** ~ **I see him, the** ~ **I like him** più lo vedo, più mi piace

moreover /mɔː'rəʊvə(r)/ *adv* inoltre

morgue /mɔːg/ *n* obitorio *m*

moribund /'mɒrɪbʌnd/ *a* moribondo

morning /'mɔːnɪŋ/ *n* mattino *m*, mattina *f*; **in the** ~ del mattino; (*tomorrow*) domani mattina

Morocc|o /mə'rɒkəʊ/ *n* Marocco *m* ● *a* ~**an** *a & n* marocchino, -a *f*

moron /'mɔːrɒn/ *n fam* deficiente *mf*

morose /mə'rəʊs/ *a* scontroso

morphine /'mɔːfiːn/ *n* morfina *f*

Morse /mɔːs/ *n* ~ [**code**] [codice *m*] Morse *m*

morsel /'mɔːsl/ *n* (*food*) boccone *m*

mortal /'mɔːtl/ *a & n* mortale *mf*. ~**ity** /mɔː'tælətɪ/ *n* mortalità *f*. ~**ly** *adv* (*wounded, offended*) a morte; (*afraid*) da morire

mortar /'mɔːtə(r)/ *n* mortaio *m*

mortgage /'mɔːgɪdʒ/ *n* mutuo *m*; (*on property*) ipoteca *f vt* ipotecare

mortuary /'mɔːtjʊərɪ/ *n* camera *f* mortuaria

mosaic /məʊ'zeɪɪk/ *n* mosaico *m*

Moscow /'mɒskəʊ/ *n* Mosca *f*

Moslem /'mʊzlɪm/ *a & n* musulmano, -a *mf*

mosque /mɒsk/ *n* moschea *f*

mosquito /mɒs'kiːtəʊ/ *n* (*pl* **-es**) zanzara *f*

moss /mɒs/ *n* muschio *m*. ~**y** *a* muschioso

most /məʊst/ *a* (*majority*) la maggior parte di; **for the** ~ **part** per lo più ● *adv* più, maggiormente; (*very*) estremamente, molto; **the** ~ **interesting day** la giornata più interessante; **a** ~ **interesting day** una giornata estremamente interessante; **the** ~ **beautiful woman in the world** la donna più bella del mondo; ~ **unlikely** veramente improbabile ● *pron* ~ **of them** la maggior parte di loro; **at** [**the**] ~ al massimo; **make the** ~ **of** sfruttare al massimo; ~ **of the time** la maggior parte del tempo. ~**ly** *adv* per lo più

MOT *n Br* revisione *f* obbligatoria di autoveicoli

motel /məʊ'tel/ *n* motel *m inv*

moth /mɒθ/ *n* falena *f*; [**clothes-**] ~ tarma *f*

moth: ~**ball** *n* pallina *f* di naftalina. ~**-eaten** *a* tarmato

mother /'mʌðə(r)/ *n* madre *f*; **M~'s Day** la festa della mamma ● *vt* fare da madre a

mother: ~**board** *n Comput* scheda *f* madre. ~**hood** *n* maternità *f*. ~**-in-law** *n* (*pl* ~**s-in-law**) suocera *f*. ~**ly** *a* materno. ~**-of-pearl** *n* madreperla *f*. ~**-to-be** *n* futura mamma *f*. ~** tongue** *n* madrelingua *f*

mothproof /'mɒθ-/ *a* antitarmico

motif /məʊ'tiːf/ *n* motivo *m*

motion /'məʊʃn/ *n* moto *m*; (*proposal*) mozione *f*; (*gesture*) gesto *m* ● *vt/i* ~ [**to**] **sb to come in** fare segno a qcno di entrare. ~**less** *a* immobile. ~**lessly** *adv* senza alcun movimento

motivat|e /'məʊtɪveɪt/ *vt* motivare. ~**ion** /-'veɪʃn/ *n* motivazione *f*

motive /'məʊtɪv/ *n* motivo *m*

motley /'mɒtlɪ/ *a* disparato

motor /'məʊtə(r)/ *n* motore *m*; (*car*) macchina *f* ● *a* a motore; *Anat* motore ● *vi* andare in macchina

Motorail /'məʊtəreɪl/ *n* treno *m* per trasporto auto

motor: ~ **bike** *n fam* moto *f inv*. ~ **boat** *n* motoscafo *m*. ~**cade** /-keɪd/ *n Am* corteo *m* di auto. ~ **car** *n* automobile *f*. ~ **cycle** *n* motocicletta *f*. ~**cyclist** *n* motociclista *mf*. ~**ing** *n* automobilismo *m*. ~**ist** *n* automobilista *mf*. ~ **racing** *n* corse *fpl* automobilistiche. ~

vehicle n autoveicolo m. ~way n autostrada f

mottled /'mɒtld/ a chiazzato

motto /'mɒtəʊ/ n (pl -es) motto m

mould¹ /məʊld/ n (fungus) muffa f

mould² n stampo m; fig foggiare; fig formare. ~ing n Archit cornice f

mouldy /'məʊldɪ/ a ammuffito; (fam: worthless) ridicolo

moult /məʊlt/ vi (bird:) fare la muta; (animal:) perdere il pelo

mound /maʊnd/ n mucchio m; (hill) collinetta f

mount /maʊnt/ n (horse) cavalcatura f; (of jewel, photo, picture) montatura f ●vt montare a (horse); salire su (bicycle); incastonare (jewel); incorniciare (photo, picture) ●vi aumentare. mount up vi aumentare

mountain /'maʊntɪn/ n montagna f. ~ bike n mountain bike f inv

mountaineer /maʊntɪ'nɪə(r)/ n alpinista mf. ~ing n alpinismo m

mountainous /'maʊntɪnəs/ a montagnoso

mourn /mɔːn/ vt lamentare ●vi ~ for piangere la morte di. ~er n persona f che participa a un funerale. ~ful a triste. ~ing n in ~ing in lutto

mouse /maʊs/ n (pl mice) topo m; Comput mouse m inv. ~trap n trappola f [per topi]

mousse /muːs/ n Culin mousse f inv

moustache /mə'stɑːʃ/ n baffi mpl

mousy /'maʊsɪ/ a (colour) grigio topo

mouth¹ /maʊð/ vt ~ sth dire qcsa silenziosamente muovendo solamente le labbra

mouth² /maʊθ/ n bocca f; (of river) foce f

mouth: ~ful n boccone m. ~organ n armonica f [a bocca]. ~piece n imboccatura f; (fig: person) portavoce m inv. ~wash n acqua f dentifricia. ~watering a che fa venire l'acquolina in bocca

movable /'muːvəbl/ a movibile

move /muːv/ n mossa f; (moving house) trasloco m; on the ~ in movimento; get a ~ on fam darsi una mossa ●vt muovere; (emotionally) commuovere; spostare (car, furniture); (transfer) trasferire; (propose) proporre; ~ house traslocare ●vi muoversi; (move house) traslocare. move along vi andare avanti ●vt muovere in avanti. move away vi allontanarsi; (move house) trasferirsi ●vt allontanare. move forward vi avanzare ●vt spostare avanti. move in

vi (to a house) trasferirsi. move off vi (vehicle:) muoversi. move out vi (of house) andare via. move over vi spostarsi ●vt spostare. move up vi muoversi; (advance, increase) avanzare

movement /'muːvmənt/ n movimento m

movie /'muːvɪ/ n film m inv; go to the ~s andare al cinema

moving /'muːvɪŋ/ a mobile; (touching) commovente

mow /məʊ/ vt (pt mowed, pp mown or mowed) tagliare (lawn). mow down vt (destroy) sterminare

mower /'məʊə(r)/ n tosaerba m inv

MP n abbr Member of Parliament

Mr /'mɪstə(r)/ n (pl Messrs) Signor m

Mrs /'mɪsɪz/ n Signora f

Ms /mɪz/ n Signora f (modo m formale di rivolgersi ad una donna quando non si vuole connotarla come sposata o nubile)

much /mʌtʃ/ a, adv & pron molto; ~ as per quanto; I love you just as ~ as before him ti amo quanto prima/lui; as ~ as £5 million ben cinque milioni di sterline; as ~ as that così tanto; very ~ tantissimo, moltissimo; the same quasi uguale

muck /mʌk/ n (dirt) sporcizia f; (farming) letame m; (fam: filth) porcheria f. muck about vi fam perder tempo; ~ about with trafficare con. muck up vt fam rovinare; (make dirty) sporcare

mucky /'mʌkɪ/ a (-ier, -iest) sudicio

mucus /'mjuːkəs/ n muco m

mud /mʌd/ n fango m

muddle /'mʌdl/ n disordine m; (mix-up) confusione f ●vt ~ [up] confondere (dates)

muddy /'mʌdɪ/ a (-ier, -iest) (path) fangoso; (shoes) infangato

'mudguard n parafango m

muesli /'muːzlɪ/ n muesli m inv

muffle /'mʌfl/ vt smorzare (sound). muffle [up] vt (for warmth) imbaccucare

muffler /'mʌflə(r)/ n sciarpa f; Am Auto marmitta f

mug¹ /mʌg/ n tazza f; (for beer) boccale m; (fam: face) muso m; (fam: simpleton) pollo m

mug² vt (pt/pp mugged) aggredire e derubare. ~ger n assalitore, -trice mf. ~ging n aggressione f per furto

muggy /'mʌgɪ/ a (-ier, -iest) afoso

mule /mjuːl/ n mulo m

mull /mʌl/ vt ~ over rimuginare su

mulled /mʌld/ a ~ **wine** vin brûlé m inv

multi /'mʌltɪ/: ~**coloured** a variopinto. ~**lingual** /-'lɪŋgwəl/ a multilingue inv. ~ **media** n multimedia mpl ● a multimediale. ~'**national** a multinazionale ● n multinazionale f

multiple /'mʌltɪpl/ a multiplo

multiplication /mʌltɪplɪ'keɪʃn/ n moltiplicazione f

multiply /'mʌltɪplaɪ/ v (pt/pp -**ied**) ● vt moltiplicare (**by** per) ● vi moltiplicarsi

multi'storey a ~ **car park** parcheggio m a più piani

mum[1] /mʌm/ a **keep** ~ fam non aprire bocca

mum[2] n fam mamma f

mumble /'mʌmbl/ vt/i borbottare

mummy[1] /'mʌmɪ/ n fam mamma f

mummy[2] n Archaeol mummia f

mumps /mʌmps/ n orecchioni mpl

munch /mʌntʃ/ vt/i sgranocchiare

mundane /mʌn'deɪn/ a (everyday) banale

municipal /mjʊ'nɪsɪpl/ a municipale

mural /'mjʊərəl/ n dipinto m murale

murder /'mɜːdə(r)/ n assassinio m ● vt assassinare; (fam: ruin) massacrare. ~**er** n assassino, -a mf. ~**ous** /-rəs/ a omicida

murky /'mɜːkɪ/ a (-**ier**, -**iest**) oscuro

murmur /'mɜːmə(r)/ n mormorio m ● vt/i mormorare

muscle /'mʌsl/ n muscolo m ● **muscle in** vi sl intromettersi (**on** in)

muscular /'mʌskjʊlə(r)/ a muscolare; (strong) muscoloso

muse /mjuːz/ vi meditare (**on** su)

museum /mjʊ'zɪəm/ n museo m

mushroom /'mʌʃrʊm/ n fungo m ● vi fig spuntare come funghi

music /'mjuːzɪk/ n musica f; (written) spartito m.

musical /'mjuːzɪkl/ a musicale; (person) dotato di senso musicale ● n commedia f musicale. ~ **box** n carillon m inv. ~ **instrument** n strumento m musicale

music: ~ **box** n carillon m inv. ~ **centre** n impianto m stereo; '~-**hall** n teatro m di varietà

musician /mjʊ'zɪʃn/ n musicista mf

Muslim /'mʊzlɪm/ a & n musulmano, -a mf

mussel /'mʌsl/ n cozza f

must /mʌst/ v aux (solo al presente) dovere; **you ~ not be late** non devi essere in ritardo; **she ~ have finished by now** (probability) deve aver finito ormai ● n a ~ fam una cosa da non perdere

mustard /'mʌstəd/ n senape f

musty /'mʌstɪ/ a (-**ier**, -**iest**) stantio

mutation /mjuː'teɪʃn/ n Biol mutazione f

mute /mjuːt/ a muto

muted /'mjuːtɪd/ a smorzato

mutilat|**e** /'mjuːtɪleɪt/ vt mutilare. ~**ion** /-'leɪʃn/ n mutilazione f

mutin|**ous** /'mjuːtɪnəs/ a ammutinato. ~**y** n ammutinamento m ● vi (pt/pp -**ied**) ammutinarsi

mutter /'mʌtə(r)/ vt/i borbottare

mutton /'mʌtn/ n carne f di montone

mutual /'mjuːtjʊəl/ a reciproco; (fam: common) comune. ~**ly** adv reciprocamente

muzzle /'mʌzl/ n (of animal) muso m; (of firearm) bocca f; (for dog) museruola f ● vt fig mettere il bavaglio a

my /maɪ/ poss a il mio m, la mia f, i miei mpl, le mie fpl; **my mother/father** mia madre/mio padre

myself /maɪ'self/ pers pron (reflexive) mi; (emphatic) me stesso; (after prep) me; **I've seen it ~** l'ho visto io stesso; **by ~** da solo; **I thought to ~** ho pensato tra me e me; **I'm proud of ~** sono fiero di me

mysterious /mɪ'stɪərɪəs/ a misterioso. ~**ly** adv misteriosamente

mystery /'mɪstərɪ/ n mistero m; ~ |**story**| racconto m del mistero

mystic|**al** /'mɪstɪk[l]/ a mistico. ~**cism** -sɪzm/ n misticismo m

mystified /'mɪstɪfaɪd/ a disorientato

mystify /'mɪstɪfaɪ/ vt (pt/pp -**ied**) disorientare

mystique /mɪ'stiːk/ n mistica f

myth /mɪθ/ n mito m. ~**ical** a mitico

mythology /mɪ'θɒlədʒɪ/ n mitologia f

Nn

nab /næb/ vt (pt/pp **nabbed**) fam beccare

naff /næf/ a Br fam banale

nag¹ /næg/ n (horse) ronzino m

nag² v (pt/pp **nagged**) ● vt assillare ● vi essere insistente ● n (person) brontolone, -a mf. **~ging** a (pain) persistente

nail /neɪl/ n chiodo m; (of finger, toe) unghia f ● **nail down** vt inchiodare; **~ sb down to a time/price** far fissare a qcno un'ora/un prezzo

nail: **~-brush** n spazzolino m da unghie. **~-file** n limetta f da unghie. **~ polish** n smalto m [per unghie]. **~ scissors** npl forbicine fpl da unghie. **~ varnish** n smalto m [per unghie]

naïve /naɪˈiːv/ a ingenuo. **~ty** /-ətɪ/ n ingenuità f

naked /ˈneɪkɪd/ a nudo; **with the ~ eye** a occhio nudo

name /neɪm/ n nome m; **what's your ~?** come ti chiami?; **my ~ is Matthew** mi chiamo Matthew; **I know her by ~** la conosco di nome; **by the ~ of Bates** di nome Bates; **call sb ~s** fam insultare qcno ● vt (to position) nominare; chiamare (baby); (identify) citare; **be ~d after** essere chiamato col nome di. **~less** a senza nome. **~ly** adv cioè

name: **~-plate** n targhetta f. **~sake** n omonimo, -a

nanny /ˈnænɪ/ n bambinaia f. **~-goat** n capra f

nap /næp/ n pisolino m; **have a ~** fare un pisolino ● vi (pt/pp **napped**) **catch sb ~ping** cogliere qcno alla sprovvista

nape /neɪp/ n **~ [of the neck]** nuca f

napkin /ˈnæpkɪn/ n tovagliolo m

Naples /ˈneɪplz/ n Napoli f

nappy /ˈnæpɪ/ n pannolino m

narcotic /nɑːˈkɒtɪk/ a & n narcotico m

narrate /nəˈreɪt/ vt narrare. **~ion** /-eɪʃn/ n narrazione f

narrative /ˈnærətɪv/ a narrativo ● n narrazione f

narrator /nəˈreɪtə(r)/ n narratore, -trice mf

narrow /ˈnærəʊ/ a stretto; (fig: views) ristretto; (margin, majority) scarso ● vi restringersi. **~ly** adv **~ly escape death** evitare la morte per un pelo. **~-'minded** a di idee ristrette

nasal /ˈneɪzl/ a nasale

nastily /ˈnɑːstɪlɪ/ adv (spitefully) con cattiveria

nasty /ˈnɑːstɪ/ a (-ier, -iest) (smell, person, remark) cattivo; (injury, situation, weather) brutto; **turn ~** (person:) diventare cattivo

nation /ˈneɪʃn/ n nazione f

national /ˈnæʃənl/ a nazionale ● n cittadino, -a mf

national: **~ 'anthem** n inno m nazionale. **N~ 'Health Service** n servizio m sanitario britannico. **N~ In'surance** n Previdenza f sociale

nationalism /ˈnæʃənəlɪzm/ n nazionalismo m

nationality /næʃəˈnælətɪ/ n nazionalità f inv

national|ization /næʃənəlaɪˈzeɪʃn/ n nazionalizzazione. **~ize** /ˈnæʃənəlaɪz/ vt nazionalizzare. **~ly** /ˈnæʃənəlɪ/ adv a livello nazionale

'nation-wide a su scala nazionale

native /ˈneɪtɪv/ a nativo; (innate) innato ● n nativo, -a mf; (local inhabitant) abitante mf del posto; (outside Europe) indigeno, -a mf; **she's a ~ of Venice** è originaria di Venezia

native: **~ 'land** n paese m nativo. **~ 'language** n lingua f madre

Nativity /nəˈtɪvɪtɪ/ n **the ~** la Natività f. **~ play** n rappresentazione f sulla nascita di Gesù

natter /ˈnætə(r)/ vi fam chiacchierare

natural /ˈnætʃrəl/ a naturale

natural: **~ 'gas** n metano m. **~ 'history** n storia f naturale

naturalist /ˈnætʃ(ə)rəlɪst/ n naturalista mf

natural|ization /nætʃ(ə)rəlaɪˈzeɪʃn/ n naturalizzazione f. **~ize** /ˈnætʃ(ə)rəlaɪz/ vt naturalizzare

naturally /ˈnætʃ(ə)rəlɪ/ adv (of course) naturalmente; (by nature) per natura

nature /ˈneɪtʃə(r)/ n natura f; **by ~** per natura. **~ reserve** riserva f naturale

naughtily /ˈnɔːtɪlɪ/ adv male

naughty /ˈnɔːtɪ/ a (-ier, -iest) monello; (slightly indecent) spinto

nausea /ˈnɔːzɪə/ n nausea f

nause|ate /ˈnɔːzɪeɪt/ vt nauseare. **~ating** a nauseante. **~ous** /-ɪəs/ a I feel **~ous** ho la nausea

nautical /ˈnɔːtɪkl/ a nautico. **~ mile** n miglio m marino

naval /ˈneɪvl/ a navale

nave /neɪv/ n navata f centrale

navel /ˈneɪvl/ n ombelico m

navigable /ˈnævɪgəbl/ a navigabile

navigat|e /ˈnævɪgeɪt/ vi navigare; Auto fare da navigatore ● vt navigare su ⟨river⟩. **~ion** /-ˈgeɪʃn/ n navigazione f. **~or** n navigatore m

navy /ˈneɪvɪ/ n marina f ● **~ [blue]** a blu scuro inv ● n blu m inv scuro

Neapolitan /nɪəˈpɒlɪtən/ a & n napoletano, -a mf

near /nɪə(r)/ a vicino; ⟨future⟩ prossimo; **the ~est bank** la banca più vicina ● adv vicino; **draw ~** avvicinarsi; **~ at hand** a portata di mano ● prep vicino a; **he was ~ to tears** aveva le lacrime agli occhi ● vt avvicinarsi a

near: **~by** a & adv vicino. **~ly** adv quasi; **it's not ~ly enough** non è per niente sufficiente. **~ness** n vicinanza f. **~ side** a Auto ⟨wheel⟩ (left) sinistro; (right) destro. **~-sighted** a Am miope

neat /niːt/ a (tidy) ordinato; (clever) efficace; (undiluted) liscio. **~ly** adv ordinatamente; (cleverly) efficacemente. **~ness** n (tidiness) ordine m

necessarily /nesəˈserɪlɪ/ adv necessariamente

necessary /ˈnesəsərɪ/ a necessario

necessit|ate /nɪˈsesɪteɪt/ vt rendere necessario. **~y** n necessità f inv

neck /nek/ n collo m; (of dress) colletto m; **~ and ~** testa a testa

necklace /ˈneklɪs/ n collana f

neck: **~line** n scollatura f. **~tie** n cravatta f

neé /neɪ/ a **~ Brett** nata Brett

need /niːd/ n bisogno m; **be in ~ of** avere bisogno di; **if ~ be** se ce ne fosse bisogno; **there is a ~ for** c'è bisogno di; **there is no ~ for that** non ce n'è bisogno; **there is no ~ for you to go** non c'è bisogno che tu vada ● vt aver bisogno di; **I ~ to know** devo saperlo; **it ~s to be done** bisogna farlo ● v aux

you ~ not go non c'è bisogno che tu vada; **~ I come?** devo [proprio] venire?

needle /ˈniːdl/ n ago m; (for knitting) uncinetto m; (of record player) puntina f ● vt (fam: annoy) punzecchiare

needless /ˈniːdlɪs/ a inutile

needlework n cucito m

needy /ˈniːdɪ/ a (-ier, -iest) bisognoso

negation /nɪˈgeɪʃn/ n negazione f

negative /ˈnegətɪv/ a negativo ● n negazione f; Phot negativo m; **in the ~** Gram alla forma negativa

neglect /nɪˈglekt/ n trascuratezza f; **state of ~** stato m di abbandono ● vt trascurare; **he ~ed to write** non si è curato di scrivere. **~ed** a trascurato. **~ful** a negligente; **be ~ful of** trascurare

négligée /ˈneglɪʒeɪ/ n négligé m inv

negligen|ce /ˈneglɪdʒəns/ n negligenza f. **~t** a negligente

negligible /ˈneglɪdʒəbl/ a trascurabile

negotiable /nɪˈgəʊʃəbl/ a ⟨road⟩ transitabile; Comm negoziabile; **not ~** ⟨cheque⟩ non trasferibile

negotiat|e /nɪˈgəʊʃɪeɪt/ vt negoziare; Auto prendere ⟨bend⟩ ● vi negoziare. **~ion** /-ˈeɪʃn/ n negoziato m. **~or** n negoziatore, -trice m

Negro /ˈniːgrəʊ/ a & n (pl **-es**) negro, -a mf

neigh /neɪ/ vi nitrire

neighbour /ˈneɪbə(r)/ n vicino, -a mf. **~hood** n vicinato m; **in the ~hood of** nei dintorni di; fig circa. **~ing** a vicino. **~ly** a amichevole

neither /ˈnaɪðə(r)/ a & pron nessuno dei due, né l'uno né l'altro ● adv... **~ nor**... né... né ● conj nemmeno, neanche; **~ do/did I** nemmeno io

neon /ˈniːɒn/ n neon m. **~ light** n luce f al neon

nephew /ˈnevjuː/ n nipote m

nerve /nɜːv/ n nervo m; (fam: courage) coraggio m; (fam: impudence) faccia f tosta; **lose one's ~** perdersi d'animo. **~-racking** a logorante

nervous /ˈnɜːvəs/ a nervoso; **he makes me ~** mi mette in agitazione; **be a ~ wreck** avere i nervi a pezzi. **~ breakdown** n esaurimento m nervoso. **~ly** adv nervosamente. **~ness** n nervosismo m; (before important event) tensione f

nervy /ˈnɜːvɪ/ a (-ier, -iest) nervoso; (Am: impudent) sfacciato

nest /nest/ n nido m ● vi fare il nido. **~-egg** n gruzzolo m

nestle /'nesl/ *vi* accoccolarsi
net[1] /net/ *n* rete *f* • *vt* (*pt/pp* netted)
(*catch*) prendere (*con la rete*)
net[2] *a* netto • *vt* (*pt/pp* netted) incassare un utile netto di
'netball *n sport m inv femminile, simile a pallacanestro*
Netherlands /'neðələndz/ *npl* the ~ i Paesi Bassi
netting /'netɪŋ/ *n* 〈wire〉 ~ reticolato *m*
nettle /'netl/ *n* ortica *f*
'network *n* rete *f*
neuralgia /njʊə'rældʒə/ *n* nevralgia *f*
neurolog|ist /njʊə'rɒlədʒɪst/ *n* neurologo, -a *mf*
neur|osis /njʊə'rəʊsɪs/ *n* (*pl* -oses /-siːz/) nevrosi *f inv*. ~otic /-'rɒtɪk/ *a* nevrotico
neuter /'njuːtə(r)/ *a Gram* neutro • *n Gram* neutro *m* • *vt* sterilizzare
neutral /'njuːtrəl/ *a* neutro; 〈country, person〉 neutrale • *n* in ~ *Auto* in folle. ~ity /-'trælətɪ/ *n* neutralità *f*. ~ize *vt* neutralizzare
never /'nevə(r)/ *adv* [non...] mai; 〈fam: expressing disbelief〉 ma va; ~ again mai più; well I ~! chi l'avrebbe detto!. ~-ending *a* interminabile
nevertheless /nevəðə'les/ *adv* tuttavia
new /njuː/ *a* nuovo
new: ~born *a* neonato. ~comer *n* nuovo, -a arrivato, -a *mf*. ~fangled /-'fæŋgld/ *a pej* modernizzante. ~-laid *a* fresco
'newly *adv* (*recently*) di recente; ~-built costruito di recente. ~-weds *npl* sposini *mpl*
new: ~ 'moon *n* luna *f* nuova. ~ness *n* novità *f*
news /njuːz/ *n* notizie *fpl; TV* telegiornale *m; Radio* giornale *m* radio; piece of ~ notizia *f*
news: ~agent *n* giornalaio, -a *mf*. ~bulletin *n* notiziario *m*. ~caster *n* giornalista *mf* televisivo, -a/radiofonico, -a. ~flash *n* notizia *f* flash. ~letter *n* bollettino d'informazione. ~paper *n* giornale *m*; (*material*) carta *f* di giornale. ~reader *n* giornalista *mf* televisivo, -a/radiofonico, -a
new: ~ year *n* (*next year*) anno *m* nuovo; N~ Year's Day *n* Capodanno *m*. N~ Year's 'Eve *n* vigilia *f* di Capodanno. N~ Zealand /'ziːlənd/ *n* Nuova Zelanda *f*. N~ Zealander *n* neozelandese *mf*
next /nekst/ *a* prossimo; (*adjoining*) vi-

cino; who's ~? a chi tocca?; ~ door accanto; ~ to nothing quasi niente; the ~ day il giorno dopo; ~ week la settimana prossima; the week after ~ fra due settimane • *adv* dopo; when will you see him ~? quando lo rivedi la prossima volta?; ~ to accanto a • *n* seguente *mf*. ~ of kin parente *m* prossimo
NHS *n abbr* National Health Service
nib /nɪb/ *n* pennino *m*
nibble /'nɪbl/ *vt/i* mordicchiare
nice /naɪs/ *a* 〈day, weather, holiday〉 bello; 〈person〉 gentile, simpatico; 〈food〉 buono; it was ~ meeting you è stato un piacere conoscerla. ~ly *adv* gentilmente; (*well*) bene. ~ties /'naɪsətɪz/ *npl* finezze *fpl*
niche /niːʃ/ *n* nicchia *f*
nick /nɪk/ *n* tacca *f*; (*on chin etc*) taglietto *m*; 〈fam: prison〉 gattabuia *f*; 〈fam: police station〉 centrale *f* [di polizia]; in the ~ of time *fam* appena in tempo • *vt* intaccare; 〈fam: steal〉 fregare; 〈fam: arrest〉 beccare; ~ one's chin farsi un taglietto nel mento
nickel /'nɪkl/ *n* nichel *m; Am* moneta *f* da cinque centesimi
'nickname *n* soprannome *m* • *vt* soprannominare
nicotine /'nɪkətiːn/ *n* nicotina *f*
niece /niːs/ *n* nipote *f*
Nigeria /naɪ'dʒɪərɪə/ *n* Nigeria *f*. ~n *a & n* nigeriano, -a *mf*
niggling /'nɪglɪŋ/ *a* 〈detail〉 insignificante; 〈pain〉 fastidioso; 〈doubt〉 persistente
night /naɪt/ *n* notte *f*; (*evening*) sera *f*; at ~ la notte, di notte; (*in the evening*) la sera, di sera; Monday ~ lunedì notte/sera • *a* di notte
night: ~cap *n* papalina *f*; (*drink*) bicchierino *m* bevuto prima di andare a letto. ~-club *n* locale *m* notturno, night[-club] *m inv*. ~-dress *n* camicia *f* da notte. ~fall *n* crepuscolo *m*. ~-gown *n*, ~ie /'naɪtɪ/ *n* camicia *f* da notte
nightingale /'naɪtɪŋgeɪl/ *n* usignolo *m*
night: ~-life *n* vita *f* notturna. ~ly *a* di notte, di sera • *adv* ogni notte, ogni sera. ~mare *n* incubo *m*. ~-school *n* scuola *f* serale. ~-time *n* at ~-time di notte, la notte. ~-'watchman *n* guardiano *m* notturno
nil /nɪl/ *n* nulla *m; Sport* zero *m*
nimble /'nɪmbl/ *a* agile. ~y *adv* agilmente

nine /naɪn/ a nove inv ● n nove m.
~ 'teen a diciannove inv ● n diciannove
m. **~ 'teenth** a & n diciannovesimo, -a
mf

ninetieth /'naɪntɪɪθ/ a & n novantesi-
mo, -a mf

ninety /'naɪntɪ/ a novanta inv ● n novanta m

ninth /naɪnθ/ a & n nono, -a mf

nip /nɪp/ n pizzicotto m; (bite) morso m
● vt pizzicare; (bite) mordere; **~ in the
bud** fig stroncare sul nascere ● vi (fam:
run) fare un salto

nipple /'nɪpl/ n capezzolo m; (Am: on
bottle) tettarella f

nippy /'nɪpɪ/ a (-ier, -iest) fam (cold)
pungente; (quick) svelto

nitrogen /'naɪtrədʒn/ n azoto m

nitwit /'nɪtwɪt/ n fam imbecille mf

no /nəʊ/ adv no ● n (pl noes) no m inv
● a nessuno; **I have no time** non ho
tempo; **in no time** in un baleno; **'no
parking'** 'sosta vietata'; **'no smoking'**
'vietato fumare'; **no one = nobody**

nobility /nəʊ'bɪlətɪ/ n nobiltà f

noble /'nəʊbl/ a nobile. **~man** n nobile m

nobody /'nəʊbədɪ/ pron nessuno; **he
knows ~** non conosce nessuno ● n
he's a ~ è nessuno

nocturnal /nɒk'tɜːnl/ a notturno

nod /nɒd/ n cenno m del capo ● v (pt/pp
nodded) ● vi fare un cenno col capo; (in
agreement) fare di sì col capo ● vt **~
one's head** fare di sì col capo. **nod off**
vi assopirsi

nodule /'nɒdjuːl/ n nodulo m

noise /nɔɪz/ n rumore m; (loud) rumore
m, chiasso m. **~less** a silenzioso.
~lessly adv silenziosamente

noisy /'nɔɪzɪ/ a (-ier, -iest) rumoroso

nomad /'nəʊmæd/ n nomade mf. **~ic**
/-'mædɪk/ a nomade

nominal /'nɒmɪnl/ a nominale

nominate /'nɒmɪneɪt/ vt proporre
come candidato; (appoint) designare.
~ion /-'neɪʃn/ n nomina f; (person
nominated) candidato, -a mf

nominative /'nɒmɪnətɪv/ a & n Gram
~ [case] nominativo m

nominee /nɒmɪ'niː/ n persona f nomi-
nata

nonchalant /'nɒnʃələnt/ a disinvolto

non-com'missioned /nɒn-/ a **~
officer** sottufficiale m

non-com'mittal a che non si sbilan-
cia

nondescript /'nɒndɪskrɪpt/ a qualunque

none /nʌn/ pron (person) nessuno;
(thing) niente; **~ of us** nessuno di noi;
~ of this niente di questo; **there's ~
left** non ce n'è più ● adv **she's ~ too
pleased** non è per niente soddisfatta;
I'm ~ the wiser non so più di prima

nonentity /nɒ'nentətɪ/ n nullità f inv

non-event n delusione f

non-ex'istent a inesistente

non-'fiction n saggistica f

non-'iron a che non si stira

nonplussed /nɒn'plʌst/ a perplesso

nonsens|e /'nɒnsəns/ n sciocchezze
fpl. **~ical** /-'sensɪkl/ a assurdo

non-'smoker n non fumatore, -trice
mf; (compartment) scompartimento m
non fumatori

non-'stick a antiaderente

non-'stop a **~ 'flight** volo m diretto
● adv senza sosta; (fly) senza scalo

non-'violent a non violento

noodles /'nuːdlz/ npl taglierini mpl

nook /nʊk/ n cantuccio m

noon /nuːn/ n mezzogiorno m; **at ~** a
mezzogiorno

noose /nuːs/ n nodo m scorsoio

nor /nɔː(r)/ adv & conj né; **~ do I** neppure io

Nordic /'nɔːdɪk/ a nordico

norm /nɔːm/ n norma f

normal /'nɔːml/ a normale. **~ity**
/-'mælətɪ/ n normalità f. **~ly** adv
(usually) normalmente

north /nɔːθ/ n nord m; **to the ~ of** a
nord di ● a del nord, settentrionale
● adv a nord

north: N~ America n America f del
Nord. **~-bound** a Auto in direzione
nord. **~-east** a di nord-est,
nordorientale ● n nord-est m ● adv a
nord-est; (travel) verso nord-est

norther|ly /'nɔːðəlɪ/ a (direction) nord;
(wind) del nord. **~n** a del nord, settentrionale. **N~n Ireland** n Irlanda f del
Nord

north: N~ 'Pole n polo m nord. **N~
'Sea** n Mare m del Nord. **~ward[s]**
/-wəd[z]/ adv verso nord. **~-west** a di
nord-ovest, nordoccidentale ● n nord-
ovest m ● adv a nord-ovest; (travel) verso nord-ovest

Nor|way /'nɔːweɪ/ n Norvegia f.
~wegian /-'wiːdʒn/ a & n norvegese mf

nose /nəʊz/ n naso m

nose: ~bleed n emorragia f nasale. **~-
dive** n Aeron picchiata f

nostalg|ia /nɒ'stældʒɪə/ n nostalgia f.
~ic a nostalgico

nostril /'nɒstrəl/ n narice f

nosy /'nəʊzi/ a (-ier, -iest) fam ficcanaso inv

not /nɒt/ adv non; **he is ~ Italian** non è italiano; **I hope ~** spero di no; **~ all of us have been invited** non siamo stati tutti invitati; **if ~** se no; **~ at all** niente affatto; **~ a bit** per niente; **~ even** neanche; **~ yet** non ancora; **~ only... but also...** non solo... ma anche...

notabl|e /'nəʊtəbl/ a (remarkable) notevole. **~y** adv (in particular) in particolare

notary /'nəʊtəri/ n notaio m; **~ 'public** notaio m

notch /nɒtʃ/ n tacca f ● **notch up** vt (score) segnare

note /nəʊt/ n nota f; (short letter, banknote) biglietto m; (memo, written comment etc) appunto m; **of ~** (person) di spicco; (comments, event) degno di nota; **make a ~ of** prendere nota di; **take ~ of** (notice) prendere nota di ● vt (notice) notare; (write) annotare. **note down** vt annotare

'notebook n taccuino m; Comput notebook m inv

noted /'nəʊtɪd/ a noto, celebre (**for** per)

note-: **~paper** n carta f da lettere. **~worthy** a degno di nota

nothing /'nʌθɪŋ/ pron niente, nulla ● adv niente affatto; **for ~** (free, in vain) per niente; (with no reason) senza motivo; **~ but** nient'altro che; **~ much** poco o nulla; **~ interesting** niente di interessante; **it's ~ to do with you** non ti riguarda

notice /'nəʊtɪs/ n (on board) avviso m; (review) recensione f; (termination of employment) licenziamento m; [advance] ~ preavviso m; **two months' ~** due mesi di preavviso; **at short ~** con breve preavviso; **until further ~** fino nuovo avviso; **give [in one's] ‹**employee:**›** dare le dimissioni; **give an employee ~** dare il preavviso a un impiegato; **take no ~ of** non fare caso a; **take no ~!** non farci caso! ● vt notare. **~able** /-əbl/ a evidente. **~ably** adv sensibilmente. **~-board** n bacheca f

noti|fication /nəʊtɪfɪ'keɪʃn/ n notifica f. **~fy** /'nəʊtɪfaɪ/ vt (pt/pp -ied) notificare

notion /'nəʊʃn/ n idea f, nozione f; **~s** pl (Am: haberdashery) merceria f

notoriety /nəʊtə'raɪətɪ/ n notorietà f

notorious /nəʊ'tɔːrɪəs/ a famigerato; **be ~ for** essere tristemente famoso per

notwith'standing prep malgrado ● adv ciononostante

nougat /'nuːgɑː/ n torrone m

nought /nɔːt/ n zero m

noun /naʊn/ n nome m, sostantivo m

nourish /'nʌrɪʃ/ vt nutrire. **~ing** a nutriente. **~ment** n nutrimento m

novel /'nɒvl/ a insolito ● n romanzo m. **~ist** n romanziere, -a mf. **~ty** n novità f; **~ties** pl (objects) oggettini mpl

November /nəʊ'vembə(r)/ n novembre m

novice /'nɒvɪs/ n novizio, -a mf

now /naʊ/ adv ora, adesso; **by ~** ormai; **just ~** proprio ora; **right ~** subito; **~ and again, ~ and then** ogni tanto; **~, ~!** su! ● conj [that] ora che, adesso che

'nowadays adv oggigiorno

nowhere /'nəʊ-/ adv in nessun posto, da nessuna parte

noxious /'nɒkʃəs/ a nocivo

nozzle /'nɒzl/ n bocchetta f

nuance /'njuːɒs/ n sfumatura f

nuclear /'njuːklɪə(r)/ a nucleare

nucleus /'njuːklɪəs/ n (pl -lei /-lɪaɪ/) nucleo m

nude /njuːd/ a nudo ● n nudo m; **in the ~** nudo

nudge /nʌdʒ/ n colpetto m di gomito ● vt dare un colpetto col gomito a

nudism /'njuːdɪzm/ n nudismo m

nud|ist /'njuːdɪst/ n nudista mf. **~ity** n nudità f

nugget /'nʌgɪt/ n pepita f

nuisance /'njuːsns/ n seccatura f; (person) piaga f; **what a ~!** che seccatura!

null /nʌl/ a **~ and void** nullo

numb /nʌm/ a intorpidito; **~ with cold** intirizzito dal freddo

number /'nʌmbə(r)/ n numero m; **a ~ of people** un certo numero di persone ● vt numerare; (include) annoverare. **~-plate** n targa f

numeral /'njuːmərəl/ n numero m, cifra f

numerate /'njuːmərət/ a **be ~** saper fare i calcoli

numerical /njuː'merɪkl/ a numerico; **in ~ order** in ordine numerico

numerous /'njuːmərəs/ a numeroso

nun /nʌn/ n suora f

nurse /nɜːs/ n infermiere, -a mf; **children's ~** bambinaia f ● vt curare

nursery /'nɜːsərɪ/ n stanza f dei bambini; (for plants) vivaio m; [day] ~ asilo *m.* ~ **rhyme** *n* filastrocca *f.* ~ **school** *n* scuola *f* materna

nursing /'nɜːsɪŋ/ *n* professione *f* d'infermiere. ~ **home** *n* casa *f* di cura per anziani

nurture /'nɜːtʃə(r)/ *vt* allevare; *fig* coltivare

nut /nʌt/ *n* noce *f*; *Techn* dado *m*; (*fam: head*) zucca *f*; ~ **s** *npl* frutta *f* secca; **be** ~**s** *fam* essere svitato. ~**crackers** *npl*

schiaccianoci *m inv.* ~**meg** *n* noce *f* moscata

nutrit|ion /njuː'trɪʃn/ *n* nutrizione *f.* ~**ious** /-ʃəs/ *a* nutriente

'**nutshell** *n* **in a** ~ *fig* in parole povere

nuzzle /'nʌzl/ *vt* (*horse, dog:*) strofinare il muso contro

nylon /'naɪlɒn/ *n* nailon *m*; ~**s** *pl* calze *fpl* di nailon ● *a* di nailon

O /əʊ/ *n Teleph* zero *m*

oaf /əʊf/ *n* (ploafs) zoticone, -a *mf*

oak /əʊk/ *n* quercia *f*● *attrib* di quercia

OAP *n abbr* (old-age pensioner) pensionato, -a *mf*

oar /ɔː(r)/ *n* remo *m.* ~**sman** *n* vogatore *m*

oasis /əʊ'eɪsɪs/ *n* (ploases /-siːz/) oasi *f inv*

oath /əʊθ/ *n* giuramento *m*; (*swearword*) bestemmia *f*

oatmeal /'əʊt-/ *n* farina *f* d'avena

oats /əʊts/ *npl* avena *fsg*; *Culin* [rolled] ~ fiocchi *mpl* di avena

obedien|ce /ə'biːdɪəns/ *n* ubbidienza *f.* ~**t** *a* ubbidiente

obes|e /ə'biːs/ *a* obeso. ~**ity** *n* obesità *f*

obey /ə'beɪ/ *vt* ubbidire a; osservare (*instructions, rules*) ● *vi* ubbidire

obituary /ə'bɪtjʊərɪ/ *n* necrologio *m*

object[1] /'ɒbdʒɪkt/ *n* oggetto *m*; *Gram* complemento *m* oggetto; **money is no** ~ i soldi non sono un problema

object[2] /əb'dʒekt/ *vi* (*be against*) opporsi (**to** a); ~ **that**... obiettare che...

objection /əb'dʒekʃn/ *n* obiezione *f*; **have no** ~ non avere niente in contrario. ~**able** /-əbl/ *a* discutibile; (*person*) sgradevole

objective /əb'dʒektɪv/ *a* oggettivo● *n* obiettivo *m.* ~**ely** *adv* obiettivamente. ~**ity** /-'tɪvəti/ *n* oggettività *f*

obligation /ɒblɪ'geɪʃn/ *n* obbligo *m*; **be under an** ~ avere un obbligo; **without** ~ senza impegno

obligatory /ə'blɪgətrɪ/ *a* obbligatorio

oblig|e /ə'blaɪdʒ/ *vt* (*compel*) obbligare;

much ~**ed** grazie mille. ~**ing** *a* disponibile

oblique /ə'bliːk/ *a* obliquo; *fig* indiretto● *n* ~ [stroke] barra *f*

obliterate /ə'blɪtəret/ *vt* obliterare

oblivion /ə'blɪvɪən/ *n* oblio *m*

oblivious /ə'blɪvɪəs/ *a* be ~ essere dimentico (**of, to** di)

oblong /'ɒblɒŋ/ *a* oblungo ● *n* rettangolo *m*

obnoxious /əb'nɒkʃəs/ *a* detestabile

oboe /'əʊbəʊ/ *n* oboe *m inv*

obscen|e /əb'siːn/ *a* osceno; (*profits, wealth*) vergognoso. ~**ity** /-'senəti/ *n* oscenità *f inv*

obscur|e /əb'skjʊə(r)/ *a* oscuro ● *vt* oscurare; (*confuse*) mettere in ombra. ~**ity** *n* oscurità *f*

obsequious /əb'siːkwɪəs/ *a* ossequioso

observa|nce /əb'zɜːvəns/ *n* (*of custom*) osservanza *f.* ~**nt** *a* attento. ~**tion** /ɒbzə'veɪʃn/ *n* osservazione *f*

observatory /əb'zɜːvətrɪ/ *n* osservatorio *m*

observe /əb'zɜːv/ *vt* osservare; (*notice*) notare; (*keep, celebrate*) celebrare. ~ **r** *n* osservatore, -trice *mf*

obsess /əb'ses/ *vt* be ~**ed by** essere fissato con. ~**ion** /-eʃn/ *n* fissazione *f.* ~**ive** /-ɪv/ *a* ossessivo

obsolete /'ɒbsəliːt/ *a* obsoleto; (*word*) desueto

obstacle /'ɒbstəkl/ *n* ostacolo *m*

obstetrician /ɒbstə'trɪʃn/ *n* ostetrico, -a *mf.* **obstetrics** /əb'stetrɪks/ *n* ostetricia *f*

obstina|cy /'ɒbstɪnəsɪ/ *n* ostinazione *f*. **~te** /-ət/ *a* ostinato

obstreperous /əb'strepərəs/ *a* turbolento

obstruct /əb'strʌkt/ *vt* ostruire; *(hinder)* ostacolare. **~ion** /-ʌkʃn/ *n* ostruzione *f*; *(obstacle)* ostacolo *m*. **~ive** /-ɪv/ *a* be **~ive** *(person:)* creare dei problemi

obtain /əb'teɪn/ *vt* ottenere. **~able** /-əbl/ *a* ottenibile

obtrusive /əb'truːsɪv/ *a* *(object)* stonato

obtuse /əb'tjuːs/ *a* ottuso

obvious /'ɒbvɪəs/ *a* ovvio. **~ly** *adv* ovviamente

occasion /ə'keɪʒn/ *n* occasione *f*; *(event)* evento *m*; **on** ~ talvolta; **on the ~ of** in occasione di

occasional /ə'keɪʒənl/ *a* saltuario; **he has the ~ glass of wine** ogni tanto beve un bicchiere di vino. **~ly** *adv* ogni tanto

occult /ɒ'kʌlt/ *a* occulto

occupant /'ɒkjʊpənt/ *n* occupante *mf*; *(of vehicle)* persona *f* a bordo

occupation /ɒkjʊ'peɪʃn/ *n* occupazione *f*; *(job)* professione *f* **~al** *a* professionale

occupier /'ɒkjʊpaɪə(r)/ *n* residente *mf*

occupy /'ɒkjʊpaɪ/ *vt* *(pt/pp* **occupied**) occupare; *(keep busy)* tenere occupato

occur /ə'kɜː(r)/ *vi* *(pt/pp* **occurred**) accadere; *(exist)* trovarsi; **it ~red to me that** mi è venuto in mente che. **~rence** /ə'kʌrəns/ *n* evento; *(fact)* fatto *m*

ocean /'əʊʃn/ *n* oceano *m*

o'clock /ə'klɒk/ *adv* **it's 7 ~** sono le sette; **at 7 ~** alle sette;

octave /'ɒktɪv/ *n Mus* ottava *f*

October /ɒk'təʊbə(r)/ *n* ottobre *m*

octopus /'ɒktəpəs/ *n* *(pl* **-puses**) polpo *m*

odd /ɒd/ *a* *(number)* dispari; *(not of set)* scompagnato; *(strange)* strano; **forty ~** quaranta e rotti; **~ jobs** lavoretti *mpl*; **the ~ one out** l'eccezione *f*; **at ~ moments** a tempo perso; **have the ~ glass of wine** avere un bicchiere di vino ogni tanto

odd|ity /'ɒdɪtɪ/ *n* stranezza *f*. **~ly** *adv* stranamente; **~ly enough** stranamente. **~ment** /-mənt/ *n* *(of fabric)* scampolo *m*

odds /ɒdz/ *npl* *(chances)* probabilità *fpl*; **at ~** in disaccordo; **~ and ends** cianfrusaglie *fpl*; **it makes no ~** non fa alcuna differenza

ode /əʊd/ *n* ode *f*

odour /'əʊdə(r)/ *n* odore *m*. **~less** *a* inodore

of /ɒv/, /əv/ *prep* di; **a cup of tea/coffee** una tazza di tè/caffè; **the hem of my skirt** l'orlo della mia gonna; **the summer of 1989** l'estate del 1989; **the two of us** noi due; **made of** di; **that's very kind of you** è molto gentile da parte tua; **a friend of mine** un mio amico; **a child of three** un bambino di tre anni; **the fourth of January** il quattro gennaio; **within a year of their divorce** a circa un anno dal loro divorzio; **half of it** la metà; **the whole of the room** tutta la stanza

off /ɒf/ *prep* da; *(distant from)* lontano da; **take £10 ~ the price** ridurre il prezzo di 10 sterline; **~ the coast** presso la costa; **a street ~ the main road** una traversa della via principale; *(near)* una strada vicino alla via principale; **get ~ the ladder** scendere dalla scala; **get ~ the bus** uscire dall'autobus; **leave the lid ~ the saucepan** lasciare la pentola senza il coperchio ● *adv* *(button, handle)* staccato; *(light, machine)* spento; *(brake)* tolto; *(tap)* chiuso; **'off'** *(on appliance)* 'off'; **2 kilometres ~** a due chilometri di distanza; **a long way ~** molto distante; *(time)* lontano; **~ and on** di tanto in tanto; **with his hat/coat ~** senza il cappello/cappotto; **with the light ~** a luce spenta; **20% ~** 20% di sconto; **be ~** *(leave)* andar via; *Sport* essere partito; *(food:)* essere andato a male; *(all gone)* essere finito; *(wedding, engagement:)* essere cancellato; **I'm ~ alcohol** ho smesso di bere; **be ~ one's food** non avere appetito; **she's ~ today** *(on holiday)* è in ferie oggi; *(ill)* è malata oggi; **I'm ~ home** vado a casa; **you'd be better ~ doing...** faresti meglio a fare...; **have a day ~** avere un giorno di vacanza; **drive/sail ~** andare via

offal /'ɒfl/ *n Culin* frattaglie *fpl*

'off-beat *a* insolito

'off-chance *n* possibilità *f* remota

off-colour *a* *(not well)* giù di forma; *(joke, story)* sporco

offence /ə'fens/ *n* *(illegal act)* reato *m*; **give ~** offendere; **take ~** offendersi *(* **at** per*)*

offend /ə'fend/ *vt* offendere. **~er** *n Jur* colpevole *mf*

offensive /ə'fensɪv/ *a* offensivo ● *n* offensiva *f*

offer /'ɒfə(r)/ *n* offerta *f* ● *vt* offrire; opporre ⟨resistance⟩; ~ **sb sth** offrire qcsa a qcno; ~ **to do sth** offrirsi di fare qcsa. ~**ing** n offerta f

off'**hand** a ⟨casual⟩ spiccio ● adv su due piedi

office /'ɒfɪs/ n ufficio m; ⟨post. job⟩ carica f. ~ **hours** pl orario m di ufficio

officer /'ɒfɪsə(r)/ n ufficiale m; ⟨police⟩ agente m [di polizia]

official /ə'fɪʃl/ a ufficiale ● n funzionario, -a mf, Sport dirigente m. ~**ly** adv ufficialmente

officiate /ə'fɪʃɪeɪt/ vi officiare

offing **in the** ~ in vista

off-licence n negozio m per la vendita di alcolici

off'**load** vt scaricare

off'**putting** a fam scoraggiante

offset /'ɒfset/ vt (pt/pp -set, pres p -setting) controbilanciare

offshoot n ramo m; fig diramazione f

off'**shore** a ⟨wind⟩ di terra; ⟨company, investment⟩ offshore inv. ~ **rig** n piattaforma f petrolifera, off-shore m inv

off'**side** a Sport [in] fuori gioco; ⟨wheel etc⟩ ⟨left⟩ sinistro; ⟨right⟩ destro

offspring n prole m

off'**stage** adv dietro le quinte

off-'**white** a bianco sporco

often /'ɒfn/ adv spesso; **how** ~ ogni quanto; **every so** ~ una volta ogni tanto

ogle /'əʊgl/ vt mangiarsi con gli occhi

oh /əʊ/ int oh!; ~ **dear** oh Dio!

oil /ɔɪl/ n olio m; ⟨petroleum⟩ petrolio m; ⟨for heating⟩ nafta f ● vt oliare

oil: ~**field** n giacimento m di petrolio. ~**-painting** n pittura f a olio. ~ **refinery** n raffineria f di petrolio. ~ **rig** piattaforma f petrolifera. ~**skins** npl vestiti mpl di tela cerata. ~**-slick** n chiazza f di petrolio. ~**-tanker** n petroliera f. ~ **well** n pozzo m petrolifero

oily /'ɔɪlɪ/ a (-ier, -iest) unto; fig untuoso

ointment /'ɔɪntmənt/ n pomata f

OK /əʊ'keɪ/ int va bene, o.k. ● a if that's **OK with you** se ti va bene; **she's OK** ⟨well⟩ sta bene; **is the milk still OK?** il latte è ancora buono? ● adv ⟨well⟩ bene ● vt ⟨anche **okay**⟩ (pt/pp **OK'd**, **okayed**) dare l'o.k. a

old /əʊld/ a vecchio; ⟨girlfriend⟩ ex; **how** ~ **is she?** quanti anni ha?; **she is ten years** ~ ha dieci anni

old: ~ **age** n vecchiaia f. ~**-age** '**pensioner** n pensionato, -a mf. ~ **boy** n Sch ex-allievo m. ~'**fashioned** a anti-

quato. ~ **girl** n Sch ex-allieva f. ~ '**maid** n zitella f

olive /'ɒlɪv/ n ⟨fruit, colour⟩ oliva f; ⟨tree⟩ olivo m ● a d'oliva; ⟨colour⟩ olivastro. ~ **branch** n fig ramoscello m d'olivo. ~ '**oil** n olio m di oliva

Olympic /ə'lɪmpɪk/ a olimpico; ~**s**, ~ **Games** Olimpiadi fpl

omelette /'ɒmlɪt/ n omelette f inv

omen /'əʊmən/ n presagio m

ominous /'ɒmɪnəs/ a sinistro

omission /ə'mɪʃn/ n omissione f

omit /ə'mɪt/ vt (pt/pp **omitted**) omettere; ~ **to do sth** tralasciare di fare qcsa

omnipotent /ɒm'nɪpətənt/ a onnipotente

on /ɒn/ prep su; ⟨on horizontal surface⟩ su, sopra; **on Monday** lunedì; **on Mondays** di lunedì; **on the first of May** il primo di maggio; **on arriving** all'arrivo; **on one's finger** ⟨cut⟩ nel dito; ⟨ring⟩ al dito; **on foot** a piedi; **on the right/left** a destra/sinistra; **on the Rhine/Thames** sul Reno/Tamigi; **on the radio/television** alla radio/televisione; **on the bus/train** in autobus/treno; **go on the bus/train** andare in autobus/treno; **get on the bus/train** salire sull'autobus/sul treno; **on me** ⟨with me⟩ con me; **it's on me** fam tocca a me ● adv ⟨further on⟩ dopo; ⟨switched on⟩ acceso; ⟨brake⟩ inserito; ⟨in operation⟩ in funzione; '**on**' ⟨on machine⟩ on; **he had his hat/coat on** portava il cappello/cappotto; **with his hat/coat on** senza cappello/cappotto; **with/without the lid on** con/senza coperchio; **be on** ⟨film, programme, event⟩ esserci; **it's not on** fam non è giusto; **be on at** fam tormentare ⟨to **per**⟩; **on and off** senza sosta; **on and off** a intervalli; **and so on** e così via; **go on** continuare; **drive on** spostarsi ⟨con la macchina⟩; **stick on** attaccare; **sew on** cucire

once /wʌns/ adv una volta; ⟨formerly⟩ un tempo; ~ **upon a time there was** c'era una volta; **at** ~ subito; ⟨at the same time⟩ contemporaneamente; ~ **and for all** una volta per tutte ● conj [non] appena. ~**-over** n fam give **sb/sth the** ~**-over** ⟨look, check⟩ dare un'occhiata veloce a qcsa/qcsa

oncoming a che si avvicina dalla direzione opposta

one /wʌn/ a un, una; **not** ~ **person** nemmeno una persona ● n uno m ● pron uno; ⟨impersonal⟩ si; ~ **another**

l'un l'altro; ~ **by** (a) uno a uno; ~ **never knows** non si sa mai

one: ~**-eyed** a con un occhio solo. ~**-off** a unico. ~**-parent 'family** n famiglia f con un solo genitore. ~**self** pron (reflexive) si; (emphatic) sé, se stesso; **by** ~**self** da solo; **be proud of** ~**self** essere fieri di sé. ~**-sided** a unilaterale. ~**-way** a (street) a senso unico; (ticket) di sola andata

onion /'ʌnjən/ n cipolla f

'onlooker n spettatore, -trice mf

only /'əʊnlɪ/ a solo; ~ **child** figlio, -a mf unico, -a ● adv & conj solo, solamente; ~ **just** appena

on/'off switch n pulsante m di accensione

'onset n (beginning) inizio m

'onslaught /'ɒnslɔːt/ n attacco m

onus /'əʊnəs/ n **the** ~ **is on me** spetta a me la responsabilità (**to** di)

onward[s] /'ɒnwəd[z]/ adv in avanti; **from then** ~ da allora [in poi]

ooze /uːz/ vi fluire

opal /'əʊpl/ n opale f

opaque /əʊ'peɪk/ a opaco

open /'əʊpən/ a aperto; (free to all) pubblico; (job) vacante; **in the** ~ **air** all'aperto ● **in the** ~ **all'aperto**; fig alla luce del sole ● vt aprire ● vi aprirsi; (shop:) aprire; (flower:) sbocciare. **open up** vt aprire ● vi aprirsi

open: ~**-air 'swimming pool** n piscina f all'aperto. ~ **day** n giorno m di apertura al pubblico

opener /'əʊpənə(r)/ n (for tins) apriscatole m inv; (for bottles) apribottiglie m inv

opening /'əʊpənɪŋ/ n apertura f; (beginning) inizio m; (job) posto m libero; ~ **hours** npl orario m d'apertura

openly /'əʊpənlɪ/ adv apertamente

open: ~**-'minded** a aperto; (broadminded) di vedute larghe. ~**-plan** a a pianta aperta. ~ **'sandwich** n tartina f. ~ **secret** n segreto m di Pulcinella. ~ **ticket** n biglietto m aperto. **O** ~ **University** corsi mpl universitari per corrispondenza

opera /'ɒpərə/ n opera f

operable /'ɒpərəbl/ a operabile

opera: ~**-glasses** npl binocolo msg da teatro. ~**-house** n teatro m lirico. ~**-singer** n cantante mf lirico, -a

operate /'ɒpəreɪt/ vt far funzionare (machine, lift); azionare (lever, brake); mandare avanti (business) ● vi Techn funzionare; (be in action) essere in fun-

zione; Mil, fig operare; ~ **on** Med operare

operatic /ɒpə'rætɪk/ a lirico, operistico

operation /ɒpə'reɪʃn/ n operazione f; Tech funzionamento m; **in** ~ Techn in funzione; **come into** ~ fig entrare in funzione; (law:) entrare in vigore; **have an** ~ Med subire un'operazione. ~**al** a operativo; (law etc) in vigore

operative /'ɒpərətɪv/ a operativo

operator /'ɒpəreɪtə(r)/ n (user) operatore, -trice mf; Teleph centralinista mf

operetta /ɒpə'retə/ n operetta f

opinion /ə'pɪnjən/ n opinione f; **in my** ~ secondo me. ~**ated** a dogmatico

opponent /ə'pəʊnənt/ n avversario, -a mf

opportun|e /'ɒpətjuːn/ a opportuno. ~**ist** /-'tjuːnɪst/ n opportunista mf. ~**istic** a opportunistico

opportunity /ɒpə'tjuːnətɪ/ n opportunità f inv

oppos|e /ə'pəʊz/ vt opporsi a; **be** ~**ed to sth** esssere contrario a qcsa; **as** ~**ed to** al contrario di. ~**ing** a avversario; (opposite) opposto

opposite /'ɒpəzɪt/ a opposto; (house) di fronte; ~ **number** fig contraparte f; **the** ~ **sex** l'altro sesso ● n contrario m ● adv di fronte ● prep di fronte a

opposition /ɒpə'zɪʃn/ n opposizione f

oppress /ə'pres/ vt opprimere. ~**ion** /-eʃn/ n oppressione f. ~**ive** /-ɪv/ a oppressivo; (heat) opprimente. ~**or** n oppressore m

opt /ɒpt/ vi ~ **for** optare per; ~ **out** dissociarsi (**of** da)

optical /'ɒptɪkl/ a ottico; ~ **illusion** illusione f ottica

optician /ɒp'tɪʃn/ n ottico, -a mf

optimis|m /'ɒptɪmɪzm/ n ottimismo m. ~**t** /-mɪst/ n ottimista mf. ~**tic** /-'mɪstɪk/ a ottimistico

optimum /'ɒptɪməm/ a ottimale ● n (pl -**ima**) optimum m

option /'ɒpʃn/ n scelta f; Comm opzione f. ~**al** a facoltativo; ~**al extras** optional m inv

opulen|ce /'ɒpjʊləns/ n opulenza f. ~**t** a opulento

or /ɔː(r)/ conj o, oppure; (after negative) né; **or** [**else**] se no; **in a year or two** un anno o due

oracle /'ɒrəkl/ n oracolo m

oral /'ɔːrl/ a orale ● n fam esame m orale. ~**ly** adv oralmente

orange /'ɒrɪndʒ/ n arancia f; (colour)

arancione *m* ●*a* arancione. ~ade /-'dʒeid/ *n* aranciata *f*. ~ juice *n* succo *m* d'arancia

orator /'ɒrətə(r)/ *n* oratore, -trice *mf*

oratorio /ɒrə'tɔ:rɪəʊ/ *n* oratorio *m*

oratory /'ɒrətərɪ/ *n* oratorio *m*

orbit /'ɔ:bɪt/ *n* orbita *f*. ●*vt* orbitare. ~al *a* ~al road tangenziale *f*

orchard /'ɔ:tʃəd/ *n* frutteto *m*

orches|tra /'ɔ:kɪstrə/ *n* orchestra *f*. ~tral /-'kestrəl/ *a* orchestrale. ~trate *vt* orchestrare

orchid /'ɔ:kɪd/ *n* orchidea *f*

ordain /ɔ:'deɪn/ *vt* decretare; *Relig* ordinare

ordeal /ɔ:'di:l/ *n fig* terribile esperienza *f*

order /'ɔ:də(r)/ *n* ordine *m*; *Comm* ordinazione *f*; **out of** ~ ⟨machine⟩ fuori servizio; **in** ~ **that** affinché; **in** ~ **to** per. ●*vt* ordinare

orderly /'ɔ:dəlɪ/ *a* ordinato. ●*n Mil* attendente *m*; *Med* inserviente *m*

ordinary /'ɔ:dɪnərɪ/ *a* ordinario

ordination /ɔ:dɪ'neɪʃn/ *n Relig* ordinazione *f*

ore /ɔ:(r)/ *n* minerale *m* grezzo

organ /'ɔ:gən/ *n Anat, Mus* organo *m*

organic /ɔ:'gænɪk/ *a* organico; ⟨without chemicals⟩ biologico. ~ally *adv* organicamente; ~ally grown coltivato biologicamente

organism /'ɔ:gənɪzm/ *n* organismo *m*

organist /'ɔ:gənɪst/ *n* organista *mf*

organization /ɔ:gənaɪ'zeɪʃn/ *n* organizzazione *f*

organize /'ɔ:gənaɪz/ *vt* organizzare. ~r *n* organizzatore, -trice *mf*

orgasm /'ɔ:gæzm/ *n* orgasmo *m*

orgy /'ɔ:dʒɪ/ *n* orgia *f*

Orient /'ɔ:rɪənt/ *n* Oriente *m*. o~al /-'entl/ *a* orientale ●*n* orientale *mf*

orient|ate /'ɔ:rɪənteɪt/ *vt* ~ate oneself orientarsi. ~ation /-'teɪʃn/ *n* orientamento *m*

origin /'ɒrɪdʒɪn/ *n* origine *f*

original /ə'rɪdʒən(ə)l/ *a* originario; ⟨not copied, new⟩ originale. ●*n* originale *m*; **in the** ~ in versione originale. ~ity /-'nælətɪ/ *n* originalità *f*. ~ly *adv* originariamente

originate /ə'rɪdʒɪneɪt/ *vi* ~e in avere origine in. ~or *n* ideatore, -trice *mf*

ornament /'ɔ:nəmənt/ *n* ornamento *m*; ⟨on mantelpiece etc⟩ soprammobile *m*. ~al /-'mentl/ *a* ornamentale. ~ation /-'teɪʃn/ *n* decorazione *f*

ornate /ɔ:'neɪt/ *a* ornato

orphan /'ɔ:fn/ *n* orfano, -a *mf* ●*vt* rendere orfano; **be ~ed** rimanere orfano. ~age /-ɪdʒ/ *n* orfanotrofio *m*

orthodox /'ɔ:θədɒks/ *a* ortodosso

orthopaedic /ɔ:θə'pi:dɪk/ *a* ortopedico

oscillate /'ɒsɪleɪt/ *vi* oscillare

ostensibl|e /ɒ'stensəbl/ *a* apparente. ~y *adv* apparentemente

ostentat|ion /ɒsten'teɪʃn/ *n* ostentazione *f*. ~ious /-ʃəs/ *a* ostentato

osteopath /'ɒstɪəpæθ/ *n* osteopata *mf*

ostracize /'ɒstrəsaɪz/ *vt* bandire

ostrich /'ɒstrɪtʃ/ *n* struzzo *m*

other /'ʌðə(r)/ *a, pron & n* altro, -a *mf*; **the ~** ⟨one⟩ l'altro, -a *mf*; **the ~ two** gli altri due; **two ~s** altri due; ~ **people** gli altri; **any ~ questions?** altre domande?; **every ~ day** ⟨alternate days⟩ a giorni alterni; **the ~ day** l'altro giorno; **the ~ evening** l'altra sera; **someone/something or ~** qualcuno/ qualcosa. ●*adv* ~ **than him** tranne lui; **somehow or ~** in qualche modo; **somewhere or ~** da qualche parte

otherwise *adv* altrimenti; ⟨differently⟩ diversamente

otter /'ɒtə(r)/ *n* lontra *f*

ouch /aʊtʃ/ *int* ahi!

ought /ɔ:t/ *v aux* I/we ~ **to stay** dovrei/dovremmo rimanere; **he ~ not to have done it** non avrebbe dovuto farlo; **that ~ to be enough** questo dovrebbe bastare

ounce /aʊns/ *n* oncia *f* (= 28, 35 g)

our /aʊə/ *poss a* il nostro *m*, la nostra *f*, i nostri *mpl*, le nostre *fpl*; ~ **mother/ father** nostra madre/nostro padre

ours /aʊəz/ *poss pron* il nostro *m*, la nostra *f*, i nostri *mpl*, le nostre *fpl*; **a friend of** ~ un nostro amico; **friends of** ~ dei nostri amici; **that is** ~ quello è nostro; ⟨as opposed to yours⟩ quello è il nostro

ourselves /aʊə'selvz/ *pers pron* ⟨reflexive⟩ ci; ⟨emphatic⟩ noi, noi stessi; **we poured ~ a drink** ci siamo versati da bere; **we heard it ~** l'abbiamo sentito noi stessi; **we are proud of ~** siamo fieri di noi; **by ~** da soli

out /aʊt/ *adv* fuori; ⟨not alight⟩ spento; **be ~** ⟨flower:⟩ essere sbocciato; ⟨workers:⟩ essere in sciopero; ⟨calculation:⟩ essere sbagliato; *Sport* essere fuori; ⟨unconscious⟩ aver perso i sensi; ⟨fig: not feasible⟩ fuori questione; **the sun is ~** è uscito il sole; ~ **and about** in piedi; **get ~** *fam* fuori!; **you should get**

~ **more** dovresti uscire più spesso; ~ **with it!** *fam* sputa il rospo!; ● *prep* ~ **of** fuori da; ~ **of date** non aggiornato; ⟨*passport*⟩ scaduto; ~ **of order** guasto; ~ **of print/stock** esaurito; **be** ~ **of bed/the room** fuori dal letto/dalla stanza; ~ **of breath** senza fiato; ~ **of danger** fuori pericolo; **nine** ~ **of ten** nove su dieci; **be** ~ **of sugar/bread** rimanere senza zucchero/pane; **go** ~ **of the room** uscire dalla stanza

out'bid *vt* (*pt/pp* **-bid**, *pres p* **-bidding**) ~ **sb** rilanciare l'offerta di qcno

'outboard *a* ~ **motor** motore *m*

'outbreak *n* (*of war*) scoppio *m*; (*of disease*) insorgenza *f*

'outbuilding *n* costruzione *f* annessa

'outburst *n* esplosione *f*

'outcome *n* risultato *m*

'outcry *n* protesta *f*

out'dated *a* sorpassato

out'do *vt* (*pt* **-did**, *pp* **-done**) superare

'outdoor *a* ⟨*life, sports*⟩ all'aperto; ~ **clothes** *pl* vestiti per uscire; ~ **swimming pool** piscina *f* scoperta

out'doors *adv* all'aria aperta; **go** ~ uscire [all'aria aperta]

'outer *a* esterno

'outfit *n* equipaggiamento *m*; (*clothes*) completo *m*; (*fam: organization*) organizzazione *f*. **~ter** *n* men's **~ter's** negozio *m* di abbigliamento maschile

'outgoing *a* ⟨*president*⟩ uscente; (*mail*) in partenza; (*sociable*) estroverso ● *npl* **~s** uscite *fpl*

out'grow *vi* (*pt* **-grew**, *pp* **-grown**) diventare troppo grande per

'outhouse *n* costruzione *f* annessa

'outing /'aʊtɪŋ/ *n* gita *f*

out'landish /aʊt'lændɪʃ/ *a* stravagante

'outlaw *n* fuorilegge *mf inv* ● *vt* dichiarare illegale

'outlay *n* spesa *f*

'outlet *n* sbocco *m*; *fig* sfogo *m*; *Comm* punto *m* [di] vendita

'outline *n* contorno *m*; (*summary*) sommario *m* ● *vt* tracciare il contorno di; (*describe*) descrivere

out'live *vt* sopravvivere a

'outlook *n* vista *f*; (*future prospect*) prospettiva *f*; (*attitude*) visione *f*

'outlying *a* ~ **areas** zone *fpl* periferiche

out'number *vt* superare in numero

'out-patient *n* paziente *mf* esterno, -a; **~s' department** ambulatorio *m*

'output *n* produzione *f*

'outrage *n* oltraggio *m* ● *vt* oltraggiare. **~ous** /-'reɪdʒəs/ *a* oltraggioso; ⟨*price*⟩ scandaloso

'outright¹ *a* completo; ⟨*refusal*⟩ netto

out'right² *adv* completamente; (*at once*) immediatamente; (*frankly*) francamente

'outset *n* inizio *m*; **from the** ~ fin dall'inizio

'outside¹ *a* esterno ● *n* esterno *m*; **from the** ~ dall'esterno; **at the** ~ al massimo

out'side² *adv* all'esterno, fuori; (*out of doors*) fuori; **go** ~ andare fuori ● *prep* fuori da; (*in front of*) davanti a

out'sider *n* estraneo, -a *mf*

'outskirts *npl* sobborghi *mpl*

out'spoken *a* schietto

out'standing *a* eccezionale; ⟨*landmark*⟩ prominente; (*not settled*) in sospeso

out'stretched *a* allungato

out'strip *vt* (*pt/pp* **-stripped**) superare

out'vote *vt* mettere in minoranza

'outward /-wəd/ *a* esterno; (*journey*) di andata ● *adv* verso l'esterno. **~ly** *adv* esternamente. **~s** *adv* verso l'esterno

out'weigh *vt* aver maggior peso di

out'wit *vt* (*pt/pp* **-witted**) battere in astuzia

oval /'əʊvl/ *a* ovale ● *n* ovale *m*

ovary /'əʊvərɪ/ *n Anat* ovaia *f*

ovation /əʊ'veɪʃn/ *n* ovazione *f*

oven /ʌvn/ *n* forno *m*. **~-ready** *a* pronto da mettere in forno

over /'əʊvə(r)/ *prep* sopra; (*across*) al di là di; (*during*) durante; (*more than*) più di; ~ **the phone** al telefono; ~ **the page** alla pagina seguente; **all** ~ **Italy** in tutta [l']Italia; ⟨*travel*⟩ per l'Italia ● *adv Math* col resto di; (*ended*) finito; ~ **again** un'altra volta; ~ **and** ~ più volte; ~ **and above** oltre a; ~ **here** there qui/là; **all** ~ (*everywhere*) dappertutto; **it's all** ~ è tutto finito; **I ache all** ~ ho male dappertutto; **come/bring** ~ venire/portare; **turn** ~ girare

over- *pref* (*too*) troppo

overall¹ /'əʊvərɔːl/ *n* grembiule *m*; **~s** *pl* tuta *fsg* [da lavoro]

overall² /əʊvər'ɔːl/ *a* complessivo; (*general*) generale ● *adv* complessivamente

over'balance *vi* perdere l'equilibrio

over'bearing *a* prepotente

'overboard *adv Naut* in mare

'overcast *a* coperto

over'charge *vt* ~ **sb** far pagare più

del dovuto a qcno ● *vi* far pagare più del dovuto

'over**coat** *n* cappotto *m*

over**come** *vt* (*pt* **-came**, *pp* **-come**) vincere; **be ~ by** essere sopraffatto da

over**crowded** *a* sovraffollato

over**do** *vt* (*pt* **-did**, *pp* **-done**) esagerare; ⟨*cook too long*⟩ stracuocere; **~ it** ⟨*fam: do too much*⟩ strafare

'over**dose** *n* overdose *f inv*

'over**draft** *n* scoperto *m*; **have an ~** avere il conto scoperto

over**draw** *vt* (*pt* **-drew**, *pp* **-drawn**) **~ one's account** andare allo scoperto; **be ~n by** ⟨*account:*⟩ essere [allo] scoperto di

over**due** *a* in ritardo

over**estimate** *vt* sopravvalutare

'over**flow**[1] *n* ⟨*water*⟩ acqua *f* che deborda; ⟨*people*⟩ pubblico *m* in eccesso; ⟨*outlet*⟩ scarico *m*

over**flow**[2] *vi* debordare

over**grown** *a* ⟨*garden*⟩ coperto di erbacce

'over**haul**[1] *n* revisione *f*

over**haul**[2] *vt* Techn revisionare

over**head** *adv* in alto

'over**head**[2] *a* aereo; ⟨*railway*⟩ sopraelevato; ⟨*lights*⟩ da soffitto ● *npl* **~s** spese *fpl* generali

over**hear** *vt* (*pt/pp* **-heard**) sentire per caso ⟨*conversation*⟩

over**heat** *vi* Auto surriscaldarsi ● *vt* surriscaldare

over**joyed** *a* felicissimo

'over**land** *a* & *adv* via terra; **~ route** via *f* terrestre

over**lap** *v* (*pt/pp* **-lapped**) ● *vi* sovrapporsi ● *vt* sovrapporre

over**leaf** *adv* sul retro

over**load** *vt* sovraccaricare

over**look** *vt* dominare; ⟨*fail to see, ignore*⟩ lasciarsi sfuggire

'over**ly** /'əuvəli/ *adv* eccessivamente

over**night**[1] *adv* per la notte; **stay ~** fermarsi a dormire

'over**night**[2] *a* notturno; **~ bag** piccola borsa *f* da viaggio; **~ stay** sosta *f* per la notte

'over**pass** *n* cavalcavia *m inv*

over**pay** *vt* (*pt/pp* **-paid**) strapagare

over**populated** *a* sovrappopolato

over**power** *vt* sopraffare. **~ing** *a* insostenibile

over**priced** *a* troppo caro

overpro**duce** *vt* produrre in eccesso

over**rate** *vt* sopravvalutare. **~d** *a* sopravvalutato

over**reach** *vt* **~ oneself** puntare troppo in alto

overre**act** *vi* avere una reazione eccessiva. **~ion** *n* reazione *f* eccessiva

over**rid|e** *vt* (*pt* **-rode**, *pp* **-ridden**) passare sopra a. **~ing** *a* prevalente

over**rule** *vt* annullare ⟨*decision*⟩

over**run** *vt* (*pt* **-ran**, *pp* **-run**, *pres p* **-running**) invadere; oltrepassare ⟨*time*⟩; **be ~ with** essere invaso da

over**seas**[1] *adv* oltremare

'over**seas**[2] *a* d'oltremare

over**see** *vt* (*pt* **-saw**, *pp* **-seen**) sorvegliare

over**shadow** *vt* adombrare

over**shoot** *vt* (*pt/pp* **-shot**) oltrepassare

'over**sight** *n* disattenzione *f*; **an ~** una svista

over**sleep** *vi* (*pt/pp* **-slept**) svegliarsi troppo tardi

over**step** *vt* (*pt/pp* **-stepped**) **~ the mark** oltrepassare ogni limite

over**t** /əu'vɜːt/ *a* palese

over**tak|e** *vt/i* (*pt* **-took**, *pp* **-taken**) sorpassare. **~ing** *n* sorpasso *m*; **no ~ing** divieto di sorpasso

over**tax** *vt fig* abusare di

'over**throw**[1] *n* Pol rovesciamento *m*

over**throw**[2] *vt* (*pt* **-threw**, *pp* **-thrown**) Pol rovesciare

'over**time** *n* lavoro *m* straordinario ● *adv* **work ~** fare lo straordinario

over**tired** *a* sovraffaticato

'over**tone** *n fig* sfumatura *f*

over**ture** /'əuvətjuə(r)/ *n* Mus preludio *m*; **~s** *pl fig* approccio *msg*

over**turn** *vt* ribaltare ● *vi* ribaltarsi

over**weight** *a* sovrappeso

over**whelm** /-'welm/ *vt* sommergere ⟨**with** di⟩; ⟨*with emotion*⟩ confondere. **~ing** *a* travolgente; ⟨*victory, majority*⟩ schiacciante

over**work** *n* lavoro *m* eccessivo ● *vt* far lavorare eccessivamente ● *vi* lavorare eccessivamente

ow**|e** /əu/ *vt also fig* dovere (⟨|**to**| *sb* a qcno); **~e** *sb sth* dovere qcsa a qcno. **~ing** *a* **be ~ing** ⟨*money:*⟩ essere da pagare ● *prep* **~ing to** a causa di

owl /aul/ *n* gufo *m*

own[1] /əun/ *a* proprio ● *pron* **a car of my ~** una macchina per conto mio; **on one's ~** da solo; **hold one's ~ with** tener testa a; **get one's ~ back** *fam* prendersi una rivincita

own[2] *vt* possedere; ⟨*confess*⟩ ammettere;

I don't ~ it non mi appartiene. **own up**
vi confessare **(to sth** qcsa)
owner /'əʊnə(r)/ *n* proprietario, -a *mf*.
~ship *n* proprietà *f*
ox /ɒks/ *n* (*pl* **oxen**) bue *m* (*pl* buoi)
oxide /'ɒksaɪd/ *n* ossido *m*

oxygen /'ɒksɪdʒən/ *n* ossigeno *m*. ~
mask *n* maschera *f* a ossigeno
oyster /'ɔɪstə(r)/ *n* ostrica *f*
ozone /'əʊzəʊn/ *n* ozono *m*. ~-'friendly
a che non danneggia l'ozono. ~ **layer** *n*
fascia *f* d'ozono

Pp

PA *abbr* (**per annum**) all'anno
pace /peɪs/ *n* passo *m*; (*speed*) ritmo *m*;
keep ~ with camminare di pari passo
con ● *vi* ~ **up and down** camminare
avanti e indietro. ~-**maker** *n Med*
pacemaker *m*; (*runner*) battistrada *m*
Pacific /pə'sɪfɪk/ *a* & *n* **the** ~ (**Ocean**)
l'oceano *m* Pacifico, il Pacifico
pacifier /'pæsɪfaɪə(r)/ *n Am* ciuccio *m*,
succhiotto *m*
pacifist /'pæsɪfɪst/ *n* pacifista *mf*
pacify /'pæsɪfaɪ/ *vt* (*pt/pp* -**ied**) placare
⟨*person*⟩; pacificare ⟨*country*⟩
pack /pæk/ *n* (*of cards*) mazzo *m*; (*of
hounds*) muta *f*; (*of wolves, thieves*)
branco *m*; (*of cigarettes etc*) pacchetto
m; **a ~ of lies** un mucchio di bugie ● *vt*
impacchettare ⟨*article*⟩; fare ⟨*suitcase*⟩;
mettere in valigia ⟨*swimsuit etc*⟩; (*press
down*) comprimere; **~ed** [**out**]
(*crowded*) pieno zeppo ● *vi* fare i bagagli; **send sb ~ing** *fam* mandare qcno a
stendere. **pack up** *vt* impacchettare
● *vi fam* ⟨*machine:*⟩ piantare in asso
package /'pækɪdʒ/ *n* pacco *m* ● *vt* impacchettare. ~ **deal** offerta *f* tutto compreso. ~ **holiday** *n* vacanza *f* organiz-
zata. ~ **tour** viaggio *m* organizzato
packaging /'pækɪdʒɪŋ/ *n* confezione *f*
packed 'lunch *n* pranzo *m* al sacco
packet /'pækɪt/ *n* pacchetto *m*; **cost a
~** *fam* costare un sacco
packing /'pækɪŋ/ *n* imballaggio *m*
pact /pækt/ *n* patto *m*
pad[1] /pæd/ *n* imbottitura *f*; (*for
writing*) bloc-notes *m inv*, taccuino *m*;
(*fam: home*) [piccolo] appartamento *m*
● *vt* (*pt/pp* **padded**) imbottire. **pad out**
vt gonfiare
pad[2] *vi* (*pt/pp* **padded**) camminare con
passo felpato

padded /'pædɪd/ *a* ~ **bra** reggiseno *m*
imbottito
padding /'pædɪŋ/ *n* imbottitura *f*; (*in
written work*) fronzoli *mpl*
paddle[1] /'pæd(ə)l/ *n* pagaia *f* ● *vt* (*row*)
spingere remando
paddle[2] *vi* (*wade*) sguazzare
paddock /'pædək/ *n* recinto *m*
padlock /'pædlɒk/ *n* lucchetto *m* ● *vt*
chiudere con lucchetto
paediatrician /piːdɪə'trɪʃn/ *n* pedia-
tra *mf*
paediatrics /piːdɪ'ætrɪks/ *n* pediatria *f*
page[1] /peɪdʒ/ *n* pagina *f*
page[2] *n* (*boy*) paggetto *m*; (*in hotel*) fat-
torino *m* ● *vt* far chiamare ⟨*person*⟩
pageant /'pædʒənt/ *n* parata *f*. ~**ry** *n*
cerimoniale *m*
pager /'peɪdʒə(r)/ *n* cercapersone *m inv*
paid /peɪd/ *see* **pay** ● *a* ~ **employment**
lavoro *m* remunerato; **put ~ to** mettere
un termine a
pail /peɪl/ *n* secchio *m*
pain /peɪn/ *n* dolore *m*; **be in** ~ soffrire;
take ~s to fare il possibile per; ~ **in
the neck** *fam* spina *f* nel fianco
pain: ~**ful** *a* doloroso; (*laborious*) penoso. ~-**killer** *n* calmante *m*. ~**less** *a* in-
dolore
painstaking /'peɪnzteɪkɪŋ/ *a* minuzioso
paint /peɪnt/ *n* pittura *f*; ~**s** *pl* colori
mpl ● *vt/i* pitturare; ⟨*artist:*⟩ dipingere.
~**brush** *n* pennello *m*. ~**er** *n* pittore,
-trice *mf*; (*decorator*) imbianchino *m*.
~**ing** *n* pittura *f*; (*picture*) dipinto *m*.
~**work** *n* pittura *f*
pair /peə(r)/ *n* paio *m*; (*of people*) coppia
f; ~ **of trousers** paio *m* di pantaloni; ~
of scissors paio *m* di forbici
pajamas /pə'dʒɑːməz/ *npl Am* pigiama
msg

Pakistan /pɑːkɪˈstɑːn/ n Pakistan m. **~i** a pakistano ● n pakistano, -a mf

pal /pæl/ n fam amico, -a mf

palace /ˈpælɪs/ n palazzo m

palatable /ˈpælətəbl/ a gradevole (al gusto)

palate /ˈpælət/ n palato m

palatial /pəˈleɪʃl/ a sontuoso

palaver /pəˈlɑːvə(r)/ n (fam: fuss) storie fpl

pale /peɪl/ a pallido

Palestin|e /ˈpælɪstaɪn/ n Palestina f. **~ian** /pælɪˈstɪnɪən/ a palestinese ● n palestinese mf

palette /ˈpælɪt/ n tavolozza f

pall|id /ˈpælɪd/ a pallido. **~or** n pallore m

palm /pɑːm/ n palmo m; (tree) palma f; **P~ 'Sunday** n Domenica f delle Palme ● **palm off** vt~ **sth off on sb** rifilare qcsa a qcno

palpable /ˈpælpəbl/ a palpabile; (perceptible) tangibile

palpitat|e /ˈpælpɪteɪt/ vi palpitare. **~ions** /-ˈteɪʃnz/ npl palpitazioni fpl

paltry /ˈpɔːltrɪ/ a (-ier, -iest) insignificante

pamper /ˈpæmpə(r)/ vt viziare

pamphlet /ˈpæmflɪt/ n opuscolo m

pan /pæn/ n tegame m, pentola f; (for frying) padella f; (of scales) piatto m ● vt (pt/pp panned) (fam: criticize) stroncare

panache /pəˈnæʃ/ n stile m

pancake n crêpe f inv, frittella f

pancreas /ˈpæŋkrɪəs/ n pancreas m inv

panda /ˈpændə/ n panda m inv. **~ car** n macchina f della polizia

pandemonium /pændɪˈməʊnɪəm/ n pandemonio m

pander /ˈpændə(r)/ vi~ **to sb** compiacere qcno

pane /peɪn/ n~ [of glass] vetro m

panel /ˈpænl/ n pannello m; (group of people) giuria f; **~ of experts** gruppo m di esperti. **~ling** n pannelli mpl

pang /pæŋ/ n~s **of hunger** morsi mpl della fame; **~s of conscience** rimorsi mpl di coscienza

panic /ˈpænɪk/ n panico m ● vi (pt/pp panicked) lasciarsi prendere dal panico. **~-stricken** a in preda al panico

panoram|a /pænəˈrɑːmə/ n panorama m. **~ic** /-ˈræmɪk/ a panoramico

pansy /ˈpænzɪ/ n viola f del pensiero; (fam: effeminate man) finocchio m

pant /pænt/ vi ansimare

panther /ˈpænθə(r)/ n pantera f

panties /ˈpæntɪz/ npl mutandine fpl

pantomime /ˈpæntəmaɪm/ n pantomima f

pantry /ˈpæntrɪ/ n dispensa f

pants /pænts/ npl (underwear) mutande fpl; (woman's) mutandine fpl; (trousers) pantaloni mpl

pantyhose n Am collant m inv

papal /ˈpeɪpl/ a papale

paper /ˈpeɪpə(r)/ n carta f; (wallpaper) carta f da parati; (newspaper) giornale m; (exam) esame m; (treatise) saggio m; **~s** pl (documents) documenti mpl; (for identification) documento m [d'identità]; **on ~** in teoria; **put down on ~** mettere per iscritto ● attrib di carta ● vt tappezzare

paper: **~back** n edizione f economica. **~-clip** n graffetta f. **~-knife** n tagliacarte m inv. **~weight** n fermacarte m inv. **~work** n lavoro m d'ufficio

par /pɑː(r)/ n (in golf) par m inv; **on a ~ with** alla pari con; **feel below ~** essere un po' giù di tono

parable /ˈpærəbl/ n parabola f

parachut|e /ˈpærəʃuːt/ n paracadute m inv ● vi lanciarsi col paracadute. **~ist** n paracadutista mf

parade /pəˈreɪd/ n (military) parata f militare ● vi sfilare ● vt (show off) far sfoggio di

paradise /ˈpærədaɪs/ n paradiso m

paradox /ˈpærədɒks/ n paradosso m. **~ical** /-ˈdɒksɪkl/ a paradossale. **~ically** adv paradossalmente

paraffin /ˈpærəfɪn/ n paraffina f

paragon /ˈpærəgən/ n~ **of virtue** modello m di virtù

paragraph /ˈpærəgrɑːf/ n paragrafo m

parallel /ˈpærəlel/ a & adv parallelo. **~ bars** npl parallele fpl. **~ port** n Comput porta f parallela ● n Geog, fig parallelo m; (line) parallela f ● vt essere paragonabile a

paralyse /ˈpærəlaɪz/ vt also fig paralizzare

paralysis /pəˈræləsɪs/ n (pl -ses) /-siːz/ paralisi f inv

parameter /pəˈræmɪtə(r)/ n parametro m

paramount /ˈpærəmaʊnt/ a supremo; **be ~** essere essenziale

paranoia /pærəˈnɔɪə/ n paranoia f

paranoid /ˈpærənɔɪd/ a paranoico

paraphernalia /pærəfəˈneɪlɪə/ n armamentario m

paraphrase /ˈpærəfreɪz/ n parafrasi f inv ● vt parafrasare

paraplegic /ˌpærəˈpliːdʒɪk/ a paraplegico ●n paraplegico, -a mf

parasite /ˈpærəsaɪt/ n parassita mf

parasol /ˈpærəsɒl/ n parasole m

paratrooper /ˈpærətruːpə(r)/ n paracadutista m

parcel /ˈpɑːsl/ n pacco m

parch /pɑːtʃ/ vt disseccare; **be ~ed** ⟨person:⟩ morire dalla sete

pardon /ˈpɑːdn/ n perdono m; Jur grazia f; **~ ?** prego?; **I beg your ~?** fml chiedo scusa?; **I do beg your ~** ⟨sorry⟩ chiedo scusa! ●vt perdonare; Jur graziare

pare /peə(r)/ vt ⟨peel⟩ pelare

parent /ˈpeərənt/ n genitore, -trice mf; **~s** pl genitori mpl. **~al** /pəˈrentl/ a dei genitori

parenthesis /pəˈrenθəsɪs/ n (pl **-ses** /-siːz/) parentesi m inv

Paris /ˈpærɪs/ n Parigi f

parish /ˈpærɪʃ/ n parrocchia f. **~ioner** /pəˈrɪʃənə(r)/ n parrocchiano, -a mf

Parisian /pəˈrɪzɪən/ n parigino, -a mf

parity /ˈpærətɪ/ n parità f

park /pɑːk/ n parco m ●vt/i Auto posteggiare, parcheggiare; **~ oneself** fam installarsi

parka /ˈpɑːkə/ n parka m inv

parking /ˈpɑːkɪŋ/ n parcheggio m, posteggio m; **'no ~'** 'divieto di sosta'. **~-lot** n Am posteggio m, parcheggio m. **~-meter** n parchimetro m. **~ space** n posteggio m, parcheggio m

parliament /ˈpɑːləmənt/ n parlamento m. **~ary** /-ˈmentərɪ/ a parlamentare

parlour /ˈpɑːlə(r)/ n salotto m

parochial /pəˈrəʊkɪəl/ a parrocchiale; fig ristretto

parody /ˈpærədɪ/ n parodia f ●vt (pt/pp -ied) parodiare

parole /pəˈrəʊl/ n **on ~** in libertà condizionale ●vt mettere in libertà condizionale

parquet /ˈpɑːkeɪ/ n **~ floor** parquet m inv

parrot /ˈpærət/ n pappagallo m

parry /ˈpærɪ/ vt (pt/pp -ied) parare ⟨blow⟩; ⟨in fencing⟩ eludere

parsimonious /ˌpɑːsɪˈməʊnɪəs/ a parsimonioso

parsley /ˈpɑːslɪ/ n prezzemolo m

parsnip /ˈpɑːsnɪp/ n pastinaca f

parson /ˈpɑːsn/ n pastore m

part /pɑːt/ n parte f; ⟨of machine⟩ pezzo m; **for my ~** per quanto mi riguarda; **on the ~ of** da parte di; **take sb's ~**

prendere le parti di qcno; **take ~ in** prendere parte a ●adv in parte ●vt **~ one's hair** farsi la riga ●vi ⟨people:⟩ separare; **~ with** separarsi da

part-ex'change n take in **~** prendere indietro

partial /ˈpɑːʃl/ a parziale; **be ~ to** aver un debole per. **~ly** adv parzialmente

particip|ant /pɑːˈtɪsɪpənt/ n partecipante mf. **~ate** /-peɪt/ vi partecipare (**in** a). **~ation** /-ˈpeɪʃn/ n partecipazione f

participle /ˈpɑːtɪsɪpl/ n participio m; **present/past ~** participio m presente/passato

particle /ˈpɑːtɪkl/ n Phys, Gram particella f

particular /pəˈtɪkjʊlə(r)/ a particolare; ⟨precise⟩ meticoloso; pej noioso; **in ~** in particolare. **~ly** adv particolarmente. **~s** npl particolari mpl

parting /ˈpɑːtɪŋ/ n separazione f; ⟨in hair⟩ scriminatura f ●attrib di commiato

partisan /pɑːtɪˈzæn/ n partigiano, -a mf

partition /pɑːˈtɪʃn/ n ⟨wall⟩ parete f divisoria; Pol divisione f ●vt dividere ⟨in parti⟩. **partition off** vt separare

partly /ˈpɑːtlɪ/ adv in parte

partner /ˈpɑːtnə(r)/ n Comm socio, -a mf; ⟨sport, in relationship⟩ compagno, -a mf. **~ship** n Comm società f inv

partridge /ˈpɑːtrɪdʒ/ n pernice f

part-'time a & adv part time; **be or work ~** lavorare part time

party /ˈpɑːtɪ/ n ricevimento m, festa f; ⟨group⟩ gruppo m; Pol partito m; Jur parte f ⟨in causa⟩; **be ~ to** essere parte attiva in

'party line[1] n Teleph duplex m inv

party 'line[2] n Pol linea f del partito

pass /pɑːs/ n lasciapassare m inv; ⟨in mountains⟩ passo m; Sport passaggio m; Sch ⟨mark⟩ ⟨voto m⟩ sufficiente m; **make a ~ at** fam fare delle avances a ●vt passare; ⟨overtake⟩ sorpassare; ⟨approve⟩ far passare; fare ⟨remark⟩; Jur pronunciare ⟨sentence⟩; **~ the time** passare il tempo ●vi passare; ⟨in exam⟩ essere promosso. **pass away** vi mancare. **pass down** vt passare; fig trasmettere. **pass out** vi fam svenire. **pass round** vt far passare. **pass through** vt attraversare. **pass up** vt passare; ⟨fam: miss⟩ lasciarsi scappare

passable /ˈpɑːsəbl/ a ⟨road⟩ praticabile; ⟨satisfactory⟩ passabile

passage /ˈpæsɪdʒ/ n passaggio m;

(*corridor*) corridoio *m*; (*voyage*) traversata *f*

passenger /ˈpæsɪndʒə(r)/ *n* passeggero, -a *mf*. ~ **seat** *n* posto *m* accanto al guidatore

passer-by /pɑːsəˈbaɪ/ *n* (*pl* ~**s-by**) passante *mf*

passing place *n* piazzola *f* di sosta *per consentire il transito dei veicoli nei due sensi*

passion /ˈpæʃn/ *n* passione *f*. ~**ate** /-ət/ *a* appassionato

passive /ˈpæsɪv/ *a* passivo ● *n* passivo *m*. ~**ness** *n* passività *f*

pass-mark *n* Sch [voto *m*] sufficiente *m*

Passover /ˈpɑːsəʊvə(r)/ *n* Pasqua *f* ebraica

pass: ~**port** *n* passaporto *m*. ~**word** *n* parola *f* d'ordine

past /pɑːst/ *a* passato; (*former*) ex: **in the** ~ **few days** nei giorni scorsi; **that's all** ~ tutto questo è passato; **the** ~ **week** la settimana scorsa ● *n* passato *m* ● *prep* oltre; **at ten** ~ **two** alle due e dieci ● *adv* oltre; **go/come** ~ passare

pasta /ˈpæstə/ *n* pasta[sciutta] *f*

paste /peɪst/ *n* pasta *f*; (*dough*) impasto *m*; (*adhesive*) colla *f* ● *vt* incollare

pastel /ˈpæstl/ *n* pastello *m* ● *attrib* pastello

pasteurize /ˈpɑːstʃəraɪz/ *vt* pastorizzare

pastille /ˈpæstɪl/ *n* pastiglia *f*

pastime /ˈpɑːstaɪm/ *n* passatempo *m*

pastoral /ˈpɑːstərəl/ *a* pastorale

pastrami /pæˈstrɑːmɪ/ *n* carne *f* di manzo affumicata

pastry /ˈpeɪstrɪ/ *n* pasta *f*. ~**ies** *pl* pasticcini *mpl*

pasture /ˈpɑːstʃə(r)/ *n* pascolo *m*

pasty¹ /ˈpæstɪ/ *n* pasticcio *m*

pasty² /ˈpeɪstɪ/ *a* smorto

pat /pæt/ *n* buffetto *m*; (*of butter*) pezzetto *m* ● *adv* **have sth off** ~ conoscere qcsa a menadito ● *vt* (*pt/pp* **patted**) dare un buffetto a; ~ **sb on the back** *fig* congratularsi con qcno

patch /pætʃ/ *n* toppa *f*; (*spot*) chiazza *f*; (*period*) periodo *m*; **not a** ~ **on** *fam* molto inferiore a ● *vt* mettere una toppa su. **patch up** *vt* riparare alla bell'e meglio; appianare (*quarrel*)

patchy /ˈpætʃɪ/ *a* incostante

pâté /ˈpæteɪ/ *n* pâté *m inv*

patent /ˈpeɪtnt/ *a* palese ● *n* brevetto *m* ● *vt* brevettare. ~ **leather shoes** *npl* scarpe *fpl* di vernice. ~**ly** *adv* in modo palese

patern|al /pəˈtɜːnl/ *a* paterno. ~**ity** *n* paternità *f*

path /pɑːθ/ *n* (*pl* ~**s** /pɑːðz/) sentiero *m*; (*orbit*) traiettoria *m*; *fig* strada *f*

pathetic /pəˈθetɪk/ *a* patetico; (*fam: very bad*) penoso

patholog|ical /pæθəˈlɒdʒɪkl/ *a* patologico. ~**ist** /pəˈθɒlədʒɪst/ *n* patologo, -a *mf*. ~**y** *n* patologia *f*

pathos /ˈpeɪθɒs/ *n* pathos *m*

patience /ˈpeɪʃns/ *n* pazienza *f*; (*game*) solitario *m*

patient /ˈpeɪʃnt/ *a* paziente ● *n* paziente *mf*. ~**ly** *adv* pazientemente

patio /ˈpætɪəʊ/ *n* terrazza *f*

patriot /ˈpætrɪət/ *n* patriota *mf*. ~**ic** /-ˈɒtɪk/ *a* patriottico. ~**ism** *n* patriottismo *m*

patrol /pəˈtrəʊl/ *n* pattuglia *f* ● *vt/i* pattugliare. ~ **car** *n* autopattuglia *f*

patron /ˈpeɪtrən/ *n* patrono *m*; (*of charity*) benefattore, -trice *mf*; (*of the arts*) mecenate *mf*; (*customer*) cliente *mf*

patroniz|e /ˈpætrənaɪz/ *vt* frequentare abitualmente; *fig* trattare con condiscendenza. ~**ing** *a* condiscendente. ~**ingly** *adv* con condiscendenza

patter¹ /ˈpætə(r)/ *n* picchiettio *m* ● *vi* picchiettare

patter² *n* (*of salesman*) chiacchiere *fpl*

pattern /ˈpætn/ *n* disegno *m* (*stampato*); (*for knitting, sewing*) modello *m*

paunch /pɔːntʃ/ *n* pancia *f*

pause /pɔːz/ *n* pausa *f* ● *vi* fare una pausa

pave /peɪv/ *vt* pavimentare; ~ **the way** preparare la strada (**for** a). ~**ment** *n* marciapiede *m*

pavilion /pəˈvɪljən/ *n* padiglione *m*

paw /pɔː/ *n* zampa *f* ● *vt fam* mettere le zampe addosso a

pawn¹ /pɔːn/ *n* (*in chess*) pedone *m*; *fig* pedina *f*

pawn² *vt* impegnare ● *n* **in** ~ in pegno. ~**broker** *n* prestatore, -trice *mf* su pegno. ~**shop** *n* monte *m* di pietà

pay /peɪ/ *n* paga *f*; **in the** ~ **of** al soldo di ● *v* (*pt/pp* **paid**) *vt* pagare; pagare (*attention*); fare (*compliment, visit*); ~ **cash** pagare in contanti ● *vi* pagare; (*be profitable*) rendere; **it doesn't** ~ **to...** *fig* è fatica sprecata...; ~ **for sth** pagare per qcsa. **pay back** *vt* ripagare. **pay in** *vt* versare. **pay off** *vt* saldare (*debt*) ● *vi fig* dare dei frutti. **pay up** *vi* pagare

payable /ˈpeɪəbl/ *a* pagabile; **make** ~ **to** intestare a

payee /per'i:/ n beneficiario m (di una somma)

payment /'peɪmənt/ n pagamento m

pay: ~ **packet** n busta f paga. ~ **phone** n telefono m pubblico

PC n abbr (**personal computer**) PC m inv

pea /pi:/ n pisello m

peace /pi:s/ n pace f; ~ **of mind** tranquillità f

peace|able /'pi:səbl/ a pacifico. ~**ful** a calmo, sereno. ~**fully** adv in pace. ~**maker** n mediatore, -trice mf

peach /pi:tʃ/ n pesca f; (tree) pesco m

peacock /'pi:kɒk/ n pavone m

peak /pi:k/ n picco m; fig culmine m. ~**ed** `cap n berretto m a punta. ~ **hours** npl ore fpl di punta

peaky /'pi:kɪ/ a malaticcio

peal /pi:l/ n (of bells) scampanio m; ~**s of laughter** pl fragore m di risate

peanut /'pi:nʌt/ n nocciolina f (americana); ~**s** pl fam miseria f

pear /peə(r)/ n pera f; (tree) pero m

pearl /pɜ:l/ n perla f

peasant /'peznt/ n contadino, -a mf

pebble /'pebl/ n ciottolo m

peck /pek/ n beccata f; (kiss) bacetto m ● vt beccare; (kiss) dare un bacetto a. ~**ing order** n gerarchia f. **peck at** vt beccare

peckish /'pekɪʃ/ a **be ~** fam avere un languorino [allo stomaco]

peculiar /pɪ'kju:lɪə(r)/ a strano; (special) particolare; ~ **to** tipico di. ~**ity** /-'ærətɪ/ n stranezza f; (feature) particolarità f inv

pedal /'pedl/ n pedale m ● vi pedalare. ~ **bin** n pattumiera f a pedale

pedantic /pɪ'dæntɪk/ a pedante

pedestal /'pedɪstl/ n piedistallo m

pedestrian /pɪ'destrɪən/ n pedone m ● a fig scadente. ~ **crossing** n passaggio m pedonale. ~ **precinct** n zona f pedonale

pedicure /'pedɪkjʊə(r)/ n pedicure f inv

pedigree /'pedɪgri:/ n pedigree m inv; (of person) lignaggio m ● attrib (animal) di razza, con pedigree

pee /pi:/ vi (pt/pp **peed**) fam fare [la] pipì

peek /pi:k/ vi fam sbirciare

peel /pi:l/ n buccia f ● vt sbucciare ● vi (nose etc:) spellarsi; (paint:) staccarsi

peep /pi:p/ n sbirciata f ● vi sbirciare

peer[1] /pɪə(r)/ vi ~ **at** scrutare

peer[2] n nobile m; his ~**s** pl (in rank) i

suoi pari; (in age) i suoi coetanei. ~**age** n nobiltà f

peeved /pi:vd/ a fam irritato

peg /peg/ n (hook) piolo m; (for tent) picchetto m; (for clothes) molletta f; **off the ~** fam prêt-à-porter

pejorative /pɪ'dʒɒrətɪv/ a peggiorativo

pelican /'pelɪkən/ n pellicano m

pellet /'pelɪt/ n pallottola f

pelt /pelt/ vt bombardare ● vi (fam: run fast) catapultarsi; ~ **[down]** (rain:) venir giù a fiotti

pelvis /'pelvɪs/ n Anat bacino m

pen[1] /pen/ n (for animals) recinto m

pen[2] n penna f; (ball-point) penna f a sfera

penal /'pi:nl/ a penale. ~**ize** vt penalizzare

penalty /'penltɪ/ n sanzione f; (fine) multa f; (in football) ~ **[kick]** [calcio m di] rigore m; ~ **area** o **box** area f di rigore

penance /'penəns/ n penitenza f

pence /pens/ see penny

pencil /'pensl/ n matita f. ~**-sharpener** n temperamatite m inv

pendant /'pendənt/ n ciondolo m

pending /'pendɪŋ/ a in sospeso ● prep in attesa di

pendulum /'pendjʊləm/ n pendolo m

penetrat|e /'penɪtreɪt/ vt/i penetrare. ~**ing** a acuto; (sound, stare) penetrante. ~**ion** /-'treɪʃn/ n penetrazione f

penfriend n amico, -a mf di penna

penguin /'pengwɪn/ n pinguino m

penicillin /penɪ'sɪlɪn/ n penicillina f

peninsula /pɪ'nɪnsjʊlə/ n penisola f

penis /'pi:nɪs/ n pene m

peniten|ce /'penɪtəns/ n penitenza f. ~**t** a penitente ● n penitente mf

penitentiary /penɪ'tenʃərɪ/ n Am penitenziario m

pen: ~**knife** n temperino m. ~**-name** n pseudonimo m

pennant /'penənt/ n bandiera f

penniless /'penɪlɪs/ a senza un soldo

penny /'penɪ/ n (pl **pence**; single coins **pennies**) penny m; Am centesimo m; **spend a ~** fam andare in bagno

pension /'penʃn/ n pensione f. ~**er** n pensionato, -a mf

pensive /'pensɪv/ a pensoso

Pentecost /'pentɪkɒst/ n Pentecoste f

pent-up /'pentʌp/ a represso

penultimate /pɪ'nʌltɪmət/ a penultimo

people /'pi:pl/ npl persone fpl, gente

fsg; ⟨*citizens*⟩ popolo *msg*; **a lot of ~** una marea di gente; **the ~** la gente; **English ~** gli inglesi; **~ say** si dice; **for four ~** per quattro ● *vt* popolare

pepper /'pepǝ(r)/ *n* pepe *m*; ⟨*vegetable*⟩ peperone *m* ● *vt* ⟨*season*⟩ pepare

pepper: **~corn** *n* grano *m* di pepe. **~mill** macinapepe *m inv*. **~mint** *n* menta *f* peperita; ⟨*sweet*⟩ caramella *f* alla menta. **~pot** *n* pepiera *f*

per /pɜː(r)/ *prep* per; **~ annum** all'anno; **~ cent** percento

perceive /pǝ'siːv/ *vt* percepire; ⟨*interpret*⟩ interpretare

percentage /pǝ'sentɪdʒ/ *n* percentuale *f*

perceptible /pǝ'septǝbl/ *a* percettibile; ⟨*difference*⟩ sensibile

percept|ion /pǝ'sepʃn/ *n* percezione *f*. **~ive** /-tɪv/ *a* perspicace

perch /pɜːtʃ/ *n* pertica *f* ● *vi* ⟨*bird:*⟩ appollaiarsi

percolator /'pɜːkǝleɪtǝ(r)/ *n* caffettiera *f* a filtro

percussion /pǝ'kʌʃn/ *n* percussione *f*. **~ instrument** *n* strumento *m* a percussione

peremptory /pǝ'remptǝrɪ/ *a* perentorio

perennial /pǝ'renɪǝl/ *a* perenne ● *n* pianta *f* perenne

perfect¹ /'pɜːfɪkt/ *a* perfetto ● *n Gram* passato *m* prossimo

perfect² /pǝ'fekt/ *vt* perfezionare. **~ion** /-ekʃn/ *n* perfezione *f*; **to ~ion** alla perfezione. **~ionist** *n* perfezionista *mf*

perfectly /'pɜːfɪktlɪ/ *adv* perfettamente

perforat|e /'pɜːfǝreɪt/ *vt* perforare. **~ed** *a* perforato; ⟨*ulcer*⟩ perforante. **~ion** *n* perforazione *f*

perform /pǝ'fɔːm/ *vt* compiere, fare; eseguire ⟨*operation, sonata*⟩; recitare ⟨*role*⟩; mettere in scena ⟨*play*⟩ ● *vi* *Theat* recitare; *Techn* funzionare. **~ance** *n* esecuzione *f*; ⟨*at theatre, cinema*⟩ rappresentazione *f*; *Techn* rendimento *m*. **~er** *n* artista *mf*

perfume /'pɜːfjuːm/ *n* profumo *m*

perfunctory /pǝ'fʌŋktǝrɪ/ *a* superficiale

perhaps /pǝ'hæps/ *adv* forse

peril /'perɪl/ *n* pericolo *m*. **~ous** /-ǝs/ *a* pericoloso

perimeter /pǝ'rɪmɪtǝ(r)/ *n* perimetro *m*

period /'pɪǝrɪǝd/ *n* periodo *m*; ⟨*menstruation*⟩ mestruazioni *fpl*; *Sch*

ora *f* di lezione; ⟨*full stop*⟩ punto *m* fermo ● *attrib* ⟨*costume*⟩ d'epoca; ⟨*furniture*⟩ in stile. **~ic** /-'ɒdɪk/ *a* periodico. **~ical** /-'ɒdɪkl/ *n* periodico *m*, rivista *f*

peripher|al /pǝ'rɪfǝrǝl/ *a* periferico. **~y** *n* periferia *f*

periscope /'perɪskǝʊp/ *n* periscopio *m*

perish /'perɪʃ/ *vi* ⟨*rot*⟩ deteriorarsi; ⟨*die*⟩ perire. **~able** /-ǝbl/ *a* deteriorabile

perjur|e /'pɜːdʒǝ(r)/ *vt* **~e oneself** spergiurare. **~y** *n* spergiuro *m*

perk /pɜːk/ *n fam* vantaggio *m*

perk up *vt* tirare su ● *vi* tirarsi su

perky /'pɜːkɪ/ *a* allegro

perm /pɜːm/ *n* permanente *f* ● *vt* **~ sb's hair** fare la permanente a qno

permanent /'pɜːmǝnǝnt/ *a* permanente; ⟨*job, address*⟩ stabile. **~ly** *adv* stabilmente

permeate /'pɜːmɪeɪt/ *vt* impregnare

permissible /pǝ'mɪsǝbl/ *a* ammissibile

permission /pǝ'mɪʃn/ *n* permesso *m*

permissive /pǝ'mɪsɪv/ *a* permissivo

permit¹ /pǝ'mɪt/ *vt* ⟨*pt/pp* -mitted⟩ permettere; **~ sb to do sth** permettere a qcno di fare qcosa

permit² /'pɜːmɪt/ *n* autorizzazione *f*

perpendicular /pɜːpǝn'dɪkjʊlǝ(r)/ *a* perpendicolare ● *n* perpendicolare *f*

perpetual /pǝ'petjʊǝl/ *a* perenne. **~ly** *adv* perennemente

perpetuate /pǝ'petjʊeɪt/ *vt* perpetuare

perplex /pǝ'pleks/ *vt* lasciare perplesso. **~ed** *a* perplesso. **~ity** *n* perplessità *f inv*

persecut|e /'pɜːsɪkjuːt/ *vt* perseguitare. **~ion** /-'kjuːʃn/ *n* persecuzione *f*

perseverance /pɜːsɪ'vɪǝrǝns/ *n* perseveranza *f*

persever|e /pɜːsɪ'vɪǝ(r)/ *vi* perseverare. **~ing** *a* assiduo

Persian /'pɜːʃn/ *a* persiano

persist /pǝ'sɪst/ *vi* persistere; **~ in doing sth** persistere nel fare qcosa. **~ence** *n* persistenza *f*. **~ent** *a* persistente. **~ently** *adv* persistentemente

person /'pɜːsn/ *n* persona *f*; **in ~** di persona

personal /'pɜːsǝnl/ *a* personale. **~ hygiene** *n* igiene *f* personale. **~ly** *adv* personalmente. **~ organizer** *n Comput* agenda *f* elettronica

personality /pɜːsǝ'nælǝtɪ/ *n* personalità *f inv*; ⟨*on TV*⟩ personaggio *m*

personnel /pɜːsəˈnel/ n personale m

perspective /pəˈspektɪv/ n prospettiva f

persp|iration /pɜːspɪˈreɪʃn/ n sudore m. ~**ire** /ˈspaɪə(r)/ vi sudare

persua|de /pəˈsweɪd/ vt persuadere. ~**sion** /-eɪʒn/ n persuasione f; (belief) convinzione f

persuasive /pəˈsweɪsɪv/ a persuasivo. ~**ly** adv in modo persuasivo

pertinent /ˈpɜːtɪnənt/ a pertinente (**to** a)

perturb /pəˈtɜːb/ vt perturbare

peruse /pəˈruːz/ vt leggere

perva|de /pəˈveɪd/ vt pervadere. ~**sive** /-sɪv/ a pervasivo

perverse /pəˈvɜːs/ a irragionevole. ~**ion** /-ʃn/ n perversione f

pervert /ˈpɜːvɜːt/ n pervertito, -a mf

perverted /pəˈvɜːtɪd/ a perverso

pessimis|m /ˈpesɪmɪzm/ n pessimismo m. ~**t** /-mɪst/ n pessimista mf. ~**tic** /-ˈmɪstɪk/ a pessimistico. ~**tically** adv in modo pessimistico

pest /pest/ n piaga f; (fam: person) peste f

pester /ˈpestə(r)/ vt molestare

pesticide /ˈpestɪsaɪd/ n pesticida m

pet /pet/ n animale m domestico; (favourite) cocco, -a mf ● a prediletto ● v (pt/pp petted) ● vt coccolare ● vi (couple:) praticare il petting

petal /ˈpetl/ n petalo m

peter /ˈpiːtə(r)/ vi ~ **out** finire

petite /pəˈtiːt/ a minuto

petition /pəˈtɪʃn/ n petizione f

pet 'name n vezzeggiativo m

petrif|y /ˈpetrɪfaɪ/ vt (pt/pp -ied) pietrificare. ~**ied** a (frightened) pietrificato

petrol /ˈpetrəl/ n benzina f

petroleum /pɪˈtrəʊlɪəm/ n petrolio m

petrol: ~-**pump** n pompa f di benzina. ~ **station** n stazione f di servizio. ~ **tank** n serbatoio m della benzina

'pet shop n negozio m di animali [domestici]

petticoat /ˈpetɪkəʊt/ n sottoveste f

petty /ˈpetɪ/ a (-ier, -iest) insignificante; (mean) meschino. ~ '**cash** n cassa f per piccole spese

petulant /ˈpetjʊlənt/ a petulante

pew /pjuː/ n banco m (di chiesa)

pewter /ˈpjuːtə(r)/ n peltro m

phallic /ˈfælɪk/ a fallico

phantom /ˈfæntəm/ n fantasma m

pharmaceutical /fɑːməˈsjuːtɪkl/ a farmaceutico

pharmac|ist /ˈfɑːməsɪst/ n farmacista mf. ~**y** n farmacia f

phase /feɪz/ n fase f ● vt phase in/out introdurre/eliminare gradualmente

Ph.D. n abbr (Doctor of Philosophy) dottorato m di ricerca

pheasant /ˈfeznt/ n fagiano m

phenomen|al /fɪˈnɒmɪnl/ a fenomenale; (incredible) incredibile. ~**ally** adv incredibilmente. ~**on** n (pl -na) fenomeno m

philanderer /fɪˈlændərə(r)/ n donnaiolo m

philanthrop|ic /fɪlənˈθrɒpɪk/ a filantropico. ~**ist** /fɪˈlænθrəpɪst/ n filantropo, -a mf

philatel|y /fɪˈlætəlɪ/ n filatelia f. ~**ist** n filatelico, -a mf

philharmonic /fɪlhɑːˈmɒnɪk/ n (orchestra) orchestra f filarmonica ● a filarmonico

Philippines /ˈfɪlɪpiːnz/ npl Filippine fpl

philistine /ˈfɪlɪstaɪn/ n filisteo, -a mf

philosoph|er /fɪˈlɒsəfə(r)/ n filosofo, -a mf. ~**ical** /fɪləˈsɒfɪkl/ a filosofico. ~**ically** adv con filosofia. ~**y** n filosofia f

phlegm /flem/ n Med flemma f

phlegmatic /flegˈmætɪk/ a flemmatico

phobia /ˈfəʊbɪə/ n fobia f

phone /fəʊn/ n telefono m; **be on the** ~ avere il telefono; (be phoning) essere al telefono ● vt telefonare a ● vi telefonare. **phone back** vt/i richiamare. ~**book** n guida f del telefono. ~ **box** n cabina f telefonica. ~ **card** n scheda f telefonica. ~ **call** telefonata f. ~-**in** n trasmissione f con chiamate in diretta. ~**number** n numero m telefonico

phonetic /fəˈnetɪk/ a fonetico. ~**s** n fonetica f

phoney /ˈfəʊnɪ/ a (-ier, -iest) fasullo

phosphorus /ˈfɒsfərəs/ n fosforo m

photo /ˈfəʊtəʊ/ n foto f. ~ **album** album m inv di fotografie. ~-**copier** n fotocopiatrice f. ~-**copy** n fotocopia f ● vt fotocopiare

photogenic /fəʊtəʊˈdʒenɪk/ a fotogenico

photograph /ˈfəʊtəgrɑːf/ n fotografia f ● vt fotografare

photograph|er /fəˈtɒgrəfə(r)/ n fotografo, -a mf. ~**ic** /fəʊtəˈgræfɪk/ a fotografico. ~**y** n fotografia f

phrase /freɪz/ n espressione f ● vt esprimere. ~-**book** n libro m di fraseologia

physical /ˈfɪzɪkl/ *a* fisico. ~ **edu'cation** *n* educazione *f* fisica. ~**ly** *adv* fisicamente

physician /fɪˈzɪʃn/ *n* medico *m*

physic|ist /ˈfɪzɪsɪst/ *n* fisico, -a *mf*. ~ *n* fisica *f*

physiology /fɪzɪˈɒlədʒɪ/ *n* fisiologia *f*

physio'therap|ist /fɪzɪəʊ-/ *n* fisioterapista *mf*. ~**y** *n* fisioterapia *f*

physique /fɪˈziːk/ *n* fisico *m*

pianist /ˈpɪənɪst/ *n* pianista *mf*

piano /pɪˈænəʊ/ *n* piano *m*

pick[1] /pɪk/ *n* (tool) piccone *m*

pick[2] *n* scelta *f*; **take your** ~ prendi quello che vuoi ●*vt* (select) scegliere; cogliere (flowers); scassinare (lock); borseggiare (pockets); ~ **and choose** fare il difficile; ~ **one's nose** mettersi le dita nel naso; ~ **a quarrel** attaccar briga; ~ **holes in** fam criticare; ~ **at one's food** spilluzzicare. **pick on** *vt* (fam: nag) assillare; **he always ~s on me** ce l'ha con me. **pick out** *vt* (identify) individuare. **pick up** *vt* sollevare; (off the ground, information) raccogliere; prendere in braccio (baby); (learn) imparare; prendersi (illness); (buy) comprare; captare (signal); (collect) andare/venire a prendere; prendere (passengers, habit); (police:) arrestare (criminal); fam rimorchiare (girl); ~ **oneself up** riprendersi ●*vi* (improve) recuperare; (weather:) rimettersi

'pickaxe *n* piccone *m*

picket /ˈpɪkɪt/ *n* picchettista *mf* ●*vt* picchettare. ~ **line** *n* picchetto *m*

pickle /ˈpɪkl/ *n* ~**s** *pl* sottaceti *mpl*. **in a** ~ *fig* nei pasticci ●*vt* mettere sottaceto

pick: ~**pocket** *n* borsaiolo *m*. ~**-up** *n* (truck) furgone *m*; (on record-player) pickup *m inv*

picnic /ˈpɪknɪk/ *n* picnic *m* ●*vi* (pt/pp **-nicked**) fare un picnic

picture /ˈpɪktʃə(r)/ *n* (painting) quadro *m*; (photo) fotografia *f*; (drawing) disegno *m*; (film) film *m inv*; **put sb in the** ~ *fig* mettere qcno al corrente; **the** ~**s** il cinema ●*vt* (imagine) immaginare

picturesque /pɪktʃəˈresk/ *a* pittoresco

pie /paɪ/ *n* torta *f*

piece /piːs/ *n* pezzo *m*; (in game) pedina *f*; **a** ~ **of bread/paper** un pezzo di pane/carta; **a** ~ **of news/advice** una notizia/un consiglio; **take to ~s** smontare. ~**meal** *adv* un po' alla volta.

~**work** *n* lavoro *m* a cottimo ● **piece together** *vt* montare; *fig* ricostruire

pier /pɪə(r)/ *n* molo *m*; (pillar) pilastro *m*

pierc|e /pɪəs/ *vt* perforare; ~**e a hole in sth** fare un buco in qcsa. ~**ing** *a* penetrante

pig /pɪg/ *n* maiale *m*

pigeon /ˈpɪdʒɪn/ *n* piccione *m*. ~**-hole** *n* casella *f*

piggy /ˈpɪgɪ/ ~**back** *n* **give sb a** ~**back** portare qcno sulle spalle. ~**bank** *n* salvadanaio *m*

pig'headed *a* fam cocciuto

pig: ~**skin** *n* pelle *f* di cinghiale. ~**tail** *n* (plait) treccina *f*

pile /paɪl/ *n* (heap) pila *f* ●*vt* ~ **sth on to sth** appilare qcsa su qcsa. **pile up** *vt* accatastare ●*vi* ammucchiarsi

piles /paɪlz/ *npl* emorroidi *fpl*

'pile-up *n* tamponamento *m* a catena

pilfering /ˈpɪlfərɪŋ/ *n* piccoli furti *mpl*

pilgrim /ˈpɪlgrɪm/ *n* pellegrino, -a *mf*. ~**age** /-ɪdʒ/ *n* pellegrinaggio *m*

pill /pɪl/ *n* pillola *f*

pillage /ˈpɪlɪdʒ/ *vt* saccheggiare

pillar /ˈpɪlə(r)/ *n* pilastro *m*. ~**-box** *n* buca *f* delle lettere

pillion /ˈpɪljən/ *n* sellino *m* posteriore; **ride** ~ viaggiare dietro

pillory /ˈpɪlərɪ/ *vt* (pt/pp **-ied**) *fig* mettere alla berlina

pillow /ˈpɪləʊ/ *n* guanciale *m*. ~**case** *n* federa *f*

pilot /ˈpaɪlət/ *n* pilota *mf* ●*vt* pilotare. ~**-light** *n* fiamma *f* di sicurezza

pimp /pɪmp/ *n* protettore *m*

pimple /ˈpɪmpl/ *n* foruncolo *m*

pin /pɪn/ *n* spillo *m*; Electr spinotto *m*; Med chiodo *m*; **I have ~s and needles in my leg** fam mi formicola una gamba ●*vt* (pt/pp **pinned**) appuntare (**to** on su); (sewing) fissare con gli spilli; (hold down) immobilizzare; ~ **sb down to a date** ottenere un appuntamento da qcno; ~ **sth on sb** fam addossare a qcno la colpa di qcsa. **pin up** *vt* appuntare; (on wall) affiggere

pinafore /ˈpɪnəfɔː(r)/ *n* grembiule *m*. ~ **dress** *n* scamiciato *m*

pincers /ˈpɪnsəz/ *npl* tenaglie *fpl*

pinch /pɪntʃ/ *n* pizzicotto *m*; (of salt) presa *f*; **at a** ~ fam in caso di bisogno ●*vt* pizzicare; (fam: steal) fregare ●*vi* (shoe:) stringere

'pincushion *n* puntaspilli *m inv*

pine[1] /paɪn/ *n* (tree) pino *m*

pine[2] *vi* **she is pining for you** le manchi molto. **pine away** *vi* deperire

pineapple /'paɪn-/ *n* ananas *m inv*

ping /pɪŋ/ *n* rumore *m* metallico

'ping-pong *n* ping-pong *m*

pink /pɪŋk/ *a* rosa *inv*

pinnacle /'pɪnəkl/ *n* guglia *f*

PIN number *n* codice *m* segreto

pin: ~**point** *vt* definire con precisione.
~**stripe** *a* gessato

pint /paɪnt/ *n* pinta *f* (= 0,571, Am: 0,47
l); **a** ~ *fam* una birra media

'pin-up *n* ragazza *f* da copertina,
pin-up *f inv*

pioneer /paɪə'nɪə(r)/ *n* pioniere, -a *mf*
● *vt* essere un pioniere di

pious /'paɪəs/ *a* pio

pip /pɪp/ *n* (*seed*) seme *m*

pipe /paɪp/ *n* tubo *m*; (*for smoking*) pipa
f; **the** ~**s** *Mus* la cornamusa ● *vt* far arrivare con tubature (*water, gas etc*).
pipe down *vi fam* abbassare la voce

pipe: ~**-cleaner** *n* scovolino *m*.
~**-dream** *n* illusione *f*. ~**line** *n*
conduttura *f*; **in the** ~**line** *fam* in cantiere

piper /'paɪpə(r)/ *n* suonatore *m* di cornamusa

piping /'paɪpɪŋ/ *a* ~ **hot** bollente

pirate /'paɪrət/ *n* pirata *m*

Pisces /'paɪsiːz/ *n Astr* Pesci *mpl*

piss /pɪs/ *vi sl* pisciare

pistol /'pɪstl/ *n* pistola *f*

piston /'pɪstn/ *n Techn* pistone *m*

pit /pɪt/ *n* fossa *f*; (*mine*) miniera *f*; (*for
orchestra*) orchestra *f* ● *vt* (*pt/pp
pitted*) *fig* opporre (**against** a)

pitch¹ /pɪtʃ/ *n* (*tone*) tono *m*; (*level*) altezza *f*; (*in sport*) campo *m*; (*fig: degree*)
grado *m* ● *vt* montare (*tent*). **pitch in** *vi
fam* mettersi sotto

pitch² *n* ~**-black** *a* nero come la pece.
~**-dark** *a* buio pesto

'pitchfork *n* forca *f*

piteous /'pɪtɪəs/ *a* pietoso

'pitfall *n fig* trabocchetto *m*

pith /pɪθ/ *n* (*of lemon, orange*) interno
m della buccia

pithy /'pɪθɪ/ *a* (**-ier, -iest**) *fig* conciso

piti|ful /'pɪtɪfl/ *a* pietoso. ~**less** *a* spie-
tato

pittance /'pɪtns/ *n* miseria *f*

pity /'pɪtɪ/ *n* pietà *f*; [**what a**] ~! che
peccato!; **take** ~ **on** avere compassione
di ● *vt* aver pietà di

pivot /'pɪvət/ *n* perno *m*; *fig* fulcro *m*
● *vi* imperniarsi (**on** su)

pizza /'piːtsə/ *n* pizza *f*

placard /'plækɑːd/ *n* cartellone *m*

placate /plə'keɪt/ *vt* placare

place /pleɪs/ *n* posto *m*; (*fam: house*)
casa *f*; (*in book*) segno *m*; **feel out of** ~
sentirsi fuori posto; **take** ~ aver luogo;
all over the ~ dappertutto ● *vt* collocare; (*remember*) identificare; ~ **an
order** fare un'ordinazione; **be** ~**d** (*in
race*) piazzarsi. ~**-mat** *n* sottopiatto *m*

placid /'plæsɪd/ *a* placido

plagiar|ism /'pleɪdʒərɪzm/ *n* plagio *m*.
~**ize** *vt* plagiare

plague /pleɪg/ *n* peste *f*

plaice /pleɪs/ *n inv* platessa *f*

plain /pleɪn/ *a* chiaro; (*simple*) semplice; (*not pretty*) scialbo; (*not patterned*)
normale; (*chocolate*) fondente; **in** ~
clothes in borghese ● *adv* (*simply*)
semplicemente ● *n* pianura *f*. ~**ly** *adv*
francamente; (*simply*) semplicemente;
(*obviously*) chiaramente

plaintiff /'pleɪntɪf/ *n Jur* parte *f* lesa

plaintive /'pleɪntɪv/ *a* lamentoso

plait /plæt/ *n* treccia *f* ● *vt* intrecciare

plan /plæn/ *n* progetto *m*, piano *m* ● *vt*
(*pt/pp* **planned**) progettare; (*intend*)
prevedere

plane¹ /pleɪn/ *n* (*tree*) platano *m*

plane² *n* aeroplano *m*

plane³ *n* (*tool*) pialla *f* ● *vt* piallare

planet /'plænɪt/ *n* pianeta *m*

plank /plæŋk/ *n* asse *f*

planning /'plænɪŋ/ *n* pianificazione *f*.
~ **permission** *n* licenza *f* edilizia

plant /plɑːnt/ *n* pianta *f*; (*machinery*)
impianto *m*; (*factory*) stabilimento *m*
● *vt* piantare. ~**ation** /plæn'teɪʃn/ *n*
piantagione *f*

plaque /plɑːk/ *n* placca *f*

plasma /'plæzmə/ *n* plasma *f*

plaster /'plɑːstə(r)/ *n* intonaco *m*; *Med*
gesso *m*; (*sticking* ~) cerotto *m*; ~ **of
Paris** gesso *m* ● *vt* intonacare (*wall*);
(*cover*) ricoprire. ~**ed** *a sl* sbronzo. ~**er**
n intonacatore *m*

plastic /'plæstɪk/ *n* plastica *f* ● *a* pla-
stico

Plasticine® /'plæstɪsiːn/ *n* plastilina® *f*

plastic: ~ **'surgeon** *n* chirurgo *m* pla-
stico. ~ **surgery** *n* chirurgia *f* plastica

plate /pleɪt/ *n* piatto *m*; (*flat sheet*) placca *f*; (*gold and silverware*) argenteria *f*;
(*in book*) tavola *f* [fuori testo] ● *vt*
(*cover with metal*) placcare

plateau /'plætəʊ/ *n* (*pl* ~**x** /-əʊz/)
altopiano *m*

platform /'plætfɔːm/ *n* (*stage*) palco *m*;
Rail marciapiede *m*; *Pol* piattaforma *f*;
~ **5** binario 5

platinum /ˈplætɪnəm/ n platino m ● a di platino

platitude /ˈplætɪtjuːd/ n luogo m comune

platonic /pləˈtɒnɪk/ a platonico

platoon /pləˈtuːn/ n Mil plotone m

platter /ˈplætə(r)/ n piatto m da portata

plausible /ˈplɔːzəbl/ a plausibile

play /pleɪ/ n gioco m; *Theat, TV* rappresentazione f; *Radio* sceneggiato m radiofonico; ~ **on words** gioco m di parole ● vt giocare a; (*act*) recitare; suonare (*instrument*); giocare (*card*) ● vi giocare; *Mus* suonare; ~ **safe** non prendere rischi. **play down** vt minimizzare. **play up** vi fam fare i capricci

play: ~**boy** n playboy m inv. ~**er** n giocatore, -trice mf. ~**ful** a scherzoso. ~**ground** n Sch cortile m (per la ricreazione). ~**group** n asilo m

playing: ~-**card** n carta f da gioco. ~-**field** n campo m da gioco

play: ~**mate** n compagno, -a mf di gioco. ~-**pen** n box m inv. ~**thing** n giocattolo m. ~**wright** /-raɪt/ n drammaturgo, -a mf

plc n abbr (**public limited company**) s.r.l.

plea /pliː/ n richiesta f; **make a ~ for** fare un appello a

plead /pliːd/ vi fare appello (**for** a); ~ **guilty** dichiararsi colpevole; ~ **with sb** implorare qcno

pleasant /ˈplez(ə)nt/ a piacevole. ~**ly** adv piacevolmente; (*say, smile*) cordialmente

pleas|e /pliːz/ adv per favore; ~**e do** prego ● vt far contento; ~**e oneself** fare il proprio comodo; ~**e yourself!** come vuoi!; *pej* fai come ti pare!. ~**ed** a lieto; ~**ed with/about** contento di. ~**ing** a gradevole

pleasurable /ˈpleʒərəbl/ a gradevole

pleasure /ˈpleʒə(r)/ n piacere m; **with** ~ con piacere, volentieri

pleat /pliːt/ n piega f ● vt pieghettare. ~**ed 'skirt** n gonna f a pieghe

pledge /pledʒ/ n pegno m; (*promise*) promessa f ● vt impegnarsi a; (*pawn*) impegnare

plentiful /ˈplentɪfl/ a abbondante

plenty /ˈplentɪ/ n abbondanza f; ~ **of money** molti soldi; ~ **of people** molta gente; **I've got** ~ ne ho in abbondanza

pliable /ˈplaɪəbl/ a flessibile

pliers /ˈplaɪəz/ npl pinze fpl

plight /plaɪt/ n condizione f

plimsolls /ˈplɪmsəlz/ npl scarpe fpl da ginnastica

plinth /plɪnθ/ n plinto m

plod /plɒd/ vi (pt/pp **plodded**) trascinarsi; (*work hard*) sgobbare

plonk /plɒŋk/ n fam vino m mediocre

plot /plɒt/ n complotto m; (*of novel*) trama f; ~ **of land** appezzamento m [di terreno] ● vt/i (pt/pp **plotted**) complottare

plough /plaʊ/ n aratro m ● vt/i arare. **plough back** vt Comm reinvestire

ploy /plɔɪ/ n fam manovra f

pluck /plʌk/ n fegato m ● vt strappare; depilare (*eyebrows*); spennare (*bird*); cogliere (*flower*). **pluck up** vt ~ **up courage** farsi coraggio

plucky /ˈplʌkɪ/ a (-**ier**, -**iest**) coraggioso

plug /plʌg/ n tappo m; *Electr* spina f; *Auto* candela f; (*fam: advertisement*) pubblicità f inv ● vt (pt/pp **plugged**) tappare; (*fam: advertise*) pubblicizzare con insistenza. **plug in** vt Electr inserire la spina di

plum /plʌm/ n prugna f; (*tree*) prugno m

plumage /ˈpluːmɪdʒ/ n piumaggio m

plumb /plʌm/ a verticale ● adv esattamente ● **plumb in** vt collegare

plumb|er /ˈplʌmə(r)/ n idraulico m. ~**ing** n impianto m idraulico

'plumb-line n filo m a piombo

plume /pluːm/ n piuma f

plummet /ˈplʌmɪt/ vi precipitare

plump /plʌmp/ a paffuto ● **plump for** vt scegliere

plunge /plʌndʒ/ n tuffo m; **take the** ~ fam buttarsi ● vt tuffare; fig sprofondare ● vi tuffarsi

plunging /ˈplʌndʒɪŋ/ a (*neckline*) profondo

plu'perfect /pluː-/ n trapassato m prossimo

plural /ˈplʊərəl/ a plurale ● n plurale m

plus /plʌs/ prep più ● a in più; **500** ~ più di 500 ● n più m; (*advantage*) extra m inv

plush /plʌʃ[ɪ]/ a lussuoso

plutonium /pluːˈtəʊnɪəm/ n plutonio m

ply /plaɪ/ vt (pt/pp **plied**) ~ **sb with drink** continuare a offrire da bere a qcno. ~**wood** n compensato m

p.m. abbr (**post meridiem**) del pomeriggio

PM n abbr **Prime Minister**

pneumatic /njuːˈmætɪk/ a pneumatico. ~ **drill** n martello m pneumatico

pneumonia /njuːˈməʊnɪə/ n polmonite f

P.O. abbr Post Office

poach /pəʊtʃ/ vt Culin bollire; cacciare di frodo ⟨deer⟩; pescare di frodo ⟨salmon⟩; ~**ed egg** uovo m in camicia. ~**er** n bracconiere m

pocket /ˈpɒkɪt/ n tasca f; **be out of** ~ rimetterci ● vt intascare. ~**-book** n taccuino m; ⟨wallet⟩ portafoglio m. ~**-money** n denaro m per le piccole spese

pod /pɒd/ n baccello m

podgy /ˈpɒdʒɪ/ a (**-ier, -iest**) grassoccio

poem /ˈpəʊɪm/ n poesia f

poet /ˈpəʊɪt/ n poeta m. ~**ic** /ˈetɪk/ a poetico

poetry /ˈpəʊɪtrɪ/ n poesia f

poignant /ˈpɔɪnjənt/ a emozionante

point /pɔɪnt/ n punto m; ⟨sharp end⟩ punta f; ⟨meaning, purpose⟩ senso m; Electr presa f [di corrente]; ~**s** pl Rail scambio m; ~ **of view** punto m di vista; **good/bad** ~**s** aspetti mpl positivi/negativi; **what is the** ~? a che scopo?; **the** ~ **is** il fatto è; **I don't see the** ~ non vedo il senso; **up to a** ~ fino a un certo punto; **be on the** ~ **of doing sth** essere sul punto di fare qcsa ● vt puntare (**at verso**) ● vi ⟨with finger⟩ puntare il dito; ~ **at/to** ⟨person:⟩ mostrare col dito; ⟨indicator:⟩ indicare. **point out** vt far notare qcsa a qcno

point-blank a a bruciapelo

pointed /ˈpɔɪntɪd/ a appuntito; ⟨question⟩ diretto. ~**ers** npl ⟨advice⟩ consigli mpl. ~**less** a inutile

poise /pɔɪz/ n padronanza f. ~**d** a in equilibrio; ~**d to** sul punto di

poison /ˈpɔɪzn/ n veleno m ● vt avvelenare. ~**ous** a velenoso

poke /pəʊk/ n [piccola] spinta f ● vt spingere; ⟨fire⟩ attizzare; ⟨put⟩ ficcare; ~ **fun at** prendere in giro. **poke about** vi frugare

poker[1] /ˈpəʊkə(r)/ n attizzatoio m

poker[2] n ⟨card game⟩ poker m

poky /ˈpəʊkɪ/ a (**-ier, -iest**) angusto

Poland /ˈpəʊlənd/ n Polonia f

polar /ˈpəʊlə(r)/ a polare. ~ **bear** n orso m bianco. ~**ize** vt polarizzare

Pole /pəʊl/ n polacco, -a mf

pole[1] n palo m

pole[2] n Geog, Electr polo m

'pole-star n stella f polare

'pole-vault n salto m con l'asta

police /pəˈliːs/ npl polizia f ● vt pattugliare ⟨area⟩

police: ~**man** n poliziotto m. ~ **state** n stato m militarista. ~ **station** n commissariato m. ~**woman** n donna f poliziotto

policy[1] /ˈpɒlɪsɪ/ n politica f

policy[2] n ⟨insurance⟩ polizza f

polio /ˈpəʊlɪəʊ/ n polio f

Polish /ˈpəʊlɪʃ/ a polacco ● n ⟨language⟩ polacco m

polish /ˈpɒlɪʃ/ n ⟨shine⟩ lucentezza f; ⟨substance⟩ lucido m; ⟨for nails⟩ smalto m; fig raffinatezza f ● vt lucidare; fig smussare. **polish off** vt fam finire; far fuori ⟨food⟩

polished /ˈpɒlɪʃt/ a ⟨manner⟩ raffinato; ⟨performance⟩ senza sbavature

polite /pəˈlaɪt/ a cortese. ~**ly** adv cortesemente. ~**ness** n cortesia f

politic /ˈpɒlɪtɪk/ a prudente

political /pəˈlɪtɪkl/ a politico. ~**ally** adv dal punto di vista politico. ~**ian** /pɒlɪˈtɪʃn/ n politico m

politics /ˈpɒlɪtɪks/ n politica f

poll /pəʊl/ n votazione f; ⟨election⟩ elezioni fpl; |**opinion**| ~ sondaggio m d'opinione; **go to the** ~**s** andare alle urne ● vt ottenere ⟨votes⟩

pollen /ˈpɒlən/ n polline m

polling /ˈpəʊlɪŋ/: ~**-booth** n cabina f elettorale. ~**-station** n seggio m elettorale

'poll tax n imposta f locale sulle persone fisiche

pollutant /pəˈluːtənt/ n sostanza f inquinante

pollute /pəˈluːt/ vt inquinare. ~**ion** /-ʃn/ n inquinamento m

polo /ˈpəʊləʊ/ n polo m. ~**-neck** n collo m alto. ~ **shirt** n dolcevita f

polyester /pɒlɪˈestə(r)/ n poliestere m

polystyrene® /pɒlɪˈstaɪriːn/ n polistirolo m

polytechnic /pɒlɪˈteknɪk/ n politecnico m

polythene /ˈpɒlɪθiːn/ n politene m. ~ **bag** n sacchetto m di plastica

polyun'saturated a polinsaturo

pomegranate /ˈpɒmɪɡrænɪt/ n melagrana f

pomp /pɒmp/ n pompa f

pompon /ˈpɒmpɒn/ n pompon m

pompous /ˈpɒmpəs/ a pomposo

pond /pɒnd/ n stagno m

ponder /ˈpɒndə(r)/ vt/i ponderare

pong /pɒŋ/ n fam puzzo m

pontiff /ˈpɒntɪf/ n pontefice m

pony /ˈpəʊnɪ/ n pony m inv. **~-tail** n
coda f di cavallo. **~-trekking** n escursioni fpl col pony

poodle /ˈpuːdl/ n barboncino m

pool[1] /puːl/ n (of water, blood) pozza f.
[swimming] ~ piscina f

pool[2] n (common fund) cassa f comune;
(in cards) piatto m; (game) biliardo m a
buca. **~s** npl ≈ totocalcio msg ● vt mettere insieme

poor /pʊə(r)/ a povero; (not good) scadente; **in ~ health** in cattiva salute
● npl **the ~** i poveri. **~ly** a **be ~ly** non
stare bene ● adv male

pop[1] /pɒp/ n botto m; (drink) bibita f
gasata ● v (pt/pp popped) ● vt (fam:
put) mettere; (burst) far scoppiare ● vi
(burst) scoppiare. **pop in out** vi fare
un salto/un salto fuori

pop[2] n fam musica f pop ● attrib pop
inv

popcorn /ˈpɒpkɔːn/ n popcorn m inv

pope /pəʊp/ n papa m

poplar /ˈpɒplə(r)/ n pioppo m

poppy /ˈpɒpɪ/ n papavero m

popular /ˈpɒpjʊlə(r)/ a popolare;
(belief) diffuso. **~ity** /-ˈlærətɪ/ n popolarità f

populate /ˈpɒpjʊleɪt/ vt popolare.
~ion /-ˈleɪʃn/ n popolazione f

porcelain /ˈpɔːsəlɪn/ n porcellana f

porch /pɔːtʃ/ n portico m; Am veranda f

porcupine /ˈpɔːkjʊpaɪn/ n porcospino m

pore[1] /pɔː(r)/ n poro m

pore[2] vi **~ over** immergersi in

pork /pɔːk/ n carne f di maiale

porn /pɔːn/ n fam porno m. **~o** a fam
porno inv

pornograph|ic /pɔːnəˈgræfɪk/ a pornografico. **~y** /-ˈnɒgrəfɪ/ n pornografia f

porous /ˈpɔːrəs/ a poroso

porpoise /ˈpɔːpəs/ n focena f

porridge /ˈpɒrɪdʒ/ n farinata f di fiocchi d'avena

port[1] /pɔːt/ n porto m

port[2] n (Naut: side) babordo m

port[3] n (wine) porto m

portable /ˈpɔːtəbl/ a portatile

porter /ˈpɔːtə(r)/ n portiere m; (for
luggage) facchino m

portfolio /pɔːtˈfəʊlɪəʊ/ n cartella f;
Comm portafoglio m

porthole n oblò m inv

portion /ˈpɔːʃn/ n parte f; (of food) porzione f

portly /ˈpɔːtlɪ/ a (-ier, -iest) corpulento

portrait /ˈpɔːtrɪt/ n ritratto m

portray /pɔːˈtreɪ/ vt ritrarre;
(represent) descrivere; (actor:) impersonare. **~al** n ritratto m

Portug|al /ˈpɔːtjʊgl/ n Portogallo m.
~uese /-ˈgiːz/ a portoghese ● n portoghese mf; (language) portoghese m

pose /pəʊz/ n posa f ● vt porre
(problem, question) ● vi (for painter)
posare; ~ **as** atteggiarsi a

posh /pɒʃ/ a fam lussuoso; (people)
danaroso

position /pəˈzɪʃn/ n posizione f; (job)
posto m; (status) ceto m [sociale] ● vt
posizionare

positive /ˈpɒzɪtɪv/ a positivo; (certain)
sicuro; (progress) concreto ● n positivo
m. **~ly** adv positivamente; (decidedly)
decisamente

possess /pəˈzes/ vt possedere. **~ion**
/pəˈzeʃn/ n possesso m; **~ions** pl beni
mpl

possess|ive /pəˈzesɪv/ a possessivo.
~iveness n carattere m possessivo.
~or n possessore, -ditrice mf

possibility /pɒsəˈbɪlətɪ/ n possibilità f
inv

possib|le /ˈpɒsəbl/ a possibile. **~ly** adv
possibilmente; **I couldn't ~ly accept**
non mi è possibile accettare; **he can't
~ly be right** non è possibile che abbia
ragione; **could you ~ly...?** potrebbe
per favore...?

post[1] /pəʊst/ n (pole) palo m ● vt affiggere (notice)

post[2] n (place of duty) posto m ● vt appostare; (transfer) assegnare

post[3] n (mail) posta f; **by ~** per posta
● vt spedire; (put in letter-box) imbucare; (as opposed to fax) mandare per posta; **keep sb ~ed** tenere qcno al corrente

post- pref dopo

postage /ˈpəʊstɪdʒ/ n affrancatura f. **~
stamp** n francobollo m

postal /ˈpəʊstl/ a postale. **~ order** n
vaglia m inv postale

post: **~-box** n cassetta f delle lettere.
~card n cartolina f. **~code** n codice m
postale. **~-date** vt postdatare

poster /ˈpəʊstə(r)/ n poster m inv;
(advertising, election) cartellone m

posterior /pɒˈstɪərɪə(r)/ n fam posteriore m

posterity /pɒˈsterətɪ/ n posterità f

posthumous /ˈpɒstjʊməs/ a postumo.
~ly adv dopo la morte

post: ~**man** n postino m. ~**mark** n timbro m postale

post-mortem /-'mɔːtəm/ n autopsia f

'post office n ufficio m postale

postpone /pəʊst'pəʊn/ vt rimandare. ~**ment** n rinvio m

posture /'pɒstʃə(r)/ n posizione f

post-'war a del dopoguerra

pot /pɒt/ n vaso m; (for tea) teiera f; (for coffee) caffettiera f; (for cooking) pentola f; ~**s of money** fam un sacco di soldi; **go to** ~ fam andare in malora

potassium /pə'tæsɪəm/ n potassio m

potato /pə'teɪtəʊ/ n (pl -es) patata f

poten|t /'pəʊtənt/ a potente. ~**tate** n potentato m

potential /pə'tenʃl/ a potenziale ●n potenziale m. ~**ly** adv potenzialmente

pot: ~**-hole** n cavità f inv; (in road) buca f. ~**-holer** n speleologo, -a mf. ~**-luck** n take ~**-luck** affidarsi alla sorte. ~ **'plant** n pianta f da appartamento. ~**-shot** n take a ~**-shot at** sparare a casaccio a

potted /'pɒtɪd/ a conservato; (shortened) condensato. ~ **'plant** n pianta f da appartamento

potter[1] /'pɒtə(r)/ vi ~ [about] gingillarsi

potter[2] n vasaio, -a mf. ~**y** n lavorazione f della ceramica; (articles) ceramiche fpl; (place) laboratorio m di ceramiche

potty /'pɒtɪ/ a (-ier, -iest) fam matto ●n vasino m

pouch /paʊtʃ/ n marsupio m

pouffe /puːf/ n pouf m inv

poultry /'pəʊltrɪ/ n pollame m

pounce /paʊns/ vi balzare; ~ **on** saltare su

pound[1] /paʊnd/ n libbra f (= 0,454 kg); (money) sterlina f

pound[2] vt battere ●vi (heart:) battere forte; (run heavily) correre pesantemente

pour /pɔː(r)/ vt versare ●vi riversarsi; (with rain) piovere a dirotto. **pour out** vi riversarsi fuori ●vt versare (drink); sfogare (troubles)

pout /paʊt/ vi fare il broncio ●n broncio m

poverty /'pɒvətɪ/ n povertà f

powder /'paʊdə(r)/ n polvere f; (cosmetic) cipria f ●vt polverizzare; (face) incipriare. ~**y** a polveroso

power /'paʊə(r)/ n potere m; Electr corrente f [elettrica]; Math potenza f. ~ **cut** n interruzione f di corrente. ~**ed** a ~**ed by electricity** dotato di corrente

[elettrica]. ~**ful** a potente. ~**less** a impotente. ~**-station** n centrale f elettrica

PR n abbr **public relations**

practicable /'præktɪkəbl/ a praticabile

practical /'præktɪkl/ a pratico. ~ **'joke** n burla f. ~**ly** adv praticamente

practice /'præktɪs/ n pratica f; (custom) usanza f; (habit) abitudine f; (exercise) esercizio m; Sport allenamento m; **in** ~ (in reality) in pratica; **out of** ~ fuori esercizio; **put into** ~ mettere in pratica

practise /'præktɪs/ vt fare pratica in; (carry out) mettere in pratica; esercitare (profession) ●vi esercitarsi; (doctor:) praticare. ~**d** a esperto

pragmatic /præg'mætɪk/ a pragmatico

praise /preɪz/ n lode f ●vt lodare. ~**worthy** a lodevole

pram /præm/ n carrozzella f

prance /prɑːns/ vi saltellare

prank /præŋk/ n tiro m

prattle /'prætl/ vi parlottare

prawn /prɔːn/ n gambero m. ~ **'cocktail** n cocktail m inv di gamberetti

pray /preɪ/ vi pregare. ~**er** n /preə(r)/ n preghiera f

preach /priːtʃ/ vt/i predicare. ~**er** n predicatore, -trice mf

preamble /priː'æmbl/ n preambolo m

pre-ar'range /priː-/ vt predisporre

precarious /prɪ'keərɪəs/ a precario. ~**ly** adv in modo precario

precaution /prɪ'kɔːʃn/ n precauzione f; **as a** ~ per precauzione. ~**ary** a preventivo

precede /prɪ'siːd/ vt precedere

preceden|ce /'presɪdəns/ n precedenza f. ~**t** n precedente m

preceding /prɪ'siːdɪŋ/ a precedente

precinct /'priːsɪŋkt/ n (traffic-free) zona f pedonale; (Am: district) circoscrizione f

precious /'preʃəs/ a prezioso; (style) ricercato ●adv fam ~ **little** ben poco

precipice /'presɪpɪs/ n precipizio m

precipitate /prɪ'sɪpɪteɪt/ vt precipitare

précis /'preɪsiː/ n (pl précis /-siːz/) sunto m

precis|e /prɪ'saɪs/ a preciso. ~**ely** adv precisamente. ~**ion** /-'sɪʒn/ n precisione f

precursor /priː'kɜːsə(r)/ n precursore m

predator /'predətə(r)/ n predatore, -trice mf. ~**y** a rapace

413

predecessor /'pri:dɪsesə(r)/ n predecessore, -a mf

predicament /prɪ'dɪkəmənt/ n situazione f difficile

predicat|e /'predɪkət/ n Gram predicato m. **~ive** /prɪ'dɪkətɪv/ a predicativo

predict /prɪ'dɪkt/ vt predire. **~able** /-əbl/ a prevedibile. **~ion** /-'dɪkʃn/ n previsione f

pre'domin|ant /prɪ-/ a predominante. **~ate** vi predominare

pre-'eminent /prɪ-/ a preminente

preen /pri:n/ vt lisciarsi; **~** oneself fig farsi bello

pre|'fab /'pri:fæb/ n fam casa f prefabbricata. **~'fabricated** a prefabbricato

preface /'prefɪs/ n prefazione f

prefect /'pri:fekt/ n Sch studente, -tessa mf della scuola superiore con responsabilità disciplinari ecc

prefer /prɪ'fɜ:(r)/ vt (pt/pp **preferred**) preferire

prefera|ble /'prefərəbl/ a preferibile (to a). **~bly** adv preferibilmente

preferen|ce /'prefərəns/ n preferenza f. **~tial** /-'renʃl/ a preferenziale

prefix /'pri:fɪks/ n prefisso m

pregnan|cy /'pregnənsɪ/ n gravidanza f. **~t** a incinta

prehi'storic /pri:-/ a preistorico

prejudice /'predʒʊdɪs/ n pregiudizio m ●vt influenzare (against contro); (harm) danneggiare. **~d** a prevenuto

preliminary /prɪ'lɪmɪnərɪ/ a preliminare

prelude /'prelju:d/ n preludio m

pre-'marital a prematrimoniale

premature /'premətjʊə(r)/ a prematuro

pre'meditated /pri:-/ a premeditato

premier /'premɪə(r)/ a primario ●n Pol primo ministro m, premier m inv

première /'premɪeə(r)/ n prima f

premises /'premɪsɪz/ npl locali mpl; on the **~** sul posto

premium /'pri:mɪəm/ n premio m; **be at a ~** essere una cosa rara

premonition /premə'nɪʃn/ n presentimento m

preoccupied /pri:'ɒkjʊpaɪd/ a preoccupato

prep /prep/ n Sch compiti mpl

preparation /prepə'reɪʃn/ n preparazione f. **~s** pl preparativi mpl

preparatory /prɪ'pærətrɪ/ a preparatorio ●adv **~ to** per

prepare /prɪ'peə(r)/ vt preparare ●vi prepararsi (for per); **~d to** disposto a

pre'pay /pri:-/ vt (pt/pp -paid) pagare in anticipo

preposition /prepə'zɪʃn/ n preposizione f

prepossessing /pri:pə'zesɪŋ/ a attraente

preposterous /prɪ'pɒstərəs/ a assurdo

prerequisite /pri:'rekwɪzɪt/ n condizione f sine qua non

prescribe /prɪ'skraɪb/ vt prescrivere

prescription /prɪ'skrɪpʃn/ n Med ricetta f

presence /'prezns/ n presenza f; **~** of mind presenza f di spirito

present¹ /'preznt/ a presente ●n presente m; **at ~** attualmente

present² n (gift) regalo m; **give sb sth as a ~** regalare qcsa a qcno

present³ /prɪ'zent/ vt presentare; **~ sb with an award** consegnare un premio a qcno. **~able** /-əbl/ a **be ~able** essere presentabile

presentation /prezn'teɪʃn/ n presentazione f

presently /'prezntlɪ/ adv fra poco; (Am: now) attualmente

preservation /prezə'veɪʃn/ n conservazione f

preservative /prɪ'zɜ:vətɪv/ n conservante m

preserve /prɪ'zɜ:v/ vt preservare; (maintain, Culin) conservare ●n (in hunting & fig) riserva f; (jam) marmellata f

preside /prɪ'zaɪd/ vi presiedere (over a)

presidency /'prezɪdənsɪ/ n presidenza f

president /'prezɪdənt/ n presidente m. **~ial** /-'denʃl/ a presidenziale

press /pres/ n (machine) pressa f; (newspapers) stampa f ●vt premere; pressare (flower); (iron) stirare; (squeeze) stringere ●vi (urge) incalzare. **press for** vi fare pressione per; **be ~ed for** essere a corto di. **press on** vi andare avanti

press: ~ conference n conferenza f stampa. **~ cutting** n ritaglio m di giornale. **~ing** a urgente. **~-stud** n [bottone m] automatico m. **~-up** n flessione f

pressure /'preʃə(r)/ n pressione f ●vt = pressurize. **~-cooker** n pentola f a pressione. **~ group** n gruppo m di pressione

pressurize /'preʃəraɪz/ vt far pressione su. **~d** a pressurizzato

prestig|e /pre'stiː3/ n prestigio m. **~ious** /-'stɪdʒəs/ a prestigioso

presumably /prɪ'zjuː'məblɪ/ adv presumibilmente

presume /prɪ'zjuːm/ vt presumere; **~ to do sth** permettersi di fare qcsa

presumpt|ion /prɪ'zʌmpʃn/ n presunzione f; (boldness) impertinenza f. **~uous** /-'zʌmptjʊəs/ a impertinente

presup'pose /priː-/ vt presupporre

pretence /prɪ'tens/ n finzione f; (pretext) pretesto m: **it's all ~** è tutta una scena

pretend /prɪ'tend/ vt fingere; (claim) pretendere ● vi fare finta

pretentious /prɪ'tenʃəs/ a pretenzioso

pretext /'priːtekst/ n pretesto m

pretty /'prɪtɪ/ a (-ier, -iest) carino ● adv (fam: fairly) abbastanza

prevail /prɪ'veɪl/ vi prevalere; **~ on sb to do sth** convincere qcno a fare qcsa. **~ing** a prevalente

prevalen|ce /'prevələns/ n diffusione f. **~t** a diffuso

prevent /prɪ'vent/ vt impedire; **~ sb [from] doing sth** impedire a qcno di fare qcsa. **~ion** /-enʃn/ n prevenzione f. **~ive** /-ɪv/ a preventivo

preview /'priːvjuː/ n anteprima f

previous /'priːvɪəs/ a precedente. **~ly** adv precedentemente

pre-'war /priː-/ a anteguerra

prey /preɪ/ n preda f; **bird of ~** uccello m rapace ● vi **~ on** far preda di; **~ on sb's mind** attanagliare qcno

price /praɪs/ n prezzo m ● vt Comm fissare il prezzo di. **~less** a inestimabile; (fam: amusing) spassosissimo. **~y** a fam caro

prick /prɪk/ n puntura f ● vt pungere. **prick up** vt **~ up one's ears** rizzare le orecchie

prickl|e /'prɪkl/ n spina f; (sensation) formicolio m. **~y** a pungente; (person) irritabile

pride /praɪd/ n orgoglio m ● vt **~ oneself on** vantarsi di

priest /priːst/ n prete m

prim /prɪm/ a (primmer, primmest) perbenino

primarily /'praɪmərɪlɪ/ adv in primo luogo

primary /'praɪmərɪ/ a primario; (chief) principale. **~ school** n scuola f elementare

prime¹ /praɪm/ a principale, primo;

prime² vt preparare (surface, person)

Prime Minister n Primo Ministro m

primeval /praɪ'miːvl/ a primitivo

primitive /'prɪmɪtɪv/ a primitivo

primrose /'prɪmrəʊz/ n primula f

prince /prɪns/ n principe m

princess /prɪn'ses/ n principessa f

principal /'prɪnsəpl/ a principale ● n Sch preside m

principality /prɪnsɪ'pælətɪ/ n principato m

principally /'prɪnsəplɪ/ adv principalmente

principle /'prɪnsəpl/ n principio m; **in ~** in teoria; **on ~** per principio

print /prɪnt/ n (mark, trace) impronta f; Phot copia f; (picture) stampa f; **in ~** (printed out) stampato; (book) in commercio; **out of ~** esaurito ● vt stampare; (write in capitals) scrivere in stampatello. **~ed matter** n stampe fpl

print|er /'prɪntə(r)/ n stampante f; Typ tipografo. **-a** mf. **~er port** n Comput porta f per la stampante. **~ing** n tipografia f

'printout n Comput stampa f

prior /'praɪə(r)/ a precedente. **~ to** prep prima di

priority /praɪ'ɒrətɪ/ n precedenza f; (matter) priorità f inv

prise /praɪz/ vt **~ open|up** forzare

prison /'prɪz(ə)n/ n prigione f. **~er** n prigioniero, -a mf

privacy /'prɪvəsɪ/ n privacy f

private /'praɪvət/ a privato; (car, secretary, letter) personale ● n Mil soldato m semplice; **in ~** in privato. **~ly** adv (funded, educated etc) privatamente; (in secret) in segreto; (confidentially) in privato; (inwardly) interiormente

privation /praɪ'veɪʃn/ n privazione f. **~s** pl stenti mpl

privatize /'praɪvətaɪz/ vt privatizzare

privilege /'prɪvəlɪdʒ/ n privilegio m. **~d** a privilegiato

privy /'prɪvɪ/ a **be ~ to** essere al corrente di

prize /praɪz/ n premio m ● a (idiot etc) perfetto ● vt apprezzare. **~-giving** n premiazione f. **~-winner** n vincitore, -trice mf. **~-winning** a vincente

pro /prəʊ/ n (fam: professional) professionista mf; **the ~s and cons** il pro e il contro

probability /prɒbə'bɪlətɪ/ n probabilità f inv

415

probabl|e /ˈprɒbəbl/ a probabile. ~**y**
adv probabilmente

probation /prəˈbeɪʃn/ n prova f; Jur libertà f vigilata. ~**ary** a in prova; ~**ary
period** periodo m di prova

probe /prəʊb/ n sonda f; (fig:
investigation) indagine f ● vt sondare;
(investigate) esaminare a fondo

problem /ˈprɒbləm/ n problema m ● a
difficile. ~**atic** /-ˈmætɪk/ a problematico

procedure /prəˈsiːdʒə(r)/ n procedimento m

proceed /prəˈsiːd/ vi procedere ● vt ~
to do sth proseguire facendo qcsa

proceedings /prəˈsiːdɪŋz/ npl
(report) atti mpl; Jur azione fsg legale

proceeds /ˈprəʊsiːdz/ npl ricavato
msg

process /ˈprəʊses/ n processo m; (procedure) procedimento m; **in the** ~ nel
far ciò ● vt trattare; Admin occuparsi
di; Phot sviluppare

procession /prəˈseʃn/ n processione f

proclaim /prəˈkleɪm/ vt proclamare

procure /prəˈkjʊə(r)/ vt ottenere

prod /prɒd/ n colpetto m ● vt (pt/pp
prodded) punzecchiare; fig incitare

prodigal /ˈprɒdɪɡl/ a prodigo

prodigious /prəˈdɪdʒəs/ a prodigioso

prodigy /ˈprɒdɪdʒɪ/ n [infant] ~ bambino m prodigio

produce[1] /ˈprɒdjuːs/ n prodotti mpl; ~
of Italy prodotto in Italia

produce[2] /prəˈdjuːs/ vt produrre;
(bring out) tirar fuori; (cause) causare;
(fam: give birth to) fare. ~**r** n produttore m

product /ˈprɒdʌkt/ n prodotto m. ~**ion**
/prəˈdʌkʃn/ n produzione f; Theat spettacolo m

productiv|e /prəˈdʌktɪv/ a produttivo.
~**ity** /-ˈtɪvətɪ/ n produttività f

profan|e /prəˈfeɪn/ a profano;
(blasphemous) blasfemo. ~**ity** /-ˈfænətɪ/
n (oath) bestemmia f

profession /prəˈfeʃn/ n professione f.
~**al** a professionale; (not amateur) professionista; (piece of work) da professionista; (man) di professione ● n professionista mf. ~**ally** adv professionalmente

professor /prəˈfesə(r)/ n professore m
[universitario]

proficien|cy /prəˈfɪʃnsɪ/ n competenza f. ~**t** a **be** ~**t in** essere competente in

profile /ˈprəʊfaɪl/ n profilo m

profit /ˈprɒfɪt/ n profitto m ● vi ~ **from**

trarre profitto da. ~**able** /-əbl/ a proficuo. ~**ably** adv in modo proficuo

profound /prəˈfaʊnd/ a profondo. ~**ly**
adv profondamente

profus|e /prəˈfjuːs/ a ~**e apologies**
una profusione di scuse. ~**ion** /-ˈjuːʒn/ n
profusione f; **in** ~**ion** in abbondanza

progeny /ˈprɒdʒənɪ/ n progenie f inv

prognosis /prɒgˈnəʊsɪs/ n (pl -**oses**)
prognosi f inv

program /ˈprəʊɡræm/ n programma m
● vt (pt/pp **programmed**) programmare

programme /ˈprəʊɡræm/ n Br programma m. ~**r** n Comput programmatore, -trice mf

progress[1] /ˈprəʊɡres/ n progresso m;
in ~ in corso; **make** ~ fig fare progressi

progress[2] /prəˈɡres/ vi progredire; fig
fare progressi

progressive /prəˈɡresɪv/ a progressivo; (reforming) progressista. ~**ly** adv
progressivamente

prohibit /prəˈhɪbɪt/ vt proibire. ~**ive**
/-ɪv/ a proibitivo

project[1] /ˈprɒdʒekt/ n progetto m; Sch
ricerca f

project[2] /prəˈdʒekt/ vt proiettare (film,
image) ● vi (jut out) sporgere

projectile /prəˈdʒektaɪl/ n proiettile m

projector /prəˈdʒektə(r)/ n proiettore m

prolific /prəˈlɪfɪk/ a prolifico

prologue /ˈprəʊlɒɡ/ n prologo m

prolong /prəˈlɒŋ/ vt prolungare

promenade /prɒməˈnɑːd/ n lungomare m inv

prominent /ˈprɒmɪnənt/ a prominente; (conspicuous) di rilievo

promiscu|ity /prɒmɪˈskjuːətɪ/ n promiscuità f. ~**ous** /prəˈmɪskjʊəs/ a
promiscuo

promis|e /ˈprɒmɪs/ n promessa f ● vt
promettere; ~**e sb that** promettere a
qcno che; **I** ~**ed to** l'ho promesso. ~**ing**
a promettente

promot|e /prəˈməʊt/ vt promuovere;
be ~**ed** Sport essere promosso. ~**ion**
/-əʊʃn/ n promozione f

prompt /prɒmpt/ a immediato;
(punctual) puntuale ● adv in punto ● vt
incitare (**to** a); Theat suggerire a ● vi
suggerire. ~**er** n suggeritore, -trice mf.
~**ly** adv puntualmente

Proms /prɒmz/ npl rassegna f di concerti estivi di musica classica presso
l'Albert Hall a Londra

prone /prəʊn/ a be ~ to do sth essere incline a fare qcsa

prong /prɒŋ/ n dente m (di forchetta)

pronoun /ˈprəʊnaʊn/ n pronome m

pronounce /prəˈnaʊns/ vt pronunciare; (declare) dichiarare. ~d a (noticeable) pronunciato

pronunciation /prənʌnsɪˈeɪʃn/ n pronuncia f

proof /pruːf/ n prova f; Typ bozza f, prova f • a ~ against a prova di

prop¹ /prɒp/ n puntello m • vt (pt/pp **propped**) ~ **open** tenere aperto; ~ **against** (lean) appoggiare a. **prop up** vt sostenere

prop² n Theat, fam accessorio m di scena

propaganda /prɒpəˈgændə/ n propaganda f

propel /prəˈpel/ vt (pt/pp **propelled**) spingere. ~**ler** n elica f

proper /ˈprɒpə(r)/ a corretto; (suitable) adatto; (fam: real) vero [e proprio]. ~**ly** adv correttamente. ~ '**name**, ~ '**noun** n nome m proprio

property /ˈprɒpətɪ/ n proprietà f inv. ~ **developer** n impresario m edile. ~ **market** n mercato m immobiliare

prophecy /ˈprɒfəsɪ/ n profezia f

prophesy /ˈprɒfɪsaɪ/ vt (pt/pp -**ied**) profetizzare

prophet /ˈprɒfɪt/ n profeta m. ~**ic** /prəˈfetɪk/ a profetico

proportion /prəˈpɔːʃn/ n proporzione f; (share) parte f; ~**s** pl (dimensions) proporzioni fpl. ~**al** a proporzionale. ~**ally** adv in proporzione

proposal /prəˈpəʊzl/ n proposta f; (of marriage) proposta f di matrimonio

propose /prəˈpəʊz/ vt proporre; (intend) proporsi • vi fare una proposta di matrimonio

proposition /prɒpəˈzɪʃn/ n proposta f; (fam: task) impresa f

proprietor /prəˈpraɪətə(r)/ n proprietario, -a mf

prosaic /prəˈzeɪɪk/ a prosaico

prose /prəʊz/ n prosa f

prosecut|e /ˈprɒsɪkjuːt/ vt intentare azione contro. ~**ion** /-ˈkjuːʃn/ n azione f giudiziaria; **the** ~**ion** l'accusa f. ~**or** n [**Public**] **P**~**or** Pubblico Ministero m

prospect¹ /ˈprɒspekt/ n (expectation) prospettiva f

prospect² /prəˈspekt/ vi ~ **for** cercare

prospect|ive /prəˈspektɪv/ a (future) futuro; (possible) potenziale. ~**or** n cercatore m

prospectus /prəˈspektəs/ n prospetto m

prosper /ˈprɒspə(r)/ vi prosperare; (person:) stare bene finanziariamente. ~**ity** /-ˈsperətɪ/ n prosperità f

prosperous /ˈprɒspərəs/ a prospero

prostitut|e /ˈprɒstɪtjuːt/ n prostituta f. ~**ion** /-ˈtjuːʃn/ n prostituzione f

prostrate /ˈprɒstreɪt/ a prostrato; ~ **with grief** fig prostrato dal dolore

protagonist /prəʊˈtægənɪst/ n protagonista mf

protect /prəˈtekt/ vt proteggere (**from** da). ~**ion** /-ekʃn/ n protezione f. ~**ive** /-ɪv/ a protettivo. ~**or** n protettore, -trice mf

protégé /ˈprɒtɪʒeɪ/ n protetto m

protein /ˈprəʊtiːn/ n proteina f

protest¹ /ˈprəʊtest/ n protesta f

protest² /prəˈtest/ vi protestare

Protestant /ˈprɒtɪstənt/ a protestante • n protestante mf

protester /prəˈtestə(r)/ n contestatore, -trice mf

protocol /ˈprəʊtəkɒl/ n protocollo m

prototype /ˈprəʊtə-/ n prototipo m

protract /prəˈtrækt/ vt protrarre

protrude /prəˈtruːd/ vi sporgere

proud /praʊd/ a fiero (**of** di). ~**ly** adv fieramente

prove /pruːv/ vt provare • vi ~ **to be a lie** rivelarsi una bugia. ~**n** a dimostrato

proverb /ˈprɒvɜːb/ n proverbio m. ~**ial** /prəˈvɜːbɪəl/ a proverbiale

provide /prəˈvaɪd/ vt fornire; ~ **sb with sth** fornire qcsa a qcno • vi ~ **for** (law:) prevedere

provided /prəˈvaɪdɪd/ conj ~ [**that**] purché

providen|ce /ˈprɒvɪdəns/ n provvidenza f. ~**tial** /-ˈdenʃl/ a provvidenziale

providing /prəˈvaɪdɪŋ/ conj = **provided**

provinc|e /ˈprɒvɪns/ n provincia f; fig campo m. ~**ial** /prəˈvɪnʃl/ a provinciale

provision /prəˈvɪʒn/ n (of food, water) approvvigionamento m (**of** di); (law) disposizione f; ~**s** pl provviste fpl. ~**al** a provvisorio

proviso /prəˈvaɪzəʊ/ n condizione f

provocat|ion /prɒvəˈkeɪʃn/ n provocazione f. ~**ive** /prəˈvɒkətɪv/ a provocatorio; (sexually) provocante. ~**ively** adv in modo provocatorio

provoke /prəˈvəʊk/ vt provocare

prow /praʊ/ n prua f

prowess /ˈpraʊɪs/ n abilità f inv

prowl /praʊl/ *vi* aggirarsi ● *n* on the ~ in cerca di preda. **~er** *n* tipo *m* sospetto

proximity /prɒk'sɪmətɪ/ *n* prossimità *f*

proxy /'prɒksɪ/ *n* procura *f*; (*person*) persona *f* che agisce per procura

prude /pruːd/ *n* be a ~ essere eccessivamente pudico

pruden|ce /'pruːdəns/ *n* prudenza *f*. **~t** *a* prudente; (*wise*) oculatezza *f*

prudish /'pruːdɪʃ/ *a* eccessivamente pudico

prune[1] /pruːn/ *n* prugna *f* secca

prune[2] *vt* potare

pry /praɪ/ *vi* (*pt/pp* **pried**) ficcare il naso

psalm /sɑːm/ *n* salmo *m*

pseudonym /'sjuːdənɪm/ *n* pseudonimo *m*

psychiatric /saɪkɪ'ætrɪk/ *a* psichiatrico

psychiatr|ist /saɪ'kaɪətrɪst/ *n* psichiatra *mf*. **~y** *n* psichiatria *f*

psychic /'saɪkɪk/ *a* psichico; **I'm not** ~ non sono un indovino

psycho|analyse /saɪkəʊ-/ *vt* psicanalizzare. **~a'nalysis** *n* psicanalisi *f*. **~'analyst** *n* psicanalista *mf*

psychological /saɪkə'lɒdʒɪkl/ *a* psicologico

psycholog|ist /saɪ'kɒlədʒɪst/ *n* psicologo, -a *mf*. **~y** *n* psicologia *f*

psychopath /'saɪkəpæθ/ *n* psicopatico, -a *mf*

P.T.O. *abbr* (**please turn over**) vedi retro

pub /pʌb/ *n* fam pub *m* inv

puberty /'pjuːbətɪ/ *n* pubertà *f*

public /'pʌblɪk/ *a* pubblico ● *n* the ~ il pubblico; **in** ~ in pubblico

publican /'pʌblɪkən/ *n* gestore, -trice *mf*/proprietario, -a *mf* di un pub

publication /pʌblɪ'keɪʃn/ *n* pubblicazione *f*

public: ~ **con'venience** *n* gabinetti *mpl* pubblici. ~ **'holiday** *n* festa *f* nazionale. ~ **'house** *n* pub *m* inv

publicity /pʌb'lɪsətɪ/ *n* pubblicità *f*

publicize /'pʌblɪsaɪz/ *vt* pubblicizzare

public 'library *n* biblioteca *f* pubblica

publicly /'pʌblɪklɪ/ *adv* pubblicamente

public: ~ **re'lations** pubbliche relazioni *fpl*. ~ **school** *n* scuola *f* privata; *Am* scuola *f* pubblica. **~-'spirited** *a* be ~spirited essere dotato di senso civico. ~ **'transport** *n* mezzi *mpl* pubblici

publish /'pʌblɪʃ/ *vt* pubblicare. **~er** *n* editore *m*; (*firm*) editore *m*, casa *f* editrice. **~ing** *n* editoria *f*

pudding /'pʊdɪŋ/ *n* dolce *m* cotto a vapore; (*course*) dolce *m*

puddle /'pʌdl/ *n* pozzanghera *f*

pudgy /'pʌdʒɪ/ *a* (-**ier**, -**iest**) grassoccio

puff /pʌf/ *n* (*of wind*) soffio *m*; (*of smoke*) tirata *f*; (*for powder*) piumino *m* ● *vt* sbuffare. **puff at** *vt* tirare boccate da ⟨*pipe*⟩. **puff out** *vt* lasciare senza fiato ⟨*person*⟩; spegnere ⟨*candle*⟩. **~ed** *a* (*out of breath*) senza fiato. ~ **pastry** *n* pasta *f* sfoglia

puffy /'pʌfɪ/ *a* gonfio

pull /pʊl/ *n* trazione *f*; (*fig: attraction*) attrazione *f*; (*fam: influence*) influenza *f* ● *vt* tirare; estrarre ⟨*tooth*⟩; stirarsi ⟨*muscle*⟩; ~ **faces** far boccace; ~ **oneself together** cercare di controllarsi; ~ **one's weight** mettercela tutta; ~ **sb's leg** *fam* prendere in giro qcno. **pull down** *vt* (*demolish*) demolire. **pull in** *vi* Auto accostare. **pull off** *vt* togliere; *fam* azzeccare. **pull out** *vt* tirar fuori ● *vi* Auto spostarsi; (*of competition*) ritirarsi. **pull through** *vi* (*recover*) farcela. **pull up** *vt* sradicare ⟨*plant*⟩; (*reprimand*) rimproverare ● *vi* Auto fermarsi

pulley /'pʊlɪ/ *n* Techn puleggia *f*

pullover /'pʊləʊvə(r)/ *n* pullover *m* inv

pulp /pʌlp/ *n* poltiglia *f*; (*of fruit*) polpa *f*; (*for paper*) pasta *f*

pulpit /'pʊlpɪt/ *n* pulpito *m*

pulsate /pʌl'seɪt/ *vi* pulsare

pulse /pʌls/ *n* polso *m*

pulses /'pʌlsɪz/ *npl* legumi *mpl* secchi

pulverize /'pʌlvəraɪz/ *vt* polverizzare

pumice /'pʌmɪs/ *n* pomice *f*

pummel /'pʌml/ *vt* (*pt/pp* **pummelled**) prendere a pugni

pump /pʌmp/ *n* pompa *f* ● *vt* pompare; ~ **sb for sth** *fam* cercare di estorcere qcsa da qcno. **pump up** *vt* (*inflate*) gonfiare

pumpkin /'pʌmpkɪn/ *n* zucca *f*

pun /pʌn/ *n* gioco *m* di parole

punch[1] /pʌntʃ/ *n* pugno *m*; (*device*) pinza *f* per forare ● *vt* dare un pugno a; forare ⟨*ticket*⟩; perforare ⟨*hole*⟩

punch[2] *n* (*drink*) ponce *m* inv

punch: ~ **line** *n* battuta *f* finale. **~-up** *n* rissa *f*

punctual /'pʌŋktjʊəl/ *a* puntuale. **~ity** /-'ælətɪ/ *n* puntualità *f*. **~ly** *adv* puntualmente

punctuat|e /'pʌŋktjʊeɪt/ *vt* punteggiare. **~ion** /-'eɪʃn/ *n* punteggiatura *f*. **~ion mark** *n* segno *m* di interpunzione

puncture /'pʌŋktʃə(r)/ *n* foro *m*; (*tyre*) foratura *f* ● *vt* forare

pungent /'pʌndʒənt/ a acre
punish /'pʌnɪʃ/ vt punire. ~**able** /-əbl/ a punibile. ~**ment** n punizione f
punitive /'pju:nɪtɪv/ a punitivo
punk /pʌŋk/ n punk m inv
punnet /'pʌnɪt/ n cestello m (per frutta)
punt /pʌnt/ n (boat) barchino m
punter /'pʌntə(r)/ n (gambler) scommettitore, -trice mf; (client) consumatore, -trice mf
puny /'pju:nɪ/ a (-ier, -iest) striminzito
pup /pʌp/ n = **puppy**
pupil /'pju:pl/ n alunno, -a mf; (of eye) pupilla f
puppet /'pʌpɪt/ n marionetta f; (glove ~, fig) burattino m
puppy /'pʌpɪ/ n cucciolo m
purchase /'pɜ:tʃəs/ n acquisto m; (leverage) presa f ● vt acquistare. ~r n acquirente mf
pure /pjʊə(r)/ a puro
purée /'pjʊəreɪ/ n purè m inv
purely /'pjʊəlɪ/ adv puramente
purgatory /'pɜ:gətrɪ/ n purgatorio m
purge /pɜ:dʒ/ Pol n epurazione f ● vt epurare
puri|fication /pjʊərɪfɪ'keɪʃn/ n purificazione f. ~**fy** /'pjʊərɪfaɪ/ vt (pt/pp -ied) purificare
puritan /'pjʊərɪtən/ n puritano, -a mf. ~**ical** a puritano
purity /'pjʊərɪtɪ/ n purità f
purple /'pɜ:pl/ a viola inv
purpose /'pɜ:pəs/ n scopo m; (determination) fermezza f; **on** ~ apposta. ~-**built** a costruito ad hoc. ~**ful** a deciso. ~**fully** adv con decisione. ~**ly** adv apposta
purr /pɜ:(r)/ vi (cat:) fare le fusa
purse /pɜ:s/ n borsellino m; (Am: handbag) borsa f ● vt increspare (lips)
pursue /pə'sju:/ vt inseguire; fig proseguire. ~**r** /-ə(r)/ n inseguitore, -trice mf
pursuit /pə'sju:t/ n inseguimento m; (fig: of happiness) ricerca f; (pastime) attività f inv; **in** ~ all'inseguimento
pus /pʌs/ n pus m
push /pʊʃ/ n spinta f; (fig: effort) sforzo m; (drive) iniziativa f; **at a** ~ in caso di bisogno; **get the** ~ fam essere licenziato ● vt spingere; premere (button); (pressurize) far pressione su; **be** ~**ed for time** fam non avere tempo ● vi spingere. **push aside** vt scostare. **push back** vt respingere. **push off** vt togliere ● vi (fam: leave) levarsi dai

piedi. **push on** vi (continue) continuare. **push up** vt alzare (price)
push: ~-**button** n pulsante m. ~-**chair** n passeggino m. ~-**over** n fam bazzecola f. ~-**up** n flessione f
pushy /'pʊʃɪ/ a fam troppo intraprendente
puss /pʊs/ n, **pussy** /'pʊsɪ/ n micio m
put /pʊt/ vt (pt/pp put, pres p **putting**) mettere; ~ **the cost at 5 million** valutare il costo a 5 milioni ● vi ~ **to sea** salpare. **put aside** vt mettere da parte. **put away** vt mettere via. **put back** vt rimettere; mettere indietro (clock). **put by** vt mettere da parte. **put down** vt mettere giù; (suppress) reprimere; (kill) sopprimere; (write) annotare; ~ **one's foot down** fam essere fermo; Auto dare un'accelerata; ~ **down to** (attribute) attribuire. **put forward** vt avanzare; mettere avanti (clock). **put in** vt (insert) introdurre; (submit) presentare ● vi ~ **in for** far domanda di. **put off** vt spegnere (light); (postpone) rimandare; ~ **sb off** tenere a bada qcno; (deter) smontare qcno; (disconcert) distrarre qcno; ~ **sb off sth** (disgust) disgustare qcno di qcsa. **put on** vt mettersi (clothes); mettere (brake); Culin mettere su; accendere (light); mettere in scena (play); prendere (accent); ~ **on weight** mettere su qualche chilo. **put out** vt spegnere (fire, light); tendere (hand); (inconvenience) creare degli inconvenienti a. **put through** vt far passare; Teleph **I'll** ~ **you through to him** glielo passo. **put up** vt alzare; erigere (building); montare (tent); aprire (umbrella); affiggere (notice); aumentare (price); ospitare (guest); ~ **sb up to sth** mettere qcsa in testa a qcno ● vi (at hotel) stare; ~ **up with** sopportare ● a **stay** ~! rimani lì!
putty /'pʌtɪ/ n mastice m
put-up /'pʊtʌp/ a ~ **job** truffa f
puzzl|e /'pʌzl/ n enigma m; (jigsaw) puzzle m inv ● vt lasciare perplesso ● vi ~**e over** scervellarsi su. ~**ing** a inspiegabile
pygmy /'pɪgmɪ/ n pigmeo, -a mf
pyjamas /pə'dʒɑ:məz/ npl pigiama msg
pylon /'paɪlən/ n pilone m
pyramid /'pɪrəmɪd/ n piramide f
python /'paɪθn/ n pitone m

Qq

quack¹ /kwæk/ n qua qua m inv ● vi
fare qua qua
quack² n (doctor) ciarlatano m
quad /kwɒd/ n (fam: court) =
quadrangle. **~s** pl = **quadruplets**
quadrangle /'kwɒdræŋgl/ n quadran-
golo m; (court) cortile m quadrangolare
quadruped /'kwɒdrʊped/ n quadrupe-
de m
quadruple /'kwɒdrʊpl/ a quadruplo
● vt quadruplicare ● vi quadruplicarsi.
~ts /-plɪts/ npl quattro gemelli mpl
quagmire /'kwɒgmaɪə(r)/ n pantano m
quaint /kweɪnt/ a pittoresco; (odd) bizzarro
quake /kweɪk/ n fam terremoto m ● vi
tremare
qualification /kwɒlɪfɪ'keɪʃn/ n qualifica f. **~ied** /-faɪd/ a qualificato;
(limited) con riserva
qualify /'kwɒlɪfaɪ/ v (pt/pp -ied) ● vt
(course:) dare la qualifica a (as di);
(entitle) dare diritto a; (limit) precisare
● vi ottenere la qualifica; Sport qualifi-
carsi
quality /'kwɒlətɪ/ n qualità f inv
qualm /kwɑ:m/ n scrupolo m
quandary /'kwɒndərɪ/ n dilemma m
quantity /'kwɒntətɪ/ n quantità f inv;
in ~ in grande quantità
quarantine /'kwɒrəntiːn/ n quarante-
na f
quarrel /'kwɒrəl/ n lite f ● vi (pt/pp
quarrelled) litigare. **~some** a litigio-
so
quarry¹ /'kwɒrɪ/ n (prey) preda f
quarry² n cava f
quart /kwɔːt/ n 1.14 litro
quarter /'kwɔːtə(r)/ n quarto m; (of
year) trimestre m; Am 25 centesimi mpl;
~s pl Mil quartiere msg; **at |a| ~ to
six** alle sei meno un quarto ● vt dividere in quattro. **~-'final** n quarto m di finale
quarterly /'kwɔːtəlɪ/ a trimestrale
● adv trimestralmente
quartet /kwɔː'tet/ n quartetto m
quartz /kwɔːts/ n quarzo m. **~ watch** n
orologio m al quarzo

quash /kwɒʃ/ vt annullare; soffocare
(rebellion)
quaver /'kweɪvə(r)/ vi tremolare
quay /kiː/ n banchina f
queasy /'kwiːzɪ/ a **I feel ~** ho la nausea
queen /kwiːn/ n regina f. **~ mother** n
regina f madre
queer /kwɪə(r)/ a strano; (dubious) sospetto; (fam: homosexual) finocchio ● n
fam finocchio m
quell /kwel/ vt reprimere
quench /kwentʃ/ vt **~ one's thirst**
dissetarsi
query /'kwɪərɪ/ n domanda f; (question
mark) punto m interrogativo ● vt (pt/pp
-ied) interrogare; (doubt) mettere in
dubbio
quest /kwest/ n ricerca f (for di)
question /'kwestʃn/ n domanda f; (for
discussion) questione f; **out of the ~**
fuori discussione; **without ~** senza
dubbio; **in ~** in questione ● vt interrogare; (doubt) mettere in dubbio. **~able**
/-əbl/ a discutibile. **~ mark** n punto m
interrogativo
questionnaire /kwestʃə'neə(r)/ n
questionario m
queue /kjuː/ n coda f, fila f ● vi [up]
mettersi in coda (for per)
quick /kwɪk/ a veloce; **be ~!** sbrigati!;
have a ~ meal fare uno spuntino
● adv in fretta ● n **be cut to the ~** fig
essere punto sul vivo. **~ly** adv in fretta.
~-tempered a collerico
quid /kwɪd/ n inv fam sterlina f
quiet /'kwaɪət/ a (calm) tranquillo;
(silent) silenzioso; (voice, music) basso;
keep ~ about fam non raccontare a
nessuno ● n quiete f; **on the ~** di nascosto. **~ly** adv (peacefully) tranquilla-
mente; (say) a bassa voce
quieten /'kwaɪətn/ vt calmare.
quieten down vi calmarsi. **~ness** n
quiete f
quilt /kwɪlt/ n piumino m. **~ed** a
trapuntato
quins /kwɪnz/ npl fam = **quintuplets**
quintet /kwɪn'tet/ n quintetto m

quintuplets /'kwɪntjʊplɪts/ *npl* cinque gemelli *mpl*

quip /kwɪp/ *n* battuta *f*

quirk /kwɜːk/ *n* stranezza *f*

quit /kwɪt/ *v* (*pt/pp* **quitted, quit**) ● *vt* lasciare; (*give up*) smettere (**doing** di fare) ● *vi* (*fam: resign*) andarsene; *Comput* uscire; **give sb notice to ~** ⟨*landlord:*⟩ dare a qcno il preavviso di sfratto

quite /kwaɪt/ *adv* (*fairly*) abbastanza; (*completely*) completamente; (*really*)

veramente; **~** [**so**]**!** proprio così!; **~ a few** parecchi

quits /kwɪts/ *a* pari

quiver /'kwɪvə(r)/ *vi* tremare

quiz /kwɪz/ *n* (*game*) quiz *m inv* ● *vt* (*pt/pp* **quizzed**) interrogare

quota /'kwəʊtə/ *n* quota *f*

quotation /kwəʊ'teɪʃn/ *n* citazione *f*; (*price*) preventivo *m*; ⟨*of shares*⟩ quota *f*. **~ marks** *npl* virgolette *fpl*

quote /kwəʊt/ *n fam* = **quotation; in ~s** tra virgolette ● *vt* citare; quotare ⟨*price*⟩

⋯⋯⋯⋯⋯⋯⋯⋯⋯⋯⋯⋯⋯⋯⋯⋯⋯⋯⋯⋯⋯⋯⋯⋯⋯⋯⋯

Rr

⋯⋯⋯⋯⋯⋯⋯⋯⋯⋯⋯⋯⋯⋯⋯⋯⋯⋯⋯⋯⋯⋯⋯⋯⋯⋯⋯

rabbi /'ræbaɪ/ *n* rabbino *m*; (*title*) rabbi

rabbit /'ræbɪt/ *n* coniglio *m*

rabble /'ræbl/ *n* **the ~** la plebaglia

rabies /'reɪbiːz/ *n* rabbia *f*

race[1] /reɪs/ *n* (*people*) razza *f*

race[2] *n* corsa *f* ● *vi* correre ● *vt* gareggiare con; fare correre ⟨*horse*⟩

race: ~course *n* ippodromo *m*. **~horse** *n* cavallo *m* da corsa. **~track** *n* pista *f*

racial /'reɪʃl/ *a* razziale. **~ism** *n* razzismo *m*

racing /'reɪsɪŋ/ *n* corse *fpl*; (*horse-*) corse *fpl* dei cavalli. **~ car** *n* macchina *f* da corsa. **~ driver** *n* corridore *m* automobilistico

racis|m /'reɪsɪzm/ *n* razzismo *m*. **~t** /-ɪst/ *a* razzista ● *n* razzista *mf*

rack[1] /ræk/ *n* (*for bikes*) rastrelliera *f*; (*for luggage*) portabagagli *m inv*; (*for plates*) scolapiatti *m inv* ● *vt* **~ one's brains** scervellarsi

rack[2] *n* **go to ~ and ruin** andare in rovina

racket[1] /'rækɪt/ *n Sport* racchetta *f*

racket[2] *n* (*din*) chiasso *m*; (*swindle*) truffa *f*; (*crime*) racket *m inv*, giro *m*

radar /'reɪdɑː(r)/ *n* radar *m*

radian|ce /'reɪdɪəns/ *n* radiosità *f*. **~t** *a* raggiante

radiat|e /'reɪdɪeɪt/ *vt* irradiare ● *vi* ⟨*heat:*⟩ irradiarsi. **~ion** /-'eɪʃn/ *n* radiazione *f*

radiator /'reɪdɪeɪtə(r)/ *n* radiatore *m*

radical /'rædɪkl/ *a* radicale ● *n* radicale *mf*. **~ly** *adv* radicalmente

radio /'reɪdɪəʊ/ *n* radio *f inv*

radio'active *a* radioattivo. **~ac'tivity** *n* radioattività *f*

radiograph|er /reɪdɪ'ɒgrəfə(r)/ *n* radiologo, -a *mf*. **~y** *n* radiografia *f*

radio'therapy *n* radioterapia *f*

radish /'rædɪʃ/ *n* ravanello *m*

radius /'reɪdɪəs/ *n* (*pl* **-dii** /-dɪaɪ/) raggio *m*

raffle /'ræfl/ *n* lotteria *f*

raft /rɑːft/ *n* zattera *f*

rafter /'rɑːftə(r)/ *n* trave *f*

rag /ræg/ *n* straccio *m*; (*pej: newspaper*) giornalaccio *m*; **in ~s** stracciato

rage /reɪdʒ/ *n* rabbia *f*; **all the ~** *fam* all'ultima moda ● *vi* infuriarsi; ⟨*storm:*⟩ infuriare; ⟨*epidemic:*⟩ imperversare

ragged /'rægɪd/ *a* logoro; ⟨*edge*⟩ frastagliato

raid /reɪd/ *n* (*by thieves*) rapina *f*; *Mil* incursione *f*, raid *m inv*; (*police*) irruzione *f* ● *vt Mil* fare un'incursione in; ⟨*police, burglars:*⟩ fare irruzione in. **~er** *n* (*of bank*) rapinatore, -trice *mf*

rail /reɪl/ *n* ringhiera *f*; (*hand-*) ringhiera *f*; *Naut* parapetto *m*; **by ~** per ferrovia

'railroad *n Am* = **railway**

'railway *n* ferrovia *f*. **~man** *n* ferroviere *m*. **~ station** *n* stazione *f* ferroviaria

rain /reɪn/ *n* pioggia *f* ● *vi* piovere

rain: ~bow *n* arcobaleno *m*. **~coat** *n* impermeabile *m*. **~fall** *n* precipitazione *f* [atmosferica]

rainy /'reɪnɪ/ *a* (**-ier, -iest**) piovoso

raise /reɪz/ *n Am* aumento *m* ● *vt* alza

re; levarsi ⟨*hat*⟩; allevare ⟨*children, animals*⟩; sollevare ⟨*question*⟩; ottenere ⟨*money*⟩

raisin /ˈreɪzn/ *n* uva *f* passa

rake /reɪk/ *n* rastrello *m* ●*vt* rastrellare. **rake up** raccogliere col rastrello; *fam* rivangare

rally /ˈrælɪ/ *n* raduno *m*; *Auto* rally *m inv*; *Tennis* scambio *m* ●*v* (*pt/pp* -**ied**) ●*vt* radunare ●*vi* radunarsi; (*recover strength*) riprendersi

ram /ræm/ *n* montone *m*; *Astr* Ariete *m* ●*vt* (*pt/pp* **rammed**) cozzare contro

RAM /ræm/ *n* (*memoria f*) RAM *f*

ramble /ˈræmbl/ *n* escursione *f* ●*vi* gironzolare; (*in speech*) divagare. ~**er** *n* escursionista *mf*; (*rose*) rosa *f* rampicante. ~**ing** *a* (*in speech*) sconnesso; ⟨*club*⟩ escursionistico

ramp /ræmp/ *n* rampa *f*; *Aeron* scaletta *f* mobile (*di aerei*)

rampage /ˈræmpeɪdʒ/ *n* be/go on the ~ scatenarsi ●*vi* ~ **through the streets** scatenarsi per le strade

rampant /ˈræmpənt/ *a* dilagante

rampart /ˈræmpɑːt/ *n* bastione *f*

ramshackle /ˈræmʃækl/ *a* sgangherato

ran /ræn/ *see* **run**

ranch /rɑːntʃ/ *n* ranch *m inv*

rancid /ˈrænsɪd/ *a* rancido

rancour /ˈræŋkə(r)/ *n* rancore *m*

random /ˈrændəm/ *a* casuale; ~ **sample** campione *m* a caso ●*n* at a ~ a casaccio

randy /ˈrændɪ/ *a* (-**ier, -iest**) *fam* eccitato

rang /ræŋ/ *see* **ring**²

range /reɪndʒ/ *n* serie *f*; *Comm, Mus* gamma *f*; (*of mountains*) catena *f*; (*distance*) raggio *m*; (*for shooting*) portata *f*; (*stove*) cucina *f* economica; **at a** ~ **of** a una distanza di ●*vi* estendersi; ~ **from... to...** andare da... a.... ~**r** *n* guardia *f* forestale

rank /ræŋk/ *n* (*row*) riga *f*; *Mil* grado *m*; (*social position*) rango *m*; **the** ~ **and file** la base; **the** ~**s** *pl Mil* i soldati semplici ●*vt* (*place*) annoverare (**among** tra) ●*vi* (*be placed*) collocarsi

rankle /ˈræŋkl/ *vi fig* bruciare

ransack /ˈrænsæk/ *vt* rovistare; (*pillage*) saccheggiare

ransom /ˈrænsəm/ *n* riscatto *m*; **hold sb to** ~ tenere qcno in ostaggio (*per il riscatto*)

rant /rænt/ *vi* ~ [**and rave**] inveire;

what's he ~**ing on about?** cosa sta blaterando?

rap /ræp/ *n* colpo *m* [secco]; *Mus* rap *m* ●*v* (*pt/pp* **rapped**) ●*vt* dare colpetti a ●*vi* ~ **at** bussare a

rape /reɪp/ *n* (*sexual*) stupro *m* ●*vt* violentare, stuprare

rapid /ˈræpɪd/ *a* rapido. ~**ity** /rəˈpɪdətɪ/ *n* rapidità *f*. ~**ly** *adv* rapidamente

rapids /ˈræpɪdz/ *npl* rapida *fsg*

rapist /ˈreɪpɪst/ *n* violentatore *m*

rapport /ræˈpɔː(r)/ *n* rapporto *m* di intesa

rapture /ˈræptʃə(r)/ *n* estasi *f*. ~**ous** /-rəs/ *a* entusiastico

rare¹ /reə(r)/ *a* raro. ~**ly** *adv* raramente

rare² *a Culin* al sangue

rarefied /ˈreərɪfaɪd/ *a* rarefatto

rarity /ˈreərətɪ/ *n* rarità *f inv*

rascal /ˈrɑːskl/ *n* mascalzone *m*

rash¹ /ræʃ/ *n Med* eruzione *f*

rash² *a* avventato. ~**ly** *adv* avventatamente

rasher /ˈræʃə(r)/ *n* fetta *f* di pancetta

rasp /rɑːsp/ *n* (*noise*) stridio *m*. ~**ing** *a* stridente

raspberry /ˈrɑːzbərɪ/ *n* lampone *m*

rat /ræt/ *n* topo *m*; (*fam: person*) carogna *f*; **smell a** ~ *fam* sentire puzzo di bruciato

rate /reɪt/ *n* (*speed*) velocità *f inv*; (*of payment*) tariffa *f*; (*of exchange*) tasso *m*; ~**s** *pl* (*taxes*) imposte *fpl* comunali sui beni immobili; **at any** ~ in ogni caso; **at this** ~ di questo passo ●*vt* stimare; ~ **among** annoverare tra ●*vi* ~ **as** essere considerato

rather /ˈrɑːðə(r)/ *adv* piuttosto; ~! eccome!; ~ **too...** un po' troppo...

ratification /rætɪfɪˈkeɪʃn/ *n* ratifica *f*. ~**fy** /ˈrætɪfaɪ/ *vt* (*pt/pp* -**ied**) ratificare

rating /ˈreɪtɪŋ/ *n* ~**s** *pl Radio, TV* indice *m* d'ascolto, audience *f inv*

ratio /ˈreɪʃɪəʊ/ *n* rapporto *m*

ration /ˈræʃn/ *n* razione *f* ●*vt* razionare

rational /ˈræʃənl/ *a* razionale. ~**ize** *vt/i* razionalizzare

rat race *n fam* corsa *f* al successo

rattle /ˈrætl/ *n* tintinnio *m*; (*toy*) sonaglio *m* ●*vi* tintinnare ●*vt* (*shake*) scuotere; *fam* innervosire. **rattle off** *vt fam* scrionare

rattlesnake *n* serpente *m* a sonagli

raucous /ˈrɔːkəs/ *a* rauco

rave /reɪv/ *vi* vaneggiare; ~ **about** andare in estasi per

raven /ˈreɪvn/ n corvo m imperiale

ravenous /ˈrævənəs/ a ‹person› affamato

ravine /rəˈviːn/ n gola f

raving /ˈreɪvɪŋ/ a ~ **mad** fam matto da legare

ravishing /ˈrævɪʃɪŋ/ a incantevole

raw /rɔː/ a crudo; ‹not processed› grezzo; ‹weather› gelido; ‹inexperienced› inesperto; **get a ~ deal** fam farsi fregare. **~ ma'terials** npl materie fpl prime

ray /reɪ/ n raggio m; ~ **of hope** barlume m di speranza

raze /reɪz/ vt ~ **to the ground** radere al suolo

razor /ˈreɪzə(r)/ n rasoio m. **~ blade** n lametta f da barba

re /riː/ prep con riferimento a

reach /riːtʃ/ n portata f; **within ~** a portata di mano; **out of ~ of** fuori dalla portata di; **within easy ~** facilmente raggiungibile ● vt arrivare a ‹place, decision›; ‹contact› contattare; ‹pass› passare; **I can't ~ it** non ci arrivo ● vi arrivare (**to** a); ~ **for** allungare la mano per prendere

re'act /rɪ-/ vi reagire

re'action /rɪ-/ n reazione f. **~ary** a & n reazionario, -a mf

reactor /rɪˈæktə(r)/ n reattore m

read /riːd/ vt ⟨pt/pp read⟩ red/› leggere; Univ studiare ● vi leggere; ‹instrument› indicare. **read out** vt leggere ad alta voce

readable /ˈriːdəbl/ a piacevole a leggersi; ‹legible› leggibile

reader /ˈriːdə(r)/ n lettore, -trice mf; ‹book› antologia f

readily /ˈredɪlɪ/ adv volentieri; ‹easily› facilmente. **~ness** n disponibilità f; **in ~ness** pronto

reading /ˈriːdɪŋ/ n lettura f

rea'djust /riː-/ vt regolare di nuovo ● vi riabituarsi (**to** a)

ready /ˈredɪ/ a ‹-ier, -iest› pronto; ‹quick› veloce; **get ~** prepararsi

ready: **~-'made** a confezionato. **~ money** n contanti mpl. **~-to-'wear** a prêt-à-porter

real /riːl/ a vero; ‹increase› reale ● adv Am fam veramente. **~ estate** n beni mpl immobili

realism /ˈriəlɪzm/ n realismo m. **~t** -lıst- n realista mf. **~tic** /-ˈlɪstɪk/ a realistico

reality /rɪˈælətɪ/ n realtà f inv

realization /rɪəlaˈzeɪʃn/ n realizzazione f

realize /ˈrɪəlaɪz/ vt realizzare

really /ˈrɪəlɪ/ adv davvero

realm /relm/ n regno m

realtor /ˈrɪəltə(r)/ n Am agente mf immobiliare

reap /riːp/ vt mietere

reap'pear /riː-/ vi riapparire

rear[1] /rɪə(r)/ a posteriore; Auto di dietro; **~ end** fam didietro m● n **the ~** ‹of building› il retro; ‹of bus, plane› la parte posteriore; **from the ~** da dietro

rear[2] vt allevare ● vi ~ **[up]** ‹horse:› impennarsi

'rear-light n luce f posteriore

re'arm /riː-/ vt riarmare ● vi riarmarsi

rear'range /riː-/ vt cambiare la disposizione di

rear-view 'mirror n Auto specchietto m retrovisore

reason /ˈriːzn/ n ragione f; **within ~** nei limiti del ragionevole ● vi ragionare; ~ **with** cercare di far ragionare. **~able** /-əbl/ a ragionevole. **~ably** /-əblɪ/ adv ‹in reasonable way, fairly› ragionevolmente

reas'sur|ance /riː-/ n rassicurazione f. **~e** vt rassicurare; **~e sb of sth** rassicurare qcno su qcsa. **~ing** a rassicurante

rebate /ˈriːbeɪt/ n rimborso m; ‹discount› deduzione f

rebel[1] /ˈrebl/ n ribelle mf

rebel[2] /rɪˈbel/ vi ⟨pt/pp rebelled⟩ ribellarsi. **~lion** /-jən/ n ribellione f. **~lious** /-jəs/ a ribelle

re'bound[1] /rɪ-/ vi rimbalzare; fig ricadere

'rebound[2] /riː-/ n rimbalzo m

rebuff /rɪˈbʌf/ n rifiuto m

re'build /riː-/ vt ⟨pt/pp -built⟩ ricostruire

rebuke /rɪˈbjuːk/ vt rimproverare

rebuttal /rɪˈbʌtl/ n rifiuto m

re'call /rɪ-/ n richiamo m; **beyond ~** irrevocabile ● vt richiamare; riconvocare ‹diplomat, parliament›; ‹remember› rievocare

recap /ˈriːkæp/ vt/i fam = **recapitulate** ● n ricapitolazione f

recapitulate /riːkəˈpɪtjʊleɪt/ vt/i ricapitolare

re'capture /riː-/ vt riconquistare; ricatturare ‹person, animal›

reced|e /rɪˈsiːd/ vi allontanarsi. **~ing** a ‹forehead, chin› sfuggente; **have ~ing hair** essere stempiato

receipt /rɪˈsiːt/ n ricevuta f; ‹receiving› ricezione f; **~s** pl Comm entrate fpl

receive /rɪˈsiːv/ vt ricevere. ~**r** n Teleph ricevitore m; Radio, TV apparecchio m ricevente; (of stolen goods) ricettatore, -trice mf

recent /ˈriːsnt/ a recente. ~**ly** adv recentemente

receptacle /rɪˈseptəkl/ n recipiente m

reception /rɪˈsepʃn/ n ricevimento m; (welcome) accoglienza f; Radio ricezione f; ~ **|desk|** (in hotel) reception f inv. ~**ist** n persona f alla reception

receptive /rɪˈseptɪv/ a ricettivo

recess /rɪˈses/ n rientranza f; (holiday) vacanza f; Am Sch intervallo m

recession /rɪˈseʃn/ n recessione f

reˈcharge /riː-/ vt ricaricare

recipe /ˈresəpɪ/ n ricetta f

recipient /rɪˈsɪpɪənt/ n (of letter) destinatario, -a mf; (of money) beneficiario, -a mf

reciproˈcal /rɪˈsɪprəkl/ a reciproco. ~**cate** /-keɪt/ vt ricambiare

recital /rɪˈsaɪtl/ n recital m inv

recite /rɪˈsaɪt/ vt recitare; (list) elencare

reckless /ˈreklɪs/ a (action, decision) sconsiderato; **be a ~ driver** guidare in modo spericolato. ~**ly** adv in modo sconsiderato. ~**ness** n sconsideratezza f

reckon /ˈrekn/ vt calcolare; (consider) pensare. **reckon on/with** vt fare i conti con

reˈclaim /rɪ-/ vt reclamare; bonificare (land)

reclin|e /rɪˈklaɪn/ vi sdraiarsi. ~**ing** a (seat) reclinabile

recluse /rɪˈkluːs/ n recluso, -a mf

recognition /rekəɡˈnɪʃn/ n riconoscimento m; **beyond ~** irriconoscibile

recognize /ˈrekəɡnaɪz/ vt riconoscere

reˈcoil /rɪ-/ vi (in fear) indietreggiare

recollect /rekəˈlekt/ vt ricordare. ~**ion** /-ekʃn/ n ricordo m

recommend /rekəˈmend/ vt raccomandare. ~**ation** /-ˈdeɪʃn/ n raccomandazione f

recompense /ˈrekəmpens/ n ricompensa f

reconˈcile /ˈrekənsaɪl/ vt riconciliare; conciliare (facts); ~**cile oneself to** rassegnarsi a. ~**ciliation** /-sɪlɪˈeɪʃn/ n riconciliazione f

reconˈdition /riː-/ vt ripristinare. ~**ed engine** n motore m che ha subito riparazioni

reconnaissance /rɪˈkɒnɪsns/ n Mil ricognizione f

reconnoitre /rekəˈnɔɪtə(r)/ vi (pres p -**tring**) fare una recognizione

reconˈsider /riː-/ vt riconsiderare

reconˈstruct /riː-/ vt ricostruire. ~**ion** n ricostruzione f

record[1] /rɪˈkɔːd/ vt registrare; (make a note of) annotare

record[2] /ˈrekɔːd/ n (file) documentazione f; Mus disco m; Sport record m inv; ~**s** pl (files) schedario msg; **keep a ~ of** tener nota di; **off the ~** in via ufficiosa; **have a |criminal| ~** avere la fedina penale sporca

recorder /rɪˈkɔːdə(r)/ n Mus flauto m dolce

recording /rɪˈkɔːdɪŋ/ n registrazione f

ˈrecord-player n giradischi m inv

recount /rɪˈkaʊnt/ vt raccontare

reˈcount[1] /riː-/ vt ricontare (votes etc)

ˈre-count[2] /riː-/ n Pol nuovo conteggio m

recoup /rɪˈkuːp/ vt rifarsi di (losses)

recourse /rɪˈkɔːs/ n **have ~ to** ricorrere a

reˈcover /riː-/ vt rifoderare

recover /rɪˈkʌvə(r)/ vt/i recuperare. ~**y** n recupero m; (of health) guarigione f

recreation /rekrɪˈeɪʃn/ n ricreazione f. ~**al** a ricreativo

recrimination /rɪkrɪmɪˈneɪʃn/ n recriminazione f

recruit /rɪˈkruːt/ n Mil recluta f; **new ~** (member) nuovo, -a adepto, -a mf; (worker) neoassunto, -a mf • vt assumere (staff). ~**ment** n assunzione f

rectang|le /ˈrektæŋgl/ n rettangolo m. ~**ular** /-ˈtæŋɡjʊlə(r)/ a rettangolare

rectify /ˈrektɪfaɪ/ vt (pt/pp -**ied**) rettificare

recuperate /rɪˈkuːpəreɪt/ vi ristabilirsi

recur /rɪˈkɜː/ vi (pt/pp **recurred**) ricorrere; (illness:) ripresentarsi

recurren|ce /rɪˈkʌrəns/ n ricorrenza f; (of illness) ricomparsa f. ~**t** a ricorrente

recycle /riːˈsaɪkl/ vt riciclare

red /red/ a (**redder, reddest**) rosso • n rosso m; **in the ~** (account) scoperto. **R~ Cross** n Croce f rossa

redd|en /ˈredn/ vt arrossare • vi arrossire. ~**ish** a rossastro

reˈdecorate /riː-/ vt (paint) ridipingere; (wallpaper) ritappezzare

redeem /rɪˈdiːm/ vt ~**ing quality** unico aspetto m positivo

redemption /rɪˈdempʃn/ n riscatto m

redeˈploy /riː-/ vt ridistribuire

red: ~**-haired** *a* con i capelli rossi. ~**-handed** *a* **catch sb** ~**-handed** cogliere qcno con le mani nel sacco. ~'**herring** *n* diversione *f*. ~**-hot** *a* rovente

red: ~ '**light** *n* Auto semaforo *m* rosso

re'double /ri:-/ *vt* raddoppiare

redress /rɪ'dres/ *n* riparazione *f* ● *vt* ristabilire ⟨*balance*⟩

red 'tape *n fam* burocrazia *f*

reduce /rɪ'dju:s/ *vt* ridurre; *Culin* far consumare. ~**tion** /-'dʌkʃn/ *n* riduzione *f*

redundan|cy /rɪ'dʌndənsɪ/ *n* licenziamento *m*; ⟨*payment*⟩ cassa *f* integrazione. ~**t** *a* superfluo; **make** ~**t** licenziare; **be made** ~**t** essere licenziato

reed /ri:d/ *n Bot* canna *f*

reef /ri:f/ *n* scogliera *f*

reek /ri:k/ *vi* puzzare (**of** di)

reel /ri:l/ *n* bobina *f* ● *vi* ⟨*stagger*⟩ vacillare. **reel off** *vt fig* snocciolare

refectory /rɪ'fektərɪ/ *n* refettorio *m*; *Univ* mensa *f* universitaria

refer /rɪ'fɜ:(r)/ *v* ⟨*pt/pp* **referred**⟩ ● *vt* rinviare ⟨*matter*⟩ (**to** a); indirizzare ⟨*person*⟩ ● *vi* ~ **to** fare allusione a; ⟨*consult*⟩ rivolgersi a ⟨*book*⟩

referee /refə'ri:/ *n* arbitro *m*; ⟨*for job*⟩ garante *mf* ● *vt/i* ⟨*pt/pp* **refereed**⟩ arbitrare

reference /'refərəns/ *n* riferimento *m*; ⟨*in book*⟩ nota *f* bibliografica; ⟨*for job*⟩ referenza *f*; *Comm* '**your** ~' 'riferimento'; **with** ~ **to** con riferimento a; **make** |a| ~ **to** fare riferimento a. ~ **book** *n* libro *m* di consultazione. ~ **number** *n* numero *m* di riferimento

referendum /refə'rendəm/ *n* referendum *m inv*

re'fill[1] /ri:-/ *vt* riempire di nuovo; ricaricare ⟨*pen, lighter*⟩

'**refill**[2] /ri:-/ *n* ⟨*for pen*⟩ ricambio *m*

refine /rɪ'faɪn/ *vt* raffinare. ~**d** *a* raffinato. ~**ment** *n* raffinatezza *f*; *Techn* raffinazione *f*. ~**ry** /-ərɪ/ *n* raffineria *f*

reflect /rɪ'flekt/ *vt* riflettere; **be** ~**ed in** essere riflesso in ● *vi* ⟨*think*⟩ riflettere (**on su**); ~ **badly on sb** *fig* mettere in cattiva luce qcno. ~**ion** /-ekʃn/ *n* riflessione *f*; ⟨*image*⟩ riflesso *m*; **on** ~**ion** dopo riflessione. ~**ive** /-ɪv/ *a* riflessivo. ~**or** *n* riflettore *m*

reflex /'ri:fleks/ *n* riflesso *m* ● *attrib* di riflesso

reflexive /rɪ'fleksɪv/ *a* riflessivo

reform /rɪ'fɔ:m/ *n* riforma *f* ● *vt* riformare ● *vi* correggersi. **R**~**ation** /refə'meɪʃn/ *n Relig* Riforma *f*. ~**er** *n* riformatore, -trice *mf*

refrain[1] /rɪ'freɪn/ *n* ritornello *m*

refrain[2] /rɪ'freɪn/ *vi* astenersi (**from** da)

refresh /rɪ'freʃ/ *vt* rinfrescare. ~**ing** *a* rinfrescante. ~**ments** *npl* rinfreschi *mpl*

refrigerat|e /rɪ'frɪdʒəreɪt/ *vt* conservare in frigo. ~**or** *n* frigorifero *m*

re'fuel /ri:-/ *v* ⟨*pt/pp* **-fuelled**⟩ ● *vt* rifornire ⟨*di carburante*⟩ ● *vi* fare rifornimento

refuge /'refju:dʒ/ *n* rifugio *m*; **take** ~ rifugiarsi

refugee /refjʊ'dʒi:/ *n* rifugiato, -a *mf*

'**refund**[1] /'ri:-/ *n* rimborso *m*

re'fund[2] /rɪ-/ *vt* rimborsare

refurbish /ri:'fɜ:bɪʃ/ *vt* rimettere a nuovo

refusal /rɪ'fju:zl/ *n* rifiuto *m*

refuse[1] /rɪ'fju:z/ *vt/i* rifiutare; ~ **to do sth** rifiutare di fare qcsa

refuse[2] /'refju:s/ *n* rifiuti *mpl*. ~ **collection** *n* raccolta *f* dei rifiuti

refute /rɪ'fju:t/ *vt* confutare

re'gain /rɪ-/ *vt* riconquistare

regal /'ri:gl/ *a* regale

regalia /rɪ'geɪlɪə/ *npl* insegne *fpl* reali

regard /rɪ'gɑ:d/ *n* ⟨*heed*⟩ riguardo *m*; ⟨*respect*⟩ considerazione *f*; ~**s** *pl* saluti *mpl*; **send/give my** ~**s to your brother** salutami tuo fratello ● *vt* ⟨*consider*⟩ considerare (**as** come); **as** ~**s** riguardo a. ~**ing** *prep* riguardo a. ~**less** *adv* lo stesso; ~ **of** senza badare a

regatta /rɪ'gætə/ *n* regata *f*

regenerate /rɪ'dʒenəreɪt/ *vt* rigenerare ● *vi* rigenerarsi

regime /reɪ'ʒi:m/ *n* regime *m*

regiment /'redʒɪmənt/ *n* reggimento *m*. ~**al** /-'mentl/ *a* reggimentale. ~**ation** /-mən'teɪʃn/ *n* irreggimentazione *f*

region /'ri:dʒən/ *n* regione *f*; **in the** ~ **of** *fig* approssimativamente. ~**al** *a* regionale

register /'redʒɪstə(r)/ *n* registro *m* ● *vt* registrare; mandare per raccomandata ⟨*letter*⟩; assicurare ⟨*luggage*⟩; immatricolare ⟨*vehicle*⟩; mostrare ⟨*feeling*⟩ ● *vi* ⟨*instrument:*⟩ funzionare; ⟨*student:*⟩ iscriversi (**for** a); ~ **with** iscriversi nella lista di ⟨*doctor*⟩

registrar /redʒɪ'strɑ:(r)/ *n* ufficiale *m* di stato civile

registration /redʒɪ'streɪʃn/ *n* ⟨*of vehicle*⟩ immatricolazione *f*; ⟨*of letter*⟩ raccomandazione *f*; ⟨*of luggage*⟩ assicurazione *f*; ⟨*for course*⟩ iscrizione *f*. ~ **number** *n Auto* [numero *m* di] targa *f*

425

registry office /'redʒɪstrɪ-/ n anagrafe f

regret /rɪ'gret/ n rammarico m ● vt (pt/pp **regretted**) rimpiangere; **I ~ that** mi rincresce che. **~fully** adv con rammarico

regrettab|le /rɪ'gretəbl/ a spiacevole. **~ly** adv spiacevolmente; (before adjective) deplorevolmente

regular /'regjʊlə(r)/ a regolare; (usual) abituale ● n cliente mf abituale. **~ity** /-'lærətɪ/ n regolarità f. **~ly** adv regolarmente

regulat|e /'regjʊleɪt/ vt regolare. **~ion** /-'leɪʃn/ n (rule) regolamento m

rehabilitat|e /ri:hə'bɪlɪteɪt/ vt riabilitare. **~ion** /-'teɪʃn/ n riabilitazione f

rehears|al /rɪ'hɜːsl/ n Theat prova f. **~e** vt/i provare

reign /reɪn/ n regno m ● vi regnare

reimburse /ri:ɪm'bɜːs/ vt **~ sb for sth** rimborsare qcsa a qcno

rein /reɪn/ n redine f

reincarnation /ri:ɪnkɑː'neɪʃn/ n reincarnazione f

reinforce /ri:ɪn'fɔːs/ vt rinforzare. **~d 'concrete** n cemento m armato. **~ment** n rinforzo m

reinstate /ri:ɪn'steɪt/ vt reintegrare

reiterate /ri:'ɪtəreɪt/ vt reiterare

reject /rɪ'dʒekt/ vt rifiutare. **~ion** /-ekʃn/ n rifiuto m; Med rigetto m

rejoic|e /rɪ'dʒɔɪs/ vi liter rallegrarsi. **~ing** n gioia f

rejuvenate /rɪ'dʒu:vəneɪt/ vt ringiovanire

relapse /rɪ'læps/ n ricaduta f ● vi ricadere

relate /rɪ'leɪt/ vt (tell) riportare; (connect) collegare ● vi **~ to** riferirsi a; identificarsi con (person). **~d** a imparentato (to a); (ideas etc) affine

relation /rɪ'leɪʃn/ n rapporto m; (person) parente mf. **~ship** n rapporto m (blood tie) parentela f; (affair) relazione f

relative /'relətɪv/ n parente mf ● a relativo. **~ly** adv relativamente

relax /rɪ'læks/ vt rilassare; allentare (pace, grip) ● vi rilassarsi. **~ation** /ri:læk'seɪʃn/ n rilassamento m, relax m; (recreation) svago m. **~ing** a rilassante

relay¹ /ri:'leɪ/ vt (pt/pp **-layed**) ritrasmettere; Radio, TV trasmettere

relay² /'ri:leɪ/ n Electr relais m inv; **work in ~s** fare i turni. **~ [race]** n [corsa f a] staffetta f

release /rɪ'li:s/ n rilascio m; (of film) distribuzione f ● vt liberare; lasciare (hand); togliere (brake); distribuire (film); rilasciare (information etc)

relegate /'relɪgeɪt/ vt relegare; **be ~d** Sport essere retrocesso

relent /rɪ'lent/ vi cedere. **~less** a inflessibile; (unceasing) incessante. **~lessly** adv incessantemente

relevan|ce /'reləvəns/ n pertinenza f. **~t** a pertinente (to a)

reliab|ility /rɪlaɪə'bɪlətɪ/ n affidabilità f. **~le** /-'laɪəbl/ a affidabile. **~ly** adv in modo affidabile; **be ~ly informed** sapere da fonte certa

relian|ce /rɪ'laɪəns/ n fiducia f (on in). **~t** a fiducioso (on in)

relic /'relɪk/ n Relig reliquia f; **~s** pl resti mpl

relief /rɪ'li:f/ n sollievo m; (assistance) soccorso m; (distraction) diversivo m; (replacement) cambio m; (in art) rilievo m; **in ~** in rilievo. **~ map** n carta f in rilievo. **~ train** n treno m supplementare

relieve /rɪ'li:v/ vt alleviare; (take over from) dare il cambio a; **~ of** liberare da (burden)

religion /rɪ'lɪdʒən/ n religione f

religious /rɪ'lɪdʒəs/ a religioso. **~ly** adv (conscientiously) scrupolosamente

relinquish /rɪ'lɪŋkwɪʃ/ vt abbandonare; **~ sth to sb** rinunciare a qcsa in favore di qcno

relish /'relɪʃ/ n gusto m; Culin salsa f ● vt fig apprezzare

relo'cate /ri:-/ vt trasferire

reluctan|ce /rɪ'lʌktəns/ n riluttanza f. **~t** a riluttante. **~tly** adv a malincuore

rely /rɪ'laɪ/ vi (pt/pp **-ied**) **~ on** dipendere da; (trust) contare su

remain /rɪ'meɪn/ vi restare. **~der** n resto m. **~ing** a restante. **~s** npl resti mpl; (dead body) spoglie fpl

remand /rɪ'mɑːnd/ n **on ~** in custodia cautelare ● vt **~ in custody** rinviare con detenzione provvisoria

remark /rɪ'mɑːk/ n osservazione f ● vt osservare. **~able** /-əbl/ a notevole. **~ably** adv notevolmente

remarry /ri:-/ vi (pt/pp **-ied**) risposarsi

remedial /rɪ'mi:dɪəl/ a correttivo; Med curativo

remedy /'remədɪ/ n rimedio m (for contro) ● vt (pt/pp **-ied**) rimediare a

remember /rɪ'membə(r)/ vt ricordare,

ricordarsi; ~ **to do sth** ricordarsi di fare qcsa; ~ **me to him** salutamelo ● *vi* ricordarsi

remind /rɪ'maɪnd/ *vt* ~ **sb of sth** ricordare qcsa a qcno. ~**er** *n* ricordo *m*; (*memo*) promemoria *m inv*; (*letter*) lettera *f* di sollecito

reminisce /remɪ'nɪs/ *vi* rievocare il passato. ~**nces** /-ənsɪz/ *npl* reminiscenze *fpl*. ~**nt** *a* **be** ~**nt of** richiamare alla memoria

remiss /rɪ'mɪs/ *a* negligente

remission /rɪ'mɪʃn/ *n* remissione *f*; (*of sentence*) condono *m*

remit /rɪ'mɪt/ *vt* (*pt/pp* **remitted**) rimettere ⟨*money*⟩. ~**tance** *n* rimessa *f*

remnant /'remnənt/ *n* resto *m*; (*of material*) scampolo *m*; (*trace*) traccia *f*

remonstrate /'remənstreɪt/ *vi* fare rimostranze (**with sb** a qcno)

remorse /rɪ'mɔːs/ *n* rimorso *m*. ~**ful** *a* pieno di rimorso. ~**less** *a* spietato. ~**lessly** *adv* senza pietà

remote /rɪ'məʊt/ *a* remoto; (*slight*) minimo. ~ **access** *n* Comput accesso *m* remoto. ~ **con'trol** *n* telecomando *m*. ~-**con'trolled** *a* telecomandato. ~**ly** *adv* lontanamente; **be not** ~**ly...** non essere lontanamente...

re'movable /rɪ-/ *a* rimovibile

removal /rɪ'muːvl/ *n* rimozione *f*; (*from house*) trasloco *m*. ~ **van** *n* camion *m inv* da trasloco

remove /rɪ'muːv/ *vt* togliere; togliersi ⟨*clothes*⟩; eliminare ⟨*stain, doubts*⟩

remuneration /rɪmjuːnə'reɪʃn/ *n* remunerazione *f*. ~**ive** /-'mjuːnərətɪv/ *a* rimunerativo

render /'rendə(r)/ *vt* rendere ⟨*service*⟩

rendering /'rend(ə)rɪŋ/ *n* Mus interpretazione *f*

renegade /'renɪɡeɪd/ *n* rinnegato, -a *mf*

renew /rɪ'njuː/ *vt* rinnovare ⟨*contract*⟩. ~**al** *n* rinnovo *m*

renounce /rɪ'naʊns/ *vt* rinunciare a

renovate /'renəveɪt/ *vt* rinnovare. ~**ion** /-'veɪʃn/ *n* rinnovo *m*

renown /rɪ'naʊn/ *n* fama *f*. ~**ed** *a* rinomato

rent /rent/ *n* affitto *m* ● *vt* affittare; ~ ⌊**out**⌋ dare in affitto. ~**al** *n* affitto *m*

renunciation /rɪnʌnsɪ'eɪʃn/ *n* rinuncia *f*

re'open /riː-/ *vt/i* riaprire

re'organize /riː-/ *vt* riorganizzare

rep /rep/ *n* Comm fam rappresentante *mf*; Theat ≈ teatro *m* stabile

repair /rɪ'peə(r)/ *n* riparazione *f*; in

good/bad ~ in buone/cattive condizioni ● *vt* riparare

repatriat|e /riː'pætrɪeɪt/ *vt* rimpatriare. ~**ion** /-'eɪʃn/ *n* rimpatrio *m*

re'pay /riː-/ *vt* (*pt/pp* **-paid**) ripagare. ~**ment** *n* rimborso *m*

repeal /rɪ'piːl/ *n* abrogazione *f* ● *vt* abrogare

repeat /rɪ'piːt/ *n* TV replica *f* ● *vt/i* ripetere; ~ **oneself** ripetersi. ~**ed** *a* ripetuto. ~**edly** *adv* ripetutamente

repel /rɪ'pel/ *vt* (*pt/pp* **repelled**) respingere; *fig* ripugnare. ~**lent** *a* ripulsivo

repent /rɪ'pent/ *vi* pentirsi. ~**ance** *n* pentimento *m*. ~**ant** *a* pentito

repercussions /riːpə'kʌʃnz/ *npl* ripercussioni *fpl*

repertoire /'repətwɑː(r)/ *n* repertorio *m*

repetit|ion /repɪ'tɪʃn/ *n* ripetizione *f*. ~**ive** /rɪ'petɪtɪv/ *a* ripetitivo

re'place /rɪ-/ *vt* (*put back*) rimettere a posto; (*take the place of*) sostituire; ~ **sth with sth** sostituire qcsa con qcsa. ~**ment** *n* sostituzione *f*; (*person*) sostituto, -a *mf*. ~**ment part** *n* pezzo *m* di ricambio

'replay /riː-/ *n* Sport partita *f* ripetuta; ⌊**action**⌋ ~ replay *m inv*

replenish /rɪ'plenɪʃ/ *vt* rifornire ⟨*stocks*⟩; (*refill*) riempire di nuovo

replica /'replɪkə/ *n* copia *f*

reply /rɪ'plaɪ/ *n* risposta *f* (**to** a) ● *vt/i* (*pt/pp* **replied**) rispondere

report /rɪ'pɔːt/ *n* rapporto *m*; TV, Radio servizio *m*; Journ cronaca *f*; Sch pagella *f*; (*rumour*) diceria *f* ● *vt* riportare; ~ **sb to the police** denunciare qcno alla polizia ● *vi* riportare; (*present oneself*) presentarsi (**to** a). ~**edly** *adv* secondo quanto si dice. ~**er** *n* cronista *mf*, reporter *m inv*

repose /rɪ'pəʊz/ *n* riposo *m*

repos'sess /riː-/ *vt* riprendere possesso di

reprehensible /reprɪ'hensəbl/ *a* provevole

represent /reprɪ'zent/ *vt* rappresentare

representative /reprɪ'zentətɪv/ *a* rappresentativo ● *n* rappresentante *mf*

repress /rɪ'pres/ *vt* reprimere. ~**ion** /-eʃn/ *n* repressione *f*. ~**ive** /-ɪv/ *a* repressivo

reprieve /rɪ'priːv/ *n* commutazione *f* della pena capitale; (*postponement*) sospensione *f* della pena capitale; *fig* tregua f ● vt sospendere la sentenza a; *fig* risparmiare

reprimand /'reprɪmɑːnd/ n rimprovero m ● vt rimproverare

reprint[1] /'riː-/ n ristampa f

reprint[2] /riː-/ vt ristampare

reprisal /rɪ'praɪzl/ n rappresaglia f; **in ~ for** per rappresaglia contro

reproach /rɪ'prəʊtʃ/ n ammonimento m ● vt ammonire. **~ful** a riprovevole. **~fully** adv con aria di rimprovero

repro'duc|e /riː-/ vt riprodurre ● vi riprodursi. **~tion** /-'dʌkʃn/ n riproduzione f. **~tive** /-'dʌktɪv/ a riproduttivo

reprove /rɪ'pruːv/ vt rimproverare

reptile /'reptaɪl/ n rettile m

republic /rɪ'pʌblɪk/ n repubblica f. **~an** a repubblicano ● n repubblicano, -a m.f

repudiate /rɪ'pjuːdɪeɪt/ vt ripudiare; respingere ⟨view, suggestion⟩

repugnan|ce /rɪ'pʌgnəns/ n ripugnanza f. **~t** a ripugnante

repuls|ion /rɪ'pʌlʃn/ n repulsione f. **~ive** /-ɪv/ a ripugnante

reputable /'repjʊtəbl/ a affidabile

reputation /repjʊ'teɪʃn/ n reputazione f

repute /rɪ'pjuːt/ n reputazione f. **~d** /-ɪd/ a presunto; **he is ~d to be** si presume che sia. **~dly** adv presumibilmente

request /rɪ'kwest/ n richiesta f ● vt richiedere. **~ stop** n fermata f a richiesta

require /rɪ'kwaɪə(r)/ vt (need) necessitare di; (demand) esigere. **~d** a richiesto; **I am ~d to do** si esige che io faccia. **~ment** n esigenza f; (condition) requisito m

requisite /'rekwɪzɪt/ a necessario ● n **toilet/travel ~s** pl articoli mpl da toilette/viaggio

re'sale /'riː-/ n rivendita f

rescue /'reskjuː/ n salvataggio m ● vt salvare. **~r** n salvatore, -trice mf

research /rɪ'sɜːtʃ/ n ricerca f ● vt fare ricerche su; *Journ* fare un'inchiesta su ● vi **~ into** fare ricerche su. **~er** n ricercatore, -trice mf

resem|blance /rɪ'zembləns/ n rassomiglianza f. **~ble** /-bl/ vt rassomigliare a

resent /rɪ'zent/ vt risentirsi per. **~ful** a pieno di risentimento. **~fully** adv con risentimento. **~ment** n risentimento m

reservation /rezə'veɪʃn/ n (booking) prenotazione f; (doubt, enclosure) riserva f

reserve /rɪ'zɜːv/ n riserva f; (shyness) riserbo m ● vt riservare; riservarsi ⟨right⟩. **~d** a riservato

reservoir /'rezəvwɑː(r)/ n bacino m idrico

re'shape /riː-/ vt ristrutturare

re'shuffle /riː-/ n *Pol* rimpasto m ● vt *Pol* rimpastare

reside /rɪ'zaɪd/ vi risiedere

residence /'rezɪdəns/ n residenza f; (stay) soggiorno m. **~ permit** n permesso m di soggiorno

resident /'rezɪdənt/ a residente ● n residente mf. **~ial** /-'denʃl/ a residenziale

residue /'rezɪdjuː/ n residuo m

resign /rɪ'zaɪn/ vt dimettersi da; **~ oneself to** rassegnarsi a ● vi dare le dimissioni. **~ation** /rezɪg'neɪʃn/ n rassegnazione f; (from job) dimissioni fpl. **~ed** a rassegnato

resilient /rɪ'zɪlɪənt/ a elastico; *fig* con buone capacità di ripresa

resin /'rezɪn/ n resina f

resist /rɪ'zɪst/ vt resistere a ● vi resistere. **~ance** n resistenza f. **~ant** a resistente

resolut|e /'rezəluːt/ a risoluto. **~ely** adv con risolutezza. **~ion** /-'luːʃn/ n risolutezza f

resolve /rɪ'zɒlv/ vt **~ to do** decidere di fare

resonan|ce /'rezənəns/ n risonanza f. **~t** a risonante

resort /rɪ'zɔːt/ n (place) luogo m di villeggiatura; **as a last ~** come ultima risorsa ● vi **~ to** ricorrere a

resound /rɪ'zaʊnd/ vi risonare (with di). **~ing** (success) risonante

resource /rɪ'sɔːs/ n **~s** pl risorse fpl. **~ful** a pieno di risorse; (solution) ingegnoso. **~fulness** n ingegnosità f

respect /rɪ'spekt/ n rispetto m; (aspect) aspetto m; **with ~ to** per quanto riguarda ● vt rispettare

respectability /rɪspektə'bɪlətɪ/ n rispettabilità f

respect|able /rɪ'spektəbl/ a rispettabile. **~ably** adv rispettabilmente. **~ful** a rispettoso

respective /rɪ'spektɪv/ a rispettivo. **~ly** adv rispettivamente

respiration /respɪ'reɪʃn/ n respirazione f

respite /'respaɪt/ n respiro m

respond /rɪ'spɒnd/ vi rispondere; (react) reagire (**to** a); (patient:) rispondere (**to** a)

response /rɪ'spɒns/ n risposta f; ⟨reaction⟩ reazione f

responsibility /rɪspɒnsɪ'bɪlətɪ/ n responsabilità f inv

responsib|le /rɪ'spɒnsəbl/ a responsabile; ⟨job⟩ impegnativo

responsive /rɪ'spɒnsɪv/ a be ~ ⟨audience etc.⟩ reagire; ⟨brakes.⟩ essere sensibile

rest[1] /rest/ n riposo m; Mus pausa f; **have a ~**riposarsi ●vt riposare; ⟨lean⟩ appoggiare (**on** su); ⟨place⟩ appoggiare ●vi riposarsi; ⟨elbows.⟩ appoggiarsi; ⟨hopes.⟩ riposare; **it ~s with you**sta a te

rest[2]n the ~ il resto m; ⟨people⟩ gli altri

restaurant /'restərɒnt/ n ristorante m. **~ car**n vagone m ristorante

restful /'restfl/ a riposante

restive /'restɪv/ a irrequieto

restless /'restlɪs/ a nervoso

restoration /restə'reɪʃn/ n ⟨of building⟩ restauro m

restore /rɪ'stɔ:(r)/ vt ristabilire; restaurare ⟨building⟩; ⟨give back⟩ restituire

restrain /rɪ'streɪn/ vt trattenere; ~ **oneself** controllarsi. **~ed** a controllato. **~t** n restrizione f; ⟨moderation⟩ ritegno m

restrict /rɪ'strɪkt/ vt limitare; ~ **oneself to** limitarsi a. **~ion** /-ɪkʃn/ n limite m; ⟨restraint⟩ restrizione f. **~ive** /-ɪv/ a limitativo

'rest room n Am toilette f inv

result /rɪ'zʌlt/ n risultato m; **as a ~** a causa di ●vi ~ **from** risultare da; ~ **in** portare a

resume /rɪ'zju:m/ vt/i riprendere

résumé /'rezjʊmeɪ/ n riassunto m; Am curriculum vitae m inv

resumption /rɪ'zʌmpʃn/ n ripresa f

resurgence /rɪ'sɜ:dʒəns/ n rinascita f

resurrect /rezə'rekt/ vt fig risuscitare. **~ion** /-ekʃn/ n the R~ion Relig la Risurrezione

resuscitat|e /rɪ'sʌsɪteɪt/ vt rianimare. **~ion** /-'teɪʃn/ n rianimazione f

retail /'ri:teɪl/ n vendita f al minuto o al dettaglio ●a & adv al minuto ●vt vendere al minuto ●vi ~ **at** essere venduto al pubblico al prezzo di. **~er** n dettagliante mf

retain /rɪ'teɪn/ vt conservare; ⟨hold back⟩ trattenere

retaliat|e /rɪ'tælɪeɪt/ vi vendicarsi. **~ion** /-'eɪʃn/ n rappresaglia f; **in ~ion for**per rappresaglia contro

retarded /rɪ'tɑ:dɪd/ a ritardato

retentive /rɪ'tentɪv/ a ⟨memory⟩ buono

rethink /ri:'θɪŋk/ vt (pt/pp **rethought**) ripensare

reticen|ce /'retɪsəns/ n reticenza f. **~t** a reticente

retina /'retɪnə/ n retina f

retinue /'retɪnju:/ n seguito m

retire /rɪ'taɪə(r)/ vi andare in pensione; ⟨withdraw⟩ ritirarsi ●vt mandare in pensione ⟨employee⟩. **~d** a in pensione. **~ment**n pensione f; **since my ~ment** da quando sono andato in pensione

retiring /rɪ'taɪərɪŋ/ a riservato

retort /rɪ'tɔ:t/ n replica f ●vt ribattere

re'touch /ri:-/ vt Phot ritoccare

re'trace /rɪ-/ vt ripercorrere; ~ **one's steps**ritornare sui propri passi

retract /rɪ'trækt/ vt ritrattare ⟨statement, evidence⟩ ●vi ritrarsi

re'train /ri:-/ vt riqualificare ●vi riqualificarsi

retreat /rɪ'tri:t/ n ritirata f; ⟨place⟩ ritiro m ●vi ritirarsi; Mil battere in ritirata

re'trial /ri:-/ n nuovo processo m

retribution /retrɪ'bju:ʃn/ n castigo m

retrieval /rɪ'tri:vl/ n recupero m

retrieve /rɪ'tri:v/ vt recuperare

retrograde /'retrəgreɪd/ a retrogrado

retrospect /'retrəspekt/ n **in ~** guardando indietro. **~ive** /-'spektɪv/ a retrospettivo; ⟨legislation⟩ retroattivo ●n retrospettiva f

return /rɪ'tɜ:n/ n ritorno m; ⟨giving back⟩ restituzione f; Comm profitto m; ⟨ticket⟩ biglietto m di andata e ritorno; **by ~** ⟨of post⟩ a stretto giro di posta; **in ~** in cambio ⟨for di⟩; **many happy ~s!** cento di questi giorni! ●vi ritornare ●vt ⟨give back⟩ restituire; ricambiare ⟨affection, invitation⟩; ⟨put back⟩ rimettere; ⟨send back⟩ mandare indietro; ⟨elect⟩ eleggere

return: ~ **flight** n volo m di andata e ritorno. ~ **match** n rivincita f. ~ **ticket**n biglietto m di andata e ritorno

reunion /ri:'ju:nɪən/ n riunione f

reunite /ri:jʊ'naɪt/ vt riunire

re'us|able /ri:-/ a riutilizzabile. **~e**vt riutilizzare

rev /rev/ n Auto, fam giro m ⟨di motore⟩ ●v (pt/pp **revved**) ●vt ~ ⟨**up**⟩far andare su di giri ●vi andare su di giri

reveal /rɪ'vi:l/ vt rivelare; ⟨dress.⟩ scoprire. **~ing**a rivelatore; ⟨dress⟩ osé inv

revel /'revl/ vi (pt/pp **revelled**) ~ **in sth**godere di qcsa

revelation /revəˈleɪʃn/ n rivelazione f

revelry /ˈrevlrɪ/ n baldoria f

revenge /rɪˈvendʒ/ n vendetta f; Sport rivincita f; **take ~** vendicarsi ●vt vendicare

revenue /ˈrevənjuː/ n reddito m

reverberate /rɪˈvɜːbəreɪt/ vi riverberare

revere /rɪˈvɪə(r)/ vt riverire. **~nce** /ˈrevərəns/ n riverenza f

Reverend /ˈrevərənd/ a reverendo

reverent /ˈrevərənt/ a riverente

reverse /rɪˈvɜːs/ a opposto; **in ~ order** in ordine inverso ●n contrario m; (back) rovescio m; Auto marcia indietro ●vt invertire; **~ the car into the garage** entrare in garage a marcia indietro; **~ the charges** Teleph fare una telefonata a carico del destinatario ●vi Auto fare marcia indietro

revert /rɪˈvɜːt/ vi **~ to** tornare a

review /rɪˈvjuː/ n (survey) rassegna f; (re-examination) riconsiderazione f; Mil rivista f; (of book, play) recensione f ●vt riesaminare (situation); Mil passare in rivista; recensire (book, play). **~er** n critico, -a mf

revile /rɪˈvaɪl/ vt ingiuriare

revis|e /rɪˈvaɪz/ vt rivedere; (for exam) ripassare. **~ion** /-ˈvɪʒn/ n revisione f; (for exam) ripasso m

revival /rɪˈvaɪvl/ n ritorno m; (of patient) recupero m; (from coma) risveglio m

revive /rɪˈvaɪv/ vt resuscitare; rianimare (person) ●vi riprendersi; (person): rianimarsi

revoke /rɪˈvəʊk/ vt revocare

revolt /rɪˈvəʊlt/ n rivolta f ●vi ribellarsi ●vt rivoltare. **~ing** a rivoltante

revolution /revəˈluːʃn/ n rivoluzione f; Auto **~s per minute** giri mpl al minuto. **~ary** /-ərɪ/ a & n rivoluzionario, -a mf. **~ize** vt rivoluzionare

revolve /rɪˈvɒlv/ vi ruotare; **~ around** girare intorno a

revolv|er /rɪˈvɒlvə(r)/ n rivoltella f, revolver m inv. **~ing** a ruotante

revue /rɪˈvjuː/ n rivista f

revulsion /rɪˈvʌlʃn/ n ripulsione f

reward /rɪˈwɔːd/ n ricompensa f ●vt ricompensare. **~ing** a gratificante

re·write /riː-/ vt (pt rewrote, pp rewritten) riscrivere

rhapsody /ˈræpsədɪ/ n rapsodia f

rhetoric /ˈretərɪk/ n retorica f. **~al** /rɪˈtɒrɪkl/ a retorico

rheuma|tic /rʊˈmætɪk/ a reumatico. **~tism** /ˈruːmətɪzm/ n reumatismo m

Rhine /raɪn/ n Reno m

rhinoceros /raɪˈnɒsərəs/ n rinoceronte m

rhubarb /ˈruːbɑːb/ n rabarbaro m

rhyme /raɪm/ n rima f; (poem) filastrocca f ●vi rimare

rhythm /ˈrɪðm/ n ritmo m. **~ic[al]** a ritmico. **~ically** adv con ritmo

rib /rɪb/ n costola f

ribald /ˈrɪbld/ a spinto

ribbon /ˈrɪbən/ n nastro m; **in ~s** a brandelli

rice /raɪs/ n riso m

rich /rɪtʃ/ a ricco; (food) pesante ●n **the ~** pl i ricchi; **~es** pl ricchezze fpl. **~ly** adv riccamente; (deserve) largamente

rickety /ˈrɪkɪtɪ/ a malfermo

ricochet /ˈrɪkəʃeɪ/ vi rimbalzare ●n rimbalzo m

rid /rɪd/ vt (pt/pp rid, pres p ridding) sbarazzare (of di); **get ~ of** sbarazzarsi di

riddance /ˈrɪdns/ n **good ~!** che liberazione!

ridden /ˈrɪdn/ see ride

riddle /ˈrɪdl/ n enigma m

riddled /ˈrɪdld/ a **~ with** crivellato di

ride /raɪd/ n (on horse) cavalcata f; (in vehicle) giro m; (journey) viaggio m; **take sb for a ~** fam prendere qcno in giro ●v (pt rode, pp ridden) ●vt montare (horse); andare su (bicycle) ●vi andare a cavallo; (jockey, showjumper): cavalcare; (cyclist:) andare in bicicletta; (in vehicle) viaggiare. **~r** n cavallerizzo, -a mf; (in race) fantino m; (on bicycle) ciclista mf; (in document) postilla f

ridge /rɪdʒ/ n spigolo m; (on roof) punta f; (of mountain) cresta f

ridicule /ˈrɪdɪkjuːl/ n ridicolo m ●vt mettere in ridicolo

ridiculous /rɪˈdɪkjʊləs/ a ridicolo

riding /ˈraɪdɪŋ/ n equitazione f ●attrib d'equitazione

rife /raɪf/ a **be ~** essere diffuso; **~ with** pieno di

riff-raff /ˈrɪfræf/ n marmaglia f

rifle /ˈraɪfl/ n fucile m. **~-range** n tiro m al bersaglio ●vt ~ [through] mettere a soqquadro

rift /rɪft/ n fessura f; fig frattura f

rig¹ /rɪg/ n equipaggiamento m; (at sea) piattaforma f [per trivellazioni subacquee] ●rig out vt (pt/pp rigged) equipaggiare. **rig up** vt allestire

rig[2] *vt* (*pt/pp* **rigged**) manovrare ⟨*election*⟩

right /raɪt/ *a* giusto; (*not left*) destro; **be ~** ⟨*person:*⟩ aver ragione; ⟨*clock:*⟩ essere giusto; **put ~** mettere all'ora ⟨*clock*⟩; correggere ⟨*person*⟩; rimediare a ⟨*situation*⟩; **that's ~**! proprio così! ● *adv* (*correctly*) bene; (*not left*) a destra; (*directly*) proprio; (*completely*) completamente; **~ away** immediatamente ● *n* giusto *m*; (*not left*) destra *f*; (*what is due*) diritto *m*; **on/to the ~** a destra; **be in the ~** essere nel giusto; **know ~ from wrong** distinguere il bene dal male; **by ~s** secondo giustizia; **the R~** *Pol* la destra ● *vt* raddrizzare; **~ a wrong** *fig* riparare a un torto. **~ angle** *n* angolo *m* retto

rightful /'raɪtfl/ *a* legittimo

right: **~-handed** *a* che usa la mano destra. **~-hand 'man** *n fig* braccio *m* destro

rightly /'raɪtlɪ/ *adv* giustamente

right: **~ of way** *n* diritto *m* di transito; (*path*) passaggio *m*; *Auto* precedenza *f*. **~-'wing** *a Pol* di destra ● *n Sport* ala *f* destra

rigid /'rɪdʒɪd/ *a* rigido. **~ity** /-'dʒɪdətɪ/ *n* rigidità *f*

rigmarole /'rɪgmərəʊl/ *n* trafila *f*; (*story*) tiritera *f*

rigorous /'rɪgərəs/ *a* rigoroso

rile /raɪl/ *vt fam* irritare

rim /rɪm/ *n* bordo *m*; (*of wheel*) cerchione *m*

rind /raɪnd/ *n* (*on fruit*) scorza *f*; (*on cheese*) crosta *f*; (*on bacon*) cotenna *f*

ring[1] /rɪŋ/ *n* (*circle*) cerchio *m*; (*on finger*) anello *m*; (*boxing*) ring *m inv*; (*for circus*) pista *f*; **stand in a ~** essere in cerchio

ring[2] *n* suono *m*; **give sb a ~** *Teleph* dare un colpo di telefono a qcno ● *v* (*pt* **rang**, *pp* **rung**) ● *vt* suonare; **~ [up]** *Teleph* telefonare a ● *vi* suonare; *Teleph* **~ [up]** telefonare. **ring back** *vt/i Teleph* richiamare. **ring off** *vi Teleph* riattaccare

ring: **~leader** *n* capobanda *m*. **~ road** *n* circonvallazione *f*

rink /rɪŋk/ *n* pista *f* di pattinaggio

rinse /rɪns/ *n* risciacquo *m*; (*hair colour*) cachet *m inv* ● *vt* sciacquare

riot /'raɪət/ *n* rissa *f*; (*of colour*) accozzaglia *f*; **~s** *pl* disordini *mpl*; **run ~** impazzare ● *vi* creare disordini. **~er** *n* dimostrante *mf*. **~ous** /-əs/ *a* sfrenato

rip /rɪp/ *n* strappo *m* ● *vt* (*pt/pp* **ripped**)

strappare; **~ open** aprire con uno strappo. **rip off** *vt fam* fregare

ripe /raɪp/ *a* maturo; ⟨*cheese*⟩ stagionato

ripen /'raɪpn/ *vi* maturare; ⟨*cheese:*⟩ stagionarsi ● *vt* far maturare; stagionare ⟨*cheese*⟩

ripeness /'raɪpnɪs/ *n* maturità *f*

'rip-off *n fam* frode *f*

ripple /'rɪpl/ *n* increspatura *f*; (*sound*) mormorio *m* ●

rise /raɪz/ *n* (*of sun*) levata *f*; (*fig: to fame, power*) ascesa *f*; (*increase*) aumento *m*; **give ~ to** dare adito a ● *vi* (*pt* **rose**, *pp* **risen**) alzarsi; ⟨*sun:*⟩ sorgere; ⟨*dough:*⟩ lievitare; ⟨*prices, water level:*⟩ aumentare; (*to power, position*) arrivare (**to** a). **~r** *n* **early ~r** persona *f* mattiniera

rising /'raɪzɪŋ/ *a* ⟨*sun*⟩ levante; **~ generation** nuova generazione *f* ● *n* (*revolt*) sollevazione *f*

risk /rɪsk/ *n* rischio *m*; **at one's own ~** a proprio rischio e pericolo ● *vt* rischiare

risky /'rɪskɪ/ *a* (**-ier**, **-iest**) rischioso

risqué /'rɪskeɪ/ *a* spinto

rite /raɪt/ *n* rito *m*; **last ~s** estrema unzione *f*

ritual /'rɪtjʊəl/ *a* rituale ● *n* rituale *m*

rival /'raɪvl/ *a* rivale ● *n* rivale *mf*; **~s** *pl Comm* concorrenti *mpl* ● *vt* (*pt/pp* **rivalled**) rivaleggiare con. **~ry** *n* rivalità *f inv*; *Comm* concorrenza *f*

river /'rɪvə(r)/ *n* fiume *m*. **~-bed** *n* letto *m* del fiume

rivet /'rɪvɪt/ *n* rivetto *m* ● *vt* rivettare; **~ed by** *fig* inchiodato da

Riviera /rɪvɪ'eərə/ *n* **the Italian ~** la riviera ligure

road /rəʊd/ *n* strada *f*, via *f*; **be on the ~** viaggiare

road: **~-block** *n* blocco *m* stradale. **~-hog** *n fam* pirata *m* della strada. **~-map** *n* carta *f* stradale. **~ safety** *n* sicurezza *f* sulle strade. **~ sense** *n* prudenza *f* (*per strada*). **~side** *n* bordo *m* della strada. **~-sign** *n* cartello *m* stradale. **~way** *n* carreggiata *f*, corsia *f*. **~-works** *npl* lavori *mpl* stradali. **~worthy** *a* sicuro

roam /rəʊm/ *vi* girovagare

roar /rɔː(r)/ *n* ruggito *m*; **~s of laughter** scroscio *msg* di risa ● *vi* ruggire; ⟨*lorry, thunder:*⟩ rombare; **~ with laughter** ridere fragorosamente. **~ing** *a* **do a ~ing trade** *fam* fare affari d'oro

roast /rəʊst/ *a* arrosto; **~ pork** arrosto

m di maiale ● *n* arrosto *m* ● *vt* arrostire 〈*meat*〉 ● *vi* arrostirsi

rob /rɒb/ *vt* 〈*pt/pp* robbed〉 derubare 〈of di〉; svaligiare 〈*bank*〉. **~ber** *n* rapinatore *m*. **~bery** *n* rapina *f*

robe /rəʊb/ *n* tunica *f*; 〈*Am: bathrobe*〉 accappatoio *m*

robin /ˈrɒbɪn/ *n* pettirosso *m*

robot /ˈrəʊbɒt/ *n* robot *m inv*

robust /rəʊˈbʌst/ *a* robusto

rock[1] /rɒk/ *n* roccia *f*; 〈*in sea*〉 scoglio *m*; 〈*sweet*〉 zucchero *m* candito. **on the ~s** 〈*ship*〉 incagliato; 〈*marriage*〉 finito; 〈*drink*〉 con ghiaccio

rock[2] *vt* cullare 〈*baby*〉; 〈*shake*〉 far traballare; 〈*shock*〉 scuotere ● *vi* dondolarsi

rock[3] *n* Mus rock *m*

rock-'bottom *a* bassissimo ● *n* livello *m* più basso

rockery /ˈrɒkərɪ/ *n* giardino *m* roccioso

rocket /ˈrɒkɪt/ *n* razzo *m* ● *vi* salire alle stelle

rocking /ˈrɒkɪŋ/: **~-chair** *n* sedia *f* a dondolo. **~-horse** *n* cavallo *m* a dondolo

rocky /ˈrɒkɪ/ *a* (**-ier, -iest**) roccioso; *fig* traballante

rod /rɒd/ *n* bacchetta *f*; 〈*for fishing*〉 canna *f*

rode /rəʊd/ *see* ride

rodent /ˈrəʊdnt/ *n* roditore *m*

roe /rəʊ/ *n* 〈*pl* roe *or* roes〉 **~[-deer]** capriolo *m*

rogue /rəʊg/ *n* farabutto *m*

role /rəʊl/ *n* ruolo *m*

roll /rəʊl/ *n* rotolo *m*; 〈*bread*〉 panino *m*; 〈*list*〉 lista *f*; 〈*of ship, drum*〉 rullio *m* ● *vi* rotolare; **be ~ing in money** *fam* nuotare nell'oro ● *vt* spianare 〈*lawn, pastry*〉. **roll over** *vi* rigirarsi. **roll up** *vt* arrotolare; rimboccarsi 〈*sleeves*〉 ● *vi fam* arrivare

'roll-call *n* appello *m*

roller /ˈrəʊlə(r)/ *n* rullo *m*; 〈*for hair*〉 bigodino *m*. **~ blind** *n* tapparella *f*. **~-coaster** *n* montagne *fpl* russe. **~-skate** *n* pattino *m* a rotelle

'rolling-pin *n* mattarello *m*

Roman /ˈrəʊmən/ *a* romano ● *n* romano, -a *mf*. ● **Catholic** *a* cattolico ● *n* cattolico, -a *mf*

romance /rəʊˈmæns/ *n* 〈*love-affair*〉 storia *f* d'amore; 〈*book*〉 romanzo *m* rosa

Romania /rəʊˈmeɪnɪə/ *n* Romania *f*. **~n** *a* rumeno ● *n* rumeno, -a *mf*; 〈*language*〉 rumeno *m*

romantic /rəʊˈmæntɪk/ *a* romantico.

~ally *adv* romanticamente. **~ism** /-tɪsɪzm/ *n* romanticismo *m*

Rome /rəʊm/ *n* Roma *f*

romp /rɒmp/ *n* gioco *m* rumoroso ● *vi* giocare rumorosamente. **~ers** *npl* pagliaccetto *msg*

roof /ruːf/ *n* tetto *m*; 〈*of mouth*〉 palato *m* ● *vt* mettere un tetto su. **~-rack** *n* portabagagli *m inv*. **~-top** *n* tetto *m*

rook /rʊk/ *n* corvo *m*; 〈*in chess*〉 torre *f*

room /ruːm/ *n* stanza *f*; 〈*bedroom*〉 camera *f*; 〈*for functions*〉 sala *f*; 〈*space*〉 spazio *m*. **~y** *a* spazioso; 〈*clothes*〉 ampio

roost /ruːst/ *vi* appollaiarsi

root[1] /ruːt/ *n* radice *f*; **take ~** metter radici ● **root out** *vt fig* scovare

root[2] *vi* **~ about** grufolare; **~ for sb** *Am fam* fare il tifo per qcno

rope /rəʊp/ *n* corda *f*; **know the ~s** *fam* conoscere i trucchi del mestiere ● **rope in** *vt fam* coinvolgere

rosary /ˈrəʊzərɪ/ *n* rosario *m*

rose[1] /rəʊz/ *n* rosa *f*; 〈*of watering-can*〉 bocchetta *f*

rose[2] *see* rise

rosé /ˈrəʊzeɪ/ *n* [vino *m*] rosé *m inv*

rosemary /ˈrəʊzmərɪ/ *n* rosmarino *m*

rosette /rəʊˈzet/ *n* coccarda *f*

roster /ˈrɒstə(r)/ *n* tabella *f* dei turni

rostrum /ˈrɒstrəm/ *n* podio *m*

rosy /ˈrəʊzɪ/ *a* (**-ier, -iest**) roseo

rot /rɒt/ *n* marciume *m*; 〈*fam: nonsense*〉 sciocchezze *fpl* ● *vi* 〈*pt/pp* rotted〉 marcire

rota /ˈrəʊtə/ *n* tabella *f* dei turni

rotary /ˈrəʊtərɪ/ *a* rotante

rotate /rəʊˈteɪt/ *vt* far ruotare; avvicendare 〈*crops*〉 ● *vi* ruotare. **~ion** /-eɪʃn/ *n* rotazione *f*; **in ~ion** a turno

rote /rəʊt/ *n* **by ~** meccanicamente

rotten /ˈrɒtn/ *a* marcio; *fam* schifoso; 〈*person*〉 penoso

rotund /rəʊˈtʌnd/ *a* paffuto

rough /rʌf/ *a* 〈*not smooth*〉 ruvido; 〈*ground*〉 accidentato; 〈*behaviour*〉 rozzo; 〈*sport*〉 violento; 〈*area*〉 malfamato; 〈*crossing, time*〉 brutto; 〈*estimate*〉 approssimativo ● *adv* 〈*play*〉 grossolanamente; **sleep ~** dormire sotto i ponti ● *vt* **~ it** vivere senza confort. **rough out** *vt* abbozzare

roughage /ˈrʌfɪdʒ/ *n* fibre *fpl*

rough 'draft *n* abbozzo *m*

rough|ly /ˈrʌflɪ/ *adv* rozzamente; 〈*more or less*〉 pressappoco. **~ness** *n* ruvidità *f*; 〈*of behaviour*〉 rozzezza *f*

rough paper *n* carta *f* da brutta

roulette /ruːˈlet/ *n* roulette *f*

round /raʊnd/ a rotondo ● n tondo m; (slice) fetta f; (of visits, drinks) giro m; (of competition) partita f; (boxing) ripresa f, round m inv; **do one's ~s** ⟨doctor:⟩ fare il giro delle visite ● prep intorno a; **open ~ the clock** aperto ventiquattr'ore ● adv **all ~** tutt'intorno; **ask sb ~** invitare qcno; **go/come ~ to** ⟨a friend etc⟩ andare da; **turn/look ~** girarsi; **~ about** (approximately) intorno a ● vt arrotondare; girare ⟨corner⟩. **round down** vt arrotondare (per difetto). **round off** vt (end) terminare. **round on** vt aggredire. **round up** vt radunare; arrotondare ⟨prices⟩

roundabout /raʊndəbaʊt/ a indiretto ● n giostra f; (for traffic) rotonda f

round: **~ 'trip** n viaggio m di andata e ritorno

rous|e /raʊz/ vt svegliare; risvegliare ⟨suspicion, interest⟩. **~ing** a di incoraggiamento

route /ruːt/ n itinerario m; Naut, Aeron rotta f; (of bus) percorso m

routine /ruːˈtiːn/ a di routine ● n routine f inv; Theat numero m

rov|e /rəʊv/ vi girovagare. **~ing** a ⟨reporter, ambassador⟩ itinerante

row[1] /rəʊ/ n (line) fila f; **three years in a ~** tre anni di fila

row[2] vi (in boat) remare

row[3] /raʊ/ n fam (quarrel) litigata f; (noise) baccano m ● vi fam litigare

rowdy /ˈraʊdɪ/ a (-ier, -iest) chiassoso

rowing boat /ˈrəʊɪŋ-/ n barca f a remi

royal /ˈrɔɪəl/ a reale

royal|ty /ˈrɔɪəltɪ/ n appartenenza f alla famiglia reale; (persons) i membri della famiglia reale. **~ies** npl (payments) diritti mpl d'autore

rpm abbr revolutions per minute

rub /rʌb/ n **give sth a ~** dare una sfregata a qcsa ● vt (pt/pp rubbed) sfregare. **rub in** vt **don't ~ it in** fam non rigirare il coltello nella piaga. **rub off** vt mandar via sfregando ⟨stain⟩; (from blackboard) cancellare ● vi andar via; **~ off on** essere trasmesso a. **rub out** vt cancellare

rubber /ˈrʌbə(r)/ n gomma f; (eraser) gomma f [da cancellare]. **~ band** n elastico m. **~y** a gommoso

rubbish /ˈrʌbɪʃ/ n immondizie fpl; (fam: nonsense) idiozie fpl; (fam: junk) robaccia f ● vt fam fare a pezzi. **~ bin** n pattumiera f. **~ dump** n discarica f; (official) discarica f comunale

rubble /ˈrʌbl/ n macerie fpl

ruby /ˈruːbɪ/ n rubino m ● attrib di rubini; ⟨lips⟩ scarlatta

rucksack /ˈrʌksæk/ n zaino m

rudder /ˈrʌdə(r)/ n timone m

ruddy /ˈrʌdɪ/ a (-ier, -iest) rubicondo; fam maledetto

rude /ruːd/ a scortese; (improper) spinto. **~ly** adv scortesemente. **~ness** n scortesia f

rudiment /ˈruːdɪmənt/ n **~s** pl rudimenti mpl. **~ary** /-ˈmentərɪ/ a rudimentale

rueful /ˈruːfl/ a rassegnato

ruffian /ˈrʌfɪən/ n farabutto m

ruffle /ˈrʌfl/ n gala f ● vt scompigliare ⟨hair⟩

rug /rʌɡ/ n tappeto m; (blanket) coperta f

rugby /ˈrʌɡbɪ/ n **~ [football]** rugby m

rugged /ˈrʌɡɪd/ a ⟨coastline⟩ roccioso

ruin /ˈruːɪn/ n rovina f; **in ~s** in rovina ● vt rovinare. **~ous** /-əs/ a estremamente costoso

rule /ruːl/ n regola f; (control) ordinamento m; (for measuring) metro m; **~s** pl regolamento msg; **as a ~** generalmente ● vt governare; dominare ⟨colony, behaviour⟩; **~ that** stabilire che ● vi governare. **rule out** vt escludere

ruled /ruːld/ a ⟨paper⟩ a righe

ruler /ˈruːlə(r)/ n capo m di Stato; (sovereign) sovrano, -a mf; (measure) righello m, regolo m

ruling /ˈruːlɪŋ/ a ⟨class⟩ dirigente; ⟨party⟩ di governo ● n decisione f

rum /rʌm/ n rum m inv

rumble /ˈrʌmbl/ n rombo m; (of stomach) brontolio m ● vi rombare; ⟨stomach:⟩ brontolare

rummage /ˈrʌmɪdʒ/ vi rovistare (in/through in)

rummy /ˈrʌmɪ/ n ramino m

rumour /ˈruːmə(r)/ n diceria f ● vt **it is ~ed that** si dice che

rump /rʌmp/ n natiche fpl. **~ steak** n bistecca f di girello

rumpus /ˈrʌmpəs/ n fam baccano m

run /rʌn/ n (on foot) corsa f; (distance to be covered) tragitto m; (outing) giro m; Theat rappresentazioni fpl; (in skiing) pista f, (Am: ladder) smagliatura f (in calze); **at a ~** di corsa; **~ of bad luck** periodo m sfortunato; **on the ~** in fuga; **have the ~ of** avere a disposizione; **in the long ~** a lungo termine ● v (pt ran, pp run, pres p running) ● vi correre; ⟨river:⟩ scorrere; ⟨nose, makeup:⟩ colare; ⟨bus:⟩ fare servizio; ⟨play:⟩ essere in cartellone; ⟨colours:⟩ sbiadire; (in *election*) presentarsi [come candidato] ● *vt* (*manage*) dirigere; tenere ⟨*house*⟩; ⟨*drive*⟩ dare un passaggio a; correre ⟨*risk*⟩; *Comput* lanciare; *Journ* pubblicare ⟨*article*⟩; ⟨*pass*⟩ far scorrere ⟨*eyes, hand*⟩; ~ **a bath** far scorrere l'acqua per il bagno. **run across** *vi* ⟨*meet, find*⟩ imbattersi in. **run away** *vi* scappare [via]. **run down** *vi* scaricarsi; ⟨*clock:*⟩ scaricarsi; ⟨*stocks:*⟩ esaurirsi ● *vt Auto* investire; ⟨*reduce*⟩ esaurire; ⟨*fam: criticize*⟩ denigrare. **run in** *vi* entrare di corsa. **run into** *vi* ⟨*meet*⟩ imbattersi in; ⟨*knock against*⟩ urtare. **run off** *vi* andare via di corsa ● *vt* stampare ⟨*copies*⟩. **run out** *vi* uscire di corsa; ⟨*supplies, money:*⟩ esaurirsi; ~ **out of** rimanere senza. **run over** *vi* correre; ⟨*overflow*⟩ traboccare ● *vt Auto* investire. **run through** *vi* scorrere. **run up** *vi* salire di corsa; ⟨*towards*⟩ arrivare di corsa ● *vt* accumulare ⟨*debts, bill*⟩; ⟨*sew*⟩ cucire

'**runaway** *n* fuggitivo, -a *mf*

run·'down *a* ⟨*area*⟩ in abbandono; ⟨*person*⟩ esaurito ● *n* analisi *f*

rung[1] /rʌŋ/ *n* ⟨*of ladder*⟩ piolo *m*

rung[2] *see* **ring**[2]

runner /'rʌnə(r)/ *n* podista *mf*; ⟨*in race*⟩ corridore, -trice *mf*; ⟨*on sledge*⟩ pattino *m*. ~ **bean** *n* fagiolino *m*. ~**-up** *n* secondo, -a *mf* classificato, -a

running /'rʌnɪŋ/ *a* in corsa; **four times** ~ quattro volte di

seguito ● *n* corsa *f*; ⟨*management*⟩ direzione *f*; **be in the** ~ essere in lizza. ~ '**commentary** *n* cronaca *f*

runny /'rʌnɪ/ *a* semiliquido; ~ **nose** naso che cola

run: ~**-of-the-'mill** *a* ordinario. ~**-up** *n* *Sport* rincorsa *f*; **the** ~**-up to** il periodo precedente. ~**way** *n* pista *f*

rupture /'rʌptʃə(r)/ *n* rottura *f*; *Med* ernia *f* ● *vt* rompere; ~ **oneself** farsi venire l'ernia ● *vi* rompersi

rural /'rʊərəl/ *a* rurale

ruse /ru:z/ *n* astuzia *f*

rush[1] /rʌʃ/ *n Bot* giunco *m*

rush[2] *n* fretta *f*; **in a** ~ di fretta ● *vi* precipitarsi ● *vt* far premura a; ~ **sb to hospital** trasportare qcno di corsa all'ospedale. ~**-hour** *n* ora *f* di punta

rusk /rʌsk/ *n* biscotto *m*

Russia /'rʌʃə/ *n* Russia *f*. ~**n** *a & n* russo, -a *mf*; ⟨*language*⟩ russo *m*

rust /rʌst/ *n* ruggine *f* ● *vi* arrugginirsi

rustic /'rʌstɪk/ *a* rustico

rustle /'rʌsl/ *vi* frusciare ● *vt* far frusciare; *Am* rubare ⟨*cattle*⟩. **rustle up** *vt fam* rimediare

'**rustproof** *a* a prova di ruggine

rusty /'rʌstɪ/ *a* (-**ier**, -**iest**) arrugginito

rut /rʌt/ *n* solco *m*; **in a** ~ *fam* nella routine

ruthless /'ru:θlɪs/ *a* spietato. ~**ness** *n* spietatezza *f*

rye /raɪ/ *n* segale *f*

Ss

---

sabbath /'sæbəθ/ *n* domenica *f*; ⟨*Jewish*⟩ sabato *m*

sabbatical /sə'bætɪkl/ *n Univ* anno *m* sabbatico

sabot|age /'sæbətɑːʒ/ *n* sabotaggio *m* ● *vt* sabotare. ~**eur** /-'tɜː(r)/ *n* sabotatore, -trice *mf*

saccharin /'sæʃeɪ/ *n* saccarina *f*

sachet /'sæʃeɪ/ *n* bustina *f*; ⟨*scented*⟩ sacchetto *m* profumato

sack[1] /sæk/ *vt* ⟨*plunder*⟩ saccheggiare

sack[2] *n* sacco *m*; **get the** ~ *fam* essere licenziato ● *vt fam* licenziare. ~**ing** *n* tela *f* per sacchi; ⟨*fam: dismissal*⟩ licenziamento *m*

sacrament /'sækrəmənt/ *n* sacramento *m*

sacred /'seɪkrɪd/ *a* sacro

sacrifice /'sækrɪfaɪs/ *n* sacrificio *m* ● *vt* sacrificare

sacrilege /'sækrɪlɪdʒ/ *n* sacrilegio *m*

sad /sæd/ *a* (**sadder, saddest**) triste. ~**den** *vt* rattristare

saddle /'sædl/ *n* sella *f* ● *vt* sellare; **I've been** ~**d with...** *fig* mi hanno affibbiato...

sadis|m /'seɪdɪzm/ *n* sadismo *m*. ~**t** /-dɪst/ *n* sadico, -a *mf*. ~**tic** /sə'dɪstɪk/ *a* sadico

sad|ly /'sædlɪ/ *adv* tristemente; ⟨*unfor-*

tunately) sfortunatamente. **~ness** *n* tristezza *f*

safe /seɪf/ *a* sicuro; (*out of danger*) salvo; (*object*) al sicuro; **~ and sound** sano e salvo ●*n* cassaforte *f*. **~guard** *n* protezione *f* ●*vt* proteggere. **~ly** *adv* in modo sicuro; (*arrive*) senza incidenti; (*assume*) con certezza

safety /'seɪftɪ/ *n* sicurezza *f*. **~-belt** *n* cintura *f* di sicurezza. **~-deposit box** *n* cassetta *f* di sicurezza. **~-pin** *n* spilla *f* di sicurezza o da balia. **~-valve** *n* valvola *f* di sicurezza

sag /sæg/ *vi* (*pt/pp* **sagged**) abbassarsi

saga /'sɑːgə/ *n* saga *f*

sage /seɪdʒ/ *n* (*herb*) salvia *f*

Sagittarius /sædʒɪ'teərɪəs/ *n* Sagittario *m*

said /sed/ *see* **say**

sail /seɪl/ *n* vela *f*; (*trip*) giro *m* in barca a vela ●*vi* navigare; *Sport* praticare la vela; (*leave*) salpare ●*vt* pilotare

sailboard *n* tavola *f* del windsurf. **~ing** *n* windsurf *m inv*

sailing /'seɪlɪŋ/ *n* vela *f*. **~-boat** *n* barca *f* a vela. **~-ship** *n* veliero *m*

sailor /'seɪlə(r)/ *n* marinaio *m*

saint /seɪnt/ *n* santo, -a *mf*. **~ly** *a* da santo

sake /seɪk/ *n* **for the ~ of** (*person*) per il bene di; (*peace*) per amor di; **for the ~ of it** per il gusto di farlo

salad /'sæləd/ *n* insalata *f*. **~ bowl** *n* insalatiera *f*. **~ cream** *n* salsa *f* per condire l'insalata. **~-dressing** *n* condimento *m* per insalata

salary /'sælərɪ/ *n* stipendio *m*

sale /seɪl/ *n* vendita *f*; (*at reduced prices*) svendita *f*; **for on ~** in vendita. **'for ~'** 'vendesi'

salesman /'seɪlzmæn/ *n* venditore *m*; (*traveller*) rappresentante *m*. **~woman** *n* venditrice *f*

salient /'seɪlɪənt/ *a* saliente

saliva /sə'laɪvə/ *n* saliva *f*

sallow /'sæləʊ/ *a* giallastro

salmon /'sæmən/ *n* salmone *m*

saloon /sə'luːn/ *n* *Auto* berlina *f*; (*Am: bar*) bar *m*

salt /sɔːlt/ *n* sale *m* ●*a* salato; (*fish*, *meat*) sotto sale ●*vt* salare; (*cure*) mettere sotto sale. **~-cellar** *n* saliera *f*. **~water** *n* acqua *f* di mare. **~y** *a* salato

salutary /'sæljʊtərɪ/ *a* salutare

salute /sə'luːt/ *n* *Mil* saluto *m* ●*vt* salutare ●*vi* fare il saluto

salvage /'sælvɪdʒ/ *n* *Naut* recupero *m* ●*vt* recuperare

salvation /sæl'veɪʃn/ *n* salvezza *f*. **S~ Army** *n* Esercito *m* della Salvezza

salvo /'sælvəʊ/ *n* salva *f*

same /seɪm/ *a* stesso (**as** di) ●*pron* **the ~** lo stesso; **be all the ~** essere tutti uguali ●*adv* **the ~** nello stesso modo; **all the ~** (*however*) lo stesso; **the ~ to you** altrettanto

sample /'sɑːmpl/ *n* campione *m* ●*vt* testare

sanatorium /sænə'tɔːrɪəm/ *n* casa *f* di cura

sanctimonious /sæŋktɪ'məʊnɪəs/ *a* moraleggiante

sanction /'sæŋkʃn/ *n* (*approval*) autorizzazione *f*; (*penalty*) sanzione *f* ●*vt* autorizzare

sanctity /'sæŋktətɪ/ *n* santità *f*

sanctuary /'sæŋktjʊərɪ/ *n* *Relig* santuario *m*; (*refuge*) asilo *m*; (*for wildlife*) riserva *f*

sand /sænd/ *n* sabbia *f* ●*vt* **~** [**down**] carteggiare

sandal /'sændl/ *n* sandalo *m*

sand: **~bank** *n* banco *m* di sabbia. **~paper** *n* carta *f* vetrata ●*vt* cartavetrare. **~-pit** *n* recinto *m* contenente sabbia dove giocano i bambini

sandwich /'sænwɪdʒ/ *n* tramezzino *m* ●*vt* **~ed between** schiacciato tra

sandy /'sændɪ/ *a* (**-ier, -iest**) (*beach*, *soil*) sabbioso; (*hair*) biondiccio

sane /seɪn/ *a* (*not mad*) sano di mente; (*sensible*) sensato

sang /sæŋ/ *see* **sing**

sanitary /'sænɪtərɪ/ *a* igienico; (*system*) sanitario. **~ napkin** *n Am*, **~ towel** *n* assorbente *m* igienico

sanitation /sænɪ'teɪʃn/ *n* impianti *mpl* igienici

sanity /'sænətɪ/ *n* sanità *f* di mente; (*common sense*) buon senso *m*

sank /sæŋk/ *see* **sink**

sapphire /'sæfaɪə(r)/ *n* zaffiro *m* ●*a* blu zaffiro *inv*

sarcasm /'sɑːkæzm/ *n* sarcasmo *m*. **~tic** /-'kæstɪk/ *a* sarcastico

sardine /sɑː'diːn/ *n* sardina *f*

Sardinia /sɑː'dɪnɪə/ *n* Sardegna *f*. **~n** *a* & *n* sardo, -a *mf*

sardonic /sɑː'dɒnɪk/ *a* sardonico

sash /sæʃ/ *n* fascia *f*; (*for dress*) fusciacca *f*

sat /sæt/ *see* **sit**

satanic /sə'tænɪk/ *a* satanico

satchel /'sætʃl/ *n* cartella *f*

satellite /'sætəlaɪt/ *n* satellite *m*. **~**

dish n antenna f parabolica. ~ **television** n televisione f via satellite

satin /'sætɪn/ n raso m ● attrib di raso

satire /'sætaɪə(r)/ n satira f

satirical /sə'tɪrɪkl/ a satirico

satir|ist /'sætɪrɪst/ n scrittore, -trice mf satirico, -a; (comedian) comico, -a mf satirico, -a. ~**ize** vt satireggiare

satisfaction /sætɪs'fækʃn/ n soddisfazione f; **be to sb's** ~ soddisfare qcno

satisfactor|y /sætɪs'fæktərɪ/ a soddisfacente. ~**ily** adv in modo soddisfacente

satisf|y /'sætɪsfaɪ/ vt (pp/pp -ied) soddisfare; (convince) convincere; **be** ~**ied** essere soddisfatto. ~**ying** a soddisfacente

saturat|e /'sætʃəreɪt/ vt inzuppare (with di); Chem, fig saturare (with di). ~**ed** a saturo

Saturday /'sætədeɪ/ n sabato m

sauce /sɔ:s/ n salsa f; (cheek) impertinenza f. ~**pan** n pentola f

saucer /'sɔ:sə(r)/ n piattino m

saucy /'sɔ:sɪ/ a (-ier, -iest) impertinente

Saudi Arabia /saʊdɪə'reɪbɪə/ n Arabia f Saudita

sauna /'sɔ:nə/ n sauna f

saunter /'sɔ:ntə(r)/ vi andare a spasso

sausage /'sɒsɪdʒ/ n salsiccia f; (dried) salame m

savage /'sævɪdʒ/ a feroce; (tribe, custom) selvaggio ● n selvaggio, -a mf ● vt fare a pezzi. ~**ry** n ferocia f

save /seɪv/ n Sport parata f ● vt salvare (from da); (keep, collect) tenere; risparmiare (time, money); (avoid) evitare; Sport parare (goal); Comput salvare, memorizzare ● vi |up| risparmiare ● prep salvo

saver /'seɪvə(r)/ n risparmiatore, -trice mf

savings /'seɪvɪŋz/ npl (money) risparmi mpl. ~ **account** n libretto m di risparmio. ~ **bank** n cassa f di risparmio

saviour /'seɪvjə(r)/ n salvatore m

savour /'seɪvə(r)/ n sapore m ● vt assaporare. ~**y** a salato; fig rispettabile

saw[1] /sɔ:/ see **see**[1]

saw[2] n sega f ● vt/i (pt sawed, pp sawn or sawed) segare. ~**dust** n segatura f

saxophone /'sæksəfəʊn/ n sassofono m

say /seɪ/ n have one's ~ dire la propria; **have a** ~ avere voce in capitolo ● vt/i (pt/pp said) dire; **that is to** ~ cioè; **that goes without** ~**ing** questo è

ovvio; **when all is said and done** alla fine dei conti. ~**ing** n proverbio m

scab /skæb/ n crosta f; pej crumiro m

scaffold /'skæfəld/ n patibolo m. ~**ing** n impalcatura f

scald /skɔ:ld/ vt scottare; (milk) scaldare ● n scottatura f

scale[1] /skeɪl/ n (of fish) scaglia f

scale[2] n scala f; **on a grand** ~ su vasta scale ● vt (climb) scalare. **scale down** vt diminuire

scales /skeɪlz/ npl (for weighing) bilancia fsg

scallop /'skɒləp/ n (shellfish) pettine m

scalp /skælp/ n cuoio m capelluto

scalpel /'skælpl/ n bisturi m inv

scam /skæm/ n fam fregatura f

scamper /'skæmpə(r)/ vi ~ **away** sgattaiolare via

scampi /'skæmpɪ/ npl scampi mpl

scan /skæn/ n Med scanning m inv. scansioscintigrafia f ● vt (pt/pp scanned) scrutare; (quickly) dare una scorsa a; Med fare uno scanning di

scandal /'skændl/ n scandalo m; (gossip) pettegolezzi mpl. ~**ize** /-d(ə)laɪz/ vt scandalizzare. ~**ous** /-əs/ a scandaloso

Scandinavia /skændɪ'neɪvɪə/ n Scandinavia f. ~**n** a & n scandinavo, -a mf

scanner /'skænə(r)/ n Comput scanner m inv

scant /skænt/ a scarso

scant|y /'skæntɪ/ a (-ier, -iest) scarso; (clothing) succinto. ~**ily** adv scarsamente; (clothed) succintamente

scapegoat /'skeɪpgəʊt/ n capro m espiatorio

scar /skɑ:(r)/ n cicatrice f ● vt (pt/pp scarred) lasciare una cicatrice a

scarc|e /skeəs/ a scarso; fig raro; **make oneself** ~**e** fam svignarsela. ~**ely** adv appena; ~**ely anything** quasi niente. ~**ity** n scarsezza f

scare /skeə(r)/ n spavento m; (panic) panico m ● vt spaventare; **be** ~**d** aver paura (**of** di)

scarecrow /'skeəkrəʊ/ n spaventapasseri m inv

scarf /skɑ:f/ n (pl scarves) sciarpa f; (square) foulard m inv

scarlet /'skɑ:lət/ a scarlatto. ~ **fever** n scarlattina f

scary /'skeərɪ/ a **be** ~ far paura

scathing /'skeɪðɪŋ/ a mordace

scatter /'skætə(r)/ vt spargere; (disperse) disperdere ● vi disperdersi. ~**-brained** a fam scervellato. ~**ed** a sparso

scatty /'skætɪ/ a (-ier, -iest) fam svitato

scavenge /'skævɪndʒ/ vi frugare nella spazzatura. ~r n persona f che fruga nella spazzatura

scenario /sɪ'nɑːrɪəʊ/ n scenario m

scene /siːn/ n scena f; (quarrel) scenata f; behind the ~s dietro le quinte

scenery /'siːnərɪ/ n scenario m

scenic /'siːnɪk/ a panoramico

scent /sent/ n odore m; (trail) scia f; (perfume) profumo m. ~ed a profumato (with di)

sceptic|al /'skeptɪkl/ a scettico. ~ism /-tɪsɪzm/ n scetticismo m

schedule /'ʃedjuːl/ n piano m, programma m; (of work) programma m; (timetable) orario m; behind ~ in indietro; on ~ nei tempi previsti; according to ~ secondo i tempi previsti ● vt prevedere. ~d flight n volo m di linea

scheme /skiːm/ n (plan) piano m, (plot) macchinazione f ● vi pej macchinare

schizophren|ia /skɪtsə'friːnɪə/ n schizofrenia f. ~ic /-'frenɪk/ a schizofrenico

scholar /'skɒlə(r)/ n studioso, -a mf. ~ly a erudito. ~ship n erudizione f; (grant) borsa f di studio

school /skuːl/ n scuola f; (in university) facoltà f; (of fish) branco m

school: ~boy n scolaro m. ~girl n scolara f. ~ing n istruzione f. ~-teacher n insegnante mf

sciatica /saɪ'ætɪkə/ n sciatica f

scien|ce /'saɪəns/ n scienza f; ~ce fiction fantascienza f. ~tific /-'tɪfɪk/ a scientifico. ~tist n scienziato, -a mf

scintillating /'sɪntɪleɪtɪŋ/ a brillante

scissors /'sɪzəz/ npl forbici fpl

scoff¹ /skɒf/ vi ~ at schernire

scoff² vt fam divorare

scold /skəʊld/ vt sgridare. ~ing n sgridata f

scone /skɒn/ n pasticcino m da tè

scoop /skuːp/ n paletta f; Journ scoop m inv ● scoop out vt svuotare. scoop up vt tirar su

scope /skəʊp/ n portata f; (opportunity) opportunità f inv

scorch /skɔːtʃ/ vt bruciare. ~er n fam giornata f torrida. ~ing a caldissimo

score /skɔː(r)/ n punteggio m; Mus partitura f; (for film, play) musica f; a ~ [of] (twenty) una ventina [di]; keep [the] ~ tenere il punteggio; on that ~ a questo proposito ● vt segnare (goal); (cut) incidere ● vi far punti; (in football etc) segnare; (keep score) tenere il punteggio. ~r n segnapunti m inv; (of goals) giocatore, -trice mf che segna

scorn /skɔːn/ n disprezzo m ● vt disprezzare. ~ful a sprezzante

Scorpio /'skɔːpɪəʊ/ n Astr Scorpione m

scorpion /'skɔːpɪən/ n scorpione m

Scot /skɒt/ n scozzese mf

Scotch /skɒtʃ/ a scozzese ● n (whisky) whisky m [scozzese]

scotch vt far cessare

scot-'free a get off ~ cavarsela impunemente

Scot|land /'skɒtlənd/ n Scozia f. ~s, ~tish a scozzese

scoundrel /'skaʊndrəl/ n mascalzone m

scour¹ /'skaʊə(r)/ vt (search) perlustrare

scour² vt (clean) strofinare

scourge /skɜːdʒ/ n flagello m

scout /skaʊt/ n Mil esploratore m ● vi ~ for andare in cerca di

Scout n (Boy) ~ [boy]scout m inv

scowl /skaʊl/ n sguardo m torvo ● vi guardare [di] storto

Scrabble® /'skræbl/ n Scarabeo® m

scraggy /'skrægɪ/ a (-ier, -iest) pej scarno

scram /skræm/ vi fam levarsi dai piedi

scramble /'skræmbl/ n (climb) arrampicata f ● vi (clamber) arrampicarsi; ~ for azzuffarsi per ● vt Teleph creare delle interferenze in; (eggs) strapazzare

scrap¹ /skræp/ n (fam: fight) litigio m

scrap² n pezzetto m; (metal) ferraglia f; ~s pl (of food) avanzi mpl ● vt (pt/pp scrapped) buttare via

'scrap-book n album m inv

scrape /skreɪp/ vt raschiare; (damage) graffiare. **scrape through** vi passare per un pelo. **scrape together** vt racimolare

scraper /'skreɪpə(r)/ n raschietto m

scrappy /'skræpɪ/ a frammentario

'scrap-yard n deposito m di ferraglia; (for cars) cimitero m delle macchine

scratch /skrætʃ/ n graffio m; (to relieve itch) grattata f; start from ~ partire da zero; up to ~ (work) all'altezza ● vt graffiare; (to relieve itch) grattare ● vi grattarsi

scrawl /skrɔːl/ n scarabocchio m ● vt/i scarabocchiare

scrawny /'skrɔːnɪ/ a (-ier, -iest) pej magro

scream /skriːm/ n strillo m ●vt/i strillare

screech /skriːtʃ/ n stridore m ●vi stridere ●vt strillare

screen /skriːn/ n paravento m; Cinema, TV schermo m ●vt proteggere; (conceal) riparare; proiettare (film); (candidates) passare al setaccio; Med sottoporre a visita medica. **~ing** n Med visita f medica; (of film) proiezione f. **~play** n sceneggiatura f

screw /skruː/ n vite f ●vt avvitare. **screw up** vt (crumple) accartocciare; strizzare (eyes); storcere (face); (sl: bungle) mandare all'aria

'**screwdriver** n cacciavite m inv

screwy /'skruːɪ/ a (-ier, -iest) fam svitato

scribble /'skrɪbl/ n scarabocchio m ●vt/i scarabocchiare

script /skrɪpt/ n scrittura f (a mano); (of film) sceneggiatura f

'**script-writer** n sceneggiatore, -trice m f

scroll /skrəʊl/ n rotolo m (di pergamena); (decoration) voluta f

scrounge /skraʊndʒ/ vt/i scroccare. **~r** n scroccone, -a mf

scrub[1] /skrʌb/ n (land) boscaglia f

scrub[2] /skrʌb/ vt (pt/pp **scrubbed**) strofinare; (fam: cancel) cancellare (plan)

scruff /skrʌf/ n by the **~** of the neck per la collottola

scruffy /'skrʌfɪ/ a (-ier, -iest) trasandato

scrum /skrʌm/ n (in rugby) mischia f

scruple /'skruːpl/ n scrupolo m

scrupulous /'skruːpjʊləs/ a scrupoloso

scrutin|ize /'skruːtɪnaɪz/ vt scrutinare. **~y** n (look) esame m minuzioso

scuffle /'skʌfl/ n tafferuglio m

sculpt /skʌlpt/ vt/i scolpire. **~or** /'skʌlptə(r)/ n scultore m. **~ure** /-tʃə(r)/ n scultura f

scum /skʌm/ n schiuma f; (people) feccia f

scurrilous /'skʌrɪləs/ a scurrile

scurry /'skʌrɪ/ vi (pt/pp -ied) affrettare il passo

scuttle /'skʌtl/ vi (hurry) **~ away** correre via

sea /siː/ n mare m; at **~** in mare; fig confuso; by **~** via mare. **~board** n costiera f. **~food** n frutti mpl di mare. **~gull** n gabbiano m

seal[1] /siːl/ n Zool foca f

seal[2] /siːl/ n sigillo m; Techn chiusura f ermetica ●vt sigillare; Techn chiudere ermeticamente. **seal off** vt bloccare (area)

'**sea-level** n livello m del mare

seam /siːm/ n cucitura f; (of coal) strato m

'**seaman** n marinaio m

seamless /'siːmlɪs/ a senza cucitura

seamy /'siːmɪ/ a sordido; (area) malfamato

seance /'seɪɑːns/ n seduta f spiritica

sea: **~plane** n idrovolante m. **~port** n porto m di mare

search /sɜːtʃ/ n ricerca f; (official) perquisizione f; **in ~** of alla ricerca di ●vt frugare (for alla ricerca di); perlustrare (area); (officially) perquisire ●vi **~ for** cercare. **~ing** a penetrante

search: **~light** n riflettore m. **~-party** n squadra f di ricerca

sea: **~sick** a be/get **~** avere il mal di mare. **~side** n at/to the **~side** al mare. **~side resort** n stazione f balneare. **~side town** n città f di mare

season /'siːzn/ n stagione f ●vt (flavour) condire. **~able** /-əbl/ a, **~al** a stagionale. **~ing** n condimento m

'**season ticket** n abbonamento m

seat /siːt/ n (chair) sedia f; (in car) sedile m; (place to sit) posto m [a sedere]; (bottom) didietro m; (of government) sede f; **take a ~** sedersi ●vt mettere a sedere; (have seats for) avere posti [a sedere] per; **remain ~ed** mantenere il proprio posto. **~-belt** n cintura f di sicurezza

sea: **~weed** n alga f marina. **~worthy** a in stato di navigare

secateurs /sekə'tɜːz/ npl cesoie fpl

seclu|ded /sɪ'kluːdɪd/ a appartato. **~sion** /-ʒn/ n isolamento m

second[1] /sɪ'kɒnd/ vt (transfer) distaccare

second[2] /'sekənd/ a secondo; **on ~ thoughts** ripensandoci meglio ●n secondo m; **~s** pl (goods) merce fsg di seconda scelta; **have ~s** (at meal) fare il bis; **John the S~** Giovanni Secondo ●adv (in race) al secondo posto ●vt assistere; appoggiare (proposal)

secondary /'sekəndrɪ/ a secondario. **~ school** n scuola f media (inferiore e superiore)

second: **~-best** a secondo dopo il migliore; **be ~-best** pej essere un ripiego. **~ class** adv (travel, send) in seconda classe. **~-class** a di seconda classe

'**second hand** n (on clock) lancetta f dei secondi

second-'hand a & adv di seconda mano

secondly /'sekəndlɪ/ adv in secondo luogo

second-'rate a di second'ordine

secrecy /'si:krəsɪ/ n segretezza f; **in ~** in segreto

secret /'si:krɪt/ a segreto • n segreto m

secretarial /sekrə'teərɪəl/ a (work, staff) di segreteria

secretary /'sekrətərɪ/ n segretario, -a mf

secret|e /sɪ'kri:t/ vt secernere (poison). **~ion** /-i:ʃn/ n secrezione f

secretive /'si:krətɪv/ a riservato. **~ness** n riserbo m

secretly /'si:krɪtlɪ/ adv segretamente

sect /sekt/ n setta f. **~arian** a settario

section /'sekʃn/ n sezione f

sector /'sektə(r)/ n settore m

secular /'sekjʊlə(r)/ a secolare; (education) laico

secure /sɪ'kjʊə(r)/ a sicuro • vt proteggere; chiudere bene (door); rendere stabile (ladder); (obtain) assicurarsi. **~ly** adv saldamente

security /sɪ'kjʊərətɪ/ n sicurezza f; (for loan) garanzia f. **~ies** npl titoli mpl

sedate¹ /sɪ'deɪt/ a posato

sedate² vt somministrare sedativi a

sedation /sɪ'deɪʃn/ n somministrazione f di sedativi; **be under ~** essere sotto l'effetto di sedativi

sedative /'sedətɪv/ a sedativo • n sedativo m

sedentary /'sedəntərɪ/ a sedentario

sediment /'sedɪmənt/ n sedimento m

seduce /sɪ'dju:s/ vt sedurre

seduct|ion /sɪ'dʌkʃn/ n seduzione f. **~ive** /-tɪv/ a seducente

see /si:/ v (pt saw, pp seen) • vt vedere; (understand) capire; (escort) accompagnare; **go and ~** andare a vedere; (visit) andare a trovare; **~ you!** ci vediamo!; **~ you later!** a più tardi!; **~ing that** visto che ● vi vedere; (understand) capire; **~ about** occuparsi di. **see off** vt veder partire; (chase away) mandar via. **see through** vi vedere attraverso; (fig non farsi ingannare da • vt portare a buon fine. **see to** vi occuparsi di

seed /si:d/ n seme m; Tennis testa f di serie; **go to ~** fare seme; fig lasciarsi andare. **~ed player** n Tennis testa f di serie. **~ling** n pianticella f

seedy /'si:dɪ/ a (-ier, -iest) squallido

seek /si:k/ vt (pt/pp sought) cercare

seem /si:m/ vi sembrare. **~ingly** adv apparentemente

seen /si:n/ see **see¹**

seep /si:p/ vi filtrare

see-saw /'si:sɔ:/ n altalena f

seethe /si:ð/ vi **~ with anger** ribollire di rabbia

'see-through a trasparente

segment /'segmənt/ n segmento m; (of orange) spicchio m

segregat|e /'segrɪgeɪt/ vt segregare. **~ion** /-'geɪʃn/ n segregazione f

seize /si:z/ vt afferrare; Jur confiscare. **seize up** vi Techn bloccarsi

seizure /'si:ʒə(r)/ n Jur confisca f; Med colpo m [apoplettico]

seldom /'seldəm/ adv raramente

select /sɪ'lekt/ a scelto; (exclusive) esclusivo ● vt scegliere; selezionare (team). **~ion** /-ekʃn/ n selezione f. **~ive** /-ɪv/ a selettivo. **~or** n Sport selezionatore, -trice mf

self /self/ n io m

self: **~-ad'dressed** a con il proprio indirizzo. **~-ad'hesive** a autoadesivo. **~-as'surance** n sicurezza f di sé. **~-as'sured** a sicuro di sé. **~-'catering** a in appartamento attrezzato di cucina. **~-'centred** a egocentrico. **~-'confidence** n fiducia f in se stesso. **~-'confident** a sicuro di sé. **~-'conscious** a impacciato. **~-con'tained** a (flat) con ingresso indipendente. **~-con'trol** n autocontrollo m. **~-de'fence** n autodifesa f; Jur legittima difesa f. **~-de'nial** n abnegazione f. **~-determi'nation** n autodeterminazione f. **~-em'ployed** a che lavora in proprio. **~-e'steem** n stima f di sé. **~-'evident** a ovvio. **~-'governing** a autonomo. **~-'help** n iniziativa f personale. **~-in'dulgent** a indulgente con se stesso. **~-'interest** n interesse m personale

selfish /'selfɪʃ/ a egoista. **~ishness** n egoismo m. **~less** a disinteressato

self: **~-'made** a che si è fatto da sé. **~-'pity** n autocommiserazione f. **~-'portrait** n autoritratto m. **~-pos'sessed** a padrone di sé. **~-'preser'vation** n istinto m di conservazione. **~-re'spect** n amor m proprio. **~-'righteous** a presuntuoso. **~-'sacrifice** n abnegazione f. **~-'satisfied** a compiaciuto di sé. **~-'service** n self-service m inv ● attrib self-service. **~-suf·fi·cient** *a* autosufficiente. **~-willed** *a* ostinato

sell /sel/ *v* (*pt/pp* sold) ● *vt* vendere; be **sold out** essere esaurito ● *vi* vendersi. **sell off** *vt* liquidare

seller /'selə(r)/ *n* venditore, -trice *mf*

Sellotape® /'seləʊ-/ *n* nastro *m* adesivo, scotch® *m*

'sell-out *n* (*fam: betrayal*) tradimento *m*; be a **~** (*concert:*) fare il tutto esaurito

selves /selvz/ *pl of* self

semblance /'sembləns/ *n* parvenza *f*

semen /'si:mən/ *n* Anat liquido *m* seminale

semester /sɪ'mestə(r)/ *n Am* semestre *m*

semi /'semɪ/: **~breve** /'semibri:v/ *n* semibreve *f*. **~circle** /'semɪsɜ:k(ə)l/ *n* semicerchio *m*. **~circular** *a* semicircolare. **~colon** *n* punto e virgola *m*. **~-detached** *a* gemella ● *n* casa *f* gemella. **~·final** *n* semifinale *f*

seminar /'semɪnɑ:(r)/ *n* seminario *m*. **~y** /-nərɪ/ *n* seminario *m*

semolina /semə'li:nə/ *n* semolino *m*

senate /'senət/ *n* senato *m*. **~or** *n* senatore *m*

send /send/ *vt/i* (*pt/pp* sent) mandare; **~ for** mandare a chiamare (*person*); far venire (*thing*). **~er** *n* mittente *mf*. **~-off** *n* commiato *m*

senile /'si:naɪl/ *a* arteriosclerotico; Med senile. **~ity** /sɪ'nɪlətɪ/ *n* senilismo *m*

senior /'si:nɪə(r)/ *a* più vecchio; (*in rank*) superiore ● *n* (*in rank*) superiore *mf*; (*in sport*) senior *mf*; she's two years my **~** è più vecchia di me di due anni. **~ citizen** *n* anziano, -a *mf*

seniority /si:nɪ'ɒrətɪ/ *n* anzianità *f* di servizio

sensation /sen'seɪʃn/ *n* sensazione *f*. **~al** *a* sensazionale. **~ally** *adv* in modo sensazionale

sense /sens/ *n* senso *m*; (*common ~*) buon senso *m*; in a **~** in un certo senso; **make ~** aver senso ● *vt* sentire. **~less** *a* insensato; (*unconscious*) privo di sensi

sensible /'sensəbl/ *a* sensato; (*suitable*) appropriato. **~y** *adv* in modo appropriato

sensitive /'sensɪtɪv/ *a* sensibile; (*touchy*) suscettibile. **~ely** *adv* con sensibilità. **~ity** /-'tɪvɪtɪ/ *n* sensibilità *f inv*

sensory /'sensərɪ/ *a* sensoriale

sensual /'sensjʊəl/ *a* sensuale. **~ity** /-'ælətɪ/ *n* sensualità *f inv*

sensuous /'sensjʊəs/ *a* voluttuoso

sent /sent/ *see* send

sentence /'sentəns/ *n* frase *f*; Jur sentenza *f*; (*punishment*) condanna *f* ● *vt* **~ to** condannare a

sentiment /'sentɪmənt/ *n* sentimento *m*; (*opinion*) opinione *f*; (*sentimentality*) sentimentalismo *m*. **~al** /-'mentl/ *a* sentimentale; *pej* sentimentalista. **~ality** /-'tælətɪ/ *n* sentimentalità *f inv*

sentry /'sentrɪ/ *n* sentinella *f*

separable /'sepərəbl/ *a* separabile

separate¹ /'sepərət/ *a* separato. **~ly** *adv* separatamente

separate² /'sepəreɪt/ *vt* separare ● *vi* separarsi. **~ion** /-'reɪʃn/ *n* separazione *f*

September /sep'tembə(r)/ *n* settembre *m*

septic /'septɪk/ *a* settico; go **~** infettarsi. **~ tank** *n* fossa *f* biologica

sequel /'si:kwəl/ *n* seguito *m*

sequence /'si:kwəns/ *n* sequenza *f*

sequin /'si:kwɪn/ *n* lustrino *m*, paillette *f inv*

serenade /serə'neɪd/ *n* serenata *f* ● *vt* fare una serenata a

serene /sɪ'ri:n/ *a* sereno. **~ity** /-'renətɪ/ *n* serenità *f inv*

sergeant /'sɑ:dʒənt/ *n* sergente *m*

serial /'sɪərɪəl/ *n* racconto *m* a puntate; *TV* sceneggiato *m* a puntate; *Radio* commedia *f* radiofonica a puntate. **~ize** *vt* pubblicare a puntate; *Radio, TV* trasmettere a puntate. **~ killer** *n* serial killer *mf inv*. **~ number** *n* numero *m* di serie. **~ port** *n Comput* porta *f* seriale

series /'sɪəri:z/ *n* serie *f inv*

serious /'sɪərɪəs/ *a* serio; (*illness, error*) grave. **~ly** *adv* seriamente; (*ill*) gravemente; **take ~ly** prendere sul serio. **~ness** *n* serietà *f*; (*of situation*) gravità *f*

sermon /'sɜ:mən/ *n* predica *f*

serpent /'sɜ:pənt/ *n* serpente *m*

serrated /se'reɪtɪd/ *a* dentellato

serum /'sɪərəm/ *n* siero *m*

servant /'sɜ:vənt/ *n* domestico, -a *mf*

serve /sɜ:v/ *n Tennis* servizio *m* ● *vt* servire; scontare (*sentence*); **~ its purpose** servire al proprio scopo; **it ~s you right!** ben ti sta!; **~s two** per due persone ● *vi* prestare servizio; *Tennis* servire. **~ as** servire da

server /'sɜ:və(r)/ *n Comput* server *m inv*

service /'sɜ:vɪs/ *n* servizio *m*; Relig funzione *f*; (*maintenance*) revisione *f*. **~s** *pl* forze *fpl* armate; (*on motorway*) area *f* di servizio; **in the ~s** sotto le armi; **of ~ to** utile a; **out of ~** ~

⟨*machine:*⟩ guasto • *vt* Techn revisionare. ~**able** /-əbl/ *a* utilizzabile; ⟨*hardwearing*⟩ resistente; ⟨*practical*⟩ pratico

service: ~ **area** *n* area *f* di servizio. ~ **charge** *n* servizio *m*. ~**man** *n* militare *m*. ~ **provider** *n* fornitore, -trice *m* di servizi. ~ **station** *n* stazione *f* di servizio

serviette /sɜːvɪˈet/ *n* tovagliolo *m*

servile /ˈsɜːvaɪl/ *a* servile

session /ˈseʃn/ *n* seduta *f*; Jur sessione *f*; Univ anno *m* accademico

set /set/ *n* serie *f inv*, set *m inv*; ⟨*of crockery, cutlery*⟩ servizio *m*; TV, Radio apparecchio *m*; Math insieme *m*; Theat scenario *m*; Cinema, Tennis set *m inv*; ⟨*of people*⟩ circolo *m*; ⟨*of hair*⟩ messa *f* in piega • *a* ⟨*ready*⟩ pronto; ⟨*rigid*⟩ fisso; ⟨*book*⟩ in programma; **be ~ on doing sth** essere risoluto a fare qcsa; **be ~ in one's ways** essere abitudinario • *v* (*pt/pp* **set**, *pres p* **setting**) • *vt* mettere, porre; mettere ⟨*alarm clock*⟩; assegnare ⟨*task, homework*⟩; fissare ⟨*date, limit*⟩; chiedere ⟨*questions*⟩; montare ⟨*gem*⟩; assestare ⟨*bone*⟩; apparecchiare ⟨*table*⟩; ~ **fire to** dare fuoco a; ~ **free** liberare • *vi* ⟨*sun:*⟩ tramontare; ⟨*jelly, concrete:*⟩ solidificare; ~ **about doing sth** mettersi a fare qcsa. **set back** *vt* mettere indietro; ⟨*hold up*⟩ ritardare; ⟨*fam: cost*⟩ costare a. **set off** *vi* partire • *vt* avviare; mettere ⟨*alarm*⟩; fare esplodere ⟨*bomb*⟩. **set out** *vi* partire; ~ **out to do sth** proporsi di fare qcsa • *vt* disporre; ⟨*state*⟩ esporre. **set to** *vi* mettersi all'opera. **set up** *vt* fondare ⟨*company*⟩; istituire ⟨*committee*⟩

'set-back *n* passo *m* indietro

set 'meal *n* menù *m inv* fisso

settee /seˈtiː/ *n* divano *m*

setting /ˈsetɪŋ/ *n* scenario *m*; ⟨*position*⟩ posizione *f*; ⟨*of sun*⟩ tramonto *m*; ⟨*of jewel*⟩ montatura *f*

settle /ˈsetl/ *vt* ⟨*decide*⟩ definire; risolvere ⟨*argument*⟩; fissare ⟨*date*⟩; calmare ⟨*nerves*⟩; saldare ⟨*bill*⟩ • *vi* ⟨*to live*⟩ stabilirsi; ⟨*snow, dust, bird:*⟩ posarsi; ⟨*subside*⟩ assestarsi; ⟨*sediment:*⟩ depositarsi. **settle down** *vi* sistemarsi; ⟨*stop making noise*⟩ calmarsi. **settle for** *vt* accontentarsi di. **settle up** *vi* regolare i conti

settlement /ˈsetlmənt/ *n* ⟨*agreement*⟩ accordo *m*; ⟨*of bill*⟩ saldo *m*; ⟨*colony*⟩ insediamento *m*

settler /ˈsetlə(r)/ *n* colonizzatore, -trice *mf*

'set-to *n fam* zuffa *f*; ⟨*verbal*⟩ battibecco *m*

'set-up *n* situazione *f*

seven /ˈsevn/ *a & n* sette *m*. ~**teen** *a & n* diciassette *m*. ~**'teenth** *a & n* diciassettesimo, -a *mf*

seventh /ˈsevnθ/ *a & n* settimo, -a *mf*

seventieth /ˈsevntɪɪθ/ *a & n* settantesimo, -a *mf*

seventy /ˈsevntɪ/ *a & n* settanta *m*

sever /ˈsevə(r)/ *vt* troncare ⟨*relations*⟩

several /ˈsevrəl/ *a & pron* parecchi

sever|e /sɪˈvɪə(r)/ *a* severo; ⟨*pain*⟩ violento; ⟨*illness*⟩ grave; ⟨*winter*⟩ rigido. ~**ely** *adv* severamente; ⟨*ill*⟩ gravemente. ~**ity** /-ˈverətɪ/ *n* severità *f*; ⟨*of pain*⟩ violenza *f*; ⟨*of illness*⟩ gravità *f*; ⟨*of winter*⟩ rigore *m*

sew /səʊ/ *vt/i* (*pt* **sewed**, *pp* **sewn** or **sewed**) cucire. **sew up** *vt* ricucire

sewage /ˈsuːɪdʒ/ *n* acque *fpl* di scolo

sewer /ˈsuːə(r)/ *n* fogna *f*

sewing /ˈsəʊɪŋ/ *n* cucito *m*; ⟨*work*⟩ lavoro *m* di cucito. ~ **machine** *n* macchina *f* da cucire

sewn /səʊn/ *see* **sew**

sex /seks/ *n* sesso *m*; **have ~** avere rapporti sessuali. ~**ist** *a* sessista. ~ **offence** *n* delitto *m* a sfondo sessuale

sexual /ˈseksjʊəl/ *a* sessuale. ~ '**intercourse** *n* rapporti *mpl* sessuali. ~**ity** /-ˈælətɪ/ *n* sessualità *f*. ~**ly** *adv* sessualmente

sexy /ˈseksɪ/ *a* (**-ier, -iest**) sexy *inv*

shabby /ˈʃæbɪ/ *a* (**-ier, -iest**) scialbo; ⟨*treatment*⟩ meschino. ~**iness** *n* trasandatezza *f*; ⟨*of treatment*⟩ meschinità *f inv*

shack /ʃæk/ *n* catapecchia *f* • **shack up with** *vt fam* vivere con

shade /ʃeɪd/ *n* ombra *f*; ⟨*of colour*⟩ sfumatura *f*; ⟨*for lamp*⟩ paralume *m*; ⟨*Am: for window*⟩ tapparella *f*; **a ~ better** un tantino meglio • *vt* riparare dalla luce; ⟨*draw lines on*⟩ ombreggiare. ~**s** *npl fam* occhiali *mpl* da sole

shadow /ˈʃædəʊ/ *n* ombra *f*; **S~ Cabinet** governo *m* ombra • *vt* ⟨*follow*⟩ pedinare. ~**y** *a* ombroso

shady /ˈʃeɪdɪ/ *a* (**-ier, -iest**) ombroso; ⟨*fam: disreputable*⟩ losco

shaft /ʃɑːft/ *n* Techn albero *m*; ⟨*of light*⟩ raggio *m*; ⟨*of lift, mine*⟩ pozzo *m*

shaggy /ˈʃægɪ/ *a* (**-ier, -iest**) irsuto; ⟨*animal*⟩ dal pelo arruffato

shake /ʃeɪk/ *n* scrollata *f* • *v* (*pt* **shook**, *pp* **shaken**) • *vt* scuotere; agitare ⟨*bottle*⟩; far tremare ⟨*building*⟩; ~ **hands with** stringere la mano a • *vi* tremare. **shake off** *vt* scrollarsi di dosso. **~-up** n Pol rimpasto m; Comm ristrutturazione f

shaky /ˈʃeɪkɪ/ a (-ier, -iest) tremante; ⟨table etc⟩ traballante; ⟨unreliable⟩ vacillante

shall /ʃæl/ v aux I ~ go andrò; we ~ see vedremo; what ~ I do? cosa faccio?; I'll come too, ~ I? vengo anch'io, no?; thou shalt not kill liter non uccidere

shallow /ˈʃæləʊ/ a basso, poco profondo; ⟨dish⟩ poco profondo; fig superficiale

sham /ʃæm/ a falso ● n finzione f; ⟨person⟩ spaccone, -a mf ● vt ⟨pt/pp shammed⟩ simulare

shambles /ˈʃæmblz/ n baraonda fsg

shame /ʃeɪm/ n vergogna f; it's a ~ that è un peccato che; what a ~! che peccato! **~-faced** a vergognoso

shame|ful /ˈʃeɪmfl/ a vergognoso. **~less** a spudorato

shampoo /ʃæmˈpuː/ n shampoo m inv ● vt fare uno shampoo a

shandy /ˈʃændɪ/ n bevanda f a base di birra e gassosa

shan't /ʃɑːnt/ = shall not

shanty town /ˈʃæntɪtaʊn/ n bidonville f inv, baraccopoli f inv

shape /ʃeɪp/ n forma f; ⟨figure⟩ ombra f; take ~ prendere forma; get back in ~ ritornare in forma ● vt dare forma a ⟨into di⟩ ● vi ~ [up] mettere la testa a posto; ~ up nicely mettersi bene. **~less** a informe

shapely /ˈʃeɪplɪ/ a (-ier, -iest) ben fatto

share /ʃeə(r)/ n porzione f; Comm azione f ● vt dividere; condividere ⟨views⟩ ● vi dividere. **~holder** n azionista mf

shark /ʃɑːk/ n squalo m, pescecane m; fig truffatore, -trice mf

sharp /ʃɑːp/ a ⟨knife etc⟩ tagliente; ⟨pencil⟩ appuntito; ⟨drop⟩ a picco; ⟨reprimand⟩ severo; ⟨outline⟩ marcato; ⟨alert⟩ acuto; ⟨unscrupulous⟩ senza scrupoli; ~ pain fitta f ● adv in punto; Mus fuori tono; look ~! sbrigati! ● n Mus diesis m inv. **~en** vt affilare ⟨knife⟩; appuntire ⟨pencil⟩

shatter /ˈʃætə(r)/ vt frantumare; fig mandare in frantumi; **~ed** ⟨fam: exhausted⟩ a pezzi ● vi frantumarsi

shav|e /ʃeɪv/ n rasatura f; have a ~e farsi la barba ● vt radere ● vi radersi. **~er** n rasoio m elettrico. **~ing-brush** n pennello m da barba; **~ing foam** n schiuma f da barba; **~ing soap** n sapone m da barba

shawl /ʃɔːl/ n scialle m

she /ʃiː/ pers pron lei

sheaf /ʃiːf/ n ⟨pl sheaves⟩ fascio m

shear /ʃɪə(r)/ vt ⟨pt sheared, pp shorn or sheared⟩ tosare

shears /ʃɪəz/ npl ⟨for hedge⟩ cesoie fpl

sheath /ʃiːθ/ n ⟨pl ~s /ʃiːðz/⟩ guaina f

shed¹ /ʃed/ n baracca f; ⟨for cattle⟩ stalla f

shed² vt ⟨pt/pp shed, pres p shedding⟩ perdere; versare ⟨blood, tears⟩; ~ light on far luce su

sheen /ʃiːn/ n lucentezza f

sheep /ʃiːp/ n inv pecora f. **~-dog** n cane m da pastore

sheepish /ˈʃiːpɪʃ/ a imbarazzato. **~ly** adv con aria imbarazzata

'sheepskin n [pelle f di] montone m

sheer /ʃɪə(r)/ a puro; ⟨steep⟩ a picco; ⟨transparent⟩ trasparente ● adv a picco

sheet /ʃiːt/ n lenzuolo m; ⟨of paper⟩ foglio m; ⟨of glass, metal⟩ lastra f

shelf /ʃelf/ n ⟨pl shelves⟩ ripiano m; ⟨set of shelves⟩ scaffale m

shell /ʃel/ n conchiglia f; ⟨of egg, snail, tortoise⟩ guscio m; ⟨of crab⟩ corazza f; ⟨of unfinished building⟩ ossatura f; Mil granata f ● vt sgusciare ⟨peas⟩; Mil bombardare. **shell out** vi fam sborsare

'shellfish n inv mollusco m; Culin frutti mpl di mare

shelter /ˈʃeltə(r)/ n rifugio m; ⟨air raid ~⟩ rifugio m antiaereo ● vt riparare ⟨from da⟩; fig mettere al riparo; ⟨give lodging to⟩ dare asilo a ● vi rifugiarsi. **~ed** ⟨spot⟩ riparato; ⟨life⟩ ritirato

shelve /ʃelv/ vt accantonare ⟨project⟩

shelves /ʃelvz/ see shelf

shelving /ˈʃelvɪŋ/ n ⟨shelves⟩ ripiani mpl

shepherd /ˈʃepəd/ n pastore m ● vt guidare. **~'s pie** n pasticcio m di carne tritata e patate

sherry /ˈʃerɪ/ n sherry m inv

shield /ʃiːld/ n scudo m; ⟨for eyes⟩ maschera f; Techn schermo m ● vt proteggere ⟨from da⟩

shift /ʃɪft/ n cambiamento m; ⟨in position⟩ spostamento m; ⟨at work⟩ turno m ● vt spostare; ⟨take away⟩ togliere; riversare ⟨blame⟩ ● vi spostarsi; ⟨wind:⟩ cambiare; ⟨fam: move quickly⟩ darsi una mossa

'shift work n turni mpl

shifty /ˈʃɪftɪ/ a (-ier, -iest) pej losco; ⟨eyes⟩ sfuggente

shilly-shally /ˈʃɪlɪʃælɪ/ vi titubare

shimmer /ˈʃɪmə(r)/ n luccichio m •vi luccicare

shin /ʃɪn/ n stinco m

shine /ʃaɪn/ n lucentezza f; give sth a ~ dare una lucidata a qcsa •v (pt/pp shone) •vi splendere; (reflect light) brillare; ⟨hair, shoes:⟩ essere lucido •vt ~ a light on puntare una luce su

shingle /ˈʃɪŋgl/ n (pebbles) ghiaia f

shingles /ˈʃɪŋglz/ n Med fuochi mpl di Sant'Antonio

shiny /ˈʃaɪnɪ/ a (-ier, -iest) lucido

ship /ʃɪp/ n nave f •vt (pt/pp shipped) spedire; (by sea) spedire via mare

ship: ~ment n spedizione f; (consignment) carico m. ~per n spedizioniere m. ~ping n trasporto m; (traffic) imbarcazioni fpl. ~shape a & adv in perfetto ordine. ~wreck n naufragio m. ~wrecked a naufragato. ~yard n cantiere m navale

shirk /ʃɜːk/ vt scansare. ~er n scansafatiche mf inv

shirt /ʃɜːt/ n camicia f; in ~-sleeves in maniche di camicia

shit /ʃɪt/ vulg n & int merda f •vi (pt/pp shit) cagare

shiver /ˈʃɪvə(r)/ n brivido m •vi rabbrividire

shoal /ʃəʊl/ n (of fish) banco m

shock /ʃɒk/ n (impact) urto m; Electr scossa f [elettrica]; fig colpo m, shock m inv; Med shock m inv; get a ~ Electr prendere la scossa •vt scioccare. ~ing a scioccante; (fam: weather, handwriting etc) tremendo

shod /ʃɒd/ see shoe

shoddy /ˈʃɒdɪ/ a (-ier, -iest) scadente

shoe /ʃuː/ n scarpa f; (of horse) ferro m •vt (pt/pp shod, pres p shoeing) ferrare ⟨horse⟩

shoe: ~horn n calzante m. ~lace n laccio m da scarpa. ~maker n calzolaio m. ~shop n calzoleria f. ~string n on a ~string fam con una miseria

shone /ʃɒn/ see shine

shoo /ʃuː/ vt ~ away cacciar via •int sciò

shook /ʃʊk/ see shake

shoot /ʃuːt/ n Bot germoglio m; (hunt) battuta f di caccia •v (pt/pp shot) •vt sparare; girare ⟨film⟩ •vi (hunt) andare a caccia. **shoot down** vt abbattere. **shoot out** vi (rush) precipitarsi fuori. **shoot up** vi (grow) crescere in fretta; ⟨prices:⟩ salire di colpo

'shooting-range n poligono m di tiro

shop /ʃɒp/ n negozio m; (workshop) of-

ficina f; talk ~ fam parlare di lavoro •vi (pt/pp shopped) far compere; go ~ping andare a fare compere. **shop around** vi confrontare i prezzi

shop: ~ assistant n commesso, -a mf. ~keeper n negoziante mf. ~-lifter n taccheggiatore, -trice mf. ~-lifting n taccheggio m; ~per n compratore, -trice mf

shopping /ˈʃɒpɪŋ/ n compere fpl; (articles) acquisti mpl; do the ~ fare la spesa. ~ bag n borsa f per la spesa. ~ centre n centro m commerciale. ~ trolley n carrello m

shop: ~-steward n rappresentante mf sindacale. ~-window n vetrina f

shore /ʃɔː(r)/ n riva f

shorn /ʃɔːn/ see shear

short /ʃɔːt/ a corto; (not lasting) breve; ⟨person⟩ basso; (curt) brusco; a ~ time ago poco tempo fa; be ~ of essere a corto di; be in ~ supply essere scarso; fig essere raro; Mick is ~ for Michael Mick è il diminutivo di Michael •adv bruscamente; in ~ in breve; in ~ of doing a meno di fare; go ~ essere privato (di); stop ~ of doing sth non arrivare fino a fare qcsa; cut ~ interrompere ⟨meeting, holiday⟩; to cut a long story ~ per farla breve

shortage /ˈʃɔːtɪdʒ/ n scarsità f inv

short: ~bread n biscotto m di pasta frolla. ~ circuit n corto m circuito. ~coming n difetto m. ~ cut n scorciatoia f

shorten /ˈʃɔːtn/ vt abbreviare; accorciare ⟨garment⟩

short: ~hand n stenografia f. ~-handed a corto di personale. ~hand typist n stenodattilografo, -a mf. ~ list n lista f dei candidati selezionati per un lavoro. ~-lived /-lɪvd/ a di breve durata

short|ly /ˈʃɔːtlɪ/ adv presto; ~ly before/after poco prima/dopo. ~ness n brevità f inv; (of person) bassa statura f

short-range a di breve portata

shorts /ʃɔːts/ npl calzoncini mpl corti

short: ~-sighted a miope. ~-sleeved a a maniche corte. ~-staffed a a corto di personale. ~ story n racconto m, novella f. ~-tempered a irascibile. ~-term a a breve termine. ~ wave n onde fpl corte

shot /ʃɒt/ see shoot •n colpo m; (person) tiratore m; Phot foto f inv; (injection) puntura f; (fam: attempt) pro-

va f; **like a ~** fam come un razzo. **~gun**
n fucile m da caccia

should /ʃʊd/ v aux **I ~** go dovrei andare; **I ~ have seen him** avrei dovuto ve-
derlo; **I ~ like** mi piacerebbe; **this ~**
be enough questo dovrebbe bastare; **if**
he ~ come se dovesse venire

shoulder /'ʃəʊldə(r)/ n spalla f ● vt mettersi in spalla; fig accollarsi. **~-bag** n
borsa f a tracolla. **~-blade** n scapola f.
~-strap n spallina f; (of bag) tracolla f

shout /ʃaʊt/ n grido m ● vt/i gridare.
shout at vi alzar la voce con. **shout**
down vt azzittire gridando

shouting /'ʃaʊtɪŋ/ n grida fpl

shove /ʃʌv/ n spintone m ● vt spingere;
(fam: put) ficcare ● vi spingere. **shove**
off vi fam togliersi di torno

shovel /'ʃʌvl/ n pala f ● vt (pt/pp
shovelled) spalare

show /ʃəʊ/ n (display) manifestazione
f; (exhibition) mostra f; (ostentation)
ostentazione f; Theat, TV spettacolo m;
(programme) programma m; **on ~**
esposto ● v (pt showed, pp shown)
● vt mostrare; (put on display) esporre;
proiettare (film) ● vi (film:) essere pro-
iettato; **your slip is ~ing** ti si vede la
sottoveste. **show in** vt far accomodare.
show off vi fam mettersi in mostra
● vt mettere in mostra. **show up** vi risaltare; (fam: arrive) farsi vedere ● vt
(fam: embarrass) far fare una brutta
figura a

'show-down n regolamento m dei conti

shower /'ʃaʊə(r)/ n doccia f; (of rain)
acquazzone m; **have a ~** fare la doccia
● vt ~ **with** coprire di ● vi fare la doccia. **~proof** a impermeabile. **~y** a da
acquazzoni

'show-jumping n concorso m ippico

shown /ʃəʊn/ see show

'show-off n esibizionista mf

showy /'ʃaʊ/ a appariscente

shrank /ʃræŋk/ see shrink

shred /ʃred/ n brandello m; fig briciolo
m ● vt (pt/pp shredded) fare a brandelli; Culin tagliuzzare. **~der** n distruttore
m di documenti

shrewd /ʃruːd/ a accorto. **~ness** n accortezza f

shriek /ʃriːk/ n strillo m ● vt/i strillare

shrift /ʃrɪft/ n **give sb short ~** liquidare qcno rapidamente

shrill /ʃrɪl/ a penetrante

shrimp /ʃrɪmp/ n gamberetto m

shrine /ʃraɪn/ n (place) santuario m

shrink /ʃrɪŋk/ vi (pt shrank, pp
shrunk) restringersi; (draw back) ritrarsi (from da)

shrivel /'ʃrɪvl/ vi (pt/pp shrivelled)
raggrinzare

shroud /ʃraʊd/ n sudario m; fig manto m

Shrove /ʃrəʊv/ n **~ Tuesday** martedì
m grasso

shrub /ʃrʌb/ n arbusto m

shrug /ʃrʌg/ n scrollata f di spalle
● vt/i (pt/pp shrugged) **~ |one's**
shoulders scrollare le spalle

shrunk /ʃrʌŋk/ see shrink   **~en** a
rimpicciolito

shudder /'ʃʌdə(r)/ n fremito m ● vi fre-
mere

shuffle /'ʃʌfl/ vi strascicare i piedi ● vt
mescolare (cards)

shun /ʃʌn/ vt (pt/pp shunned) rifuggi-
re

shunt /ʃʌnt/ vt smistare

shush /ʃʊʃ/ int zitto!

shut /ʃʌt/ v (pt/pp shut, pres p
shutting) ● vt chiudere ● vi chiudersi;
(shop:) chiudere. **shut down** vt/i chiudere. **shut up** vt chiudere; fam far tacere ● vi fam stare zitto; **~ up!** stai zitto!

'shut-down n chiusura f

shutter /'ʃʌtə(r)/ n serranda f; Phot ot-
turatore m

shuttle /'ʃʌtl/ n navetta f ● vi far la
spola

shuttle: ~cock n volano m. **~**
service n servizio m pendolare

shy /ʃaɪ/ a (timid) timido. **~ness** n timidezza f

Siamese /saɪə'miːz/ a siamese

sibling /'sɪblɪŋ/ n (brother) fratello m;
(sister) sorella f; **~ s** pl fratelli mpl

Sicily /'sɪsɪlɪ/ n Sicilia f. **~ian** a & n si-
ciliano, -a mf

sick /sɪk/ a ammalato; (humour) macabro; **be ~** (vomit) vomitare; **be ~ of**
sth fam essere stufo di qcsa; **feel ~**
aver la nausea

sicken /'sɪkn/ vt disgustare ● vi be
~ing for something covare qualche
malanno. **~ing** a disgustoso

sick|ly /'sɪklɪ/ a (-ier, -iest) malaticcio.
~ness n malattia f; (vomiting) nausea f.
~ness benefit n indennità f di malattia

side /saɪd/ n lato m; (of person,
mountain) fianco m; (of road) bordo m;
on the ~ (as sideline) come attività secondaria; **~ by ~** fianco a fianco; **take**
~s immischiarsi; **take sb's ~** prende-

re le parti di qcno; **be on the safe ~**
andare sul sicuro ● *attrib* laterale ● *vi*
~ with parteggiare per

side: **~board** *n* credenza *f*. **~s** *npl*
basette *fpl*. **~-effect** *n* effetto *m*
collaterale. **~lights** *npl* luci *fpl* di posizione. **~line** *n* attività *f inv* complementare. **~show** *n* attrazione *f*.
~-step *vt* schivare. **~-track** *vt* sviare.
~walk *n Am* marciapiede *m*. **~ways**
adv obliquamente

siding /'saɪdɪŋ/ *n* binario *m* di raccordo

sidle /'saɪdl/ *vi* camminare furtivamente (**up to verso**)

siege /siːdʒ/ *n* assedio *m*

sieve /sɪv/ *n* setaccio *m* ● *vt* setacciare

sift /sɪft/ *vt* setacciare; **~ |through|** *fig*
passare al setaccio

sigh /saɪ/ *n* sospiro *m* ● *vi* sospirare

sight /saɪt/ *n* vista *f*; (*on gun*) mirino *m*;
the ~s *pl* le cose da vedere; **at first ~** a
prima vista; **be within/out of ~**
essere/non essere in vista; **lose ~ of**
perdere di vista; **know by ~** conoscere
di vista. **have bad ~** vederci male ● *vt*
avvistare

'sightseeing *n* **go ~** andare a visitare
posti

sign /saɪn/ *n* segno *m*; (*notice*) insegna *f*
● *vt/i* firmare. **sign on** *vi* (*as
unemployed*) presentarsi all'ufficio di
collocamento; *Mil* arruolarsi

signal /'sɪgnl/ *n* segnale *m* ● *v* (*pt/pp
signalled*) *vt* segnalare ● *vi* fare se-
gnali; **~ to sb** far segno a qcno (**to do**).
~-box *n* cabina *f* di segnalazione

signature /'sɪgnətʃə(r)/ *n* firma *f*. **~
tune** *n* sigla *f* [musicale]

signet-ring /'sɪgnɪt-/ *n* anello *m* con sigillo

significa|nce /sɪg'nɪfɪkəns/ *n* signifi-
cato *m*. **~t** *a* significativo

signify /'sɪgnɪfaɪ/ *vt* (*pt/pp* -**ied**) indicare

sign-language *n* linguaggio *m* dei se-
gni

signpost /'saɪn-/ *n* segnalazione *f* stradale

silence /'saɪləns/ *n* silenzio *m* ● *vt* far
tacere. **~r** *n* (*on gun*) silenziatore *m*;
Auto marmitta *f*

silent /'saɪlənt/ *a* silenzioso; (*film*)
muto; **remain ~** rimanere in silenzio.
~ly *adv* silenziosamente

silhouette /sɪlu'et/ *n* sagoma *f*, silhouette *f inv* ● *vt* **be ~d** profilarsi

silicon /'sɪlɪkən/ *n* silicio *m*. **~ chip**
piastrina *f* di silicio

silk /sɪlk/ *n* seta *f* ● *attrib* di seta.
~worm *n* baco *m* da seta

silky /'sɪlkɪ/ *a* (-**ier**, -**iest**) come la seta

sill /sɪl/ *n* davanzale *m*

silly /'sɪlɪ/ *a* (-**ier**, -**iest**) sciocco

silo /'saɪləʊ/ *n* silo *m*

silt /sɪlt/ *n* melma *f*

silver /'sɪlvə(r)/ *a* d'argento; (*paper*)
argentato ● *n* argento *m*; (*silverware*)
argenteria *f*

silver: **~-plated** *a* placcato d'argento.
~ware *n* argenteria *f*. **~ 'wedding** *n*
nozze *fpl* d'argento

similar /'sɪmɪlə(r)/ *a* simile. **~ity**
/-'lærətɪ/ *n* somiglianza *f*. **~ly** *adv* in
modo simile

simile /'sɪmɪlɪ/ *n* similitudine *f*

simmer /'sɪmə(r)/ *vi* bollire lentamente ● *vt* far bollire lentamente. **simmer
down** *vi* calmarsi

simple /'sɪmpl/ *a* semplice; (*person*)
semplicotto. **~-'minded** *a* sempliciotto

simplicity /sɪm'plɪsətɪ/ *n* semplicità *f*

simpli|fication /sɪmplɪfɪ'keɪʃn/ *n*
semplificazione *f*. **~fy** /'sɪmplɪfaɪ/ *vt*
(*pt/pp* -**ied**) semplificare

simply /'sɪmplɪ/ *adv* semplicemente

simulat|e /'sɪmjʊleɪt/ *vt* simulare.
~ion /-'leɪʃn/ *n* simulazione *f*

simultaneous /sɪml'teɪnɪəs/ *a* simul-
taneo

sin /sɪn/ *n* peccato *m* ● *vi* (*pt/pp
sinned*) peccare

since /sɪns/ *prep* da ● *adv* da allora
● *conj* da quando; (*because*) siccome

sincere /sɪn'sɪə(r)/ *a* sincero. **~ly** *adv*
sinceramente; **Yours ~ly** distinti saluti

sincerity /sɪn'serətɪ/ *n* sincerità *f*

sinful /'sɪnfl/ *a* peccaminoso

sing /sɪŋ/ *vt/i* (*pt* **sang**, *pp* **sung**) cantare

singe /sɪndʒ/ *vt* (*pres p* **singeing**) bru-
ciacchiare

singer /'sɪŋə(r)/ *n* cantante *mf*

single /'sɪŋgl/ *a* solo; (*not double*) semplice; (*unmarried*) celibe; (*woman*) nubile; (*room*) singolo; (*bed*) a una piazza
● *n* (*ticket*) biglietto *m* di sola andata;
(*record*) singolo *m*; **~s** *pl Tennis* singolo
m ● **single out** *vt* scegliere; (*distinguish*) distinguere

single: **~-breasted** *a* a un petto.
~-handed *a & adv* da solo. **~-minded** *a*
risoluto. **~ 'parent** *n* genitore *m* che alleva il figlio da solo

singly /'sɪŋglɪ/ *adv* singolarmente

singular /'sɪŋgjʊlə(r)/ *a Gram* singolare ● *n* singolare *m*. ~**ly** *adv* singolarmente

sinister /'sɪnɪstə(r)/ *a* sinistro

sink /sɪŋk/ *n* lavandino *m* ● *v* (*pt* sank, *pp* sunk) ● *vi* affondare ● *vt* affondare ⟨ship⟩; scavare ⟨shaft⟩; investire ⟨money⟩. **sink in** *vi* penetrare; **it took a while to ~ in** ⟨*fam*: *be understood*⟩ c'è voluto un po' a capirlo

sinner /'sɪnə(r)/ *n* peccatore, -trice *mf*

sinus /'saɪnəs/ *n* seno *m* paranasale. ~**itis** *n* sinusite *f*

sip /sɪp/ *n* sorso *m* ● *vt* (*pt/pp* sipped) sorseggiare

siphon /'saɪfn/ *n* ⟨bottle⟩ sifone *m* ● **siphon off** *vt* travasare ⟨con sifone⟩

sir /sɜː(r)/ *n* signore *m*; S~ ⟨title⟩ Sir *m*; Dear S~s Spettabile ditta

siren /'saɪrən/ *n* sirena *f*

sissy /'sɪsɪ/ *n* femminuccia *f*

sister /'sɪstə(r)/ *n* sorella *f*; ⟨nurse⟩ [infermiera *f*] caposala *f*. ~**-in-law** *n* (*pl* ~**s-in-law**) cognata *f*. ~**ly** *a* da sorella

sit /sɪt/ *v* (*pt/pp* sat, *pres p* sitting) ● *vi* essere seduto; ⟨sit down⟩ sedersi; ⟨committee⟩ riunirsi ● *vt* sostenere ⟨exam⟩. **sit back** *vi fig* starsene con le mani in mano. **sit down** *vi* mettersi a sedere. **sit up** *vi* mettersi seduto; ⟨not slouch⟩ star seduto diritto; ⟨stay up⟩ stare alzato

site /saɪt/ *n* posto *m*; Archaeol sito *m*; ⟨building ~⟩ cantiere *m* ● *vt* collocare

sit-in /'sɪtɪn/ *n* occupazione *f* ⟨di fabbrica ecc⟩

sitting /'sɪtɪŋ/ *n* seduta *f*; ⟨for meals⟩ turno *m*. ~**-room** *n* salotto *m*

situat|e /'sɪtjʊeɪt/ *vt* situare. ~**ed** *a* situato. ~**ion** /-'eɪʃn/ *n* situazione *f*; ⟨location⟩ posizione *f*; ⟨job⟩ posto *m*

six /sɪks/ *a & n* sei *m*. ~**teen** *a & n* sedici *m*. ~**teenth** *a & n* sedicesimo, -a *mf*

sixth /sɪksθ/ *a & n* sesto, -a *mf*

sixtieth /'sɪkstɪɪθ/ *a & n* sessantesimo, -a *mf*

sixty /'sɪkstɪ/ *a & n* sessanta *m*

size /saɪz/ *n* dimensioni *fpl*; ⟨of clothes⟩ taglia *f*, misura *f*; ⟨of shoes⟩ numero *m*; **what ~ is the room?** che dimensioni ha la stanza? ● **size up** *vt fam* valutare

sizeable /'saɪzəbl/ *a* piuttosto grande

sizzle /'sɪzl/ *vi* sfrigolare

skate¹ /skeɪt/ *n inv* ⟨fish⟩ razza *f*

skate² /skeɪt/ *n* pattino *m* ● *vi* pattinare

skateboard /'skeɪtbɔːd/ *n* skate-board *m inv*

skater /'skeɪtə(r)/ *n* pattinatore, -trice *mf*

skating /'skeɪtɪŋ/ *n* pattinaggio *m*. ~**-rink** *n* pista *f* di pattinaggio

skeleton /'skelɪtn/ *n* scheletro *m*. ~'**key** *n* passe-partout *m inv*. ~ 'staff *n* personale *m* ridotto

sketch /sketʃ/ *n* schizzo *m*; Theat sketch *m inv* ● *vt* fare uno schizzo di

sketch|y /'sketʃɪ/ *a* (-**ier**, -**iest**) abbozzato. ~**ily** *adv* in modo abbozzato

skewer /'skjʊə(r)/ *n* spiedo *m*

ski /skiː/ *n* sci *m inv* ● *vi* (*pt/pp* skied, *pres p* skiing) sciare; **go ~ing** andare a sciare

skid /skɪd/ *n* slittata *f* ● *vi* (*pt/pp* skidded) slittare

skier /'skiːə(r)/ *n* sciatore, -trice *mf*

skiing /'skiːɪŋ/ *n* sci *m*

skilful /'skɪlfl/ *a* abile

'**ski-lift** *n* impianto *m* di risalita

skill /skɪl/ *n* abilità *f inv*. ~**ed** *a* dotato; ⟨worker⟩ specializzato

skim /skɪm/ *vt* (*pt/pp* skimmed) schiumare; scremare ⟨milk⟩. **skim off** *vt* togliere. **skim through** *vt* scorrere

skimp /skɪmp/ *vi* ~ **on** lesinare su

skimpy /'skɪmpɪ/ *a* (-**ier**, -**iest**) succinto

skin /skɪn/ *n* pelle *f*; ⟨on fruit⟩ buccia *f* ● *vt* (*pt/pp* skinned) spellare

skin: ~-**deep** *a* superficiale. ~-**diving** *n* nuoto *m* subacqueo

skinflint /'skɪnflɪnt/ *n* miserabile *mf*

skinny /'skɪnɪ/ *a* (-**ier**, -**iest**) molto magro

skip¹ /skɪp/ *n* ⟨container⟩ benna *f*

skip² /skɪp/ *n* salto *m* ● *v* (*pt/pp* skipped) ● *vi* saltellare; ⟨with rope⟩ saltare la corda ● *vt* omettere

skipper /'skɪpə(r)/ *n* skipper *m inv*

skipping-rope /'skɪpɪŋrəʊp/ *n* corda *f* per saltare

skirmish /'skɜːmɪʃ/ *n* scaramuccia *f*

skirt /skɜːt/ *n* gonna *f* ● *vt* costeggiare

skit /skɪt/ *n* bozzetto *m* comico

skittle /'skɪtl/ *n* birillo *m*

skive /skaɪv/ *vi fam* fare lo scansafatiche

skulk /skʌlk/ *vi* aggirarsi furtivamente

skull /skʌl/ *n* cranio *m*

skunk /skʌŋk/ *n* moffetta *f*

sky /skaɪ/ *n* cielo *m*. ~'**light** *n* lucernario *m*. ~'**scraper** *n* grattacielo *m*

slab /slæb/ *n* lastra *f*; ⟨slice⟩ fetta *f*; ⟨of chocolate⟩ tavoletta *f*

slack /slæk/ *a* lento; ⟨person⟩ fiacco ● *vi* fare lo scansafatiche. **slack off** *vi* rilassarsi

slacken /'slækn/ *vi* allentare; ~ [off]

⟨trade:⟩ rallentare; ⟨speed, rain:⟩ diminuire ● vt allentare; diminuire ⟨speed⟩

slacks /slæks/ npl pantaloni mpl sportivi

slag /slæg/ n scorie fpl ● **slag off** vt (pt/pp **slagged**) Br fam criticare

slain /sleɪn/ see **slay**

slam /slæm/ v (pt/pp **slammed**) ● vt sbattere; ⟨fam: criticize⟩ stroncare ● vi sbattere .

slander /'slɑːndə(r)/ n diffamazione f ● vt diffamare. ~**ous** /-rəs/ a diffamatorio

slang /slæŋ/ n gergo m. ~**y** a gergale

slant /slɑːnt/ n pendenza f; ⟨point of view⟩ angolazione f; **on the** ~ in pendenza ● vt pendere; fig distorcere ⟨report⟩ ● vi pendere

slap /slæp/ n schiaffo m ● vt (pt/pp **slapped**) schiaffeggiare; ⟨put⟩ schiaffare ● adv in pieno

slap: ~**-dash** a fam frettoloso. ~**-up** a fam di prim'ordine

slash /slæʃ/ n taglio m ● vt tagliare; ridurre drasticamente ⟨prices⟩

slat /slæt/ n stecca f

slate /sleɪt/ n ardesia f ● vt fam fare a pezzi

slaughter /'slɔːtə(r)/ n macello m; ⟨of people⟩ massacro m ● vt macellare; massacrare ⟨people⟩. ~**house** n macello m

Slav /slɑːv/ a slavo ● n slavo. ·a mf

slave /sleɪv/ n schiavo, ·a mf ● vi ~ |**away**| lavorare come un negro. ~**-driver** n schiavista mf

slav|ery /'sleɪvərɪ/ n schiavitù f. ~**ish** a servile

Slavonic /slə'vɒnɪk/ a slavo

slay /sleɪ/ vt (pt slew, pp slain) ammazzare

sleazy /'sliːzɪ/ a (-ier, -iest) sordido

sledge /sledʒ/ n slitta f. ~**-hammer** n martello m

sleek /sliːk/ a liscio, lucente; ⟨well-fed⟩ pasciuto

sleep /sliːp/ n sonno m; **go to** ~ addormentarsi; **put to** ~ far addormentare ● v (pt/pp **slept**) ● vi dormire ● vt ~**s** six ha sei posti letto. ~**er** n Rail treno m con vagoni letto; ⟨compartment⟩ vagone m letto; **be a light/heavy** ~**er** avere il sonno leggero/pesante

sleeping: ~**-bag** n sacco m a pelo. ~**-car** n vagone m letto. ~**-pill** n sonnifero m

sleep: ~**less** a insonne. ~**lessness** n insonnia f. ~**-walker** n sonnambulo, ·a mf. ~**-walking** n sonnambulismo m

sleepy /'sliːpɪ/ a (-ier, -iest) assonnato; **be** ~ aver sonno

sleet /sliːt/ n nevischio m ● vi **it is** ~**ing** nevischia

sleeve /sliːv/ n manica f; ⟨for record⟩ copertina f. ~**less** a senza maniche

sleigh /sleɪ/ see **slitta** f

sleight /slaɪt/ n ~ **of hand** gioco m di prestigio

slender /'slendə(r)/ a snello; ⟨fingers, stem⟩ affusolato; fig scarso; ⟨chance⟩ magro

slept /slept/ see **sleep**

sleuth /sluːθ/ n investigatore m, detective m inv

slew[1] /sluː/ vi girare

slew[2] see **slay**

slice /slaɪs/ n fetta f ● vt affettare; ~**d bread** pane m a cassetta

slick /slɪk/ a liscio; ⟨cunning⟩ astuto ● n ⟨of oil⟩ chiazza f di petrolio

slid|e /slaɪd/ n scivolata f; ⟨in playground⟩ scivolo m; ⟨for hair⟩ fermaglio m ⟨per capelli⟩; Phot diapositiva f ● v (pt/pp **slid**) ● vi scivolare ● vt far scivolare. ~**-rule** n regolo m calcolatore. ~**ing** a ⟨door, seat⟩ scorrevole. ~**ing scale** n scala f mobile

slight /slaɪt/ a leggero; ⟨importance⟩ poco; ⟨slender⟩ esile. ~**est** minimo; **not in the** ~**est** niente affatto ● vt offendere ● n offesa f. ~**ly** adv leggermente

slim /slɪm/ a (**slimmer, slimmest**) snello; fig scarso; ⟨chance⟩ magro ● vi dimagrire

slim|e /slaɪm/ n melma f. ~**y** a melmoso; fig viscido

sling /slɪŋ/ n Med benda f al collo ● vt (pt/pp **slung**) fam lanciare

slip /slɪp/ n scivolata f; ⟨mistake⟩ lieve errore m; ⟨petticoat⟩ sottoveste f; ⟨for pillow⟩ federa f; ⟨paper⟩ scontrino m; **give sb the** ~ fam sbarazzarsi di qcno; ~ **of the tongue** lapsus m inv ● v (pt/pp **slipped**) ● vi scivolare; ⟨go quickly⟩ sgattaiolare; ⟨decline⟩ retrocedere ● vt he ~**ped it into his pocket** se l'è infilato in tasca; ~ **sb's mind** sfuggire di mente a qcno. **slip away** vi sgusciar via; ⟨time:⟩ sfuggire. **slip into** vi infilarsi ⟨clothes⟩. **slip up** vi fam sbagliare

slipped 'disc n Med ernia f del disco

slipper /'slɪpə(r)/ n pantofola f

slippery /'slɪpərɪ/ a scivoloso

slip-road n bretella f

slipshod /'slɪpʃɒd/ a trascurato

'slip-up n fam sbaglio m

slit /slɪt/ n spacco m; (tear) strappo m; (hole) fessura f ● vt (pt/pp **slit**) tagliare

slither /'slɪðə(r)/ vi scivolare

sliver /'slɪvə(r)/ n scheggia f

slobber /'slɒbə(r)/ vi sbavare

slog /slɒg/ n (hard) ~ sgobbata f ● vi (pt/pp **slogged**) (work) sgobbare

slogan /'sləʊgən/ n slogan m inv

slop /slɒp/ v (pt/pp **slopped**) ● vt versare. **slop over** vi versarsi

slop|e /sləʊp/ n pendenza f; (ski ~) pista f ● vi essere inclinato. inclinarsi. ~ing a in pendenza

sloppy /'slɒpɪ/ a (-ier, -iest) (work) trascurato; (worker) negligente; (in dress) sciatto; (sentimental) sdolcinato

slosh /slɒʃ/ vi fam (person, feet:) sguazzare; (water:) scrosciare ● vt (fam: hit) colpire

sloshed /slɒʃt/ a fam sbronzo

slot /slɒt/ n fessura f; (time-~) spazio m ● v (pt/pp **slotted**) ● vt infilare. **slot in** vi incastrarsi

'slot-machine n distributore m automatico; (for gambling) slot-machine f inv

slouch /slaʊtʃ/ vi (in chair) stare scomposto

slovenl|y /'slʌvnlɪ/ a sciatto. ~iness n sciatteria f

slow /sləʊ/ a lento; **be ~** (clock:) essere indietro; **in ~ motion** al rallentatore ● adv lentamente ● **slow down, up** vt/i rallentare

slow: ~coach n fam tartaruga f. ~ly adv lentamente. ~ness n lentezza f

sludge /slʌdʒ/ n fanghiglia f

slug /slʌg/ n lumacone m; (fam: bullet) pallottola f

sluggish /'slʌgɪʃ/ a lento

sluice /sluːs/ n chiusa f

slum /slʌm/ n (house) tugurio m; ~s pl bassifondi mpl

slumber /'slʌmbə(r)/ vi dormire

slump /slʌmp/ n crollo m; (economic) depressione f ● vi crollare

slung /slʌŋ/ see **sling**

slur /slɜː(r)/ n (discredit) calunnia f ● vt (pt/pp **slurred**) biascicare

slurp /slɜːp/ vt/i bere rumorosamente

slush /slʌʃ/ n pantano m nevoso; fig sdolcinatezza f. ~ **fund** n fondi mpl neri

slushy /'slʌʃɪ/ a fangoso; (sentimental) sdolcinato

slut /slʌt/ n sgualdrina f

sly /slaɪ/ a (-er, -est) scaltro ● n **on the ~** di nascosto

smack¹ /smæk/ n (on face) schiaffo m;

(on bottom) sculaccione m ● vt (on face) schiaffeggiare; (on bottom) sculacciare; ~ **one's lips** far schioccare le labbra ● adv fam in pieno

smack² vi ~ **of** fig sapere di

small /smɔːl/ a piccolo; **be out work until the ~ hours** fare le ore piccole ● adv **chop up** ~ fare a pezzettini ● n **the ~ of the back** le reni

small: ~ **ads** npl annunci mpl [commerciali]. ~ **change** n spiccioli mpl. ~**holding** n piccola tenuta f. ~**pox** n vaiolo m. ~ **talk** n chiacchiere fpl

smarmy /'smɑːmɪ/ a (-ier, -iest) fam untuoso

smart /smɑːt/ a elegante; (clever) intelligente; (brisk) svelto; **be** ~ (fam: cheeky) fare il furbo ● vi (hurt) bruciare

smarten /'smɑːtn/ vt ~ **oneself up** farsi bello

smash /smæʃ/ n fragore m; (collision) scontro m; Tennis schiacciata f ● vt spaccare; Tennis schiacciare ● vi spaccarsi; (crash) schiantarsi (into contro). ~ [**hit**] n successo m. ~**ing** a fam fantastico

smattering /'smætərɪŋ/ n infarinatura f

smear /smɪə(r)/ n macchia f; Med striscio m ● vt imbrattare; (coat) spalmare (with di); fig calunniare

smell /smel/ n odore m; (sense) odorato m ● v (pt/pp **smelt** or **smelled**) ● vt odorare; (sniff) annusare ● vi odorare (of di)

smelly /'smelɪ/ a (-ier, -iest) puzzolente

smelt¹ /smelt/ see **smell**

smelt² vt fondere

smile /smaɪl/ n sorriso m ● vi sorridere; ~ **at** sorridere a (sb); sorridere di (sth)

smirk /smɜːk/ n sorriso m compiaciuto

smithereens /smɪðə'riːnz/ npl **to in** ~ in mille pezzi

smitten /'smɪtn/ a ~ **with** tutto preso da

smock /smɒk/ n grembiule m

smog /smɒg/ n smog m inv

smoke /sməʊk/ n fumo m ● vt/i fumare. ~**less** a senza fumo; (fuel) che non fa fumo

smoker /'sməʊkə(r)/ n fumatore, -trice mf; Rail vagone m fumatori

'smoke-screen n cortina f di fumo

smoking /'sməʊkɪŋ/ n fumo m; 'no ~' 'vietato fumare'

smoky /'sməʊkɪ/ a (-ier, -iest) fumoso; ⟨taste⟩ di fumo

smooth /smuːð/ a liscio; ⟨movement⟩ scorrevole; ⟨sea⟩ calmo; ⟨manners⟩ mellifluo ● vt lisciare. **smooth out** vt lisciare. ~**ly** adv in modo scorrevole

smother /'smʌðə(r)/ vt soffocare

smoulder /'sməʊldə(r)/ vi fumare; ⟨with rage⟩ consumarsi

smudge /smʌdʒ/ n macchia f ● vt/i imbrattare

smug /smʌg/ a (smugger, smuggest) compiaciuto. ~**ly** adv con aria compiaciuta

smuggl|e /'smʌgl/ vt contrabbandare. ~**er** n contrabbandiere, -a mf. ~**ing** n contrabbando m

smut /smʌt/ n macchia f di fuliggine; fig sconcezza f

smutty /'smʌtɪ/ a (-ier, -iest) fuligginoso; fig sconcio

snack /snæk/ n spuntino m. ~**-bar** n snack bar m inv

snag /snæg/ n ⟨problem⟩ intoppo m

snail /sneɪl/ n lumaca f; at a ~'s pace a passo di lumaca

snake /sneɪk/ n serpente m

snap /snæp/ n colpo m secco; ⟨photo⟩ istantanea f ● attrib ⟨decision⟩ istantaneo ● v (pt/pp **snapped**) ● vi ⟨break⟩ spezzarsi; ~ **at** ⟨dog:⟩ cercare di azzannare; ⟨person:⟩ parlare seccamente a ● vt ⟨break⟩ spezzare; ⟨say⟩ dire seccamente; Phot fare un'istantanea di. **snap up** vt afferrare

snappy /'snæpɪ/ a (-ier, -iest) scorbutico; ⟨smart⟩ elegante; **make it ~!** sbrigati!

'snapshot n istantanea f

snare /sneə(r)/ n trappola f

snarl /snɑːl/ n ringhio m ● vi ringhiare

snatch /snætʃ/ n strappo m; ⟨fragment⟩ brano m; ⟨theft⟩ scippo m; **make a ~ at sth** cercare di afferrare qcsa ● vt strappare [di mano] (from a); ⟨steal⟩ scippare; rapire ⟨child⟩

sneak /sniːk/ n fam spia m/f ● vi ⟨fam: tell tales⟩ fare la spia ● vt ⟨take⟩ rubare; ~ **a look at** dare una sbirciata a. **sneak in/out** vi sgattaiolare dentro/fuori

sneakers /'sniːkəz/ npl Am scarpe fpl da ginnastica

sneaking /'sniːkɪŋ/ a furtivo; ⟨suspicion⟩ vago

sneaky /'sniːkɪ/ a sornione

sneer /snɪə(r)/ n ghigno m ● vi sogghignare; ⟨mock⟩ ridere di

sneeze /sniːz/ n starnuto m ● vi starnutire

snide /snaɪd/ a fam insinuante

sniff /snɪf/ n ⟨of dog⟩ annusata f ● vi tirare su col naso ● vt odorare ⟨flower⟩; sniffare ⟨glue, cocaine⟩; ⟨dog:⟩ annusare

snigger /'snɪgə(r)/ n risatina f soffocata ● vi ridacchiare

snip /snɪp/ n taglio m; ⟨fam: bargain⟩ affare m ● vt/i (pt/pp **snipped**) ~ [**at**] tagliare

snipe /snaɪp/ vi ~ **at** tirare su; fig sparare a zero su. ~**r** n cecchino m

snippet /'snɪpɪt/ n a ~ **of information/news** una breve notizia/informazione

snivel /'snɪvl/ vi (pt/pp **snivelled**) piagnucolare. ~**ling** a piagnucoloso

snob /snɒb/ n snob mf inv. ~**bery** n snobismo m. ~**bish** a da snob

snooker /'snuːkə(r)/ n snooker m

snoop /snuːp/ n spia f ● vi fam curiosare

snooty /'snuːtɪ/ a fam sdegnoso

snooze /snuːz/ n sonnellino m ● vi fare un sonnellino

snore /snɔː(r)/ vi russare

snorkel /'snɔːkl/ n respiratore m

snort /snɔːt/ n sbuffo m ● vi sbuffare

snout /snaʊt/ n grugno m

snow /snəʊ/ n neve f ● vi nevicare; ~**ed under with** fig sommerso di

snow: ~**ball** n palla f di neve ● vi fare a palle di neve. ~**-drift** n cumulo m di neve. ~**drop** n bucaneve m inv. ~**fall** n nevicata f. ~**flake** n fiocco m di neve. ~**man** n pupazzo m di neve. ~**-plough** n spazzaneve m inv. ~**storm** n tormenta f. ~**y** a nevoso

snub /snʌb/ n sgarbo m ● vt (pt/pp **snubbed**) snobbare

'snub-nosed a dal naso all'insù

snuff /snʌf/ n tabacco m da fiuto

snug /snʌg/ a (snugger, snuggest) comodo; ⟨tight⟩ aderente

snuggle /'snʌgl/ vi rannicchiarsi (**up to** accanto a)

so /səʊ/ adv così; **so far** finora; **so am I** anch'io; **so I see** così pare; **that is so** è così; **so much** così tanto; **so much the better** tanto meglio; **so it is** proprio così; **if so** se è così; **so as to** in modo da; **so long!** fam a presto! ● pron **I hope/think/am afraid so** spero/penso/temo di sì; **I told you so** te l'ho detto; **because I say so** perché lo dico io; **I did so!** è vero!; **so saying/doing,...** così dicendo/facendo,...; **or so**

circa; **very much so** sì, molto; **and so forth** or **on** e così via ● *conj* (*therefore*) perciò; (*in order that*) così; **so that** affinché; **so there!** ecco!; **so what?** e allora?; **so where have you been?** allora, dove sei stato?

soak /səʊk/ *vt* mettere a bagno ● *vi* stare a bagno; ~ **into** (*liquid:*) penetrare. **soak up** *vt* assorbire

soaking /ˈsəʊkɪŋ/ *n* ammollo *m* ● *a* & *adv* ~ |**wet**| *fam* inzuppato

so-and-so /ˈsəʊənsəʊ/ *n* Tal dei Tali *mf*; (*euphemism*) specie *f* di imbecille

soap /səʊp/ *n* sapone *m*. ~ **opera** *n* telenovella *f*, soap opera *f inv*. ~ **powder** *n* detersivo *m* in polvere

soapy /ˈsəʊpɪ/ *a* (-**ier**, -**iest**) insaponato

soar /sɔː(r)/ *vi* elevarsi; (*prices:*) salire alle stelle

sob /sɒb/ *n* singhiozzo *m* ● *vi* (*pt/pp* **sobbed**) singhiozzare

sober /ˈsəʊbə(r)/ *a* sobrio; (*serious*) serio ● **sober up** *vi* ritornare sobrio

so-called *a* cosiddetto

soccer /ˈsɒkə(r)/ *n* calcio *m*

sociable /ˈsəʊʃəbl/ *a* socievole

social /ˈsəʊʃl/ *a* sociale; (*sociable*) socievole

socialis|m /ˈsəʊʃəlɪzm/ *n* socialismo *m*. ~**t** /-ɪst/ *a* socialista ● *n* socialista *mf*

socialize /ˈsəʊʃəlaɪz/ *vi* socializzare

socially /ˈsəʊʃəlɪ/ *adv* socialmente; **know sb** ~ frequentare qcno

social: ~ **se'curity** *n* previdenza *f* sociale. ~ **work** *n* assistenza *f* sociale. ~ **worker** *n* assistente *mf* sociale

society /səˈsaɪətɪ/ *n* società *f inv*

sociolog|ist /ˈsəʊsɪˈɒlədʒɪst/ *n* sociologo, -a *mf*. ~**y** *n* sociologia *f*

sock[1] /sɒk/ *n* calzino *m*; (*kneelength*) calza *f*

sock[2] *fam* *n* pugno *m* ● *vt* dare un pugno a

socket /ˈsɒkɪt/ *n* (*wall plug*) presa *f* [di corrente]; (*for bulb*) portalampada *m inv*

soda /ˈsəʊdə/ *n* soda *f*; *Am* gazzosa *f*. ~ **water** *n* seltz *m inv*

sodden /ˈsɒdn/ *a* inzuppato

sodium /ˈsəʊdɪəm/ *n* sodio *m*

sofa /ˈsəʊfə/ *n* divano *m*. ~ **bed** *n* divano *m* letto

soft /sɒft/ *a* morbido, soffice; (*voice*) sommesso; (*light, colour*) tenue; (*not strict*) indulgente; (*fam: silly*) stupido; **have a** ~ **spot for sb** avere un debole per qcno. ~ **drink** *n* bibita *f* analcolica

soften /ˈsɒfn/ *vt* ammorbidire; *fig* attenuare ● *vi* ammorbidirsi

softly /ˈsɒftlɪ/ *adv* (*say*) sottovoce; (*treat*) con indulgenza; (*play music*) in sottofondo

soft: ~ **toy** *n* pupazzo *m* di peluche. ~**ware** *n* software *m*

soggy /ˈsɒgɪ/ *a* (-**ier**, -**iest**) zuppo

soil[1] /sɔɪl/ *n* suolo *m*

soil[2] *vt* sporcare

solar /ˈsəʊlə(r)/ *a* solare

sold /səʊld/ *see* **sell**

solder /ˈsəʊldə(r)/ *n* lega *f* da saldatura ● *vt* saldare

soldier /ˈsəʊldʒə(r)/ *n* soldato *m* ● **soldier on** *vi* perseverare

sole[1] /səʊl/ *n* (*of foot*) pianta *f*; (*of shoe*) suola *f*

sole[2] *n* (*fish*) sogliola *f*

sole[3] *a* unico, solo. ~**ly** *adv* unicamente

solemn /ˈsɒləm/ *a* solenne. ~**ity** /səˈlemnətɪ/ *n* solennità *f inv*

solicit /səˈlɪsɪt/ *vt* sollecitare ● *vi* (*prostitute:*) adescare

solicitor /səˈlɪsɪtə(r)/ *n* avvocato *m*

solid /ˈsɒlɪd/ *a* solido; (*oak, gold*) massiccio ● *n* (*figure*) solido *m*; ~**s** *pl* (*food*) cibi *mpl* solidi

solidarity /sɒlɪˈdærətɪ/ *n* solidarietà *f inv*

solidify /səˈlɪdɪfaɪ/ *vi* (*pt/pp* -**ied**) solidificarsi

soliloquy /səˈlɪləkwɪ/ *n* soliloquio *m*

solitaire /sɒlɪˈteə(r)/ *n* solitario *m*

solitary /ˈsɒlɪtrɪ/ *a* solitario; (*sole*) solo. ~ **con'finement** *n* cella *f* di isolamento

solitude /ˈsɒlɪtjuːd/ *n* solitudine *f*

solo /ˈsəʊləʊ/ *n* Mus assolo *m* ● *a* (*flight*) in solitario ● *adv* in solitario. ~**ist** *n* solista *mf*

solstice /ˈsɒlstɪs/ *n* solstizio *m*

soluble /ˈsɒljʊbl/ *a* solubile

solution /səˈluːʃn/ *n* soluzione *f*

solve /sɒlv/ *vt* risolvere

solvent /ˈsɒlvənt/ *a* solvente ● *n* solvente *m*

sombre /ˈsɒmbə(r)/ *a* tetro; (*clothes*) scuro

some /sʌm/ *a* (*a certain amount of*) del; (*a certain number of*) qualche, alcuni; ~ **day** un giorno o l'altro; **I need** ~ **money/books** ho bisogno di soldi/ libri; **do** ~ **shopping** fare qualche acquisto ● *pron* (*a certain amount*) un po'; (*a certain number*) alcuni; **I want** ~ ne voglio

some: ~**body** /-bədɪ/ *pron* & *n* qualcuno *m*. ~**how** *adv* in qualche modo; ~**how or other** in un modo o nell'altro. ~**one** *pron & n* = **somebody**

somersault /'sʌməsɔːlt/ *n* capriola *f*; **turn a ~** fare una capriola

'**something** *pron* qualche cosa, qualcosa; ~ **different** qualcosa di diverso; ~ **like** un po' come; (*approximately*) qualcosa come; **see ~ of sb** vedere qcno un po'

some: ~**time** *adv* un giorno o l'altro; ~**time last summer** durante l'estate scorsa. ~**times** *adv* qualche volta. ~**what** *adv* piuttosto. ~**where** *adv* da qualche parte ●*pron* ~**where to eat** un posto in cui mangiare

son /sʌn/ *n* figlio *m*

sonata /sə'nɑːtə/ *n* sonata *f*

song /sɒŋ/ *n* canzone *f*

sonic /'sɒnɪk/ *a* sonico. ~ '**boom** *n* bang *m inv* sonico

son-in-law *n* (*pl* ~**s-in-law**) genero *m*

sonnet /'sɒnɪt/ *n* sonetto *m*

soon /suːn/ *adv* presto; (*in a short time*) tra poco; **as ~ as** [non] appena; **as ~ as possible** il più presto possibile; ~**er or later** prima o poi; **the ~er the better** prima è, meglio è; **no ~er had I arrived than...** ero appena arrivato quando...; **I would ~er go** preferirei andare; ~ **after** subito dopo

soot /sʊt/ *n* fuliggine *f*

sooth|e /suːð/ *vt* calmare

sooty /'sʊti/ *a* fuligginoso

sophisticated /sə'fɪstɪkeɪtɪd/ *a* sofisticato

soporific /sɒpə'rɪfɪk/ *a* soporifero

sopping /'sɒpɪŋ/ *a & adv* **be ~** [**wet**] essere bagnato fradicio

soppy /'sɒpi/ *a* (**-ier, -iest**) *fam* svenevole

soprano /sə'prɑːnəʊ/ *n* soprano *m*

sordid /'sɔːdɪd/ *a* sordido

sore /sɔː(r)/ *a* dolorante; (*Am: vexed*) arrabbiato; **it's ~** fa male; **have a ~ throat** avere mal di gola ●*n* piaga *f*. ~**ly** *adv* (*tempted*) seriamente

sorrow /'sɒrəʊ/ *n* tristezza *f*. ~**ful** *a* triste

sorry /'sɒri/ *a* (**-ier, -iest**) (*sad*) spiacente; (*wretched*) pietoso; **you'll be ~**! te ne pentirai!; **I am ~** mi dispiace; **be or feel ~ for** provare compassione per; ~!**scusa**!; (*more polite*) scusi!

sort /sɔːt/ *n* specie *f*; (*fam: person*) tipo *m*; **it's a ~ of fish** è un tipo di pesce; **be out of ~s** (*fam: unwell*) stare poco bene ●*vt* classificare. **sort out** *vt* sele-

zionare (*papers*); *fig* risolvere (*problem*); occuparsi di (*person*)

'**so-so** *a & adv* così così

sought /sɔːt/ *see* **seek**

soul /səʊl/ *n* anima *f*

sound¹ /saʊnd/ *a* sano; (*sensible*) saggio; (*secure*) solido; (*thrashing*) clamoroso ●*adv* ~ **asleep** profondamente addormentato

sound² *n* suono *m*; (*noise*) rumore *m*; **I don't like the ~ of it** *fam* non mi suona bene ●*vi* suonare; (*seem*) aver l'aria ●*vt* (*pronounce*) pronunciare; *Med* auscultare (*chest*). ~ **barrier** *n* muro *m* del suono. ~ **card** *n* Comput scheda *f* sonora. ~**less** *a* silenzioso. **sound out** *vt fig* sondare

soundly /'saʊndli/ *adv* (*sleep*) profondamente; (*defeat*) clamorosamente

'**sound:** ~**proof** *a* impenetrabile al suono. ~**-track** *n* colonna *f* sonora

soup /suːp/ *n* minestra *f*. ~**ed-up** *fam* (*engine*) truccato

soup: ~**plate** *n* piatto *m* fondo. ~**-spoon** *n* cucchiaio *m* da minestra

sour /'saʊə(r)/ *a* agro; (*not fresh & fig*) acido

source /sɔːs/ *n* fonte *f*

south /saʊθ/ *n* sud *m*; **to the ~ of** a sud di ●*a* del sud, meridionale ●*adv* verso il sud

south: S~ 'Africa *n* Sudafrica *f*. S~ A'merica *n* America *f* del Sud. S~ American *a & n* sud-americano, -a *mf*. ~-'east *n* sud-est *m*

southerly /'sʌðəli/ *a* del sud

southern /'sʌðən/ *a* del sud, meridionale; ~ **Italy** il Mezzogiorno. ~**er** *n* meridionale *mf*

South 'Pole *n* polo *m* Sud

'**southward**[**s**] /-wəd[z]/ *adv* verso sud

souvenir /suːvə'nɪə(r)/ *n* ricordo *m*, souvenir *m inv*

sovereign /'sɒvrɪn/ *a* sovrano ●*n* sovrano, -a *mf*. ~**ty** *n* sovranità *f inv*

Soviet /'səʊvɪət/ *a* sovietico; ~ **Union** Unione *f* Sovietica

sow¹ /saʊ/ *n* scrofa *f*

sow² /səʊ/ *vt* (*pt* **sowed**, *pp* **sown** or **sowed**) seminare

soya /'sɔɪə/ *n* ~ **bean** soia *f*

spa /spɑː/ *n* stazione *f* termale

space /speɪs/ *n* spazio *m* ●*a* (*research etc*) spaziale ●*vt* ~ **out** distanziare

space: ~**ship** *n* astronave *f*. ~ **shuttle** *n* navetta *f* spaziale

spacious /'speɪʃəs/ *a* spazioso

spade /speɪd/ *n* vanga *f*; (*for child*) pa-

letta f; ~s pl (in cards) picche fpl.
~work n lavoro m preparatorio
Spain /speɪn/ n Spagna f
span[1] /spæn/ n spanna f; (of arch) luce
f; (of time) arco m; (of wings) apertura f
● vt (pt/pp spanned) estendersi su
span[2] see **spick**
Span|iard /ˈspænjəd/ n spagnolo, -a
mf. ~ish a spagnolo ● n (language) spagnolo m; the ~ish pl gli spagnoli
spank /spæŋk/ vt sculacciare. ~ing n
sculacciata f
spanner /ˈspænə(r)/ n chiave f inglese
spar /spɑː(r)/ vi (pt/pp sparred)
(boxing) allenarsi; (argue) litigare
spare /speə(r)/ a (surplus) in più;
(additional) di riserva ● n (part) ricambio m ● vt risparmiare; (do without)
fare a meno di; can you ~ five
minutes? avresti cinque minuti?; to ~
(surplus) in eccedenza. ~ part n pezzo
m di ricambio. ~ time n tempo m libero. ~ wheel n ruota f di scorta
sparing /ˈspeərɪŋ/ a parco (with di).
~ly adv con parsimonia
spark /spɑːk/ n scintilla f. ~ing-plug n
Auto candela f
sparkl|e /ˈspɑːkl/ n scintillio m ● vi
scintillare. ~ing a frizzante; (wine)
spumante
sparrow /ˈspærəʊ/ n passero m
sparse /spɑːs/ a rado. ~ly adv scarsamente; ~ly populated a bassa densità
di popolazione
spartan /ˈspɑːtn/ a spartano
spasm /ˈspæzm/ n spasmo m. ~odic
/-ˈmɒdɪk/ a spasmodico
spastic /ˈspæstɪk/ a spastico ● n
spastico, -a mf
spat /spæt/ see **spit**[1]
spate /speɪt/ n (series) successione f;
be in full ~ essere in piena
spatial /ˈspeɪʃl/ a spaziale
spatter /ˈspætə(r)/ vt schizzare
spatula /ˈspætjʊlə/ n spatola f
spawn /spɔːn/ n uova fpl (di pesci, rane
ecc) ● vi deporre le uova ● vt fig generare
spay /speɪ/ vt sterilizzare
speak /spiːk/ v (pt spoke, pp spoken)
● vi parlare (to a); ~ing! Teleph sono
io! ● vt dire; ~ one's mind dire quello
che si pensa. **speak for** vi parlare a
nome di. **speak up** vi parlare più forte;
~ up for oneself farsi valere
speaker /ˈspiːkə(r)/ n parlante mf; (in
public) oratore, -trice mf; (of stereo) cassa f

spear /spɪə(r)/ n lancia f
spec /spek/ n on ~ fam senza certezza
special /ˈspeʃl/ a speciale. ~ist n specialista mf. ~ity /-ʃɪˈælətɪ/ n specialità
f inv
special|ize /ˈspeʃəlaɪz/ vi specializ-
zarsi. ~ly adv specialmente; (particu-
larly) particolarmente
species /ˈspiːʃiːz/ n specie f inv
specific /spəˈsɪfɪk/ a specifico. ~ally
adv in modo specifico
specifications /spesɪfɪˈkeɪʃnz/ npl
descrizione f
specify /ˈspesɪfaɪ/ vt (pt/pp -ied) speci-
ficare
specimen /ˈspesɪmən/ n campione m
speck /spek/ n macchiolina f; (particle) granello m
speckled /ˈspekld/ a picchiettato
specs /speks/ npl fam occhiali mpl
spectacle /ˈspektəkl/ n (show) spettacolo m. ~s npl occhiali mpl
spectacular /spekˈtækjʊlə(r)/ a
spettacolare
spectator /spekˈteɪtə(r)/ n spettatore,
-trice mf
spectre /ˈspektə(r)/ n spettro m
spectrum /ˈspektrəm/ n (pl -tra) spettro m; fig gamma f
speculat|e /ˈspekjʊleɪt/ vi speculare.
~ion /-ˈleɪʃn/ n speculazione f. ~ive
/-ɪv/ a speculativo. ~or n speculatore,
-trice mf
sped /sped/ see **speed**
speech /spiːtʃ/ n linguaggio m; (address) discorso m. ~less a senza parole
speed /spiːd/ n velocità f inv; (gear)
marcia f; at ~ a tutta velocità ● vi
(pt/pp sped) andare veloce; (pt/pp
speeded) (go too fast) andare a velocità
eccessiva. **speed up** (pt/pp speeded
up) vt/i accelerare
speed: ~boat n motoscafo m. ~ing n
eccesso m di velocità. ~ limit n limite
m di velocità
speedometer /spiːˈdɒmɪtə(r)/ n tachimetro m
speed|y /ˈspiːdɪ/ a (-ier, -iest) rapido.
~ily adv rapidamente
spell[1] /spel/ n (turn) turno m; (of
weather) periodo m
spell[2] v (pt/pp spelled or spelt) ● vt
how do you ~...? come si scrive...?;
could you ~ that for me? me lo può
compitare?; ~ disaster essere disa-
stroso ● vi he can't ~ fa molti errori
d'ortografia

spell³ *n* (*magic*) incantesimo *m*. ~**bound** *a* affascinato

spelling /'spelɪŋ/ *n* ortografia *f*

spelt /spelt/ *see* **spell**²

spend /spend/ *vt/i* (*pt/pp* **spent**) spendere; passare ⟨*time*⟩

spent /spent/ *see* **spend**

sperm /spɜːm/ *n* spermatozoo *m*; (*semen*) sperma *m*

spew /spjuː/ *vt/i* vomitare

spher|e /sfɪə(r)/ *n* sfera *f*. ~**ical** /'sferɪkl/ *a* sferico

spice /spaɪs/ *n* spezia *f*; *fig* pepe *m*

spick /spɪk/ *a* ~ **and span** lindo

spicy /'spaɪsɪ/ *a* piccante

spider /'spaɪdə(r)/ *n* ragno *m*

spik|e /spaɪk/ *n* punta *f*; *Bot, Zool* spina *f*; (*on shoe*) chiodo *m*. ~**y** *a* ⟨*plant*⟩ pungente

spill /spɪl/ *v* (*pt/pp* **spilt** *or* **spilled**) ● *vt* versare ⟨*blood*⟩ ● *vi* rovesciarsi

spin /spɪn/ *v* (*pt/pp* **spun**, *pres p* **spinning**) ● *vt* far girare; filare ⟨*wool*⟩; centrifugare ⟨*washing*⟩ ● *vi* girare; ⟨*washing machine*⟩ centrifugare ● *n* rotazione *f*; (*short drive*) giretto *m*. **spin out** *vt* far durare

spinach /'spɪnɪdʒ/ *n* spinaci *mpl*

spinal /'spaɪnl/ *a* spinale. ~ **'cord** *n* midollo *m* spinale

spindl|e /'spɪndl/ *n* fuso *m*. ~**y** *a* affusolato

spin-'drier *n* centrifuga *f*

spine /spaɪn/ *n* spina *f* dorsale; (*of book*) dorso *m*; *Bot, Zool* spina *f*. ~**less** *a fig* smidollato

spinning /'spɪnɪŋ/ *n* filatura *f*. ~-**wheel** *n* filatoio *m*

spin-off *n* ricaduta *f*

spiral /'spaɪrəl/ *a* a spirale ● *n* spirale *f* ● *vi* (*pt/pp* **spiralled**) formare una spirale. ~ **'staircase** *n* scala *f* a chiocciola

spire /'spaɪə(r)/ *n* guglia *f*

spirit /'spɪrɪt/ *n* spirito *m*; (*courage*) ardore *m*; ~**s** *pl* (*alcohol*) liquori *mpl*; **in good ~s** di buon umore; **in low ~s** abbattuto

spirited /'spɪrɪtɪd/ *a* vivace; (*courageous*) pieno d'ardore

spirit: ~-**level** *n* livella *f* a bolla d'aria. ~ **stove** *n* fornellino *m* [da campeggio]

spiritual /'spɪrɪtjʊəl/ *a* spirituale ● *n* spiritual *m*. ~**ism** /-lɪzm/ *n* spiritismo *m*. ~**ist** /-ɪst/ *n* spiritista *mf*

spit¹ /spɪt/ *n* (*for roasting*) spiedo *m*

spit² /spɪt/ *n* sputo *m* ● *vt/i* (*pt/pp* **spat**, *pres p* **spitting**) sputare; ⟨*cat:*⟩ soffiare; ⟨*fat:*⟩ sfrigolare; **it's ~ting** [**with rain**] pioviggina; **the ~ting image of** il ritratto spiccicato di

spite /spaɪt/ *n* dispetto *m*; **in ~ of** malgrado ● *vt* far dispetto a. ~**ful** *a* indispettito

spittle /'spɪtl/ *n* saliva *f*

splash /splæʃ/ *n* schizzo *m*; (*of colour*) macchia *f*; ⟨*fam: drop*⟩ goccio *m*. ● *vt* schizzare; ~ **sb with sth** schizzare qcno di qcsa ● *vi* schizzarsi. **splash about** *vi* schizzarsi. **splash down** *vi* ⟨*spacecraft:*⟩ ammarare

spleen /spliːn/ *n Anat* milza *f*

splendid /'splendɪd/ *a* splendido

splendour /'splendə(r)/ *n* splendore *m*

splint /splɪnt/ *n Med* stecca *f*

splinter /'splɪntə(r)/ *n* scheggia *f* ● *vi* scheggiarsi

split /splɪt/ *n* fessura *f*; (*quarrel*) rottura *f*; (*division*) scissione *f*; (*tear*) strappo *m* ● *v* (*pt/pp* **split**, *pres p* **splitting**) ● *vt* spaccare; (*share, divide*) dividere; (*tear*) strappare ● *vi* spaccarsi; (*tear*) strapparsi; (*divide*) dividersi; ~ **on sb** *fam* denunciare qcno ● *vi* **a ~ second** una frazione di secondo. **split up** *vt* dividersi ● *vi* ⟨*couple:*⟩ separarsi

splutter /'splʌtə(r)/ *vi* farfugliare

spoil /spɔɪl/ *n* ~**s** *pl* bottino *msg* ● *v* (*pt/pp* **spoilt** *or* **spoiled**) ● *vt* rovinare; viziare ⟨*person*⟩ ● *vi* andare a male. ~**sport** *n* guastafeste *mf inv*

spoke¹ /spəʊk/ *n* raggio *m*

spoke², **spoken** /'spəʊkn/ *see* **speak**

'spokesman *n* portavoce *m inv*

sponge /spʌndʒ/ *n* spugna *f* ● *vt* pulire (con la spugna) ● *vi* ~ **on** *fam* scroccare da. ~-**cake** *n* pan *m* di Spagna

spong|er /'spʌndʒə(r)/ *n* scroccone, -a *mf*. ~**y** *a* spugnoso

sponsor /'spɒnsə(r)/ *n* garante *mf*; *Radio, TV* sponsor *m inv*; (*god-parent*) padrino *m*, madrina *f*; (*for membership*) socio, -a *mf* garante ● *vt* sponsorizzare. ~**ship** *n* sponsorizzazione *f*

spontaneous /spɒn'teɪnɪəs/ *a* spontaneo

spoof /spuːf/ *n fam* parodia *f*

spooky /'spuːkɪ/ *a* (-**ier**, -**iest**) *fam* sinistro

spool /spuːl/ *n* bobina *f*

spoon /spuːn/ *n* cucchiaio *m* ● *vt* mettere col cucchiaio. ~-**feed** *vt* (*pt/pp* -**fed**) *fig* imboccare. ~**ful** *n* cucchiaiata *f*

sporadic /spə'rædɪk/ *a* sporadico

sport /spɔːt/ *n* sport *m inv* ● *vt* sfoggiare. ~**ing** *a* sportivo; ~**ing chance** possibilità *f inv*

sports: ~**car** *n* automobile *f* sportiva. ~ **coat** *n*, ~ **jacket** *n* giacca *f* sportiva. ~**man** *n* sportivo *m*. ~**woman** *n* sportiva *f*

sporty /'spɔːtɪ/ *a* (‑**ier**, ‑**iest**) sportivo

spot /spɒt/ *n* macchia *f*; (*pimple*) brufolo *m*; (*place*) posto *m*; (*in pattern*) pois *m inv*; (*of rain*) goccia *f*; (*of water*) goccio *m*; ~**s** *pl* (*rash*) sfogo *msg*; **a ~ of** *fam* un po' di; **a ~ of bother** qualche problema; **on the ~** sul luogo; (*immediately*) immediatamente; **in a** [**tight**] ~ *fam* in difficoltà ● *vt* (*pt/pp* **spotted**) macchiare; (*fam: notice*) individuare

spot: ~ 'check *n* (*without warning*) controllo *m* a sorpresa; **do a ~ check on sth** dare una controllata a qcsa. ~**less** *a* immacolato. ~**light** *n* riflettore *m*

spotted /'spɒtɪd/ *a* (*material*) a pois

spotty /'spɒtɪ/ *a* (‑**ier**, ‑**iest**) (*pimply*) brufoloso

spouse /spaʊz/ *n* consorte *mf*

spout /spaʊt/ *n* becco *m* ● *vi* zampillare (**from** da)

sprain /spreɪn/ *n* slogatura *f* ● *vt* slogare

sprang /spræŋ/ *see* **spring**²

sprawl /sprɔːl/ *vi* (*in chair*) stravaccarsi; (*city etc.*) estendersi; **go ~ing** (*fall*) cadere disteso

spray /spreɪ/ *n* spruzzo *m*; (*preparation*) spray *m inv*; (*container*) spruzzatore *m* ● *vt* spruzzare. ~**-gun** *n* pistola *f* a spruzzo

spread /spred/ *n* estensione *f*; (*of disease*) diffusione *f*; (*paste*) crema *f*; (*fam: feast*) banchetto *m* ● *v* (*pt/pp* **spread**) ● *vt* spargere; spalmare (*butter, jam*); stendere (*cloth, arms*); diffondere (*news, disease*); dilazionare (*payments*); ~ **sth with** spalmare qcsa di ● *vi* spargersi; (*butter:*) spalmarsi; (*disease:*) diffondersi. ~**sheet** *n* Comput foglio *m* elettronico. **spread out** *vt* spargagliare ● *vi* sparpagliarsi

spree /spriː/ *n fam* **go on a ~** far baldoria; **go on a shopping ~** fare spese folli

sprig /sprɪg/ *n* rametto *m*

sprightly /'spraɪtlɪ/ *a* (‑**ier**, ‑**iest**) vivace

spring¹ /sprɪŋ/ *n* primavera *f* ● *attrib* primaverile

spring² *n* (*jump*) balzo *m*; (*water*) sor‑

gente *f*; (*device*) molla *f*; (*elasticity*) elasticità *f* ● *v* (*pt* **sprang**, *pp* **sprung**) ● *vi* balzare; (*arise*) provenire (**from** da) ● *vt* **he just sprang it on me** me l'ha detto a cose fatte compiuto. **spring up** balzare; *fig* spuntare

spring: ~**board** *n* trampolino *m*. ~‑'cleaning *n* pulizie *fpl* di Pasqua. ~**time** *n* primavera *f*

sprinkle /'sprɪŋkl/ *vt* (*scatter*) spruzzare (*liquid*); spargere (*flour, cocoa*); ~ **sth with** spruzzare qcsa di (*liquid*); cospargere qcsa di (*flour, cocoa*). ~**er** *n* sprinkler *m inv*; (*for lawn*) irrigatore *m*. ~**ing** *n* (*of liquid*) spruzzatina *f*; (*of pepper, salt*) pizzico *m*; (*of flour, sugar*) spolveratina *f*; (*of knowledge*) infarinatura *f*; (*of people*) pugno *m*

sprint /sprɪnt/ *n* sprint *m inv* ● *vi* fare uno sprint; *Sport* sprintare. ~**er** *n* sprinter *f inv*

sprout /spraʊt/ *n* germoglio *m*; [**Brussels**] ~**s** *pl* cavolini *mpl* di Bruxelles ● *vi* germogliare

spruce /spruːs/ *a* elegante ● *n* abete *m*

sprung /sprʌŋ/ *see* **spring**² ● *a* molleggiato

spud /spʌd/ *n fam* patata *f*

spun /spʌn/ *see* **spin**

spur /spɜː(r)/ *n* sperone *m*; (*stimulus*) stimolo *m*; (*road*) svincolo *m* ● **on the ~ of the moment** su due piedi ● *vt* (*pt/pp* **spurred**) ~ [**on**] *fig* spronare [a]

spurious /'spjʊərɪəs/ *a* falso

spurn /spɜːn/ *vt* sdegnare

spurt /spɜːt/ *n* getto *m*; *Sport* scatto *m*; **put on a ~** fare uno scatto ● *vi* sprizzare; (*increase speed*) scattare

spy /spaɪ/ *n* spia *f* ● *v* (*pt/pp* **spied**) ● *vi* spiare ● *vt* (*fam: see*) spiare. **spy on** *vi* spiare

spying /'spaɪɪŋ/ *n* spionaggio *m*

squabble /'skwɒbl/ *n* bisticcio *m* ● *vi* bisticciare

squad /skwɒd/ *n* squadra *f*

squadron /'skwɒdrən/ *n* Mil squadrone *m*; Aeron, Naut squadriglia *f*

squalid /'skwɒlɪd/ *a* squallido

squalor /'skwɒlə(r)/ *n* squallore *m*

squander /'skwɒndə(r)/ *vt* sprecare

square /skweə(r)/ *a* quadrato; (*meal*) sostanzioso; (*fam: old-fashioned*) vecchio stampo ● *n* ~ *fam* pari ● *n* quadrato *m*; (*in city*) piazza *f*; (*on chessboard*) riquadro *m* ● *vt* (*settle*) far quadrare; *Math* elevare al quadrato ● *vi* (*agree*) armonizzare

squash /skwɒʃ/ *n* (*drink*) spremuta *f*;

(*sport*) squash *m*; (*vegetable*) zucca *f* ● *vt* schiacciare; soffocare ‹*rebellion*›

squat /skwɒt/ *a* tarchiato ● *n fam* edificio *m* occupato abusivamente ● *vi* (*pt/pp* **squatted**) accovacciarsi; ~ in occupare abusivamente. **~ter** *n* occupante *mf* abusivo, -a

squawk /skwɔːk/ *n* gracchio *m* ● *vi* gracchiare

squeak /skwiːk/ *n* squittio *m*; (*of hinge, brakes*) scricchiolio *m* ● *vi* squittire; ‹*hinge, brakes*:› scricchiolare

squeal /skwiːl/ *n* strillo *m*; (*of brakes*) cigolio *m* ● *vi* strillare; *sl* spifferare

squeamish /ˈskwiːmɪʃ/ *a* dallo stomaco delicato

squeeze /skwiːz/ *n* stretta *f*; (*crush*) pigia pigia *m inv* ● *vt* premere; (*to get juice*) spremere; stringere ‹*hand*›; (*force*) spingere a forza; (*fam: extort*) estorcere (**out of** da). **squeeze in/out** *vi* sgusciare dentro/fuori. **squeeze up** *vi* stringersi

squelch /skweltʃ/ *vi* sguazzare

squid /skwɪd/ *n* calamaro *m*

squiggle /ˈskwɪgl/ *n* scarabocchio *m*

squint /skwɪnt/ *n* strabismo *m* ● *vi* essere strabico

squire /ˈskwaɪə(r)/ *n* signorotto *m* di campagna

squirm /skwɜːm/ *vi* contorcersi; (*feel embarrassed*) sentirsi imbarazzato

squirrel /ˈskwɪrəl/ *n* scoiattolo *m*

squirt /skwɜːt/ *n* spruzzo *m*; (*fam: person*) presuntuoso *m* ● *vt/i* spruzzare

St *abbr* (**Saint**) S; *abbr* **Street**

stab /stæb/ *n* pugnalata *f*, coltellata *f*; (*sensation*) fitta *f*; (*fam: attempt*) tentativo *m* ● *vt* (*pt/pp* **stabbed**) pugnalare, accoltellare

stability /stəˈbɪlɪtɪ/ *n* stabilità *f inv*

stabilize /ˈsteɪbɪlaɪz/ *vt* stabilizzare ● *vi* stabilizzarsi

stable¹ /ˈsteɪbl/ *a* stabile

stable² *n* stalla *f*; (*establishment*) scuderia *f*

stack /stæk/ *n* catasta *f*; (*of chimney*) comignolo *m*; (*chimney*) ciminiera *f*; (*fam: large quantity*) montagna *f* ● *vt* accatastare

stadium /ˈsteɪdɪəm/ *n* stadio *m*

staff /stɑːf/ *n* (*stick*) bastone *m*; (*employees*) personale *m*; (*teachers*) corpo *m* insegnante; *Mil* Stato *m* Maggiore ● *vt* fornire di personale. **~-room** *n Sch* sala *f* insegnanti

stag /stæg/ *n* cervo *m*

stage /steɪdʒ/ *n* palcoscenico *m*; (*profession*) teatro *m*; (*in journey*) tappa *f*; (*in process*) stadio *m*; **go on the ~** darsi al teatro; **by** *or* **in ~s** a tappe ● *vt* mettere in scena; (*arrange*) organizzare

stage: ~ door *n* ingresso *m* degli artisti. **~ fright** *n* panico *m* da scena. **~ manager** *n* direttore, -trice *mf* di scena

stagger /ˈstægə(r)/ *vi* barcollare ● *vt* sbalordire; scaglionare ‹*holidays etc*›; **I was ~ed** sono rimasto sbalordito ● *n* vacillamento *m*. **~ing** *a* sbalorditivo

stagnant /ˈstægnənt/ *a* stagnante

stagnat|e /stægˈneɪt/ *vi fig* [ri]stagnare. **~ion** /-ˈneɪʃn/ *n fig* inattività *f*

'stag party *n* addio *m* al celibato

staid /steɪd/ *a* posato

stain /steɪn/ *n* macchia *f*; (*for wood*) mordente *m* ● *vt* macchiare; (*wood*) dare il mordente a; **~ed glass** vetro *m* colorato; **~ed-glass window** vetrata *f* colorata. **~less** *a* senza macchia; (*steel*) inossidabile. **~ remover** *n* smacchiatore *m*

stair /steə(r)/ *n* gradino *m*; **~s** *pl* scale *fpl*. **~case** *n* scala *fpl*

stake /steɪk/ *n* palo *m*; (*wager*) posta *f*; *Comm* partecipazione *f*; **at ~** in gioco ● *vt* puntellare; (*wager*) scommettere

stale /steɪl/ *a* stantio; (*air*) viziato; (*uninteresting*) trito [e ritrito]. **~mate** *n* (*in chess*) stallo *m*; (*deadlock*) situazione *f* di stallo

stalk¹ /stɔːk/ *n* gambo *m*

stalk² *vt* inseguire ● *vi* camminare impettito

stall /stɔːl/ *n* box *m inv*; **~s** *pl Theat* platea *f*; (*in market*) bancarella *f* ● *vi* ‹*engine*:› spegnersi; *fig* temporeggiare ● *vt* far spegnere ‹*engine*›; tenere a bada ‹*person*›

stallion /ˈstæljən/ *n* stallone *m*

stalwart /ˈstɔːlwət/ *a* fedele

stamina /ˈstæmɪnə/ *n* [capacità *f inv* di] resistenza *f*

stammer /ˈstæmə(r)/ *n* balbettio *m* ● *vt/i* balbettare

stamp /stæmp/ *n* (*postage ~*) francobollo *m*; (*instrument*) timbro *m*; *fig* impronta *f* ● *vt* affrancare ‹*letter*›; timbrare ‹*bill*›; battere ‹*feet*›. **stamp out** *vt* spegnere; *fig* soffocare

stampede /stæmˈpiːd/ *n* fuga *f* precipitosa, fuggi-fuggi *m inv fam* ● *vi* fuggire precipitosamente

stance /stɑːns/ *n* posizione *f*

stand /stænd/ *n* (*for bikes*) rastrelliera *f*; (*at exhibition*) stand *m inv*; (*in market*) bancarella *f*; (*in stadium*) gradinata *f*; *fig* posizione *f* ● *v* (*pt/pp* **stood**) ● *vi* stare in piedi; (*rise*) alzarsi [in piedi]; (*be*) trovarsi; (*be candidate*) essere candidato (**for** a); (*stay valid*) rimanere valido; ~ **still** non muoversi; **I don't know where I** ~ non so qual'è la mia posizione; ~ **firm** *fig* tener duro; ~ **together** essere solidali; ~ **to lose/gain** rischiare di perdere/vincere; ~ **to reason** essere logico ● *vt* (*withstand*) resistere a; (*endure*) sopportare; (*place*) mettere; ~ **a chance** avere una possibilità; ~ **one's ground** tener duro; ~ **the test of time** superare la prova del tempo; ~ **sb a beer** offrire una birra a qcno. **stand by** *vi* stare a guardare; (*be ready*) essere pronto ● *vt* (*support*) appoggiare. **stand down** *vi* (*retire*) ritirarsi. **stand for** *vt* (*mean*) significare; (*tolerate*) tollerare. **stand in for** *vt* sostituire. **stand out** *vi* spiccare. **stand up** *vi* alzarsi [in piedi]. **stand up for** *vt* prendere le difese di; ~ **up for oneself** farsi valere. **stand up to** *vt* affrontare

standard /'stændəd/ *a* standard; **be** ~ **practice** essere pratica corrente ● *n* standard *m inv*; *Techn* norma *f*; (*level*) livello *m*; (*quality*) qualità *f inv*; (*flag*) stendardo *m*; ~**s** *pl* (*morals*) valori *mpl*; ~ **of living** tenore *m* di vita. ~**ize** *vt* standardizzare

'**standard lamp** *n* lampada *f* a stelo

'**stand-by** *n* riserva *f*; **on** ~ (*at airport*) in lista d'attesa

'**stand-in** *n* controfigura *f*

standing /'stændɪŋ/ *a* (*erect*) in piedi; (*permanent*) permanente ● *n* posizione *f*; (*duration*) durata *f*. ~ **order** *n* addebitamento *m* diretto. ~**-room** *n* posti *mpl* in piedi

stand: ~**-offish** /stænd'ɒfɪʃ/ *a* scostante. ~**point** *n* punto *m* di vista. ~**still** *n* come to a ~**still** fermarsi; **at a** ~**still** in un periodo di stasi

stank /stæŋk/ *see* **stink**

staple[1] /'steɪpl/ *n* (*product*) prodotto *m* principale

staple[2] *n* graffa *f* ● *vt* pinzare. ~**r** *n* pinzatrice *f*, cucitrice *f*

star /stɑ:(r)/ *n* stella *f*; (*asterisk*) asterisco *m*; *Theat, Cinema, Sport* divo, -a *mf*, stella *f* ● *vi* (*pt/pp* **starred**) essere l'interprete principale

starboard /'stɑ:bəd/ *n* tribordo *m*

starch /stɑ:tʃ/ *n* amido *m* ● *vt* inamidare. ~**y** *a* ricco di amido; *fig* compito

stare /steə(r)/ *n* sguardo *m* fisso ● *vi*

it's rude to ~ è da maleducati fissare la gente; ~ **at** fissare; ~ **into space** guardare nel vuoto

'**starfish** *n* stella *f* di mare

stark /stɑ:k/ *a* austero; (*contrast*) forte ● *adv* completamente; ~ **naked** completamente nudo

starling /'stɑ:lɪŋ/ *n* storno *m*

'**starlit** *a* stellato

starry /'stɑ:rɪ/ *a* stellato

start /stɑ:t/ *n* inizio *m*; (*departure*) partenza *f*; (*jump*) sobbalzo *m*; **from the** ~ [fin] dall'inizio; **for a** ~ tanto per cominciare; **give sb a** ~ *Sport* dare un vantaggio a qcno ● *vi* [in]cominciare; (*set out*) avviarsi; (*engine, car*) partire; (*jump*) trasalire; **to** ~ **with,...** tanto per cominciare,... ● *vt* [in]cominciare; (*cause*) dare inizio a; (*found*) mettere su; mettere in moto (*car*); mettere in giro (*rumour*). ~**er** *n* *Culin* primo *m* [piatto *m*]; (*in race: giving signal*) starter *m inv*; (*participant*) concorrente *mf*; *Auto* motorino *m* d'avviamento. ~**ing-point** *n* punto *m* di partenza

startle /'stɑ:tl/ *vt* far trasalire; (*news*) sconvolgere

starvation /stɑ:'veɪʃn/ *n* fame *f*

starve /stɑ:v/ *vi* morire di fame ● *vt* far morire di fame

stash /stæʃ/ *vt* *fam* ~ [away] nascondere

state /steɪt/ *n* stato *m*; (*grand style*) pompa *f*; ~ **of play** punteggio *m*; **be in a** ~ (*person*) essere agitato; **lie in** ~ essere esposto ● *attrib* di Stato; *Sch* pubblico; (*with ceremony*) di gala ● *vt* dichiarare; (*specify*) precisare. ~**less** *a* apolide

stately /'steɪtlɪ/ *a* (**-ier, -iest**) maestoso. ~ **home** *n* dimora *f* signorile

statement /'steɪtmənt/ *n* dichiarazione *f*; *Jur* deposizione *f*; (*in banking*) estratto *m* conto; (*account*) rapporto *m*

'**statesman** *n* statista *m*

static /'stætɪk/ *a* statico

station /'steɪʃn/ *n* stazione *f*; (*police*) commissariato *m* ● *vt* appostare (*guard*); **be** ~**ed in Germany** essere di stanza in Germania. ~**ary** /-ərɪ/ *a* immobile

stationer /'steɪʃənə(r)/ *n* ~**'s** [**shop**] cartoleria *f*. ~**y** *n* cartoleria *f*

'**station-wagon** *n* *Am* familiare *f*

statistic|al /stə'tɪstɪkl/ *a* statistico. ~**s** *n & pl* statistica *f*

statue /'stætju:/ *n* statua *f*

stature /'stætʃə(r)/ *n* statura *f*

status /'steɪtəs/ n condizione f; (high rank) alto rango m. **~ symbol** n status symbol m inv

statut|e /'stætjuːt/ n statuto m. **~ory** a statutario

staunch /stɔːntʃ/ a fedele. **~ly** adv fedelmente

stave /steɪv/ vt **~ off** tenere lontano

stay /steɪ/ n soggiorno m ● vi restare, rimanere; (reside) alloggiare; **~ the night** passare la notte; **~ put** non muoversi ● vt **~ the course** resistere fino alla fine. **stay away** vi stare lontano. **stay behind** vi non andare con gli altri. **stay in** vi (at home) stare in casa; Sch restare a scuola dopo le lezioni. **stay up** vi stare su; (person:) stare alzato

stead /sted/ n **in his ~** in sua vece; **stand sb in good ~** tornare utile a qcno. **~fast** a fedele; (refusal) fermo

steadily /'stedɪlɪ/ adv (continually) continuamente

steady /'stedɪ/ a (-ier, -iest) saldo, fermo; (breathing) regolare; (job, boyfriend) fisso; (dependable) serio

steak /steɪk/ n (for stew) spezzatino m; (for grilling, frying) bistecca f

steal /stiːl/ v (pt stole, pp stolen) ● vt rubare (from da). **steal in/out** vi entrare/uscire furtivamente

stealth /stelθ/ n **by ~** di nascosto. **~y** a furtivo

steam /stiːm/ n vapore m; **under one's own ~** fam da solo ● vt Culin cucinare a vapore ● vi fumare. **steam up** vi appannarsi

'steam-engine n locomotiva f

steamer /'stiːmə(r)/ n piroscafo m; (saucepan) pentola f a vapore

'steamroller n rullo m compressore

steamy /'stiːmɪ/ a appannato

steel /stiːl/ n acciaio m ● vt **~ oneself** temprarsi

steep¹ /stiːp/ vt (soak) lasciare a bagno

steep² a ripido; (fam: price) esorbitante. **~ly** adv ripidamente

steeple /'stiːpl/ n campanile m. **~chase** n corsa f ippica a ostacoli

steer /stɪə(r)/ vt/i guidare; **~ clear of** stare alla larga da. **~ing** n Auto sterzo m. **~ing-wheel** n volante m

stem¹ /stem/ n stelo m; (of glass) gambo m; (of word) radice f ● vi (pt/pp stemmed) **~ from** derivare da

stem² vt (pt/pp stemmed) contenere

stench /stentʃ/ n fetore m

step /step/ n passo m; (stair) gradino m; **~s** pl (ladder) scala f portatile; **in ~** al passo; **be out of ~** non stare al passo; **~ by ~** un passo alla volta ● vi (pt/pp stepped) **~ into** entrare in; **~ out of** uscire da; **~ out of line** sgarrare. **step down** vi fig dimettersi. **step forward** vi farsi avanti. **step in** vi fig intervenire. **step up** vt (increase) aumentare

step: ~brother n fratellastro m. **~child** n figliastro, -a mf. **~daughter** n figliastra f. **~father** n patrigno m. **~-ladder** n scala f portatile. **~mother** n matrigna f

'stepping-stone n pietra f per guadare; fig trampolino m

step: ~sister n sorellastra f. **~son** n figliastro m

stereo /'sterɪəʊ/ n stereo m; **in ~** in stereofonia. **~phonic** /-'fɒnɪk/ a stereofonico

stereotype /'sterɪətaɪp/ n stereotipo m. **~d** a stereotipato

steril|e /'steraɪl/ a sterile. **~ity** /stə'rɪlətɪ/ n sterilità f

sterilization /sterɪlaɪ'zeɪʃn/ n sterilizzazione f. **~e** /'ster-/ vt sterilizzare

sterling /'stɜːlɪŋ/ a fig apprezzabile; **~ silver** argento m pregiato ● n sterlina f

stern¹ /stɜːn/ a severo

stern² n (of boat) poppa f

stethoscope /'steθəskəʊp/ n stetoscopio m

stew /stjuː/ n stufato m; **in a ~** fam agitato ● vt/i cuocere in umido; **~ed fruit** frutta f cotta

steward /'stjuːəd/ n (at meeting) organizzatore, -trice mf; (on ship, aircraft) steward m inv. **~ess** n hostess f inv

stick¹ /stɪk/ n bastone m; (of celery, rhubarb) gambo m; Sport mazza f

stick² v (pt/pp stuck) ● vt (stab) [con]ficcare; (glue) attaccare; (fam: put) mettere; (fam: endure) sopportare ● vi (adhere) attaccarsi (to a); (jam) bloccarsi; **~ to** attenersi a (facts); mantenere (story); perseverare in (task); **~ at it** fam tener duro; **~ at nothing** fam non fermarsi di fronte a niente; **be stuck** (vehicle, person:) essere bloccato; (drawer:) essere incastrato; **be stuck with sth** fam farsi incastrare con qcsa. **stick out** vi (project) sporgere; (fam: catch the eye) risaltare ● vt fam fare (tongue). **stick up for** vt fam difendere

sticker /'stɪkə(r)/ n autoadesivo m

'sticking plaster n cerotto m

stick-in-the-mud n retrogrado m

stickler /'stɪklə(r)/ n **be a ~ for** tenere molto a

sticky /'stɪkɪ/ a (-ier, -iest) appiccicoso; ⟨adhesive⟩ adesivo; ⟨fig: difficult⟩ difficile

stiff /stɪf/ a rigido; ⟨brush, task⟩ duro; ⟨person⟩ controllato; ⟨drink⟩ forte; ⟨penalty⟩ severo; ⟨price⟩ alto; **bored ~** fam annoiato a morte; **~ neck** torcicollo m. **~en** vt irrigidire ● vi irrigidirsi. **~ness** n rigidità f

stifl|e /'staɪfl/ vt soffocare. **~ing** a soffocante

stigma /'stɪgmə/ n marchio m

stiletto /stɪ'letəʊ/ n stiletto m; **~ heels** tacchi mpl a spillo; **~s** ⟨pl: shoes⟩ scarpe fpl coi tacchi a spillo

still[1] /stɪl/ n distilleria f

still[2] a fermo; ⟨drink⟩ non gasato; **keep/stand ~** stare fermo ● n quiete f; ⟨photo⟩ posa f ● adv ancora; ⟨nevertheless⟩ nondimeno, comunque; **I'm ~ not sure** non sono ancora sicuro

'**stillborn** a nato morto

still 'life n natura f morta

stilted /'stɪltɪd/ a artificioso

stilts /stɪlts/ npl trampoli mpl

stimulant /'stɪmjʊlənt/ n eccitante m

stimulat|e /'stɪmjʊleɪt/ vt stimolare. **~ion** /-'leɪʃn/ n stimolo m

stimulus /'stɪmjʊləs/ n (pl -li /-laɪ/) stimolo m

sting /stɪŋ/ n puntura f; ⟨organ⟩ pungiglione m ● v (pt/pp **stung**) ● vt pungere; ⟨jellyfish:⟩ pizzicare ● vi ⟨insect:⟩ pungere. **~ing nettle** n ortica f

stingy /'stɪndʒɪ/ a (-ier, -iest) tirchio

stink /stɪŋk/ n puzza f ● vi (pt **stank**, pp **stunk**) puzzare

stint /stɪnt/ n lavoro m; **do one's ~** fare la propria parte ● vt **~ on** lesinare su

stipulat|e /'stɪpjʊleɪt/ vt porre come condizione. **~ion** /-'leɪʃn/ n condizione f

stir /stɜː(r)/ n mescolata f; ⟨commotion⟩ trambusto m ● v (pt/pp **stirred**) ● vt muovere; ⟨mix⟩ mescolare ● vi muoversi

stirrup /'stɪrəp/ n staffa f

stitch /stɪtʃ/ n punto m; ⟨in knitting⟩ maglia f; ⟨pain⟩ fitta f; **have sb in ~es** fam far ridere qcno a crepapelle ● vt cucire

stock /stɒk/ n ⟨for use or selling⟩ scorta f, stock m inv; ⟨livestock⟩ bestiame m; ⟨lineage⟩ stirpe f; Fin titoli mpl; Culin brodo m; **in ~** disponibile, out of **~** esaurito; **take ~** fig fare il punto ● a solito ● vt ⟨shop:⟩ vendere; approvvigio-

nare ⟨shelves⟩. **stock up** vi far scorta ⟨with di⟩

stock: ~broker n agente m di cambio. **~ cube** n dado m [da brodo]. **S~ Exchange** n Borsa f Valori

stocking /'stɒkɪŋ/ n calza f

stockist /'stɒkɪst/ n rivenditore m

stock: ~market n mercato m azionario. **~pile** vt fare scorta di ● n riserva f. **~-still** a immobile. **~-taking** n Comm inventario m

stocky /'stɒkɪ/ a (-ier, -iest) tarchiato

stodgy /'stɒdʒɪ/ a indigesto

stoic /'stəʊɪk/ n stoico, -a mf. ● al a stoico. **~ism** /-sɪzm/ stoicismo m

stoke /stəʊk/ vt alimentare

stole[1] /stəʊl/ n stola f

stole[2], **stolen** /'stəʊln/ see **steal**

stolid /'stɒlɪd/ a apatico

stomach /'stʌmək/ n pancia f; Anat stomaco m ● vt fam reggere. **~-ache** n mal m di pancia

stone /stəʊn/ n pietra f; ⟨in fruit⟩ nocciolo m; Med calcolo m; ⟨weight⟩ 6,348 kg ● a di pietra; ⟨wall, Age⟩ della pietra ● vt snocciolare ⟨fruit⟩. **~-cold** a gelido. **~-'deaf** a fam sordo come una campana

stony /'stəʊnɪ/ a pietroso; ⟨glare⟩ glaciale

stood /stʊd/ see **stand**

stool /stuːl/ n sgabello m

stoop /stuːp/ n curvatura f ● vi stare curvo; ⟨bend down⟩ chinarsi; fig abbassarsi

stop /stɒp/ n ⟨break⟩ sosta f; ⟨for bus, train⟩ fermata f; Gram punto m; **come to a ~** fermarsi; **put a ~ to sth** mettere fine a qcsa ● v (pt/pp **stopped**) ● vt fermare; arrestare ⟨machine⟩; ⟨prevent⟩ impedire; **~ sb doing sth** impedire a qcno di fare qcsa; **~ doing sth** smettere di fare qcsa; **~ that!** smettila! ● vi fermarsi; ⟨rain:⟩ smettere ● int fermo!. **stop off** vi fare una sosta. **stop up** vt otturare ⟨sink⟩; tappare ⟨hole⟩. **stop with** vi ⟨fam: stay with⟩ fermarsi da

stop: ~gap n palliativo m; ⟨person⟩ tappabuchi m inv. **~-over** n sosta f; Aeron scalo m

stoppage /'stɒpɪdʒ/ n ostruzione f; ⟨strike⟩ interruzione f; ⟨deduction⟩ trattenute fpl

stopper /'stɒpə(r)/ n tappo m

stop: ~-press n ultimissime fpl. **~-watch** n cronometro m

storage /'stɔːrɪdʒ/ n deposito m; ⟨in

warehouse) immagazzinaggio *m*; *Comput* memoria *f*

store /stɔː(r)/ *n* (*stock*) riserva *f*; (*shop*) grande magazzino *m*; (*depot*) deposito *m*; **in ~** in deposito; **what the future has in ~ for me** cosa mi riserva il futuro; **set great ~ by** tenere in gran conto ●*vt* tenere; (*in warehouse, Comput*) immagazzinare. **~-room** *n* magazzino *m*

storey /ˈstɔːrɪ/ *n* piano *m*

stork /stɔːk/ *n* cicogna *f*

storm /stɔːm/ *n* temporale *m*; (*with thunder*) tempesta *f* ●*vt* prendere d'assalto. **~y** *a* tempestoso

story /ˈstɔːrɪ/ *n* storia *f*; (*in newspaper*) articolo *m*

stout /staʊt/ *a* (*shoes*) resistente; (*fat*) robusto; (*defence*) strenuo

stove /stəʊv/ *n* stufa *f*; (*for cooking*) cucina *f* [economica]

stow /stəʊ/ *vt* metter via. **~away** *n* passeggero, -a *mf* clandestino, -a

straddle /ˈstrædl/ *vt* stare a cavalcioni su; (*standing*) essere a cavallo su

straggl|e /ˈstrægl/ *vi* crescere disordinatamente; (*dawdle*) rimanere indietro. **~er** *n* persona *f* che rimane indietro. **~y** *a* in disordine

straight /streɪt/ *a* diritto, dritto; (*answer, question, person*) diretto; (*tidy*) in ordine; (*drink, hair*) liscio ●*adv* diritto, dritto; (*directly*) direttamente; **~ away** immediatamente; **~ on** *or* **ahead** diritto; **~ out** *fig* apertamente; **go ~** *fam* rigare diritto; **put sth ~** mettere qcsa in ordine; **sit/stand up ~** stare diritto

straighten /ˈstreɪtn/ *vt* raddrizzare ●*vi* raddrizzarsi; **~ |up|** (*person:*) mettersi diritto. **straighten out** *vt fig* chiarire (*situation*)

straightforward *a* franco; (*simple*) semplice

strain[1] /streɪn/ *n* (*streak*) vena *f*; *Bot* varietà *f inv*; (*of virus*) forma *f*

strain[2] *n* tensione *f*; (*injury*) stiramento *m*; **~s** *pl* (*of music*) note *fpl* ●*vt* tirare; sforzare (*eyes, voice*); stirarsi (*muscle*); *Culin* scolare ●*vi* sforzarsi. **~ed** *a* (*relations*) teso. **~er** *n* colino *m*

strait /streɪt/ *n* stretto *m*; **in dire ~s** in serie difficoltà. **~-jacket** *n* camicia *f* di forza. **~-laced** *a* puritano

strand[1] /strænd/ *n* (*of thread*) gugliata *f*; (*of beads*) filo *m*; (*of hair*) capello *m*

strand[2] *vt* be **~ed** rimanere bloccato

strange /streɪndʒ/ *a* strano; (*not*

known) sconosciuto; (*unaccustomed*) estraneo. **~ly** *adv* stranamente; **~ly enough** curiosamente. **~r** *n* estraneo, -a *mf*

strangle /ˈstræŋgl/ *vt* strangolare; *fig* reprimere

strangulation /stræŋgjʊˈleɪʃn/ *n* strangolamento *m*

strap /stræp/ *n* cinghia *f*; (*to grasp in vehicle*) maniglia *f*; (*of watch*) cinturino *m*; (*shoulder ~*) bretella *f*, spallina *f* ●*vt* (*pt/pp* **strapped**) legare; **~ in** *or* **down** assicurare

strapping /ˈstræpɪŋ/ *a* robusto

strata /ˈstrɑːtə/ *npl see* **stratum**

stratagem /ˈstrætədʒəm/ *n* stratagemma *f*

strategic /strəˈtiːdʒɪk/ *a* strategico

strategy /ˈstrætədʒɪ/ *n* strategia *f*

stratum /ˈstrɑːtəm/ *n* (*pl* **strata**) strato *m*

straw /strɔː/ *n* paglia *f*; (*single piece*) fuscello *m*; (*for drinking*) cannuccia *f*; **the last ~** l'ultima goccia

strawberry /ˈstrɔːbərɪ/ *n* fragola *f*

stray /streɪ/ *a* (*animal*) randagio ●*n* randagio *m* ●*vi* andarsene per conto proprio; (*deviate*) deviare (**from** da)

streak /striːk/ *n* striatura *f*; (*fig: trait*) vena *f* ●*vi* sfrecciare. **~y** *a* striato; (*bacon*) grasso

stream /striːm/ *n* ruscello *m*; (*current*) corrente *f*; (*of blood, people*) flusso *m*; *Sch* classe *f* ●*vi* scorrere. **stream in/out** *vi* entrare/uscire a fiotti

streamer /ˈstriːmə(r)/ *n* (*paper*) stella *f* filante; (*flag*) pennone *m*

streamline *vt* rendere aerodinamico; (*simplify*) snellire. **~d** *a* aerodinamico

street /striːt/ *n* strada *f*. **~car** *n Am* tram *m inv*. **~lamp** *n* lampione *m*

strength /streŋθ/ *n* forza *f*; (*of wall, bridge etc*) solidità *f*; **~s** *pl* punti *mpl* forti; **on the ~ of** grazie a. **~en** *vt* rinforzare

strenuous /ˈstrenjʊəs/ *a* faticoso; (*attempt, denial*) energico

stress /stres/ *n* (*emphasis*) insistenza *f*; *Gram* accento *m* tonico; (*mental*) stress *m inv*; *Mech* spinta *f* ●*vt* (*emphasize*) insistere su; *Gram* mettere l'accento [tonico] su. **~ed** *a* (*mentally*) stressato. **~ful** *a* stressante

stretch /stretʃ/ *n* stiramento *m*; (*period*) periodo *m* di tempo; (*of road*) tratto *m*; (*elasticity*) elasticità *f* ●*a* di fila; **have a ~** stirarsi ●*vt* tirare; allargare (*shoes, arms etc*); (*person:*) allungare ● *vi* (*become wider*) allargarsi; (*extend*) estendersi; (*person:*) stirarsi. ~**er** *n* barella *f*

strew /struː/ *vt* (*pp* **strewn** or **strewed**) sparpagliare

stricken /'strɪkn/ *a* prostrato; ~ **with** affetto da (*illness*)

strict /strɪkt/ *a* severo; (*precise*) preciso. ~**ly** *adv* severamente; ~**ly speaking** in senso stretto

stride /straɪd/ *n* [lungo] passo *m*; **take sth in one's** ~ accettare qcsa con facilità ● *vi* (*pt* **strode**, *pp* **stridden**) andare a gran passi

strident /'straɪdənt/ *a* stridente; (*colour*) vistoso

strife /straɪf/ *n* conflitto *m*

strike /straɪk/ *n* sciopero *m*; *Mil* attacco *m*; **on** ~ in sciopero ● *v* (*pt*/*pp* **struck**) ● *vt* colpire; accendere (*match*); trovare (*oil, gold*); (*delete*) depennare; (*occur to*) venire in mente a; *Mil* attaccare ● *vi* (*lightning:*) cadere; (*clock:*) suonare; *Mil* attaccare; (*workers:*) scioperare; ~ **lucky** azzeccarla. **strike off**, **strike out** *vt* eliminare. **strike up** *vt* fare (*friendship*); attaccare (*conversation*). ~**-breaker** *n* persona *f* che non aderisce a uno sciopero

striker /'straɪkə(r)/ *n* scioperante *mf*

striking /'straɪkɪŋ/ *a* impressionante; (*attractive*) affascinante

string /strɪŋ/ *n* spago *m*; (*of musical instrument, racket*) corda *f*; (*of pearls*) filo *m*; (*of lies*) serie *f*; **the** ~**s** *pl Mus* gli archi; **pull** ~**s** *fam* usare le proprie conoscenze ● *vt* (*pt*/*pp* **strung**) (*thread*) infilare (*beads*). ~**ed** *a* (*instrument*) a corda

stringent /'strɪndʒnt/ *a* rigido

strip /strɪp/ *n* striscia *f* ● *v* (*pt*/*pp* **stripped**) ● *vt* spogliare; togliere le lenzuola da (*bed*); scrostare (*wood, furniture*); smontare (*machine*); (*deprive*) privare (**of** di) ● *vi* (*undress*) spogliarsi. ~ **cartoon** *n* striscia *f*. ~ **club** *n* locale *m* di strip-tease

stripe /straɪp/ *n* striscia *f*; *Mil* gallone *m*. ~**d** *a* a strisce

striplight *n* tubo *m* al neon

stripper /'strɪpə(r)/ *n* spogliarellista *mf*; (*solvent*) sverniciatore *m*

strip-'tease *n* spogliarello *m*, striptease *m inv*

strive /straɪv/ *vi* (*pt* **strove**, *pp* **striven**) sforzarsi (**to** di); ~ **for** sforzarsi di ottenere

strode /strəʊd/ *see* **stride**

stroke[1] /strəʊk/ *n* colpo *m*; (*of pen*) tratto *m*; (*in swimming*) bracciata *f*; *Med* ictus *m inv*; ~ **of luck** colpo *m* di fortuna; **put sb off his** ~ far perdere il filo a qcno

stroke[2] *vt* accarezzare

stroll /strəʊl/ *n* passeggiata *f* ● *vi* passeggiare. ~**er** *n* (*Am: push-chair*) passeggino *m*

strong /strɒŋ/ *a* (**-er** /-gə(r)/, **-est** /-gɪst/) forte; (*argument*) valido

strong: ~**-box** *n* cassaforte *f*. ~**hold** *n* roccaforte *f*. ~**ly** *adv* fortemente. ~**-minded** *a* risoluto. ~**-room** *n* camera *f* blindata

stroppy /'strɒpɪ/ *a* scorbutico

strove /strəʊv/ *see* **strive**

struck /strʌk/ *see* **strike**

structural /'strʌktʃərəl/ *a* strutturale. ~**ly** *adv* strutturalmente

structure /'strʌktʃə(r)/ *n* struttura *f*

struggle /'strʌgl/ *n* lotta *f*; **with a** ~ con difficoltà ● *vi* lottare; ~ **for breath** respirare con fatica; ~ **to do sth** fare fatica a fare qcsa; ~ **to one's feet** alzarsi con fatica

strum /strʌm/ *vt*/*i* (*pt*/*pp* **strummed**) strimpellare

strung /strʌŋ/ *see* **string**

strut[1] /strʌt/ *n* (*component*) puntello *m*

strut[2] *vi* (*pt*/*pp* **strutted**) camminare impettito

stub /stʌb/ *n* mozzicone *m*; (*counterfoil*) matrice *f* ● *vt* (*pt*/*pp* **stubbed**) ~ **one's toe** sbattere il dito del piede (**on** contro). **stub out** *vt* spegnere (*cigarette*)

stubble /'stʌbl/ *n* barba *f* ispida. ~**ly** *a* ispido

stubborn /'stʌbən/ *a* testardo; (*refusal*) ostinato

stubby /'stʌbɪ/ *a* (**-ier**, **-iest**) tozzo

stucco /'stʌkəʊ/ *n* stucco *m*

stuck /stʌk/ *see* **stick**[2]. ~**-up** *a fam* snob *inv*

stud[1] /stʌd/ *n* (*on boot*) tacchetto *m*; (*on jacket*) borchia *f*; (*for ear*) orecchino *m* [a bottone]

stud[2] *n* (*of horses*) scuderia *f*

student /'stjuːdənt/ *n* studente *m*, studentessa *f*; (*school child*) scolaro, -a *mf*. ~ **nurse** *n* studente, studentessa infermiere, -a

studied /'stʌdɪd/ *a* intenzionale; (*politeness*) studiato

studio /'stjuːdɪəʊ/ *n* studio *m*

studious /'stjuːdɪəs/ *a* studioso; (*attention*) studiato

study /'stʌdɪ/ n studio m ● vt/i (pt/pp **studied**) studiare

stuff /stʌf/ n materiale m; (fam: things) roba f ● vt riempire; (with padding) imbottire; Culin farcire; ~ **sth into a drawer/one's pocket** ficcare qcsa alla rinfusa in un cassetto/in tasca. ~**ing** n (padding) imbottitura f; Culin ripieno m

stuffy /'stʌfɪ/ a (**-ier, -iest**) che sa di chiuso; (old-fashioned) antiquato

stumbl|e /'stʌmbl/ vi inciampare; ~**e across** or **on** imbattersi in. ~**ing-block** n ostacolo m

stump /stʌmp/ n ceppo m; (of limb) moncone m. ~**ed** a fam perplesso ● **stump up** vt/i fam sganciare

stun /stʌn/ vt (pt/pp **stunned**) stordire; (astonish) sbalordire

stung /stʌŋ/ see **sting**

stunk /stʌŋk/ see **stink**

stunning /'stʌnɪŋ/ a fam favoloso; (blow, victory) sbalorditivo

stunt¹ /stʌnt/ n fam trovata f pubblicitaria

stunt² vt arrestare lo sviluppo di.~**ed** a stentato

stupendous /stju:'pendəs/ a stupendo. ~**ly** adv stupendamente

stupid /'stju:pɪd/ a stupido. ~**ity** /-'pɪdətɪ/ n stupidità f. ~**ly** adv stupidamente

stupor /'stju:pə(r)/ n torpore m

sturdy /'stɜ:dɪ/ a (**-ier, -iest**) robusto; (furniture) solido

stutter /'stʌtə(r)/ n balbuzie f ● vt/i balbettare

sty, stye /staɪ/ n (pl**styes**) Med orzaiolo m

style /staɪl/ n stile m; (fashion) moda f; (sort) tipo m; (hair~) pettinatura f; **in ~** in grande stile

stylish /'staɪlɪʃ/ a elegante. ~**ly** adv con eleganza

stylist /'staɪlɪst/ n stilista mf; (hair~) parrucchiere, -a mf. ~**ic** /-'lɪstɪk/ a stilistico

stylized /'staɪlaɪzd/ a stilizzato

stylus /'staɪləs/ n (on record player) puntina f

suave /swɑ:v/ a dai modi garbati

sub'conscious /sʌb-/ a subcosciente ● n subcosciente m. ~**ly** adv in modo inconscio

subcon'tract vt subappaltare (**to** a). ~**or** n subappaltatore m

'subdivi|de vt suddividere. ~**sion** n suddivisione f

subdue /səb'dju:/ vt sottomettere; (make quieter) attenuare. ~**d** a (light) attenuato; (person, voice) pacato

subhuman /sʌb'hju:mən/ a disumano

subject¹ /'sʌbdʒɪkt/ a~ **to** soggetto a; (depending on) subordinato a; ~ **to availability** nei limiti della disponibilità ● n soggetto m; (of ruler) suddito, -a mf; Sch materia f

subject² /səb'dʒekt/ vt (to attack, abuse) sottoporre; assoggettare (country)

subjective /səb'dʒektɪv/ a soggettivo. ~**ly** adv soggettivamente

subjugate /'sʌbdʒʊgeɪt/ vt soggiogare

subjunctive /səb'dʒʌŋktɪv/ a & n congiuntivo m

sub'let vt (pt/pp -**let**, pres p -**letting**) subaffittare

sublime /sə'blaɪm/ a sublime. ~**ly** adv sublimemente

subliminal /sə'blɪmɪnl/ a subliminale

sub-ma'chine-gun n mitraglietta f

submarine /'sʌbməri:n/ n sommergibile m

submerge /səb'mɜ:dʒ/ vt immergere; **be ~d** essere sommerso ● vi immergersi

submiss|ion /səb'mɪʃn/ n sottomissione f. ~**ive** /-sɪv/ a sottomesso

submit /səb'mɪt/ v (pt/pp -**mitted**, pres p -**mitting**) ● vt sottoporre ● vi sottomettersi

subordinate /sə'bɔ:dɪnət/ vt subordinare (**to** a)

subscribe /səb'skraɪb/ vi contribuire; ~ **to** abbonarsi a (newspaper); sottoscrivere (fund); fig aderire a. ~**r** n abbonato, -a mf

subscription /səb'skrɪpʃn/ n (to club) sottoscrizione f; (to newspaper) abbonamento m

subsequent /'sʌbsɪkwənt/ a susseguente. ~**ly** adv in seguito

subservient /səb'sɜ:vɪənt/ a subordinato; (servile) servile. ~**ly** adv servilmente

subside /səb'saɪd/ vi sprofondare; (ground:) avvallarsi; (storm:) placarsi

subsidiary /səb'sɪdɪərɪ/ a secondario ● n ~ [**company**] filiale f

subsid|ize /'sʌbsɪdaɪz/ vt sovvenzionare. ~**y** n sovvenzione f

subsist /səb'sɪst/ vi vivere (**on** di). ~**ence** n sussistenza f

substance /'sʌbstəns/ n sostanza f

sub'standard a di qualità inferiore

substantial /səb'stænʃl/ a solido; (meal) sostanzioso; (considerable) note-

461

vole. **~ly** adv notevolmente; (essentially) sostanzialmente

substantiate /səbˈstænʃɪeɪt/ vt comprovare

substitut|e /ˈsʌbstɪtjuːt/ n sostituto m ●vt **~e A for B** sostituire B con A ●vi **~e for sb** sostituire qcno. **~ion** /-ˈtjuːʃn/ n sostituzione f

subterranean /sʌbtəˈreɪnɪən/ a sotterraneo

'subtitle n sottotitolo m

sub|tle /ˈsʌtl/ a sottile; ⟨taste, perfume⟩ delicato. **~tlety** n sottigliezza f. **~tly** adv sottilmente

subtract /səbˈtrækt/ vt sottrarre. **~ion** /-ækʃn/ n sottrazione f

suburb /ˈsʌbɜːb/ n sobborgo m; **in the ~s** in periferia. **~an** /səˈbɜːbən/ a suburbano. **~ia** /səˈbɜːbɪə/ n sobborghi mpl

subversive /səbˈvɜːsɪv/ a sovversivo

'subway n sottopassaggio m; (Am: railway) metropolitana f

succeed /səkˈsiːd/ vi riuscire; (follow) succedere a; **~ in doing** riuscire a fare ●vt succedere a ⟨king⟩. **~ing** a successivo

success /səkˈses/ n successo m; **be a ~** (in life) aver successo. **~ful** a riuscito; ⟨businessman, artist etc⟩ di successo. **~fully** adv con successo

succession /səkˈseʃn/ n successione f; **in ~** di seguito

successive /səkˈsesɪv/ a successivo. **~ly** adv successivamente

successor /səkˈsesə(r)/ n successore m

succinct /səkˈsɪŋkt/ a succinto

succulent /ˈsʌkjʊlənt/ a succulento

succumb /səˈkʌm/ vi soccombere (**to** a)

such /sʌtʃ/ a tale; **~ a book** un libro di questo genere; **~ a thing** una cosa di questo genere; **~ a long time ago** tanto tempo fa; **there is no ~ thing** non esiste una cosa così; **there is no ~ person** non esiste una persona così ●pron as a **~** come tale; **~ as** chi; **and ~** e simili; **~ as it is** così com'è. **~like** pron fam di tal genere

suck /sʌk/ vt succhiare. **suck up** vt assorbire. **suck up to** vt fam fare il lecchino con

sucker /ˈsʌkə(r)/ n Bot pollone m; (fam: person) credulone, -a mf

suction /ˈsʌkʃn/ n aspirazione f

sudden /ˈsʌdn/ a improvviso ●n **all of a ~** all'improvviso. **~ly** adv improvvisamente

sue /suː/ ●v (pres p **suing**) ●vt fare causa a (**for** per) ●vi fare causa

suede /sweɪd/ n pelle f scamosciata

suet /ˈsuːɪt/ n grasso m di rognone

suffer /ˈsʌfə(r)/ vi soffrire (**from** per) ●vt soffrire; subire ⟨loss etc⟩; (tolerate) subire. **~ing** n sofferenza f

suffice /səˈfaɪs/ vi bastare

sufficient /səˈfɪʃənt/ a sufficiente. **~ly** adv sufficientemente

suffix /ˈsʌfɪks/ n suffisso m

suffocat|e /ˈsʌfəkeɪt/ vt/i soffocare. **~ion** /-ˈkeɪʃn/ n soffocamento m

sugar /ˈʃʊɡə(r)/ n zucchero m ●vt zuccherare. **~ basin**, **~-bowl** n zuccheriera f. **~y** a zuccheroso; fig sdolcinato

suggest /səˈdʒest/ vt suggerire; (indicate, insinuate) fare pensare a. **~ion** /-estʃən/ n suggerimento m; (trace) traccia f. **~ive** /-ɪv/ a allusivo. **~ively** adv in modo allusivo

suicidal /suːɪˈsaɪdl/ a suicida

suicide /ˈsuːɪsaɪd/ n suicidio m; (person) suicida mf; **commit ~** suicidarsi

suit /suːt/ n vestito m; (woman's) tailleur m inv; (in cards) seme m; Jur causa f; **follow ~** fig fare lo stesso ●vt andar bene a; (adapt) adattare (**to** a); (be convenient) andare bene per; **be ~ed to or for** essere adatto a; **~ yourself!** fa' come vuoi!

suitab|le /ˈsuːtəbl/ a adatto. **~y** adv convenientemente

'suitcase n valigia f

suite /swiːt/ n suite f inv; (of furniture) divano m e poltrone fpl assortiti

sulk /sʌlk/ vi fare il broncio. **~y** a imbronciato

sullen /ˈsʌlən/ a svogliato

sulphur /ˈsʌlfə(r)/ n zolfo m. **~ic** /-ˈfjuːrɪk/ **~ic acid** n acido m solforico

sultana /sʌlˈtɑːnə/ n uva f sultanina

sultry /ˈsʌltrɪ/ a (**-ier, -iest**) ⟨weather⟩ afoso; fig sensuale

sum /sʌm/ n somma f; Sch addizione f ●**sum up** ●v (pt/pp **summed**) ●vi riassumere ●vt valutare

summar|ize /ˈsʌməraɪz/ vt riassumere. **~y** n sommario m ●a sommario; ⟨dismissal⟩ sbrigativo

summer /ˈsʌmə(r)/ n estate f. **~-house** n padiglione m. **~-time** n (season) estate f

summery /ˈsʌmərɪ/ a estivo

summit /ˈsʌmɪt/ n cima f. **~ conference** n vertice m

summon /ˈsʌmən/ vt convocare; Jur citare. **summon up** vt raccogliere (strength); rievocare (memory)

summons /'sʌmənz/ n Jur citazione f ● vt citare in giudizio

sump /sʌmp/ n Auto coppa f dell'olio

sumptuous /'sʌmptjʊəs/ a sontuoso. **~ly** adv sontuosamente

sun /sʌn/ n sole m ● vt (pt/pp sunned) **~ oneself** prendere il sole

sun: ~bathe vi prendere il sole. **~-bed** n lettino m solare. **~burn** n scottatura f (solare). **~burnt** a scottato (dal sole)

sundae /'sʌndeɪ/ n gelato m guarnito

Sunday /'sʌndeɪ/ n domenica f

'sundial n meridiana f

sundry /'sʌndrɪ/ a svariati; **all and ~** tutti quanti

'sunflower n girasole m

sung /sʌŋ/ see sing

'sun-glasses npl occhiali mpl da sole

sunk /sʌŋk/ see sink

sunken /'sʌŋkn/ a incavato

'sunlight n luce f del] sole m

sunny /'sʌnɪ/ a (-ier, -iest) assolato

sun: ~rise n alba f. **~-roof** n Auto tettuccio m apribile. **~set** n tramonto m. **~shade** n parasole m. **~shine** n [luce f del] sole m. **~stroke** n insolazione f. **~-tan** n abbronzatura f. **~-tanned** a abbronzato. **~-tan oil** n olio m solare

super /'su:pə(r)/ a fam fantastico

superb /su:'pɜ:b/ a splendido

supercilious /su:pə'sɪliəs/ a altezzoso. **~ly** adv superciliosamente

superficial /su:pə'fɪʃl/ a superficiale. **~ly** adv superficialmente

superfluous /su'pɜ:flʊəs/ a superfluo

super'human a sovrumano

superintendent /su:pərɪn'tendənt/ n (of police) commissario m di polizia

superior /su:'pɪərɪə(r)/ a superiore ● n superiore, -a mf. **~ity** /-'ɒrətɪ/ n superiorità f

superlative /su:'pɜ:lətɪv/ a eccellente ● n superlativo m

'superman n superuomo m

'supermarket n supermercato m

'supermodel n top model f inv

super'natural a soprannaturale

'superpower n superpotenza f

supersede /su:pə'si:d/ vt rimpiazzare

super'sonic a supersonico

superstition /su:pə'stɪʃn/ n superstizione f. **~ous** /-'stɪʃəs/ a superstizioso

supervise /'su:pəvaɪz/ vt supervisionare. **~ion** /-'vɪʒn/ n supervisione f. **~or** n supervisore m

supper /'sʌpə(r)/ n cena f

supple /'sʌpl/ a slogato

supplement /'sʌplɪmənt/ n supplemento ● vt integrare. **~ary** /-'mentərɪ/ a supplementare

supplier /sə'plaɪə(r)/ n fornitore, -trice mf

supply /sə'plaɪ/ n fornitura f; (in economics) offerta f; **supplies** pl Mil approvvigionamenti mpl ● vt (pt/pp -ied) fornire; **~ sb with sth** fornire qcsa a qcno

support /sə'pɔ:t/ n sostegno m; (base) supporto m; (keep) sostentamento m ● vt sostenere; mantenere (family); (give money to) mantenere finanziariamente; Sport fare il tifo per. **~er** n sostenitore, -trice mf; Sport tifoso, -a mf. **~ive** /-ɪv/ a incoraggiante

suppose /sə'pəʊz/ vt (presume) supporre; (imagine) pensare; **be ~d to** do dover fare; **not be ~d to** fam non avere il permesso di; **I ~ so** suppongo di sì. **~dly** /-ɪdlɪ/ adv presumibilmente

suppress /sə'pres/ vt sopprimere. **~ion** /-eʃn/ n soppressione f

supremacy /su:'preməsɪ/ n supremazia f

supreme /su:'pri:m/ a supremo

surcharge /'sɜ:tʃɑ:dʒ/ n supplemento m

sure /ʃʊə(r)/ a sicuro, certo; **make ~** accertarsi; **be ~ to do it** mi raccomando di farlo ● adv Am fam certamente; **~ enough** infatti. **~ly** adv certamente; (Am: gladly) volentieri

surety /'ʃʊərətɪ/ n garanzia f; **stand ~ for** garantire per

surf /sɜ:f/ n schiuma f ● vt Comput **the Net** surfare in Internet

surface /'sɜ:fɪs/ n superficie f; **on the ~** fig in apparenza ● vi (emerge) emergere. **~ mail** n **by ~ mail** per posta ordinaria

'surfboard n tavola f da surf

surfing /'sɜ:fɪŋ/ n surf m inv

surge /sɜ:dʒ/ n (of sea) ondata f; (of interest) aumento m; (in demand) impennata f; (of anger, pity) impeto m ● vi riversarsi; **~ forward** buttarsi in avanti

surgeon /'sɜ:dʒən/ n chirurgo m

surgery /'sɜ:dʒərɪ/ n chirurgia f; (place, consulting room) ambulatorio m; (hours) ore fpl di visita; **have ~** subire un'intervento [chirurgico]

surgical /'sɜ:dʒɪkl/ a chirurgico

surly /'sɜ:lɪ/ a (-ier, -iest) scontroso

surmise /sə'maɪz/ vt pensare

surmount /sə'maʊnt/ vt sormontare

surname /'sɜ:neɪm/ n cognome m

surpass /sə'pɑːs/ vt superare

surplus /'sɜːpləs/ a d'avanzo ●n sovrappiù m

surpris|e /sə'praɪz/ n sorpresa f ●vt sorprendere; **be ~ed** essere sorpreso (**at** da). **~ing** a sorprendente. **~ingly** adv sorprendentemente

surrender /sə'rendə(r)/ n resa f ●vi arrendersi ●vt cedere

surreptitious /sʌrəp'tɪʃəs/ a & adv di nascosto

surrogate /'sʌrəgət/ n surrogato m. **~ mother** n madre f surrogata

surround /sə'raʊnd/ vt circondare. **~ing** a circostante. **~ings** npl dintorni mpl

surveillance /sə'veɪləns/ n sorveglianza f

survey[1] /'sɜːveɪ/ n sguardo m; (poll) sondaggio m; (investigation) indagine f; (of land) rilevamento m; (of house) perizia f

survey[2] /sə'veɪ/ vt esaminare; fare un rilevamento di (land); fare una perizia di (building). **~or** n perito m; (of land) topografo, -a mf

survival /sə'vaɪvl/ n sopravvivenza f; (relic) resto m

surviv|e /sə'vaɪv/ vt sopravvivere a ●vi sopravvivere. **~or** n superstite mf; **be a ~or** fam riuscire sempre a cavarsela

susceptible /sə'septəbl/ a influenzabile; **~ to** sensibile a

suspect[1] /'sə'spekt/ vt sospettare; (assume) supporre

suspect[2] /'sʌspekt/ a & n sospetto, -a mf

suspend /sə'spend/ vt appendere; (stop, from duty) sospendere. **~er belt** n reggicalze m inv. **~ers** npl giarrettiere fpl; (Am: braces) bretelle fpl

suspense /sə'spens/ n tensione f; (in book etc) suspense f

suspension /sə'spenʃn/ n Auto sospensione f. **~ bridge** n ponte m sospeso

suspici|on /sə'spɪʃn/ n sospetto m; (trace) pizzico m; **under ~on** sospettato. **~ous** /-ɪʃəs/ a sospettoso; (arousing suspicion) sospetto. **~ously** adv sospettosamente; (arousing suspicion) in modo sospetto

sustain /sə'steɪn/ vt sostenere; mantenere (life); subire (injury)

sustenance /'sʌstɪnəns/ n nutrimento m

swab /swɒb/ n Med tampone m

swagger /'swægə(r)/ vi pavoneggiarsi

swallow[1] /'swɒləʊ/ vt/i inghiottire. **swallow up** vt divorare; (earth, crowd:) inghiottire

swallow[2] n (bird) rondine f

swam /swæm/ see swim

swamp /swɒmp/ n palude f ●vt fig sommergere. **~y** a paludoso

swan /swɒn/ n cigno m

swap /swɒp/ n fam scambio m ●vt (pt/pp swapped) fam scambiare (for con) ●vi fare cambio

swarm /swɔːm/ n sciame m ●vi sciamare; **be ~ing with** brulicare di

swarthy /'swɔːðɪ/ a (-ier, -iest) di carnagione scura

swastika /'swɒstɪkə/ n svastica f

swat /swɒt/ vt (pt/pp swatted) schiacciare

sway /sweɪ/ n fig influenza f ●vi oscillare; (person:) ondeggiare ●vt (influence) influenzare

swear /sweə(r)/ v (pt swore, pp sworn) ●vt giurare ●vi giurare; (curse) dire parolacce; **~ at** sbimprecare contro qcno; **~ by** fam credere ciecamente in. **~word** n parolaccia f

sweat /swet/ n sudore m ●vi sudare

sweater /'swetə(r)/ n golf m inv

sweaty /'swetɪ/ a sudato

swede /swiːd/ n rapa f svedese

Swed|e n svedese mf. **~en** n Svezia f. **~ish** a n (language) svedese m

sweep /swiːp/ n spazzata f, spazzata f; (curve) curva f; (movement) movimento m ampio; **make a clean ~** fig fare piazza pulita ●v (pt/pp swept) ●vt scopare, spazzare; (wind:) spazzare ●vi (go swiftly) andare rapidamente; (wind:) soffiare. **sweep away** vt fig spazzare via. **sweep up** vt spazzare

sweeping /'swiːpɪŋ/ a (gesture) ampio; (statement) generico; (changes) radicale

sweet /swiːt/ a dolce; **have a ~ tooth** essere goloso ●n caramella f; (dessert) dolce m. **~ corn** n mais m

sweet: ~heart n innamorato, -a mf; **hi, ~heart** ciao, tesoro. **~ness** n dolcezza f. **~ pea** n pisello m odoroso. **~shop** n negozio m di dolciumi

swell /swel/ ●v (pt swelled, pp swollen or swelled) ●vi gonfiarsi; (increase) aumentare ●vt (increase) far salire. **~ing** n gonfiore m

swelter /'sweltə(r)/ vi soffocare [dal caldo]

swept /swept/ see sweep

swerve /swɜːv/ vi deviare bruscamente

swift /swɪft/ a rapido. ~**ly** adv rapidamente

swig /swɪg/ n fam sorso m ● vt (pt/pp **swigged**) fam scolarsi

swill /swɪl/ n (for pigs) brodaglia f ● vt ~ [**out**] risciacquare

swim /swɪm/ n have a ~ fare una nuotata ● v (ptswam, ppswum) vi nuotare; (room:) girare; **my head is** ~**ming** mi gira la testa ● vt percorrere a nuoto. ~**mer** n nuotatore, ·trice mf

swimming /'swɪmɪŋ/ n nuoto m. ~-**baths** npl piscina fsg. ~ **costume** n costume m da bagno. ~-**pool** n piscina f. ~ **trunks** npl calzoncini mpl da bagno

'swim-suit n costume m da bagno

swindle /'swɪndl/ n truffa f ● vt truffare. ~**r** n truffatore, ·trice mf

swine /swaɪn/ n fam porco m

swing /swɪŋ/ n oscillazione f; (shift) cambiamento m; (seat) altalena f; Mus swing m; **in full** ~ in piena attività ● v (pt/pp swung) ● vi oscillare; (on swing, sway) dondolare; (dangle) penzolare; (turn) girare ● vt oscillare; far deviare (vote). ~-**door** n porta f a vento

swingeing /'swɪndʒɪŋ/ a (increase) drastico

swipe /swaɪp/ n fam botta f ● vt fam colpire; (steal) rubare; far passare nella macchinetta (credit card)

swirl /swɜːl/ n (of smoke, dust) turbine m ● vi (water:) fare mulinello

swish /swɪʃ/ a fam chic ● vi schioccare

Swiss /swɪs/ a & n svizzero, ·a mf; **the** ~ **pl** gli svizzeri. ~ '**roll** n rotolo m di pan di Spagna ripieno di marmellata

switch /swɪtʃ/ n interruttore m; (change) mutamento m ● vt cambiare; (exchange) scambiare ● vi cambiare; ~ **to passare a**. **switch off** vt spegnere. **switch on** vt accendere

switch: ~**back** n montagne fpl russe. ~**board** n centralino m

Switzerland /'swɪtsələnd/ n Svizzera f

swivel /'swɪvl/ v (pt/pp swivelled) ● vt girare ● vi girarsi

swollen /'swəʊlən/ see swell ● a gonfio. ~-'**headed** a presuntuoso

swoop /swuːp/ n (by police) incursione

f ● vi ~ [**down**] (bird:) piombare; fig fare un'incursione

sword /sɔːd/ n spada f

swore /swɔː(r)/ see swear

sworn /swɔːn/ see swear

swot /swɒt/ n fam sgobbone, ·a mf ● vt (pt/ppswotted) fam sgobbare

swum /swʌm/ see swim

swung /swʌŋ/ see swing

syllable /'sɪləbl/ n sillaba f

syllabus /'sɪləbəs/ n programma m [dei corsi]

symbol /'sɪmbl/ n simbolo m (**of** di). ~**ic** /·'bɒlɪk/ a simbolico. ~**ism** /-ɪzm/ n simbolismo m. ~**ize** vt simboleggiare

symmetr|ical /sɪ'metrɪkl/ a simmetrico. ~**y** /'sɪmətrɪ/ n simmetria f

sympathetic /sɪmpə'θetɪk/ a (understanding) comprensivo; (showing pity) compassionevole. ~**ally** adv con comprensione/compassione

sympathize /'sɪmpəθaɪz/ vi capire; (in grief) solidarizzare; ~ **with sb** capire qcno/solidarizzare con qcno. ~**r** n Pol simpatizzante mf

sympathy /'sɪmpəθɪ/ n comprensione f; (pity) compassione f; (condolences) condoglianze fpl; **in** ~ **with** (strike) per solidarietà con

symphony /'sɪmfənɪ/ n sinfonia f

symptom /'sɪmptəm/ n sintomo m. ~**atic** /·'mætɪk/ a sintomatico (**of** di)

synagogue /'sɪnəgɒg/ n sinagoga f

synchronize /'sɪŋkrənaɪz/ vt sincronizzare

syndicate /'sɪndɪkət/ n gruppo m

syndrome /'sɪndrəʊm/ n sindrome f

synonym /'sɪnənɪm/ n sinonimo m. ~**ous** /·'nɒnɪməs/ a sinonimo

synopsis /sɪ'nɒpsɪs/ n (pl -**opses** /-siːz/) (of opera, ballet) trama f; (of book) riassunto m

syntax /'sɪntæks/ n sintassi f inv

synthesize /'sɪnθəsaɪz/ vt sintetizzare. ~**r** n Mus sintetizzatore m

synthetic /sɪn'θetɪk/ a sintetico ● n fibra f sintetica

Syria /'sɪrɪə/ n Siria f. ~**n** a & n siriano, ·a mf

syringe /sɪ'rɪndʒ/ n siringa f

syrup /'sɪrəp/ n sciroppo m; Br tipo m di melassa

system /'sɪstəm/ n sistema m. ~**atic** /·'mætɪk/ a sistematico

Tt

tab /tæb/ n linguetta f; (with name) etichetta f; **keep ~s on** fam sorvegliare; **pick up the ~** fam pagare il conto

tabby /'tæbɪ/ n gatto m tigrato

table /'teɪbl/ n tavolo m; (list) tavola f; **at** [the] **~** a tavola; **~ of contents** tavola f delle materie; **~** vt proporre. **~-cloth** n tovaglia f. **~spoon** n cucchiaio m da tavola. **~spoon[ful]** n cucchiaiata f

tablet /'tæblɪt/ n pastiglia f; (slab) lastra f; **~ of soap** saponetta f

'**table tennis** n tennis m da tavolo; (everyday level) ping pong m

tabloid /'tæblɔɪd/ n [giornale m formato] tabloid m inv; pej giornale m scandalistico

taboo /tə'buː/ a tabù inv ● n tabù m inv

tacit /'tæsɪt/ a tacito

taciturn /'tæsɪtɜːn/ a taciturno

tack /tæk/ n (nail) chiodino m; (stitch) imbastitura f; Naut virata f; fig linea f di condotta ● vt inchiodare; (sew) imbastire ● vi Naut virare

tackle /'tækl/ n (equipment) attrezzatura f; (football etc) contrasto m, tackle m inv ● vt affrontare

tacky /'tækɪ/ a (paint) non ancora asciutto; (glue) appiccicoso; fig pacchiano

tact /tækt/ n tatto m. **~ful** a pieno di tatto; (remark) delicato. **~fully** adv con tatto

tactic|al /'tæktɪkl/ a tattico. **~s** npl tattica fsg

tactless /'tæktlɪs/ a privo di tatto. **~ly** adv senza tatto. **~ness** n mancanza f di tatto; (of remark) indelicatezza f

tadpole /'tædpəʊl/ n girino m

tag[1] /tæg/ n (label) etichetta f ● vt (pt/pp tagged) attaccare l'etichetta a. **tag along** vi seguire passo passo

tag[2] n (game) acchiapparello m

tail /teɪl/ n coda f; **~s** pl (tailcoat) frac m inv ● vt (fam: follow) pedinare. **tail off** vi diminuire

tail: **~back** n coda f. **~-end** n parte f finale; (of train) coda f. **~ light** n fanalino m di coda

tailor /'teɪlə(r)/ n sarto m. **~-made** a fatto su misura

'**tail wind** n vento m di coda

taint /teɪnt/ vt contaminare

take /teɪk/ n Cinema ripresa f ● v (pt took, pp taken) ● vt prendere; (to a place) portare (person, object); (endure) sopportare; (require) occorrere; (teach) insegnare; (study) studiare (subject); fare (exam, holiday, photograph, walk, bath); sentire (pulse); misurare (sb's temperature); ~ prisoner fare prigioniero qcno; **be ~n ill** ammalarsi; **~ sth calmly** prendere con calma qcsa ● vi (plant:) attecchire. **take after** vt assomigliare a. **take away** vt (with one) portare via; (remove) togliere; (subtract) sottrarre; '**to ~ away**' 'da asporto'. **take back** vt riprendere; ritirare (statement); (return) riportare [indietro]. **take down** vt portare giù; (remove) tirare giù; (write down) prendere nota di. **take in** vt (bring indoors) portare dentro; (to one's home) ospitare; (understand) capire; (deceive) ingannare; riprendere (garment); (include) includere. **take off** vt togliersi (clothes); (deduct) togliere; (mimic) imitare; **~ time off** prendere delle vacanze; **~ oneself off** andarsene ● vi Aeron decollare. **take on** vt farsi carico di; assumere (employee); (as opponent) prendersela con. **take out** vt portare fuori; togliere (word, stain); (withdraw) ritirare (money, books); **~ out a subscription to sth** abbonarsi a qcsa; **~ it out on sb** fam prendersela con qcno. **take over** vt assumere il controllo di (firm) ● vi **~ over from sb** sostituire qcno; (permanently) succedere a qcno. **take to** vt (as a habit) darsi a; **I took to her** (liked) mi è piaciuta. **take up** vt portare su; accettare (offer); intraprendere (profession); dedicarsi a (hobby); prendere (time); occupare (space); tirare su (floor-boards); accorciare (dress); **~ sth up with sb** discutere qcsa con qcno ● vi **~ up with sb** legarsi a qcno

take: **~-away** n (meal) piatto m da asporto; (restaurant) ristorante m che prepara piatti da asporto. **~-off** n

Aeron decollo *m*. **~-over** *n* rilevamento *m*. **~-over bid** *n* offerta *f* di assorbimento

takings /'teɪkɪŋz/ *npl* incassi *mpl*

talcum /'tælkəm/ *n* **~ |powder|** talco *m*

tale /teɪl/ *n* storia *f*; *pej* fandonia *f*

talent /'tælənt/ *n* talento *m*. **~ed** *a* [ricco] di talento

talk /tɔːk/ *n* conversazione *f*; *(lecture)* conferenza *f*; *(gossip)* chiacchiere *fpl*. **make small ~** parlare del più e del meno ● *vi* parlare ● *vt* parlare di *(politics etc)*; **~ sb into sth** convincere qcno di qcsa. **talk over** *vt* discutere

talkative /'tɔːkətɪv/ *a* loquace

talking-to *n* sgridata *f*

talk show *n* talk show *m inv*

tall /tɔːl/ *a* alto. **~boy** *n* cassettone *m*. **~ order** *n* impresa *f* difficile. **~ story** *n* frottola *f*

tally /'tælɪ/ *n* conteggio *m*; **keep a ~ of** tenere il conto di ● *vi* coincidere

tambourine /tæmbə'riːn/ *n* tamburello *m*

tame /teɪm/ *a* *(animal)* domestico; *(dull)* insulso ● *vt* domare. **~ly** *adv* docilmente. **~r** *n* domatore, -trice *mf*

tamper /'tæmpə(r)/ *vi* **~ with** manomettere

tampon /'tæmpɒn/ *n* tampone *m*

tan /tæn/ *a* marrone rossiccio ● *n* marrone *m* rossiccio; *(from sun)* abbronzatura *f* ● *v* *(pt/pp* **tanned**) ● *vt* conciare *(hide)* ● *vi* abbronzarsi

tang /tæŋ/ *n* sapore *m* forte; *(smell)* odore *m* penetrante

tangent /'tændʒənt/ *n* tangente *f*

tangible /'tændʒɪbl/ *a* tangibile

tangle /'tæŋgl/ *n* groviglio *m*; *(in hair)* nodo *m* ● *vt* **~ |up|** aggrovigliare ● *vi* aggrovigliarsi

tango /'tæŋgəʊ/ *n* tango *m inv*

tank /tæŋk/ *n* contenitore *m*; *(for petrol)* serbatoio *m*; *(fish ~)* acquario *m*; *Mil* carro *m* armato

tankard /'tæŋkəd/ *n* boccale *m*

tanker /'tæŋkə(r)/ *n* nave *f* cisterna; *(lorry)* autobotte *f*

tanned /tænd/ *a* abbronzato

tantaliz|e /'tæntəlaɪz/ *vt* tormentare. **~ing** *a* allettante; *(smell)* stuzzicante

tantamount /'tæntəmaʊnt/ *a* **~ to** equivalente a

tantrum /'tæntrəm/ *n* scoppio *m* d'ira

tap /tæp/ *n* rubinetto *m*; *(knock)* colpo *m*; **on ~** *fig* a disposizione ● *v* *(pt/pp* **tapped**) ● *vt* dare un colpetto a; sfruttare *(resources)*; mettere sotto controllo

(telephone) ● *vi* picchiettare. **~-dance** *n* tip tap *m* ● *vi* ballare il tip tap

tape /teɪp/ *n* nastro *m*; *(recording)* cassetta *f* ● *vt* legare con nastro; *(record)* registrare

'**tape: ~ backup drive** *n Comput* unità *f* di backup a nastro. **~-deck** *n* piastra *f*. **~-measure** *n* metro *m* [a nastro]

taper /'teɪpə(r)/ *n* candela *f* sottile ● **taper off** *vi* assottigliarsi

'**tape: ~ recorder** *n* registratore *m*. **~ recording** *n* registrazione *f*

tapestry /'tæpɪstrɪ/ *n* arazzo *m*

tap water *n* acqua *f* del rubinetto

tar /tɑː(r)/ *n* catrame *m* ● *vt* *(pt/pp* **tarred**) incatramare

tardy /'tɑːdɪ/ *a* (-ier, -iest) tardivo

target /'tɑːgɪt/ *n* bersaglio *m*; *fig* obiettivo *m*

tariff /'tærɪf/ *n* *(price)* tariffa *f*; *(duty)* dazio *m*

Tarmac® /'tɑːmæk/ *n* macadam *m* al catrame. **tarmac** *n Aeron* pista *f* di decollo

tarnish /'tɑːnɪʃ/ *vi* ossidarsi ● *vt* ossidare; *fig* macchiare

tarpaulin /tɑː'pɔːlɪn/ *n* telone *m* impermeabile

tart¹ /tɑːt/ *a* aspro; *fig* acido

tart² *n* crostata *f*; *(individual)* crostatina *f*; *(sl: prostitute)* donnaccia *f* ● **tart up** *vt fam* **~ oneself up** agghindarsi

tartan /'tɑːtn/ *n* tessuto *m* scozzese, tartan *m inv* ● *attrib* di tessuto scozzese

tartar /'tɑːtə(r)/ *n* *(on teeth)* tartaro *m*

tartar 'sauce /tɑːtə-/ *n* salsa *f* tartara

task /tɑːsk/ *n* compito *m*; **take sb to ~** riprendere qcno. **~ force** *n Pol* commissione *f*; *Mil* task-force *f inv*

tassel /'tæsl/ *n* nappa *f*

taste /teɪst/ *n* gusto *m*; *(sample)* assaggio *m*; **get a ~ of sth** *fig* assaporare il gusto di qcsa ● *vt* sentire il sapore di; *(sample)* assaggiare ● *vi* sapere (**of** di); **it ~s lovely** è ottimo. **~ful** *a* di [buon] gusto. **~fully** *adv* con gusto. **~less** *a* senza gusto. **~lessly** *adv* con cattivo gusto

tasty /'teɪstɪ/ *a* (-ier, -iest) saporito

tat /tæt/ *see* **tit²**

tatter|ed /'tætəd/ *a* cencioso; *(pages)* stracciato. **~s** *npl* **in ~s** a brandelli

tattoo¹ /tæ'tuː/ *n* tatuaggio *m* ● *vt* tatuare

tattoo² *n Mil* parata *f* militare

tatty /'tætɪ/ *a* (-ier, -iest) *(clothes, person)* trasandato; *(book)* malandato

taught /tɔːt/ *see* **teach**

taunt /tɔːnt/ *n* scherno *m* ● *vt* schernire

Taurus /'tɔːrəs/ n Astr Toro m

taut /tɔːt/ a teso

tawdry /'tɔːdrɪ/ a (-ier, -iest) pacchiano

tax /tæks/ n tassa f; (on income) imposte fpl; before ● (price) tasse escluse; (salary) lordo ● vt tassare; fig mettere alla prova; ~ **with** accusare di. ~**able** /-əbl/ a tassabile. ~**ation** /-'seɪʃn/ n tasse fpl. ~ **evasion** n evasione f fiscale. ~**-free** a esentasse. ~ **haven** n paradiso m fiscale

taxi /'tæksɪ/ n taxi m inv ● vi (pt/pp taxied, pres p taxiing) (aircraft:) rullare. ~ **driver** n tassista mf. ~ **rank** n posteggio m per taxi

taxpayer n contribuente mf

tea /tiː/ n tè m inv. ~**-bag** n bustina f di tè. ~**-break** n intervallo m per il tè

teach /tiːtʃ/ vt/i (pt/pp taught) insegnare; ~ **sb sth** insegnare qcsa a qcno. ~**er** n insegnante mf; (primary) maestro, -a mf. ~**ing** n insegnamento m

tea: ~**-cloth** n (for drying) asciugapiatti m inv. ~**cup** n tazza f da tè

teak /tiːk/ n tek m

tea-leaves npl tè m inv sfuso; (when infused) fondi mpl di tè

team /tiːm/ n squadra f; fig èquipe f inv ● **team up** vi unirsi

team-work n lavoro m di squadra; fig lavoro m d'équipe

teapot n teiera f

tear[1] /teə(r)/ n strappo m ● v (pt tore, pp torn) ● vt strappare ● vi strappare; (material:) strapparsi; (run) precipitarsi. **tear apart** vt (fig: criticize) fare a pezzi; (separate) dividere. **tear away** vt ~ **oneself away** andare via; ~ **oneself away from** staccarsi da (television). **tear open** vt aprire strappando. **tear up** vt strappare; rompere (agreement)

tear[2] /tɪə(r)/ n lacrima f. ~**ful** a (person) in lacrime; (farewell) lacrimevole. ~**fully** adv in lacrime. ~**gas** n gas m lacrimogeno

tease /tiːz/ vt prendere in giro (person); tormentare (animal)

tea: ~**-set** n servizio m da tè. ~ **shop** n sala f da tè. ~**spoon** n cucchiaino m [da tè]. ~**spoon|ful** n cucchiaino m

teat /tiːt/ n capezzolo m; (on bottle) tettarella f

tea-towel n strofinaccio m [per i piatti]

technical /'teknɪkl/ a tecnico. ~**ity** /-'kælətɪ/ n tecnicismo m; Jur cavillo m giuridico. ~**ly** adv tecnicamente; (strictly) strettamente

technician /tek'nɪʃn/ n tecnico, -a mf

technique /tek'niːk/ n tecnica f

technological /teknə'lɒdʒɪkl/ a tecnologico

technology /tek'nɒlədʒɪ/ n tecnologia f

teddy /'tedɪ/ n ~ |**bear**| orsacchiotto m

tedious /'tiːdɪəs/ a noioso

tedium /'tiːdɪəm/ n tedio m

tee /tiː/ n (in golf) tee m inv

teem /tiːm/ vi (rain) piovere a dirotto; be ~**ing with** (full of) pullulare di

teenage /'tiːneɪdʒ/ a per ragazzi; ~ **boy/girl** adolescente mf. ~**r** n adolescente mf

teens /tiːnz/ npl the ~ l'adolescenza fsg; be in one's ~ essere adolescente

teeny /'tiːnɪ/ a (-ier, -iest) piccolissimo

teeter /'tiːtə(r)/ vi barcollare

teeth /tiːθ/ see tooth

teeth|e /tiːð/ vi mettere i [primi] denti. ~**ing troubles** npl fig difficoltà fpl iniziali

teetotal /tiː'təʊtl/ a astemio. ~**ler** n astemio, -a mf

telecommunications /telɪkəmjuːnɪ'keɪʃnz/ npl telecomunicazioni fpl

telegram /'telɪgræm/ n telegramma m

telegraph /'telɪgrɑːf/ n telegrafo m. ~**ic** /-'græfɪk/ a telegrafico. ~ **pole** n palo m del telegrafo

telepathy /tɪ'lepəθɪ/ n telepatia f

telephone /'telɪfəʊn/ n telefono m; be on the ~ avere il telefono; (be telephoning) essere al telefono ● vt telefonare a ● vi telefonare

telephone: ~ **book** n elenco m telefonico. ~ **booth** n, ~ **box** n cabina f telefonica. ~ **directory** n elenco m telefonico. ~ **number** n numero m di telefono

telephonist /tɪ'lefənɪst/ n telefonista mf

telephoto /'telɪ-/ a ~ **lens** teleobiettivo m

telescope /'telɪskəʊp/ n telescopio m. ~**ic** /-'skɒpɪk/ a telescopico

televise /'telɪvaɪz/ vt trasmettere per televisione

television /'telɪvɪʒn/ n televisione f; watch ~ guardare la televisione. ~ **set** n televisore m

telex /'teleks/ n telex m inv

tell /tel/ vt (pt/pp told) dire; raccontare (story); (distinguish) distinguere (**from** da); ~ **sb sth** dire qcsa a qcno; ~ **the time** dire l'ora; **I couldn't** ~ **why...** non sapevo perché... ● vi (produce an effect) avere effetto; **time will** ~ il tempo ce lo dirà; **his age is beginning to**

~ l'età comincia a farsi sentire [per lui];
you mustn't ~ non devi dire niente.
tell off vt sgridare

teller /'telə(r)/ n (in bank) cassiere, -a mf

telling /'telɪŋ/ a significativo; (argument) efficace

telly /'telɪ/ n fam tv f inv

temerity /tɪ'merətɪ/ n audacia f

temp /temp/ n fam impiegato, -a mf temporaneo, -a

temper /'tempə(r)/ n (disposition) carattere m; (mood) umore m; (anger) collera f; **lose one's** ~ arrabbiarsi; **be in a** ~ essere arrabbiato; **keep one's** ~ mantenere la calma

temperament /'tempərəmənt/ n temperamento m. **~al** /-'mentl/ a (moody) capriccioso

temperate /'tempərət/ a (climate) temperato

temperature /'temprətʃə(r)/ n temperatura f; **have a** ~ avere la febbre

tempest /'tempɪst/ n tempesta f. **~uous** /-'pestjʊəs/ a tempestoso

temple[1] /'templ/ n tempio m

temple[2] n Anat tempia f

tempo /'tempəʊ/ n ritmo m; Mus tempo m

temporary /'tempərərɪ/ a temporaneo; (measure, building) provvisorio. **~ily** adv temporaneamente; (introduced, erected) provvisoriamente

tempt /tempt/ vt tentare; sfidare (fate); ~ **sb** to indurre qcno a; **be** ~**ed** essere tentato (to di); **I am** ~**ed by the offer** l'offerta mi tenta. **~ation** /-'teɪʃn/ n tentazione f. **~ing** a allettante; (food, drink) invitante

ten /ten/ a & n dieci m

tenable /'tenəbl/ a fig sostenibile

tenaci|ous /tɪ'neɪʃəs/ a tenace. **~ty** /-'næsətɪ/ n tenacia f

tenant /'tenənt/ n inquilino, -a mf; Comm locatario, -a mf

tend[1] /tend/ vt (look after) prendersi cura di

tend[2] vi **to do sth** tendere a far qcsa

tendency /'tendənsɪ/ n tendenza f

tender[1] /'tendə(r)/ n Comm offerta f; **be legal** ~ avere corso legale ● vt offrire; presentare (resignation)

'tender[2] a tenero; (painful) dolorante. **~ly** adv teneramente. **~ness** n tenerezza f; (painfulness) dolore m

tendon /'tendən/ n tendine m

tenement /'tenəmənt/ n casamento m

tenner /'tenə(r)/ n fam biglietto m da dieci sterline

tennis /'tenɪs/ n tennis m. **~-court** n

campo m da tennis. **~ player** n tennista mf

tenor /'tenə(r)/ n tenore m

tense[1] /tens/ n Gram tempo m

tense[2] a teso ● vt tendere (muscle). **tense up** vi tendersi

tension /'tenʃn/ n tensione f

tent /tent/ n tenda f

tentacle /'tentəkl/ n tentacolo m

tentative /'tentətɪv/ a provvisorio; (smile, gesture) esitante. **~ly** adv timidamente; (accept) provvisoriamente

tenterhooks /'tentəhʊks/ npl **be on** ~ essere sulle spine

tenth /tenθ/ a decimo ● n decimo, -a mf

tenuous /'tenjʊəs/ a fig debole

tepid /'tepɪd/ a tiepido

term /tɜːm/ n periodo m; Sch Univ trimestre m; (expression) termine m; ~s pl (conditions) condizioni fpl; ~ **of office** carica f; **in the short/long** ~ a breve/lungo termine; **be on good/bad** ~s essere in buoni/cattivi rapporti; **come to** ~s **with** accettare (past, fact); **easy** ~s facilità f di pagamento

terminal /'tɜːmɪn(ə)l/ a finale; Med terminale ● n Aeron terminal m inv; Rail stazione f di testa; (of bus) capolinea m; (on battery) morsetto m; Comput terminale m. **~ly** adv **be** ~**ly ill** essere in fase terminale

terminate /'tɜːmɪneɪt/ vt terminare; rescindere (contract); interrompere (pregnancy) ● vi terminare; ~e **in** finire in. **~ion** /-'neɪʃn/ n termine m; Med interruzione f di gravidanza

terminology /tɜːmɪ'nɒlədʒɪ/ n terminologia f

terminus /'tɜːmɪnəs/ n (pl -ni /-naɪ/) (for bus) capolinea m; (for train) stazione f di testa

terrace /'terəs/ n terrazza f; (houses) fila f di case a schiera; **the** ~s pl Sport le gradinate. **~d house** n casa f a schiera

terrain /te'reɪn/ n terreno m

terrible /'terəbl/ a terribile. **~y** adv terribilmente

terrier /'terɪə(r)/ n terrier m inv

terrific /tə'rɪfɪk/ a fam (excellent) fantastico; (huge) enorme. **~ally** adv fam terribilmente

terri|fy /'terɪfaɪ/ vt (pt/pp -ied) atterrire; **be** ~**fied** essere terrorizzato. **~fying** a terrificante

territorial /terɪ'tɔːrɪəl/ a territoriale

territory /'terɪtərɪ/ n territorio m

terror /'terə(r)/ n terrore m. **~ism**

/·ɪzm/ n terrorismo m. ~ist /·ɪst/ n terrorista mf. ~ize vt terrorizzare

terse /tɜːs/ a conciso

test /test/ n esame m; (in laboratory) esperimento m; (of friendship, machine) prova f; (of intelligence, aptitude) test m inv; **put to the ~** mettere alla prova ●vt esaminare; provare (machine)

testament /'testəmənt/ n testamento m; **Old/New T~** Antico/Nuovo Testamento m

testicle /'testɪkl/ n testicolo m

testify /'testɪfaɪ/ vt/i (pt/pp -ied) testimoniare

testimonial /testɪ'məʊnɪəl/ n lettera f di referenze

testimony /'testɪmənɪ/ n testimonianza f

'**test: ~ match** n partita f internazionale. **~tube** n provetta f. **~tube 'baby** n fam bambino, -a mf in provetta

tetanus /'tetənəs/ n tetano m

tether /'teðə(r)/ n **be at the end of one's ~** non poterne più

text /tekst/ n testo m. **~book** n manuale m

textile /'tekstaɪl/ a tessile ●n stoffa f

texture /'tekstʃə(r)/ n (of skin) grana f, (of food) consistenza f; **of a smooth ~** (to the touch) soffice al tatto

Thai /taɪ/ a & n tailandese mf. **~land** n Tailandia f

Thames /temz/ n Tamigi m

than /ðən/, accentato /ðæn/ conj che; (with numbers, names) di; **older ~ me** più vecchio di me

thank /θæŋk/ vt ringraziare; **~ you [very much]** grazie [mille]. **~ful** a grato. **~fully** adv con gratitudine; (happily) fortunatamente. **~less** a ingrato

thanks /θæŋks/ npl ringraziamenti mpl; **~!** fam grazie!; **~ to** grazie a

that /ðæt/ a & pron (pl **those**) quel, quei pl; (before s + consonant, gn, ps and z) quello, quegli pl; (before vowel) quell' mf, quegli mpl; quella fpl; **~ one** quello; **I don't like those** quelli non mi piacciono; **~ is** cioè; **is ~ you?** sei tu?; **who is ~?** chi è?; **what did you do after ~?** cosa hai fatto dopo?; **like ~** in questo modo, così; **a man like ~** un uomo così; **~ is why** ecco perché; **~'s it!** (you've understood) ecco!; (I've finished) ecco fatto!; (I've had enough) basta così!; (there's nothing more) tutto qui!; **~'s ~!** (with job) ecco fatto!; (with relationship) è tutto finito!; **and ~'s ~!** punto e basta! **all ~ I know** tutto quello che so ●adv così; **it wasn't ~ good** non era poi così buono ●rel pron che; **the man ~ I spoke to**

l'uomo con cui ho parlato; **the day ~ I saw him** il giorno in cui l'ho visto; **all ~ I know** tutto quello che so ●conj che; **I think ~ ...** penso che...

thatch /θætʃ/ n tetto m di paglia. **~ed** a coperto di paglia

thaw /θɔː/ n disgelo m ●vt fare scongelare (food) ●vi (food:) scongelarsi; **it's ~ing** sta sgelando

the /ðə/, di fronte a una vocale /ðiː/ def art il, la f; i mpl, le fpl; (before s + consonant, gn, ps and z) lo, gli mpl; (before vowel) l' mf, gli mpl, le fpl; **at ~ cinema/station** al cinema/alla stazione; **from ~ cinema/station** dal cinema/dalla stazione ●adv **~ more ~ better** più ce n'è meglio è; (with reference to pl) più ce ne sono, meglio è; **~ better** tanto meglio

theatre /'θɪətə(r)/ n teatro m; Med sala f operatoria

theatrical /θɪ'ætrɪkl/ a teatrale; (showy) melodrammatico

theft /θeft/ n furto m

their /ðeə(r)/ poss a il loro m, la loro f, i loro mpl, le loro fpl; **~ mother/father** la loro madre/il loro padre

theirs /ðeəz/ poss pron il loro m, la loro f, i loro mpl, le loro fpl; **a friend of ~** un loro amico; **friends of ~** dei loro amici; **those are ~** quelli sono loro; (as opposed to ours) quelli sono i loro

them /ðem/ pron (direct object) li m, le f; (indirect object) gli, loro fml; (after prep: with people) loro; (after preposition: with things) essi; **we haven't seen ~** non li/le abbiamo visti/viste; **give ~ the money** dai loro or dagli i soldi; **give it to ~** dagli elo; **I've spoken to ~** ho parlato con loro; **it's ~** sono loro

theme /θiːm/ n tema m. **~ song** n motivo m conduttore

them'selves pers pron (reflexive) si; (emphatic) se stessi; **they poured ~ a drink** si sono versati da bere; **they said so ~** lo hanno detto loro stessi; **they kept it to ~** se lo sono tenuti per sé; **by ~** da soli

then /ðen/ adv allora; (next) poi; **by ~** (in the past) ormai; (in the future) per allora; **since ~** sin da allora; **before ~** prima di allora; **from ~ on** da allora in poi; **now and ~** ogni tanto; **there and ~** all'istante ●a di allora

theologian /θɪə'ləʊdʒɪən/ n teologo, -a mf. **~y** /-'ɒlədʒɪ/ n teologia f

theorem /'θɪərəm/ n teorema m

theoretical /θɪə'retɪkl/ a teorico

theory /ˈθɪərɪ/ *n* teoria *f*; in ~ in teoria

therapeutic /θerəˈpjuːtɪk/ *a* terapeutico

therap|ist /ˈθerəpɪst/ *n* terapista *mf*. ~y *n* terapia *f*

there /ðeə(r)/ *adv* là, lì; down/up ~ laggiù/lassù; ~ is/are c'è/ci sono; ~ he/she is eccolo/eccola ● *int* ~, ~! dai, su!

there: ~abouts *adv* |or| ~abouts (*roughly*) all'incirca. ~after *adv* dopo di che. ~by *adv* in tal modo. ~fore /-fɔ:(r)/ *adv* perciò

thermal /ˈθɜ:m(ə)l/ *a* termale; ~ underwear *n* biancheria *f* che mantiene la temperatura corporea

thermometer /θəˈmɒmɪtə(r)/ *n* termometro *m*

Thermos® /ˈθɜ:məs/ *n* ~ |flask| termos *m inv*

thermostat /ˈθɜ:məstæt/ *n* termostato *m*

thesaurus /θɪˈsɔ:rəs/ *n* dizionario *m* dei sinonimi

these /ði:z/ *see* this

thesis /ˈθi:sɪs/ *n* (*pl* -ses /-si:z/) tesi *f inv*

they /ðeɪ/ *pron* loro; ~ are tired sono stanchi; we're going, but ~ are not noi andiamo, ma loro no; ~ say (*generalizing*) si dice; ~ are building a new road stanno costruendo una nuova strada

thick /θɪk/ *a* spesso; (*forest*) fitto; (*liquid*) denso; (*hair*) folto; (*fam: stupid*) ottuso; (*fam: close*) molto unito; be 5 mm ~ essere 5 mm di spessore ● *adv* densamente ● *n* in the ~ of nel mezzo di. ~en *vt* ispessire (*sauce*) ● *vi* ispessirsi; (*fog*) infittirsi. ~ly *adv* densamente; (*cut*) a fette spesse. ~ness *n* spessore *m*

thick: ~set *a* tozzo. ~-skinned *a fam* insensibile

thief /θi:f/ *n* (*pl* thieves) ladro, -a *mf*

thieving /ˈθi:vɪŋ/ *a* ladro ● *n* furti *mpl*

thigh /θaɪ/ *n* coscia *f*

thimble /ˈθɪmbl/ *n* ditale *m*

thin /θɪn/ *a* (thinner, thinnest) sottile; (*shoes, sweater*) leggero; (*liquid*) liquido; (*person*) magro; (*fig: excuse, plot*) inconsistente ● *adv* = thinly ● *v* (*pt/pp* thinned) ● *vt* diluire (*liquid*) ● *vi* diradarsi. thin out *vi* diradarsi. ~ly *adv* (*populated*) scarsamente; (*disguised*) leggermente; (*cut*) a fette sottili

thing /θɪŋ/ *n* cosa *f*; ~s *pl* (belongings) roba *fsg*; for one ~ in primo luogo; the right ~ la cosa giusta; just the ~! pro-

prio quel che ci vuole!; how are ~s? come vanno le cose?; the latest ~ *fam* l'ultima cosa; the best ~ would be la cosa migliore sarebbe; poor ~! poveretto!

think /θɪŋk/ *vt/i* (*pt/pp* thought) pensare; (*believe*) credere; I ~ so credo di sì; what do you ~? (*what is your opinion?*) cosa ne pensi?; ~ of/about pensare a; what do you ~ of it? cosa ne pensi di questo?. think over *vt* riflettere su. think up *vt* escogitare

third /θɜ:d/ *a & n* terzo, -a *mf*. ~ly *adv* terzo. ~-rate *a* scadente

thirst /θɜ:st/ *n* sete *f*. ~ily *adv* con sete. ~y *a* assetato; be ~y aver sete

thirteen /θɜ:ˈti:n/ *a & n* tredici *m*. ~th *a & n* tredicesimo, -a *mf*

thirtieth /ˈθɜ:tɪɪθ/ *a & n* trentesimo, -a *mf*

thirty /ˈθɜ:tɪ/ *a & n* trenta *m*

this /ðɪs/ *a* (*pl* these) questo; ~ man/woman quest'uomo/questa donna; these men/women questi uomini/queste donne; ~ one questo; ~ morning/evening stamattina/stasera ● *pron* (*pl* these) questo; we talked about ~ and that abbiamo parlato del più e del meno; like ~ così; ~ is Peter; *Teleph* sono Peter; who is ~? chi è?; *Teleph* chi parla? ● *adv* così; ~ big così grande

thistle /ˈθɪsl/ *n* cardo *m*

thorn /θɔ:n/ *n* spina *f*. ~y *a* spinoso

thorough /ˈθʌrə/ *a* completo; (*knowledge*) profondo; (*clean, search, training*) a fondo; (*person*) scrupoloso

thorough: ~bred *n* purosangue *m inv*. ~fare *n* via *f* principale; 'no ~fare' 'strada non transitabile'

thorough|ly /ˈθʌrəlɪ/ *adv* (*clean, search, know sth*) a fondo; (*extremely*) estremamente. ~ness *n* completezza *f*

those /ðəʊz/ *see* that

though /ðəʊ/ *conj* sebbene; as ~ come se ● *adv fam* tuttavia

thought /θɔ:t/ *see* think ● *n* pensiero *m*; (*idea*) idea *f*. ~ful *a* pensieroso; (*considerate*) premuroso. ~fully *adv* pensierosamente; (*considerately*) premurosamente. ~less *a* (*inconsiderate*) sconsiderato. ~lessly *adv* con noncuranza

thousand /ˈθaʊznd/ *a* one ~ mille *m inv* ● *n* mille *m inv*; ~s of migliaia *fpl* di. ~th *a* millesimo ● *n* millesimo, -a *mf*

thrash /θræʃ/ *vt* picchiare; (*defeat*) sconfiggere. thrash out *vt* mettere a punto

thread /θred/ *n* filo *m*; (of screw) filetto

m ● *vt* infilare ⟨*beads*⟩; ~ **one's way through** farsi strada fra. ~**bare** *a* logoro

threat /θret/ *n* minaccia *f*

threaten /'θretn/ *vt* minacciare (**to do** di fare) ● *vi* fig incalzare. ~**ing** *a* minaccioso; ⟨*sky, atmosphere*⟩ sinistro

three /θriː/ *a* & *n* tre *m.* ~**fold** *a* & *adv* triplo. ~**some** /-səm/ *n* trio *m*

thresh /θreʃ/ *vt* trebbiare

threshold /'θreʃəʊld/ *n* soglia *f*

threw /θruː/ *see* throw

thrift /θrɪft/ *n* economia *f.* ~**y** *a* parsimonioso

thrill /θrɪl/ *n* emozione *f*; (*of fear*) brivido *m* ● *vt* entusiasmare; **be** ~**ed with** essere entusiasta di. ~**er** *n* (*book*) [romanzo *m*] giallo *m*; (*film*) [film *m*] giallo *m.* ~**ing** *a* eccitante

thrive /θraɪv/ *vi* (*pt* **thrived** *or* **throve**, *pp* **thrived** *or* **thriven** /'θrɪvn/) ⟨*business:*⟩ prosperare; ⟨*child, plant:*⟩ crescere bene; **I** ~ **on pressure** mi piace essere sotto tensione

throat /θrəʊt/ *n* gola *f*; **sore** ~ mal *m* di gola

throb /θrɒb/ *n* pulsazione *f*; (*of heart*) battito *m* ● *vi* (*pt*/*pp* **throbbed**) ⟨*vibrate*⟩ pulsare; ⟨*heart:*⟩ battere

throes /θrəʊz/ *npl* **in the** ~ **of** fig alle prese con

thrombosis /θrɒm'bəʊsɪs/ *n* trombosi *f*

throne /θrəʊn/ *n* trono *m*

throng /θrɒŋ/ *n* calca *f*

throttle /'θrɒtl/ *n* (*on motorbike*) manopola *f* di accelerazione ● *vt* strozzare

through /θruː/ *prep* attraverso; (*during*) durante; (*by means of*) tramite; (*thanks to*) grazie a; **Saturday** ~ **Tuesday** *Am* da sabato a martedì incluso ● *adv* attraverso; ~ **and** ~ fino in fondo; **wet** ~ completamente bagnato; **read sth** ~ dare una lettura a qcsa; **let** ~ lasciar passare ⟨*sb*⟩ ● *a* ⟨*train*⟩ diretto; **be** ~ (*finished*) aver finito; *Teleph* avere la comunicazione

throughout /θruː'aʊt/ *prep* per tutto ● *adv* completamente; (*time*) per tutto il tempo

throw /θrəʊ/ *n* tiro *m* ● *vt* (*pt* **threw**, *pp* **thrown**) lanciare; (*throw away*) gettare; azionare ⟨*switch*⟩; disarcionare ⟨*rider*⟩; (*fam: disconcert*) disorientare; *fam* dare ⟨*party*⟩. **throw away** *vt* gettare via. **throw out** *vt* gettare via; rigettare ⟨*plan*⟩; buttare fuori ⟨*person*⟩. **throw up** *vt* alzare ● *vi* (*vomit*) vomitare

throw-away *a* ⟨*remark*⟩ buttato lì; ⟨*paper cup*⟩ usa e getta *inv*

thrush /θrʌʃ/ *n* tordo *m*

thrust /θrʌst/ *n* spinta *f* ● *vt* (*pt*/*pp* **thrust**) (*push*) spingere; (*insert*) conficcare; ~ |**up**|**on** imporre a

thud /θʌd/ *n* tonfo *m*

thug /θʌg/ *n* delinquente *m*

thumb /θʌm/ *n* pollice *m*; **as a rule of** ~ come regola generale; **under sb's** ~ succube di qcno ● *vt* ~ **a lift** fare l'autostop. ~-**index** *n* indice *m* a rubrica. ~**tack** *n Am* puntina *f* da disegno

thump /θʌmp/ *n* colpo *m*; (*noise*) tonfo *m* ● *vt* battere su ⟨*table, door*⟩; battere ⟨*fist*⟩; colpire ⟨*person*⟩ ● *vi* battere (**on** su); ⟨*heart:*⟩ battere forte. **thump about** *vi* camminare pesantemente

thunder /'θʌndə(r)/ *n* tuono *m*; (*loud noise*) rimbombo *m* ● *vi* tuonare; (*make loud noise*) rimbombare. ~**clap** *n* rombo *m* di tuono. ~**storm** *n* temporale *m.* ~**y** *a* temporalesco

Thursday /'θɜːzdeɪ/ *n* giovedì *m inv*

thus /ðʌs/ *adv* così

thwart /θwɔːt/ *vt* ostacolare

thyme /taɪm/ *n* timo *m*

Tiber /'taɪbə(r)/ *n* Tevere *m*

tick /tɪk/ *n* (*sound*) ticchettio *m*; (*mark*) segno *m*; (*fam: instant*) attimo *m* ● *vi* ticchettare. **tick off** *vt* spuntare; *fam* sgridare. **tick over** *vi* ⟨*engine:*⟩ andare al minimo

ticket /'tɪkɪt/ *n* biglietto *m*; (*for item deposited, library*) tagliando *m*; (*label*) cartellino *m*; (*fine*) multa *f.* ~-**collector** *n* controllore *m.* ~-**office** *n* biglietteria *f*

tick|le /'tɪkl/ *n* solletico *m* ● *vt* fare il solletico a; (*amuse*) divertire ● *vi* fare prurito. ~**lish** /'tɪklɪʃ/ *a* che soffre il solletico

tidal /'taɪdl/ *a* ⟨*river, harbour*⟩ di marea. ~ **wave** *n* onda *f* di marea

tiddly-winks /'tɪdlɪwɪŋks/ *n* gioco *m* delle pulci

tide /taɪd/ *n* marea *f*; (*of events*) corso *m*; **the** ~ **is in** out ⟨*c'è alta/bassa marea*⟩ ● **tide over** *vt* ~ **sb over** aiutare qcno a andare avanti

tidily /'taɪdɪlɪ/ *adv* in modo ordinato

tidiness /'taɪdɪnɪs/ *n* ordine *m*

tidy /'taɪdɪ/ *a* (**-ier, -iest**) ordinato; ⟨*fam: amount*⟩ bello ● *vt* (*pt*/*pp* **-ied**) ~ |**up**| ordinare; ~ **oneself up** mettersi in ordine

tie /taɪ/ *n* cravatta *f*; (*cord*) legaccio *m*; (*fig: bond*) legame *m*; (*restriction*) impedimento *m*; *Sport* pareggio *m* ● *v* (*pres p* **tying**) ● *vt* legare; fare ⟨*knot*⟩; **be** ~**d**

(*in competition*) essere in parità ● *vi* pareggiare. **tie in with** *vt* corrispondere a. **tie up** *vt* legare; vincolare ⟨*capital*⟩; **be ~d up** ⟨*busy*⟩ essere occupato

tier /tɪə(r)/ *n* fila *f*; (*of cake*) piano *m*; (*in stadium*) gradinata *f*

tiff /tɪf/ *n* battibecco *m*

tiger /'taɪgə(r)/ *n* tigre *f*

tight /taɪt/ *a* stretto; ⟨*taut*⟩ teso; (*fam: drunk*) sbronzo; (*fam: mean*) spilorcio; **~ corner** *fam* brutta situazione *f* ● *adv* strettamente; ⟨*hold*⟩ forte; ⟨*closed*⟩ bene

tighten /'taɪtn/ *vt* stringere; avvitare ⟨*screw*⟩; intensificare ⟨*control*⟩ ● *vi* stringersi

tight: **~-'fisted** *a* tirchio. **~-fitting** *a* aderente. **~ly** *adv* strettamente; ⟨*hold*⟩ forte; ⟨*closed*⟩ bene. **~rope** *n* fune *f* (*da funamboli*)

tights /taɪts/ *npl* collant *m inv*

tile /taɪl/ *n* mattonella *f*; (*on roof*) tegola *f* ● *vt* rivestire di mattonelle ⟨*wall*⟩

till[1] /tɪl/ *prep & conj* = **until**

till[2] *n* cassa *f*

tiller /'tɪlə(r)/ *n* barra *f* del timone

tilt /tɪlt/ *n* inclinazione *f*; **at full ~** a tutta velocità ● *vt* inclinare ● *vi* inclinarsi

timber /'tɪmbə(r)/ *n* legname *m*

time /taɪm/ *n* tempo *m*; (*occasion*) volta *f*; (*by clock*) ora *f*; **two ~s four** due volte quattro; **at any ~** in qualsiasi momento; **this ~** questa volta; **at ~s, from ~ to ~** ogni tanto; **~ and again** cento volte; **two at a ~** due alla volta; **on ~** in orario; **in ~** in tempo; (*eventually*) col tempo; **in no ~ at all** velocemente; **in a year's ~** fra un anno; **behind ~** in ritardo; **behind the ~s** antiquato; **for the ~ being** per il momento; **what is the ~?** che ora è?; **by the ~ we arrive** quando arriviamo; **did you have a nice ~?** ti sei divertito?; **have a good ~!** divertiti! ● *vt* scegliere il momento per; cronometrare ⟨*race*⟩; **be well ~d** essere ben calcolato

time: **~ bomb** *n* bomba *f* a orologeria. **~-lag** *n* intervallo *m* di tempo. **~less** *a* eterno. **~ly** *a* opportuno. **~-switch** *n* interruttore *m* a tempo. **~-table** *n* orario *m*

timid /'tɪmɪd/ *a* (*shy*) timido; (*fearful*) timoroso

timing /'taɪmɪŋ/ *n* *Sport, Techn* cronometraggio *m*; **the ~ of the election** il momento scelto per le elezioni

tin /tɪn/ *n* stagno *m*; (*container*) barattolo *m* ● *vt* (*pt/pp* **tinned**) inscatolare. **~ foil** *n* [carta *f*] stagnola *f*

tinge /tɪndʒ/ *n* sfumatura *f* ● *vt* **~d with** *fig* misto a

tingle /'tɪŋgl/ *vi* pizzicare

tinker /'tɪŋkə(r)/ *vi* armeggiare

tinkle /'tɪŋkl/ *n* tintinnio *m*; (*fam: phone call*) colpo *m* di telefono ● *vi* tintinnare

tinned /tɪnd/ *a* in scatola

'tin opener *n* apriscatole *m inv*

tinsel /'tɪnsl/ *n* filo *m* d'argento

tint /tɪnt/ *n* tinta *f* ● *vt* tingersi ⟨*hair*⟩

tiny /'taɪnɪ/ *a* (**-ier, -iest**) minuscolo

tip[1] /tɪp/ *n* punta *f*

tip[2] *n* (*money*) mancia *f*; (*advice*) consiglio *m*; (*for rubbish*) discarica *f* ● *v* (*pt/pp* **tipped**) ● *vt* (*tilt*) inclinare; (*overturn*) capovolgere; (*pour*) versare; (*reward*) dare una mancia a ● *vi* inclinarsi; (*overturn*) capovolgersi. **tip off** *vt* **~ sb off** (*inform*) fare una soffiata a qcno. **tip out** *vt* rovesciare. **tip over** *vt* capovolgere ● *vi* capovolgersi

'tip-off *n* soffiata *f*

tipped /tɪpt/ *a* ⟨*cigarette*⟩ col filtro

tipsy /'tɪpsɪ/ *a fam* brillo

tiptoe /'tɪptəʊ/ **non ~** in punta di piedi

tiptop /tɪp'tɒp/ *a fam* in condizioni perfette

tire /'taɪə(r)/ *vt* stancare ● *vi* stancarsi. **~d** *a* stanco; **~d of** stanco di; **~d out** stanco morto. **~less** *a* instancabile. **~some** /-səm/ *a* fastidioso

tiring /'taɪərɪŋ/ *a* stancante

tissue /'tɪʃuː/ *n* tessuto *m*; (*handkerchief*) fazzolettino *m* di carta. **~-paper** *n* carta *f* velina

tit[1] /tɪt/ *n* (*bird*) cincia *f*

tit[2] *n* **~ for tat** pan per focaccia

title /'taɪtl/ *n* titolo *m*. **~-deed** *n* atto *m* di proprietà. **~-role** *n* ruolo *m* principale

tittle-tattle /'tɪtltætl/ *n* pettegolezzi *mpl*

to /tuː/, *atono* /tə/ *prep* **a**; (*to countries*) in; (*towards*) verso; (*up to, until*) fino a; **I'm going to John's/the butcher's** vado da John/dal macellaio; **come/go to sb** venire/andare da qcno; **to Italy/Switzerland** in Italia/Svizzera; **I've never been to Rome** non sono mai stato a Roma; **go to the market** andare al mercato; **to the toilet/my room** in bagno/camera mia; **to an exhibition** a una mostra; **to university** all'università; **twenty/quarter to eight** le otto meno venti/un quarto; **5 to 6 kilos** da 5 a 6 chili; **to the end** alla fine; **to this day** fino a oggi; **to the best of my recollection** per quanto mi possa ricordare; **give/say sth to sb** dare/dire qcsa a qcno; **give it to me** dammelo; **there's nothing to it** è una cosa da niente ● *verbal constructions*

to go andare; **learn to swim** imparare a nuotare; **I want to go** voglio/devo andare; **it's easy to forget** è facile da dimenticare; **too ill/tired to go** troppo malato/stanco per andare; **you have to** devi; **I don't want to** non voglio; **live to be 90** vivere fino a 90 anni; **he was the last to arrive** è stato l'ultimo ad arrivare; **to be honest,...** per essere sincero,... ● *adv* **pull to** chiudere; **to and fro** avanti e indietro

toad /təʊd/ *n* rospo *m*. ~**stool** *n* fungo *m* velenoso

toast /təʊst/ *n* pane *m* tostato; (*drink*) brindisi *m inv* ● *vt* tostare (*bread*); (*drink a ~ to*) brindare a. ~**er** *n* tostapane *m inv*

tobacco /tə'bækəʊ/ *n* tabacco *m*. ~**nist's** [**shop**] *n* tabaccheria *f*

toboggan /tə'bɒgən/ *n* toboga *m inv* ● *vi* andare in toboga

today /tə'deɪ/ *a & adv* oggi *m*; **a week ~** una settimana a oggi; ~**'s paper** il giornale di oggi

toddler /'tɒdlə(r)/ *n* bambino, -a *mf* ai primi passi

to-do /tə'duː/ *n fam* baccano *m*

toe /təʊ/ *n* dito *m* del piede; (*of footwear*) punta *f*; **big ~** alluce *m* ● *vt* ~ **the line** rigar diritto. ~**nail** *n* unghia *f* del piede

toffee /'tɒfɪ/ *n* caramella *f* al mou

together /tə'geðə(r)/ *adv* insieme; (*at the same time*) allo stesso tempo; ~ **with** insieme a

toilet /'tɔɪlɪt/ *n* (*lavatory*) gabinetto *m*. ~ **paper** *n* carta *f* igienica

toiletries /'tɔɪlɪtrɪz/ *npl* articoli *mpl* da toilette

toilet: ~ **roll** *n* rotolo *m* di carta igienica. ~ **water** *n* acqua *f* di colonia

token /'təʊkən/ *n* segno *m*; (*counter*) gettone *m*; (*voucher*) buono *m* ● *attrib* simbolico

told /təʊld/ *see* **tell** ● **all** ~ in tutto

tolerable /'tɒl(ə)rəbl/ *a* tollerabile; (*not bad*) discreto. ~**y** *adv* discretamente

toleran|ce /'tɒl(ə)r(ə)ns/ *n* tolleranza *f*. ~**t** *a* tollerante. ~**tly** *adv* con tolleranza

tolerate /'tɒlərett/ *vt* tollerare

toll¹ /təʊl/ *n* pedaggio *m*; **death** ~ numero *m* di morti

toll² *vi* suonare a morto

tom /tɒm/ *n* (*cat*) gatto *m* maschio

tomato /tə'mɑːtəʊ/ *n* (*pl -es*) pomodoro *m*. ~ **ketchup** *n* ketchup *m*. ~ **purée** *n* concentrato *m* di pomodoro

tomb /tuːm/ *n* tomba *f*

tomboy /'tɒmbɔɪ/ *n* maschiaccio *m*

tombstone /'tuːmstəʊn/ *n* pietra *f* tombale

tom-cat *n* gatto *m* maschio

tomfoolery /tɒm'fuːlərɪ/ *n* stupidaggini *fpl*

tomorrow /tə'mɒrəʊ/ *a & adv* domani; ~ **morning** domani mattina; **the day after** ~ dopodomani; **see you** ~! a domani!

ton /tʌn/ *n* tonnellata *f* (*= 1,016 kg.*); ~**s of** *fam* un sacco di

tone /təʊn/ *n* tono *m*; (*colour*) tonalità *f inv* ● **tone down** *vt* attenuare. **tone up** *vt* tonificare (*muscles*)

toner /'təʊnə(r)/ *n* toner *m*

tongs /tɒnz/ *npl* pinze *fpl*

tongue /tʌn/ *n* lingua *f*; ~ **in cheek** (*fam: say*) ironicamente. ~-**twister** *n* scioglilingua *m inv*

tonic /'tɒnɪk/ *n* tonico *m*; (*for hair*) lozione *f* per i capelli; *fig* toccasana *m inv*; ~ [**water**] acqua *f* tonica

tonight /tə'naɪt/ *adv* stanotte; (*evening*) stasera ● *n* questa notte *f*; (*evening*) questa sera *f*

tonne /tʌn/ *n* tonnellata *f* metrica

tonsil /'tɒnsl/ *n Anat* tonsilla *f*. ~**litis** /-sə'laɪtɪs/ *n* tonsillite *f*

too /tuː/ *adv* troppo; (*also*) anche; ~ **many** troppi; ~ **much** troppo; ~ **little** troppo poco

took /tʊk/ *see* **take**

tool /tuːl/ *n* attrezzo *m*

toot /tuːt/ *n* suono *m* di clacson ● *vi Auto* clacsonare

tooth /tuːθ/ *n* (*pl* **teeth**) dente *m*

tooth: ~**ache** *n* mal *m* di denti. ~**brush** *n* spazzolino *m* da denti. ~**less** *a* sdentato. ~**paste** *n* dentifricio *m*. ~**pick** *n* stuzzicadenti *m inv*

top¹ /tɒp/ *n* (*toy*) trottola *f*

top² *n* cima *f*; *Sch* primo, -a *mf*; (*upper part or half*) parte *f* superiore; (*of page, list, street*) inizio *m*; (*upper surface*) superficie *f*; (*lid*) coperchio *m*; (*of bottle*) tappo *m*; (*garment*) maglia *f*; (*blouse*) camicia *f*; *Auto* marcia *f* più alta; **at the ~** fig al vertice; **at the ~ of one's voice** a squarciagola; **on ~/on** ~ **of** sopra; **on ~ of that** (*besides*) per di più; **from** ~ **to bottom** da cima a fondo ● *a* in alto; (*official, floor of building*) superiore; (*pupil, musician etc*) migliore; (*speed*) massimo ● *vt* (*pt/pp* **topped**) essere in testa a (*list*); (*exceed*) sorpassare; ~**ped with ice-cream** ricoperto di gelato. **top up** *vt* riempire

top: ~ **floor** *n* ultimo piano *m*. ~ **hat** *n*

cilindro *m*. ~**-heavy** *a* con la parte superiore sovraccarica

topic /'tɒpɪk/ *n* soggetto *m*; (*of conversation*) argomento *m*. ~**al** *a* d'attualità

top: ~**less** *a* & *adv* topless. ~**most** *a* più alto

topple /'tɒpl/ *vt* rovesciare ●*vi* rovesciarsi. **topple off** *vi* cadere

top-'secret *a* segretissimo, top secret *inv*

topsy-turvy /tɒpsɪ'tɜːvɪ/ *a* & *adv* sottosopra

torch /tɔːtʃ/ *n* torcia *f* [elettrica]; (*flaming*) fiaccola *f*

tore /tɔː(r)/ *see* **tear**[1]

torment[1] /'tɔːment/ *n* tormento *m*

torment[2] /tɔː'ment/ *vt* tormèntare

torn /tɔːn/ *see* **tear**[1] ●*a* bucato

tornado /tɔː'neɪdəʊ/ *n* (*pl* **-es**) tornado *m inv*

torpedo /tɔː'piːdəʊ/ *n* (*pl* **-es**) siluro *m* ●*vt* silurare

torrent /'tɒrənt/ *n* torrente *m*. ~**ial** /tə'renʃl/ *a* (*rain*) torrenziale

torso /'tɔːsəʊ/ *n* torso *m*; (*in art*) busto *m*

tortoise /'tɔːtəs/ *n* tartaruga *f*

tortuous /'tɔːtʃʊəs/ *a* tortuoso

torture /'tɔːtʃə(r)/ *n* tortura *f* ●*vt* torturare

Tory /'tɔːrɪ/ *a* & *n fam* conservatore, -trice *mf*

toss /tɒs/ *vt* gettare; (*into the air*) lanciare in aria; (*shake*) scrollare; (*horse*) disarcionare; mescolare (*salad*); rivoltare facendo saltare in aria (*pancake*); ~ **a coin** fare testa o croce ●*vi* ~ **and turn** (*in bed*) rigirarsi; **let's ~ for it** facciamo testa o croce

tot[1] /tɒt/ *n* bimbetto, -a *mf*. (*fam: of liquor*) goccio *m*

tot[2] *vt* (*pt/pp* **totted**) ~ **up** *fam* fare la somma di

total /'təʊtl/ *a* totale ●*n* totale *m* ●*vt* (*pt/pp* **totalled**) ammontare a; (*add up*) sommare

totalitarian /təʊtælɪ'teərɪən/ *a* totalitario

totally /'təʊtəlɪ/ *adv* totalmente

totter /'tɒtə(r)/ *vi* barcollare; (*government:*) vacillare

touch /tʌtʃ/ *n* tocco *m*; (*sense*) tatto *m*; (*contact*) contatto *m*; (*trace*) traccia *f*; (*of irony, humour*) tocco *m*; **get/be in ~** mettersi/essere in contatto ●*vt* toccare; (*lightly*) sfiorare; (*equal*) eguagliare; (*fig: move*) commuovere ●*vi* toccarsi. **touch down** *vi* Aeron

atterrare. **touch on** *vt fig* accennare a. **touch up** *vt* ritoccare (*painting*)

touch|ing /'tʌtʃɪŋ/ *a* commovente. ~**y** *a* permaloso; (*subject*) delicato

tough /tʌf/ *a* duro; (*severe, harsh*) severo; (*durable*) resistente; (*resilient*) forte

toughen /'tʌfn/ *vt* rinforzare. **toughen up** *vt* rendere più forte (*person*)

tour /tʊə(r)/ *n* giro *m*; (*of building, town*) visita *f*; Theat, Sport tournée *f inv*; (*of duty*) servizio *m* ●*vt* visitare ●*vi* fare un giro turistico; Theat essere in tournée

touris|m /'tʊərɪzm/ *n* turismo *m*. ~**t** /-rɪst/ *n* turista *mf* ●*attrib* turistico. ~**t office** *n* ufficio *m* turistico

tournament /'tʊənəmənt/ *n* torneo *m*

'tour operator *n* tour operator *mf inv*, operatore, -trice *mf* turistico, -a

tousle /'taʊzl/ *vt* spettinare

tout /taʊt/ *n* (*ticket* ~) bagarino *m*; (*horse-racing*) informatore *m* ●*vi* ~ **for** sollecitare

tow /təʊ/ *n* rimorchio *m*; **'on** ~' *a* rimorchio'; **in** ~ *fam* al seguito ●*vt* rimorchiare. **tow away** *vt* portare via col carro attrezzi

toward[s] /tə'wɔːd(z)/ *prep* verso (*with respect to*) nei riguardi di

towel /'taʊəl/ *n* asciugamano *m*. ~**ling** *n* spugna *f*

tower /'taʊə(r)/ *n* torre *f* ●*vi* ~ **above** dominare. ~ **block** *n* palazzone *m*. ~**ing** *a* torreggiante; (*rage*) violento

town /taʊn/ *n* città *f inv*. ~ **'hall** *n* municipio *m*

tow: ~**-path** *n* strada *f* alzaia. ~**-rope** *n* cavo *m* da rimorchio

toxic /'tɒksɪk/ *a* tossico

toxin /'tɒksɪn/ *n* tossina *f*

toy /tɔɪ/ *n* giocattolo *m*. ~**shop** *n* negozio *m* di giocattoli. **toy with** *vt* giocherellare con

trace /treɪs/ *n* traccia *f* ●*vt* seguire le tracce di; (*find*) rintracciare; (*draw*) tracciare; (*with tracing-paper*) ricalcare

track /træk/ *n* traccia *f*; (*path, Sport*) pista *f*; Rail binario *m*; **keep ~ of** tenere d'occhio ●*vt* seguire le tracce di. **track down** *vt* scovare

'track: ~**ball** *n* Comput trackball *f inv*. ~**suit** *n* tuta *f* da ginnastica

tractor /'træktə(r)/ *n* trattore *m*

trade /treɪd/ *n* commercio *m*; (*line of business*) settore *m*; (*craft*) mestiere *m*; **by** ~ di mestiere ●*vt* commerciare; ~ **sth for sth** scambiare qcsa per qcsa ●*vi* commerciare. **trade in** *vt* (*give in* *part exchange*) dare in pagamento parziale

'**trade mark** *n* marchio *m* di fabbrica

trader /'treɪdə(r)/ *n* commerciante *mf*

trade: ~**sman** *n* (*joiner etc*) operaio *m*. ~ '**union** *n* sindacato *m*. ~ '**unionist** *n* sindacalista *mf*

trading /'treɪdɪŋ/ *n* commercio *m*. ~ **estate** *n* zona *f* industriale

tradition /tra'dɪʃn/ *n* tradizione *f*. ~**al** *a* tradizionale. ~**ally** *adv* tradizionalmente

traffic /'træfɪk/ *n* traffico *m* ● *vi* (*pt/pp* **trafficked**) trafficare

traffic: ~ **circle** *n* *Am* isola *f* rotatoria. ~ **jam** *n* ingorgo *m*. ~ **lights** *npl* semaforo *msg*. ~ **warden** *n* vigile *m* [urbano]; (*woman*) vigilessa *f*

tragedy /'trædʒədɪ/ *n* tragedia *f*

tragic /'trædʒɪk/ *a* tragico. ~**ally** *adv* tragicamente

trail /treɪl/ *n* traccia *f*; (*path*) sentiero *m* ● *vi* strisciare; (*plant*) arrampicarsi; ~ [**behind**] rimanere indietro; (*in competition*) essere in svantaggio ● *vt* trascinare

trailer /'treɪlə(r)/ *n* *Auto* rimorchio *m*; (*Am: caravan*) roulotte *f inv*; (*film*) presentazione *f* (*di un film*)

train /treɪn/ *n* treno *m*; ~ **of thought** filo *m* dei pensieri ● *vt* formare professionalmente; *Sport* allenare; (*aim*) puntare; educare ⟨*child*⟩; addestrare ⟨*animal, soldier*⟩ ● *vi* fare il tirocinio; *Sport* allenarsi. ~**ed** *a* ⟨*animal*⟩ addestrato (**to do** *a* fare)

trainee /treɪ'niː/ *n* apprendista *mf*

train|er /'treɪnə(r)/ *n* *Sport* allenatore, ·trice *mf*; (*in circus*) domatore, ·trice *mf*; (*of dog, race-horse*) addestratore, ·trice *mf*; ~**ers** *pl* scarpe *fpl* da ginnastica. ~**ing** *n* tirocinio *m*; *Sport* allenamento *m*; (*of animal, soldier*) addestramento *m*

traipse /treɪps/ *vi* ~ **around** *fam* andare in giro

trait /treɪt/ *n* caratteristica *f*

traitor /'treɪtə(r)/ *n* traditore, ·trice *mf*

tram /træm/ *n* tram *m inv*. ~·**lines** *npl* rotaie *fpl* del tram

tramp /træmp/ *n* (*hike*) camminata *f*; (*vagrant*) barbone, ·a *mf*; (*of feet*) calpestio *m* ● *vi* camminare con passo pesante; (*hike*) percorrere a piedi

trample /'træmpl/ *vt/i* ~ [**on**] calpestare

trampoline /'træmpəliːn/ *n* trampolino *m*

trance /trɑːns/ *n* trance *f inv*

tranquil /'træŋkwɪl/ *a* tranquillo. ~**lity** /·'kwɪlətɪ/ *n* tranquillità *f*

tranquillizer /'træŋkwɪlaɪzə(r)/ *n* tranquillante *m*

transact /træn'zækt/ *vt* trattare. ~**ion** /·ækʃn/ *n* transazione *f*

transatlantic /trænzət'læntɪk/ *a* transatlantico

transcend /træn'send/ *vt* trascendere

transfer[1] /'trænsfɜː(r)/ *n* trasferimento *m*; *Sport* cessione *f*; (*design*) decalcomania *f*

transfer[2] /træns'fɜː(r)/ *v* (*pt/pp* **transferred**) ● *vt* trasferire; *Sport* cedere ● *vi* trasferirsi; (*when travelling*) cambiare. ~**able** /·əbl/ *a* trasferibile

transform /træns'fɔːm/ *vt* trasformare. ~**ation** /·fə'meɪʃn/ *n* trasformazione *f*. ~**er** *n* trasformatore *m*

transfusion /træns'fjuːʒn/ *n* trasfusione *f*

transient /'trænzɪənt/ *a* passeggero

transistor /træn'zɪstə(r)/ *n* transistor *m inv*; (*radio*) radiolina *f* a transistor

transit /'trænzɪt/ *n* transito *m*; **in** ~ (*goods*) in transito

transition /træn'zɪʃn/ *n* transizione *f*. ~**al** *a* di transizione

transitive /'trænzɪtɪv/ *a* transitivo

transitory /'trænzɪtərɪ/ *a* transitorio

translat|e /trænz'leɪt/ *vt* tradurre. ~**ion** /·'leɪʃn/ *n* traduzione *f*. ~**or** *n* traduttore, ·trice *mf*

transmission /trænz'mɪʃn/ *n* trasmissione *f*

transmit /trænz'mɪt/ *vt* (*pt/pp* **transmitted**) trasmettere. ~**ter** *n* trasmettitore *m*

transparen|cy /træn'spærənsɪ/ *n* *Phot* diapositiva *f*. ~**t** *a* trasparente

transpire /træn'spaɪə(r)/ *vi* emergere; (*fam: happen*) accadere

transplant[1] /'trænsplɑːnt/ *n* trapianto *m*

transplant[2] /træns'plɑːnt/ *vt* trapiantare

transport[1] /'trænspɔːt/ *n* trasporto *m*

transport[2] /træn'spɔːt/ *vt* trasportare. ~**ation** /·teɪʃn/ *n* trasporto *m*

transvestite /trænz'vestaɪt/ *n* travestito, ·a *mf*

trap /træp/ *n* trappola *f*; (*fam: mouth*) boccaccia *f* ● *vt* (*pt/pp* **trapped**) intrappolare; schiacciare (*finger in door*). ~'**door** *n* botola *f*

trapeze /trə'piːz/ *n* trapezio *m*

trash /træʃ/ *n* robaccia *f*; (*rubbish*) spazzatura *f*; (*nonsense*) schiocchezze *fpl*. ~**can** *n* *Am* secchio *m* della spazzatura. ~**y** *a* scadente

trauma /'trɔːmə/ *n* trauma *m*. ~**tic**

/-'mætɪk/ a traumatico. ~**tize** /-taɪz/ traumatizzare

travel /'trævl/ n viaggi mpl ● v (pt/pp **travelled**) vi viaggiare; (to work) andare ● vt percorrere (distance). ~ **agency** n agenzia f di viaggi. ~ **agent** n agente mf di viaggio

traveller /'trævələ(r)/ n viaggiatore, -trice mf; Comm commesso m viaggiatore; ~**s** pl (gypsies) zingari mpl. ~'s **cheque** n traveller's cheque m inv

trawler /'trɔːlə(r)/ n peschereccio m

tray /treɪ/ n vassoio m; (for baking) teglia f; (for documents) vaschetta f sparticarta; (of printer, photocopier) vassoio m

treacherous /'tretʃərəs/ a traditore; (weather, currents) pericoloso. ~y n tradimento m

treacle /'triːkl/ n melassa f

tread /tred/ n andatura f; (step) gradino m; (of tyre) battistrada m inv ● v (pt trod, pp trodden) ● vi (walk) camminare. **tread on** vt calpestare (grass); pestare (foot)

treason /'triːzn/ n tradimento m

treasure /'treʒə(r)/ n tesoro m ● vt tenere in gran conto. ~**r** n tesoriere, -a mf

treasury /'treʒərɪ/ n the **T**~ il Ministero del Tesoro

treat /triːt/ n piacere m; (present) regalo m; **give sb a** ~ fare una sorpresa a qcno ● vt trattare; Med curare; ~ **sb to sth** offrire qcsa a qcno

treatise /'triːtɪz/ n trattato m

treatment /'triːtmənt/ n trattamento m; Med cura f

treaty /'triːtɪ/ n trattato m

treble /'trebl/ a triplo ● n Mus (voice) voce f bianca ● vt triplicare ● vi triplicarsi. ~ **clef** n chiave f di violino

tree /triː/ n albero m

trek /trek/ n scarpinata f; (as holiday) trekking m inv ● vi (pt/pp **trekked**) farsi una scarpinata; (on holiday) fare trekking

tremble /'trembl/ vi tremare

tremendous /trɪ'mendəs/ a (huge) enorme; (fam: excellent) formidabile. ~**ly** adv (very) straordinariamente; (a lot) enormemente

tremor /'tremə(r)/ n tremito m; (earth) ~ **scossa** f [sismica]

trench /trentʃ/ n fosso m; Mil trincea f. ~ **coat** n trench m inv

trend /trend/ n tendenza f; (fashion) moda f. ~**y** a (-ier, -iest) fam di o alla moda

trepidation /trepɪ'deɪʃn/ n trepidazione f

trespass /'trespəs/ vi ~ **on** introdursi abusivamente in; fig abusare di. ~**er** n intruso, -a mf

trial /'traɪəl/ n Jur processo m; (test, ordeal) prova f; **on** ~ in prova; Jur in giudizio; **by** ~ **and error** per tentativi

triangle /'traɪæŋgl/ n triangolo m. ~**ular** /-'æŋgjʊlə(r)/ a triangolare

tribe /traɪb/ n tribù f inv

tribulation /trɪbjʊ'leɪʃn/ n tribolazione f

tribunal /traɪ'bjuːnl/ n tribunale m

tributary /'trɪbjʊtərɪ/ n affluente m

tribute /'trɪbjuːt/ n tributo m; **pay** ~ rendere omaggio

trice /traɪs/ n **in a** ~ in un attimo

trick /trɪk/ n trucco m; (joke) scherzo m; (in cards) presa f; **do the** ~ fam funzionare; **play a** ~ **on** fare uno scherzo a ● vt imbrogliare

trickle /'trɪkl/ vi colare

trickster /'trɪkstə(r)/ n imbroglione, -a mf. ~**y** a (-ier, -iest) (operation) complesso; (situation) delicato

tricycle /'traɪsɪkl/ n triciclo m

tried /traɪd/ see try

trifle /'traɪfl/ n inezia f; Culin zuppa f inglese. ~**ing** a insignificante

trigger /'trɪgə(r)/ n grilletto m ● vt ~ [off] scatenare

trigonometry /trɪgə'nɒmɪtrɪ/ n trigonometria f

trim /trɪm/ a (trimmer, trimmest) curato; (figure) snello ● n (of hair, hedge) spuntata f; (decoration) rifinitura f; **in good** ~ in buono stato; (person) in forma ● vt (pt/pp **trimmed**) spuntare (hair etc); (decorate) ornare; Naut orientare. ~**ming** n bordo m; ~**mings** pl (decorations) guarnizioni fpl; **with all the** ~**mings** Culin guarnito

trinket /'trɪŋkɪt/ n ninnolo m

trio /'triːəʊ/ n trio m

trip /trɪp/ n (excursion) gita f; (journey) viaggio m; (stumble) passo m falso ● v (pt/pp **tripped**) ● vt far inciampare ● vi inciampare (on/over in). **trip up** vt far inciampare

tripe /traɪp/ n trippa f; (sl: nonsense) fesserie fpl

triple /'trɪpl/ a triplo ● vt triplicare ● vi triplicarsi

triplets /'trɪplɪts/ npl tre gemelli mpl

triplicate /'trɪplɪkət/ n **in** ~ in triplice copia

tripod /'traɪpɒd/ n treppiede m inv

tripper /'trɪpə(r)/ n gitante mf

trite /traɪt/ a banale

triumph /'traɪʌmf/ n trionfo m ●vi trionfare (over su). ~ant /-'ʌmf(ə)nt/ a trionfante. ~antly adv (exclaim) con tono trionfante

trivial /'trɪvɪəl/ a insignificante. ~ity /-'ælətɪ/ n banalità f inv

trod, trodden /trɒd, 'trɒdn/ see tread

trolley /'trɒlɪ/ n carrello m; (Am: tram) tram m inv. ~ bus n filobus m inv

trombone /trɒm'bəʊn/ n trombone m

troop /truːp/ n gruppo m; ~s pl truppe fpl ●vi ~ in/out entrare/uscire in gruppo

trophy /'trəʊfɪ/ n trofeo m

tropic /'trɒpɪk/ n tropico m; ~s pl tropici mpl. ~al a tropicale

trot /trɒt/ n trotto m ●vi (pt/pp trotted) trottare

trouble /'trʌbl/ n guaio m; (difficulties) problemi mpl; (inconvenience, Med) disturbo m; (conflict) conflitto m; be in ~ essere nei guai; (swimmer, climber:) essere in difficoltà; get into ~ finire nei guai; get sb into ~ mettere qcno nei guai; take the ~ to do sth darsi la pena di far qcsa ●vt (worry) preoccupare; (inconvenience) disturbare; (conscience, old wound:) tormentare; why don't ~! non ti disturbare!. ~maker n be a ~-maker seminare zizzania. ~some /-səm/ a fastidioso

trough /trɒf/ n trogolo m; (atmospheric) depressione f

trounce /traʊns/ vt (in competition) schiacciare

troupe /truːp/ n troupe f inv

trousers /'traʊzəz/ npl pantaloni mpl

trout /traʊt/ n inv trota f

trowel /'traʊəl/ n (for gardening) paletta f; (for builder) cazzuola f

truant /'truːənt/ n play ~ marinare la scuola

truce /truːs/ n tregua f

truck /trʌk/ n (lorry) camion m inv

trudge /trʌdʒ/ n camminata f faticosa ●vi arrancare

true /truː/ a vero; come ~ avverarsi

truffle /'trʌfl/ n tartufo m

truism /'truːɪzm/ n truismo m

truly /'truːlɪ/ adv veramente; Yours ~ distinti saluti

trump /trʌmp/ n (in cards) atout m inv

trumpet /'trʌmpɪt/ n tromba f. ~er n trombettista mf

truncheon /'trʌntʃn/ n manganello m

trunk /trʌŋk/ n (of tree, body) tronco m; (of elephant) proboscide f; (for travelling, storage) baule m; (Am: of car) bagagliaio m; ~s pl calzoncini mpl da bagno

truss /trʌs/ n Med cinto m erniario

trust /trʌst/ n fiducia f; (group of companies) trust m inv; (organization) associazione f; on ~ sulla parola ●vt fidarsi di; (hope) augurarsi ●vi ~ in credere in; ~ to affidarsi a. ~ed a fidato

trustee /trʌs'tiː/ n amministratore, -trice mf fiduciario, -a

trust|ful /'trʌstfl/ a fiducioso. ~ing a fiducioso. ~worthy a fidato

truth /truːθ/ n (pl -s /truːðz/) verità f inv. ~ful a veritiero. ~fully adv sinceramente

try /traɪ/ n tentativo m, prova f; (in rugby) meta f ●v (pt/pp tried) vt provare; (be a strain on) mettere a dura prova; Jur processare (person); discutere (case); ~ to do sth provare a fare qcsa ●vi provare. **try on** vt provarsi (garment). **try out** vt provare

trying /'traɪɪŋ/ a duro; (person) irritante

T-shirt /'tiː-/ n maglietta f

tub /tʌb/ n tinozza f; (carton) vaschetta f; (bath) vasca f da bagno

tuba /'tjuːbə/ n Mus tuba f

tubby /'tʌbɪ/ a (-ier, -iest) tozzo

tube /tjuːb/ n tubo m; (of toothpaste) tubetto m; Rail metro f

tuber /'tjuːbə(r)/ n tubero m

tuberculosis /tjuːbɜːkjʊ'ləʊsɪs/ n tubercolosi f

tubular /'tjuːbjʊlə(r)/ a tubolare

tuck /tʌk/ n piega f ●vt (put) infilare. **tuck in** vt rimboccare; ~ sb in rimboccare le coperte a qcno ●vi (fam: eat) mangiare con appetito. **tuck up** vt rimboccarsi (sleeves); (in bed) rimboccare le coperte a

Tuesday /'tjuːzdeɪ/ n martedì m inv

tuft /tʌft/ n ciuffo m

tug /tʌg/ n strattone m; Naut rimorchiatore m ●v (pt/pp tugged) vt tirare ●vi dare uno strattone. ~ of war n tiro m alla fune

tuition /tjuː'ɪʃn/ n lezioni fpl

tulip /'tjuːlɪp/ n tulipano m

tumble /'tʌmbl/ n ruzzolone m ●vi ruzzolare. ~down a cadente. ~-drier n asciugabiancheria f

tumbler /'tʌmblə(r)/ n bicchiere m (senza stelo)

tummy /'tʌmɪ/ n fam pancia f

tumour /'tjuːmə(r)/ n tumore m

tumult /'tjuːmʌlt/ n tumulto m. ~uous /-'mʌltjʊəs/ a tumultuoso

tuna /'tjuːnə/ n tonno m

tune /tjuːn/ n motivo m; **out of/in ~** ⟨instrument⟩ scordato/accordato; ⟨person⟩ stonato/intonato; **to the ~ of** fam per la modesta somma di ● vt accordare ⟨instrument⟩; sintonizzare ⟨radio, TV⟩; mettere a punto ⟨engine⟩. **tune in** vt sintonizzare ● vi sintonizzarsi (**to** su). **tune up** vi Mus accordare gli strumenti

tuneful /'tjuːnfl/ a melodioso

tuner /'tjuːnə(r)/ n accordatore, -trice mf; Radio, TV sintonizzatore m

tunic /'tjuːnɪk/ n tunica f; Mil giacca f; Sch grembiule m

Tunisia /tjuˈnɪzɪə/ n Tunisia f. **~n** a & n tunisino, -a mf

tunnel /'tʌnl/ n tunnel m inv ● vi (pt/pp **tunnelled**) scavare un tunnel

turban /'tɜːbən/ n turbante m

turbine /'tɜːbaɪn/ n turbina f

turbulen|ce /'tɜːbjʊləns/ n turbolenza f. **~t** a turbolento

turf /tɜːf/ n erba f; ⟨segment⟩ zolla f erbosa ● **turf out** vt fam buttar fuori

Turin /tjʊˈrɪn/ n Torino f

Turk /tɜːk/ n turco, -a mf

turkey /'tɜːkɪ/ n tacchino m

Turk|ey n Turchia f. **~ish** a turco

turmoil /'tɜːmɔɪl/ n tumulto m

turn /tɜːn/ n (rotation, short walk) giro m; (in road) svolta f, curva f; (development) svolta f; Theat numero m; (fam: attack) crisi f inv; **a ~ for the better/worse** un miglioramento/peggioramento; **do sth a good ~** rendere un servizio a qcno; **take ~s** fare a turno; **in ~** a turno; **out of ~** ⟨speak⟩ a sproposito; **it's your ~** tocca a te ● vt girare; voltare ⟨back, eyes⟩; dirigere ⟨gun, attention⟩ ● vi girare; ⟨person:⟩ girarsi; ⟨leaves:⟩ ingiallire; ⟨become⟩ diventare; **~ right/left** girare a destra/sinistra; **~ sour** inacidirsi; **~ to sb** rivolgersi a qcno; fig rivolgersi a qcno. **turn against** vi diventare ostile a ● vt mettere contro. **turn away** vt mandare via ⟨people⟩ ● vi girarsi dall'altra parte ⟨head⟩ ● vi girarsi dall'altra parte. **turn down** vt piegare ⟨collar⟩; abbassare ⟨heat, gas, sound⟩; respingere ⟨person, proposal⟩. **turn in** vt ripiegare in dentro ⟨edges⟩; consegnare ⟨lost object⟩ ● vi (fam: go to bed) andare a letto; **~ into the drive** entrare nel viale. **turn off** vt spegnere; chiudere ⟨tap, water⟩ ● vi ⟨car:⟩ girare. **turn on** vt accendere; aprire ⟨tap, water⟩; (fam: attract) eccitare ● vi ⟨attack⟩ attaccare. **turn out** vt (expel) mandar via; spegnere ⟨light,

gas⟩; (produce) produrre; (empty) svuotare ⟨room, cupboard⟩ ● vi ⟨transpire⟩ risultare; **~ out well/badly** ⟨cake, dress:⟩ riuscire bene/male; ⟨situation:⟩ andare bene/male. **turn over** vt girare ● vi girarsi; **please ~ over** vedi retro. **turn round** vt girarsi; ⟨car:⟩ girare. **turn up** vt tirare su ⟨collar⟩; alzare ⟨heat, gas, sound, radio⟩ ● vi farsi vedere

turning /'tɜːnɪŋ/ n svolta f. **~-point** n svolta f decisiva

turnip /'tɜːnɪp/ n rapa f

turn: ~-out n (of people) affluenza f. **~over** n Comm giro m d'affari; (of staff) ricambio m. **~pike** n Am autostrada f. **~stile** n cancelletto m girevole. **~table** n piattaforma f girevole; (on record-player) piatto m (di giradischi). **~-up** n (of trousers) risvolto m

turpentine /'tɜːpəntaɪn/ n trementina f

turquoise /'tɜːkwɔɪz/ a (colour) turchese ● n turchese m

turret /'tʌrɪt/ n torretta f

turtle /'tɜːtl/ n tartaruga f acquatica

tusk /tʌsk/ n zanna f

tussle /'tʌsl/ n zuffa f ● vi azzuffarsi

tutor /'tjuːtə(r)/ n insegnante mf privato, -a; Univ insegnante mf universitario, -a che segue individualmente un ristretto numero di studenti. **~ial** /-'tɔːrɪəl/ n discussione f col tutor

tuxedo /tʌkˈsiːdəʊ/ n Am smoking m inv

TV n abbr (**television**) tv f inv, tivù f inv

twaddle /'twɒdl/ n scemenze fpl

twang /twæŋ/ n (in voice) suono m nasale ● vt far vibrare

tweed /twiːd/ n tweed m inv

tweezers /'twiːzəz/ npl pinzette fpl

twelfth /twelfθ/ a & n dodicesimo, -a mf

twelve /twelv/ a & n dodici m

twentieth /'twentɪɪθ/ a & n ventesimo, -a mf

twenty /'twentɪ/ a & n venti m

twerp /twɜːp/ n fam stupido, -a mf

twice /twaɪs/ adv due volte

twiddle /'twɪdl/ vt giocherellare con; **~ one's thumbs** fig girarsi i pollici

twig[1] /twɪg/ n ramoscello m

twig[2] /twɪg/ vt/i (pt/pp **twigged**) fam intuire

twilight /'twaɪ-/ n crepuscolo m

twin /twɪn/ n gemello, -a mf ● attrib gemello. **~ beds** npl letti mpl gemelli

twine /twaɪn/ n spago m ● vi intrecciarsi; ⟨plant:⟩ attorcigliarsi ● vt intrecciare

twinge /twɪndʒ/ n fitta f; **~ of conscience** rimorso m di coscienza

twinkle /'twɪŋkl/ n scintillio m ● vi scintillare

twin 'town n città f inv gemellata

twirl /twɜːl/ vt far roteare ● vi volteggiare ● n piroetta f

twist /twɪst/ n torsione f; (curve) curva f; (in rope) attorcigliata f; (in book, plot) colpo m di scena ● vt attorcigliare ⟨rope⟩; torcere ⟨metal⟩; girare ⟨knob, cap⟩; (distort) distorcere; ~ **one's ankle** storcersi la caviglia ● vi attorcigliarsi ⟨road⟩ essere pieno di curve

twit /twɪt/ n fam cretino. ·a mf

twitch /twɪtʃ/ n tic m inv; (jerk) strattone m ● vi contrarsi

twitter /'twɪtə(r)/ n cinguettio m ● vi cinguettare; ⟨person⟩ cianciare

two /tuː/ a & n due m

two: ~**-faced** a falso. ~**-piece** a (swimsuit) due pezzi m inv; (suit) comple-

to m. ~**some** /-səm/ n coppia f. ~**-way** a ⟨traffic⟩ a doppio senso di marcia

tycoon /taɪˈkuːn/ n magnate m

tying /'taɪɪŋ/ see **tie**

type /taɪp/ n tipo m; (printing) carattere m [tipografico] ● vt/i scrivere a macchina. ~**writer** n macchina f da scrivere. ~**written** a dattiloscritto

typhoid /'taɪfɔɪd/ n febbre f tifoidea

typical /'tɪpɪkl/ a tipico. ~**ly** adv tipicamente; (as usual) come al solito

typify /'tɪpɪfaɪ/ vt (pt/pp -ied) essere tipico di

typing /'taɪpɪŋ/ n dattilografia f

typist /'taɪpɪst/ n dattilografo, -a mf

typography /taɪˈpɒɡrəfɪ/ n tipografia f

tyrannical /tɪˈrænɪkl/ a tirannico

tyranny /'tɪrənɪ/ n tirannia f

tyrant /'taɪrənt/ n tiranno, -a mf

tyre /'taɪə(r)/ n gomma f, pneumatico m

Uu

ubiquitous /juːˈbɪkwɪtəs/ a onnipresente

udder /'ʌdə(r)/ n mammella f (di vacca, capra etc)

ugl|iness /'ʌɡlɪnɪs/ n bruttezza f. ~**y** a (-ier, -iest) brutto

UK n abbr **United Kingdom**

ulcer /'ʌlsə(r)/ n ulcera f

ulterior /ʌlˈtɪərɪə(r)/ a ~ **motive** secondo fine m

ultimate /'ʌltɪmət/ a definitivo; (final) finale; (fundamental) fondamentale. ~**ly** adv alla fine

ultimatum /ʌltɪˈmeɪtəm/ n ultimatum m inv

ultrasound /'ʌltrə-/ n Med ecografia f

ultra'violet a ultravioletto

umbilical /ʌmˈbɪlɪkl/ a ~ **cord** cordone m ombelicale

umbrella /ʌmˈbrelə/ n ombrello m

umpire /'ʌmpaɪə(r)/ n arbitro ● vt/i arbitrare

umpteen /ʌmpˈtiːn/ a fam innumerevole. ~**th** a fam ennesimo; **for the ~th time** per l'ennesima volta

UN n abbr (**United Nations**) ONU f

un'able /ʌn-/ a **be ~ to do sth** non po-

tere fare qcsa; (not know how) non sapere fare qcsa

una'bridged a integrale

unac'companied a non accompagnato; ⟨luggage⟩ incustodito

unac'countable a inspiegabile. ~**y** adv inspiegabilmente

unac'customed a insolito; **be ~ to** non essere abituato a

una'dulterated a ⟨water⟩ puro; ⟨wine⟩ non sofisticato; fig assoluto

un'aided a senza aiuto

unanimity /juːnəˈnɪmɪtɪ/ n unanimità f

unanimous /juːˈnænɪməs/ a unanime. ~**ly** adv all'unanimità

un'armed a disarmato. ~ **combat** n lotta f senza armi

unas'suming a senza pretese

unat'tached a staccato; ⟨person⟩ senza legami

unat'tended a incustodito

unau'thorized a non autorizzato

una'voidable a inevitabile

una'ware a **be ~ of sth** non rendersi conto di qcsa. ~**s** /-eəz/ adv **catch sb ~s** prendere qcno alla sprovvista

un'balanced a non equilibrato; (mentally) squilibrato

un'bearabl|e *a* insopportabile. **~y** *adv* insopportabilmente

unbeat|able /ʌn'bi:təbl/ *a* imbattibile. **~en** *a* imbattuto

unbeknown /ʌnbɪ'nəʊn/ *a fam* ~ **to me** a mia insaputa

unbe'lievable *a* incredibile

un'bend *vi* (*pt/pp* -bent) (*relax*) distendersi

un'biased *a* obiettivo

un'block *vt* sbloccare

un'bolt *vt* togliere il chiavistello di

un'breakable *a* infrangibile

unbridled /ʌn'braɪdld/ *a* sfrenato

un'burden *vt* ~ **oneself** *fig* sfogarsi (**to** con)

un'button *vt* sbottonare

uncalled-for /ʌn'kɔ:ldfɔ:(r)/ *a* fuori luogo

un'canny *a* sorprendente; (*silence, feeling*) inquietante

un'ceasing *a* incessante

uncere'monious *a* (*abrupt*) brusco. **~ly** *adv* senza tante cerimonie

un'certain *a* incerto; (*weather*) instabile; **in no** ~ **terms** senza mezzi termini. **~ty** *n* incertezza *f*

un'changed *a* invariato

un'charitable *a* duro

uncle /'ʌŋkl/ *n* zio *m*

un'comfortabl|e *a* scomodo; imbarazzante (*silence, situation*); **feel** ~ **e** *fig* sentirsi a disagio. **~y** *adv* (*sit*) scomodamente; (*causing alarm etc*) spaventosamente

un'common *a* insolito

un'compromising *a* intransigente

uncon'ditional *a* incondizionato. **~ly** *adv* incondizionatamente

un'conscious *a* privo di sensi; (*unaware*) inconsapevole; **be** ~ **of sth** non rendersi conto di qcsa. **~ly** *adv* inconsapevolmente

uncon'ventional *a* poco convenzionale

unco'operative *a* poco cooperativo

un'cork *vt* sturare

un'couth /ʌn'ku:θ/ *a* zotico

un'cover *vt* scoprire; portare alla luce (*buried object*)

unde'cided *a* indeciso; (*not settled*) incerto

undeniabl|e /ʌndɪ'naɪəbl/ *a* innegabile. **~y** *adv* innegabilmente

under /'ʌndə(r)/ *prep* sotto; (*less than*) al di sotto di; ~ **there** lì sotto; ~ **repair/construction** in riparazione/ costruzione; ~ **way** *fig* in corso ● *adv*

(~ *water*) sott'acqua; (*unconscious*) sotto anestesia

'undercarriage *n Aeron* carrello *m*

'underclothes *npl* biancheria *fsg* intima

under'cover *a* clandestino

'undercurrent *n* corrente *f* sottomarina; *fig* sottofondo *m*

under'cut *vt* (*pt/pp* -cut) *Comm* vendere a minor prezzo di

'underdog *n* perdente *m*

under'done *a* (*meat*) al sangue

under'estimate *vt* sottovalutare

under'fed *a* denutrito

under'foot *adv* sotto i piedi; **trample** ~ calpestare

under'go *vt* (*pt* -went, *pp* -gone) subire (*operation, treatment*); ~ **repair** essere in riparazione

under'graduate *n* studente, -tessa *mf* universitario, -a

'underground[1] *adv* sottoterra

'underground[2] *a* sotterraneo; (*secret*) clandestino ● *n* (*railway*) metropolitana *f*. ~ **car park** *n* parcheggio *m* sotterraneo

'undergrowth *n* sottobosco *m*

'underhand *a* subdolo

'underlay *n* strato *m* di gomma o feltro posto sotto la moquette

under'lie *vt* (*pt* -lay, *pp* -lain, *pres p* -lying) *fig* essere alla base di

under'line *vt* sottolineare

underling /'ʌndəlɪŋ/ *n pej* subalterno, -a *mf*

under'lying *a fig* fondamentale

under'mine *vt fig* minare

underneath /ʌndə'ni:θ/ *prep* sotto; ~ **it** sotto ● *adv* sotto

under'paid *a* mal pagato

'underpants *npl* mutande *fpl*

'underpass *n* sottopassaggio *m*

under'privileged *a* non abbiente

under'rate *vt* sottovalutare

'underseal *n Auto* antiruggine *m inv*

'undershirt *n Am* maglia *f* della pelle

under'staffed /-'sta:ft/ *a* a corto di personale

under'stand *vt* (*pt/pp* -stood) capire; **I** ~ **that...** (*have heard*) mi risulta che... ● *vi* capire. **~able** /-əbl/ *a* comprensibile. **~ably** /-əblɪ/ *adv* comprensibilmente

under'standing *a* comprensivo ● *n* comprensione *f*; (*agreement*) accordo *m*; **on the** ~ **that** a condizione che

'understatement *n* understatement *m inv*

'understudy *n Theat* sostituto, -a *mf*

under'take *vt* (*pt* -took, *pp* -taken)

intraprendere; ~ **to do sth** impegnarsi a fare qcsa

'**undertaker** n impresario m di pompe funebri; [**firm of**] ~**s** n impresa f di pompe funebri

under'taking n impresa f; ⟨promise⟩ promessa f

'undertone n fig sottofondo m; **in an** ~ sottovoce

under'value vt sottovalutare

'underwater¹ a subacqueo

'under'water² adv sott'acqua

'underwear n biancheria f intima

'under'weight a sotto peso

'underworld n ⟨criminals⟩ malavita f

'underwriter n assicuratore m

unde'sirable a indesiderato; ⟨person⟩ poco raccomandabile

undies /'ʌndɪz/ npl fam biancheria fsg intima ⟨da donna⟩

un'dignified a non dignitoso

un'do vt ⟨pt -did, pp -done⟩ disfare; slacciare ⟨dress, shoes⟩; sbottonare ⟨shirt⟩; fig, Comput annullare

un'done a ⟨shirt, button⟩ sbottonato; ⟨shoes, dress⟩ slacciato; ⟨not accomplished⟩ non fatto; **leave** ~ ⟨job⟩ tralasciare

un'doubted a indubbio. ~**ly** adv senza dubbio

un'dress vt spogliare; **get** ~**ed** spogliarsi ● vi spogliarsi

un'due a eccessivo

undulating /'ʌndjʊleɪtɪŋ/ a ondulato; ⟨country⟩ collinoso

un'duly adv eccessivamente

un'dying a eterno

un'earth vt dissotterrare; fig scovare; scoprire ⟨secret⟩. ~**ly** a soprannaturale; **at an** ~**ly hour** fam a un'ora impossibile

un'ease n disagio m. ~**y** a a disagio; ⟨person⟩ inquieto; ⟨feeling⟩ inquietante; ⟨truce⟩ precario

un'eatable a immangiabile

uneco'nomic a poco remunerativo

uneco'nomical a poco economico

unem'ployed a disoccupato ● npl **the** ~ i disoccupati

unem'ployment n disoccupazione f. ~ **benefit** n sussidio m di disoccupazione

un'ending a senza fine

un'equal a disuguale; ⟨struggle⟩ impari; **be** ~ **to a task** non essere all'altezza di un compito

unequivocal /ʌnɪ'kwɪvəkl/ a inequivocabile; ⟨person⟩ esplicito

unerring /ʌn'ɜːrɪŋ/ a infallibile

un'ethical a immorale

un'even a irregolare; ⟨distribution⟩ ineguale; ⟨number⟩ dispari

unex'pected a inaspettato. ~**ly** adv inaspettatamente

un'failing a infallibile

un'fair a ingiusto. ~**ly** adv ingiustamente. ~**ness** n ingiustizia f

un'faithful a infedele

unfa'miliar a sconosciuto; **be** ~ **with** non conoscere

un'fasten vt slacciare; ⟨detach⟩ staccare

un'favourable a sfavorevole; ⟨impression⟩ negativo

un'feeling a insensibile

un'finished a da finire; ⟨business⟩ in sospeso

un'fit a inadatto; ⟨morally⟩ indegno; Sport fuori forma; ~ **for work** non in grado di lavorare

unflinching /ʌn'flɪntʃɪŋ/ a risoluto

un'fold vt spiegare; ⟨spread out⟩ aprire; fig rivelare ● vi ⟨view:⟩ spiegarsi

unfore'seen a imprevisto

unfor'gettable /ʌnfə'getəbl/ a indimenticabile

unfor'givable /ʌnfə'gɪvəbl/ a imperdonabile

un'fortunate a sfortunato; ⟨regrettable⟩ spiacevole; ⟨remark, choice⟩ infelice. ~**ly** adv purtroppo

un'founded a infondato

unfurl /ʌn'fɜːl/ vt spiegare

un'furnished a non ammobiliato

ungainly /ʌn'geɪnlɪ/ a sgraziato

ungodly /ʌn'gɒdlɪ/ a empio; ~ **hour** fam ora f impossibile

un'grateful a ingrato. ~**ly** adv senza riconoscenza

un'happily adv infelicemente; ⟨unfortunately⟩ purtroppo. ~**ness** n infelicità f

un'happy a infelice; ⟨not content⟩ insoddisfatto ⟨with di⟩

un'harmed a incolume

un'healthy a poco sano; ⟨insanitary⟩ malsano

un'hook vt sganciare

un'hurt a illeso

unhy'gienic a non igienico

unification /juːnɪfɪ'keɪʃn/ n unificazione f

uniform /'juːnɪfɔːm/ a uniforme ● n uniforme f. ~**ly** adv uniformemente

unify /'juːnɪfaɪ/ vt ⟨pt/pp -ied⟩ unificare

uni'lateral /juːnɪ-/ a unilaterale

uni'maginable a inimmaginabile

unim'portant a irrilevante

unin'habited a disabitato

unin'tentional *a* involontario. ~ly *adv* involontariamente

union /'ju:nɪən/ *n* unione *f*; ⟨trade ~⟩ sindacato *m*. U~ Jack *n* bandiera *f* del Regno Unito

unique /ju:'ni:k/ *a* unico. ~ly *adv* unicamente

unison /'ju:nɪsn/ *n* in ~ all'unisono

unit /'ju:nɪt/ *n* unità *f inv*; ⟨department⟩ reparto *m*; ⟨of furniture⟩ elemento *m*

unite /ju:'naɪt/ *vt* unire ● *vi* unirsi

united /ju:'naɪtɪd/ *a* unito. U~ 'Kingdom *n* Regno *m* Unito. U~ 'Nations *n* [Organizzazione *f* delle] Nazioni Unite *fpl*. U~ 'States [of America] *n* Stati *mpl* Uniti [d'America]

unity /'ju:nətɪ/ *n* unità *f*; ⟨agreement⟩ accordo *m*

universal /ju:nɪ'vɜ:sl/ *a* universale. ~ly *adv* universalmente

universe /'ju:nɪvɜ:s/ *n* universo *m*

university /ju:nɪ'vɜ:sətɪ/ *n* università *f inv* ● *attrib* universitario

un'just *a* ingiusto

unkempt /ʌn'kempt/ *a* trasandato; ⟨hair⟩ arruffato

un'kind *a* scortese. ~ly *adv* in modo scortese. ~ness *n* mancanza *f* di gentilezza

un'known *a* sconosciuto

un'lawful *a* illecito, illegale

unleaded /ʌn'ledɪd/ *a* senza piombo

un'leash *vt fig* scatenare

unless /ən'les/ *conj* a meno che; ~ I am mistaken se non mi sbaglio

un'like *a* (not the same) diversi ● *prep* diverso da; that's ~ him non è da lui; ~ me, he... diversamente da me, lui...

un'likely *a* improbabile

un'limited *a* illimitato

un'load *vt* scaricare

un'lock *vt* aprire (con chiave)

un'lucky *a* sfortunato; it's ~ to... porta sfortuna...

un'manned *a* senza equipaggio

un'married *a* non sposato. ~ 'mother *n* ragazza *f* madre

un'mask *vt fig* smascherare

unmistakabl|e /ʌnmɪ'steɪkəbl/ *a* inconfondibile. ~y *adv* chiaramente

un'mitigated *a* assoluto

un'natural *a* innaturale; *pej* anormale. ~ly *adv* in modo innaturale; *pej* in modo anormale

unneces'sarily *adv* inutilmente

un'necessary *a* inutile

un'noticed *a* inosservato

unob'tainable *a* ⟨products etc⟩ introvabile; ⟨telephone number⟩ non ottenibile

unob'trusive *a* discreto. ~ly *adv* in modo discreto

unof'ficial *a* non ufficiale. ~ly *adv* ufficiosamente

un'pack *vi* disfare le valigie ● *vt* svuotare ⟨parcel⟩; spacchettare ⟨books⟩; ~ one's case disfare la valigia

un'paid *a* da pagare; ⟨work⟩ non retribuito

un'palatable *a* sgradevole

un'paralleled *a* senza pari

un'pick *vt* disfare

un'pleasant *a* sgradevole; ⟨person⟩ maleducato. ~ly *adv* sgradevolmente; ⟨behave⟩ maleducatamente. ~ness *n* ⟨bad feeling⟩ tensioni *fpl*

un'plug *vt* (*pt/pp* -plugged) staccare

un'popular *a* impopolare

un'precedented *a* senza precedenti

unpre'dictable *a* imprevedibile

unpre'meditated *a* involontario

unpre'pared *a* impreparato

unpre'tentious *a* senza pretese

un'principled *a* senza principi; ⟨behaviour⟩ scorretto

unpro'fessional *a* non professionale; it's ~ è una mancanza di professionalità

un'profitable *a* non redditizio

un'qualified *a* non qualificato; ⟨fig: absolute⟩ assoluto

un'questionable *a* incontestabile

un'quote *vi* chiudere le virgolette

unravel /ʌn'rævl/ *vt* (*pt/pp* -ravelled) districare; ⟨in knitting⟩ disfare

un'real *a* irreale; *fam* inverosimile

un'reasonable *a* irragionevole

unre'lated *a* ⟨fact⟩ senza rapporto (to con); ⟨person⟩ non imparentato (to con)

unre'liable *a* inaffidabile; ⟨person⟩ inaffidabile, che non dà affidamento

unrequited /ʌnrɪ'kwaɪtɪd/ *a* non corrisposto

unreservedly /ʌnrɪ'zɜ:vɪdlɪ/ *adv* senza riserve; ⟨frankly⟩ francamente

un'rest *n* fermenti *mpl*

un'rivalled *a* ineguagliato

un'roll *vt* srotolare ● *vi* srotolarsi

unruly /ʌn'ru:lɪ/ *a* indisciplinato

un'safe *a* pericoloso

un'said *a* inespresso

un'salted *a* non salato

unsatis'factory *a* poco soddisfacente

un'savoury *a* equivoco

unscathed /ʌn'skeɪðd/ *a* illeso

un'screw *vt* svitare

un'scrupulous *a* senza scrupoli

un'seemly *a* indecoroso

un'selfish *a* disinteressato

un'settled *a* in agitazione; ⟨*weather*⟩ variabile; ⟨*bill*⟩ non saldato

unshakeable /ʌnˈʃeɪkəbl/ *a* categorico

unshaven /ʌnˈʃeɪvn/ *a* non rasato

unsightly /ʌnˈsaɪtlɪ/ *a* brutto

un'skilled *a* non specializzato. ~ worker *n* manovale *m*

un'sociable *a* scontroso

unso'phisticated *a* semplice

un'sound *a* ⟨*building, reasoning*⟩ poco solido; ⟨*advice*⟩ poco sensato; **of ~ mind** malato di mente

unspeakable /ʌnˈspiːkəbl/ *a* indicibile

un'stable *a* instabile; ⟨*mentally*⟩ squilibrato

un'steady *a* malsicuro

un'stuck *a* **come ~** staccarsi; ⟨*fam: project*⟩ andare a monte

unsuc'cessful *a* fallimentare; be ~ ⟨*in attempt*⟩ non aver successo. ~ly *adv* senza successo

un'suitable *a* ⟨*inappropriate*⟩ inadatto; ⟨*inconvenient*⟩ inopportuno

unsu'specting *a* fiducioso

unthinkable /ʌnˈθɪŋkəbl/ *a* impensabile

un'tidiness *n* disordine *m*

un'tidy *a* disordinato

un'tie *vt* slegare

until /ənˈtɪl/ *prep* fino a; **not ~** non prima di; **~ the evening** fino alla sera; **~ his arrival** fino al suo arrivo ● *conj* finché, fino a quando; **not ~ you've seen it** non prima che l'abbia visto

untimely /ʌnˈtaɪmlɪ/ *a* inopportuno; ⟨*premature*⟩ prematuro

un'tiring *a* instancabile

un'told *a* ⟨*wealth*⟩ incalcolabile; ⟨*suffering*⟩ indescrivibile; ⟨*story*⟩ inedito

unto'ward *a* **if nothing ~ happens** se non capita un imprevisto

un'true *a* falso; **that's ~** non è vero

unused[1] /ʌnˈjuːzd/ *a* non [ancora] usato

unused[2] /ʌnˈjuːst/ *a* **be ~ to** non essere abituato a

un'usual *a* insolito. ~ly *adv* insolitamente

un'veil *vt* scoprire

un'wanted *a* indesiderato

un'warranted *a* ingiustificato

un'welcome *a* sgradito

un'well *a* indisposto

unwieldy /ʌnˈwiːldɪ/ *a* ingombrante

un'willing *a* riluttante. ~ly *adv* malvolentieri

un'wind *v* (*pt/pp* unwound) ● *vt* svolgere, srotolare ● *vi* svolgersi, srotolarsi; ⟨*fam: relax*⟩ rilassarsi

un'wise *a* imprudente

unwitting /ʌnˈwɪtɪŋ/ *a* involontario; ⟨*victim*⟩ inconsapevole. ~ly *adv* involontariamente

un'worthy *a* non degno

un'wrap *vt* (*pt/pp* -wrapped) scartare ⟨*present, parcel*⟩

un'written *a* tacito

up /ʌp/ *adv* su; ⟨*not in bed*⟩ alzato; ⟨*road*⟩ smantellato; ⟨*theatre curtain, blinds*⟩ alzato; ⟨*shelves, tent*⟩ montato; ⟨*notice*⟩ affisso; ⟨*building*⟩ costruito; **prices are up** i prezzi sono aumentati; **be up for sale** essere in vendita; **up here/there** quassù/lassù; **time's up** tempo scaduto; **what's up?** *fam* cosa è successo?; **up to** ⟨*as far as*⟩ fino a; **be up to** essere all'altezza di ⟨*task*⟩; **what's he up to?** *fam* cosa sta facendo?; ⟨*plotting*⟩ cosa sta combinando?; **I'm up to page 100** sono arrivato a pagina 100; **feel up to it** sentirsela; **be one up on sb** *fam* essere in vantaggio su qcno; **go up** salire; **lift up** alzare; **up against** *fig* alle prese con ● *prep* su; **the cat ran is up the tree** il gatto è salito di corsa/è sull'albero; **further up this road** più avanti su questa strada; **row up the river** risalire il fiume; **go up the stairs** salire su per le scale; **be up the pub** *fam* essere al pub; **be up on** *or* **in sth** essere bene informato su qcsa ● *n* **ups and downs** *npl* alti *mpl* e bassi

upbringing *n* educazione *f*

up'date[1] *vt* aggiornare

'update[2] *n* aggiornamento *m*

up'grade *vt* promuovere ⟨*person*⟩; modernizzare ⟨*equipment*⟩

upgradeable /ʌpˈgreɪdəbl/ *a* Comput upgradabile

upheaval /ʌpˈhiːvl/ *n* scompiglio *m*

up'hill *a* in salita; *fig* arduo ● *adv* in salita

up'hold *vt* (*pt/pp* upheld) sostenere ⟨*principle*⟩; confermare ⟨*verdict*⟩

upholster /ʌpˈhəʊlstə(r)/ *vt* tappezzare. ~er *n* tappezziere, -a *mf*. ~y *n* tappezzeria *f*

'upkeep *n* mantenimento *m*

up-'market *a* di qualità

upon /əˈpɒn/ *prep* su; **~ arriving home** una volta arrivato a casa

upper /ˈʌpə(r)/ *a* superiore ● *n* ⟨*of shoe*⟩ tomaia *f*

upper: **~ circle** *n* seconda galleria *f*. **~ class** *n* alta borghesia *f*. **~ hand** *n* **have the ~ hand** avere il sopravvento.

~most *a* più alto; that's ~most in my mind è la mia preoccupazione principale

'upright *a* dritto; ⟨piano⟩ verticale; ⟨honest⟩ retto ●*n* montante *m*

'uprising *n* rivolta *f*

'uproar *n* tumulto *m*; be in an ~ essere in trambusto

up'root *vt* sradicare

up'set[1] *vt* ⟨pt/pp upset, pres p upsetting⟩ rovesciare; sconvolgere ⟨plan⟩; ⟨distress⟩ turbare; get ~ about sth prendersela per qcsa; be very ~ essere sconvolto; have an ~ stomach avere l'intestino disturbato

'upset[2] *n* scombussolamento *m*

'upshot *n* risultato *m*

upside 'down *adv* sottosopra; turn ~ ~ capovolgere

up'stairs[1] *adv* [al piano] di sopra

'upstairs[2] *a* del piano superiore

'upstart *n* arrivato, -a *mf*

'upstream *adv* controcorrente

'upsurge *n* ⟨in sales⟩ aumento *m* improvviso; ⟨of enthusiasm, crime⟩ ondata *f*

'uptake *n* be slow on the ~ essere lento nel capire; be quick on the ~ capire le cose al volo

up'tight *a* teso

up-to-'date *a* moderno; ⟨news⟩ ultimo; ⟨records⟩ aggiornato

'upturn *n* ripresa *f*

'upward /ʌpwəd/ *a* verso l'alto, in su; ~ slope salita *f* ●*adv* ~[s] verso l'alto; ~s of oltre

uranium /jʊ'reɪnɪəm/ *n* uranio *m*

urban /'ɜːbən/ *a* urbano

urge /ɜːdʒ/ *n* forte desiderio *m* ●*vt* esortare (to a). urge on *vt* spronare

urgen|cy /'ɜːdʒənsɪ/ *n* urgenza *f*. ~t *a* urgente

urinate /'jʊərɪneɪt/ *vi* urinare

urine /'jʊərɪn/ *n* urina *f*

urn /ɜːn/ *n* urna *f*; ⟨for tea⟩ contenitore *m* munito di cannella che si trova nei self-service, mense ecc

us /ʌs/ *pers pron* ci; ⟨after prep⟩ noi; they know us ci conoscono; give us

the money dateci i soldi; give it to us dateglielo; they showed it to us ce l'hanno fatto vedere; they meant us, not you intendevano noi, non voi; it's us siamo noi; she hates us ci odia

US[A] *n[pl] abbr* ⟨United States [of America]⟩ U.S.A. *mpl*

usable /'juːzəbl/ *a* usabile

usage /'juːsɪdʒ/ *n* uso *m*

use[1] /juːs/ *n* uso *m*; be of ~ essere utile; be of no ~ essere inutile; make ~ of usare; ⟨exploit⟩ sfruttare; it is no ~ è inutile; what's the ~? a che scopo?

use[2] /juːz/ *vt* usare. use up *vt* consumare

used[1] /juːzd/ *a* usato

used[2] /juːst/ *pt* be ~ to sth essere abituato a qcsa; get ~ to abituarsi a; he ~ to live here viveva qui

useful /'juːsfl/ *a* utile. ~ness *n* utilità *f*

useless /'juːslɪs/ *a* inutile; ⟨fam: person⟩ incapace

user /'juːzə(r)/ *n* utente *mf*. ~-'friendly *a* facile da usare

usher /'ʌʃə(r)/ *n* Theat maschera *f*; Jur usciere *m*; ⟨at wedding⟩ persona *f* che accompagna gli invitati a un matrimonio ai loro posti in chiesa ● usher in *vt* fare entrare

usherette /ʌʃə'ret/ *n* maschera *f*

usual /'juːʒʊəl/ *a* usuale; as ~ come al solito. ~ly *adv* di solito

usurp /jʊ'zɜːp/ *vt* usurpare

utensil /jʊ'tensl/ *n* utensile *m*

uterus /'juːtərəs/ *n* utero *m*

utilitarian /jʊtɪlɪ'teərɪən/ *a* funzionale

utility /jʊ'tɪlətɪ/ *n* servizio *m*. ~ room *n* stanza *f* in casa privata per il lavaggio, la stiratura dei panni ecc

utilize /'juːtɪlaɪz/ *vt* utilizzare

utmost /'ʌtməʊst/ *a* estremo ●*n* one's ~ tutto il possibile

utter[1] /'ʌtə(r)/ *a* totale. ~ly *adv* completamente

utter[2] *vt* emettere ⟨sigh, sound⟩; proferire ⟨word⟩. ~ance /-əns/ *n* dichiarazione *f*

U-turn /'juː-/ *n* Auto inversione *f* a U; *fig* marcia *f* in dietro

Vv

vacan|cy /'veɪk(ə)nsɪ/ n (job) posto m vacante; (room) stanza f disponibile. **~t** a libero; (position) vacante; (look) assente
vacate /və'keɪt/ vt lasciare libero
vacation /və'keɪʃn/ n Univ & Am vacanza f
vaccinat|e /'væksɪneɪt/ vt vaccinare. **~ion** /-'neɪʃn/ n vaccinazione f
vaccine /'væksi:n/ n vaccino m
vacuum /'vækjʊəm/ n vuoto m ● vt passare l'aspirapolvere in/su. **~ cleaner** n aspirapolvere m inv. **~ flask** n thermos® m inv. **~-packed** a confezionato sottovuoto
vagabond /'vægəbɒnd/ n vagabondo, -a mf
vagina /və'dʒaɪnə/ n Anat vagina f
vagrant /'veɪgrənt/ n vagabondo, -a mf
vague /veɪg/ a vago; (outline) impreciso; (absent-minded) distratto; **I'm still ~ about it** non ho ancora le idee chiare in proposito. **~ly** adv vagamente
vain /veɪn/ a vanitoso; (hope, attempt) vano; **in ~** invano. **~ly** adv vanamente
valentine /'væləntaɪn/ n (card) biglietto m di San Valentino
valiant /'vælɪənt/ a valoroso
valid /'vælɪd/ a valido. **~ate** vt (confirm) convalidare. **~ity** /və'lɪdətɪ/ n validità f
valley /'vælɪ/ n valle f
valour /'vælə(r)/ n valore m
valuable /'væljʊəbl/ a di valore; fig prezioso. **~s** npl oggetti mpl di valore
valuation /væljʊ'eɪʃn/ n valutazione f
value /'vælju:/ n valore m; (usefulness) utilità f ● vt valutare; (cherish) apprezzare. **~ 'added tax** n imposta f sul valore aggiunto
valve /vælv/ n valvola f
vampire /'væmpaɪə(r)/ n vampiro m
van /væn/ n furgone m
vandal /'vændl/ n vandalo, -a mf. **~ism** /-ɪzm/ n vandalismo m. **~ize** vt vandalizzare
vanilla /və'nɪlə/ n vaniglia f
vanish /'vænɪʃ/ vi svanire
vanity /'vænətɪ/ n vanità f. **~ bag or case** n beauty-case m inv

vantage-point /'vɑːntɪdʒ-/ n punto m d'osservazione; fig punto m di vista
vapour /'veɪpə(r)/ n vapore m
variable /'veərɪəbl/ a variabile; (adjustable) regolabile
variance /'veərɪəns/ n **be at ~** essere in disaccordo
variant /'veərɪənt/ n variante f
variation /veərɪ'eɪʃn/ n variazione f
varicose /'værɪkəʊs/ a **~ veins** vene fpl varicose
varied /'veərɪd/ a vario; (diet) diversificato; (life) movimentato
variety /və'raɪətɪ/ n varietà f inv
various /'veərɪəs/ a vario
varnish /'vɑːnɪʃ/ n vernice f; (for nails) smalto m ● vt verniciare; **~ one's nails** mettersi lo smalto
vary /'veərɪ/ vt/i (pt/pp -ied) variare. **~ing** a variabile; (different) diverso
vase /vɑːz/ n vaso m
vast /vɑːst/ a vasto; (difference, amusement) enorme. **~ly** adv (superior) di gran lunga; (different, amused) enormemente
vat /væt/ n tino m
VAT /vi:eɪ'ti:, væt/ n abbr (value added tax) I.V.A. f
vault[1] /vɔːlt/ n (roof) volta f; (in bank) caveau m inv; (tomb) cripta f
vault[2] n salto m ● vt/i ~ [over] saltare
VDU n abbr (visual display unit) VDU m
veal /vi:l/ n carne f di vitello ● attrib di vitello
veer /vɪə(r)/ vi cambiare direzione; Naut, Auto virare
vegetable /'vedʒtəbl/ n (food) verdura f; (when growing) ortaggio m ● attrib (oil, fat) vegetale
vegetarian /vedʒɪ'teərɪən/ a & n vegetariano, -a mf
vegetat|e /'vedʒɪteɪt/ vi vegetare. **~ion** /-'teɪʃn/ n vegetazione f
vehemen|ce /'vi:əməns/ n veemenza f. **~t** a veemente. **~tly** adv con veemenza
vehicle /'vi:ɪkl/ n veicolo m; (fig: medium) mezzo m
veil /veɪl/ n velo m ● vt velare

vein /veɪn/ n vena f; (*mood*) umore m; (*manner*) tenore m. **~ed** a venato

Velcro® /'velkrəʊ/ n ~ **fastening** chiusura f con velcro"

velocity /vɪ'lɒsətɪ/ n velocità f

velvet /'velvɪt/ n velluto m. **~y** a vellutato

vendetta /ven'detə/ n vendetta f

vending-machine /'vendɪŋ-/ n distributore m automatico

veneer /vəˈnɪə(r)/ n impiallacciatura f; *fig* vernice f. **~ed** a impiallacciato

venereal /vɪ'nɪərɪəl/ a ~ **disease** malattia f venerea

Venetian /vəˈniːʃn/ a & n veneziano, -a mf. **v~ blind** n persiana f alla veneziana

vengeance /'vendʒəns/ n vendetta f; **with a ~** fam a più non posso

Venice /'venɪs/ n Venezia f

venison /'venɪsn/ n Culin carne f di cervo

venom /'venəm/ n veleno m. **~ous** /-əs/ a velenoso

vent[1] /vent/ n presa f d'aria; **give ~ to** *fig* dar libero sfogo a ● vt *fig* sfogare (*anger*)

vent[2] n (*in jacket*) spacco m

ventilat|e /'ventɪleɪt/ vt ventilare. **~ion** /-'leɪʃn/ n ventilazione f; (*installation*) sistema m di ventilazione. **~or** n ventilatore m

ventriloquist /ven'trɪləkwɪst/ n ventriloquo, -a mf

venture /'ventʃə(r)/ n impresa f ● vt azzardare ● vi avventurarsi

venue /'venjuː/ n luogo m (*di convegno, concerto, ecc.*)

veranda /vəˈrændə/ n veranda f

verb /vɜːb/ n verbo m. **~al** a verbale

verbatim /vɜː'beɪtɪm/ a letterale ● adv parola per parola

verbose /vɜː'bəʊs/ a prolisso

verdict /'vɜːdɪkt/ n verdetto m; (*opinion*) parere m

verge /vɜːdʒ/ n orlo m; **be on the ~ of doing sth** essere sul punto di fare qcsa ● **verge on** vt *fig* rasentare

verger /'vɜːdʒə(r)/ n sagrestano m

verify /'verɪfaɪ/ vt (*pt/pp* -**ied**) verificare; (*confirm*) confermare

vermin /'vɜːmɪn/ n animali mpl nocivi

vermouth /'vɜːməθ/ n vermut m inv

vernacular /vəˈnækjʊlə(r)/ n vernacolo m

versatil|e /'vɜːsataɪl/ a versatile. **~ity** /-'tɪlətɪ/ n versatilità f

verse /vɜːs/ n verso m; (*of Bible*) versetto m; (*poetry*) versi mpl

versed /vɜːst/ a **~ in** versato in

version /'vɜːʃn/ n versione f

versus /'vɜːsəs/ prep contro

vertebra /'vɜːtɪbrə/ n (*pl-brae* /-briː/) *Anat* vertebra f

vertical /'vɜːtɪkl/ a & n verticale m

vertigo /'vɜːtɪgəʊ/ n Med vertigine f

verve /vɜːv/ n verve f

very /'verɪ/ adv molto; **~ much** molto; **~ little** pochissimo; **~ many** moltissimi; **~ few** pochissimi; **~ probably** molto probabilmente; **~ well** benissimo; **at the ~ most** tutt'al più; **at the ~ latest** al più tardi ● a **the ~ first** il primissimo; **the ~ thing** proprio ciò che ci vuole; **at the ~ end/beginning** proprio alla fine/all'inizio; **that ~ day** proprio quel giorno; **the ~ thought** la sola idea; **only a ~ little** solo un pochino

vessel /'vesl/ n nave f

vest /vest/ n maglia f della pelle; (*Am: waistcoat*) gilè m inv. **~ed interest** n interesse m personale

vestige /'vestɪdʒ/ n (*of past*) vestigio m

vestment /'vestmənt/ n Relig paramento m

vestry /'vestrɪ/ n sagrestia f

vet /vet/ n veterinario, -a mf ● vt (*pt/pp* vetted) controllare minuziosamente

veteran /'vetərən/ n veterano, -a mf

veterinary /'vetərɪnərɪ/ a veterinario. **~ surgeon** n medico m veterinario

veto /'viːtəʊ/ n (*pl-es*) veto m ● vt proibire

vex /veks/ vt irritare. **~ation** /-'seɪʃn/ n irritazione f. **~ed** a irritato; **~ed question** questione f controversa

VHF n abbr (**very high frequency**) VHF

via /'vaɪə/ prep via; (*by means of*) attraverso

viable /'vaɪəbl/ a (*life form, relationship, company*) in grado di sopravvivere; (*proposition*) attuabile

viaduct /'vaɪədʌkt/ n viadotto m

vibrat|e /vaɪ'breɪt/ vi vibrare. **~ion** /-'breɪʃn/ n vibrazione f

vicar /'vɪkə(r)/ n parroco m (*protestante*). **~age** /-rɪdʒ/ n casa f parrocchiale

vicarious /vɪ'keərɪəs/ a indiretto

vice[1] /vaɪs/ n vizio m

vice[2] n Techn morsa f

vice 'chairman n vicepresidente mf

vice 'president n vicepresidente mf

vice versa /vaɪs'vɜːsə/ adv viceversa

vicinity /vɪ'sɪnətɪ/ n vicinanza f; **in the ~ of** nelle vicinanze di

vicious /'vɪʃəs/ a cattivo; (*attack*) brutale: ⟨animal⟩ pericoloso. ~ **circle** n circolo m vizioso. ~**ly** adv ⟨attack⟩ brutalmente

victim /'vɪktɪm/ n vittima f. ~**ize** vt fare delle rappresaglie contro

victor /'vɪktə(r)/ n vincitore m

victorious /vɪk'tɔːrɪəs/ a vittorioso. ~**y** /'vɪktərɪ/ n vittoria f

video /'vɪdɪəʊ/ n video m; ⟨cassette⟩ videocassetta f; ⟨recorder⟩ videoregistratore m ●attrib video ● vt registrare

video: ~ **card** n Comput scheda f video. ~ **cas'sette** n videocassetta f. ~**conference** n videoconferenza f. ~ **game** n videogioco m. ~ **recorder** n videoregistratore m. ~**-tape** n videocassetta f

vie /vaɪ/ vi ⟨pres p vying⟩ rivaleggiare

view /vjuː/ n vista f; ⟨photographed, painted⟩ veduta f; ⟨opinion⟩ visione f. **look at the** ~ guardare il panorama: **in my** ~ secondo me; **in** ~ **of** in considerazione di; **on** ~ esposto: **with a** ~ **to** con l'intenzione di ● vt visitare ⟨house⟩; ⟨consider⟩ considerare ● vi TV guardare. ~**er** n TV telespettatore. ·trice mf, Phot visore m

view: ~**finder** n Phot mirino m. ~**point** n punto m di vista

vigil /'vɪdʒɪl/ n veglia f

vigilance /'vɪdʒɪləns/ n vigilanza f. ~**t** a vigile

vigorous /'vɪgərəs/ a vigoroso

vigour /'vɪgə(r)/ n vigore m

vile /vaɪl/ a disgustoso; ⟨weather⟩ orribile; ⟨temper, mood⟩ pessimo

villa /'vɪlə/ n ⟨for holidays⟩ casa f di villeggiatura

village /'vɪlɪdʒ/ n paese m. ~**r** n paesano. ·a mf

villain /'vɪlən/ n furfante m; ⟨in story⟩ cattivo m

vindicate /'vɪndɪkeɪt/ vt ⟨from guilt⟩ discolpare; **you are ~d** ti sei dimostrato nel giusto

vindictive /vɪn'dɪktɪv/ a vendicativo

vine /vaɪn/ n vite f

vinegar /'vɪnɪgə(r)/ n aceto m

vineyard /'vɪnjɑːd/ n vigneto m

vintage /'vɪntɪdʒ/ a ⟨wine⟩ d'annata ● n ⟨year⟩ annata f

viola /vɪ'əʊlə/ n Mus viola f

violate /'vaɪəleɪt/ vt violare. ~**ion** /·'leɪʃn/ n violazione f

violence /'vaɪələns/ n violenza f. ~**t** a violento

violet /'vaɪələt/ a violetto ● n ⟨flower⟩ violetta f; ⟨colour⟩ violetto m

violin /vaɪə'lɪn/ n violino m. ~**ist** n violinista mf

VIP n abbr ⟨very important person⟩ vip mf

virgin /'vɜːdʒɪn/ a vergine ● n vergine f. ~**ity** /·'dʒɪnətɪ/ n verginità f

Virgo /'vɜːgəʊ/ n Astr Vergine f

virile /'vɪraɪl/ a virile. ~**ity** /·'rɪlətɪ/ n virilità f

virtual /'vɜːtjʊəl/ a effettivo. ~ **reality** n realtà f virtuale. ~**ly** adv praticamente

virtue /'vɜːtjuː/ n virtù f inv; ⟨advantage⟩ vantaggio m; **by** or **in** ~ **of** a causa di

virtuoso /vɜːtʊ'əʊzəʊ/ n ⟨pl **-si** /·'ziː⟩ virtuoso m

virtuous /'vɜːtjʊəs/ a virtuoso

virulent /'vɪrʊlənt/ a virulento

virus /'vaɪərəs/ n virus m inv

visa /'viːzə/ n visto m

vis-à-vis /viːzɑː'viː/ prep rispetto a

viscount /'vaɪkaʊnt/ n visconte m

viscous /'vɪskəs/ a vischioso

visibility /vɪzə'bɪlətɪ/ n visibilità f

visible /'vɪzəbl/ a visibile. ~**y** adv visibilmente

vision /'vɪʒn/ n visione f; ⟨sight⟩ vista f

visit /'vɪzɪt/ n visita f ● vt andare a trovare ⟨person⟩; andare da ⟨doctor etc⟩; visitare ⟨town, building⟩. ~**or** n ospite mf; ⟨of town, museum⟩ visitatore. ·trice mf; ⟨in hotel⟩ cliente mf

visor /'vaɪzə(r)/ n visiera f; Auto parasole m

vista /'vɪstə/ n ⟨view⟩ panorama m

visual /'vɪzjʊəl/ a visivo. ~ **aids** npl supporto m visivo. ~ **dis play unit** n visualizzatore m. ~**ly** adv visualmente; ~**ly handicapped** non vedente

visualize /'vɪzjʊəlaɪz/ vt visualizzare

vital /'vaɪtl/ a vitale. ~**ity** /vaɪ'tælətɪ/ n vitalità f. ~**ly** /'vaɪtəlɪ/ adv estremamente

vitamin /'vɪtəmɪn/ n vitamina f

vivacious /vɪ'veɪʃəs/ a vivace. ~**ty** /·'væsətɪ/ n vivacità f

vivid /'vɪvɪd/ a vivido. ~**ly** adv in modo vivido

vocabulary /və'kæbjʊlərɪ/ n vocabolario m; ⟨list⟩ glossario m

vocal /'vəʊkl/ a vocale; ⟨vociferous⟩ eloquente. ~ **cords** npl corde fpl vocali

vocalist /'vəʊkəlɪst/ n vocalista mf

vocation /və'keɪʃn/ n vocazione f. ~**al** a di orientamento professionale

vociferous /və'sɪfərəs/ a vociante

vodka /'vɒdkə/ n vodka f inv

vogue /vəʊg/ n moda f; **in** ~ in voga

voice /vɔɪs/ n voce f ● vt esprimere. **~mail** n posta f elettronica vocale

void /vɔɪd/ a (not valid) nullo; ~ of privo di ● n vuoto m

volatile /ˈvɒlətaɪl/ a volatile; ⟨person⟩ volubile

volcanic /vɒlˈkænɪk/ a vulcanico

volcano /vɒlˈkeɪnəʊ/ n vulcano m

volition /vəˈlɪʃn/ n of his own ~ di sua spontanea volontà

volley /ˈvɒlɪ/ n (of gunfire) raffica f; Tennis volée f inv

volt /vəʊlt/ n volt m inv. **~age** /-ɪdʒ/ n Electr voltaggio m

voluble /ˈvɒljʊbl/ a loquace

volume /ˈvɒljuːm/ n volume m; (of work, traffic) quantità f inv. **~ control** n volume m

voluntar|y /ˈvɒləntərɪ/ a volontario. **~y work** n volontariato m. **~ily** adv volontariamente

volunteer /vɒlənˈtɪə(r)/ n volontario, -a mf ● vt offrire volontariamente ⟨information⟩ ● vi offrirsi volontario; Mil arruolarsi come volontario

voluptuous /vəˈlʌptjʊəs/ a voluttuoso

vomit /ˈvɒmɪt/ n vomito m ● vt/i vomitare

voracious /vəˈreɪʃəs/ a vorace

vot|e /vəʊt/ n voto m; (ballot) votazione f; (right) diritto m di voto; **take a ~e on** votare su ● vi votare ● vt **~e sb president** eleggere qcno presidente. **~er** n elettore, -trice mf. **~ing** n votazione f

vouch /vaʊtʃ/ vi **for** garantire per. **~er** n buono m

vow /vaʊ/ n voto m ● vt giurare

vowel /ˈvaʊəl/ n vocale f

voyage /ˈvɔɪɪdʒ/ n viaggio m [marittimo]; (in space) viaggio m [nello spazio]

vulgar /ˈvʌlgə(r)/ a volgare. **~ity** /-ˈgærətɪ/ n volgarità f inv

vulnerable /ˈvʌlnərəbl/ a vulnerabile

vulture /ˈvʌltʃə(r)/ n avvoltoio m

vying /ˈvaɪɪŋ/ see vie

Ww

wad /wɒd/ n batuffolo m; (bundle) rotolo m. **~ding** n ovatta f

waddle /ˈwɒdl/ vi camminare ondeggiando

wade /weɪd/ vi guadare; ~ **through** fam procedere faticosamente in ⟨book⟩

wafer /ˈweɪfə(r)/ n cialda f, wafer m inv; Relig ostia f

waffle[1] /ˈwɒfl/ vi fam blaterare

waffle[2] n Culin cialda f

waft /wɒft/ vt trasportare ● vi diffondersi

wag /wæg/ v (pt/pp wagged) ● vt agitare ● vi agitarsi

wage[1] /weɪdʒ/ vt dichiarare ⟨war⟩; lanciare ⟨campaign⟩

wage[2] n, & ~s pl salario msg. **~ packet** n busta f paga

waggle /ˈwægl/ vt dimenare ● vi dimenarsi

wagon /ˈwægən/ n carro m; Rail vagone m merci

wail /weɪl/ n piagnucolio m; (of wind) lamento m; (of baby) vagito m ● vi piagnucolare; ⟨wind:⟩ lamentarsi; ⟨baby:⟩ vagire

waist /weɪst/ n vita f. **~coat** /ˈweɪskəʊt/ n gilè m inv; (of man's suit) panciotto m. **~line** n vita f

wait /weɪt/ n attesa f; lie in ~ **for** appostarsi per sorprendere ● vi aspettare; ~ **for** aspettare ● vt ~ **one's turn** aspettare il proprio turno. **wait on** vt servire

waiter /ˈweɪtə(r)/ n cameriere m

waiting: **~-list** n lista f d'attesa. **~-room** n sala f d'aspetto

waitress /ˈweɪtrɪs/ n cameriera f

waive /weɪv/ vt rinunciare a ⟨claim⟩; non tener conto di ⟨rule⟩

wake[1] /weɪk/ n veglia f funebre ● v (pt woke, pp woken) ~ [up] ● vt svegliare ● vi svegliarsi

wake[2] n Naut scia f; in the ~ of fig nella scia di

waken /ˈweɪkn/ vt svegliare ● vi svegliarsi

Wales /weɪlz/ n Galles m

walk /wɔːk/ n passeggiata f; (gait) andatura f; (path) sentiero m; go for a ~ andare a fare una passeggiata ● vi camminare; (as opposed to drive etc) andare a piedi; (*ramble*) passeggiare ● *vt* portare a spasso (*dog*); percorrere (*streets*). **walk out** *vi* (*husband, employee:*) andarsene; (*workers:*) scioperare. **walk out on** *vt* lasciare

walker /'wɔːkə(r)/ *n* camminatore, -trice *mf*; (*rambler*) escursionista *mf*

walking /'wɔːkɪŋ/ *n* camminare *m*; (*rambling*) fare *m* delle escursioni. **~-stick** *n* bastone *m* da passeggio

'Walkman® *n* Walkman *m inv*

walk: **~-out** *n* sciopero *m*. **~-over** *n fig* vittoria *f* facile

wall /wɔːl/ *n* muro *m*; **go to the ~** *fam* andare a rotoli; **drive sb up the ~** *fam* far diventare matto qcno ● **wall up** *vt* murare

wallet /'wɒlɪt/ *n* portafoglio *m*

wallop /'wɒləp/ *n fam* colpo *m* ● *vt* (*pt/pp* **walloped**) *fam* colpire

wallow /'wɒləʊ/ *vi* sguazzare; (*in self-pity, grief*) crogiolarsi

'wallpaper *n* tappezzeria *f* ● *vt* tappezzare

walnut /'wɔːlnʌt/ *n* noce *f*

waltz /wɔːlts/ *n* valzer *m inv* ● *vi* ballare il valzer

wan /wɒn/ *a* esangue

wand /wɒnd/ *n* (*magic ~*) bacchetta *f* [magica]

wander /'wɒndə(r)/ *vi* girovagare; (*fig: digress*) divagare. **wander about** *vi* andare a spasso

wane /weɪn/ *n* **be on the ~** essere in fase calante ● *vi* calare

wangle /'wæŋgl/ *vt fam* rimediare (*invitation, holiday*)

want /wɒnt/ *n* (*hardship*) bisogno *m*; (*lack*) mancanza *f* ● *vt* volere; (*need*) aver bisogno di; **~** [**to have**] **sth** volere qcsa; **~ to do sth** voler fare qcsa; **we ~ to stay** vogliamo rimanere; **I ~ you to go** voglio che tu vada; **it ~s painting** ha bisogno d'essere dipinto; **you ~ to learn to swim** bisogna che impari a nuotare ● *vi* **~ for** mancare di. **~ed** *a* ricercato. **~ing** *a* **be ~ing** mancare; **be ~ing in** mancare di

wanton /'wɒntən/ *a* (*cruelty, neglect*) gratuito; (*morally*) debosciato

war /wɔː(r)/ *n* guerra *f*; *fig* lotta *f* (**on** contro); **at ~** in guerra

ward /wɔːd/ *n* (*in hospital*) reparto *m*; (*child*) minore *m* sotto tutela ● **ward off** *vt* evitare; parare (*blow*)

warden /'wɔːdn/ *n* guardiano, -a *mf*

warder /'wɔːdə(r)/ *n* guardia *f* carceraria

wardrobe /'wɔːdrəʊb/ *n* guardaroba *m*

warehouse /'weəhaʊs/ *n* magazzino *m*

war: **~fare** *n* guerra *f*. **~head** *n* testata *f*

warily /'weərɪlɪ/ *adv* cautamente

warlike /'wɔːlaɪk/ *a* bellicoso

warm /wɔːm/ *a* caldo; (*welcome*) caloroso; **be ~** (*person:*) aver caldo; **it is ~** (*weather*) fa caldo ● *vt* scaldare. **warm up** *vt* scaldare ● *vi* scaldarsi; (*fig*) animarsi. **~-hearted** *a* espansivo. **~ly** *adv* (*greet*) calorosamente; (*dress*) in modo pesante

warmth /wɔːmθ/ *n* calore *m*

warn /wɔːn/ *vt* avvertire. **~ing** *n* avvertimento *m*; (*advance notice*) preavviso *m*

warp /wɔːp/ *vt* deformare; *fig* distorcere ● *vi* deformarsi

'war-path *n* **on the ~** sul sentiero di guerra

warped /wɔːpt/ *a fig* contorto; (*sexuality*) deviato; (*view*) distorto

warrant /'wɒrənt/ *n* (*for arrest, search*) mandato *m* ● *vt* (*justify*) giustificare; (*guarantee*) garantire

warranty /'wɒrəntɪ/ *n* garanzia *f*

warring /'wɔːrɪŋ/ *a* in guerra

warrior /'wɒrɪə(r)/ *n* guerriero, -a *mf*

'warship *n* nave *f* da guerra

wart /wɔːt/ *n* porro *m*

'wartime *n* tempo *m* di guerra

wary /'weərɪ/ *a* (**-ier**, **-iest**) (*careful*) cauto; (*suspicious*) diffidente

was /wɒz/ *see* **be**

wash /wɒʃ/ *n* lavata *f*; (*clothes*) bucato *m*; (*in washing machine*) lavaggio *m*; **have a ~** darsi una lavata ● *vt* lavare; (*sea:*) bagnare; **~ one's hands** lavarsi le mani ● *vi* lavarsi. **wash out** *vt* sciacquare (*soap*); sciacquarsi (*mouth*). **wash up** *vt* lavare ● *vi* lavare i piatti; *Am* lavarsi

washable /'wɒʃəbl/ *a* lavabile

wash: **~-basin** *n* lavandino *m*. **~ cloth** *n Am* guanto *m* da bagno

washed 'out *a* (*faded*) scolorito; (*tired*) spossato

washer /'wɒʃə(r)/ *n Techn* guarnizione *f*; (*machine*) lavatrice *f*

washing /'wɒʃɪŋ/ *n* bucato *m*. **~-machine** *n* lavatrice *f*. **~-powder** *n* detersivo *m*. **~-'up** *n* **do the ~-up** lavare i piatti. **~-'up liquid** *n* detersivo *m* per i piatti

wash: **~-out** *n* disastro *m*. **~-room** *n* bagno *m*

wasp /wɒsp/ *n* vespa *f*

wastage /'weɪstɪdʒ/ *n* perdita *f*

waste /weɪst/ *n* spreco *m*; (*rubbish*) rifiuto *m*; ~ **of time** perdita *f* di tempo ●*a* ⟨*product*⟩ di scarto; ⟨*land*⟩ desolato; **lay ~** devastare ●*vt* sprecare. **waste away** *vi* deperire

waste: ~**-disposal unit** *n* eliminatore *m* di rifiuti. ~**ful** *a* dispendioso. ~ **paper** *n* carta *f* straccia. ~**-paper basket** *n* cestino *m* per la carta [straccia]

watch /wɒtʃ/ *n* guardia *f*; ⟨*period of duty*⟩ turno *m* di guardia; ⟨*timepiece*⟩ orologio *m*; **be on the ~** stare all'erta ●*vt* guardare ⟨*film, match, television*⟩; ⟨*be careful of, look after*⟩ stare attento a ●*vi* guardare. **watch out** *vi* ⟨*be careful*⟩ stare attento (**for** a). **watch out for** *vt* ⟨*look for*⟩ fare attenzione all'arrivo di ⟨*person*⟩

watch: ~**-dog** *n* cane *m* da guardia. ~**ful** *a* attento. ~**maker** *n* orologiaio. *a mf.* ~**man** *n* guardiano *m*. ~**-strap** *n* cinturino *m* dell'orologio. ~**word** *n* motto *m*

water /'wɔ:ta(r)/ *n* acqua *f* ●*vt* annaffiare ⟨*garden, plant*⟩; ⟨*dilute*⟩ annacquare ●*vi* ⟨*eyes:*⟩ lacrimare; **my mouth was** ~**ing** avevo l'acquolina in bocca. **water down** *vt* diluire; *fig* attenuare

water: ~**-colour** *n* acquerello *m*. ~**cress** *n* crescione *m*. ~**fall** *n* cascata *f*

watering-can *n* annaffiatoio *m*

water: ~**-lily** *n* ninfea *f*. ~ **logged** *a* inzuppato. ~**-main** *n* conduttura *f* dell'acqua. ~ **polo** *n* pallanuoto *f*. ~**-power** *n* energia *f* idraulica. ~**proof** *a* impermeabile. ~**shed** *n* spartiacque *m* *inv*; *fig* svolta *f*. ~**-skiing** *n* sci *m* nautico. ~**tight** *a* stagno; *fig* irrefutabile. ~**way** *n* canale *m* navigabile

watery /'wɔ:tarı/ *a* acquoso; ⟨*eyes:*⟩ lacrimoso

watt /wɒt/ *n* watt *m* *inv*

wave /weɪv/ *n* onda *f*; ⟨*gesture*⟩ cenno *m*; *fig* ondata *f* ●*vt* agitare; ~ **one's hand** agitare la mano ●*vi* far segno; ⟨*flag:*⟩ sventolare. ~**length** *n* lunghezza *f* d'onda

waver /'weɪva(r)/ *vi* vacillare; ⟨*hesitate*⟩ esitare

wavy /'weɪvɪ/ *a* ondulato

wax[1] /wæks/ *vi* ⟨*moon:*⟩ crescere; ⟨*fig: become*⟩ diventare

wax[2] *n* cera *f*; ⟨*in ear*⟩ cerume *m* ●*vt* dare la cera a. ~**works** *n* museo *m* delle cere

way /weɪ/ *n* percorso *m*; ⟨*direction*⟩ direzione *f*; ⟨*manner, method*⟩ modo *m*; ~ *spl* ⟨*customs*⟩ abitudini *fpl*; **be in the ~** essere in mezzo; **on the ~ to Rome** an-

dando a Roma; **I'll do it on the ~** lo faccio mentre vado; **it's on my ~** è sul mio percorso; **a long ~ off** lontano; **this ~** da questa parte; ⟨*like this*⟩ così; **by the ~** a proposito; **by ~ of** come; ⟨*via*⟩ via; **either ~** ⟨*whatever we do*⟩ in un modo o nell'altro; **in some ~s** sotto certi aspetti; **in a ~** in un certo senso; **in a bad ~** ⟨*person*⟩ molto grave; **out of the ~** fuori mano; **under ~** in corso; **lead the ~** far strada; *fig* aprire la strada; **make ~** far posto (**for** a); **give ~** *Auto* dare la precedenza; **go out of one's ~** *fig* scomodarsi (**to** per); **get one's |own| ~** averla vinta ●*adv* ~ **behind** molto indietro. ~**in** *n* entrata *f*

way 'out *n* uscita *f*. *fig* via *f* d'uscita

way-'out *a fam* eccentrico

wayward /'weɪwad/ *a* capriccioso

WC *n abbr* WC; **the WC** il gabinetto

we /wi:/ *pers pron* noi; **we're the last** siamo gli ultimi; **they're going, but we're not** loro vanno, ma noi no

weak /wi:k/ *a* debole; ⟨*liquid*⟩ leggero. ~**en** *vt* indebolire ●*vi* indebolirsi. ~**ling** *n* smidollato, -a *mf.* ~**ness** *n* debolezza *f*; ⟨*liking*⟩ debole *m*

wealth /welθ/ *n* ricchezza *f*; *fig* gran quantità *f.* ~**y** *a* (**-ier, -iest**) ricco

wean /wi:n/ *vt* svezzare

weapon /'wepan/ *n* arma *f*

wear /wea(r)/ *n* ⟨*clothing*⟩ abbigliamento *m*; **for everyday ~** da portare tutti i giorni; ~ |**and tear**| usura *f* ●*v* (*pt* **wore**, *pp* **worn**) ●*vt* portare; ⟨*damage*⟩ consumare; ~ **a hole in** sth logorare qcsa fino a fare un buco; **what shall I ~?** cosa mi metto? ●*vi* consumarsi; ⟨*last*⟩ durare. **wear off** *vi* scomparire; ⟨*effect:*⟩ finire. **wear out** *vt* consumare [fino in fondo]; ⟨*exhaust*⟩ estenuare ●*vi* estenuarsi

wearable /'wearabl/ *a* portabile

weary /'wɪarɪ/ *a* (**-ier, -iest**) sfinito ●*v* (*pt/pp* **wearied**) ●*vt* sfinire ●*vi* ~**y of** stancarsi di. ~**ily** *adv* stancamente

weasel /'wi:zl/ *n* donnola *f*

weather /'weða(r)/ *n* tempo *m*; **in this ~** con questo tempo; **under the ~** *fam* giù di corda ●*vt* sopravvivere a ⟨*storm*⟩

weather: ~**-beaten** *a* ⟨*face*⟩ segnato dalle intemperie. ~**cock** *n* gallo *m* segnavento. ~ **forecast** *n* previsioni *fpl* del tempo

weave[1] /wi:v/ *vi* (*pt/pp* **weaved**) ⟨*move*⟩ zigzagare

491

weave² *n* tessuto *m* ● *vt* (*pt* **wove**, *pp* **woven**) tessere; intrecciare ⟨*flowers etc*⟩; intrecciare le fila di ⟨*story etc*⟩. ~r *n* tessitore, -trice *mf*

web /web/ *n* rete *f*; ⟨*of spider*⟩ ragnatela *f*. ~**bed feet** *npl* piedi *mpl* palmati. ~ **page** *n* Comput pagina *f* web; ~ **site** *n* Comput sito *m* web

wed /wed/ *vt* (*pt/pp* **wedded**) sposare ● *vi* sposarsi. ~**ding** *n* matrimonio *m*

wedding: ~ **cake** *n* torta *f* nuziale. ~ **day** *n* giorno *m* del matrimonio. ~ **dress** *n* vestito *m* da sposa. ~**-ring** *n* fede *f*

wedge /wedʒ/ *n* zeppa *f*; ⟨*for splitting wood*⟩ cuneo *m*; ⟨*of cheese*⟩ fetta *f* ● *vt* ⟨*fix*⟩ fissare

wedlock /ˈwedlɒk/ *n* **born out of** ~ nato fuori dal matrimonio

Wednesday /ˈwenzdeɪ/ *n* mercoledì *m inv*

wee¹ /wiː/ *a fam* piccolo

wee² *vi fam* fare la pipì

weed /wiːd/ *n* erbaccia *f*; ⟨*fam: person*⟩ mollusco *m* ● *vt* estirpare le erbacce da ● *vi* estirpare le erbacce. **weed out** *vt fig* eliminare

weed-killer *n* erbicida *m*

weedy /ˈwiːdɪ/ *a fam* mingherlino

week /wiːk/ *n* settimana *f*. ~**day** *n* giorno *m* feriale. ~**end** *n* fine *m* settimana

weekly /ˈwiːklɪ/ *a* settimanale ● *n* settimanale *m* ● *adv* settimanalmente

weep /wiːp/ *vi* (*pt/pp* **wept**) piangere

weigh /weɪ/ *vt/i* pesare; ~ **anchor** levare l'ancora. **weigh down** *vt fig* piegare. **weigh up** *vt fig* soppesare; valutare ⟨*person*⟩

weight /weɪt/ *n* peso *m*; **put on/lose** ~ ingrassare/dimagrire. ~**ing** *n* ⟨*allowance*⟩ indennità *f inv*

weight: ~**lessness** *n* assenza *f* di gravità. ~**-lifting** *n* sollevamento *m* pesi

weighty /ˈweɪtɪ/ *a* (**-ier, -iest**) pesante; ⟨*important*⟩ di un certo peso

weir /wɪə(r)/ *n* chiusa *f*

weird /wɪəd/ *a* misterioso; ⟨*bizarre*⟩ bizzarro

welcome /ˈwelkəm/ *a* benvenuto; **you're ~!** prego!; **you're ~ to have it**/**to come** prendilo/vieni pure ● *n* accoglienza *f* ● *vt* accogliere; ⟨*appreciate*⟩ gradire

weld /weld/ *vt* saldare. ~**er** *n* saldatore *m*

welfare /ˈwelfeə(r)/ *n* benessere *m*; ⟨*aid*⟩ assistenza *f*. **W~ State** *n* Stato *m* assistenziale

well¹ /wel/ *n* pozzo *m*; ⟨*of staircase*⟩ tromba *f*

well² *adv* (**better, best**) bene; **as** ~ anche; **as** ~ **as** ⟨*in addition*⟩ oltre a; ~ **done!** bravo!; **very** ~ benissimo ● *a* **he is not** ~ non sta bene; **get** ~ **soon!** guarisci presto! ● *int* beh!; ~ **I never!** ma va!

well: ~**-behaved** *a* educato. ~**-being** *n* benessere *m*. ~**-bred** *a* beneducato. ~**-heeled** *a fam* danaroso

wellingtons /ˈwelɪŋtənz/ *npl* stivali *mpl* di gomma

well: ~**-known** *a* famoso. ~**-meaning** *a* con buone intenzioni. ~**-meant** *a* con le migliori intenzioni. ~**-off** *a* benestante. ~**-read** *a* colto. ~**-to-do** *a* ricco

Welsh /welʃ/ *a & n* gallese; ⟨*language*⟩ gallese *m*; **the** ~ *pl* i gallesi. ~**man** *n* gallese *m*. ~ **rabbit** *n* toast *m inv* al formaggio

went /went/ *see* **go**

wept /wept/ *see* **weep**

were /wɜː(r)/ *see* **be**

west /west/ *n* ovest *m*; **to the** ~ **of** a ovest di; **the W~** l'Occidente *m* ● *a* occidentale ● *adv* verso occidente; **go** ~ *fam* andare in malora. ~**erly** *a* verso ovest; occidentale ⟨*wind*⟩. ~**ern** *a* occidentale ● *n* western *m inv*

West: ~ **Germany** *n* Germania *f* Occidentale. ~ **Indian** *a & n* antillese *mf*. ~ **Indies** /ˈɪndɪz/ *npl* Antille *fpl*

westward[s] /-wəd[z]/ *adv* verso ovest

wet /wet/ *a* (**wetter, wettest**) bagnato; fresco ⟨*paint*⟩; ⟨*rainy*⟩ piovoso; ⟨*fam: person*⟩ smidollato; **get** ~ bagnarsi ● *vt* (*pt/pp* **wet, wetted**) bagnare. ~ **blanket** *n* guastafeste *mf inv*

whack /wæk/ *n fam* colpo *m* ● *vt fam* dare un colpo a. ~**ed** *a fam* stanco morto. ~**ing** *a* ⟨*fam: huge*⟩ enorme

whale /weɪl/ *n* balena *f*; **have a** ~ **of a time** *fam* divertirsi un sacco

wham /wæm/ *int* bum

wharf /wɔːf/ *n* banchina *f*

what /wɒt/ *pron* che, [che] cosa; ~ **for?** perché?; ~ **is that for?** a che cosa serve?; ~ **is it?** com'è?; ~ **is your name?** come ti chiami?; ~ **is the weather like?** com'è il tempo?; ~ **is the film about?** di cosa parla il film?; ~ **is he talking about?** di cosa sta parlando?; **he asked me** ~ **she had said** mi ha chiesto cosa ha detto; ~ **about going to the cinema?** e se andassimo al cinema?; ~ **about the children?** (*what will they do*) e i bambini?; ~ **if it rains?** e se piove? ● *a* quale, che; **take** ~ **books you want** prendi tutti i libri che vuoi; ~ **kind of** a che tipo di; **at** ~ **time?** a che ora? ● *adv* che; ~ **a lovely day!** che bella giornata! ● *int* ~! [che] cosa!; ~? [che] cosa?

what'ever *a* qualunque ● *pron* qualsiasi cosa, ~ **is it?** cos'è?; ~ **he does** qualsiasi cosa faccia; ~ **happens** qualunque cosa succeda; **nothing** ~ proprio niente

whatso'ever *a & pron* = whatever

wheat /wi:t/ *n* grano *m*, frumento *m*

wheedle /'wi:d(ə)l/ *vt* ~ **sth out of sb** ottenere qcsa da qualcuno con le lusinghe

wheel /wi:l/ *n* ruota *f*; (*steering* ~) volante *m*; **at the** ~ al volante ● *vt* (*push*) spingere ● *vi* (*circle*) ruotare; ~ (*round*) ruotare

wheel: ~barrow *n* carriola *f*. ~chair *n* sedia *f* a rotelle. ~-clamp *n* ceppo *m* bloccaruote

wheeze /wi:z/ *vi* ansimare

when /wen/ *adv & conj* quando; **the day** ~ il giorno in cui; ~ **swimming/reading** nuotando/leggendo

when'ever *adv & conj* in qualsiasi momento; (*every time that*) ogni volta che; ~ **did it happen?** quando è successo?

where /weə(r)/ *adv & conj* dove; **the street** ~ **I live** la via in cui abito; ~ **do you come from?** da dove vieni?

whereabouts¹ /weərə'baʊts/ *adv* dove

'whereabouts² *n* **nobody knows his** ~ nessuno sa dove si trova

where'as *adv* dal momento che; (*in contrast*) mentre

where'by *adv* attraverso il quale

whereu'pon *adv* dopo di che

wher'ever *adv & conj* dovunque; ~ **is he?** dov'è mai?; ~ **possible** dovunque sia possibile

whet /wet/ *vt* (*pt/pp* whetted) aguzzare (*appetite*)

whether /'weðə(r)/ *conj* se; ~ **you like it or not** che ti piaccia o no

which /wɪtʃ/ *a & pron* quale; ~ **one?** quale?; ~ **one of you?** chi di voi?; ~ **way?** (*direction*) in che direzione? ● *rel pron* (*object*) che; ~ **he does frequently** cosa che fa spesso; **after** ~ dopo di che; **on/in** ~ su/in cui

which'ever *a & pron* qualunque; ~ **it is** qualunque sia; ~ **one of you** chiunque tra voi

whiff /wɪf/ *n* zaffata *f*; **have a** ~ **of sth** odorare qcsa

while /waɪl/ *n* **a long** ~ un bel po'; **a little** ~ un po' ● *conj* mentre; (*as long as*) finché; (*although*) sebbene ● **while away** *vt* passare (*time*)

whilst /waɪlst/ *conj* see while

whim /wɪm/ *n* capriccio *m*

whimper /'wɪmpə(r)/ *vi* piagnucolare; (*dog:*) mugolare

whimsical /'wɪmzɪkl/ *a* capriccioso; (*story*) fantasioso

whine /waɪn/ *n* lamento *m*; (*of dog*) guaito *m* ● *vi* lamentarsi; (*dog:*) guaire

whip /wɪp/ *n* frusta *f*; (*Pol: person*) parlamentare *mf* incaricato, -a di assicurarsi della presenza dei membri del suo partito alle votazioni ● *vt* (*pt/pp* whipped) frustare; *Culin* sbattere; (*snatch*) afferrare; (*fam: steal*) fregare. **whip up** *vt* (*incite*) stimolare; *fam* improvvisare (*meal*). ~ped 'cream *n* panna *f* montata

whirl /wɜːl/ *n* (*movement*) rotazione *f*; **my mind's in a** ~ ho le idee confuse ● *vi* girare rapidamente ● *vt* far girare rapidamente. ~ **pool** *n* vortice *m*. ~ **wind** *n* turbine *m*

whirr /wɜː(r)/ *vi* ronzare

whisk /wɪsk/ *n Culin* frullino *m* ● *vt Culin* frullare. **whisk away** *vt* portare via

whisker /'wɪskə(r)/ *n* ~s baffi *mpl*; (*on man's face*) basette *fpl*; **by a** ~ per un pelo

whisky /'wɪskɪ/ *n* whisky *m inv*

whisper /'wɪspə(r)/ *n* sussurro *m*; (*rumour*) diceria *f* ● *vt/i* sussurrare

whistle /'wɪsl/ *n* fischio *m*; (*instrument*) fischietto *m* ● *vt* fischiettare ● *vi* fischiettare; (*referee:*) fischiare

white /waɪt/ *a* bianco; **go** ~ (*pale*) sbiancare ● *n* bianco *m*; (*of egg*) albume *m*; (*person*) bianco, -a *mf*

white: ~ 'coffee *n* caffè *m inv* macchiato. ~-'collar worker *n* colletto *m* bianco

'Whitehall *n* strada *f* di Londra, sede degli uffici del governo britannico; *fig* amministrazione *f* britannica

white 'lie *n* bugia *f* pietosa

whiten /'waɪtn/ *vt* imbiancare ● *vi* sbiancare

whiteness /'waɪtnɪs/ *n* bianchezza *f*

'whitewash *n* intonaco *m*; *fig* copertura *f* ● *vt* dare una mano d'intonaco a; *fig* coprire

Whitsun /'wɪtsn/ *n* Pentecoste *f*

whittle /'wɪtl/ *vt* ~ **down** ridurre

whiz[z] /wɪz/ *vi* (*pt/pp* **whizzed**) sibilare. **~-kid** *n fam* giovane *m* prodigio

who /hu:/ *inter pron* chi ● *rel pron* che; **the children, ~ were all tired,...** i bambini, che erano tutti stanchi,...

who'ever *pron* chiunque; **~ he is** chiunque sia; **~ can that be?** chi può mai essere?

whole /həʊl/ *a* tutto; (*not broken*) intatto; **the ~ truth** tutta la verità; **the ~ world** il mondo intero; **the ~ lot** (*everything*) tutto; (*pl*) tutti; **the ~ lot of you** tutti voi ● *n* tutto *m*; **as a ~** nell'insieme; **on the ~** tutto considerato; **the ~ of Italy** tutta l'Italia

whole: **~food** *n* cibo *m* macrobiotico. **~-'hearted** *a* di tutto cuore. **~meal** *a* integrale

wholesale *a & adv* all'ingrosso; *fig in* massa. **~r** *n* grossista *mf*

wholesome /'həʊlsəm/ *a* sano

wholly /'həʊlɪ/ *adv* completamente

whom /hu:m/ *rel pron* che; **the man ~ I saw** l'uomo che ho visto; **to/with ~** a/con cui ● *inter pron* chi; **to ~ did you speak?** con chi hai parlato?

whooping cough /'hu:pɪŋ/ *n* pertosse *f*

whopping /'wɒpɪŋ/ *a fam* enorme

whore /hɔ:(r)/ *n* puttana *f vulg*

whose /hu:z/ *rel pron* il cui; **people ~ name begins with D** le persone i cui nomi cominciano con la D ● *inter pron* di chi; **~ is that?** di chi è quello? ● *a* **~ car did you use?** di chi è la macchina che hai usato?

why /waɪ/ *adv* (*inter*) perché; **the reason ~** la ragione per cui; **that's ~** per questo ● *int* diamine

wick /wɪk/ *n* stoppino *m*

wicked /'wɪkɪd/ *a* cattivo; (*mischievous*) malizioso

wicker /'wɪkə(r)/ *n* vimini *mpl* ● *attrib* di vimini

wide /waɪd/ *a* largo; (*experience, knowledge*) vasto; (*difference*) profondo; (*far from target*) lontano; **10 cm ~** largo 10 cm; **how ~ is it?** quanto è largo? ● *adv* (*off target*) lontano dal bersaglio; **~ awake** del tutto sveglio; **~ open** spalancato; **far and ~** in lungo e in largo. **~ly** *adv* largamente; (*known, accepted*) generalmente; (*different*) profondamente

widen /'waɪdn/ *vt* allargare ● *vi* allargarsi

widespread *a* diffuso

widow /'wɪdəʊ/ *n* vedova *f*. **~ed** *a* vedovo. **~er** *n* vedovo *m*

width /wɪdθ/ *n* larghezza *f*; (*of material*) altezza *f*

wield /wi:ld/ *vt* maneggiare; esercitare (*power*)

wife /waɪf/ *n* (*pl* **wives**) moglie *f*

wig /wɪg/ *n* parrucca *f*

wiggle /'wɪgl/ *vi* dimenarsi ● *vt* dimenare

wild /waɪld/ *a* selvaggio; (*animal, flower*) selvatico; (*furious*) furibondo; (*applause*) fragoroso; (*idea*) folle; (*with joy*) pazzo; (*guess*) azzardato; **be ~ about** (*keen on*) andare pazzo per ● *adv* **run ~** crescere senza controllo ● *n* **in the ~** allo stato naturale; **the ~s** *pl* le zone sperdute

wilderness /'wɪldənɪs/ *n* deserto *m*; (*fig: garden*) giungla *f*

wildfire *n* **spread like ~** allargarsi a macchia d'olio

wild: **~-'goose chase** *n* ricerca *f* inutile. **~life** *n* animali *mpl* selvatici

wilful /'wɪlfl/ *a* intenzionale; (*person, refusal*) ostinato. **~ly** *adv* intenzionalmente; (*refuse*) ostinatamente

will[1] /wɪl/ *v aux* **he ~ arrive tomorrow** arriverà domani; **I won't tell him** non glielo dirò; **you ~ be back soon, won't you?** tornerai presto, no?; **he ~ be there, won't he?** sarà là, no?; **she ~ be there by now** sarà là ormai; **~ you go?** (*do you intend to go*) pensi di andare?; **~ you go to the baker's and buy...?** puoi andare dal panettiere a comprare...?; **~ you be quiet!** vuoi stare calmo!; **~ you have some wine?** vuoi del vino?; **the engine won't start** la macchina non parte

will[2] *n* volontà *f inv*; (*document*) testamento *m*

willing /'wɪlɪŋ/ *a* disposto; (*eager*) volonteroso. **~ly** *adv* volentieri. **~ness** *n* buona volontà *f*

willow /'wɪləʊ/ *n* salice *m*

will-power *n* forza *f* di volontà

willy-'nilly *adv* (*at random*) a casaccio; (*wanting to or not*) volente o nolente

wilt /wɪlt/ *vi* appassire

wily /'waɪlɪ/ *a* (**-ier, -iest**) astuto

wimp /wɪmp/ *n* rammollito, -a *mf*

win /wɪn/ *n* vittoria *f*; **have a ~** riportare una vittoria ● *v* (*pt/pp* **won**; *pres p* **winning**) ● *vt* vincere; conquistare (*fame*) ● *vi* vincere. **win over** *vt* convincere

wince /wɪns/ vi contrarre il viso

winch /wɪntʃ/ n argano m

wind¹ /wɪnd/ n vento m; (breath) fiato m; (fam: flatulence) aria f; **get/have the ~ up** fam aver fifa; **get ~ of** aver sentore di; **in the ~** nell'aria ● vt ~ **sb** lasciare qcno senza fiato

wind² /waɪnd/ v (pt/pp wound) ● vt (wrap) avvolgere; (move by turning) far girare; caricare (clock) ● vi (road:) serpeggiare. **wind up** vt caricare (clock); concludere (proceedings); fam prendere in giro (sb)

wind /wɪnd/: **~fall** n fig fortuna f inaspettata

winding /'waɪndɪŋ/ a tortuoso

wind: **~instrument** n strumento m a fiato. **~mill** n mulino m a vento

window /'wɪndəʊ/ n finestra f; (of car) finestrino m; (of shop) vetrina f

window: **~box** n cassetta f per i fiori. **~cleaner** n (person) lavavetri m inv. **~dresser** n vetrinista mf. **~dressing** n vetrinistica f; fig fumo m negli occhi. **~pane** n vetro m. **~shopping** n: **go ~shopping** andare in giro a vedere le vetrine. **~sill** n davanzale m

windscreen n, Am **windshield** n parabrezza m inv. **~washer** n getto m d'acqua. **~wiper** n tergicristallo m

wind: **~surfing** n windsurf m inv. **~swept** a esposto al vento; (person) scompigliato

windy /'wɪndɪ/ a (-ier, -iest) ventoso

wine /waɪn/ n vino m

wine: **~bar** n ≈ enoteca f. **~glass** n bicchiere m da vino. **~list** n carta f dei vini

winery /'waɪnərɪ/ n Am vigneto m

wine-tasting n degustazione f di vini

wing /wɪŋ/ n ala f; Auto parafango m; **~s** pl Theat quinte fpl. **~er** n Sport ala f

wink /wɪŋk/ n strizzata f d'occhio; **not sleep a ~** non chiudere occhio ● vi strizzare l'occhio; (light:) lampeggiare

winner /'wɪnə(r)/ n vincitore, -trice mf

winning /'wɪnɪŋ/ a vincente; (smile) accattivante. **~post** n linea f d'arrivo. **~s** npl vincite fpl

wint|er /'wɪntə(r)/ n inverno m. **~ry** a invernale

wipe /waɪp/ n passata f; (to dry) asciugata f ● vt strofinare; (dry) asciugare. **wipe off** vt asciugare; (erase) cancellare. **wipe out** vt annientare; eliminare (village); estinguere (debt). **wipe up** vt asciugare (dishes)

wire /'waɪə(r)/ n fil m di ferro; (electrical) filo m elettrico

wireless /'waɪəlɪs/ n radio f inv

wire netting n rete f metallica

wiring /'waɪərɪŋ/ n impianto m elettrico

wiry /'waɪərɪ/ a (-ier, -iest) (person) dal fisico asciutto; (hair) aspido m

wisdom /'wɪzdəm/ n saggezza f; (of action) sensatezza f. **~ tooth** n dente m del giudizio

wise /waɪz/ a saggio; (prudent) sensato. **~ly** adv saggiamente; (act) sensatamente

wish /wɪʃ/ n desiderio m; **make a ~** esprimere un desiderio; **with best ~es** con i migliori auguri ● vt desiderare; **~ sb well** fare tanti auguri a qcno; **I ~ you every success** ti auguro buona fortuna; **I ~ you could stay** vorrei che tu potessi rimanere ● vi **~ for sth** desiderare qcsa. **~ful** a **~ful thinking** illusione f

wishy-washy /'wɪʃɪwɒʃɪ/ a (colour) spento; (personality) insignificante

wisp /wɪsp/ n (of hair) ciocca f; (of smoke) filo m; (of grass) ciuffo m

wistful /'wɪstfl/ a malinconico

wit /wɪt/ n spirito m; (person) persona f di spirito; **be at one's ~s' end** non saper che pesci pigliare

witch /wɪtʃ/ n strega f. **~craft** n magia f. **~hunt** n caccia f alle streghe

with /wɪð/ prep con; (fear, cold, jealousy etc) di; **I'm not ~ you** fam non ti seguo; **can I leave it ~ you?** (task) puoi occupartene tu?; **~ no regrets/money** senza rimpianti/soldi; **be ~ it** fam essere al passo coi tempi; (alert) essere concentrato

with'draw v (pt -drew, pp -drawn) ● vt ritirare; prelevare (money) ● vi ritirarsi. **~al** n ritiro m; (of money) prelevamento m; (from drugs) crisi f inv di astinenza; Psych chiusura f in se stessi. **~al symptoms** npl sintomi mpl da crisi di astinenza

with'drawn see **withdraw** ● a (person) chiuso in se stesso

wither /'wɪðə(r)/ vi (flower:) appassire

with'hold vt (pt/pp -held) rifiutare (consent) (from a); nascondere (information) (from a); trattenere (smile)

with'in prep in; (before the end of) entro; **~ the law** legale ● adv all'interno

with'out prep senza; **~ stopping** senza fermarsi

with'stand vt (pt/pp -stood) resistere a

witness /'wɪtnɪs/ n testimone mf ● vt autenticare (signature); essere testimone di ⟨accident⟩. **~-box** Am **~-stand** n banco m dei testimoni

witticism /'wɪtɪsɪzm/ n spiritosaggine f

wittingly /'wɪtɪŋlɪ/ adv consapevolmente

witty /'wɪtɪ/ a (-ier, -iest) spiritoso

wives /waɪvz/ see **wife**

wizard /'wɪzəd/ n mago m. **~ry** n stregoneria f

wobb|le /'wɒbl/ vi traballare. **~ly** a traballante

wodge /wɒdʒ/ n fam mucchio m

woe /wəʊ/ n afflizione f

woke, woken /wəʊk, 'wəʊkn/ see **wake**[1]

wolf /wʊlf/ n (pl **wolves** /wʊlvz/) lupo m; ⟨fam: womanizer⟩ donnaiolo m ● vt **~ (down)** divorare. **~ whistle** n fischio m ● vi **~-whistle at sb** fischiare dietro a qcno

woman /'wʊmən/ n (pl **women**) donna f. **~izer** n donnaiolo m. **~ly** a femmineo

womb /wuːm/ n utero m

women /'wɪmɪn/ see **woman**. **W~'s Libber** /'lɪbə(r)/ n feminista f. **W~'s Liberation** n movimento m femminista

won /wʌn/ see **win**

wonder /'wʌndə(r)/ n meraviglia f; ⟨surprise⟩ stupore m; **no ~!** non c'è da stupirsi!; **it's a ~ that...** è incredibile che... ● vi restare in ammirazione; ⟨be surprised⟩ essere sorpreso; **I ~** è quello che mi chiedo; **I ~ whether she is ill** mi chiedo se è malata?. **~ful** a meraviglioso. **~fully** adv meravigliosamente

won't /wəʊnt/ = **will not**

woo /wuː/ vt corteggiare; fig cercare di accattivarsi ⟨voters⟩

wood /wʊd/ n legno m; ⟨for burning⟩ legna f; ⟨forest⟩ bosco m; **out of the ~** fig fuori pericolo; **touch ~!** tocca ferro!

wood: **~ed** /-ɪd/ a boscoso. **~en** a di legno; fig legnoso. **~ wind** n strumenti mpl a fiato. **~ work** n ⟨wooden parts⟩ parti fpl in legno; ⟨craft⟩ falegnameria f. **~worm** n tarlo m. **~y** a legnoso; ⟨hill⟩ boscoso

wool /wʊl/ n lana f ● attrib di lana. **~len** a di lana. **~lens** npl capi mpl di lana

woolly /'wʊlɪ/ a (-ier, -iest) ⟨sweater⟩ di lana; fig confuso

word /wɜːd/ n parola f; ⟨news⟩ notizia f; **by ~ of mouth** a viva voce; **have a ~ with** dire due parole; **have ~s** bisticciare; **in other ~s** in altre parole. **~ing** n parole fpl. **~ processor** n programma m di videoscrittura, word processor m inv

wore /wɔː(r)/ see **wear**

work /wɜːk/ n lavoro m; ⟨of art⟩ opera f; **~s** pl ⟨factory⟩ fabbrica fsg; ⟨mechanism⟩ meccanismo msg; **at ~** al lavoro; **out of ~** disoccupato ● vi lavorare; ⟨machine, ruse⟩ funzionare; ⟨study⟩ studiare ● vt far funzionare ⟨machine⟩; far lavorare ⟨employee⟩; far studiare ⟨student⟩. **work off** vt sfogare ⟨anger⟩; lavorare per estinguere ⟨debt⟩; fare sport per smaltire ⟨weight⟩. **work out** vt elaborare ⟨plan⟩; risolvere ⟨problem⟩; calcolare ⟨bill⟩; **I ~ed out how he did it** ho capito come l'ha fatto ● vi evolvere. **work up** vt **I've ~ed up an appetite** mi è venuto appetito; **don't get ~ed up** ⟨anxious⟩ non farti prendere dal panico; ⟨angry⟩ non arrabbiarti

workable /'wɜːkəbl/ a ⟨feasible⟩ fattibile

workaholic /wɜːkə'hɒlɪk/ n staccanovista mf

worker /'wɜːkə(r)/ n lavoratore, -trice mf; ⟨manual⟩ operaio, -a mf

working /'wɜːkɪŋ/ a ⟨clothes etc⟩ da lavoro; ⟨day⟩ feriale; **in ~ order** funzionante. **~ class** n classe f operaia. **~-class** a operaio

work: **~man** n operaio m. **~manship** n lavorazione f. **~out** n allenamento m. **~shop** n officina f; ⟨discussion⟩ dibattito m

world /wɜːld/ n mondo m; **a ~ of difference** una differenza abissale; **out of this ~** favoloso; **think the ~ of sb** andare matto per qcno. **~ly** a materiale; ⟨person⟩ materialista. **~-wide** a mondiale ● adv mondialmente

worm /wɜːm/ n verme m ● vt **~ one's way into sb's confidence** conquistarsi la fiducia di qcno in modo subdolo. **~-eaten** a tarlato

worn /wɔːn/ see **wear** ● a sciupato. **~-out** a consumato; ⟨person⟩ sfinito

worried /'wʌrɪd/ a preoccupato

worry /'wʌrɪ/ n preoccupazione f ● v (pt/pp **worried**) ● vt preoccupare; ⟨bother⟩ disturbare ● vi preoccuparsi. **~ing** a preoccupante

worse /wɜːs/ a peggiore ● adv peggio ● n peggio m

worsen /'wɜːsn/ vt/i peggiorare

worship /'wɜːʃɪp/ n culto m; ⟨service⟩ funzione f; **Your/His W~** ⟨to judge⟩ signor giudice/il giudice ● v (pt/pp **-shipped**) ● vt venerare ● vi andare a messa

worst /wɜːst/ a peggiore ● adv peggio

[di tutti]● *n* the ~ il peggio; get the ~ of it avere la peggio; if the ~ comes to the ~ nella peggiore delle ipotesi

worth /wɜːθ/ *n* valore *m*; £10 ~ of petrol 10 sterline di benzina ● *a* be ~ valere; be ~ it *fig* valerne la pena; it's ~ trying vale la pena di provare; it's ~ my while mi conviene. ~less *a* senza valore. ~while *a* che vale la pena; ⟨cause⟩ lodevole

worthy /'wɜːðɪ/ *a* degno; ⟨cause, motive⟩ lodevole

would /wʊd/ *v aux* I ~ do it lo farei; ~ you go? andresti?; ~ you mind if I opened the window? ti dispiace se apro la finestra?; he ~ come if he could verrebbe se potesse; he said he ~n't ha detto di no; ~ you like a drink? vuoi qualcosa da bere?; what ~ you like to drink? cosa prendi da bere?; you ~n't, ~ you? non lo faresti, vero?

wound[1] /'wuːnd/ *n* ferita *f* ● *vt* ferire

wound[2] /waʊnd/ *see* wind[2]

wove, woven /wəʊv, 'wəʊvn/ *see* weave[2]

wrangle /'ræŋgl/ *n* litigio *m* ● *vi* litigare

wrap /ræp/ *n* ⟨shawl⟩ scialle *m* ● *vt* (*pt/pp* wrapped) ~ [up] avvolgere; incartare ⟨present⟩; be ~ped up in *fig* essere completamente preso da ● *vi* ~ up warmly coprirsi bene. ~per *n* ⟨for sweet⟩ carta *f* [di caramella]. ~ping *n* materiale *m* da imballaggio. ~ping paper *n* carta *f* da pacchi; ⟨for gift⟩ carta *f* da regalo

wrath /rɒθ/ *n* ira *f*

wreak /riːk/ *vt* ~ havoc with sth scombussolare qcsa

wreath /riːθ/ *n* (*pl* ~s /-ðz/) corona *f*

wreck /rek/ *n* ⟨of ship⟩ relitto *m*; ⟨of car⟩ carcassa *f*; ⟨person⟩ rottame *m* ● *vt* far naufragare; demolire ⟨car⟩. ~age /-ɪdʒ/ *n* rottami *mpl*; *fig* brandelli *mpl*

wrench /rentʃ/ *n* ⟨injury⟩ slogatura *f*; ⟨tool⟩ chiave *f* inglese; ⟨pull⟩ strattone *m* ● *vt* ⟨pull⟩ strappare; slogarsi ⟨wrist, ankle etc⟩

wrest /rest/ *vt* strappare (from a)

wrestl|e /'resl/ *vi* lottare corpo a cor-

po; *fig* lottare. ~er *n* lottatore, -trice *mf*. ~ing *n* lotta *f* libera; ⟨all-in⟩ catch *m*

wretch /retʃ/ *n* disgraziato, -a *mf*. ~ed /-ɪd/ *a* odioso; ⟨weather⟩ orribile; feel ~ed ⟨unhappy⟩ essere triste; ⟨ill⟩ sentirsi malissimo

wriggle /'rɪgl/ *n* contorsione *f* ● *vi* contorcersi; ⟨move forward⟩ strisciare; ~ out of sth *fam* sottrarsi a qcsa

wring /rɪŋ/ *vt* (*pt/pp* wrung) torcere ⟨sb's neck⟩; strizzare ⟨clothes⟩; ~ one's hands torcersi le mani; ~ing wet inzuppato

wrinkle /'rɪŋkl/ *n* grinza *f*; ⟨on skin⟩ ruga *f* ● *vt/i* raggrinzire. ~d *a* ⟨skin, face⟩ rugoso; ⟨clothes⟩ raggrinzito

wrist /rɪst/ *n* polso *m*. ~-watch *n* orologio *m* da polso

writ /rɪt/ *n* Jur mandato *m*

write /raɪt/ *vt/i* (*pt* wrote, *pp* written, *pres p* writing) scrivere. write down *vt* annotare. write off *vt* cancellare ⟨debt⟩; distruggere ⟨car⟩

'write-off *n* ⟨car⟩ rottame *m*

writer /'raɪtə(r)/ *n* autore, -trice *mf*; she's a ~ è una scrittrice

'write-up *n* ⟨review⟩ recensione *f*

writhe /raɪð/ *vi* contorcersi

writing /'raɪtɪŋ/ *n* ⟨occupation⟩ scrivere *m*; ⟨words⟩ scritte *fpl*; ⟨handwriting⟩ scrittura *f*; in ~ per iscritto. ~-paper *n* carta *f* da lettera

written /'rɪtn/ *see* write

wrong /rɒŋ/ *a* sbagliato; be ~ ⟨person:⟩ sbagliare; what's ~? cosa c'è che non va? ● *adv* sbagliato; go ~ ⟨person:⟩ sbagliare; ⟨machine:⟩ funzionare male; ⟨plan:⟩ andar male ● *n* ingiustizia *f*; in the ~ dalla parte del torto; know right from ~ distinguere il bene dal male ● *vt* fare torto a. ~ful *a* ingiusto. ~ly *adv* in modo sbagliato; ⟨accuse, imagine⟩ a torto; ⟨informed⟩ male

wrote /rəʊt/ *see* write

wrought 'iron /rɔːt-/ *n* ferro *m* battuto ● *attrib* di ferro battuto

wrung /rʌŋ/ *see* wring

wry /raɪ/ *a* (-er, -est) ⟨humour, smile⟩ beffardo

Xx

Xmas /'krɪsməs/ *n fam* Natale *m*
'X-ray *n (picture)* radiografia *f*; **have**
an ~ farsi fare una radiografia ● *vt*
passare ai raggi X

Yy

yacht /jɒt/ *n* yacht *m inv*; *(for racing)*
barca *f* a vela. ~**ing** vela *f*
Yank /jæŋk/ *n fam* americano, -a *mf*
yank *vt fam* tirare
yap /jæp/ *vi (pt/pp yapped)* ⟨*dog:*⟩ guaire
yard¹ /jɑːd/ *n* cortile *m*; *(for storage)* deposito *m*
yard² *n* iarda *f* (= 91,44 cm). ~**stick** *n*
fig pietra *f* di paragone
yarn /jɑːn/ *n* filo *m*; *(fam: tale)* storia *f*
yawn /jɔːn/ *n* sbadiglio *m* ● *vi* sbadi-
gliare. ~**ing** *a* ~**ing gap** sbadiglio *m*
year /jɪə(r)/ *n* anno *m*; *(of wine)* annata *f*;
for ~**s** *fam* da secoli. ~**book** *n* annuario
m. ~**ly** *a* annuale ● *adv* annualmente
yearn /jɜːn/ *vi* struggersi. ~**ing** *n* desiderio *m* struggente
yeast /jiːst/ *n* lievito *m*
yell /jel/ *n* urlo *m* ● *vi* urlare
yellow /'jeləʊ/ *a & n* giallo *m*
yelp /jelp/ *n (of dog)* guaito *m* ● *vi*
⟨*dog:*⟩ guaire
yen /jen/ *n* forte desiderio *m* (**for** di)
yes /jes/ *adv* sì ● *n* sì *m inv*
yesterday /'jestədeɪ/ *n & adv* ieri *m*
inv; ~**'s paper** il giornale di ieri; **the
day before** ~ l'altroieri
yet /jet/ *adv* ancora; **as** ~ fino ad ora;
not ~ non ancora; **the best** ~ il migliore finora ● *conj* eppure
yew /juː/ *n* tasso *m (albero)*
yield /jiːld/ *n* produzione *f*; *(profit)* reddito *m* ● *vt* produrre; fruttare ⟨*profit*⟩
● *vi* cedere; *Am Auto* dare la precedenza
yodel /'jəʊdl/ *vi (pt/pp yodelled)* cantare jodel

yoga /'jəʊgə/ *n* yoga *m*
yoghurt /'jɒgət/ *n* yogurt *m inv*
yoke /jəʊk/ *n* giogo *m*; *(of garment)*
carré *m inv*
yokel /'jəʊkl/ *n* zotico, -a *mf*
yolk /jəʊk/ *n* tuorlo *m*
you /juː/ *pers pron (subject)* tu, voi *pl*;
(formal) lei, voi *pl*; *(direct/indirect object)*
ti, vi *pl*; *(formal: direct object)* la; *(formal:
indirect object)* le; *(after prep)* te, voi *pl*;
(formal: after prep) lei; ~ **are very kind**
(sg) sei molto gentile; *(formal)* è molto
gentile; *(pl & formal pl)* siete molto genti-
li; ~ **can stay, but he has to go** *(sg)* tu
puoi rimanere, ma lui deve andarsene;
(pl) voi potete rimanere, ma lui deve andarsene; **all of** ~ tutti voi; **I'll give** ~
the money *(sg)* ti darò i soldi; *(pl)* vi
darò i soldi; **I'll give it to** ~ *(sg)* te/*(pl)* ve
lo darò; **it was** ~! *(sg)* eri tu!; *(pl)* eravate
voi!; ~ **have to be careful** *(one)* si deve
fare attenzione
young /jʌŋ/ *a* giovane ● *npl (animals)*
piccoli *mpl*; **the** ~ *(people)* i giovani. ~
lady *n* signorina *f*. ~ **man** *n* giovanotto
m. ~**ster** *n* ragazzo, -a *mf*; *(child)* bambino, -a *mf*
your /jɔː(r)/ *poss a* il tuo *m*, la tua *f*, i
tuoi *mpl*, le tue *fpl*; *(formal)* il suo *m*, la
sua *f*, i suoi *mpl*, le sue *fpl*; *(pl & formal
pl)* il vostro *m*, la vostra *f*, i vostri *mpl*,
le vostre *fpl*; ~ **mother/father** tua
madre/tuo padre; *(formal)* sua
madre/suo padre; *(pl & formal pl)* vostra madre/vostro padre
yours /jɔːz/ *poss pron* il tuo *m*, la tua *f*, i
tuoi *mpl*, le tue *fpl*; *(formal)* il suo *m*, la

sua *f*. i suoi *mpl*, le sue *fpl*; (*pl & formal pl*) il vostro *m*, la vostra *f*. i vostri *mpl*, le vostre *fpl*; **a friend of ~** un tuo/suo/vostro amico; **friends of ~** dei tuoi/vostri/suoi amici; **that is ~** quello è tuo/vostro/suo; (*as opposed to mine*) quello è il tuo/il vostro/il suo

your'self *pers pron* (*reflexive*) ti; (*formal*) si; (*emphatic*) te stesso; (*formal*) sé, se stesso; **do pour ~ a drink** versati da bere; (*formal*) si versi da bere; **you said so ~** lo hai detto tu stesso; (*formal*) lo ha detto lei stesso; **you can**

be proud of ~ puoi essere fiero di te/di sé; **by ~** da solo

your'selves *pers pron* (*reflexive*) vi; (*emphatic*) voi stessi; **do pour ~ a drink** versatevi da bere; **you said so ~** lo avete detto voi stessi; **you can be proud of ~** potete essere fieri di voi; **by ~** da soli

youth /juːθ/ *n* (*pl* **youths** /-ðːz/) gioventù *f inv*; (*boy*) giovanetto *m*; **the ~** (*young people*) i giovani. **~ful** *a* giovanile. **~ hostel** *n* ostello *m* [della gioventù]

Yugoslav /ˈjuːɡəslɑːv/ *a & n* jugoslavo, -a *mf*

Yugoslavia /-ˈslɑːvɪə/ *n* Jugoslavia *f*

Zz

zany /ˈzeɪnɪ/ *a* (**-ier, -iest**) demenziale

zeal /ziːl/ *n* zelo *m*

zealous /ˈzeləs/ *a* zelante. **~ly** *adv* con zelo

zebra /ˈzebrə/ *n* zebra *f*. **~'crossing** *n* passaggio *m* pedonale. zebre *fpl*

zero /ˈzɪərəʊ/ *n* zero *m*

zest /zest/ *n* gusto *m*

zigzag /ˈzɪɡzæɡ/ *n* zigzag *m inv* ● *vi* (*pt/pp* **-zagged**) zigzagare

zilch /zɪltʃ/ *n fam* zero *m* assoluto

zinc /zɪŋk/ *n* zinco *m*

zip /zɪp/ *n* ~ |**fastener**| cerniera *f* |lampo] ● *vt* (*pt/pp* **zipped**) ~ |**up**| chiudere con la cerniera [lampo]

'**Zip code** *n Am* codice *m* postale

zipper /ˈzɪpə(r)/ *n Am* cerniera *f* [lampo]

zodiac /ˈzəʊdɪæk/ *n* zodiaco *m*

zombie /ˈzɒmbɪ/ *n fam* zombi *mf inv*

zone /zəʊn/ *n* zona *f*

zoo /zuː/ *n* zoo *m inv*

zoolog|ist /zəʊˈɒlədʒɪst/ *n* zoologo, -a *mf*. **~y** zoologia *f*

zoom /zuːm/ *vi* sfrecciare. **~ lens** *n* zoom *m inv*

ITALIAN VERB TABLES

REGULAR VERBS:

1. in -are (*eg* compr|are)

   Present ~o, ~i, ~a, ~iamo, ~ate, ~ano
   Imperfect ~avo, ~avi, ~ava, ~avamo, ~avate, ~avano
   Past historic ~ai, ~asti, ~ò, ~ammo, ~aste, ~arono
   Future ~erò, ~erai, ~erà, ~eremo, ~erete, ~eranno
   Present subjunctive ~i, ~i, ~i, ~iamo, ~iate, ~ino
   Past subjunctive ~assi, ~assi, ~asse, ~assimo, ~aste, ~assero
   Present participle ~ando
   Past participle ~ato
   Imperative ~a (*fml* ~i), ~iamo, ~ate
   Conditional ~erei, ~eresti, ~erebbe, ~eremmo, ~ereste, ~erebbero

2. in -ere (*eg* vend|ere)

   Pres ~o, ~i, ~e, ~iamo, ~ete, ~ono
   Impf ~evo, ~evi, ~eva, ~evamo, ~evate, ~evano
   Past hist ~ei *or* ~etti, ~esti, ~è *or* ~ette, ~emmo, ~este, ~erono *or* ~ettero
   Fut ~erò, ~erai, ~erà, ~eremo, ~erete, ~eranno
   Pres sub ~a, ~a, ~a, ~iamo, ~iate, ~ano
   Past sub ~essi, ~essi, ~esse, ~essimo, ~este, ~essero
   Pres part ~endo
   Past part ~uto
   Imp ~i (*fml* ~a), ~iamo, ~ete
   Cond ~erei, ~eresti, ~erebbe, ~eremmo, ~ereste, ~erebbero

3. in -ire (*eg* dorm|ire)

   Pres ~o, ~i, ~e, ~iamo, ~ite, ~ono
   Impf ~ivo, ~ivi, ~iva, ~ivamo, ~ivate, ~ivano
   Past hist ~ii, ~isti, ~ì, ~immo, ~iste, ~irono
   Fut ~irò, ~irai, ~irà, ~iremo, ~irete, ~iranno
   Pres sub ~a, ~a, ~a, ~iamo, ~iate, ~ano
   Past sub ~issi, ~issi, ~isse, ~issimo, ~iste, ~issero
   Pres part ~endo
   Past part ~ito
   Imp ~i (*fml* ~a), ~iamo, ~ite
   Cond ~irei, ~iresti, ~irebbe, ~iremmo, ~ireste, ~irebbero

Notes

- Many verbs in the third conjugation take *isc* between the stem and the ending in the first, second, and third person singular and in the third person plural of the present, the present subjunctive, and the imperative: fin|ire **Pres** ~isco, ~isci, ~isce, ~iscono. **Pres sub** ~isca, ~iscano **Imp** ~isci.

- The three forms of the imperative are the same as the corresponding forms of the present for the second and third conjugation. In the first conjugation the forms are also the same except for the second person singular: present *compri*, imperative *compra*. The negative form of the second person singular is formed by putting *non* before the infinitive for all conjugations: *non comprare*. In polite forms the third person of the present subjunctive is used instead for all conjugations: *compri*.

IRREGULAR VERBS:

Certain forms of all irregular verbs are regular (except for *essere*). These are: the second person plural of the present, the past subjunctive, and the present participle. All forms not listed below are regular and can be derived from the parts given. Only those irregular verbs considered to be the most useful are shown in the tables.

accadere	*as* **cadere**
accendere	• **Past hist** accesi, accendesti • **Past part** acceso
affliggere	• **Past hist** afflissi, affliggesti • **Past part** afflitto
ammettere	*as* **mettere**
andare	• **Pres** vado, vai, va, andiamo, andate, vanno • **Fut** andrò *etc* • **Pres sub** vada, vadano • **Imp** va', vada, vadano
apparire	• **Pres** appaio *or* apparisco, appari *or* apparisci, appare *or* apparisce, appaiono *or* appariscono • **Past hist** apparvi *or* apparsi, apparisti, apparve *or* appari *or* apparse, apparvero *or* apparirono *or* apparsero • **Pres sub** appaia *or* apparisca
aprire	• **Pres** apro • **Past hist** aprii, apristi • **Pres sub** apra • **Past part** aperto
avere	• **Pres** ho, hai, ha, abbiamo, hanno • **Past hist** ebbi, avesti, ebbe, avemmo, aveste, ebbero • **Fut** avrò *etc* • **Pres sub** abbia *etc* • **Imp** abbi, abbia, abbiate, abbiano
bere	• **Pres** bevo *etc* • **Impf** bevevo *etc* • **Past hist** bevvi *or* bevetti, bevesti • **Fut** berrò *etc* • **Pres sub** beva *etc* • **Past sub** bevessi *etc* • **Pres part** bevendo • **Cond** berrei *etc*
cadere	• **Past hist** caddi, cadesti • **Fut** cadrò *etc*
chiedere	• **Past hist** chiesi, chiedesti • **Pres sub** chieda *etc* • **Past part** chiesto *etc*
chiudere	• **Past hist** chiusi, chiudesti • **Past part** chiuso
cogliere	• **Pres** colgo, colgono • **Past hist** colsi, cogliesti • **Pres sub** colga • **Past part** colto
correre	• **Past hist** corsi, corresti • **Past part** corso
crescere	• **Past hist** crebbi • **Past part** cresciuto
cuocere	• **Pres** cuocio, cuociamo, cuociono • **Past hist** cossi, cocesti • **Past part** cotto
dare	• **Pres** do, dai, dà, diamo, danno • **Past hist** diedi *or* detti, desti • **Fut** darò *etc* • **Pres sub** dia *etc* • **Past sub** dessi *etc* • **Imp** da' (*fml* dia)

dire	• **Pres** dico, dici, dice, diciamo, dicono • **Impf** dicevo *etc* • **Past hist** dissi, dicesti • **Fut** dirò *etc* • **Pres sub** dica, diciamo, diciate, dicano • **Past sub** dicessi *etc* • **Pres part** dicendo • **Past part** detto • **Imp** di' (*fml* dica)
dovere	• **Pres** devo *or* debbo, devi, deve, dobbiamo, devono *or* debbono • **Fut** dovrò *etc* • **Pres sub** deva *or* debba, dobbiamo, dobbiate, devano *or* debbano • **Cond** dovrei *etc*
essere	• **Pres** sono, sei, è, siamo, siete, sono • **Impf** ero, eri, era, eravamo, eravate, erano • **Past hist** fui, fosti, fu, fummo, foste, furono • **Fut** sarò *etc* • **Pres sub** sia *etc* • **Past sub** fossi, fossi, fosse, fossimo, foste, fossero • **Past part** stato • **Imp** sii (*fml* sia), siate • **Cond** sarei *etc*
fare	• **Pres** faccio, fai, fa, facciamo, fanno • **Impf** facevo *etc* • **Past hist** feci, facesti • **Fut** farò *etc* • **Pres sub** faccia *etc* • **Past sub** facessi *etc* • **Pres part** facendo • **Past part** fatto • **Imp** fa' (*fml* faccia) • **Cond** farei *etc*
fingere	• **Past hist** finsi, fingesti, finsero • **Past part** finto
giungere	• **Past hist** giunsi, giungesti, giunsero • **Past part** giunto
leggere	• **Past hist** lessi, leggesti • **Past part** letto
mettere	• **Past hist** misi, mettesti • **Past part** messo
morire	• **Pres** muoio, muori, muore, muoiono • **Fut** morirò *or* morrò *etc* • **Pres sub** muoia • **Past part** morto
muovere	• **Past hist** mossi, movesti • **Past part** mosso
nascere	• **Past hist** nacqui, nascesti • **Past part** nato
offrire	• **Past hist** offersi *or* offrii, offristi • **Pres sub** offra • **Past part** offerto
parere	• **Pres** paio, pari, pare, pariamo, paiono • **Past hist** parvi *or* parsi, paresti • **Fut** parrò *etc* • **Pres sub** paia, paiamo *or* pariamo, pariate, paiano • **Past part** parso
piacere	• **Pres** piaccio, piaci, piace, piacciamo, piacciono • **Past hist** piacqui, piacesti, piacque, piacemmo, piaceste, piacquero • **Pres sub** piaccia *etc* • **Past part** piaciuto
porre	• **Pres** pongo, poni, pone, poniamo, ponete, pongono • **Impf** ponevo *etc* • **Past hist** posi, ponesti • **Fut** porrò *etc* • **Pres sub** ponga, poniamo, poniate, pongano • **Past sub** ponessi *etc*
potere	• **Pres** posso, puoi, può, possiamo, possono • **Fut** potrò *etc* • **Pres sub** possa, possiamo, possiate, possano • **Cond** potrei *etc*
prendere	• **Past hist** presi, prendesti • **Past part** preso
ridere	• **Past hist** risi, ridesti • **Past part** riso

rimanere	• **Pres** rimango, rimani, rimane, rimaniamo, rimangono • **Past hist** rimasi, rimanesti • **Fut** rimarrò *etc* • **Pres sub** rimanga • **Past part** rimasto • **Cond** rimarrei
salire	• **Pres** salgo, sali, sale, saliamo, salgono • **Pres sub** salga, saliate, salgano
sapere	• **Pres** so, sai, sa, sappiamo, sanno • **Past hist** seppi, sapesti • **Fut** saprò *etc* • **Pres sub** sappia *etc* • **Imp** sappi (*fml* sappia), sappiate • **Cond** saprei *etc*
scegliere	• **Pres** scelgo, scegli, sceglie, scegliamo, scelgono • **Past hist** scelsi, scegliesti *etc* • **Past part** scelto
scrivere	• **Past hist** scrissi, scrivesti *etc* • **Past part** scritto
sedere	• **Pres** siedo *or* seggo, siedi, siede, siedono • **Pres sub** sieda *or* segga
spegnere	• **Pres** spengo, spengono • **Past hist** spensi, spegnesti • **Past part** spento
stare	• **Pres** sto, stai, sta, stiamo, stanno • **Past hist** stetti, stesti • **Fut** starò *etc* • **Pres sub** stia *etc* • **Past sub** stessi *etc* • **Past part** stato • **Imp** sta' (*fml* stia)
tacere	• **Pres** taccio, tacciono • **Past hist** tacqui, tacque, tacquero • **Pres sub** taccia
tendere	• **Past hist** tesi • **Past part** teso
tenere	• **Pres** tengo, tieni, tiene, tengono • **Past hist** tenni, tenesti • **Fut** terrò *etc* • **Pres sub** tenga
togliere	• **Pres** tolgo, tolgono • **Past hist** tolsi, tolse, tolsero • **Pres sub** tolga, tolgano • **Past part** tolto • **Imp** *fml* tolga
trarre	• **Pres** traggo, trai, trae, traiamo, traete, traggono • **Past hist** trassi, traesti • **Fut** trarrò *etc* • **Pres sub** tragga • **Past sub** traessi *etc* • **Past part** tratto
uscire	• **Pres** esco, esci, esce, escono • **Pres sub** esca • **Imp** esci (*fml* esca)
valere	• **Pres** valgo, valgono • **Past hist** valsi, valesti • **Fut** varrò *etc* • **Pres sub** valga, valgano • **Past part** valso • **Cond** varrei *etc*
vedere	• **Past hist** vidi, vedesti • **Fut** vedrò *etc* • **Past part** visto *or* veduto • **Cond** vedrei *etc*
venire	• **Pres** vengo, vieni, viene, vengono • **Past hist** venni, venisti • **Fut** verrò *etc*
vivere	• **Past hist** vissi, vivesti • **Fut** vivrò *etc* • **Past part** vissuto • **Cond** vivrei *etc*
volere	• **Pres** voglio, vuoi, vuole, vogliamo, volete, vogliono • **Past hist** volli, volesti • **Fut** vorrò *etc* • **Pres sub** voglia *etc* • **Imp** vogliate • **Cond** vorrei *etc*

English irregular verbs

Infinitive Infinito	Past Tense Passato	Past Participle Participio passato	Infinitive Infinito	Past Tense Passato	Past Participle Participio passato
arise	arose	arisen	**feed**	fed	fed
awake	awoke	awoken	**feel**	felt	felt
be	was	been	**fight**	fought	fought
bear	bore	borne	**find**	found	found
beat	beat	beaten	**flee**	fled	fled
become	became	become	**fling**	flung	flung
begin	began	begun	**fly**	flew	flown
behold	beheld	beheld	**forbid**	forbade	forbidden
bend	bent	bent	**forget**	forgot	forgotten
beseech	beseeched	beseeched	**forgive**	forgave	forgiven
	besought	besought	**forsake**	forsook	forsaken
bet	bet,	bet,	**freeze**	froze	frozen
	betted	betted	**get**	got	got,
bid	bade,	bidden,			gotten *Am*
	bid	bid	**give**	gave	given
bind	bound	bound	**go**	went	gone
bite	bit	bitten	**grind**	ground	ground
bleed	bled	bled	**grow**	grew	grown
blow	blew	blown	**hang**	hung,	hung,
break	broke	broken		hanged (*vt*)	hanged
breed	bred	bred	**have**	had	had
bring	brought	brought	**hear**	heard	heard
build	built	built	**hew**	hewed	hewed,
burn	burnt,	burnt,			hewn
	burned	burned	**hide**	hid	hidden
burst	burst	burst	**hit**	hit	hit
bust	busted,	busted,	**hold**	held	held
	bust	bust	**hurt**	hurt	hurt
buy	bought	bought	**keep**	kept	kept
cast	cast	cast	**kneel**	knelt	knelt
catch	caught	caught	**know**	knew	known
choose	chose	chosen	**lay**	laid	laid
cling	clung	clung	**lead**	led	led
come	came	come	**lean**	leaned,	leaned,
cost	cost,	cost,		leant	leant
	costed (*vt*)	costed	**leap**	leapt,	leapt,
creep	crept	crept		leaped	leaped
cut	cut	cut	**learn**	learnt,	learnt,
deal	dealt	dealt		learned	learned
dig	dug	dug	**leave**	left	left
do	did	done	**lend**	lent	lent
draw	drew	drawn	**let**	let	let
dream	dreamt,	dreamt,	**lie**	lay	lain
	dreamed	dreamed	**light**	lit,	lit,
drink	drank	drunk		lighted	lighted
drive	drove	driven	**lose**	lost	lost
dwell	dwelt	dwelt	**make**	made	made
eat	ate	eaten	**mean**	meant	meant
fall	fell	fallen	**meet**	met	met

Infinitive / *Infinito*	Past Tense / *Passato*	Past Participle / *Participio passato*	Infinitive / *Infinito*	Past Tense / *Passato*	Past Participle / *Participio passato*
mow	mowed	mown, mowed	spend	spent	spent
			spill	spilt, spilled	spilt, spilled
overhang	overhung	overhung	spin	spun	spun
pay	paid	paid	spit	spat	spat
put	put	put	split	split	split
quit	quitted, quit	quitted, quit	spoil	spoilt, spoiled	spoilt, spoiled
read	read /red/	read /red/	spread	spread	spread
rid	rid	rid	spring	sprang	sprung
ride	rode	ridden	stand	stood	stood
ring	rang	rung	steal	stole	stolen
rise	rose	risen	stick	stuck	stuck
run	ran	run	sting	stung	stung
saw	sawed	sawn, sawed	stink	stank	stunk
			strew	strewed	strewn, strewed
say	said	said	stride	strode	stridden
see	saw	seen	strike	struck	struck
seek	sought	sought	string	strung	strung
sell	sold	sold	strive	strove	striven
send	sent	sent	swear	swore	sworn
set	set	set	sweep	swept	swept
sew	sewed	sewn, sewed	swell	swelled	swollen, swelled
shake	shook	shaken	swim	swam	swum
shear	sheared	shorn, sheared	swing	swung	swung
shed	shed	shed	take	took	taken
shine	shone	shone	teach	taught	taught
shit	shit	shit	tear	tore	torn
shoe	shod	shod	tell	told	told
shoot	shot	shot	think	thought	thought
show	showed	shown	thrive	thrived, throve	thrived, thriven
shrink	shrank	shrunk			
shut	shut	shut	throw	threw	thrown
sing	sang	sung	thrust	thrust	thrust
sink	sank	sunk	tread	trod	trodden
sit	sat	sat	understand	understood	understood
slay	slew	slain	undo	undid	undone
sleep	slept	slept	wake	woke	woken
slide	slid	slid	wear	wore	worn
sling	slung	slung	weave	wove	woven
slit	slit	slit	weep	wept	wept
smell	smelt, smelled	smelt, smelled	wet	wet, wetted	wet, wetted
sow	sowed	sown, sowed	win	won	won
			wind	wound	wound
speak	spoke	spoken	wring	wrung	wrung
speed	sped, speeded	sped, speeded	write	wrote	written
spell	spelled, spelt	spelled, spelt			